Cross-Border Transactions

KT-511-871

Law of International Trade:
Cross-Border Commercial Transactions
Fifth Edition

by

Prof. J.C.T. Chuah
Head of Academic Law, The City Law School,
City University London

SWEET & MAXWELL  **THOMSON REUTERS**

First Edition 1998
Second Edition 2001
Reprinted in 2003
Third Edition 2005
Fourth Edition 2009
Fifth Edition 2013

Published in 2013 by Sweet & Maxwell, 100 Avenue Road, London NW3 3PF
part of Thomson Reuters (Professional) UK Limited
(Registered in England & Wales, Company No 1679046.
Registered Office and address for service:
Aldgate House, 33 Aldgate High Street, London EC3N 1DL)

For further information on our products and services, visit
www.sweetandmaxwell.co.uk

Typeset by Interactive Sciences Limited, Gloucester
Printed and bound by CPI Group (UK) Ltd, Croydon CR0 4YY

No natural forests were destroyed to make this product; only farmed timber was
used and replanted.

A CIP catalogue record for this book is available from the British Library.

ISBN: 978-0-414-02325-3

PREFACE

This book is now fifteen years old and in its fifth edition. I am grateful for the continued support of law teachers, students, practitioners and other readers to whom the law relating to cross border commercial transactions from the lenses of English private law holds some interest. This edition has retained the same breadth and scope of coverage as the last edition. As a textbook for both undergraduate and postgraduate courses on private international trade law, it tries to reflect as closely as possible the conventional syllabi of my law teaching colleagues. A word of thanks is due to those who responded to my request for their course syllabus.

The purpose of this textbook, like previous editions, is to provide the reader with a reasonably comprehensive package of the law into which he or she might dip. There is no requirement for the reader to start with Chapter 1 and conclude with Chapter 15. The chapters are written to be fairly self-contained, although ample cross-referencing is provided to enable the reader to make the relevant connections. Footnote references have been updated to reflect the growing literature on the subject.

I am grateful to my readers, especially colleagues, who tell me that the chapter on the Vienna Convention on the Contracts for the International Sale of Goods (CISG) which was new in the fourth edition is particularly useful to their postgraduate students. The chapter on alternative dispute resolution has been expanded, again on the basis of comments from my esteemed colleagues who teach the law of international trade in UK universities. I have tried to ensure that the larger coverage remains closely focused on dispute resolution in the area of international commerce.

The text has incorporated numerous recent cases both in the UK and elsewhere, and, legal and commercial developments. A few of the notable legal and commercial developments discussed include:

- INCOTERMS 2010;

- Late payment interest;

- The ESS CargoDocs;

- BIMCO Piracy Clause for Time Charter Parties 2009;

- Reform of Insurance law in the UK;

- ICC Uniform Rules for Demand Guarantees 2010 (No.758);

- ICC Uniform Rules on Forfaiting 2013 (No.800);

- Recast of the Brussels I Regulation; and

- ICC Arbitration Rules 2012.

As with previous editions, I would like to acknowledge my gratitude to scholarship of many others. Also, I could not have written this book without drawing from my experience working with the chambers of commerce, export-ers, freight professionals, bankers, insurers, lawyers and civil servants. I am indebted to all of them. Many of them, if they read this book, will recognise immediately their own contributions. I should like to ask them to treat this discovery as a heartfelt thank-you from me to them.

I am especially grateful to my research student, Petya Ilieva, for her help with Chapters 5 and 15. I would like to thank the team at Sweet & Maxwell for their help in bringing to fruition this new edition. Special thanks, as always, must go to Mark Herrett.

Jason C.T. Chuah
April 2013

ACKNOWLEDGMENTS

Grateful acknowledgment is made to the following organisations and publishers for their permission to quote from their works:

- UK Chamber of Shipping, Common Short Form Bill of Lading
- Zurich International, Certificate of Insurance
- Lloyd's, Certificate of Insurance
- The Observer, "Global trade in phantom cargoes swindles banks of £500 million"
- The International Chamber of Commerce for their assistance regarding the Quick Reference Chart to the INCOTERMS® 2010 Rules

The author is also grateful to the following reports for their assistance in writing this book: All E.R., I.C.L.R. and Lloyd's Law Reports.

While every care has been taken to establish and acknowledge copyright, and contact the copyright owners, the publishers tender their apologies for any accidental infringement. They would be pleased to come to a suitable arrangement with the rightful owners in each case.

CONTENTS

TABLE OF CASES

TABLE OF STATUTES

TABLE OF STATUTORY INSTRUMENTS

TABLE OF COURT RULES

CHAPTER 1

INTRODUCTION AND CONTEXT

Of all the economic activities, it is hard to imagine one more relevant to the **1–001** prosperity of the country than international trade. International trade allows countries to enjoy goods which they would not have been able, for lack of indigenous raw materials or technology, to produce, and to earn vital foreign exchange by selling goods which they are able to produce or manufacture at an advantage over other countries. The mutual demand and supply for goods in turn stimulates the economy, resulting in growth and employment. The fact is that no country is wholly self-sufficient. The movement of goods generates the movement of capital, and capital enables a global financial system to remain stable. Indeed, despite some of the difficulties globalisation has brought into the international trading system, international trade by and large remains a significant key to economic success and development.

The importance of international trading inevitably invites governments and international organisations to want to develop laws to manage and control it. Indeed, there are many legal rules, whether international, supra-national or national, that apply to the public or economic aspects of international trade. These may include, for example, instruments such as the World Trade Organisation Agreements, bilateral Free Trade Agreements, the European Union Treaty, the World Customs Organization's legal rules, etc. It is clearly needful, given the public and economic importance of international trade, that such instruments are in place to ensure that factors which distort trade or unfairly harm developing countries are properly controlled. There is however another aspect of international trade which deserves no less recognition—the private aspects of international trade. Although international trade is sometimes expressed in terms of trade between countries, in reality, the majority of the traders are corporate entities or businesses. These entities or persons make contracts for the sale and purchase of goods across borders which they would like see recognised and enforced by nation states. Their relationship would only work if other commercial arrangements were in place to facilitate the cross border sale and purchase of the goods. These private commercial arrangements are essentially subject to national law. This book is thus primarily concerned with how English law governs these relationships and transactions. In short, the subject under consideration is international commerce on English law terms although some reference to transnational legal instruments (such as the Uniform Customs and Practice Publication No.600, the INCO-TERMS 2010, the Uniform Rules for Demand Guarantees) and international legal instruments (such as the Vienna Convention on Contracts for the International Sale of Goods and the Rotterdam Rules etc).

In particular, the book will examine how English law facilitates and enforces the international sale relationship. In any sale, it is imperative for the goods to be shipped or delivered. This is made all the more complex in international trade because of the distances involved. The goods have to be transported, usually, by a commercial carrier. The carrier would insist on a contract of carriage with either the buyer or seller. It is therefore of some importance to discuss this contract in some detail. In the meantime, the seller or buyer would wish to protect themselves against any risk of loss, damage or delay caused to the goods as a result of the distances the goods have to be carried over. The most conventional form of protection is the insurance. The law relating to insurance contracts requires the insured person and the insurer to act towards each other in good faith, and places a number of conditions on the insured person before a claim would be paid out, given that abuse might arise. Other than the requirement to pay for the goods, there may also be the need to raise finance (for both the seller and buyer) from banks using the sale contract. Here, an evaluation of the law relating to payment and trade finance is necessary. Last, but not least, disputes inevitably do happen. The book thus examines the issue as to where to sue and which country's laws will apply to the contract, in the light of the international element in the contracts. There is also the ever important role alternative dispute resolution methods play in helping commercial parties resolve their disputes. The book ends with a chapter covering different methods of non-judicial resolution of disputes—in particular, commercial negotiation and arbitration.

What Governs the Relationships in International Trade?

1–002 Without delving into the genesis and history of English international commercial law,[1] it suffices to observe that the following might be said to be its main characteristics:

- to ensure certainty in the regulation of the parties' rights and obligations by ensuring the law is consistent with precedent and predictable[2];

- to provide sufficient flexibility to the parties' need to do business by permitting the recognition of trade custom and usage;

- to give primacy to the parties' agreement by preferring not to re-write the terms of the contract without sufficient proof of the parties presumed intention[3];

[1] See C.M. Schmitthoff, *Commercial Law in a Changing Economic Climate*, 2nd edn (London: Sweet & Maxwell, 1981), Chs 1 and 2 for a general account of the historical development of commercial law.

[2] As Lord Salmon said in *Mardorf Peach & Co Ltd v Attica Sea Carriers Corp of Liberia (The Laconia)* [1977] A.C. 850 at 878: "Certainty is of the primary importance in all commercial transactions".

[3] In *Exxonmobil Sales and Supply Corp v Texaco Ltd* [2003] EWHC 1964, for example, the court refused to allow proof of custom or usage to override a contractual clause tacitly excluding such custom or usage. The problem though is always one of construction of the clause but in that case, given the commercial background, the court was persuaded that the clause (known as an "entire agreement" clause) was sufficiently wide to exclude custom and usage.

- to provide an efficient system for the resolution of commercial disputes through the workings of the commercial court, the recognition and enforcement of arbitral awards, the facilitation of other forms of alternative dispute resolution (including mediation, conciliation, etc) and the recognition and enforcement of foreign judicial awards; and

- to recognise the international dimension of commerce by the application of specialised rules of conflict of laws, the admittance of practice and rules of international organisations (such as the International Chamber of Commerce, the UNCITRAL) as guiding the interpretation and application of commercial law, and the use of foreign law as a guide.

The functions of international commercial law are necessarily linked to their sources. One of its most important sources is the commercial contract. That shall be the starting point in this next section. In turn, the contract can only have existence and enforceability because it is underpinned by national law. However, that relationship between the contract and national law must not be treated in isolation. EU and international legal influences also have an impact.

Contract

Where the performance of a duty is provided for by contract, unless the provision   **1–003**
contradicts the law or public policy of the country, that contractual provision shall be binding as between the parties. In the examination of the relationship between the parties, it is therefore necessary to extract the contents of the contract and then properly to construe them to determine the extent of that relationship. The contents of the contractual relationship may be found either in the expressly stated terms of the contract or may be elicited by the court from the surrounding facts or legal environment.

The terms of the contract must be sufficiently certain; in *Schweppe v Harper* [2008] EWCA Civ 442, whether there is certainty can sometimes be a difficult matter of judgment. There, in a 2–1 decision, the Court of Appeal held that the financing contract was uncertain given that there were no clear terms as to the amount of finance sought, the rate or rates of interest and any other consideration to be provided, the length of the finance and how repayment was to be made. In general, the courts would try to save a commercial deal as the presumption is that there is intention to be legally bound in a commercial relationship. Indeed, the courts, where appropriate, would imply reasonable terms into the contract to make it enforceable. However, the contract also has to be capable of being performed and this is where the courts might find the gaps in the "contract" too cavernous to fill.

Express terms

(a) **Generally**   It is customary practice in international commerce for parties   **1–004**
to adopt commonly recognised or standard terms. These standardised contracts are very much the result of the growth of large-scale enterprises with mass production and mass distribution. According to Kessler:

"The stereotyped contract of today reflects the impersonality of the market. It has reached its greatest perfection in the different types of contracts used on the various exchanges. Once the usefulness of these contracts was discovered and perfected in the transportation, insurance, and banking business, their use spread into all other fields of large scale enterprise, into international as well as national trade . . . ".[4]

The benefits of using these standardised terms include:

(i) as far as the trader or businessman is concerned, the risk factor is extremely important in any business venture. Hence with the uniformity of terms and predictability of consequences from the contractual arrangement being made pellucid right at the outset, he is able to calculate the precise risks involved. Take for example standard form insurance contracts, the commonly used terms of the cover and excepted perils make the computation of risks more efficient for both the insurer and the insured;

(ii) standard form contracts are also useful in excluding or controlling the "illogical factor" of judicial reasoning in litigation: the conviction that being codified terms will make the contract so limpid that the court or arbitrator will have little choice but to adhere to the expressed terms. Clarity in standard form contracts is no less an important factor in its appeal to the business person. Decision makers entrusted with the task of construing the standard form contract can take comfort in the fact that these terms are not novel, but have been addressed by precedent or practice; and

(iii) the use of standard form contracts also contributes to the reduction in cost and increase in efficiency of transaction. The time and cost saved from extensive negotiation and personalised drafting of the contract are not insubstantial especially in respect of large-scale enterprises.

1–005   While the recognition of the standard form clauses is widespread, a distinction must be made between those that have been agreed to by parties of equal bargaining power and those imposed on persons on a "take it or leave it" basis. In the words of Lord Diplock in *A. Schroeder Music Publishing Co Ltd v Macaulay* [1974] 3 All E.R. 616:

"Standard forms of contracts are of two kinds. The first, of very ancient origin, are those which set out the terms on which mercantile transactions of common occurrence are to be carried out. Examples are bills of lading, charterparties, policies of insurance, contracts of sale in the commodity markets. The standard clauses in these contracts have been settled over the years by negotiation by representatives of the commercial interests involved and have been widely adopted because experience has shown that they facilitate the conduct of trade. . . . If fairness or reasonableness were relevant to their enforceability the fact that they are widely used by parties whose bargaining power is fairly matched would raise a strong presumption that their terms are fair and reasonable.

The same presumption, however, does not apply to the other kind of standard form of contract. This is of comparatively modern origin. It is the

---

[4] Kessler, "Contracts of Adhesion—some Thoughts about Freedom of Contract" (1943) Col. L.R. 629, at 631.

result of the concentration of particular kinds of business in relatively few hands. The ticket cases in the 19th century provide what are probably the first examples. The terms of this kind of standard form of contract have not been the subject of negotiation between the parties to it, or approved by any organisation representing the interests of the weaker party".

In international commerce, the standard form contract used is usually of the **1–006** former. The latter is frequently subject to consumer protection legislation, for example, the Unfair Contract Terms Act 1977 and the Unfair Terms in Consumer Contracts Regulations 1999; the rationale being that as stated by Lord Diplock. An international trade contractual relationship is normally exempt from these consumer protection provisions. For example, the Unfair Contracts Terms Act 1977 does not apply to "international supply contracts". Section 26 of the Act defines this to be contracts for the sale of goods where the seller and buyer are based in different jurisdictions and one of the following conditions applies:

1. the goods are to be carried from one state to another;

2. the acts constituting the offer and acceptance have been done in different territories; or

3. the goods are to be delivered to a territory other than that which the offer and acceptance took place.

Yuanda (UK) Co Ltd v WW Gear Construction Ltd [2011] 1 All E.R. (Comm) 550   **1–007**
Facts:
The parties had entered into a contract for the provision of glazed curtain walling. Yuanda is a subsidiary of a large Chinese company registered in England. Gear was a company incorporated in Cyprus but appeared to have had several places of business. The curtain walling was to furnish a hotel in England which was being project managed by GC, a company controlled by Gear. It was intended that the curtain walling system would be manufactured in China.

Gear wanted to rely on a clause in the contract which carried a late payment interest rate which was much lower than the statutory rate under the Late Payment of Commercial Debts (Interest) Act 1998. The question was whether the clause was reasonable in the light of s.3 of the Unfair Contract Terms Act 1977. Section 3 of the 1977 Act provides that where the contract is made on the basis of one party's written standard terms of business, that person

"cannot by reference to any contract term—(a) when himself in breach of contract, exclude or restrict any liability of his in respect of the breach . . . except in so far as . . . the contract term satisfies the requirement of reasonableness".

Much, therefore, depended on whether the contract in question was an international supply of goods contract. If it was, the Unfair Contract Terms Act 1977 would not apply.
Held:
The High Court held that s.26(3)(b) applied because Yuanda's place of business was in England whilst Gear probably had its place of business in Cyprus. Section 26(4) was also satisfied because the substantial parts of the curtain walling system were to be manufactured in China and it was self-evident that the goods had to be transported from the territory of one state (China) to the territory of another (England). The Unfair Contract Terms Act 1977 therefore could not apply.

The court also found that Yuanda had not dealt on the back of Gear's standard form contract. Section 3 did not apply, even if this was not an international supply contract.

1–008   Express promises must be incorporated into the contract before they could be treated as the binding express terms of the contract. Naturally, if the party concerned has signed attesting to his consent to a set of standard terms, he is bound and there is no defence in saying that he had not read the terms. In *L'Estrange v Graucob Ltd* [1934] 2 K.B. 394 the claimant had bought an automatic slot machine from the defendants signing an order form which contained in small print a number of terms. That was sufficient to bind her to the terms, regardless of whether she had read them or not. Scrutton J. said:

> "[W]hen a document is signed, then, in the absence of fraud, or, I will add, misrepresentation, the party signing it is bound, and it is wholly immaterial whether he has read the document or not".

It should also be borne in mind that although such cases should normally be read in the light of the Unfair Contract Terms Act 1977 (s.6(3) and Sch.2 para.(c), and possibly the Unfair Terms in Consumer Contract Regulations 1999), those legislative provisions have no effect on international supply contracts as discussed above. This raises the stakes for the trader—he must be particularly careful in what he signs.

In international commerce, the problem is made complicated by the fact that the transaction might be found in a lengthy exchange of standard conditions between the parties—the battle of the forms, as some term it. Identifying exactly what was agreed and when it was agreed is a serious problem for lawyers.

1–009   *Butler Machine Tool Co Ltd v Ex-Cell-O Corp Ltd* [1979] 1 All E.R. 965
Facts:
On May 23, 1969, the sellers made an offer to sell a machine tool to the buyers for £75,535 delivery in 10 months' time. The offer was stated to be subject to certain terms and conditions which "shall prevail over any terms and conditions in the Buyers' order". The conditions contained a price variation clause providing for the goods to be charged at the price ruling on the date of delivery. On May 27, the buyers placed an order and that order was stated to be subject to certain terms and conditions. These were very different from those stated in the sellers' offer. At the foot of the buyers' order was a tear-off acknowledgement slip stating "we accept your order on the Terms and Conditions stated thereon". The sellers signed and returned the acknowledgement slip with a letter stating that "this is being entered in accordance with our . . . quotation of May 23 for delivery in 10/11 months". At delivery, the sellers demanded an increase in the price of £2,892 on the basis of the price variation clause in their offer.
Held:
The correct approach, said Lord Denning M.R., was to look at all the documents passing between the parties and glean from them, and/or from the conduct of the parties, whether they have reached agreement on all material points, even though there may be differences between the forms and conditions printed on the back of them. Using this rule, it would usually be the case that in a battle of the forms, the contract is made as soon as the last of the forms is sent and received without objection. The court took the view that the sellers had signed the acknowledgement slip agreeing to the terms set out by the buyers and were, as such, bound by the buyers' terms. They were thus not entitled to rely on the price variation clause.

1–010   It might be noted that in *Butler Machine Tool* the court dismissed the sellers' argument that the acknowledgement slip had been qualified by the letter which purported to revive the terms set out in the "quotation" of May 23. The court was of the opinion that the letter only referred to the price and identity of the machine and not ancillary terms set out in the initial quotation, and was therefore irrelevant. In the ultimate analysis, it boiled down to a matter of construction. It is obvious that there need to be proper rules governing the process of contract construction.

Where there is a battle of the forms, the circumstances surrounding the exchange of the forms are particularly relevant. In *LIDL UK GmbH v Hertford Foods Ltd* [2001] EWCA Civ 938, H and L had made an oral agreement for the delivery of several consignments of corned beef. That oral agreement was confirmed by the exchange between the parties of a number of documents. H claimed that its terms governed the contract; whilst L contended that its own terms did. Chadwick L.J. held that the common background knowledge that H and L brought to the negotiations which culminated in the agreement was vital. It is a question of proof whether there was knowledge or notice of the relevant set of terms by the parties. Where it could not be proved that the parties had relied on one or the other set of terms, the court will have no choice but to find either that there was no contract or that neither set of terms would apply. In the case of the latter, express terms which are ascertainable and implied terms would be given effect to (*GHSP Inc v AB Electronics* [2010] EWHC 1828 (Comm)).

In a battle of forms case, the traditional analysis (namely, the one based on offer and acceptance) should be used, unless the parties' conduct and the documents passing between them showed that their common intention was that some other terms were to prevail. It would be difficult to displace that traditional analysis unless there was a clear course of dealing between the parties (*Tekdata Interconnections Ltd v Amphenol Ltd* [2009] EWCA Civ 1209; also *Trebor Bassett Holdings Ltd v ADT Fire and Security Plc* [2011] EWHC 1936 (TCC)).

(b) Rules of construction The centrality of contractual terms means that the rights and obligations of the parties are very much dependent on what the contract is perceived as saying and what the courts consider to be the proper way to construe it. As for Lord Goff: **1–011**

> "[T]here is only one principle of construction so far as commercial documents are concerned: and that is to make, so far as possible, commercial sense of the provision in question, having regard to the words used, the remainder of the document in which they are set, the nature of the transaction, and the legal and factual matrix".[5]

"Commercial sense" refers to acknowledged trade usage or practice in the industry and the objectively determined presumed business intentions of the parties. Giving the contract or other commercial documents their commercial sense also implies that they should be construed so as to give them reasonable business efficacy where that is admissible on the language (*BWE International Ltd v Jones* [2003] EWCA Civ 298). The court should also be concerned to ensure that the construction taken should not detract from the need to guarantee

---

[5] Goff, "Commercial Contracts and the Commercial Court" [1984] L.M.C.L.Q. 382, 388; see also McLauchlan, "Common Intention and Contract Interpretation" [2011] L.M.C.L.Q. 30.

certainty in commercial transactions.[6] The importance of the commercial purpose or object of the contract must be given due weight. In *Antaios Cia Naviera SA v Salen Rederierna AB, The Antaios* [1985] A.C. 191, the court was faced with the dilemma of adopting either a literal reading or a purposive construction of the NYPE time charter form. Lord Diplock decided on the latter because it would better serve the commercial purpose of the contract. The commercial purpose is to be ascertained from what risks and burdens prudent commercial men in the situation would have been prepared to assume.[7]

Hence, it is an objective test based on the commercial environment. The objectivity is seen in *Miramar Maritime Corporation v Holborn Oil Trading Ltd* [1984] A.C. 676, where the court had first to consider the literal analysis of the words as expressed in the contract, and then to set this interpretation against the yardstick of commercial purpose. Where the literal reading will flout the commercial purpose, the contract must be construed to yield to business sense. In that case, the Exxonvoy 1969 form (a standard form charterparty) had to be given a purposive reading because, had the provision been taken literally, it would have been likely that a financial liability of unknown extent must be absorbed by the contracting party. Such an assumption of risk of an unknown extent must surely be outside the commercial purpose of a prudent commercial person.

1–012 It should however be pointed out that the courts are not suggesting that the purposive rule be resorted to before a literal approach has been applied. The literal reading means according to Lord Diplock in the above mentioned case, "a detailed semantic and syntactical analysis" of the words. It was affirmed in *Multiplex Constructions v Cleveland Bridge* [2007] EWCA Civ 1372 that the court will not readily accept that people have made linguistic mistakes, particularly in formal documents. If the ordinary meaning of the words makes sense in relation to the rest of the document and the factual background, the court will give effect to that language, even though the consequences may appear hard to one side or the other. This is not to say however that English law is not liberal in its approach to the construction of contracts. Lord Blackburn's judgment in the old case of *River Wear Commissioners v Adamson* (1877) 2 App. Cas. 743 posits the approach as

" . . . enquir[ing] beyond the language and see[ing] what the circumstances were with reference to which the words were used, and the object, appearing from those circumstances, which the person using them had in view".

The circumstances under which the words are used can include how the market conducts itself. It was held in *Thomas Crema v Cenkos Security* [2010] EWCA

---

[6] Indeed, as is stated in *Vallejo v Wheeler* (1774) 1 Cowp. 143: "In all mercantile transactions the great object should be certainty: and therefore, it is of more consequence that a rule should be certain, than whether the rule is established one way or the other. Because speculators in trade then know what ground to go upon".

[7] As Lord Halsbury commented in *Glynn v Margetson & Co* [1893] A.C. 351, "that a business sense will be given to business documents". The business sense is that which businessmen, in the course of their ordinary dealings, would give the document. It is likely to be a reasonably straightforward sense since, as Lord Mansfield famously observed (*Hamilton v Mendes* (1761) 2 Burr 1198), "the daily negotiations and property of merchants ought not to depend upon subtleties and niceties; but upon rules, easily learned and easily retained, because they are the dictates of common sense, drawn from the truth of the case". See also *British Energy Power & Trading v Credit Suisse* [2008] EWCA Civ 53.

Civ 1444 that even though a practice of the market had not established itself as a trade usage or custom, it could legitimately be relied on as part of the factual background to guide the interpretation of the contract.

Lord Blackburn's words could not be taken as permitting the evidence of prior **1–013** negotiations. In *Prenn v Simmonds* [1971] 3 All E.R. 237, Lord Wilberforce refused to interpret a vague contractual clause in the light of prior negotiations on the basis that at that stage, the parties could not be deemed to have reached consensus. Such representations may go some limited way to explaining the objective of the parties during the negotiations stage but they cannot be adequately held to reflect the common intention. The court is entitled however "to place itself in the same factual matrix as that in which the parties were" to ascertain the contract's true meaning (*Reardon Smith v Hanen-Tangen* [1976] 1 W.L.R. 989; *The Karen Oltmann* [1976] 2 Lloyd's Rep. 708). The Court of Appeal attempted a definition in *Scottish Power PLC v Britoil Ltd* (*The Times*, December 2, 1997) stating, "the factual matrix to which a court was to have regard in construing a contract meant the immediate context of the contract". Nevertheless, only where the literal words offer no assistance could the court have regard to surrounding circumstances or the factual matrix (*New Hampshire Insurance v MGN Ltd* [1996] C.L.C. 692).

All this was thrown into some confusion following *Investors Compensation Scheme v West Bromwich Building Society* [1998] 1 W.L.R. 896, HL where Lord Hoffmann remarked that the "factual matrix" included "absolutely anything which would have affected the way in which the language of the document would have been understood by a reasonable man". His Lordship went on to say that the meaning which a document would convey to a reasonable man is not the same thing as the meaning of its words:

"The meaning of words is a matter of dictionaries and grammars; the meaning of the document is what the parties using those words against the relevant background would reasonably have been understood to mean".

There was some disquiet (see for example *National Bank of Sharjah v Delbourg* (July 9, 1997, CA)) over this approach in that it seemed to admit "absolutely anything" as the factual matrix.

The matter was revisited by the House of Lords in *BCCI v Munawar Ali* [2001] **1–014** UKHL 8. Upon his redundancy, M signed a document releasing B, his employer, from "all claims . . . that exist or may exist". At that time, he and B were unaware of a claim he could bring against B. That claim was unrelated to his redundancy. The House of Lords (4–1) held that the document could not be construed as depriving M of his claim given that factual matrix at the time the release was signed. In *BCCI*, Lord Hoffmann took the opportunity to explain what was meant by "absolutely anything":

"I did not think it necessary to emphasise that I meant anything which a reasonable man would have regarded as *relevant*. I was merely saying that there is no conceptual limit to what can be regarded as background . . . I was certainly not encouraging a trawl through 'background' which could not have made a reasonable person think that the parties must have departed from conventional usage".

The distinction between conventional and unconventional however is a difficult one to make as the House of Lords emphasised in *Amoco (UK) Exploration Co v Teesside Gas Transportation Ltd* [2001] UKHL 18. It held that where the terms in question could be given either their technical or commercial meaning, the latter sense must predominate. The Court of Appeal agreed with counsel that there was nothing unreasonable in a provision by which liability for payment could be retrospectively invalidated by the discovery of a latent defect in the gas facility. The House of Lords disagreed finding that such an approach was contrary to conventional practice.

Extrinsic aid to construction

1-015 As to whether extrinsic evidence might be adduced to help construe the contract, it is a well known principle that where a contract is, viewed without any assistance from extrinsic evidence, uncertain as to the precise identity of the subject matter, extrinsic evidence may be admissible to establish it. Thus, for example, in *MacDonald v Longbottom* (1860) 1 El. & El. 988, where the only definition of the subject matter of the sale was "your wool", extrinsic evidence was admissible to show what wool the seller then owned. The principle is explained by Griffiths L.J. in *Scarfe v Adams* [1981] 1 All E.R. 843 as

" . . . if the terms of the transfer clearly define the land or interest transferred extrinsic evidence is not admissible to contradict the transfer. In such a case, if the transfer does not truly express the bargain between vendor and purchaser, the only remedy is by way of rectification of the transfer. But, if the terms of the transfer do not clearly define the land or interest transferred, then extrinsic evidence is admissible so that the court may (to use the words of Lord Parker in *Eastwood v Ashton* [1915] AC 900 at 913) 'do the best it can to arrive at the true meaning of the parties upon a fair consideration of the language used'".

A question which has caused some considerable difficulty in this connection is whether prior negotiations might be introduced as extrinsic evidence to explain the choice of terminology used in the contract and to interpret that terminology. This has sometimes been termed the "private dictionary principle". Kerr J. in *The Karen Oltmann* [1976] 2 Lloyd's Rep. 708 held

"if a contract contains words which, in their context, are fairly capable of bearing more than one meaning, and if it is alleged that the parties have in effect negotiated on an agreed basis that the words bore only one of the two possible meanings, then it is permissible for the court to examine the extrinsic evidence relied upon to see whether the parties have in fact used the words in question in one sense only, so that they have in effect given their own dictionary meaning to the words as the result of their common intention".

In *Chartbrook Ltd v Persimmon Homes Ltd* [2007] EWHC 409 (Ch); [2008] EWCA Civ 183 and *euNetworks Fiber Ltd v Abovenet Communications* [2007] EWHC 3099 (Ch), both cases decided by Briggs J., the judge questioned whether the private dictionary principle was really a principle of construction at all, rather than an aspect of the law of rectification. The judge held in *Chartbrook* that the adverse effect on third party rights was a compelling reason for not admitting evidence of prior negotiations. If the parties' negotiations were to be routinely admissible as an aid to contractual construction, then third parties reading, dealing with or having transferred to them rights or obligations under the contract could not make any safe assumptions about its meaning without themselves carrying out an inquiry as to those negotiations, so as to put themselves in the same state of knowledge as the parties to the contract. The Court of Appeal concurred.

In *euNetworks*, Briggs J. reasoned that, even if the principle was a principle of   **1–016** construction, it should not be used for the construction of words, phrases or terms which have already been defined in the contract in question. The existence of definitions is a clear signal to any third parties that the meaning of the word, phrase or term in question is to be found within, rather than without, the four corners of the contract itself. Even where there are no prescribed definitions in the contract, the private dictionary principle should nevertheless be restrictively applied especially where there are third parties involved or likely to be involved in the contractual relationship. Indeed, as Creswell J. reminded us in *Proforce Recruit v Rugby Group Ltd* [2007] EWHC 1621 (QB), the principle is an exceptional principle and it would seldom arise in the interpretation of commercial contracts.

It should also be noted that there is no material difference in the manner of construction between commercial contracts and commercial notices. Notices in international trade are very important—many a duty will not arise unless an appropriate notice had been served. Lord Hoffmann commented in *West Bromwich* that he could see no reason why the two should be treated differently when it comes to reliance on the commercial background to construe them. There is support for such a position in Lord Steyn's judgment in *Mannai Investment Co Ltd v Eagle Star Life Assurance Co Ltd* [1997] 1 E.G.L.R. 57 where His Lordship said, "in determining the meaning of the language of . . . unilateral notices, the law therefore generally favours a commercially sensible construction". It should follow that a commercially sensible construction would necessarily take account of the commercial background to the notice.[8]

Best endeavour clauses

Express undertakings to perform a thing will be construed strictly against the   **1–017** promisor. Therefore the agreement will qualify the undertaking by taking some form of "endeavours" to achieve the outcome. For example, the promise to take best endeavours or reasonable endeavours or all reasonable endeavours to bring about the desired outcome. How should such clauses be construed?

The leading case of *Rhodia International Holdings Ltd v Huntsman International LLC* [2007] EWHC 292 (Comm). The judge acknowledged that different forms of endeavours will carry a varying degree of strictness. For example, "best endeavours" must mean what the words say; they do not mean "second best endeavours". In *Jet2.com v Blackpool Airport* [2012] EWCA Civ 417 the Court of Appeal by a majority held that the use of terms such as "best endeavours" and "all reasonable endeavours" are sufficiently certain for recognition and enforcement by the courts. However, much depends on the context in

---

[8] See also *Barclays Bank Plc v Bee* [2001] EWCA Civ 1126.

which that expression is used. An important part of the context is the objective towards which the endeavours are to be directed. If the endeavours are directed towards a result which can be identified with certainty, then whether the endeavours satisfy the obligation can also be decided (perhaps, if need be, by expert evidence). In *The Talisman* [1989] 1 Lloyd's Rep. 535, for example, where the question was whether the skipper of a fishing boat had used reasonable endeavours to prevent the boat from sinking. The object of the endeavours was clearly defined. In that context, as Lord Keith explained, the test was

" . . . an objective one, directed to ascertaining what an ordinarily competent fishing boat skipper might reasonably be expected to do in the same circumstances".

In *Little v Courage Ltd* (1995) 70 P. & C.R. 469 the lease contained an option to renew which was conditional on the parties having agreed a business plan. No business plan had in fact been agreed. The tenant argued that the parties had an obligation to use their best endeavours to reach an agreement. This court rejected that argument. Millett L.J. said:

"An undertaking to use one's best endeavours to obtain planning permission or an export licence is sufficiently certain and is capable of being enforced: an undertaking to use one's best endeavours to agree, however, is no different from an undertaking to agree, to try to agree, or to negotiate with a view to reaching agreement; all are equally uncertain and incapable of giving rise to an enforceable legal obligation.".

Thus, we have in that case an objective towards which the endeavours were to be directed was too uncertain to enforce.

1–018   "Reasonable endeavours" has been interpreted in *Rhodia* to mean that a party may only need to take one course of action and not explore further options. This obviously means that "reasonable endeavours" is less stringent than "best endeavours". "All reasonable endeavours" is taken by the judge in *Rhodia* to equate to using "best endeavours" because both require all courses of action to be pursued. Although financial loss is not an excuse for failing to deliver, the promisor can rely on its own commercial interests and position when pursuing all reasonable endeavours to bring about the agreed outcome to qualify and limit the scope of its obligation—for instance, they certainly would not need to take action resulting in "the certain ruin of the Company or . . . the utter disregard for the interests of shareholders" (*Terrell v Mabie Todd and Co Limited* [1952] 69 RPC 234).

Parties may wish to clarify and narrow the scope of their endeavours clause by:

● making it clear whether the promisor would bear any costs when taking steps to bring about the desired outcome and, if so, how much;

● the period for which he should pursue that objective; and

● what steps he must take to achieve the objective, including any legal actions or processes he should follow in order to bring about the desired consequence.

Implied terms

These are terms which the court will read into the contract when the express   **1–019**
terms are inadequate to explain any duties or rights which either party claims to
exist.

There are three types of implied terms:

* terms implied in fact;

* terms implied in law; and

* terms implied by custom or usage.

(a) **Implied in fact**   The courts may be prepared to imply into a contract   **1–020**
terms which in their mind are vital to give "business efficacy" to the contract; i.e.
to enable the contract to work in the manner it must have been intended to. In *The
Moorcock* [1886–1890] All E.R. 530, the claimants had agreed to discharge and
load cargo at a wharf owned and managed by the defendants. It was known to the
parties that the vessel would take the ground at low tide. When it did, the vessel
was damaged as a result of the uneven river bed. The condition of the river bed
was a fact which the defendants could have ascertained, although the area was
outside their control. The Court of Appeal held the defendants liable for the
damage caused, because both parties must have contemplated that the wharf
should be safe for the vessel especially in the light of the fact that both parties
knew that at low tide, the vessel would take ground:

> " . . . [I]n business transactions what the law desires to effect by the
> implication is to give such business efficacy to the transaction as must have
> been intended by both parties; not to impose on one side all the perils of the
> transaction or to emancipate one side from all the burdens, but to make each
> party promise in law as much, at all events, as it must have been in the
> contemplation of both parties that he should be responsible for".

The rule is often cited in the context of MacKinnon L.J.'s so-called "officious
bystander" test (*Shirlaw v Southern Foundries (1926) Ltd* [1939] 2 K.B. 206).
The duty or right must be one which is so obvious that it goes without saying.
Thus if, while the parties were making the contract, an officious bystander were
to suggest that some provision be expressly stated, they would testily suppress
him with a common, "Oh, of course". It should be noted, though, that the
application of the test has not been at all smooth or consistent.[9]

The courts have consistently held that in order for a term to be properly   **1–021**
implied, it must be justifiable on grounds of commercial common sense and that
even though the term proposed to be implied is fair and equitable, the court
would not do so unless it was necessary to give business efficacy. In *Mousaka Inc
v Golden Seagull Maritime Inc* [2002] 1 Lloyd's Rep. 797, it was argued by the
claimant that there was an implied term to the form of security for the release of
an arrested ship could be changed from time to time and that the claimant was not
bound by the initial form of security used. The court rejected that argument

---

[9] See, e.g. cases like *Shell UK Ltd v Lostock Garage Ltd* [1977] 1 All E.R. 481; *Liverpool City
Council v Irwin* [1976] 2 All E.R. 39; *Ashmore v Corporation of Lloyds (No.2), The Times,* July 17,
1992; *Trollope and Colls Ltd v North West Metropolitan Regional Hospital Board* [1973] 2 All E.R.
260.

stating that to permit such a term would be to permit the constant renegotiation of the identity of the security. That would be contrary to common sense and sensible commercial practice. The other implied term argued for by the claimant was for the reduction of the quantum of security if it became obvious that the amount of compensation was to be less than the quantum secured. Although the agreement without such a term might be less than fair, and the term proposed was not unjust or inequitable, those were not sufficiently sound reasons for implying the term. It might also be pointed out that if the court yielded to such a plea, it would clearly have implications for other similar disputes in the future and it would weaken the commercial legal underpinnings in place to permit such a state of uncertainty.

The test as to whether the term to be implied is necessary does not mean necessity under the circumstances but necessity to effect the presumed mutual intentions of the parties. As Lord Bingham M.R. in *Philips Electronique v BSB* [1995] E.M.L.R. 472 said:

"The question of whether a term should be implied, and if so what, almost inevitably arises after a crisis has been reached in the performance of the contract. So the court comes to the task of implication with the benefit of hindsight, and it is tempting for the court then to fashion a term which will reflect the merits of the situation as they then appear. Tempting, but wrong".

The touchstone is the test of necessity: that is a question of asking whether the proposed implied term was necessary to make the contract work or, put another way, whether in the absence of the implied term the contract failed to deliver the bargain which the parties had agreed (see Lord Steyn's speech in *Equitable Life Assurance Society v Hyman* [2002] 1 A.C. 408; also *Meridian International Services v Richardson* [2008] EWCA Civ 609). The courts are, therefore, particularly slow to imply terms into a contract particularly where there were already detailed terms and conditions (*Leander Construction v Mulalley & Co* [2011] EWHC 3449 (TCC)).

Finally, for a term to be implied, it must be clear or sufficiently certain. In *Socimer International Bank v Standard Bank* [2008] EWCA Civ 116, it was argued that it was an implied term of the forward sale agreement that, on termination, one of the sellers had to carry out a reasonable, objective valuation of the assets. However the Court of Appeal concluded a reasonable valuation is not the same as an objective valuation. The implied term was therefore too uncertain to enforce.

1–022   **(b) Implied in law** The law may impose certain terms on particular classes of contracts. Hence, where the contract in question falls within a certain class of contracts, it too will be subject to terms normally applicable to that class of contracts. The courts have however been unequivocal in rejecting the formulation that an implication should be made where to do so would be reasonable. Reasonableness is not sufficient, the implication must be necessary or imperative (*Scally v Southern Health and Social Services Noard* [1991] 4 All E.R. 563, see especially Lord Bridge's speech).

It has been suggested that the test is subject to "wider considerations" than business efficacy. In deciding to imply a term on this basis, the court must assess broader issues of policy circumstances surrounding the particular category or class of contracts in question, and not merely the circumstances of the particular contract in question.[10] Therefore, a contractual term may be incorporated through this mechanism only if the contract in question belongs to a definable category. In *Scally*, the claimants had missed the opportunity to buy "added years" in their statutory pension scheme because their employers had failed to comply with the government's circular by not informing them of their right to do so. The claimants' claim was that their employers had breached the contract of employment by not informing them of their right to purchase "added years". The question for the court was whether there was such a term implied into the contract. The House of Lords held the employers would be liable if the term was "a necessary incident of a definable category of contractual relationship". From the facts, it was absolutely necessary for the employer to take reasonable steps to bring the term in the contract in question to the attention of the employee so that he may be in a position to enjoy its benefits.

Terms, as pointed out before, may also be implied into contracts by statute law. This includes not only national legislation and subsidiary legislation, but certain EC legislative provisions (e.g. Regulations and Treaty provisions in particular). These statutory provisions regulate the operation of those commercial contracts that fall within their purview. The parties are sometimes prohibited from modifying or excluding these terms. Be that as it may, the general tenor of these statutes is that as implied terms, the provisions should preferably be subject to the parties' common intention. For example, the Sale of Goods Act 1979 s.55 permits the exclusion or variation of any right, duty or liability implied by law by express agreement, or by the course of dealings between the parties, or by usage binding on the parties. That freedom of contract is of paramountcy in international commerce as evidenced by s.26 of the Unfair Contract Terms Act 1977 where the terms of an international supply contract are not subject to any requirement of reasonableness under the Act.

The next chapter will consider the area of sale and supply of goods in relation to these statutorily implied terms in greater detail.

(c) Implied by custom or course of dealings[11]   The rule is that a term may   **1–023** be implied into the contract where it is proved that there is a course of dealings between the parties showing the existence of that duty or right. In *McCutcheon v David Macbrayne Ltd* [1964] 1 W.L.R. 125, the House of Lords was unequivocal in requiring evidence of consistency in the alleged course of dealings. Consistency evinces the common intention of the parties to be bound by the term. Consistency of practice also goes some way at clarifying the precise nature of the right or obligation being implied into the contract. Besides clarity, the law also insists that the term implied in this manner be not inconsistent with any express terms of the contract. The latter must prevail, unless as a matter of construction the two terms can be reconciled (*Les Affreteurs Reunis Societe Anonyme v Walford* [1919] A.C. 801).

In *Lovell & Christmas Ltd v Wall* (1911) 104 L.T. 85 Cozens-Hardy M.R. made it clear that where a word has acquired a secondary meaning within the

---

[10] Phang, "Implied terms in English Law—some recent developments" (1993) J.B.L. 242.
[11] See, in particular, C. Schmitthoff, *International Trade Usages* (Paris: Institute of International Business Law, 1987).

particular trade, that secondary meaning should generally be given effect to. Hence, the well-known example used was where in a particular trade 1000 rabbits meant 1200, that secondary meaning should be accepted as binding between the parties even though the term was "inconsistent" with the expressly stated figure of 1000. Trade custom had in this case been used to explain and qualify an express term and because that secondary meaning had wide recognition in the trade, it reflected the objective intention of the contract.

The usage or custom must also be tested against the nature of the contract as a whole. It must not fly in the face of the contract (*London Export Corporation Ltd v Jubilee Coffee Roasting Co* [1958] 1 W.L.R. 661).

Parties dealing within a particular industry or trade or commercial sector may be presumed to have contracted with each on the basis of certain accepted trade usage or customs. Again these must be clear and consistent. In *Kum v Wah Tat Bank Ltd* [1971] 1 Lloyd's Rep. 439, the Judicial Committee of the Privy Council held that for a trade custom to be incorporated into the contract as an implied term, that custom must be generally accepted by those doing business in the particular trade in the particular place, and be so generally known that an outsider making reasonable enquiries could not fail to discover it. It therefore follows that the custom will become immediate binding on the newcomer to the trade in the particular place.

1–024   A custom or usage must be reasonable before the courts will permit its application. Keating J. in *Paxton v Courtnay* (1860) 2 F. & F. 131, stated that it is reasonable only if it is fair and proper and such as reasonable, honest and right-minded men would adopt. In *North and South Trust Co v Berkeley* [1971] 1 W.L.R. 470, the practice amongst Lloyd's underwriters to use Lloyd's insurance brokers as their agents when dealing with claims assessors was not reasonable and thus could not be given effect to as legally accepted usage. It was held to be unreasonable because it conflicted with the legal rule that an agent cannot act for two opposing principals. (Bear in mind that a "broker" is an agent in law.) A fortiori, therefore, the custom concerned must not be unlawful (*Daun v City of London Brewery Co* (1869) L.R. 8 Eq. 155).

Custom may also form a source of law, especially in commercial transactions. For example, the *Uniform Customs and Practice for Documentary Credits* (2007 Revision, ICC Publication No.600) has been incorporated into virtually all letters of credit used in international trade financing. They have been described by Professor Goode as "the most successful harmonising measure in the history of international commerce". The Rules in mirroring customary practice are however subject to the same considerations discussed above.

A question of some importance arose in the case of *Exxonmobil Sales and Supply v Texaco Ltd* [2003] EWHC (Comm) 1964. The parties' contract was for the sale of 15,000 tonnes of diesel CIF Cardiff. There was a clause in the contract which provided that the contract

"contains the entire agreement of the parties . . . and there is no other promise, representation, warranty, usage or course of dealing affecting it".

The defendant however wanted to rely on a custom or usage for the retention of samples of oil being tested. The claimants contended that the contract did not permit the admittance of such a term. The court agreed with the claimants stating the words are clear in the "entire agreement" clause that custom and usage would be excluded. The court, however, also went on to say that where it was necessary to imply a term into a contract on the grounds of business efficacy, it is conceivably arguable that such a term may not be excluded by an "entire agreement" clause because such a term could not be said to be found in the document or documents forming part of the contract. The same could not be said of an implied term by usage or custom. Although the reason for the distinction given by the court is principally one based on construction of the "entire agreement" clause, it should also be highlighted that it is contrary to the presumed intention of the parties to exclude all implied terms, especially those which are vital to the commercially sound functioning of the contract, without words to that effect. There thus appears to be a hierarchy of implied terms—those implied by law being at the pinnacle of importance, followed by those terms implied by fact, whilst those implied by custom or usage being the at the foot.

Municipal law

National legislation, both primary and secondary, and judicial activism go a long way in reflecting the concern of the government over the once popular laissez-faire basis in commercial transactions, including those with an international flavour. Legislative intervention, which is a more formal and direct mode of intrusion, can broadly be categorised into two types of regulation—economic and social. **1–025**

Regulation is the state's attempt at plugging the failings of the market. In social regulation, for example, two types of market failure are emphasised:

1. the failure of the market in providing sufficient or adequate information on the quality of the goods or services being offered, as a result of which the market fails to meet customers' preferences; and

2. the failure of the market to provide goods or services of an optimal standard.

The response from the state is based on the degree of intervention required to rectify these failures. Unfortunately, very often this is a decision made on very subjective and qualitative factors, leading to objections from the market. Social regulation is manifest in consumer protection legislation such as the Consumer Protection Act 1987, the Unfair Contract Terms Act 1977, the Sale of Goods Act 1979 and other similar instruments.

Economic regulation is born of a similar cause—the failure of the market affecting the economic interests of the state. It applies primarily to the regulation of monopolistic or oligopolistic firms in the market. The objective of economic regulation is to ensure that the market (monopolistic or oligopolistic) does not operate in such a way as to affect the greater good of the economy and the interests of the consumer. Competition law is set in place to counteract the destructive monopolistic tendencies of enterprises.

International and European law

International trade law cannot be emancipated from European or international law by virtue of the relationships it engenders and also the fact that English law is now irrevocably tied to EU law and various international provisions. **1–026**

European Union law

1–027 The European Union has its genesis in the Treaty of European Economic Community of 1957 (also known as the Treaty of Rome or the Treaty) which had as its main objective the creation of a common market. The original membership of six (Belgium, West Germany, the Netherlands, France, Italy and Luxembourg) has now grown to 27; given this large membership, it cannot be denied that this closer and larger economic and political union would have a tremendous impact on international trade, whether it be trade between the members of the Community or between Member States and non-Member States. The Community committed itself to achieving the free movement of people, goods, services and capital and to eradicating the barriers to the establishment of business.

The EU has seven major organs or "institutions"; they are the Council of the EU, the Commission, the European Council, the European Parliament, the Court of Justice of the EU, the European Central Bank and the Court of Auditors. The Council is the main law-making body in the EU, it has the duty of ensuring

"co-ordination of the general economic policies of the Member States, the power to take decisions, the liberty to approve proposed legislative acts and other ancillary powers and responsibilities".

According to art.17, TEU, the Commission shall ensure that the all legislative provisions are adhered to by the subjects of EU law in order to promote the general interest of the Union. It also has the power to make proposals for legislative measures as it sees fit. These proposals should then be vetted and approved by the Parliament and Council.

1–028 The European Parliament was established originally with the task of

"participating in the process leading up to the adoption of Community acts by requiring consultation and/or approval before the adoption of an act is finalised" (art.251 and 252, former TEC).

Its powers have since been expanded, especially with the advent of the "ordinary legislative procedure" which puts it on equal footing with the Council (art.289, TFEU).

The Court of Justice of the EU (CJEU) shall ensure that in the interpretation and application of the Treaties, the law is observed. This "law" refers to the law as provided for in the Community's primary (Treaty law) and secondary legislation (legislative acts made under art.288, TFEU, e.g. regulations, directives and decisions), and general principles common to the laws of the Member States (art.340, TFEU).

The Court of Auditors shall, as is expressed very briefly in the Treaty (art.285, TFEU), "carry out the audit" of the EU.

As far as English law is concerned, EU law is primary as a source of law. Section 2 of the European Communities Act 1972 provides that EU law shall have effect in this country as if it were made by the United Kingdom Parliament. This implies that EU law is supreme over national law; where there is a conflict between national and EU law, EU law must prevail and the national law in question shall be void to that extent (*R. v Secretary of State for Transport Ex p. Factortame Ltd (No.2)* [1991] 1 A.C. 603).

There are three types of EU legislation: regulations, directives and decisions. **1–029** A regulation is binding in its entirety, directly applicable to all Member States and is of general application. A directive on the other hand is binding on the Member States only as to the result to be achieved, and every Member State shall have the liberty to choose the form and methods to implement it. A decision is binding in its entirety upon those to whom it is addressed.

The supremacy of EU law is evident in the fact that although private individuals are not signatories to the Treaty, the Treaty allows them to claim and enforce any rights pertaining to them (*Van Gend en Loos v Nederlandse Administratie der Belastingen* (26/62) [1963] E.C.R. 1). The pervasiveness of EU law is further reflected in the principle of direct effect where directives which are not directly applicable in a Member State will have direct effect as long as the following conditions are met (*Van Duyn v Home Office* (41/74) [1974] E.C.R. 1337):

- the deadline for implementation of the Directive has lapsed;

- the provisions upon which the claimant seeks to rely are clear, unambiguous and certain; and

- the claimant has complied with all the requirements or conditions set out in the Directive.

The European Court of Justice in *Francovich v Italian State* (6/90 and 9/90) [1993] 2 C.M.L.R. 66 has now made it possible for an individual to sue a Member State for a loss suffered as a result of the Member State failing to implement a directive.

In international trade law the pervasiveness of European law is felt not only in areas of jurisdiction and conflict of laws, but in consumer protection, insurance, banking and credit arrangements, competition law, customs and excise regulations, etc. It would be impossible to enumerate an exhaustive list of the areas affected by EU law in international trade. However, throughout the book, it will be pellucid how extensive the influence of EU law is on the subject matter, but, unfortunately, not always for the better.

International law

In international trade, there have been many attempts at harmonising trade law **1–030** and practice either by treaty or model codes. The former is only applicable as law in this country if it has been formally incorporated into national law by legislation.

Model codes on the other hand are not binding until they have been brought into the contract as an express or implied term. They are merely the codification of current trade practice and usage.[12] Some examples of model codes are the INCOTERMS (2010 Revision), the UCP Rules on Documentary Credit (2007 Revision, Publication No.600) and the Uniform Rules for Demand Guarantees (1992) introduced under the auspices of the International Chamber of Commerce (ICC).

---

[12] For a detailed account of the genesis of such international efforts, see Schmitthoff, "The Unification of the Law of International Trade" (1968) J.B.L. 105.

Harmonisation of Commercial Law

1–031   International and European manoeuvres have tended to favour the harmonisation
of rules and regulations in international trade and finance to ensure that certainty
in legal application and efficiency in international trade relations are optimally
maintained. Despite these so-called obvious advantages, traders and lawyers are
slow to support the process of harmonisation.

The proponents of harmonisation are frequently enamoured by the idealism
that uniformity of principle would result in the diminishing of barriers to trade
because the market will be a level playing field because traders would be rid of
the complexities of different legal regimes. International traders, however, often
want to "legislate" their own rights and obligations; and indeed, many prefer to
use standards from contracts drawn up by their own trade association, etc.
Although there is some weight in the argument that the harmonisation process,
say of international sales law such as the Vienna Convention on Contracts for the
International Sale of Goods (CISG) 1980 does not remove the right of the trading
parties to make their own contracts, it is needful to bear in mind that commercial
law is not merely about the application of principles (or theories), but the
interpretation of contracts using methods entrenched in a state's own domestic
legal culture. It is the latter which is difficult to harmonise as it entails language,
cultural, socio-economic, regional and political factors which are sui generis to
that country. Additionally, some states already have such an established and
sophisticated system of international commercial law (such as the United
Kingdom) that to introduce something alien to the system would simply serve to
cause uncertainty for international traders who have long relied on the system.

Harmonisation generally entails the adoption of similar rules—however, no
legal rule can be so pellucid that it is not subject to different and, indeed,
conflicting interpretations. Different countries will apply the "harmonised" rules
differently and this thus defeats the intended object of some proponents of
harmonisation to reduce the problems caused by the conflict of laws. The CISG
is a good example of such conflict; although a number of countries have adopted
the convention, they have quite different approaches to its interpretation.
Common law jurisdictions, for instance, tend to take a more discursive approach
to its construction and application, giving lengthy reasons for the judgment,
whilst civil law jurisdictions prefer a more succinct and pithy approach to its
application. That said, some international conventions do exhort contracting
states to adopt an international approach[13] and indeed, the English courts have
been very astute in taking account of foreign jurisprudence on the application of
international transport conventions.[14]

1–032   Harmonisation has also been objected to on the ground that it is a very costly
exercise requiring lengthy negotiations between state representatives. Also, the
risk of failure or collapse is not negligible, with negotiating states having their
own agenda. Thus, given that international traders seem content to work out their
own contractual rights and obligations in reliance on a chosen domestic law and
trade practice and custom, the benefits harmonisation promises seem too modest
for some states to invest in it.

---

[13] See, for example, the Convention on the Law Applicable to Contracts for the International Sale
of Goods, The Hague, 1985.
[14] *Quantum Corp Inc v Plane Trucking Ltd* [2002] EWCA Civ 350; see below para.9–024.

In addition, many attempts at harmonising certain aspects of international trade have resulted in poor coverage of the issues, partly because other areas remain unregulated or are regulated in a tenor quite contrary to the international measure.[15] The CISG, for instance, leaves out issues of contractual validity, formality and property rights to national rules resulting in a diluted form of harmonisation. Furthermore, the spirit of its provisions on formation and implied duties could very well conflict with the spirit and method of the remnant of national law on those omitted issues; thus, a national court in attempting to apply the convention provisions faces the problem of applying those provisions without infringing the sensibility of their own existing laws.

Nonetheless, harmonisation proponents have never been so active. International intergovernmental organisations such as UNIDROIT and UNCITRAL have been proposing new harmonised rules on a host of activities, ranging from banking to the carriage of goods. These measures are intended to be adopted and ratified by Member States as law. Legal harmonisation endeavours are perhaps less popular than non-legal Model Contracts, or Standard Terms. Non-governmental trade organisations such as the ICC for example have been in the forefront of promoting their Model Contracts for adoption by traders with or without variation. Fields of activity that these organisations have ventured into include bills of exchange, documentary credits, performance guarantees, insurance, etc. States are more receptive to these measures because there is no resulting "loss" of sovereignty in that the laws of the state on civil and contractual relations are not derogated from. The state's courts retain judicial control in the interpretation, application and enforcement of these Model Contracts.

The Structure and Characteristics of International Trade

The law of comparative advantage

The acquisition and exchange of goods across national boundaries have taken **1–033** place since time immemorial. Besides the need to import goods which cannot be obtained or manufactured locally, the economic rationale for importing goods from abroad can be explained by the law of comparative costs. This theory states that some goods cannot be produced locally in sufficient quantities to meet demand as a result of the lack of certain production factors. For example, a country may lack the distinct technology required for the production of the goods, or it could be because the climate is not suitable. Hence, according to this line of economic thought, a country should concentrate on those products which it can produce at a maximum cost advantage in contrast to other countries. While there are exceptions to this theory, it has frequently been used to explain the need for international trading.

The chief benefit from international trade, as clearly emphasised by the theory, is the fact that consumers in a domestic market will have wider access to a variety of goods at a competitive price. Not only are consumers the beneficiaries, but producers or entrepreneurs are able to buy production ingredients from outside their own countries to better their products and thus become more competitive, and to sell to a bigger market.

---

[15] Munday, "The Uniform Interpretation of International Conventions" [1978] I.C.L.Q. 450.

The elaborate outworking of the theory can be explained in a simple example. For instance, the UK could produce X amount of beer with the labour of 1000 workers and Y amount of washing-up liquid with 1500 workers. Germany on the other hand needs only 900 workers to produce X amount of beer and 800 workers to produce Y amount of washing-up liquid. In this respect, Germany has an "absolute advantage" over the UK in the production of these items since it is able to produce the same quantity with a lower labour input. However, trade was still advantageous to both states, in that when the UK exported to Germany the beer produced by the labour force of 1000 in exchange for washing-up liquid produced by 800 German workers, the UK has imported washing-up liquid which would have required 1500 workers to produce. Germany on the other hand would have gained by her 800 workforce beer which would have taken 900 of her labourers to produce had it not been for international trade. (This is assuming that both countries have full employment.)

1–034   This theory makes the implicit assumption that the parties in a trading relationship are countries. This is rarely the case. Trade is most usually conducted between private individuals or legal entities situated in different countries. Hence, taken in its most basic form, this theory tells us that international trade broadens the business opportunities for private traders in any one country and through their exchanges of services and goods, there are economic gains for the nations as a whole.

How international trade is structured

1–035   The structure of international trade refers to the mechanisms in place for trading to take place. It should not be confused with the channels for the distribution of goods. The latter refers to the way goods traded are transported and carried to their destinations. The structure is more than mere direct exporting although this is and has been one of the most popular and important forms of trading. It comprises countertrade, commodity trading, multinational operations, subsidiaries and joint ventures.

Direct exporting

1–036   Direct exporting is the transfer of the property in the goods to the buyer by shipping the goods to him or his agent, payment being made to the seller either directly or through a bank payment system. Very often the transfer of property in the goods takes place through the assignment or transfer of the document of title relating to the goods to the buyer or his agent in place of the actual delivery of the goods themselves.

Counter-trade

1–037   Counter-trade is ideal for countries which do not have easy access to liquidity or foreign currency to play an active role in international trade.[16] Counter-trade may take any of the following forms below.

---

[16] See Sumer & Chuah, "Emerging legal challenges for countertrade techniques in international trade" (2007) Int.T.L.R. 111.

(i) Barter.

(ii) Counter-purchase.

(iii) Offset.

(iv) Buy-back.

(v) Switch trading.

(vi) Evidence accounts.

Counter-trade has the appeal of being convenient to the extent that no payment of money mechanism needs to be set up. The trader also finds appeal in the flexibility in these transactions.

The risks involved in counter-trade include the likelihood that the value of the goods counter-traded is not comparable to those exported and the gap of time between export and purchase. This gap is usually bridged by the provision of credit; this is not conventional prudence though as the risk is substantial.

(i) Barter   Barter trade is characterised by the exchange of goods for goods.   **1–038**
There is in theory no money settlement or consideration involved. The transaction is contained in a single contract, there is no distinct sale agreement as against a purchase agreement.

(ii) Counter-purchase   There are, in a counter-purchase arrangement, two   **1–039**
distinct contracts as against barter trade. The first contract details all the incidences of export sale, for example, time of delivery, any credit period and mode of delivery. The second provides for the purchase or the intention to purchase by the exporter of agreed goods or services from the buyer's country. This may be for a value equal to or greater than that in the first contract. The commitment to counter-purchase is the pre-requisite or pre-condition to the original export order.

(iii) Offset   Offset enables the importer to commit the exporter to using local   **1–040**
production forces or factors when the former "buys" large, costly plants, factories, systems or other similar goods. In the public sector, the purchase of such items can attract much publicity as to the ill effects it will have on the community—for example, the loss of jobs, the purchase of expensive technology from abroad, etc. To mitigate against these probable criticisms, the government buyer may insist that the seller buy locally made components in the project and/ or provide technological know-how through co-operative ventures. This should offset the cost of import and the travails of unemployment.

(iv) Buy-back   This refers to the undertaking made by the exporter to accept   **1–041**
as payment, either in part or in entirety, the goods produced by the plant or factory (the plant having been purchased by the importer, usually the government of a lesser developed country) and bought back from the importing country. If the cost of production is very much lower than that in the exporting country, the exporter by buying the goods back on such an arrangement stands to gain financially. The major risk is that the time involved in the building of the factory or plant may be longer than expected. Where this is the case, production cannot commence and neither can "repayment". Hence, to the exporter of the plant, the

sale is on very extended credit terms making the entire transaction quite hazardous. The buy-back mode was extremely popular in the former Soviet Union, although direct exporting and other forms have taken on greater importance since her dismantling.

1–042   **(v) Switch trading**   In conventional trading, exports are paid for out of the foreign exchange earned by the importing country on a multinational trading basis. Some state trading nations have in the past found it more convenient and strategically sound to enter into bilateral agreements whereby goods exported to the corresponding country will be paid for from the proceeds of the sale of goods from that country. For example, the sale of goods from Uzbekistan to Pakistan will be paid for out of the proceeds of goods sold to Uzbekistan from Pakistan.

This ensures that the balance of trade between the two countries remains stable throughout. However, it is quite foreseeable that the balance can be undulated as a result of unforeseen demand or supply patterns within either country. It is also anticipated that some third countries trading with the two states concerned will participate in the agreement. The funds are then "switched" between the countries.

1–043   **(vi) Evidence accounts**   Where switch trading is popular in state trading nations, evidence accounts, which works on a similar basis, is used by some exporters in capitalist economies. The exporter undertakes to purchase goods from the importing state at an agreed quantity or rate, in consideration of the importing state reducing or removing certain trade restraints. This arrangement obliges the exporter to maintain an evidence account through which all exports and imports of a specified period will be passed. It is anticipated that the flow of imports and exports over this specified period will achieve a balance or level condign to the purposes of both parties.

CHAPTER 2

INTERNATIONAL SALE OF GOODS

It goes without saying that the centrepiece of international trade is the sale of **2–001** goods contract. This contract between the buyer and seller is mostly likely to have been made on their behalf by agents. For example, the buyer might have sought the services of a confirming house to obtain the undertaking from the seller. Similarly, the seller might rely on his commercial agent to market the goods to the buyer. Be that as it may, the relationship in question is one between the seller and buyer, generally. However what makes the sale an international rather than domestic sale?

By and large a sale might be said to be possessed of an international character where:

1. the transaction involves the carriage of the goods from one country to another; or

2. the transaction is entered into between parties who are situated in different countries, the place where the goods are situated and where they are to be delivered is immaterial.

The first type however might nevertheless not attract the application of any private international law rules because if the buyer and seller are both situated in the same country, say England, it is very likely that the applicable law to the contract will be English law, and the place where any legal dispute is brought will be England. The second appears to be the definition applied by the Vienna Convention on Contracts for the International Sale of Goods 1980 (CISG). Article 1 states that the Convention will apply to contracts of sale between parties whose places of business are in different states. For example, if S is situated in France and B is in England but the contract calls for the delivery of goods from London to Liverpool, this might well constitute a sale to which the Convention would apply. It should however be stressed that the Convention does not actually define international sale—all it does is to specify what type of international sale of goods contracts would fall within its governance. It should also be stated that the United Kingdom has not implemented the Convention.

2–002   One important aspect of the characterisation of a contract as an international sale of goods contract lies in the fact that under the Unfair Contract Terms Act 1977 (UCTA) certain contracts are excluded from its application. The Act's provisions on reasonableness of a pre-imposed term will not apply to international supply of goods contracts. This is a critical provision because the 1977 Act contains some very potent rules on nullifying the effect of an "unreasonable" or "unfair" term. Such terms in an international supply contract would not be struck down by the Act. An international supply contract must meet the following requirements (s.26(3)):

- it is a contract where possession or ownership of goods passes; and
- it is made by parties with their places of business in territories of different states.

In addition, *one* of the following conditions should be satisfied (s.26(4)):

- the goods are, at the time of the contract, in the course of carriage or will be carried from one state to another; or
- the offer and acceptance have been done in the territories of different states,
- the contract provides for the delivery to a state other than that within whose territory the offer and acceptance were done.

2–003   *Air Transworld Limited v Bombardier Inc* [2012] EWHC 243 (Comm)
Facts:
Bombardier, a Canadian company, sold an aircraft to Angoil, an Angolan company controlled by M. A representative of M signed the purchase agreement and faxed it to Bombardier in Canada. The next day, Bombardier signed the agreement and sent it back to M's representative.
    Some 14 months after delivery, the aircraft developed a serious fault with the main engine driven pump. The contract contained a limitation of liability clause which Bombardier wanted to rely on. If the contract was an international supply contract within the terms of s.26 of the UCTA, the clause would not be subject to the reasonableness test of the UCTA 1977. Naturally Bombardier wanted to persuade the court that the contract was indeed an international supply contract.
Held:
The relevant starting point had to be the second condition where offer and acceptance were "done" in different territories. A distinction has to be made between the place where the offer/acceptance is made and the place where it is communicated—which, under common law rules, happens in the place of receipt where there is instantaneous communication.
    When M faxed the contract to Canada, he was making an offer in the UK, but communicated to Canada. When Bombardier signed and returned the contract, the acceptance was made in Canada, but communicated in the UK.
2–004   The judge considered that "the acts constituting the offer and acceptance" took place in different countries, whether one looked at the making of the offer/acceptance or the place of communication. In the judge's view, "the act constituting the offer and acceptance" referred to the totality of acts which constituted the offer and acceptance, including both the making and receiving of each. What was at issue was the "international" nature of the contract. What that condition (s.26(4)(b)) was intended to exclude, as an international supply contract, were cases where there was an international element in the formation of the contract, so that all elements of the offer and acceptance had to occur in the same state if the provisions of the UCTA were to apply.

Thus, if any of the elements including the making of the offer, making the acceptance, communication of the offer, or communication of the acceptance happened in different Member States, then the contract was capable of being an international supply contract under this condition.

As to the condition that the goods had been carried from one state to another, case law showed that the requirements of this condition (s.26(4)(a)) would be satisfied even though there was no express obligation to deliver the goods to another state. There simply had to be an intention on the part of the parties that the goods will be used in another country.[1] The contract here contemplated delivery in Canada, and even if the agreement did not expressly so provide, the intention of the purchaser was to use the aircraft elsewhere, probably in Africa.

Lastly, as to the requirement that the offer and acceptance were made in one state whilst delivery was made to another, the court held that as the section requires delivery "to" the territory of another state, not delivery "in" another state, this subsection would not apply if offer and acceptance had been in the UK, with delivery to be in Canada where the aircraft was manufactured.

It appears from this case that as long as the parties are from different states, if **2–005** any part of the contract process happens in different countries, the contract is likely to be an international supply contract.

Section 26(4) is problematic and cannot be said to have been properly thought through, despite the laudable intentions of the legislators. Indeed, as Mance L.J. said in *Amiri v BAE Systems* [2004] 1 All E.R. 385, "[s.26(4) is] open to the comment that it has not been fully worked out". This is because the common or classical forms of international trading such as CIF, FOB, FAS, etc which should be excluded from the Act, might fall foul of the wording in s.26(4). After all, s.26(4)(a) requires the court to determine whether, at the moment of contract, the goods supplied under it were still in the course of carriage from the territory of one state to the territory of another. Take the case where there is a *string* of CIF sales (namely that a sale is made on the basis of the bill of lading and other documents)[2] and the last sale is made when the vessel is within the territory of the state where the cargo is to be discharged. On one view the goods are not then in the course of carriage from one state to another. Such a view is surely inappropriate.

A better view is that the goods can be said to be in the course of carriage from one state to another (just as a passenger may be said to be in the course of carriage from London to Paris when the Eurostar stops and even is delayed for several hours at Lille). In *Balmoral Group Ltd v Borealis (UK) Ltd* [2006] EWHC 1900 (Comm) (see also *Kingspan Environmental Ltd v Borealis A/S* [2012] EWHC 1147 (Comm)), the invoices had described Great Britain as the "place of despatch", the goods had originally been carried from Norway to Great Britain. The warehouses where the goods were kept when they arrived in Great Britain before further despatch were no more than transhipment centres. The contracts were, therefore, international supply of goods contracts.

Without the application of the UCTA, the legal response to the use of terms **2–006** which are said to be unfair depends on whether the term in question has in fact been *properly* incorporated into the contract and the clarity with which the term has been set out. The more unusual a term is, the higher is the threshold for

---

[1] See *Trident Turboprop (Dublin) Ltd v First Flight Couriers Ltd* [2010] Q.B. 86 and *Amiri v BAE* [2003] 2 Lloyd's Rep. 767.
[2] See below, paras 2–064—2–096.

incorporation (*Thornton v Shoe Lane Parking* [1971] 1 All E.R. 686; *A Schroeder Music Publishing v Macaulay* [1974] 1 W.L.R. 1308). On the issue of interpretation, the House of Lords held in *Photo Productions Ltd v Securicor Transport Ltd* [1980] A.C. 827 that the term should be given a strict and narrow reading, but if the term is sufficiently clear, it would be enforced. Recourse could not be had to the reasonableness of the term in question. However, where an ambiguity exists, the court would insist on a *contra proferentem* interpretation.

Freedom of contract or party autonomy is deemed by the law to be exceedingly important in international commercial contracts. That freedom must necessarily include the independence to negotiate.

Negotiating the Contract[3]

2–007   It is probably universally accepted that clear and effective communication between buyer and seller is the cornerstone of a successful contract of sale. The intentions of the parties should be unequivocal and clear to each other. This is to ensure that the emerging contract accurately reflects the parties' bargain despite the fact that the law is concerned with the presumed intent, rather than the parties' subjective intent. This should warn traders to be careful when relying on previous conduct and other tacit promises. An express provision would save much time and costs later. The now-defunct Simpler Trade Procedures Board (SITPRO) and other trade facilitation organisations have introduced certain pro-forma documents (including a pro-forma invoice, bill of lading, export order form, etc) to remind traders of the essentials of the contract of sale.

An effectual communication should contain the following information in order to avoid confusion or incompleteness:

1. terms of sale or trade, including any special conditions of sale;

2. terms of payment;

3. country of origin of the goods;

4. name, address of seller's bank and account number, sort code, etc;

5. whether insurance is arranged or not arranged, and what kind of insurance;

6. methods of shipment (i.e. sea/air/road/rail/post) to named port or place of destination as reflected in the terms of sale;

7. product or goods description, including any technical literature;

8. quantity, pack size, part or code number;

9. price and currency of sale; and

10. special stowage requirements, e.g. temperature control during and after transit, dangerous goods information, possible hazards as may be caused by the goods.

---

[3] See generally, N. Horn, *Adaptation and Renegotiation of Contracts in International Trade and Finance* (London: Kluwer, Deventer, 1985).

It is also important not to forget issues of foreign law and requirements—it can be all too easy to concentrate entirely on the legal and commercial requirements in the country of export and fail to look at such requirements in the country of import. For example, it is vital to ensure that the importer has the legal capacity to import under the laws of his home country. In *Continental Enterprises Ltd v Shandong Zhucheng Foreign Trade Group Co* [2005] EWHC 92, the Commercial Court held that a contract for the import of soy bean into China which was entered into by an importer who did not have an import licence or the power under its articles of association to apply for an import licence was void for want of capacity. Although the decision was controversial as a matter of law with regard to whether or not failure to obtain an import licence under Chinese law constitutes lack of legal capacity, it serves as a reminder that the exporter should take care in such matters.

In general, the astute lawyer organising the international business negotiation should ensure that the procedure adopted should: **2–008**

1. allow room to work out problems, especially, those of a technical nature;

2. provide opportunities to clarify issues;

3. create future business opportunities if the negotiation in question falls through;

4. not engender intimidation and confrontation—courtesy should be maintained at all times;

5. be free from interruptions;

6. set clear objectives for what should be achieved;

7. adhere to the agenda although ensuring that there is some flexibility for compromise; and

8. observe cultural differences.[4]

Cultural and language differences between the negotiating opposites can be stumbling blocks for a successful relationship. The parties should therefore make advance inquiries as to the cultural values and distinctiveness of the other. Parties should recognise that delays may not always mean "no": they might mean "maybe, but ... " or "not today because it's not an auspicious day" or something else. As far as language is concerned, avoid jargon, slang and figurative language. For example, the English penchant for using terms such as "level playing field" or "grasp the nettle", etc, are frequently misunderstood and such figures of speech are not always sympathetically appreciated. What is

---

[4] For more on cultural factors and negotiation, see Brett, "Culture and Negotiation" (2000) 35(2) International Journal of Psychology 97. The author finds: "Cultural values and norms also may affect negotiators' strategic negotiation processes. For example, negotiators from cultures where direct, explicit communications are preferred may share information by stating and reciprocating preferences and priorities, by commenting on similarities and differences, and by giving direct feedback. Negotiators from cultures where the norm is to communicate indirectly and infer meaning may share information by making multi-issue proposals and inferring priorities from subtle changes in proposals. In our research contrasting US and Japanese negotiators, we found that the Japanese were using a relatively large number of proposals, compared to the US negotiators, and the US negotiators were using a whole array of direct communications relatively more frequently than the Japanese."

important is the use of simple, nonfigurative and declarative sentences, possibly bolstered by the use of charts, diagrams and statistics.

Flexibility is important to the parties; so it is not unusual for the parties to agree to negotiate changes to the deal or a new bargain in the event of intervening developments (such a change in the market or logistics). The promise is sometimes expressed as an agreement to negotiate in good faith.[5] However, the English law position is that such agreements cannot be enforced because they lack certainty (*Walford v Miles* [1992] 2 A.C. 128). However, an agreement to negotiate may be enforceable if the parties have set out objective criteria (*Petromec v Petroleo* [2006] 1 Lloyd's Rep. 121), or machinery for resolving any disagreement (*Barbudev v Eurocom Cable Management Bulgaria* [2011] EWHC 1560 (Comm)). It might, however, be said that in reality is the court completing the parties' agreement by reference to the objective criteria or the machinery rather than by enforcing the agreement to negotiate.

Role of Agents in International Sales

Agents important in international sales include:

Factors

2–009   A factor is a person in possession of goods belonging to his principal to be sold for the benefit of the latter. It is customary for factors to sell those goods in his own name without disclosing the identity of the principal. It was however held in *Stevens v Biller* (1883) 25 Ch.D. 31 that where he does disclose the identity of his principal by selling in the latter's name, that fact alone does not mean that he would cease to be a factor. Under the Factors Act 1889, a factor who in the customary course of his business has authority to sell goods, or to consign goods for sale, or to buy goods or to raise money on the security of goods, is termed a mercantile agent. The Act warrants that where a mercantile agent, with the consent of the principal is in possession of goods or documents of title to the goods, any sale or other disposition transacted by him in the ordinary course of business in respect of these goods is as valid as if it were expressly authorised by the principal, provided the third party did not know of the agent's lack of authority (ss.2(1), 9).

In *Lloyd's Bank v Bank of America National Trust and Savings Association* [1937] 2 K.B. 631, the buyers had been given an advance for the purchase of certain goods on the security of the bills of lading relating to the goods. The bills were subsequently returned to the buyers to enable them to sell the goods on. The buyers gave an undertaking to the bank that they were to hold the bills of lading in trust for the bank. The buyers then pledged the bills in breach of their undertaking to the Bank of America. The court held that the buyers had received the documents of title as mercantile agents of Lloyd's Bank and as such the pledging of the documents with the Bank of America was binding on their principal, Lloyd's Bank.

---

[5] As to whether there is a general duty of good faith in English law, see below, para.2–058.

Brokers

A broker negotiates on behalf buyers and sellers. He is, however, not in **2–010** possession of the goods. His business is to introduce customers to sellers, and vice versa. He manages the signing of the contract between the two parties but does not actually sell or buy in his own name.

Commission agents

A commission agent or merchant enters into contracts with third parties in his **2–011** own name, although he does so as an agent. He therefore is privy to the contract with the third party and as far as the third party is concerned, recourse may be had to the commission agent. Professor Schmitthoff warns against confusing the commission agent with the civil law term "commissionaires":

> "A commissionaire is a person who internally, *i.e.* in his relationship to his principal, is an agent but externally, *i.e.*, in his relationship to the third party, is a seller or buyer in his own name. Where a commissionaire has acted for the principal, no privity of contract can be constituted between the principal and the third party. As an agent, the commissionaire is accountable to his principal for the profit from the transaction, must use reasonable diligence in the performance of his duties, and must not make an undisclosed profit or take a bribe. The principal, on the other hand, cannot claim the price from the third-party directly nor is he liable in contract for any defects of the goods . . . [A] distinction is drawn between direct and indirect agency. A direct agent is an agent who discloses his agency quality to the third party, an indirect agent is a person who, though being an agent, treats with the third party in his own name. The commissionaire is an indirect agent".[6]

In English law, the commission agent is different from the commissionaire in that he remains an agent. There is in effect only one contract—that between his principal and the third party. The commissionaire arrangement involves two separate and distinct relationships—the contract of sale between the commissionaire and the third party, and the agency contract between the principal and the commissionaire.

Confirming houses

A confirming house takes on the role of an agent for an overseas buyer who is **2–012** interested in buying goods from a seller in the country. While in a sense the confirming house might be perceived as a buying agent, this is not altogether a correct observation. This is because instead of simply adopting the task of buying goods on behalf of the overseas buyer, the confirming house can in fact buy in its own name as a principal and then resell the goods to the buyer.

Frequently the confirming house takes on greater responsibility than that of a mere buying agent; in *Sobell Industries Ltd v Cory Bros & Co* [1955] 2 Lloyd's Rep. 82 for example, the confirming house had acted not only as an agent for the overseas buyer, but as guarantor of the buyer's bona fides and solvency in the

---

[6] C. Schmitthoff, *Export Trade*, 11th edn (London: Sweet & Maxwell, 2007), para.27–015.

sale transaction. This act of confirming the sale is the main appeal of a confirming house as an agent.

Del credere agent

2-013   The *del credere* agent takes on additional risks, like the confirming house. He is prepared, upon the payment of a satisfactory commission, to indemnify the principal if the transaction falls through and the principal suffers loss as a result. The terms of the *del credere* agency are such that the agent only agrees to indemnify the principal in the event of the buyer not taking delivery of the goods or becoming insolvent and unable to settle the purchase price. The *del credere* remains an agent throughout; he is therefore not to be held liable for non-performance of the contract by his principal (*Churchill & Sim v Goddard* [1937] 1 K.B. 92).

There are no formal requirements to the formation or creation of a *del credere* agency. Its existence can be implied from the parties' conduct as is demonstrated in *Shaw v Woodcock* (1827) 7 B&C 73. The *del credere* agency's primary appeal is the comfort for principals that the transaction will be performed. That attraction of the *del credere* agency is now suitably substituted by modern mechanisms including the documentary credit system and the performance bond.

Commercial agents

2-014   Commercial agents are a relatively new legal phenomenon in England and Wales. Until the Commercial Agents Regulations 1993 (which were required to be introduced by EU Directive 86/653, the so-called self-employed commercial agents directive), English law did not treat commercial agents (as defined by the EU Directive) as anything other than ordinary agents whose rights and obligations are entirely governed by the agency contract. Following the Directive (and the making of the 1993 Regulations), there is a legal definition for commercial agents and certain statutory rights and obligations which may not be derogated from have been introduced.

A commercial agent is defined by the 1993 Regulations as a self-employed individual, partnership or company who has continuing authority to negotiate the sale or purchase of goods on behalf of the principal. A commercial agent does not need to be authorised to conclude sales on behalf of their principal and it is usually sufficient that they are authorised to introduce customers to the business. A party that buys products from a business and then resells them would not generally be a commercial agency. Also, agents who sell services rather than goods, or are just instructed to conclude a single transaction, are not subject to the 1993 Regulations.

Where the principal terminates the contract, the agent is entitled to receive his commission/remuneration for the remainder of the contract until the date of termination and also to be paid "compensation" (or "an indemnity" if the contract so provides). This is to recognise the goodwill and business that the agent has built up for the principal. In *Lonsdale v Howard & Hallam* [2007] UKHL 32, Lord Hoffmann (with whom the other Law Lords agreed) said that the agent is entitled to be compensated for the deprivation of his right to future commissions. Like any other exercise in valuation, much depends on the value of the agent's business (which is being terminated) at the time the agency agreement was terminated. The likely future performance of the agent's business will also be factored into the valuation—so if the business is likely to decline anyway, that will mean a reduction in the compensation award. However, the fact that the agent may have found additional work is not relevant. The agent may also be entitled to recover any expenses incurred as a result of following the principal's advice.

An indemnity is payable in place of compensation where this is provided for **2–015** in the contract; under the 1993 Regulations, a commercial agent is entitled to an indemnity if and to the extent that he fulfils two tests. First, the agent must have introduced to the principal new customers or significant new business with existing customers and the principal must continue to benefit from this business. Secondly, the payment of an indemnity must be equitable having regard to all of the circumstances (which includes any commission lost by the agent on such business). The agent's indemnity entitlement is capped at one year's average commission, calculated by reference to the preceding five years.

The agent must give the principal notice of his intention to claim compensation/an indemnity within one year of termination or he will lose this entitlement. If the principal terminates the agency agreement because the agent has committed a serious breach of contract, the principal may be able to avoid paying the compensation/indemnity.

However, if the agent terminates the agency agreement he has no right to compensation or an indemnity, unless:

(a) he is terminating the agency because of age, infirmity or ill-health;

(b) the agency comes to the end of its fixed term; or

(c) the agent terminates because the principal has committed a serious breach of contract.

The compensation or indemnity includes the amount of commission the agent has lost.

Processing the Export Order

Once the offer to sell overseas has been accepted, the trader will put his **2–016** management plan into action. A management plan ensures that the order is properly processed, i.e. the manufacture or acquisition of the goods according to contract description, quality control, packing for export, pre-shipment inspection, shipping, complete and accurate documentation, export invoicing, banking facilities, and insurance if required are vital elements of the process. A good management plan would also ensure that payment for the goods is made promptly and that legal action is taken when problems arise.

Trade Terms

There are a number of special trade terms, such as INCOTERMS 2010, that **2–017** traders can apply to their contract of sale. These terms have been laid down by the relevant trade association, such as the International Chamber of Commerce (or ICC, which sponsors the INCOTERMS). Traders, simply by referring to them, could legitimately be deemed to have adopted the full range of duties and rights these "trade terms" imply. For example, a trader may describe quite simply in his contract that delivery is, say, "DDP Singapore (INCOTERMS 2010)" without needing to set out in full the duties and rights of both parties because the full range of duties and rights attendant to this special term " DDP" would have been conveniently set out in INCOTERMS 2010. Thus, as far as the courts are concerned, this description will be taken to mean that the traders have agreed to be governed by the published terms, INCOTERMS 2010, applicable to DDP contracts. Any variation of the duties or rights adumbrated in INCO-TERMS 2010 must be clear and precise. Otherwise, the presumption will be that no variation was intended. In some countries, such pre-designated trade terms (such as INCOTERMS 2010) form part of their national law and cannot thus be departed from. In the United Kingdom however, these are but pure contractual terms which may be varied subject to evidence of the parties' intention to do so.

INCOTERMS or similar special trade terms not only make clear to the parties where delivery of the goods is to take place but are also important in aiding the calculation of the purchase price. For example, where the contract calls for "Delivery CIF Singapore", the seller's invoice would account for all incidental charges incurred up until the delivery of the goods at Singapore, including premium for the insurance and freight charges.

INCOTERMS were first published in 1936 under the auspices of the ICC.[7] The newest set, INCOTERMS 2010, were published on January 1, 2011. For contracts entered into pre-September 2010, INCOTERMS 2000 will continue to apply even if performance of the contracts was made in 2011. For contracts entered into between September 16, 2010 and December 31, 2011, the parties should specify which set of INCOTERMS is to apply. From January 1, 2011 the presumption is that any reference to INCOTERMS in the contract is a reference to INCOTERMS 2010.

They might be contrasted against trade terms established by common law and trade practice.

---

[7] For a general analysis, see J. Ramberg, *Guide to INCOTERMS 2010* (Paris: ICC, 2011); Oduntan, "'C.I.F. Gatwick' and other such nonsense upon stilts: INCOTERMS and the Law, Jargon and Practice of International Business Transactions" (2010) I.C.C.L.R. 6.

TRADITIONAL TERMS

2–018

Examples of some common terms	Duties
Ex Works	Buyer or agent has to collect goods from seller's factory or warehouse.
FAS Port of Shipment (FREE ALONGSIDE)	Seller is responsible for delivering the goods to alongside the ship so that they can be loaded by the buyer or his agents.
FOB Port of Shipment (FREE ON BOARD)	Seller is responsible for placing goods on board ship and paying all charges up to the point the goods are loaded over the rails of the ship.
FOB Airport	Seller is responsible for delivering goods into the charge of the air carrier or his agent or any other person named by the buyer.
CIF Port of Discharge (COST, INSURANCE & FREIGHT)	Seller is to arrange and pay for contracts of freight and insurance for the goods. He should produce an invoice for the agreed sales price, an insurance policy and a clean bill of lading.
C&F Port of Discharge (COST & FREIGHT)	Seller is to arrange and pay for the carriage of the goods to the destination port. He should also provide an effective notice of shipment to the buyer to enable him to arrange appropriate insurance for the goods. The seller is also responsible for the issue of a sales invoice and a clean bill of lading.
Delivered Free, or Free Delivery, or Franco Domicile	Seller is responsible for all charges up to the delivery of the goods at the buyer's address. This will include import duties unless specifically excluded by contract.
Ex Ship/Arrival	Seller to deliver goods to buyer from a ship that has arrived at the port of delivery.

Examples of some common terms	Duties
Ex Quay/Port of discharge	Seller to deliver goods to buyer from a ship that has arrived at the agreed port, and additionally to pay import duties and unloading charges payable at the port.

INCOTERMS 2010

2–019　The pre-defined trade terms in the INCOTERMS 2010 are grouped into two categories depending on the mode of transport being used. The first group applies to sale of goods to be carried by any mode of transport. The second applies only to goods carried by sea or inland waterway.

2–020

Any mode of transport	EXW—Ex Works (named place of delivery). The buyer is to take delivery of the goods at the seller's premises. The seller must ensure that the goods are made available at his premises (shop, factory, warehouse, etc) for collection at the agreed time. The term is usually used when making an initial quotation for the sale of goods without any costs included. The buyer pays all carriage costs; he is responsible for carrying the goods to the final place of discharge and as such, the risks of the voyage are borne by him. The contract may, however, make the seller responsible for loading the goods, but this must be made explicit.
	FCA—Free Carrier (named place of delivery). The seller undertakes to ensure that the goods are cleared for export and delivered to the first carrier chosen by the buyer. The seller is responsible for the cost of carriage to that named point of delivery. As soon as the goods are handed over to the first carrier, the risk will also pass to the buyer.
	CPT—Carriage Paid To (named place of destination). The seller is responsible for the cost of carriage. Risk transfers to the buyer upon handing goods over to the first carrier at the place of import/destination.
	CIP—Carriage and Insurance Paid to (named place of destination). The seller will be responsible for carriage and insurance[8] to the named destination point, but risk

---

[8] In *Geofizika v MMB International* [2010] EWCA Civ 459, the seller was held to have failed to obtain a conforming insurance cover for the buyer under the CIP contract. However, they were not liable to compensate the buyer for the loss in question because even if they had obtained the ICC(C) policy, the buyer's loss would not have been covered. That was because the goods had been carried below deck and it was a warranty of the insurance that goods carried below deck were not covered.

passes when the goods are handed over to the first carrier.

DAT—Delivered at Terminal (named terminal at place of destination). The seller will cover the cost of carriage to the terminal. However, the buyer will take on the costs related to import clearance. The risk up to the point that the goods are unloaded at the terminal will remain with the seller. This new term replaces the old INCOTERM DEQ (Delivered ex Quay). The view was that DAT is more useful than DEQ in the case of containers that might be unloaded and then loaded into a container stack at the terminal, awaiting shipment. Previously there was no term which expressly dealt with containers that were not at the buyer's premises.

DAP—Delivered at Place (named place of destination). The seller pays for carriage to the named place. However, the buyer will take on the costs related to import clearance. The risk up to the point that the goods are unloaded at the terminal will remain with the seller.

DDP—Delivered Duty Paid (named place of destination). The seller must deliver the goods to the named place in the buyer's country. He also pays the costs of conveying the goods to the destination; including import duties and taxes. The buyer will arrange for the unloading of the goods.

Sea and inland waterway transport	FAS—Free Alongside Ship (named port of shipment). The seller must deliver the goods to alongside the ship at the named port. He is also required to clear the goods for export. Heavy-lift or bulk cargo is likely to adopt this trade term.

FOB—Free on Board (named port of shipment). The seller is required to load the goods on board the vessel nominated by the buyer. The traditional description about the goods crossing the ship's rail is removed. Delivery is now signified by the placing of the goods on board. The seller must clear the goods for export. The buyer is required to inform the seller of his nominated ship and port of loading. The ICC has also made clear that this term should not be used for container goods carried on a multimodal contract. The more appropriate INCOTERM for container shipments is FCA.

> CFR—Cost and Freight (named port of destination). The seller is to pay the costs and freight to bring the goods to the port of destination. However, risk passes to the buyer when the goods are loaded on the vessel.
>
> CIF—Cost, Insurance and Freight (named port of destination). Essentially the same duties as CFR apply except that the seller must, in addition, obtain and pay for an appropriate insurance cover.

The following are some suggestions as to how traders might be able to substitute certain traditional terms with the new INCOTERMS 2010:

TRADE TERMS

2–021

Traditional Terms		INTERCOMS 2010
In regular use		Possible alternative/s
Ex Works	_____	EXW—Ex Works
FOB	_____	FCA—Free Carrier
		CFR—Cost & Freight
C&F	_____	or
		CPT—Carriage Paid To
CIF	_____	CIP—Carriage and Insurance Paid To
Franco Domicile	_____	DDP—Delivered Duty Paid

QUICK REFERENCE CHART TO THE INCOTERMS® 2010 RULES

SERVICES	Rules for any mode or modes of transport							Rules for sea and inland waterway transport			
	EXW Ex Works	FCA Free Carrier	CPT Carriage Paid To	CIP Carriage & Insurance Paid To	DAT Delivered at Terminal	DAP Delivered at Place	DDP Delivered Duty Paid	FAS Free Alongside Ship	FOB Free on Board	CFR Cost & Freight	CIF Cost, Insurance & Freight
	Who Pays	Who Pays	Who Pays	Who Pays	Who Pays	Who Pays	Who Pays	Who Pays	Who Pays	Who Pays	Who Pays
Export Packing	Seller	Seller	Seller	Seller	Seller	Seller	Seller	Seller	Seller	Seller	Seller
Marking & Labeling	Seller	Seller	Seller	Seller	Seller	Seller	Seller	Seller	Seller	Seller	Seller
Block and Brace	1	1	1	1	1	1	1	1	1	1	1
Export Clearance (License, EEI/AES)	Buyer	Seller	Seller	Seller	Seller	Seller	Seller	Seller	Seller	Seller	Seller
Freight Forwarder Documentation Fees	Buyer	Buyer	Seller	Seller	Seller	Seller	Seller	Seller	Seller	Seller	Seller
Inland Freight to Main Carrier	Buyer	2	Seller	Seller	Seller	Seller	Seller	Seller	Seller	Seller	Seller
Origin Terminal Charges	Buyer	Buyer	Seller	Seller	Seller	Seller	Seller	Buyer	Seller	Seller	Seller
Vessel Loading Charges	Buyer	Buyer	Seller	Seller	Seller	Seller	Seller	Buyer	Seller	Seller	Seller
Ocean Freight / Air Freight	Buyer	Buyer	Seller	Seller	Seller	Seller	Seller	Buyer	Buyer	Seller	Seller
Nominate Export Forwarder	Buyer	Buyer	Seller	Seller	Seller	Seller	Seller	Buyer	Buyer	Seller	Seller
Marine Insurance	3	3	3	Seller	3	3	3	3	3	3	Seller
Unload Main Carrier Charges	Buyer	Buyer	4	4	Seller	Seller	Seller	Buyer	Buyer	4	4
Destination Terminal Charges	Buyer	Buyer	4	4	4	Seller	Seller	Buyer	Buyer	4	4
Nominate On-Carrier	Buyer	Buyer	5	5	5	5	Seller	Buyer	Buyer	Buyer	Buyer
Security Information Requirements	Buyer	Buyer	Buyer	Buyer	Buyer	Buyer	Seller	Buyer	Buyer	Buyer	Buyer
Customs Broker Clearance Fees	Buyer	Buyer	Buyer	Buyer	Buyer	Buyer	Seller	Buyer	Buyer	Buyer	Buyer
Duty, Customs Fees, Taxes	Buyer	Buyer	Buyer	Buyer	Buyer	Buyer	Seller	Buyer	Buyer	Buyer	Buyer
Delivery to Buyer Destination	Buyer	Buyer	Buyer	Buyer	Buyer	Buyer	Seller	Buyer	Buyer	Buyer	Buyer
Delivering Carrier Unloading	Buyer	Buyer	Buyer	Buyer	Buyer	Buyer	Buyer	Buyer	Buyer	Buyer	Buyer

Notes:
1 – Incoterms® 2010 do not deal with the parties' obligations for stowage within a container and therefore, where relevant, the parties should deal with this in the the sales contract.
2 – FCA Seller's Facility – Buyer pays inland freight; other FCA qualifiers; other FCA qualifier, Seller arranges and loads pre-carriage carrier and pays inland freight to the "F" delivery place
3 – Incoterms® 2010 does not obligate the buyer nor must the seller to insure the goods, therefore this issue be addressed elsewhere in the sales contract.
4 – Charges paid by Buyer or Seller depending on contract of carriage.
5 – Charges paid by Seller if through Bill of Lading or door-to-door rate to Buyer's destination

INCOTERMS® IS A REGISTERED TRADEMARK OF THE INTERNATIONAL CHAMBER OF COMMERCE. THIS DOCUMENT IS NOT INTENDED AS LEGAL ADVICE BUT IS BEING PROVIDED FOR REFERENCE PURPOSES ONLY. USERS SHOULD SEEK SPECIFIC GUIDANCE FROM INCOTERMS® 2010 AVAILABLE THROUGH THE INTERNATIONAL CHAMBER OF COMMERCE AT WWW.ICCBOOKS.COM

We now turn to a few of the more commonly used terms and examine the law that relates to them.

Ex Works

An ex works contract requires the seller to deliver the goods to the buyer at the **2–023** place of manufacture or storage of the goods, namely the seller's works, factory or store. This feature suggests that this mode of delivery is perhaps more akin to a domestic sale since the point of delivery is at the seller's premises. This has the important implication that it may under certain circumstances not be classed as an international supply contract under s.26 of the Unfair Contract Terms Act 1977. Section 26(4) states that for a contract to qualify as an international supply contract, it must meet any of the following conditions:

1. the goods in question are, at the time of the conclusion of the contract, in the course of carriage, or will be carried, from the territory of one State to the territory of another; or

2. the acts constituting the offer and acceptance have been done in territories of different states; or

3. the contract provides for the goods to be delivered to the territory of a State other than that within whose territory those acts were done.

For the purposes of the Act, it is not sufficient that the seller is aware of the buyer's intention to take the goods abroad, the contract must have been made with that intention in mind and must objectively reflect that fact. The likelihood of an ex works contract not meeting these requirements is therefore great. Hence, under certain circumstances, it may not have the status of an international supply contract and will be subject the terms of the Unfair Contract Terms Act 1977.

2–024 *Amiri Flight Authority v BAE Systems Plc* [2004] 1 All E.R. (Comm.) 385
Facts:
The contract between the parties was for the manufacture and delivery of an aircraft. The aircraft was manufactured and delivered in England. The buyer was established in Abu Dhabi and the aircraft was intended to be flown back to Abu Dhabi. Under the contract, the defendant was also to supply a maintenance programme and services for the aircraft. The fuel tanks were subsequently found to suffer from serious corrosion. The claimant sought damages on the basis that the corrosion had occurred as a result of negligent maintenance by the seller. The contract contained an exemption of liability clause dealing with such liability. The question was whether the contract was an international supply contract for the purposes of the Unfair Contract Terms Act 1977. If it was, the exemption clause would not be subject to the Act, to the detriment of the buyer. The lower court held that the contract was for the international supply of goods and the Act therefore would not apply as a result of s.26(4).
Held:
The Court of Appeal reversed Tomlinson J.'s decision, stating that the clear words of s.26(4) clearly envisaged movement of goods from one country to another. In this case, there was no such movement. It was understandable for the lower court to assume that given the international character of the contract, it was an international supply contract but it could not be ignored that the contract clearly provided for the manufacture and delivery of the aircraft in England. It was, thus, a domestic sale of goods. If the contract had been made with the offer being made in England and the acceptance, in Abu Dhabi, then it would have qualified as an international supply contract, but the acts of offer and acceptance were made entirely in one jurisdiction.

Under an ex works contract, the seller is duty bound to supply the goods in conformity with the contract of sale and trade usage suggests that where documentation is used for the sale, there must be proper documentation certifying or declaring that the goods are in conformity with the contract. Such documentation usually takes the form of a bill of lading or way bill, depending on the type of carriage required.

Other terms are similar to those of a domestic sale of goods contract. The ex works contract is sometimes referred to as ex factory, ex warehouse or ex store.

Ex Ship

The ex ship clause indicates that delivery of the goods to the buyer will take place **2–025** at the ship upon her arrival. The "ex ship" contract is also referred to as an "arrival" contract. The duty on the seller, as defined in *Yangtsze Insurance Association v Lukmanjee* [1918] A.C. 585 by the Privy Council, involves

" ... [causing] delivery to be made to the buyer from a ship which has arrived at the port of delivery and has reached a place therein which is usual for the delivery of goods of the kind in question. The seller has therefore to pay the freight, or otherwise release the shipowner's lien and to furnish the buyer with an effectual direction to the ship to deliver. Until this is done, the buyer is not bound to pay for the goods".

That "effectual direction" usually takes the form of a delivery order (fig.2–028). The delivery order is defined as an "order by the owner of goods to a person holding them on his behalf, to deliver them to a person named". The delivery order does not take the place of the goods and is not the subject matter of the ex ship contract. It should be noted that discharge of the ex ship contract is entirely based on the actual delivery of the goods. Everything hinges on the correct delivery of the goods. Where documents are used, they are to be treated as of performing little more than administrative functions. They do not take the place of the goods. That is the distinction between a CIF contract and an ex ship contract.

The risk and property of the goods remain with the seller until delivery has been made.

Yangtsze Insurance Association v Lukmanjee [1918] A.C. 585   **2–026**
Facts:
The contract expressed as an ex ship contract called for the delivery of timber. The timber was to be made into rafts and floated from the ship to shore for delivery. The sellers had taken out a cargo insurance policy on the goods. Some of the timber was lost while being made into rafts. The buyers attempted to claim under the policy taken out by the sellers.
Held:
The buyers were not entitled to claim under the policy because property in the goods had not passed to them. Under an ex ship contract, property passes when the buyer takes actual delivery of the goods. Here the risk and property in goods were still with the sellers. The insurance taken out could not be properly said to have been taken out for the buyers' benefit because the nature of the ex ship contract is such that the buyer is not intended to receive any right over the goods until actual delivery.

Free Alongside Ship

In this contract, the seller only has to deliver the goods "alongside the vessel" so **2–027** that the buyer could load them. The seller's task is naturally dependent on where the ship is berthed. Where it is berthed by the quay or wharf, then all the seller has to do is to deliver the goods up to the ship's anchorage or so near thereto so that the goods could be effectively loaded. On the other hand where the ship could not berth by the quay but is stationed at some point outside the quay side, the seller's duty is to ensure that the goods are placed on lighters and carried by these lighters to the ship's side at sea.

While it is clear that the seller is not directly responsible for the export itself and hence, for the acquisition of any export licences, there is a convention that he should render the buyer at the latter's request every assistance in obtaining the licence or any other governmental authorisation. There is obiter dictum in *Anglo-Russian Merchant Traders Ltd v Batt* [1917] 2 K.B. 679 that this might even amount to an implied term of co-operation. This is to say that there might exist a term to the effect that the seller, though not directly responsible to obtain the export licence, should offer reasonable assistance so as to enable the buyer to take delivery of the goods and thus, encourage survival of the contract.

As evidence of performance of the contract, the seller should provide at his own expense the customary clean document in proof of delivery of the goods alongside the named vessel. Although this is not an implied term of the contract, as a matter of prudence the seller does well to ensure that he receives some form of documentation that the goods had been delivered alongside the named vessel.

2–028

COLLECTION/DELIVERY ORDER

Exporter **A**	Exporter's reference **U N I C** Forwarder's reference
Collection address if different from A **B**	

Other UK transport details e.g. delivery address **C**	Haulier **D**

Vessel/flight no. and date	Port/airport of loading
Port/airport of discharge	

DANGEROUS GOODS
Specify proper shipping name, hazard class, UN No. flashpoint (deg C) Shipper must provide the appropriate Dangerous Goods Declaration

Shipping marks, container number	Number and kind of packages, description of goods	Gross weight (kg)	Cube (m3)

IMPORTANT - DOCUMENTS TO BE COLLECTED

Collect documents from **A B**

Deliver documents to **C D** or :-

		Total gross weight of goods	Total cube of goods

Prefix and container/trailer number(s)	Seal number(s)	Container/trailer size(s) and type(s)	Tare wt (kg) as marked on CSC plate	Weight of container and goods (kg)

Received the above number of packages/containers/trailers in apparent good order unless stated hereon	For and on behalf of
Haulier's name	
Vehicle reg. no	Date
Driver's signature / Signature and date	

The buyer on the other hand must give the seller good and sufficient notice of the vessel's name and berth. He should ensure that the delivery date is made known to the seller to enable the seller to expedite delivery per contract. Where the name of the ship had been agreed to at the outset, it is up to the buyer to make an effective nomination. Once the goods have been delivered alongside the vessel, the responsibility to load passes to the buyer and so does the risk of the goods.

Free on Board

Introduction

2–029 The FOB contract has been used in international trade in Great Britain for around two centuries. The use of the term has not been confined to sea-borne commerce. It has also been of some importance to the carriage of goods by air, land or rail, however it has to be said that INCOTERMS 2010 do not encourage use of the FOB contract in sales involving non-sea or waterway transport. A general simplification of the term is provided for by Lord Brougham in the old case of *Cowasjee v Thompson* (1845) 5 Moore P.C. 165:

> "It is proved beyond all doubt, indeed it is not denied that when goods are sold in London 'free on board', the cost of shipping them falls on the seller, but the buyer is considered the shipper".

While it will be shown later that this statement is not invariably true of all FOB contracts, as a general rule, it should stand. In order to understand the role and position of FOB contracts today, a tour of some early common law decisions on the matter would be most useful and illuminating. We start with an examination of *Cowasjee v Thompson*.

2–030 *Cowasjee v Thompson* (1845) 5 Moore P.C. 165
Facts:
The contract provided that the goods were to be sold and delivered "free on board" to be paid for by means of cash or bills, at the option of the buyers. The goods were then delivered on board, and receipts were taken from the ship's mate by the lighterman who was employed by the sellers. The sellers then informed the buyers that the goods had been delivered. The buyers then paid by bill of exchange. Although the sellers had retained the mate's receipt for the goods, the master signed the bills of lading in the name of the buyers' name. The buyers then became insolvent during the period of the currency of the bill of exchange. Realising that the bills were not likely to be honoured, the sellers attempted to stop the goods which they claimed were "in transitu".
Held:
Although the bills of lading were not issued in exchange for the mate's receipt, the Judicial Committee of the Privy Council, reversing the decision of the Supreme Court of Bombay, stated that no action in trover would lie for the goods since, once the goods were delivered on board the ship, they were no longer "in transitu" so as to be stopped by the sellers. The retention of the receipts by the sellers was irrelevant because once the goods went over the rails of the ship, the property had passed.

It is clear that in this case, while it might be economically unjust to the seller to have to suffer at the insolvency of the buyers, the court's chief concern was with the certainty of the point of performance or completion of the sale. The same could be said of *Brown v Hare* (1858) 27 L.J. Ex. 377.

2–031 *Brown v Hare* (1858) 27 L.J. Ex. 377
Facts:
The defendants who were Bristol merchants had bought from the plaintiffs in Rotterdam, 10 tons of the "best refined rape oil to be shipped free on board at Rotterdam in September 1857 at £48.15s. per ton to be paid for on delivery to" the claimants of the bills of lading by bill of exchange. The buyers then requested that the goods be shipped on the first vessel from Rotterdam, *The Sophie*. The sellers then wrote to notify the buyers that five tons

would be shipped immediately and the bill of lading, invoice and bill of exchange drawn on the buyers were enclosed. The bill of lading was made deliverable to the seller's "order or assigns". Two hours after receiving the bill of lading, the buyers found out that the goods had been lost. They returned the bill of lading to the sellers and refused to pay. They argued that they were not liable for payment because the goods had not been delivered free on board as the contract stipulated as the bill of lading had been made deliverable to the seller/shipper. It was further argued that the seller had control of the oil and that the contract of carriage had been made with him, therefore, consequently he must bear the risk of the loss.

Held:

The majority of the Court of Exchequer found for the claimants. Pollock C.B. delivering the judgment of the majority held that the meaning of the term "free on board" was that property was to pass to the defendants when the goods were delivered on board. The bill of lading was not issued by the seller in the form in question to retain the property in the goods, but simply in order to secure the payment of the price.

Another important nineteenth century case is *Stock v Inglis* (1884) 12 Q.B.D.   **2–032** 573. In that case Brett M.R. made it clear that under a FOB contract, the risk of loss is on the buyer from the time of delivery of the goods at the FOB point. His Lordship's dictum goes:

"If the goods dealt with by the contract are specific goods it is not denied but that the words 'free on board' according to the general understanding of merchants would mean more than merely that the shipper was to put them on board at his expense; they would mean that he was to put them on board at his expense on account of the person for whom they were shipped; and in that case the goods so put on board under such a contract would be at the risk of the buyer; whether they were lost or not on the voyage. Now that is the meaning of these words 'free on board' in a contract with regard to specific goods, and in that case the goods are at the purchaser's risk even though the payment is not to be made on the delivery of the goods on board, but at some other time, and although the bill of lading is sent forward by the seller with the documents attached in order that the goods shall not be finally delivered to the purchaser until he has either accepted bills or paid cash".[9]

These cases demonstrate the complication caused by documentation, especially the bill of lading. The role of the bill of lading will be examined in greater detail in the next chapter. In this chapter it suffices to note that the basic principles of a FOB contract, as established by these authorities, are:

1. the seller's duty is to deliver the goods over the rails[10] of the ship, the issue of a bill of lading or mate's receipt is irrelevant to the issue of property and risk;

2. the buyer's duty is to ensure that the seller is properly notified as to the vessel to ship the goods;

---

[9] See also *The Parchim* [1918] A.C. 157 (below at para.2–035) although it should be remembered that that case is to be read in the light of its special facts and prevailing circumstances of the time.

[10] Readers should note that under the new INCOTERMS 2010, this anachronistic reference to the ship's rail has been abolished. In the case of CIF, FOB and CFR contracts, the goods are now delivered when they are "on board".

3. the buyer remains the legal shipper of the goods, he is the main contracting party in the contract of carriage;

4. property and risk pass when the goods are taken over the rails of the ship; and

5. when the risk passes, this means that the buyer has an insurance interest in the goods and is entitled to insure them.

2–033   These are not strict immutable obligations. The FOB contract is in fact a flexible instrument[11] which allows the parties to agree to different terms as they see fit.[12] For example, the seller might offer to arrange the insurance for the buyer; or the buyer might agree to assist with the task of delivering the goods over the ship's rail. This element of flexibility is perhaps what makes the FOB contract so popular. Judicial recognition and response to this characteristic of the FOB contract has been somewhat slower than mercantile practice, and was not fully expressed until *Pyrene Co Ltd v Scindia Navigation Co Ltd* [1954] 2 Q.B. 402. Devlin J. held:

"The FOB contract has become a flexible instrument. In what counsel called the classic type as described, for example, in *Wimble, Sons & Co. v Rosenberg & Sons* [1913] 3 K.B. 743, the buyer's duty is to nominate the ship, and the seller's to put the goods on board for account of the buyer and procure a bill of lading in terms usual in the trade. In such a case the seller is directly a party to the contract of carriage at least until he takes out a bill of lading in the buyer's name. Probably the classic type is based on the assumption that the ship nominated will be willing to load any goods brought down to the berth or at least those of which she is notified. Under present conditions, when space often has to be booked well in advance, the contract of carriage comes into existence at an earlier point in time. Sometimes the seller is asked to make the necessary arrangements; and the contract may then provide for his taking the bill of lading in his own name and obtaining payment against the transfer, as in a CIF contract. Sometimes the buyer engages his own forwarding agent at the port of loading to book space and to procure the bill of lading; if freight has to be paid in advance this method may be the most convenient. In such a case the seller discharges his duty by putting the goods on board, getting the mate's receipt and handing it to the forwarding agent to enable him to obtain the bill of lading".

Two further cases in which judicial recognition was given to the flexibility of the FOB contract are *NV Handel Ny J. Smits Import-Export v English Exporters (London) Ltd* [1957] Lloyd's Rep. 517 and *Ian Stach Ltd v Baker Bosley Ltd* [1958] Lloyd's Rep. 127. In *NV Handel*, the sellers had agreed to do their best to secure shipping space for a cargo to be delivered FOB Rotterdam. The sellers failed to nominate a ship. The court decided that the mere fact that the sellers were burdened with the limited obligation of doing their best to secure shipping space did not prevent the contract from being on FOB terms. These terms remained effective to specify the exact price, and what was to be included in that

---

[11] That flexibility is qualified or limited in some respects if INCOTERMS 2010 are adopted.
[12] See Evans, "FOB and CIF Contracts" [1993] A.L.J. 844.

price and were equally apt to address the issue of when and where property will pass. However, the sellers had expressly undertaken to secure shipping space and failed to do so, their claim was to be dismissed.

It was argued in *Ian Stach Ltd v Baker Bosley Ltd* [1958] Lloyd's Rep. 127 that **2–034** as the buyer had stipulated the shipping date under a "classic FOB contract" the documentary credit need only be opened a reasonable time *before* the date of shipment nominated by the buyer and not the *start* of the shipment period since the buyer is the shipper of the goods. The court recognised that there are variants to the FOB contract but felt that no distinction needed to be made in regards to documentary credit on the ground that in international commercial contracts certainty is absolutely vital and the best way to ensure certainty is to insist that the documentary credit be opened at the very latest by the earliest shipping date (i.e. at the start of the agreed shipment period). In this respect, no distinction is to be made between a FOB and CIF contract.

The flexibility inherent in a FOB contract can also be its greatest disadvantage from a legal point of view. Taking an extended FOB contract which requires the seller to arrange shipping space and prepay insurance on the goods to be carried, it is extremely difficult to differentiate that from a CIF contract. The problem becomes manifest when the court has to determine whether the seller had undertaken to perform these duties as principal or agent for the buyer. The use of the FOB label by traders does not necessarily signify their intention to be governed by the legal obligations relating to FOB contracts. It may simply denote their calculation of the price of the goods. It could be said that the distinction between the CIF sale and the extended FOB contract is that for a sale to be on FOB terms, services that are connected with the provision of the vessel and prepayment of freight and insurance must be treated as having been provided on account of the buyer. Nonetheless, there is much difficulty and little clarity in this area of law.

The Parchim [1918] A.C. 157 **2–035**
Facts:
The contract for the sale and delivery of Chilean saltpetre was expressed as C&F Taltal, Chile. The saltpetre was to be delivered to a range of possible European ports. The contract provided that the buyers were to assume the charter of the ship from the sellers. They were also to nominate the port of discharge and where necessary, to supply a substitute vessel to carry the goods. The issue for the Judicial Committee of the Privy Council was whether property in the goods passed in this case on shipment or when the documents had been accepted.
Held:
The Privy Council was of the opinion that this "C&F contract" was in effect an extended FOB contract. The terms are consistent with it as being a FOB contract, hence, property was to pass on shipment and not upon the tender of shipping documents.

It is not always helpful to term the contract in question as a classic, strict or extended FOB; the reality of practice and usage is that most contracts may possess terms capable of being construed one way or the other. It is perhaps more important to concentrate on the construction of the contract in question as to what the parties have undertaken to perform and the validity of these undertakings than to be over swayed by the labels applied. As said before, traders often apply these trade terms more so for accounting business than legal purposes. Be that as it may, the promoters of export like UK Trade and Investment (UKTI), the Institute of Export, the British International Freight Association, etc, have been encouraging and educating traders in the choice and use of trade terms as given effect to by the law.

Duties of the classic FOB seller

1. To make available at the port of loading and to ship free on board goods answering in all respects the description in the contract of sale

2–036   This description of the seller's duty begs the question as to what constitutes "the description in the contract of sale" of the goods. It is generally discussed in Chapter 3 that the description of the goods does not only refer to statements made about the physical condition of the goods. In international commerce particularly, it may also apply to the statement about where the goods are to be delivered to. In the case of an FOB contract, this is synonymous with the place of shipment. Hence, where the seller defaults in sending the goods to the agreed, named port of shipment, he commits a breach of a condition. In short, the port of delivery in an FOB contract is a condition of the contract. In *Petrograde Inc v Stinnes GmbH* [1995] 1 Lloyd's Rep. 142, the defendants were entitled to refuse delivery at a port other than the one specified in the contract.

In FOB contracts it is axiomatic that the seller must ship the goods at the latest by the end of the period specified for shipment in the contract. If the time for shipment is expressly at the buyer's option (or the contract is silent on the point) the buyer is normally entitled to call for shipment at any time during the period. In most contracts, where the time for delivery is not stated, the seller is required to send the goods to the buyer within a reasonable time (s.29(3) Sale of Goods Act 1979). However in an FOB context, where it is for the buyer to ensure that the ship is sent first to the port of shipment, the seller's duty to ship would not arise until the buyer has performed his part of the bargain. That means, s.29(3) does not come into effect until the buyer has nominated the ship (and/or port where applicable).

Where the shipment period is not explicitly stated, the courts would look to the factual matrix of the contract to see if one could be implied. In *Cereal Investments v ED&F Man Sugar* [2007] EWHC 2843, the FOB contract stated "One vessel only presenting October 2006 Shipment at Buyer's Option, with 10 days pre-advise of vessel arrival". The judge thought that a commercial and grammatical reading must lead to two severed parts—"one vessel only presenting October 2006" and "Shipment at Buyer's Option, with 10 days pre-advise of vessel arrival". Shipment was thus in October 2006. However, as to how much time the seller had to load the goods, the clause was silent. That said, although the contract did not specify an end period with a fixed date, it was not uncommon for contracts of this kind simply to require a party to make a reasonable estimate of the time needed for a particular purpose. Thus, in this case the buyer would have to make a reasonable estimate of when shipment would be complete.

2–037   It should also be noted that in the common law the seller would not be deemed to be making delivery unless the carrier he uses fully intends and is aware that the delivery he is making is in relation to the seller's contract. In *Albright & Wilson UK v Biachem Ltd* [2002] UKHL 37, the buyer was expecting two deliveries—one from X and the other from Y. The same carrier was used by X and Y. The carrier had mixed up the consignment notes and delivered X's goods as Y's. The Court of Appeal and the High Court held that although obviously the delivery of one load could not be the performance of two contracts (each for one load), a single delivery could amount to *purported* performance of two contracts. The House of Lords disagreed and held that where a carrier had delivered goods on behalf of one consignor to the consignee under a delivery or consignment note relating to goods on behalf of another consignor who coincidentally had contracted with the same carrier to supply different goods to that consignee, the carrier could not be said to be performing *both* contracts at the same time. Thus, in relation to Y's liability, it would not be appropriate to treat the events as constituting his performance.

The goods brought to meet the ship must meet their contractual description and be of satisfactory quality at the time of shipment.[13] In *KG Bominflot Bunkergesellschaft fur Mineraloele mbh v Petroplus Marketing AG (The Mercini Lady)* [2009] EWHC 1088 (Comm); part reversed in [2010] EWCA Civ 1145, the buyer had bought oil from P under an FOB contract. Before shipment, the oil was tested and found to meet the contractual specifications, but once it had reached its destination, four days later and after an incident-free voyage, the buyer alleged that it ceased to conform. The High Court held that there was indeed a breach of s.14(2) of the Sale of Goods Act 1979 (implied term of description), and s.14(3) (an implied term that it would be reasonably fit for purpose following such a voyage). That decision was reversed in part by the Court of Appeal on appeal. On the issue of whether there was a requirement that the specifications would continue to be satisfied after shipment (delivery), the Court of Appeal held that the contract made it very clear that:

(a) the specification had to be met at the time of delivery;

(b) the intention was that the gasoil should be inspected by an independent inspector prior to loading; and

(c) the inspector's determination was to be final and binding in the absence of fraud or manifest error.

It is obvious from Rix L.J.'s judgment that where the documents ascertaining and verifying the description of the goods were intended to be conclusive and final at the time of shipment, the court would not be too swift to depart from them.

The description attached to the FOB term as to where the goods are to be **2–038** delivered may either refer to a specific port or several possible ports. Whatever form that description may take, it must be certain and ascertainable. In *Boyd & Co Ltd v Louca* [1973] 1 Lloyd's Rep. 209 this was reiterated. There, the contract stated that goods were to be delivered "FOB stowed good Danish port". The

---

[13] In the case of the CIF and CFR contracts, where the seller knows the destination of the goods, the time taken to complete a normal voyage formed the basic measure of what was a reasonable time. However, in an FOB contract, where the seller did not know the destination of the goods, it was not appropriate to adopt the same measure. A FOB buyer was entitled to expect that he would receive goods that would be of satisfactory quality for a sufficient time to enable him to have some beneficial use of the goods or to sell them on (*Navigas Ltd of Gibraltar v Enron Liquid Fuels Inc* [1997] 2 Lloyd's Rep. 759). What constituted a reasonable time would depend on the circumstances of the contract in question, including the fact that it would be likely that the goods would be carried by sea before resale or use, the nature of the goods and whether the seller knew that the buyer would be selling the goods on or using them itself (*The Mercini Lady* [2009] EWHC 1088).

question was whether this rendered the contract so unclear that it could not be performed. The buyer insisted that it was not unclear and the contract in these terms conferred on them the right to nominate whichever port in Denmark to receive delivery of the goods, so long as the nominated port was a good port. The court agreed stating that, where possible, the priority of the law is to rescue rather than to dash the contract on grounds of uncertainty of intention. From the term "FOB good Danish port" the court agreed with the buyer that it was clear to the extent that the contract intended to use any suitable Danish port and that it was implicit in the FOB term that the buyer was to make a selection of the port of shipment. After all the buyer is essentially the shipper in a strict or classic FOB contract.

This nomination or description is binding on both the sellers and the buyers. In *Modern Transport Co Ltd v Ternstrom & Roos* (1924) 19 Ll. L. Rep. 345, it was held that the buyer had no right to demand that the seller delivers the goods to another place other than the agreed port, even though under the FOB contract he has the right to nominate the port of shipment generally. Similarly in *Peter Turnbull & Co Pty Ltd v Mundas Trading Co (Australasia) Pty Ltd* [1954] 2 Lloyd's Rep. 198, the Australian High Court held that the sellers were obliged to deliver to the Port of Sydney in spite of the fact that the buyers had failed to nominate an appropriate vessel to take delivery at Sydney. The sellers had also attempted to resist performance by alleging that it was impossible for them to secure delivery goods to Sydney without considerable cost and expense. Impossibility of performance is however not proved merely on the ground that performance is extremely difficult.

It might be noted in passing that although in an FOB contract the buyer should be given the right to nominate the FOB port, the situation is less straightforward in the case of other modes of transport. In *Zenziper Grains & Feed Stuffs v Bulk Trading Corp Ltd* [2000] All E.R. (D) 2139, the Court of Appeal overruled that High Court's decision that in a "free on truck" contract for the sale of goods to be imported by the seller that allowed for delivery at a range of places in the country of destination, the right and duty to nominate the place of delivery lay with the buyer. The Court of Appeal held that that duty and right should go to the seller because the mechanics of the contract would work far better if it was the seller (who made all the shipping arrangements) who selected the place for delivery and duly informed the buyer. The Court of Appeal considered that no analogy should be drawn from an FOB contract. The buyer had submitted that, if an analogy is to be sought, such an FOT contract is more akin to (albeit not the same as) an "ex ship" or "arrival" contract, than an FOB contract. Whether or not the judge was right to assert that an FOT contract is "essentially derived" from an FOB contract,[14] any analogy based on the practicalities so far as nominating the place of delivery is concerned, can only sensibly be applied to an FOT contract where the place of delivery is in the country of origin and not the country of destination. It might also be noted that the chartering of a ship is radically different from the hiring of a truck. It is likely to be a more straightforward task for a buyer to hire trucks to take delivery of goods at a place selected by the seller than to charter a ship to load a cargo. Secondly, the choice of loading ports under an FOB contract will normally be constrained by the

---

[14] It should, however, be noted that no authority was advanced for that proposition by counsel in that case.

physical characteristics of the ocean vessel on which the goods are to be loaded (for example, her length and draught) which the buyer has chartered, as to which the seller will usually have no knowledge. Thus, it would be sensible for the buyer to select the loading port. However, under an FOT contract for the delivery not in the country of origin, but in the country of destination, the goods will be delivered by an ocean vessel *chartered by the seller*, at a discharge port agreed between the seller and the ship owner. Here, as the selection of the discharge port is conditioned by the physical attributes of the ship, the same considerations should apply making it only sensible to confer on the seller the right to choose the delivery port under the FOT contract. Third, the goods which are the subject of an FOT sale may form only part of a large single cargo also the subject of several FOT sales to different buyers. In such a situation, it would be commercially impractical if each buyer were entitled to call for delivery to be made at a different port.

The seller is also duty bound to ensure that he gets the goods to alongside the   **2–039** ship with sufficient time to complete loading within the shipment period. In *All Russian Co-operative Society Ltd v Benjamin Smith & Sons* (1923) 14 Ll. L. Rep. 351, the seller was only able to get the goods to the ship 15 minutes before expiry of the shipment period. While the court noted that the buyers should co-operate within reasonable bounds with the loading to ensure that shipment was within the contracted time, under the circumstances the seller was in breach for failing to ensure sufficient time for loading.

The seller is also required to give notice to the buyer under s.32(3) of the Sale of Goods Act 1979 to enable the buyer to arrange any necessary insurance cover. In *Wimble, Sons & Co Ltd v Rosenberg & Sons* [1913] 3 K.B. 743, the Court of Appeal held that although this was a statutory imposition on the seller, it would be deemed to have been complied with if the buyer was already in possession of the relevant information to enable him to arrange cargo insurance. The rationale of the section is to ensure that the seller is placed a duty to provide the buyer with that information through the notice. It might be observed that the exception to the statutory rule seems to be that the buyer should have relevant information to arrange his own cargo insurance, not merely enough information to secure general insurance.

Notice of readiness[15] to load is also crucial to the buyer. He needs the information to nominate a suitable vessel to collect and take delivery of the goods. Where there is an absence of notice or a short notice, the buyer's duty to make a nomination will not arise. On the other hand, where, as in *Harlow & Jones v Panex Ltd* [1967] 2 Lloyd's Rep. 509, the seller had given proper notice and the buyer failed to arrange for the nominated ship to be ready to take the shipment on that date, the buyer would be held liable. As the FOB contract is flexible, it may be that the seller arranges for shipment. In such a case, the notice of readiness to load could be dispensed with.

The seller's duty to load is usually pre-determined by contract. His duty is   **2–040** treated with the strictness as is common in mercantile contracts. It is performed by the seller seeing to it that the goods are placed onboard the correct ship using the prescribed method of loading and the contractual loading rate. The loading rate stipulation is usually treated as a warranty; where, for example, the seller

---

[15] See Chapter 7 paras 7–120—7–125 for the shipping/charterparty context of notice of readiness.

completes loading within shipment period but fails to adhere to the contracted loading rate, the buyer cannot reject the goods. His remedy lies in damages (*Tradax Export v Italgrani di Francesco Ambrosio* [1983] 2 Lloyd's Rep. 109).

2. To pay all handling and transport charges in connection with delivering the goods to the port of loading to be taken over the ship's rails[16]

2–041 The seller is generally responsible for the payment of handling and transport charges incurred by the delivery of the goods to the ship. Furthermore, where he has undertaken to obtain the relevant documentation for export on behalf of the buyer, he may be accountable for any charge/fee incurred from obtaining relevant documentation. Such documentation may include:

● certificates of origin;

● movement certificates;

● invoices of value and origin;

● pre-shipment inspection certification;

● Standard Shipping Notes (SSN);

● Dangerous Goods Note (DGN); and

● certificates of health.

All documents or certificates required should be specified in the contract properly as the courts are very slow to imply the requirement of any particular document (*Wilmar Oleo Pte Ltd v Vinmar Chemicals & Polymers* [2011] EWHC 2067). Where a dispute arises as to whether a document tendered or produced was compliant with the contract, the court will treat that as a matter of contractual interpretation. In *RG Grain Trade LLP (UK) v Feed Factors International Ltd* [2011] EWHC 1889 (Comm), for example, the court found that the certificates of quality issued were not final and binding because they did not conform to the contract's conditions for what would constitute a final and binding certificate.

2–042 There are no general rules[17] at common law as to who is directly responsible for the payment of these charges or the securing of the documentation. Export licences are highly illustrative of the problem. It may be thought that in a FOB contract the buyer being the shipper of goods is directly responsible for obtaining the export licence. Indeed in *Brandt & Co v Morris & Co Ltd* [1917] 2 K.B. 784, the court held that although the sellers had applied for the export licence but failed, the primary duty of obtaining the licence rests with the buyers who were the shippers. As shippers, they were responsible in taking delivery of the goods over the rails of their chosen vessel; without obtaining the export licence, they have breached that responsibility. Scrutton L.J. said

" . . . the obtaining of a licence to export is the buyer's concern. It is their concern to have the ship sent out of the country after the goods have been put

---

[16] The reference to the ship's rail has now been abolished in contracts governed by INCOTERMS 2010 (see para.2–020 above).

[17] Unless INCOTERMS 2010 are used where some guidance is offered.

on board and the fact that . . . a prohibition against export includes a prohibition against bringing the goods on to the quay or other place to be shipped for exportation does not cast a duty of obtaining the licence on the sellers. Bringing the goods on to quay is merely subsidiary to the export which is the gist of the licence".

A contrast may, however, be had in *AV Pound & Co v Hardy & Co Inc* [1956] 1 A.C. 588.

AV Pound & Co v Hardy & Co Inc [1956] 1 A.C. 588   **2–043**
Facts:
Under a FAS contract for the delivery of turpentine, a Portuguese export licence was required. The seller attempted to secure an export licence through their supplier in Portugal. The authorities would have granted the licence but for the destination being in East Germany. The buyers refused to nominate a substitute for that destination.
Held:
Lord Somervell felt unable to support Scrutton L.J.'s proposition that it was the duty of the buyer in a FOB (or FAS) contract to obtain the licence for export. Viscount Kilmuir explained that the distinction between the present case and *Brandt v Morris* was that in the latter, both the seller and buyer were British traders albeit that the buyer was securing goods for an overseas merchant. Where a British buyer has bought goods from a British seller for export, he is to apply for the export licence because he alone knows the full facts regarding the destination of the goods and other information surrounding the purported export. In the present case, the parties were not based in Portugal. The seller had a supplier in Portugal and both of them were in a better position than the buyer to obtain the licence. Practical convenience dictated that the seller be responsible for the export licence. It must have been in the contemplation of the parties that this was to be so.

Where the undertaking to obtain the licence is deemed to have been assumed by the seller, the general rule in *Overseas Buyers Ltd v Granadex SA* [1980] 2 Lloyd's Rep. 608 is that he needs merely to use the best of his endeavours to do so. It is only an absolute duty where it is pellucid from the contractual terms and circumstances that he had indeed assumed an undertaking of that magnitude. Sellers often rely on a "subject to licence" clause in the contract of sale to support the position that they have not assumed an absolute duty to secure the export licence. The judgment in *Vidler & Co (London) Ltd v Silcock & Sons Ltd* [1960] 1 Lloyd's Rep. 509 indicates that the seller who defends his inaction or want of reasonable effort by alleging that nothing could or would have changed matters, should have a heavy burden to prove his allegation. And, of course self-induced impossibility is not frustration of the contract but a breach of the same (see, *Maritime National Fish Ltd v Ocean Trawlers Ltd* [1935] A.C. 524; *Agroexport State Enterprise for Foreign Trade v Compagnie Européene de Céréales* [1974] 1 Lloyd's Rep. 499).

3. To complete all declarations required by HM Revenue and Customs

Where the goods are from bond or under drawback, there are declarations that   **2–044**
must be completed. The seller under the FOB contract is responsible in ensuring that these declarations are properly made. Customs may insist on a bond on certain goods; goods liable for duty but for the fact they have been imported on a temporary basis and are to be re-exported for example, may be subject to a bond. Other goods placed in warehouses waiting for transhipment may in like

manner be under bond as well. The signatories to the bond bind themselves to pay to Customs any monies due should any of the conditions stated in the bond not be fulfilled. Goods under drawback are goods for which an amount of excise or import duty is remitted or paid back when the goods are exported.

The buyer's duty as shipper

2–045 In the strict FOB contract, the buyer is responsible as shipper of the goods for the following duties:

1. to fix the dates within the agreed shipment period when the goods are to be loaded;

2. to procure space on a vessel fit to carry the goods;

3. to allow the seller enough time to get the goods to port by issuing a valid nomination of the vessel and the date the vessel will be ready to collect; and

4. to make a second nomination substituting an earlier but unsuitable vessel provided there is sufficient time left for loading and the seller is given good and reasonable notice.

Where the FOB contract imposes extended tasks on the seller, the above duties should be construed and applied accordingly.

Notice of readiness and time of shipment

2–046 Time of shipment in an FOB contract is usually of the essence. This means that the goods must have been placed onboard the ship by the last day of the shipment period. This in turn means that the buyer needs to get the vessel to the loading port in sufficient time for such loading to occur. There will often be contractual provisions whereby, if a shipment period is designated, the buyer must give a certain number of days notice stating the time of probable arrival of the vessel. This is to give the seller ample time to load before the end of the shipment period.

It follows that a provision calling for a notice of probable readiness to load be given on or before a certain day is a condition of the contract. If the relevant party does not comply with the time obligation, the "innocent" party can treat the omission as a repudiatory breach and can accept the repudiation by bringing the contract to an end and sue for damages, if he has suffered any loss.

2–047 *Bunge Corporation v Tradax Export SA* [1981] 2 All E.R. 513
Facts:
The contract of sale called for the delivery of 15,000 tonnes of soya bean meal FOB an American port in the Gulf of Mexico to be nominated by the sellers. The buyers were to nominate an effective ship to take delivery of the goods and to give the sellers at least 15 days notice of readiness of the vessel to load. The notice was given but it was four days late. The sellers treated the contract as repudiated.
Held:
The buyers attempted to rely on Roskill L.J.'s dictum in *Cehave NV v Bremer Handelsgesellschaft mbH (The Hansa Nord)* [1975] 3 All E.R. 739 that

"a court should not be over ready, unless required by statute or authority so to do, to construe a term in a contract as a 'condition'".

Lord Wilberforce rejected this argument stating

"the fundamental fallacy of the appellants' argument lies in attempting to apply this analysis to a time clause such as the present in a mercantile contract, which is totally different in character".[18]

The House of Lords gave judgment in favour of the sellers. The court was concerned that in mercantile contracts such as the present where certainty of rights and duties is central that time clauses should be enforced strictly. The parties need to know precisely their full rights and duties, given that in many FOB contracts, the parties are engaged in a series of mutually dependent rights and duties. Time being of the essence also conforms to established mercantile and business practices.

The time of the essence finding in *Bunge Corporation v Tradax* was used in **2–048** *Thai Maparn Trading Co v Louis Dreyfus Commodities (The Med Salvador and The Goa)* [2011] EWHC 2494 (Comm) by the sellers to treat the contract as having been repudiated by the buyers who gave short notice. In that case, the FOB contract expressly required the buyers to give a vessel nomination notice seven working days before the vessel's estimated time of arrival (or readiness to load). The sellers argued that strict compliance with the notice of readiness provisions by the buyers was a condition precedent to their being obliged to have cargo ready to load during the shipment periods and, as the buyers had failed to serve contractual notices, the sellers were not in default for failing to produce the cargo to meet the vessel. The court ruled that the sellers were not entitled to reject the notice given by the buyers even though it was short notice. It should be noted that in *Bunge v Tradax* the breach was not because the notice was short. The breach occurred because notice was given after the last date on which it could legitimately have been given (the required 15-day notice would have lapsed after the last possible date for shipment).

The court did not accept the argument that a timely nomination notice was a condition precedent to the sellers' own obligation to provide and load a full cargo. Moreover, contractually, the sellers' duty to provide and load the cargo would not have commenced until the expiry of seven working days from the notice of readiness (not the nomination itself) had been given. It should not be assumed that this case departs from the *Bunge v Tradax* insistence on time being of the essence. The facts are different.

Parties who are concerned about the strictures of time and notices may wish to provide specifically for a procedure to extend time whilst preserving the importance of a time stipulation. In *Pec Ltd v Thai Maparn Trading Co* [2011] EWHC 3306 (Comm), for example, the contract allowed the FOB buyer to extend the time for delivery and in order to do so, it must serve a notice on the sellers informing the latter of their intention.[19] However, such a provision must

---

[18] See also G. Treitel "Time of shipment in F.O.B. contracts" [1991] L.M.C.L.Q. 147.

[19] The contractual stipulation was one commonly found in GAFTA contracts. In that case, it was GAFTA Form 120, cl.7 which provided that the contract period of delivery would be extended by an additional period of not more than 21 days, provided that the buyer served notice claiming extension not later than the next business day following the last day of the delivery period.

be interpreted narrowly and in a commercial manner. There, the buyers' notice merely stated that they were ready to extend the delivery period by 21 days and that if they did not receive any reply regarding the cargo readiness for loading from the sellers within two days they would treat it as in default. The court construed the message as simply suggesting that the buyers were "prepared" to extend not that they were actually doing so. Moreover, it was dependent on the sellers' response—the buyers' readiness to extend the delivery period was qualified by a statement that if the sellers failed to advise within two days the readiness of the cargo it would put the seller in default. The effect was to make the extension conditional on the sellers confirming the readiness of the cargo, which never happened.

It is always a possibility, given the flexibility of the FOB term, for the parties to make time not of the essence. This can be achieved normally by means of explicit words in the contract but it is not unknown that the use of certain less explicit language could result in the same conclusion, as long as the factual matrix supports such a construction.

2–049 *ERG Raffinerie Mediterranee SpA v Chevron USA Inc* [2007] EWCA Civ 494
Facts:
The contract was for the sale of gasoline,

> "FOB ISAB refinery north site (Priolo Terminal—Augusta Bay) in a single lot by m/t 'tbn'/subs[20] to be nominated by buyer and to be acceptable to seller in the period 27–30/05/2004".

The contract provided for loading during a four-day delivery period, which could be narrowed to a two-day laycan.[21] The Buyer nominated a vessel and narrowed the laycan to a two-day date range. The seller started to blend the cargo but encountered technical problems. The vessel arrived before the laycan period and gave notice of readiness, but because of the problems at the plant it could not then load. After waiting for six days the buyer ordered the vessel away from port, claiming that the seller's failure to commence loading was a repudiatory breach.
Held:
The court held that the use of a laycan clause which entitled the tanker to present at any moment up to the end of the delivery period, made the contract a nontraditional FOB contract in that the time of delivery had become an obligation that was not of the essence of the contract. Longmore L.J. had this to say as regards a laycan clause in the FOB contract:

> "[T]he seller knows that he has to have his goods available for loading during whatever period the contract specifies but may stipulate for a narrowing of that period by requiring the buyer to nominate a shorter period within which he will make the ship available to take the goods. If, however, that period of availability is close to the end of the delivery period, that narrowing may have the consequence that, if the vessel presents towards the end of the narrowed period, the goods will not be shipped by the end of the shipment period. If this is the case, the natural conclusion might be . . . that it cannot have been the parties' intention that there would be a breach of condition if the goods have not been shipped by the end of that delivery period".

---

[20] m/t 'tbn'/subs—"merchant tanker 'to be nominated' or substitutes".
[21] See paras 7–122—7–125; also 2–099.

This case demonstrates that the borrowing of words, especially those relating to the presentation or sailing of the ship, from conventional shipping contracts such as charterparties, for the purposes of the sale contract should be carefully thought through.

Once the notice of readiness to load is properly given by the buyer, the seller **2–050** must comply with that date.[22] Failure to do so constitutes a failure to deliver; Lord Ackner held in *Compagnie Commerciale Sucres et Denrees v Czarnikow Ltd (The Naxos)* [1990] 1 W.L.R. 1337 that an FOB seller has to have cargo available to load without delay "as soon as the vessel is ready to load the cargo in question".

In an FOB contract, the buyer will usually charter the ship to take delivery of the goods. They are, thus, potentially rendering themselves liable for demurrage (a sum in liquidated damages to be paid to the shipowners for use of the vessel at the port of loading or unloading longer than permitted by the charterparty); but it is of course the sellers who in practical terms have to put the goods on board the vessel. If the buyer is liable for demurrage because the seller has taken too long to load the vessel, the buyer will wish to make the seller responsible for indemnifying him in respect of that demurrage liability. The contract of sale will, therefore, normally reflect the buyer's obligations to the shipowners.

The courts are sensitive to the buyer's obligations to the carrier under these circumstances. They will hold the seller responsible for the buyer's demurrage liabilities and other costs if the seller fails to comply with the notice of readiness (*SK Shipping v BP Energy (Asia) Pte Ltd* [2000] 1 All E.R. (Comm) 810).

If after serving a notice of readiness to load the ship is required to be cleaned, **2–051** maintained or repaired, what impact will that have on the seller's duty to load? Of course if the buyer agrees that the holds need to be cleaned or the engine be repaired, he will negotiate for some time with the seller. However if the seller is the one who is insisting that the ship be cleaned or repaired, and the buyer disagrees, the impasse might result in the goods not being delivered within the contractual delivery period. If the goods are then not shipped, can the buyer sue the seller for non-delivery?

Soufflet Negoce SA v Bunge SA [2010] EWCA Civ 1102   **2–052**
Facts:
S had entered an FOB contract to sell 15,000 tons of feed barley to B for delivery onto a vessel between October 9 and October 22, 2006. The contract (in GAFTA Contract Form 49) provided the vessel was to be presented at the loading port in readiness to load within the delivery period (as notified in the notice of readiness). B had chartered a vessel and the shipowners served a notice of readiness on the last day of the delivery period. On that day B's surveyors issued a certificate of cleanliness for the vessel but S's surveyors found that the cargo holds were unclean and not suitable to receive the cargo. The following day S declared that B were in default due to the fact that the vessel was not presented ready to load.

The issue for the court was whether B could sue S for non-delivery of goods on the basis that S were under a duty to load where it was physically and legally possible for them to do so.

---

[22] In *Tradox v Italgrani (The Belgrano)* [1986] 1 Lloyd's Rep. 112 (*Financial Times*, November 26, 1985), it was held that the strict rule in *Bunge v Tradax* meant that as long as the buyer had complied with his side of the bargain in nominating the vessel and time for shipment in time, the seller must be prepared to load by that nominated time even though it is before the end of the shipment period generally provided for in the contract.

Held:

The buyer's obligation was merely to present the ship in readiness to load. That required no more than that the ship should be ready in the sense of it being lawful and possible for loading to take place. S could not use the fact that the holds needed cleaning as indicating that the ship had not "arrived" during the contractual delivery period. If B was prepared to assume the risk of loading the goods into unclean holds, that was entirely their prerogative. It was not conceivable that S had any real legitimate interest in the state of the holds. After all, their duty is merely to deliver the goods FOB.

If S were genuinely concerned about the state of the holds and the negative effect that might have on them (such as being exposed to tortious claims by third parties or loss of reputation), they should have insisted on making provision to inspect the holds in the sale contract.

Where no notice of readiness has been given, the seller who takes his goods to port before time does so at his own peril, as is seen in *J & J Cunningham Ltd v Munro Ltd* (1922) 28 Com. Cas. 42.

2–053 *J & J Cunningham Ltd v Munro Ltd* (1922) 28 Com. Cas. 42

Facts:

The contract was for the sale of bran, delivery FOB Rotterdam October shipment. The sellers had carried the goods to port by mid-October but the buyers had not yet given any notice of readiness to load. They were only able to procure shipping space much later, although it was within the shipment period. The bran had in the meantime deteriorated and the sellers argued that the risk in the goods had shifted to the buyers from the time the cargo was brought to Rotterdam.

Held:

The court held that the first step to the performance of the FOB contract is to be initiated by the buyer, not the seller. Here, the seller had gone ahead with the delivery of the goods to port without first receiving a notice of readiness from the buyers. The FOB contract guarantees the buyers the prerogative to choose the loading date; the sellers must not therefore be allowed to deprive the buyers of that right and duty. On the question of whether the sellers would be left without a remedy where the buyers substitutes the nominated loading date and the sellers in reliance on that notice, had brought the goods to port and the goods had subsequently deteriorated as a result of the buyers' change of mind, Hewart L.C.J. turned to a version of "promissory estoppel" which His Lordship felt would place the risk with the buyers.

2–054   As a matter of estoppel, the buyers could not be held to the original nomination (of date of shipment or of loading vessel) unless the contract otherwise stipulates. The seller who acts in reliance on that nomination as if it were final does so at his own peril, but where there is some express or implied representation from the buyer that he would not change his mind, the buyer would be estopped from so doing.

As with the reasonableness of the shipment date, the buyer's duty to nominate a vessel implies that the vessel nominated must be suitable for the performance of the FOB contract. Suitability refers, inter alia, to the following conditions, not merely the physical attributes of the ship to take delivery of the goods:

1. the ship must have the requisite administrative clearance to enter port and take delivery of the goods;

2. the ship's crew and management must be competent for the loading and processing of the cargo;

3. the named ship must not belong to an enemy of the country of shipment/ loading; and

4. the ship's ability to arrive on time for the delivery to take place.

A seller is entitled to reject a nominated vessel which does not comply with the port's load restrictions. In *Richco International v Bunge and Co (The New Propser)* [1991] 2 Lloyd's Rep. 93, that entitlement applied even though it would have been impossible for the buyer to nominate a vessel that complied with the contract because no vessel could load the amount of goods in question while complying with the restrictions of port/s to be used under the contract. The doctrine of strict performance is not to be detracted from under such circumstances.

The duty to nominate is a contractual term, as such it would appear possible **2–055** for the parties to waive the nomination and use of a suitable vessel.[23]

The FOB buyer has the right, unless the contract provides otherwise, to make a second nomination to substitute a vessel which for one reason or another is rendered unsuitable. Besides undertaking to pay the additional costs and expense in making a second nomination, the buyers should act with the least possible delay to allow the sellers sufficient time to load and perform other duties within the shipment period.

Agricultores Federatos Argentinos v Ampro SA [1965] 2 Lloyd's Rep. 157 **2–056**
Facts:
The contract called for the shipment of maize on FOB terms between September 20 and 29. The buyers' first nomination turned out to be unsuitable. They then made a second nomination at 1630 on September 29. The sellers refused to load claiming that the buyers had breached the contract. The buyers sued the sellers for nonperformance. On the facts, it would have been possible to complete loading before the end of September 29 if workers were to work overtime. Indeed, the buyers had already permission for overtime loading and obtaining labour was not difficult.
Held:
The sellers were not entitled to treat the contract as repudiated. The buyers' right to make a second nomination is valid so long as the goods could be shipped within the shipment period by the substitute vessel. The fact that the vessel had to work overtime to complete loading was immaterial to the issue of the buyers' right to make a substitute nomination. The buyers' right to make a substitute need not be founded on any serious grounds; it is his prerogative to replace the original vessel as sees fit. It is for the sellers to prove the substitute was unsuitable.

An implied term of co-operation?

We have seen in *All Russian Cooperative Society Ltd v Benjamin Smith & Sons* **2–057** (1923) 14 Ll. L. Rep. 351 that there appears to be in general law an implied duty to co-operate to ensure the performance of the contract. This would apply here where the seller could be required to put reasonable effort to assist the buyers in completing loading within the shipment period.

In line with the business efficacy test in *Liverpool City Council v Irwin* [1977] A.C. 239, in general law, it now is reasonably well-established that business

---

[23] *Compagnie de Renflouement de Récuperation et de Travaux Sous-Marins VS Baroukh et Cie v W Seymour Plant Sales and Hire Ltd* [1981] 2 Lloyd's Rep. 466.

efficacy requires a certain degree of co-operation between the parties. In *Mackay v Dick* [1881] 6 App.Cas. 251, a contract for the sale of a digging machine was subject to a condition precedent that it should be shown to be capable of excavating a specified quantity of clay in a fixed time at a defined site. If the machine failed the test, the buyer was entitled to return the digger within two months and the buyer would not have to pay. The buyer however did not co-operate with the testing by refusing to provide the necessary facilities for the test. It then rejected the digger. The House of Lords gave judgment to the seller. Lord Blackburn held that there was an implied term of co-operation and the buyer was in breach of that duty. His Lordship ruled that the effect of the buyer's refusal to co-operate in doing the test was that the seller would be entitled to payment even though the digger may not have satisfied the requirements of the contract. Although tempting, the implied duty of co-operation should not be thought to equate to a general duty of good faith, which as we know, is not a precept contained in English contract law. Although *Mackay v Dick* was decided under Scots law, the principle was considered to be equally settled under English law in *Colley v Overseas Exporters* [1921] 8 Ll. L. Rep. 127.

Hence, the duty of co-operation was held to entail an implied obligation to exercise due diligence or best endeavours to obtain a consent, approval or licence where such consent, approval or licence from a third party is essential to the performance of the contract (*Anglo-Russian Merchant Traders Ltd v Batt* [1917] 2 K.B. 679 (CA); *Brauer & Co (Great Britain) Ltd v James Clark (Brush Materials) Ltd* [1952] 2 All E.R. 497; *CPC Group Ltd v Qatari Diar Real Estate Investment Co.* [2010] EWHC 1535 (Ch)).

2–058   *Is there in English law a general duty of good faith?*

In *Yam Seng Pte Ltd v International Trade Corp. Ltd* [2013] EWHC 111 (QB), the parties in question had committed themselves to a long-term commercial relationship. ITC was found to have misled Y about the legal, commercial and logistical issues and had repeatedly missed deadlines for supplying Manchester United branded goods to Y. ITC had also unjustifiably threatened to replace Y with another distributor in Singapore. Y sued for breach of contract. Leggatt J. found in favour of Y. The judgment was especially noteworthy—the judge reasoned that the contract was subject to an *implied* duty on the parties to act in "good faith" which ITC had breached. That implied duty in an ordinary commercial contract is founded on the presumed intentions of the parties, rather than simply as a matter of law. Although the reference to "good faith" by English judges is not especially unique, the way Leggatt J. constructed the reasoning around a principle of good faith is particularly ground-breaking. English courts have always developed a good faith concept in a piecemeal fashion and have resisted saying that there is a general good faith principle. Here, the judge started by stressing the importance of implied good faith in long-term agreements requiring extensive cooperation. He then pointed out that other common law countries have changed their views on a rejection of a good faith principle and have developed the common law to accommodate such a principle. The judge also looked to some more recent English decisions on fair dealing and an expectation of honesty in business relations. He further justified the use of a good faith principle on the grounds that a contract can never cater for every eventuality, and, in the absence of express language, a reasonable construction which promotes its values and purposes should be adopted—referring to the UK Supreme Court's decision in *Rainy Sky v Kookmin Bank* [2011] UKSC 50. He also said:

"In refusing, however, if indeed it does refuse, to recognise any such general obligation of good faith, this jurisdiction would appear to be swimming against the tide. . . . Attempts to harmonise the contract law of EU member states, such as the Principles of European Contract Law proposed by the Lando Commission and the European Commission's proposed Regulation for a Common European Sales Law on which consultation is currently taking place, also embody a general duty to act in accordance with good faith and fair dealing. There can be little doubt that the penetration of this principle into English law and the pressures towards a more unified European law of contract in which the principle plays a significant role will continue to increase. It would be a mistake, moreover, to suppose that willingness to recognise a doctrine of good faith in the performance of contracts reflects a divide between civil law and common law systems or between continental paternalism and Anglo-Saxon individualism. Any such notion is gainsaid by that fact that such a doctrine has long been recognised in the United States."

This judgment shows a gradual narrowing of the gap between English common law and European civil laws. The case may or may not be supported by the higher courts but it has thrown down the gauntlet for the adoption of a good faith principle, which the judge was entirely convinced, is not contrary to the content and spirit of the common law.

The duty to co-operate would also encompass a duty to work together to   **2–059** resolve the problems that would almost certainly occur in the course of the contract (especially where it is a long-term contract), and it requires the parties not to take unreasonable actions that might damage their working relationship, *Anglo Group Plc v Winther Browne & Co Ltd* 72 Con. L.R. 118. Indeed, the substance and scope of the term of co-operation (implied or express) are more pronounced in long-term contracts than one-off contracts (*Compass Group v Mid Essex Hospital Services* [2012] EWHC 781 (QB)).

On the other hand where the seller is required to put in special effort and/or expense to ensure that loading is completed within time, the second nomination will be treated as a repudiatory breach of the contract by the buyer even though the seller had attempted to load. In *Bunge & Co Ltd v Tradax England Ltd* [1975] 2 Lloyd's Rep. 235, the sellers had commenced the loading process although they had serious misgivings about whether the loading would be completed within the agreed shipment period following a late nomination from the buyers. When it became clear that the loading could not be completed within the shipment period, the sellers stopped loading, deemed the contract to have been repudiated and sued for the price and damages for non-acceptance. The buyers argued that the sellers should be barred from claiming because they had accepted the breach by attempting to perform. The court rejected the buyers' contention and awarded the sellers damages for non-acceptance. The sellers' *action for the price* could however not be sustained when property in the goods had not passed in accordance with s.49(1) of the Sale of Goods Act 1979.

Where the contract expressly provides that the first nomination is to be final and binding then, as was pointed out in *Cargill v Continental C/A* [1989] 1 Lloyd's Rep. 193, the buyer is irrevocably bound by his first nomination. In that case, the contractual notice supplied by the buyers stipulated that it was to be treated as "final notice" of the nomination. This declaration was sufficient to deprive the buyers of any contractual right to make a substitution.[24]

The first nomination remains binding if the substitution is unsuitable or ineffective. The way *Coastal (Bermuda) Petroleum Ltd v VTT Vulcan Petroleum SA (The Marine Star)* [1993] 1 Lloyd's Rep. 329 takes and applies this proposition is of some interest.

2–060   *Coastal (Bermuda) Petroleum Ltd v VTT Vulcan Petroleum SA (The Marine Star)*
[1993] 1 Lloyd's Rep. 329
Facts:
Under a CIF contract, the sellers who had the duty of nominating a vessel to take delivery of oil from the Black Sea had substituted "The Marine Star" so that it could be used to take delivery of another cargo. The sellers alleged that as the substitute vessel was not possible to perform the contract as a result of frustrating circumstances, they were right to treat the entirety of the contract as having been rendered impossible. The force majeure clause should therefore apply.
Held:
The court disagreed holding that the sellers were barred from claiming impossibility of the CIF contract simply because their second nomination had failed. The original nomination could not be ignored and the substitution was not caused by an frustrating event falling within the ambit of the force majeure clause. The force majeure clause did not therefore avail the sellers.

That proposition should apply mutatis mutandis to the buyer in a FOB contract who has the duty and right of nominating a vessel.

The buyer's duty to pay

2–061   The buyer's duty to pay is usually prescribed by contract. The methods of payment in international sales will be discussed in a later chapter. It would however be useful to consider here when payment should be effected. The general rule is that where no time for payment has been pre-arranged, the price falls due as soon as the contract is concluded provided that the seller is ready and willing to deliver the goods according to contract. In the case of a documentary sale, the duty to pay is activated when the buyer is delivered the appropriate documents relating to the goods. In the norm, this refers to the bill of lading, although where trade custom admits any other document such as the mate's receipt, the courts will give effect to that custom accordingly. In *Kum v Wah Tat Bank Ltd* [1971] 1 Lloyd's Rep. 439, the custom of merchants shipping goods between Sarawak and Singapore was that a mate's receipt not marked "non-negotiable" and naming the consignee would be treated as negotiable and sufficient as a demand for payment. There are two conditions for the incorporation of trade usage in a contract; first, the usage must not be illegal or contrary

---

[24] It was also held that the buyer's failure to comply with the vessel nomination clause allows the seller to refuse to perform irrespective of the seller's motives. It is obvious in that case that the sellers declined to deliver because there was an upward movement in the market price of the goods.

to public policy and secondly, it must be reasonable and not contradict the express terms of the contract.

Where payment of the price is not dependent on the presentment of documents and the time for payment has been set, it was held in *Pearl Mill Co Ltd v Ivy Tannery Co Ltd* [1919] 1 K.B. 78 that this in itself is not a condition of the contract but the presence of unreasonable delay may signify an intention not to perform the contract. The unreasonable delay when coupled with some other objective evidence that the buyer wishes to abandon the contract allows the seller to resell the goods without notice to the buyer. Support for this proposition may be had in *Allied Marine Transport Ltd v Vale do Rio Doce Navegacao (The Leonidas D)* [1985] 2 All E.R. 796. Robert Goff L.J. adopted the following test as to when an intention to abandon contract may be implied

"to enable one party (the sellers) to rely on abandonment, it was enough for them to show that the buyers so conducted themselves as to entitle the sellers to assume, and that the sellers did assume, that the contract was agreed to be abandoned *sub silentio*".

It should be remembered that in the light of this decision, mere silence or omission is not sufficient because it is not conclusive as to the intention to abandon contract, only indicative. The equivocal nature of silences and omissions makes it unjust for the sellers to take the unilateral action of reselling the goods in the context of *Pearl Mill Co Ltd v Ivy Tannery Co Ltd.*

Cost, Insurance and Freight

An appropriate starting point for our discussion is Lord Wright's description of the CIF contract in *Smyth & Co Ltd v Bailey Son & Co Ltd* [1940] 3 All E.R. 60:   **2–062**

"The initials [CIF] indicate that the price is to include cost, insurance and freight. It is a type of contract which is more widely and more frequently in use than any other contract used for the purposes of sea-borne commerce. An enormous number of transactions, in value amounting to untold sums, are carried out every year under CIF contracts. The essential characteristics of this contract have often been described. The seller has to ship or acquire after that shipment the contract goods, as to which, if unascertained, he is generally required to give a notice of appropriation. On or after shipment, he has to obtain proper bills of lading and proper policies of insurance. He fulfils his contract by transferring the bills of lading and the policies to the buyer. As a general rule, he does so only against payment of the price, less the freight which the buyer has to pay. In the invoice which accompanies the tender of the documents on the 'prompt'—that is, the date fixed for payment—the freight is deducted, for this reason. In this course of business, the general property remains in the seller until he transfers the bill of lading . . . By mercantile law, the bills of lading are the symbols of the goods. The general property in the goods must be in the seller if he is to be able to pledge them. The whole system of commercial credits depends upon the seller's ability to give a charge on the goods and the policies of insurance".

The term "CIF" also indicates where delivery is to be made; hence, if the contract provides for delivery CIF Colombo this means that the seller will have to bear the cost, freight and insurance to enable delivery of the goods at Colombo. His undertaking under the contract is to ensure that the goods are delivered to the port of discharge, thus enabling him to buy goods afloat if he is not already in possession of the contracted goods. It is however not particularly common nowadays for sellers to rely on procuring goods afloat to satisfy their sale contracts. Furthermore, there are practical difficulties in buying goods afloat. This is recognised by modern case law.

In *Tradax André et Cie SA* [1976] 1 Lloyd's Rep. 416 the sellers attempted to rely on a force majeure clause in the contract to exempt them from delivering the goods as a result of a supervening impossibility. The buyers contended that the force majeure clause did not apply because there was no frustrating event; the sellers could have bought goods afloat to satisfy the contract even though this would be at the sellers' considerable cost and difficulty. Although the court recognised that possibility as not being inconsistent with CIF contracts, it was held that buying afloat was not an option because to force the sellers so to act would result in many buyers chasing after very few such cargoes at sea bearing in mind the world trade situation in that commodity. This was affirmed later by Lord Wilberforce in *Bremer v Vanden Avenne* [1978] 2 Lloyd's Rep. 109. An exception must be regarded though. In *Bunge SA v Deutsche Conti* [1979] 2 Lloyd's Rep. 435 and *André et Cie v Tradax Export* [1983] 1 Lloyd's Rep. 254 where it is proved that the contemplation of the parties is that goods should be bought from other suppliers to meet the contract before or after shipment, that term of the contract will be binding and the courts will give effect to it accordingly.

2–063   The CIF contract being girded by documents is also ideal where string transactions are envisaged. This means that before and after shipment, title in the goods is intended to pass from one buyer to another several times before the goods finally arrive at the port of call, all through the transfer of the bill of lading or similar documents of title. Hence, it is important, when considering the duties of the seller and buyer, to note that the roles change as often as the document of title changes hands.

The seller is usually duty bound:

1. to ship goods meeting the contract description at the port of shipment as agreed or to procure goods already afloat to meet the contractual requirements;

2. to enter into a contract of carriage with a carrier who is able to deliver the goods to the port of discharge as agreed and secure a bill of lading in relation to the goods;

3. to make sure that the goods are properly insured under a contract of insurance to which the buyer may avail;

4. to append a commercial invoice which conforms to the contractual description of the goods; and

5. to tender the bill of lading, the insurance policy, the invoice and other documents as provided for in the contract such as a certificate of origin, a certificate of quality, etc.

The buyer, on the other hand, should:

1. accept the documents as tendered if they conform to the contract;

2. take delivery of the goods when they arrive at the agreed port of discharge:

3. settle all customs dues at port of entry; and

4. obtain any import licences, if required.

Documentation and CIF sales

The documents mentioned above, the bill of lading, the insurance policy and **2–064** the commercial invoice, are central to the optimal discharge of the CIF contract. They are extremely important to the seller who relies on them to be paid; and for the buyer, they allow him to claim protection for and property in the goods. Where the buyer relies on his bank to settle the invoice at first instance, the bank will want proof that the contract has been performed to the satisfaction of the contract or else they in turn could be refused payment by the buyer. Equally important for the bank, the documents will serve as security for money advanced. It is therefore imperative that the seller ensures that the documents as tendered conform to the contractual requirements in order to be paid. It was suggested by Scrutton J. in *Arnold Karberg & Co v Blythe, Green, Jourdain & Co* [1915] 2 K.B. 379 that the CIF contract might more appropriately be termed a contract for the sale of documents relating to the goods rather than one for the sale of goods.[25] Although this description has been criticised for not being an accurate portrayal of the law by the Court of Appeal when the case went on appeal,[26] it really quite nicely captures the centrality of documents in the CIF contract.

As McCardie J. quite rightly suggested in *Manbre Saccharine Co Ltd v Corn Products Co Ltd* [1919] 1 K.B. 198 the difference between the Court of Appeal's approach and Scrutton J.'s description is one of phraseology only. In reality, according to McCardie J. "the obligation of the vendor is to deliver documents rather than goods—to transfer symbols rather than the physical property represented thereby". The judge went on to say:

"[I]f the vendor fulfils his contract by shipping the appropriate goods in the appropriate manner under a proper contract of carriage, and if he obtains the proper documents for tender to the purchaser, I am unable to see how the rights and duties of either party are affected by the loss of ship or goods, or by knowledge of such loss by the vendor, prior to actual tender of the documents. If the ship be lost prior to tender but without the knowledge of the seller it was,

---

[25] For an analysis of this suggestion, see Odeke, "The Nature of CIF Contract—is it a sale of documents or a sale of goods?" [1993] *Journal of Contract Law* 158.

[26] [1916] 1 K.B. 495, 510 and 514.

2–065

Shipper	VAT no.		COMMON SHORT FORM BILL OF LADING	B/L no.

Shippers reference

Forwarder's reference

Consignee	VAT no.

Name of Carrier

Notify party and address

The contract evidenced by this Short Form Bill of Lading is subject to the exceptions, limitations, conditions and liberties (including those relating to pre-carriage and on-carriage) set out in the Carrier's Standard Conditions applicable to the voyage covered by this Short Form Bill of Lading and operative on its date of issue. If the carriage is one where the provisions of the Hague Rules contained in the International Convention for unification of certain rules relating to Bills of Lading dated Brussels on 25th August 1924 as amended by the Protocol signed at Brussels on 23rd February 1968 (the Hague Visby Rules) are compulsorily applicable under Article X the said Standard Conditions contain or shall be deemed to contain a Clause giving effect to the Hague Visby Rules. Otherwise except as provided below, the said Standard conditions contain or shall be deemed to contain a Clause giving effect to the provisions of the Hague Rules.

The Carrier hereby agrees that to the extent of any inconsistency the said Clause shall prevail over the exceptions, limitations, conditions and liberties set out in the Standard Conditions in respect of any period to which the Hague Rules or the Hague Visby Rules by their terms apply. Unless the Standard Conditions expressly provide otherwise, neither the Hague Rules nor the Hague Visby Rules shall apply to this contract where the goods carried hereunder consist of live animals or cargo which by this contract is stated as being carried on deck and is so carried.

Notwithstanding anything contained in the said Standard Conditions the term Carrier in this Short Form Bill of Lading shall mean the Carrier named on the front thereof.

A copy of the Carrier's said Standard Conditions applicable hereto may be inspected or will be supplied on request at the office of the Carrier or the Carrier's Principal Agents.

Pre-Carriage by#	Place of receipt by pre-carrier#
Vessel	Port of loading
Port of discharge	Place of delivery by on-carrier#

Shipping marks: container number	Number and kind of packages: description of goods	Gross weight	Measurement

Freight details: charges etc.	

RECEIVED FOR CARRIAGE as above in apparent good order and condition, unless otherwise stated hereon, the goods described in the above particulars.

IN WITNESS whereof the number of original bills of lading stated below have been signed, all of this tenor and date, one of which being accomplished the others to stand void.

C of S
CSF
BL
1987

Ocean freight payable at	Place and date of issue
Number of original Bs/L	Signature for carrier, carrier's principal place of business

Authorised and licensed by the
Chamber of Shipping © 1979/1987/1992

I assume, always clear that he could make an effective proffer of the documents to the buyer. In my opinion it is also clear that he can make an effective tender even though he possesses at the time of tender actual knowledge of the loss of the ship or goods. For the purchaser in case of loss will get the documents he bargained for; and if the policy be that required by the contract, and if the loss be covered thereby, he will secure the insurance moneys. The contingency of loss is within and not outside the contemplation of the parties . . . ".

It is therefore vital that the documents correspond to the contract. But what constitutes a conforming document? In Chapter 6, we will assess the effects of a bill of lading as a document of title, a receipt for goods, evidence of the contract of carriage and indeed the contract of carriage itself. Here we will consider the role of that bill of lading in the sale transaction and examine what makes it conforming *for purposes of the sale of goods*.

The bill of lading must meet the following requirements or else it could be rejected for nonconformity:

It must provide continuous cover

The bill of lading must cover the entirety of the transit of the goods; any break **2–066** in cover might mean that the buyer is left without a right of suit against an errant carrier. The bill of lading should therefore be issued at time of shipment and refers to the whole of the voyage to be undertaken. In *Hansson v Hamel & Horley Ltd* [1922] 2 A.C. 36, the House of Lords made it clear that this is a requirement at law and any derogation from it is untenable and can result in repudiation of the contract.

Hansson v Hamel & Horley Ltd [1922] 2 A.C. 36 **2–067**
Facts:
The contract provided that the cargo of cod guano was to be shipped CIF Kobe or Yokohama from Norway. There were, however, no ships sailing directly from Norway to Japan. Transshipment had to be organised and the goods were placed on a local ship to be carried to Hamburg before transhipped to Japan. The bill of lading issued at the port of Hamburg referring to the carrying vessel as *The Atlas Maru* makes no reference of the leg between Norway and Hamburg.
Held:
Lord Summer, whose speech found concurrence with the House, said:

"A [CIF] seller, as often been pointed out, has to cover the buyer by procuring and tendering documents which will be available for his protection from shipment to destination".

The ocean bill of lading (i.e. a bill of lading covering the ocean leg of the shipment) in this case afforded the buyer no protection in regard to the first voyage. Although the bill of lading as issued was labelled a "through bill of lading" it was not really so because it gave the buyer no protection for the first leg of the voyage. It was further held that it was immaterial that no loss or damage had occurred during the first part of the voyage.

Where the contract provides for transshipment, it is the seller's responsibility to procure a through bill of lading, i.e. one that covers the whole voyage. In commerce it is quite likely that a bill of lading having retrospective effect may be issued. The validity of such bills of lading was considered by Lord Summer who held that bills of lading with retrospective cover issued subsequent to the commencement of voyage are valid provided that they had been issued within a reasonable time after commencement of the voyage. Whilst the courts may be inclined to allow some latitude of time, any delayed issue of the bill of lading has to be reasonable. In *Foreman & Ellams Ltd v Blackburn* [1928] 2 K.B. 60, the contract called for delivery of frozen rabbits CIF Liverpool from Sydney. Seven weeks after the ship had set sail from Sydney a bill of lading was issued. This the court thought was excessively delayed. It was not regular in that trade for the issue of a bill of lading after such long lapse of time from shipment.

2–068   A possible exception is where there exists a local trade custom that the subsequent bill of lading be issued in exchange for the original bill of lading covering only the first leg of the voyage. In *Meyer v Aune* (1939) 55 T.L.R. 876, the CIF contract provided for the delivery of copra from Sibu, Borneo (now the state of Sarawak in Malaysia). The copra was first shipped to the Philippines from Sibu. The bill of lading issued in Sibu covered the voyage to the Philippines but not beyond. At port in the Philippines, that bill of lading was surrendered for a bill of lading backdated to the original date of shipment. The buyers in Marcé rejected the documents for loss of continuous cover. The court however took into account the fact that the practice of not issuing through bills in the region for local shipment was so notorious and common that the buyers must be deemed to have notice of the custom. For that reason the rejection was not justified.

The consignees in *Foreman & Ellams Ltd v Blackburn* [1928] 2 K.B. 60 encountered a different situation. There the goods were shipped within shipment period but a bill of lading was not issued until the ship had returned to port after making several domestic ports of call. They were, according to the court, deprived of cover between the original shipment date and the time the ship finally set sail for England. Continuous cover is a cardinal requisite of the CIF contract.

The subsequent issue of the bill of lading is not only inconsistent with the rule that it should provide continuous cover for the buyer but also may fall foul of the rule that the terms on its face will be treated as conclusive. In *Landauer v Craven* [1912] 2 K.B. 94 the contract stated that delivery was CIF London from Hong Kong or the Philippines, "direct or indirect" voyage. Shipment was to be effected between October 1 and December 31. The goods were shipped from Manila, the Philippines to Hong Kong on December 28 which was properly within shipment period. The goods then were transshipped from Hong Kong on March 25 and a bill of lading dated March 25 was issued. The buyers were not happy with the bill of lading and paid under protest. The court held the bill of lading untenable because it was dated March 25 which was outside shipment period. Extraneous evidence that the goods had in fact been shipped in December was not admissible to rebut the description on the face of the bill. Of course, it is also obvious that there was no bill of lading cover for the leg between Manila and Hong Kong.

The bill must be genuine

2–069   The bill of lading must be genuine in that it must accurately portray the actual state of affairs at the time of shipment. In *Landauer v Craven* we have seen how important it is to ensure that the date of shipment evidenced in the bill of lading coincides with the contractual time of shipment. There the bill was properly rejected because by law it had designated conclusively that the date of shipment was March 25. That date was however outside the agreed time of shipment. This naturally wields tremendous pressure on sellers to procure bills of lading that suggest that shipment was on time. Occasion for fraud or forgery in the dating of the bill of lading is abetted by the fact that frequently the buyer has no control over the issue of the bill of lading and he is not at the port of shipment to know that goods have been shipped late. Carriers may also contrive to issue false bills of lading so as to avoid liability for late delivery.

In *Finlay v Kwik Hoo Tong* [1929] 1 K.B. 400, the CIF contract provided for shipment to be in September. When the bills of lading were tendered, nothing suggested that shipment was outside September. The bill of lading was in fact inaccurate. The inaccuracy was discovered two years later by which time the buyers had entered into subcontracts for the delivery of those goods. The sub-buyers refused to take delivery alleging that the goods had been shipped outside shipment period and that the bill of lading was not genuine. The court held that in their undertaking to supply a conforming bill of lading, the original sellers are deemed to have promised to state truly in the bill the date of shipment. The fact that they had not done so meant that the buyers had lost their right to reject the documents for which damages ought to be payable to compensate for this loss of right.

In *Foreman & Ellams Ltd v Blackburn* [1928] 2 K.B. 60, the bill of lading representing the frozen rabbits stated "shipment on the SS Suffolk now lying in Sydney". It was issued on August 17. The ship had actually loaded the goods in June and had left Sydney to collect other consignments at other ports in Australia. It then returned to Sydney where the bill was issued and then finally sailed for Liverpool. The court found the bill to be inaccurate because it did not refer to the initial shipment of the goods in June.

The bill must be unaltered

The law recognises the paramountcy of security in documentary sales by **2–070** providing that the bills as procured must not contain any alterations. The presumption is that where there are entered on the face of a bill altered terms the bill will not be valid. In *SIAT v Tradax* [1980] 1 Lloyd's Rep. 53, the bill of lading was altered by the shipmaster who visited the various persons in possession of the bills and cancelled out the destination shown and substituting it with "Venezia". It was agreed that an altered bill of lading has little value in international commerce. The sellers recognised this and attempted to rely on a clause in the contract permitting them to require the buyers to accept the documents if they, as sellers, gave adequate notice to the buyers that the shipment had been in accordance with the contract. The court in commenting on the altered bill said that the bill of lading must provide for the carriage to the agreed destination and although the original charterparty did allow goods to be delivered to either Ravenna or Venice, the terms on the bill could not be varied by extraneous evidence such as the charterparty. On whether the sellers could rely on the standard trade clause allowing them to demand acceptance of the documents (and goods) regardless of the state of the bill of lading, the court held that such clauses must be construed narrowly. In the present context, since the letter of guarantee issued by the sellers could not really guarantee that performance had indeed been consistent with the original contract, it could not assist them.

The bill must be effective as a contract of carriage

2–071 The bill of lading as the contract of carriage itself has to be fully effective as such before the buyers are required to accept it. It must be effective not only at the time of shipment or when it was issued but at the time of tender. In *Arnold Karberg v Blythe, Green, Jourdain & Co* [1916] 1 Q.B. 495, we have seen how the bill was ineffective because the contract of carriage contained in it has become illegal. The sellers had argued in that case that in a CIF contract the buyer should bear any war risk and as such the bill should be accepted and paid for. To this Bankes L.J. said:

> "I quite accept the contention that certain risks do fall on the buyer, as the parties have agreed that the seller shall be under no obligation to obtain policies covering war risks. I agree also that the condition of the goods at the time of the tender of the shipping documents is not material nor is the value of the documents at the time of tender material. In all such matters the risk is on the buyer. He may be obliged to pay for goods although they may be at the bottom of the sea, or although through some unforeseen circumstance they may never arrive, or although they may have been lost owing to some cause not covered by the agreed form of policy. All these risks, however are risks affecting the goods. In effect the contention of the appellants appears to me to be a contention that one of the risks undertaken by the buyer is a risk affecting this contract, and not the goods the subject-matter of the contract. I cannot agree with this view. It appears to me that the question of the construction of the contract must depend on the language used, and not upon any such considerations as these. In the present case it is not disputed that the outbreak of war dissolved the contract of affreightment, and that in so far as any further prosecution of the voyage was concerned the bill of lading was no longer an effective document".

Although the effectiveness of the bill of lading may be affected by considerations of public policy and illegality, it is not vitiated by the loss of goods or ship. As was pointed out by Bankes L.J. the latter are factors impacting on the goods and *not the contract*. This was reiterated in *Manbre Saccharine Co Ltd v Corn Products Co Ltd* [1919] 1 K.B. 198 where McCardie J. quoted *Scrutton on Charterparties*, 8th edn:

> "[T]here may be cases in which the buyer must pay the full price for delivery of the documents, though he can get nothing out of them, and though in any intelligible sense no property in the goods can ever pass to him—*i.e.*, if the goods have been lost by a peril excepted by the bill of lading, and by a peril not insured by the policy, the bill of lading and the policy yet being in the proper commercial form called for by the contract".

The bill must be effective as a document of title

2–072 As a document of title, it must be legally effective to pass title in the goods to the buyer. The requirements of the Carriage of Goods by Sea Act 1992 must therefore be satisfied.[27]

---

[27] See Ch.6 on Bills of Lading for a fuller account.

The bill must be clean on its face

It must be clear from the face of the bill that the goods have been received for   **2–073**
shipped and shipped in apparent good order and condition. Any clause or
qualification in the bill that the goods are not in good order and condition would
render the bill unclean. Such a clause is documentary evidence that the contract
of sale had not been performed as regards quality and possibly, description. A
seller who tenders a bill of lading which is claused need not be paid. We shall see
in Chapter 6 that the statement of the condition of the goods refers to the state of
the goods at the time of shipment and not subsequent to shipment.[28] In *The
Galatia* [1980] 1 All E.R. 501 for example, the 200 tonnes of sugar were
damaged by fire after they had been put on board "The Galatia". The shipmaster
had initially indicated in the bill of lading that the goods had been received and
shipped in good order and condition. Following the fire, he typed on the bill "Bill
of lading has been discharged as a result of damage". This, the court held, was
immaterial and did not render the bill unclean. The clausing or qualification was
added after the goods had been shipped by which time the bill of lading would
have been operational and the clause added or detracted nothing from it.

The bill should be freely transferable

Subject to the terms of the contract, it is conventional that the bill of lading be   **2–074**
made "to order", so as to entitle the consignor to transfer the rights represented
by the bill of lading to a sub-buyer or any other person simply by "indorsement"
(i.e. writes or prints on the bill that the document is "indorsed" to a named
person) or mere delivery. It is of course possible for the sale agreement merely
to envisage the issue of a straight consigned bill of lading. This happens where
the consignee of the goods and the bill of lading has no intention to pass on his
rights in the goods and the bill to any third party. Where a buyer is buying for his
own consumption and does not need trade finance from a bank, for example,
there is usually no need for a "to order" bill. A bill of lading which is issued
specifically to a named consignee is not freely transferable. It is called a straight
consigned bill of lading.[29]

Although the "to order" bill of lading makes it easily transferable, it would not
be right to call the "to order" bill a negotiable instrument. It does not satisfy the
requirements for negotiability at common law. The Privy Council had this to say
in *Henderson v The Comptoire d'Escompte de Paris* (1873) L.R. 5 P.C. 253:

> "It appears that a bill of lading was made out, which is in the usual form, with
> this difference, that the words 'or order or assigns' are omitted. It has been
> argued that, notwithstanding the omission of these words, this bill of lading
> was a negotiable instrument, and there is some authority at *nisi prius* for that
> proposition; but, undoubtedly, the general view of the mercantile world has

---

[28] paras 6–024—6–026.

[29] It should however not be assumed that a straight bill is not a bill of lading; although it is not
freely transferable, in the hands of the named consignee it remains a good document of title (*The
Rafaela S* [2005] UKHL 11). A straight bill of lading should be distinguished from a sea waybill. The
sea waybill is not a document of title, and is frequently used for short sea journeys. It does not entitle
the holder to take delivery of the goods on its presentation to the carrier. The carrier would require
proof of identity before releasing the goods.

been for some time that, in order to make bills of lading negotiable, some such words as 'or order or assigns' ought to be in them. For the purposes of this case, in the view their Lordships take, it may be assumed that this bill of lading is not a negotiable instrument".

In *International Air and Sea Cargo v Owners of the Ship "Chitral"* [2000] 1 All E.R. (Comm) 932 the court was urged to accept a straight consigned bill of lading as a "to order" or "negotiable" bill. The defendants argued that there was a phrase within the printed section of the bill to the effect that delivery was to be "unto the above-mentioned consignee or to his or their assigns". This was said to have the impact of rendering the box for inserting the name of the consignee as if the words "or order" had been added. The court refused to accept that submission, stating:

"a. The printed box for naming of the consignee specifically provides 'if order state notify party' (and no such notify party was so stated).

b. It follows that the form contemplates that it may be used both as a straight consigned bill and as negotiable bill as might be required by the shipper.

c. The Defendants' construction would eliminate these alternative uses.

d. A more comfortable construction of the printed term is that is intended as a general description of the shipowners' obligations in performing the carriage with delivery to the consignee or his assigns 'if applicable'."

The defendants further relied upon the fact that the consignee had purported to indorse the bill to a third party. But an "indorsement" of a non-negotiable bill must, by definition, be ineffective. Where the form of the bill enables the shipper to elect whether to have a sea waybill or a bill of lading properly so-called, the notation simply begs the question, it does not provide the confirmation that it is indeed freely transferable.

The bill must not be a forgery

2–075 If the bill of lading had been forged, it is not to be treated as a bill of lading. It is ineffective ab initio and cannot be conferred any legal force for obvious reasons. It is a non-instrument. In *Motis Exports Ltd v Dampskibsselskabet AF 1912, Aktieselskabet Dampskibsselskabet Svendborg* [2000] 1 Lloyd's Rep. 211, the claimant was the shipper of various consignments under a number of Maersk Line bills of lading. The question for the court was whether the carriers were liable for the loss of the goods caused by their releasing the goods against valid delivery orders obtained by rogues producing forged bills of lading. The carrier's defence was that they were innocent and were as much the victims as the claimant. The question was whether the exemption of liability clause in the agreement protected them. That clause read:

"Where the carriage called for commences at the port of loading and/or finishes at the port of discharge, the Carrier shall have no liability whatsoever for any loss or damage to the goods while in its actual or constructive possession before loading and after discharge over the ship's rail, or if applicable, on the ship's ramp, however caused".

They argued that the clause applied because the goods had already crossed the ship's rail when they were delivered against the fraudulently obtained delivery orders.

The bill of lading serves an important general role in representing and securing both title to and physical possession of goods.[30] Mummery L.J. observed that although skilled fraud may not be uncommon, the carrier's construction of the exemption clause would appear to go to the extreme of protecting against any misdelivery, however negligent, and to undervalue the importance which both parties must be taken to have attached to the ship's obligation to deliver against presentation of original bills of lading. It should however be noted that in the light of *Photo Productions v Securicor Transport Ltd* [1980] A.C. 827, it should not be presumed that a wide exemption clause would not be effective at common law, especially, given that the Unfair Contract Terms Act 1977 has no place in international supply and, possibly, international carriage contracts.[31]

The Court of Appeal dismissed the carrier's appeal stating that the natural subject matter of the exemption clause consisted in loss or damage caused to the goods while in the carrier's custody but not the deliberate delivery up of the goods. Having disposed of the exemption clause, the court then went on to hold that this was a case of misdelivery. A forged bill of lading is a nullity in the eyes of the law. It was, according to the Court of Appeal, simply a piece of paper with writing on it, which had no effect whatsoever. It was no defence for the carrier to say that he was the victim of the fraud himself.

Time of tender

Assuming that the bill of lading obtained by the seller is conforming, he should **2–076** ensure that it is tendered within a reasonable time after shipment of the goods. Whether the goods arrive before or after the presentment of the bill of lading is immaterial as long as the seller had made the tender within reasonable time. In *Sanders Brothers v Maclean & Co* (1883) 11 Q.B.D. 327, Brett M.R. said:

> "I quite agree that [the seller] has no right to keep the bill of lading in his pocket, and when it is said that he should do what is reasonable, it is obvious that the reasonable thing is he should make every reasonable exertion to send forward the bill of lading as soon as possible after he has destined the cargo to the particular vendee or consignee. If that be so, the question whether he has used such reasonable exertion will depend upon the particular circumstances of each case".

These circumstances could include the nature of the goods shipped, the distances involved, the existence of string contracts, administrative charges involved in late delivery, etc. For example, where the goods are perishable the reasonable thing for him to do is to make even a greater exertion than he would in another situation. Where the documents are tendered late, the buyer is entitled to reject them according to the Court of Appeal's decision in *Toepfer v Lenersan-Poortman NV* [1980] 1 Lloyd's Rep. 143.

---

[30] See Todd, [1999] L.M.C.L.Q. 449 on reservations expressed on this elevation of the bill of lading.

[31] s.26 and Sch.1 of the Unfair Contract Terms Act 1977.

2–077	*Toepfer v Lenersan-Poortman NV* [1980] 1 Lloyd's Rep. 143
Facts:
The CIF contract required that payment be made no later than 20 days after the date of the bill of lading. The bills of lading were issued on December 11. Nine days later the ship ran aground. The goods were rescued and placed onto another vessel which did not discharge the goods until April. In the meantime the sellers had tendered the delivery orders to the buyers in February. The buyers rejected the delivery orders alleging that they were out of time.
Held:
The Court of Appeal held that the requirement that payment be made within 20 days after the issue of the bills of lading did not only grant the sellers a right to be paid within that time but had also imposed on them a duty to tender conforming documents in time so that the buyers could make prompt payment on the agreed date. The time of tender in a mercantile contract is generally a condition.

The buyer's two rights—right to conforming documents and right to conforming goods

2–078	The CIF contract gives rise to two distinct rights: the right to call for conforming documents and the right to conforming goods. This binomial nature of the CIF contract is a source of major legal difficulties. First, the two rights must be distinct in the contract; a general reference in a trade term calling for the use of documents does not necessarily mean that it is a CIF contract. Secondly, there is the problem of working out how one right affects the other. For example, how does the parties' conduct vis-à-vis one right affect their entitlement to the other in the same contract?

On the first issue, it is perhaps understandable that some non-CIF contracts which nevertheless make express reference to documents have been mis-described as CIF sales. In *Comptoir d'Achat et de Vente du Boerenbond Belge SA v Luis de Ridder Ltd* [1949] A.C. 293, it was clear that although the parties had termed their contract CIF, it was in fact an arrival or ex ship contract.

2–079	*Comptoir d'Achat et de Vente du Boerenbond Belge SA v Luis de Ridder Ltd (The Julia)* [1949] A.C. 293
Facts:
The contract for the delivery of a cargo of rye was described as CIF Antwerp, Belgium. It contemplated that the buyers were to pay against a bill of lading or a delivery order. The buyers then paid against a delivery order. Under the contract the sellers had undertaken to pay for any deficiency in weight or quality on arrival, and any averages arising from the shipment. Subsequent to that Belgium was invaded by Germany and it became impossible for the ship to enter port under those circumstances. The goods were discharged in Portugal instead. The buyers sued to recover the moneys paid claiming that consideration for the contract had totally collapsed. The sellers alleged that the contract was on CIF terms which meant that all they had to do was to tender conforming documents.
Held:
The House of Lords disagreed with the construction applied to the contract by the sellers. Lord Porter considered the main issue to be whether under those circumstances, the buyers had undertaken to pay for the documents representing the goods or for the delivery of the goods themselves. While recognising that commercial realities might make it necessary to substitute the bill of lading with a delivery order as a document against which payment is to be made or the insurance policy with an insurance certificate, the law must take into account the presumed intention of the parties as evidenced by the circumstances surrounding the contract. The present agreement however referred to the seller's duty to

account for the landed weight on the ship's arrival at Antwerp. The contract as a whole was therefore an arrival contract and not one on CIF terms.

Similarly in *Scottish & Newcastle International Ltd v Ghalanos* [2008] UKHL 11 the House of Lords made it clear that the label used in the contract would not trump the substance of the contract. In that case, the contract for the sale of cider was labelled "CFR Limassol, Cyprus". However, as the contract provided for the buyer's right to designate a vessel to take delivery of the cider at Liverpool, England, it could not be properly treated as a CFR contract where it would be the seller who should arrange for carriage. Thus, although it was labelled CFR, the true nature of the contract called for delivery FOB Liverpool.

It is important to be able to identify the CIF contract and distinguish it from **2–080** contracts under other trade terms because it is in the CIF contract where there is that splendid distinction between the seller's obligation to ship conforming goods and the buyer's duty to pay against conforming documents. The majority of the Court of Appeal in *Gill & Duffus SA v Berger & Co Inc (No.2)* [1983] 1 Lloyd's Rep. 622 erroneously held that the buyers were entitled to justify a wrongful rejection of documents on the basis that the goods that finally arrived were not in conformity. The House of Lords dismissed this approach as being an absolute contradiction to the essence of a CIF contract.[32] The fact that the goods delivered could have been rejected on the basis of non-conformity does not and cannot retrospectively validate a wrongful rejection of the documents. The duties are distinct and separate.

The distinctiveness of the two duties can raise difficult problems for the buyer who has accepted documents which appear conforming but are in fact defective, and subsequently the goods where he has no means of discovering whether the goods had been shipped according to contractual requirements.[33] As payment of the price would have taken place during the tender of the documents, the buyer is compelled to take delivery of the goods even though they are not in conformity. The goods are his only security. In *Taylor & Sons Ltd v Bank of Athens* (1922) Com. Cas. 142, the buyers who in reliance on the misdated bill of lading, had taken delivery of goods shipped outside shipment period, claimed for damages alleging that the goods were not in conformity. They were awarded only nominal damages. The court held that it was only a breach of warranty and damages were to be based on the difference between the goods actual value as shipped and the market value of goods shipped within the contracted shipment period. Since there was no difference between the two values, the buyers were awarded a mere nominal sum—they had suffered no actual loss, only a loss of right.

In *Finlay v Kwik Hoo Tong* [1929] 1 K.B. 400 the sellers were to perform two specific duties, (a) to ship the goods meeting the contractual description and (b) to tender conforming and genuine documents. There they had failed to perform both. The buyers, however, attempted to claim damages for the defective documents instead of late shipment of the goods. Their argument was that by the defective and inaccurate bill of lading they had forfeited their right to reject the documents and in turn had to accept the goods when the market for those goods was falling.

---

[32] See [1984] A.C. 382 for the HL judgment.
[33] Feltham, "The Appropriation in a CIF contract of goods lost or damaged at sea" [1975] J.B.L. 273.

2–081 *Finlay v Kwik Hoo Tong* [1929] 1 K.B. 400
Facts:
The bill of lading had stated not fraudulently but inaccurately that shipment had taken place within shipment period. The buyers accepted the documents without notice of the fact that the goods had been shipped outside shipment period. On the strength and in reliance on the documents they had then entered into several subcontracts. Their subpurchasers refused to take delivery of the goods alleging that the goods did not meet their contractual description, i.e. they were not shipped within shipment period (see *Bowes v Shand* [1877] A.C. 455, below). If the buyers were aware of the defect in the documents, they could have rejected them and avoided the falling market price in the goods. They sued to recover damages for this loss.
Held:
The Court of Appeal gave judgment for the buyers and held that the failure to tender genuine documents had deprived the buyers of their right of rejection which they would have exercised without a doubt in the falling market. The buyers were awarded damages which restored them to the position had they been able to reject the documents; namely the difference between the contract price and market price. It was also held that the computation of damages may take into account the commercial morality of the sellers' conduct and the buyers' business reputation.

Where the defect in the documents is discovered before taking delivery of the goods, the buyers are entitled to reject the consignment even though the goods had been paid for and property in them had passed to the buyers.[34] In *Kwei Tek Chao v British Traders & Shippers Ltd* [1954] 2 Q.B. 459 under the contract of sale, delivery of the chemical was to be made in Hong Kong. Property in the goods passed to the buyers when they were paid for in exchange for the bills of lading. It was later discovered by the buyers that the goods had been shipped outside shipment period. The bills of lading had been forged without the sellers' complicity. Devlin J. held that the buyers were entitled to reject the goods, the title of which was defeasible. The right of rejection may be activated unless the buyers had accepted the goods in accordance with the provisions of s.35 of the Sale of Goods Act 1979. Under s.35, the buyer is deemed to have accepted the goods when he intimates to the seller that he has accepted them or when he does any act to goods delivered to him which is inconsistent with the ownership of the seller. Furthermore, where the goods are delivered to the buyer and he has not previously examined them, he is not deemed to have accepted them until he has had a reasonable opportunity to examine them to ascertain whether they are in conformity with the contract.

2–082 In the CIF contract, it is envisaged that property in the goods passes on the tender of documents but that passage is subject to the condition that they re-vest if upon examination the buyer finds them not to be in accordance with the contract. This means that he gets only conditional property in the goods. Thus, the buyer's dealings with the documents are merely dealings with that conditional property in the goods. It therefore must follow that there can be no dealing which is inconsistent with the seller's ownership in the goods. The buyer who transfers the documents on in exchange for payment is merely selling on his conditional property in the goods; the seller retains a reversionary interest in the goods.[35]

---

[34] Treitel, "Rights of rejection under CIF sales" [1984] L.M.C.L.Q. 565.
[35] Crawford, "Analysis and operation of a CIF contract" [1995] Tulane L. Rev. 396.

In *Hardy & Co v Hillerns and Fowler* [1923] 2 K.B. 490, we see an example of a buyer acting in a manner inconsistent with his conditional property. The seller's reversionary interest in the goods becomes operative immediately following the buyer's act of examining the goods upon their landing at the port of discharge. Although the pledge or transfer of documents relating to the goods does not constitute an act inconsistent with the seller's reversionary interest, the actual physical dispatch of some of the goods to a sub-buyer by the buyer during the time he was given to examine the goods does.

This principle of the buyer's conditional property was applied in *Kwei Tek Chao v British Traders & Shippers Ltd* to enable the buyers to claim damages for the loss of right to reject the documents even though they had taken delivery of the goods knowing that the goods had been shipped outside shipment period. The prudence in the buyer's act, to wit, in ensuring that he retains some security having paid in full for the documents (as in *Taylor & Sons Ltd v Bank of Athens*), was held to be acceptable and should not be construed as a bar to the buyer's claim.

Both *Finlay v Kwik Hoo Tong* and *Kwei Tek Chao v British Traders &* **2–083** *Shippers* enfold a buyer who has suffered loss as a result of two breaches by the seller—the failure of the seller to ship within shipment period and the failure to tender a genuine document. Where the documents are not genuine but the goods have been shipped within shipment period and are conforming in all other respect, the Court of Appeal held in *Procter & Gamble Philippine Manufacturing Corp v Kurt A. Becher GmbH* [1988] 2 Lloyd's Rep. 21 that the buyer would not be entitled to claim any more than nominal damages even though by the time of the goods landing market price had fallen. While it is recognised that the bill of lading should carry a correct date and be genuine as a condition of the contract, the bills of lading in the present case did not conceal a failure to ship goods in accordance with their contractual description. In *Finlay v Kwik Hoo Tong*, the bill of lading, if correctly dated, would have entitled the buyer to avoid the loss occasioned by the falling market but not in *Proctor & Gamble*. It may be observed that while the award of market loss damages could discourage lax practices in the trade, it could surely not be warranted where the seller is not aware or to be blamed for the misdating.

The rule in *Procter & Gamble Corp v Kurt A Becher GmbH*, however, should not exclude the buyer's right to claim damages for loss other than the market loss suffered by reason of the false bill of lading.[36] Where the buyer is unable to fulfil a pre-existing subsale contract as a result of the false bill of lading or is locked in on a falling market, he could recover damages from the seller for such loss. The buyer is of course not restrained by the *Procter & Gamble* rule from suing the carrier in the tort of deceit for having been deprived of the right to reject the goods and/or documents (*The Saudi Crown* [1986] 1 Lloyd's Rep. 261).

The buyer could lose his right to reject nonconforming documents if he waives his right or does an act which would bar him from enforcing his right later on. In *Panchaud Frères SA v Etablissements General Grain Co* [1970] 1 Lloyd's Rep. 53.

---

[36] Treitel, "Damages for breach of a CIF contract" [1988] L.M.C.L.Q. 457.

2–084   *Panchaud Frères SA v Etablissements General Grain Co* [1970] 1 Lloyd's Rep. 53
Facts:
Shipment was to be June/July 1965. The bill of lading stated that shipment had taken place
on July 31, 1965. The certificate of quality on the other hand suggested that the goods had
been loaded between August 10 and 12, 1965. The issue for the court was whether the
buyers by taking up the documents and paying for them should be precluded from
complaining of late shipment or the defect in the documents.
Held:
Lord Denning M.R. opined that if the buyer who is entitled to reject so conducts himself
as to lead the other party to believe that he is not relying on that ground, he cannot
afterwards set it up as a ground of rejection. The judge also felt disposed to state that the
buyers should have examined the documents carefully before accepting the goods
afterwards. Winn L.J. on the other hand saw it as a requirement of fair conduct "an
inchoate doctrine . . . negating any liberty to blow hot and cold in commercial conduct".
His Lordship was also apprehensive as to any introduction of constructive notice as an
element in the waiver into commercial transactions and as such did not venture to find
estoppel or waiver in the circumstances. Judgment was therefore given to the sellers.

A related case, *Procter & Gamble Philippine Manufacturing Corp v Peter
Cremer GmbH & Co (The Manila)* [1988] 3 All E.R. 843 raises the issue as to
whether a CIF buyer who has taken up documents for goods shipped late can
reject the goods although the documents only disclosed the possibility of late
shipment. Under the CIF contract, the buyers had paid 98 per cent of the price
despite the fact that a survey report stated that loading was not completed until
eleven days after the issue of the bill of lading. The buyers then wanted to
repudiate the contract. The court held that the arbitrator's finding that the survey
report which was not required under the contract could not cast doubt on the bill
of lading which must be taken as conclusive on its face. Hirst J. referred to
Panchaud Frères SA v Etablissements General Grain Co and reviewed the law
on estoppel and waivers. The judge found that no distinctive principle may be
derived from the speeches in *Panchaud Frères SA v Etablissements General
Grain Co* but if he had to choose, he would apply Lord Denning M.R.'s analysis.
Estoppel may be applied to prevent the buyer from blowing hot and cold but
there is no evidence of estoppel on the facts here. Moreover, the present case
according to Hirst J. was different from *Panchaud Frères SA v Etablissements
General Grain Co* in that the survey report was not part of the contractually
required documents and as such no reliance could be placed on it when deciding
whether the goods had been shipped within shipment period. The bill of lading
must be taken on its face.

2–085   We shall now examine how and when an estoppel and/or waiver might apply.
A waiver occurs when a party who is entitled to a right under contract expresses
either in words or conduct that he will not seek to exercise that right and this
undertaking of his is not supported by consideration from the promisee. Where
the promisee then acts in reliance on this undertaking, the promisor is estopped
from resiling from his promise. Where a party has the option to exercise one of
two alternative rights, the fact that he opts for one and not the other is a waiver
of that other. His act of election, as this sort of waiver is known, are governed by
the following rules:

1. the promisor has full knowledge of the circumstances giving rise to his rights
   (in *The Manila* Hirst J. opined that constructive knowledge is insufficient,
   only actual notice will do);

2. the election need not be supported by consideration;

3. it need not take any specific form, for example it need not be in writing or under seal;

4. there is no need to show reliance by one party on the election;

5. the election, once made, is final; and

6. the promisor could only be bound by his election if the alternative rights involved had in fact been in existence at the time of the election.

An estoppel is different in that it requires a representation from one party that he will not insist on his legal rights against the other party. Furthermore, the law will only bind the promisor to that promise if the promisee had relied on the promise and it would be inequitable to allow the promisor to go back on his promise. Knowledge, whether constructive or actual, does not come into the equation at all. In *Motor Oil Hellas (Corinth) Refineries SA v Shipping Corp of India (The Kanchenjunga)* [1990] 1 Lloyd's Rep. 391, Lord Goff said:

"No question arises of any particular knowledge on the part of the representor, and the estoppel may be suspensory only. Furthermore, the representation itself is different in character [from election]. The party making his election is communicating his choice whether or not to exercise a right which has become available to him. The party to an equitable estoppel is representing that he will not in the future enforce his legal rights. His representation is therefore in the nature of a promise which, though unsupported by consideration, can have legal consequences; hence it is sometimes referred to as promissory estoppel".

Where the goods shipped are defective, does the buyer have a right to claim damages in a CIF sale assuming that the documents tendered were in conformity? It is quite possible that certain defects or nonconformity in the goods would not have been apparent on the face of the documents, hence to deprive the buyer of the right to reject the goods simply because he had accepted the documents would seem quite unjust (*Kwei Tek Chao v British Traders & Shippers Ltd*). The measure of damages is to be calculated according to the formula in s.53(3) of the Sale of Goods Act 1979. That provision allows the buyer to claim damages to the difference between the value of the goods at the time of delivery and the value of the goods if they had been conforming. This is yet another argument why the CIF contract is a sale of goods rather than a sale of documents contract.

Other documents

Besides the bill of lading, the seller has to tender the commercial invoice and the **2–086** insurance policy if he wishes to be paid. Some contracts also call for the presentation of certificates of origin and movement certificates. Very briefly, the invoice is the demand for payment and therefore must refer to the goods as evidenced in the corresponding bill of lading. Any inconsistency would mean rejection and a legitimate right to refuse payment. The certificate of origin is a frequently called for document. It may be required either by the buyer who wishes to have a certification as to the originating point of the goods or the laws of the importing country. Some overseas countries require the certificate of origin to be legalised by their UK consulates or legations before the certificate becomes acceptable. For such a service, a legalisation fee is normally payable.

Another document of some importance for traders is a certificate of quality or a survey report relating to the condition of the goods issued by an agreed third party. As regards the issuer's duty of care, clearly a duty is owed to the parties to whom the certificate is directed. For example, where the buyer and seller agree to the nomination of a particular issuer, that issuer will owe both the buyer and seller a duty of care as there is quite obviously a relationship of proximity (*Hedley Byrne v Heller* [1964] A.C. 465). Conversely, if the certificate is relied on by a stranger, say a person who comes across the document by accident, it is unlikely that the issuer would owe this person a duty of care as there is no relationship of proximity (*Caparo v Dickman* [1990] 2 A.C. 605). As to whether other individuals such as buyers who have not been identified in the contract between the seller and the issuer, or sub-buyers down the supply chain, the position is less clear. It is quite fact dependent as to whether the court would be able safely to say that there exists a relationship of sufficient proximity and reasonable foreseeability of harm *(AIC Ltd v ITS Testing Services (UK) Ltd (The Kriti Palm)* [2007] 1 Lloyd's Rep. 555).

The duty to take reasonable care is also an implied term of the contract between the certifier and the traders. However, it is less clear whether the duty to take reasonable care included a duty to carry out re-tests should the need arise and consequently to disclose the re-test results to all concerned. In *The Kriti Palm* the majority of the Court of Appeal held that, under the circumstances of that case, there was a duty of disclosure. Rix L.J. who gave the dissenting judgment was on the other hand concerned that such a conclusion might give rise to an erroneous general principle. His Lordship reasoned that as a general proposition, any provider of goods or services who has reason to think that the goods or services provided have some flaw or defect would have a duty to disclose his suspicion or concern, and to investigate it and report it to his buyers and any sub-buyers. That would surely be inviting trouble to established jurisprudence. Buxton L.J. however made clear that no general proposition of law was being proferred:

"[T]he existence of such a duty is a matter of commonsense . . . Not only as a matter of law, but also commercially, it really challenges reality to think that a certifier, armed with tests that suggested that the tests used to complete the certificate had or might have produced incorrect results, could nonetheless simply do nothing about it; and in particular could properly say nothing about those tests to those who had employed him to certify . . . That obligation, of not sitting on material of one's own creation that is known to be inconsistent with the certificate, does not lead to the endless uncertainty that Rix LJ fears . . . It is for the holder of the certificate to decide what he does with the information once he receives it. What I cannot accept is that considerations of

2–087

INVOICE　RECHNUNG　FACTURE　FACTURA　فاتـــــورة

U
N
I
C

Invoice number		
Invoice date (tax point)	Seller's reference	
Buyer's reference	Other reference	

Consignee　　　　　VAT no	Buyer (if not consignee)　　　VAT no
	Country of origin of goods　　　Country of destination
	Terms of delivery and payment

Vessel/flight no. and date	Port/airport of loading
Port/airport of discharge	Place of delivery

Shipping marks, container number	No. and kind of packages description of goods	Commodity code	Total gross wt (Kg)	Total cube (m3)
			Total net wt(Kg)	

Item/packages	Gross/net/cube	Description	Quantity	Unit price	Amount
					Invoice total

Name of signatory

Place and date of issue

It is hereby certified that this invoice shows the actual price of the goods described, that no other invoice has been or will be issued, and that all particulars are true and correct.

Signature

certainty empower the certifier to take that decision for the holder by withholding relevant information from him. Nor does such a duty create a continuing duty of review and disclosure under every conceivable kind of contract . . . . This is the specific case of a certificate, where the certifier was in possession of material of his own creation that cast doubt on the certificate that he had given".

The concern of both Rix and Buxton L.JJ. should be heeded. A duty of disclosure in general commercial law would give rise to much uncertainty. *The Kriti Palm* should therefore be confined to its own distinctive facts.

Special rules for the insurance policy

The policy must refer to and cover the buyer

2–088   As an example, in *Manbre Saccharine v Corn Products* [1919] 1 K.B. 196, the insurance policy was lawfully rejected by the buyer because it referred to a quantity of goods not evidenced on the bill of lading. A similar situation arose in *Hickox v Adams* (1876) 34 L.T. 404.

2–089   *Hickox v Adams* (1876) 34 L.T. 404
Facts:
The seller had arranged to deliver CIF 1,000 units of a cargo of 2,000 units to the buyer. The 2,000 units were delivered to K who was asked by the seller to hand over 1,000 units to the buyer. The seller had taken a single insurance policy covering the entire cargo of 2,000 units.
Held:
The buyer need not take delivery of the goods from K. The seller was in breach of the contract for two reasons. First, the tender was bad because the seller had not tendered an insurance policy. Secondly, even if they had, the policy would be ineffectual because it did not refer to the buyer's 1,000 units but the entire cargo of 2,000 units to be delivered to K.

The policy must specify clearly the protection available to the buyer. In *Malmberg v Evans* (1924) 29 Com. Cas. 235, the document tendered purported to be an insurance policy but did not specify the risks insured against. The buyers refused to accept it as an effective policy. The buyers had also argued that the seller should have tendered a policy issued in England. The court stated that where goods are sold on CIF terms by a foreign seller to English buyers, the buyers cannot call for a policy issued in England. The only operative aspect of the duty is that the policy be valid and effective. In this case, the foreign policy was not valid not because it was issued outside England but because it did not specify clearly the risks covered. The buyers should not be subject to uncertainty when it comes to the protection of his interests in the goods. By the same token, in *Comptoir d'Achat et de Vente du Boerenbond Belge SA v Luis de Ridder Limitada (The Julia)* [1949] A.C. 293, the insurance taken out by the seller was not consistent with the provisions of a CIF contract because it had not been taken out for the exclusive protection or on behalf of the buyers. The sellers had effected insurance on the entire consignment of 700,000 tons of rye while the buyers were only to take delivery of 500,000 tons. The insurance was not therefore for the exclusive benefit of the buyers.

It must be for continuous cover

In *Belgian Grain & Produce v Co* (1919) 1 Ll. L. Rep. 256, the rule was that any **2–090** policy taken out by the sellers would not be effective if it did not sufficiently cover all transhipments. In that case though the policies which incorporated the ICC terms had extended protection to transhipments as were contemplated by the bill of lading and as such transhipments were usual in the course of the voyage, the policies were good. The Court of Appeal considered, in obiter, in *Lindon v White* [1975] 1 Lloyd's Rep. 384, that the insurance policy should have been extended to cover the arrival of the goods at the buyer's warehouse because the contract was described as CIF customer's warehouse. It had only referred to the port of arrival. There the sellers had delivered the goods in error to the buyer's office instead of his warehouse and the tender of the insurance policy was ineffective because it did not cover the entirety of the transit.

The policy should be effective

It would be pointless for the buyer if the seller tendered an insurance policy **2–091** which is ineffective to protect his interest in the cargo. In *Cantiere Meccanico Brindisino v Janson* (1912) 17 Com. Cas. 182, a policy of insurance had been taken out on a floating dock which was to be towed away under a CIF contract of sale. The seller had honestly believed that the dock was fit for the voyage. It was not. It sank and the buyers attempted to claim from the insurers who successfully defended their refusal to pay on the ground that the seller who had taken out the insurance ought to know that the dock was not properly enforced and should have disclosed that fact to the underwriters when taking out the cover. The court held that the buyers had not been given an effective insurance policy from the seller under the CIF sale. The seller was in breach and must therefore compensate the buyers.

A valid insurance policy does not mean that the seller is to effect cover of the goods against every risk. It depends entirely on the contract of sale what type of insurance the seller is obliged to procure for the buyer's protection. In *Groom v Barber* [1915] 1 K.B. 316, the CIF buyers argued that the sellers had breached the contract by not procuring a war risk insurance cover for them. The ship was torpedoed and the goods lost. The court held in construing the clause "war risk for buyer's account" in the contract as simply meaning no more than that the buyers could if they wanted to insure on war risk. It did not create a duty or right; it was simply a liberty clause. Although war risk cover had become a customary practice when the contract was to be performed, it was not so when the contract was made. It is the latter that should dictate whether or not a custom should be implied into the contract. That custom could not therefore be read into the contract.

Certificates of insurance are usually not sufficient

In *Phoenix v de Monchy* (1929) 37 Com. Cas. 69, insurance was taken out against **2–092** leakage. The certificate of insurance read, "This Certificate represents and takes the place of the policy . . . ". In the policy there was a clause which stipulated that no action may be lodged after one year of loss. The stipulation was absent in the certificate. On the question as to whether the holder of the certificate is bound by the limitation clause in the policy, Viscount Dunedin had this to say

" . . . the certificate is the determinative of the two instruments. The condition in question is a collateral stipulation imposing a condition precedent. It has nothing to do with insurance but might be applied to any contract . . . Common sense revolts against the idea of this being enforced against the holder of the certificate. Neither the holder nor a possible indorsee could ever have seen the policy".

As a general rule, the buyer is entitled to a policy of insurance and nothing less will suffice. McCardie J., in *Diamond Alkali Export Corp v Bourgeois* [1921] 3 K.B. 443, held that the buyer would have no way of determining the terms of his cover unless he had in possession the policy of insurance itself. A certificate or broker's note would not contain the same comprehensive terms generally. Furthermore, under s.50(3) of the Marine Insurance Act 1906 assignment of insurance rights is by way of indorsement of policies, not certificates or cover notes. This is, however, very much a general rule which could be varied by contract and given the prevalence of the certificate in international mercantile use, such an insistence on the policy should perhaps be reviewed. The Law Commission in its review of insurance law more generally has also recommended that the need for a document such as a policy should be questioned.[37] The policy's elevated status by marine insurance law has much to do with the fact that the government used to impose stamp duty on insurance policies. However with the abolition of that stamp duty and the rise of electronic commerce it is questioned whether the policy should continue to remain so central in international trade, especially documentary sales.

Indeed, where the sale is to be paid for by a letter of credit governed by the UCP 600, art.28(d) of the UCP allows for the substitution of a policy with a certificate of insurance or even a declaration under an open cover. The parties' agreement to use the UCP 600 is thus also agreement to the variation of the rule in *Diamond Alkali*, unless a contrary intention is explicitly expressed in the letter of credit. Cover notes though are not acceptable (art.28(c)).

---

[37] *http://www.lawcommission.justice.gov.uk/areas/insurance-contract-law.htm* (Issues Paper No 9, Oct 2010), [accessed April 8, 2013].

2–093

CERTIFICATE OF INSURANCE

Exporter	CERTIFICATE NO. ZINT	
	Exporter's reference
	Forwarder's reference

Consignee	CONDITIONS OF INSURANCE
	☐ Institute Cargo Clauses (A)
	☐ Institute Cargo Clauses (B)
Selling agent	☐ Institute Cargo Clauses (C)
	☐ Institute Cargo Clauses (Air) (Excluding sendings by Post)
Other UK transport details	Further subject to Institute War Clauses and Institute Strikes Clauses (Cargo) (Air Cargo)
	Institute Classification Clause
	Institute Radioactive Contamination Exclusion Clause

| Vessel | Port of loading | Other Special Conditions (see reverse) | |
| Port of discharge | Final destination | Insured value | Premium |

| Shipping marks, container numbers | Number and kind of packages; description of goods | Gross Weight | Cube (m³) |

PROCEDURE IN EVENT OF CLAIM

1 It is the duty of the Assured and their agents to take such measures as may be reasonable for the purpose of averting or minimising a loss and to ensure that all rights against Carriers Bailees or other third parties are properly preserved and exercised.

2 Follow the procedures stated overleaf.

3 Apply immediately for survey of damaged goods to the Agent stated below or if none stated to the nearest Institute of London Underwriters or Lloyds Agent or to Zurich International Head Office as shown on reverse.

Claims Payable at:

By:

For Zurich International (UK) Limited

Dennis W. White, Managing Director

This is to certify that Zurich International has insured the above mentioned goods for the voyage and value stated on behalf of:

Under Policy No:

This Certificate is not valid unless counter-signed
This Certificate requires endorsement by the Assured

Signatory's company:

Name of signatory:

Dated:

Signed:

ZURICH INTERNATIONAL UK

Curing a defective tender

2–094   Consider the following situation. The seller makes tender of documents. The documents are defective; for example, the description of the goods in the bill of lading is not in line with the contract. He then makes a second tender with conforming documents this time. The question is whether the buyer is obliged to accept these documents if the second tender is within time.

The authority for the general rule that a seller is entitled to make a subsequent tender to cure the defective first tender is the Court of Appeal's judgment in *Borrowman Phillips & Co v Free & Hollis* (1878) 4 Q.B.D. 500.

2–095   *Borrowman Phillips & Co v Free & Hollis* (1878) 4 Q.B.D. 500
Facts:
The suppliers attempted to deliver maize on the Charles Platt to the buyers but were unable to secure documents relating to the goods. Following an arbitrator's finding that the tender was not acceptable, the suppliers made a second tender of goods on board the Maria D and documents relating to that consignment. The buyers rejected the second tender on the ground that the suppliers were not entitled under contract to substitute other goods for those represented by the first tender.
Held:
The Court of Appeal held that the suppliers were entitled to make a second tender of documents and goods meeting the contractual description so long as time permitted and the second tender is not inconsistent with the contract. The contract did not bind the suppliers to deliver goods on board the Charles Platt. The buyers therefore had to pay damages for non-acceptance of good and documents.

It is controversial whether there exists a general right to cure a defective tender. Although the rule in *Borrowman Phillips & Co v Free & Hollis* has frequently been thought of and accepted as a proposition that there is such a right, academic opinion has cast doubt on the issue.[38] It is submitted that it might be more useful to consider not whether there exists a right to cure but how the general contractual principles on discharge and performance of contracts might be applied in such a situation. The general rule is that a breach does not automatically terminate or discharge the contract. This translated means that the buyer's rejection does not automatically bring an end to the contract as long as the seller does not signify that any rejection by the buyer will be treated by them as repudiation. In *Borrowman Phillips & Co v Free & Hollis*, Brett L.J. said:

> "It has been argued by the defendants' counsel that the claimants could not lawfully tender the cargo of the Maria D, because they had already tendered that of the Charles Platt, and had *insisted upon* that tender" (emphasis added).

That qualification is vital to the buyers' argument in that case—without proof of the sellers' insistence on the first tender, the sellers are free to make a corrective tender as long as there is time for them so to do. Any such insistence on the sellers' part could be construed as an election to bind themselves to the tender and they could not later on claim the right of a further tender of performance.

---

[38] See, e.g. Ahdar, "Seller cure in the Sale of Goods" [1990] L.M.C.L.Q. 364, Apps, "The right to cure defective performance" [1994] L.M.C.L.Q. 525 and Mak, "The Seller's Right to Cure defective performance—A Reappraisal" [2007] L.M.C.L.Q. 409.

From the facts the Court of Appeal found that the suppliers had not bound themselves to the cargo on the Charles Platt and were therefore free to make a second tender.

Secondly, where the conduct of either party amounts to repudiation then the **2–096** contract comes to an end and the right and/or duty to cure a defective tender expires. For example, the seller is not entitled to make numerous tenders of performance; his numerous attempts at performing the contract would make a farce of his undertaking to perform the contract within the time of performance. This might be construed by the courts as his intention not to see his contractual obligations to fruition, and consequently an anticipatory breach of the contract. His anticipatory breach could then be accepted and acknowledged by the buyer and the contract comes to an end. The seller's right (or duty) to re-tender comes to an end. The buyer could then sue for nondelivery or failure to perform the contract. It would seem that under general law of contract, even a single bad tender could constitute an anticipatory breach of condition under certain circumstances; for example where the defect is so grave that the seller could not have intended to carry on with the contract or where the defective tender had been made very close to the due date that it would have been impossible to cure the tender. The buyer, under these circumstances, may justifiably treat the contract as having come to an end. The seller could not argue that he had a right to cure his defective tender of performance. What constitutes such a repudiation of the contract is naturally a matter of fact.[39]

It is perhaps important to note too that the buyer may call for a second tender if the seller's first attempt fails. On the other hand if he does not call for a fresh tender, his conduct might cost him his right to reject the tender. In *Motor Oil Hellas (Corinth) Refineries SA v Shipping Corp of India (The Kanchenjunga)* [1990] 1 Lloyd's Rep. 391, Lord Goff of Chiveley had this to say about the tender of performance:

"The other party is entitled to reject the tender of performance as uncontractual; and, subject to the terms of the contract, he can then, if he wishes, call for a fresh tender of performance in its place. But if, with knowledge of the facts giving rise to his right to reject, he nevertheless unequivocally elects not to do so, his election will be final and binding upon him and he will have waived his right to reject the tender as uncontractual".

As we have seen in *Borrowman Phillips & Co v Free & Hollis*, the same applies to the seller who elects not to make a second tender. His election binds him and he could not subsequently resile from it.

As for instalment deliveries of goods, special rules apply. Section 31 of the Sale of Goods Act 1979 provides:

1. unless otherwise agreed, the buyer of goods is not bound to accept delivery of them by instalments;

2. where there is a contract for the sale of goods to be delivered by stated instalments, which are to be separately paid for, and the seller makes defective deliveries in respect of one or more instalments or the buyer neglects of refuses to take delivery of or pay for one or more instalments, it is a question

---

[39] See *Vitol SA v Norelf* [1996] 3 All E.R. 193.

in each case depending on the terms of the contract and the circumstances of the case whether the breach of contract is a repudiation of the whole contract or whether it is a severable breach giving rise to a claim for compensation but not to a right to treat the whole contract as repudiated.

The test is not easy:

" . . . Has the buyer evinced an intention to abandon or to refuse to perform the contract? In answering this question, the law has regard to such factors as the degree to which the delivery of one instalment is linked with another, the proportion of the contract which has been affected by the allegedly repudiatory breach and the probability that the breach will be repeated. However, these are merely part of the raw material for answering the question. They cannot be conclusive in themselves." (per Donaldson J. in *Warinco AG v Samor SpA* [1977] 2 Lloyd's Rep. 582).

Shipment of the goods and bills of lading

2–097 Section 32(1) Sale of Goods Act 1979 provides that where, in pursuance of a contract, the seller is authorised or required to send the goods to the buyer, delivery of the goods to a carrier (whether named by the buyer or not) for the purpose of transmission to the buyer is prima facie deemed to be a delivery of the goods to the buyer. This rule is subject to contractual modification—in an FOB contract, for example, whilst it is true to say that delivery of the goods by the seller to the carrier is prima facie delivery of the goods to the buyer under s.32(1), the contract may require additional specific obligations (e.g. a requirement to stow the goods, to obtain documents from a named carrier, to deliver to a named carrier, etc) before delivery is said to have been properly made. As far as the CIF contract is concerned, the seller "must make such contract with the carrier on behalf of the buyer as may be reasonable" (s.32(2)). What is reasonable depends on the nature of the goods and other circumstances of the case. Section 32(2) further provides that if the seller fails to do so, and the goods are lost or damaged in the course of transit, the buyer may decline to treat delivery to the carrier as delivery to himself or may hold the seller responsible in damages.[40] It would appear that the contract of carriage is not made by the seller as the buyer's agent; the CIF seller acts as a principal (*Houlder Bros v Commissioner of Public Works* [1908] A.C. 276) despite the words "on behalf of the buyer" in s.32(2). As regards the duty of a seller to give notice of shipment to the buyer to enable him to secure insurance under s.32(3) which we considered earlier in the context of the FOB contract (para.2–039), it should be said that the duty does not apply to the CIF seller. It does however apply to a CFR seller.

Both FOB and CIF contracts require that the goods be shipped. In an FOB contract, the concept of shipment is perhaps a little less problematic in that the seller's duty is to load the goods free on board the buyer's nominated vessel. Shipment in that context should thus mean the loading of the goods on board the nominated ship. In a CIF contract, the shipping documents used are very much underpinned by the actual shipment of goods. Indeed, as we shall see, the bill of lading must state that the goods have been shipped in accordance with the terms

---

[40] See Lorenzon, "When is a CIF seller's carriage contract unreasonable? Section 32(2) of the Sale of Goods Act 1979" (2007) 13 J.I.M.L. 241.

of the contract of sale. The carrier, thus, needs to know when shipment takes place to be able to issue a bill of lading or some other shipping document reflecting the apparent condition of the goods at shipment. Similarly, the seller and buyer need to be certain that the goods have actually been shipped. What does shipment mean? Does it import a legal or simply a factual meaning?

The Exchequer Chamber defined it in *Alexander v Vanderzee* (1872) L.R. 7 C.P. 530 as referring to the act of completing loading and the ship finally setting sail with the goods. In that case the CIF contract required that the grain be shipped in June/July 1869 at the seller's option. The loading commenced in May and was completed in June. The bills of lading were dated June 4 and June 6. The buyers alleged that as more than half the cargo had already been loaded in May, shipment had actually taken place in May and therefore the sellers were in breach. The court disagreed with the buyer's interpretation and found for the sellers.

In *Bowes v Shand* (1877) 2 App. Cas. 455, the House of Lords was **2–098** unequivocal in holding that *Alexander v Vanderzee* did not lay down any general proposition of law. Indeed the court in *Alexander v Vanderzee* referred to the "ordinary business sense of the word". In *Bowes v Shand*, shipment was fixed for March/April. The entirety of the cargo of rice had been put onboard in February save 50 bags. These 50 bags were finally put onboard in March and a March bill of lading was issued. The question for the House of Lords was whether the sellers had performed their duty to ship within shipment period. The buyer's contention that they did not was approved by the House of Lords. The House of Lords held that whether shipment had taken place is a question of fact and *Alexander v Vanderzee* could be distinguished on the ground that, in that case, there was continuous loading until the period of completion. Here it was evident that the loading process had been completed; the nominal saving of the 50 bags was intended simply to procure a bill of lading meeting the March shipment requirement. The House of Lords also considered that trade custom may only be admissible to prove the fact of shipment where that usage is infamous, clear and consistent.

In *Mowbray v Rosser* (1922) 91 L.J.K.B. 524, the sellers had purported to rely on trade usage to prove their performance of the contract within shipment period. It was alleged by the sellers that in the United States, shipment meant the loading of goods on railway wagons to be carried to port as much as it meant the actual loading on to the designated ship. The Court of Appeal rejected the sellers' contention stating that custom was not admissible when it contradicted the contract and did not explain it.

It should not be forgotten that shipment is a matter of contract, as well as a matter of fact. Where there is a reference in the contract to shipment, the court will give effect to it. However where the term referring to shipment is unclear, the court will construe it according to the commercial realities of international sales.

SHV Gas Supply v Naftomar [2005] EWHC 2528   **2–099**
Facts:
The contract called for delivery of butane "CIF a Tunisian port". The contract contained a force majeure clause and a "laycan" provision indicating a *three-day period* and giving notice of the estimated time of arrival of the vessel at the discharge port. Bad weather prevented the vessel chartered by the seller to carry the cargo from loading until after the laycan period had expired. The buyer cancelled the contract relying on the seller's failure to ship within the agreed period. The seller disputed the claim that there was an agreed

shipping or loading period. The buyer claimed that the seller was been in breach of the obligation to ship within the three-day laycan period and/or alternatively, under s.29 Sale of Goods Act 1979, there was an implied term that the goods would be shipped within a reasonable time, which had expired.

Held:

The court clarified what "laycan" meant. The term is usually used in the negotiation of charterparties, to refer to the earliest date at which the laydays can commence and the date after which the charter can be cancelled if the vessel has not by then arrived. In FOB sales, the term refers to the time the seller can cancel the contract if the vessel, which it is the buyer's duty to procure, does not arrive at the port by the cancellation date. A laycan provision did not thus fit easily into a CIF contract where it was the seller's obligation to make the contract of carriage, ship the goods on board and tender the customary documents. The "laycan" term is much better suited to FOB contracts. That said, it could be applied to CIF contracts.

The parties had specifically chosen the word "laycan", not shipment, to refer to the three-day period. The word "laycan" did not mean shipment. If the shipment period had been guaranteed, a notice of the estimated time of arrival at the discharge port would not be necessary.

If the word "laycan" did not provide for a shipment period, one would be implied. That implied term lies in the Sale of Goods Act 1979 s.29(3) which provides that the seller should ship within a reasonable time. As the seller could not be blamed for the weather or for berthing difficulties and there was no evidence that it was in any way dilatory in shipping the cargo (*Hick v Raymond* (1893) A.C. 22), it was not in breach of s.29(3).

In the alternative, even if the seller was in breach of s.29(3), the force majeure clause would render the contract discharged.

2–100   As regards s.29(3), it should be remembered that what is a reasonable time depends on the circumstances as they existed at the time in question. Lord Herschell L.C. in *Hick v Raymond* [1893] A.C. 22 made clear that:

> "I would observe, in the first place, that there is of course no such thing as a reasonable time in the abstract. It must always depend on the circumstances. Upon "the ordinary circumstances" say the learned counsel for the appellant. But what may without impropriety be termed the ordinary circumstances differ in particular ports at different times of the year. As regards the practicability of discharging a vessel they may differ in summer and winter. Again, weather increasing the difficulty of, though not preventing, the discharge of a vessel may continue for so long a period that it may justly be termed extraordinary. Could it be contended that in so far as it lasted beyond the ordinary period the delay caused by it was to be excluded in determining whether the cargo had been discharged within a reasonable time? It appears to me that the appellant's contention would involve constant difficulty and dispute, and that the only sound principle is that the "reasonable time" should depend on the circumstances which actually exist. If the cargo has been taken with all reasonable despatch under those circumstances I think the obligation of the consignee has been fulfilled. When I say the circumstances which actually exist, I, of course, imply that those circumstances, in so far as they involve delay, have not been caused or contributed to by the consignee".

Given these uncertainties, most CIF traders will specify the shipment period in the contract. However, whilst defining the shipment period is generally a good thing, defining facts constituting shipment can cause problems of interpretation. The contract should not be over-prescriptive. Hence, where the contract states that shipment would only take place once the goods have been loaded on a specific vessel, loading of the goods onto a comparable vessel would not amount to shipment. However, given the unusual nature of the term, the courts would not enforce such a stipulation unless the words are clear and explicit to that effect.

In *PT Putrabali Adyamulia v Societe est Epices (The Intan 6 V.360A SN)* [2003] 2 Ll. L.R. 700 the parties had entered into a contract of sale of goods which incorporated the International General Produce Association (IGPA) contract form No.5. A declaration of shipment was made stating the name of the vessel for shipment. That vessel was an unpowered barge. The barge sank and the goods were lost. The buyer refused to pay against the documents on the basis that the declaration of shipment required by the contract was defective as the vessel was not a contractual ship. The contract called for a "first class ship". The court found that although the vessel was not a first class ship, there was nothing in the contract to preclude the seller from shipping the goods on an unpowered vessel. As such, effective shipment had taken place. It is clear from this case that whether shipment was compliant depends on the precise terms of the contract; where it is provided that the goods are to be shipped on a specific vessel, that must take place. However, where the contract is unclear, the court would not be too ready to imply a contrary intention. Furthermore, there is no general presumption that the goods would be carried on an ocean going vessel, unless the circumstances clearly require the use of such a vessel.

This takes us to another issue: does the failure to ship within time permit the **2–101** buyer to reject the *goods* when they arrive? In *Bowes v Shand*, the House of Lords treated the violation as a breach of condition. In this connection s.10(2) of the Sale of Goods Act 1979 provides that whether a stipulation as to time is of the essence of a contract of sale depends on the terms of the contract. The fact that the contract is in essence a commercial transaction signifies the importance of time. Incidentally it might be observed that s.10(1) provides that unless a different intention appears from the terms of the contract, stipulations as to time of payment are not of the essence of a contract of sale. The presumption here is that time of payment is not a condition. That presumption may however be rebutted.

There is, however, some suggestion in *HongKong Fir Shipping Co v Kawasaki Kisen Kaisha* [1962] 2 Q.B. 26 that the time stipulation might in fact be an innominate or intermediate term; the consequences of the breach becoming central to the founding of the claimant's right to repudiate the contract. In a case dealing with the failure of the seller in meeting contractual description, *Reardon Smith Line Ltd v Yngvar Hansen-Tangen* [1976] 1 W.L.R. 989, Lord Wilberforce said:

"The general law of contract has developed, along more rational lines (*e.g. HongKong Fir Shipping Co. Ltd v Kawasaki Kisen Kaisha Ltd* [1962] 2 Q.B. 26) in attending to the nature and gravity of a breach or departure rather than in accepting rigid categories which do or do not automatically give a right to rescind, and if the choice were between extending cases under the Sale of Goods Act 1893 into other fields, or allowing more modern doctrine to infect those cases, my preference would be clear".

It might be argued therefore that while His Lordship preferred the "more **2–102** rational lines" evidenced by *HongKong Fir Shipping Co Ltd*, where the failure to ship within time constitutes a breach of contractual description, s.13(2) of the Sale of Goods Act 1979 states in no uncertain terms that the breach shall be one of condition. Other time stipulations not falling within s.13 might be more problematic—should they be treated as innominate terms or as conditions? The House of Lords seemed to have laid the matter to rest in *Bunge Corp v Tradax SA* [1981] 1 W.L.R. 711. It was held there that the failure of the FOB buyers to provide a 15-day notice informing the sellers as to the readiness of their vessel to load was a breach of condition and that in general time stipulations in a mercantile contract are to be treated as conditions for the reasons discussed (see FOB contracts).

Another aspect of the seller's duty to ship goods meeting the contract is to ensure that the goods are shipped by a route is usual or customary where there is no express condition made as to the route. In *Tsakiroglou & Co Ltd v Noblee Thorl GmbH* [1962] A.C. 93 the sellers argued that the CIF Hamburg contract had been frustrated because the Suez Canal which was the intended route had been closed to sea traffic. The alternative route is via the Cape of Good Hope, a journey about 6,000 miles longer than the route through the Suez. The sellers further contended that this was an untenable risk which the contracting parties had not intended or anticipated. The House of Lords first held that there is a duty on the CIF seller who has undertaken shipment of the goods to use a route which is usual or customary at the time of shipment. The fact that at the time of contracting the route was not within contemplation is immaterial. The contractual duty arises when the goods are ready to be shipped at the agreed shipment period. In deciding whether the route via the Cape is a "usual or customary route", the court considered two legal questions:

● whether there is an express stipulation in the contract preventing the alternative route; and

● whether from the facts it may be inferred a prohibition as to the alternative route.[41]

It was held that the longer route would not be detrimental to the goods and that as there was no stipulation as to time of delivery the contract of sale had not been frustrated. Additional costs and expense could not be sufficient to frustrate the contract of sale even though it might not have been foreseen by the parties. Although the court did consider it possible that a charterparty might be frustrated by the closure of the canal (*Société Franco Tunisienne v Sidermar* [1961] 2 Q.B. 278), the position here is very different—the subject matter in this instance was a contract of sale where the subject matter was the delivery of the goods not the voyage. The consequences are simply that the sellers had to pay more freight and the buyers had to wait longer for his goods. These are not fundamental to the contract of sale unless specifically stipulated.

2–103   Although the CIF seller need not ensure delivery of the goods at port of destination, he must not do any act which would prevent the delivery of the goods at the agreed port of discharge. This duty is a corollary of the seller's duty to obtain a valid contract of carriage. The Court of Appeal in *Lecky v Ogilvy*

---

[41] These facts may include any specific term in the contract as to time of delivery, the inherent condition of the goods in withstanding the alternative journey, the seasonal nature of the goods, etc.

(1897) 3 Com. Cas. 29 held that the sellers had an absolute duty to procure shipment under a bill of lading which would, subject to the exceptions contained therein, ensure the delivery of the goods at the port of destination. There, although the sellers had arranged, without negligence, for the goods to be shipped to Tripoli in Libya, the bill of lading issued was for shipment of the goods to Tripoli in Syria. The goods were, as a result, delivered to Syria instead of to Libya. It was held that the buyers were entitled to sue for nondelivery. The bill of lading as issued would not have seen to it that the goods were taken to the agreed port of discharge.

This duty to secure an effective contract of carriage also means that where the seller had chartered or used a ship which is incapable of entering the contractual port of discharge, the buyer may repudiate the contract. In *Marshall v Arcos* (1932) 44 Ll.L. Rep. 384, the CIF sellers had contracted to deliver the goods to the buyers' wharf. The vessel they had chartered was too large to approach the buyers' wharf. The sellers had then offered to reimburse the buyers if the latter took delivery of the good. The buyers rejected the offer and subsequently the documents. The bill of lading, namely the contract of carriage, was ineffective at ensuring delivery of the goods at the agreed destination. The sellers had to sell the goods by public tender and the buyers were invited to tender which they did at a price lower than the contract price. The questions for the court were:

- whether the buyers were entitled to reject documents; and

- if so, on what basis were they entitled to claim damages.

The court held that the documents could be rejected. The bill of lading which incorporated the charterparty provided for delivery "such spot or as near thereto as a named ship might safely get" must conform precisely. There is no room for variation, however minor. On whether and to what extent the buyer's conduct should be taken into account to mitigate the sum of damages payable, that was according to the court a matter of fact which should be referred to arbitration in line with the contract.

The buyer's duty to take delivery of the goods

We have alluded to the buyer's obligation to take delivery of the goods when they   **2–104** arrive; this is corollary of the buyer's twin rights—his right in relation to the documents and his right in respect of the physical goods. In a CIF contract, the seller would have arranged for shipment of the goods.When the ship arrives at the port of discharge, he will normally be contract bound to give a notice of readiness to the buyer enabling the latter to organise for the receipt and onward carriage of the goods. As with the notice of readiness to load (in the FOB context), the notice requirement is likely to be strictly applied and time will be treated as of the essence.

Construing a notice of readiness stipulation depends on the factual matrix—so a similar requirement in a FOB contract, for example, would be interpreted differently in a CIF contract. In a CIF contract, the seller's duty is to arrange for shipment to the CIF port/place/berth. The precise scope of that duty will, in part, guide the interpretation of the notice of readiness duty in the sale contract.

2–105   *Suek v Glencore International* [2011] EWHC 1361 (Comm).

Facts:

S had entered into a CIF contract with G. When the vessel arrived at the discharge port, the berth was occupied by another vessel so it could not reach the berth. In addition, the weather conditions were such that the vessel could not reach the berth. The master gave notice of readiness in accordance with a clause in the contract of sale which stipulated that "in case the berth was occupied on arrival, the vessel could tender notice of readiness at the usual waiting place . . . whether in berth or not". The issue was whether the clause should be interpreted as leaving the responsibility for delay with the buyer who did not have the berth available or with the seller whose vessel could not access the berth. G argued that the clause could only be used if the only cause of the delay was the unavailability of a berth. It argued that if there was a weather problem, the vessel would have to wait until conditions cleared, and only if the berth was then unavailable could the master give notice of readiness.

Held:

The court took the view that the seller's primary obligation was to nominate a carrying vessel and ship the coal to port and not to take active steps to impede delivery. If anyone, it was the buyer, whose obligation is to provide a safe berth and to whom notice is to be given, who can take steps to make the berth available. There might be some inconvenience to the buyer if notice of readiness was given at a time when both causes were in place at the time of the vessel's arrival at the port and the berth became available before the weather conditions lifted, but it was for the buyer to provide a berth. The master was thus entitled to give notice of readiness to unload despite the berth being unavailable.

It is very important to note that that case concerns terms which are also commonly used in charterparties; but the context is different. Here we are dealing with a CIF contract and not a charterparty.[42]

International Sale Contracts and Frustration

Application of the doctrine

2–106   Frustration occurs when, through no fault of the parties, the performance of the contract has been rendered impossible by circumstances extraordinary and usually unforeseeable by the parties. The contract is thus brought to an end automatically, and this discharge of the contract is not dependent on the parties' intention. Bingham L.J. in *J Lauritzen AS v Wijsmuller BV (The Super Servant II)* [1990] 1 Lloyd's Rep. 1 considered that this aspect of the doctrine of frustration had been evolved to mitigate the rigour of the common law's insistence on literal performance of absolute promises. His Lordship also saw the object of the doctrine as giving effect to the demands of justice, namely to achieve a just and reasonable result, to do what is reasonable and fair, as an expedient to escape from the injustice which would result from enforcing the literal terms later a significant change in circumstances has taken place.

However, given the far-reaching effect of the doctrine, it should not be lightly invoked and must be kept within very narrow bounds. The courts will look at the intent and circumstances of the contract when determining whether a significant

---

[42] For how the notice of readiness requirements are reconciled with laytime and demurrage provisions in a charterparty see Chapter 7 generally and *Bulk Transport Group Shipping Co Ltd v Seacrystal Shipping Ltd (The Kyzikos)* [1987] 1 Lloyd's Rep. 48.

change in circumstances has occurred rendering the contract impossible; and this will be done guided by the overriding concern to preserve the commercial contract rather than to kill it.

Thus in *Intertradax v Lesieur* [1978] 2 Lloyd's Rep. 509, the seller's reliance on frustration failed when he could not deliver as a result of breakdown of machinery and raw materials shortages because the court considered that these events are common place in the world of business and could therefore have been anticipated. Furthermore, the seller had not sufficiently proved that the cause of the failure to deliver was the breakdown of machinery. The court will not be swayed by tenuous evidence. The causal link between the alleged frustrating event and the impossibility of performance must first be firmly established.

It is seen therefore that shortages and failure of production processes could not be easily pleaded as frustrating events because these events are foreseeable and should have been considered by the seller when contracting. Hardship without more is not enough to bring an end to the contract.[43] Where the impossibility is caused by an externality beyond the anticipation of the parties, the courts would be slightly more disposed to extend the doctrine of frustration. A good case study is *Re Badische Co Ltd* [1921] 2 Ch. 331.

Re Badische Co Ltd [1921] 2 Ch. 331   **2–107**
Facts:
An enemy enterprise registered in England was wound up by emergency legislation when war broke out. The company had contracted to deliver a cargo of unascertained goods to the applicant who claimed damages for nondelivery when the company was wound up. The controller (liquidator) resisted the claim on the following grounds:

• the contract was dissolved at the outbreak of war;

• the contract would have been suspended if any contingency beyond the parties' control arises (e.g. fire, accidents, war, strikes, etc).

Held:
The Chancery Court held that the German company though registered in England assumed every character of an enemy enterprise since the persons controlling it are persons from an enemy state. The contract to supply goods from Germany had to be illegal under these circumstances. The contracts had been made on the basis that the existing commercial conditions would continue and this basis having ceased to exist by war, the commercial object of the contract had been frustrated at the outbreak of war. Contracts for the sale of unascertained goods are not immune in this respect to the doctrine of frustration.

---

[43] The position is different in the CISG and other European instruments. Article 79 of the CISG relieves a party from paying damages only if the breach of contract was due to an *impediment* beyond its control. The question as to what it means by impediment and whether economic hardship should amount to an impediment is left unattended, at least in express terms. In judicial and arbitration decisions however, art.79 has been recognised as extending to cases of hardship. Once the notion of impediment can be overcome to extend to hardship, the tenor and structure of art.79 is similar to the other international instruments. They all require:
  (a) the impediment is beyond the party's control; and
  (b) it could not reasonably be expected to have taken the impediment into account at the time of the conclusion of the contract; and
  (c) it could not reasonably be expected to have avoided or overcome it or its consequences.
Art. 6.2.2 of the UNICTRAL Principles of International Commercial Contracts 2004, Art. 6.111 of the Principles of European Contract Law 1999, Art. III–1.110 of the Draft Frame of Reference 2008 and Art. 89(3) of the draft European Sales Law Regulation are expressed along similar lines.

2–108   In *Lewis Emmanuel & Son Ltd v Sammut* [1959] 2 Lloyd's Rep. 629, for example, the CIF London contract was not frustrated simply because the seller could not find suitable shipping space for the cargo of potatoes during the narrowly defined shipment period. The seller had taken on the risk of finding shipping space and must therefore be held answerable for the failure to procure shipping space. The courts would not question the prudence of the narrowly defined shipment period and indeed any other term of the contract. The parties' freedom to contract on any legal basis must not be constrained.

Be that as it may, there could be instances where the courts would find the contract frustrated. Frustration occurs when, as Lord Wright said in *Denny, Mott & Dickson Ltd v James B Fraser & Co* [1944] A.C. 265:

> "The parties did not anticipate fully and completely, if at all, or provide for what actually happened. It is not possible to my mind to say that, if they had thought of it, they would have said, 'Well, if that happens, all is over between us'. On the contrary, they would have almost certainly on the one side or the other have sought to introduce reservations of qualifications or compensations".

2–109   The reluctance of the courts to find the contract frustrated reflects the common law's respect for freedom of contract. Commercial parties are expected to be conscious of the probable impediments to trade and if they do not provide for contingencies in the event of these impediments occurring, the courts would not reward them for this failing by finding the contract to be frustrated. There is thus a strict construction of what frustrating event is within the anticipation of the parties. In *The Mary Nour* [2008] EWCA Civ 856, the "FOB the Mary Nour, Padang, Indonesia" contract for the delivery of cement was found to have been frustrated by the arbitrators. The buyers had intended to ship the cement to Mexico; a shipment intended to break a cartel controlled by a local Mexican company, Cemex. The sellers were owned by Gresik, an Indonesian company. Gresik, not wanting to offend Cemex and also feeling the pressure from Cemex which had used its influence to persuade a supplier in Taiwan to withdraw its offer of a cargo to Gresik, put a stop on the sellers from making delivery. The arbitrators were not persuaded that the parties had foreseen, or must be taken to have foreseen, that any action Cemex might take to interfere with the supply of cargo would make it impossible to perform the contract on terms which bore any real commercial resemblance to those agreed. They therefore held that in what they described as "the altogether exceptional circumstances of the case" it would be positively unjust to hold the parties bound and that the contract was therefore frustrated. At the court of first instance, Field J. disagreed. The Judge said

> " . . . where a seller makes an unqualified promise to sell he bears the risk of a failure of his contemplated source of supply where that source is not the specified source or the goods are not specific goods and the supplier is not excused by frustration, e.g. it is physically and legally possible for the supplier to make delivery but he chooses not to. This is because there is always a risk of supplier failure and as between the buyer and the seller, it is the seller who is in a position to guard against the risk either by making a binding and enforceable contract with the supplier with an appropriate jurisdiction or arbitration clause, or, as Lord Denning said in [*Intertradex SA v Lesieur*

Tourteaux SARL [1978] 2 Lloyds Rep. 509] by protecting himself by making his promise conditional on the goods being available for delivery. This is no more than good sense and common justice. In a commercial age in which wealth is made up largely of promises, it is of the greatest importance that contractual obligations are enforced in accordance with their terms save only in a most limited range of circumstances".

Although the courts should normally accept the arbitrators' finding of fact, here it was the law which the arbitrators had erred on. The Court of Appeal affirmed Field J.'s decision, stating that the contract will not be frustrated if, although delivery remains physically and legally possible, the seller's supplier chooses (for whatever reason) not to make the goods available. Here we have an FOB contract, the seller's duty is to load the goods on board the vessel designated by the buyer. The goods are available and there was no legal or regulatory prohibition; only a commercial one. That was not enough therefore to constitute frustration.

Effects of frustration

The effects of frustration are generally dependent on whether the Law Reform   **2–110**
(Frustrated Contracts) Act 1943 applies to the facts. Where the Act does not apply, regard must be had to common law rules. At common law, the contract comes to an end automatically when the frustrating event takes place. This would mean that the obligations of the parties under the contract cease immediately. Once the contract is set aside, the natural approach of the common law is to let the loss lie where it falls. This can however lead to unjust results where for example buyers who have made pre-payment could not recover anything and the sellers are unjustly enriched. This harshness of the common law survived until the 1943 case of *Fibrosa Spolka Akcyjna v Fairbairn Lawson Combe Barbour Ltd* [1943] A.C. 32.

Fibrosa Spolka Akcyjna v Fairbairn Lawson Combe Barbour Ltd [1943] A.C. 32   **2–111**
Facts:
The contract was for delivery of machinery CIF Gydnia. At the time of the contract, July 1939, the buyers made an advance payment of £1,000. However before the sellers were able to manufacture the machinery, the contract was frustrated as a result of Poland being occupied by Germany. The buyers sued to recover the £1,000.
Held:
The House of Lords held that they were entitled to succeed because there had been a total failure of consideration. The total failure of consideration however meant that the sellers could not recover expenses incurred in attempting to perform the contract (including any manufacturing costs and expenses already incurred).

The Law Reform (Frustrated Contracts) Act 1943 does not apply to: **2–112**

1. any charterparty, except a time charterparty or demise charterparty (s.2(5)(a));

2. any contract of carriage of goods by sea (s.2(5)(a));

3. any contract of insurance (s.2(5)(b)); or

4. any contract to which s.7 Sale of Goods Act 1979 applies or any other contract for the sale of specific goods where the frustrating event is the perishing of the goods (s.2(5)(c)).

It becomes immediately important to note the provisions of s.7 Sale of Goods Act 1979. That section reads:

"Where there is an agreement to sell specific goods, and subsequently the goods, without any fault on the part of the seller or buyer, perish before the risk passes to the buyer, the agreement is thereby avoided".

The scope of s.7 is extremely narrow—it applies only to specific goods where property and risk have not passed and not to cases where only part of the goods have perished. However as far the Law Reform (Frustrated Contracts) Act 1943 is concerned, even where the perishing of the goods has taken place not within the contemplation of s.7 Sale of Goods Act 1979, the 1943 Act will not apply as long as the goods perished are specific goods according to the second limb of s.2(5)(c).

2–113

> N.B. Specific goods are defined as "goods identified and agreed on at the time a contract of sale is made", according to s.61(1) Sale of Goods Act 1979. Where goods under the court are specific goods, specific performance of the contract may be ordered by the courts under s.52 of the Act. In *Re Wait* [1927] 1 Ch. 606, a sale of 5,000 tons of a cargo of 10,000 tons of wheat on a specific ship was not considered by the court to be a sale in specific goods. See paras 3–014—3–016.

"Perishing" does not mean the physical destruction of the goods alone; in an insurance case, *Asfar & Co Ltd v Blundell* [1896] 1 Q.B. 123, in deciding whether the goods have perished or lost for the purposes of the Marine Insurance Act 1906, Lord Esher M.R. considered that not only should the court take into account the physical destruction of the goods but, equally important, whether the goods as salvaged had lost their original character so as to render their intended commercial purpose defeated. The dates in that case as salvaged from the bottom of the sea could be used to make industrial alcohol but were totally unsuitable for human consumption, which was their original commercial purpose. His Lordship decided that the nature of the goods had altered so drastically that they must be deemed to be a total loss.

Any other contract for the sale of goods will be governed by the Act including a contract for the sale of specific goods which is frustrated otherwise than by the goods perishing. Where the 1943 Act applies, the following rules will determine the effects of a frustrated contract.

1. Section 1(2) of the Act states that all sums paid to any party under that contract shall be recoverable. Where money is payable under the contract, the duty to pay ceases.

2–114   *Example*: the seller delivers first instalment of a cargo of unascertained goods to buyer; the contract being one for delivery of goods by instalments. The contract becomes frustrated after the first delivery. If payment for that instalment had been paid, the buyer could recover the money paid. Where payment should be due, the buyer does not have to make payment.

2. However, having considered all the circumstances of the case it may be just to allow the party to whom payment is to be made or has been made, retain or recover such sums as to cover his expenses incurred before the contract became frustrated.

Example: where it is in the contemplation of the contract in the example above that the buyer were to reimburse the seller for cost of transport, the seller could retain part of the payment made to cover this expense. Where he has yet to receive payment, the buyer would be obliged to reimburse him for the expense.

3. Section 1(3) provides,

> "where any party to the contract has, by reason of anything done by any other party thereto in, or for the purpose of, the performance of the contract, obtained a valuable benefit (other than a payment of money [described above]) before the time of discharge, there shall be recoverable from him by the said other party such sum (if any), not exceeding the value of the said benefit to the party obtaining it, as the Court considers just, having regard to all the circumstances of the case . . . ".

Example: where the buyer in the contract above has disposed of the goods in the first instalment, he must pay for that instalment. It would seem that the mere acceptance of the goods delivered in part would be sufficient to activate this provision. Hence, a buyer who has taken delivery of a part of the goods is obliged to pay for that part. However, where it is not a benefit to him to have possession of that portion, it is not clear whether he has to pay for them. Although there is dictum in *BP Exploration Co (Libya) Ltd v Hunt* [1979] 1 W.L.R. 783 (see also, the House of Lords' decision in [1982] 1 W.L.R. 253) that where the buyer receives no benefit from the receipt of the goods he should not have to pay for them, the position is not entirely clear. An illustration is where the buyer has taken delivery of a portion of the goods but since then, there is a supervening illegality on the further and subsequent disposal of the goods. The goods have now become a burden on the buyer—should he be compelled to pay the seller? On the one hand it might be argued that the Act tries to ensure that the loss is distributed fairly and hence, where the goods have been taken delivery of by the buyer, they should be paid for by the buyer. The fact of frustration must be an accepted fact of commercial life. On the other is the stipulation in the Act "valuable benefit", which suggests that the law would only insist on the payment where there has been a benefit in a real sense. The inherent value in the goods will not do; the law should consider the circumstances in determining whether there has been received by the buyer any real advantage or benefit.

Force majeure clauses and shipment of goods

In the large majority of documentary sales (especially the CIF and its variant contracts) frustration would be difficult to establish. In this light, commercial people have thought it necessary in many cases to insert a force majeure clause. **2–115**

The object is to specify what events would bring the contract to an end and free the parties from performance, thereby overcoming the general reluctance of the law to find impossibility or frustration. The courts have generally treated these clauses with circumspect because usually they are inserted by the stronger bargaining party and the weaker party has little say in the matter. It is also usually to the advantage of the seller. For example, it is typical for a force majeure clause to release the seller from performing the contract if there is a shortage of goods, breakdown of machinery, strikes, governmental action or other similar events which the courts would not consider to be frustrating events. Although seen in this light, the force majeure clause resembles an exemption of liability clause, it has been ruled in *Trade & Transport Inc v Iino Kaiun Kaisha Ltd* [1973] 1 W.L.R. 210 that that is not the case. Therefore, a force majeure clause could not be stretched to protect a seller from his failure to perform the contract as a result of his own negligence or wilful default (*Gyllenhammar & Partners International Ltd v Sour B Industrija* [1989] 2 Lloyd's Rep. 403).

The approach of the courts when confronted by a force majeure clause is to construe it narrowly and to cast the burden of proof on the party pleading it. In *Channel Island Ferries Ltd v Sealink UK Ltd* [1988] 1 Lloyd's Rep. 145, Parker L.J. held that it is for the party relying on the force majeure clause to prove the facts giving rise to his plea within that clause. Where the clause provided that the party is to be relieved of liability if he is "prevented" from carrying out his obligations under the contract. He must show that performance has become physically or legally impossible, and not merely more difficult, inconvenient or unprofitable. This approach attempts to prevent that party from avoiding the normal incidences of strict contractual performance when he could not plead frustration in law. He must further prove that:

- his failure to perform was not caused by his own fault or actions;

- his nonperformance was due to circumstances beyond his control; and

- he could not have taken any reasonable steps to avoid or mitigate the supervening circumstances or events.

2–116   The standard approach to force majeure clauses is one of strictness, that is to say, the terms of the clause will be read as supporting performance instead of exempting it. In *Agrokor AG v Tradigrain SA* [2000] 1 Lloyd's Rep. 497, the force majeure clause provided:

> "In case of prohibition of export, restricting export, whether partially or otherwise, any such restriction shall be deemed by both parties to apply to the contract and to the extent of such total or partial restriction to prevent fulfilment whether by shipment or by any other means whatsoever and to that extent this contract or any unfulfilled proportion thereof shall be cancelled".

Soon after the contract was made, the Croatian Government imposed an export ban on wheat and wheat flour from Croatia. The arbitrators found that the force majeure clause did not exempt the sellers from delivering the contracted wheat on the basis that the sellers could deliver wheat of any European origin under the contract. The clause was to be construed generally against the party attempting to get out of performing the strict terms of the contract. This was upheld by the Commercial Court which stated that it was for the sellers to show not merely that there was a ban which restricted the export of wheat but also that the ban had the effect of restricting the performance of the actual contract with the buyer. That, they failed to do.

As far as the ICC is concerned, the use of force majeure clauses is good, sound **2–117** mercantile practice and should be encouraged.[44] The organisation has introduced a model clause (ICC Publication No.421) which could be incorporated into any international contract of sale. The clause provides that a party is not liable to perform his contractual obligations if he succeeds in proving:

- that the failure was due to an impediment beyond his control;

- that he could not reasonably be expected to have taken the impediment and its effects upon his ability to perform the contract into account at the time of the conclusion of the contract; and

- that he could not reasonably have avoided or overcome it or at least its effects.

The ICC conditions are not dissimilar to the English law approach. On the first condition that the impediment is beyond the party's control, we see a similar requirement in *Lebeaupin v Crispin & Co* [1920] 2 K.B. 714. The suppliers of tinned salmon failed in invoking the force majeure clause because it was their fault that they waited too long before harvesting the fish crop by which time the crop had run out. The depletion of the salmon run was therefore self induced and could not constitute force majeure. Additionally, it must be within the suppliers' contemplation that if they waited, they risked not being able to perform the contract. The "impediment" must have been within his contemplation; again reflecting a parallel with the ICC second condition. On the third condition, the English courts are equally strict about the party's duty to attempt to overcome the effects of the "impediment". In *Joseph Pyke & Son (Liverpool) Ltd v Richard Cornelius & Co* [1955] 2 Lloyd's Rep. 747 for example, the sellers were prevented from relying on the force majeure clause because they could have obtained the contracted goods from another supplier although their intended supplier was no longer suitable.

All depends, however, on the construction of the contract within its own particular set of circumstances. In the following case we see how the court found that the force majeure clause actually availed the sellers.

Walton (Grain & Shipping) v British Italian Trade Co [1959] 1 Lloyd's Rep. 223 **2–118**
Facts:
The sellers were obliged under a CIF contract to deliver a cargo of groundnut oil. There was a force majeure clause in the contract:

---

[44] The ICC also envisages hardship as a possible excuse for non-performance or revised performance unlike English contract law. The ICC model hardship clause thus provides: "Where a party to a contract proves that: (2) (a) the continued performance of its contractual duties has become excessively onerous due to an event beyond its reasonable control which it could not reasonably have been expected to have taken into account at the time of the conclusion of the contract; and that (b) it could not reasonably have avoided or overcome the event or its consequences, the parties are bound, within a reasonable time of the invocation of this Clause, to negotiate alternative contractual terms which reasonably allow for the consequences of the event."

"Should the shipment be delayed . . . by any executive or legislative act . . . time of shipment to be extended by two months. Should shipment not be possible within these two months, contract to be void".

Subsequent to the contract, the Indian Government issued an edict refusing to grant any export licence for groundnut oil. The buyers sued for delivery and/or damages for non-delivery. The sellers attempted to rely on the force majeure clause and argued that there exists an implied term in the contract that shipment is subject to licence. The buyers on the other hand contended that under a CIF contract, it was the duty of the sellers to secure the export licence. That duty was an ordinary commercial risk. The force majeure clause could only apply where the event is

"something of the kind not in the knowledge of the parties at the time of the contract and which occurs *after* making the contract".

In the present case, there was no supervening illegality since it was illegal to export without an export licence in the first place, and this was known to the parties at the time of the contract. All that happened was that the sellers' expectations were not fulfilled. There was thus no force majeure.

Held:

The court gave judgment in favour of the sellers. Construing the force majeure clause, it is clear that the facts fell squarely within the parameters of the clause. There is an implied condition in every contract that at the time of performance, it should be legal for the promisor to carry out his contractual obligations. The contract is therefore accordingly discharged when the sellers attempted but could not secure the export licence. As for the definition of "supervening", a common sense approach should be adopted. The buyers' contention that force majeure did not arise because there was a pre-existing illegality on shipment without licence could not be accepted.

2–119   In the context of CIF contracts, it was contended in *Tradax Export SA v André et Cie* [1976] 1 Lloyd's Rep. 416 that in a series of string contracts for the delivery of soya bean meal, there could be no force majeure because under a CIF contract the sellers could find and buy goods, pro rata, afloat to overcome the embargo issued by the US Government and satisfy the contracts. The Court of Appeal considered this to be quite untenable because it would mean many buyers chasing after very limited supplies afloat. That would be highly impractical and quite unworkable.[45]

In the case where the seller has enough goods to satisfy only a few of his many contracts, the issue is whether he needs:

1. to allocate and distribute pro rata the goods to meet every contract; or

2. to satisfy in full only a few and plead force majeure with the rest.

Both options are open to him subject to any express or implied terms of the contract. In *Pool Shipping v London Coal Co of Gibraltar* [1939] 2 All E.R. 432, the contract provided for the delivery of coal "as were normally required". There was also a force majeure clause which referred to the prevention of "the normal working of the contract". The suppliers were unable to meet all their contracts as a result of government pressure on collieries. The court held that the suppliers

---

[45] See Lorenzon, Skajaa, Baatz and Nicoll, *C.I.F. and F.O.B. Contracts*, 5th edn (London: Sweet & Maxwell, 2012), para.4–003.

were entitled to equalise the shortage of delivery among their contracts, provided that the shortage was due to causes beyond their control. In *Intertradex SA v Lesieur Tourteaux SARL* [1978] 2 Lloyd's Rep. 509, he could allocate the available goods in any way which the trade would consider reasonable and proper between his many contracts. This could be done on the basis of pro rata sharing or any other method recognised in the trade. This should, however, be contrasted against *The Superservant II* [1990] 1 Lloyd's Rep. where the contract was held to have been breached and not frustrated when the defendants allocated their sole available tug to a third party and not to the claimants because the second tug had broken down. As for option two, everything hinges on the construction of the force majeure clause. It has been held that a clause that referred to the seller's being "prevented" from performing the contract would be sufficient even though, *in stricto senso*, he was only prevented because he had allocated the goods to another or other contracts and not to the buyer in question. Where the force majeure clause uses a wide term like "being hindered from performing" instead of "being prevented from performing", the courts would grant it the breadth of scope that it calls for.

CHAPTER 3

TERMS UNDER THE SALE OF GOODS ACT 1979

Where the international sales contract is expressed to be governed by English law **3–001** or where under the rules of private international law, it is determined that English law is the applicable law, then English domestic law relating to the sale and supply goods becomes immediately relevant. The law of sale of goods in England and Wales is generally governed by the Sale of Goods Act 1979 (which consolidates and amends the Sale of Goods Act 1893), the Supply of Goods and Services Act 1982 and the Sale and Supply of Goods Act 1994. The Sale of Goods Act 1893 was intended to codify the law relating to the sale of goods. As such it is subject to slightly different rules of interpretation. As Lord Herschell states in *Bank of England v Vagliano Bros* [1891] A.C. 107:

> "[T]he proper course is in the first instance to examine the language of the statute and to ask what is its natural meaning, uninfluenced by any considerations derived from the previous state of the law, and not to start with inquiring how the law previously stood, and then, assuming that it was probably intended to leave it unaltered, to see if the words of the enactment will bear an interpretation in conformity with this view. If a statute, intended to embody in a code a particular branch of the law, is to be treated in this fashion, it appears to me that its utility will be almost entirely destroyed, and the very nature with which it was enacted will be frustrated. The purpose of such a statute surely was that on any point specifically dealt with by it, the law should be ascertained by interpreting the language used instead of, as before, by roaming over a vast number of authorities in order to discover what the law was, extracting it by a minute critical examination of the prior decisions".

In certain cases where the provisions of the codifying Act are ambiguous, the courts may be entitled to refer to previously decided cases for assistance. Moreover, where there are technical terms employed by the Act or the provisions may carry a technical meaning, it would be useful to turn to earlier decisions.

While Lord Herschell's exhortation has commonly been cited, it is not an immutable rule. For example, Lord Diplock in *Ashington Piggeries Ltd v Christopher Hill Ltd* [1972] A.C. 441 stated that the Act "ought not to be construed so narrowly as to force on parties to contracts for the sale of goods promises and consequences different from what they must reasonably have intended" in relation to implied terms under the Act. Under certain circumstances, departure from Lord Herschell's prescription may be justified by the words in s.62(2) of the Act itself. Section 62(2) provides that:

"The rules of the common law, including the law merchant except in so far as they are inconsistent with the provisions of this Act and in particular the rules relating to the law of principal and agent and the effect of fraud, misrepresentation, duress or coercion, mistake, or other invalidating cause, apply to contracts for the sale of goods".

3–002 There is uncertainty as to which rules of the common law are "inconsistent with the provisions of the Act". In *Re Wait* [1927] 1 Ch. 606, Atkin L.J. was clear about the terms of the codifying Act.

In that case, Wait had contracted to buy 1000 tons of wheat. The cargo was to arrive at Avonmouth from the USA on the *MV Challenger*. The following day, he agreed to sell 500 tons of the wheat to H & B who paid him in advance. Before the arrival of the ship, Wait went bankrupt. Some of the goods had been disposed of but the remainder was held by Wait's trustee in bankruptcy. On whether H & B have a claim to part of the cargo held by the trustee, the Court of Appeal held that they could not succeed. They could only prove in Wait's bankruptcy for the return of the price. The 500 tons which was to be used to meet H & B's contract had not been identified and hence, they had no right to the goods held. In rejecting the argument that H & B might be able to assert a claim of a proprietary nature to their share of the wheat based on equitable principles, Atkin L.J. said:

"The Code was passed at a time when the principles of equity and equitable remedies were recognized and given effect to in all our Courts, and the particular equitable remedy of specific performance is specially referred to in section 52. The total sum of legal relations (meaning by the word 'legal' existing in equity as well as in common law) arising out of the contract for the sale of goods may well be regarded as defined by the Code. It would have been futile in a code intended for commercial men to have created an elaborate structure of rules dealing with rights at law, if at the same time it was intended to leave, subsisting with the legal rights, equitable rights inconsistent with, more extensively, and coming into existence earlier than the rights so carefully set out in the various sections of the Code. The rules for transfer of property as between seller and buyer . . . appear to be complete and exclusive statements of the legal relations both in law and equity".

This is clearly consistent with the dicta of Lord Herschell. Indeed, Atkin L.J. also stated that

"inasmuch as we are now bound by the plain language of the Code I do not think that decisions in cases before 1893 are of much value".

The Contract of Sale

3–003 Section 2(1) of the 1979 Act defines the contract of sale of goods as:

"[A] contract by which the seller transfers or agrees to transfer the property in goods to the buyer for a money consideration called the price".

The intention to sell and buy

It is immediately evident that there are two parties to that contract for the sale of **3–004** goods—the buyer and the seller. Under normal contractual conditions, the seller and buyer must have full capacity to contract. They must be committed to the transfer of property in the goods for a money consideration. This commitment must be made clear. While the courts' prevailing attitude is to save a commercial contract, it would not do so if the terms are too unclear. For example, in *G Scammell & Nephew Ltd v Ouston* [1941] A.C. 25, the House of Lords held that an agreement to acquire goods "on hire-purchase" was too vague since there were many kinds of hire-purchase agreements in widely different terms, so it was impossible to specify the terms on which the parties had agreed.

The law of contract recognises the existence of an agreement when an offer to enter into legal relations has been accepted unequivocally by the promisee. Consistent with the requirement that there be a clearly expressed intention to sell and buy, or the intention to create legal relations, the trader needs to decide whether the terms of the offer are clear and whether they suggest the preparedness of the offeror to enter into legal relations with him. Without such clarity, the offer is not capable of being accepted. Frequently this is a matter of construction of the language and circumstances of the purported offer. In *Grainger v Gough* [1896] A.C. 325, the wine catalogue was held not to constitute an offer. In that case two chief reasons were supplied by the court:

- it was not conceivable that with his limited stock, the offeror would expose himself to more acceptors than practically possible; and

- it was clearly not his intention to bind himself to contracts with acceptors whose creditworthiness he has no knowledge of.

This case shows us that the primary concern of the law in establishing the existence of an offer is to look to the presumed intention of the offeror. Where the circumstances and language of the offer are such that it is not conceivable that he must have made such an offer, the law would not recognise it as an offer.

It is important to consider the entirety of the circumstances and not be unduly **3–005** swayed by any one isolated piece of evidence when attempting to establish the existence of an offer. This is especially so in the case of international commerce. In *J Evans & Sons (Portsmouth) Ltd v Andrea Merzario Ltd* [1976] 2 All E.R. 930, the importers of machinery parts had frequently used the services of the defendant freight forwarding agents to arrange carriage of the goods to England. These contracts were expressed in the trade's standard terms. Up until 1967, the defendants had always arranged for the crates or trailers to hold the machinery and to be kept under deck where the goods would be protected. In 1967, following a "courtesy call" to the importers, the defendants suggested the machinery should in the future be carried in containers and gave assurances to the claimants that the containers will be stowed below deck so that the goods would not rust. In reliance on this proposition, the importers agreed that the consignment in question be shipped in container. The container was inadvertently placed on deck and not below deck. It was not fastened properly and the container fell overboard. The primary question for the court was whether the "courtesy call" was legally binding. The Court of Appeal held that it was, overruling Kerr J. It was a legally binding offer which was properly accepted for the following reasons:

- the defendants had suggested a change in pre-existing practice between the parties—they wanted to use containers instead of trailers;

- the claimants would not have agreed without assurances that the goods would be shipped under deck;

- the fact that the offer was couched in "courtesy" terms does not negate the intention to create legal relations; and

- the reality of the courtesy call was that "if the plaintiffs continued to give the defendants their business, the defendants will ensure that those goods in containers are shipped under deck".

3–006   Where the price of the goods is concerned, s.8(1) of the Sale of Goods Act 1979 provides that the price:

1. may be fixed by the contract (for example, the contract stating that the price is to be £3000); or

2. may be determined by the course of dealing between the parties; or

3. may be left to be fixed in a manner agreed by the contract. (For example, in *Foley v Classique Coaches Ltd* [1934] 2 K.B. 1, an agreement to supply petrol "at a price to be agreed by the parties" was held to be a valid contract.)

The major difficulty with this last provision is whether the courts will read the agreement to agree as a binding contract. This will usually depend on whether from the circumstances there is an intention to create legal relations and sufficient clarity of terms (see for example, *Courtney & Fairburn Ltd v Tolaini Bros (Hotels) Ltd* [1975] 1 All E.R. 716, and the problematic case of *May & Butcher v The King* [1934] 2 K.B. 17n). In *May & Butcher v The King*, the House of Lords held that an agreement for the sale of goods at a price to be determined later could not be enforced because

"The Sale of Goods Act 1893 says that if the price is not mentioned and settled in the contract it is to be a reasonable price. The simple answer in this case is that the Sale of Goods Act provides for silence on the point and here there is no silence, because there is a provision that the two parties *are to agree . . .* there was clearly no contract." (emphasis added).

This is however not a general principle as was pointed out by *Hillas & Co Ltd v Arcos Ltd* (1932) 147 L.T. 503.

3–007   *Hillas & Co Ltd v Arcos Ltd* (1932) 147 L.T. 503
Facts:
An option to buy more timber provided that the price was to accord with "fair specification" to be arrived at later. The buyers purported to exercise the option but the sellers had sold the goods to someone else. The sellers argued that they were not bound by the option because the price was not fixed and the offer was therefore void for uncertainty.

Held:
The majority in the Court of Appeal had felt bound by the House of Lords' judgment in *May & Butcher v The King* and held therefore that there was no contract. The House of Lords however allowed the appeal, implying that no general principle may be derived from *May & Butcher v The King*. The House of Lords held, distinguishing *May & Butcher v The King*, that the parties had been trading with each other and were familiar with "fair specification" as a mode of price determination and as such the price could be determined according to their previous course of dealing.

Where the price cannot be determined according to s.8(1), s.8(2) states that the buyer will have to pay a reasonable price. What is reasonable is a question of fact dependent on the circumstances of each particular case. In the old case of *Acebal v Levy* (1834) 10 Bing. 376, while reference to the market price should help in the determination of what is reasonable, market price per se may or may not be a reasonable price.

The law also acknowledges the fact that under certain circumstances, it may be **3–008** necessary to have an independent third party to fix the price by valuation. Section 9 provides that where the person appointed to make the valuation fails to make the valuation, the contract is avoided. It is of course possible to circumscribe this contingency by express stipulation in the contract. Where goods or any part of them have been delivered to the buyer before the agreement is avoided as a result of the failure of valuation, the buyer is required to pay a reasonable price for what he has received.

In general, the courts seem quite prepared, on the authority of *Sudbrook Trading Estate Ltd v Eggleton* [1983] 1 A.C. 444, to find a contract where there exists a recognition, express or otherwise, that the price to be fixed in the future, especially where part of that contract has been performed (e.g. where part of all of the goods have been delivered on the strength of that acknowledgement).

Sudbrook Trading Estate Ltd v Eggleton [1983] 1 A.C. 444   **3–009**
Facts:
The contractual leases relate to certain industrial premises in Gloucester. Clause 11 entitled the lessees to purchase the reversion in fee simple, on certain conditions (which were all satisfied),

"at such price not being less than Seventy five thousand pounds as may be agreed upon by two valuers one to be nominated by the Lessor and the other by the Lessee or in default of such agreement by an Umpire appointed by the said Valuers . . ."

The lessors argued that the clause and indeed the options to purchase were void for uncertainty because

"they contain no formula by which the price Court of Appeal be fixed in the event of no agreement being reached, and that they were no more than agreements to agree".

They had further refused to appoint their valuer which in turn rendered the price fixing machinery inoperable.
Held:
While the price is an essential term of the contract, the mechanism for arranging the price was clear and valid. Hence, the lessor's default should not be allowed to defeat the operation of the price fixing mechanism. The court will order an inquiry to determine the reasonable price for the reversion on the basis that the stipulation that a price is to be fixed by valuers must indicate that a fair and reasonable price should be paid. Furthermore, as Lord Fraser of Tullybelton said:

"[W]hen the option was exercised, there was constituted a complete contract for sale, and the clause should be construed as meaning that the price was to be a fair price".

This dictum tells us that the contract had been partly performed; and it would therefore not be fair to deprive the lessees of any redress.

3–010   Parties to the contract must also be careful with expressing their contracts as being subject to the satisfaction of any condition/s. In *Astra Trust v Adams & Williams* [1969] 1 Lloyd's Rep. 81, the contract for the sale of a boat was made subject to "satisfactory survey". It was held that there was no contract because there was no commitment evident from the terms that the buyer would make the purchase. The terms of the contract were uncertain.

It is, however, safe to say that where possible the courts will endeavour to save a contract rather than to strike it down on the basis of uncertainty. In *Hillas & Co Ltd v Arcos Ltd*, Lord Wight put it in the following terms:

> "Businessmen often record the most important agreements in crude and summary fashion; modes of expression sufficient and clear to them in the course of their business may appear to those unfamiliar with the business far from complete or precise. It is accordingly the duty of the court to construe such documents fairly and broadly, without being too astute or subtle in finding defects; but, on the contrary, the court should seek to apply the old maxim of English law, *verba ita sunt intelligenda ut res magis valeat quam pereat*".

Indeed the court in *David T Boyd & Co v Louis Louca* [1973] 1 Lloyd's Rep. 209 in an attempt to resolve the uncertainty held that a contract containing an uncertainty may be binding because there is placed on one party the duty to clarify the duty. In that case, the contract was expressed as "free on board . . . good Danish port". The court held that the contract was not too vague and as it was an FOB contract, the buyer was duty bound to name the port of shipment.

3–011   This commitment to sell and buy distinguishes the sale contract from a hire-purchase arrangement. The hire-purchase contract is a contract of bailment or hire with the option of purchase at the end of the hire period. The parties are not committed to sell or buy until the option is exercised by the hirer at the end of the hire period. A contract of hire purchase should not be confused with a conditional sale contract. The latter allows the buyer to pay by instalments for the goods and the contract carries a stipulation that no property will pass until all the instalments have been paid.

Finally, on this point of the commitment to sell and buy, a "sale or return" contract may pose certain difficulties. In a "sale or return" contract, the buyer who intends to resell the goods he has received from the seller is entitled to return the goods if the resale falls through. However, if the buyer does anything to show that he has asserted proprietary rights over the goods, he is presumed to have bought the goods and must pay the seller. An example is where he has applied the goods to his own use or has resold them. Where an "agent" is involved though, the major difficulty is deciding whether the contract is in fact an agency or a sale or return contract.

In *Weiner v Harris* [1910] 1 K.B. 285, a jewellery manufacturer delivered goods to a dealer "on sale for cash only or return". The object was to retain property in the goods until the goods have been sold or returned. The dealer was contractually entitled to receive half the profit from any resale and was required to keep the jewellery separate from his own goods. On resale, he was to pay the cost price and half the profit to the manufacturer. The court held that the dealer was the manufacturer's agent and hence, any person buying the goods from the dealer obtained a good title even if the dealer failed to pay the manufacturer.

Sale and the "agreement to sell"

It is necessary to make the distinction between the sale and the agreement to sell. **3–012**
This is because a sale of goods is both a contract and a conveyance (see *Mischeff v Springett* [1942] 2 K.B. 331) whereas the agreement to sell is simply a contract. This means that if one party to an agreement to sell defaults performance, the other party has recourse only to a personal remedy. Where there is in fact a sale, the buyer may also have proprietary remedies in respect of the goods themselves and the seller may be entitled to sue for the price.
    Further, under s.20(1) of the Act

"unless otherwise agreed, the goods remain at the seller's risk until the property in term is transferred to the buyer, but when the property in them is transferred to the buyer, the goods are at the buyer's risk whether delivery has been made or not".

As a general rule, therefore, the risk of loss, damage or deterioration lies on the owner of the goods at any given time. Thus, it usually falls on the seller under an agreement to sell but where there has been a sale, the prima facie assumption is that the buyer now has the risk.

Subject matter of the Sale of Goods contract

First, it should be pointed out that "goods" is defined in s.61(1) as including "all **3–013**
personal chattels other than things in action and money" and in particular as including

"emblements, industrial growing crops and things attached to or forming part of the land which are agreed to be severed before sale or under the contract of sale".

Section 5(1) of the Act then subdivides goods into *existing goods*, owned or possessed by the seller, or goods to be manufactured or acquired by him after the making of the contract of sale, also known as *future goods*. The Act further classifies goods as:

- *specific goods*;
- *unascertained goods*;
- *ascertained goods*.

In international trade law, these categories are essential to the determination of the rules on passing of property, risk and the remedy of specific performance.

Thus, it would be useful to appreciate their definitions and how they interact with the other provisions of the Act.

3–014 "Existing goods" according to s.5(1) are goods already in the ownership or possession of the seller. They may however be specific or unascertained. This distinction is important to the determination of where risk falls and when property passes. Section 16, for example, states that property in unascertained goods cannot pass to the buyer, until they have first been ascertained.

Future goods refer to goods which are not yet in existence or existing goods not yet acquired by the seller. Where the contract is expressed as on for the sale of future goods, it is merely an agreement to sell the goods and not a proper sale. Future goods usually are unascertained goods and therefore property in them cannot pass. Before the 1893 Act though, equity provided that a beneficial interest passed to the buyer as soon as the goods become present goods and the contract could then be enforced by specific performance (*Holroyd v Marshall* (1862) 10 H.L.C. 191).

"Specific goods" is defined by s.61(1) as goods identified and agreed on at the time a contract of sale is made. Specific goods are usually goods properly designated or identified. Further, they should be capable of being designated or identified when the contract is made. For example, when seller agrees to sell "his Ford Escort", the car in question is to be treated as specific goods because it can be properly identified as the subject matter for the sale when the contract is made. The court will look at how substitutable the goods are when deciding whether they are specific goods—in *Aercap Partners v Avia Asset* [2010] EWHC 2431, the court found that given that the contract clearly envisaged the possibility of the goods being replaced by an engine of the same type, model, thrust rating and same or better age, the goods could not be said to be specific goods. It also made commercial sense that some other engine could be used to assemble the contracted airframe; the specified engine was not so unique that it could not be substituted. It was therefore not specific goods.

3–015 Other examples may include "the only yellow car in the parking bay", "the book you have in your hand", "my entire collection of Elvis CDs", etc. There is however no provision in the Act which states that specific goods must be in existence at the time of the contract. Where for instance the contract was for the sale of the entire future crop of a particular piece of land, it has been argued that this would have been for specific goods.[1]

Where the contract is for a specified quantity, the situation is less clear. In *Howell v Coupland* (1876) 1 Q.B.D. 258, for example, the contract was for the sale of a quantity of potatoes to be grown on a designated plot of land. The court held that the failure of the crop resulted in the frustration of the contract because the goods described in the contract were specific and no substitute would suffice. However, this pre-1893 case was not followed in *Re Wait* [1927] 1 Ch. 606. There, it was held that a contract for a specified quantity of goods from a particular mass was not a contract for specific goods. Support may also be had from *Blackburn Bobbin Co v Allen* [1918] 2 K.B. 467 where the Court of Appeal was clearly of the opinion that a contract for the sale of a quantity of timber from Finland was not one for the sale of specific goods. In the light of ss.6 and 7, which deal with the perishing of goods, it has been said that the intention of the Act is to confine specific goods to existing goods and not otherwise. It would

---

[1] See, *Benjamin's Sale of Goods* paras 1–113, 1–114.

therefore follow that future goods are not capable of being labelled as specific goods.

Pragmatism, however, would suggest that it is in fact possible to have future goods which are specific. Where A and B agree that A will buy five scarves from a boutique where A, as a valued customer, is entitled to a special discount so that she could then resell two of the scarves to B, it is immediately clear that this is a contract for future goods. The goods (i.e. the two scarves) have, however, been properly identified by the parties and they are already in existence.

Be that as it may, it would be safe to say that in international trade, future **3–016** goods are very seldom specific. Where the issue is on the perishing of goods (i.e. ss.6 and 7), the doubt remains but only as a rare situation.

On the other hand, there is no definition of "unascertained goods" or "ascertained goods" even though these terms are used in the Act for different purposes (see for example, ss.16, 17 and 52). In *Re Wait* [1927] 1 Ch. 606, Atkin L.J. thought that ascertained "probably means identified in accordance with the agreement after the time a contract of sale is made". Unascertained goods fall into three general categories:

1. generic goods sold by description (for example, 100kg of Siamese rice, a new Ford Escort, 1000 second-hand bicycles);

2. goods not yet in existence (for example, goods to be manufactured in the future or something to be grown); or

3. a part to be ascertained or identified from a specific mass or bulk (for example, six potatoes from the sack in your shop, 100kg of sugar from the 1000kg now in your warehouse).

Terms of the Contract

Conditions, warranties and representations

In the run up to the conclusion of a sale contract, it is inevitable that certain **3–017** promises and statements will be made to attract the other party into making the contract. Where such statements or promises have been made, it is vital to know which category of promises they fall into. The legal consequences of the failure of any of these statements or promises are dependent on the type of promise they are.

Statements of opinion and puffs

Puffs do not bind the maker because they are usually too vague or extravagant to **3–018** found any basis of liability. For example, in *Chalmers v Harding* (1868) 17 L.T. 571, the statement by the seller that he is selling a "very good second-hand reaper" should not be made binding because it was clear that it was not so intended. *Simplex commendatio non obligat.*

If it is a statement of opinion, the consequence is less equivocal. It depends to a certain extent on who the maker of the opinion is. Where the statement is made by a professional person regarding his field of expertise or where it is represented that the opinion is sound and based on facts, then the courts are more ready to find an enforceable promise in the statement of opinion.[2]

Actionable statements

3–019 Two of the more popularly known actionable promises are conditions and warranties. These are regarded as promises that the maker must be made to fulfil. A condition as defined by Lord Diplock in *Photo Production Ltd v Securicor Transport Ltd* [1980] A.C. 826, is a promise in respect of which the parties have agreed, whether by express words or by implication, that any failure of performance by one party, irrespective of gravity of the event that has resulted in the breach, shall entitle the other party to treat the contract as discharged. A warranty is defined in s.61(1) of the Sale of Goods Act 1979 as

> "an agreement with reference to goods which are the subject of the contract of sale, but collateral to the main purpose of such contract, the breach of which gives rise to a claim for damages, but not the right to reject the goods or treat the contract as repudiated".

In addition, it is important to note the provisions of s.11(3) of the Act:

> "Whether a stipulation in a contract of sale is a condition, the breach of which may give rise to a right to treat the contract as repudiated, or a warranty, the breach of which may give rise to a claim in damages but not to a right to reject the goods and treat the contract as repudiated, depends in each case on the construction of the contract; and a stipulation may be a condition, though called a warranty in the contract".

It was stated in *Wickham Machine Tool Sales Ltd v L. Schuler AG* [1974] A.C. 235 that a stipulation described as a condition may not in fact be one. Labels are not conclusive whether they are applied to warranties or conditions.

There is a third type of terms—innominate or intermediate terms. These may or may not give rise to a right to repudiate the contract depending on the seriousness of the breach. In *Cehave NV v Bremer Handelsgeselschaft GmbH (The Hansa Nord)* [1976] Q.B. 44, the court held, in relying on *Hong Kong Fir Shipping Co Ltd v Kawasaki Kisen Kaisha Ltd* [1962] 2 Q.B. 26, that the term "shipment to be made in good condition" was not a condition but an innominate term. The consequences of its breach depended on the nature and effect of the breach.

3–020 There is yet another group of statements which may be treated as actionable. There are misrepresentations of fact which do not constitute a contractual promise as such but are treated by law as binding on the maker. At common law these statements are not actionable because they do not form part of the contractual promise made. However, equity does provide that the claimant may be entitled to rescind the agreement and claim an indemnity according to the rule in *Redgrave v Hurd* (1881) 20 Ch D 1. It is also clear that from *Leaf v International Galleries* [1950] 2 K.B. 86 and the more recent case of *Royscot*

---

[2] See *Andrews v Hopkinson* [1957] 1 Q.B. 229; *Porter v General Guarantee Corp Ltd* [1982] R.T.R. 384.

Trust Ltd v Rogerson [1991] Q.B. 297 that this equitable rule will extend to cases covered by the Sale of Goods Act 1979.

This right to reject must be very clearly expressed. In *Grimoldby v Wells* (1875) L.R. 10 C.P. 391, it was clear that where it is not clear that the plaintiff had intended to reject the goods, the seller may treat his inaction or equivocality as either a waiver or an affirmation of the contract. Either will result in the buyer losing his right to reject. Section 11(2) of the Sale of Goods Act 1979 provides that where the buyer may waive the condition to be performed by the seller or may elect to treat the breach of the condition as a breach of warranty and not as a ground for treating the contract as repudiated. According to the international sales case of *Kwei Tek Chao v British Traders and Shippers Ltd* [1954] 2 Q.B. 459, the buyer will lose his right to recover money *in restitution* if he waives the condition or if he elects to treat the contract as not having been repudiated.

In this connection regard should also be had to s.11(4) of the Act. That section provides that where the contract is not severable and the buyer has accepted the goods or part of them, the buyer may not reject the goods or treat the contract as having been repudiated. This is subject however to any express or implied term to the contrary, and s.35A of the Act.

Following the Misrepresentation Act 1967, the claimant who has entered into **3–021** the contract as a result of the misrepresentation may rescind the contract and this right to rescind cannot be restricted (s.1(b)). Further, the claimant may claim damages in lieu of rescission and he has a statutory right of action against a party who has made the misrepresentation negligently (s.2). Section 3 (as amended by s.8 of the Unfair Contract Terms Act 1977) prohibits terms excluding liability for misrepresentation.[3]

Any damages succeeded on a claim in misrepresentation will be based on the tortious principle of restitutio in integrum; which means that the award of damages will try to put the claimant in the position which he would have been had he never entered into the contract (*Royscot Trust Ltd v Rogerson* [1991] 2 Q.B. 297). This may be contrasted against a claim founded on a contractual promise (i.e. a condition, warranty or innominate term). The measure of damages will be to place the claimant in the position at which he would have been if the contractual promise had been fulfilled. This may include the difference between the value of the goods as indicated in the contract and the actual value when they were delivered. The claimant may also claim loss of profit (see also, s.53 of the Sale of Goods Act 1979).

Implied conditions and warranties under the Act

Implied term to pass a good title

Under s.12(1) of the Act, there is an implied condition on the seller that in the **3–022** case of a sale, he has a right to sell the goods and in the case of an agreement to sell, he will have such a right at the time when the property in the goods is to pass to the buyer. Section 12(1) is breached if the seller at the relevant time does not have the power to transfer the property or title in the goods to the buyer. There

---

[3] See *Skipskredittforeningen v Emperor Navigation* [1998] 1 Lloyd's Rep. 66 on how an anti set-off clause applied in relation to a claim for damages based on misrepresentation is to be appraised in the light of the Misrepresentation Act 1967 and the Unfair Contract Terms Act 1977.

need not be any other interference with the buyer's possession of the goods, the mere absence of a right to sell is sufficient to activate s.12(1).

Further, in *Niblett v Confectioners' Materials Co Ltd* [1921] 3 K.B. 387, the seller was held to have no right to sell because his right could be lawfully restrained by a third party who held the trade mark to the goods. Thus, the seller was in breach of s.12(1). According to Scrutton L.J., if the seller can be stopped from selling by process of law, then he does not have the right to sell.

3–023 *Great Elephant Corp v Trafigura Beheer* [2012] EWHC 1745 (Comm)
Facts:
V agreed to sell C crude oil. Whilst the tanker was preparing to load the crude oil at a floating terminal off Port Harcourt, Nigeria, the representative of the Nigerian Department of Petroleum Resources (D) was not on board the terminal. Subsequently, when D's representative arrived on board, he did not require the loading operation to stop. D then refused to allow the ship to leave. D required the operator to explain its apparent breach of the Nigerian Procedure Guide for Terminal Operations by commencing loading without clearance. The Minister of Petroleum Resources required the operator to pay a "fine" of $12 million before D completed the cargo documents and the vessel was allowed to leave some weeks later. The issue was whether the fact that D had the power to prevent the cargo from leaving port meant that V had no right to sell the cargo for the purposes of s.12(1).
Held:
Although the buyer's possession of the goods had been disturbed, it should be noted that s.12(1) is concerned with defects in title and not with the case where a good title is passed to the buyer but for some reason the buyer's right to quiet possession is subsequently interfered with. The latter case is the subject of s.12(2)(b) which provides for an implied term that the buyer will enjoy quiet possession of the goods.

In *Niblett's* case the third-party trade mark holder had a superior title (in the sense that the seller could have been restrained by injunction from selling the goods). In this case, however, D did not have a superior title to V in the same sense. A third-party right which merely interferes with the possession of the buyer was not sufficient to prevent the seller from having the "right to sell". Whilst it might be true that D could have obtained an injunction restraining the cargo from leaving Nigeria, that could not mean that V had no right to sell the cargo in breach of s.12(1).

3–024   In *Karlshamns Oljefabriker v Eastport Navigation Corp (The Elafi)* [1986] 1 All E.R. 208, it was held that the seller does not need to have ownership at any time, all the contract of sale requires is that the seller will have the power to vest those rights of ownership on the buyer at the agreed time. He could therefore simply cause the transfer of those rights from a third party to the buyer directly.

The consequences of a breach of s.12(1) may be seen in the case of *Rowland v Divall* [1923] 2 K.B. 500. The claimant had purchased a car from the defendant for £334. He then resold it to A for £400 who used it for four months. It soon transpired that the defendant had bought the car from someone without a good title. The original owner sought the return of the car. The claimant then refunded A the full purchase price and claimed the return of £334 from the defendant. On whether the defendant was entitled to set-off against the claim the depreciation of the car for the four months' use, it was held that there had been a total failure of consideration resulting from the breach of s.12(1). The buyer had not received any part of that which contracted to receive, namely the property and right to possession. Nothing therefore could be set-off against the claim.

In *Butterworth v Kingsway Motors Ltd* [1954] 1 W.L.R. 1286, A was paying for a car under a contract of hire purchase. She erroneously thought that she had a right to sell the car if she carried on paying the instalments. She then sold the car to B, who sold it to C. C then sold it to the defendant who subsequently sold it to the claimant for £1,275. After using the car for about a year, the claimant received notification from the original hirers claiming possession of the car. The claimant claimed the return of the full purchase price from the defendant. A week later, A paid off the hire. The defendant was still held liable for the return of the full purchase price even though the acquisition of a good title by A would have fed the defective titles down the chain. The court also refused to consider the fact that the claimant had used the car for almost a year. The defendant was held to have breached s.12(1), and as a result of the total failure of consideration he was obliged to return the full purchase price. Meanwhile the market price of the car had fallen to £800 and the refunding of the full purchase meant that the claimant succeeded in making a profit of £475.

It might be noted that the Law Reform Committee suggested that a buyer in these circumstances should be entitled to recover no more than his actual loss taking into consideration any benefit he may have derived from the goods when they remained in his possession.[4]   **3–025**

Section 12(2) makes the warranty (a) that the goods sold are free from any charge or encumbrance not disclosed to the buyer before the contract is made and, (b) that the buyer is to enjoy quiet possession of the goods. Where there has been a breach of s.12(1), it would appear inescapable that s.12(2)(b) may be activated as well (*Niblett v Confectioners' Materials Ltd* [1921] 3 K.B. 387). A frequently cited case on s.12(2)(b) is *Microbeads AC v Vinhurst Roadmarkings* [1975] 1 W.L.R. 218.

There, the seller sold the buyer some road marking machines in pursuant to a contract entered into before May 1970. Unknown to them, another company involved in the making of road marking machines had patented their design. Under the law, they had the right to enforce their patent with effect from November 1970. In 1972, the company brought a patent action against the buyer. On whether the buyer had a legitimate claim against the seller under s.12, the court held that while the seller was not in breach of the implied warranty as to title because at the time of the contract, they had every right to sell. However, they were in breach of the warranty as to quiet possession because there was implied an undertaking as to the future.

In an international trade case, *The Playa Larga* [1983] 2 Lloyd's Rep. 171, the seller was held to have breached s.12(2)(b). In that case, the seller, the Cuban state sugar trading agency, had sold sugar to a buyer in Chile. The cargo was being shipped to Chile when the Chilean Government was overthrown and replaced. In response, the Cuban Government ordered the seller to terminate all trading relations with Chile. The seller then ordered the ship not to discharge its cargo. It is clear in this case that s.12(2)(b) protects the buyer from interference from the seller himself.   **3–026**

Another example of how the warranty might be breached in an international commercial context is where the seller is contractually or legally (under English or foreign law) bound not to sell to the buyer. In *Louis Dreyfus Trading Ltd v Reliance Trading Ltd* [2004] EWHC 525, the contract for the sale of sugar

---

[4] Law Reform Comm., "Transfer of Title to Chattels" (1967) (12th Report) Cmnd. 2658.

anticipated that the buyer would subsequent re-sell the sugar. Payment was made but when the sugar was being discharged, M, a third party, obtained an injunction in the Gambian courts restraining further discharge on the basis that the seller was in breach of an exclusivity agreement whereby M would be the only consignee in the Gambia. The injunction was not lifted until after a month. There, the claim for damages for breach of the warranty of quiet possession was proved.

Implied term of description

3–027 Section 13(1) provides that in a sale of goods by description, there is an implied condition that the goods shall correspond with the description. Broadly speaking, goods are sold by description when the buyer contracts on the basis of the description. It used to be thought that the term "sale by description" should be distinct from the sale of specific goods. In the latter, the principle of caveat emptor was particularly to be venerated since in most cases, the buyer would have had the opportunity of inspecting the goods. On the other hand, in the sale of generic goods, the buyer does not have the same opportunity to assess the quality and nature of the goods. All that he has is the description of the goods afforded to him by the seller, hence, the bindingness of the description. The significance of that rationale has now diminished. In *Varley v Whipp* [1900] 1 Q.B. 513, for example, the term "sale by description" was quite generously extended to a second-hand reaping machine, that is to say, specific goods, and in *Grant v Australian Knitting Mills Ltd* [1936] A.C. 85, to specific goods (woollen undergarments) which have been seen and inspected by the buyer.

According to Lord Wright, there is a sale by description even though the buyer is buying something displayed before him on the counter. A thing is sold by description, even though it is specific, so long as it is sold not merely as the specific thing but as a thing corresponding to a description, e.g. woollen undergarments. A fortiori, by virtue of s.13(3) a sale is not prevented from being a sale by description by reason only that, being exposed for sale or hire, the goods are selected by the buyer.

However, the intention of the parties to "sell and buy by description" may be derived from the buyer's reliance on the words used. Where there is some reliance on the description which leads to the buyer to contract with the seller, the courts would be more willing to treat those words as forming the essence of s.13.

3–028 That said, the court will need to be convinced of the parties' intention to treat certain words as descriptive words; where there are words uttered which, from the facts, could not be taken as binding, the court will not give the benefit of the doubt to the buyer. In *Richard Drake v Thos Agnew & Sons Ltd* [2002] EWHC 294, it was claimed by the buyer that the sellers had warranted to him that the painting sold to him was by Van Dyck. The court however noted that although the sellers had given the buyer an impression that the painting might have been painted by Van Dyck, the fact that they had deliberately avoided stating that as a matter of fact showed that they had merely expressed an opinion and should be taken as such. The buyer was thus not entitled to succeed as it was obvious that mere opinion could not be taken as binding.

In the context of international commerce, it is important to note the dominant criterion of certainty of transactions. Thus, in the somewhat heavily criticised case of *Re Moore & Co Ltd v Landauer & Co's Arbitration* [1921] 2 K.B. 519, the Court of Appeal had allowed the buyer to repudiate the contract on the basis of s.13 even though the goods had been delivered in good condition and quality. In that case, while the entire consignment of Australian canned fruits had been shipped, only half had been packed in cases of 30 tins each. The others were packed in cases of 24 each, contrary to the description of the contract. Scrutton L.J. quoting McCardie J. in *Manbre Saccharine Co Ltd v Corn Products Ltd* [1919] 1 K.B. 198 stated that commercial men do not waste their time including immaterial provisions in their contract. There is thus a virtual presumption that words used in a commercial agreement are for a purpose, and are normally to be taken seriously.

In *Arcos v Ronaasen* [1933] A.C. 470, the contract was for the sale of barrel staves, CIF River Thames, the thickness of the staves to be half an inch. The House of Lords allowed the buyers to reject the goods on the ground that a large proportion of the staves were slightly thicker than half an inch even though the staves were fit for the purpose of the contract. Again the approach of the House of Lords may be justified on the ground of certainty in mercantile relations. The buyers were entitled to demand the very goods they had contracted to buy and need not accept others, even though these are fit for the purpose and are of merchantable quality.

The case of *Bowes v Shand* demonstrates a further aspect of the court's attitude   **3–029** to contract description in international trade. In that case, the House of Lords treated all parts of the description as being of equal importance, the breach of which must entail the right of rejection. There, the contract stated that the 300 tons of Madras rice were to be shipped from Madras or coast to London on board The Rajah of Cochin between the months of March and April. Every one of these items was to be treated as forming the description. In determining whether any particular form of words is part of the description, the court will examine objectively the intention of the parties in employing those words and the weight placed on them by the parties.

We might observe Salmond J.'s statement in the New Zealand case of *Taylor v Combined Buyers* (1922) N.Z.L.R. 627 which highlights the distinctiveness of unascertained goods. The judge said:

"For this purpose every description and every part of the description is material, whether it relates to kind or quality, to essential or inessential attributes. The buyer is not bound to accept any goods which fail in any respect whatever to conform to the contractual description of the goods bargained for".

The court is, however, bound to consider the circumstances of the case in deciding whether that virtual presumption of description could be rebutted. Where for example, the contract is for the sale of specific goods as in *Reardon Smith Line Ltd v Yngvar Hansen-Tangen* [1976] 1 W.L.R. 989, the use of certain descriptive words may not give rise to a sale by description. In that case, the contract was for the delivery of an 8000 ton tanker to be built in Yard 354 at Osaka Zosen but the ship was in fact constructed in another yard as Yard 354 was not large enough for an 8,000-ton vessel. The House of Lords held that "Yard 354" did not form part of the description. Lord Wilberforce considered that the true test is whether a particular item in a description constitutes a substantial ingredient of the "identity" of the thing sold, and only if it does, will the item be treated as a condition.

3–030   A distinction should be made between words used to state an essential part of the description of the goods (namely to identify the goods) and those used to provide one party with a specific indication (identification) of the goods so that he can find them and if he wishes sub-dispose of them. Where the words used in the contract bear the former sense, those words form the description of the contract. Where the words are simply intended for identification and not identity, all that the law requires is that the words are capable of fulfilling that function. Such words may therefore be more liberally construed, in contrast to words used to set out essential elements of description.

Perhaps a workable test might be borrowed from Lord Wilberforce in *Ashington Piggeries Ltd v Christopher Hill Ltd* [1972] A.C. 441 who said

> " . . . the Sale of Goods Act was [not] designed to provoke metaphysical discussions as to the nature of what is delivered in comparison with what is sold. The test of description, at least where commodities are concerned, is intended to be a broader, more common sense, test of a mercantile character. The question whether that is what the buyer bargained for, has to be answered according to such tests as men in the market would apply, leaving more delicate questions of conditions, or quality to be determined under other clauses of the contract or sections of the Act".

Shipping terms are often treated as forming part of the description in international sale. It would be useful to consider a few of the more popular terms:

3–031   **The name of the vessel to be used**   Where the contract specifies that a particular vessel will be used for the carriage of the goods, that term is a contractual description of the goods, generally speaking (*Bowes v Shand* (1877) 2 App. Cas. 455). In *Thomas Borthwick Ltd v Bunge Ltd* (1969) 1 Ll.R. 17 it is clear that this is subject to the contract. There, Browne J. held that on a proper construction of the contract, the sellers were entitled to substitute the named vessel with another because the originally named vessel was unable to load within the shipment period.

3–032   **Time of shipment**   In *Ashmore v Cox* [1899] 1 Q.B. 436, it seems that not only does this form part of the description and hence, a condition, but it is a condition precedent to the corresponding party's duty to perform his part of the contract. In *Ashmore v Cox*, the buyer was entitled to reject the goods and refuse to pay because the seller had shipped the goods outside the agreed time for shipment. This precept prevents the seller in this case from pleading that the damages should be reduced as a result of the buyer's failure to perform his part of the bargain.

3–033   **Place of shipment and discharge**   In *Gill & Duffus v Société pour l'Exportation des Sucres* [1985] 1 Lloyd's Rep. 621, where the contract specifically stipulates a place of shipment, the shipper was obliged not to ship the goods from elsewhere. Failure to do so would mean that the goods did not meet their description.

Route to be used   The route to be used by the vessel, where stated in the   **3–034**
contract, is usually a part of the description. In *Bergerco USA v Vegoil* [1984] 1
Lloyd's Rep. 440, the contract referred to the direct shipment of the goods. The
shipper, however, had used a vessel that had called at a number of transit or
intermediate ports. This was held to be in breach of the buyer's right to have the
contractual description satisfied.

As with all terms, the description which is actionable at law may be introduced
into the contract at any time before discharge and subject to existing terms of the
contract. Hence, where the contract allows one party to make subsequent
nominations of port of shipment, port of discharge, time for shipment, etc, any
properly made nomination will be binding. In *Boyd v Louca* [1973] 1 Lloyd's
Rep. 209, where the FOB buyer had the right and duty to nominate the port of
shipment, any such nomination will form part of the description of the contract
and hence, contractually binding.

Satisfactory goods

Section 14(2) provides that it is an implied term that all goods sold in the course   **3–035**
of a business must be of satisfactory quality. Section 14(2A) states that the goods
are of satisfactory quality if they meet the standard that a reasonable person
would regard as satisfactory, taking account of any description of the goods, the
price (if relevant) and all other relevant circumstances.

The implied term of satisfactory quality does not extend to the following
situations:

1. where the buyer's attention has been specifically drawn to the unsatisfactory
   quality in the goods before the contract is made;

2. where the buyer has examined the goods before the contract is made which
   that examination ought to reveal any unsatisfactory quality; or

3. in the case of a contract for the sale by sample, where any matter making the
   quality unsatisfactory would have been apparent on a reasonable examination of the sample.

Subsection (2B) further provides that the quality of the goods includes their state
and condition and the following may be treated as aspects of "quality" in
appropriate cases:

1. fitness for all the purposes for which the goods of the kind in question are
   commonly supplied;

2. appearance and finish;

3. freedom from minor defects;

4. safety;

5. durability.

That new section was grafted onto the Act by the Sale and Supply of Goods Act
1994 and it replaces the old provision on merchantable quality. Although the
older provisions on merchantable quality and fitness for purpose have been

rendered obsolete, case law on those concepts should remain useful in the interpretation of these new provisions. It is in this spirit that we shall consider the operation of the new s.14.

The crucial elements in s.14 are:

"Sells goods in the course of a business"

3–036   This requirement, which was also in the original provision, has been left intact. In the realm of international trade law, this requirement should not be a serious issue given the nature of international sale transactions.

"Satisfactory quality"

3–037   While the statutory provision attempts to provide some guidance on the application of the term of "satisfactory quality", there is much room for interpretative manoeuvring. The statements made about the standards of quality and aspects of quality are not exhaustive; this means that the court may inquire into any other relevant circumstance. The test seems to be one based on reasonableness of trade practice and consumer behaviour more than anything else.

Section 14(2A) refers to the factors that the court will consider when making an assessment on whether the goods are of satisfactory quality. The first of these is "any description of the goods". It should be mentioned that this seems to refer to descriptive words which are contractual rather than representations which are not. Where a non-contractual representation is misleading, it may be actionable under the Misrepresentation Act 1967. Under the Act, the buyer may be entitled to rescind the contract or where the misrepresentation was fraudulent or negligent, to claim compensation.

Under the old provision on merchantable quality, the description applied to the goods is of paramount importance as is evident in *Harlingdon & Leinster Enterprises Ltd v Christopher Hull Fine Art Ltd* [1991] 1 Q.B. 564 where a painting sold as by Gabriele Münter turned out to be a forgery. Slade L.J. in discussing the operation of the former provision on merchantable quality, stated:

> "The complaint, and only complaint as to the quality of picture, relates to the identity of the artist. There is no other complaint of any kind as to its condition or quality. If the verdict of the experts had been that the artist was in truth Gabriele Münter, the claim would not have arisen. *Having concluded that this was not a contract for the sale of goods by description because it was not a term of the contract that she was the artist, I see no room for the application of section 14*. If the plaintiffs fail to establish a breach of contract through the front door of section 13(1), they cannot succeed through the back door of section 14" (emphasis added).

3–038   A similar position is taken in a more recent case involving the new s.14(2). In *Clegg v Andersson* [2003] EWCA Civ 320, the claimant had bought a yacht with a keel "in accordance with the manufacturer's standard specification". At the time of delivery, the seller informed the buyer that the keel was substantially heavier than the manufacturer's standard specification. The buyer rejected the yacht three weeks later. The Court of Appeal held that a reasonable person would consider that the yacht as delivered was not of satisfactory quality because of the overweight keel, the adverse effect it had on rig safety and the need for more than remedial work.

The second reference is to "price (if relevant)". This is self-explanatory. A buyer who contracted to take delivery of goods sold at an unusually low price must be subject to the caveat emptor principle. The relevance of the price element is frequently dependent on the description applied to the goods and the intention of the parties in the contract. Where goods are sold at "bargain" prices (for example at liquidation sales or the sale of salvaged goods), it is the presumed intention that the quality of the goods should be at least equivalent to the price stated, if not greater.

"Other relevant circumstances" is the third mentioned criterion. This again is to be reinforced by the notion of reasonableness. An interesting case that reflects such circumstances is *Aswan Engineering Establishment Co v Lupdine Ltd* [1987] 1 W.L.R. 1. The buyer bought a consignment of liquid waterproofing compound. The compound, which was packed in plastic pails, was stacked five or six high in shipping containers. Upon arrival in Kuwait, the pails were left standing on the quayside. The temperature in the pails became so high that they collapsed and were damaged. The Court of Appeal held that they were merchantable as "heavy duty pails suitable for export" and Lloyd L.J.'s dictum is of particular interest:

"One must assume that the hypothetical buyer knows not only that the goods on offer are defective, but also what the nature of the particular defect is; so that in the present case one must assume that the hypothetical buyer knows that the pails are incapable of withstanding temperatures in excess of 60 centigrade when stacked five or six high, or perhaps two or three high, without separation".

It seems clear that where the buyer buys goods to be used in circumstances **3–039** which are unsuitable for such use and this fact is not known to the seller, he would not be able to claim that the goods are not of satisfactory quality.

In international commerce, frequently the goods bought need to meet various regulatory and/or commercial requirements—for example, an airplane that must meet the regulations relating to airworthiness, foodstuffs that should satisfy the quality classification for import under the law, or paper that meets the local industry standards, etc. Of course, if these requirements are communicated to the supplier there is no excuse for the supplier not to comply. Unfortunately where these requirements are not made explicit, a dispute may arise as to whether the goods meet the satisfactory quality test in s.14(2). It seems incontrovertible that if the attributes of the goods breach legal requirements, the goods could not be said to be of satisfactory quality. In *Keith Lowe v W Machell Joinery* [2011] EWCA Civ 794, for example, the staircase supplied, if installed, would have been in breach of building regulations. The court held that the goods were, therefore, not of satisfactory quality.

Of course it should not be ignored that if the goods bought and sold under the contract are illegal, the contract of sale itself will be illegal and cannot be enforced (*Activa DPS Europe v Pressure Seal Solutions* [2012] EWCA Civ 943).

The courts will, however, show some degree of common sense when deciding how strict these legal requirements or specifications would affect the useability of the goods. In *Bramhill v Edwards* [2004] EWCA Civ 403, the goods supplied were a second hand motor-home, imported from North America. The vehicle was 102 inches wide, which exceeded the maximum permitted by the Road Vehicles (Construction and Use) Regulations 1986. The purchasers contended that the seller was in breach of s.14(2) because, they said, the vehicle could not be insured and it could not be driven lawfully on the roads in the UK. The evidence accepted by the judge, however, showed that there was no problem in practice about obtaining insurance, and that the authorities turned a blind eye to the minor excess over the prescribed maximum width, which was common in relation to vehicles imported from North America, so that there was, in reality, no risk of prosecution. In *Activa DPS Europe*, the court considered that the buyer could not complain about lack of conformity with legal requirements if it could (and did) resell the same goods bought from the seller to its own customers.

3–040   In *Jewson Ltd v Boyhan* [2003] EWCA Civ 1030, K, the buyer, had bought a number of electric boilers to heat a number of flats which he was developing. It was intended that the electric boilers should be able to perform the task as well as gas boilers. The sales representative had assured him that the boilers were perfect for K's specific requirements as they were more efficient and cost less to run than gas boilers. K was also told that the boilers complied with all relevant regulations and legislation. Unfortunately, the boilers were not particularly energy efficient and that resulted in generating a low energy efficiency rating for the flats. The buyer argued that the boilers were not of satisfactory quality.

The High Court agreed with him and held that a reasonable buyer would regard the boilers as of unsatisfactory quality if their installation in the flats resulted in an energy efficiency rating (so called Standard Assessment Procedure [SAP] rating) which was so low that a proposed purchaser might delay purchasing the flats or pull out of the purchase.

The Court of Appeal disagreed and stated that that was not the correct application and reading of s.14(2). In general, a particular purpose (i.e. that the boilers should meet a certain energy efficiency rating) which is not one of the ordinary uses for which goods of the relevant type are generally supplied is irrelevant. The question in most cases would be whether the goods are intrinsically satisfactory and fit for all purposes for which goods of the kind in question are supplied. In the present case, as the boilers were satisfactory as boilers, they were of satisfactory quality.

3–041   The Act is not categorical as to the point in time that the implied term of satisfactory quality should be satisfied. However, cases like *Cordova Land Co Ltd v Victor Bus Inc* [1966] 1 W.L.R. 793 and *Lambert v Lewis* [1981] 1 All E.R. 1185 have made it quite clear that the implied terms of s.14 will relate to the goods at the time of delivery. Once the breach has become evident, the buyer is estopped from relying on the implied condition to secure an indemnity against any liability which he may attract in the subsequent resale of the goods.

The seller should not be made liable for any damage to the goods between the time of sale and the time of delivery which occurs without fault on the part of the seller and at a time when the risk has passed to the buyer. This does not, however, excuse the seller from putting into transit goods which he knows or ought to know will have deteriorated by the time they reach the buyer when the voyage was within the bounds of the contract. According to Diplock J. in *Mash & Murrell Ltd v Emanuel Ltd* [1961] 1 All E.R. 485, where goods are sold under a contract such as a CIF or FOB contract, which involves transit before use there is an implied warranty not only that the goods are to be merchantable at the time they are put on the vessel, but that they shall be in such a state that they can endure the normal journey and be in a merchantable condition on arrival.

This however must not be taken to mean that the implied term of satisfactory quality is a continuing one. It only turns on the occasion where the goods as delivered have not survived the transit and have deteriorated as a result, and are simply not of satisfactory quality at the time of delivery.

Although the new provision makes reference to durability as an aspect of quality, it is submitted that this does not change the state of the law as it stood before the amendment. As before, durability as a matter of quality affects the situation at the time of supply; it does not mean that there is a continuing obligation of satisfactory quality.[5] Where the goods become defective or unsatisfactory after a short while, the durability aspect as introduced by the new law does not mean that there is a warranty that the goods are durable. It only raises a rebuttable presumption that the goods must have been of inferior quality *at the time of supply*. In *Ward v MGM* ([2012] EWHC 4093 (QB)), the luxury yacht which burst into flames 15 minutes after delivery, almost killing the buyer and his partner, was found not to be of satisfactory quality. The court concluded that the accident had been caused by a defective engine and held that the yacht lacked the necessary safety and durability required by s.14(2). **3–042**

A further issue in the buyer's right to reject the goods for not being of satisfactory quality is the state of knowledge against which the quality has to be tested. This is best illustrated by a case. In *Henry Kendall & Sons v William Lillico & Sons Ltd* [1969] 2 A.C. 31, the buyer had refused to take delivery of a consignment of Brazilian groundnut meal on the basis that it was not of merchantable quality and was therefore not saleable. At a later date but before the trial date, it was discovered that the meal, though toxic, could be safely introduced into cattle feed in small quantities, which meant that it was saleable. The issue was whether the buyer was entitled to rescind the contract when he did. The majority view in the House of Lords was that since it had been proved as a fact that the goods were actually merchantable, it would be unreal to exclude this piece of fact from the inquiry. Lord Pearce, one of the minority, however, held that the real question was whether the hypothetical buyer had rightfully rejected the goods. As it was to be a hypothetical exercise, it was important to create a hypothetical market. Furthermore, according his Lordship:

"Suppose the goods contained a hidden deadly poison to which there was discovered by scientists two years after delivery a simple, easy, inexpensive antidote which could render the goods harmless. They would be unmarketable at the date of delivery if the poison was brought to light, since no purchaser could then have known the antidote to the poison".

It would not be fair to the parties to assess the quality on subsequent permutations of evidence; the parties need to know their legal position at the time when their contractual rights are called into question (i.e. the time of delivery). On this basis it has been suggested that "after-acquired" evidence should not be relevant to the determination of "satisfactory quality".

---

[5] Law Commission, "Report on Sale and Supply of Goods", No.160 (1987) para.3.54.

"Fitness for purpose"

3–043   Section 14(3) provides that where the seller sells goods in the course of a business and the buyer, expressly or by implication, makes known to the seller or his agent any particular purpose for which the goods are being bought, there is an implied term that the goods will be reasonably fit for that purpose, whether or not that is a purpose for which such goods are commonly supplied. The buyer will not however be able to rely on this provision where circumstances show that the buyer does not rely or that it is unreasonable for him to rely on the skill or judgement of the seller. This section also applies where the purchase price or part of it is payable by instalments and the goods were previously sold to the seller by a credit-broker, provided the buyer had made known to that credit broker the particular purpose for which the goods had been purchased.

There is some overlap between ss.14(2) and (3) as amended, but they perform different functions. The function of s.14(2) is to establish a general standard which goods are required to meet, whereas the function of s.14(3) is to impose a particular (and usually different if not higher) standard which is appropriate where the buyer, to the seller's knowledge, buys goods for a particular purpose and relies on the seller's skill and judgment for that purpose. Goods are satisfactory if they meet the standard which a reasonable person would regard as satisfactory. In determining the standard that a reasonable person would regard as satisfactory, the circumstances which have to be taken into account include the description of the goods, the price and all other relevant circumstances as we have seen in the discussion above. Although in some cases those circumstances would also include the fitness of the goods in relation to the purposes for which goods of the kind in question are normally supplied, that is not the same inquiry which has to be had as regards s.14(3).[6]

3–044   **Particular purpose**   "Particular purpose" means that the purpose for which the goods are being purchased has been specified; it does not necessarily refer to any special or extraordinary purpose. This provision may be distinguished from the satisfactory quality condition on the fact that certain goods may be of satisfactory quality but if they do not meet the purpose for which they have been purchased they are of little use to the buyer. The classic example is that found in *Ashington Piggeries Ltd v Christopher Hill Ltd* [1972] A.C. 441 where cattle feed suitable for most livestock was bought for the particular purpose of being given to mink, and turned out to be harmful to mink.

In *B S Brown & Sons Ltd v Craiks Ltd* [1969] S.L.T. 107, if the buyer intends to use the goods for an extraordinary purpose, he has the duty to ensure that this is communicated to the seller before the contract is made or else he would not be entitled to plead s.14(3). He is, however, not obliged to specify all the particular uses to which he might intend to apply the goods, so long as these particularities fall within the general ambit of the purpose stated. In *Ashington Piggeries*, herring meal was commonly used both as an animal food and as a fertilizer. The sellers were aware that the meal was bought to be used as animal feed but did not know that it would be fed to mink. The House of Lords held that as a general rule, if the sellers had not known the purpose for which the meal was bought, there could be no implying of the fitness condition at all. However, according to the

---

[6] *Jewson Ltd v Boyhan* [2003] EWCA Civ 1030.

majority, as the buyers had communicated to the sellers that it was to be used as animal feed, they were not bound to go further and specify all the different kinds of animal to which the feed was to be given. It was sufficient as long as herring meal was commonly fed to mink.

Section 14(3) requires that the buyer "expressly or by implication" make known to the seller "the particular purpose for which the goods are required". In *Hamilton v Papakura DC* [2002] UKPC 9, the Privy Council applied the test in *Ashington Piggeries* to a claim by the buyer that the water sold to him for the cultivation of tomatoes was not fit for the purpose. The water had caused damage to the tomatoes. The buyer argued that as the sellers knew that the water was meant for crop cultivation, it did not matter that it was not specifically made known to the seller that it was for tomatoes, a crop particularly sensitive to water. The court held that the correct test was whether, on the evidence, using the water purchased for cultivating tomatoes or cherry tomatoes was a normal use for which the seller should reasonably have contemplated that "it was not unlikely" the water would be used. The court was persuaded on the evidence that the sellers could not reasonably have contemplated that the water would be used for cultivation of *that kind*. The legal test has the semblance of certainty but as these two cases demonstrate, it is not always easy to predict the end result.

It also seems to be the principle from *Henry Kendall & Sons v William Lillico* **3–045**
& Sons Ltd [1969] 2 A.C. 31 that the required purpose must be stated with sufficient particularity to show the buyer's reasonable reliance on the seller's skill and judgment. In *Teheran-Europe Co Ltd v S T Belton (Tractors) Ltd* [1968] 2 Q.B. 545, the Court of Appeal stated that "so as to show that the buyer relies on the seller's skill or judgment" means that "the buyer makes the particular purpose known to the seller in such a way that the seller knows that he is being relied upon". In that case, an English company had sold mobile air-compressors to Teheran-Europe Ltd, a company based in Persia (Iran). The buyers had made known to the sellers that the compressors were to be resold as "new and unused" machines in Persia. On the issue of reliance, the court held that the sellers did not know that they were being relied on for the purported resale in Persia. As far as the court was concerned, the buyers knew all about the conditions in Persia, had seen the goods, and had read the description accompanying the compressors. They relied on their own skill and judgment to see what was suitable for resale in Persia and not on the seller's. At all events, the court found that they did not make the purpose known to the seller in such circumstances as to show him that they relied on the seller's skill and judgment. The mere communication of the purpose for which the goods were purchased was not sufficient to raise the implied term of fitness. Reasonable reliance on the seller's skill or judgment must be demonstrated as well. This however may be presumed, unless rebutted, when the evidence shows that there has been the effective communication of the particular purpose for which the goods would be applied (*Kendall v Lillico*).

The court in *IBC Vehicles Ltd v Durr Ltd* (March 17, 2000) re-emphasised the point of reliance. In that case, the defendant sold a colour paint oven to the claimant and also undertook to ensure that specialist fitters would attend to any technical repairs or re-calibration which might be needed. A motor needed to be replaced in the oven. IBC, without wishing to call out a specialist to do the job, decided to have its maintenance staff undertake the task in reliance on the basic training given to them by the defendant. The oven exploded causing damage to the factory. Garland J. held that IBC had at the time been perfectly content with the level of training offered by the seller, who had never professed to offer in-depth instruction or training in relation to matters which clearly fell within the expertise of specialised subcontractors. There had been no mechanical failure of the oven, only a serious failure to re-assemble a simple linkage correctly which was followed by the thoroughly ill-advised attempt to restart the oven. The change from a safe to an unsafe condition was brought about by IBC's staff whose reliance on the basic training given was clearly misplaced and not by any breach of the terms of fitness for purpose or merchantability.

Where the buyer relied on the seller's skill or judgment in some aspects of the goods and not others can be problematic in an attempt to rely on s.14(3). The rule from *Ashington Piggeries Ltd v Christopher Hill Ltd* seems to be that although the buyers may have relied on their own expertise in some areas, the sellers would still be liable where the buyer's reliance on them had been in those aspects which resulted in the unfitness. In that case, while Ashington Piggeries had relied on their own expertise to ensure that no idiosyncratic nature of the minks made the feed unsuitable, they had relied on the seller's skill or judgment to obtain the ingredients, mix them correctly and ensure that they did not contain a toxin rendering the compound unsafe for feeding to animals generally. Christopher Hill Ltd had failed to supply a compound fit for the required purpose.

3–046   On the other hand, in *Jewson Ltd v Boyhan* [2003] EWCA Civ 1030, it might be recalled that the boilers were alleged to be unsatisfactory because they reduced the energy efficiency rating (a standard requirement for new properties) for the flats. In relation to a claim by the buyer under s.14(3), the Court of Appeal gave judgment to the sellers. The court held that it was a case of partial reliance[7]—although the buyer had relied on the sellers as regards the intrinsic qualities of the boilers, he had not relied on their skill and judgment in relation to the suitability of the boilers to provide a superior energy efficiency rating. The question whether they were suitable for a good energy efficiency rating could only be properly ascertained in relation to the specifications of the flats being developed. It was thus a matter for the buyer and his building advisers. On those aspects on which the buyer relied on the sellers, the goods were reasonably fit for their purpose. On those where there was no reliance (namely, the energy efficiency rating), clearly s.14(3) would not apply.

In international sales where chain contracts are common, it is not necessary for the buyer to rely upon the skill and judgement of his immediate seller if he relied upon that of a person further up the line (*Britvic Soft Drinks Ltd v Messer UK Ltd* [2002] 1 Lloyd's Rep. 20; also *Webster Thompson v JG Pears (Newark) Ltd* [2009] EWHC 1070 (Comm)).

3–047   **Reasonably fit for that purpose**   In *Bristol Tramways v Fiat Motors Ltd* [1910] 2 K.B. 831, the Court of Appeal held that since the omnibuses as delivered were not fit to perform the duty required of them, namely "the purpose of conveying passengers in and near Bristol, a heavy traffic in a hilly district", the seller's were in breach of s.14(3). The purpose conveyed to the seller is of utmost importance, the seller will not be liable for the failure of the goods to meet an unspecified purpose. In *Bristol Tramways*, the omnibuses were not sufficiently powerful for use in hilly areas. Where the purpose is narrowly set out as in this case, the less circumscribed the range of goods which are reasonably fit for such

---

[7] The law does not require exclusive reliance, partial reliance is enough (*BSS v Makers Ltd* [2011] EWCA Civ 809).

purpose. The purpose of a car to drive on the road will be satisfied by almost any car so long as it will function reasonably; but the narrower purpose of an omnibus suitable to the crowded streets of a city or the hilly districts can only be achieved by a narrower range of vehicles.

The duty to supply goods that are reasonably fit for their purpose is a contractual duty and is in no way connected with any notions of negligence or fault. In *Randall v Newson* (1877) 2 Q.B.D. 102, it is no defence to plead that the seller had not been negligent or that he had exercised due diligence. In *Bigge v Parkinson* (1862) 7 H & N 955, Cockburn C.J. said:

"Where a person undertakes to supply provisions, and they are supplied in cases hermetically sealed, but turn out to be putrid, it is no answer to say that he has been deceived by the person from whom he got them".

In deciding the question of fact as to whether the goods are reasonably fit for their purpose, the risk of their unsuitability would be weighed against the gravity of the consequences. For example, where food sold was merely unpalatable or useless on rare occasions, it might well be reasonably suitable for food. But it would certainly not be reasonably suitable if even on the very rare occasions it killed the customer. Goods will not be fit if they have hidden limitations or defects requiring special precautions unknown to the buyer or seller. In *Henry Kendall & Sons v William Lillico & Sons Ltd* [1969] 2 A.C. 31, the groundnut meal delivered was not fit for the purpose of reselling in small lots to compounders of food for cattle and poultry. It was highly toxic. According to Lord Pearce:

"It is quite unsuitable that [the buyer] should get toxic meal which can only be used by inserting it in quantities so abnormally small that the dilution of other compounds removes its lethal effect".

The lower courts were right to hold that the meal was not reasonably fit for the purpose for which it was supplied by Kendall.

It should also be noted that in considering whether goods are reasonably fit for **3–048** their purpose the instructions accompanying the goods must be taken into account (*Wormell v RHM Agriculture (East) Ltd* [1987] 1 W.L.R. 1091).

Similar to the term on satisfactory quality, the provision on fitness for purpose is not a continuing duty (*Rogers v Parish Ltd* [1987] Q.B. 933), but where the goods become defective or fail to perform the purposes for which they have been bought only after a short time, this may be evidence of its unfitness at the date of delivery (*Lambeth v Lewis* [1981] 1 All E.R. 1185).

Certification of quality

In many contracts for bulk goods, the matter of quality is usually left to be **3–049** ascertained and verified by some independent expert and the certification provided by the third party will be taken as the final say on the issue of quality. This is to avoid any lengthy and costly dispute over quality. For example, a few of the standard GAFTA (Grain and Feed Trade Association) contracts provide that a certificate of inspection issued by the superintendent, at time of loading into the ocean carrying vessel, shall be final as to quality. However, this is has not been entirely trouble free. Some parties may quibble over the appointment of the superintendent or inspector, and some may dispute over whether the certificate was in fact a certificate of inspection or quality, whilst others may fight over how the certification was to be carried out and at which stage the certification had taken place.

In *RG Grain Trade LLP (UK) v Feed Factors International Ltd* [2011] EWHC 1889 (Comm), the contract provided that quality and condition was to be tested by a GAFTA-approved supervisor appointed by G, with F having the right to appoint its own GAFTA-approved supervisor. Further analysis, if required, was to be carried out by an analytical chemist (S). F exercised its option to appoint its own supervisor and a joint sampling was carried out. G's inspector (X) certified that the cargo was in accordance with the contract specifications. However, on loading, F's analysis suggested that the cargo did not comply with the protein and fibre content specifications. F sent samples to S for analysis. S certified that the protein and fibre content was not within the levels specified in the contract. F rejected the goods, which were subsequently sold to another party. G's claim for the balance of the purchase price succeeded before the first-tier arbitrators but the GAFTA Board of Appeal found that S's analysis superseded X's certification and allowed F's appeal. The court agreed that S's analysis was final and binding; however if F had decided not to appoint S, then the certification by X would have been final and binding.

It should also be noted that even if the certificate showed that there was non-compliance (for example, that the goods contained impurities, etc) that assertion does not necessarily mean that the goods are not of satisfactory quality. The certificate merely states what is in the goods—the failure to conform may or may not give rise to a breach of the satisfactory quality condition. Indeed, the level of non-conformity may be such that it only amounts to a warranty or an innominate term (*RG Grain v Feed Factors* [2011] EWHC 1889 (Comm)). In *RG Grain*, for example, the parties had relied on GAFTA Form 119 which provides:

> "Warranted to contain not less than x % of oil and protein combined and not more than 1.5% of sand and/or silica. Should the whole, or any portion, not turn out equal to warranty, the goods must be taken at an allowance to be agreed or settled by arbitration as provided for below. . . . Should the goods contain over 3% of sand and/or silica the Buyers shall be entitled to reject the goods, in which case the contract shall be null and void, for such quantity rejected. . . . The right of rejection provided by this Clause shall be limited to the mark/parcel or marks/parcels found to be defective."

3–050   It is, therefore, readily seen that only where the impurities are above a certain threshold could the buyer reject the goods/documents. In any other case, the buyers are not permitted to reject but are entitled only to a monetary allowance as compensation.

The courts are particularly slow to override certificates or documents agreed by the parties to be final and conclusive using the implied terms of the Sale of Goods Act 1979. In *KG Bominflot Bunkergesellschaft fur Mineraloele mbh v Petroplus Marketing AG (The Mercini Lady)* [2010] EWCA Civ 1145), it was argued that after delivery (the shipment of the goods under an FOB contract) the goods should remain to satisfy the contract specifications, under s.14(2) Sale of

Goods Act 1979. The Court of Appeal rejected that submission. Rix L.J. held that the contract required the issue of a final and conclusive certificate of inspection *at the time of delivery* certifying that the goods met the contract specifications. That had been done. Subsequent events should not be allowed to derogate from the finality of that document.

Sale by sample

Section 15 provides that a contract of sale is a contract for sale by sample where there is an express or implied term to that effect in the contract. In the case of a contract for sale by sample there is an implied term:

    3–051

1. that the bulk will correspond with the sample in quality;

2. that the goods will be free from any defect making their quality unsatisfactory which would not be apparent on reasonable examination of the sample.

The function of a sample is very similar to that of a contractual description. In *Drummond v Van Ingen* (1887) 12 App. Cas. 284, Lord Macnaghten said:

> "After all the offer of a sample is to present to the eye the real meaning and intention of the parties with regard to the subject matter of the contract which, owing to the imperfection of language, it may be difficult or impossible to express in words. The sample speaks for itself. But it cannot be treated as saying more than such a sample would tell a merchant of the class to which the buyer belongs, using due care and diligence, and appealing to it in the ordinary way and with the knowledge possessed by merchants of that class at the time. No doubt the sample might be made to say a great deal more. Pulled to pieces and examined by unusual tests which curiosity or suspicion might suggest, it would doubtless reveal every secret of its construction. But that is not the way in which business is done in this country. Some confidence there must be between merchant and manufacturer".

It is therefore impractical to insist that correspondence with sample means compliance of the bulk with the sample in every aspect. As long as the bulk goods are similar to the sample in terms of quality and condition which an ordinary comparison or inspection would reveal, the condition is met.

In *Steels & Busks Ltd v Bleecker Bik & Co Ltd* [1956] 1 Lloyd's Rep. 228, Sellers J. held that in assessing the quality of goods and their state and condition on delivery for the purposes of s.15, normal market standard and normal tests should be applied. In that case, the sample was rubber delivered under previous contracts. The consignment in question contained an invisible preservative, PNP, which was unsuitable for the buyer's use of the rubber to manufacture corsets. Sellers J. decided that there was no breach of s.15 because it was market practice to assess the quality of rubber by visual inspection of samples drawn in the wharves after rubber has been landed, such inspection had never been extended to running chemical tests on the rubber.

    3–052

It should also be borne in mind that under s.35 of the Sale of Goods Act 1979 where goods are delivered to the buyer in pursuant to a sale by sample, and he has not previously them, he is not deemed to have accepted the goods until he has had a reasonable opportunity of examining them for the purpose of comparing the bulk with the sample.

3–053   **Effect of Sale and Supply of Goods Act 1994 on the right to reject**   The Sale and Supply of Goods Act 1994 introduces into the Sale of Goods Act 1979 a new section, s.15A. That section, which applies only to non-consumer sales, states that the buyer will forfeit his right to reject the goods even though the implied conditions under ss.13–15 have been breached if the breach is so slight that it would be unreasonable for him to reject the goods. We will examine in greater detail how this provision applies to international sale contracts in the next chapter.[8]

It suffices to say at this stage that the use of standard trade terms in international sales which call for strict performance of the contract should be effective in excluding the operation of s.15A. Section 15A(2) provides that the provision will not apply where a contrary intention *appears in, or is to be implied* from the contract. It could therefore be argued that the new statutory provision does not affect international sale contracts where the strict performance of certain obligations is considered an implied term of the contract. The use of INCO-TERMS, for example, should also be indicative of the contract requiring strict performance.

Excluding or limiting the Implied Terms

3–054   Section 55(1) of the Sale of Goods Act 1979 provides that, subject to the Unfair Contract Terms Act 1977 (UCTA), an implied term may be negative or varied by express agreement, or by the course of dealings between the parties or by such usage as binds both parties to the contract. An express term however will not negative a term implied by the Act unless inconsistent with it. Under s.6(1) UCTA 1977, s.12 of the Sale of Goods Act 1979 on the seller's undertakings as regards passing of title, etc cannot be excluded. Section 6(3) allows the Sale of Goods Act's implied terms under ss.13,14 and 15 to be excluded or restricted subject to satisfying the reasonableness requirement. Section 11(1) of the UCTA provides:

> "The term shall have been a reasonable one to be included having regard to the circumstances which were or ought reasonably to have been known to or in the contemplation of the parties when the contract was made."

The Guidelines in Schedule 2 should be referred to for guidance as to how the test of reasonableness should be evaluated. An example of how the UCTA reasonableness requirement was applied is seen in *Kingsway Hall Hotel Ltd v Red Sky IT (Hounslow) Ltd* [2010] EWHC 965 (TCC). In that case, the hotel had bought a defective IT system from Red Sky. However, the IT company argued that their standard form contract had the effect of limiting or excluding the operation of s.14 of the Sale of Goods Act 1979. In reliance on the Sch.2 Guidelines in UCTA 1977, they reasoned that the exclusion clauses were reasonable. They claimed the following.

---

[8] See paras 4–003—4–004.

(a) That the parties were of equal bargaining power relative to each other. There were over 30 property management systems competing in this highly competitive market.

(b) The customer received a significant inducement to agree to the terms in that a significant discount was given and concessions were made on payment terms despite the fact that the contract price was very modest.

(c) There was a long course of dealing between the parties so that the hotel ought to have become aware of the existence of and extent of the terms.

(d) Although the system was not bespoke software, it had been adapted to the special order of the customer in that it would be configured for the particular customer. The system was used by a wide range of customers and the consequences of a breach would differ widely depending on which customers were using the software.

They also turned to s.11(4) of the UCTA which provides that in considering **3–055** whether or not a clause or clauses in a contract satisfy the requirement of reasonableness, regard shall be had to

"a. the resources which he could expect to be available to him for the purpose of meeting liability, should it arise.

b. how far it was open to him to cover himself by insurance."

The court disagreed finding that the clauses were unreasonable and therefore the implied terms prevailed. Judge Toulmin QC held that the exclusion clause needed to be construed *contra proferentem*. Apart from the price, the contract had not been a freely negotiated contract. The system had clearly been supplied off the shelf; it was not a bespoke system specially tailored for the customer. The standard terms had been predicated on the basis that a customer would carry out its own inquiry before purchasing, however in this case, the customer had clearly sought and received advice from the supplier. As such, the seller was not entitled to rely on the clauses to exclude their liability under the Sale of Goods Act 1979.

CHAPTER 4

REMEDIES IN INTERNATIONAL SALES

Where there has been a breach of the contract of sale by one party, the natural **4–001** expectation is that there should be available a right to damages. The role of damages is to reinstate the claimant to the position he would have been if not for the breach. Additionally, the claimant may also be entitled to bring the contract to an end where a condition or fundamental term of the contract of sale has been broken. In the sale of goods, there are also remedies against the goods themselves. For the buyer, he may under certain circumstances insist on the specific performance of the contract. For the seller who is unpaid, he may exercise a lien over the goods, stop goods in transit to the buyer or exercise a limited right of resale. Where property in the goods has passed to the buyer, the seller also is entitled to bring an action for the price.

Given the caution that traders exercise in international sales, it is not unusual for these commercial people to set up specific mechanisms for preventing the failure to pay. Some sellers insist on a "retention of title" clause, also known as a "Romalpa" clause[1] which would allow them to reserve ownership rights over the goods until they have been paid for. Others may require a deposit to be paid so as to deter buyers from resiling from performance. Others may demand that the buyer to secure a performance bond or guarantee from a bank which would mean that the bank will have to pay if the buyer defaults.

Buyer's Remedies

It is trite law that the buyer may reject the goods on arrival if they: **4–002**

1. had been sold by a seller who had no title in the goods (see also s.12 Sale of Goods Act 1979);

2. do not meet contractual description (including time of shipment) (s.13); or

3. are not of satisfactory quality (s.14).

---

[1] Named after the case of *Aluminium Industrie Vaassen BV v Romalpa Aluminium Ltd* [1976] 2 All E.R. 552.

The buyer forfeits his right to reject the goods if, for all intents and purposes, his conduct shows that he has accepted the goods. Section 35(1) of the Sale of Goods Act 1979 provides that the buyer will be deemed to have accepted the goods when he intimates to the seller that he has accepted them or when the goods have been delivered to him he does any act which is inconsistent with the seller's ownership. However, if the buyer had not previously examined the goods delivered to him, he is not deemed to have accepted them until he has had a reasonable opportunity to examine them (s.35(2)). Section 35(4) provides that the buyer is also deemed to have accepted the goods when after the lapse of reasonable time, he retains the goods without intimating to the seller that he has rejected them. It should be noted that for the purposes of s.35(4), what is a reasonable time depends on whether the buyer has had a reasonable opportunity of examining the goods to ascertain whether they are in conformity.[2] Rougier J. had this to say about what constitutes reasonable time in a commercial context:

> "What is a reasonable practical interval in commercial terms between a buyer receiving the goods and his ability to send them back, taking into consideration from his point of view the nature of the goods and their function, and from the point of view of the seller the commercial desirability of being able to close his ledger reasonably soon after the transaction is complete".

Where the buyer had merely asked for or agreed to the repair of the goods by the seller or some other person arranged by the seller, that could not be treated as acceptance by the buyer (s.35(6)(a)). It would also not be acceptance if the goods have been delivered to another person under a subsale or some other disposition (s.35(6)(b)). In *Clegg v Andersson* [2003] EWCA Civ 320, the buyer in question did not reject the goods until three weeks after the date of delivery. However, the Court of Appeal found that there was no acceptance under s.35 because the buyer had merely sought information from the seller about the suitability of the goods under EU rules to help him decide between acceptance or rejection. It would not be reasonable to assume that his act was tantamount to acceptance. Even if he had agreed to the remedial works mentioned by the seller, that would not be acceptance.

4–003   Following the passage of the Sale and Supply of Goods Act 1994, the Sale of Goods Act 1979 has been distended to accommodate a new section, s.15A. This new section, which has no effect on consumer sales, would seem to wield serious consequences on nonconsumer contracts in whose class international sale contracts belong. That section provides that the buyer forfeits his right to reject the goods even though the implied conditions under ss.13–15 of the Sale of Goods Act 1979 have been breached where he does not deal as a consumer and the breach is so slight that it would be unreasonable for him to reject the goods.

It is difficult to know exactly how these provisions will affect international trade practice. We have seen how international trade contracts call for the utmost precision in performance. For instance, the failure to ship within shipment period is considered to be a repudiatory breach and cannot be excused generally (*Kwei*

---

[2] In the case of sale by sample, whether they are in conformity by comparing them with the sample. See paras 3–051—3–052.

Tek Chao v British Traders & Shippers Ltd [1954] 2 Q.B. 459). Where, for example, the contract calls for shipment in April and the goods were in fact shipped on May 1, that will be a serious breach of the term of description upon which the buyer can repudiate the contract. Will such strict performance be derogated from as a result of s.15A?

Section 15A as introduced by the Sale and Supply of Goods Act 1994 stipulates:

(1) Where in the case of a contract of sale:

    (a) the buyer would, apart from this subsection, have the right to reject goods by reason of a breach on the part of the seller of a term implied by ss.13, 14 or 15 above; but

    (b) the breach is so slight that it would be unreasonable for him to reject them, then, if the buyer does not deal as consumer, the breach is not be treated as a breach of condition but may be treated as breach of warranty.

(2) This section applies unless a contrary intention appears in, or is to be implied from, the contract.

(3) It is for the seller to show that a breach fell within subs.(1)(b) above.

It might be argued that the use of standard trade terms could be construed as **4–004** excluding the operation of the section. Section 15A(2) provides that the section applies unless a contrary intention appears in, or is to be implied from the contract. It could therefore be argued that the new statutory provision affects little international sale contracts expressed in standard terms calling for utmost precision in performance. For example, where these contracts follow the INCOTERMS model, performance of certain obligations is expressly stated as being strict. It is also correct to say that where the contracts are expressed in any of the standard trade terms, the strict performance of certain tasks is necessarily an implied term. Of course it is open to the parties to insert a clause in their contract excluding the operation of s.15A.

In a case of a breach of s.30, i.e. where the seller makes a short delivery or delivers a larger quantity than is originally agreed, the 1994 Act states:

"A buyer who does not deal as consumer may not—

    (a) where the seller delivers a quantity of goods less than he contracted to sell, reject the goods, . . .

    (b) where the seller delivers a quantity of goods larger than he contracted to sell, reject the whole [consignment] . . . , if the shortfall or, as the case may be, excess is so slight that it would be unreasonable for him to do so".

This provision is now contained in s.30(2A) of the Sale of Goods Act 1979. It is however the onus of the seller to show that the buyer contracted as a non consumer and that the rejection was unreasonable.

In *Moralice (London) Ltd v ED & F Man* [1954] 2 Lloyd's Rep. 526, McNair **4–005** J. had held that where the price is payable by means of a documentary credit against shipping documents as is typical in many international sale contracts, the de minimis rule has no application as between the seller and the bank. The bank may legitimately call for strict compliance with the terms in the letter of credit. Be that as it may, art.30(b) of the UCP 600 permits a tolerance of five per cent more or less than the contract quantity unless the letter of credit makes it clear that that is not permissible. In this context, s.30(2A) seems to mirror trade practice.

We should also not forget the role of s.35A of the Sale of Goods Act 1979 in this regard. That section provides that the buyer does not lose his right to reject some goods as part of a larger bulk which are defective because he has accepted other goods in the larger bulk which are not defective.

Example: Seller delivers 100 sacks of flour; 30 sacks are defective but the remaining 70 are not. Section 35A allows the buyer to reject the 30 sacks and keep the 70 which are of satisfactory quality.

On whether the buyer has a right to claim specific performance of the contract, s.52 provides that the court may make an order for specific performance of a contract for the sale of specific or ascertained goods if it thinks fit. The decree may be made with or without conditions as seem just to the court. Section 52 does not refer to unascertained goods but in *Sky Petroleum v VIP Petroleum* [1974] 1 All E.R. 954, the court saw no exception in unascertained goods and granted specific performance of a contract for the delivery of unascertained goods. No explicit reference was however made to s.52.

Buyer's action for damages for nondelivery

4–006   Where damages are sought for nondelivery of the goods, the buyer's quantum of damages depends on s.51. Section 51 provides:

"(1) Where the seller wrongfully neglects or refuses to deliver the goods to the buyer, the buyer may maintain an action against the seller for damages for non-delivery.

(2) The measure of damages is the estimated loss directly and naturally resulting, in the ordinary course of events, from the seller's breach of contract.

(3) Where there is an available market for the goods in question, the measure of damages is prima facie to be ascertained by the difference between the contract price and the market or current price of the goods at the time or times when they ought to have been delivered or (if no time was fixed) at the time of the refusal to deliver."

In *The Mary Nour* [2007] EWHC 2340, the sellers had failed to load the goods. The contract had called for the delivery of cement FOB The Mary Nour, Padang, Indonesia. The cement was intended by the buyers to be imported into Mexico to break a cartel held by a company, Cemex. The buyers had to satisfy their contract by buying from a Russian supplier because suppliers elsewhere in Asia declined to sell to them as they feared offending Cemex. The sellers contended in the arbitration that the buyers had suffered no loss because there was an available market for cement in Padang at the same price as the contract price. They also contended that they had not undertaken to supply cement that was capable of being imported into Mexico and the losses claimed by the buyers were not losses directly and naturally resulting from a failure to supply cement FOB

Indonesia. Rather, they were all losses following from the buyers' desire to obtain a cargo capable of being exported to Mexico and the need (given the refusal of other Asian suppliers to sell) of shipping a cargo other than from Indonesia. The arbitrators ruled that the sellers' argument could not be sustained because the sellers' breach was not simply a failure to supply cement FOB Indonesia but was a failure to supply cement "FOB the Mary Nour" in Indonesia. The identity of the carrying vessel was inextricably linked with the FOB sale contract. Given that it seemed to be clear beyond doubt that there was no available source of supply for the contractual cement cargo to be shipped on the Mary Nour in Indonesia or elsewhere in Asia, the sellers were in breach and the extra costs and expense arising from the buyers needing to buy from Russia are losses directly and naturally resulting, in the ordinary course of events, from the seller's breach of contract (s.51(2) Sale of Goods Act 1979).

Where the buyer has rejected the goods on the basis of a breach of condition, he is additionally entitled to claim damages. There has been some confusion as to the correct measure of damages for such a claim. That matter was addressed in *A.C. Daniels & Co Ltd v Jungwoo Logic* (April 14, 2000). There, the buyers had legitimately rejected delivery of a mould which was designed and manufactured by the defendant. They then went on to claim the return of the price of the mould (£45,000) and damages for breach of contract. It was raised by the defence that the true measure of damages as set out in *Cullinane v British "Rema" Manufacturing Co Ltd* [1954] 1 Q.B. 292 was that it should be based on the cost of restoring the claimant to the position it would have occupied if there had been no contract. Judge Hicks QC held that that was a misreading of *Cullinane*. The true measure was based on the cost of restoring the claimant to the position he would have occupied if the contract had been properly performed.

In applying s.51(2), namely to ascertain what flowed directly and naturally from the defendant's breach, it is important first to try and ascertain the natural market loss. That is where s.51(3) becomes relevant. It states that damages will normally be the difference between contract price and market price; the proviso being that there must be an available market.

In *Air Studios Limited v Lombard North Central Plc* [2012] EWHC 3162 **4–007** (QB), the supplier had failed to deliver some highly specialist second-hand equipment to the buyer. As to whether s.51(3) could be relied on in assessing the damages due to the buyer, it was argued that there was no available market for such specialist second hand equipment. The court was not prepared to confine itself to looking at the market in goods meeting the precise description. It held that as long as other equipment was capable of performing the same functions, the market in those goods could be deemed as the "available market". That said, the court concluded that whilst there was a market in similar goods capable of performing a comparable function as the contracted goods, that market lacked the requisite flexibility and was not one in which "a would-be buyer could be confident of being able to purchase appropriate replacement equipment within a reasonable time". The judge considered both the time it would take to acquire replacement equipment and the need for assistance from a specialist to be relevant.

Where there is no available market, it would not be appropriate to try and calculate damages on the basis of the difference between the value of the cargo when it should have been delivered and its value when actually delivered in the absence of an available market (*Contigroup Companies Inc v Glencore AG*

[2004] EWHC 2750). The court would have to take into account other relevant factors in assessing the value of the goods, in such a case—namely, s.51(2) will apply without the benefit of the presumption in s.51(3).

Section 51 is not intended to produce outcomes which depart significantly from the common law rule on the measure of damages. In particular, where there is no available market in goods of the contractual specification, a claimant may not substitute more valuable goods as the benchmark under s.51(3). Section 51(3) could not be used to achieve a windfall; it is only intended to *simplify* the common law rule on measure of damages by presumptively fixing the damages as the difference between contract price and market price. It might also be noted that s.51(2) loss of profit would not be used as a benchmark if and where some other measure would be more appropriate.

4-008 To what extent can a buyer claim redress for the loss of a subsale? It is common in international commerce for a buyer to buy goods to be resold. Suppose S has agreed to deliver to B goods priced at £10,000, and B has contracted to sell the goods on to SB for £15,000. Where it occurs that S fails to deliver the said goods to B and as a result B loses his potential profit from the contract with SB, can B recover the loss of profit from S? For the provisions of the Sale of Goods Act 1979 to apply B must show that this was a loss in "the usual course of events". He could demonstrate this if it is obvious that B is a dealer or S is aware of the subsale.

4-009 *Re Hall (R&H) Ltd and WH Pim Jr & Co's Arbitration* [1928] All E.R. 763
Facts:
The contract price was 51s 9d per quarter of specific cargo of corn. The buyers had contracted to resell at 56s 9d per quarter. The sellers failed to deliver and at the agreed time of delivery, market price was 53s 9d per quarter. The buyers claimed to be entitled of the difference between contract price and subsale price, i.e. (56s 9d—51s 9d) per quarter.
Held:
It was clear that they were entitled to the difference between contract price and market price at time of delivery, i.e. (53s 9d—51s 9d) per quarter. The House of Lords however held that they could claim the difference between contract price and subsale price because the contract called for the delivery of specific goods and it was clear that the contract of sale anticipated that the goods will be resold by the buyer.

Similarly, in *Truk (UK) Ltd v Tokmakidis GmbH* [2000] 1 Lloyd's Rep. 543, it was held that the buyer was right to refuse delivery of goods which did not satisfy the requirements of the contract and was entitled to damages on the basis of whatever profit they would have made on the resale as it was obvious to the seller that the goods were bought for resale. The fact that defect was not discovered six months after delivery did not prevent the claimant from succeeding because as soon as they discovered the fault, they had it verified and promptly took action to return the goods. They had not affirmed the contract.

It should also follow that if the buyer had had to pay compensation to or to settle a claim by a sub-buyer, that should be recoverable from the seller. The buyer's success, however, depends on the general rules of remoteness of damage—that is to say, the subsale is within the parties' reasonable contemplation at the time of the contract and it is clear that if the goods are late or to delivered, the buyer would be liable to his sub-buyers on that basis. The court has also permitted the buyer to claim, not only the compensation he has paid to his sub-buyer, but also any reasonable costs he had expended to settle his liability with his sub-buyer (*Contigroup Companies Inc v Glencore AG* [2004] EWHC 2750).

Quantum is also dependent on the extent the claimant could mitigate his loss.

Payzu v Saunders [1919] 2 K.B. 581 CA.   **4–010**
Facts:
The defendant had contracted to deliver a consignment of silk to the claimants. The contract also stated that payment may be postponed. However, the defendant subsequently refused to deliver unless the claimants were prepared to pay cash. This was of course in breach of the contract and entitled the buyers to repudiate the contract. They then claimed damages to be based at the difference between contract price and the market price which at the time of the repudiation had risen sharply.
Held:
The court was persuaded by the defendant's argument that it would have been cheaper for the buyers to accept the seller's offer to deliver against cash at the contract price. The buyers' conduct was unreasonable and they were therefore not entitled to the difference between market price and contract price. On this point, Bankes L.J. said:

> "[T]he question what is reasonable for a person to do in mitigation of his damages cannot be a question of law, but must be one of fact in the circumstances of each particular case. There may be cases where as matter of fact it would be unreasonable to expect a plaintiff in view of the treatment he has received from the defendant to consider an offer made".

Damages could also be claimed for late delivery. The normal measure of damages for late delivery applied to a contract for the sale of goods is the difference in value of the goods at the contractual delivery date and their value on the date on which they were actually delivered.[3] The value of the goods, both at the time of contractual delivery and actual delivery, must necessarily entail an evaluation of the market price of the goods.

Buyer's action for damages for breach of defective goods

Section 53 of the Sale of Goods Act 1979 provides that: **4–011**

"(2) The measure of damages for breach of warranty is the estimated loss directly and naturally resulting, in the ordinary course of events, from the breach of warranty.

(3) In the case of breach of a warranty of quality such loss is prima facie the difference between the value of the goods at the time of delivery to the buyer and the value they would have had if they had answered the warranty".

It is important to bear in mind that this rule is only a prima facie rule. In appropriate circumstances a different date may be taken. Much depends on what

---

[3] See *Hadley v Baxendale* [1854] 156 E.R. 145.

the parties' original presumed intention as regards the warranty of quality. Indeed, in an FOB sale, for example, the value may be taken at a place other than the place of shipment. In *Van den Hurk v R Martens & Co Ltd* [1920] 1 K.B. 850 the defendants sold and delivered sodium sulphide in drums to the claimant in Manchester. They sold it either ex store or FOB. It was impracticable to open the drums until they reached the actual user and not customary in the trade to sample them before then. The drums were resold by the claimant and did not reach their ultimate consignees at Lyons and Genoa until some months later. They were then found to be of inferior quality and were rejected. Bailhache J. held that the damages were to be assessed at the date when the drums were opened by the ultimate consignees at those two places.

In *Obaseki Bros v Reif & Sons Ltd* [1952] 2 Lloyd's Rep. 364 logs were sold FOB Sapele (in Nigeria). The contract required that the logs be graded by a Brokers' Panel when they arrived in the UK and the price would be then based on the results. When they arrived the buyers rejected them on quality grounds. The umpire awarded damages by reference to the market value at the UK destination of goods of fair average quality as called for by the contract and the market value of the goods as delivered. Lord Goddard C.J. upheld the award, observing that it was inappropriate to fix the value of the goods in West Africa when the buyers wanted them in England, their ultimate destination. He rejected the contention that the award was wrong because it was made on a CIF basis and held that the correct date was the date when the Broker's Panel examined the goods before which no right of rejection would arise.

4–012   The circumstances under which the prima facie rule is to displaced can be controversial as we shall see in the discussion below on the relevance of a sub-sale, for example. However, what might be taken at this stage is that s.53(2) and (3) are not exhaustive rules. They merely guide how damages are to be measured following a breach of warranty.

In addition to claiming damages, the buyer may set up the breach of warranty in diminution or extinction of the price (s.53(1)); the fact that the buyer has set up the breach in diminution or extinction of the price does not prevent him from bringing an action for the same breach of warranty if he has suffered further damage (s.53(4)). It also goes without saying that the buyer must try to mitigate his damage or loss; that is the common law principle which must apply alongside s.53.

As regards the prima facie rule (s.53(2)) it is important to show what the value of the goods is if they were compliant, and the value of the defective goods. In ascertaining the value of the goods if they had been compliant with the contract, their market price would be a good starting point. However, where there is no available market, other evidence would be admitted to show the value of the goods in their warranted state, including the contract price and resale price. These are merely relevant factors and are not conclusive one way or another.[4] In ascertaining the value of the goods in their defective state, naturally the market price for goods in that state would be relevant.[5] However, it is often the case that there is no available market for defective goods. In such a case, the court may

---

[4] *Loder v Kekulé* (1857) 3 C.B.N.S. 128.
[5] *Biggin & Co Ltd v Permanite Ltd* [1951] 1 K.B. 422.

award damages looking at the cost of the repairs which are necessary to bring the goods to a standard where they will become saleable.[6]

Relevance of sub-sales in measure of damages

The prima facie measure of damages under s.53(3) is displaced where the seller **4–013** and buyer contemplate when they enter into the contract of sale that it is not unlikely that the buyer will sub-sell the goods on the same or similar warranties as to the condition and description of the goods (*Choil Trading SA v Sahara Energy* [2010] EWHC 374), and that a breach of warranty by the seller will put the buyer in breach of warranty in his sub-sale. In such a case the buyer's claim for damages must be assessed by reference to the sub-sale and not according to s.53(3) of the Sale of Goods Act 1979 (*Kwei Tek Chao v British Traders & Shippers Ltd* [1954] 2 Q.B. 459, 489; *Bence Graphics International v Fasson UK Ltd* [1998] Q.B. 877).

In general, the buyer's damages should not be reduced simply because he has been able to deliver the goods a third party on subsale (*Slater v Hoyle & Smith Ltd* [1920] 2 K.B. 11).[7] In *Louis Dreyfus Trading Ltd v Reliance Trading Ltd* [2004] EWHC 525, a case involving the warranty of quiet possession, the contract of sale of sugar clearly anticipated that the buyer would subsequently re-sell the sugar. The delivery of the cargo was disrupted and by the time delivery resumed, the market price had fallen to $224.00 per m.t. The seller brought an action to compel the buyer to take delivery of the goods. The buyer refused and counter-claimed, arguing that the disruption was caused by the seller and as such, the seller was liable in damages for the breach of the warranty of quiet possession. The buyer's claim for damages was on the basis of the difference between the contract price ($257.43 per m.t.) and the value when they eventually became available ($224.00). The seller argued that the buyer had suffered no loss. They pointed out that the buyer was to receive in their subsale a substantial profit. The buyer, on the other hand, contended that the subsale was *res inter alios acta* and had no bearing on the assessment of damages. They submitted that a seller could not rely on a subsale in order to reduce the buyer's damages unless the parties contemplated that the only possible (inevitable) loss that the buyer might suffer was by way of his liability to his sub-buyer.

The Commercial Court held that as to the issue of quantum, s.53(2), (3)[8] would apply: the principle of remoteness of damage looked to consequences of a breach that the parties were to be taken to have contemplated as serious possibilities, or not unlikely results, and not to inevitabilities. The buyer's submission was therefore to be rejected as a matter of principle. The prima facie measure of

---

[6] *Minster Trust Ltd v Traps Tractors Ltd* [1954] 1 W.L.R. 963. See also *Ali Reza-Delta Transport Co v United Arab Shipping Co* [2003] EWCA Civ 684, a case not involving the sale of goods but where the defendant carrier had damaged the claimant's cargo-handling equipment. It was held that regard should be had to the fact that the equipment had been transported from Europe to Saudi Arabia and tropicalised at great cost, in assessing the market value of the damaged equipment. It was not appropriate to rely on the market value prevailing in Europe.

[7] But see *Bence Graphics International Ltd v Fasson UK Ltd* [1998] Q.B. 87 where the Court of Appeal declined to follow *Slater v Hoyle & Smith*; the Court of Appeal's case was criticised by Treitel, (1997) 113 L.Q.R. 188.

[8] Although s.53(3) refers to the case where there is a breach of warranty of quality, it is right to treat the breach of the warranty of quiet possession on a similar footing.

damages in such a case should be the difference between the value of the goods as and when delivered and the value of the goods had the contract been observed. If either the buyer or seller wants to depart from the prima facie presumption, it is then up to them to rebut it. It was open to the seller to demonstrate that the impact of the subsale was such that the prima facie measure of damages was inappropriate in that it did not result in the award of damages compensating the buyer for the loss that they suffered. The fact that the seller had shown that the subsale would have brought substantial profits to the buyer was ineffectual; those considerations did not necessarily mean that the amount of the buyer's loss did not reflect the difference between the market value of the sugar as warranted and its value as and when it was in fact delivered. The arbitral tribunal, according to the court, should additionally have considered whether or not the seller had rebutted the presumption that the damages should be assessed on the basis set out in s.53(3).

4-014   In summing up, it is useful to refer to what Devlin J. said in *Kwei Tek Chao v British Traders and Shippers Ltd* [1954] 2 Q.B. 459:

> "It is perfectly true that the defendants knew that the plaintiffs were merchants who had bought for re-sale, but everyone who sells to a merchant knows that he bought for re-sale, and it does not, as I understand it, make any difference to the ordinary measure of damage where there is a market. What is contemplated is that the merchant buys for re-sale, but if the goods are not delivered to him he will go out into the market and buy similar goods and honour his contract in that way. If the market has fallen, he has suffered no damage; if the market has risen the measure of damage is the difference in the market price. There are, of course, cases where that prima facie measure of damage is not applicable because something different is contemplated. If, for example, a man sells goods of a special manufacture and it is known that they are to be re-sold, it must also be known that they cannot be bought in the market, being specially manufactured by the seller. In such a case the loss of profit becomes the appropriate measure of damage. Similarly, it may very well be that in the case of string contracts, if the seller knows that the merchant is not buying merely for re-sale generally, but upon a string contract where he will re-sell those specific goods and where he could only honour his contract by delivering those goods and no others, the measure of loss or profit on re-sale is the right measure".

Where the buyer has himself paid damages to his sub-buyer as a result of the defective goods, it seems only equitable that he should be able to claim that back from the seller (*Hammond & Co v Bussey* (1887) 20 Q.B.D. 79). However, it should not be too remote—that is to say, the parties should have contemplated that the buyer would or probably would resell the goods and that the terms of the subsale would be largely similar to those in the original sale contract. It is also vital to show that it is not unlikely that the seller's breach will result in the buyer's liability to his sub-buyers.[9]

---

[9] In the case of string contracts, it does not matter how many subsales occur in the string: *Biggin & Co Ltd v Permanite Ltd* [1951] 1 K.B. 422.

Reduction of damages by apportionment?

Where the seller and a third party are both factually responsible for the breach of   **4–015**
implied term (such as S sells a defective plumbing system to B but S had sourced
some of the defective parts from T), the question of apportionment of damages
might be thought to arise. It is, however, trite law that where the claim is founded
on one of the implied terms in the Sale of Goods Act 1979 by the buyer, the seller
cannot reduce their liability by an apportionment to take account of the
negligence of the third party, *Barclays Bank Plc v Fairclough Building Ltd (No.1)*
[1995] Q.B. 214; also *Hi-Lite v Wolseley* [2011] EWHC 2153 (TCC). In *Hi-Lite
v Wolseley,* for example, the drainage pipe had been supplied by W to H who in
turn supplied it to O. The pipe was defective but the fitting performed by H at O's
premises was also unsatisfactory. Any negligence on H's part cannot give rise to
apportionment between W and H. The liability under s.14(2) Sale of Goods Act
1979 (failure to supply goods of a satisfactory quality) is strict.

Reliance on a liquidated damages clause

It is also possible for the parties to pre-agree to the amount payable following a   **4–016**
breach of the contract. Such contractual clauses (known generally as liquidated
damages or agreed damages clauses) will usually be given effect to by a court of
law as long as they have been freely entered into and represent a genuine attempt
at quantifying the potential loss or damage. The courts however would not
enforce a clause which is in effect a penalty clause. Where the sum stipulated is
extravagantly greater than the damage which could conceivably follow a breach,
that will likely be held to be a penalty clause. In *Dunlop Pneumatic Tyre Co Ltd
v New Garage and Motor Co Ltd* [1915] A.C. 79, the House of Lords held that
there is a presumption that a clause requiring the payment of "a single lump sum
on the occurrence of one or more or all of several events, some of which may
occasion serious, and others but trifling, damage" is a penalty. This is, however,
a mere presumption which could be rebutted. In *Cenargo Ltd v Empresa
Nacional Bazan de Construcciones Navales Militares SA* [2002] C.L.C. 1151, the
Court of Appeal, relying on *Robophone v Blank* [1966] 1 W.L.R. 1428, stated
that when assessing whether a clause was penal, the court should consider the
range of losses which it could have been anticipated at the time that the contract
was made would be covered by the clause. This is significant because the clause
must be construed and applied in the light of what the presumed intention of the
parties was at the time the contract was made.[10]

Seller's Remedies

Action for the price

The seller is entitled to sue for the price if property in the goods has passed to the   **4–017**
buyer. Section 49(1) of the Sale of Goods Act 1979 provides that where the

---

[10] See also *Philips (HK) Ltd v The Att Gen of Hong Kong* (1993) 61 B.L.R. 49.

property has passed to the buyer and the buyer wrongfully neglects or refuses to pay for the goods according to the terms of the contract, the seller may maintain an action against them for the price. Crucial to the action for the price is therefore the passing of property. This can clearly be a problem where there is a retention of title clause.[11] In *FG Wilson v John Holt* [2012] EWHC 2477 (Comm) the parties had agreed to the following clause:

> "Notwithstanding delivery and the passing of risk in the products, title shall not pass to Buyer until Seller has received payment in full for the products and all other goods or services agreed to be sold by Seller to Buyer for which payment is then due. Until such time as title passes, Buyer shall hold the products as Seller's fiduciary agent and shall keep them separate from Buyer's other goods. Prior to title passing Buyer shall be entitled to resell or use the products in the ordinary course of business and shall account to the Seller for the proceeds of sale. If the Buyer fails to comply with a demand from the Seller to return products to which title has not passed, Seller may forthwith enter any premises where the products are stored and repossess them."

The question was therefore whether title in the goods had passed to the buyer so as to permit the unpaid seller to sue for the price. The court found that despite the retention of title clause, property had passed to the buyer. The court emphasised the fact that the trading history of the parties was such that the intention was always for the buyer to pass a good title to the sub-buyer. The court also dismissed the argument that the retention of title clause meant that the buyer was selling the goods as the seller's fiduciary agent. Popplewell J. said:

> "The inclusion in the clause of an express obligation on the buyer to account for the proceeds of sale is at best neutral as to the capacity in which he sells. It is consistent with his selling as principal."

That reading coincides with the emerging view in some case law that a retention of title clause will not work well if a resale is intended by the seller and buyer.

4–018   Be that as it may, the court went on to say that even if the buyer had sold the goods as agent, s.49(1) has still been met. The Judge relied on the rationale for s.49(1) as permitting him to take the view that the seller had done all that is necessary to enable the buyer to pass on good title:

> "The rationale for s.49(1) is that an action for the price will lie when the seller has delivered the goods to the buyer and conferred on him the ability freely to deal with the goods as his own. Whilst the goods remain in the hands of the buyer, to whom property has not yet passed by reason of a retention of title clause, an action for the price will not lie because the buyer's freedom to deal with the goods as his own is constrained: the seller is free to retake possession of the goods in which he retains property. But once the goods are sold on, with the consent of the seller conferred by the retention of title clause, the seller has done all that is necessary for the buyer to have dealt with the goods as his own and transfer property in the goods to the third parties. The rationale of s.49(1) is fulfilled."

---

[11] See below (paras 4–033—4–041) for the law relating to retention of title clauses.

Interestingly, this view might be supported by a reading of s.25, Sale of Goods Act 1979.[12] That section allows a buyer in possession of goods, with the seller's consent, to confer good title to a bona fide purchaser without notice. The section provides that the mechanism by which the purchaser acquires title is by treating the buyer in possession (who has no title) as agent for the seller. The Judge thought that s.25 is, therefore, akin to the position created by the retention of title clause in the present case. The Judge went on to add, "it would in my view be remarkable if, in a case governed by s.25, the seller were unable to sue the buyer for the price."

Section 49(2) states that where the price is payable on a certain day irrespective of delivery and the buyer wrongfully neglects or refuses to pay the price, the seller may sue for the price even though property in the goods has not passed.[13] In *Workman Clark v Lloyd Brazileno* (1908) 24 T.L.R. 458, the ship building contract that provided for the payment of 20 per cent of the purchase price "on the laying of the keel" was held to be for payment on a day certain because when the duty to pay arose, the day on which it fell due became certain.

The provision, however, is not intended to have a wide effect as is seen in *Otis Vehicle Rentals Ltd v Ciceley Commercials Ltd* [2002] 2 All E.R. (D) 203; indeed, in general, no action for the price can be maintained outside the parameters and conditions established in s.49(1).[14] In that case, A obtained a number of vehicles from B. B then sold the vehicles to C who agreed to pay A a "buy-back" price to repurchase the vehicles after two or three years. C then refused to pay the buy-back price and A disposed of the vehicles elsewhere. A then sued claiming the buy-back price from C. C admitted liability but argued that A was not entitled to the buy-back price, merely damages for breach of contract. **4–019**

The court held that under these circumstances, s.49(2) did not apply. The mechanics of the buy-back agreement would have involved payment of the buy-back price by C against an arranged re-delivery of the vehicles to C. As such the agreement was for the payment of the buy-back price to take place two or three years after the date of the original sale. That being so, it was not an agreement that the price was payable on a day certain irrespective of delivery. The commercial reality was that payment and delivery would have been co-ordinated so as to have simultaneous effect. Even if that was not the case, the seller's entitlement to sue for the price under s.49(2) depended on his continued willingness and ability to deliver the goods to the buyer which he no longer had.

Late Payment Interest

Where the buyer fails to make payment when the time for payment of the purchase price is due, he may be liable to pay statutory interest on top of the debt. **4–020**

---

[12] See generally Davies, "Transferability and Sale of Goods" (1987) 7 Legal Studies 1; Rutherford and Todd, "Section 25(1) of the Sale of Goods Act 1893; The Reluctance to create a Mercantile Agency" (1979) 38(2) C.L.J. 345.

[13] On the issue of when property passes, see below para.4–042 et seq.

[14] See also *FG Wilson v John Holt* [2012] EWHC 2477 (Comm); for a contrary view see *Chitty on Contracts,* edited by H.G. Beale, 31st edn (London: Sweet & Maxwell, 2012), Vol 2 para.43–396, *Benjamin's Sale of Goods,* edited by M.Bridge, 8th edn (London: Sweet & Maxwell, 2012) para.16–028, and Goode on Commercial Law, 4th edn (London: Lexis Nexis, 2012) pp.427–428.

In an action for the price, this additional statutory interest will usually be included in the claim.

The duty to pay statutory interest for having not made timely payment is an implied term by law—the relevant law being the Late Payment of Commercial Debts (Interest) Act 1998. For business commercial transactions,[15] statutory interest will accrue as of the day after the agreed date for payment.[16] The agreed date for payment may be ascertained by reference to the happening of an event or the failure of the happening of an event.[17] In any other case, that is to say where no date of payment had been agreed, under s.4(5) the statutory interest will commence a day after

> "the last day of the period of 30 days beginning with—
>
> (a) the day on which the obligation of the supplier to which the debt relates is performed; or
>
> (b) the day on which the purchaser has notice of the amount of the debt or (where that amount is unascertained) the sum which the supplier claims is the amount of the debt,
>
> whichever is the later."

4–021   As to what constitutes good notice, the courts seem to adopt a fairly generous outlook. In *Ruttle Plant Hire v Secretary of State for Environment, Food and Rural Affairs* [2009] EWCA Civ 97, the lower court had held that as the invoices tendered to the buyer referred to the wrong price, there was no effective notice. That view was rejected by the Court of Appeal. The Court of Appeal held that the requirement of notice was essentially directed at the presence of an outstanding contractual debt; the precise amount was less important than the fact of an outstanding debt. To hold otherwise would be somewhat disproportionate (see also *E-Nik Ltd v Secretary of State for Communities and Local Government* [2012] EWHC 3027 (Comm)).

It is also accepted that where a single contract created several invoices (debts), statutory interest should be calculated with reference to each invoice separately.[18]

Once statutory interest begins to run in relation to a qualifying debt, the supplier shall be entitled to a fixed sum (this is in addition to the statutory interest on the debt).

This sum serves as compensation and shall be:

(a) for a debt less than £1000, the sum of £40;

(b) for a debt of £1000 or more, but less than £10,000, the sum of £70; and

(c) for a debt of £10,000 or more, the sum of £100.

4–022   Section 5 of the Act permits the suspension or partial remission or entire remission of statutory interest where it is in the interests of justice to do so. Section 5(4) further provides that:

---

[15] See s.2(1).
[16] S.4(2).
[17] S.4(3).
[18] See the High Court's decision in *Ruttle Plant Hire v Secretary of State for Environment, Food and Rural Affairs* [2008] All ER (D) 191, a point which was not in dispute.

"Remission of statutory interest under this section may be required—

(a) by reason of conduct at any time (whether before or after the time at which the debt is created); and

(b) for the whole period for which statutory interest would otherwise run or for one or more parts of that period."

It should be noted that "conduct" will include any act or omission.

In *Banham Marshalls Services v Lincolnshire CC* [2007] EWHC 402 (QB) the court regretted that the law provided little guidance on what is meant by the "interests of justice". Starting with first principles, such a term would usually confer wide discretion on the judge. The court could inquire into the conduct of the parties (especially the claimant), any inexplicable delays, the presence of a genuine dispute over the performance of the contract, etc. That is not to say that just because there is a dispute between the parties, statutory interest can be withheld or suspended.

Section 8 renders any contract term void to the extent that it attempts to exclude or vary the right to statutory interest unless there is a substantial contractual remedy for late payment of the debt. This means that the statutory interest may be replaced contractually by the parties provided the contractual remedy is a substantial remedy. A substantial remedy is one which at least judged at the date of the contract would provide adequate compensation for late payment (*Water Lily & Co Ltd v Giles Patrick Cyril Mackay, DMW Developments* [2012] EWHC 1773 (TCC)). What is adequate depends on the commercial circumstances of the case. In *Yuanda (UK) Co Ltd v WW Gear* [2011] 1 All E.R. (Comm) 550, the contract provided for the payment of an interest rate of 0.5 per cent over the base rate for late payment. The court held that the amount was not a substantial remedy given that statutory interest rate was 8 per cent over the base rate at the relevant time.[19]

Damages for non-acceptance

Where the buyer wrongfully neglects or refuses to accept and pay for the goods, the seller may maintain an action against him for damages for non-acceptance. The measure of damages is the estimated loss directly and naturally resulting, *in the ordinary course of events*, from the buyer's breach. The ordinary course of events could, it is foreseeable, lead to many different loss or damage scenarios. For example, where the goods are defective, they could cause damage to person or property; or late delivery could result in loss of profit which the goods were intended to generate and this is reasonably foreseeable. **4–023**

Where there is an available market for the goods, the measure of damages is prima facie to be ascertained by the difference between the contract price and the market or current price at the time when the goods ought to have been accepted or (if no time was fixed for acceptance) at the time of the refusal to accept.

In *Bem Dis A Turk Ticaret v International Agri Trade* [1999] 1 All E.R. (Comm) 619 the goods were sold on C&F Turkey terms. The sellers had made the necessary shipping arrangements, which involved chartering a ship. The

---

[19] See Barber, "Late Payment of Commercial Debts (Interest) Act 1998—No Laughing Matter" (2007) 23 Const. L. J. 331.

buyers defaulted as a result of a subsequent prohibition on import of the commodity into Turkey. That led to the sellers cancelling the charterparty. The arbitrators found that the cancellation costs were costs naturally flowing from the buyer's breach of contract. There was however at the date of breach no difference between the contract price and the market price. The buyers thus argued that s.50(3) had the effect that in such circumstances the sellers could not recover the cancellation costs. Unsurprisingly the arbitrators, the Commercial Court, and the Court of Appeal rejected that argument. Hirst L.J. observed that that would equate to putting the cart before the horse. Section 50(2) lays down the general rule. Section 50(3) only provides the prima facie measure, and in particular does not exclude where appropriate the recovery of additional costs occasioned by the buyer's breach over and above the difference between contract price and market price.

4–024   It is trite law that subsequent action or inaction by the seller in relation to that transaction is irrelevant because it was not something caused by the buyer's original breach (*Westbrook Resources v Globe Metallurgical* [2008] EWHC 241, following the original breach, the sellers sold the manganese on to a third party). Additional loss was incurred because they changed the delivery terms from FOB to C&F (making themselves the shippers). The court held that is a matter entirely independent of the buyer's original breach and rejected the seller's argument that the change was an act to mitigate further loss. The court held that it was concerned with placing the seller at the same financial position he would have been if the contract had been performed. The amount of damages is the difference between the contract price and the price obtainable in the market at the time of the breach. That might amount to a loss on the contract in terms of price realised as compared with the cost of acquisition but that is irrelevant. If the seller had to go into the market to acquire goods in order to fulfil the contract of sale, that cost was disregarded. If it was taken into account it would have the effect of either increasing or diminishing the buyer's liability in a wholly arbitrary manner which had nothing to do with the contract that it had breached.

Damages for breach of warranty

4–025   Where the seller alleges that the buyer has breached a warranty or where the seller elects to treat a breach of condition as a breach of warranty, the measure of damages is to be determined according to the normal rules of contract law. At common law, the seller's damages are based on the following principles enunciated in *Victoria Laundry (Windsor) Ltd v Newman Industries Ltd; Coulson & Co Ltd (third parties)* [1949] 2 K.B. 528:

1. The governing purpose of damages is to put the party whose rights have been violated in the same position, so far as money can do so, as if his rights had been observed. This purpose, if appropriately pursued, would provide him with a complete indemnity for the entirety of his loss.

2. The aggrieved party is only entitled to recover such part of the loss actually resulting as was at the time of the contract reasonably foreseeable as liable to result from the breach. What was reasonably foreseeable depends on the knowledge of the parties or at all events, by the party who later commits the breach at that time.

The seller's right to damages is, however, subject to the overriding principle that he must attempt to mitigate his damage or loss.

Pre-agreed remedies

The seller may also take advantage of pre-agreed remedies as could the buyer (as **4–026** discussed above in para.4–016). The seller could require that the buyer puts down a deposit or agrees to a liquidated damages clause in the contract. The deposit or earnest money is paid by the buyer to demonstrate his intention to commit himself to the purchase. The law allows that sum to be forfeited if the buyer refuses to proceed with the purchase.[20] Similarly, the parties could agree in the contract that a sum, payable as a lump sum or on a scale proportionate to the breach, be paid by the buyer (or the seller) following a failure to proceed with the contract. Both measures must not be penal in nature. As far as a liquidated damages clause is concerned, it would not be applied if the court finds that it is not a genuine pre-estimate of the damage suffered as a result of the breach.[21]

It is not uncommon for sellers to require the buyers to purchase a minimum quantity in medium- to long-term agreements. If the buyers fail to place an order for the contractual minimum quantity, they will be required to pay for those minimum quantities even though they had not ordered the goods. Such a contractual clause is known as a "take or pay" clause. Are such clauses a penalty? In *M&J Polymers Ltd v Imerys* [2008] EWHC 344, Burton J. made it clear that for a clause to qualify as a penalty clause, first there must be a breach of contract. Where there is no breach, there is no penalty. For example, where the clause provided for payment of money upon the happening of an event other than a breach, there is no penalty. On the other hand, if the clause applies only when the buyer breaches the contract by failing to order minimum quantities, it might run foul of the law against penalties.[22] In that case though, the court found that the take or pay clause was commercially justifiable (*Murray v Leisureplay* [2005] EWCA Civ 963). It did not amount to oppression. It was negotiated and freely entered into between parties of comparable bargaining power, and did not have the predominant purpose of deterring a breach of contract nor amount to a provision "*in terrorem*".

Seller's remedies against the goods themselves

Where the seller has not been paid, not only does he have an action in contract **4–027** for damages or for the price (if property in the goods has passed to the buyer) he may exercise any of the following rights:

1. a lien for the price;

2. if the buyer is insolvent, a right of stoppage in transit after he has parted with possession of the goods;

3. a right of resale.

---

[20] *Workers Trust & Merchant Bank Ltd v Dojap Investments Ltd* [1993] A.C. 573.
[21] *Dunlop Pneumatic Tyre Co Ltd v New Garage and Motor Co Ltd* [1915] A.C. 79.
[22] See also *Export Credits Guarantee Department v Universal Oil Products Co* [1983] 1 W.L.R. 399 and *Euro London Appointments Ltd v Claessens International Ltd* [2006] EWCA Civ 385.

A lien is a right to retain possession of the goods until payment is exacted from the buyer where the conditions in s.41 of the Sale of Goods Act 1979 exist:

1. where the goods have been sold without any stipulation as to credit;
2. where the goods have been sold on credit but the term of credit has expired;
3. where the buyer becomes insolvent.

The lien, however, terminates when:

1. the seller delivers the goods to a carrier or other bailee or custodier for the purpose of transmission to the buyer without reserving the right of disposal of the goods;
2. when the buyer or his agent lawfully obtains possession of the goods;
3. the seller has waived his lien or his right of retention.

4–028   The seller, however, does not lose his lien simply because he has obtained judgment for the price of the goods. These conditions suggest that the lien means that the potency of the unpaid seller's lien has very little relevance in international sales where there is usually some stipulation as to credit provision, and carriage by a third party is always envisaged.

The right to stop goods in transit might be thought to be of more relevance to international sales but it is limited in one major respect. It is only workable where the buyer is insolvent. Section 44 of the Sale of Goods Act 1979 provides that when the buyer becomes insolvent the unpaid seller who has parted with the possession of the goods has the right of stopping them in transit. This is to say that the seller may resume possession of the goods which are in transit by giving notice to the carrier of the goods. Once notice has been issued, the carrier must redeliver the goods to the seller whose obligation it is to pay any expenses of the redelivery (s.46). The seller then retains possession of them until payment is made.

4–029   The right of stoppage can only be used when the goods are in transit, that is to say, the time when the goods are delivered to a carrier by land or water, or other bailee for the purpose of transmission to the buyer, until the buyer or his agent takes delivery of the goods from the carrier or bailee (s.45). If the buyer rejects the goods upon arrival, the goods will carry on being in transit. If the buyer obtains delivery of the goods before their arrival at the agreed destination, the transit comes to an end.

When the goods are delivered to a ship chartered by the buyer the question whether they are in the possession of the master as a carrier or as agent to the buyer is dependent on the circumstances. Where the ship taking delivery of the goods is owned by the buyer, delivery of the goods to the ship master is clearly delivery of the goods to the buyer. Transit thus ends. Again, where there is a demise charter taken out by the buyer, delivery of the goods to the vessel will bring transit to an end. However, where the ship is on a time or voyage charter to the buyer, delivery to the shipmaster does not signify an end to transit because the shipmaster is not the employee or agent of the buyer unlike the other two situations mentioned. Transit does not end when goods are delivered to a shipmaster who does not act as the buyer's agent. It is clear from *Ex parte*

Rosevear China Clay Co Ltd (1879) 11 Ch. D. 560 that the delivery of goods to a shipmaster under an FOB contract does not exclude the seller's right of stoppage if the buyer becomes insolvent. The carrier who takes instructions from the buyer as to the voyage to be taken need not necessarily be in an agency relationship with the buyer. In that case, delivery to the shipmaster was not the end of transit. On the other hand, where the buyer gives instructions that the goods are to be delivered to a particular place to be kept until he gives fresh orders as to their new destination, the original transit is at an end when the goods reach that place.

It has been opined that where the bill of lading is involved, transfer of the bill of lading to the buyer should terminate the right of stoppage. It is unclear at English law whether there is such a cessation of the right when the bill of lading is transferred. Both Professors Schmitthoff and Atiyah were of the opinion that the mere transfer of the bill of lading to the buyer does not extinguish the seller's right of stoppage. Professor Atiyah said:

"Both section 39(1) (which says that the seller's real rights exist even though property may have passed), and section 47(2) (which postulates a transfer of the bill of lading to the buyer and further dealings with the bill by the buyer), seem to assume that the right may continue even after the bill is transferred to the buyer".

It might be added that the right of stoppage refers to the transit of the goods; **4–030** it applies as long as the goods are in transit. The right of stoppage is not linked with the passing of property in the goods but the transfer of control of the goods during transit. This means that although property might pass when the bill of lading is transferred to the buyer, the right of stoppage does not become extinguished.

The right of stoppage depends on three conditions as was pointed out in *The Tigress* (1863) 32 L.J.P.M. & A. 97:

"First, the vendor must be unpaid; secondly the vendee must be insolvent; thirdly, the vendee must not have indorsed over for value".

This third condition is now provided for in s.47(2):

"[W]here a document of title [including a bill of lading] to goods has been lawfully transferred to any person as buyer or owner of the goods, and that person transfers the document to a person who takes it in good faith and for valuable consideration"

then the right of stoppage lapses.

The rule in s.47(2) is nicely illustrated in *Leask v Scott Bros* (1877) 2 Q.B.D. 376.

Leask v Scott Bros (1877) 2 Q.B.D. 376 **4–031**
Facts:
In pursuant to the contract of sale of a cargo of nuts, the sellers delivered to the buyers a bill of lading representing the goods. The buyers then handed the bill of lading over to his lenders to secure a loan. The buyers then became insolvent and the goods were not paid for. The sellers attempted to exercise their right of stoppage.

Held:
The court decided that once the buyer had negotiated the bill of lading to the lenders, the sellers' right of stoppage was defeated.

The right of stoppage applies only in relation to the price of the goods in question. It may not be extended to claim insurance monies for goods damaged in transit.

4–032   *Berndtson v Strang* (1868) L.R. 3 Ch. App. 588
Facts:
The contract was for the delivery of timber to a buyer in England. The timber was then shipped from Sweden to London but was damaged during transit. The insolvent buyer had earlier taken out an insurance policy covering the goods. They were unable to pay for the goods. The sellers purported to extend the right of stoppage to claim money owing under the insurance policy.
Held:
Lord Cairns L.C. held that the sellers could not succeed because the right of stoppage did not entitle them to go beyond a claim for possession of the goods. There is no implied corollary in the right of stoppage that the goods are to arrive at their destination in good condition. Of course, where the international sale involves the taking out of an insurance policy by the seller (as in CIF sales and many FOB contracts today) the problem would not arise.

Under the Sale of Goods Act 1979 there is a limited right of re-sale available to the unpaid seller.

When the unpaid seller exercises his right to stop goods in transit or his lien over the goods, the contract does not come to an end. Under s.48(2) however, if the seller does resell the goods to a third party, that third party acquires a better interest to the goods than the original buyer. The unpaid seller has a right to resell the goods under s.48(3):

1. where the goods are of a perishable nature;

2. where he gives notice to the buyer of his intention to re-sell and the buyer does not pay the price within a reasonable time; and

3. where the seller has expressly reserved a right of re-sale in the event of the buyer's default.

Any profit made by the seller on re-sale may be retained. The original buyer has no entitlement to any profit made on the re-sale. Where the seller suffers a loss on the re-sale, he may hold the original buyer accountable for his loss. He could bring an action against the buyer to recover that loss as damages.

Reservation of Title

4–033   Sellers also exploit the provisions of ss.17–19 to ensure that their right to be paid is not lost when the goods are delivered to the buyer by inserting a clause in the contract stating that title in the goods is retained by the seller until payment has been made. Section 17 guarantees them this right to determine when property should pass. Not only are they permitted to change the standard rules on the passing of property, sellers are expressly permitted by s.19 to retain title in the goods until certain conditions have been met. A reservation of the right of disposal is common in international sale transactions because the clause enables the seller to reclaim his goods should the buyer go into receivership or become bankrupt.

While the practicality of such a clause seems incontrovertible, the legal issues may be less so. We shall consider some of the issues it raises in the context of international trade.

First we need to distinguish the simple retention of title clause from a security agreement. The latter will not be subject to the rules on sale and must be registered under the Companies Acts (where the transaction involves companies). It was argued in *Armour v Thyssen Edelstahlwerke AG* [1990] 3 W.L.R. 810 that such a retention of title clause rendered the transaction a security agreement (or a charge) instead of a sale. The House of Lords rejected this argument saying that:

> "[We are] ... unable to regard a provision reserving title to the seller until payment of all debts due to him by the buyer as amounting to the creation by the buyer of a right to security in favour of the seller. Such a provision does in a sense give the seller security for the unpaid debts of the buyer. But it does so by way of a legitimate retention of title, not by virtue of any right over his own property conferred by the buyer".

A charge may be defined generally as a proprietary right in a specified property granted by a debtor in favour of another person as security for a debt. A charge over a company's assets gives to the creditor a prior claim over other creditors to payment of his debt out of the liquidation of those assets.

There are two types of charges that we need to concern ourselves with **4–034** —specific or fixed charges and floating charges. In *Illingworth v Houldsworth* [1904] A.C. 355 Lord Macnaghten compared the two types of charges:

> "[S]pecific charge ... is one that without more fastens on ascertained and defined property or property capable of being ascertained and defined; a floating charge, on the other hand, is ambulatory and shifting in its nature, hovering over and so to speak floating with the property which it is intended to affect until some event occurs or some act is done which causes it to settle and fasten on the subject of the charge within its reach and grasp".

We should, however, be careful to note that there is no single exhaustive definition of the floating charge.

Lord Macnaghten also approved the description of the floating charge provided by Romer L.J. when the case was heard by the Court of Appeal. According to Romer L.J., a charge is likely to be treated as a floating charge:

1. if it is a charge on a class of assets of a company present and future;

2. if that class is one which, in the ordinary course of the business of the company would be changing from time to time; and

3. if the contemplation of the parties is that until some future step is taken by one or on behalf of those interested in the charge, the company may carry on its business in the ordinary way as far as concerns that particular class of assets.

A floating charge may therefore be defined as a charge on a class of assets of a company, present or future, which changes in the ordinary course of the company's business—until the holders enforce the charge the companymay carry on business and deal with the assets charged. It is not restricted to current assets such as book debts or stock in trade. A floating charge over "undertaking and assets" (a common stipulation in the charge) of a company applies to both fixed and current assets. It attaches to the assets only on crystallization (e.g. when the company becomes liquidated, when the company stops trading, the appointment of a receiver over the assets of the company, if the charge so provides, etc).

4–035   In company law, there exists a system of registration of charges the effect of which is to serve as notice to any subsequent buyer or chargee of the existence of the charge. Failure to register a charge when it is registrable means that the chargee may be lawfully ignored by the holder of a registered subsequent charge or a subsequent buyer.

A simple reservation of title clause is not a charge according to the House of Lords because the buyer had never owned the goods as the retention of title was imposed right at the outset. Where he was never an owner, he could not grant any proprietary right in those goods. Where the clause is more elaborately devised, it may be found to be a charge and must be registered for full effect.

The case from which the retention of title clause takes its name is *Aluminium Industrie Vaassen BV v Romalpa Aluminium Ltd* [1976] 2 All E.R. 552. In that case, the contract for the sale of aluminium foil stated:

1. that ownership of the aluminium foil is to be transferred only when the buyers have met all that is owing to the sellers;

2. the buyers are required to store the foil in such a way that it is clear for all to see that the goods do not belong to them until payment has been made;

3. if the buyers manufacture products using the foil, property in these products will vest in the sellers as security for payment and if required, the products will be kept separate from the buyers' own materials and goods. Until the buyers have satisfied the debt, they hold the goods as "fiduciary owners" for the seller;

4. if the buyers sell the manufactured goods onto third parties, they are to hand the proceeds over to the sellers when requested.

4–036   Romalpa, the buyers, went into receivership. The main issue for the court was whether the sellers could defeat the receiver's claim over the goods using the retention of title clause.

The Court of Appeal allowed the sellers to rely on the retention of title clause. Provision 1. was of course a simple reservation of title clause and was perfectly valid in the light of ss.17 and 19 of the Sale of Goods Act 1979. Provision 2. expedited the operation of provision 1. by imposing on the buyer the duty to ensure that goods belonging to the sellers were set apart. It also signified the clear intention of the sellers to retain title in the goods. The stipulation also placed the buyer in a fiduciary relationship with the seller.

There are two situations worth considering. First, where the goods are still in the seller's possession. Here the position is fairly straightforward; the seller's interest can be quite easily protected under the clause. The second is when the goods have been re-sold. In *Romalpa*, where the goods have been re-sold, the proceeds are to be handed over to the original seller. However, what if the seller seeks, not the proceeds but the return of the goods themselves?

In *Four Point Garage Ltd v Carter* [1985] 3 All E.R. 12, it was contended that **4–037** the simple retention of title clause had the effect of preserving title, despite the sale to an ultimate customer. However Simon Brown J. held that there is usually an implied right to sell the goods on. It would be commercially unrealistic to prevent the buyer from selling the goods on. Further, in most cases, where there has been a re-sale, the ultimate buyer will be able to rely on s.2 Factors Act 1889 or s.25 Sale of Goods Act 1979, or alternatively be able to rely on an estoppel, as recognised by s.21 of the Sale of Goods Act 1979. That section provides:

"Subject to this Act, where goods are sold by a person who is not their owner, and who does not sell them under the authority or with the consent of the owner, the buyer acquires no better title to the goods than the seller had unless the owner of the goods is, by his conduct, precluded from denying the sellers authority to sell".

In *Fairfax Gerard Holdings v Capital Bank Plc* [2007] EWCA Civ 1226, F gave finance to D to buy machinery from China to be sold to C. The finance agreement between F and D contained a simple reservation of title clause stipulating that F

"shall open Letters of Credit on your suppliers in our name and sell the machines to you with the reservation of title and subject to the terms of our Standard Trust receipt. You will invoice your customers with the debt assigned to us with the following assignment notice printed on them . . . ".

C argued that the clause showed that F had authorised D to pass on a good title to them. The Court of Appeal held that the clause recognised that prior to payment, title would be passed at least to the customers identified in the letter. The only purpose of including a requirement that invoices to customers bear the assignment notice could be that the proceeds of sale could be passed on to F.

In *Re Andrabell Ltd* [1984] 3 All E.R. 407, one of the factors relied on by Peter **4–038** Gibson J. in rejecting the application of the suppliers was that the goods had been intermingled and it was therefore not possible to identify clearly which goods were subject to the *Romalpa* clause. It must be said that where there exists a specific clause instructing the buyer to keep the goods separate and proceeds of any sale in a separate account, that should avail the seller. Without stipulation to that effect the court would consider whether there is a fiduciary relationship between the parties from the facts. Where there is such a relationship, the seller may trace his proprietary interest to the proceeds of any sale of the goods. The case has also been often cited as support for the proposition that any provision of credit is inconsistent with the equitable duty to account. In that case, the seller had granted the buyers 45 days' credit. It is, however, submitted that the fiduciary relationship is not necessarily removed by the provision of credit; the effect of the credit stipulation merely suspends the duty to account until the end of the credit term.

The importance of an appropriately drafted clause is seen in *Borden (UK) Ltd v Scottish Timber Products Ltd* [1981] Ch. 25 where the goods sold had been incorporated with other materials in the manufacture of chipboards.

4–039 *Borden (UK) Ltd v Scottish Timber Products Ltd* [1981] Ch. 25
Facts:
Resin was sold to Scottish Timber Ltd under a term that property in the resin will not pass
to the buyers until full payment had been made. The resin was then mixed with hardeners
and wood chippings to make chipboard. The buyers went into receivership. The sellers
wanted to trace their interest in the resin to the finished chipboard and any proceeds of sale
of the chipboard.
Held:
It is clear that the simple clause does not provide for the contingency of the resin being
incorporated with other materials. The Court of Appeal held that there is no general
principle of law that would assist the seller because the resin had ceased to exist after it
had been incorporated to make chipboard. Property in the resin did not mean ownership
of the chipboard. Buckley L.J. commented:

> "The manufacture had amalgamated the resin and the other ingredients into a new
> product by an irreversible process and the resin, as resin, could not be recovered for any
> purpose; for all practical purposes it had ceased to exist and the ownership in that resin
> must also have ceased to exist".

The sellers were unable to trace their proprietary interest in the resin to the chipboard
because according to the court:

> "[I]t is a fundamental feature of the doctrine of tracing that the property to be traced can
> be identified at every stage of its journey through life, and that it can be identified as
> property to which a fiduciary obligation still attaches in favour of the [seller]".

We should also consider *Re Peachdart Ltd* [1984] 1 Ch. 131.

4–040 *Re Peachdart Ltd* [1984] 1 Ch. 131
Facts:
The sellers sold leather to Peachdart Ltd to be made into handbags. There was a retention
of title clause in the contract of sale which stated that ownership in the leather remains
with the sellers until full payment of the purchase price is paid and that the buyers are
accountable to the sellers for any proceeds of sale of the leather or goods made out of
it.
Held:
There was no doubt that property in any remaining leather held in stock vested in the seller
by virtue of the *Romalpa* clause. However, as for the leather applied to make handbags,
Vinelott J. held that the sellers' claim could not be sustained. Once the leather was
processed to make into handbags, title in the goods passed to the buyer subject to a
charge.

It may be raised in criticism that in *Re Peachdart Ltd*, the explicit terms of the
Romalpa clause had been ignored. In that case, the clause reads

> " . . . ownership of the Products shall remain with the Seller which reserves the
> right to dispose of the products until payment in full for all the Products has
> been received . . . If any of the Products are incorporated in or used as
> materials for other goods before such payment the property in the whole of
> such goods shall be and remain with the Seller until such payment has been
> made . . . Until the Seller is paid in full for all the Products the relationship of
> the Buyer to the Seller shall be fiduciary in respect of the Products".

It is not easy to reconcile this case with *Aluminium Industrie Vaassen BV v
Romalpa Aluminium Ltd* given the specific stipulation in the contract.

While comprehensive drafting has much to be commended, it might, however, **4–041**
raise special difficulties, especially when the intention of the clause is not entirely
clear as was highlighted in *Re Bond Worth Ltd* [1980] Ch. 228. There the seller
stipulated that the equitable and beneficial ownership in the goods and additionally, the beneficial interest in any finished product made out of the fibre and
proceeds of any sale, are to remain with him until the price is paid. This implied
that the buyer was to have legal ownership. The fact that property in the goods
has passed to the buyer with the seller retaining an equitable title suggests that a
charge has been generated, i.e. the buyer who has legal title allowing the seller
to hold the equitable title.

A point on drafting might be made. Where the clause provides that:

1. property will not pass until full payment of the goods;

2. the buyer may not sell the goods as principal but must hold the proceeds of
   any sale of the goods for the seller;

3. the buyer holds the goods as bailee for the seller;

it should constitute a registrable charge.[23] This charge would be void unless it has
been properly registered (*Tatung (UK) Ltd v Galex Telesure Ltd* [1988] 5 B.C.C.
325).[24]

Summary of the principles:

- a simple *Romalpa* clause provides that property in goods will remain with seller
  until full payment of the goods has been made;

- a simple retention of title clause differs from a floating charge on the ground that the
  buyer never had property in the goods at the outset; a clause that grants back
  beneficial or equitable title to the seller on the other hand implies that property in the
  goods has passed to the buyer and is therefore a charge (*Re Bond Worth Ltd*). A
  charge must be registered for full effect (ss.395–399 of the Companies Act
  1989);

- a *Romalpa* clause may be effective even though the goods have been resold or
  incorporated into the buyer's own goods/products provided there is express
  provision that they can be used in this way before property has passed (*Borden (UK)
  Ltd; Aluminium Industrie Vaassen BV*);

- where the retention of property clause refers to other duties of the buyer, for
  example, the duty to account, it is always a matter of construction as to what the
  duties and rights of the parties are (*Re Andrabell Ltd*); and

- where the circumstances and contract reveal a fiduciary relationship between the
  parties, generally the seller would have a right to trace his proprietary interest (*Re
  Peachdart Ltd; Borden (UK) Ltd*).

---

[23] See Fisher & Lightwood, *Law of Mortgages*, 10th edn (London: Lexis Nexis), Ch.27;
McCormack, *Reservation of Title*, 2nd edn (London: Sweet & Maxwell, 1995), Chs 2 and 3; R.
Goode, *Commercial Law*, 2nd edn (London: Penguin, 1995), pp.654–657.

[24] Also *E. Pfeiffer Weinkellerei-Weinenkauf GmbH v Arbuthnot Factors Ltd* [1988] 1 W.L.R. 150;
Compaq Computer Ltd v Abereon Group Ltd [1993] B.C.L.C. 602.

Property in Goods

4–042 Property in goods is central to the sale transaction. Indeed the Sale of Goods Act 1979 makes it an implied condition to the contract of sale that title in the goods is passed to the buyer. Furthermore, English law has always maintained the proposition that the seller could only sustain an action for the price where property in the goods has passed to the buyer. Related to this is the time when property passes. We have seen in the discussion of retention of title clauses how no charge may be created unless the chargor first has ownership in the goods. We have also witnessed how the retention of title clause operates in conjunction with the concept of passing of property. In the realm of general law, legal and equitable incidences apply and attach on the owner of goods—for example, who in a transaction has the right to sue in relation to goods, priorities in goods in the event of insolvency, etc. The importance of the passing of property cannot thus be overstated.

Sections 16 to 19 of the Sale of Goods Act 1979 on the passage of property apply to both domestic and international sale contracts. The passage of property in goods depends on two important factors:

1. the parties' intention as objectively determined; and

2. the type of goods involved.

Where as in many international sale transactions the parties either expressly or by implication indicate their intention as to when property should pass, the law will have to give effect to that intention. Section 17 provides that where there is a contract for the sale of specific or ascertained goods the property in them is transferred at such time as the parties intend it to pass.

The court will look at the terms of the contract, the conduct of the parties and other circumstances of the case in determining when the parties intend property to pass (s.17(2)). A good illustration of this rule is *Stora Enso Oyj v Port of Dundee* [2006] CSOH 40. There, the contract called for the delivery of wood pulp "CIP Dundee Incoterms 2000". The contract was expressed to be in accordance with the General Trade Rules for Wood Pulp. CIP stands for "carriage and insurance paid". Under the General Trade Rules for Wood Pulp, delivered pulp was to remain the property of the seller until it had been paid for in full. Before the pulp was paid for, a fire destroyed it. The Outer House held that the expression "CIP" in the contract did not qualify or negate the clear provisions of the General Trade Rules. The parties' use of that term was only a shorthand way of recording their agreement as to what was included in the price of the pulp. It was not used to provide for the time property and risk pass.

4–043 International sales usually involve unascertained goods rather than specific goods. Thus, we should start by considering the operation of s.16 of the Sale of Goods Act 1979. That section provides that property in unascertained goods shall not pass until they have been ascertained. An example of how unascertained goods become ascertained is in *David Peters v Revenue and Customs* [2012] UKFTT 124 (TC). There, the court accepted the argument that as the plant and materials had been selected by the customer and were clearly identifiable from their serial numbers and invoice numbers, they were ascertained goods. Section 16 should not however be read as saying that property will pass when the goods are ascertained; it simply states that property cannot pass until the goods have been ascertained.

The Sale of Goods Act 1979 does not define the term "unascertained goods". In *Re Wait* [1927] 1 Ch. 606, Atkin L.J. described unascertained as "probably [meaning] identified in accordance with the agreement after the time a contract of sale is made". For our purposes we may consider unascertained goods as falling into any of the following categories:

1. future goods—goods that will be brought into existence to meet the contract will usually be unascertained at the time of the contract because they have yet to come into existence. However, in *Howell v Coupland* (1876) 1 Q.B.D. 258 the court felt that the goods to be delivered under the contract were in fact specific even though when the contract was made the potatoes had yet to be grown. The court considered as relevant the fact that the contract referred to a "specific quantity of potatoes to be grown in a specific plot of land". It would seem that *Howell v Coupland* is not good law in the light of the wording in ss.5, 6 and 7 of the Act, which suggest that for goods to be treated as specific goods, they should be in existence at the time of the contract;

N.B. The Act defines specific goods as those "identified and agreed on at the time a contract is made" (s.61(1)).

2. generic goods—for example, where the contract calls for the delivery of "100 tons of wheat";

3. portion of goods from an ascertained whole—In *Re Wait* [1927] 1 Ch. 606, it was held that a specified quantity from an ascertained whole could not be treated as specific goods and was in fact unascertained.

Where there is no express or standard practice as to the presumed intention of the parties (for example where there is no clear contract terms between the parties as in *David Peters v Revenue and Customs* [2012] UKFTT 124 (TC)), the courts would turn to the specific rules in s.18 for assistance in establishing when property in goods should pass. These rules carry only presumptive force and may be rebutted by evidence. Bearing in mind the nature of standard trade terms where the passing of property is subject to specific rules as matter of the presumed intention of the parties, the rules in s.18 are of limited assistance. However, they should be of relevance in helping us assess how the courts approach the matter of intention and in setting the context of the law on property in movables. The Rules are as follows.

Rule 1

Where there is an unconditional contract for the sale of specific goods in a **4–044** deliverable state property in the goods passes when the contract is made. It is not relevant whether the time of payment or the time of delivery, or both had been postponed. A good illustrative case is *Kursell v Timber Operators and Contractors Ltd* [1927] 1 K.B. 298.

4–045   *Kursell v Timber Operators and Contractors Ltd* [1927] 1 K.B. 298
Facts:
The contract of sale called for the delivery of all the timber in a Latvian forest which
conformed with certain specified measurements. A specific delivery date had been fixed.
Soon after the conclusion of the contract, the seller's rights in the forest were revoked. The
issue for the court was whether property in the timber had passed under r.1 when the
contract was made.
Held:
The court held that the goods were not specific goods under r.1. Scrutton L.J. said:

> "Specific goods are defined as goods identified and agreed upon at the time a contract
> of sale is made. It appears to me these goods were neither identified nor agreed upon.
> Not every tree in the forest passed, but only those complying with a certain
> measurement not then made. How much of each tree passed depended on where it was
> cut, how far from the ground. Nor does the timber seem to be in a deliverable state until
> the buyer has severed it. He cannot under the definition be bound to take delivery of an
> undetermined part of a tree not yet identified".

"Deliverable state" therefore means: "in a such a state that the buyer would
under the contract be bound to take delivery of them". In *Underwood v Burgh
Castle Brick and Cement Syndicate* [1922] 1 K.B. 243 the contract was for the
delivery Free on Rails (FOR) of machinery which must be dismantled and broken
into parts. A part of the machinery was damaged when it was being loaded on a
railway wagon. The sellers could not plead r.1 successfully because the machine
was not in a deliverable state (the machinery had yet to be dismantled and broken
into parts) when the contract was made.

Rule 2

4–046   This Rule states that where there is a contract for the sale of specific goods and
the seller is required to do something to the goods in order to put them into a
deliverable state, property shall not pass until that thing has been done and the
buyer has notice that it has indeed been completed. The rule considers the thing
to be done to be a condition of the contract. Where it is only incidental or
supplementary to the contract, r.2 does not apply. It is always a matter of
construction whether the thing required is a condition or not.

Rule 3

4–047   By this Rule, where there is a contract for the sale of specific goods in a
deliverable state but the seller is bound to weigh, measure, test or do some other
act or thing to ascertain the price of the goods, property does not pass until the
act or thing is done and the buyer has notice that it has been done.
  Where the measurement or weighing is to be done by the buyer, the passage
of property is not suspended as was held in *Turley v Bates* (1863) 2 H.&C.
200.

Rule 4

4–048   Where goods are delivered to the buyer on approval or on sale or return or other
similar terms:

(a) the property in the goods passes to the buyer when he signifies his approval or acceptance to the seller or does any act adopting the transaction;

(b) if he does not signify his approval or acceptance to the seller but retains the goods without giving the seller a notice of rejection, property passes to him when the time to return the goods expires. Where the time for return has not been fixed, he is deemed to have property in the goods after a reasonable time.

Rule 5

Rule 5 comes in four limbs. Limb 1 of r.5 provides that in general property in **4–049** unascertained goods passes to the buyer when the goods are unconditionally appropriated to the contract where there is assent from the parties. This assent may be implied or express. Either party may appropriate the goods to the contract as long as there is assent from the other party.

For r.5(1) to apply, there must thus also be real evidence of the parties' intention to pass property in the goods at the relevant time. In *Rohit Kulkarni v Manor Credit (Davenham) Ltd* [2010] EWCA Civ 69, K had ordered a car from a company (G), knowing that G had no such car but intended to source one. G bought the car from M under a hire purchase agreement and delivered it to K. However, three days earlier G had given K the car's registration number so he could insure it. M discovered G's fraud and repossessed the car. The lower court found that the parties had intended property in the car to pass to K when he had been given the registration number and that K's insurance of the car amounted to an assent to G's appropriation of it. The Court of Appeal however disagreed stating that the judge had erred by deciding the case on the basis of r.5(1) before assuring himself that there was actually intention for property in the car to pass *before* actual delivery. That was a significant preliminary step which the judge should have considered before embarking on an analysis of r.5(1). After all, s.18 does begin with these words "unless a different intention appears".

Limb 2 states that where the seller delivers to the buyer or a carrier or other bailee for the transmission of the goods to the buyer and does not reserve his right of disposal, he is to be taken to have unconditionally appropriated the goods to the contract.

Rule 5(1) refers to unconditional appropriation. This is explained by Pearson **4–050** J. in *Carlos Federspiel & Co v Charles Twigg* [1957] 1 Lloyd's Rep. 240:

> "[A] mere setting apart or selection of the seller of the goods which he expects to use in performance of the contract is not enough. If that is all, he can change his mind and use those goods in performance of some other contract and use some other goods in performance of this contract".

In order for appropriation to occur, the judge went on to say, "the parties must have had or be reasonably supposed to have had an intention to attach the contract irrevocably to those goods".

In *Re London Wine (Shippers) Co* (1986) P.C.C. 121, each wine purchaser was given a document stating that he was the owner of the quantity he had ordered and which was stored by the wine dealer for him until the wine is ready for delivery. There was no appropriation because there was no action to attach irrevocably the contract to the quantity of wine ordered. It was impossible to say who owned which particular case/s of wine.

Another condition to unconditional appropriation is that the other party must assent. Assent need not be express; it can be implied from the facts. In *Aldridge v Johnson* [1857] 26 L.J.Q.B. 296, the buyer had supplied sacks to the seller to be filled with barley from a bulk. The act of supplying the sacks would constitute assent from the buyer. Where the assent is given only after appropriation, property will pass not at appropriation but at the time assent is given. In *Pignataro v Gilroy* [1919] 1 K.B. 459, the sellers set aside the buyers' rice and then sent the buyers, at the latters' request, a delivery order to collect the rice. The buyers did not turn up. His asking for the delivery order however constituted assent. Thus, property did pass but not at the time the rice was packed and set aside, but when at a reasonable time after the buyers' lack of response.

4–051   Rule 5(2) is particularly relevant where the goods are to be delivered by a carrier. It states that goods will normally be considered to have been unconditionally appropriated when they are handed over to the carrier. However there are two conditions:

(a)   there should be no reservation of the right of disposal by the seller (s.19); and

(b)   the goods must be ascertained goods (s.16).

In *Healy v Howlett* [1917] 86 L.J.K.B. 337, the seller had sold 20 boxes of mackerel on FOR terms. He was also dispatching 190 boxes on the rail to other consignees at the same time. Ridley J. held that the placing of all 190 boxes on the rail was not unconditional appropriation because it could not be said which box was set apart for which customer. There was therefore no passing of property.

Rule 5(3) provides that where there is a contract for the sale of a specified quantity of unascertained goods in a deliverable state forming part of a bulk which is identified either in the contract or by subsequent agreement between the parties and the bulk is reduced to (or to less than) that quantity, then, if the buyer under that contract is the only buyer to whom goods are due out of the bulk:

(a)   the remaining goods are to be taken as appropriated to that contract at the time when the bulk is so reduced; and

(b)   the property in those goods then passes to that buyer.

Rule 5(4) states that the above provision will also apply where a bulk is reduced to (or to less than) the aggregate of the quantities due to a single buyer under separate contracts relating to that bulk and he is the only buyer to whom goods are then due out of that bulk.

4–052   These two paragraphs were added to the Sale of Goods Act 1979 by Sale of Goods (Amendment) Act 1995 and effectively gives statutory recognition to the principle espoused in *The Elafi* [1982] 1 All E.R. 208. In that case, the buyers had bought 6,000 tons of copra CIF Karlshamns. The sellers shipped 16,000 tons on a single vessel, 6,000 tons were intended for the buyers and the rest for other buyers, including a small quantity for F. F sold his lot to the buyers. Thus, the buyers were given bills of lading relating to 6,000 tons and F's lot respectively. The court held that no property could be said to pass on shipment because the goods were a single undivided bulk. However, by the time the ship left Hamburg after calling at several other ports, the goods left onboard were destined for the buyers. Therefore, Mustill J. held that at that stage property could pass. The goods had become ascertained by "exhaustion". This case demonstrates that although the buyers had paid against the bills of lading, property did not pass at the delivery of the bills of lading. The lesson is thus—where the bills of lading covered only part of a larger bulk cargo, no unqualified property can pass until the goods become ascertained (see also s.16).

Unascertained goods from a bulk

Section 16, as might be recalled, provides that no property could pass until **4–053** unascertained goods have become ascertained. This fairly unremarkable rule however could cause tremendous difficulties for commercial sales. In *Re Goldcorp Exchange Ltd* [1994] 2 All E.R. 806 the contract provided for the sale of gold bullions which the seller would keep for the buyer who has pre-paid. Although ownership certificates were issued to the buyers, as the goods were all put in a mixed bulk, the Privy Council held that there was no ascertainment and therefore appropriation. As such, property had not passed to the buyer. The seller had become insolvent but the buyer, as a non-owner, was no better than an unsecured creditor. There was also no equitable assignment because such an equitable principle did not apply following the codification of sale of goods law (per Atkin L.J. in *Re Wait* [1927] 1 Ch. 606).

The Sale of Goods (Amendment) Act 1995 was passed to ameliorate just such an injustice. A new section was introduced to the Sale of Goods Act 1979—s.20A. Section 20A(1) provides:

"This section applies to a contract for the sale of a specified quantity of unascertained goods if the following conditions are met:

(a) the goods or some of them form part of a bulk which is identified either in the contract or by subsequent agreement between the parties; and

(b) the buyer has paid the price for some or all of the goods which are the subject of the contract and which form part of the bulk".

The effect of s.20A is that as soon as the buyer pays the price (or part of it), he immediately acquires property in an undivided share in the bulk. He effectively becomes an owner in common of the bulk.[25]

Another condition, other than payment of the price, before the buyer could benefit from s.20A is that there is no agreement between the parties to derogate from s.20A. That derogation may either be for the non-application of the section or that property in the undivided share will pass at some particular point in time after payment.

Section 20A(4) then provides that where the aggregate of the undivided shares **4–054** of all the buyers of the bulk would exceed the whole of the bulk, the undivided share of each buyer will be reduced proportionately. This is applicable when the bulk quantity had been reduced. Example: A, B and C have each paid for 10kg

---

[25] See Burns, "Better late than never: the reform of the law on the sale of goods forming part of a bulk" (1996) 59 M.L.R. 260.

of goods weighing 30kg. If the bulk suffers wastage and is reduced to 27kg, the effect of s.20A(4) is that A, B and C will now own 9kg each.

What happens if the seller sold quantity in excess of what is in the bulk? Suppose A has 100kg of goods, and sells 50kg to B, 50kg to C and 50kg to D. B, C and D have all paid. It is obvious that the seller had sold 150kg when he only had 100kg. If A delivers to B the 50kg, the question is what happens to C and D's share? Will they be diluted? It would appear so. If C takes the goods in good faith and for valuable consideration, property will pass to him under s.24. Section 20A(4) suggests that C and D's rights could now only be applied to the remaining quantity—50kg—namely, that they will take only 25kg each.

A third condition before s.20A could apply is that the contract must be for a specified quantity of goods forming part of an identified bulk. It would not be enough if the parties had simply intended for the goods to come from a general source—for example, if A agrees to sell B 5000 gallons of oil. Section 61 Sale of Goods Act 1979 defines bulk as:

"[A] mass or collection of goods of the same kind which (a) is contained within a confined space or area, and (b) is such that any goods in the bulk are interchangeable with any other goods therein of the same number or quantity".

The contract calling for 5000 gallons of oil would not satisfy s.61 as the oil could be sourced from anywhere; there is no particular or identified bulk from which it should derive. It should also be remembered that the contract must be for a specified quantity—if the contract is for one-fifth of the sugar in warehouse X, that is not a contract coming under s.20A. Instead, that would be a contract for the sale of specific goods.

Passing of Property in FOB Contracts

4–055   The paradigm rule is that in an FOB sale, property passes on shipment, i.e. when the goods are over the ship's rail and the risk in each parcel of the cargo will pass when the parcel crosses the same (*Colonial Insurance Co of New Zealand v Adelaide Marine Insurance* (1886) 12 App. Cas. 128). This rule is consistent with the seller's duty in any sale to relinquish risk and property when the goods are delivered to the buyer. Once the goods have crossed the ship's rail, the seller is deemed to have delivered the goods to the buyer. It is open to the parties to exclude the general presumption that property in the goods will pass at shipment but it is not always clear when and whether this is indeed the case when reliance is made on some implied waiver of the general rule.[26]

As may be recalled, s.18 r.5 of the Sale of Goods Act 1979 states that where the seller delivers the goods to the buyer or a carrier or other bailee or custodier (whether named by the buyer or not) for the purpose of transmission to the buyer, and does not reserve the right of disposal, he is to be taken to have unconditionally appropriated the goods to the contract. Where, as in *Inglis v Stock* (1885) 10 App. Cas. 263, the goods are shipped in bulk and the goods have

---

[26] See, e.g., *Transpacific Eternity SA v Kanematsu Corp (The Antares III)* [2002] 1 Lloyd's Rep. 233.

yet to be ascertained, property will not pass on shipment. (Note discussion above on the Sale of Goods (Amendment) Act 1995 which provides that if the owner of part of an undivided bulk sells it to a buyer who pays the price, property in an undivided share of the bulk can pass to the buyer if the parties so agree.[27])

Where the FOB sale is characterised by documents, the intention of the parties could be presumed to exclude the passing of property on shipment. The act of retaining the documents signifies the intention of the seller not to dispose of ownership in the goods. Where payment is only to be made against conforming documents, the contract would usually have stipulated that the bill of lading is made deliverable to the seller or to his order as security for payment. Sections 19(1) and (2) are particularly relevant if this is the case (see, *Mitsui & Co Ltd v Flota Mercante Grancolumbiana SA (The Ciudad de Pasto)* [1989] 1 All E.R. 951). Section 19(2) provides that

"where goods are shipped, and by the bill of lading the goods are deliverable to the order of the seller or his agent, the seller is prima facie to be taken to reserve the right of disposal".

The seller in reserving the right of disposal makes it clear that the goods have not been unconditionally appropriated to the contract and consequently, property is not to pass on shipment (s.19(1)). The seller has first to be paid before property in the goods can pass. It is apparent that the provisions of s.19(2) do not apply where the bill of lading is made out in the buyer's name or to his order; where this is the case, r. 5(2) of s.18 suggests that delivery of the goods to the carrier will be deemed an unconditional appropriation of the goods.

In *The Seven Pioneer* [2001] 2 Lloyd's Rep. 57, the contract for the sale of **4–056** cement was on FOB Jakarta, Indonesia terms. The contract provided for payment against bills of lading but the bills of lading were never sent and the claimants never paid the sellers for the shipment. The goods were damaged, it was alleged, due to poor stowage. The claimants sued the carrier. The carrier argued that the claimants had never acquired a sufficient proprietary or possessory interest in the goods to found a claim in tort.[28] The dispute was governed by New Zealand law. The New Zealand High Court held that the sellers having delivered the goods to a carrier for the purpose of transmission to the buyer were deemed to have unconditionally appropriated the goods to the contract unless they had reserved the right of disposal (s.20 r.(5)(2) of New Zealand's Sale of Goods Act 1908, which is identical to s.18 r.(5)(2) of the English Act) which means that under r.5(1) property would have effectively passed to the buyer. The court however found that although the bills of lading had been made out to the claimants as consignee and buyer, the bills had never been sent on to the claimants. The natural inference there was that the claimants had not acquired any rights to the bills of lading until payment was made. That being the case, the claimants did not have a sufficient interest in the goods at the time they were damaged to found a claim in negligence.

---

[27] Paragraph 4–053; also, Reynolds, "Stowing, trimming and their effects on delivery, risk and property in sales 'f.o.b.s.', 'f.o.b.t.' and 'f.o.b.s.t.'" [1994] L.M.C.L.Q. 119.

[28] The claimants also attempted to sue in contract but as they were not privy to the contract of carriage and had not received the bills of lading, that action failed.

It is, however, quite conceivable that the seller might not wish to reserve the right of disposal by retaining possession of the bill of lading. Where his clear intention is to pass it on to the buyer at the first opportune occasion, *The Albazero* [1977] A.C. 744 held that he would be deemed to have retained the bill of lading as the buyer's agent and was not acting in his own capacity. This and other circumstances are supportive of the suggestion that property in the goods was intended to pass on shipment.

A case involving an FAS contract might be instructive as to how difficult it can be to ascertain the appropriate intention when, although the contract envisages the use of documents, the documents turn out to be invalid.

4–057 *Transpacific Eternity SA v Kanematsu Corp (The Antares III)* [2002] 1 Lloyd's Rep. 233
Facts:
N agreed to sell on FAS terms, a large consignment of soya bean extraction and flake to S. S then agreed to sell the same to K. The cargo was to be shipped on a ship owned by T. The ship was chartered to M, a company associated with S. S defaulted on payment. Bills of lading issued were invalid for various reasons. The issue was whether N or K had title to the goods. N claimed that they were the true owners because property had never passed to S, S never having paid for them. As such, K could not get any title. K, on the other hand, submitted that the presumption that property would not pass until payment was displaced in all the circumstances of the case, in particular in the context of an FAS contract, where the mate's receipt had named S as consignee. The presumed intention was therefore that property should pass at ship's rail.
Held:
David Steel J. rejected K's argument stating that the presumption in s.19 that property did not pass until the conditions imposed by the seller were fulfilled clearly applied to an FOB contract but there was no justification in practice or principle for treating an FAS contract in any different way. The mate's receipt could not be relied on to alter the construction of the contracts of carriage. In order to displace the presumption, K needed to show in a clear and unequivocal way that that was indeed the parties' intention.

Much hinges on that elusive presumed intention of the parties. At which stage the property is to pass and whether the seller has reserved the right of disposal are fundamentally determined by the presumed intention of the parties evidenced in the contract. That intention is not easily identifiable as we see in *Mitsui & Co Ltd v Flota Mercante Grancolumbiana SA (The Ciudad de Pasto)* [1989] 1 All E.R. 951.

4–058 *Mitsui & Co Ltd v Flota Mercante Grancolumbiana SA (The Ciudad de Pasto)* [1989] 1 All E.R. 951
Facts:
The buyers had paid up to 80 per cent of the full purchase price of a consignment of prawns by documentary credit. The sellers had retained the bill of lading. The question was whether it was the intention of the parties that property in the goods should pass when the balance is paid or when the goods are shipped. It was argued that the fact that the contract provided for the payment of the full purchase price through documentary credit *before* shipment must surely mean that property was to pass then and not when documents are tendered.
Held:
The Court of Appeal was not persuaded and held that without any stipulations to the contrary in the contract, property in an FOB contract will not pass until the full purchase price is paid and the bill of lading is delivered to the buyers.

This case might be criticised on the ground that if the sellers were to become insolvent, the buyers would be left without a remedy. Property has not passed but yet they had paid 80 per cent of the price. On the other hand, of course, it could be said that if property were deemed to have passed on shipment, this leaves the sellers exposed to the risk of the buyers' absconding and not paying the balance of the full purchase price.

The passing of property is essential if the seller wishes to bring an action for the price of the goods. In *Colley v Overseas Exporter Ltd* [1921] 3 K.B. 302, Colley had agreed to sell leather belting to the defendant company on FOB terms. The buyers were to nominate a vessel to take delivery of the goods. They failed to do so. It was held that the sellers could not sue for the price of the goods even though the buyers were in breach of the contract. Their only remedy lay in damages. The reason supplied by the court was that the property has not passed to the buyers.

Passing of Property in CIF Sales

As before, the first general point to make is that under s.16 of the Sale of Goods Act 1979 no ownership in the goods will pass until the goods have been ascertained. The facts of *Re Wait* [1927] 1 Ch. 606 come to mind immediately. There, the buyers had received no title, legal or beneficial, where the goods, although paid for, formed a part of a larger unidentified bulk and therefore were not yet identified and ascertained for the purposes of the contract. **4–059**

Where the goods have become ascertained, property in them passes according to the presumed intention of the parties. This raises specific difficulties in a CIF contract. The intention behind a CIF contract is that even though goods are lost after shipment, the seller can still insist on payment because there exists insurance covering the cargo.[29] As long as the seller is able to tender conforming documents he is entitled to be paid. As far as the buyer is concerned, he should have adequate protection under the insurance policy secured on his account by the seller. This feature of the CIF contract makes it impractical to rely entirely on the presumptions in s.18 of the 1979 Act. What is the presumed intention of the parties in a CIF contract as to the transfer of ownership? Could we make any general observation as to the nature of that intention when the documents play such a central role in the transaction?

The presumed intention of the parties is invariably a question of fact and construction of the contract. However, although it is a matter of fact and construction, it might be submitted that trade practice seems to indicate that the traders would expect property to pass upon the transfer of the documents in exchange for payment of the price. For after all, the bill of lading represents title in the goods, hence the transfer of the bill of lading should mean the transfer of property in the goods. Indeed in *Mitsui & Co Ltd v Flota Mercante Grancolumbiana SA* above, the court indicated that where the international sale contract (whether FOB or CIF) is characterised by the transfer of documents, property is to pass on tender of documents and payment of the price.

---

[29] Murray, "Risk at loss of goods in transit: a comparison of the 1990 Incoterms with terms from other voices" (1991) 23 University of Miami Inter-American L. Rev. 93 offers an interesting analysis of Anglo-American law on this issue.

4–060 Sections 19(1) and (2) of the Sale of Goods Act 1979 will apply where the bill of lading issued is made out to the order of the seller or his agent. This means that there is a statutory inference that the seller has reserved his right of disposal. Property will not pass until the conditions set by the seller have been fulfilled—usually referring to full payment of the price. Under s.19(3) where the seller presents the buyer with a bill of exchange and the bill of lading relating to the goods, the buyer must return the bill of lading if he does not pay or accept the bill of exchange. Property cannot pass until he has accepted or paid the bill of exchange. If the buyer does not accept or make payment of the bill of exchange, the seller retains his right of disposal (property in the goods) even though the bill of exchange drawn on the buyer has been discounted to a bank.

The general practice is that there is no intention to pass property in the goods in the transfer of the documents if there no reciprocal payment of the price from the buyer. In *Leigh & Sillivan Ltd v Aliakmon Shipping Co Ltd (The Aliakmon)* [1986] A.C. 785, the C&F contract called for the delivery of a cargo of steel coils from Korea to Humberside. The steel was damaged whilst being stowed on the Aliakmon. The seller had not yet been paid but the documents relating to the goods had been transferred to the buyer's agent. The House of Lords held that the mere transfer of the bills of lading would not signify the passing of property when the terms of the C&F contract in question clearly envisaged property to pass on payment of the price.

It is important to note that although the general intention of the parties in a CIF agreement is to pass property in the goods when the documents are exchanged in payment of the price, there may be special cases calling for a different finding. A case where the general rule was deviated from is *The Albazero* [1977] A.C. 774. There the sale agreement was between two companies within the same corporate group. The issue was which company had the locus standi as owners to take action following the loss of the goods. The court held that property passed when the bill of lading was posted; payment need not have been effected. There was no serious issue as to the security of payment afforded by the documents, that is to say, there was no implicit condition that property hinges on payment. The sale was one between allied firms.

4–061 In CIF contracts, we often see a contractual term requiring the seller to give a "notice of appropriation". This is a notice given to the buyer informing him that the goods have been appropriated to the contract[30] but it should be noted that the notice does not constitute *unconditional* appropriation. The intention behind the notice is not to attach the goods irrevocably to the contract (see Pearson J.'s explanation of "unconditional appropriation" in *Carlos Federspiel & Co v Charles Twigg* [1957] 1 Lloyd's Rep. 240). Moreover, the appropriation served by the notice is conditional on the buyer taking up and paying against shipping documents.

It is also important to remind ourselves that s.18 r.5(3) and (4), and *The Elafi* [1982] 1 All E.R. 208 mean that a quantity of goods represented by a bill of lading can become unconditionally appropriated by "exhaustion". There is no passing of property in the CIF contract despite the bill of lading having been delivered to the buyer where the goods form part of a bulk which have yet to become ascertained (*The Elafi*).

---

[30] Davies, "Continuing dilemmas with passing of property in part of a bulk" [1991] J.B.L. 111.

The transfer of property in the documents is conditional. We have seen in *Kwei Tek Chao v British Traders and Shippers Ltd* [1954] 1 All E.R. 779 that the buyer who has paid for and accepted documents which appear to be conforming could still reject the goods if they do not conform to the contract. If he rejects the goods and signifies his rejection to the seller, ownership in the goods returns to the seller.

Risk and Property

The general statement of law is found in s.20 of the Sale of Goods Act 1979:   **4–062**

"(1) Unless otherwise agreed, the goods remain at the seller's risk until the property in them is transferred to the buyer, but when the property in them is transferred to the buyer the goods are at the buyer's risk whether delivery has been made or not.

(2) But where delivery has been delayed through the fault of either buyer or seller the goods are at the risk of the party at fault as regards any loss which might not have occurred but for such fault".

Under an FOB contract, risk passes on shipment. It is, however, only mere coincidence that this is also when property generally passes. Where the passing of property has been postponed as a result of the seller reserving his right of disposal (e.g. bills of lading having been made out in the seller's name), risk will still pass on shipment. In *Stock v Inglis* (1885) 10 App. Cas. 263, the contract called for the delivery of sugar FOB Hamburg. The sugar sold was part of a bulk and had yet to be ascertained. This meant that property in the goods did not pass to the buyer when the goods were shipped. The sugar was subsequently lost. The buyers claimed under the insurance policy. The insurers defended the claim on the ground that the buyers had not suffered any loss because they were not the owners of the goods. The court rejected their contention and stated that although property had not passed to the buyers, the risk in the goods had.

The passing of risk in a CIF contract is not governed by s.20. The passing of risk takes place upon shipment while property passes, as we have seen above, at a later stage in time, when the documents are taken up and paid for. The position is best explained in the Kennedy L.J.'s words in *Biddell Bros v E Clemens Horst Co* [1911] 1 K.B. 934:

" . . . the goods are at the risk of the purchaser [at time of shipment], against which he has protected himself by the stipulation in his CIF contract that the vendor shall, at his own cost, provide him with a proper policy of marine insurance intended to protect the buyer's interest, and available for his use if the goods should be lost in transit".

A related issue is whether the seller under a CIF contract is obliged to notify the buyer of any change of risk. Section 32(3) of the Sale of Goods Act 1979 seems to impose such a duty on the seller; it provides that, unless otherwise agreed, where goods are sent by the seller to the buyer by a route involving sea transit, under circumstances in which it is usual to insure, the seller must give such notice to the buyer as may enable him to insure them during their sea transit. It further states that if the seller fails to notify the buyer, the goods are at his risk during the sea transit. The approach of Hamilton L.J.'s judgment in *Wimble v Rosenberg* [1913] 3 K.B. 743 seems to be that s.32(3) has no application in CIF contracts, for after all there is always an express arrangement as to insurance in the CIF contract. Support for this proposition may be found in Rowlatt J.'s judgment in *Law & Bonar v American Tobacco Co Ltd* [1916] 2 K.B. 605. It was decided there that the seller under a CIF contract need not inform the buyer as to any change of risk. The CIF contract only obliges him to take out insurance as is usual to the trade; the fact the circumstances of the transaction may involve special or extraordinary risks is irrelevant. If the buyer wants this added protection, he needs to ensure that special cover is taken out. Section 32(3) does not avail him.

4–063   It is open to the parties to an international sale agreement to lay down their own arrangement for the allocation of risk. Common clauses used are the so-called landed/out-turn quantity clause and the landed quality clause.[31] The former stipulates that where there is a difference between the weight or quantity of the goods at the time of shipment and the time of arrival, that would not be paid for by the buyer. A landed quality clause on the other hand provides that the buyer will pay a lower price if there is a difference in the quality of the goods between the time of shipment and time of arrival. Outturn clauses are commonplace in the oil and gas trade. Such clauses though generally helpful to the buyer could well cause difficulties for him but as the law on the passing of risk is not displaced, such clauses might actually operate to the disadvantage of the buyer. In the case of out-turn quantity clauses, for example, the buyer nonetheless continues to bear the risk of a total loss or deterioration of the goods. The clause does not after all relate to quality. As for the landed quality clause, the buyer would not be covered if there was a total loss of the goods or where part of the goods have disappeared.

A CIF out-turn contract is not necessarily a contradiction in terms. According to Phillips J. in *CEP Interagra SA v Select Energy Trading* (November 14, 1990), a CIF out-turn is not necessarily a contradiction in terms despite the fact that the passing of risk may have been varied. The CIF contract is, after all, a creature of contract. This is especially so in the bulk goods and oil trade.[32] A commercial justification might be that it is not uncommon for oil cargoes sold on CIF terms to reach their destination before the seller can tender the bill of loading. The ship may then give delivery to the buyer in exchange for an indemnity and the buyer may pay the seller against a letter of indemnity. Payment may therefore precede

---

[31] The following is an example of a CIF outturn/CFR outturn clause:
"(a) For the purpose of determining the compliance of the Product with the quantity and quality provisions of the Special Conditions, the quality shall be determined at the Port of Loading, in accordance with Articles 3.2.1 to Article 3.2.5, and the quantity measurement shall be carried out at the Port of Destination, in accordance with Article 4.2.;
(b) In the event of a total loss of the Cargo or where the discharge quantity determined by the Independent Inspector in accordance with Article 4.2.4 is less than 99.5% of the loaded quantity determined in accordance with Article 3.2.2, then the quantity invoiced by the Seller shall be 99.5% of the quantity specified on the certificate(s) of quantity (or the equivalent document) issued at the Port of Loading."
(*http://www.statoil.com/en/OurOperations/TradingProducts/NGL/ConditionsOfSales/Downloads/ Statoil%20ASA%20General%20Terms%20and%20Conditions%20for%20Sales%202011%20ver sion%206%20May.pdf.* [Accessed April 8, 2013])
[32] *Produce Brokers New Co v Wray Sanderson & Co* (1931) 39 Ll.L. Rep. 257; *Plaimar Ltd v Waters Trading Co Ltd* (1945) 72 C.L.R. 304.

delivery. A CIF out-turn clause would permit such variations to the classic CIF transaction.[33] That said, it is uncertain if such a liberal reading of a CIF contract can be justified in the light of *Law & Bonar*, which held that a clause stating risk remained with the seller until actual delivery was repugnant to a CIF contract.

---

[33] per Phillips J. in *CEP Interagra SA v Select Energy Trading GmbH* (November 14, 1990).

CHAPTER 5

THE VIENNA CONVENTION ON CONTRACTS FOR THE INTERNATIONAL SALE OF GOODS

Attempts were made as long ago as the 1920s to harmonise or unify the law **5–001** relating to international sale of goods by the International Institute for the Unification of Private Law (UNIDROIT) working in collaboration with lawyers in the League of Nations. Two conventions were completed in 1964—the Convention relating to a Uniform Law on the International Sale of Goods (The Hague, 1964) and the Convention relating to a Uniform Law on the Formation of Contracts for the International Sale of Goods (The Hague, 1964). These conventions did not command wide acceptance, internationally.

In 1966 the United Nations established the UN Commission on International Trade Law (UNCITRAL). This is a commission which is set up, as expressed by UN Resolution 2205 (XXI) of December 17, 1966, "to promote the progressive harmonization and unification of international trade law". One of the major achievements of UNCITRAL is the Vienna Convention on Contracts for the International Sale of Goods 1980 (CISG). Unlike the many non binding codes published by UNCITRAL, the CISG is an international convention.[1] It becomes binding once the legislature of a country formally adopts it as forming part of national law.

The United Kingdom has not ratified the Convention. However, where the contract of sale selects as its applicable law the law of a country which has adopted the CISG, then, if the dispute comes before an English court, the court would in general need to apply it. Under the new Rome I Regulation (art.3 and recital 12, of the Preamble to the Regulation), it will also be possible the parties to choose the CISG as the applicable law of the sale contract. In such a case too, if the dispute comes before the English court, it will have to apply the CISG. The CISG may also be a source of inspiration and guidance for an English court attempting to develop the parameters of new jurisprudence. In *Square Mile Partnership Ltd v Fitzmaurice McCall Ltd* [2005] EWHC 1565 (Ch) and *ProForce Recruit Ltd v The Rugby Group Ltd* [2006] EWCA Civ 69 for example, we see the English courts clearly drawing from CISG and UNIDROIT principles

---

[1] See generally, Barry, "The Vienna Convention on International Sales Law" (1989) 105 L.Q.R. 201.

to evaluate how the matter of pre-contractual negotiations should be relevant to the issue of construction of contracts.[2]

Application and Field of Operation of the CISG

5–002   The CISG only applies to contracts of sale of goods between parties whose places of business are in different states when the states are contracting states (art.1(1)(a)) or when the rules of private international law lead to the application of the law of a contracting state (art.1(1)(b)). It is interesting to observe that in *Cedar Petrochemicals, Inc v Dongbu Hannong Chemical Co Ltd*[3] the New York court ruled that the CISG would only apply between the contracting parties and did not apply to any third parties to the contract although they might have a nationality of a country member to the Convention.

Article 1(2) goes on to state that

> "the fact that the parties have their places of business in different States is to be disregarded whenever this fact does not appear either from the contract or from any dealings between, or from information disclosed by, the parties at any time before or at the conclusion of the contract".

Nationality or residence is not relevant, generally.

Example: A has its place of business in the United Kingdom. B has its place of business in Germany. The United Kingdom is not a contracting state but Germany is. A and B make a contract of sale. The contract does not contain a choice of law clause. A dispute has broken and proceedings are commenced in Italy. In reliance on art.1(1), the Italian court should:

- find that the parties have their places of business in different states;

- find that only one state is a contracting state;

- apply its private international law (the Rome Convention) to ascertain the applicable law of the contract;

- apply the CISG if it finds that the applicable law is German law;

- apply English law and thus, not apply the CISG, if the applicable law is English law.

Article 95 allows contracting states to make reservation to limit the application of art.1(1)(b).

5–003   As regards its field of operation, the CISG does not apply to all sales. The following are excluded (art.2): goods bought for personal, family or household use, unless the seller, at any time before or at the conclusion of the contract, neither knew nor ought to have known that the goods were bought for any such use. The intention is to exclude consumer sales from the Convention. In

---

[2] Bonell, "The UNIDROIT Principles and CISG—Sources of Inspiration for English Courts?" (2007) 19 Pace Int'l L. Rev. 9; Rogowska, "CISG in UK: How does the CISG govern the contractual relations of English businessmen?" (2007) 18(7) I.C.C.L.R. 226–230; Berg, "Thrashing through the undergrowth" (2006) 122 L.Q.R. 354.

[3] United States, July 19, 2007 Federal District Court NY (*http://cisgw3.law.pace.edu/cases/070719u1.html*) [accessed April 9, 2013].

particular, if it is made known to the seller that the purchase is for personal or family purposes, it would follow that the sale would not come under the CISG.

Article 3(1) provides that contracts for the supply of goods to be manufactured or produced are considered sales unless the party who orders the goods undertakes to supply a substantial part of the materials necessary for such manufacture or production. So, if A supplies to B all the leather used for making a consignment of handbags which in turn will be supplied to A, this is not a sale. The main problem here is obvious—what does substantial mean? If A supplied 30 per cent of the leather needed, will that be substantial enough?

On the scope of its application, it should be pointed out that the CISG does not cover every aspect of the sale relationship. Article 4 provides that the CISG will only govern the formation of the sale contract and the rights and obligations of the buyer and seller arising from the contract. It is not concerned with:

1. the validity of the contract or of any of its provisions or of any usage;

2. the effect which the contract may have on the property in the goods sold.

Last but not least, art.6 allows the parties to the contract to exclude the application of the Convention. It also provides that the parties may, subject to art.12, derogate from or vary the effect of the CISG provisions. Many trade associations have excluded the application of the Convention in favour of English law (such as the Grain and Feed Trade Association). This provision is important for English traders who do not wish to be caught by the application of the CISG through art.1(1)(b).

Problems of interpretation

Although the CISG is an international treaty, it is invariably applied and **5–004** interpreted by national courts. Given the many different courts and tribunals involved, it is very likely that there will be many different interpretations and approaches being applied to the common text. In order to ensure that this risk is minimised, the CISG provides for certain guidelines on how the provisions should be interpreted and applied.

Article 7(1) thus provides that in the interpretation of the Convention, regard should be had to "its international character and to the need to promote uniformity in its application and the observance of good faith in international trade". In this connection, contracting states should construe the provisions by drawing from precedents and norms adopted in other contracting states. Clearly, precedents or norms from other contracting states are not binding but the court dealing with the dispute in question should have proper regard to the need for uniformity.

The second limb to art.7(1) relates to the so-called universal principle of good faith. The duty is placed on the courts of the contracting states to ensure that the principle of good faith is observed in its decisions. It might be noted that art.7(1) places the duty only on the court to interpret the provisions of the CISG in good faith; it should not be treated as a provision imposing a general duty of good faith on the parties. It should also be added that as there is no definition of good faith in the CISG, this makes art.7(1) a difficult provision to give practical effect to. It has however been argued that by not providing for a single standard of good faith as an interpretive aid, the CISG requires courts to apply so-called autonomous concepts. Courts, according to some jurists, should take an autonomous approach—namely, an interpretation that excludes domestic law as an influence on the interpretation process.[4] It is submitted that rather than excluding domestic law, a better approach would be to refer to both domestic law and other systems of law (for example, the UNIDROIT Principles) to develop an international jurisprudence. In the car amplifiers case[5] for example, the US court commented that "furthermore, in applying the CISG, courts may inform their analysis by looking to parallel [US Uniform Commercial Code] provisions" and there is no shortage of CISG cases which have applied the UNIDROIT Principles.[6] Naturally a major difficulty with an autonomous approach is the fact that the CISG is law for a large conglomerate of nation states with different linguistic and cultural norms.

5-005   A further tool to interpretation is laid down in art.7(2). It states:

"Questions concerning matters governed by this Convention which are not expressly settled in it are to be settled in conformity with the general principles on which it is based or, in the absence of such principles, in conformity with the law applicable by virtue of the rules of private international law".

A starting point has to be that when a court has to decide which matters are "matters governed by this Convention which are not expressly settled" it should naturally refer to issues explicitly excluded from the CISG. Article 7(2) refers to two possible gaps—one where the CISG governs the issue but does not make provisions for, and the other where the issue is outside its scope. The latter is fairly straightforward. Matters falling within art.4 (validity and property rights issues), art.5 (personal injury) and art.6 (parties' derogation from the text). Other non-explicitly excluded matters such as documentary sales (these are alluded to but no express provisions are made for them) could well fall within the scope of art.7(2). For such matters, the court is required by art.7(2) to give regard to "general principles" on which the matter is based—this could encompass domestic principles, international autonomous concepts, academic commentaries to the CISG, the Principles of European Contract Law and the UNIDROIT Principles of International Commercial Contracts 1994.[7] The worry here is that the sources of "general principles" are not exhaustive and whilst a number of commentators see this as advancing flexibility and the development of international legal norms, commercial parties are naturally concerned that there is a

---

[4] Salama, "Pragmatic Responses to Interpretive Impediments: Article 7 of the CISG, An Inter-American Application" (2006) 28 University of Miami Inter-American Law Review 225; see also Ferrari, "Applying the CISG in a truly uniform manner: Tribunale di Vigevano" (2001) NS Vol.6, Uniform Law Review/Revue de Droit Uniforme, 203.

[5] US, March 21, 2012; Federal District Court [Illinois] (*http://cisgw3.law.pace.edu/cases/120321u1.html*) [accessed April, 9, 2013].

[6] Netherlands, February 10, 2005 Netherlands Arbitration Institute (interim award) (*http://cisgw3.law.pace.edu/cases/050210n1.html*) [accessed April 9, 2013]; China, September 2004 CIETAC Arbitration proceeding (*Steel products case*) [English text] (*http://cisgw3.law.pace.edu/cases/040900c1.html*) [accessed April 9, 2013].

[7] On the relevance of the UNIDROIT Principles to interpretation of art.80 CISG, see F. Schafer, "Editorial remarks on whether and the extent to which the UNIDROIT Principles may be used to help interpret Article 80 of the CISG", (Pace Law School Institute of International Commercial Law, 2004) *http://www.cisg.law.pace.edu/cisg/biblio/schafer.html*.

loss of legal certainty. Indeed, as is evident in US case law,[8] the US judiciary when dealing with art.7(2) has turned to US jurisprudence to provide a source of "general principles". Whilst many have decried this as being US-centric and insular, there is much to be said for the desire to provide traders in the United States with some degree of legal certainty and familiarity.

Article 7(2) also stresses that only where there are no general principles is the court permitted to turn to private international law. This is of course consistent with the CISG's objective to reduce the role of private international law and to promote the development of a unified international jurisprudence.

The CISG's proponents are aware of the difficulties in interpretation of the Convention by national courts and tribunals and are determined that some positive effort should be taken to provide for a body of relevant literature[9] that decision takers can consult. In this connection, the UNCITRAL plays an important role in making public decisions on the CISG made by national courts (the Case Law on UNCITRAL Texts (CLOUT) service).[10] Indeed, it might be thought, with such a resource, there should be less force justifying nonratification principally on the argument that an established, trade-friendly system of law (such as English law) would find it difficult to adopt an international approach. That said, it might be argued that a uniform international jurisprudence on international sales leads inevitably to a minimum compromise position (in the words of Hobhouse J., "a multicultural compromise"[11]), and lacks the pragmatism the common law embodies.

The Convention also contains specific rules on how contracts should be interpreted. On ascertaining the parties intention, the CISG admits both a subjective and objective element. Article 8(1) states that a party's statements or conduct "are to be interpreted according to his intent", but this is only confined to the case where "the other party knew or could not have been unaware what that intent was". It is thus a rare situation that an inquiry into the party's subjective intention would be made. It would appear where the parties have established practices between themselves and know each other well or that the statements are so very clear that the other side could not have been unaware of the intention. A US decision[12] suggests that art.8(1) does permit

5–006

"a substantial inquiry into the parties' subjective intent, even if the parties did not engage in any objectively ascertainable means of registering this intent".

---

[8] *Zapata Hermanos Sucesores, S.A. v Hearthside Baking Co*, 313 F.3d 385, 388 (7th Cir. 2002); *Schmitz-Werke GmbH & Co v Rockland Indus., Inc*, 37 F. App'x 687, 692 (4th Cir. 2002); *Chicago Prime Packers, Inc v Northam Food Trading Co*, 408 F.3d 894 (7th Cir. 2005); *Delchi Carrier S.p.A. v Rotorex Corp*, 71 F.3d 1024, 1027–28 (2nd Cir. 1995); *Comark v Merch, Inc v Highland Group, Inc*, 932 F.2d 1196 (7th Cir. 1991); *Alberts Bonnie Brad, Inc v Ferral*, 544 N.E.2d 422, 423 (Ill. App. 4th 1989).

[9] Sometimes called a "global jurisconsultorium"; see Andersen, "The Global Jurisconsultorium of the CISG Revisited" (2009) 13(1) Vindobona Journal of International Commercial Law & Arbitration 43–70.

[10] Readers may also wish to consult websites maintained by the University of Tromso (*http://www.lexmercatoria.com*) and Pace Law School in New York (*http://www.cisg.law.pace.edu*).

[11] Hobhouse J., (1990) 106 L.Q.R. 530.

[12] CLOUT case No.222 [United States *MCC-Marble Ceramic Center v Ceramica Nuova D'Agostino*, [Federal Appellate Court] [11th Cir.] June 29, 1998; *http://cisgw3.law.pace.edu/cases/980629u1.html* [accessed April 9, 2013].

Article 8(2) takes on the more common situation. It provides that in cases not falling within art.8(1), the statements or conduct are to be interpreted

> "according to the understanding that a reasonable person of the same kind as the other party would have had in the same circumstances".

For example, if Buyer is an expert and he knew that he was accepting an old machine from Seller, a court is entitled to find that Seller was entitled to expect that Buyer concluded the contract in full knowledge of the machine's technical limitations. The test is that of a similar, reasonable expert buyer. The objective test advocated here however allows the court to give due consideration to

> "all relevant circumstances of the case including negotiations, any practices which the parties have established between themselves, usages and any subsequent conduct of the parties" (art.8(3)).

This rule of interpretation is clearly wider than the English equivalent where evidence of prior negotiations normally (*Prenn v Simmonds* [1971] 3 All E.R. 237) and of subsequent conduct (*James Miller & Partners v Whitworth Street Estates (Manchester) Ltd* [1970] A.C. 583) would be excluded. There is some controversy as to whether art.8 rejects the parol evidence rule. It would be useful for contracting parties fearing a rejection of the parol evidence rule to provide for a so-called "merger clause" in their contract. Such a clause normally states that any and all prior agreements and understandings not expressed in writing are expressly excluded. Another issue of some concern for common lawyers is whether art.8(3) might lead to silence being treated as acceptance.[13]

5–007   In conclusion, the courts are also entitled under art.9(1) to give effect to "any usage to which [the parties] have agreed and by any practices which they have established between themselves". The references in art.9(1) to "have agreed" and "established between themselves" were to allay concerns that trade usages might be imposed on developing countries by developed countries without the former's consent. However, such a restriction would obviously derogate from the need to fill gaps in the contract using established trade practice. The whole idea of wishing to resort to trade practice or usage is because the parties do not wish to have to refer to every usage there is and seek express agreement. Hence, art.9(2) provides that unless otherwise agreed, the parties will be presumed to have agreed to

> "a usage of which the parties knew or ought to have known, and which in international trade is widely known to, and regularly observed by, parties to contracts of the type involved".

It is obvious that the geographic area where the parties operate is an important factor to the question of whether the practice in question is one which the parties

---

[13] CLOUT case No.23 [United States *Filanto v Chilewich* Federal District Court [New York] April 14, 1992 *http://cisgw3.law.pace.edu/cases/920414u1.html* [accessed April 9, 2013].

knew or ought to have known. What about INCOTERMS?[14] Can it be said that these are incorporated by implication through art.9(2)? In a case from the United States,[15] it was stated that as

> "the aim of INCOTERMS, which stands for international commercial terms, is to provide a set of international rules for the interpretation of the most commonly used trade terms in foreign trade",

it should be concluded that they are incorporated into the parties' sale contract under art.9(2).[16] That appears to be the case even when INCOTERMS have not been expressly referred to as long as the trade term used is one which is clearly derived from INCOTERMS. For example, where the contract called for delivery FOB, it would seem permissible for the court to refer to INCOTERMS to flesh out the duties and rights of the parties as indicating what the parties have agreed, in reliance on art.9(2).

Formation of the Contract of Sale

On the whole, the CISG requires evidence of offer and acceptance before there could be said to exist a contract. Article 14(1) states that: **5–008**

> "[A] proposal for concluding a contract addressed to one or more specific persons constitutes an offer if it is sufficiently definite and indicates the intention of the offeror to be bound in case of acceptance".

The immediate question, naturally, is when is a proposal "sufficiently definite"? This is particularly a problem where the price for the goods has yet to be agreed. As far as the common law is concerned, the lack of a price in an offer does not necessarily mean that it would fail for lack of certainty. The CISG's solution is provided for in the second limb to art.14(1). It states that a proposal is sufficiently definite if it indicates the goods and expressly or implicitly fixes or makes provision for determining the quantity and the price. Article 55 however goes on to provide that where a contract had been validly made, but there is no price provision, the parties will be deemed impliedly to have agreed to a price "generally charged at the time of the conclusion of the contract for such goods sold under comparable circumstances in the trade concerned". This is further subject to the absence of any indication to the contrary from the facts. There is

---

[14] It might be noted that UNICITRAL has endorsed the texts of the latest INCOTERMS 2010 and UNIDROIT Principles of International Commercial Contracts 2010, which could be used in the gap-filling process of the CISG. See also: *http://www.uncitral.org/uncitral/en/other_organizations_texts.html*; *http://www.iccwbo.org/News/Articles/2012/UN-endorses-Incoterms-2010,-ICC-rules-for-international-trade/* [accessed April 9, 2013].

[15] *St Paul Insurance Company v Neuromed Medical Systems & Support* Federal District Court [New York] March 26, 2002; *http://cisgw3.law.pace.edu/cases/020326u1.html* [accessed April 9, 2013].

[16] See also United States February 7, 2006 Federal District Court [Texas] (*China North Chemical Industries Corporation v Beston Chemical Corporation*) (*http://cisgw3.law.pace.edu/cases/060207u1.html*) and United States July 19, 2007 Federal District Court [New York] (*Cedar Petrochemicals, Inc v Dongbu Hannong Chemical Co, Ltd*) (*http://cisgw3.law.pace.edu/cases/070719u1.html*) [accessed April 9, 2013].

a bit of a circuitous problem here, though. Article 55 refers to "a contract has been validly concluded" but, as noted earlier, art.14(1) would not consider that a contract had been validly made without a price or price-setting provision. In a Hungarian case,[17] it was held that an offer which did not contain the price for the aircraft engines for sale could not be a legal offer under art.14(1) and art.55 could not apply. Article 55, according to the Hungarian court, did not prevail over art.14. On the other hand, a Swiss court[18] held that art.55 operated as an exception to art.14 and would apply despite the fact that under art.14 there would have been no validly concluded contract. Although that clearly went against the literal reading of art.14, there is a view that to do otherwise would be to ignore commercial realities.[19] It is of course possible contractually to exclude the operation of Pt II (where art.14 is) or Pt III (where art.55 is held) as the parties see fit.

There is a further limitation in art.14(1)—it states that an offer should be "addressed to one or more specific persons". Proposals made to nonspecific persons, such as through a catalogue or a webpage, would not constitute an offer, only an invitation to treat offers (art.14(2)). However, where the offeror makes it plain that he does intend to make an offer to the public, art.14(2) allows that to be given proper effect to.

5–009   An offer can be withdrawn. Withdrawing an offer however is not the same as the revocation of an offer, under the CISG. A withdrawal becomes effective as soon as it reaches the offeree before or at the same time as the offer (art.15(2)), whilst a revocation is effective if it reaches the offeree before he has dispatched an acceptance (art.16(1)). These are fairly uncontroversial provisions. However, art.16(2) introduces a concept alien to the English lawyer—an irrevocable offer. An irrevocable offer is not binding, in English law, because it is not supported by consideration.

Article 16(2) provides that an offer:

(a) if it indicates, whether by stating a fixed time for acceptance or otherwise, that it is irrevocable; or

(b) if it was reasonable for the offeree to rely on the offer as being irrevocable and the offeree has acted in reliance on the offer.

It should not be thought that art.16(2)(a) simply means that an offer will endure for a fixed period of time before it lapses or is revoked. That, of course, is no different to the concept of a standing offer in the common law. However, art.16(2)(a) seems to be far more robust than that. That said, a proposal by West Germany during the negotiations to make it clear that an offer is actually irrevocable (meaning no revocation) until the lapse of the fixed period was rejected. That said, so was the United Kingdom's proposal for a more common law based interpretation. The net result is thus uncertainty. For pragmatic reasons, offerors would do well to make things clear when making proposals.

---

[17] CLOUT case No.53 (September 25, 1992; Hungary Supreme Court) (*http://cisgw3.law. pace.edu/cases/920925h1.html* [accessed April 9, 2013]).

[18] CLOUT case No.215; Switzerland, Bezirksgericht [District Court] St Gallen July 3, 1997 (*http:/ /cisgw3.law.pace.edu/cases/970703s1.html* [accessed April 9, 2013]).

[19] See also, ICC International Court of Arbitration, case No.9819 of 1999; *http://cisgw3.law. pace.edu/cases/999819i1.html* [accessed April 9, 2013].

The rule for acceptance is that it becomes effective when it reaches the offeror as long as it does so within the time he has fixed or, if no time is fixed, within a reasonable time (art.18(2)). Late acceptance is usually of no effect but art.21(1) provides that the offeror may nevertheless make it effective by so informing the offeree without delay. Article 21(2) makes special provisions where the transmission of the acceptance had been unduly interrupted—that is to say, where under normal conditions the acceptance would have reached the offeror. When this occurs, the onus is on the offeror to inform the offeree without delay that he considers his offer to have lapsed. This is to pass the risk to the offeror.

As far as acceptance by conduct is concerned, it was noted by a Californian court[20] that the CISG recognises a party's conduct as a form of acceptance. In that case, the Australian seller had sent a sales quote identifying the goods, quantity and price to the US buyer. The buyer then incorporated the sales quote into its presentation to a third party buyer in California which later agreed to buy the goods. The buyer then placed the order with the Australian seller for direct delivery to the sub-buyer. The court held that the buyer's conduct represented acceptance of the seller's general terms and conditions. **5–010**

International commercial contracts are frequently made through the exchange of correspondence and communications. This potentially raises the difficulty in ascertaining when the offer and acceptance had taken place. The battle of forms is only very nominally referred to in the CISG. Article 19(1) adopts the traditional "mirror image" rule, that an acceptance which adds to or modifies the terms of the offer constitutes only a counter-offer. The "mirror image" rule is however qualified by art.19(2) and (3) in these terms:

"(2) However, a reply to an offer which purports to be an acceptance but contains additional or different terms which do not materially alter the terms of the offer constitutes an acceptance, unless the offeror, without undue delay, objects orally to the discrepancy or dispatches a notice to that effect. If he does not so object, the terms of the contract are the terms of the offer with the modifications contained in the acceptance.

(3) Additional or different terms relating, among other things, to the price, payment, quality and quantity of the goods, place and time of delivery, extent of one party's liability to the other or the settlement of disputes are considered to alter the terms of the offer materially".

It has also been reported in an Austrian decision that regard should be had to the presumed intentions of parties and relevant trade usage as to what is a material modification.[21] An issue of some importance has arisen as to jurisdiction clauses—do they form a material modification if one's party's form refers to a jurisdiction choice different from that contained in the other party? In a US case, *CSS Antenna Inc v Amphenol-Tuchel Electronics GmbH* 764 F Supp. 2d 745 (D. Md. 2011), the court held that a forum selection provision relates to "settlement of disputes" therefore it should be treated as a material alteration. In *Belcher-Robinson LLC v Linamar Corp*, 699 F. Supp 2d 1329 (M.D. Ala. 2010) the

---

[20] *Golden Valley Grape Juice v Centrisys Corp* No CV F 09-1424 LJO GSA 2010 US Dist LEXIS 11884 (e.d. Cal. Jan 21, 2010).

[21] CLOUT case No.189 Austria Oberster Gerichtshof [Supreme Court] March 20, 1997 (*http://cisgw3.law.pace.edu/cases/970320a3.html* [accessed April 9, 2013]).

Alabama court was less convinced that a forum selection provision always works as a material alteration. It might be said that the *Antenna* case more closely reflects the tenor of art.19(3).

5–011 The following have been considered in existing case law as not being material modifications:

1. a reply that modified the offer by stating that the price would be modified by increases as well as decreases in the market price[22];

2. deferring delivery of one item of the bulk[23];

3. a standard term reserving the right to change the delivery date[24];

4. a request that the buyer draft a formal termination agreement[25];

5. a request to treat the contract as confidential until a joint public announcement is made[26]; and

6. a requirement that the buyer should reject the goods within a stated period.[27]

An interesting question has arisen as to whether a modification which is to the benefit of the offeror should be considered as a material modification.[28] It is however questioned as to whether that which the offeror had not specified for could properly be described as for his benefit, commercially speaking.

Other than art.19, there is nothing else in the CISG dealing with the battle of the forms. However, given the international nature of the convention, it may be permissible for national courts to consider the UNIDROIT Principles. Article 2.19 of the Principles permits contracts to be made by conduct. Moreover, art.2.22 of the 1994 Principles, states that:

> "[W]here both parties use standard terms and reach agreement except on those terms, a contract is concluded on the basis of the agreed terms and of any standard terms which are common in substance unless one party clearly indicates in advance, or later and without undue delay informs the other party, that it does not intend to be bound by such a contract".

[22] CLOUT case No.158 France Cour d'appel [Appellate Court] Paris April 22, 1992, *http://cisgw3.law.pace.edu/cases/920422f1.html, affirmed*, CLOUT case No.155 [France Cour de Cassation [Supreme Court] January 4, 1995, *http://cisgw3.law.pace.edu/cases/950104f1.html*] [accessed April 9, 2013].

[23] CLOUT case No.158 France Cour d'appel [Appellate Court] Paris April 22, 1992, *http://cisgw3.law.pace.edu/cases/920422f1.html, affirmed*, CLOUT case No.155 [France Cour de Cassation [Supreme Court] January 4, 1995, *http://cisgw3.law.pace.edu/cases/950104f1.html*] [accessed April 9, 2013].

[24] CLOUT case No.362 Germany Oberlandesgericht [Appellate Court] Naumburg April 27, 1999, *http://cisgw3.law.pace.edu/cases/990427g1.html* [accessed April 9, 2013].

[25] China CIETAC Arbitration Award case No.75 of April 1, 1993, *http://cisgw3.law.pace.edu/cases/930401c1.html* [accessed April 9, 2013].

[26] Hungary Fováosi Bíróság [Metropolitan Court] Budapest January 10, 1992, *http://cisgw3.law.pace.edu/cases/920110h1.html* [accessed April 9, 2013].

[27] CLOUT case No.50 Germany Landgericht [District Court] Baden-Baden August 14, 1991, *http://cisgw3.law.pace.edu/cases/910814g1.html* [accessed April 9, 2013].

[28] See CLOUT case No.189 Austria Oberster Gerichtshof [Supreme Court] March 20, 1997, *http://cisgw3.law.pace.edu/cases/970320a3.html* [accessed April 9, 2013].

The provision clearly envisages the likelihood that there may not be a "mirror image" in all cases involving the battle of the forms. A distinction is made between the conclusion of the agreement and the agreement as to the precise contents of the agreement. It would appear that as regards content, the terms which are common in substance will be binding but conflicting terms will not. Those areas where the conflicting terms relate would not be resolved using the contract, but by reference to the Principles and the applicable law of the contract. It would seem to follow that any "last shot" principle, as alluded to in an old English case *British Road Services Ltd v Arthur V Crutchley & Co* [1968] 1 All E.R. 811,[29] would be rejected by this approach.

Article 2.22 lays down this proviso: "unless one party clearly indicates *in advance* ... that it does not intend to be bound" (emphasis added). The commentary to the Principles states that a "clear indication" is not just given by a respective standard clause in terms of business or its interpretation, it should be an explicit special declaration.

The Parties' Rights and Obligations

Delivery of goods

A central duty of the seller in a contract of sale is necessarily the duty to deliver the goods (or documents relating to the goods). Article 30 states: **5–012**

> "The seller must deliver the goods, hand over any document relating to them and transfer the property in the goods, as required by the contract and this Convention".

However, given that art.4 is not concerned with "the effect which the contract may have on the property of the goods sold", what the seller must do to discharge his obligation in art.30 to transfer property to the buyer is a matter for the applicable law of the contract. In this regard, thus, the CISG makes room for the role of the applicable law of the contract.

Articles 31–34 provide detailed rules on the performance of the general obligation in art.30, including provisions on the handing over of any documents relating to the goods. Article 33 requires delivery to be made in accordance with the time stated in the contract and, where this is not stated, within a reasonable time.

A US case showing how reasonableness might be ascertained is *Alpha Prime v Holland Loader* (C.A. No 09-cv-01763-WYD-KMT, 2010 US Dist LEXIS 67591 (D. Colo. July 6, 2010). There, the court found that there was substantial dispute over whether the seller's delivery of the refurbished loader 10 months after the conclusion of the contract was reasonable under art.33. It stressed that reasonableness had to be decided based on what is "acceptable commercial conduct in the circumstances".[30]

---

[29] The principle states that the party who makes the most recent reference to his set of terms shall be treated as the offeror and as long as the other party has demonstrated some sign of assent, the contract is presumed to have been made on the terms of the party delivering the "last shot". But now, see *Butler Machine Tool v Ex-Cell-O Corp Ltd* [1979] 1 All E.R. 965.

[30] The court cited the Official Commentary to the CISG 109.

Late delivery is a breach of contract and if the delivery date was essential, it will constitute a fundamental breach (art.25) for which a declaration of avoidance may be possible (art.26). Unlike English law, time is not necessarily of the essence in international sales. Hence, if the parties wish to ensure that time is of the essence, they should make clear that a breach of time of delivery shall be treated as a fundamental breach. Naturally, where the seller pre-signifies to the buyer that he will not be delivering goods at the time of delivery, that would be an anticipatory breach (art.71).

Conformity of goods

5–013   Article 35 states that the seller must deliver goods which are of the quantity, quality and description required by the contract and which are contained or packaged in the manner required by the contract. Conformity is then further described in art.35(2) (subject to any agreement to the contrary)[31] as the goods should:

(a) be fit for the purpose for which goods of the same description would ordinarily be used;

(b) be fit for any particular purpose expressly or impliedly made known to the seller unless under the circumstances, the buyer did not rely on the seller's skill and judgment, or it was unreasonable for the buyer to do so;

(c) possess the qualities of goods which the seller has held out to the buyer as a sample or model;

(d) be contained or packaged in the manner usual for such goods or where there is no such manner, in a manner adequate to preserve and protect the goods.

Additionally, the seller would not be in breach if at the time of the contract, the buyer knew or could not have been unaware of the lack of conformity.

On the question of whether there is a requirement under art.35(2)(a) that goods exported should meet the requirements of the importing country where that is the place the goods will subsequently be marketed and sold, there has been some confusion. The question is whether "ordinarily be used" refers to circumstances and conditions at the importing country or somewhere else more generally. In a case from Germany[32] it was considered that it was not reasonable to expect a seller to know what local requirements are and as such, there was no breach of art.35(1) and art.35(2)(a) if the goods are acceptable in some countries but not the importing state. There, it was ruled that the fact that mussels sold to the buyer's country contained cadmium levels exceeding the recommendations of the buyer's country's health regulations did not mean the mussels failed to conform.

---

[31] The implied warranties of merchantability and fitness under the CISG may be disclaimed or excluded; see also art.6 which permits the parties to "derogate from or vary the effect of any of [the CISG's] provisions" and that should include art.35. See also the US case of *Norfolk S Ry v Power Source Supply* C.A. no 06-58 J, 2008 US Dis LECIS 56942 (W.D. Pa July 25, 2008).

[32] CLOUT case No.123 Germany Bundesgerichtshof [Supreme Court] March 8, 1995 (*http://cisgw3.law.pace.edu/cases/950308g3.html* [accessed April 9, 2013]).

In another case,[33] a seller who delivered video recorders to a Swiss buyer with instructions only in German and not in the other languages spoken in Switzerland, was held to have delivered nonconforming goods. The difference lies very much in what is reasonable under the circumstances and what is known to the seller. In the latter, it was reasonable that, given the close proximity between the German seller and Swiss buyer, the seller would know that instructions should be provided in the main languages spoken in Switzerland. On the other hand, it was not reasonable to expect the seller in the mussels case to know what the local health requirements were.

A similar issue arises in art.35(2)(d). That article refers to packaging in the "manner usual for such goods". The question is whether the seller is required to package the goods in a manner required by the laws of the importing country (which may be unique to that country). In a French case,[34] it was held that the seller was in breach where the cheese sold had been packaged in a manner inconsistent with the importing country's food labelling laws. It would appear that the appropriate approach should be what is reasonable and consistent with the other terms of the contract.

An American case[35] suggests to us that the burden is on the buyer to show the lack of conformity. The appellate court reasoned that although the CISG is silent on this issue, a comparison with the US Uniform Commercial Code (UCC) indicates that the burden should rest with the buyer. The reference and reliance to the UCC is somewhat controversial because some commentators are of the view that domestic law should not be relied on in the interpretation of the CISG.[36] **5–014**

Article 36(1) lays down the general rule that the seller is liable for a lack of conformity that exists at the time the risk passes to the buyer. The relevant time is the time when the loss of conformity comes into existence, not the time it is discovered or indeed, the time when it ought to have been discovered. Evidence showing the lack of conformity at the time the risk passes is therefore critical. It thus becomes imperative also to ascertain who actually bears the burden of proof. There is no guidance on how best to resolve this issue.

The seller will also continue to be liable for conformity if he had guaranteed the future fitness of the goods (art.36(2)). It is unclear to what extent such a guarantee might be implied from the circumstances of the case.

The buyer must examine the goods within a short period of time (art.38(1)). This provision received much support from developing countries. The consequences of failing to do this can be devastating. The time when a buyer is required to examine the goods is closely linked to the time when the buyer "ought to have discovered" a lack of conformity under art.39. Under art.39, the buyer loses his right to rely on the lack of conformity if he does not give notice to the seller about the lack of conformity within a reasonable time after *he has discovered or ought to have discovered the nonconformity.* Therefore, a buyer who does not examine the goods within a short period of time could thus fail to give the requisite notice under art.39 thereby costing him his right to rely on non- **5–015**

---

[33] CLOUT case No.343 Germany Landgericht [District Court] Darmstadt May 9, 2000, *http://cisgw3.law.pace.edu/cases/000509g1.html* [accessed April 9, 2013].

[34] CLOUT case No.202 France Cour d'appel [Appellate Court] Grenoble September 13, 1995, *http://cisgw3.law.pace.edu/cases/950913f1.htm* [accessed April 9, 2013].

[35] *Chicago Prime Packers v Northam Food Trading* 408 F 3d 894 (7th Cir 2005).

[36] See para.5–005 where we disagree with this view.

conformity. In a somewhat controversial US case, there is dicta that where the seller is already aware of the non-conformity, then no notice from the buyer is necessary (In *Re Siskiyou Evergreens Inc* (No 02–66975-fra11, 2004 Bankr LEXIS 1044 (Bankr. D. Or. Mar 29, 2004). In the interest of certainty, a better view would be to insist strictly on the notice although it has to be said that the Oregon Bankruptcy Court's decision focuses mainly on the purposive reading of art.39. There is some comfort for the buyer though in that art.44 at least allows him to reduce the price (in accordance with art.55) or claim for damages if he has a reasonable excuse for his failure to give the requisite notice.

There is however no provision in the CISG detailing how an examination should be carried out. Cases have diverged, for example, on whether sampling would be appropriate and to what extent.[37] It has been suggested that how the examination should be carried would largely depend on the parties' commercial practices, trade usage and reasonableness of the circumstances. It is submitted that as art.38 could quite easily cost the buyer his right to rely on nonconformity, it should be construed generally in favour of the buyer, rather than the seller.

Duty to pay and take delivery

5–016   The buyer is required by art.53 to pay the price for the goods and take delivery of them as required by the contract and the Convention. This duty will necessarily entail taking appropriate steps and complying with such formalities as may be required under the contract or any laws and regulations to enable payment to be made (art.54). Plainly, art.54 will be breached if the buyer failed to open a letter of credit in time or to authorise properly a money transfer. What about situations where government approval is required for the fund transfer and the buyer fails to obtain this? One view is that as long as the buyer has taken all steps required by the government concerned to secure the approval, he would have met the requirements of art.54. After all, he cannot singularly influence the decision of the authorities. On the other hand, it might be argued that by promising to pay, he had undertaken an absolute duty, subject only to the government's refusal falling to be considered as a frustrating event under art.79.

Article 58(1) requires the buyer to pay the price when the seller places either the goods or documents controlling their disposition at his disposal, subject only to the contract requiring him to pay at a specific time. This reference in art.58(1)

---

[37] CLOUT case No.230 Germany Oberlandesgericht [Appellate Court] Karlsruhe June 25, 1997, *http://cisgw3.law.pace.edu/cases/970625g1.html* [accessed April 9, 2013]; CLOUT case No.232 Germany Oberlandesgericht [Appellate Court] München March 11, 1998 *http://cisgw3.law.pace.edu/ cases/980311g1.html* [accessed April 9, 2013]; CLOUT case No.98 Netherlands Rechtbank [District Court] Roermond December 19, 1991, *http://cisgw3.law.pace.edu/cases/911219n1.html* [accessed April 9, 2013]; Austria Obester Gerichtshof [Supreme Court] August 27, 1999, *http://cisgw3.law. pace.edu/cases/990827a3.html* [accessed April 9, 2013]; CLOUT case No.292 Germany Oberlandesgericht [Appellate Court] Saarbrücken January 13, 1993, *http://cisgw3.law.pace.edu/cases/ 930113g1.html* [accessed April 9, 2013]; CLOUT case No.285 Germany Oberlandesgericht [Appellate Court] Koblenz September 11, 1998, *http://cisgw3.law.pace.edu/cases/980911g1.html* [accessed April 9, 2013]; CLOUT case No.251 Switzerland Handelsgericht [Commercial Court] Zürich November 30, 1998, *http://cisgw3.law.pace.edu/cases/981130s1.html* [accessed April 9, 2013]; CLOUT case No.81 Germany Oberlandesgericht [Appellate Court] Düsseldorf February 10, 1994, *http://cisgw3.law.pace.edu/cases/940210g1.html* [accessed April 9, 2013]; CLOUT case No.4 Germany Landgericht [District Court] Stuttgart August 31, 1989, *http://cisgw3.law.pace.edu/cases/ 890831g1.html* [accessed April 9, 2013].

to "specific time" has been problematic. Can a "specific time" be time range or the occurrence of certain events? In a Swiss case,[38] the parties had agreed that payment of 30 per cent of the price would be made at the time of the order, 30 per cent at the start of assembly, 30 per cent at the completion of installation, and 10 per cent after successful start-up of the facility. The Swiss Supreme Court held that payment was to be made at a specific time and not when the goods are placed at the buyer's disposal.

In sales involving a transport contract, art.58(2) provides that the seller may dispatch the goods on terms whereby the goods or documents will not be handed over until payment is made. If the parties wish for payment to be made on different conditions, they should exclude art.58(2) from their contract (art.6).

Article 58(3) provides that the buyer is not bound to pay until he has had an **5–017** opportunity to examine the goods, unless the procedures for delivery or payment agreed upon by the parties are inconsistent with his having such an opportunity. The provision is silent as to whether a buyer may suspend payment of the price in the event that examination reveals that the goods are not in conformity. It is open to the parties to exclude art.58(3) from applying to them (art.6). Thus, might it be said that a CIF or CFR contract, by implication, dispenses with the right to examine the goods?

As regards taking delivery, art.60 states that the buyer's duty consists in doing all the acts which could reasonably be expected of him in order to enable the seller to make delivery and in actually taking over the goods. Again, it should be clear that where the contract is made on CIF or CFR terms, this duty is dispensed with. It has also frequently been said art.60 envisages the buyer undertaking a duty to cooperate. An example would be that the buyer should make sure that his workers are on site to open the premises to the seller's lorries. The qualification is "reasonably be expected of him"—where the seller is acting in breach he will not be entitled to expect the buyer to bend over backwards to take delivery. For example, if the contract requires the seller to provide the workers to unload the goods, they cannot then expect the buyer to provide the staff to carry the goods if the seller's workers happen to be ill. Whether the duty is wider than the English law implied term of cooperation (*All Russian Cooperative Society v Benjamin Smith* (1923) 14 Ll. L. Rep. 351) remains to be seen.

Remedies of the Buyer and Seller

General concepts

An essential concept relevant to remedies under the Convention is the concept of **5–018** a fundamental breach. Article 25 states:

"A breach of contract committed by one of the parties is fundamental if it results in such detriment to the other party as substantially to deprive him of what he is entitled to expect under the contract, unless the party in breach did

---

[38] CLOUT case No.194 Switzerland Bundesgericht [Supreme Court] January 18, 1996, *http://cisgw3.law.pace.edu/cases/960118s1.html* [accessed April 9, 2013].

not foresee and a reasonable person of the same kind in the same circumstances would not have foreseen such a result".

Thus, whether a contract may be avoided depends on whether the breach will substantially deprive the aggrieved party of what he is entitled to expect under the contract. The test is based on the presumed intention of the parties. In cases of non conformity of goods, much depends on the seriousness of the breach. In *Banks Hardwoods Florida LLC v Maderas Iglesias SA* (No 08-23497-CIV, 2009 WL 3618011 (S.D. Fla. Oct 29, 2009), the buyer in Florida had rejected the timber as non-conforming but had sold some of it eventually and made part payment to the seller. The court felt unable to find at summary judgment stage whether the breach was slight or not. Material factual issues had to be resolved and these could only be done at trial. On the other hand, the US court in *Doolim Corp v R Doll* (No 08 Civ 1587(BSJ)(HBP) 2009 WL 1514913 (S.D.N.Y May 29, 2009) observed that a buyer's failure to pay for more than a "small fraction" of the goods constituted fundamental breach of the contract. The buyer had paid only $200,000 which the court noted was less than 20 per cent of the purchase price. There was also persistent refusal to the seller's demands for payment. That meant that the buyer had "substantially deprived [the seller] of the performance that it had a right to expect from [the buyer]" namely, full payment within 15 days of delivery. The seller was allowed therefore to avoid the contract.

There is however a further criterion to the concept of a fundamental breach. It requires that the party at fault did not foresee the result. However as Bridge noted:

"[G]iven the stringency of the test of substantial impairment, it would be a strangely unimaginative contract breaker who failed to foresee effects of such magnitude".[39]

5–019   Article 25 is particularly silent as to *when* the requirement of foresight is to be applied. Should the person in breach foresee the consequences of the breach at the time of the breach or at the time the contract was made? It has been argued that since the detriment is defined in terms of expectation under the contract, it might seem that the conclusion of the contract, not the moment of breach, should be the determining time.[40]

It might also be said that under art.25, the burden of proof is with the person in breach. He has to prove that he did not foresee the consequences of his breach and that a reasonable person of the same kind in the same circumstances would not have foreseen such an effect. The aggrieved party on the other hand has to prove that the breach deprived him substantially of what he was entitled to expect under the contract.

The aggrieved party, following a fundamental breach, may terminate the contract but in order to do so, he must give a notice of avoidance to the other party (art.26). There is no such thing as an automatic termination, under the Convention. The provision unfortunately is silent as to what constitutes effective notice. What if the buyer simply turns away the goods? Is that notice of

---

[39] M. Bridge, *The International Sale of Goods*, 2nd edn (Oxford: Oxford University Press, 2007) para.12.25.
[40] Barry, "The Vienna Convention on International Sales Law" (1989) 105 L.Q.R. 201.

avoidance? It would appear that something more explicit is needed given the need for legal certainty in international commercial relationships.

Under certain circumstances, a contracting party has the right to suspend performance (as against terminating the contract) when the other side appears not to be honouring his part of the bargain. Article 71(1) provides that a party may suspend performance if it becomes apparent that the other party will not perform a substantial part of the contract as a result of:

- serious deficiency in his ability to perform;

- lack of creditworthiness;

- his conduct in preparing to perform or in the actual performance.

An example might be seen in the US case of *Doolim Corp v R Doll* (above) where the seller was entitled under art.71 to withhold shipment of the knit garments when the buyer had failed to obtain a letter of credit to be issued in the seller's favour. The magistrate judge found that the seller had "well grounded fears" about the buyer's performance under the contract.

The right to suspend under art.71 must be distinguished from the right to avoid **5–020** the contract under art.72 for an anticipatory breach. An anticipatory breach under art.72(1) requires that it should be "clear that one of the parties will commit a fundamental breach". Article 71 on the other hand refers to "becomes apparent". A criticism though is that whilst there is a discernible difference in theory, it is exceedingly difficult to make a practical distinction between "clear" and "apparent". If a party wishes to suspend performance, he must give notice immediately to the other side. Again, there is no provision in the CISG on what constitutes effective notice for this purpose.

The Convention also makes provision for special remedies for the innocent parties. Articles 45 and 61 provide, respectively, that the buyer and seller are conferred certain remedies. In the event of a breach by the seller, the buyer may:

- exercise the rights in arts 46–52;

- claim damages as provided in arts 74–77.

As for the seller, he may:

- exercise his rights under arts 62–65;

- claim damages as provided in arts 74–77.

Buyer's right to repair or delivery of substitute goods

Under art.46(2), in case of lack of conformity the buyer may request the seller to repair the goods, unless this is in all the circumstances unreasonable. If, however, the lack of conformity constitutes a fundamental breach, he may request the seller to substitute the goods. In either case, the buyer's request is dependent on the service of the notice of lack of conformity required by art.39. It should be noted that the buyer would not be deprived of his right to damages by invoking art.46 (indeed, any of the remedies in arts 46–52) (art.45(2)).

Seller's right to cure

5–021   Article 48(1) provides that the seller may, even after the date for delivery, remedy at his own expense any failure to perform his obligations, if he can do so without unreasonable delay and without causing the buyer unreasonable inconvenience or uncertainty of reimbursement by the seller of expenses advanced by the buyer. However, the buyer retains any right to claim damages under the Convention. The seller can ask the buyer whether he will accept late performance within a specified period. If the buyer fails to respond within a reasonable time, the seller is entitled to proceed with performance. During this time, the buyer is not permitted to seek any remedy inconsistent with the seller's performance (art.48(2)).

Parties' right to extra time for performance

5–022   This has sometimes been described as *Nachfrist* ("the period after"). In general, it is the right of either party to set an additional period of time of reasonable length for performance by the other party (arts 47(1), 49(1)(b), 63(1), 64(1)(b)). There is a duty on the party fixing the period not to resort to any remedy for breach of contract during this additional period of time. Of course, the bets are off if the party given extra time indicates to the other party that he will not perform during that time. There are basically three situations which could conceivably invoke *nachfrist*:

- failure by the seller to deliver; or

- failure by the buyer to take delivery; or

- failure by the buyer to pay the price.

The extra time fixed should of a reasonable length. In a German case[41] involving art.47(1) which provides that the buyer may fix an additional period of time of reasonable length to enable the seller to perform or complete performance, an extension by two weeks for the delivery of three printing machines from Germany to Egypt was deemed to be too short, whereas a period of seven weeks was regarded as reasonable. This is essentially a question of fact.

Buyer's right to price reduction

5–023   Article 50 entitles the buyer, in case of nonconformity of the goods, to reduce the price

> "in the same proportion as the value that the goods actually delivered had at the time of delivery bears to the value that conforming goods would have had at that time".

This remedy is applicable regardless of whether the nonconformity is a fundamental or a simple breach, whether or not the seller was negligent or

---

[41] CLOUT case No.136 Germany Oberlandesgericht [Appellate Court] Celle May 24, 1995, *http://cisgw3.law.pace.edu/cases/950524g1.html* [accessed April 9, 2013].

whether the seller was excused from liability under art.79 (frustration-type events). In the case of art.79 (namely where the seller is unable to perform due to an impediment beyond his control), the buyer would not be able to claim in damages. However, art.50 at least offers him a remedy to reduce the price accordingly. The remedy also does not depend on whether the buyer has paid or not. Resort to the remedy is not an obstacle to a claim for damages (art.45(2) for example).

The reduction should take into account the value of the delivered goods compared with the value conforming goods would have. Thus, usually, a relevant date for the comparison of values is the date of actual delivery at the place of delivery.[42]

The parties' right to avoid the contract

The parties may declare the contract avoided: **5–024**

1. if a failure by the other party to perform any of his obligations amounts to a fundamental breach; or

2. if a party fails to perform within a *Nachfrist* fixed by the other party; or

3. if, during the *Nachfrist*, a party declares that he will not perform.

Avoidance, according to art.81, releases both parties from their obligations subject to any damages which may be due.

It is possible for restitution to be made when the contract is avoided. Article 81(2) states that a party who has performed in whole or in part may claim restitution of anything supplied or paid. This may involve requiring the seller to ask for the goods back or the buyer to seek a refund of deposits. Article 84(1) states that if a price refund is payable, the seller must also pay interest on it, from the date on which the price was paid. It is submitted that "price" includes also a deposit, as part of the price. In the case of the buyer making restitution of the goods, art.84(2), he must also "account to the seller" for all benefits it derived from the goods before making such restitution.

One difficult issue has arisen in relation to art.81(2)—where should the restitution be made? This is of course an important question because it in turn leads to the issue as to who bears the risk. Consider the following example, A and B have avoided the contract. A places the goods at the berth where the goods were originally delivered. B insists that the goods should be returned to the original port of shipment. The goods are then stolen. Who bears the risk? In a German case,[43] it was held that as the CISG is silent on this, reliance should be made on the national law which governs the enforcement of a judgment ordering such restitution. This is consistent with art.28 which provides that a court is not bound to enter a judgment for specific performance unless it would do so under its own law in respect of similar contracts of sale not governed by the CISG. That

---

[42] See, for example, CLOUT case No.56 Switzerland Pretore [District Court] Canton of Ticino, Locarno Campagna April 27, 1992, *http://cisgw3.law.pace.edu/cases/920427s1.html* [accessed April 9, 2013]; CLOUT case No.175 Austria Oberlandesgericht [Appellate Court] Graz November 9, 1995, *http://cisgw3.law.pace.edu/cases/951109a3.html* [accessed April 9, 2013].

[43] Germany Landgericht [District Court] Landshut April 5, 1995, *http://cisgw3.law.pace.edu/cases/950405g1.html* [accessed April 9, 2013].

said, it is a little disappointing that on such an important remedy, the CISG passes it back to national law for a determination.

Before these restitutionary remedies are resorted to, the contract must first be properly avoided. Avoidance is a precondition to restitution under the CISG.

The parties' remedy in cases of partial performance or excess performance

5–025   Articles 51 and 52 envisage four situations—where the seller:

1. delivers only part of the goods;

2. delivers all the goods but some are nonconforming;

3. delivers before the time of delivery; or

4. delivers more than agreed.

In the case of partial performance (1. and 2.), art.51 provides that the remedies mentioned above shall apply in respect of the part which is not conforming or not delivered.

Example: Under a contract, A delivers 100 cars to B. Five cars are not of satisfactory quality. This would clearly fall within 2. above. Under art.51, B should be entitled to:

1. require A to repair or substitute the cars;

2. ask for a price reduction;

3. avoid the contract for the five cars (partial avoidance).

It is immediately obvious that in English law, there is no such thing as a partial avoidance. Indeed, although it is an available remedy under the CISG, it is not one which could be easily invoked because the buyer will need to demonstrate that defectiveness of the five cars is such as to deprive buyer of what he is entitled to expect with respect to the five cars and that the circumstances are such that substitution or repair would not be reasonable. Of course, where if it is proved that the failure to deliver the five conforming cars constitute *a fundamental breach* (art.25), the buyer may avoid the *entire* contract (art.51(2)). In the case of contracts requiring delivery by instalments, the rules of avoidance would apply to each individual delivery. So, where a contract calls for 10 instalments and one turns out to be nonconforming, the aggrieved party may avoid the contract with respect to that shipment. That is to say, a fundamental breach has been committed in relation to that shipment. However, the single instalment would render the entire contract unacceptable, the buyer would have cause to treat that breach as a fundamental breach of the entire contract.

5–026   In the case of a delivery made too early, the buyer can refuse to take delivery (art.52(1). If he decides to reject, he may be required to

"take possession of them on behalf of the seller, provided that this can be done without payment of the price and without unreasonable inconvenience or unreasonable expense" (art.86(2)) and "to preserve them as are reasonable in the circumstances" (art.86(1)).

As regards a delivery made in excess of the quantity ordered, the buyer is entitled to accept or reject the excess quantity. If he takes delivery of all or part of the excess quantity, he must pay for it at the contract rate (art.52(2)).

Seller's right to make specification

Article 65 tries to remedy a situation where the buyer is given the right to make specifications for the goods but fails to do so within a reasonable or contractual time. At common law, such a failure by the buyer would constitute a breach of contract and all the incidences of a breach would attach. In contradistinction, art.65(1) provides that the seller may continue with the contract by making the specification himself in accordance with the requirements of the buyer that may be known to him. Article 65(2) requires the seller to inform the buyer and fix a reasonable time within which the buyer may make a different specification. If the buyer fails to respond properly, the specifications chosen by the seller will become binding. It must be said that this provision conflicts with accepted international commercial practice and flies in the face of any principle requiring the plaintiff/claimant (the seller) to mitigate his loss. **5–027**

The parties' entitlement to damages

The standard principle is set out in art.74:

> "Damages for breach of contract by one party consist of a sum equal to the loss, including loss of profit, suffered by the other party as a consequence of the breach. Such damages may not exceed the loss which the party in breach foresaw or ought to have foreseen at the time of the conclusion of the contract, in the light of the facts and matters of which he then knew or ought to have known, as a possible consequence of the breach of contract".

This, it has to be said, is largely comparable the English remoteness of damage rule in *Hadley v Baxendale* (1854) 9 Exch. 341.

However, art.74 is to be applied alongside another noteworthy provision —art.77. Article 77 states that a party who relies on a breach of contract must take reasonable measures to mitigate the loss but it is silent as to when the aggrieved party should take such measures. In the context of the CISG, the period before avoidance of the contract but after the breach (for example, the *Nachfrist* or the time given for making repairs or delivery of substitute goods) can cause peculiar problems. In English law, where there is no such legally nebulous period, the issue as to when the duty to mitigate attaches does not arise. In a couple of CISG cases,[44] it has been held that the aggrieved party is not obliged to mitigate in the period before the contract is avoided.

A related problem is in relation to anticipatory breaches. Would the aggrieved party who failed to accept the repudiation be held to have failed to mitigate his **5–028**

---

[44] CLOUT case No.361 Germany Oberlandesgericht [Appellate Court] Braunschweig October 28, 1999, *http://cisgw3.law.pace.edu/cases/991028g1.html* [accessed April 9, 2013]; CLOUT case No.130 Germany Oberlandesgericht [Appellate Court] Düsseldorf January 14, 1994, *http://cisgw3 .law.pace.edu/cases/940114g1.html* [accessed April 9, 2013].

loss if the events were such that had he accepted the anticipatory breach earlier on, the loss would have been smaller? Honnold gives the following example:

"On June 1 A and X made a contract for A to sell and deliver to X on August 1 1,000 bales of cotton at $50 per bale. Both A and X were merchants engaged in the purchase and resale of cotton. Shortly after June 1 cotton prices fell and on July 1, when the market price was $40 per bale, buyer X repudiated the contract and requested A to resell the cotton before the market could decline further. A replied that A expected X to receive and pay for the cotton in accordance with the contract; X thereupon repeated its repudiation. By August 1, the agreed delivery date, the price had fallen to $30; X again refused to receive and pay for the goods. A thereupon declared the contract avoided, resold the goods for $30 per bale ($30,000) and claimed damages from X of $20,000 ($50,000–$30,000). X contended that on July 1, when X repudiated, A should have mitigated loss by selling the cotton at $40, a step that would have reduced damages from $20,000 to $10,000".[45]

It might be argued that in such a case, there was nothing wasteful or unreasonable in A's refusal to accept X's repudiation. On that basis, A should not be held to have failed to comply with art.77.

Another problematic provision to be applied alongside art.74 is art.78. That article provides that if a party fails to pay the price or any arrears, the other party is entitled to interest on it, without prejudice to any claim for damages recoverable under art.74. Article 74 however specifies neither the amount of interest nor the way interest is to be calculated (for example, when should interest commence). It simply confers on the aggrieved party a general right to interest. This then begs the question as to whether the award of interest is a matter which is mentioned in the convention but not expressly settled by the Convention, or simply, one that is not governed by the Convention at all. The implications of this issue of characterisation is important. Under the Convention, the former is to be dealt with quite differently from the latter. It may be recalled that under art.7(2) the former will have to be settled in conformity with the general principles on which the Convention is based or, in the absence of those principles, in conformity with the law applicable by virtue of the rules of private international law. Conversely, if the matter is outside the Convention's scope, it must be resolved using the law applicable by virtue of the rules of private international law, without any recourse to the "general principles" of the Convention. It appears that the practice is to apply the rate provided for by the applicable law of the contract of sale, if the contract had not been governed by the CISG. In short, the application of the putative proper law.

Impossibility of performance

5–029 As with any good system of contract law, the CISG provides for events rendering the contract impossible to perform. Article 79 states:

"A party is not liable for a failure to perform any of his obligations if he proves that the failure was due to an impediment beyond his control and that he could

---

[45] J. O. Honnold, *Uniform Law for International Sales under the 1980 United Nations Convention*, 3rd edn (New York: Aspen Publishers, 1999) p.419.1.

not reasonably be expected to have taken the impediment into account at the time of the conclusion of the contract or to have avoided or overcome it or its consequences".

Article 79(5) explains the "not liable" in these terms: "nothing in this article prevents either party from exercising any right other than to claim damages under this Convention". What is important thus is that art.79 does not end the contract merely to provide the nonperforming party with a defence against a claim for damages. The parties' obligations are therefore not discharged.

Another critical implication is that art.79 refers to being exempt from performing "any of his obligations", not just the contract as whole. Given that the CISG allows for partial breaches or nonperformance, this provision could be used as defence against a claim for damages for partial nonperformance.

In English law, hardship alone will not discharge the contract. Under art.79, it is arguable that hardship might be sufficient. However, there is a large body of cases suggesting the disinclination of tribunals to allow a party to resile from its obligations on the basis of increased financial or economic hardship.[46]

Article 79(2) introduces a novel concept—where the party's failure to perform **5–030** was due to the failure of a third party whom he has engaged to perform the contract. There is some question as to whether the third party should be the nonperforming party's subcontractor or whether that third party might have been asked by the other party to work with the nonperforming party. For example, if A asks C to help B in the manufacture of goods to satisfy a sale contract between A and B, should C be treated as a third person for the purposes of art.79(2)? It would seem that the word "engaged" should be read as indicating a direct relationship between B and C. A subcontractor or an independent contractor with a direct relationship would seem to fall within art.79(2) but a supplier does not. It has been held in a German case[47] that where S had asked his supplier, M, to send the goods directly to B, in the event of M's failure to perform, the relevant provision as far as S was concerned was art.79(1) and not art.79(2).

Article 79(2) stresses that for the exemption to apply, the conditions under art.79(1) be satisfied with respect to both the party claiming exemption *and* the third party. This is the case even though the third party is not involved in the dispute and not claiming to be exempt. Indeed, it does not even matter that the third party's relationship with the person seeking the exemption is not subject to the CISG.

In conclusion, art.79 like other parts of the CISG can be contracted out of art.6; the parties might wish to provide for their own force majeure clause.

---

[46] See UNCITRAL Digest of CISG case law 2012 (2012) http://*www.ucitral.org*, pp.390–391.

[47] CLOUT case No.272 Germany Oberlandesgericht [Appellate Court] Zweibrücken March 31, 1998, *http://cisgw3.law.pace.edu/cases/980331g1.html* [accessed April 9, 2013].

CHAPTER 6

BILLS OF LADING

In Chapter 2, we saw how essential documents are in the conduct of international **6–001** trade. One of the most important of these documents is the bill of lading. The bill of lading is a creature more of mercantile usage than the law; hence while there are express references in the law (see, e.g. the Carriage of Goods by Sea Act 1971, Carriage of Goods by Sea Act 1992, Bills of Lading Act 1855 and other statutes) on its role, status and effect, there is no prescriptive legal definition as to what it is. It is presumed by law that if a document is accepted by the trade to be a bill of lading and performs the following functions, it should be treated as a bill of lading:

- a receipt for goods shipped;

- evidence of the contract of carriage;

- a document of title.

It was not until the late eighteenth century, several centuries after they came into general use by merchants, that the common law courts first made a pronouncement as to their nature.[1] The court in *Lickbarrow v Mason* (1794) 5 T.R. 683 acknowledged that trade custom has established the bill of lading as a document of title to the goods agreed to be delivered to the consignee. The Bills of Lading Act 1855, the predecessor of the Carriage of Goods by Sea Act 1992, was subsequently enacted to give statutory recognition to this trade custom. Section 1 of that Act gives the indorsee or named consignee a statutory right to sue in his own name simply by virtue of his possession of the bill. That has been retained by the 1992 Act, with some important modifications.[2]

Bills of Lading in Trade Practice

Bills of lading are usually issued in sets by an agent of the shipowner (normally **6–002** the ship master). Each bill of lading in the set is sufficient and valid to induce delivery of the goods. One is kept on board the vessel whilst the others will be

---

[1] See W.P. Bennett, *The History and Present Position of the Bill of Lading as a Document of Title to Goods* (Cambridge: CUP, 1914).

[2] Paras 6–038—6–051.

remitted to consignees of goods or any banks issuing letters of credit for the goods. There is usually a clause in the bill of lading to the effect that once one of the set has been activated to demand delivery of the goods, the others are to "stand void". It is trite law that the carrier need not make inquiries as to whether the holder of the bill of lading is legitimately entitled to it.

6–003   *Glyn Mills Currie & Co v The East & West Indies Dock Co* (1882) 7 App. Cas. 591
Facts:
The seller had pledged one of three bills of lading issued in a set to the bank, Glyn Mills Currie & Co and had retained the other two. When the goods arrived in London, they were placed in a warehouse. The warehouseman then delivered the goods to a person tendering one of the remaining two bills. The bill was unendorsed. In the meantime the seller had become insolvent and the bank attempted to seek damages from the warehouse for misdelivery.
Held:
The House of Lords held that the warehouse was not liable to the bank. They had acted in good faith and without notice of the bank's prior claim. The clause in the bill of lading "one of which bills being accomplished, the others to stand void" must be taken to enable delivery of the goods to the first person to produce the relevant bill of lading in demand of the goods.

The fact that any one bill issued in a set is capable of inducing delivery of goods is obviously a potential aperture for fraud or sharp dealing. The common law however takes the position that certainty in commercial transactions and the sanctity of documents are two corner stones of international trade law which should not be derogated from, especially so when commercial people should be aware of the risks involved in export-import and as such, by entering into these contracts, they are deemed to have voluntarily assumed the appending risks.[3] It is therefore not open to consignees to act as the buyers did in *Sanders Bros v Maclean & Co* (1883) 11 Q.B.D. 327.

6–004   *Sanders Bros v Maclean & Co* (1883) 11 Q.B.D. 327
Facts:
The CIF buyers refused to accept the bills of lading on the basis that the contract anticipated the issue of a set of three bills of lading and they had only been offered two.
Held:
The Court of Appeal was asked whether the buyers were entitled to demand the entire set. Bowen L.J. rejected the buyers' claim on the basis that it was not a term of the contract, implied or otherwise, for the seller to tender the entire set where bills were issued in sets. His Lordship said:

> "[I]t is plain that the purpose and idea of drawing bills of lading in sets—whatever the present advantage or disadvantage of the plan—is that the whole set should not remain always in the same hands".

The shipper or his vendees, according to His Lordship, may prefer to retain one of the originals for their own protection against loss, or to transfer it to their correspondents. The habit of merchants seemed to be that

---

[3] Crawford, "Analysis and Operation of a CIF Contract" (1954–55) 29 Tulane L. Rev. 396.

"the remainder of the set are effective documents and sufficient for all purposes of negotiating the goods comprised in the bill of lading".

It is important to bear in mind that the object of mercantile usage is as described by the old saying **6–005**

"credit, not distrust, is the basis of commercial dealings; mercantile genius consists principally in knowing whom to trust and with whom to deal and commercial intercourse and communication is no more based on the supposition of fraud than it is on the supposition of forgery".

Banks are, however, slightly more cautious. Under their code of practice in documentary credits, the UCP 600, they insist that when the credit calls for a bill of lading, they will only accept a document which consists of a sole original bill of lading or, if issued in more than one original, the full set as so issued (art.20(a)(iv)). It is of course available to traders to make this a condition of their contract of sale.

The normal procedure for the consignee of the goods to secure delivery is to tender the bill of lading at the port of destination to the ship master or shipowner's agent in exchange for a delivery order enabling him to demand delivery. Freight may be payable by the consignee.[4] Where the journey is relatively short, it would be impractical to send the bill of lading separated from the goods; the object being to enable the buyer to take delivery of the goods as soon as possible. There are two ways around the problem. First, the shipmaster would carry the bill of lading in the ship's bag on board the carrying vessel and hand it over to the consignee upon arrival subject to the latter producing proof of identity. The second, which is gaining more popularity, is by means of electronic data transfer. It is also a distinct advantage of electronic bills of lading that they are never issued in sets. This would reduce the potential for fraud à la *Glyn Mills Currie & Co v The East & West Indies Dock Co*. The Comité Maritime Internationale (CMI) predicts that electronic bills of lading are likely to grow, not diminish, in importance and use. Electronic bills are also much faster and their increased use should render the current reliance on letters of indemnity (to induce release of goods without production of the bill of lading) less needful. Letters of indemnity always involve a third party—a guarantor. Removing that need means less hassle for the traders, for the carrier (who would be concerned that the wording in the indemnity is right) and less cost for all concerned. Another advantage with electronic bills of lading is that ships will no longer need to wait hours at port of loading awaiting cargo documents to be brought onboard— thereby reducing the risk of incurring demurrage.

In order to facilitate this the use of electronic bills,[5] it has devised a set of rules on good practice in this field. The CMI Rules for Electronic Bills of Lading provide in Rule 4 that:

"(a) The carrier, upon receiving the goods from the shipper, shall give notice of the receipt of the goods to the shipper by a message at the electronic address specified by the shipper.

---

[4] See paras 7–086—7–089.
[5] Walden and Savage, "The legal problems of paperless transactions" [1989] J.B.L. 102 explores some of the legal impediments to this development.

(b) This receipt message shall include:

(i) the name of the shipper;
(ii) the description of the goods, with any representations and reservations, in the same tenor as would be required if a paper bill of lading were issued;
(iii) the date and place of the receipt of the goods;
(iv) a reference to the carrier's terms and conditions of carriage; and
(v) the Private Key to be used in subsequent Transmissions.

The shipper must confirm this receipt message to the carrier, upon which Confirmation the shipper shall be the holder.

(c) Upon demand of the Holder, the receipt message shall be updated with the date and place of shipment as soon as the goods have been loaded on board.

(d) The information contained in (ii), (iii) and (iv) . . . above including the date and place of shipment if updated in accordance with paragraph (c) of this Rule, shall have the same force and effect as if the receipt message were contained in a paper bill of lading".

6–006   The rights and obligations of the parties are comparable to those operating under a paper bill of lading. An additional obligation relates to the Private Key. Rule 8 states that the Private Key is unique to each successive holder. It is not transferrable by the holder. The carrier and the holder shall each maintain security of the Private Key. The carrier is only obliged to send a confirmation of an electronic message to the last holder to whom it issued a Private Key, when the holder secures the transmission containing the electronic message by use of the Private Key. This Private Key enables the holder and only the holder to access the information contained in the electronic message.

When the carrier notifies the holder of the place and time of intended delivery of the goods, the holder is obliged under Rule 9 to nominate a consignee to collect the goods. The holder is further obliged to supply the carrier with adequate delivery instructions with verification by the Private Key. If he does not make the nomination, he (the holder) will be deemed to be the consignee of the goods. Once the carrier has received this confirmation and nomination (if any) attested and verified by the Private Key, he shall deliver the goods to the person supplying him with proper identification at the place of destination. As with the common law rule in *Glyn Mills Currie & Co*, upon the delivery to the person with proof of identity, the Private Key shall automatically be cancelled and any other demand for delivery need not be honoured.

The Electronic Bill of Lading Project—BOLERO

6–007   The CMI Rules for Electronic Bills of Lading are lacking in that they do not deal with generally with the conduct of an entire chain sale transaction on-line, without the actual transfer of documents, electronic or otherwise. It is in this connection that the Bolero project fills a gap. The project not only purports to replace the paper bill of lading and waybill with an electronic bill (known as the Bolero bill) in a transferable or non-transferable form, it also provides for a registry system where every "indorsement" of the Bolero bill is monitored and properly recorded.

The Bolero project was the initiative of the International Chamber of Commerce and is sponsored by Society for Worldwide Interbank Financial Telecommunications (SWIFT) and the Through-transport Club (TTC). The technical infrastructure of Bolero went on-line on December 1, 1998 and the first "live" trade was carried out in February 2000 through the agency of Bolero.net, the operating system.

The main objectives of the Bolero service are to:

- provide a central registry for the electronic storage and associated maintenance of shipping and trade documentation;

- provide a central registry for all aspects of trade from pre-booking to inward goods clearance;

- provide a central registry for the validation of documents which relate to the progress and movement of the consignment;

- ensure that security and authentication requirements are met so as to engender trust between participants;

- provide a global, electronic infrastructure for international traders and shippers;

- provide an open system with a simple interface using internationally recognised standards.

A description of the first "live" transaction in February 2000 might be helpful in understanding how Bolero actually works.

The importer (Federated Merchandising Group Inc) bought a consignment of **6–008** women's knitwear under a letter of credit from Peninsula Knitters (the sellers) in Hong Kong. Citibank acted as both the Issuing Bank and Advising Bank. The shipment was from Hong Kong to the United States. The required electronic documents included the invoice, the bill of lading (issued by the carrier) and the forwarder's cargo receipt. The full set of documents was presented to Citibank electronically by Peninsula for negotiation of the letter of credit. Citibank made payment to Peninsula on the basis of the documents as submitted electronically and a payment pre-advice from Federated authorising that payment. It goes without saying that the transaction required a great deal of co-operation and trust between the parties (the seller, buyer, bank, freight forwarder and carrier).

The essence of the Bolero system lies in its "Core Messaging Platform". This application is vital for the secure transmission of trade documents between participants. Such secure transmission relies chiefly on the use of digital signatures and encryption. The proponents of Bolero argue that the electronic system is far more secure than its paper-based equivalent because while it is possible for a confidential paper document to be copied, forged and presented to third parties without knowledge of the originator, Bolero's security encryption means that a document could only be viewed by the intended recipient and its use of digital signatures ensures that electronically signed documents cannot be altered or forged generally.

The Core Messaging Platform overcomes the problem of the absence of acknowledgement of receipt which is usually suffered by e-mail. For example, it is difficult for the sender to tell whether an e-mail has been received or read by the corresponding party. The Bolero system addresses this problem by the adoption of a unique messaging protocol. When a message is transmitted, the Bolero system provider (for example, Bolero.net) acknowledges receipt immediately and then forwards the message to the receiver. As soon as it is received (downloaded) by the receiver, an automatic acknowledgement of receipt is transmitted to Bolero. Bolero will then transmit that acknowledgement to the sender.

6–009   When trade documents are transmitted, it is crucial that all interested parties are convinced that the documents are original and have not been tampered with. With Bolero, the system matches the original content against the forwarding content. Where an inconsistency is found, the document will be rejected. The Core Messaging Platform also maintains a log of all transmissions made.

Another major imperative of the Bolero project is that the electronic system should be a fully functional equivalent to the paper document. As far as the project is concerned, this means that the rights represented by the electronic bill of lading should be capable of being created, transferred, pledged, amended and surrendered. In order that this (especially its capacity for pledging) could be achieved, the system employs a mechanism called "Title Registry". That said, unlike the conventional system, the Bolero system does not actually cause the transfer of a document, it merely treats each transmission as a new transaction.

The Title Registry is an IT application which enables the recording and transferring of any rights and obligations under the Bolero bill of lading. The Title Registry maintains an indorsement chain (a chain of persons being consigned the bill of lading) and registers every transfer that takes place. There is also a time stamp of each electronic indorsement in the indorsement chain so that the time of every transaction can be ascertained with accuracy. The Title Registry also maintains a full log of all Bolero bill of lading transactions and these logs could subsequently be checked against the digitally signed messages maintained by the Core Messaging Platform to prove transaction integrity. It therefore provides legal certainty of ownership at every stage of the trade chain.

6–010   It is clear, therefore, that in the eyes of the law, the Bolero title registry system does not actually offer complete legal equivalence to the electronic bill of lading. Whilst it achieves the main functions of the bill of lading in reality, it is not a true equivalent to the paper bill because it requires the involvement of the carrier or the registrar upon each transfer in order to achieve, by attornment and novation, the same result as would be achieved by a paper bill.[6] Attornment occurs when one party accepts and acknowledges implicitly or expressly that a particular right had been transferred. Under Bolero, the carrier who is the bailee agrees that the shipper can transfer the right to give orders to the carrier to another party. The carrier agrees to take instructions only from the person holding the "key" (the unique electronic message). Therefore the carrier by advising the party holding the key that he now holds the cargo to that person's order, the carrier is

---

[6] See Electronic Commerce—Formal Requirements in Commercial Transactions: Advice from the Law Commission, Law Commission, December 2001, available at *http://www.lawcom.gov.uk/docs/ecommerce.pdf* (Part 4, 23–24), [accessed April 9, 2013].

effectively acknowledging that the rights in the goods have been transferred to the new consignee. That is attornment.

Further, under the Bolero Rulebook, the new consignee acquires his rights against the carrier by novation. The carrier's contract with the shipper is "extinguished and a new contract on the same terms is created between the carrier and the consignee"[7]; that means, a new party is substituted for the original shipper and a new contract is brought into existence between the substituted party and the carrier.

In short, attornment and novation in the Bolero system are represented by the acknowledgement by the carrier that it now holds goods to the order of a new transferee, and a separate but new contract based on the same original terms between the carrier and the consignee. It is not like a paper bill of lading where the rights are transferred by mere delivery of the bill (ss.2–3 Carriage of Goods by Sea Act 1992); there is no need for any acknowledgement by the carrier. For English law to provide for full legal equivalence, the law will therefore need to be changed. Section 1(5) Carriage of Goods by Sea Act envisages the potential need for some regulatory and legal change—it enables the Secretary of State to introduce regulations to deal with electronic shipping transport documents. If new Regulations are indeed to be introduced under s.1(5), those regulations must ensure that the holder is given exclusive control of the transport document in question at any one time. Guidance perhaps might be sought from the Rotterdam Rules. In short provisions need to be made as regards how the electronic transport record may be issued (art.1(10), (21)[8] of the Rotterdam Rules), transferred (art.1(22))[9] and held (art.9)[10] but they should essentially be technology neutral—which means, whilst they should provide for objectives to be met by the electronic systems, they should not legislate how those systems should work technologically. Article 9 of the Rotterdam Rules is a good example of this technology neutral approach—although it provides for certain procedures which must be met in the use of an electronic transport document, it does not set out the technical details of what those procedures should have. Any regulations changing the law on electronic shipping or transport documents must also provide a commercially workable definition of electronic transport records.[11]

---

[7] Rule 3.5.1(3) of the Bolero Rulebook.

[8] Article 1(21) "The 'issuance' of a negotiable electronic transport record means the issuance of the record in accordance with procedures that ensure that the record is subject to exclusive control from its creation until it ceases to have any effect or validity."

[9] Article 1(22) provides, "the 'transfer' of a negotiable electronic transport record means the transfer of exclusive control over the record."

[10] Article 9(1) provides "The use of a negotiable electronic transport record shall be subject to procedures that provide for: (a) The method for the issuance and the transfer of that record to an intended holder; (b) An assurance that the negotiable electronic transport record retains its integrity; (c) The manner in which the holder is able to demonstrate that it is the holder; and (d) The manner of providing confirmation that delivery to the holder has been effected, or that . . . the electronic transport record has ceased to have any effect or validity."

[11] As for the Rotterdam Rules' definition, art.1(18) provides: "Electronic transport record" means information in one or more messages issued by electronic communication under a contract of carriage by a carrier, including information logically associated with the electronic transport record by attachments or otherwise linked to the electronic transport record contemporaneously with or subsequent to its issue by the carrier, so as to become part of the electronic transport record, that: (a) Evidences the carrier's or a performing party's receipt of goods under a contract of carriage; and (b) evidences or contains a contract of carriage. That definition would include sea waybills.

The ESS CargoDocs system

6–011   Another commercial provider is Electronic Shipping Solutions (ESS) which is backed by two investment funds. Its system, called ESS Databridge, facilitates many shipping documents apart from bills of lading, on which live transactions began in 2009. ESS cargo and transport documents work similarly to Bolero —their system allows electronic messages from the "relevant party" to be sent through a secure central title registry/server. In the Bolero system, we have seen how the relevant parties must become members of Bolero and are, as such, governed by the Rulebook which sets out their rights and obligations as regards title transfer and other aspects of trading. The Bolero system works on the basis that possession of a paper bill is replaced by "exclusive control" of an electronic record through a title registry. ESS Databridge achieves exclusive control through limiting access to the electronic record in question. It works on a token system but has an advantage over Bolero in that it allows users to upload documents which look and feel like a traditional bill of lading.

CargoDocs, the ESS Databridge's solution, is a web-based solution enabling users to replace paper documentation relating to shipping cargo in containers with original, negotiable electronic documents. The service is structured to enable and facilitate the electronic creation, signing, issuing and filing of bills of lading and associated documents.[12]

It allows the trader to upload bill of lading data directly from the trader's own operational systems or to enter data directly onto a CargoDocs web interface. ESS then recreates the carriers' bill of lading templates, so the electronic version looks just like the original paper documents. ESS will then ensure that the shipper and carrier are able to verify the authenticity of the paperless bill of lading. There is no printing, faxing or scanning required. The system also allows for the signing of multi-electronic bills of lading. There is an option to issue electronic bills of lading automatically on completion of certain steps. The system allows also for the re-production of the data in various formats to satisfy requirements from customs and other authorities. The documents can also be endorsed electronically and online which means that it is compliant with the standards laid down for the use of electronic letters of credit.[13]

6–012   They also claim to be committed to providing a 12-year secure online access and storage for all eDocs. CargoDocs can also be used directly by the designated agent of the carrier, as applicable. There is always only one electronic bill of lading issued, and it resides on the ESS-Databridge with access given only to authorised parties.

All CargoDocs users must agree to the ESS-Databridge Services & Users Agreement (DSUA) before being permitted to use live electronic documents. The DSUA is a multi-partite agreement which binds all CargoDocs users to each other and to ESS, similar to the Bolero Rulebook.

---

[12] Associated documents include shipping lists, commercial invoices, certificates of quality etc.

[13] See eUCP art.e3 . . . "'electronic record' means data created, generated, sent, communicated, received, or stored by electronic means that is capable of being authenticated as to the apparent identity of a sender and the apparent source of the data contained in it, and as to whether it has remained complete and unaltered, and is capable of being examined for compliance with the terms and conditions of the eUCP Credit."; more on the eUCP see Davidson, *http://www.uncitral.org/* . . . */UNCITRAL-paper_Feb2011-Alan-Davidson.pdf.*

ESS has not disclosed in full how its products work to the public; it is understandably protective of its trade and commercial secrets. However, its publicity material has stressed the company's expectations that the product will be advantageous to the oil and energy sector, in particular. There is also planned expansion into the container and ARA[14] barge markets.[15]

Legal implications

The EU Electronic Commerce Directive

The optimal functioning of such a project depends very much on the under-pinning of the law on three areas: **6–013**

1. the provision of such services;

2. the recognition of electronic transactions (especially, contractual transactions); and

3. the regulation of providers of such services (such as Bolero.net and other similar organisations).

As far as the European Union is concerned, there is now in place a Directive on Certain Legal Aspects of Information Society Services, in particular Electronic Commerce in the Internal Market (Directive 2000/31/EC). Under the Directive (which has been implemented in the United Kingdom though the Electronic Commerce (EC Directive) Regulations 2002 SI 2002/2013), the liability of Bolero.net or other similar information society service providers[16] is generally set out in s.4. Article 12 (or reg.17 SI 2002/2013) in s.4 provides that where the information society service provider acts merely as a conduit of the data, it shall not be liable for the information transmitted as long as the provider:

1. does not initiate the transmission;

2. does not select the receiver of the transmission; and

3. does not select or modify the information contained in the transmission.

It is uncertain, though, given the nature of the Core Messaging Platform application whether the service provider (Bolero.net) could properly be excluded as not having initiated the transmission for after all, they could choose not to transmit having received the electronic document from the sender.

Similarly, although art.13 (or reg.18 SI 2002/2013) exempts the provider from liability for the automatic, intermediate and temporary storage of data (caching of data) generally, the same provisos apply. Under art.14 (or reg.19 SI 2002/2013), a service provider is not liable for the information stored at the request of a recipient of the service, on condition that: **6–014**

---

[14] Stands for Amsterdam, Rotterdam, Antwerp region.

[15] See *http://www.essdoc.com*.

[16] "Information Society Service Provider" is defined in art.2 of the Directive as any natural or legal person providing an information society service; whilst "information society service" is defined by art.1(2) of Directive 98/34 as "any service normally provided for remuneration at a distance, by means of electronic equipment, for the processing and storage of data and at the individual request of a recipient of a service". See also reg.2 SI 2002/2013.

1. the provider does not have actual knowledge or awareness of illegal activity or information and, as regards claims for damages, is not aware of facts or circumstances from which the illegal activity or information is apparent; or

2. the provider, upon obtaining such knowledge or awareness, acts expeditiously to remove or disable access to the information. Article 14 is particularly relevant when third parties, such as banks and potential sub-buyers, access the relevant documents stored by Bolero electronically and the information held could give rise to an illegality. Although this provision is clearly more directed at service providers hosting web sites with illegal (and often, objectionable) information or pictures, it is submitted that the terms of art.14 are wide enough to cover other means of electronic hosting of information.

As far as the recognition of electronic documents is concerned, the Electronic Commerce Directive is not particularly instructive. Whilst art.9 allows for the conclusion of contracts electronically, there is no provision in the Directive sanctioning the recognition of a contract reduced to and evidenced by an electronic instrument. There is however no impediment at English law to the recognition of an electronic document as evidence of the legal rights it purports to hold. In a Scottish case, *Rollo v GM Advocate* [1996] S.C.C.R. 875, the police intended to use certain information stored in the accused's electronic notepad which was seized. The seizure was made under a search warrant. The warrant referred specifically to the recovery of any "document directly or indirectly relating to, or connected with a transaction". The question was whether the electronic notepad was a document. Lord Milligan said:

> "[T]he essential essence of a document is that it is something containing recorded information of some sort. It does not matter if, to be meaningful, the information requires to be processed in some way such as translation, decoding or electronic retrieval".

Similarly, in *Leicester Building Society v Ghahremani* [1992] R.V.R. 198, the accused had deleted a part of a word processed file in a computer. The court held that that was an act done with reference to a "document" after discovery of documents had been ordered. It was therefore an act in contempt of court.

The Electronic Communications Act 2000

6–015 As we have seen, the use of electronic signatures, the need for encryption technology and reliance on third parties (such as Bolero.net) are absolutely vital for a true paperless international trade transaction to succeed. The Electronic Communications Act 2000 should be sufficiently reliable to support these needs. There are four key areas of legislative coverage in the Act:

1. a voluntary register for the providers of cryptography services;

2. the removal of issues relating to access to encryption keys;

3. the definition of an electronic signature;

4. the right of the government to introduce secondary legislation to approximate statutes which would require amendment to allow for the recognition of electronic signature and various aspects of electronic commerce.

Part I of the Act regulates the provision of "cryptographic support services". This is, under s.6,

"any service which is provided to the senders or recipients of electronic communications, or to those storing electronic data and is designed to facilitate the use of cryptographic techniques for the purpose of:

    (a) securing that such communications or data can be accessed, or can be put into an intelligible form, only by certain persons; or

    (b) securing that the authenticity or integrity of such communications or data is capable of being ascertained".

For the Act to apply, these service providers must have a connection with the jurisdiction—the service must be provided from premises in the United Kingdom or to persons carrying on a business in the United Kingdom. Under the Act, the government will maintain an approvals and register system. This ensures that all cryptography service providers are subject to some form of control. Without the full complement of procedures and standards in place, it remains to be seen how the new regulatory regime will work. Much will also fall to within the domain of self-regulation. It is probable that a service provider such as Bolero.net would be deemed a provider of cryptographic support services.

Part II refers generally to the "Facilitation of Electronic Commerce, Data **6–016** Storage etc". There is in fact very little on the regulation of electronic commerce. This Part is primarily concerned with electronic signatures which the Parliament considers to be the fulcrum in electronic commerce. Section 7(1) provides that in any legal proceedings:

(a) an electronic signature incorporated into or logically associated with a particular electronic communication or particular electronic data; and

(b) the certification by any person of such a signature,

shall each be admissible in evidence in relation to any question as to the authenticity of the communication or data or as to the integrity of the communication or data.

For the purposes of this section an electronic signature is so much of *anything* in electronic form as:

(a) is incorporated into or otherwise logically associated with any electronic communication or electronic data; and

(b) purports to be so incorporated or associated for the purpose of being used in establishing the authenticity of the communication or data, the integrity of the communication or data, or both.

This provision does not add very much to the working of electronic bills of lading, such as under the Bolero Project, but it should be welcome as formal support of electronic commerce. The Government is convinced that the Act is compatible with the EU Directive on Electronic Signatures and as it is fully compliant, there is no further need for any formal "transposition" of the EU Directive. The devil, however, seems to be in the detail.[17]

The UNCITRAL Model Law on Electronic Commerce (as amended 1998)

6–017   The UNCITRAL Model Law on Electronic Commerce is the culmination of the concerns of the international community to ensure that electronic commerce, with its cross-border influence and impact, should at least be subject to certain common definitions and standards. It is indeed a major success—its provisions have largely found their way into national laws. The Model Law by itself, however, does not have any legal effect. It serves only as a guide as to what might be incorporated into national or regional laws.

One of the more important provisions of the Model Law is its express recognition of electronic data as being of the same standing as information in writing. Article 6 states:

> "Where the law requires information to be in writing, that requirement is met by a data message if the information contained therein is accessible so as to be usable for subsequent reference".

In addition, it reduces signature to its indorsement or authentication character in art.7(1):

> "Where the law requires a signature of a person, that requirement is met in relation to a data message if:
>
> (a) a method is used to identify that person and to indicate that person's approval of the information contained in the data message; and
> (b) that method is as reliable as was appropriate for the purpose for which the data message was generated or communicated, in the light of all the circumstances, including any relevant agreement".

6–018   The Model Law gives special treatment to, inter alia, carriage of goods and the use of electronic transport documents. Article 17 permits the use of electronic documentation in any action in connection with, or in pursuance of, a contract of carriage, including but not limited to:

(a) (i) furnishing the marks, number, quantity or weight of goods;
    (ii) stating or declaring the nature or value of goods;
    (iii) issuing a receipt for goods;
    (iv) confirming that goods have been loaded;

(b) (i) notifying a person of terms and conditions of the contract;
    (ii) giving instructions to a carrier;

(c) (i) claiming delivery of goods;
    (ii) authorising release of goods;
    (iii) giving notice of loss of, or damage to, goods;

(d) giving any other notice or statement in connection with the performance of the contract;

---

[17] See Blythe, "Digital Signature Law of the UN, EU, UK and US" (2005) 11 Rich. J.L. & Tech. 6.

(e)　undertaking to deliver goods to a named person or a person authorised to claim delivery;

(f)　granting, acquiring, renouncing, surrendering, transferring or negotiating rights in goods;

(g)　acquiring or transferring rights and obligations under the contract.

This provision would clearly apply to the use of electronic bills of lading to conduct a complete sale and purchase, such as Bolero. Article 17 makes it perfectly legal for parties to replace paper document with an electronic document for the purposes set out above.[18]

Article 17(3) provides that a right is to be granted to, or an obligation is to be acquired by, one person and no other person, and if the law requires that, in order to effect this, the right or obligation must be conveyed to that person by the transfer or use of a paper document (whether that is the case under ss.2 and 3 Carriage of Goods by Sea Act 1992 in England and Wales is arguable because all that the Act calls for is the transfer of the transport document, no specific reference is made of a *paper* document), that requirement is met if the right or obligation is conveyed by using one or more data messages, provided that a reliable method is used to render such data message or messages unique.[19] That is the case with Bolero—the transfer of the rights and obligations under the bill of lading is represented by an electronic indorsement made on the indorsement chain. Each message however needs to be unique if the Model Law is to be followed which is indeed the case, with the use of encryption technology (electronic signature). The standard of "reliability" required is not based on a general test of reliability as agreed by experts—it is to be assessed in the light of the purpose for which the right or obligation was conveyed and in the light of all the circumstances, including any relevant agreement between the relevant parties.[20] How this will actually be applied makes for interesting hypothesising.

With reference to the use of an electronic document (such as the bill of lading) to grant or acquire rights/obligations in the goods or under the contract, where at any stage in the chain a paper document is used to replace the electronic document/indorsement, art.17(5) states that the paper document used must state that the use of data messages has thenceforth been terminated. Electronic document should naturally be interchangeable with paper documents, and there should be no rule against the substitution of one with the other at any stage in the proceedings, provided the parties are in agreement. Bolero does not however seem to envisage this possible fact of trading.

The Rotterdam Rules[21] and electronic bills

One of the objectives of the UN Convention on Contracts for the International **6–019** Carriage of Goods Wholly or Partly by Sea 2008 (the Rotterdam Rules) is to

---

[18] Art.16.

[19] Gaskell, "Bills of Lading in an electronic age" [2010] L.M.C.L.Q. 233; Goldby, "The CMS Rules for Electronic Bills of Lading reassessed in the light of current practice" [2008] L.M.C.L.Q. 56.

[20] Art.17(4).

[21] The Rotterdam Rules have not come into force but is the first and only transport of goods convention that makes express provisions for electronic shipping documents. For more on the Rotterdam Rules generally see paras 8–103—8–125.

encourage the development and facilitation of international trade using electronic documentation. The Rotterdam Rules explicitly provide for total functional equivalence to electronic bills of lading. Article 8 states that, if the carrier and the shipper agree, a paper bill of lading can be replaced with an electronic bill of lading and that the issuance, exclusive control or transfer of an electronic bill of lading shall have the same effect as the issuance, possession or transfer of a paper bill of lading.

Article 9 then sets out a series of "procedures" for the use of negotiable electronic bills of lading. Interestingly art.9 does not mention non-negotiable electronic bills of lading—does this mean that these procedures need not be followed for non-negotiable electronic bills of lading?

Article 9 specifies that the use of negotiable electronic bills of lading must be subject to procedures that provide for:

(a) the method for the issuance and the transfer of the electronic bills of lading to a holder;

(b) an assurance that the negotiable electronic bill of lading retains its integrity;

(c) the manner in which the holder is able to demonstrate that it is the holder; and

(d) the manner of providing confirmation that delivery to the holder has been effected or that the electronic bill of lading has ceased to have any effect or validity.

These procedures must be mentioned specifically in the contract and must be readily ascertainable.

6–020   These procedures detailed in art.9 are central to how electronic bills of lading are intended to work under the Rules. For example, transfers of the electronic bill of lading (art.57(2)), the identity of the holder of an electronic bill of lading (art.1(10)) and delivery of goods covered by an electronic bill (art.47) are all inexorably linked to the procedures in art.9 having been met. Thus, there is no effective and legal transfer of an electronic bill of lading under the Rotterdam Rules unless there is compliance with the procedures in art.9.

The Rotterdam Rules do envisage the mutual substitution between paper and electronic bills (art.10). This will have the benefit of encouraging traders to use the electronic bill more widely. In the past there have been some concerns that in the case of a string contract involving parties from countries with differing standards of IT infrastructure, the use of electronic bill will mean exclusion of certain markets.

The Bill as a Receipt

6–021   The bill of lading as a receipt is an acknowledgement by the carrier (e.g. the shipowner) or his agent that the goods have been shipped or received for shipment as the case may be. This acknowledgement will also contain statements as to the apparent condition of the goods, the quantity, markings and other relevant information known to the carrier. Where the bill of lading is governed by the Hague-Visby Rules, art.III(3) imposes on the carrier the obligation to issue a bill of lading which contains the following particulars:

- the leading marks necessary for identification of the goods;
- the number of packages or pieces;
- the quantity or weight of the goods; and
- the apparent order and condition of the goods.

The carrier has the right to expect from the shipper, true and accurate information about the goods. Article III(5) makes the shipper liable to indemnify the carrier for false or inaccurate information supplied in the bill of lading which resulted in the carrier's loss, damage or expense. In practice, the shipper or his freight forwarders would fill in the details in the bill of lading and the shipmaster (the carrier's agent) signs it. The shipmaster should signify whether the goods have been merely received for shipment or have been actually loaded on board the vessel. With the former, only a "received for shipment" bill of lading ought to be issued.

As far as the shipper of goods is concerned, the bill of lading as a receipt is prima facie evidence that he has performed the contract to the extent that the goods have been shipped. For the consignee or indorsee of the bill of lading, it acts as conclusive evidence that the goods have been shipped as per contract reflecting the sanctity of documents in documentary sales.

Under art.III(4), the carrier has no duty to make statements in the bill of lading that he does not believe or could not ascertain. However, if he does issue a bill of lading with such statements, they are to be regarded as prima facie evidence of the state and condition of the goods so received. Proof to the contrary may be admitted against the shipper but this liability extinguishes when the bill of lading has been properly transferred to a third party acting in good faith.   **6–022**

In general, the position seems to be that the carrier's duty in relation to the issue of bills of lading is confined to exercising his own judgment and skill on the appearance of the cargo being loaded. If, in exercising his judgment and skill as a reasonably observant master, he honestly believes that the apparent condition of the goods is not good, he is entitled to clause the bill accordingly even though his view might not be consistent with the view of other carriers (*The David Agmashenebeli* [2003] 1 Lloyd's Rep. 92). This subject will be looked at in greater detail later on.[22]

Received bills v shipped bills

As observed, once the goods have in fact been loaded on board the contracted vessel, the shipmaster issues a shipped bill of lading signifying the event. Where the goods have only been delivered into his charge, any bill of lading issued at this stage before shipment is a received for shipment bill. It is quite pellucid from established authorities that the more effectual document is the former because it is best documentary evidence of the fact of shipment (see, e.g., *Diamond Alkali Export Corp v Bourgeois* [1921] 3 K.B. 443). The Judicial Committee of the Privy Council on the other hand had opined in *The Marlborough Hill* [1921] 1 A.C. 444 that a received bill is not dissimilar to the shipped bill. Current mercantile practice however indicates that banks treat the two documents as   **6–023**

---

[22] See para.6–028.

significantly different. Article 20(a)(ii) of the UCP 600 on Documentary Credits for example stipulates that:

"A bill of lading, however named, must appear to indicate that the goods have been shipped on board a named vessel at the port of loading stated in the credit ... ".

This loading on board may be indicated by pre-printed words on the bill of lading to that effect. The mere statement that the goods will be loaded onboard an "intended vessel" will not be sufficient; the bill of lading must indicate with certainty the date on which the goods were finally loaded on board or shipped.

A clean bill of lading

6–024 The carrier or his agent will indorse a statement to the effect that the goods have been received for shipment in good order and condition after making a superficial examination of the goods as delivered to him. This statement is of fundamental importance because as regards the consignee or any third party who has not physically examined the goods, it is principal evidence that the shipper had shipped goods in that good order and condition. When the goods arrive at the place of discharge and are found to be damaged or defective, the natural presumption must be that the damage could only have occurred during transit and as the goods were in the carrier's care and control during that time, he could be held accountable.

6–025 *The Peter der Grosse* (1875) 1 P.D. 414
Facts:
A cargo of down and feathers had been shipped from Russia to London. The contract of carriage was represented by a clean bill of lading. However when the cargo arrived, it was stained and carried a bad smell. In an attempt to avoid liability in spite of the clean bill of lading, the carriers argued that the clause "weight, contents and value unknown" in the bill of lading meant that they could not be bound by the declaration that the goods were in good order and condition.
Held:
The court rejected the carriers' defence on the basis that the stain would have been obvious to their agent and if as they alleged the damage was there pre-shipment, they should have issued a claused bill of lading. They had not successfully rebutted the prima facie presumption indicated by their declaration that the goods were received and shipped in good order and condition. The court then went on to clarify the meaning of "good order and condition". "Apparent good order and condition" according to the judge, Sir Roger Phillimore must be taken as "that apparently, and so far as met the eye, and externally, [the goods] were placed in good order on board [the] ship". It does not therefore mean that the goods are "fit for their purpose" or of sound condition.

The effect of a clean bill of lading, as far as the carrier is concerned would be that he is estopped from claiming that the goods were damaged at the time of shipment unless the damage was such that it would not have been apparent on reasonable examination at that time. This rule of estoppel was recognised in *Compañia Naviera Vasconzada v Churchill & Sim* [1906] 1 K.B. 237 by Channell J. whose judgment was subsequently affirmed by Court of Appeal in *Brandt v Liverpool, Brazil and River Plate Steam Navigation Co* [1924] 1 K.B.

575. Channell J. substantiated his finding of an estoppel in the following manner:

> "[T]he information relates to the shipowner's knowledge; he is to say what is 'apparent', that is, visible by reasonable inspection to himself and his servants, and on the faith of that statement other people are to act, and if it is wrong, act to their prejudice".

The importance of the element of reliance leading to detriment should however **6–026** not be overstated. It is submitted that while the element of reliance forms part of the rationale for the estoppel principle, the principle should be applied strictly to preserve commercial certainty and evidence should not be admitted to show lack of actual reliance. This is tantamount to saying that while the reliance notion forms a good rationale to the commercial practice of acknowledging the estoppel rule, that commercial practice has now gained such widespread acceptance and recognition that it should be applied as matter of principle. Scrutton L.J. was right to say in *Silver v Ocean Steamship Co Ltd* [1930] 1 K.B. 416 that

> "the mercantile importance of clean bills of lading is so obvious and important that the fact that [the consignee] took the bill of lading, which is in fact clean, without objection, is quite sufficient evidence that he relied on it".

The mere taking of the clean bill of lading according to Scrutton L.J. was sufficient to give rise to the estoppel against the carrier.

A related proposition is found in *Evans v James Webster & Brothers Ltd* (1928) 34 Com. Cas. 172 where it was held that an innocent indorsee for value of a bill of lading is entitled to act on the statements contained in the bill unless he has at the material time clear and definite knowledge from other sources that the statements in the bill are untrue. Any other position would derogate from the value and sanctity of the bill of lading as a document of title (an issue which we will discuss later) on the faith of which carriers and traders deal.

Extent of duty

It is clear that the carrier need not go beyond making a superficial examination **6–027** of the goods. In container transport, he may examine the items in the containers but need not remove the items' packaging to check the contents. Where the goods are labelled as "FCL/FCL" (Full Container Load/Full Container Load), (which means that the goods have been packed and sealed into containers by the shippers to be opened and unpacked by the buyer) the carrier is not duty bound to examine the contents. He is entitled to make out a bill of lading with the phrase "said to contain . . . packed by shippers". If his cursory examination of the goods reveals any sort of damage, defect, blemish or stains, he should make a note or statement of it in the bill of lading. Only a cursory examination is required. In *Silver v Ocean Steamship Co Ltd* [1930] 1 K.B. 416, for example, the carrier was not liable for failing to allude to certain defects in the metal cans containing Chinese eggs which had pinhole perforations not reasonably apparent to the carrier's servants loading at Shanghai under clusters of dim electric bulbs.

A statement in the bill of lading that the goods were damaged, defective, blemished or stained makes the bill of lading a "claused" bill of lading. This is contrasted against a clean bill of lading, which Salmon J. in *British Imex Industries Ltd v Midland Bank Ltd* [1958] 1 Q.B. 542 described as a bill of lading that does not contain any reservation as to the apparent good order and condition of the goods or the packing. Banking practice adopts a similar definition as is evident in the UCP 600. The Rules provide in art.27 that a clean transport document (including a bill of lading) is one which bears no clause or notation which expressly declares a defective condition of the goods or their packaging. The court in *Canada and Dominion Sugar Co Ltd v Canadian National (West Indies) Steamships Ltd* [1947] A.C. 46 while agreeing with the general definition prevalent in the banking industry, took a more stringent position. It held that the statement, "Signed under guarantee to produce ship's clean receipt" in the bill of lading was sufficient to qualify the "apparent good order and condition" notation. The bill of lading was deemed claused as a result. This approach clearly differs from the UCP position where unless the clause or notation *expressly declares* a defect, the bill of lading would be treated as clean. Judgments like this have been said to scare carriers into entering as little information as possible in the bill of lading, which although in itself may not be a bad thing could result in either the carrier being found liable for not performing his duties to the best of his endeavours or the aggravation of any potential damage or loss. (See e.g. *New Chinese Antimony Co Ltd v Ocean Steamship Co Ltd* [1917] 2 K.B. 664; *Ace Imports Pty Ltd v Companhia de Navegecao Lloyd Brasileiro (The Esmeralda I)* [1988] 1 Lloyd's Rep. 206 and *The Nea Thyi* [1982] 1 Lloyd's Rep. 606).

The *Canada & Dominion Sugar Co Ltd* case makes clear the proposition that where the statement is unqualified or unclear the law would not readily impose an estoppel on the carrier. The Privy Council summarised the law in this way:

> "It is true that the unqualified statement is only one step in the establishment of the estoppel. Estoppel is a complex legal notion, involving a combination of several essential elements, the statement to be acted on, action on the faith of it, resulting detriment to the actor. Estoppel is often described as a rule of evidence, as, indeed, it may be so described. But the whole concept is more correctly viewed as a substantive rule of law. The purchaser or other transferee must have acted on it to his detriment, as, for instance, he did in this case when he took up the documents and paid for them. It is also true that he cannot be said to rely on the statement if he knew that it was false: he must reasonably believe it to be true and therefore act on it. Estoppel is different from contract both in its nature and consequences. But the relationship between the parties must also be such that the imputed truth of the statement is a necessary step in the constitution of the cause of action. But the whole case of estoppel fails if the statement is not sufficiently clear and unqualified".

It should be borne in mind that the carrier's duty is only confined to defect or damage discovered during time of shipment.

6–028   *Golodetz (M) & Co Inc v Czarnikow-Rionda Co Inc (The Galatia)* [1979] 2 All E.R. 726; affd. [1980] 1 All E.R. 501
Facts:
A fire broke out on the ship. Goods on board were damaged by the fire and attempts to put the fire out. The shipmaster made a clause in the bill of lading stating the event and loss. The bill of lading was subsequently rejected for being claused.

Held:
The bill of lading was not claused because the loss or damage occurred after shipment and the notation entered by the shipmaster describing the fire did not suggest that the goods were not in good order and condition at the *time of shipment*, which was the operative time.

Thus far, we have looked at how the duty to issue bills of lading is to be carried out. What has not been examined is the issue of the standard of that duty. In *The David Agmashenebeli* [2003] 1 Lloyd's Rep. 92, the master had issued a bill of lading stating that the goods were discoloured and contained foreign particles. The court agreed with the sellers, whose bill of lading was subsequently rejected by the buyer's bank, that the master had used excessively strong language to describe the apparent condition of the goods. However, the court held that the master should not be subject to any higher duty than that of a reasonably observant master who honestly believed that the clausing was justified on his assessment of the pre-loading condition of the goods. There was no question of a liability in tort because it would not be "fair, just or reasonable"[23] to impose a duty of care where the master was required to carry out his functions quickly without detaining the vessel unduly, and where the Hague-Visby Rules were intended to be an international code of law which should not be shackled by domestic rules on tortious liability.

Indemnities and the bill of lading

In the sale transaction, the consignee or buyer is entitled to a clean bill of lading **6–029** evidencing to himself and/or any third party taking possession or delivery of the goods that the goods are in apparent good order and condition. Banks offering documentary credit facilities will also want a clean bill of lading to satisfy themselves that the goods, their security, have been shipped in good order and condition. It would therefore be fair to say that one of the overriding concerns of the shipper's is securing a clean bill of lading. The carrier may therefore in turn be put under tremendous pressure by the shipper to issue and sign a clean bill of lading. Shippers are also known to resort to various means of inducing the carrier to issue clean bills.

One of the more popular ways is offering to indemnify the carrier if the latter were to suffer loss or liability for the bill of lading issued. Pearce L.J. in *Brown Jenkinson & Co Ltd v Percy Dalton (London) Ltd* [1957] 2 Q.B. 621 anatomises the device in these terms:

"[In reliance on the indemnity] the plaintiffs issued a clean bill of lading in respect of goods contained in barrels that were to their knowledge faulty. Thereby they made a representation of fact that they knew to be false. They knew that the purpose of the representation was to procure payment by bankers, who were very often not prepared to provide the money if the bill of lading is not clean. The bankers paid the money relying, no doubt, on the plaintiffs' representation. Others besides the bankers were affected by the representation, since subsequent purchasers were entitled to rely on the bills of lading".

---

[23] As required in *Caparo v Dickman* [1990] 2 A.C. 605; see also Parker, "Liability for incorrectly clausing bills of lading" [2003] L.M.C.L.Q. 201.

His Lordship then went on to comment on the first instance judge's observation that there was no real dishonesty in the widespread practice:

"I find it difficult to see what answer the plaintiffs would have had if the purchasers had sued them in fraud. The fact that the damage was subsequently made good seemed to the judge to change the quality of the act. But it does not, in my opinion, alter the fact that the plaintiffs, by making a representation of fact that they knew to be false, with intent that it should be acted on (as in fact it was), were committing a tort. They are now seeking to recover on the indemnity in consideration of which they committed the tort. Had they been actively intending that someone should be defrauded by their misrepresentation, their case would have been unanswerable.

The real difficulty that arises . . . is due to the fact that the plaintiffs . . . appear from evidence not to have contemplated that anybody would be ultimately be defrauded. Theirs was a slipshod and unthinking extension of a known commercial practice to a point at which it constituted fraud in law . . . [I]t has become customary, in the short-sea trade in particular, for shipowners to give a clean bill of lading against an indemnity from the shippers in certain cases where there is bona fide dispute (between the shipper and carrier) as to the condition or packing of the goods. This avoids the necessity of rearranging any letter of credit, a matter which can create difficulty where the time is short".

6–030   His Lordship's concern was therefore whether the claimants had exceeded the reasonable bounds of the hitherto convenient and customary practice. In the present case, Pearce and Morris L.JJ. found that there was no bona fide dispute as to the condition of the goods (the barrels were so badly defective that "the orange juice was streaming out like water") and the representation was clearly wrong and misleading that it must be treated as tortious, making the indemnity illegal.

Lord Evershed M.R. dissented on the basis that the claimants' conduct was not dishonest because it was not their intention to defraud and as such public policy considerations did not demand that they be deprived of the benefit of the indemnity.

Statements in the bill of lading as to quantity

6–031   As was pointed earlier, where the bill of lading is governed by the Hague-Visby Rules, the position is that any statement describing:

- leading marks necessary for identification of goods;

- number of packages or pieces, or the quantity or weight;

- apparent order and condition of the goods

will be treated as prima facie evidence of the goods so described as against the carrier. No proof rebutting the statements will be allowed when the bill of lading has been transferred to a third party acting in good faith (art.III(3)). Where the bill of lading is not governed by the Hague-Visby Rules, the principle of estoppel applies, binding the maker to his statement in the bill of lading describing the apparent order and condition of the goods. The principle does not however apply to statements referring to the quantity or weight of the goods shipped or received for shipment by the carrier. The position of statements referring to quantity and weight is set out in *Grant v Norway* (1851) 10 C.B. 665.

Grant v Norway (1851) 10 C.B. 665 **6–032**
Facts:
The shipmaster signed three bills of lading for 12 bales of silk which had never been put on board and indorsed them to Biale, Koch & Co which were in turn indorsed and deposited with the claimants.
Held:
On whether the shipowner/carrier could be held liable for the non-delivery of goods, Jervis C.J. stated that the master had exceeded his authority by signing and issuing bills of lading for goods never actually placed on board his employer's vessel. It was not usual in the management of the ship for the master to give a bill of lading for goods not put on board. Any party taking the bill of lading by indorsement must be deemed to have notice of the usual powers of the shipmaster and the fact that he does not have the authority to sign bills of lading for goods not actually put on board. The indorsee of the bill of lading could not therefore bind the shipowner if he takes the bill of lading with notice of the lack of authority.

Grant v Norway therefore very effectively derogates from the sanctity of the bill of lading; necessitating the indorsee to make inquiries as to the veracity of the statements in the bill of lading as to quantity and weight. Section 3 of the Bills of Lading Act 1855 was consequently enacted to counter the effect of *Grant v Norway* and to enable traders once again to rely on the statements in the bill of lading as conclusive. Section 3 states that every bill of lading in the hands of a consignee or indorsee for valuable consideration representing goods to have been shipped on board a vessel shall be conclusive evidence of such shipment as against the master or other person signing it, regardless of the fact that the goods may not have been shipped on board. The section then sets out the following exceptions to the new rule:

- where the holder of the bill of lading has actual notice at the time of taking the bill that the goods had not been put on board;

- the shipmaster had been misrepresented to; he must further show that this was caused without any default on his part and wholly by the fraud of the shipper or of the holder, or some other person under whom the holder claims.

But does s.3 really mitigate the rule in *Grant v Norway*? It would seem not. **6–033** The section refers to estoppel as a defence, not a cause of action. Secondly, there is no reference to the estoppel being raised against the shipowner, only as against his shipmaster or person signing the bill of lading.

The limitations of s.3 are well recognised and it is no wonder that the Carriage of Goods by Sea Act 1992 which repealed the 1855 Act provides in s.4 that the lawful holder of a bill of lading shall be entitled to rely on statements in bills representing the goods to have been shipped on board a vessel, or as received for shipment on board a vessel signed by the shipmaster or by a person who has express, implied or apparent authority of the carrier to sign bills of lading as conclusive evidence against the carrier of the shipment or receipt for shipment of the goods. The Act brings statements in bills of lading falling outside the Hague-Visby Rules in line with the position of art.III(4) of the latter.

6–034   *Agrosin Pte Ltd v Highway Shipping Co Ltd (The Mata K)* [1998] 2 Lloyd's Rep. 614
Facts:
The bill of lading in question stated the gross shipped weight to be "11,000 metric tonnes" but the box marked "shipped" included the words "weight, measure, quantity, quality, condition, contents and value unknown". On discharge of the goods in Japan, a shortage was discovered. The questions for the court were:

1. whether the defendants were bound by the quantities stated on the bill of lading pursuant to s.4 of the Carriage of Goods by Sea Act 1992;

2. what the effect is of art.III(4) of the Hague Rules which were incorporated by the charter.

Held:
The court whilst acknowledging that under s.4 of the Carriage of Goods by Sea Act 1992, a bill of lading which represented that certain goods had been shipped on board a vessel and signed by the master of the vessel or a person with his express, implied or apparent authority shall be conclusive evidence against the carrier of the shipment in the favour of a person who has become the lawful holder of the bill of lading, said that a representation of "weight unknown" was not a representation as to quantity. As such s.4 did not apply. In circumstances where the bill of lading contained words to the effect of "quantity unknown", the carrier was merely accepting the weights stated for the purposes of calculating freight and was not making any representation as to the actual quantity shipped (per Longmore J. in *Noble Resources Ltd v Cavalier Shipping Corp (The Atlas)* [1996] 1 Lloyd's Rep. 642; and note also *New Chinese Antimony Co Ltd v Ocean Steamship Co Ltd* (1917) 2 K.B. 664). As for art.III(4), the presence of a "weight unknown" indorsement clearly defeated the argument that the 11,000 metric tonne entry was conclusive evidence of the quantity actually shipped.

Statements as to leading marks

6–035   The common law position, in contradistinction to art.III(4) of the Hague-Visby Rules, is that where the carrier makes a notation in the bill of lading as to the leading marks on the bill of lading, he is not estopped from adducing evidence to show that the goods received for shipment were in fact the goods delivered to the consignee. The rule must be applied in the light of *Compania Importadora de Arroces Collette y Kamp SA v P&O Steam Navigation Co* (1927) 28 Lloyd's L. Rep. 63. There, Wright J. held that statements as to leading marks, though not conclusive, were prima facie evidence to that effect. The carrier will have to show by "clear and sufficient evidence" that the bill of lading was in fact erroneous.

The basis of the rule is not entirely clear as demonstrated in *Parsons v New Zealand Shipping Co* [1901] 1 Q.B. 548.

6–036   *Parsons v New Zealand Shipping Co* [1901] 1 Q.B. 548
Facts:
The bill of lading in question described the consignment of frozen lamb as marked Sun Brand 488X and Sun Brand 622X. It turned out that the lambs had actually been marked and labelled Sun Brand 388X and Sun Brand 522X respectively. The market for lamb was falling quite sharply and the buyers refused to take delivery and sued the carriers for misdelivery.

Held:

The Court of Appeal decided unanimously in favour of the carrier. Collins and Romer L.JJ. held that the markings for book-keeping purposes on the carcasses was immaterial. Collins L.J. stated:

> "[I]t is obvious that, where marks have no market meaning and indicate nothing whatever to a buyer as to the nature, quality, or quantity of the goods which he is buying, it is absolutely immaterial to him whether the goods bear one mark or another".

The crucial issue is whether the mistaken markings affect the existence or identity of the goods or simply make identification of the consignment more difficult. If it is the latter, the carrier is entitled to produce evidence to show that the markings were mistaken but the agreed cargo had actually been shipped to the satisfaction of the contract. Smith M.R. on the other hand approached the matter on the basis that the carriers were exempt from liability simply because there was an exclusion of liability clause covering misdelivery. His Lordship did not consider the markings as being of little importance. His position was that if the contract was for ABC champagne, ABC champagne must be delivered. It is not acceptable to tender XYZ champagne which is just as good.

It is patent that Smith M.R.'s judgment was swayed by his concern to ensure **6–037** commercial certainty. Documentary sanctity is the norm; it is the backbone of the international sale transaction. Traders, banks, and insurers should need not go beyond the face of the documents. Indeed if the buyer or seller is not warranted to produce extraneous evidence to show that the bill of lading's description does refer to the contracted goods, there is no reason why the carrier should be thus entitled.[24] On that basis Smith M.R.'s approach is to an appreciable extent preferable.

Switch bills of lading:

Sometimes carriers are asked by the seller to issue a replacement bill of lading as substitute for the original bill of lading. These bills are thus issued not at the time of shipment. They are called "switch bills of lading". The seller may ask for a switch bill to conceal the identity of his suppliers from the buyers to prevent the two from conducting direct dealings with each other. Switch bills are sometimes alongside a transferable credit (see paras 11–065—11–066). Other reasons for doing so might be:

* the original bill names a port of discharge which is subsequently changed (where, for example, the seller gives the buyer a right to change the port of discharge);

* the seller had shipped the goods in small parcels and the buyer wants a single bill referring to all the parcels for his sale to a sub-buyer.

These are legitimate commercial reasons but in law, such bills of lading are highly problematic, particularly if they have been issued by charterers rather than owners.[25] In *The Atlas* [1996] 1 Lloyd's Rep. 642, for example, the switch bills were held not to constitute prima facie evidence of the quantity shipped. There is also the issue of authority. A charterer does not have apparent or ostensible authority to issue a second

---

[24] Incidentally, this case also demonstrates the difficulty in distinguishing words of description (i.e. words that go to the identity of the goods) from mere representations.

[25] Toh, "Of straight and switch bills of lading" [1996] L.M.C.L.Q. 416.

set of bills of lading on behalf of the shipowner. As such, he could not to be treated as the contractual carrier under a switch bill of lading.

As some of the information in the switch bill will inevitably be changed, this could well constitute a mis-statement of fact. This could potentially lead to claims of fraudulent misrepresentation. In turn, even if the shipper offers the carrier an indemnity, it might be unenforceable for illegality (*Brown Jenkinson v Percy Dalton* [1957] 2 Q.B. 621). One way to guard against this is to change only information that could not be said to induce the holder into incurring loss or damage. Also, where the original bills are still in circulation, this could very well lead to fraud.

There are things that the carriers and their agents could do to minimise the risk of legal exposure. They should always ensure that proper authority is given before agreeing to issue a switch bill. The bill should only be issued if the *complete* first set has been handed over so as to ensure that there is only one set of bills in circulation relating to the consignment in question. The information to be changed should not misrepresent the port of loading, the shipment date, and the condition of the goods. These are matters which when relied on by the holder of the bill could lead to his suffering damage. Naturally, it goes without saying that the terms of the indemnity would be construed very restrictively. Hence, the carrier or his agent should ensure that the letter of indemnity is set out in the clearest terms and proper authority of the giver is ascertained.

The Bill of Lading as Contract

6–038 The bill of lading through trade usage has long been recognised as not only being the evidence of the contract of carriage but as being that contract itself. This evolved character is given due recognition and effect under the Carriage of Goods by Sea Act 1992 which defines the contract of carriage in s.5(1) as "the contract contained in or evidenced by" the bill of lading. The terms contained in the bill of lading may therefore in some situations be effectively the terms of the contract or in others, merely evidence of the actual terms. The distinction is significant to the extent that as a primary and negotiable document, it is treated by the law as the actual contract once it has been indorsed to a third party. The third party may legitimately rely on it as containing the terms of the contract and any variation of the contract between the shipper and carrier could and should not bind him who cannot have notice of the variation.

The position may be summarised as such:

- in the hands of the shipper, the bill of lading represents the contract of carriage i.e. merely the evidence of the contract. The parties are free to vary and amend the contract as they so desire;

- once it has been transferred or indorsed to a third party, the bill of lading should not be treated as simply the evidence of the contract of carriage. The third party may rely on it as the contract of carriage per se.

The following case explains the basis for the rule and discusses the possible approaches to the issue.

6–039 *Leduc & Co v Ward* (1888) 20 Q.B.D. 475
Facts:
A cargo of rape seed was to be shipped on the Austria to Dunkirk. There was a liberty clause in the contract enabling the shipowner "to call at any ports in any order". Instead

of sailing directly to Dunkirk the ship called at Glasgow. The ship was lost to the perils of the sea as a result. It was alleged that the indorsee should be bound by an agreement between the shipper and carrier that the ship should proceed first to Glasgow.
Held:
Lord Esher M.R. was of the opinion that:

> "[I]f the goods have been received by the captain, [the bill of lading] is the evidence in writing of what the contract of carriage between the parties is; it may be true that the contract of carriage is made before it is given, because it would generally be made before the goods are sent down to the ship: but when the goods are put on board the captain has authority to reduce that contract into writing: and then the general doctrine of law is applicable, by which, where the contract has been reduced into a writing which is intended to constitute the contract, parol evidence to alter or qualify the effect of such writing is not admissible, and the writing is the only evidence of the contract, except where there is some usage so well established and generally known that it must be taken to be incorporated with the contract".

Without drawing from the parol evidence doctrine, Fry L.J. held that the terms represented by the bill of lading are conclusive and no evidence may be admitted to contradict or vary them, by virtue of the Bills of Lading Act 1855.

The exaltation of the parol evidence rule in Lord Esher M.R.'s dictum does not   **6–040**
coincide with current practice on parol evidence in contract and general commercial practice. The generality of Lord Esher M.R.'s dictum might also mean that the reduced to writing contract in the bill of lading is not only protected by the parol evidence rule as far as the third party holder is concerned but also the shipper. This is not consistent with the commercial norm that the bill of lading is only conclusive evidence of the terms of the contract of carriage for the third party. That character of the bill of lading was emphasised by the High Court in *SS Ardennes (Cargo Owners) v SS Ardennes (Owners)* [1951] 1 K.B. 55.

SS Ardennes (Cargo Owners) v SS Ardennes (Owners) [1951] 1 K.B. 55   **6–041**
Facts:
The shipowners had given a verbal undertaking to the shippers that they would ensure that the vessel proceeded to London directly. The bill of lading, however, contained a clause enabling the shipowner to call at transit ports and break the journey. The ship made a call at Antwerp before arriving at London. The delay resulted in the shippers having to pay more import duty. The carriers in defence alleged that the oral undertaking could not vary the terms contained in the bill of lading.
Held:
The court disagreed with the carriers and held that the bill of lading was not in itself the contract *between the shipper and carrier*, only excellent evidence of it. This meant that the parties could vary it as they did in this case through the oral undertaking. Lord Goddard C.J. alluded to *Leduc & Co v Ward* (1888) but made it quite explicit that it was Fry L.J.'s judgment on which they had relied.

It was suggested by the shipowners in *Michael S Evryalos Maritime Ltd v China Pacific Insurance Co Ltd (MV Michael S)* (December 20, 2001), that following the passage of the 1992 Act, the rule in *Leduc v Ward* that an indorsee was not affected by the terms agreed to or understandings reached between the shipper and the shipowner of which he had no notice no longer applied. They argued that s.5(1)(a) had changed all that. They contended that the words "the contract contained in or evidenced by that bill" meant that the carrier was now entitled to bind the indorsee to agreements or understandings reached between the original parties. The Commercial Court rejected that construction, and held that it was obvious that that was not the intention of the Law Commission. The court thought it more probable that the words "evidenced by" were inserted to take account of those frequent cases where there was a concluded contract of carriage before the time when the bill of lading was issued by the carrier, rather than to give effect to agreements or understandings reached by the original parties without the indorsee's knowledge.

6–042   The bill of lading is totally reliant on the existence of a contract of carriage. Although it would be treated as a contract once indorsed to a third party, it would nonetheless be a nullity if there was no contract in the first place (*Heskell v Continental Express Ltd* [1950] 1 All E.R. 1033).

As long as it is obvious that the terms and conditions are reproduced or attached to the bill of lading, it is no defence to say that they were too unclear or illegible. In *Pirelli Cables Ltd v United Thai Shipping Corp Ltd* [2000] 1 Lloyd's Rep. 663, it was argued before the court that the exclusive jurisdiction clause in the bill of lading which was indorsed on the reverse of the bill of lading could not be binding because it was so faint and in such small writing as to be effectively illegible. Langley J. rejected the argument stating:

> "Mr Macey-Dare referred me to the decision of the Court of Appeal of New South Wales in *Chellaram & Co v China-Ocean Shipping Co* ("*The Zhi Jiang Kou*") [1991] 1 Lloyd's Rep. 493 and in particular the robust approach of Kirby, P. to just this issue at page 520 of the report. I respectfully agree. This too is a case where the existence of conditions was apparent and if the claimants had been interested to know what they were they could have asked for and would have obtained a more legible copy".

Charterparties and the bill of lading

6–043   In a situation where the shipowner contracts immediately and directly with a cargo owner to carry the latter's goods in consideration of freight, the legal relationship is clearly that between carrier and shipper. Where the shipowner had first chartered the vessel to a charterer who then in turn contracts with the cargo owner, the position becomes blurred. It is immediately obvious that there may now be two contracts of carriage—the charterparty and the contract between charterer and shipper. How does one affect the other?

It might be useful to start our discussion in the context of this scenario:

Example: A, the shipowner enters into a charterparty with B, the charterer. B wants a third of the space on board the vessel for his own goods; the remainder he sells to C, who has a cargo of widgets to ship. Under the charterparty, a bill of lading could be demanded from the shipmaster, A's agent. Under the second contract of carriage, C, the shipper of widgets, also has the right to a bill of lading representing the goods. The nature of the parties' rights and obligations will depend on the underlying contractual relationship and in what capacity the ship master issued the bill of lading.

Charterer in possession of bill of lading

6–044   We consider first the situation of the charterer who is in possession of bill of lading issued to him by the shipmaster. The early case of *Rodocanachi, Sons &*

Co v Milburn Bros (1886) 18 Q.B.D. 67 makes an excellent introduction to the rule that regardless of the bill of lading and the representations in it, the charterer's rights and obligations are founded solely on the charterparty.

Rodocanachi, Sons & Co v Milburn Bros (1886) 18 Q.B.D. 67   **6–045**
Facts:
Under a charterparty for the use of the ship to carry a cargo of cotton seed, the shipmaster was to sign bills of lading representing the goods and contract. The bill contained an exemption of liability clause. The cargo was subsequently lost through the negligence of the shipmaster. The main issue was whether the charterparty must be read as incorporating the terms of the bill of lading.
Held:
The Court of Appeal held that the shipowner (as the master's agent) was not entitled to rely on the exemption clause in the bill because

> "when there is a charterparty, . . . , the bill of lading operates prima facie as a mere receipt for the goods, and a document of title which may be negotiated, and by which the property is transferred, but does not operate as a new contract, or alter the contract contained in the charterparty".

Commercial practice soon reflected this position. Shipmasters were ordered by their employers to sign bills of lading "without prejudice to the terms of the charterparty". It was once thought that the "without prejudice" clause was for the benefit of the shipowners. This was effectively rebutted in *Turner v Haji Goolam Mahomed Azam* [1904] A.C. 826, where Lord Lindley was of the opinion that

> "the words, 'without prejudice to this charter' mean that the rights of the shipowners against the . . . charterers, and *vice versa*, are to be preserved".

The shipmaster has no authority to modify or vary the charterparty; he has only to sign the bill of lading "without prejudice".

  The rule is not free from difficulty as the facts in *President of India v Metcalfe* [1970] 1 Q.B. 289 reveal.

President of India v Metcalfe [1970] 1 Q.B. 289   **6–046**
Facts:
The Indian government had chartered a ship to carry a consignment of fertilisers from the Italian sellers. The sellers obtained bills of lading from the shipmaster and then forwarded these bills to the charterer, the Indian government. That bill of lading did not contain an arbitration clause which was present in the charterparty. The Indian government sought to rely on the clause against the shipowners. The difficulty of the case is obviously the fact that the bill has been transferred back to the charterer. The shipowners argued that this meant the contract was hence contained in the bill of lading, and not the charterparty.
Held:
Lord Denning M.R. held that even though the charterer is not the shipper and takes the bill of lading as an indorsee, his relationship with the shipowner has to be governed by the charterparty. As between the shipowner and charterer, the bill of lading is only a receipt for the goods. Reliance for this judgment was placed on the Scottish decision in *Love & Stewart Ltd v Rowtor Steamship Co Ltd* [1916] S.C. 223; [1916] 2 A.C. 527.

6–047 *Love & Stewart Ltd v Rowtor Steamship Co Ltd* [1916] 2 A.C. 527
Facts:
The sale contract was for a large parcel of pit props to be delivered FOB Kristinestad,
Finland. The buyers then chartered a ship to go to Kristinestad and load the cargo and
carry it to Newport in New South Wales. The bill of lading was indorsed in the blank to
the seller. An invoice was subsequently presented to the buyer/charterers. The charterparty
allowed 13 days for loading and 13 days for discharging and allowed any days saved on
loading to be added on to the discharge time. The loading took nine days but the
shipmaster stated in the bill of lading that it took 13. At Newport, the discharge took 171/2
days. The shipowner claimed demurrage on the basis that the charterers had exceeded the
laytime by four and a half days. The charterers argued that as the loading had only taken
nine days and not 13 as represented in the bill of lading, they were only liable for a half-
day demurrage.
Held:
The House of Lords held that the shipowners could only claim for half a day demurrage;
they were bound by the "reversible" clause in the charterparty which allowed the adding-
on of the days saved during loading. They were not entitled to rely on the '13-day' clause
in the bill of lading. Lord Summer stated that the bill of lading was issued simply as a
receipt or "the symbol of the delivery of goods while afloat". Nothing had occurred by
which any contract for the carriage of goods arose between the charterers and the
shipowners other than the original charter itself. No new bargain had been made.

It must further be noted that although the bill of lading may have been issued to
the charterer, either directly or indirectly as demonstrated in the above cases, the
Hague-Visby Rules do not apply as far as the relationship between charterer and
shipowner is concerned. Article 1(b) is unequivocal in stipulating the limits of
the Rules. Where the bill of lading in question does not regulate the relations
between a carrier and the holder of the bill, the Rules do not have legal effect.

This has led to some charterers (or shipowners) insisting on the incorporation
of the Hague-Visby Rules as terms of the charterparty. This incorporation does
not restore the statutory effect of the Rules; it simply enables the parties and the
court to treat the Rules as forming the contractual terms. While the court would
be prepared to apply canons of statutory interpretation when construing the
Hague-Visby Rules as incorporated, it is conscious of the fact that these are, for
all intents and purposes, contractual terms and may have to depart from the
rigours of statutory interpretation (*Adamastos Shipping Co v Anglo Saxon
Petroleum* [1958] 1 Lloyd's Rep. 73; *The Satya Kailash* [1984] 1 Lloyd's Rep.
588).

The third party shipper in possession of the bill of lading

6–048 The third party may have contracted, as in our illustration above (para.6–043),
with the charterer to have his goods shipped by the latter using a vessel belonging
to the shipowner. He is entitled to a bill of lading which is to be issued and signed
by the shipmaster who is the shipowner's servant. The question is when loss or
damage is caused to the goods during transit, against whom does the action by
the cargo owner lie? Does he sue the charterer or the ship owner? The problem
is exacerbated where there are subcharterers and agents of the charterers, etc.
involved in the contract. Who should the cargo owner sue? One possible solution
is to join all of them to the action. This unfortunately may be an expensive way
to pursue a remedy at law.

The general rule is that despite the presence and privy of the charterer, the shipowner remains responsible for the management and control of the vessel, and the issue of the bill of lading. His duty makes him answerable to the cargo owner in the event of loss or damage resulting from the care and control of the cargo, or the issue of a bad bill of lading.

Sandeman v Scurr (1866) L.R. 2 Q.B. 86   **6–049**
Facts:
The *Village Belle* was under charter to load a cargo of wine and other merchandise in Portugal and discharge the same in the United Kingdom. The captain of the ship was authorised to "sign bills of lading at any rate of freight, without prejudice to the charter". The agents of the charterer then entered into a contract of carriage with the claimants agreeing to carry the latter's goods to the United Kingdom. The claimants were not aware that the ship was under charter. A bill of lading was issued evidencing the shipment. The goods were alleged to have been damaged as a result of bad stowage. The question was whether the claimants were right to pursue the action against the shipowners and not the charterers.
Held:
The claimants were entitled to bring an action against the shipowners. The reason was that irrespective of the question or fact of the charterer's liability, the claimants, having delivered the goods to be carried in ignorance of the charterparty and having dealt with the shipmaster "clothed with the ordinary authority of a master to receive and give bills of lading on behalf of his owners", are entitled to look to the owners as responsible for the safe carriage of the goods. The only exception to the rule is when the charter in question is a demise charter; the demise charter being a lease of the ship with full control of its crew and master to the charterer and the charterer stands entirely in the shoes of the ship-owner.

The rule was taken further in *Tillmans v Knutsford* [1908] A.C. 406 where even though the bill of lading was signed not by the shipmaster but the charterer himself, the third party shipper of goods could rely on it to sue the shipowner. It is ostensible that the charterer was representing the shipowner in the issuing and signing of the bill of lading. The existence of this general rule has led to many charters incorporating an indemnity clause. A typical indemnity clause is reproduced below:

> "The Master (although appointed by Owners) shall be under the orders and direction of Charterers as regards employment of the vessel, agency or other arrangements. Bills of Lading are to be signed as Charterers or their agents may direct, without prejudice to this Charter, the master attending as necessary at the offices of Charterers or their agents to do so. Charterers hereby indemnify Owners against all liabilities that may arise:
>
> (1) from any irregularities in papers supplied by Charterers or their agents, and
> (2) from signing of Bills of Lading in accordance with the directions of Charterers or their agents to the extent that the terms of such Bills of Lading impose more onerous liabilities than those assumed by Owners under the terms of this Charter".

Where the shipmaster had signed the bill of lading purporting to be acting for   **6–050** charterer, then it may be possible that the charterer could be bound by the shipmaster's act. That possibility was discussed by the Court of Appeal in *The*

Rewia [1991] 2 Lloyd's Rep. 325. The court was particularly sensitive to the original rationale to the rule that the shipowner should remain liable for bills issued by his shipmaster vis-à-vis the cargo owner holding that bill. In that case, bills of lading representing the cargo of nutmeg shipped to Rotterdam were issued in the name of a container line. Part of the cargo was lost at sea. In deciding whether the bills of lading were binding on the shipowners, the court had to ascertain whether from the terms of the bill of lading and other circumstances the shipmaster had signed the bills as agent for the shipowner or the charterer. Leggatt L.J. considered *Harrison v Huddersfield Steamship Co* (1903) 19 T.L.R. 386 as support for the proposition that "although the master is the owner's servant, his signature may in some cases bind the charterer and not the owner".

In *Harrison v Huddersfield Steamship*, the agreement between shipowner and charterer provides that the master was to be agent of the charterer and to have no authority to bind the shipowner by issuing bills of lading on the latter's behalf. The words "as master" which were printed on the bills of lading had been struck out and were substituted by the phrase "as agent for time charterers". Walton J. decided that the master had not signed as master of the ship; he had signed as agent for the charterers. The shipowners were therefore not liable.

It seems clear that while the general rule is that the master binds the shipowner by issuing and signing bills of lading, that rule may be displaced where it is clear from the circumstances and terms of the bill of lading and other documents that shipmaster was acting as the charterer's agent.[26] Modern bills of lading tend to carry a "demise clause" to ensure that matters as to agency and authority are made pellucid. This clause stipulates that

> "if the ship is not owned or chartered by demise to the company or line by whom [the] bill of lading is issued . . . the Bills of Lading shall take effect as a contract with the Owner or demise charterer, as the case may be, as principal made through the agency of the said company or line who act as agents only and shall be under no personal liability whatsoever in respect thereof".

This is intended to remove the liability of the party issuing the bill of lading unless he is the shipowner or the demise charterer.

6–051   Besides the problem of identifying the carrier against whom an action for breach of the contract of carriage may lie for the third party shipper, we need also to know what the terms are of this contract. To what extent is the third party shipper entitled to plead the terms of the charterparty in an action against the shipowner/carrier, bearing in mind that the bill of lading frequently contains a general clause stating that its terms are "as per charterparty". This is done by shipowners intent on protecting themselves from being exposed to greater liability for bills of lading issued by the charterers. The law is that any such purported incorporation must be "done by distinct and specific words, and not by [mere] general words". The limitation is seen in *TW Thomas & Co Ltd v Portsea Steamship Co Ltd* [1912] A.C. 1 where the House of Lords held that the words "Deck load at shipper's risk, and all other terms and conditions and exceptions of charter to be per charterparty" written in the margin of the bill of lading were

---

[26] See *The Starsin* [2003] UKHL 12 and paras 8–003—8–006 for a detailed examination of the subject of the identity of the carrier.

too general to incorporate into the bill of lading, the arbitration clause in the charterparty.

The Court of Appeal held in *Federal Bulk Carriers Inc v C Itoh & Co Ltd* (*The Federal Bulker*) [1989] 1 Lloyd's Rep. 103 that this process of incorporation is very much a matter of construction of contracts. The court is to ascertain the intention of the parties as expressed in the written agreement, namely the bill of lading. The court was deeply concerned with the importance of commercial certainty in the field. A few principles were laid down in this case:

1. In the light of ensuring that the bill of lading remains a document which could be relied simply on its face, the ordinary contract law rule of admitting the incorporation of external standard terms through the use of general words cannot be maintained.

2. The language used to incorporate the standard terms must be clear and effective.

3. The incorporated terms should be consistent with the tenor of the bill of lading contract.

4. On the authority of Lord Denning M.R. in *The Annefield* [1971] 1 Lloyd's Rep. 1,

> "[A] clause which is directly germane to the subject-matter of the bill of lading (that is to the shipment, carriage and delivery of goods) can and should be incorporated into the bill of lading contract, even though it may involve a degree of manipulation of the words in order to fit exactly the bill of lading".

This manoeuvre would presumably involve distorting certain express words to suit the incorporation. It was thus argued in *The Miramar* [1984] 2 Lloyd's Rep. 592 that the words "the charterer" could and should be replaced by "the consignee under a bill of lading issued in respect of the whole or any part of the cargo". The House of Lords disagreed. Lord Diplock held that if the proposition taken from Lord Denning M.R.'s judgment was right, it would have

> "the effect that every consignee to whom a bill of lading covering any part of the cargo is negotiated, is not only accepting personal liability to pay the owners freight, as stated in the bill of lading, but is also accepting blindfold a potential liability to pay an unknown and wholly unpredictable sum for demurrage which may, unknown to him, already have accrued or may subsequently accrue without any ability on his part to prevent it, even though that sum may actually exceed the delivered value of the goods to which the bill of lading gives title".

This fact is the overwhelming reason, according to His Lordship,

> "for not indulging in verbal manipulation of the actual contractual words used in the charterparty so as to give to them this effect when they are treated as incorporated in the bill of lading".

The presence of an incorporation clause in the bill of lading may reduce its transferability. Current financing practice as reflected in the UCP 600 for

Documentary Credits is that "a bill of lading, however named, must . . . contain no indication that it is subject to a charterparty . . . " (art.20(a)(vi)).

The Bill of Lading as a Document of Title

6–052 In an international sale transaction, the goods may take some time before arriving at their destination. This would cause considerable difficulty on the buyer who may wish to sell the goods on or to secure credit using the goods as collateral from banks and other financing institutions. Custom had therefore developed to treat the bill of lading as a document of title, thus enabling the owner of the goods (who could be either the buyer or the seller) to pass title in the goods simply by transferring or indorsing the bill of lading.

The nature of the bill of lading as a document of title is perhaps best seen in the light of the judgment of *Sanders Bros v Maclean* (1883) 11 Q.B.D. 327; part of it is reproduced below:

> "The law as to the indorsement of bills of lading is as clear as in my opinion the practice of all European merchants is thoroughly understood. A cargo at sea while in the hands of the carrier is necessarily incapable of physical delivery. During this period of transit and voyage, the bill of lading by the law merchant as universally recognised as its symbol, and the indorsement and delivery of the bill of lading operates as a symbolical delivery of the cargo. Property in the goods passes by such indorsement and delivery of the bill of lading, whenever it is the intention of the parties that the property should pass, just as under similar circumstances the property would pass by an actual delivery of the goods".

The bill of lading will only have the effect of a document of title if it is made clear on its face that it is negotiable, i.e. it must be an "order" bill as against a "straight" bill. The former is made out to a named consignee or to his "order or assigns". This means that the named consignee could transfer or assign the bill of lading on to any third party simply by delivery or indorsement. A straight bill of lading is made out to a named consignee. That means that it is not transferable, once it has been delivered to the "notify party". The House of Lords has confirmed in *The Rafaela S* [2005] UKHL 11 that the straight bill, although non-negotiable, is nonetheless a document of title in the hands of the named consignee because it entitles him to take delivery of the goods on production of the bill. Indeed, it was stressed in *The Rafaela S* that the production of the straight bill of lading (where no order bill was issued) is a prerequisite to delivery, even in cases where there was no express provision to that effect in the bill of lading (see also the Singapore case of *Voss v APL Co PTE Ltd* [2002] 2 Lloyd's Rep. 707 and the Hong Kong case of *Carewins Development (China) Ltd v Bright Fortune Shipping Ltd* (July 13, 2007)). It has been thought in some quarters that a straight bill had the same legal effect as a sea waybill[27] but as Lord Steyn

---

[27] Indeed for the purposes of the Carriage of Goods by Sea Act 1992, a straight bill be dealt with by the provisions relating to the sea waybill rather than those relating to the bill of lading (*AP Moeller Maersk A/S (trading as Maersk Line) v Sonaec Villas Cen Sad Fadoul* [2010] EWHC 355 (Comm); also *Finmoon v Baltic Reefers* [2012] EWHC 920 (Comm)).

clarified in *The Rafaela S*, a sea waybill is never a document of title. It is not a document of title because its presentation without further proof of identity would not cause the delivery of the goods by the carrier (*Soproma v Marine & Animal By-Products Corp* [1966] 1 Lloyd's Rep. 367). The differences between the documents include the fact that a straight bill of lading contains the standard terms of the carrier on the reverse side of the document but a sea waybill is blank and straight bills of lading are invariably issued in sets of three and waybills not. Also, it might be added that whilst the physical surrender of a straight bill is needed to induce delivery of the goods, there is no such requirement in the case of sea waybills.

Indemnities and delivery dispensing with the bill of lading

The general rule is that where the person calling for delivery is not in possession **6–053**
of the bill of lading, the shipmaster should not deliver the goods up to him. However, in this day and age where delays are an everyday occurrence and business depends on speed and efficiency, shipmasters (and their employers) are placed under tremendous pressure to deliver the goods even in the absence of a bill of lading. Traders resort to the device of an indemnity to induce delivery of goods without production of the bill of lading. The supplier/trader or even some third party will undertake to indemnify the carrier for loss or liability in the occasion of misdelivery. The legality and implications of an indemnity to induce the issue of a false bill of lading have been considered above[28] but here the context is different. There is no unlawful or illegal act involved (the making of a false bill of lading is to make a fraudulent representation about the goods); here the indemnity is offered to induce delivery of the goods without having sight of the bill of lading is usually not tainted by fraud or unconscionable conduct. It is, therefore, not surprising that the courts feel more inclined to be generous. In *Sze Hai Tong Bank v Rambler Cycle Co Ltd* [1959] A.C. 576, the Judicial Committee of the Privy Council held that the carriers had been liable for delivering the goods without production of the bill of lading and whilst their act was not protected by an exemption clause in the bill of lading, they were entitled to rely on the indemnity. It might also be added where the indemnity is given to a charterer instead of the shipowner, the latter can rely on the Contracts (Rights of Third Parties) Act 1999 (s.1(1)(b)) to enforce the indemnity (*Laemthong International Lines v Abdullah Mohd. Fahem* [2005] EWCA Civ 519).

Great Eastern Shipping Co Ltd v Far East Chartering Ltd & Binani Cement Ltd   **6–054**
[2011] EWHC 1372 (Comm)
Facts:
A sold coal to V who then resold to B. V owns a chartering company, F. F chartered G's vessel to carry the coal to B, in India. When the documents were delivered by A to V, V rejected them.

   B issued a letter of indemnity (as required by its contract with V) to ask F to deliver the coal to B in India without production of the bills of lading, promising to indemnify them for the act.

---

[28] See, e.g., discussion on *Brown Jenkinson & Co Ltd v Percy Dalton Ltd* [1957] 2 Q.B. 621 in paras 6–029—6–030.

The vessel arrived in India; G issued a delivery order to the port authority in favour of B and the cargo was discharged. B removed some of the cargo from the port but subsequently wrote to V rejecting the cargo on the grounds that it was below specification.

A informed G that they would sue G for damages because G had delivered the cargo to B without presentation of the bills of lading. A obtained judgment against G. V and F became insolvent; accordingly, V was unlikely to take action to obtain the bills of lading.

G, to cover its liability to A, sought to enforce the letter of indemnity under the Contracts (Rights of Third Parties) Act 1999.

B refused to pay. They argued that there was no contract between F and B which could be made the subject of the 1999 Act and that as a matter of public policy, G could not be indemnified against its own deliberate wrongdoing. B argued that once they were on notice of the supplier's claims, F and G would have known that delivery of the cargo without presentation of the bills of lading was wrongful, precluding them from enforcing the letter of indemnity.

Held:

The court held that the facts were plainly that the letter of indemnity constituted a contract capable of activating the 1999 Act. Although the letter of indemnity could be interpreted in different ways, it should be noted that in general letters of indemnity were important commercial instruments which had to be interpreted robustly and straightforwardly. They were often issued and relied upon by people for whom English was not their first language and whose opportunities for close textual analysis before committing to a wording were very limited. Moreover, it was contained in a standard form making it even more important not to depart from a straightforward reading.

There were no issues of public policy—a letter of indemnity issued on these terms was commonplace in international commerce.

6–055   On appeal, the Court of Appeal dismissed B's claim.[29] The point of public policy was clarified. The court acknowledged that where the indemnity was to induce the commission of a crime or a tort, it would not be enforceable. However, where the act underwritten by the letter of indemnity related only to a potential contractual dispute (such as who was contractually entitled to take delivery of the cargo), that letter of indemnity would be enforceable and would not be contrary to public policy.

In *The Houda* [1994] 2 Lloyd's Rep. 541, the court held that where the bill of lading has been lost, the person calling for delivery should ensure that in addition to an indemnity, a court declaration is obtained providing that on his presentment of a good indemnity to the carrier the loss of the bill of lading is not to be set up as a defence.

Although we talk about the bill of lading as being negotiable, it must not be confused with a negotiable instrument. The bill of lading is simply the document representing title to the goods and therefore, could not through the act of negotiation or indorsement pass a better title to the third party than what the holder originally possessed. A negotiable instrument on the other hand can pass a title which is indefeasible to the third party who takes it in good faith even though the original holder might not have a good title.[30]

---

[29] [2012] EWCA Civ 180.
[30] See *The Future Express* [1993] 2 Lloyd's Rep. 542 at 547 and s.38 Bills of Exchange Act 1882.

Bills of lading and the Carriage of Goods by Sea Act 1992

Holder's rights of suit and the doctrine of privity of contract

The transfer or assignment of the bill of lading is intended to generate rights and   **6–056**
obligations in the third party holder. The Bills of Lading Act 1855 was intended
to bolster the standing of the bill of lading against the constraints placed on the
transferability of contractual rights by the doctrine of privity of contract. Section
1 of that Act provides that every consignee or indorsee of a bill of lading *to whom
property in the goods shall pass* on or by reason of the consignment or
indorsement of the bill of lading, shall be vested all rights of suit and be subject
to all liabilities in respect of the goods. The law goes on to state that he will be
treated as if he had been an original party to the contract.

The fact that the doctrine of privity is routed only where there is the transfer
of property in the goods on or by reason of the transfer or indorsement of the bill
of lading means that where property in the goods has yet to pass under whatever
circumstance, there is no transfer of contractual rights or obligations through the
bill of lading.

Enichem Anic SpA v Ampelos Shipping Co Ltd (The Delfini) [1990] 1 Lloyd's Rep.   **6–057**
252
Facts:
The claimants had bought part of a cargo shipped in bulk. The appropriation of the goods
to the claimants' contract was not to take place until the goods arrive at the port of
destination. The rule in s.16 of the Sale of Goods Act 1979 provides that property in
unascertained goods will not pass until the goods become ascertained. The sale contract
stipulated that payment was to be made against the tender of conforming documents or a
letter of indemnity in the event that the bills of lading were not available at the time of
payment. The claimants then took delivery of the goods by presenting a letter of
indemnity. The goods were handed over. Subsequently, when the bill of lading was finally
delivered to the claimants, they sued the carrier for short delivery.
Held:
The claimants' contention was that under s.1 of the Bills of Lading Act 1855 when the bill
of lading was indorsed to them, they received the rights of suit against the carrier from the
shipper. The Court of Appeal decided that the claimants were not entitled to plead s.1 of
the Act because the indorsement of the bill of lading was not hinged upon the passing of
property. The passing of property took place through the actual delivery of the goods
against the letter of indemnity. They did not have any contractual rights against the carrier
because they were not privy to the contract of carriage.

The Carriage of Goods by Sea Act 1992 was enacted to counter these limitations
of the Bills of Lading Act 1855.[31] That Act came into force on September 16,
1992 and it provides that the lawful holder of a bill of lading, a sea waybill or a
delivery order acquires the right to sue the carrier in contract for loss, or damage
to the goods regardless of whether property in the goods has passed or not
(s.2(1)). It is also immaterial that the goods have ceased to exist after the issue
of the bill of lading or relevant shipping document or could not be identified for
whatever reason (s.5(4)). The holder of the bill of lading only has the title to sue
if the bill of lading had been transferred to him as a result of some contractual or
other transaction made *before* the bill ceased to function as a document of title

---

[31] See Bradgate and White, "The Carriage of Goods by Sea Act 1992" [1993] M.L.R. 188.

(s.2(2)(a)). The rationale is to avoid the open trading of bills of lading as a commodity enabling any purchaser to use them against the carrier. It should not be perceived as a right of action available to any person unrelated to the underpinning contractual arrangements. It is also intended that the Act applies not only to transferable bills of lading but these other shipping documents widely used in trade in place or in addition to bills of lading. Section 2(1)(a) applies to bills of lading, properly so called. Section 1(2) provides that a bill of lading will "not include references to a document which is incapable of transfer either by indorsement or, as a bearer bill, by delivery without indorsement". Therefore straight bills of lading do not fall under s.2(1)(a). Section 2(1)(b) on the other hand applies to the holder of a sea waybill and s.1(3) makes it plain that the term "sea waybill" will include any document (which is not a bill of lading) which is a receipt for the goods as contains, or evidences, a contract of carriage by sea and identifies the person to whom delivery is to be made by the carrier. A straight bill will therefore come under this provision instead of s.2(1)(a).

6–058   Under s.2(1)(b) of the Act, rights under a sea waybill and the contract of carriage contained in or evidenced thereby are "transferred" to the named consignee as soon as the bill is signed. But a shipper who is, and remains, party to the contract of carriage does not lose his right viz-a-viz the carrier to divert the goods, as he may wish to do if he is not paid for them (*AP Moller-Maersk v Sonaec* [2010] EWHC 355 (Comm)). Where goods are shipped by A in B's ship under a sea waybill naming C as consignee, A may exercise his power to redirect the goods by substituting D for C as consignee. Where A does this, C ceases to be, and D becomes, "the person to whom delivery . . . . is to be made by the carrier" so that rights under the contract of carriage are vested in D by virtue of s.2(1) and any rights which were previously vested in C become extinct under s.2(5).[32]

Section 2 of the Act refers to the "lawful holder" of a bill of lading. Section 5(2) defines a "lawful holder" as a holder in good faith. A holder in turn is defined as a person who:

1. holds a bill which identifies him as the consignee;

2. comes into possession of the bill as a result of delivery of the bill, of indorsement of the bill or in the case of a bearer bill, by any transfer of the bill to him;

3. comes into possession of the bill as a result of any transaction by virtue of which he would have become a holder within 1. or 2., had not the transaction been effected at a time when possession of the bill no longer have a right (as against the carrier) to possession of the goods.

These provisions, especially 1. and 2., can cause difficult interpretation problems for unusual facts.

6–059   *The Ythan* [2005] EWHC 2399
Facts:
The goods carried by the ship caused an explosion resulting in the total loss of the ship. The goods were sold by A to B. B had on-sold the goods to C. Under the terms of the

---

[32] *Carver on Bills of Lading*, 2nd edn, paras 8–013—8–014.

contract, the bill of lading should be delivered to B's bank for payment and B's bank would then deliver the bills of lading to C against C's payment.

Following the explosion, it was agreed that it would be logical for the subsale to C to be cancelled and for A to be paid by B's bank and for B to make a claim on its insurance. So A transferred the bills of lading to B's bank and was duly paid by the bank. The bank then caused the bills to be delivered to M, B's insurance agents for the purposes of the insurance claim.

Y, the shipowner, claimed that as the bills were in the possession of M, B's agents, it followed that B had become a "*lawful holder*". Further, they say that B, as lawful holder of the bills of lading, "*made a claim under the contract of carriage against*" them, as carriers of the cargo, within s.3(1)(b). Y asserted that this entitled them to sue B for damages for losses they have suffered as a result of the shipment of a dangerous cargo. *Held:*

The court held that as the goods and ship are a total loss, s.5(2)(b) could not apply. As for s.5(2)(c), Aikens J. held that "transaction" in the section referred to the physical process by which the bill is transferred from one person to another. There were two transactions in the facts—the transfer of the bills by A to B's bank, and the transfer by B's bank to M. However, the transaction relevant to the dispute is the second. That transaction was made to enable B to collect the insurance monies. Without the loss of cargo and insurance settlement B would never have had possession of the bills of lading because they would have remained in the bank's possession until C had paid for the cargo. Therefore, P did not become "holder" of the bills of lading "by virtue of" such a transaction had it occurred at a time when possession of the bills gave a right to possession of the cargo. Therefore, no rights of suit had transferred to P under s.2(1)(a).

In the alternative, under s.2(2), B did not become the "holder" of the bills as the transfer from the bank to M was effected in pursuance of a "contractual or other arrangement" that was made *after* the time when a right to possession of the cargo (as against the carrier) ceased to attach to possession of the bills. Section 2(2) required that the transaction should be pursuant to a "contractual or other arrangement" made *before* that time. The judge also held that the transaction must be the "reason or cause" for the transfer and the reason was so that the insurance monies could be paid, not because of any contractual or other arrangements in relation to the goods.

It is also important to note that once the transfer of contractual rights has taken place, it is no longer open to the transferor or consignor of the bill of lading to rely on the rights the bill represents. **6–060**

Example: Suppose A, the seller/shipper, has indorsed the bill of lading representing the goods shipped to B, the buyer. According to s.2(1), A's rights of suit against the shipowner/carrier now vest in B. A however is no longer in the position to sue based on that contract of carriage with the carrier because of the operation of s.2(5). Section 2(5) provides that where rights have been transferred by virtue of the indorsement or delivery of the bill of lading (or any other shipping document covered by the Act), that act extinguishes any entitlement to those rights which derives from a person's having been an original party to the contract of carriage.

The extinguishing of the consignor's rights will occur even where the consignor remains the owners of the goods and the consignee is merely the consignor's agent and has little interest in the goods. However, it should be noted that in the following case, the court held that the right to possession of the goods is a different matter from the right to sue under the contract of carriage.

6-061 *P&O Nedlloyd BV v Utaniko Ltd Dampskibsselskabet AF 1912 A/S (Maersk Line v East West Corp)* [2003] EWCA Civ 83.

Facts:

The claimants had agreed to sell goods to the buyers in Chile. The goods were packed into containers and shipped on the defendants' vessels. At discharge, the goods were released to the buyers without presentation of the bills of lading. The goods were subsequently consigned to the order of a few banks in Chile. The claimants then indorsed the bills of lading and sent to the banks to obtain payment from the buyers in return for the bills of lading. The banks had no property or possessory interest in the goods despite the fact that they were holders of the bills of lading. That was because they held the bills of lading to the order and direction of the sellers.

The buyers did not pay for the goods. The sellers remained the owners. The banks then returned the bills of lading to the sellers without indorsing them. The trial judge held that the 1992 Act had transferred to the banks not only the claimants' rights of suit in contract but also their right to possession of the goods, so that they had no right of action as bailors against the carrier. They, however, were entitled to sue the carrier in tort because they remained owners of the goods.

Held:

The Court of Appeal held that the sellers could not sue in contract, whether as original parties or as principals of the Chilean banks, or indeed, on any other basis because once the transfer of the bills of lading had taken place, their rights of suit were extinguished. Mance L.J. held that the 1992 Act does not expressly modify any rights other than contractual rights.

His Lordship then referred to the Law Commission's report which did not recommend an exclusion of the consignor's right to sue in tort. The sellers, however, retained the right to immediate possession of the goods. A claim in bailment against the carrier was thus permissible. Even if that assessment was incorrect, Mance L.J. thought that the sellers had a reversionary proprietary interest as owners of the goods to bring an action in bailment.

6-062   It might be argued that by allowing one person to be entitled to sue on the contract and another on tort/bailment over the same cargo, might be to expose the carrier to conflicting claims. However, as the carriers were clearly obliged to deliver the goods to the holder of the bill of lading, if they chose to deliver the goods without presentation of the bill, they must be deemed to be running the risk of being sued by either the owner of the goods or the rightful consignee.

The rule extinguishing the consignor's rights under the transferred bill might, however, be thought to raise a problem for the seller who has indorsed and delivered the bill of lading to the buyer, but subsequently has had his goods rejected by the buyer because the goods had been damaged whilst in the care and control of the shipowner. The indorsement and delivery of the bill of lading would have extinguished his original rights under the contract of carriage, and the delivery of the goods to the buyer would have resulted in the bill of lading in ceasing to be a document of title. Section 2(2)(b) comes to the rescue of a seller in such a situation:

> "Where, when a person becomes the lawful holder of a bill of lading, possession of the bill no longer gives a right (as against the carrier) to possession of the goods to which the bill of lading relates, that person shall not have any rights transferred to him by virtue of subs. (1) above unless he becomes the holder of the bill—as a result of the rejection to that person by another person of goods or documents delivered to the other person in pursuance of any such arrangements".

Another provision worth noting is s.2(4). That section provides that where a person with any interest or right in or in relation to the goods sustains loss or damage as a result of the breach of the contract of carriage, but is unable to sue because the document in question (the bill of lading, sea waybill[33] or delivery order) is vested in someone else, that other person may, if he so wishes, exercise those rights represented by the bill of lading for the benefit of the person who has suffered loss or damage. Simply put, this means that if Y is the last holder of the bill of lading but X is the one who suffered a financial loss, Y is entitled to sue the carrier in respect of X's loss.

The rule in s.2(4) seems to preserve the effect of the pre-Bills of Lading Act **6-063** 1855 case of *Dunlop v Lambert* (1839) 6 Cl. & Fin 600. It was held there that where there is a special contract made by the consignor on behalf of the consignee or any other person who might acquire an interest in the goods, with the shipowner, the consignor has a right of action against the shipowner even after property in the goods has passed. The court must satisfy itself that the "special relationship" was within the contemplation of the contracting parties as evidenced by the contract. Further, the consignor must hold any damages or proceeds of the action for the account of the consignee or any other person, the consignor is said to sue on behalf of. The converse seems to be equally applicable—where the holder of the bill is the consignee but there exists a special contract, he has the right to take action on behalf of the consignor who might have lost his right to sue following the passage of property in the goods.

The main difference between s.2(4) and *Dunlop v Lambert* seems to be this. Under the special relationship, it could be argued that the person immediately entitled to the rights of suit not only has a right but a duty, to sue and account to the other person intended to benefit from the action. Section 2(4) on the other hand does not make it a duty, only a liberty. It might therefore be suggested that banks looking to the bill of lading as security should insist on the bill being made consigned or indorsed to them so that they do not have to rely on the goodwill of the holder to take action on their behalf.

Whilst s.2(4) enables a holder of a bill to sue on behalf of the real owner of cargo, it does not create a separate cause of action (*Pace Shipping Co Ltd of Malta v Churchgate Nigeria Ltd of Nigeria* [2010] EWHC 2828 (Comm)). In that case, C was not the owner of the cargo. Nevertheless C was the last holder of the bill of lading. As such, C was entitled to claim the loss suffered by the actual cargo owner. The issue as to whether s.2(4) constituted a separate cause of action from the right of suit which C had in respect of its own financial loss was crucial to the case because, as the carrier argued, C's failure to particularise such a separate cause of action at the commencement of the arbitration proceedings could very well mean that C's claim was time-barred. Burton J. however concluded that there was no separate cause of action; C only had one cause of action under the Carriage of Goods by Sea Act 1992 (being the last lawful holder of the bill of lading). That is irrespective of whether C was making claim for its own loss or for the loss of the actual owner or indeed, for a combination of the two.

---

[33] For the purposes of the Carriage of Goods by Sea Act 1992, it appears that a straight bill of lading will be governed and covered by the provisions referring to the sea waybill (*AP Moeller-Maersk AS (trading as Maersk Line) v Sonaec Villas Cen Sad Fadoul* [2010] EWHC 355 (Comm); also *Finmoon v Baltic Reefers* [2012] EWHC 920 (Comm)).

6–064   It is, therefore, important to identify who the last lawful holder of the bill of lading is when a claimant (for example, carrier or insurer) is seeking to pursue a claim under the bill of lading. It is only that person who has the right to bring a claim under the bill of lading.

Apart from the 1992 Act, the consignee seems also able to sue the carrier on the basis of an implied contract between himself and the carrier (*Brandt v Liverpool SN Co* [1924] 1 K.B. 575).[34] Consideration for that contract is in the carrier's delivery of the goods to the consignee against the bill of lading, and the consignee paying any outstanding freight or other charges due under the original contract. The consignee takes not only the contractual rights following the transfer or consignment of the bill of lading, but also those rights which accrued at or related to events prior to the transfer of the bill. It would appear that those rights are not defeated simply because new bills are issued to replace the original bills as long as it is clear that the new bills related to the contract of carriage evidenced by the original bill of lading.[35]

Transfer of liabilities through indorsement or consignment of the bill of lading

6–065   It was intended that the holder of the bill of lading who exercises rights of suit derived from the bill of lading should also be subject to the liabilities thereunder as if he was one of the original contracting parties. The Law Commission and the Scottish Law Commission in their Joint Report, "Rights of Suit in respect of Carriage of Goods by Sea" saw no unfairness in this:

"We see in general no unfairness in making the person who either claims delivery or who takes delivery of the goods from being subject to the terms of the contract of carriage since in both cases the person is enforcing or at least attempting to enforce rights under the contract of carriage.

Furthermore it is unfair that the carrier should be denied redress against the indorsee of the bill of lading who seeks to take the benefit of the contract of carriage without the corresponding burdens".[36]

The Carriage of Goods by Sea Act 1992 thus provides in s.3 that liabilities under the contract of carriage are not transferred simultaneously with the rights of suit. Section 3 provides that a person who:

(a)   takes or demands delivery from the carrier of goods represented by the document; or

(b)   makes a claim under the contract of carriage against the carrier in respect of the goods; or

---

[34] Curwen, "The problems of transferring carriage rights: an equitable solution" [1992] J.B.L. 245.

[35] In *Rey Banano del Pacifico CA v Transportes Navieros Ecuatorianos* [2000] 2 Lloyd's Rep. 15 the court allowed the consignees who were in possession of a set of replacement bills of lading to assume the rights to sue for damage caused to a cargo of bananas even though the contract of sale between them and the original holder of the bill of lading was made after voyage had commenced.

[36] Law Com. No.196; Scot. Law Com. No.130, March 1991, at §§3.18 and §§3.22.

(c) has taken or demanded delivery of the goods before the title to sue was vested in him under s.2(1),

shall become subject to the same liabilities under that contract as if he had been party to it. The House of Lords in *Borealis AB v Stargas Ltd (The Berge Sisar)* [2001] 2 All E.R. 193 defined the term "demands delivery" in paragraph (a) as referring to a formal demand made to the carrier or his agent asserting the contractual right as the indorsee of the bill of lading to have the carrier deliver the goods to him. In *Borealis*, the claimant (Borealis) had directed the shipmaster to take the vessel to their import jetty and then, having allowed her to berth there, had taken routine samples from the cargo tanks before clearing the vessel for discharge into their terminal. The question was whether this constituted a demand under s.3(1) which would thereby make them liable for the liabilities under the original bill of lading. Lord Hobhouse felt that that was not sufficient. His Lordship said:

> "What occurred did not get even as far as the stage of Borealis expressing their willingness to receive this cargo into their terminal. It fell a long way short of amounting to any demand or request that it should be. Once Borealis knew what the true characteristics of the cargo were, they refused to accept it from the ship".

The berthing of the ship and testing of the cargo were no more than mere acts of co-operation between merchants prior to the formal delivery or demand for delivery of the cargo. The testing of the cargo, in particular, signifies the claimant's intention to confirm the true quality and quantity of the goods before calling for formal delivery. Whilst the judgment is clearly welcome given the patent uncertainty in the Act, there still remains the issue of what should happen if the holder makes a demand and his demand is rejected or denied by the carrier but instead of suing for wrongful refusal, the indorsee chooses to let the matter drop and not to make a claim. What significance of the demand remains, as far as s.3 is concerned?

As for "makes a claim under the contract of carriage" in para.(b), Lord **6–066** Hobhouse in that case said that it had to be read as referring to a formal claim against the carrier asserting the legal liability of the carrier under the contract of carriage to the holder of the bill of lading. In *The Ythan* [2005] EWHC 2399, it was held that "makes a claim" should refer to the making of a formal claim. In that case, the request for a letter of undertaking (a form of security for the cargo claim) by a holder of the bill of lading from the carrier's underwriters was not enough to trigger s.3(1)(b). The scope of para.(c) is perhaps better explained by means of an illustration:

Example: Under an international sale contract, the bill of lading relating to the goods is issued to the shipper. The cargo arrives at the port of discharge before the bill of lading. The carrier delivers the goods to the buyer against a letter of indemnity from the buyer's bank. The effect of para.(c) would be that the liabilities under the contract of carriage are transferred to the buyer even though he has yet to come into possession of the bill of lading.

Under s.1 of the now repealed Bills of Lading Act 1855, every consignee or indorsee to whom the property in the goods shall pass upon or by reason of such consignment or indorsement, "shall have transferred to and vested in him all rights of suit, and be *subject to the same liabilities* in respect of such goods as if the contract contained in the bill of lading had been made with himself".

This has clearly not been adopted by the Carriage of Goods by Sea Act 1992. The effect of this provision in the old Act was considered by the House of Lords.

6–067 *Effort Shipping Co Ltd v Linden Management SA (The Giannis NK)* [1998] A.C. 605
Facts:
The shipper had shipped a cargo of groundnuts onboard the carrier's vessel, The Giannis NK. Unknown to both the shipper and carrier, the groundnuts were infested with khapra beetles. This rendered the goods dangerous because they were likely to cause damage to other goods carried. The shippers, when sued under the Hague Rules and the contract of carriage, argued that they had transferred the bill of lading relating to the groundnuts to purchasers and as such, the third party purchasers should now be liable to the carrier under s.1 Bills of Lading Act 1855.
Held:
Lord Lloyd dismissed the shipper's appeal and said:

"Whereas the rights under the contract of carriage were to be transferred the liabilities were not. The shippers were to remain liable, but the holder of the bill of lading was to come under the same liability as the shippers. His liability was to be by way of addition, not substitution".

The concluding words in s.1 "as if the contract . . . had been made with himself" served only to underline the legislative intent, namely, to create an exception to the rule that only parties could sue on the contract. The shippers could not divest themselves of their liability for shipping dangerous goods by operation of the 1855 Act. It is swiftly seen that the Carriage of Goods by Sea Act 1992 is quite different in its treatment of the transferee of the bill of lading.

The other effect of the 1992 legislative provision is that persons holding the bill of lading as security are not necessarily possessed of any liabilities under the contract of carriage simply by virtue of their holding the bill of lading. Their liabilities under the contract of carriage would be activated only when they take or demand delivery of the goods whether in pursuance to the bill of lading or not, or when they make a claim under that contract. This provision does away with the traditional approach of linking rights and liabilities of suit with the passage of property. Although it reshapes the rule in *Sewell v Burdick* [1884] 10 App. Cas. 74 the net effect is preserved in that the holder should have asserted proprietary or contractual rights before he is possessed of the said liabilities.

6–068 *Sewell v Burdick* [1884] 10 App. Cas. 74
Facts:
The shipper of a consignment of machinery had indorsed the bill of lading in blank to the bank as security for a loan. The shipper then absconded and failed to take delivery of the goods. The carriers acting to enforce their lien over the goods auctioned the goods off. The proceeds however were insufficient to meet the freight. They then brought an action against the bank as holder and indorsee of the bill of lading for the remainder.
Held:
The House of Lords held that the Bills of Lading Act 1855 did not apply because the relationship between the shipper and the bank was that of a pledge of the goods, and not one of sale. No property had passed through the indorsement of the bill of lading, therefore the carriers were barred from taking action against the bank.

At common law, the indorser is not liable after he has indorsed over the bill of lading to another whilst the shipper remains liable as an original party to the contract. Indeed as Erle C.J. held in *Smurthwaite v Wilkins* (1862) 11 CB(ns) 842:

> "The contention is that the consignee or assignee shall always remain liable like the consignor although he has parted with all interest and property in the goods by assigning the bill of lading to a third party before the arrival of the goods. The consequences which this would lead to are so monstrous, so manifestly unjust, that I should pause before I consented to adopt this construction of the act of parliament".

Although the 1992 Act is silent on this point, Lord Hobhouse in *Borealis AB* **6–069** *v Stargas Ltd* held that there was nothing in the Commission's Report or indeed, as a matter of principle, which should prevent the rule in *Smurthwaite* to remain effective. As far as the original shipper is concerned, s.3(3) is relevant.

Section 3(3) provides that the transfer of liabilities does not result in the holder of the bill of lading being accountable for liabilities incurred *before* the bill of lading was indorsed or consigned to him. Section 3(3) states:

> "This section, so far as it imposes liabilities under any contract on any person, shall be without prejudice to the liabilities under the contract of any person as an original party to the contract".

The original party to the contract remains liable for acts and omissions done by him before the bill of lading had passed to the present holder.

The aforegoing discussion applies mutatis mutandis to sea waybills and delivery orders. As for the delivery order, s.3(2) provides that where the goods to which a ship's delivery order relates form a part only of the goods to which the contract of carriage relates, the liabilities to which any person is subject under the Carriage of Goods by Sea Act 1992 shall exclude liabilities in respect of any goods to which the order does not relate.

CHAPTER 7

CHARTERPARTIES AND COMMON LAW PRINCIPLES APPLICABLE TO CARRIAGE OF GOODS BY SEA

Carriage of Goods by Sea

It is useful to acquaint ourselves with how international shipping operates. In the main there are two types of cargo, as far as the shipping industry is concerned: **7–001**

- bulk cargo; and

- general cargo.

The type of cargo will determine the type of shipping used.

Bulk cargo forms the bulk of international shipping tonnage; bulk tonnage accounts for around three quarters of the world merchant fleet. Bulk cargo, being what it is,[1] will normally require the use of an entire vessel. This is commonly known in the shipping trade as "one ship, one cargo".[2] The types of vessels used for bulk cargo are tankers, bulk carriers, combined carriers and specialist bulk carriers. The cargo interest (meaning, generally, the person whose cargo is carried) would thus either use his own ship or charter one from the world fleet. The former is obviously an expensive option and would not be ideal where the cargo interest does not want to be involved in the running and owning of a ship. The latter is normally to be preferred because the risks of running the ship lie with the ship owner, not the cargo interest. The shipper may opt to charter the vessel for a specific term or for a specific voyage. The former is known as a time charter, whilst the latter is called a voyage charter.

---

[1] Normally 2–3,000 tons in weight.

[2] This should not be taken too literally; often a single ship may carry several different bulk cargoes in different holds.

There are three main types of bulk cargo:

- dry bulk (for example, the "five major bulk", namely, grain, coal, iron ore, phosphates, bauxite, and other minor bulk, including, cement, sugar, salt, wood chip, sulphur, etc);

- bulk liquid (crude oil, liquid chemicals, vegetable oil, etc); and

- specialist bulk (these are bulk cargoes requiring special handling and storage conditions—for example, prefabricated structures, refrigerated cargo, heavy machinery, etc).

7–002   The carriage of general cargo is an entirely different matter. The cargo interest will normally only want use of some space on the ship, not the entire ship or hold. The main types of general cargo are:

- loose cargo (individual items, pieces of equipment, parcels, etc all of which must be handled and stowed separately);

- containers (these are large standard sized units—usually 8ft wide, $8\frac{1}{2}$ft high and 20, 30 or 40ft long to be filled with cargo);

- palletized cargo;

- pre-slung cargo (e.g. planks of wood lashed together into standard sized packages);

- liquid cargo (in drums, deep tanks, etc);

- refrigerated cargo (to be held in refrigerated containers, or insulated holds); and

- wheeled cargo (heavy machinery, tractors, vehicles).

Before the introduction of containers, general cargo was especially difficult to transport. Each item had to be packed in the hold separately and dunnage (e.g. wood, burlap, hay) had to be used to ensure that the cargo was secured in place. The whole process was extremely labour intensive and time consuming, thereby leading to liners charging exorbitant shipping costs. With the use of containers, the handling and storing can be carried out some time before the ship arrives at port. That cuts down the time a ship is held at port and is less labour intensive. Shipping costs correspondingly came down.

General cargo is normally shipped by liner services. Liner services offer a regular service between specified ports with fixed prices for specified cargo. This is the main advantage of liner services—they are run almost like bus services. Whether the ship is fully loaded or not, it will sail at the advertised time and on the advertised route. Such regularity offers traders the predictability they demand. It might be observed that for a long time, the view was that as the need to maintain a regular service even when a full payload is not available despite the high overheads, the liner sector needs to be protected from undercutting by other shipowners operating on the same routes. Liner companies thus developed the "conference system"—which is essentially a cartel where all members of the conference agree to fix prices. Price fixing cartels are obviously illegal under competition law. Thus, some sort of protection from the law had to be offered. This was achieved, at EU level, by the making of Regulation 4056/86 which exempts liner conferences from the proscriptions under EU competition law.

However, the EU Commission has now removed that exemption on the basis that in general no economic sector should be protected from open competition.[3]

The carriage of goods by sea contract is made between the shipper and the carrier of the cargo. The shipper can either be the seller or the buyer as indicated earlier. The carrier on the other hand may either be the shipowner or the charterer of the vessel. The shipper usually obtains shipping space through the agency of a freight forwarder. In some instances the shipowner himself will use an agent, a loading broker to obtain cargoes for his vessel. **7–003**

The shipper will be advised by the shipowner through the agent/s as to some of the following details:

- name of the vessel;

- point of collection of the goods at port of shipment;

- time when the vessel is likely to be ready for shipment, usually stated in the "sailing card";

- the closing date, i.e. the last date when goods are received by the vessel for loading.

The shipper is contractually obliged to provide the shipowner or the carrier with shipping instructions. A similar document called the "shipping note" will be sent to the superintendent of the docks informing him as to when the ship is arriving. Material information concerning the shipment and storage of the goods is also supplied.

The place and mode of delivery of the goods to the shipowner is open to the express agreement between the parties. In the absence of such an agreement, the court will imply a term in the light of the custom of the port and/or other relevant factors. Under English law the goods are to be delivered to alongside the ship or within reach of her tackle, subject of course to the parties' express wishes or port custom.

When the goods are delivered to the shipowner, a mate's receipt will normally be issued to the shipper. The goods will be inspected by tally clerks who will then record the following details: **7–004**

- date of loading;

- identification marks;

- package quantity, weight, measurement;

- condition of packaging;

- ostensible condition of the goods.

The information on the mate's receipt will normally be transferred on to the bill of lading and if the mate's receipt is claused to reflect any ostensible deficiency

---

[3] See Chuah, "Liner conferences in the EU and the proposed review of EC Regulation 4056/86" [2005] L.M.C.L.Q. 207. Very few countries have followed suit.

in quantity or quality, so will the bill of lading. The mate's receipt has two legal effects:

1. it is an acknowledgement that the goods have been received by the shipowner in the condition described in the mate's receipt. This acknowledgement however is subject to the conditions contained in the bill of lading; and

2. it is prima facie evidence of ownership of the goods. The holder of the mate's receipt or the person named in the mate's receipt is deemed to the owner and is therefore entitled to insist on being given the bill of lading, which is the document of title relating to the goods. The mate's receipt though, is not a document of title. Its assignment or transfer will therefore not convey possession or property in the goods. In very exceptional cases, where clear, ascertainable local custom shows that the mate's receipt may operate as a document of title the courts will give effect to the custom accordingly (*Kum v Wah Tat Bank Ltd* [1971] 1 Lloyd's Rep. 439; in that case though, it was held that where the words "not negotiable" are added, the receipt could no longer be treated as a document of title despite clear evidence of such a custom).

The records taken by the tally clerks will then be submitted to the shipowner's office where they will be compared with the draft bills of lading received from the shipper. The bills of lading are then completed and signed accordingly. The bills are then handed over to the shipper when the ship sets sail.

7–005   Bills of lading are usually issued in sets. Once goods are delivered against any one of them, the others will be rendered void automatically. Where the seller and buyer have agreed that payment for the goods is to be effected through documentary credit, the full set of the bills should be tendered to the advising or paying bank (art.20(9)(iv) UCP600). The bank will then forward the documents to the issuing bank.

Where payment is not arranged through documentary credit, the bills of lading will be delivered to the buyer (consignee) using a reasonably safe and secure mode. It is usually accepted practice that at least one copy of the bill of lading reaches the consignee so that he could take delivery of the goods when they arrive.

There are instances where the shipper need not be issued his own bill of lading. This is because where freight has been arranged by a freight forwarder, the freight forwarder may have consolidated various consignments (whether belonging to the shipper in question or other shippers). This means that only one bill of lading (known as a groupage bill) or one set is issued to the freight forwarder. It would not be practicable to issue one to each and every shipper. The forwarder will then distribute the groupage consignment among the various shippers by procuring the issue of separate ship's delivery orders. The delivery order is the shipowner's undertaking to release the goods to the holder of the document. The freight forwarder could also issue his own "house" bill of lading or forwarder's certificate of transport (FCT) to enable the holder to take possession of the goods.

7–006   A house bill of lading is naturally not a proper bill of lading recognised as a bill of lading for the purposes of the Carriage of Goods by Sea Act 1992. Freight forwarders documents are in law non-negotiable, despite attempts by freight forwarders to change matters. In practice however FCTs are widely accepted to be negotiable. However, that they do not carry the same legal rights and obligations which a bill of lading can convey.

Bills of lading can sometimes become stale by the time the ship carrying the goods arrives at port of discharge. This would naturally pose a problem for the buyer who would prefer to collect his goods as soon as the ship arrives. However, without a bill of lading, he would be unable to persuade the shipmaster to release the goods. In such a situation, especially where the sea transit is likely to be short, a sea waybill is issued instead of a bill of lading. This document serves too as a receipt for the goods and evidence of the contract of carriage but unlike a bill of lading, it is not a document of title. It is therefore non-negotiable and the goods could only be released to the named consignee in the waybill. Delivery of goods need not be made against surrender of the original sea waybill. On the other hand, in the case of a bill of lading, goods can be released to a mere holder of the bill of lading. Waybills are used for short sea transits, coastal routes, deep sea transits to low-risk customers and relative small value goods (e.g. less than $500,000). Sea waybills are sometimes known as "Express Bills" in the trade as they allow the shipmaster to deliver the goods to the person named merely on proof of identity, without the presentation of a bill of lading.

Where the shipper has a large cargo, it would be natural for him to wish to use an entire ship. In such a case, chartering a vessel would be preferable to simply "buying" freight space on several ships. There are three basic forms of charterparties:

(a) Voyage charter

Under a voyage charter, the shipowner permits the charterer to use the vessel for a specific voyage, that is to say, from a specified port of loading to a named port of discharge. It is also possible for the parties to agree to nominate a port of loading or discharge from a list of pre-specified ports. The charterer undertakes to pay freight to the shipowner. A specified time for loading and discharge operations will be provided. This is called laytime; if the charterer were to exceed this pre-agreed time when loading or discharging the cargo, he is liable to pay a form of liquidated damages to the shipowner, known as demurrage. The voyage charterer therefore assumes the responsibility for delays. Nonetheless, the actual operation of the vessel remains at all times with the shipowner.

The voyage charterer might also be a person who is interested to make a profit from selling shipping space on the vessel to smaller cargo interests or shippers. The contracts of carriage he then enters into with the smaller shippers will be expressed in bills of lading incorporating the terms of the charterparty. As will be seen,[4] the bill of lading should make it clear whether the charterer is contracting with the shipper in his own capacity or whether he is doing so as the shipowner's agent. In the case of the former, the bill of lading issued would be a charterer's bill, whilst in the latter, an owner's bill would be given. The shipper's rights are dependent on who the contractual carrier is but where charter intends for the shipowner to be the contractual carrier in relation to the third party shipper, it would normally provide in a "cesser clause" that the charterer shall be relieved of responsibilities once the cargo has been loaded. The intention of the

7–007

---

[4] See paras 8–003—8–006.

arrangement is for the charterer to transfer his liabilities to the shipowner, particularly for freight, to the holder of the bill of lading.

(b) Time charter

7–008   The time charter is the hire of the vessel by the charterer for a specified period of time. Payment for the use of the vessel is by hire; and hire will be payable from the time the ship is delivered and will cease when the ship is re-delivered. When and where delivery and re-delivery should take place would normally be contractually provided for. Hire, in many cases, is pre-paid. As the ship is at the charterer's full disposal under the time charter, any loss of time would normally be borne by the charterer. However, the charter does take into account the fact that at certain times during the hire, the ship may have to be taken out of service for repairs, etc. The contract will stipulate that during such times, known as "off-hire", hire will be suspended as a result of the ship being unable to carry out normal shipping operations or functions.

Time charters are entered into where the charterer needs a vessel for a period of time without undertaking fully the financial commitments and risks of ownership or the responsibilities of navigation and ship management. He has complete use and employment of the vessel without the associated risks of ownership and management of the ship[5] but he would be responsible for bunkers, port charges, towage, etc (which, in a voyage charterparty, would be borne by the owner). It is, for example, common for an operator who finds himself temporarily short of tonnage to supplement his fleet by chartering a vessel on time charter terms. It is therefore not the intention of the charterparty to extend the liabilities under the charter to any third party. The bill of lading issued to the charterer by the shipmaster will not normally refer to any of the terms of the time charter as it is understood by all concerned that there is a time charter in place.

(c) Bareboat or demise charter

7–009   This occurs when a ship is leased to the charterer who assumes full responsibility for the crew, the equipping of the vessel, the navigation and management of the ship. He acts as the owner in all material aspects of the shipping operation. Bareboat charters are popular with governments who might from time to time need to provide ships to meet times of emergency. For example, where the navy is unable to provide sufficient capacity at times of war, the government might enter into a bareboat charter with merchant shipowners.

Charterparties naturally entail the carriage of large quantities of cargo. Where smaller cargo is being shipped, the shipper would prefer to buy shipping space on a line which serves the route in question. In such a case, the liner company will issue the shipper a bill of lading which contains the terms of the contract of carriage. The bill of lading, as we have seen, is then delivered to the consignee ("notify party") who could either seek delivery of the goods from the carrier when the ship carrying the goods arrive at the port of discharge, or to transfer it to a sub-buyer who could similarly seek delivery of the goods from the ship. The liner company selling shipping space can either be a shipowner or charterer.

---

[5] This is normally provided for in an employment clause: "the master to be under the orders of the charterers as regards employment, agency or other arrangements".

Bills of lading are not mandatory in a charterparty arrangement but where they are issued by the shipowner to the charterer, they operate as receipts for the goods shipped and as potential documents of title but are not the contract of carriage. That contract remains evidenced by the charterparty and the relationship between shipowner and charterer remains outside the purview of the Hague-Visby Rules because art.1(b) of the Hague-Visby Rules indicates that where the bill of lading does not regulate the relations between a carrier and the holder, the Rules shall have no application to that contractual arrangement. In a charterparty the bill of lading does not regulate the relations between the charterer and the shipowner. It is also open to the parties to agree that no bill of lading should be issued for the voyage being undertaken. In *Harland & Wolff Ltd v Burns & Laird Lines Ltd* (1931) 40 Ll. L. Rep. 286, the carriage was from Glasgow to Belfast and because it was such a short voyage, only the carrier's "sailing bills" were issued. No bill of lading was contemplated. There the Court of Session in Scotland held that the Carriage of Goods by Sea Act 1924 (containing the Hague Rules) did not apply because the contract was not regulated by any bill of lading.

Where the contract of carriage is not governed by statute, we need to turn to **7–010** the common law to ascertain what duties are to be imposed on the parties. Generally the common law takes a liberal approach to the freedom of contract in carriage contracts. This liberal approach means that parties are deemed to be on equal footing or bargaining positions, and the maxim caveat emptor frequently applies. In the case of a charterparty where both parties are not insubstantial for example, the common law rules will apply. The liberal approach explains why the parties are free to exclude and vary as many of the common law duties as they please. Maximum freedom is ensured.

At the turn of the twentieth century, it was acknowledged that the shipper seeking modest shipping space is invariably a smaller player in the field of international carriage compared with the shipowner and is in a vulnerable position. Consequently, international conventions were introduced to level the playing field. The first convention brought into force in this country was the Hague Rules and are contained in the Carriage of Goods by Sea Act 1924. These have now given way to the Hague-Visby Rules as contained in the Carriage of Goods by Sea Act 1971. Even more recently, we have seen the advent of the Hamburg Rules. Although the United Kingdom has not yet ratified the Hamburg Rules, it is foreseeable that there will be some contracts calling for the application of these Rules coming within the jurisdiction of English courts. In even more recent times we have seen the introduction of the Rotterdam Rules which attempt to extend the scope of sea transport law to cover door-to-door transport operations. These shifts from the common law mean that in certain areas, the carrier is not free to limit or exclude his liability for damage or loss caused except in accordance with the relevant Rules. The nature of his duties to the shipper has also taken on a different complexion.

These conventions however often provide for certain contracts to be excluded from their scope of application. In the Hague-Visby Rules for example, where the contract of carriage involves:

1. the carriage of live animals; or

2. the carriage of deck cargo; or

3. inland waterway carriage;

it will not fall to be considered under the Rules but the common law (unless the parties agree to apply the Hague-Visby Rules to their contract and even then, the Rules apply simply as contractual terms and not as law). And, of course, where the contract of carriage is a charterparty, it will usually be governed by the common law. Given the magnitude of the area falling outside the statutory provisions, a study of the common law rules is not only helpful in assisting our understanding of the "new" regime/s but is a consideration of existing and living law.

Common Carriers

7–011   The genesis of the law may be traced to the rules relating to persons termed, "common carriers". "Common carriers" are persons who hold themselves out as being prepared to carry and convey goods on behalf of some other person for a fee. The fact that these persons are deemed to have represented themselves as trustworthy men make them subject to special duties. Their duty was generally thought to be strict. If goods in their care and custody were lost or damaged, they are liable "as an insurer". Their duty is described in the following terms by Lord Mansfield:

> "... there is a further degree of responsibility (other than negligence or wilfulness) by the custom of the realm, that is, by the common law; a carrier is in the nature of an insurer. It is laid down that he is liable for every accident, except by the act of God, or the King's enemies".

In *Coggs v Bernard* (1703) 2 Ld. Raym. 909 Lord Holt described the duty of the common carrier as one which attaches with the station of one who "exercises a public employment" and this duty is

> "a politic establishment contrived by the policy of the law for the safety of all persons the necessity of whose affairs oblige them to trust these sort of persons, that they may be safe in their ways of dealing".

It is, however, not always clear who a common carrier is. Where the carrier is not a common carrier but simply a bailee, he is only required to ensure to the best of his abilities that the goods are not damaged or lost and the onus of proving that he had not been negligent lies with him (*Levinson v Patent Steam Cleaning* [1978] Q.B. 69).

7–012   Although the bailee has to discharge a particular standard of proof—in effect excluding the possibility that their breach of duty was causative of the loss of the goods—that burden is not as high as that of a common carrier. A brief account about the bailee's duty: it has long been established that a bailee is not entitled to set up as a defence *"the bare possibility of a loss, if his wrongful act had never been done"* (*Davis v Garrett* [1824–34] All E.R. Rep. 286, see also *Lilley v Doubleday* (1881) 7 Q.B.D. 510) in circumstances where the loss occurs whilst his wrongful act was in operation and in force. In *Joseph Travers v Cooper* [1915] 1 K.B. 73, goods were loaded into a barge from a ship for delivery and the barge owner's lighterman, who was in charge of the barge, negligently left her unattended at night. The barge, after taking the ground at low tide, became submerged as the tide rose and, as a result, the goods onboard were damaged. The Court of Appeal held that the onus was on the defendant barge owner to show that the negligence of his servant in leaving the barge unattended did not cause the loss. Phillimore L.J. in concluding that the defendant had failed to discharge the onus on him, clearly indicated that a bailee would be liable where the evidence showed that if the bailee had taken reasonable care of the goods, the loss might have been prevented. Moreover, as was said by Lord Loreburn, when Lord Chancellor, in *Morison Pollexfen & Blair v Walton* (May 10, 1909):

> "It is for [the bailee] to explain the loss himself, and *if he cannot satisfy the Court that it occurred from some cause independent of his own wrong-doing he must make that loss good.*" (emphasis added)

In a more modern context, in *Frans Maas v Samsung Electronics (UK) Ltd* [2004] 2 Lloyd's Rep. 251, Gross J. had to consider whether the claimant warehousemen were liable, as bailees, for the theft from the warehouse of mobile phones belonging to the defendants. Gross J. found that the theft had been caused by wilful default of the bailee's employees for which the bailee was vicariously liable and further that the theft (and hence the loss of the goods) had been caused by the claimant's negligence. Gross J. made it clear that the bailee could not rely on the fact that it could not be said with certainty that the loss would not have occurred if the bailee had taken reasonable care of the goods.

The bailee bears the burden of establishing that he took all reasonable care of the goods and that any failure to take reasonable care of the goods did not cause the loss (*Matrix Europe v Uniserve Holdings* [2009] EWHC 919 (Comm)).

Whether the sea carrier qualifies to be treated as a common carrier or simply a bailee remains an area fraught with difficulties and even when it is established that the sea carrier is indeed a common carrier, the extent of his duty is equally equivocal.

Liver Alkali Co v Johnson (1874) L.R. 9 Ex. 338   **7–013**
Facts:
The defendant had agreed to carry some salt cake belonging to the claimant from Widness to Liverpool on his flats. The flat ran aground under fog conditions and the goods were damaged. The issue was whether the defendant was under the liability of a bailee or whether he had assumed the role of a common carrier and must therefore suffer greater responsibility.
Held:
Blackburn J. decided against the defendant and held that he was a "lighterman" and as such incurred the liability of a common carrier. The court found that from the evidence, it was clear that the defendant had made it

> "his business to send out his flats under the care of his own servants, different persons as required from time to time, to carry cargoes to or from places in the Mersey, but that it always was to carry goods for one person at a time, and that he carried for any one who chose to employ him".

An express agreement was always made as to each voyage or employment of the defendant's flats which the court took to mean that the flats did not go about plying for hire, but were waiting for hire by any one. This emphasis on the public employment element was, however, not shared by Brett J. who took a somewhat radical approach to the whole issue of the common carrier. The judge held that the defendant was liable as a shipowner and the law was that every shipowner "who carries goods for hire in his ship, whether by inland navigation, or coastways, or abroad, undertakes to carry them at his own absolute risk, the act of God or of the Queen's enemies alone excepted, unless by agreement between himself and a particular freighter, on a particular voyage, or on particular voyages, he limits his liability by further exceptions".

To summarise the law so far:

— the common carrier has the duty of an insurer vis-à-vis the goods he has agreed to carry;

— the common carrier is defined as one who exercises a public employment in offering to carry goods belonging to another for a fee; and

— the main exceptions to the common carrier's duty are acts of God and acts of enemies of the Crown. Additionally, as insurers the common carrier could also plead the defences that the damage was caused by an inherent vice in the goods themselves, or that the damage or loss was the result of wrongdoing on the part of the consignor or consignee of the goods. This wrongdoing may take the form of fraudulent or negligent or intentional acts. Where the goods have been lost through a general average sacrifice, the carrier will not be held liable. This occurs when it is necessary that the goods be sacrificed to avoid peril.

7–014   Where the common carrier is also a bailee, under the law of bailment, the carrier is entitled to be remunerated for the bailment service. Where the bailment is contractual, the right to be remunerated is incontrovertible. Where the bailment is non-contractual the issue is more problematic. The general proposition at common law is nicely expressed by Bowen L.J. in *Falcke v Scottish Imperial Insurance Co* (1886) 34 Ch. D. 234:

"The general principle is, beyond all question, that work and labour done or money expended by one man to preserve or benefit the property of another do not according to English law create any lien upon the property saved or benefited, nor, even if standing alone, create any obligation to repay the expenditure. Liabilities are not to be forced upon people behind their backs any more than you can confer a benefit upon a man against his will."

However, exceptions do exist and these exceptions have become more significant than the general rule. In an old case, *Gaudet v Brown* (1873) L.R. 5 P.C. 134 (*Cargo ex Argos*), petroleum was shipped in London on the *Argos* under a bill of lading providing for delivery at Le Havre. The vessel arrived at Le Havre towards the end the Franco-Prussian war, when the port was full of munitions. As such, the landing of flammable cargoes was prohibited. The master therefore discharged the petroleum into lighters in the outer harbour, ready for collection by the shippers. But the shippers failed to present the bill of lading or to make any arrangements to receive it. Having waited for as long as the port authorities would allow him to, the master reshipped the cargo and carried it back to London. The owners successfully sued the shippers for freight for the return voyage. The case appears to have been decided on the footing that the contract of carriage was at an end when the *Argos* left Le Havre for London, either because the contractual service had been completed or because the contract was frustrated at Le Havre. The question was what was the basis of the successful claim for freight for the return voyage? The court took the view that in shipping, the master is not only empowered but duty-bound to act for the safety of the cargo especially when there is an emergency or accident. As such, he is entitled to charge the cargo owner with the expenses properly incurred in so doing.

The court held:

"In a case like the present, where the goods could neither be landed nor remain where they were, it seems to be a legitimate extension of the implied agency of the master to hold that, in the absence of all advices, he had authority to carry or send them on to such other place as in his judgment, prudently exercised, appeared to be most convenient for their owner; and if so, it will follow from established principles that the expenses properly incurred may be charged to him . . . . The authority of the master being founded on necessity would not have arisen if he could have obtained instructions from the defendant or his assignees. But under the circumstances this was not possible."

Although this case uses the language of agency and necessity, that has sometimes been doubted to represent the true legal basis of the rule.[6] Be that as it may, Lord Sumption in *ENE Kos 1 Limited v Petroleo Brasileiro SA (the Kos)* [2012] UKSC 17 opined that there is a principle that requires that a bailee of goods should have taken steps in an emergency for the sole benefit of the cargo in circumstances where it was impossible to communicate with the owners of the goods.

In *China Pacific SA v Food Corp of India (The Winson)* [1982] A.C. 939 the   **7–015** ship which was bound for Bombay with a cargo of wheat had become stranded on a reef in the South China Sea. Salvors off-loaded the wheat into barges and took it to Manila for storage in warehouses which they paid for. The owners subsequently gave notice that they were abandoning the voyage and the contract of carriage thus came to an end. The House of Lords held that the salvors, who became gratuitous bailees when they placed the goods in the warehouse,[7] were entitled to be reimbursed for the warehouse storage charges because of the reason explained by Lord Diplock below

" . . . [the salvors] under the ordinary principles of the law of bailment too well known and too well-established to call for any citation of authority, owed a duty of care to the cargo owner to take such measures to preserve the salved wheat from deterioration by exposure to the elements as a man of ordinary prudence would take for the preservation of his own property. For any breach of such duty the bailee is liable to his bailor in damages for any diminution in value of the goods consequent upon his failure to take such measures; and if he fulfils that duty he has, in my view, a correlative right to charge the owner of the goods with the expenses reasonably incurred in doing so."

Although *The Winson* was about the salvor's right to remuneration as gratuitous bailees, the Supreme Court in *The Kos* extended the principle to a gratuitous

---

[6] See Goff & Jones, *The Law of Unjust Enrichment*, 8th edn (London: Sweet & Maxwell, 2011), para.18–50.

[7] Between the time they off-loaded the goods to the time they landed the goods, the salvors were contractual bailees because there existed a salvage contract. But once they had completed the salvage, they were no longer contractual bailees.

carrier. In *The Kos*, the vessel was withdrawn legitimately by the owners but the goods were still onboard at the time of the withdrawal. The owners thus returned the goods to shore and the discharge took three days. The owners sought recovery of the costs from the cargo interest (charterers) under the law of bailment, on the premise that the contract had lapsed and they were gratuitous bailees. The Supreme Court allowed the claim, stressing that the principle was applicable regardless of whether the action was necessary. Lord Sumption thought it was more about whether that action (returning the goods back to shore) was the only reasonable and practical course of action.

Implied Duties of the Sea Carrier at Common Law

7–016   At common law where no express contractual terms have been provided for, the duties of the carrier or shipowner are generally strict—he must deliver the goods to the destination in the condition he had received them unless prevented by an act of God, acts of the Crown's enemies, inherent vice in the goods themselves, defective packaging or by an act of general average sacrifice. Considering the contractual freedom allowed by law in the absence of statutory regulation (as is the case with bill of lading contracts), shipowners and charterers/shippers have made provision for their relationship by intricate written terms. These terms are to be construed in the light of the main duties of the parties. Some of the essential duties of the shipowner include:

- duty to provide a seaworthy ship;
- duty to proceed with due despatch;
- duty to carry the goods to the appointed place of destination without deviation;
- duty to take reasonable care of the cargo; and
- duty to deliver the goods to a specified or identifiable person at the port of discharge.

Seaworthiness

7–017   While it is difficult to offer a comprehensive definition for the term "seaworthiness", we could perhaps take the general description of Field J. in *Kopitoff v Wilson* (1876) 1 Q.B.D. 377 as a starting point

> " . . . where there is no agreement to the contrary, the shipowner is, by the nature of the contract, impliedly and necessarily held to warrant that the ship is goods, and is in a condition to perform the voyage about to be undertaken, or, in ordinary language, is seaworthy, that is, fit to meet and undergo the perils of the sea and other incidental risks to which she must of necessity be exposed in the course of the voyage . . . ".

It is an absolute warranty that the ship must be fit for the prosecution of the voyage and the test is the standard of fitness required by an ordinarily careful and prudent owner for his own vessel at the commencement of the voyage, taking into account the nature and probable circumstances of the voyage (see *Virginia Carolina Chemical Co v Norfolk and North American Steam Shipping Co* [1912] 1 K.B. 229). It is also vital that seaworthiness includes the ship's to carry the *contractual* cargo. This must however be distinguished from the duty to stow and maintain the cargo properly. The cargoworthiness of the vessel refers generally on the physical attributes of the ship and is therefore a matter of seaworthiness. The care, stowage and maintenance of the cargo onboard the vessel on the other hand does not. We shall examine this distinction further in paras 7–022—7–024 below.

What is the effect of a contractual provision exempting the carrier of liability for not supplying a seaworthy ship? It is trite law from *Photo Productions* that in theory the parties are free to provide for the widest ranged exclusion clauses. The courts' attitude however would be to construe such clauses narrowly. The rule is succinctly expressed in *Owners of Cargo Onboard SS Waikato v New Zealand Shipping Co* [1899] 1 Q.B. 56:

"It is clear law that exceptions do not apply to protect the shipowner who furnishes an unseaworthy ship where the unseaworthiness causes damage, unless the exceptions are so worded as clearly to exclude or vary the implied warranty of seaworthiness".

Clarity of the terms used is of paramount importance. Where the terms of the exclusion are clear, the court will not hesitate to give condign effect to the clause as it did in *The Cargo ex Laertes* 12 P.D. 187. In that case, the words "latent defects in machinery even existing at the time of shipment" were found by the court as sufficiently protecting the shipowner from liability.

Nature of the duty

Physical condition of the vessel Clearly where the ship is physically **7–018** defective or inadequate to sail, the shipowner will be liable for failing to provide a seaworthy ship. In *Stanton v Richardson* (1875) L.R. 9 C.P. 390, the pumping equipment in the ship could not adequately deal with the surplus of water from a cargo of wet sugar and this rendered the ship unseaworthy. According to the court, the ship must be fit in design and structure and be suitably equipped to deal with the ordinary perils of the contracted sea adventure. The shipowner's failure to provide proper equipment rendered the ship unseaworthy.

Whether an act or omission renders the ship unseaworthy is usually a question of fact[8] as we see in the case of *A. Meredith Jones & Co Ltd v Vangemar Shipping Co Ltd (The Apostolis)* [1997] 2 Lloyd's Rep. 241. Welding was carried out onboard the vessel before the Apostolis had set sail. The cargo caught fire rendering the vessel incapacitated. The High Court held that the welding carried out and the threat to the cargo posed by sparks from the welding rendered the ship unseaworthy. The Court of Appeal disagreed holding that the ship was not rendered unseaworthy simply because the welding had exposed the cargo to an ephemeral risk of ignition. The holds themselves were not intrinsically unsafe

---

[8] Where there are different schools of thought and no industry standard, the court will be particularly slow to find the ship unseaworthy, per Cresswell J., *The Lendoudis Evangelos II* (June 26, 2001).

and it could not be said that the welding was taking place to render the ship seaworthy, i.e. the welding was not related to any aspect of the ship's seaworthiness. It should perhaps be mentioned that the Court of Appeal was not convinced that there was sufficient evidence to show that the fire was caused by the welding. It seems clear that any act or omission which is claimed to render the ship unseaworthy must pass the test of causation—it must be the operative and proximate cause of the ship's unseaworthiness.

7–019   **Incompetent or insufficient crew**   It is not disputed that a ship may be rendered unseaworthy by the inefficiency of the ship master or the crew. Efficiency or competence does not only refer to the crew's general competence in sailing ships; it is highly pertinent whether the crew in question is competent for the purposes of sailing the particular ship in question. Where the ship has peculiarities, the crew must be competent to tackle those peculiarities. Competence is not only to be measured by the level of training of the master and his crew but also their personal attributes and proclivities. In addition where the size of the crew is not suitable for the operations in question, that too could render a ship unseaworthy. We see these principles in action in the following cases.

7–020   *Hongkong Fir Shipping Co Ltd v Kawasaki Kisen Kaisha Ltd* [1962] 2 Q.B. 26
Facts:
The Hongkong Fir was on charter to the Kawasaki for 24 months. The charterparty provided that the vessel was to be "in every way fitted for ordinary cargo service"; a standard clause in charterparties of that kind. The engines of the ship were old and required special expertise from the crew to operate them.
Held:
The Court of Appeal found that they shipowners had employed insufficient crew to operate the engines and this was aggravated by the fact that the chief engineer was addicted to drink and had repeatedly neglected his duties. Such incompetence rendered the vessel unfit for "ordinary cargo service".

More recently, the rule was reiterated in a marine insurance case. In *Manifest Shipping & Co Ltd v Uni-Polaris Insurance Co and La Réunion Européene (The Star Sea)* [1997] 1 Lloyd's Rep. 360, the Court of Appeal, reaffirming the judgment at first instance, stated that unseaworthiness clearly included the staffing of the ship with incompetent or insufficient crew. There, the master of the ship was found to be incompetent because he lacked the knowledge to use the CO_2 fire fighting system on board the ship. The court was prepared to consider not only the navigational aspect of managing and controlling the ship, but also the important duties in ship preservation such as the crew's ability to use the fire fighting system on board.

7–021   **Inadequate documentation**   Where a vessel is unable to set sail because it does not possess the necessary documentation that could also render it unseaworthy (*The Madeleine* [1967] 2 Lloyd's Rep. 224). The courts are, however, careful not to extend the rule to nonlegal documentary requirements. In *Alfred C Toepfer Schiffahrsgesellschaft mbH v Tossa Marine Co Ltd (The Derby)* [1985] 2 Lloyd's Rep. 325, the ship was barred from discharging her cargo of timber because she did not possess an ITF blue card which signifies that conditions of employment laid down by the International Transport Workers Federation have been complied with. As a result of the temporary stoppage, the vessel was unable to proceed on time to the subcharterers. The charterers sued the shipowners for that loss of profit contending that the ship provided by the shipowner was unseaworthy because it did not possess the requisite documentation. The Court of Appeal gave judgment for the shipowners stating that the blue card was not a requirement by any law which is relevant to the ship, but a mere declaration insisted on by a self-appointed and extra legal organisation. The facts here might be contrasted with those in *The Madeleine* where the *dératisation* certificate was required by the laws of India in 1957 without which the ship could not sail to any other country.

Where the documentary requirement goes to the root of the ship's ability to sail like in *Ciampa v British Steam Navigation Co Ltd* [1915] 2 K.B. 774, its noncompliance could render the ship unseaworthy. There, the ship had set sail from Mombasa without a clean bill of health and had to be fumigated in France. The failure to supply a clean bill of health made it impossible for the vessel to perform the charterparty.

In recent times a new problem has arisen regarding documents which purport to certify that the ship meets certain commercial or regulatory requirements. Some charterparties may carry a warranty that the ship meets the approval of the charterer's customers (cargo owners for example)[9] and other stakeholders (such as government agencies). However, such a warranty has been held by the Court of Appeal in *Transpetrol v SJB (Marine Ebergy) BV Rowan* [2012] EWCA Civ 198 as a warranty that relates to the documentation of the ship rather than one that relates to the ship itself. If it were the latter, the fact that any approval expressed by any of the named customers but subsequently withdrawn could render the ship unseaworthy.

Cargoworthiness As was pointed out earlier, the fitness of the ship to   **7–022**
receive and hold the cargo or its cargoworthiness is part of the general fitness of the vessel and thus, a matter of seaworthiness. In *Owners of Cargo on Ship "Maori King" v Hughes* [1895] 2 Q.B. 550 the shipowners on being sued for damage caused by the failure of the ship's refrigeration system attempted to rely on a clause stating that the ship was not liable for damage or loss "arising from failure or breakdown of machinery, insulation or other appliances". The Court of Appeal held against them on the basis that there was an implied duty of seaworthiness meaning that the failure of the refrigeration was tantamount to unseaworthiness. Lord Esher M.R. said:

" . . . the machinery was warranted to be what might be called in nautical phraseology 'seaworthy', though it is not strictly an accurate term. But . . . [it] meant that the machinery was to be at the time of shipment fit as machinery to carry frozen meat to Europe under the ordinary conditions of an ordinary voyage".

---

[9] The Asbatankvoy Charterparty Form for example provides "Owner warrants that the Vessel is approved by the following companies and will remain so throughout the duration of this charterparty: . . . " These clauses have been quite controversial and some companies doing business with the charterer are very reluctant to be implicated in the clause. In the sinking of the *Prestige* and *Erika*, the media made a huge story about certain companies that have added their approvals to these ships. The bad publicity makes cargo owners less keen to be seen as adding their approval to the chartered ship and any commercial benefit to be involved in some prior approval of the vessel is not entirely convincing.

The duty to stow, care for and maintain the cargo on the other hand is distinct from the duty to provide a seaworthy ship. This duty does not turn on the physical attributes of the vessel but there exists opinion that bad stowage could make the vessel unseaworthy. The distinction is however not an easy one to make.

In *Kopitoff v Wilson* (1876) 1 Q.B.D. 377 a consignment of iron armour plates and bolts was lost on board the Walamo en route from Hull to Cronstadt. The heavy armour plates had been placed on the top of a quantity of railway iron and then secured there by wooded shores. The court held that as the bad stowage led to the armour plates becoming dislodged thereby causing danger to the vessel, it amounted to unseaworthiness. The test adopted was expressed in these terms:

> "Was the vessel at the time of sailing in a state, as regards the stowing and receiving of [the cargo], reasonably fit to encounter the ordinary perils that might be expected on a voyage at that season from Hull to Cronstadt?"

Where the stowage does not cause the vessel to be unsuitable for the contract voyage, then there is no breach of the duty of seaworthiness.

We see how the test operates in *The Thorsa* [1916] P. 257.

7–023   *The Thorsa* [1916] P. 257
Facts:
The ship was to carry a cargo of chocolates from Genoa to London. A cargo of gorgonzola cheese was held in the same hold. Bad weather meant that the holds had to be kept shut and as a result of poor ventilation, the chocolates were contaminated by the cheese. The owners of the chocolates argued that the ship was not seaworthy as a result of the bad stowage. The shipowners attempted to rely on a clause which provided that the ship was not liable for loss or damage arising from "any act, neglect or default in the management, loading or stowing of the ship". The clause would be inapplicable if the damage was caused not by mere stowage but also by unseaworthiness.
Held:
The Court of Appeal applying the test in *Kopitoff v Wilson* stated:

> "In the present case it is not contended that the ship was in any way defective in design or in structure, or in condition or equipment, at the time when she sailed—not the ship herself. The sole point is the way in which the cargo was stowed. It is not contended that at the date when the ship was empty and prepared to receive cargo her condition was in any way defective, nor is it contended that the cargo was so stowed, or that any part of the cargo was so stowed, as to be *a serious danger to the ship herself*" (emphasis added).

The owners of the chocolates were therefore not successful in their claim. The exemption clause applied.

A similar situation arose in the House of Lords' case of *Elder, Dempster & Co Ltd v Paterson, Zochonis & Co Ltd* [1924] A.C. 522.

7–024   *Elder, Dempster & Co Ltd v Paterson, Zochonis & Co Ltd* [1924] A.C. 522
Facts:
The Grelwen was loaded with casks of palm oil. On top of the casks were placed bags of palm kernels. When the cargo was discharged, it was found that the bags of kernels had crushed the casks and the greater part of the oil was lost or damaged. The issue for the House of Lords was whether the loss/damage was caused by bad stowage or the ship's unseaworthiness.

Held:
Viscount Cave's speech is instructive as to the test to be applied to distinguish between bad stowage and cargoworthiness.

> "At the moment when the palm oil was loaded the Grelwen was unquestionably fit to receive and carry it. She was a well built and well found ship, and lacked no equipment necessary for the carriage of palm oil; and if damage arose, it was due to the fact that after the casks of oil had been stowed in the holds the master placed upon them a weight which no casks could be expected to bear. Whether he could have stowed the cargo in a different way without endangering the safety of the ship is a matter upon which the evidence is conflicting; but if that was impossible, he could have refused to accept some part of the kernels and the oil would then have travelled safely. No doubt that course might have rendered the voyage less profitable to the charterers, but that appears to me for present purposes to be immaterial. The important thing is that at the time of loading the palm oil the ship was fit to receive and carry it without injury; and if she did not do so this was due not to any unfitness in the ship or her equipment, but to another cause".

The general rule is therefore this—bad stowage, which endangers the safety of the ship, may amount to unseaworthiness, but bad stowage which affects nothing but the cargo damaged by it, is bad stowage and nothing more, and still leaves the ship seaworthy for the adventure, even though the adventure be the carrying of that cargo.

Be that as it may, it should be borne in mind that the duty to stow properly can be varied by contract. The parties can decide who should bear that duty and to what extent. Nevertheless, as many standard charterparty forms testify, the general preference is for the shipowner to bear that duty.[10]

The duty to provide a seaworthy ship is absolute

The general rule at common law as laid down in *Steel v State Line Steamship Co*   **7–025**
(1877) 3 App. Cas. 72 is that the duty of the carrier to provide a seaworthy ship is absolute. He may not plead due diligence or non-negligence to excuse the breach. The duty however attaches only at the time when the voyage commences and does not continue after the ship has set sail.

McFadden v Blue Star Line [1905] 1 K.B. 697   **7–026**
Facts:
The *Tolosa* was contracted to carry a cargo of cotton from Wilmington to Bremen. Some time after the cotton had been loaded, the ship's engineer failed to lock the sluice door making the bulkhead watertight. He had also failed to close the sea-cock adequately. As a result the cotton became wet and damaged.
Held:
The warranty to provide a seaworthy ship is an absolute one. According to Channell J., this is to say that

> "if the ship is in fact unfit at the time when the warranty begins, it does not matter that its unfitness is due to some latent defect which the shipowner does not know of, and it

---

[10] See, e.g., the amended NYPE form. On how such a clause on the liability for careless or bad stowage on the shipowner under a charterparty is applied, see *The Shinjitsu Maru (No.5)* [1985] 1 Lloyd's Rep. 568; *The Argonaut* [1985] 2 Lloyd's Rep. 216; *The Alexandros P* [1986] 1 Lloyd's Rep. 421.

is no excuse for the existence of such a defect that he used his best endeavours to make the ship as good as it could be made".

The ordinary warranty of seaworthiness does not take effect before the ship is ready to sail nor does it continue to have effect after she has set sail. It takes effect at the time of sailing alone.

As for the cargoworthiness of the ship, the duty takes effect at the time of loading (*A E Reed & Co Ltd v Page, Son & East Ltd* [1927] 1 K.B. 743), although in *Elder, Dempster & Co* we see in Viscount Cave's speech that it might extend to the time of sailing as well. The extent and nature of the duty of seaworthiness may of course be varied by contract, as is typical of the common law duties. This practical element of the law is aided by the application of the doctrine of "stages". The doctrine attempts to obviate the difficulty that where long distances are involved and refuelling is needed, the ship because of its limited fuel at the start of the voyage will invariably be unseaworthy for the entirety of the adventure. The effect of the "doctrine" was discussed by the Court of Appeal in *The Vortigern* [1899] P. 140. A.L. Smith L.J., with whom the court agreed, said:

> "The only way in which [the] warranty can be complied with is for the shipowners to extend the existing warranty to the commencement of each stage [of the voyage], and I can see no reason why such warranty should not be implied, and I have no difficulty in making the implication, for it is the only way in which the clear intention of the parties can be carried out, and the undoubted and admitted warranty complied with. It appears to me to be no answer to say that it is a warranty subsequent to the commencement of the voyage".

This is a case where the doctrine of stages has permitted the court to imply the warranty of seaworthiness to the contract *after* the ship has sailed. But how relevant is the doctrine to pre-sailing operations?

7–027   *AE Reed & Co Ltd v Page, Son & East Ltd* [1927] 1 K.B. 743
Facts:
The appellants' barge, the *Jellicoe* had a maximum capacity of 170 tons of wood pulp but as loading progressed, more than 190 tons were placed onboard her. She sank and the cargo was lost. It was argued that at the time she sank, the duty of seaworthiness had yet to take effect since the ship had not set sail and loading was still in progress. In addition, the defendants also argued that the doctrine of stages could not apply where the cause of the loss or damage was overloading and not inadequate equipment.
Held:
The court considered that there was no good reason why the doctrine of stages should not apply to pre-shipment operations. Lord Hewart C.J. said:

> "It was argued that the doctrine of stages was only a question of difference of equipment, and that overloading was not equipment. But damages unrepaired at the commencement of a new stage, collision during loading, and starting on the voyage with that damage unrepaired, may obviously be unseaworthiness at the commencement of the voyage stage, I see no reason for defining stages only by difference of equipment. Applying the [doctrine]: the barge was sent to the ship's side to carry 170 tons, and she was fit to carry that quantity. The warranty of cargoworthiness was complied with when loading commenced. But then 190 tons were put into her, some 14 per cent more than

her proper load. With that cargo in, she had a dangerously low freeboard in calm water. I think at any rate one of her gunwales was awash, and water could continuously enter through cracks, which would be only an occasional source of leakage if she were properly loaded. She had to lie so loaded for some unascertained time in the river till a tug came ... She was exposed to all the wash of passing vessels, and the more water she took onboard, the more dangerous she would become. It is clear that she was quite unfit to lie in the river for any time exposed to the wash of passing vessels and the natural' send' of the water, It is still clearer that she was quite unfit to be towed, and that she was in such a condition that she would soon go to the bottom.... when the loading was finished and the man in charge, apparently in the ordinary course of his business, left her unattended in the river waiting for a tug, and unfit in fact either to lie in the river of be towed, there was a new stage of the adventure, a new warranty of fitness for that stage and a breach of that warranty which prevented the exceptions from applying".

Burden of proof

As with most civil actions, the party who alleges must prove. Where the claimant **7–028** claims that the ship is unseaworthy, the burden of proof is on him. This means that he has to show:

1. the ship was unseaworthy at the operative time (time when the ship sails or loading commences); and

2. it was that element of unseaworthiness that caused the loss or damage.[11]

There are instances where the courts will be prepared to presume the ship's unseaworthiness. In *Pickup v Thomas and Mersey Marine Insurance Co* (1878) 3 Q.B.D. 594, for example, where the ship sank soon after leaving port with no weather or other circumstances to account for her loss, there should be no objection to the court's dispensing with the burden.

Effect of breach

The modern position is that laid down by the Court of Appeal in *Hongkong Fir* **7–029** *Shipping Co Ltd v Kawasaki Kisen Kaisha* [1962] 2 Q.B. 26 where it was held that the breach of the warranty does not allow the claimant to repudiate the contract automatically. The term of seaworthiness is not a condition. It is to be regarded as an intermediate or innominate term; where if the breach is serious and defeats the commercial purpose of the contract of carriage, then the claimant may treat the contract as repudiated. On the other hand where the breach is of minor consequence, then a repudiation may not be exercised. The reason for so treating the warranty of seaworthiness is, in the words of Diplock L.J.:

"As my brethren have already pointed out, the shipowner's undertaking to tender a seaworthy ship has, as a result of numerous decisions as to what can amount to 'unseaworthiness', become one of the most complex of contractual undertakings. It embraces obligations with respect to every party of the hull

---

[11] *International Packers v Ocean Steamship Co* [1955] 2 Lloyd's Rep. 218 and *Kuo International Oil Ltd v Daisy Shipping Co Ltd (The Yamatogawa)* [1990] 2 Lloyd's Rep. 39.

and machinery, stores and equipment and the crew itself. It can be broken by the presence of trivial defects easily and rapidly remediable as well as by defects which must inevitably result in a total loss of the vessel".

Duty to proceed with due despatch

Nature of duty

7–030 The ship supplied by the carrier must be ready to commence the contractual voyage and then to proceed on the voyage and complete it with due despatch. The duty to proceed with due or reasonable despatch is usually expressly stipulated in the contract of carriage. Where the contract is silent, the law will imply a term that the carrier should ensure that the vessel uses reasonable time to proceed on and complete the contracted voyage. A similar term is implied as to the shipowner's duty to proceed with all reasonable despatch to the port of loading to take delivery of the charterer's or shipper's cargo.

In *Freeman v Taylor* (1831) 8 Bing. 124, for example, the shipowner had chartered the Edward Lombe to Taylor and had undertaken to "proceed with all convenient speed" from London to Bombay to take delivery of a cargo of cotton but en route, the shipowner called at the Cape of Good Hope and spent more time than necessary there. As a result the ship arrived at Bombay more than six weeks late. The charterer refused to load and assumed the contract of carriage to have been repudiated by the shipowner's delay. Tindal C.J. gave this statement of the law:

> "[I]nasmuch as the freighter might bring his action against the owner, and recover damages for any ordinary deviation, he could not, for such deviation, put an end to the contract: but if the deviation was so long and unreasonable that, in the ordinary course of mercantile concerns, it might be said to have put an end to the whole object the freighter had in view in chartering the ship, in that case the contract might be considered at an end . . . ".

It appears therefore that the legal consequences of a breach of the duty are similar to those for the seaworthiness undertaking. This means that whether or not the claimant is entitled to treat the contract as having been repudiated depends on the seriousness of the effects of the breach. (*N.B.* Although Tindal C.J. referred to "deviation", the term is used in the context of the duty to proceed with due despatch.)

The House of Lords had occasion to examine in some detail the nature of the duty to proceed with due despatch in *Kawasaki Kisen Kaisha Ltd v Whistler International Ltd* [2000] 3 W.L.R. 1954.

7–031 *Kawasaki Kisen Kaisha Ltd v Whistler International Ltd (The Hill Harmony)* [2000] 3 W.L.R. 1954.
Facts:
The Hill Harmony was chartered under a time charter, an amended New York Produce Exchange 1946 form. Under the charter, the charterers were entitled to "employ the vessel for any lawful trades, etc". They instructed the shipmaster to proceed by the "Great Circle" route on a trans-Pacific voyage. The shipmaster refused and chose to proceed by a more southerly route. This was because when the vessel had previously followed the

northerly route, she suffered severe weather damage. The southerly route was considerably longer and as such, the charterers deducted hire from the shipowners. Two vital questions were:

- whether the charterers were entitled to insist on the northerly route; and

- whether the shipowners were in breach of the due or utmost despatch clause in the charter.

Held:

The Court of Appeal held that the structure and terms of the charterparty were such that they did no more than require the master/owners to proceed in "utmost despatch" by the direct route or a usual and reasonable route and to operate the vessel in accordance with the charterer's orders as to its employment. The master had a professional right and duty to decide upon the course or courses to be followed when prosecuting the voyage as properly defined, having regard to weather conditions and other hazards of navigation. All this must be exercised in good faith. There was a clear distinction between navigation and employment; the former is the domain of the master whilst the latter belongs to the charterer.

The House of Lords, however, disagreed with the Court of Appeal. It was held that the "utmost despatch" clause was a merchant's clause with the object of giving effect to the mercantile policy of saving time. A voyage would not have been prosecuted with utmost despatch if the owners or the master unnecessarily chose a longer route which would cause the vessel's arrival at her destination to be delayed. Strict observance of time is vital. The owners had agreed in the charterparty what were to be the limits within which the charterers could order the vessel to sail (in this case, they were limits set out in the Institute Warranty Limits) and had undertaken that, barring unforeseen matters, the vessel would be fit to sail in those waters. It was therefore not open to the owners to say that the vessel was not fit to take the shorter route as directed by the charterer. It was not a good reason that he preferred to sail through calm waters or that he wanted to avoid heavy weather. Vessels were designed and built to be able to sail safely in heavy weather. There was a direct relationship between navigation and employment of the vessel. The choice between *usual* routes was a commercial one and related to the exploitation of the earning capacity of the vessel. It was therefore within the ambit of the employment clause. The charterers were therefore entitled to deduct hire from the shipowners.

The Court of Appeal's approach places much emphasis on the autonomy of the master to direct the route for his vessel. The court referred to the reasonableness of the master's decision to take the ship into a calmer route. This however misses the general paradigm in contract law which is that a party is bound by his contractual obligations strictly. There was no issue of safety in the dispute—it was clear that the vessel would have been able to navigate through the "Great Circle" safely, merchant ships are generally built to withstand heavy weather conditions. It would however cause more inconvenience and cost (in possible repairs to the ship for damage caused by heavy weather). Mere inconvenience, as we appreciate in English contract law, is rarely a good legal cause for avoiding contractual obligations. Only where safety becomes an issue, could the charterer's instructions be disregarded.[12]   **7–032**

Closely related to this duty to proceed with due despatch to the port of loading is the incorporation of an "Expected Ready to Load" clause in the contract of carriage, usually the charterparty. The nature and extent of the clause was

---

[12] This case also discusses the availability of the defence in art.IV(2)(a), Hague-Visby Rules which have been incorporated into the charterparty. See below, paras 8–053—8–055.

considered in *Maredelanto Compania Naviera SA v Bergbau-Handel GmbH (The Mihalis Angelos)* [1971] 1 Q.B. 164.

7–033 *Maredelanto Compania Naviera SA v Bergbau-Handel GmbH (The Mihalis Angelos)* [1971] 1 Q.B. 164
Facts:
The shipowners had undertaken in the charterparty that the vessel "was expected ready to load" about July 1, 1965. The vessel was to proceed to Haiphong and then load a cargo of apatite and carry it to Europe. There was a cancelling clause stating that the charterers could cancel the contract if the vessel was not placed at their disposal in Haiphong by July 20. It was found as a matter of fact that the Mihalis Angelos could not have reasonably made it to Haiphong on July 1. The earliest she could get there was July 13. On July 17, the charterers cancelled the contract on the basis that the ship could not arrive on time. The shipowners claimed damages on the footing that they had lost the charter on July 17, a premature invocation of the cancelling clause. The main issue was whether the "expected ready to load" clause was a condition, the breach of which entitled the charterers to treat the contract as repudiated.
Held:
Lord Denning M.R. held that the correct meaning of an "expected ready to load" clause was that it is an assurance from the shipowners that they honestly expect the vessel to be ready to load on that date and that their expectation is based on reasonable grounds (*Samuel Sanday & Co v Keighley Maxted & Co* (1922) 27 Com. Cas. 296). When the owners or their agent stated in a charter that the ship was "expected ready to load about July 1, 1965", they were making a representation as to their own state of mind; that is, of what they themselves expected and by inserting it in the contract as a term, they were binding themselves to the truth of the representation. Authority suggests that the term is a condition, the breach of which would free the charterers from their duties. Four reasons were supplied by Megaw L.J.:

1. Treating the representation as a condition leans towards certainty in the law. It is common ground that predictability and certainty in the law is of paramount importance in commercial law.

2. It is highly unlikely that the shipowner could legitimately feel that he had suffered an injustice if the law were to treat his undertaking as serious and binding.

3. An analogy may be drawn from cases on the sale of goods where binding authority has established that an "expected ready to load" clause is a condition, a breach of it enables the buyer to reject the goods without having to show that the dishonest or unreasonable expectation of the seller has in fact been prejudicial to the buyer (*Finnish Government v H Ford & Co Ltd* (1921) 6 Ll. L. Rep. 188). It would produce an undesirable anomaly if the clause were given a different effect and interpretation in a charterparty. The fact that the charterparty contains a cancelling clause does not justify a distinction being made.

4. The charterer has legitimate expectation that vessel is due on the "expected ready to load" date and would have conducted his affairs in reliance on that date (*Scrutton on Charterparties*, 10th edn (London: Sweet & Maxwell, 1964) p.79).

However, where the contract provides for a particular cancellation date (as opposed to simply the expected ready to load date), then the charterers must wait until that date has expired before cancelling the charter.

7–034   Where the contract is silent as to date of arrival or time the ship is expected ready to load, the implied term to proceed with due despatch remains operative. That term however is an innominate term unlike an express "expected ready to load" clause. The latter gives rise to an automatic right of cancellation. The former is dependent on the seriousness of the breach. It is not uncommon, as we have seen, for parties to enter a cancellation clause in the charterparty. That clause allows the charterer to terminate the contract after a certain date. Once this date has passed, he can legitimately terminate the charter and make alternative arrangements to have the cargo shipped. The provisions of a cancellation clause will however be construed strictly—the shipowner cannot challenge the charterer's invocation of a cancellation clause by showing that it was not his fault or breach that caused the late arrival and in like manner, the charterer cannot use the cancellation clause as giving rise to a right in damages for the delay caused. Damages will only arise where the shipowner has breached the general undertaking to proceed with due despatch and this must be proved separately. In this connection, the "expected ready to load" clause buttresses the duty by prescribing an estimated time of arrival for the vessel and allows the charterer to use the stipulated date as a guide as to what constituted reasonable despatch.

It might be noted that a cancellation clause may be invoked even when the delay was caused by an excepted peril as was the case in *Smith v Dart* (1884) 14 Q.B.D. 105.

Smith v Dart (1884) 14 Q.B.D. 105   **7–035**
Facts:
The charterparty for a cargo of oranges contained a cancellation clause allowing the charterers to terminate the charter if the ship was not ready to load by December 15. The ship was delayed as a result of bad weather conditions. There was also a clause in the charterparty excepting liability for damage, loss or delay caused by dangers and accidents of the seas.
Held:
Mathew J. held that the exception clause could not defeat the cancellation clause. The latter is an absolute right granted on the charterers. The effect of the exception under these circumstances is to afford protection against damages for the shipowner. It does not affect the absolute right under the cancellation clause.

It is important to note therefore that where there is a cancellation clause, the charterer must wait until the cancellation date before terminating the charter. Where there is no cancellation clause, but simply an "expected ready to load" clause or an "estimated time of arrival" stipulation, the charterer may treat the contract as having been repudiated at a time when it is clear that the ship will not be able to arrive on time. This was affirmed by the Court of Appeal in *Geogas SA v Trammo Gas Ltd (The Baleares)* [1993] 1 Lloyd's Rep. 215 where Neill L.J. held:

"It is clear from the decision in *The Mihalis Angelos* that a right to treat the charterparty as having been repudiated by the owners may arise before the date on which the charterers are given a contractual right to cancel. This right arises when it becomes clear that there is no reasonable prospect of the vessel being able to perform the contemplated voyage".

Where there is no express provision at all as to the time of arrival or a cancellation date, the charterer's right to either damages or repudiation will be determined by the general common law rules on the vessel's failure to proceed to the loading port with due despatch.

Duty not to deviate

Nature of the duty

7–036   At common law, the carrier must ensure that the vessel under the contract of carriage proceeds on the voyage in the usual and customary route and manner. He is not allowed to deviate from the agreed voyage unless it is to save life. The agreed route is that which is specified in the contract of carriage; where the contract does not make any express stipulation as to the route, the courts will presume that the proper route is that which is the direct geographical route between the port of loading and discharge. The courts will however take evidence and be open to persuasion as to what constitutes the customary route. The customary route may be the usual route taken by shipping lines in the particular trade; or it could be the route consistently taken by the carriers concerned.

7–037   *Reardon Smith Line Ltd v Black Sea and Baltic Insurance Co* [1939] A.C. 562
Facts:
Under a charterparty, the Indian City was to load a cargo of ore at the port of Poti at the Black Sea and carry it to Baltimore, USA. Soon after leaving Poti, the vessel called at Constantza which added about 200 miles to the voyage to take bunkers. She ran aground when she attempted to enter Constantza. Some of the cargo had to be jettisoned. She was unable to complete the voyage and the charterers thus refused to pay freight. The shipowners argued that it was customary for ships of the kind in question to call at Constantza for cheap bunkers.
Held:
It was quite clear that Constantza was treated by many shipping lines using the Black Sea as a usual and recognised bunkering port. In addition, the House of Lords recognised that the doctrine of stages permitted ocean lines to call at customary bunkering ports in order to ensure that the ship remained seaworthy for the purposes of the contract of carriage. Thus, to call at such ports has become an ordinary incident of the voyage. A shipowner is entitled to rely on his own wisdom to decide where to call at for bunkers as long as the decision is reasonable. Lord Wright said:

"The test of what is usual and reasonable in a commercial sense may arise in very different circumstances and must be decided whenever it arises by application of sound business considerations and by determining what is fair and reasonable in the interest of all concerned".

What is reasonable is naturally a question of fact—but the court will give due regard to how economical and convenient it was to make the call at the bunkering port concerned.

It is trite law that the duty not to deviate is breached only where the deviation was intentional. In *Rio Tinto Co Ltd v Seed Shipping Co* (1926) 134 L.T. 764 for example, there was no deviation where the vessel had sailed off course due to the ill shipmaster who misinterpreted navigational instructions. Similarly where the ship is blown, or forced, off course there is no deviation. In *Tait v Levi* (1811) 14 East. 481, a less than satisfactory case, the court was divided on whether there was deviation. The shipmaster had taken the vessel into Barcelona thinking that it was Tarragona. As a result the ship was captured and restrained by French forces. The case is problematic not because the court could not decide what amounted to deviation but the court was unsettled by the issue of "involuntariness". Should the shipmaster's error leading to the deviation be treated as involuntary? Interestingly, on a similar point, the House of Lords thought in *Hain Steamship Co Ltd v Tate & Lyle Ltd* [1936] 2 All E.R. 597 that it was a breach of the duty where the deviation was the consequence of the shipmaster not receiving his shipping instructions on time.

When deviation is justified

The deviation will be excused if it was necessary to save human life. This liberty **7–038** however does not extend to saving property. An authoritative statement of the law on deviation to save lives is reproduced below from *Scaramanga & Co v Stamp* (1880) 5 C.P.D. 295:

"Deviation for the purpose of saving life is protected, and involves neither forfeiture of insurance nor liability to the goods owner in respect of loss which would otherwise be within the exception of 'perils of the seas'. And, as a necessary consequence of the foregoing, deviation for the purpose of communicating with a ship in distress is allowable, inasmuch as the state of the vessel in distress may involve danger to life. On the other hand, deviation for the sole purpose of saving property is not thus privileged, but entails all the usual consequences of deviation.

If, therefore, the lives of the persons on board a disabled ship can be saved without saving the ship, as by taking them off, deviation for the purpose of saving the ship will carry with it all the consequences of an unauthorised deviation".

The Court of Appeal went on to explain why the distinction between saving life and saving property should be made. All prevailing is the perception that of sailors who have trusted themselves to the sea, it is of the utmost importance that the "promptings of humanity" to save life should not be checked or interfered with.

"It would be against the common good and shocking to the sentiments of mankind, that the shipowner should be deterred from endeavouring to save life by the fear, lest any disaster to ship or cargo, consequent on so doing, should fall on himself."

The court felt that any deviation to save property, however, falls on a totally different footing. Cockburn C.J. in response to the ship master's deviation to tow a helpless vessel, the *Arion*, into a port for a fee of 1,000 lira, said:

"There is here no moral duty to fulfil, which, though its fulfilment may have been attended with danger to life or property, remains unrewarded. There would be much force, no doubt, in the argument that it is to the common interest of merchants and insurers, as well as of shipowners, that ships and cargoes, when in danger of perishing, should be saved, and consequently that, as matter of policy, the same latitude should be allowed . . . , were it not that the law has provided another, and a very adequate motive for the saving of property, by securing to the salvor a liberal proportion of the property saved—a proportion in which not only the value of the property saved, but also the danger run by the salvor to life or property is taken into account, and in calculating which, if it be once settled that the insurance will not be protected, nor the shipowner freed from liability in respect of loss of cargo, the risk thus run will, no doubt, be included as an element. It would obviously be most unjust if the shipowner could thus take the chance of highly remunerative gain at the risk and possible loss of the merchant or the insurer, neither of whom derive any benefit from the preservation of the property saved. This is strikingly exemplified in the present case, in which, not content with what would have been awarded to him by the proper court on account of salvage, the master made his own terms, and would have been paid a very large sum had the attempt to bring the *Arion* into port proved successful".

7–039   The carrier may also deviate to avoid danger to the ship or cargo during an emergency, for example, he may have to take the ship to a port outside the usual route for emergency repairs or as was the case in *The Teutonia* (1872) L.R. 4 P.C. 171, to avoid capture by enemy forces. The liberty to take the ship to port for repairs is not confined to using the nearest port; it is always a question of fact as to what is a reasonable decision of the shipmaster. The courts will not lightly presume to possess the expertise and prudence of a shipmaster in making that decision (*Phelps, James & Co v Hill* [1891] 1 Q.B. 605). While this latitude could not be challenged; where the deviation to save ship or cargo is originally caused by the unseaworthiness of the ship, this raises the difficult question as to whether there is in fact unauthorised deviation.

In *J&E Kish v Charles Taylor, Sons & Co* [1912] A.C. 604, the House of Lords allowed the deviation even though it was caused by of a pre-existing unseawor-thiness of the vessel. Lord Atkinson relying on the dictum of Lord Watson in *Strang, Steel & Co v Scott & Co* (1889) 14 App. Cas. 601 said:

> "'it is the presence of the peril and not its causes' which justify it, and that it is, therefore immaterial whether the unseaworthiness of the ship or her negligent navigation contributed directly to the peril or not".

The rationale was that it would be unfair to put the shipmaster in the dilemma either to continue on his voyage at all hazards or to subject himself to the penalties of unauthorised deviation where the ship needs repairs whether as a result of his own fault or that of his employers, the shipowners.

Effect of deviation

7–040   The traditional common law position as set out in the old case of *Balian v Joly, Victoria Co* (1890) 6 T.L.R. 345 was that an unauthorised deviation will result in the contract of carriage being displaced, i.e. the contract will be suspended and the carrier is reduced to a "wrongful bailee". As a wrongful bailee, the carrier could not then rely on any of the exceptions and defences contained in the contract of carriage.[13]

7–041   *Joseph Thorley Ltd v Orchis Steamship Co Ltd* [1907] 1 K.B. 660
Facts:
The contract of carriage contained a clause exempting the carriers from liability for loss or damage caused by negligence of stevedores. The ship had deviated from its agreed

---

[13] Cashmore, "The Legal Nature of the Doctrine of Deviation" [1989] J.B.L. 492.

route. When the goods were being unloaded, stevedores employed by the carrier damaged the goods. In defending the action brought against them by the cargo owners, the carriers attempted to rely on the exclusion clause.

Held:

The Court of Appeal reiterated the traditional rule that the legal effect of deviation is that the contract will be displaced and the carrier will therefore not be entitled to rely on the exclusion clauses in the contract of carriage. The court held that the undertaking not to deviate has the effect of a condition, a breach of which goes to the root of the contract and brings the contract to an end. The deviation amounts to failure to comply with a condition precedent of the contract and will displace the express contract, independently of any question whether the deviation has any bearing on the particular loss or damage. It is an absolute undertaking, the breach of which however slight will allow the cargo owner to treat the contract as having been repudiated.

Fletcher Moulton L.J. said:

"The cases show that, for a long series of years, the courts have held that a deviation is such a serious matter, and changes the character of the contemplated voyage so essentially, that a shipowner who has been guilty of a deviation cannot be considered as having performed his part of the . . . contract but something fundamentally different; and therefore he cannot claim the benefit of stipulations in his favour contained in the [contract]".

Several issues arise:

1. To what extent, if at all, is the shipowner allowed to rely on exceptions and defences as regards loss or damage occurring before the deviation?

2. What are the options available to the cargo owner following an unauthorised deviation?

3. What is the legal position of a "wrongful bailee" with reference to the goods?

4. What is the shipowner's right to demurrage or dead freight accrued before the deviation?

5. What is the shipowner's right to freight following deviation?

The House of Lords' case of *Hain Steamship Co Ltd v Tate & Lyle Ltd* [1936] 2 All E.R. 597 goes some distance to resolving these issues.

Hain Steamship Co Ltd v Tate & Lyle Ltd [1936] 2 All E.R. 597   **7–042**

Facts:

As a result of poor communication, the shipmaster was not informed on time that the port of loading was to be S. Pedro de Macoris in San Domingo. As a result, the ship had set sail for another port. This was clearly a deviation. The vessel was then ordered by the charterers to proceed to the San Domingo port when the mistake was discovered. The goods were subsequently unloaded at S. Pedro but on leaving port, the ship ran aground resulting in a partial loss of the cargo.

Held:

The House of Lords considered that although the deviation, albeit not the fault of the shipmaster, had constituted a breach of condition and would have brought the contract to an end. However, the charterers by ordering the vessel to proceed to the nominated port was a waiver of the breach. Lord Atkin stated that the claimant's options when the ship deviates are to be governed by the ordinary law of contract. His Lordship said:

"The party who is affected by the breach has the right to say, I am not now bound by the contract whether it is expressed in charterparty, bill of lading or otherwise. He can, of course, claim his goods from the ship; whether and to what extent he will become liable to pay some remuneration for carriage I do not think arises in this case . . . but I am satisfied that once he elects to treat the contract as at an end he is not bound by the promise to pay the agreed freight any more than by his other promises. But on the other hand, as he can elect to treat the contract as ended, so he can elect to treat the contract as subsisting and if he does this with knowledge of his rights he must in accordance with the general law of contract be held bound. No doubt one must be careful to see that the acts of the cargo owner are not misinterpreted when he finds that his goods have been taken off on a voyage to which he did not agree. He could not reasonably be expected to recall the goods when he discovers the ship at a port of call presumably still intending to reach her agreed port of destination".

In this case, there was a waiver because the charterer had procured the ship to be recalled to the San Domingo port for the express purpose of continuing to load under the charter, a obligation which, of course, only existed under the express contract.

7–043   A few essential principles might be extracted from Lord Atkin's dicta:

1. Deviation is a fundamental term of the contract, a breach of which should bring obligations existing under the contract of carriage to an end.[14]

2. This means that the aggrieved party need not to carry on with his part of the contract, i.e. he may be entitled to refuse to pay freight.

3. Some remuneration for services already rendered (for example, freight where delivery of the goods has been effected) may have to be paid by the aggrieved party, perhaps on the basis of quantum meruit. In addition, the liabilities of the aggrieved party before the breach remain to exist. Hence, the carrier has a right to debts owing to him by the aggrieved party before the deviation.

4. On the other hand the aggrieved party can opt to carry on with the contract. This is a waiver of his right to treat the contract as having been repudiated. A waiver will be valid only if the aggrieved party had acted with knowledge of his rights. The aggrieved party's conduct in protecting his cargo should not be misconstrued as constituting a waiver. The waiver must be supported by evidence of intention on the aggrieved party's part to carry on with the contract.

Some of these principles became less clear in the light of *Photo Production v Securicor* where the House of Lords expressly rejected the notion of deviation as a fundamental breach. If *Photo Production v Securicor* is to be extended to deviation cases, everything would depend on what consequences the parties are said to have intended as regards deviation.[15] On the other hand, Lord Wilberforce suggested that the cases on deviation should be treated as a "body of authority sui generis with special rules derived from historical and commercial reasons". It remains to be seen how the courts will respond to these considerations.[16] It

---

[14] Dockray, "Deviation: a Doctrine all at sea?" [2000] L.M.C.L.Q. 76.

[15] See also *Kenya Railways v Antares Co Ltd (The Antares)* [1987] 1 Lloyd's Rep. 424.

[16] Debattista [1989] J.B.L. 22 and Hubbard [1986] Victoria University of Wellington L. Rev. 147; see also *The Kapitan Petko Voivoda* [2003] EWCA Civ 451 where the Court of Appeal expressed doubt as to the correctness of those cases on "deviation . . . decided in the nineteenth century".

might be added that the effect of deviation under the Carriage of Goods by Sea Act 1971 is entirely different.[17]

Liberty clauses

Considering the potentially devastating effect of an unauthorised deviation, it has now become general practice to insert a clause in the contract of carriage allowing the shipowner to deviate under certain circumstances. This is known as a liberty clause. Naturally the courts are somewhat mindful of the fact that these clauses should not be applied in such a way so as to destroy the object of the contract. We see this circumspection applied in *Leduc v Ward* (1888) 20 Q.B.D. 475.   **7–044**

Leduc v Ward (1888) 20 Q.B.D. 475   **7–045**
Facts:
The contract of carriage provided that rape seed was to be shipped on the Austria "now lying in the port of Fiume and bound for Dunkirk, with liberty to call at any ports in any order". The vessel deviated from the ordinary direct route to Dunkirk to call at Glasgow. It sank near Ailsa Craig. It was argued, inter alia, that the deviation was protected by the liberty clause.
Held:
Lord Esher, in holding the liberty clause ineffective to protect the shipowner, addressed the issue in two stages:

- First, the clause would be applied in the understanding that it was not the intention of the parties to defeat the commercial object of the contract. This consideration would be the overriding factor in the construction and application of the liberty clause.

- Second, the court will ascertain the contractual object of the carriage. In this case that object was that the goods carried

  "may be sold or otherwise dealt with at the place of destination; and the person who wants them at that place for sale or use there acts upon the assumption that they will arrive there at or about a certain time in the ordinary course of a voyage there from the port of shipment".

Business could not be carried out under any other terms.
Finally, the clause will be subject to the normal rules of contractual construction. As Lord Esher said:

  "[I]t is a question of the construction of a mercantile expression used in mercantile document, and I think that as such the term can have but one meaning, namely, that the ports, liberty to call at which is intended to be given, must be ports which are substantially ports which will be passed on the named voyage"

so as not to defeat the contractual object of the parties. It could not be within the contemplation of the parties to treat the words "any ports at any order" to mean, as the defendants contended, "any port in the world"; such a construction was simply too wide and not consistent with the mercantile object of the contract of carriage as stated above.

---

[17] See Ch.8, paras 8–067—8–069.

Such a restrictive approach was indorsed in the subsequent House of Lords' case of *Glynn v Margetson & Co* [1893] A.C. 351.

7–046 *Glynn v Margetson & Co* [1893] A.C. 351
Facts:
A cargo of oranges was shipped at Malaga in Spain. The bill of lading which contained the contract of carriage stated:

> "Shipped in good order and condition . . . in and upon the good steamship called the Zena, now lying in the port of Malaga, and bound for Liverpool . . . with liberty to proceed to and stay at any port or ports in any rotation in the Mediterranean, Levant, Black Sea or Adriatic, or on the coasts of Africa, Spain, Portugal, France, Great Britain and Ireland, for the purpose of delivering coals, cargo or passengers, or for any other purpose whatsoever".

The ship then instead of sailing for Liverpool headed for a port in the other direction, called Burriana. The issue for the court was whether the clause should be construed as permitting a deviation and whether there is any reason for putting a restriction on them as the claimants argued.
Held:
Again it is important to approach the matter from the standpoint of what the object of the contract was. In this case, Lord Herschell L.C. held that the object and intent of the contract of carriage was the carriage of oranges from Malaga to Liverpool. It would defeat this particular object if the shipowner's contention that the clause permitted him to take the ship anywhere he pleased, to trade in any manner that he pleased and to arrive at the port of destination for the oranges when he pleased. The construction relied on by the shipowners was unreasonable because he was effectively asking the court to acknowledge an unbridled liberty to do as he pleased with the pursuance of the contractual voyage and a liberty of such a magnitude could not have been the object of the contract. The clause must be construed within the realms of business sense and commercial realities—in this case, that meant that the clause simply permitted the shipowner to call at ports en route to Liverpool, not any port he wished. After all the clause did not refer to liberty simpliciter to proceed to any port, purposes are mentioned; one of which being "for the purpose of delivering coals, cargo or passengers". According to Lord Herschell L.C.:

> "That clause seems to throw light upon the construction which ought to be put upon the language used in the other part of the instrument, because the delivering of coals, cargo or passengers points to the carrying out of a voyage already determined upon in relation to a cargo already on board".

7–047   In another House of Lords' case, the confinement of the clause to the named purposes of the contract was applied to defeat the shipowner's claim. In *Stag Line Ltd v Foscolo, Mango & Co Ltd* [1932] A.C. 328, Lord Atkin commented:

> "Even if [the words of the liberty clause are] limited to port or ports on the geographical course of voyage, as I think on authority they clearly must be, the purpose of the call must receive some limitation. The liberty could not reasonably be intended to give the right to call at an intermediate port to land or take on board friends of the shipowner for the purposes of a pleasure trip . . .".

While it is quite clear that the courts will strive to narrow the application of a liberty clause, the fact remains that a liberty clause is a valid contractual clause.

This essentially places the cargo interest in a precarious position where the carrier or shipowner has employed clear and precise language to allow himself "to do as he pleases". Hence, a clause that provides expressly that the

> "ship has the liberty to call at any port or ports whatsoever in any order in or out of the route or in a contrary direction to or beyond the port of destination"

must be given full effect (*Connolly Shaw v Nordenfjeldske SS Co* (1934) 50 T.L.R. 418.). What the parties have expressly agreed to, whether rightly or wrongly, must be treated as sacrosanct. The *contra proferentem* rule has no place in a very clearly and precisely drafted clause.

Shipowner's duty to take reasonable care of the goods

It is conventional practice that charterparties will generally stipulate expressly that the shipowner is to exercise due diligence in the care and stowing of the goods. The Gencon Charter (as revised in 1922 and 1976), for example, provides in Clause 2: **7–048**

> "Owners are to be responsible for loss of or damage to the goods or for delays in delivery of the goods only in case the loss, damage or delay has been caused by improper or negligent stowage of the goods (unless stowage performed by Shippers/Charterers or their stevedores or servants) or by personal want of due diligence on the part of the Owners or their Manager to make the vessel in all respects seaworthy and to secure that she is properly manned, equipped and supplied or by the personal act or default of the Owners of their Manager".

It is also quite common for shippers and shipowners to agree on a "Clause Paramount" which has the effect of incorporating the Hague-Visby Rules (or the Hague Rules or Hamburg Rules) partly to stipulate expressly the duties of the carrier and partly to apply the limitation of liability provisions in the conventional rules to the contract. Where this is the case, the convention rules on care and protection of cargo (e.g. art.III(2) Hague-Visby Rules) will be given contractual force.

Where the contract of carriage or the charterparty is silent as to his duty to take care of the goods, Channell J.'s words in *McFadden v Blue Star Line* [1905] 1 K.B. 697 may be pertinent:

> "If anything happens whereby the goods are damaged during the voyage, the shipowner is liable because he is an insurer except in the event of the damage happening from some cause in respect of which he is protected by the exceptions in his [contract]".

Where the contract clearly provides that the charterer is himself responsible for the care of the goods, then the shipowner's common law duty is relieved of him. In *Transocean Liners Reederei GmbH v Euxine Shipping Co Ltd (The Imvros)* [1999] 1 Lloyd's Rep. 848, for example, the charterers were barred from suing the shipowners for the loss of their goods caused by poor loading and lashing because they had themselves issued directions as to how the goods are to be **7–049** stowed or kept and those instructions were inconsistent with standard practice as set out in the IMO Code of Practice for Ships Carrying Timber Deck Cargoes.

Duty to deliver the goods to named or identifiable person

7–050 The shipowner is duty bound to deliver the goods to the right person at the port of discharge—this is the person named either in the bill of lading, the mate's receipt or the charterparty itself (*Bourne v Gatliffe* (1841) 133 E.R. 1298). This personal duty of the shipowner entails seeing to it that the goods are delivered up to the right person; he will not be excused if he simply left the goods by the quayside. He must wait a reasonable time to enable the consignee to take delivery of the goods, failing which he needs to land the goods and leave them with a warehouse. All this will naturally be done at the consignee's expense. The Merchant Shipping Act 1894 ss.492 to 498 provide that where a consignee fails to take delivery of the goods, the shipowner may land the goods after the agreed time of delivery or, if no time is pre-arranged, after 72 hours from the vessel first reports. Upon the consignee or cargo owner failing to settle his debts, the warehouse taking possession of the goods may arrange for the goods to be sold by auction to meet debts in the following order:

● custom duties;

● sale expenses;

● storage charges; and

● freight and dues owing to the shipowner.

Where no bill of lading is issued, the goods shall be deliverable to the charterer who is usually also the consignee. The identity of the charterer will be stated in the non-negotiable receipt issued by the shipmaster when he accepts the goods for shipment. Where a bill of lading has been issued, the shipowner's primary duty is to deliver the goods to the named consignee or indorsee of the bill of lading. As a general rule, the bill of lading constitutes a contract between the shipowner and the shipper despite the presence or existence of a charterer and the acts of the charterer are usually deemed to be acts carried out on behalf of the shipowner. Thus, in *MB Pyramid Sound NV v Briese-Schiffahrts GmbH (The Sina) (The Ines)* [1995] 2 Lloyd's Rep. 144 for example, it was held that although the delivery of the goods without presentment of the bill of lading was made by the charterer's agent, that act of misdelivery was imputable on the shipowners. The implied term is that when the shipowner delivers the goods upon the presentment of a bill of lading, he will be protected from any action for misdelivery or tort. We may recall how this was explained in *Glyn Mills Currie & Co v East and West India Dock Co* (1882) 7 App. Cas. 591 (as discussed in Chapter 6). In *The Houda* [1994] 2 Lloyd's Rep. 541, the shipowners had refused to deliver the goods up to the charterers because the charterers had not been able to produce the relevant bills of lading. According to the charterers, the bills of lading had been lost during the chaos following the Iraqi invasion of Kuwait. The shipowners relied on the rule in *Barclays Bank Ltd v Commissioners of Customs and Excise* [1963] 1 Lloyd's Rep. 81 that:

"It is clear law that, where a bill of lading or order is issued in respect of a contract of carriage by sea, the shipowner is not bound to surrender possession of the goods to any person whether named as consignee or not, except on production of the bill of lading".

Although the charterers accepted this general rule, they argued that time charters must be subject to different rules. An order to deliver should fall within the terms of the employment and use of vessel clauses in the time charter for after all the time charterers were themselves the owners of the goods. This argument was accepted at first instance by Phillips J. who thought it coincided with the business efficacy test.

The Court of Appeal took a different view. It held that there was no persuasive grounds for distinguishing time charters from other contracts of carriage where in both arrangements delivery of the goods is expressly subject the presentation of the bill of lading. To adopt the view of Phillips J. would be to throw confusion on an established mercantile rule. Millett L.J. said:

"[The shipmaster] has no means of satisfying himself that it is a lawful order with which he must comply for, unless the bills of lading are produced, he cannot know for certain that the person to whom he has been ordered to deliver the cargo is entitled to it".

The shipowners were therefore not in breach for misdelivery.

The shipowner must also comply with any precise terms of the charterparty as **7–051** regards the quantity to be delivered. Where the charterers have given precise instructions as to the amount or quantity of goods to be discharged at a certain port, even though the receivers appear to act in a bona fide manner in requesting the shipmaster to vary the amount of goods to be released to them, the ship does so at her peril. In *Merit Shipping Co Inc v TK Boesen A/S (The Goodpal)* [2000] 1 Lloyd's Rep. 638, the Commercial Court held that the receivers could only be deemed to be standing in the charterer's stead to the extent of the quantities specified in the contract of carriage. In that case, the master's instructions were that he should discharge at Zhangjiagang 19,006.01 tonnes of soya bean pellets. The receivers meeting the ship requested the master to deliver to them 19,445 tonnes and offered an indemnity to the master if he complied. The master complied and as a result when the ship called subsequently at Fangcheng, he was unable to deliver the quantity demanded by the holders of the bill of lading. That failure caused the ship to be arrested and the owners' P & I club had to put up a guarantee for the release of the vessel.

The question for the court was whether the charterers could be held liable for the instructions issued by the receivers. Colman J. said no. It was, and was only, the owner's decision to accede to the requests of the receivers which caused the under-delivery at Fangcheng. The charterers were not liable for instructions given by the receivers which were clearly inconsistent with the terms of the charter. The receivers were not acting as the charterer's agents in demanding the release of the goods contrary to the charterparty. This was not a case where the master or owner might be left in doubt whether the charterers' instructions were unlawful—there simply never were any charterers' instructions.

It is of course quite possible to insert a clause excluding or limiting the shipowners' liability for misdelivery. Such a clause must however be clearly worded or else, the courts would construe it *contra proferentem*. In *MB Pyramid Sound NV v Briese Schiffahrts GmbH and Latvian Shipping Association Ltd (The Ines)* [1995] 2 Lloyd's Rep. 144, the shipowners had delivered the claimants' telephones to a third party without the production of the original bill of lading. The shipowners attempted to rely on several clauses which they claimed excused the misdelivery. One such clause reads:

"PERIOD OF RESPONSIBILITY Goods in the custody of the carrier or his agent . . . before loading and after discharge . . . are in such custody at the sole risk of the owners of the goods and thus the carrier has no responsibility whatsoever for the goods prior to the loading on and subsequent to the discharge from the ocean vessel . . . ".

7–052 The goods had been misdelivered subsequent to discharge. It was argued by the shipowners that this clause was wide enough to excuse their breach. Clarke J. did not agree. For the clause to be operative, it must be precise in its reference to misdelivery. This particular clause appears to be concerned with the loss or damage to the goods but not with misdelivery. The shipowners were therefore not entitled to plead it.

Confusio is the Latin word for the mixing of goods belonging to different owners, so that they could not be separated. How does this affect the duty of the shipowner to deliver the right goods to the right consignee? At English law where the cargoes belonging to two or more holders of relevant bills of lading have become mixed in such a way that the individual packages can no longer be identified (for example, where identification marks have become erased or obliterated), it was held in *Spence v Union Marine Insurance Co Ltd* (1868) L.R. 3 C.P. 427 that

"the owners of the goods so mixed become tenants in common of the whole in the proportions which they have severally contributed to it".

Bovill C.J. went on to say that this result would follow only in those cases where, after the adoption of all reasonable means and exertions to identify or separate the goods, it was found impracticable to do so. Furthermore the mixing of the goods must be caused by a peril excepted in the contract—in *Spence's* case, the obliteration of the marks was caused by the "action of the sea". Where the mixture of the goods was caused not by an exception, the shipowner will remain liable for failing to deliver the agreed consignment of goods to the consignee (*Frank Stewart Sandeman & Sons v Tyzack and Branfoot Steamship Co Ltd* [1913] A.C. 680). He is not entitled to insist on the consignee accept a proportion of the mixed goods.

7–053 It was argued by the cargo owners in *Indian Oil Corp Ltd v Greenstone Shipping SA (The Ypatianna)* [1987] 2 Lloyd's Rep. 286 that where their cargo had been mixed without their consent (as against a case of mere obliteration of marks), the entire cargo should belong to them. In rejecting the less than reasonable submission, Staughton J. had this to say about the principle

" . . . where B wrongfully mixes the goods of A with goods of his own, which are substantially of the same nature and quality, and they cannot in practice be separated, the mixture is held in common and A is entitled to receive out of it a quantity equal to that of his goods which went into the mixture, any doubt as to that quantity being resolved in favour of A. He is also entitled to claim damages from B in respect of any loss he may have suffered, in respect of quality or otherwise, by reason of the admixture.

Whether the same rule would apply when the goods of A and B are not substantially of the same nature and quality must be left to another case. It does not arise here. The claim based on a rule of law that the mixture becomes the property of the receivers fails".

Exceptions to Carrier's Liability at Law

Act of God

In *Nugent v Smith* (1876) 1 C.P.D. 423, the owner of two horses had shipped them **7-054** onboard a ship belonging to the defendant company from London to Aberdeen. During the voyage, one of the horses died from injuries caused by a violent storm. The defendant was not negligent on his part in the care of the horses. The issue was whether he was nonetheless strictly liable for the death of the horse as a common carrier or sea carrier. The court was swift to point out that there is no common law proposition that every carrier by sea is subject to the same liability of a common carrier. However, from the facts the defendant was clearly a common carrier and in order for the company to escape liability, they must prove that the

"damage or loss in question must have been caused directly and exclusively by such a direct and violent and sudden and irreversible act of Nature as the defendant could not, by any amount of ability, foresee would happen or, if [they] could foresee that it would happen, [they] could not by any amount of care and skill resist, so as to prevent its effect".

Act of the Queen's enemies

The other recognised exception to the strict duty is "act of the Queen's enemies". **7-055** This term must be distinguished from acts of an armed force intending to rob the carrier of goods. In *Forward v Pittard* (1785) 1 T.R. 27, Lord Mansfield commented,

"If an armed force come to rob the carrier of the goods, he is liable: and a reason is given in the books, which is a bad one, *viz.* that he ought to have sufficient force to repel it: but that would be impossible in some cases, as for instance in the riots in the year 1780. The true reason is, for fear it may give room for collusion, that the master may contrive to be robbed on purpose, and share the spoil".

Inherent vice

Where it is proved that the cargo had been lost or damaged as a result of its own **7-056** inherent nature and that this was something beyond the control of the carrier, the law will not make him liable for the loss or damage. The description of the court in *Albacora SRL v Westcott & Lawrence Line* [1966] 2 Lloyd's Rep. 53 is noteworthy. The court stated that inherent vice is "unfitness for the treatment the contract of carriage authorised or required". It was further held in *Hudson v Baxendale* (1857) 2 H.&N. 575 that in order to succeed on inherent vice or defect of the goods as an exception, the carrier must show that he himself had not been at fault.

Fault or fraud of the consignor

7-057   If the damage is caused by an act or omission of the consignor, the carrier is freed from liability. For example, where the goods had been inadequately packed and that caused the goods to be damaged, the carrier should not be held liable. Likewise where the loss or damage is caused as a result of the consignor's failure to address and label the goods, the carrier is not liable. In *Bradley v Waterhouse* (1828) 3 C.O.P. 318 the claimant had hidden money in a consignment of tea which was delivered to the common carrier. The money was subsequently stolen. Tenterden C.J. held that the claimant had brought about his own loss "by his own manner of conducting the business" and the carrier was not liable. It of course goes without say that where the consignor's fraudulent act or forgery of documents results in loss, the carrier is not liable.

A more difficult situation arose in *Gould v South Eastern and Chatham Railway Co* [1920] 2 K.B. 186.

7-058   *Gould v South Eastern and Chatham Railway Co* [1920] 2 K.B. 186
Facts:
The claimant had entered into a contract with the defendant railway company for the carriage of his glass showcase. The defendant's agent informed the claimant's when examining the showcase that it was not properly packed and might be charged at a higher rate. The claimant's asked the agent to "do his best" for him. The agent then claused the consignment noted stating that the case was not properly packed and that carriage was at the claimant's own risk. The case was badly damaged in transit.
Held:
On the issue of whether the carrier who is aware of the insufficiency of packing could cast liability back on the claimant for the latter's failure to pack the goods properly, the Court of Appeal said:

"Now does it make a difference that the faulty packing which caused the damage was manifest to the carrier at the time that the goods were delivered to him to be carried? By analogy to the exception of inherent vice it would seem that it does not. The inherent vice or natural tendency of certain kinds of goods to depreciate or become damaged may be perfectly apparent to the carrier, and in most cases would be quite apparent when he received the goods, nevertheless he is not responsible for the damage resulting from such cause, and it appears to me that there is no reason for treating the exception of damage caused by defective packing in any different way".

Limitation Clauses

7-059   Concerned with the enormity of their potential legal liability and the frailty of the common law exceptions to their generally strict liability, carriers have resorted to incorporating exclusion or limitation of liability clauses in their contracts. At law, these exclusion of liability clauses will be treated with circumspect and any ambiguities will be construed *contra proferentem*. This means that the uncertainty will be construed against the favour of the party pleading it. In *Mitsubishi Corp v Eastwind Transport Ltd* [2004] EWHC 2924, for example, the court refused to construe the exemption clause widely. There, the clause stipulated that "the carrier was not responsible for any loss or damage to or in connection with the goods, however caused". The ship's refrigeration system was not working properly, causing deterioration to the frozen goods. The Commercial Court held that it was plain that the words "however caused" did not operate to relieve the carrier from any and every breach of contract. It was only applicable, in the context, to damage caused by negligence or the unseaworthiness or uncargoworthiness of the vessel. In addition, we should note the following principles on the right to insert exclusion clauses:

1. the clause must be incorporated at time of contract; a subsequent insertion will be deemed to be a unilateral variation of the contract which will not carry any legal effect without the assent of the other party (*Chapelton v Barry UDC* [1940] 1 K.B. 532);

2. there is no general rule of law that allows the court to strike down an exclusion of liability clause that seems to forgive the breach of a term that goes to "the root of the contract". It is always a matter of construction as to whether the clause is sufficiently wide to cover the breach in question (*Photo Productions Ltd v Securicor Transport Ltd* [1980] A.C. 827).

The breadth of this freedom to contract means that it is not uncommon to set out all probable exempting events. It suffices for our purpose to note and discuss a few of the more standard exemptions.

Perils of the sea

It is common for carriers to exempt liability for damage or loss caused to goods   **7–060**
where the cause is a peril of the sea. It is good sense that the term "perils of the sea" should not cover every accident or casualty which may occur during transit of the goods. The question for us is how to limit its scope, and to what extent it should be limited.

In *The Xantho* (1887) 12 App. Cas. 503, Lord Herschell had this to say:

" . . . it is well settled that it is not every loss or damage of which the sea is the immediate cause that is covered by these words. They do not protect, for example, against that natural and inevitable action of the winds and waves, which results in what might be described as wear and tear. There must be some casualty, something which could not be foreseen as one of the necessary incidents of the adventure".

His Lordship then went to hold that although there should be some unforeseen casualty, there is no reason to treat a loss as falling outside the scope of the term "perils of the sea" *simply* because human fault was involved. In that case, the Xantho had collided with the Valuta in fog and sank. The claimants had relied on *Woodley v Michell* (1883) 11 Q.B.D. 47 as authority for their contention that where human negligence was involved in the loss or damage to ship and/or cargo, it could not be classed as "perils of the sea".

Lord Bramwell sought assistance in the law and practice of marine insurance where perils of the sea had been applied to include negligence of crew and other human default. His Lordship considered that that approach is not dissimilar to the law of carriage. His argument was:

> "It would be strange if an underwriter on cargo, suing in the name of the cargo owners on the bill of lading should say, 'I have paid for a loss by perils of the sea, and claim on you because the loss was not by perils of the sea'".

7–061   In another case decided on the same day (*Hamilton, Fraser & Co v Pandorf & Co* (1887) 12 App. Cas. 518), the House of Lords went so far to say that damage caused by sea water coming through a hole gnawed into the lead pipe by rats was covered by the exclusion of "dangers and accidents of the seas" clause. Lord Bramwell stated that the term "perils of the sea" or "dangers and accidents of the seas" must be given the same meaning in both marine insurance policies and bills of lading. Although it may be true to say that the mere fact of rats making a hole in the lead pipe is not a peril of the sea, when it leads to the incursion of sea water then it becomes a sea damage, occurring at sea with nobody's fault and consequently a peril of the sea.

Guidance might be sought from marine insurance cases. In a marine insurance case decided on that same day, July 14, 1887, *Thames and Mersey Marine Insurance Co v Hamilton, Fraser & Co* (1887) 12 App. Cas. 484, the House of Lords held that the fact that a valve in the ship's donkey-engine had become clogged up by salt and thereby causing the air chamber to split was not a peril of the sea. Lord Bramwell said:

> "The damage to the donkey-engine was not through its being in a ship or at sea. The same thing would have happened had the boilers and engines been on land, if the same management had taken place. The sea, waves and winds had nothing to do with it".

In the case against *Pandorf & Co*, on the other hand, although the rats making a hole in the lead pipe would not have ordinarily been a peril of the sea, it was treated as such because not only did it take place at sea but "the sea, waves and winds" did have something to with the ultimate damage. This was reaffirmed in *Canada Rice Mills Ltd v Union Marine and General Insurance Co Ltd* [1941] A.C. 55 by Lord Wright:

> "Where there is an accidental incursion of seawater into a vessel at a part of the vessel and in a manner, where seawater is not expected to enter in the ordinary course of things, and there is consequent damage . . . there is prima facie a loss by perils of the sea. The accident may consist in some negligent act, such as improper opening of a valve, or a hole made in a pipe by mischance, or it may be that sea water is admitted by stress of weather or some like cause bringing the sea over openings ordinarily not exposed to the sea or, even without stress of weather, by the vessel heeling over owing to some accident, or by the breaking of hatches or other coverings. These are merely a few amongst many possible instances in which there may be a fortuitous

incursion of seawater. It is the fortuitous entry of seawater which is the peril of the sea in such cases".

It seems to be the rule in the United States that the words "perils of the sea" **7–062** could not be extended to cover negligent acts leading to damage or loss (*The Burma* 187 Fed. Rep. 94 (1911)). Express words to that effect must be specifically incorporated. However, from Lord Wright's speech, the position is quite different at English law.

Summary of principles from these cases:

— It is notable that there is no invariable rule of law or presumption of fact that a particular event shall be treated as a peril of the sea.

— It is clear that while the court would not be prepared to allow the carrier to extend the scope of their protection no bounds, it would not unduly restrict it to losses "occasioned by extraordinary violence of the winds or waves". Human agency does not necessarily exclude the perils of sea as the operative and proximate cause of loss or damage. This does not however include events having no connection whatsoever with "the sea, waves and winds".

— The court would be prepared to treat the term as carrying the same import and scope as it does in the law of marine insurance. What marine insurers understand by "perils of the sea" therefore may be used when establishing whether a certain event is in fact such a peril.

— The general practice seems to be that a collision would fall within the ambit of "perils of the sea".

Arrest or restraint of princes

Frequently inserted in the contract of carriage is a clause exempting the carrier **7–063** from liability where damage or loss to the goods has been caused by "arrest or restraint of princes". This clause has, in general, been construed in the broadest sense, whether rightly or wrongly. It has been applied to allow the carrier to cover himself from liability for damage or loss caused by governmental seizure of the goods, embargoes, arrests, blockades, stoppages, searches of vessels, quarantines, etc.

There are a few limitations though. In the old case of *Atkinson v Ritchie* (1809) 10 East. 530, the restraint of princes must be an existing fact and not a mere apprehension. The carrier, in order to succeed in his defence, must show that the threat of interference from a foreign power is not only a matter of supposition but is imminent. The imminence of threat or interference does not however expect proof of immediate threat, merely a real threat.

Rickards v Forrestal [1942] A.C. 50 **7–064**
Facts:
The German carrier had to discharge the claimant's cargo at a neutral port following the outbreak of war, in compliance with orders from the German authorities. The claimant was therefore prevented from taking possession of his cargo.
Held:
It was argued by the claimant that the ship was at a neutral port which was not subject to direct control of the German government and as such the carrier should not be entitled to

plead "restraint of princes" as an exception. Lord Wright disagreed stating that it was immaterial where the vessel was or indeed, that there was no immediate threat of physical force or interference. His Lordship stated:

> "It is enough, I think, that there is an order of the state addressed to a subject of that state, acting with compelling force on him, decisively exacting his obedience and requiring him to do the act which effectively restrains the goods".

7–065   *Watts, Watts & Co Ltd v Mitsui & Co Ltd* [1917] A.C. 227
Facts:
A vessel had been chartered to proceed to Marioupol, a port in the Sea of Azov, *not* before September 1, 1914 to load a cargo of ammonia sulphate for carriage to Japan. The ship owner then invoked the cancellation clause in the charterparty and withdrew the vessel from the charter for fear that the Turkish government would close the Dardanelles (entry to the Black Sea) following the outbreak of the First World War. The cancellation clause permitted the withdrawal of the vessel where the vessel was not ready to load by September 20. The closure of the Dardanelles meant that ship would be trapped in the Black Sea. The evidence showed that even if the ship had arrived by the cancelling date, it would not have been possible to load and leave the Black Sea before the Dardanelles were closed.
Held:
While the ship owner's apprehension was reasonable, the cancellation could not be said to be justified by "restraint of princes" because, according to Lord Dunedin:

> " . . . while there was natural and great apprehension . . . , and while the decision of the British Government immediately after to exclude Black Sea voyages from the benefits of the Government insurance scheme might well deter British subjects from sending their ships to the Black Sea, yet it is clearly proved by the production of lists of ships which after that date and up to September 26 passed inwards and outwards through the Dardanelles that there was no such restraint as would have actually prevented the appellants presenting a ship at Marioupol before or by the appointed date of September 20".

The degree of the risk, it is seen, must not only be reasonable but substantially imminent to attract the application of the term "restraint of princes". In Lord Loreburn's speech, we see the following description:

> " . . . if the situation had been so menacing that a man of sound judgment would think it foolhardiness to proceed with the voyage, I should have regarded that as in fact a restraint of princes. It is true that mere apprehension will not suffice, but on the other hand it has never been held that a ship must continue her voyage till physical force is actually exercised".

7–066   A related problem is whether the carrier should be estopped from pleading the exemption clause where it is clear at the time of contracting that there is a substantial risk of the "restraint or arrest of princes". Where it is clear right at the outset that the vessel would be restrained or arrested by a foreign power, Rowlatt J. was of the opinion in *Ciampa v British India Steam Navigation Co Ltd* [1915] 2 K.B. 774 that the carrier could not plead "restraint of princes" as exempting them from liability. In that case it was pellucid that the carrier's ship had sailed from a plague ridden area and would therefore be imminently subject to the process of compulsory *dératisation* (sulphur fumigation of the ship) upon its arrival at Marseilles. Thus any damage caused by the fumigation could not be excused by the restraint of princes clause.

Strikes or lockouts

Another common exemption stipulated in a typical contract of carriage is that of **7–067**
liability for damage or loss caused as a result of strikes and/or lockouts. The term
"strikes" has been the subject of gradual evolution in the construction of
contractual clauses. "Strikes" was initially defined in *King v Parker* (1876) 34
L.T. 887 as "a concerted effort by workmen either to obtain an increase in wages
or to resist an attempt by employers to reduce their wages" or in the words of
Sankey J. in *Williams Brothers (Hull) Ltd v Naamlooze Vennootschap etc.* (1915)
21 Com. Cas. 253 as "a general concerted refusal by workmen to work in
consequence of an alleged grievance". This requirement of a grievance against
the strikers' employers was dropped in *The Laga* [1966] 1 Lloyd's Rep. 582, a
case which, although not dealing with a contractual exemption for strike action,
nevertheless gave a workable definition for the term.

The Laga [1966] 1 Lloyd's Rep. 582   **7–068**
Facts:
Workmen at the port of Nantes refused to unload vessels intending to discharge coal there.
The refusal to work was not because of any industrial dispute the workmen had with their
employers but was a show of support for French miners who were then on strike. One of
the issues for the court in establishing laytime was whether there had indeed been a
strike.
Held:
McNair J. extended the strike definition to sympathetic strikes. He said:

> " ... since ... one has had the great development of sympathetic strikes, when one has
> had, at any rate in this country, and, indeed, elsewhere, the general strike in which many
> of those out on strike had no grievance at all against an employer. And, in my judgment,
> it would be extremely difficult to say in a charter-party such as this that a sympathetic
> strike or a general strike which had the effect of causing the loss of time was not a strike
> within the meaning of this charter-party".

The general definition developed in *The Laga* was taken even further in *The New
Horizon* [1975] 2 Lloyd's Rep. 314 by Lord Denning M.R. who held that the
withdrawal of good faith by workers, though not in breach of their contracts of
employment was tantamount to a strike. The dock workers at St Nazaire in that
case had refused shift work although in the past they had done so even though it
was not contractually required. This meant that work was done only during the
day and not continuously for 24 hours as anticipated by their employers. Two
issues arise:

1. whether it is material that the action taken was not in breach of contract;

2. whether the fact that the stoppage only took place for eight hours during the
   night meant that it was not strike action.

To this Lord Denning M.R. said: **7–069**

> "They did it so as to get an improvement in their terms and conditions of work.
> They were not in breach of contract. But it is none the less a strike. Many a

strike takes place after lawful notice; but it is still a strike. It was discontinuous. At work during the day-time, off work at night. But a strike need not be continuous. It can be discontinuous and the periods may be added up . . . So it seems to me that it was a 'strike' and the charterers were entitled to an extension of laytime".

Even where "strike" has been established it must be shown to have brought about the loss or damage in question. This is of course a matter of causation; a none too simple matter. In *Leonis v Rank (No.2)* (1908) 13 Com. Cas. 295, it was held that the exception clause covers not only direct damage or loss caused by the strike but also loss/damage brought about by the after effects of the strike or lockout.

Negligence and navigational errors

7–070   It is common for carriers to insert a clause in the contract of carriage exempting themselves from liability for damage or loss caused as a result of "errors in navigation". Others may insist on an exemption clause providing that the carriers shall not be liable for loss or damage caused by "want of due diligence" or "negligence". The courts are understandably careful not to allow the exemption clauses as worded to go beyond the natural boundaries of the clause. As a matter of construction of the relevant clause, the court will adopt a *contra proferentem* approach where the wording of the clause is ambiguous. Bowen L.J.'s approach in *Burton & Co v English* (1883) 12 Q.B.D. 218 is perhaps one of the most instructive:

> "There is . . . another rule of construction which one would bring to bear upon this charterparty, and that is, that one must see if this stipulation which we have got to construe is introduced by way of exception or in favour of one of the parties to the contract, and if so, we must take care not to give it an extension beyond what is fairly necessary, because those who wish to introduce words in a contract in order to shield themselves ought to do so in clear words".

We have been referred to *Photo Productions v Securicor* earlier which allows the inclusion of exclusion clauses that might go to the root the contract. Given the current legal position of exemption clauses in commercial contracts, it is not surprising to expect the courts to adopt a strict approach to the construction and application of an exclusion of liability clause, especially one worded in generality.

The *Emmanuel C* [1983] 1 Lloyd's Rep. 310 is a good example of how the court addressed the contractual exception of "errors of navigation". The Emmanuel C had been chartered under a time charter. The charterparty provided that the carrier shall not be liable for "errors of navigation". The ship ran aground by reason of negligent navigation. The shipowners tried to rely on the exemption clause. It is worth setting out the shipowners' reasons as to why the clause was applicable:

1. The expression "errors of navigation" is plainly wide enough to include negligent errors. It is only a legal refinement to make the distinction between negligent and non-negligent errors;

2. It was the normal working assumption in shipping circles that liability for negligent navigation would be excepted;

3. Unless "errors of navigation" were construed to include negligent errors the reference lacked substance because it was very hard to conceive of an error of navigation which was not negligent and which would not be covered by "perils of the sea".

Bingham J. was however unconvinced. He held that the reference to "errors of **7–071** navigation" was necessarily neutral; it could refer to either negligent or non-negligent errors and quoted from the findings of the arbitrator:

"In the shipping commercial world it is not unusual to see exemption clauses which clearly expressly exclude liability for negligence so that, in general, there is no, and never has been any, reluctance to use appropriate language to make it abundantly clear that negligence is being excepted".

In the light of the neutrality of the clause, it must be construed against the party attempting to rely on it.

Fire

It is also a common occurrence that carriers protect themselves against loss or **7–072** damage caused to goods as a result of fire. While they may generally rely on statutory exceptions like the recent Merchant Shipping Act 1995, these are usually subject to important qualifications. These qualifications are as set out in s.186:

- it only applies to an owner of a UK ship;

- the fire must be on board the vessel;

- loss or damage resulting from personal acts or omissions of the shipowner is not covered.

It might thus be more advantageous to rely on a more protective device like a wide exclusion clause.

But what does "loss or damage by fire" mean? Kelly C.B. in the old insurance case of *Stanley v Western Insurance Co* (1868) L.R. 3 Ex. 71 defined it in these terms:

" . . . any loss resulting from an apparently necessary and bona fide effort to put out a fire, whether it be by spoiling the goods by water, or throwing the articles of furniture out of the window, or even the destroying of a neighbouring house by an explosion for the purpose of checking the progress of the flames, in a word, every loss that clearly and proximately results, whether directly or indirectly, from the fire, is within the policy".

It would seem therefore to include smoke damage (*The Diamond* [1906] P. 282).

Shipper's Duty Not to Ship Dangerous Goods

Concept of dangerous goods

7–073   The shipper is bound at common law not to ship dangerous goods without first seeking the assent of the shipowner. What, however, is classed as "dangerous goods"? Where the goods are intrinsically dangerous, such as explosives, radioactive agents or easily combustible materials, it is not difficult to attribute the label "dangerous" to such goods. Where the goods are in themselves not intrinsically dangerous but could cause hazard to ship, crew or cargo if used or dealt with wrongly, should they be treated as "dangerous goods"?

Example: Carrier agrees to carry a cargo of wine. Wine is not generally dangerous but if it were to leak, it could quite easily contaminate other goods or cause damage to the ship's equipment. Does this render the cargo of wine dangerous? If it does, the carrier could escape liability if the shipper had not first informed him of the "dangerous goods".

The rationale behind the duty not to ship dangerous goods is that the contract does not anticipate the undertaking of any out of ordinary risks by the carrier. It is not within the contemplation of the parties that the carrier should carry dangerous goods without first having been offered the opportunity to refuse to accommodate the risk. Furthermore it cannot be in the interest of the shipper to unnecessarily put the adventure in jeopardy. It could surely not be right to simply approach the concept of dangerous goods from a linguistic standpoint. The rationale of the duty demands that the law take a teleological assessment of the concept. As Mustill J. said in the *Athanasia Comninos* [1990] 1 Lloyd's Rep. 277:

> "[I]t is essential . . . to remember that we are here concerned, not with the labelling in the abstract of goods as 'dangerous' or 'safe' but with the distribution of risk for the consequences of a dangerous situation arising during the voyage".

7–074   It becomes, therefore, important to examine not only whether the carrier was aware of the natural and intrinsic dangerous qualities of the goods being shipped, but also how the goods should be kept and cared. Where special procedures are required to ensure that the goods do not become dangerous, the shipper has a duty to inform the carrier. Failure to do so would be in breach of the common law duty not to ship dangerous goods.

Hence, in *Mitchell, Cotts & Co v Steel Brothers & Co Ltd* [1916] 2 K.B. 611, this broad concept was applied to goods which in themselves were not dangerous but because they were not accompanied with the requisite documentation caused the ship to be detained. In that case, the charterparty provided for the carriage of rice from Burma to Alexandria. En route, the charterers instructed the vessel to discharge the cargo at Piraeus instead. Consent from the British authorities was required for the discharge at Piraeus as the charterers knew. The shipowners were not aware of the required consent and as a result the ship was detained at Port Said for 22 days. In giving judgment for the shipowners, Atkin J. commented that the loading of unlawful cargo which may result in the detention or seizure of the ship was analogous to the shipment of dangerous cargo which might cause destruction of the ship.

This generous approach was recently confirmed by the House of Lords in *Effort Shipping Co Ltd v Linden Management SA (The Giannis NK) The Times*, January 29, 1998, albeit a case involving the Hague Rules (art.IV Rule 6), where Lord Lloyd said:

" ... it was settled law that the word 'dangerous' ... must be given a broad meaning. Dangerous goods were not confined to goods of an inflammable or explosive nature or their like. Goods could be dangerous ... if they were dangerous to other goods, even though they were not dangerous to the vessel itself. 'Dangerous' was not to be confined to goods which were liable to cause direct physical damage to other goods".

That case concerned the construction of "dangerous goods" in the Hague Rules where art.IV Rule 6 covers "goods of an inflammable, explosive or dangerous nature". Given these apparent restrictions, it must surely be right to say that the broad meaning approach adopted by the House of Lords applies with equal, if not greater, force to the common law concept of "dangerous goods".

Nature of the duty

1. Where the risk is clearly obvious to any reasonable shipowner, it appears that   **7–075**
   the shipper need not make the requisite disclosure. The shipowner's act of accepting the goods must be presumed to be an acceptance of the risk. In *General Feeds Inc v Burnham Shipping Corp (The Amphion)* [1991] 2 Lloyd's Rep. 101, Evans J. after careful deliberation stated:

   "If there is a known risk of danger to the ship, which cannot be altogether avoided by strict compliance with the rules of safe carriage, then by agreeing to carry the goods of that description the shipowner may be held to have accepted that risk for himself".

2. Where neither party is aware (or ought to be aware) of the dangerous propensity of the goods, the majority in *Brass v Maitland* (1856) 26 L.J.Q.B. 49 decided that liability on the shipper is strict and could not be excused or justified on grounds of ignorance.

Brass v Maitland (1856) 26 L.J.Q.B. 49   **7–076**
Facts:
Maitland had shipped a cargo of bleaching powder on board the Regina. Bleaching powder contained chloride of lime which was corrosive. The powder corroded the casks in which it was held and caused damage to other goods.
Held:
Where neither party is aware or ought to be aware of the dangerous nature of the cargo, Lord Campbell C.J. felt that as a matter of the allocation of risk the shipper must be held liable. The goods before shipment were in the control of the shippers who must therefore be deemed to ensure that they are not dangerous for the contractual voyage they will be embarking on. His Lordship considered that it must be in the interest of business transactions that the duty incumbent on the shipper be regarded as strict:

"If, under these circumstances, there were not a duty incumbent on the shipper to give notice of the dangerous nature of the goods to be shipped, commerce could not be carried on. It would be strange to suppose that the master or mate, having no reason to suspect that goods offered to him for a general ship may not safely be stowed away in the hold, must ask every shipper the contents of every package. If he is not to do so, and there is no duty on the part of the shipper of a dangerous package to give notice of its contents or quality, the consequence is that, without any remedy against the shipper, although no blame is imputable to the shipowners or those employed by them, this package may cause the destruction of the ship and all her cargo and the lives of all who sail in her".

It should however be noted that on this statement of law Compton J. dissented. The judge was concerned that there was no authority in law permitting liability for dangerous cargo to be imputed on a shipper who had not been negligent or at fault. He felt that the duty should only apply where:

"[T]he shipper has knowledge, or means of knowledge, of the dangerous nature of the goods when shipped or where he has been guilty of some negligence as shipper, as by shipping without communicating danger, which he had the means of knowing, and ought to have communicated".

The position at law as to the nature of the duty on the shipper who is unaware of the danger and has not been negligent remains not entirely pellucid. Be that as it may, in *The Athanasia Comninos* [1990] 1 Lloyd's Rep. 277, a case decided in 1979 but reported only in 1990, Mustill J. held that the absolute nature of the duty should be preferred. As far as the Hague and Hague-Visby Rules are concerned it is now settled law following *Effort Shipping Co Ltd v Linden Management SA (The Giannis NK)* [1998] A.C. 605 that liability is strict and the shipper is not entitled to plead ignorance or due diligence (paras 8–031—8–034).

Shipper's or Charterer's Duty to Pay Freight

When freight is payable

7–077   The general rule is that freight is normally payable on delivery of the goods. Hence, where the goods have not been delivered for whatever reason, the duty to pay does not arise. This is so even though the failure of delivery is due to an excepted peril provided for in the contract of carriage. We observe the dictum of Lord Ellenborough in *Hunter v Prinsep* (1808) 10 East. 378:

"The ship owners undertake that they will carry the goods to the place of destination unless prevented by the dangers of the seas, or other unavoidable casualties: and the freighter undertakes that if the goods be delivered at the place of their destination he will pay the stipulated freight; but it was only in that event, *viz.* of their delivery at the place of destination, that he, the freighter, engages to pay anything. If the ship is disabled from completing her voyage, the ship owner may still entitle himself to the whole freight, by forwarding the goods by some other means to the place of destination".

The converse however is equally true. Where the goods are delivered at the place of destination, the fact that they are delivered damaged freight is payable in full. Any claim for the damage caused must be instituted as a separate action.

Dakin v Oxley (1864) 15 C.B.N.S. 646   **7-078**

Facts:

The coal carried under the charterparty was delivered at Nassau damaged due to the fault of the master and crew, and their unskilful and negligent navigation of the vessel. The coal owners then decided to abandon the coal to the shipowner and refused to pay the freight.

Held:

Willes C.J. stated;

> " . . . the true test of the right to freight is the question whether the service in respect of which the freight was contracted to be paid has been substantially performed . . . according to the law of England, as a rule, freight is earned by the carriage and arrival of the goods ready to be delivered to the merchant, though they be in a damaged state when they arrive".

The rationale for the rule seems to be the assumption that it is prudent and reasonable mercantile practice to rely on a system of insurance to ensure that damaged goods are properly provided for. The question of fortuitous damage, as the court put it, must be settled with the underwriters and where there is allegation that the shipowners are themselves culpable, then a separate action will have to be brought against them. Willes C.J. was also of the opinion that English law does not permit the deduction of a sum of money from the freight once the goods have been delivered (*Davidson v Gwynne* 12 East. 381; *Stinson v Hall* 1 Hurlst & N. 831).

That application of the rule was confirmed in *Aries Taker Corp v Total*   **7-079**
Transport Ltd (The Aries) [1977] 1 Lloyd's Rep. 334 where Lord Wilberforce refused to allow a deduction to be set-off against the freight claimed for short delivery. In His Lordship's opinion, whatever the rightness or wrongness of the rule against a deduction of the freight when the goods are tendered, the parties have contracted on this basis and must therefore be bound accordingly. Lord Salmon had this to add:

> "A rule of law, particularly a rule of commercial law which has stood so long and upon the faith of which many thousands of contracts of carriage have been made and are daily being made containing a provision that the contract shall be governed by the law of England, cannot now be successfully challenged in our Courts. The fact that . . . neither the reason nor the justification for this rule of English law has ever been defined [is beside the point]".

The rule also militates against an equitable set-off. In *The Aries* the argument that a deduction for short delivery is based on an equitable set-off was soundly rejected as having no basis in law (see also *The Dominique* [1989] 1 Lloyd's Rep. 431).

In the case of a charterparty, when the payment of freight becomes outstanding either wholly or partly, the shipowner has a right to "intercept" freight. In Greer J.'s judgment in *Molthese Rederi v Ellerman*, we find the following description of "interception of freight":

> "That [the shipowner] can intervene successfully before receipt of the freight by the agent seems to me to be the necessary consequence of holding . . . that the bill of lading contract is a contract between the shipowner and the shipper, and not a contract between the charterers and the shipper. If this be so, the legal

right to the freight is in the owner and not in the charterer, and the former can intervene at any time before the agent has received the freight, and say to him, 'I am no longer content that the charterer should collect the freight. If you collect it at all, you must collect it for me'".

7–080   Indeed, this follows from the rule that unless the contract provides otherwise, payment of freight by the shipper or cargo interest to the shipowner does not discharge the shipper's liability to pay freight (*Tradigrain SA v King Diamond Marine Ltd (The Spiros C)* [2000] 2 All E.R. (Comm) 542; *Dry Bulk Handy Holding Inc v Fayette International* [2012] EWHC 2107 (Comm)).

Where the goods delivered are no longer recognisable as those supplied under the contract, then the shipowners may be denied freight. In *Asfar v Blundell* [1896] 1 Q.B. 123, *The Govino* was submerged in water for two days as a result of a collision. Her cargo of dates was damaged and could not be sold for human consumption. They were subsequently sold for distillation into alcohol. The rule is that where there has been a total loss of the goods then there arises no entitlement to freight—there has been a total failure of consideration. Lopes L.J. said:

"[the dates] were a mixture of date pulp and sewage and in a state of fermentation and putrefaction; they had clearly lost any merchantable character as dates. In my judgment, it is idle to suggest that there was not a total loss of the dates, and that the plaintiffs were not entitled to recover as for a total loss of their freight . . . ".

7–081   *Montedison SpA v Icroma SpA (The Caspian Sea)* [1980] 1 Lloyd's Rep. 91
Facts:
The Caspian Sea was chartered to carry a cargo of "Bachaquero Crude" and/or dirty petroleum from Punta Cardon to Genoa. "Bachaquero" crude oil was shipped but when it was discharged, the charterers claimed that it had been contaminated with residues in the tanks. The charterers took delivery of the oil but refused to pay freight on the basis that the oil delivered was not described in the contract.

The issues for the court were whether the oil met the contractual description and whether a right to freight arose under these circumstances. The charterers argued that there was no immediate right to freight because what was delivered was not merchantable as "Bachaquero Crude" or alternatively was not commercially identical with the cargo loaded.
Held:
Donaldson J. was of the opinion that the fact that the oil delivered was not commercially identical with the cargo loaded did not deprive the shipowners of their right to freight. The owners will be entitled to freight as long as what they finally delivered could be in commercial terms resembled the goods as originally described. To illustrate, the judge said:

"If one takes a carboy of sulphuric acid and adds a limited quantity of water—an experiment which should be conducted with extreme care and with knowledge of the likely consequences—the resulting liquid will still be sulphuric acid, albeit, dilute sulphuric acid. But if one adds enough water, the point will be reached at which the liquid is more properly described as water contaminated with acid than as dilute acid. This is the dividing line".

It should be noted that if the amount of freight has not been specified in the contract, the person liable to pay freight will be required under an implied term to pay a reasonable amount. (*BP Oil v Target Shipping* [2012] EWHC 1590 (Comm)). What is reasonable depends on the true nature of the carriage obligation, the shipowner's actual costs and legitimate expectations of profit and market conditions.

Advance freight

It is common for shipowners and shippers of goods to specify expressly in the contract (e.g. the voyage charter) when freight is to be paid. Any such stipulation may indicate that freight is to be paid in advance. This will always be a matter of construction for the courts. The courts have always ensured that unless the terms of the payment of freight clause is clear, they would displace the general rule at common law that freight is to be paid when the goods are delivered to the port of destination. We sample a few standard clauses where advance freight is provided for: **7–082**

1. "Freight is payable on final sailing";

2. "Freight payable on the signing of bills of lading";

3. "Freight is payable on the sailing of ship";

4. "Freight payable within seven days of the master signing the bills of lading"; or

5. "Freight payable in advance subject to insurance".

Where freight is agreed to be settled in advance, it will fall due even though the goods do not reach their destination. The contract must make it express that freight is to be pre-paid, failure to make the stipulation clear would revive the general common law rule that freight is to be paid upon delivery of the goods at the port of destination. Where the contract specifies for example that "freight deemed to have been earned on shipment whether ship lost or not", it is clear that the parties intend to contract on advance freight. The provision will then specify the event at which freight becomes payable; for example, it might stipulate that freight is payable when the bills of lading are signed, or when the ship sails, etc (see above). Once freight is paid, the shipowners' right to retain it is not subject to whether the goods arrive or not (*Oriental Steamship Co Ltd v Taylor* [1893] 2 Q.B. 518).

The shipowner is not entitled to retain pre-paid freight:

1. if the event at which payment of freight is to be made did not take place. For example, if the contract stipulates that freight becomes payable when the ship leaves, and the ship has not actually done so then no freight is payable.

Roelandts v Harrison (1854) 156 E.R. 189   **7–083**
Facts:
The contract stipulated that freight was payable on "final sailing" of the ship. While the ship was being towed through a canal on its way from the docks to sea, it ran aground. The shipowner claimed freight.
Held:
The court held that "final sailing" had indeed taken place, the ship was clearly leaving port to proceed on her voyage. Freight was therefore payable.

The shipper must not do anything to hinder the event from taking place. Where bills of lading are to be tendered for signature and payment of freight is dependent on the signing, cargo owners who do not present the bills of lading cannot then avoid liability for freight (*Oriental Steamship Co Ltd v Taylor*);

2. where the goods have been lost before the event to pay advance freight occurs. In *Compania Naviera General SA v Kerametal Ltd (The Lorna I)* [1983] 1 Lloyd's Rep. 373, payment was to be made "within five days of the master signing bills of lading, . . . [of] freight non-returnable cargo and/or ship lost or not lost". The Lorna I was lost in bad sailing conditions in the Black Sea soon after setting sail but before the expiry of the five days. On whether the charterers were liable for freight, the Court of Appeal held that no freight had been earned before the expiry of the five days as the goods had been lost. There was a total failure of consideration, an event not provided for by the contract. The court held:

> "[if the advance freight] is payable, say, five days after the master signed the bill, and the cargo is lost by a frustrating event within the five days and the bill does not contain an 'earned upon shipment' or similar clause, the carrier cannot demand payment of the . . . [unpaid freight]".

In *Bank of Boston Connecticut v European Grain and Shipping Ltd (The Dominique)* [1989] 2 W.L.R. 442, the House of Lords held that where the contract was terminated by the parties after the event for which freight is payable has taken place, the fact of the termination does not defeat the accrued right to freight.

7–084   *Bank of Boston Connecticut v European Grain and Shipping Ltd (The Dominique)*
[1989] 2 W.L.R. 442
Facts:
The shipowners' vessel was arrested by creditors. It was clear that the shipowners could not secure the release of the vessel on time to perform the contract. The charterers thus accepted that as a repudiation of the charterparty. The payment of freight clauses were "confusingly drawn". Clause 16 of the standard Gencon form read:

> "Freight shall be prepaid within five days of signing and surrender of final bills of lading, full freight deemed to be earned on signing bills of lading, discountless and non-returnable, vessel and/or cargo lost or not lost and to be paid to . . . ".

Sequence of events:
• July 14, 1982—bills of lading properly signed;

• July 19, 1982—ship arrested by creditors in Colombo;

• July 22, 1982—charterparty terminated by charterers' acceptance of shipowners' breach;

• July 26, 1982—all bills of lading delivered to the shippers of goods (i.e. surrender of final bills of lading) with whom the charterers had contracted.

The charterers' argument:
The owner's right to freight accrued only after July 22, i.e. only the first limb of cl.16 prevails. Freight was not payable until five days after all signed bills had been delivered to shippers, that is to say, five days after July 26.

The owners' argument:
Consistent with the two limbs to cl.16, the right to freight accrued on completion of the signing of the bills of lading, but payment was postponed until five days after the bills of lading, having been signed, were delivered to the shippers.
Held:
The court held that the owners' right to freight had accrued, i.e. earned when the bills were signed. The fact that payment was not due until five days after the surrender of the bills to shippers was only a contractual postponement of the debt. Time for payment and time when freight is earned are two different questions and must be treated separately. Advance freight becomes payable, namely the debt to pay, arises as soon as the event for which freight has been earned takes place; the time for payment is simply a reference to the manner of paying the debt.

The effects of termination of a contract are, as stated in *McDonald v Dennys* **7–085**
Lascelles Ltd (1933) 48 C.L.R. 457:

"When a party to a simple contract, upon a breach by the other party of a condition of the contract, elects to treat the contract as no longer binding upon him, the contract is not rescinded as from the beginning. Both parties are discharged from further performance of the contract, but rights are not divested or discharged which have already been unconditionally acquired. Rights and obligations which arise from the partial execution of the contract and causes of action which have accrued from its breach alike continue unaffected".

It may appear unjust to the cargo owner to have to pay freight when the goods have not been carried to their destination and all that remains is a cause of action against, in this case, a destitute shipowner. It must be borne in mind though that in such transactions, there should be an insurance arrangement in place to ensure that such risks are distributed in a commercially sound manner. Once the freight risk is transferred to the cargo owner, shipper or charterer, as the case may be, should have the insurable interest, when freight is accrued, to take out a suitable insurance policy.

The fact of advance or pre-paid freight is usually evidenced by a clause in the bill of lading called the freight prepaid clause. In *Cho Yang Shipping v Coral (UK)* [1997] 2 Lloyd's Rep. 641 we are reminded that the

"basic commercial function of a 'freight prepaid' clause is to assure the notify party to other consignee that as between him and the shipowner no liability for freight can be asserted".

In general "freight prepaid" does not affect the liability of the shipper if freight had not in fact been paid (*The Constanza M* [1980] 1 Lloyd's Rep. 505) although where the terms are clearly to the contrary then they must be given effect to by the courts (*Cho Yang Shipping v Coral (UK)*). A freight pre-paid indorsement in the bill of lading can also have the effect of barring the carrier from exercising his lien over the goods.[18]

---

[18] See also *Dry Bulk Handy Holding Inc v Fayette International* [2012] EWHC 2107 (Comm).

Other parties potentially liable for freight

7–086 Where the goods have been shipped under a bill of lading, it is usually the duty of the shipper to make payment for freight unless it has been made clear to the carrier at the time of shipment that the shipper of goods is simply acting as an agent for another person. This duty is nevertheless not set in stone; the bill of lading may state expressly that the shipper is to be exempt from payment.

Besides the shipper of goods, freight may be claimed against:

1. consignee or indorsee of a bill of lading;

2. a seller who stops goods in transit; or

3. the charterer.

In the case of a charterparty, it is usually the charterer who is responsible for collecting freight from the shipper rather than the shipowner himself. This does not mean that the shipowner is not entitled to pursue the shipper for freight but merely that the shipper's first priority is to the charterer even though the contract he has with the charterer is one evidenced by the bill of lading issued by the shipowners. It is normally more expedient for the shipowners to authorise the charterer to collect freight as his agent.[19] It is also possible for the charterer to collect freight in his own right (as principal), especially in the context of a time charter.

7–087 *Tradigrain SA v King Diamond Marine Ltd (The Spiros C)* [2000] 2 Lloyd's Rep. 319
Facts:
The vessel had been chartered under a time charter. The charterers then sold shipping space to various shippers. The charterers failed to make payment of hire. Under the arrangement between the shipper and the charterers, certain deductions could be made from the payment of freight The shipowners attempted to claim these deductions for himself from the shippers. The issues for the court were:

1. whether the owners were entitled to claim payment of freight from the shippers under the bill of lading contract; and

2. whether the shipowners were precluded from intercepting freight which had not been paid by the shipper but had, as between the shipper and the charterers, been treated as discharged by set off on account of other payments made by the shipper for the benefit of the charterers although the contract between the shipper and the charterers made no provision for such payments to be deducted from the freight. The bill of lading contract provided that payment of freight was "payable as per" charterparty.

The Commercial Court gave judgment for the shipowners allowing them to intercept the payment of freight. The judge, Colman J., referred to *Wehner v Dene Steam Shipping Co* [1905] 2 K.B. 92 which had stated that the owners had an entitlement to intercept the bill of lading freight provided that the obligation to pay the freight remained wholly or partly outstanding. In order to ascertain whether the obligation had been discharged, it was important to define the obligation by looking to the terms of the bill of lading. In this case, the bill of lading contract provided that freight was payable "as per charterparty". That provision could not be overridden by a stipulation in the contract between the shipper and charterers that payment of freight was to be paid to a specified account of a person other

---

[19] See *Molthes Rederi Aktieselskabet v Ellerman's Wilson Line Ltd* [1927] 1 K.B. 710.

than the owners or that payment could be set off against any benefits already received by the charterers from the shipper. All these collateral arrangements could not affect the owners' rights against the shipper, for after all, the contract was that as evidenced by the bill of lading issued by the shipowners and those terms could not be varied without the consent of the shipowners.

Held:

The Court of Appeal allowed the appeal from Colman J.'s decision. The court noted that there was no authority on the position adopted by Colman J. and further held that the lower court's judgment could very well result in the shipper having to pay the advance against freight once more. Where freight was payable as per charterparty the shipowner must be said to have intended to delegate the whole manner or mode of freight collection to the time charterer. If the time charterer was willing to accept freight not only as a direct payment to a nominated account but also in the form of cash disbursements to his shipping agents or to the master, there was no reason why the shipowner should consider such arrangements, even if different from that contemplated in his original time charterparty, were outside the scope of his delegated authority to his time charterer. The deductions agreed between the charterers and the shipper in this case were therefore binding on the owners. The owners claim for freight in the sum of the deductions failed.

This case demonstrates that the shipowner's entitlement could be seriously affected by any arrangements as to freight collection made between the charterer and the shipper, where it is within the charterer's implied or express authority under the original charter to make those arrangements. Although the Court of Appeal was reluctant to find any legal principle in the dispute and was prepared merely to confine themselves to the construction of the various agreements, it did suggest that in similar arrangements where the shipper has been permitted by the charterer to make variation to the payment of freight, it would be unjust to prevent him from relying on that promise against the shipowner even though the shipowner was not privy to that promise. The court was of the opinion that it was clear that under a time charter, generally, the shipowner is prepared or presumed to be prepared to leave all matters of freight collection to the charterer; as such, the risk of non payment of hire must surely rest on the shipowner and no one else. That is the shipowner's voluntary assumption of risk.   **7–088**

Consignee or indorsee of a bill of lading

Under the repealed Bills of Lading Act 1855, the carrier could recover freight from any consignee or indorsee of a bill of lading to whom the property in the goods had passed as the result of the indorsement. Where property had not passed as a result of the indorsement, the doctrine of privity militates against the carrier and he cannot demand payment of the freight from the consignee or indorsee. As far as the original party to the contract is concerned, it has now been confirmed by the House of Lords in *Effort Shipping Co Ltd v Linden Management SA (The Giannis NK) The Times*, January 29, 1998 that the transfer of the bill of lading to the indorsee or consignee neither exonerates nor excuses the original shipper. Lord Lloyd considered that s.1 of the 1855 Act simply made the subsequent holder of the bill of lading liable in *addition* to and not in *substitution* of the original party's liability. Although the case concerned liability for the carriage of dangerous goods, it would seem to apply mutatis mutandis to other contractual obligations undertaken by the original party to the contract.   **7–089**

The enactment of the Carriage of Goods by Sea Act 1992 (s.3(1)) means that a person who becomes the lawful holder of a bill of lading and hence becomes vested with the rights of the contract of carriage, shall be subject to the liabilities under the original contract (including the duty to pay freight) if:

(a) he takes or demands delivery from the carrier of any of the goods to which the document relates;

(b) he makes a claim under the contract of carriage against the carrier in respect of any of those goods; or

(c) he is a person who, at a time before those rights were vested in him, took or demanded delivery from the carrier of any of those goods.

It seems to follow that until the indorsee or consignee attempts to exercise his rights under the contract of carriage, no demand for freight may be made against him.[20] It should be noted that the primary duty of the original shipper to pay freight remains even though he might have transferred the bill of lading to the consignee or indorsee. Section 3(3) of the Carriage of Goods by Sea Act 1992 does not allow the shipper to escape liability to pay as "original party to the contract" by virtue of the indorsee or consignee becoming liable for freight.

Seller who stops goods in transit

7–090   The seller who exercises his right under s.39, Sale of Goods Act 1979 to stop goods in transit either by taking actual possession of the goods or by giving notice to the carrier, must bear the original freight and expenses of the re-delivery. This is the case even though he may not be liable as a shipper to pay freight.

Charterer

7–091   The charterer is the primary party responsible for the freight. Even where the charterer has subchartered or issued bills of lading to third parties requiring these third parties to pay the freight, the shipowner is not required to go beyond the charterer for full payment of the freight. Many voyage charters employ a clause which provides expressly that

> "the charterer's liability to cease under the charterparty on the cargo being loaded, the master and owners having a lien on cargo for freight and demurrage".

The first part of this clause is generally known as a cesser clause and is intended to relieve the charterer from amongst others, the duty to pay freight once the cargo is loaded. It is usually reciprocated by the second limb of the clause which allows the shipowner to exercise a lien on the goods as security. That limb is frequently referred to as a lien clause. The quid pro quo for the cesser clause is the lien clause. In *Fidelitas Shipping Co Ltd v V/O Exportchleb* [1963] 2 Lloyd's

---

[20] In *Evergreen Marine Corp v Aldgate Warehouse (Wholesale) Ltd* [2003] EWHC 667, the carriers attempted to show that the intended consignees had entered into special contracts to underwrite payment of freight because it was obvious that the intended consignees who had not even received the bill of lading were not going to accept the bill. The court however saw no evidence of such special undertakings.

Rep. 113, it was remarked that the two would usually go hand in hand. The lien conferred must be effective. For example, in *The Sinoe* [1971] 1 Lloyd's Rep. 514, the lien could not have been used at the port of discharge because the goods were consigned to the government of the place of destination and they would not have permitted the carrier to withhold the goods.

Types of freight

Lump sum freight

If the contract provides for lump sum freight, i.e. the freight is expressed as a **7–092** single sum which is not calculated on the basis of the quantity of cargo carried, then it is not necessary that the full cargo be delivered before the shipowner could call for payment of full freight. Freight falls due as soon as part of the cargo has been delivered. The ship itself need not make it to the place of destination; as long as the shipowner could deliver a part of the cargo to the cargo owner or shipper, freight is payable. The undertaking here is that the contract of carriage (usually a charterparty) will be performed whether or not the shipper uses full capacity of the ship. It is used when the nature of the goods or their quantity is not yet known. It is also possible for such contracts to specify that freight shall be payable upon the "right and true delivery of the cargo" as we see in the case below.

William Thomas & Sons v Harrowing Steamship Co [1915] A.C. 58   **7–093**
Facts:
The steamer carrying the cargo was chartered under charterparty which provided for the payment of a lump sum of 1,600 as freight

> "in full of all port charges and pilotages, in consideration of which owners place at charterers disposal the full reach of steamer, on and under decks, including spare bunkers, if any".

Another clause stated that "freight is to be paid in cash without discount (less freight advance, if any) on unloading and right delivery of the cargo". As the steamer attempted to enter the port of destination, her anchor dragged and her cables parted because of perils of the sea. She was thus driven ashore. Part of her cargo was washed overboard and the remainder was delivered to the cargo owner.
Held:
Once the remaining goods have been delivered safely at the agreed place of destination, the freight falls due where the contract of carriage expresses that freight is to be paid as a lump sum. In this particular case, the charterers tried relying on the clause that "freight was only payable on the right and true delivery of the cargo" as permitting them to refuse to pay. Lord Lindley held that the true construction of the clause was that right and true delivery of the cargo must necessarily be subject to any excepted perils. In this case, the accident was a peril of the sea. That being the case, there was no total failure of consideration and the lump sum freight had to be settled.

Pro rata freight

There may be an express or implied agreement to the effect that the charterer or **7–094** shipper pays all or part of the freight where a different port may be used as a substitute for the agreed port/s of call or port of destination. This is effectively a variation of the original contract but the right to do so is dependent on the terms of that contract. Where there is no such variation permitted under contract, the general rule of law is that even though through an excepted peril the carrier could not deliver the goods at the port of destination, there is no right to freight at all, whether in full or proportion to the amount of voyage completed.

In *Christy v Row* (1808) 127 E.R. 849, the shipowners were entitled to claim pro rata freight because the shipper of the goods (cargo owners) had taken delivery of the goods at an intermediate port, raising the presumption that they had dispensed with the necessity of carrying the goods to the ultimate port of destination. It should however be recognised that the mere act of taking delivery of the goods at an intermediate port must be accompanied by other evidence evincing the intention on both parties to relinquish the original contractual obligations. The court will insist on satisfying itself that the shipper takes delivery of the goods at the intermediate port not involuntarily and that the shipowner is prepared to dispose of the goods to the shipper in that manner. The presence of consent makes the variation binding. By the same token, where, in *Metcalfe v Brittania Ironworks Co* (1877) 2 Q.B.D. 423, the cargo owners accepted the goods at an intermediate port under protest when ice prevented the vessel from completing the voyage, that was not an agreement to pay pro rata freight.

Back freight

7–095   Briefly, when delivery of the goods has been prevented by events beyond the control of the shipowner or his master, the master is empowered to take steps in dealing with the goods. The shipowner then becomes entitled to charge the shipper or cargo owner "back freight" to cover expenses incurred by the ship-master.

Example: The shipmaster is not able to deliver the goods at the port of destination as a result of the outbreak of hostilities. Unable to contact the cargo owner, he lands the goods at a nearby port to be returned on the next available ship to port of shipment. Any warehouse charges and other expenses incurred may be recovered by the shipowner from the cargo owner as "back freight". Such an entitlement is however subject to the terms of the contract.

Dead freight

7–096   "Dead Freight" is another term for damages payable by the charterer who has failed to supply "a full and complete cargo" under the terms of the contract. The tender of the full and complete cargo must be genuine; in *AIC Ltd v Marine Pilot Ltd (The Archimidis)* [2008] EWCA Civ 175 the shipowner was entitled to dead freight because although the charterer had made a formal tender of the cargo, there was no way in reality for the loading to be completed in time for the ship's scheduled departure from port. (*N.B.* For a more detailed consideration, see discussion below paras 7–111—7–113.)

Charterer's Duty to Use a Good and Safe Port

7–097   The charterparty may provide that the charterer shall be entitled to nominate a port of destination or loading at a specified time. It is important that this allowance not be treated as being unlimited. The charterer must ensure that the nominated port is a good and safe port.[21] There is a persuasive case for making out the proposition that there should be an implied term or warranty of safety. Indeed, if a named port or anchorage is specifically identified in the charterparty this should not be read as suggesting that the shipowner is to be regarded as having *consented to the risk* that the port might prove to be unsafe (*Ullises Shipping Corporation v Fal Shipping Co Ltd (The Greek Fighter)* [2006] EWHC 172). However, that is not to say that in all cases the fact that the charterparty is silent as to a warranty of safe port, the court would necessarily imply a term of safe port. The law on implied terms must continue to be applied strictly—that is to say, the term must be reasonable and necessary for the functioning of the charterparty. In *Mediterranean Salvage & Towage Ltd v Seamar Trading & Commerce Inc* [2009] EWCA Civ 531 the Court of Appeal did not think that an implied term of a safe port was necessary in the business sense to give efficacy to the charterparty (a Gencon charter). What was especially noteworthy there was the fact that under the charterparty, the shipowner had expressly warranted that upon arrival at Chekka, the loading port, the vessel would comply with all restrictions of the port, including its berths and approaches and that the shipowner had satisfied itself with and about Chekka's specifications and restrictions. The implied term would thus be inconsistent with that clause which had clearly cast the burden on ensuring that the port of loading was safe to the shipowner.

It is also likely that where the express terms could give rise to two interpretations, one favouring the warranty of safe port and the other not, the court would prefer the former. In *AIC Ltd v Marine Pilot Ltd (The Archimidis)* [2008] EWCA Civ 175 the voyage charter stipulated, "Load one safe port Ventspils. Discharge 1/2 safe ports United Kingdom Continent Bordeaux/ Hamburg range". Following the tenor of the judgment in *The Greek Fighter*, the Court of Appeal held that those words amounted to a warranty of safe port. This particular issue had not previously come before the Court of Appeal and it has long been unclear whether there could be a safe port warranty where there is an agreed single port.[22] The duty applies both to voyage and time charters but the extent it applies may differ (see below, and *Kodros Shipping Corp v Empresa Cubana de Fletes (The Evia) (No.2)* [1983] 1 A.C. 736).

What does "good and safe port" mean? Sellers L.J. in *Leeds Shipping Co Limited v Societe Francaise Bunge* [1958] 2 Lloyd's Rep. 127 (CA) said:

> " . . . a port will not be safe unless . . . the particular ship can reach it, use it and return from it . . . without being exposed to danger which cannot be avoided by good navigation and seamanship . . . ".

A safe port however does not mean a safe berth—there is no duty at common law to nominate a safe berth where the port is named in the charter *(Mediterranean Salvage & Towage Ltd v Seamar Trading (The Reborn)* [2008] EWHC 1875). Safety includes not only physical conditions of the port concerned but other

---

[21] See Baker and David, "The Politically Unsafe Port" [1986] L.M.C.L.Q. 112 and Reynolds, "The Concept of Safe Ports" [1974] L.M.C.L.Q. 171.

[22] There may also be implications for sale contracts which use the words "safe port" where only one delivery port is named. The traders (whether a FOB seller or CIF/CFR buyer) may be found to have warranted by these words the safety of the relevant ports and thus, may need to indemnify their buyer or seller for liabilities incurred against the carrier.

factors rendering the port a danger to the ship. The political situation or any civil unrest at a particular port could render the port unsafe for the ship. The port could also become unsafe because it is not sufficiently equipped.

7–098 *Tage Berglund v Montoro Shipping Corp Ltd (The Dagmar)* [1968] 2 Lloyd's Rep. 563
Facts:
The Dagmar was chartered to load timber at Cape Chat in Quebec. The master was warned that he would have to rely on his own devices to check weather conditions because Cape Chat did not have weather forecast facilities. North winds struck and the ship was driven aground.
Held:
The port was unsafe because it was not adequately equipped to enable the ship to avoid bad weather conditions. The fact that the shipmaster[23] had to use his own devices to ascertain weather and wind conditions was proof that the port was not adequately safe for the ship.

Similarly, in *Maintop Shipping Co Ltd v Bulkindo Lines Pte Ltd (The Marinicki)* [2003] EWHC 1894, the ship was damaged by an underwater obstruction within a dredged channel leading into and out of the port of Jakarta, Indonesia. It was obvious that if the port had such obstructions, it would be an unsafe port. However, the shipowners in the time charter were unable to show when and how the obstruction came to rest in the channel. The court thus deemed, on balance, that it was an unforeseeable fortuity and the port was not unsafe simply because of the obstruction. That said, the charterers were nonetheless liable because the shipowners were able to show that the port was unsafe because there was no proper system or no system at all in the port for monitoring the safety of the entry channel to the port and warning vessels using the approaches to the port of any hazards. This case demonstrates how important it is to identify that particular aspect of the port which renders it unsafe. A general plea is insufficient.

7–099 A port however does not become unsafe simply because under certain weather conditions it might be dangerous (*The Heinrich Horn* [1971] A.M.C. 362). As we saw in *The Dagmar* bad weather conditions only make the port unsafe if the port is inadequately equipped to enable ships to avoid the dangers or if conditions at port make it impossible for a ship under the threat of hazardous weather conditions to leave. Lord Denning M.R. said in *Islander Shipping Enterprises v Empresa Maritima Del Estado (The Khian Sea)* [1979] 1 Lloyd's Rep. 545:

> "First, there must be an adequate weather-forecasting system. Second, there must be an adequate availability of pilots and tugs. Thirdly, there must be adequate sea room to manoeuvre. And fourthly, there must be an adequate system for ensuring that sea room and room for manoeuvre is always available".

The rule seems to be this: a port is safe if the ship under charter can safely enter it, lie there safely and leave it safely. It might be useful to note Sellers L.J.'s dictum in *Leeds Shipping Co Ltd v Societé Française Bunge (The Eastern City)* [1958] 2 Lloyd's Rep. 127:

> "[A] port will not be safe port unless, in the relevant periods of time, the particular ship can reach it, use it and return from it without, in the absence of

---

[23] See Herman and Goldman, "The Master's Negligence and Charterer's Warranty of Safe Port/Berth" [1983] L.M.C.L.Q. 615 on the shipmaster's role.

some abnormal occurrence, being exposed to danger which cannot be avoided by some good navigation and seamanship . . . ".

In *The Livanita* [2007] EWHC 1317, the mere fact that St Petersburg would be affected by ice in the winter months did not mean that it was an unsafe port. Indeed, in that case, the charter had specifically referred to ice. The presence of ice itself was therefore plainly contemplated by both parties. However, ice breakers at the port brought about many floating ice blocks. That created a dangerous situation for the ship, rendering the port unsafe.

The safety of the port is not compromised simply because of a temporary **7–100** hazard. In *The Hermine* [1979] 1 L.L. Rep. 212, according to the Court of Appeal, the test is this:

"[A] port will not lack the characteristics of a safe port merely because some delay, insufficient to frustrate the adventure, may be caused to the vessel in her attempt to reach, use and leave the port, by some temporary evident obstruction or hazard".

This has more recently been applied in *The Count* [2006] EWHC 3222.

It should be noted that the question as to whether a port is safe or not is one of fact, not of law. A decision by a tribunal of fact that the port is safe or unsafe is a matter which cannot be appealed against. This was stressed by Tomlinson J. in *Boulos Gad Tourism & Hotels Ltd v Uniground Shipping Co Ltd* (November 16, 2001) who stated that safety is a relative concept and all maritime adventures are subject to some degree of risk. As long as the arbitrator had applied himself properly in concluding on the evidence that the port or adventure was not unsafe, such a finding of fact cannot be reviewed.

In general, the question as to whether the port is safe refers to the safety of the port when the nomination was made; there is no implied term that the port has to remain safe when the ship is subsequently in port. In *Kodros Shipping Corp v Empresa Cubana de Fletes (The Evia) (No.2)* [1983] 1 A.C. 736 the charterparty provided that *The Evia* was to be employed "between good and safe ports". In March 1980 she was ordered to load a cargo of cement and building materials in Cuba to be carried to Iraq. After discharging her cargo on September 22, the Iraqi port was closed as a result of the Iran-Iraq war and the ship was trapped.[24] The general issue was whether the charterer was in breach for not using a safe port as provided for in the contract. In approving and applying Sellers L.J.'s test in *The Eastern City* (above), the House of Lords discussed the nature of the undertaking to nominate good and safe ports

" . . . a charterer will exercise that undoubted contractual right by giving the shipowner orders to go to a particular port or place of loading or discharge. It is clearly at that point of time when that order is given that that contractual promise to the charterer regarding the safety of that intended port or place must be fulfilled. But that contractual promise cannot mean that that port or place must be safe when that that port or place must be safe when that order is given,

---

[24] See Hibbits, "The Impact of the Iran-Iraq cases on the law of frustration of charterparties" [1985] J.M.L.C. 441 on some of the consequences of the Iran–Iraq conflict on international shipping.

for were that so, a charterer could not legitimately give orders to go to an ice-bound port which he and the owner both knew in all human probability would be ice-free by the time that vessel reached it. Nor, were that the nature of the promise, could a charterer order a ship to a port or place the approaches to which were at the time of the order blocked as a result of a collision or by some submerged wreck or obstacles even though such obstacles would in all human probability be out of the way before the ship required to enter".

7–101   The charterer's duty to nominate a safe port relates to the characteristics of the port or place in question and means that when the order is given that port is or place is *prospectively* safe for the ship to get to, stay at and leave. Where abnormal events make the port unsafe after the orders have been given, Lord Roskill was concerned that to hold the charterer liable for any resultant damage or loss would be to make the charterer

> "the insurer of such unexpected and abnormal risks which . . . should properly fall upon the ship's insurers under policies of insurance the effecting of which is the owner's responsibility".

In so deciding, the House of Lords overruled the decision of Mustill J. in *Transoceanic Petroleum Carriers v Cook Industries Inc (The Mary Lou)* [1981] 2 Lloyd's Rep. 272 where the judge had held that the charterer must warrant that the nominated port should *continue* to be safe.

The next issue for consideration is whether there exists a residual duty on the charterer after nomination. Lord Roskill stated that the issue depends on whether the charterer is under a time or a voyage charter. In the case of a time charter, the charterer is in complete control of the employment of the ship and it is in his powers to give appropriate orders timeously to prevent the ship from proceeding to or remaining at a port initially safe but since become dangerous. A voyage charterer does not have the same power. If there is a single loading or discharging port named in the voyage charterparty then, unless the charterparty specifically otherwise provides, a voyage charterer may not be able to order that ship to go elsewhere. If there is a range of ports stipulated in the voyage charterparty, once the charterer has selected the contractual port or ports of loading or discharge, the charterer then has no further right of nomination or re-nomination. Lord Roskill felt that in a time charter, the charterer has a residual duty after nomination

> "to do all he can effectively do to protect the ship from the new danger in the port which has arisen since his original order for her to go to it was given".

7–102   This means that if the ship could be ordered to go somewhere else to avoid an impending danger, the time charterer should make the order. In the case of a voyage charterer, Lord Roskill was less keen to hold him to a similar residual duty.

A breach of the duty to use a safe port is normally associated with physical harm or damage to the vessel for which the shipowner would be entitled to claim compensation. What if no physical harm was sustained? In *The Count* [2006] EWHC 3222, the court awarded damages to the owners whose ship was seriously delayed as a result of the closure of the access to the port because another ship was grounded as a result of the buoys not being in their proper position (the buoys were moved by shifting sand). There was a proved causal link between the port condition and the delay.

Contractual variations of the standard duty

"Due Diligence in Employment of Vessel between Safe Ports" clause

Where there is a clause that the charterer is to use due diligence to ensure that the **7–103** ship is employed between safe and good ports as in *K/S Penta Shipping A/S v Ethiopian Shipping Lines Corp (The Saga Cob)* [1992] 2 Lloyd's Rep. 545, the Court of Appeal did not seem to treat the qualification "due diligence" as markedly different from the standard contractual requirement to use only good and safe ports. The port in that case was found not to be prospectively unsafe because the risk of guerrilla attacks was not a normal characteristic of the port. Furthermore, the port will only be regarded as unsafe where "the political risk is sufficient for a reasonable shipowner or master to decline to send his vessel there" (see also *The Chemical Venture* [1993] 1 Lloyd's Rep. 508). *Dow Europe SA v Novoklav Inc* [1998] 1 Lloyd's Rep. 306 states that "due diligence" in the Shelltime 4 form was not to be construed as referring to personal liability alone, without clear words to that effect. That obligation is delegable.

It is becoming more common for charterparties expressly to grant the shipowner or shipmaster the right to decline a nomination if the port nominated is considered by the shipowner or shipmaster as dangerous.[25] The breadth of this discretion was discussed in *Abu Dhabi National Timber Co v Product Star Shipping Ltd (The Product Star) (No.2)* [1993] 1 Lloyd's Rep. 397. The Court of Appeal held that where such a discretion is conferred under the charter, the shipowner or shipmaster should exercise his discretion "honestly and in good faith" and "having regard to the provisions of the contract by which it is conferred, it must not be exercised arbitrarily, capriciously or unreasonably". Where as in that case, the owners had not consulted the master as to the invocation of the refusal of nomination clause, although that omission does not invalidate his refusal of the nomination it calls into question the owners' good faith and strongly suggests that their refusal was arbitrary. It should however not be thought that just because the shipmaster and owners disagree on what constitutes a good and safe port necessarily points to an unjustified refusal of the nomination. The Court of Appeal was concerned with the fact that there had been no consultation with the master, not that there might be a difference of opinion. Additionally, where the risk has not changed materially, then the refusal becomes highly questionable.

In conclusion, it should be added that where the nominated port (whether of loading or discharge) is not unsafe, there is a contentious issue as to whether the charterer is entitled to change the nomination. In *Antiparos ENE v SK Shipping* [2008] EWHC 1139, Andrew Smith J. thought that an unlimited right to change nominations could have far reaching consequences, especially where the charter

---

[25] See Baker, "The safe port/berth obligation and employment and indemnity clauses" [1988] L.M.C.L.Q. 43; Davenport, "Unsafe ports again" [1993] L.M.C.L.Q. 150.

provided for several alternative port ranges at a considerable distance from each other. The judge held that without an express term, the parties could not be taken to have intended to confer such a right. On the other hand, there is the view of some commentators that such a right to substitute should exist for commercial practicalities. It is therefore best for the charterparty to make explicitly clear whether the charterer should have such a right. Such a right may be subject to an implied term that the charterer should cover the extra expenses incurred by the shipowner (such as costs sustained as a result of having to change bunkering ports as in *Antiparos ENE v SK Shipping*).

A "near clause"

7–104 The "near clause" allows the shipowner to discharge the cargo at a place other than the nominated port if the ship is unable to safely discharge the cargo there. The clause entitles the shipowner to unload the cargo at a place "so near thereto as she may safely get and lie always afloat". An excellent example of such a clause is *The Athamas (Owners) v Dig Vijay Cement Co Ltd* [1963] 1 Lloyd's Rep. 287. The charterparty there provided that:

" . . . being so loaded the vessel shall proceed . . . safely to, and to enter and discharge the balance of the cargo at one safe place always afloat, PNOM-PENH, or so near thereto as she may safely get and lie always afloat and there deliver the cargo . . . ".

The relevant law is set out in *The Varing* [1931] P. 79 where Scrutton L.J. said

" . . . when you are chartered to go to a discharging place and cannot get there, you are bound to wait a reasonable time before having recourse to the clause 'or as near thereto as she can safely get'. You cannot arrive and, when you find that you cannot get in on the exact day you desire, immediately go off to a place which you describe as 'so near thereto as she can safely get'. When a reasonable time has elapsed, and when there is no chance of your getting in to your discharging place within a reasonable time, the ship is at liberty to go to a reasonable discharging place—'as near thereto as she can safely get'—and can call upon the consignee to take delivery at the substituted place".

The shipowner must make up his mind as to what he wishes to do. Notice must be given to the charterer and consignee that he is invoking the contractual clause to discharge the goods somewhere else. These legal principles were later affirmed by the Court of Appeal in *The Athamas*. In that case it was argued by the charterer that the shipowner should not have discharged the cargo at Saigon which was about 250 miles from Phnom-Penh. The court found that while distance is a relevant factor in deciding whether the substitute place of discharge is "as near thereto as she may safely get", it is not the overriding consideration. The size and other physical specifications of the vessel must further be considered. In that case, the arbitrators found as a matter of fact that *The Athamas* could not get to Phnom-Penh within a reasonable time and that Saigon was the appropriate alternative or substituted place of delivery under the charterparty.

War risk clauses

A war risk clause will give the shipowner the power to cancel a contract of **7–105** carriage or refuse to comply with the charterer's instructions on the basis of a risk of war or threat of war. The term "war" is defined usually to include

> "act of war; civil war; hostilities; revolution; rebellion; civil commotion; warlike operations; laying of mines; acts of piracy; acts of terrorists; acts of hostility or malicious damage; blockades . . . ; by any person, body, terrorist or political group, or the Government of any state whatsoever".

There are two commonly used war risk clauses in the industry—BIMCO's Conwartime 2004 (for time charters) and Voywar 2004 (for voyage charterparties).[26] It should be noted that not only does the clause entitle the shipowner to refuse to send the ship to an unsafe port, it allows him not to use a particular route if that route is likely to be subject to a war risk.

A Conwartime 2004 clause was tested recently in the case of *Taokas Navigation v Komrowski Bulk Shipping* [2012] EWHC 1888. It seemed implicit from the judgment that the exercise of judgement by the shipowner as to whether a port was under a threat or risk of "war" should be made in good faith—this is somewhat controversial given that there is no real guidance as to what might constitute good faith in this context. A better view might be to require that the judgment be informed (*ENE Kos 1 v Petroleo Brasileiro SA* [2012] 2 W.L.R. 976) and honestly made.

In *Pacific Basin IHX Ltd v Bulkhandling Handymax AS (The Triton Lark)* **7–106** [2012] 1 Lloyd's Rep. 151 the bulk carrier was ordered to load a cargo of bulk potash in Hamburg for carriage to China via Suez and the Gulf of Aden. The master feared an attack by pirates if that route was taken. His concerns were heightened due to the fact that a few days before the charterers' instructed the master to proceed via Suez and the Gulf of Aden, four pirate attacks had taken place. Despite the master's concerns, the charterers insisted that the vessel should proceed via Suez at night (given that no vessels at that time had been hijacked at night-time) through "the safe MSPA channel".[27] The owners refused, asking for additional conditions to be met including the appointment of a second master on board to be paid for by the charterers and if the ship was seized, the charterers should compensate the owners for loss of hire. The charterers did not agree. Teare J. remitted the case back to the arbitrators to decide there was a "real likelihood", in the sense of real danger, that the vessel would be exposed to piracy. A distinction must be made between whether there is a risk that a serious event will occur and whether there is a serious risk that an event will occur. The latter is the true test. It suggests, therefore, that the court seemed to favour a narrow test—one which is more favourable to the charterers.

An important question is what happens if, at the time the charterparty was made, the risk was known to the owners. Will that knowledge be taken as

---

[26] *https://www.bimco.org/en/Chartering/~/ . . . /SC2004_12_03.ashx* [accessed April 13, 2013].

[27] The Maritime Security Patrol Area (MSPA) is zone in the Gulf of Aden forming a narrow, rectangular corridor between Somalia and Yemen patrolled by the Combined Task Force 150, (CTF 150). The CTF 150 was established by a coalition of states to protect ships from pirate attacks in the area. However, the taskforce comprises only 12–15 vessels which have to cover well over 2.4 million square miles of sea. It is thus unwise to assume that the risk of a pirate attack was entirely removed by the presence of the task force.

the owner's acceptance of the risk, despite the presence of a war risk clause? In *The Product Star (No.2)* [1993] 1 Lloyd's Rep. 397 the position was that where it is proved that the owners had, by the terms of the charterparty construed in its factual context, accepted a particular war risk clause involved in trading to a port or area, the liberty to refuse to trade to such port or area is not available unless they can show that there has been an escalation in the relevant war risk since the date of the charter. Similarly, if at the time the clause was made the owners and charterers were aware of the risks, without a material change (reduction) in those risks between the time of the charterparty and the time of the instructions, the owners can continue to rely on the clause not to comply with the charterers' instructions (*Taokas Navigation v Komrowski Bulk Shipping* [2012] EWHC 1888).

Duty to Engage in Lawful Trades

7–107   It goes without saying that the charterer or shipper of goods is subject to the normal requirements of contractual validity, and in this instance, to use the ship only in lawful trades. This is an absolute duty. It makes no difference whether or not the charterer is aware of the illegality. In *The Greek Fighter* [2006] EWHC 1729 the court held that where the charterer's loading of contraband oil on the vessel would expose the vessel to seizure by the authorities, the charterer would be in breach of the duty not to engage in unlawful trades even though they did not know the oil was contraband. The charterparty may be illegal at the outset, that is to say, the terms of the contract themselves are illegal, or the illegality may arise as a result of the manner of performance as intended by both or one of the parties. Where the terms are illegal at the outset, the contract is unenforceable and void, regardless of whether the parties were aware of the law or not. Where the manner of performance but not the substance of the contract is illegal, it is customary to distinguish between a situation where the illegality is known to both parties and a case where only one party is aware of the illegality.

Where both parties are aware of the illegality or *in pari delicto*, the contract is unenforceable. In a case concerning the carriage of goods by road, *Ashmore, Benson, Pease & Co Ltd v AV Dawson Ltd* [1973] 1 W.L.R. 828, the parties had agreed to transport two boilers on a lorry which was not lawfully authorised to carry boilers. In the course of transit the boilers were damaged, but the claimant was not entitled to bring an action to recover the damage because he was privy to the illegality. The claimant had not only known that the boilers were to be carried in an illegal manner but had actually been privy to the illegality by assisting the defendant carrier to perform the contract in that illegal manner.

Where the party performing the contract had committed an incidental act which is illegal, that fact alone does not deprive him of a remedy under the contract. Therefore in *St John Shipping Corp v Joseph Rank Ltd* [1957] 1 Q.B. 267, the carrier was entitled to claim freight even though it had illegally overloaded its vessel. It should however be borne in mind that the claimant would not have been entitled to recover freight if it is proved that he had planned at the outset to perform the contract in an illegal manner.

7–108   Where only one party is aware of the illegality, the "innocent" party is not deprived a remedy in contract. In another carriage case, *Archbolds (Freightage) Ltd v S. Spanglett Ltd* [1961] 1 Q.B. 374, the vehicle used to carry the claimant's goods was not properly licensed. This was not known to the claimant whom the court held was not precluded from bringing an action for nondelivery even though the performance of the contract would have been illegal because he was not privy to the unlawfulness. However, once the "innocent" party discovers the illegal object of the other party, he must refuse to assist in the unlawful performance of the contract. Any expense or cost already incurred by the 'innocent' party may be recovered under the quantum meruit rule.

At this point it is perhaps necessary to note that where the contract of carriage is to be governed by a foreign law and not English law and that it is invalid under that law, arts 10–12 Rome I Regulation require an English court to give effect to that foreign law rendering the contract invalid, unless that foreign law is manisfestly incompatible with public policy. Where one party claims to be ignorant of the foreign law or of the intention of the other party to use an illegal manner of performance, it should be noted that the existence of the foreign law is treated as a matter of fact not of law. Thus ignorance of the content of that law will be treated as mistake of fact and not of law. This was applied in *Fielding & Platt Ltd v Najjar* [1969] 1 W.L.R. 25. There it was pleaded that the parties had intended to use false invoices to deceive Lebanese authorities and this rendered the contract void. In finding that it was not a term of the contract to use false invoices, the court held that the claimant suppliers were entitled to be paid. The court must be satisfied that sufficient evidence is adduced to show that the claimants (suppliers of goods) were aware of the illegality or had intended to participate in it—the illegality could not be presumed.

In the above cases, the charterer is taken to warrant that the adventure would be lawful. However, where the illegality arises only after the charterparty has been made, it may be open to the charterer (and the owner) to rely on the doctrine of frustration of contracts. The success of such a plea of course depends on whether the intervening illegality was an ordinary commercial risk within the contemplation of the parties, whether the illegality was self-induced and whether it rendered performance totally incapable of legal performance. It is usually to the parties' interest to make specific provisions (such as a force majeure type clause) to deal with such eventualities or contingencies. The force majeure-type clause will provide for circumstances under which the contract might be terminated or extended. Such clauses would however be construed quite narrowly.

In *The Florida* [2006] EWHC 1137, a different type of clause was relied on by the owners. There, a liberty clause in the charterparty provided that the owner could,   **7–109**

"before loading or before the commencement of the voyage, require the shipper to take delivery and, failing that, warehouse the cargo at the cargo's expense, or alternatively, discharge the cargo elsewhere at the risk and expense of the cargo . . . *in any situation whatsoever and wheresoever occurring and whether existing or anticipated before commencement of or during the voyage*" (emphasis added).

The contract called for the carriage of goods from Dumai to Lagos, Nigeria. However soon after the contract was made, the Nigerian government banned all discharge of vegetable oil. Consequently, charterer claimed that the charterparty had been frustrated. The arbitrator ruled that the liberty clause applied and as such, the charterer could not rely on the defence of frustration. On appeal, Tomlinson J. disagreed with the arbitrator's opinion and held that the clause anticipated the presence or existence of cargo. Without the existence of a lawful cargo, the liberty clause could not be said to apply. As such, the contract was effectively frustrated.

Duty of Charterer to Provide and Load a Full and Complete Cargo

7–110   We have stated earlier that the failure of the shipper or charterer to provide adequate cargo could result in dead freight being charged. But is there a general duty on the charterer or shipper to provide a cargo for the vessel?[28] What happens if the shipper or cargo owner through no fault of his own is prevented from delivering to port the agreed cargo for loading?

7–111   *(Sueton D) Grant & Co v Coverdale, Todd & Co* (1884) 9 App. Cas. 470
Facts:
The charterparty stated that laytime was to commence once the vessel was ready to load except if frosts and other unavoidable accidents preventing loading were to occur. The full and complete cargo to be loaded was 1800 tons of iron. About half the cargo was to be brought to the ship for loading by canal. The Glamorganshire Canal unfortunately then froze over and for a fortnight, the charterers were unable to load. The shipowners sued for demurrage for the detention of the ship. The charterers attempted to rely on the exception clause.
Held:
The charterers' duty is to have the cargo ready to be loaded, and to tender it to be put on board the ship in the usual and proper manner. According to the House of Lords:

"[The] business of both parties meets and concurs in that operation of loading. When the charterer has tendered the cargo, and when the operation has proceeded to the point at which the shipowner is to take charge of it, everything after that is the shipowner's business, and everything before the commencement of the operation of loading . . . is the charterer's part only".

This places the risk of the cargo not being ready for loading on the charterer. Thus, any stipulation varying this assumption of risk will have be construed *contra proferentem*. What occurred in preventing the delivery of the cargo to the ship was not to be construed as having prevented loading. It could not have been the intention of the shipowner to agree to

"those things with which he has nothing whatever to do, which precede altogether the whole operation of loading, which are no part whatever of it, but which belong to that which is exclusively the charterer's business".

7–112   In *Hunter v Fry* (1819) 2 B. & Ald. 421, the duty on the charterer was to load a "full and complete" cargo and this was construed as filling to the full capacity of the ship even though a lower threshold is stipulated in the charterparty. This naturally only applies to the charterer who has undertaken an absolute duty to the shipowner. Other shippers of goods need only be bound by the agreed cargo

---

[28] Note that as for a time charterer, he must pay hire despite not having loaded the ship (subject only to any "off-hire" stipulations). See para.7–142.

quantity for the essence of their contract of carriage is the purchase of shipping space and not the use of the entire ship.

In *Brightman & Co v Bunge y Born Limitada Sociedad* [1924] 2 K.B. 619, the charterer who has undertaken to load a full and complete cargo of wheat and/or maize and/or rye must still load a full cargo of any one of other two named grains if he is prevented from shipping wheat. The clause cannot be construed as suggesting that the charterer is freed from loading maize or rye once he has decided to ship and load wheat instead. The duty to load a full and complete cargo does not terminate when the selection to load wheat is made. In *South African Dispatch Line v Owners of the Steamship Niki* [1960] 1 K.B. 518, that duty remains operative even though the failure to load that particular cargo was protected by an exception clause. He must still load alternative goods.

In *Reardon Smith Line Ltd v Ministry of Agriculture, Fisheries and Food* [1963] A.C. 691, where the charterer is given the right to elect conclusively the exact and particular cargo from a range of goods to be loaded, that right will be respected. Once he has made the choice, he is no longer duty bound to choose an alternative cargo (subject to any contractual requirements to the contrary). This means that his duty to load a full and complete cargo will be deemed to have been discharged. It was held that where the charter had expressly granted the charterer the right to choose conclusively between two cargoes and when the selected cargo was not available, there was no duty to load the other. It is always a matter of construction as to whether such a right exists in the charterparty. In *Reardon Smith Line Ltd*, the so-called options were subject to additional freight making it clear that there is no unfettered right to "switch" cargoes. Hence, they were not true options for the charterer.

There are occasions where the shipowner might agree with the charterer to   **7–113** help secure the relevant "approvals" from shippers to provide a full and complete cargo. Many tanker charters make such a provision. The shipowners promise to guarantee to obtain within a certain period "approval" from the petroleum companies to use the charterer's vessel. The nature of such a provision was the thrust of the dispute in *BS&N Ltd (BVI) v Micado Shipping (Malta) Ltd (The Seaflower)* [2000] 2 Lloyd's Rep. 37. It was held that such a clause, although labelled as a guarantee, should not be classed as a condition. It is a mere innominate term. Applying the strict test in *Hong Kong Fir Shipping Co Ltd v Kawasaki Kisen Kaisha Ltd* [1962] Q.B. 26, the breach of the contract in failing to obtain the relevant approval from the oil companies by the due date was not a repudiatory breach. It could not have been the intention of the parties to treat the failure as fundamental where a breach would not have "substantially deprived the charterers of the whole benefit of the contract". The true nature of the breach depended on the seriousness of the breach. In *The Seaflower*, the shipowners had successfully obtained two out of three approvals; as such it could not be said that the charterers had been substantially deprived of the benefit of the contract. The obligation to obtain the necessary approval could not thus be said to be a condition.

Responsibility for cargo operations

Under the common law, the voyage charterer is responsible for bringing the cargo   **7–114** alongside the ship to enable the shipowner to load it. This is commonly known as the "alongside rule". It is however obvious that whilst the alongside rule would apply very well in traditional cargo operations taking place at the ship's tackle, in modern cargo operations, it is not always efficient to load at the ship's tackle. For example, in cases of bulk cargo, loading is carried out by cranes, grabs and other mechanical means which are located on shore. The equipment is usually under the charterer's control; hence, it would be more appropriate contractually to treat the charterer as responsible for the loading but clear words must be used.[29] In the case of a time charter, too, it is normally provided for that the carrier, who has contractual employment and use of the vessel, is responsible for loading operations.

The contract however sometimes envisages that the shipowner will assist the charterer in cargo operations. Where this is so, it is not always clear how liability for loss or damage caused to the ship, crew or port should be allocated. In the recent Court of Appeal's case of *CV Scheepvaartonderneming Flintermar v Sea Malta Co Ltd* [2005] EWCA Civ 17, the shipowner claimed damages from the time charterer for injuries caused to his chief officer during cargo operations. The hatch cover to the ship's hold consisted of 11 interlocking but removable pontoons. The stevedores *employed by the shipowners* to carry out the removal of the pontoons were negligent. As a result, the chief officer fell into the hold and injured himself. The lower court held that although the accident was caused by the stevedores' negligence, the stevedores were performing the shipowner's work at the time in replacing the pontoons and as such, the charterers were not liable. The Court of Appeal however allowed the appeal from the shipowner, stating that contractually and customarily (in the modern context), the charterer bore primary responsibility for hatch-handling. The hatch was part of the vessel's equipment and its removal and replacement was part of cargo operations. The hatch-handling occurred within the time and space of the overall cargo operation and was conducted by the shipowner's stevedores as an integral part of that operation without extra payment and pursuant to an arrangement between the parties. Although it was for the shipmaster to decide how to load and discharge, it was for the charterer (and the stevedores assisting him) to execute the cargo operations without negligence.

The discharge of the cargo under a voyage charter is normally a joint effort between the consignee and the owner; with the owner being responsible for moving the cargo to the side of the ship most convenient for the unloading, and the consignee to take delivery of it from there. If lighters are required, the court has held in an old case, *Petersen v Freebody* [1895] 2 Q.B. 294, that that would be paid for by the charterer. Charterers and shipowners are however not prepared these days to leave it to chance and will thus explicitly provide for the allocation of these responsibilities by contract. Nonetheless, it should also be borne in mind that the courts also apply and recognise any unique port customary practice at the locality in question, provided the practice is reasonable, well known and not inconsistent with the express terms of the contract. The position under a time charter is not especially different. The time charterer who is normally responsible for full employment of the vessel will work with the consignee in cargo discharge operations.

---

[29] See *Jindal Iron and Steel Co Ltd v Islamic Solidarity Co Jordan Inc (The MV Jordan II)* [2004] UKHL 49 where the House of Lords confirmed the position that such contractual allocation is permissible even where art.III(2) and (8) of the Hague-Visby Rules apply. See para.8–039.

Laytime

Laytime commences when the ship becomes an *arrived ship* and is ready to load. **7–115** The shipowner is usually contractually bound to give the charterer a notice of readiness. Laytime is important as it represents the time within which the charterer has to load or unload under the charterparty or contract of carriage. Where laytime has not been specified in the contract as an express term, the charterer must load or unload within a reasonable time. Where laytime has been pre-set, the charterer exceeds it at the peril of having to pay liquidated damages called demurrage. A demurrage clause might look something like this:

> "Ten running days on demurrage at the rate stated . . . per day or pro rata for any part of a day, to be allowed Merchants altogether at ports of loading and discharging." (Clause 7 Gencon Charter).

This means that demurrage or liquidated damages (as against a penalty) will be charged on a daily rate for ten days after the laytime has expired. As pre-estimated damages, the sum provided need not be "right" or supported by an honest belief: it only needs to be objectively reasonable (*McAlpine v Tilebox* [2005] All E.R. (D) 396).

The arrived ship

Central to all this is, therefore, the concept of an arrived ship as laytime does not **7–116** run until the ship is an arrived ship, and demurrage cannot be imposed until laytime has expired. Whether the ship is an arrived ship depends largely on the terms of the charterparty. Where the charter specifies that the ship is to proceed to an exact loading or discharging berth (known as a berth charter), then the ship does not become arrived until it gets to that exact spot. Where, on the other hand, the charter specifies that the ship is to proceed to a named port (known as a port charter), it is not always clear when the ship becomes an arrived ship because of the large area involved. It is important, therefore, to be able to distinguish a berth charterparty from a port charterparty, especially when the charterparty refers to both berth and port. That of course is a matter of interpretation of the terms in the charterparty. In *Novologistics Sarl v Five Ocean* [2009] EWHC 3046 (Comm), the opening term in the charterparty provided "one good and safe chrts' berth terminal 4 . . . Xingang to one good and safe berth Cadiz and one good and safe berth Bilbao". The court concluded that it was a berth charterparty. The clause defined the contractual destinations, both as to place of loading and as to place/s of discharge, and it identified the destination as the berth. This, therefore, made the charter a berth charter. Also, the "chrts' berth" wording gave the charterer the right to nominate the berth at Xingang and for that reason too the charter was a berth charter.

As for a port charter, questions will arise as to whether the ship needs to be docked or berthed before it becomes an arrived ship.

EL Oldendorff & Co GmbH v Tradax Export SA (The Johanna Oldendorff) [1974]   **7–117**
A.C. 479
Facts:
Under a voyage charter, The *Johanna Oldendorff* was to load a cargo of grain in the United States and then "proceed to London or Avonmouth or Glasgow or Belfast or

Liverpool/Birkenhead (counting as one port) or Hull". The charterers gave instructions that the ship was to discharge at Liverpool/Birkenhead but no berth was named. The ship, upon clearing customs, was ordered to proceed to anchor at the bar light vessel. It was argued by the shipowners that the ship became an arrived ship when she anchored at the bar awaiting a berth because that is within the port of Liverpool and it was the usual place to await a berth. Furthermore it was a place she was ordered to by the port authorities. The charterers on the other hand argued that the anchorage was at least 17 miles away from the dock area and the ship could not be an arrived ship until she got to the unloading berth in the Birkenhead docks.

Held:

The correct test to be applied, according to Lord Reid, is the time the ship was placed at the immediate and effective disposition of the charterers. The geographical location is of secondary importance. Lord Reid said:

"Before a ship can be said to have arrived at a port she must, if she cannot proceed immediately to a berth, have reached a position within the port where she is at the immediate and effective disposition of the charterer. If she is at a place where waiting ships usually lie, she will be in such a position unless in some extraordinary circumstances proof of which would lie in the charterer. . . .

If the ship is waiting at some other place in the port then it will be for the owner to prove that she is as fully at the disposition of the charterer as she would have been if in the vicinity of the berth for loading or discharge".

The shipowners would have discharged their burden by showing that the ship is placed at the anchorage which is the customary waiting place for such vessels.

The rationale of the case may be examined using a "stages" doctrine applicable to voyage charters. It may be observed that the *voyage* charterparty is composed of mutual duties all of which are built into the four stages of the charterparty:

1. the loading voyage;

2. the loading operation;

3. the carrying voyage; and

4. the discharging operation.

7–118   It is clear that one stage does not commence until the preceding stage has been properly completed. In the case where the ship is required to proceed to a named berth, the shipowner's duty is strict—he must ensure that the ship gets to the agreed berth or dock. But if no berth is available, the voyage stage ends when the ship is moored at a convenient place within the larger port area awaiting the commencement of the loading or unloading operations. According to Lord Diplock in *The Johanna Oldendorff*, the subsequent delay while waiting for a berth does not fall within the voyage stage because that stage has ended. As a matter of the distribution of responsibilities it is trite law in voyage charterparties that the shipowner is solely responsible for the voyage stages but *jointly* and *secondarily* responsible with the charterer for the loading and unloading operations. Once the voyage stage has ended, the ship is placed at the charterer's hands for loading or unloading since this stage is in his primary control and responsibility.

As always the charter might place the waiting risk on the charterers. This is achieved through a clause phrased in the following manner:

"Laytime to commence Wipon/Wibon/Wifpon/Wccon and the Master to have the right to tender notice of readiness . . . "

These acronyms, as translated, are:

- Wipon—whether in port or not;
- Wibon—whether in berth or not;
- Wifpon—whether in free pratique[30] or not;
- Wccon—whether cleared customs or not.

In *Carboex SA v Louis Dreyfus Commodities Suisse SA* [2012] EWCA Civ 838, the court held that the purpose of a Wibon clause in a *berth* charter was to transfer the general risk of congestion from the owner to the charterer, but it was equally true to say that its function was to start the laytime clock running. The two were opposite sides of the same coin—once time started to run, the charterer bore the risk of delay. The same is true where the Wipon clause is used in relation to a port charterparty. However, what is the practical effect of a Wibon clause on a *port* charterparty?

We see such an instance in *Seacrystal Shipping Ltd v Bulk Transport Group Shipping Co Ltd (The Kyzikos)* [1989] 1 Lloyd's Rep. 1. There, two issues were discussed **7–119**

1. whether under the Wibon clause the ship could give a valid notice of readiness to discharge when, on her arrival in the discharging port, a berth was vacant but she was prevented from proceeding to it because of fog; and

2. if so, whether the ship at that place (where she was prevented from going any further) could properly be said to be at the "immediate and effective disposition of the charterers" so as to qualify her as an arrived ship under the port charterparty.

Lord Brandon, in reversing the judgment of the Court of Appeal, held that the Wibon clause should be interpreted as applying only to cases where a berth is not available and not to cases where a berth is available but is unreachable by reason of bad weather (and in that case, fog). This would answer issue 1. in the negative and issue 2. does not therefore need to be addressed. If no valid of readiness can be issued, laytime does not commence. Lord Brandon was careful to point out that it has always been understood by commercial people that "whether in berth or not" referred to the availability of the berth caused by port congestion. There

---

[30] Pratique is a licence given to the ship to enter port upon the master's or ship's agent's confirmation to the port authorities that the ship is free from contagious disease. A ship can signal a request for "pratique" by flying a solid yellow square-shaped flag (the Q flag). Such request can also be forwarded by the ship's agent. There is no general common law duty to obtain free pratique before loading or unloading but where the master has reason to believe that the vessel does not have a clean bill of health, that can give rise to liability. The charterparty, however, may make free pratique a pre-condition to loading and discharge operations. Where that is so, the notice of readiness is linked to free pratique (i.e. notice of readiness would be defective if free pratique had not been obtained by the time the ship should be ready to load) and failure of the ship to obtain free pratique can affect laytime and in turn, result in demurrage (*AET v Arcadia Petroleum* [2010] EWCA Civ 713).

is no custom that it referred to a ship being prevented from docking as a result of bad weather.

Notice of readiness

7–120 "A charterer manifestly wants, if he can get it, a fixed date for the arrival of the ship at the port of loading. He has to make arrangements to bring down the cargo and to have it ready to load when the ship arrives and he wants to know as near as he can what that date is going to be. On the other hand, it is to the interest of the shipowner, if he can have it, to have the date as flexible as possible because of the inevitable delays due to bad weather or other circumstances that there might be in the course of a voyage. He can never be sure that he can arrive at a port on a fixed and certain day. Therefore, in order to accommodate these two views as far as possible it has been the general practice for a long time past to have a clause under which the shipowner, without pledging himself to a fixed day, gives a date in the charterparty of expected readiness, that is the date when he expects that he will be ready to load."

In those simple but classic words in *Evera SA Commercial v North Shipping Co Ltd* [1956] 2 Lloyd's Rep. 367, Devlin J. put his finger on the tension between a shipowner's obligation to proceed to a loading port (duty of due despatch) and his statement about the expected time of the vessel's arrival (duty to give notice of readiness to load).

At common law, the shipowner need only to give reasonable notice of readiness at the port of loading but not the port of discharge. This old rule has now largely been displaced by an express stipulation that notice should be given at both ports. The notice is issued when or after the ship becomes an arrived ship. The shipowner would of course wish to give notice of readiness as soon as possible. The earlier notice is given, the sooner laytime will begin.

7–121 It should be remembered that the notice of readiness and the actual loading or unloading are to be treated separately. If the shipowner fails to give proper notice of readiness, laytime does not run from the actual time the cargo is loaded or unloaded but from the time the notice is finally given (*Pteroti Compania Naviera v National Coal Board* [1958] 1 Q.B. 469). The law as established in *Christensen v Hindustan Steel Ltd* [1971] 1 Lloyd's Rep. 395 is that the notice of readiness cannot be given until the vessel is actually ready to load or discharge. In *Compania de Naviera Nedelka SA v Tradax Internacional SA (The Tres Flores)* [1974] 1 Q.B. 264, the readiness of the ship may be prescribed by contract. In that case the relevant clause read:

"Before tendering notice master has to take necessary measures for holds to be clean, dry, without smell and in every way suitable to receive grain to shippers/ charterers' satisfaction".

The master had issued a notice of readiness as soon as the ship arrived at port on the Monday. The ship had to be fumigated before she could take delivery of the cargo but the inspectors of shipping at the port had been prevented from dealing with the ship by reason of bad weather. The fumigation was only completed a few days later. Lord Denning M.R. held that the fumigation was not a mere preliminary or routine matter. It was an essential step before the ship could be properly said to be ready to load, hence, a notice of readiness could not be issued when that step has yet to be taken.

A statement that a vessel will be ready only at a later date or time will not do. In *Transgrain Shipping BV v Global Transporte Oceanio SA (The Mexico I)* [1990] 1 Lloyd's Rep. 507, the Court of Appeal rejected the shipowners' contention that although the notice of readiness was given at a time when the ship was not physically ready to discharge the cargo of maize, it was an "anticipatory notice" indicating that laytime should run once the ship was *actually* ready to be unloaded. The court held that this would defeat the very purpose of the notice and could not be applied where the unloading (and loading) operations are a matter of joint responsibility between the shipowners and the charterers/shippers. The Court of Appeal then went on to hold that an invalid notice could not start laytime and a second notice must be given before laytime will start. Mustill L.J. described this duty in the following terms:

"Moreover, quite apart from the practical objection to this variant of argument, it does not meet the fundamental objection that the contract provides for laytime to be started by notice (which means a valid notice) and in no other way".

This statement raises some difficulty in the case of *The Petr Schmidt* [1997] 1 Lloyd's Rep. 284. Does it mean that any notice which does not conform to the contract is invalid and as such, a nullity and of no effect?

The Petr Schmidt [1997] 1 Lloyd's Rep. 284   **7–122**
Facts:
The notice of readiness according to the contract of carriage must be given between 0600 and 1700 hours in any day. It was in fact served at 0001 hours. The charterers argued that this was a nullity and a second notice must be given before laytime could start. The shipowners on the other hand argued that although it was not within the contracted hours, it should by necessity be deemed to be operative and effective by 6am on the relevant day.
Held:
Longmore J. rejected the charterers' argument and stated that although it might be correct to say in the light of *The Mexico I* that a notice given outside the contractual hours was invalid, it did not follow that the courts should hold that a premature notice of readiness was a nullity and of no effect. There was no good reason why the notice should not be effective as at the time which the contract fixed for it to be tendered. It was impossible to find any real prejudice in this particular premature notice on the charterers. The ship was for all intents and purposes physically ready. Moreover, the charterers were not prejudiced even if the ship through some freak of circumstance was made not ready at the contractual time of 0600 hours, the notice would be invalid in the traditional sense.

The spirit behind the judgment in *The Petr Schmidt* was an issue of contention in *Glencore Grain Ltd v Flacker Shipping (The MV Happy Day)* [2002] EWCA Civ. 1068.[31]

Glencore Grain Ltd v Flacker Shipping Ltd (The Happy Day) [2002] EWCA Civ 1068   **7–123**
Facts:
The chartered ship was unable to enter Cochin on arrival on September 25, 1998 because she missed the tide. The master however nevertheless issued a notice of readiness. It was

---

[31] See Aspragkathou, "The Happy Day and Invalidity of a Notice of Readiness under English Law" (2007) 38 J.Mar.L. & Com. 191.

obvious that the notice was invalid because as a berth charterparty, the ship had to be berthed before the notice could be given. The ship then berthed the following day. No further notice of readiness was served. Discharge was not completed until Christmas day.

The Commercial Court ruled that no demurrage was payable because no valid notice of readiness was ever given. Langley J. relied on *The Mexico I* [1990] 1 Lloyd's Rep. 507, where Mustill L.J. had stated that where the contract provided for the commencement of laytime to be activated by a valid notice of readiness and "in no other way", that contractual intent could be given effect to. It was not open to the owners to argue that the notice could be treated as "inchoate" which could subsequently be effective when the cargo was or was known to be available for discharge or loading.

Held:

The Court of Appeal allowed the appeal. Potter L.J. agreed with Langley J. that the inchoate notice argument was untenable. However, the doctrine of waiver could be invoked and applied in the circumstances. The charterer (and/or the receivers of the cargo, who for all intents and purposes were to be treated as the charterer's agents) had knowledge of the relevant facts whether to accept or reject the notice of readiness, despite its invalidity. His Lordship reasoned it like this:

> "The owners had served NOR (notice of readiness) upon the receivers' agents . . . at a time shortly before she arrived at berth. Having arrived at berth the vessel was in fact ready to commence the cargo operation required and neither the owners nor the Master received any intimation of rejection or reservation so far as the validity of the NOR was concerned. The charterers were well aware of the matters which the NOR was concerned to convey, namely the arrival of the vessel and its readiness to discharge . . . On an objective construction of those matters, although the charterers were not under a contractual duty to indicate rejection of the NOR, by their failure to do so, coupled with their assent to commencement of discharging operations, they intimated, and a reasonable shipowner would have concluded, that the charterers thereby waived reliance upon any invalidity in the NOR and any requirement for further notice . . . ".

7–124   It is clear from this judgment that the Court of Appeal had struggled to modulate the strictness of principle in *The Mexico I*—it did not seek to argue that *The Mexico I* was incorrectly decided. Indeed, that would be very difficult, especially given the fact that in commercial contracts, where the parties' agreement is clear, that must be given effect to even when it might cause serious hardship to one party. Certainty is important. The present case attempted to circumvent the problem by finding that there was a waiver of the invalid notice. The concept of a waiver is notoriously flexible and depends much on the fairness of the case, rather than any notion of commercial certainty. The conclusion is thus that this is a fair decision but it means that the burden is now very much on charterers and their receivers to respond appropriately and unequivocally to an invalid notice of readiness if they wish to be protected from a claim in demurrage.

What if the charterer receives an early notice of readiness and then orders the vessel to load and does in fact load the ship, all *before* the contractual laytime is to commence? Does this amount to free loading time? Or does laytime start to run at the end of the notice period since the time is in fact used or intended to be used for loading? These were the questions posed in *The Front Commander* [2006] EWCA Civ 944. Naturally, if the contract prohibits an early notice of readiness that would be so enforced. Where it is silent, the court held that it was incorrect to treat the said period as being free loading time. On the contrary, "if a charterer uses a vessel, known to be ready at the time of use, which has been tendered to him by a valid notice of readiness, or by an invalid notice whose invalidity is known, he must expect time to run against him, allowing for any relevant notice time".

The charterer by ordering the vessel to load before contractual laytime must be taken as sanctioning or approving an early commencement of laytime. However it should be remembered that, as Rix L.J. cautioned, all this is "subject to any express contrary agreement". In that case, the court was addressing an amended Asbatankvoy form.

It is also customary to include in the laytime clause, a cancellation clause. This **7–125** is known as a "lay/can" clause.[32] The lay/can period is the time during which loading of the goods could take place under the charter. If this period is exceeded, the shipowner is entitled to cancel the charter and/or claim demurrage (liquidated damages for unlawful detention of the vessel) for the period exceeding the lay/can range.

In *SK Shipping v BP Energy (Asia) Pte Ltd* [2000] 1 All E.R. (Comm) 810, the court held that the lay/can dates were binding on the parties and that although the contract provided that lay/can was subject to acceptance by the loading terminals, that provision could not avail the defendant who had not bothered to ask the terminals whether the dates were suitable (when those dates subsequently turned out to be unacceptable to the terminals).

Inconsistencies between notice of readiness and "reachable on arrival" clauses

In *Nereide SpA di Navigazione v Bulk Oil International Ltd (The Laura Prima)* **7–126** [1982] 1 Lloyd's Rep. 1, the vessel was chartered for a voyage from one safe berth in Libya to two safe ports in Italy. The charterparty provided, inter alia, as follows:

"6. Notice of readiness. Upon arrival at customary anchorage at each port of loading . . . the master . . . shall give the charterer . . . notice . . . that the vessel is ready to load . . . cargo, berth or no berth, and laytime . . . shall commence upon the expiration of 6 hours after receipt of such notice or upon the vessel's arrival in berth whichever first occurs. However, where delay is caused to vessel getting into berth and after giving notice of readiness for any reason over which charterers has no control, such delay shall not count as used laytime."

and

"9. Safe berthing—shifting. The vessel shall load . . . any safe place or wharf, or along side vessels . . . reachable on her arrival, which shall be designated and procured by the Charterer . . . . "

---

[32] A specimen lay/can clause might be had in cl.5, SHELLTIME 4 Form: "The vessel shall not be delivered to Charterers before . . . and Charterers shall have the option of cancelling this charter if the vessel is not ready and at their disposal on or before . . . ". On the relevance of lay/can clauses in international sales, see paras 2–049—2–099.

Clause 9 is commonly called a "reachable on arrival" clause. The ship arrived in Libya and notice of readiness was tendered but she was unable to proceed to a berth due to overcrowding. It remained so for two weeks. The charterers tried to rely on cl.6 to prevent laytime from running. The shipowners countered that cl.9 was breached since they had not found a berth which was reachable on arrival of the ship. The House of Lords held that cl.9 did prevail over cl.6 and that cl.9, therefore, required the charterers to nominate a berth which was reachable on the vessel's arrival. Lord Brandon said:

> "'Reachable on arrival' is a well-known phrase and means precisely what it says. If a berth cannot be reached on arrival, the warranty is broken unless there is some relevant protecting exception. . . . The berth is required to have two characteristics: it has to be safe and it has also to be reachable on arrival."

It should be noted that the rule established by *The Laura Prima* applies when a berth is not reachable on arrival for any reason, not just congestion (see *The Sea Queen* [1988] 1 Lloyd's Rep. 500 where there were no tugs available, and *The Fjordaas* [1988] 1 Lloyd's Rep. 336 where the weather was bad).

Suspension or interruption of laytime

7–127   In general, without contractual provisions to the contrary, laytime could be suspended or properly interrupted by any event which is outside the control of the charterer and effectively prevents loading or discharging from carrying on. It could also be suspended if the shipowner is himself responsible for the disruption—for example, where he removes the ship from the loading berth without a reasonable cause as in *The Fontevivo* [1975] 1 Lloyd's Rep. 339. Similarly, in *Alphapoint Shipping Ltd v Rotem Amfert Negev Ltd (The Agios Dimitrios)* [2004] EWHC 2232, the court held that the charterer was entitled to set off against the shipowner's claim for demurrage because the cargo holds were contaminated and laytime had been extended as a result of the suspension of loading for the holds to be cleaned properly. The court also considered that although the charterer had accepted the shipowner's notice of readiness to load without demur, that was not a waiver of their right to argue that it was the shipowner's fault which resulted in an extension of laytime. It is also not unusual for the parties to agree to the splitting of any demurrage payable as a result of any problems arising during loading and discharge as a negotiating chip.[33] Proof however can sometimes be problematic.[34]

In *Stolt Tankers Inc v Landmark Chemicals SA (The Stolt Spur)* [2002] 1 Lloyd's Rep. 786 the Commercial Court identified and affirmed another incident which had the effect the interrupting laytime, other than the shipowner's fault. In that case, the court upheld the arbitrators' finding that laytime had been interrupted when the vessel which was waiting for the charterer's berth to become available had been engaged in cargo operations in respect of another

---

[33] See, e.g. *Portolana Compania Naviera Ltd v Vitol SA Inc* [2004] EWCA Civ 864 where the Asbatankvoy form used provided that demurrage was to be halved where any delay during discharge of cargo by the consignee/receiver was caused by a breakdown of equipment.

[34] *Triton Navigation Ltd v Vitol SA* [2003] EWCA Civ 1715.

charterparty. The vessel could not berth because of port congestion. Notice of readiness was given and thus, laytime commenced. It then left the waiting anchorage for six days to discharge cargo under a concurrent charterparty and to have its tanks cleaned. The charterer argued that laytime was interrupted and in order for the shipowner to be entitled to demurrage, he was under an obligation to have the vessel ready and available to load or discharge (*Voest Alpine Intertrading v Ellis Shipping Corp* [1992] 2 Lloyd's Rep. 109). The shipowner rejected this so-called "wider principle" contending that there had to be fault on the part of the owners before laytime could be said to have been interrupted or suspended. Andrew Smith J. rejected the shipowner's submission taking a purposive approach to the issue:

> "Demurrage is payable . . . because the shipowner, having agreed freight to cover the voyage and an agreed time for loading and discharging processes, 'faces serious losses if the processes take longer than he had bargained for and the earning of freight on the ship's next engagement is postponed' and the charterer agrees to compensate him for those losses by way of demurrage. If a vessel is not available for the charterers' cargo operations but being used by the owners for their own purposes, there is no reason that they should pay compensation. She is not being detained by the charterers".

It is submitted that the "wider principle", if taken without qualification, could very well result in the charterer striving hard to find issue with whether during laytime the shipowner had been able to put the ship to some economic use. The question is what constitutes the shipowner's benefit during the time the vessel was not used by the charterer—in *The Stolt Spur*, cleaning the tanks was treated as one such benefit. What if the ship was surveyed for minor deficiencies, or was treated for rust control, etc? Are these activities for the benefit of the shipowner to the extent that laytime would be deemed to have been interrupted? Such a state of affairs surely is unhelpful, to both charterer and shipowner.

It is customary for the parties to make express provisions on when laytime **7–128** might be suspended and what implications that would have for either party as a matter of good risk management. The charterparty may, for example, provide that laytime is suspended in the event that the port is congested, or strikes, or bad weather, or riots, etc. It should be remembered that there is nothing at law preventing the parties from agreeing to a wide suspension of laytime clause—it is thus permissible to provide that "laytime may be suspended in any event beyond the control of the charterers". In *Frontier International Shipping Corp v Swissmarine Corp Inc* [2005] EWHC 8 the charterparty provided that "in case of strikes, lockout, civil commotions or other causes beyond the control of the *consignee* which delayed the discharging" (emphasis added), such time would not count towards laytime. The arbitrators found in favour of the shipowner's claim against the charterer for demurrage holding that although the strike by the consignee's employees fell within the clause and could not have been avoided by charterer, it was not beyond the consignee's control. The Commercial Court agreed with the arbitrator stating that the natural reading of the clause was that the words "beyond the control of the consignee" applied not only to "any other causes or accidents" but also to the specified events of strikes, lockouts and civil commotions. The court added that the operation of the exceptions from laytime depended on the events or causes being beyond the control of the consignee *not* *the charterer.* If the parties had intended to focus on the role of the charterer at the discharge port, they could have amended the contract to demonstrate that. It is always a question of fact whether the consignee was responsible for causing the strike.

Such a clause will only be subject to the rule of strict construction as set out in *Photo Productions v Securicor Ltd* [1980] 2 W.L.R. 283 and the *contra proferentem* rule (if the clause contains an ambiguity). In *Cero Navigation Corp v Jean Lion & Cie (The Solon)* [2000] C.L.C. 593, the owners had chartered their vessel, The Solon, to the charterers under a standard Sugar Charterparty 1969 for a voyage from Paranagua, Brazil to Algiers with a cargo of sugar. The ship arrived at Paranagua on July 30, 1996 but did not commence loading until September 8, 1996. Loading was not completed until September 26, 1996. There was an underlying factual dispute as to whether the loading port was affected by strikes and if so, when the strike occurred. The charterparty contained a clause providing for strikes and force majeure as *general* exceptions of liability under the charter. The issue was whether if the strike had occurred during laytime, laytime would be suspended until the strike had ended. The arbitrators concluded that the relevant stipulation, cl.28, operated so as to interrupt laytime in the event of a strike or other disruption, delaying the loading or discharging of the vessel.

The owners contended that as a matter of principle, general exception clauses which were claimed to operate as exception clauses for laytime and demurrage had to be clearly expressed if they were to have that effect. Such clauses were subject to the principle that an ambiguous clause was no protection where the issue was the interruption or laytime of liability for demurrage. They relied on *The Kalliopi A* [1988] 1 Lloyd's Rep. 101, *The Forum Craftsman* [1991] 1 Lloyd's Rep. 81 and *Voest Alpine Intertrading v Ellis Shipping Corp (The Lefthero)* [1992] 2 Lloyd's Rep. 169.

7–129   The owners' appeal against the arbitrator's decision was allowed by Thomas J. As a matter of principle, derived from *Photo Production Ltd v Securicor Transport Ltd* [1980] 2 W.L.R. 283, the court felt that it could not be right that less clarity was required to relieve the charterers from their primary obligation to load within laytime than the clarity required to relieve them from their secondary obligation to pay demurrage for failing to do so. The issue was whether the clause excused the charterer from his obligations under the charterparty—during laytime there was the primary obligation to load the vessel within the laydays and after expiry of the laydays, although the primary obligation continued there was the secondary obligation to pay demurrage for breach of the obligation to load within the laydays. Although the provision was wide enough to provide an exception to *laytime*, it was clear that the clause was not intended to be an exception to the *running of laytime*. The charterers could not rely on a general exception clause for a specific cause. Precise words are needed to show that laytime could be suspended.

Demurrage

7–130   Demurrage is primarily to be paid by the charterer. Again, as with all common law duties in the charterparty, it may be varied by contract. The charterparty may stipulate, especially when the charterer "sells" shipping space on the vessel to other shippers of goods, that the shippers shall themselves be responsible for demurrage since the shipment of the goods is their concern. Where this is the arrangement, the bill of lading issued to these shippers must make it clear that freight and demurrage are payable as per charter i.e. the duty of the shippers is consistent with the original duty in the charter. A cesser clause in the charterparty will usually stipulate that the charterer's liability shall cease under the charterparty upon the cargo being loaded. As with before, the quid pro quo is that the shipowner shall have a shipowner's lien on the goods for freight and demurrage.

The demurrage clause may also provide for its own suspension when certain events occur. Such terms, as to be expected, will be interpreted in a commercial way. In *Carboex SA v Louis Dreyfus Commodities Suisse SA* [2012] EWCA Civ 838, for example, the charterers were held to be able to rely on an exception in the contract which stopped time for demurrage from running when the delay was caused by strike action. In that case, the delay in question was caused by congestion. Congestion on its own would not have stopped time for demurrage from running, but because the congestion was the after-effect of a devastating strike at the port, the court ruled that the charterers were entitled to succeed.

The process of construction is to give effect to the presumed intention of the parties and to prevent an absurd outcome. In *The Miramar* [1984] A.C. 676 for example, the House of Lords had to consider whether the incorporation of a charterparty in a bill of lading was effective to incorporate laytime and discharging provisions which made demurrage payable by the "Charterer". If the incorporation of such clauses was to be effective, then the word "Charterer" would have to be manipulated so as to read "bill of lading holder". In declining to manipulate the language and thus to give effect to the incorporation of such provisions, Lord Diplock said this:

"My Lords, I venture to assert that no business man who had not taken leave of his senses would intentionally enter into a contract which exposed him to a potential liability of this kind; and this, in itself, I find to be an overwhelming reason for not indulging in verbal manipulation of the actual contractual words used in the charterparty so as to give to them this effect when they are treated as incorporated in the bill of lading. I may add that to do so would raise a whole host of questions as to how the liability is to operate as between different consignees of different parts of the cargo, to which questions no attempt has been made to vouchsafe any answer, let alone a plausible one. To give some examples: is any personal liability for demurrage incurred by consignees of cargo which has been discharged before the expiry of laytime? If the discharge of a consignee's cargo takes place after the vessel is on demurrage is his liability to pay demurrage limited to the amount of demurrage accrued after the expiry of laytime and up to the time when the discharge of his part of the cargo is complete? Is each consignee liable for all demurrage accrued while his cargo remains on board? Is the liability of each consignee to pay demurrage several? If the shipowner chooses to sue one consignee of part of the cargo for the full amount of demurrage has that consignee any right of contribution against consignees of other parts of the cargo and, if so, against which of them and upon what basis?"

Demurrage could only be claimed by a contracting carrier, not an actual **7–131** carrier, unless specifically permitted by contract. In *Electrosteel Castings Ltd v*

Scan-Trans Shipping & Chartering Sdn Bhd [2002] EWHC 1993, S argued that
they were entitled to claim demurrage for detention from the claimant cargo
interest. However, the Commercial Court found that as they had merely
contracted as "agents for the carrier", they were not the contracting carrier
entitled to claim demurrage. They had signed and declared in the signature box
in the booking note "as agents only". From the facts, the evidence was unclear
as to whether they did intend to act merely as agents but although the court
permitted S to adduce other documentary evidence to prove otherwise, it was not
prepared to countenance a different inference from the clear words in the booking
note (constituting the contract).

Demurrage, like freight, can only be claimed against the charterer or the
consignee or indorsee of the bill of lading. In *Evergreen Marine Corp v Aldgate
Warehouse (Wholesale) Ltd* [2003] EWHC 667 (Comm), the carrier brought an
action for demurrage against A, the intended consignee of the cargo. Although
the bill of lading had named A as "notify party", it had never been transferred
to A. The court ruled that the shippers were the original contracting party and the
carrier should pursue any claim for demurrage against them, instead of A, as A
had never been indorsed and delivered the bill of lading.

Given the fact that demurrage clauses as agreed damages clauses, in some
respect, tend to oust the court's jurisdiction, the court would ensure that their
invocation is carefully and closely constrained. Any procedural requirement and
time bar provisions to the owner's claim for demurrage under the charterparty
will be strictly enforced. In *Waterfront Shipping v Trafigura (The Sabrewing)*
[2007] EWHC 2482, for example, the charterparty required the owner to submit
pumping logs signed by properly authorised persons within 90 days when
submitting a claim for demurrage. That was not done. Only comparable but
unsigned surveys were submitted. Gloster J. held that that was not enough and
thus, the claim for demurrage was time barred. As to the argument that the de
minimis defence should apply, Her Ladyship held:

> "[A] real commercial purpose and importance in requiring a signed pumping
> log to support a claim in these circumstances for additional pumping time in
> excess of 24 hours, i.e. to prove that they had maintained the required average
> pressure throughout the discharge and that the fault lay with the terminal. The
> signature of a responsible officer of the Vessel was obviously important to
> show that such a person was prepared to put his name to the document to
> confirm its accuracy, to authenticate it and to prove its provenance . . . ".

Her Ladyship also expressed the view that where a document is specifically
required by the contract, it is not for the court to question its necessity.

Payment of demurrage and the *sale* contract

7-132   As between the parties to the sale contract, it is sometimes provided that one
party shall bear the payment of demurrage. This can arise when the seller acts
either as the buyer's agent in securing the contract of carriage, or where the buyer
expressly agrees to pay demurrage.[35] At the outset, it should be pointed out that
such a contractual device is permissible even if the demurrage clause in the sale

---

[35] *Ireland v Livingston* (1861) LR 5 HL 395.

contract is in excess of the seller's own liability for demurrage under the charterparty; as Lord Akinson said in *Houlder Bros v The Commissioners of Public Works* [1908] A.C. 276:

"There is, however, no rule of law that the vendor in a CIF contract may not secure for himself a profit under a demurrage clause contained in it. Neither is there any indisputable presumption of law that the parties to such a contract did not intend that he should receive such a profit".

Problems of construction can nonetheless arise because of the close association that clause in the sale contract has with the carriage contract. The principal question is to what extent is the demurrage clause in the contract of sale an indemnity clause, that is to say, are they dependent on the seller's actual liability for demurrage under the charterparty? A starting point is that laytime and demurrage clauses in the contract of sale must always be construed in that context—that is to say, the sale context.

Secondly, it is vital not to approach the demurrage clause in the sale contract with any presumption that it should either be an indemnity or an independent provision. The clause should be construed in its commercial background without reference to any particular or pre-conceived presumption of intent. In *FAL Oil Co Ltd v Petronas Trading Corp Sdn Bhd (The Devon)* [2004] EWCA Civ 822, the Court of Appeal held that that commercial context included the scope of any reference to or incorporation of the demurrage provisions of any charterparty. However, it went on to state that in the absence of any such reference, the natural inference should be that the sale contract constituted an independent code. In that case, the sale contract provided for demurrage "as per charterparty per day pro rata". The issue was whether the clause in the sale contract operated as an indemnity (that is to say, the payment is only payable when actual liability for demurrage has been settled) or an obligation to pay irrespective altogether of what the sellers' position or responsibilities may be, if in fact the vessel is kept on demurrage (a pre-estimate of potential loss). The majority of the Court of Appeal, however, found that the sale contract had been made without the knowledge of the charterparty and independently of the charterparty. The demurrage provision in the contract of sale was not to operate as an indemnity but as an independent code in its own right.[36] An independent provision can be justified as a genuine pre-estimate of the receiving party's exposure. The position is that although the demurrage clause in the contract of sale can be different and indeed higher than the seller's actual liability for demurrage, if it is excessive and punitive (or perhaps where there is collusion between the seller and the carrier to provide for an unreasonably hefty demurrage rate), the court would strike it down as a penalty.[37]

In an FOB contract, where the buyer acts as the shipper, it is open to the parties to agree in the contract of sale that the seller will pay demurrage if he takes excessively long to load. It is the position of the Court of Appeal in the following case that although the laytime in question is normally provided for in the contract

---

[36] There is dicta in *Glencore Energy v Sonol Israel* [2011] EWHC 2756 (Comm) that although we should not approach the sale demurrage or laytime clause with preconceived notions, in many cases it is usually a free-standing provision rather than an indemnity.

[37] *Gill & Duffus SA v Rionda Futures Ltd* [1994] 2 Lloyd's Rep. 67.

of sale and whilst it may often coincide with laytime in the contract of carriage, it is to be construed in the context of the sale contract.

7-133 *Kronos Worldwide Ltd v Sempra Oil Trading SARL* [2004] EWCA Civ 03
Facts:
K had contracted to sell gasoil cargoes to S on "FOB one safe port/berth" every month for a period of time. The price was to be secured by a letter of credit. The sale contract provided for a 15-day loading range to be mutually narrowed to three days with a minimum of five days between cargoes. As regards a shipment in June 2001, S nominated a vessel and stated that it intended to narrow the vessel's arrival to June 28–30. K was unable to meet that shipment slot because of problems at the refinery. The ship arrived on June 28 and a notice of readiness was issued. K asked S to open a letter of credit which they did on July 5/6. Loading then commenced on July 9 and was completed on July 11. S claimed that laytime ran from June 28–30, after which the ship was on demurrage for 11 days. K argued that as their duty to load could not commence until the letter of credit had been opened, laytime too could not commence until a reasonable time after the opening of the letter of credit. K submitted therefore that they were not liable for demurrage.
Held:
It was obvious that in the law of international sale, the letter of credit had to be opened in time, which S failed to do. The question, however, was what effect that had on when laytime commenced. The lower court had thought that to equate K's duty to load with the commencement of laytime would involve

> "an impermissible elision of S's obligation for demurrage under the charterparty at which the demurrage provision in the contract is aimed with the separate contractual obligation between S and K arising from S's failure promptly to open the letter of credit".

The Court of Appeal made clear that the provision of a letter of credit should be regarded as a condition precedent to any obligation on the seller's part to load. Thus, as far as the contract of sale was concerned, laytime depended on the opening of the letter of credit. As far as the contract of carriage is concerned, though, the provision of a letter of credit is irrelevant. The court said that there was no incongruity in recognising that laytime under the sale contract could begin at a different time to laytime under the charterparty entered into between the seller and the carrier. The fact that the running of laytime under the sale contract depended on the letter of credit, whereas laytime under charterparty did not, derived from the differences between the two contracts. The lower court's view was that the laytime provisions under all these contracts should be made to operate as far as possible back-to-back, even though the sale contract provisions relating to laytime and demurrage were not couched as an indemnity against liability under the charterparty. Such a view unfortunately overlooked the fundamental difference introduced by the require-ment that the buyer provide a letter of credit which, as a matter of law, operates as a condition precedent to the seller's duty to load.

Interruption of demurrage and laytime stipulations

7-134 The rule at common law is that "once on demurrage, always on demurrage". This means that as soon as laytime has expired and demurrage liability has commenced, it would run continuously through periods or days normally excepted from laytime, such as public holidays, Sundays (or Fridays, in some Islamic countries, bad weather working days, etc). Other laytime exceptions will also cease to operate—the period for which demurrage is payable will not suffer any breaks or interruptions. The rule is not displaced by a strike exception clause in the charter suspending laytime, for example, as is seen in *The Lefthero* [1992] 2 Lloyd's Rep. 109. In that case, it was discussed whether demurrage might be suspended for those periods when the port was on strike. The House of Lords said no. If the rule once on demurrage, always on demurrage is to be disapplied, clear language must be used in the charter. The rule however does not apply mutatis mutandis to laytime—there is no general rule that once laytime has commenced it could not be suspended (*Cero Navigation Corp v Jean Lion & Cie (The Solon)* [2000] C.L.C. 593).

Demurrage is usually stated to cover a particular period of time—in our example above (cl.7 GENCON Charter) it was for a period of 10 days. If the ship is detained longer than the 10 days, the common law rules on damages will apply.

Time Charters

Many of the duties on the carrier at common law will apply to both voyage and time charters.[38] However, it should not be forgotten that the time charter performs a different commercial function compared to the voyage charter. The time charter market is very complex and shipowners and charterers would not leave it to providence for the ascertainment of their rights and obligations. Time charters are subject to very extensive and careful negotiations between the parties but much depends on the length of time the charterer intends to use the vessel. In short-term charters, the charterer would approach a shipbroker[39] who then circulates the request to his shipowner clients specifically and also to the wider market through daily circulars in shipping press around the world. Responses (called "indications") are then received, processed and passed on to the charterer. The owner's response or offer is only valid for a very short time, normally 24 hours. During this time, the charterer may accept or make a counter offer or wait for the owners to make a further offer. In the case of a longer time charter, the charterer would not use the services of a shipbroker, preferring instead to deal directly with the shipowners. The charterer will have very specific ideas as to the type of ship he wants and the very precise knowledge of the charter status of the individual ships meeting that description in the market. As such, the market

7–135

---

[38] In *The Elli and The Frixos* [2008] EWCA Civ 584, it was argued that in a time charter the owner's duty to provide a seaworthy ship was different from that of an owner in a voyage charter. The Court of Appeal rejected the argument holding that such a proposition was not supported by case law (*Cheikh Boutros Selim El-Khoury v Ceylon Shipping Lines (The Madeleine)* (1967) 2 Lloyd's Rep. 224 Q.B.D. (Comm) and *Alfred C Toepfer Schiffahrtsgesellschaft mbH v Tossa Marine Co Ltd (The Derby)* (1985) 2 Lloyd's Rep. 325 CA (Civ Div)). It is submitted too that in terms of good commercial sense, the owner of a time chartered vessel should be made responsible for ensuring the vessel complies with mandatory regulations, both physical and documentary. After all, he has the more permanent and significant interest and responsibility for the vessel. A charterer (possibly other than a bareboat charterer) has a much more limited interest both in terms of time and control.

[39] Most charterparties negotiated by the chartering brokers would contain a clause that commission is payable to the brokers by the shipowners. Such clauses can now be enforced against the shipowners by the charterers or the brokers themselves. As for the latter, they are entitled to do so by virtue of s.1 of the Contracts (Rights of Third Parties) Act 1999 as third party beneficiary under the contract. That would also include a right to take the shipowners to arbitration under an arbitration clause in the main charterparty. See especially *Nisshin Shipping Co Ltd v Cleaves & Co Ltd* [2003] EWHC 2602.

search will be very focused and narrow. Once contract is made with an appropriate shipowner, lengthy and careful negotiations will commence.

Some of the more common clauses in the time charter deal with:

1. description of the ship;

2. the charter period; delivery and re-delivery terms;

3. employment and indemnity; and

4. hire and off-hire terms.

As regards the description of the vessel, it is seen in case law that although the courts have always stressed the importance of the descriptive words, the term is not a condition, but a warranty, generally.[40] The accuracy of the descriptive words is to be assessed at the time the vessel is delivered.[41] It is not a continuing duty; indeed some standard form time charters expressly provide that the shipowner does not undertake to warrant the accuracy of the descriptive words during the period of the charter. Further, many charters would also make the obligation less stringent by stipulating some leeway in the technical specifications—for example, instead of requiring 20 knots in the speed warranty, it would be "around 20 knots".

7-136   The contract will obviously provide for the charter period—it is a business reality that it is not always possible to prescribe precisely the ship's movements. That being the case, the courts would normally allow some allowance when construing the time provisions—especially those in relation to redelivery of the vessel. Time would not normally be presumed to be of the essence.[42] That said, where the time charter makes it clear that it shall be of the essence, the court would give it that effect accordingly.[43] It is also open to the parties to agree on the margin allowed. In *The Aspa Maria* [1976] 2 Lloyd's Rep. 643, for example, the charter period was stated to be "6 months, 30 days more or less" and the charterer had an option to extend the contract for a further period of "6 months, 30 days more or less". The Court of Appeal held that it could not have been the intention of the parties that the charterers should have the benefit of two tolerance periods in respect of one delivery. The charterers had extended the 6-month term by another 6 months but the court refused to give them a 60-day margin. The correct construction was "12 months, 30 days more or less", not "12 months, 60 days more or less".

---

[40] *French v Newgass* (1878) 3 CPD 163; *Cosmos Bulk Transport Inc v China National Foreign Trade Transportation Co* [1978] 1 Lloyd's Rep. 53; of course as a matter of contract, the term can be made of the essence, although commercial practice would suggest that given the strength of the shipowners and the narrow market, this is not easily achieved. In *Bayoil v Seawind Tankers Corp* [2000] EWHC 213, the court considered that a warranty that the ship "will" be able to prosecute the voyage at a speed of 11 knots could not be taken as an absolute undertaking.

[41] *Cosmos Bulk Transport Inc v China National Foreign Trade Transportation Co* [1978] 1 Lloyd's Rep. 53; note that the former common law rule was that the accuracy was only warranted at the time of the contract.

[42] *The Berge Tasta* [1975] 1 Lloyd's Rep. 422.

[43] *Watson v Merryweather* (1913) 12 Asp. 353, but it might be argued that, unless the words used are absolutely explicit, it would seem less than rational for the parties to agree to a precise time frame for the re-delivery of the ship given the uncertainties and unpredictability of a ship's movement. As a matter of construction, the court would take such commercial realities into consideration.

In *Petroleo Brasileiro SA v Kriti Akti Shipping Co SA* [2004] EWCA Civ 116, the contract provided that the hire period was

"11 months, 15 days more or less in Charterers' option . . . notwithstanding [which] if the vessel was upon a voyage *at the expiry of the period of the charter*, the charterers shall have use of the vessel at the same rate . . . for such extended time as may be necessary for the completion of the voyage" (emphasis added)

and that the charterers were entitled to add any off-hire time to the extension. The charterers then gave instructions to the ship for a voyage which could not be completed until well after the charter period. They then gave notice to the shipowners that they needed to extend the hire period for 36 (being off-hire time) days plus 15 days. The shipowners objected and insisted on charging a higher rate of hire. The court ruled that the phrase "at the expiry of the period of the charter" meant that the charterers were entitled to further use of the ship for 15 days until it completed the last instruction. The clause in question was different to the one in *The Aspa Maria* as it took as its starting point the time charter period and it applied whenever the vessel was on a voyage at the expiry of that period. Its effect was to enable the charterer to complete a pre-existing voyage not to order the vessel to prosecute a new voyage. Therefore, it meant that the charterers were entitled to 11 months, plus off-hire days, plus 15 days.

Naturally, exceeding the tolerance margins allowed would be a breach of contract.

Where the charterer redelivers the vessel to the owners late, they will be in **7–137** breach of contract. As to the quantum of damages, the House of Lords in *Transfield Shipping Inc v Mercator Shipping (The Achilleas)* [2008] UKHL 48 made clear that the correct test has to be the remoteness of damage rule in *Hadley v Baxendale* (1854) 9 Exch 341. The question there was whether the owners were entitled to recover damages for any loss of profit as the ship could not be made available to another charterer as a result of the ship being redelivered late. Lord Hoffmann thought that it was a matter of law as to whether there was assumption of responsibility for the type of loss in question (lost profit on the next fixture/ charter) by the charterer in the context of the prevailing market expectations. Lord Rodger, on the other hand, placed emphasis on a factual question—the fact that the freight market at the time of the late redelivery was so volatile that such a type of loss could not have been in the reasonable contemplation of the parties at the time the made the contract. Lord Rodger's position is clearly more consistent with the precedent in *Hadley v Baxendale*.

The parties are bound by the charter period; any termination of the charter before expiry of the charter period will give rise to damages. However, the parties may prescribe in the time charter events or times whereby one party may cancel the charter by giving appropriate notice. These requirements must be strictly complied with, as they allow the premature termination of the contractual relationship. Where there is a repudiatory breach of the charter period, it has been held by the House of Lords in *The Golden Victory* [2007] UKHL 7 that in quantifying the damages it is appropriate to take into account an event occurring subsequently to the termination, even though it was not clear that such an event would occur at the time of termination. In that case, the charter period was seven years. The charterers wrongfully repudiated the contract by redelivering the ship before the expiry of the charter period. The owners accepted the repudiation and claimed damages. However, soon after the redelivery was made, hostilities broke out involving the United States, the United Kingdom and Iraq. There was a clause allowing the parties to cancel the charter in the event of war involving those named countries. Thus, if the charterers had not cancelled when they did, they could have relied on the war cancellation clause to terminate the contract. The question for the court was:

"If after an accepted repudiation, an unexpected event occurred which meant that the original charter would not have run its full term, are damages still measured by reference to that full term, or by taking into account that the owners would in fact only have had the benefit of the charter for a shorter term?".

The majority of the House of Lords held that the fact that the charterers could have subsequently cancelled the contract was a relevant factor to the question of quantum (see also *The Seaflower* [2000] 2 Lloyd's Rep. 37; *The Mihalis Angelos* [1971] 1 Q.B. 164). It should be stressed that the role of the law on damages in contract was to ensure that the to restore the injured party to the same position he would have been in but for the breach, not substantially to improve upon it. Lord Scott, thus, held:

"[T]he Owners had lost a charterparty which contained a provision that would enable the Charterers to terminate the charterparty if a certain event happened. The event did happen. It happened before the damages had been assessed .... The contractual benefit... the Owners... were deprived [of] by the repudiatory breach, was the right to receive the hire rate during the currency of the charterparty. The termination of the charterparty under clause 33 [the war cancellation clause] would necessarily have brought to an end that right".

7–138   The House of Lords was clearly concerned that when awarding damages for breach of contract, the claimant should be compensated but not financially enhanced. Factual realities should be taken into account. That said, this is a novel issue for the courts and it remains to be seen how it will be developed in the future. That is especially interesting because it might be properly argued that the interests of certainty are better served by a legal principle which the loss crystallises at the time of acceptance of repudiation. That would enable the parties to know where they are and dis-enable them from waiting to see if something helpful turns up. How far should certainty be sacrificed?[44]

The general rule of damages is that damages for repudiation of a charter would normally be assessed on the basis of the difference between the contract rate and the market rate for the vessel for the balance of the charterparty period, (*Koch Marine Inc v d'Amica Societa di Navigazione arl (The Elena d'Amico)* [1980] 1 Lloyd's Rep. 75). However this only works when there is an available market. During the economic crisis in 2008–2010, market conditions were so severely depressed that it was not always possible to identify an available market. In *Zodiac Maritime Agencies Limited v Fortescue Metals Group Limited* [2010]

---

[44] See Treitel, "Assessment of damages for wrongful repudiation" (2007) 123 L.Q.R. 9.

EWHC 903 (Comm), David Steel J. took the view that an available market is one where there are available sellers and available buyers.

Where, at the date of termination, there is no market for the unexpired period and the market is only revived at a much later date, damages have to be assessed by reference to the actual loss of the owner (*Glory Wealth Shipping v Korea Line Corporation (The MV Wren)* [2011] EWHC 1819 (Comm)). The fact that the market is revived at a later stage is irrelevant (*Zodiac Maritime Agencies Limited v Fortescue Metals Group Limited*). Assessment of such damages would be subject to the usual rules, including the rule about mitigation of damage. The owner who had unreasonably failed to mitigate their losses would be stopped from claiming their self-induced loss. The question is always about how reasonable the owner conducts himself in the circumstances and prevailing market conditions. In *Isabella Shipowner v Shagang Shipping* [2012] EWHC 1077 (Comm), for example, the court was sympathetic to the owners, stating that with 94 days left of a five-year time charter in a difficult market where a substitute time charter was impossible, and trading on the spot market[45] was very difficult, it would be impossible to characterise the owner's stance in wishing to maintain the charter and a right to hire as unreasonable.[46]

Thus far we have been considering the case of an early re-delivery, which of course is a repudiation of the charter. However, it is not unusual for the ship to be re-delivered late. It is entirely reasonable for the parties to pre-agree the liquidated damages payable in the event of a late re-delivery. The amount stipulated, however, must not be punitive; if it is, it will be struck down as a penalty clause (*Lansat Shipping co Ltd v Glencore Grain BV (The Paragon)* [2009] EWHC 551 (Comm)). **7–139**

As re-delivery of the vessel at the end of the hire period is a term of the contract, it is not inconceivable that intervening circumstances might make performance of the term impossible. Where that is the case, the charterer could quite legitimately claim that the contract is frustrated and he should not be held in breach of the re-delivery term. The courts are, however, slow to find for frustration because delays in hire contracts are not an unusual commercial risk. Indeed, in *The Sea Angel* [2006] EWHC 1713 Gross J. held that although the fact that the ship was prevented (unreasonably) from leaving port by the authorities at the end of the hire period led to a serious delay for the re-delivery of the ship, the contract could not be said to have been frustrated. The reason was that as the ship was hired to carry out part of the salvage, it was quite a normal and ordinary risk that the salvor's ships, in the course of salvage operations, might be detained unreasonably by port authorities. Gross J. expressed satisfaction with the decision saying:

---

[45] The two contract types in tanker, bulk and commodity shipping are spot charters and time charters. On the spot market, the price fluctuates more or less from day-to-day. The price, "the freight rate", can vary considerably over a short period of time. On the time charter market, ships are contracted for a longer period, normally over a period of a few years, usually at a fixed price. The time charter market, therefore, frames the financial returns in a longer perspective while the spot market reflects the market situation here and now. Where prices on the spot market are high or increasing, shipping companies would be most unwilling to tie-up tonnage on long-term time charters.

[46] It should be noted that the court re-affirmed the understanding that the rule of mitigation of damages in general contract law (as espoused in *White & Carter (Councils) Ltd v McGregor* [1962] A.C. 413) is applicable to the law on charterparties. Only where the circumstances are so unusual and exceptional can the rule in *White & Carter* be departed from.

"[I]n a salvage operation of this nature, it seems to me (subject always to any specific contractual provision) more satisfactory that salvors should assume the risk of unreasonable detention of their chartered-in vessels. Such risks can always be incorporated in the price for the services and passed on [contractually]".

Much depends on the facts—there, we have a time charter to perform a salvage related operation. Would a similar decision be reached in more conventional time charters?

Employment and indemnity clause

7-140   Under the time charter, the charterer is to have full use and employment of the vessel. The extent of this right is set out in an employment clause; the clause requires the shipmaster to obey the instructions of the charterer as regards the use of the ship. The consideration for the shipowner agreeing to the employment clause is the charterer offering, in an indemnity clause, to indemnify the shipowner for any loss or damage suffered by the latter as a result of his master obeying the instructions of the charterer. A typical clause might look like this:

"The Master shall be under the orders and direction of Charterers as regards employment of the vessel, agency or other arrangements . . . Charterers hereby indemnify Owners against all consequences or liabilities that may arise . . . from the Master otherwise complying with Charterers' or their agents' orders . . . ".

For example, if the charterer orders the master to carry dangerous goods without prior consent of the shipowner, and the goods cause damage to property and crew, the charterer must indemnify the shipowner for such damage. Similarly, if the charterer requires the master to release goods without seeking the presentation of a bill, the shipowner who becomes liable to the true owner (holder of the bill) can claim to be indemnified by the charterer.

An important issue around the employment and indemnity clause arose in *The Kos* [2012] UKSC 17 as to how narrowly the clause should be construed. Here, it may be recalled, the shipowner had lawfully terminated the time charter but as the goods were still onboard, returned and re-landed the goods to shore. They then claimed compensation for the cost associated by having to unload. One ground of the claim was on the law of bailment[47] and the second was on the basis that under the indemnity clause, the shipowners were entitled to be indemnified for those costs incurred. The Supreme Court held by a majority that the clause was wide enough to assist the shipowner. It is an essential point of principle that if the costs had been incurred because the owners were merely doing what they were paid hire to do, there could be no indemnification. However, here as Lord Sumption, who gave the lead speech, held, the need to discharge the cargo under these circumstances was "not an ordinary incident of the charter or a risk they had assumed" and therefore was liable to fall within the scope of the indemnity.

---

[47] Discussed earlier in paras 7–011—7–015.

Second, and most significantly, His Lordship concluded that the "effective **7–141** cause" of shipowners' loss (that is the additional days in port and consumed bunkers) was the charterers' instruction to load the vessel, *not* the shipowners' later decision to exercise their right to withdraw the vessel upon non-payment. In so finding, the majority overturned the lower courts' decisions that the withdrawal of the vessel was an independent cause of the loss which had the effect of breaking the chain of causation.

Lord Mance dissented strongly, stating that a reasonable person in the street or a business or seafaring man would not see the charterer's original orders to load the goods as a proximate cause. It has to be said that the issue of causation as characterised by Lord Mance more closely reflects the idea of proximate causes in the law on marine insurance more generally and in turn, is more consistent with the commercial understanding of the matter of causation. A commercial test was also preferred by Colman J. in *The Greek Fighter* [2006] EWHC 1729 where the judge noted, "it is in a commercial setting improbable that a charterer would be prepared to assume the risk of eventualities remote from his own orders." Although it is true that the vessel would never have had to unload the cargo if she had never been ordered to load it in the first place, that is not a *natural* consequence of ordering it to be loaded. The true cause for the essential discharge of the cargo was the fact that the owners required the charterers to discharge the cargo. Of course it is true that that was because the charterers had failed to pay hire, but failure to make a punctual hire payment is not "an order as regards employment of the vessel . . . or other arrangements" (the wording used in the indemnity clause in the case).

The employment clause will, expressly or by implication, require the charterer to use the ship for lawful trades and to call at safe ports. It will allow the charterer to require the master to issue bills of lading. If the charterer orders the master to issue bills of lading which contradict or do not incorporate the terms of the charterparty, it is obvious that the shipowner would be liable on the bills issued on those terms because the master is his servant. In such a case, the indemnity clause will make the charterer liable to indemnify the shipowner.[48]

Payment of hire and time charters

Under a time charter, as against a voyage charter, the contract will specify in **7–142** precise terms the length of the charter period—it will normally state when hire commences and when it expires. Hire is payable throughout the charter period regardless of whether the charterer is using the vessel for his cargo or any other purposes. There is usually a provision exempting hire where the ship will be deemed contractually as not capable of earning hire from the charterer.

Where the ship goes "off-hire", hire/freight may be suspended and appropriate deductions be made but no deductions can be made for anticipatory off-hire however certain it is that the ship would be off-hire. The ship must have actually been off-hire before that right to deduct accrues (*The Li Hat* [2005] EWCH 735). A ship is "off-hire" when she is unable to perform the carriage as agreed under the charterparty. As the financial consequences can be enormous, charter will stipulate clearly what events constitute the "off-hire". The general rule is that for

---

[48] *The Brabant* [1965] 2 Lloyd's Rep. 546; *The Imvros* [1999] 1 Lloyd's Rep. 848; *Milburn v Jamaica Fruit Co* [1900] 2 Q.B. 540.

a vessel to be off-hire, the charterer must be able to bring himself within the scope of the clause defining "off-hire" (*The Mareva AS* [1977] 1 Lloyd's Rep. 368; *The Fu Ning Hai* [2006] EWHC 3250). In *Nippon Yusen Kaisha Ltd v Scindia Steam Navigation Co Ltd (The Jalagouri)* [2000] 1 Lloyd's Rep. 515, the charter provided that

> "should the vessel be seized or detained by any authority during the currency of [the] Charter Party, the Charterer's liability for seizure or detention or arrest [or] delay is ceased immediately from the time of her seizure or detention or arrest or delay and all time lost by this reason shall be treated as off-hire until the time of her release . . . ".

The vessel had a collision in Japan when she started her voyage and water entered one of the holds causing damage to the goods carried there. When she arrived at Kandla, India, she was ordered by port authorities not to complete her discharge of the cargo without a guarantee for the costs of storing the damaged parts or of clearing them from the port area. The question was whether between the time she was prevented from unloading and the time the guarantee was provided and re-berthing, she was off-hire.

7–143   The court held that the ship was off-hire for the period in dispute. It stated that there was no reason why the word "detained" should be given a restricted meaning—on the facts, until security was provided the vessel was not permitted to stay at her berth and kept from proceeding with her discharge and sent out to anchorage. This amounted to "detention" as defined by Kerr J. in *The Mareva AS* [1977] 1 Lloyd's Rep. 368.

In *The Mareva AS* cargo damage made discharge more difficult and the ship was delayed. It was accepted that the vessel had been delayed, but Kerr J. held that time had not been lost due to "detention by average accident to cargo" within cl.15 of the NYPE form. The judge defined detention as some "physical or geographical constraint upon the vessel's movements in relation to her service under the charter". He supported this view by reference to *Vogemann v Zanzibar Steamship Co Ltd* (1901) 6 Com. Cas. 253, 7 Com. Cas. 254, CA, another case under cl.15 where the vessel had sustained damage by "average accident to the ship". Commenting on that case Kerr J. said:

> "It was evidently common ground that she was detained on the way back to the port of repair in the sense in which I have sought to explain, *i.e.* that there was a constraint upon her movements in the charterers' service, since she was going back on her tracks. But once she again set off on her voyage, albeit still delayed as a result of the accident, there was no longer any detention".

7–144 | *Case study: Off hire and Piracy*

Piracy, especially around the waters near Somalia, has hit the headlines so often in recent times that few students of international trade law would be unaware of the huge cost to lives and property. Ships and crew are detained until the ransom money is found and paid. This period of detention is likely to be for an indefinite period of time. As regards ships on time charters, a contractual issue is whether the ship is off-hire when she is detained by pirates.

In *The Saldanha* [2010] EWHC 1340 (Comm) the court decided that a ship detained by Somali pirates was not off-hire for the duration of her detention. In that case the vessel had been chartered on an NYPE charter form which provided:

"That in the event of the loss of time from default and/or deficiency of men including strike of Officers and/or crew or deficiency of . . . stores, fire, breakdown or damages to hull, machinery or equipment, grounding, detention by average accidents to ship or cargo, dry-docking for the purpose of examination or painting bottom, or by any other cause preventing the full working of the vessel, the payment of hire shall cease for the time thereby lost . . . ."

Had the contract been changed to include the word "whatsoever" after "any other cause", the court thought that that would be enough to render the ship off-hire. The reference "any other cause" alone has to be read in ejusdem generis way which means, "any other cause" should be seen in the context of the physical condition or efficiency of either vessel (including its crew) or cargo (*The Laconian Confidence* [1997] 1 Lloyd's Rep. 139). For something totally extraneous to be included, the word "whatsoever" should be added to qualify "any other cause". The judge in *The Saldanha* considered the seizure of the vessel by pirates as a "classic example of a totally extraneous cause". He also added:

"Should parties be minded to treat seizures by pirates as an off-hire event under time charterparty, they can do so straightforwardly and most obviously by way of an express provision in a "seizures" or "detention" clause. Alternatively and at the very least, they can add the word "whatsoever" to the wording "any other cause", although this route will not give quite the same certainty as it presently hinges on obiter dicta, albeit of a most persuasive kind."

In *Osmium Shipping Corporation v Cargill international SA (The Captain Stefanos)* [2012] EWHC 571, the off-hire clause referred to "any accident or breakdown, . . . or capture/seizure, or detention or threatened detention by any authority including arrest". The court looked carefully at a number of factors, including the position of the comma after the words "capture/seizure" and held that this rider clause did entitle the charterers to treat the ship as off-hire for the time lost due to her capture by Somali pirates.

It should of course be noted that these decisions were concerned with charterparties made before the BIMCO Piracy Clause for Time Charter Parties 2009 was introduced (*http://www.bimco.org/en/Security/Piracy/BIMCO_Piracy_Clauses.aspx*).[49] That clause has a provision which states that: "If the Vessel is attacked by pirates any time lost shall be for the account of the Charterers and the Vessel shall remain on hire" (for a capped period). If such terms are used, it should be quite clear as to whether the ship becomes off-hire or not whilst under capture by pirates.[50]

A more conventional example of a ship going off hire is *Macieo Shipping Ltd* **7–145** *v Clipper Shipping Lines (The Clipper Sao Luis)* [2000] 1 Lloyd's Rep. 645. Fire was detected on the Clipper Sao Luis soon after the cargo holds had been sealed and just before she was to set sail for Itajai. The vessel thus remained alongside the berth so that the fire could be put out. She was then re-loaded about 20 days later and was ready to resume her voyage when she was ordered by the harbour

---

[49] More on the BIMCO clauses see Hunter, "BIMCO piracy clauses" [2009] 15 J.I.M.L. 291.
[50] On piracy and time charters, see Todd, "Ransom, piracy and time charterparties" [2012] 18 J.I.M.L. 193.

master to produce some outstanding dangerous goods documentation and participate in an inquiry into another incident at port unrelated to the fire.

The owners, whilst conceding that there was "detention", argued that as there was consensus among all concerned that the vessel should remain alongside the berth to fight the fire, there was no "off-hire". This was rejected by David Steel J. on the basis that what had to be assessed was whether the ship was able to perform the services she was chartered for and as it was plain that the ship was unable to set sail safely and without causing harm to her crew, she must be held to be off-hire. The element of consensus as to the best course of action to be taken did not alter the physical fact that the vessel was off-hire. The court also found no evidence that the ship was unable to sail the second time because the charterers had failed to obtain a dangerous goods certificate. The sole effective cause for the delay the second time was the need for two witnesses to stay for the unrelated official inquiry. As such the vessel was to be treated as off-hire during the two days the witnesses were involved.

From these authorities, it is clear that there is to be no distinction made between legal and physical detention, seizure or arrest as far as the off-hire clause is concerned (*Hyundai Merchant Marine Co Ltd v Furness Withy (The Doric Pride)* [2005] EWHC 945).

7–146   Hire is normally payable in advance and is calculated on the basis of a certain sum per tonnage of the ship deadweight for a certain time frame—for example, £x per y tons per 30 days. Currency clauses are employed in long charters to ensure that any exposure to foreign exchange risks is minimised. A simple currency clause might provide for a fixed exchange rate. Shipowners frequently provide in the charter that they would be entitled to withdraw the vessel if payment is not made on time. As time is not of the essence at common law, the courts will construe such withdrawal clauses strictly. They are however not unlawful. Occasionally, a withdrawal right is tempered with an anti-technicality clause. The clause requires the shipowner to give notice to the charterers that hire has not been paid and to warn the charterers that the vessel would be withdrawn if payment is not made within a stipulated period of time. Anti-technicality clauses will always be construed in a manner to give them the intended commercial effect. In *The North Sea* [1997] 2 Lloyd's Rep. 328, Mance J. noted that a withdrawal or cancellation clause is essentially a forfeiture clause, the effect of which may be draconian, its application should always be read narrowly and as such, the anti-technicality clause, conversely, should be applied with some degree of generosity and flexibility. In *Owneast Shipping Ltd v Qatar Navigation QSC (Qatar Star)* [2010] EWHC 1663 (Comm), for example, the charterers were given the benefit of the doubt where the anti-technicality clause was capable of two or more interpretations.

CHAPTER 8

INTERNATIONAL CONVENTIONS ON CARRIAGE OF GOODS BY SEA

As was discussed in the preceding chapter, the shipper of goods has a few options **8–001** when he decides to secure carriage for his goods. He may either charter a ship from a shipowner or simply procure shipping space from a shipowner or a charterer. Of course if it is within his means and interest, he could purchase a ship for the purposes of his trade. Where there is a charterparty, the rules of play are generally governed by the common law. At common law while there is some judicial intervention to ensure that some fair play is maintained, the law leans in favour of contractual freedom. Parties are entrusted with a substantial degree of liberty in delineating their duties and rights, and the exclusion of liabilities (*Photo Production Ltd v Securicor Transport Ltd* [1980] A.C. 827). Invariably, and rightly, concerns have been expressed about the carrier's liberty to exclude or limit their liability under the contract of carriage. Where the charterer or shipper is equally powerful in the transaction, the contractual freedom ensured by the common law works well. However, where the shipper of goods is more of a consumer than a big player, the regime would not be fair. Thus, in 1924 the draft Hague Rules by International Law Association's Maritime Law Committee (CMI) were formally adopted with some minor amendments in this country through the passage of the Carriage of Goods by Sea Act 1924. Those rules were considered to be inadequate and in 1963 substantial amendments were adopted by the CMI in Visby. The new rules are known as the Hague-Visby Rules and they were introduced into English law via the Carriage of Goods by Sea Act 1971. Since then further efforts have produced the UN Convention on Carriage of Goods by Sea 1978, more commonly known as the Hamburg Rules and in 2009, the UNCITRAL Convention on Contracts for the International Carriage of Goods wholly or partly by Sea (known as the Rotterdam Rules). These rules have no legally binding force in the United Kingdom at present.

In general, the Hague-Visby Rules provide for the application of certain duties and rights vis-à-vis the carriage and protection of the contractual cargo. They also proscribe the extent to which any party may limit his liability under the contract of carriage and the possible defences a carrier could invoke when damage or loss is claimed against him.

Contracts to which the Rules Apply

8–002 The Rules apply to any bill of lading which relates to a contract of carriage as defined in art.I. Let us paraphrase art.I. The Hague-Visby Rules will *only* apply to contracts of carriage "*covered* by a bill of lading or a similar document of title" where the bill of lading or that document of title regulates the relations between the holder and the carrier. An issue of some controversy is as to whether a straight bill of lading would qualify as "a bill of lading or similar document of title". In *The Happy Ranger* [2001] 2 Lloyd's Rep. 530, Tomlinson J. suggested, obiter, that the term "bill of lading" in art.I(b) should not be interpreted as including straight bills of lading. In reversing his decision, on other grounds, the Court of Appeal[1] reserved their opinion on the point but expressed doubt about statements to a similar effect in some textbooks. The issue was finally settled by the House of Lords in *J I MacWilliam Co Inc v Mediterranean Shipping Co SA (The Rafaela S)* [2005] UKHL 11. In that case, the contract provided for the carriage of goods from South Africa to America via England. During the leg from Felixstowe, England to Boston, USA, the goods suffered damage. The claimant was in possession of a straight bill of lading made out to the shipper by the carrier. It might be recalled that a straight bill lacks negotiability, but general commercial practice in requiring its presentation to obtain delivery of the goods is recognition of its place as a document of title. That being the case, the House of Lords found no good commercial reason for excluding it from the scope of art.I(b). There was also no rational reason for offering protection of the Hague Visby Rules to a consignee under a transferable bill but not one under a straight bill.

It would appear that art.I(b) could extend to contracts of carriage covered by a document of title recognised by trade custom and usage. In *Kum v Wah Tat Bank Ltd* [1971] 1 Lloyd's Rep. 439, the court accepted that a mate's receipt could, by virtue of established and notorious trade custom and usage, be treated as a document of title. Clearly, the burden of proving the existence of such a trade custom or usage is not light; but even leaving the issue of proof aside, it seems unlikely that in the light of how modern shipping practice is followed in many parts of the world there would still exist such a risky practice.

A charterparty is expressly excluded from the scope of the Hague-Visby Rules because the relations between the shipowner (carrier) and the charterer (holder) are not governed by the bill of lading even if a bill of lading has been issued. The Rules will however govern the relations between the charterer and a subsequent shipper of goods who holds the bill of lading issued originally by the shipowner because that contract is covered by the bill of lading. This is made explicit in art.V which states:

" . . . The provisions of these Rules shall not be applicable to charter parties, but if bills of lading are issued in the case of a ship under a charter party they shall comply with the terms of these Rules . . . ".

---

[1] [2002] 2 Lloyd's Rep. 357.

In the case of a bill of lading contract, it is very important for the cargo interest **8–003** (shipper of goods) to know with whom he is contracting. The person he is contracting with is known as the contractual carrier. The contractual carrier is not always the actual carrier. In a case, for example, where the shipowner has chartered the ship to a charterer, it is likely that the contract of carriage is made between the charterer (as principal) and the cargo interest, instead of between the shipowner and the cargo interest. In the case of the former, it is immediately obvious that the charterer is the contractual carrier but the shipowner is the actual carrier. The default position, where there is no clear evidence that the charterer is contracting as principal, is that the shipowner would be presumed to be the carrier against whom the cargo interest could sue (under the Hague-Visby Rules) and the charterer is merely the shipowner's agent. The bill of lading issued to the cargo interest in that context is a "shipowner's or owner's bill". In time charters where the existence of a charterparty is less obvious to the cargo owner/shipper of goods, this state of affairs is usually made clear in a clause called the "demise clause" in the bill of lading issued to the shipper:

"If the ocean vessel is not owned by or chartered by demise to the company or line by whom this Bill of Lading is issued (as may be the case notwithstanding anything that appeared to the contrary) this Bill of Lading shall take effect only as a contract of carriage with the owner or demise charterer as the case may be as principal made through the agency of the said company or line who act solely as agent and shall be under no personal liability whatsoever in respect thereof".

Demise clauses are intended to protect the charterer but as Colman J. pointed out in *The Owners of the Cargo Lately Laden aboard the ship "Starsin" v The Owners and/or Demise Charterer of the Ship or Vessel "Starsin"* [2000] 1 Lloyd's Rep. 85:

"[The clause] has survived from the era when a time charterer who was party to a bill of lading contract as carrier was not entitled to limit his liability under the Merchant Shipping Act. It was therefore necessary, particularly for liner companies who issued bills, to avoid being held liable as carriers. Since the enactment into English law of art. 1.2 of the Convention on Limitation of Liability for Maritime Claims, 1976 by s.186 of the Merchant Shipping Act, 1995 such precautions have become unnecessary".[2]

The extension of the right to limitation to a time charterer in fact first entered English law under s.3 of the Merchant Shipping (Liability of Shipowners and Others) Act 1958. The demise clause is there to protect a charterer who does *not* want to accept the liability of a carrier, and who therefore cautiously seeks to ensure that the mere issue of a bill of lading by himself or his agent would not have that effect. It is not, however, intended to ensure that a time charterer who *does* want to undertake the liability of a carrier and has signed as such could not do so.

---

[2] See generally *Fetim BV v Oceanspeed Shipping Ltd (The Flecha)* [1999] 1 Lloyd's Rep. 612; *MB Pyramid Sound MV v Briese Schiffahrts GmbH (The Ines)* [1995] 2 Lloyd's Rep. 144; and *Sunrise Maritime Inc v Uvisco Ltd (The Hector)* [1998] 2 Lloyd's Rep. 287.

The court's task usually is to ascertain the parties' presumed intention from the entirety of the contract and circumstances.

8–004   *Homburg Houtimport v Agrosin Private Ltd (The Starsin)* [2003] UKHL 12
Facts:
The timber carried on the Starsin deteriorated as a result of negligent stowage. The timber was carried under contracts of carriage contained in or evidenced by a series of transferable bills of lading. The respondent cargo owners were holders of the bills of lading. They made claims against the shipowners (appellants) and the charterers of the vessel. The vessel had been chartered to CPS on a time charter.

The bills were liner bills issued by CPS and signed by the port agents "as agents for CPS (the carrier)". Those words were typed in the signature box on the front of the bills. Clause 1 on the back of the bills provided that the carrier was the party on whose behalf the bill had been signed. Clause 33 was an identity of carrier clause which stated that the contract evidenced by the bill was between the merchant and the shipowner and that the line, company or agents who had executed the bill was not to be treated as a principal in the contract. The demise clause in cl.35 then provided that if the vessel was not owned by or chartered by demise to the company or line by whom the bill was issued, the bill took effect only as a contract of carriage with the owners or demise charterer as the case might be as principal made through the agency of the company or line who acted solely as agents without personal liability.

The Court of Appeal held that the bills were owners' bills.
Held:
The House of Lords allowed the appeal and held that the bills were charterers' bills. Lord Steyn considered that the form of the bill must be approached objectively—that is to ask how a reasonable person, versed in the shipping trade, would read the bill. The court thought that such a person would give greater weight to words specially chosen, such as the words which appear above the signature, rather than standard form printed conditions. Moreover, as Lord Steyn said:

"[There is] no doubt that in any event he would, as between provisions on the face of the bill and those on the reverse side of the bill, give predominant effect to those on the face of the bill".

The court also thought that given the speed at which international trade is transacted, there is little time for examining the implications of barely legible printed conditions at the time of the issue of the bill of lading. In order to find out who the carrier is it would make business common sense for a shipper to turn to the face of the bill, and in particular to the signature box, rather than clauses at the bottom of column two of the reverse side of the bill.

8–005   The judgment given by the majority of the Court of Appeal was unappealing because it would have required shipping and commercial people untrained in the law to take great care when examining the bill of lading.[3] Their approach was obviously a legalistic one—they presumed the parties to have notice of all the terms of the bill of lading. That however is to disregard the commercial reality that few reasonable commercial persons would actually read all its terms and conditions. For some things he would not go any further than what it says on the front. If the words on the front are reasonably sufficient to communicate the information in question, he would not trouble with the back. It is only if the

---

[3] See criticism of the Court of Appeal's judgment in *Debattista*, Lloyds List, (February 21, 2001) p.5.

information on the front is insufficient, or the questions which concern the reader relate to matters which do not ordinarily appear on the front, that he turns to the back and at this point, he would call in his lawyers to construe the document as a whole.

It remains possible, though less frequent, for the shipowner not to have any part in the issue of the bill of lading and for the charterer wholly to assume responsibility as carrier. Indeed in *The Venezuela* [1980] 1 Lloyd's Rep. 393 for example, the identity clause of the contract starkly referred to the charterer as "carrier" indicating that the bill of lading was not an "owner's bill" but a "charterer's bill". Where the shipper is in possession of a "charterer's bill" instead of an "owner's bill", no action in contract could be brought against the shipowners. It is naturally possible for the charterer to sue the shipowner to indemnify them from any liability the former might endure as a result of the Hague-Visby Rules.[4]

The Hague-Visby Rules shall have mandatory application where the port of shipment is a port in the United Kingdom, whether or not the carriage is between ports in two different states within the meaning of art.X (s.1(3) Carriage of Goods by Sea Act 1971). In *The Rafaela S* [2003] EWCA Civ 556 the issue as to where the UK port is a port of transshipment, whether it would be treated as a "port of shipment" for the purposes of this section was addressed by the Court of Appeal.[5] There, the goods were to be carried from Durban, South Africa to Boston, USA via Felixstowe, England. A bill of lading was issued at Durban where the goods were loaded on the Rosemary. Transshipment then took place in Felixstowe for on-carriage to Boston on the Rafaela S. The goods were damaged in the second leg of the carriage. If there were two separate contracts of carriage, it is inescapable that Felixstowe would be a port of shipment for the purposes of s.1(3) and the Hague-Visby Rules will have mandatory application. The arbitrators however held that as the bill of lading issued was a through bill, there was only one contract. The Court of Appeal however rejected that finding and held that the bill of lading clearly envisaged that separate on-carriage arrangements were to be carried out at Felixstowe and Felixstowe was, under the contract, to be treated as the port of discharge for the Rosemary.

Two other cases might be instructive. In *Stafford Allen & Sons Ltd v Pacific Steam Navigation Co* (1956) LL.LR 105 the first carrier's bill of lading provided for shipment at Corinto in Nicaragua, discharge and transshipment at Cristobal by a named "on carrier" and a final destination in London. A special clause dealt with the circumstances of transshipment, stating that the first carrier made arrangements for the transshipment and on-carriage "solely as the forwarding agent of the shipper and without any other responsibility whatsoever" and that the transshipment and on-carriage would be subject to "all the provisions of the regular form of bill of lading" of the second carrier. No further bill of lading was issued. The claimant's cargo was damaged on the second leg and it sued the

8–006

---

[4] On whether the shipper could sue the shipowner in tort, much depends on when the damage was caused. The law of negligence suggests that the tortfeasor is only liable for damage to goods to the claimant if the claimant was the owner or had a possessory title to the goods at the material time (presumably the time of the breach, but there are doubts expressed about this by the Court of Appeal in *The Starsin*). (See *The Aliakmon* [1986] 1 A.C. 785.)

[5] The case subsequently went on appeal to the House of Lords but this issue on whether there was one or two contracts was not the subject of the appeal. For an account of the House of Lords decision, see para.8–002.

second carrier. The issue was whether the regime terms of the first carrier's bill of lading applied throughout the voyage to London, or whether the terms of the second carrier's regular bill of lading applied. Sellers J. held that the second carrier's terms applied. On the other hand, in *The Anders Maersk* [1986] Lloyd's Rep. 483, a decision of the Hong Kong High Court, the bill of lading stated that the port of shipment was Baltimore and the port of discharge was Shanghai. The bill however gave the carrier a right of transshipment, which it exercised at Hong Kong. The bill also appeared to be a through bill. It made no express reference to Hong Kong at all. The claimant's cargo was damaged between Hong Kong and Shanghai. The issue was whether Hong Kong was the "port of shipment" for the purposes of the Hong Kong equivalent of the 1971 Act. Mayo J. held that transshipment was not the same as shipment, and that there had been only one port of shipment and that was Baltimore. Mayo J. said:

> "Unless reference is made to the contract between the parties, there would always be a likelihood that there would be an element of uncertainty. The shipper of goods may have no knowledge of the arrangements being made by the carrier, and it would put the shipper in an invidious position if he could only establish his rights by a subsequent re-construction of events which took place without his knowledge".

Rix L.J. considered in *The Rafaela S* that the facts in that case were more similar to *Stafford Allen & Sons Ltd* and disregarded the use of the through bill as material. His Lordship paid more attention to the fact that the contract permitted the carrier to arrange on-carriage from Felixstowe with another carrier or itself. The fact that the on-carriage was carried out by itself should not detract from the inference that the on-carriage was a separate contractual commitment. Rix L.J.'s approach was to look carefully at the terms of the contract to see what the carrier was expected to do vis-à-vis the on-carriage, despite the use of a through bill of lading. Such an approach, it is submitted, is inefficient in economic terms. Commercial men would be required to make a careful scrutiny of the bill of lading to ascertain the different ports of shipment, namely, the different countries whose carriage law would have mandatory effect. There should perhaps be a presumption that where through bills are used and only one carrier is involved, the contract of carriage would be covered by the through bill, disregarding any transshipment. That would seem to coincide with reasons of commercial efficiency.

Article X states that the Rules shall apply to every bill of lading relating to the carriage of goods between ports in two different states if:

(a) the bill of lading is issued in a contracting State; or

(b) the carriage is from a port in a contracting State; or

(c) the contract contained in or evidenced by the bill of lading provides that these Rules or legislation of any State giving effect to them are to govern the contract, whatever may be the nationality of the ship, the carrier, the shipper, the consignee or any other interested person.

8–007   This is reinforced by s.1(6) of the Carriage of Goods by Sea Act 1971 which provides that the Rules will have the force of law where the bill of lading concerned expressly provides that the Rules shall govern the contract. Furthermore, s.1(6)(b) provides that the Rules shall have the force of law in relation to

> "any receipt which is a non-negotiable document marked as such if the contract contained in or evidenced by it is a contract for the carriage of goods by sea which expressly provides that the Rules are to govern the contract as if the receipt were a bill of lading".

From this brief description of the types of contract of carriage that are to be governed by the Hague-Visby Rules, a few issues need further clarification:

1. What does "covered by a bill of lading" mean?

2. How should "the bill of lading provides that these Rules or legislation of any State giving effect to them are to govern the contract" be construed?

3. What is the effect of a document not expressly governed by the Rules providing for the inclusion or incorporation of the Hague-Visby Rules?

4. What is the period covered by the Rules?

"Covered by a bill of lading"

It was held in *Pyrene Co Ltd v Scindia Navigation Co Ltd* [1954] 2 Q.B. 402 that **8–008** a contract of carriage will be considered to be "covered by a bill of lading" and thus, falls within the governance of the Hague Rules (and by the same token, the Hague-Visby Rules) if the issue of bill of lading is contemplated when the contract was entered into. It need not actually be in existence when the damage or loss to the goods occurs or when the action was brought. In that case, when the fire tenders were being loaded, one was dropped on to the quayside and was damaged. When the bill of lading was issued, the reference to the damaged tender was deleted. The shipper attempted to rely on the Hague Rules which were then in force under the Carriage of Goods by Sea Act 1924. It was argued by the carrier that the Rules did not apply because the contract of carriage was not "covered by the bill of lading" as the fire tender in question had been deleted from the relevant bill of lading.

The court rejected the carrier's argument on the following reason:

> "The use of the word 'covered' recognises the fact that the contract of carriage is always concluded before the bill of lading, which evidences its terms, is actually issued. When parties enter into the contract of carriage in the expectation that a bill of lading will be issued to cover it, they enter into upon those terms which they know or expect the bill of lading to contain. Those terms must be in force from the inception of the contract; if it were otherwise the bill of lading would not evidence the contract but would be a variation of it. Moreover, it would be absurd to suppose that the parties intend the terms of the contract to be changed when the bill of lading is issued: for the issue of the bill of lading does not necessarily mark any stage in the development of the contract; often it is not issued till after the ship has sailed, and if there is pressure of office work on the ship's agent it may be delayed several days. . . . [W]henever a contract of carriage is concluded and it is contemplated that a

bill of lading will, in due course, be issued in respect of it, that contract is from its creation 'covered' by a bill of lading . . . ".

It follows therefore that where a bill of lading is issued but does not conform with the normal rules on bill of lading (for example, where it is not genuine or has been altered), the rules should nevertheless apply because the issuing of the bill of lading was originally intended or contemplated by the parties. It would also seem to be the case that there is no distinction made in the scope of the application of the Hague-Visby Rules whether a bill of lading is a shipped bill or a received for shipment bill. The crucial factor in determining whether the contract is covered by the bill of lading is an objective test as to whether it was the contemplation of the parties that such is to be the case. That test is not defeated simply because the bill of lading is not effective as a document of title.

8–009   Where no bill of lading is contemplated the position appears settled, namely that the Hague-Visby Rules will not apply as a result of art.I. This might seem somewhat unfair in that it does not appear to take into account some sections of modern trade where the carriage of goods by sea is for short voyages and the issue of bills of lading would simply make the process more complicated and less viable. We saw in the last chapter how the Scottish Court of Session refused to extend the application of the Hague Rules to a contract of carriage made subject to conditions contained in the carrier's "sailing bills" on the basis that there, the contract was not covered by a bill of lading (*Harland & Wolff Ltd v Burns & Laird Lines Ltd* (1931) 40 Ll. L. Rep. 286. Lord Clyde held in that case:

" . . . the contract of affreightment in the present case was a highly special one. It was not only not actually 'covered' by a bill of lading, but a bill of lading . . . was alien to its purpose".

As far as the court was concerned, the contract had not contemplated the use or issue of a bill of lading. His Lordship went on:

"That purpose [of the contract of affreightment] was not mercantile—for the goods were neither sold nor for sale—but was limited to the transport of the machinery . . . made in . . . [H&W's] Glasgow shops . . . for a particular ship [H&W] were building in their Belfast yard . . . I do not see what contractual part a bill of lading capable of being used as a document of title could have played in such a contract of affreightment, nor how the contract of carriage in this case could have been 'covered' by a bill of lading".

The Scottish case was subsequently recognised and affirmed by the House of Lords in *Vita Food Products Inc v Unus Shipping Co Ltd* [1939] A.C. 277.

It would appear that a powerful shipowner could, as the carriers did in the present case, insist that no bill of lading will be issued for a particular voyage/s and by so doing avoid the incidences of the Hague-Visby Rules. The case seems to ignore the object of the rules which is to provide some protection for the small shipper of goods. By construing the scope of the Rules strictly and literally as applying only to contracts which contemplate the issue of a bill of lading might be somewhat unjust. It might perhaps be of some comfort that the dicta of Lord Clyde make express requirement that the contract of affreightment should be of a mercantile nature (a point not expressly considered by the House of Lords in

Vita Food Products). This leaves some room for judges to hold that where (although no bill was contemplated) the contract was for the carriage of goods intended for sale or re-sale or some other mercantile purpose the Rules should apply.

Article X(c)—when the contract provides that the rules or legislation of any state giving effect to them shall apply

For art.X(c) to apply, the court must be satisfied that it is the clear intention of the parties that their contract of carriage is to be governed by the rules. In *Hellenic Steel Co v Svolamar Shipping Co Ltd (The Komninos S)* [1991] 1 Lloyd's Rep. 370, the Court of Appeal held that a choice of English law as the applicable law of the contract inferred from a choice of forum clause was not sufficient to show that it was the parties' intention to apply the Rules.

8–010

Hellenic Steel Co v Svolamar Shipping Co Ltd [1991] 1 Lloyd's Rep. 370
Facts:
The bills of lading in the provided that all disputes were "to be referred to the British courts". The goods carried from Greece to Ravenna and Ancona were damaged as a result of the ship's unseaworthiness and the crew's negligence. The bills of lading also provided for certain exceptions which would be valid unless the Hague-Visby Rules applied. It was further implied from the forum clause that the contract was to be governed by English law.
Held:
The issue was whether assuming that the English forum clause showed an intention that English law should govern the contract, the bills of lading "provided" that the legislation of the United Kingdom giving effect to the Rules should govern the contract. The Court of Appeal decided that the Rules did not apply. The following points were raised:

8–011

1. Greece was not a contracting state to the Hague-Visby Rules, so the bills were not issued in a contracting state and the carriage was not from a port in a contracting state. Therefore art.X(a) and (b) had no application.

2. The fact that the contract *implied* that it should be govern by English law is not the same thing as saying that the contract provided that the legislation of any state giving effect to the Rules are to govern it. article X(c) therefore did not apply.

Effect of a document not expressly governed by the Rules providing for their incorporation

Section 1(6)(b) of Carriage of Goods by Sea Act 1971 gives the parties the power to incorporate into their non-negotiable document the Hague-Visby Rules as if that document were a bill of lading. There are however certain provisos to the exercise of this liberty:

8–012

1. First, the non-negotiable document or receipt must be marked as being non-negotiable;

2. Secondly, the contract expressly provides that the Rules are to govern as if the receipt of non-negotiable document were a bill of lading. It is in this regard that doubts have arisen as to the scope and extent of the parties freedom to incorporate the Rules. Would it, for example, be enough that the receipt simply states that the Rules are to apply? Should there be more explicit terms before the court will consider s.1(6)(b) as having been met?

It has been suggested that even though the document might state that the Rules shall apply, this is not conclusive of its satisfying the terms of s.1(6)(b) because that section requires the express specification of the words "as if the receipt were a bill of lading". In *McCarren & Co Ltd v Humber International Transport Ltd and Trucklines Ferries (Poole) Ltd (The Vechscroon)* [1982] 1 Lloyd's Rep. 301, Lloyd J. did not find such a contention convincing. The judge said:

> "I can think of no sensible reason why Parliament should have intended to draw any distinction between a document which says 'this non-negotiable receipt shall be governed by the Hague-Visby Rules' and a document which says 'this non-negotiable receipt shall be governed by the Hague-Visby Rules as if it were a bill of lading' . . . ".

In that case, a non-negotiable commercial vehicle movement order was issued for the carriage of meat from Poole to Cherbourg and purported to incorporate the Hague-Visby Rules into the contract. The question was whether the Rules applied as a matter of law or simply as contractual terms.

It was also argued in that case that the language of s.1(6)(b) suggested that if the words "as if it were a bill of lading" were omitted, the Rules are incorporated only as contractual terms and are not intended to carry the force of law. Lloyd J. was not persuaded and held that the language of s.1(6)(b) is "perfectly general" and that it does not provide that the contract must be exclusively governed by the rules for the rules to have the force of law. Nor does the section provide that the contract is to be governed by the rules without condition or qualification.

Steyn J. took a different approach in *Browner International Ltd v Monarch Shipping Co Ltd* [1989] 2 Lloyd's Rep. 185.

8–013 *Browner International Ltd v Monarch Shipping Co Ltd (The European Enterprise)*
[1989] 2 Lloyd's Rep. 185
Facts:
The claimants were freight hauliers and contracted to carry a consignment of meat from Cork to France. They then entered into a contract of carriage with the defendant ferry owners to carry the meat from Dover to Calais. The goods were loaded on the upper deck of the ferry and were damaged by bad weather. It is the practice of English cross channel operators not to issue bills of lading for the cross channel Ro-Ro (Roll on—Roll off) ferry trade. Instead, commercial non-negotiable receipts were issued and there was a clause in these receipts stipulating that the carriage was subject to the Hague-Visby Rules. There were also exception clauses which were inconsistent with the Hague-Visby Rules.
Held:
On whether the Rules are to have the force of law in nullifying the effect of the exception clauses, the court held that the purpose of s.1(6)(b) is to confer on a voluntary consensual tie a statutory binding character but only where the formal requirements of s.1(6)(b) are met, i.e. the words "as if the receipt were a bill of lading" must not be omitted. The formal requirement of these words is to bring clearly to the minds of the parties what documents will attract the application of the rules; rules ordinarily reserved for bills of lading. Reading s.1(6)(b) with s.1(4), it seems quite obvious that the Act is not to apply to shipments where the shipper has no right to demand a bill of lading or other document of title, hence in order that a document not ordinarily covered by a bill of lading to subject itself to the legal governance of the Rules, very explicit terms must be used.

Another factor is that the contract did not incorporate the entirety of the Rules; specific exceptions and qualifications had been made. Such a partial incorporation should not have the effect of attracting statutory governance since such words would suggest that the Rules are not to govern the contract completely and should fall outside the purview of s.1(6)(b). *The Vechscroon* was therefore to be departed from.

The rules were thus of mere contractual force in this contract and did not carry the force of law.

Summarising Steyn J.'s judgment: **8–014**

1. the purpose of s.1(6)(b) as considered in the light of s.1(4) is to exclude documents not intended to operate like bills of lading from the operation of the Hague-Visby Rules;

2. section 1(6)(b) can only be activated by an express agreement between the parties to bring their contract within the scope of the Hague-Visby Rules;

3. this express agreement must be clear and adhere to the formal requirements of s.1(6)(b). The formal requirements are that the document must be marked clearly as non-negotiable and described as being governed by the Rules as if it were a bill of lading;

4. the words "as if it were a bill of lading" must not be omitted. The object of the formal requirement to insert those words is to ensure that the parties are clear in their kinds that the document has now been brought under the Rules' legal force; and

5. where the contract does not incorporate the Rules in their entirety or en bloc, it cannot be correct to say that "the contract provides that the Rules are to govern the contract".

It should be mentioned that s.1(6)(b) is an extremely complicated provision and does not appear to reflect trade practice, making it difficult for the courts to apply the provision without drastically affecting traders' legitimate expectations. Both approaches have their difficulties. With Lloyd J.'s approach, it would seem unjust for the parties who clearly intend to use the Hague-Visby Rules simply as contractual terms to have to suffer their force of law when it is clear their contract does not automatically fall within the scope of the Rules. On the other hand, Steyn J.'s conclusion that express words that the Rules are to govern the contract "as if the receipt were a bill of lading" must be made is somewhat too onerous. Surely implicit terms should be permitted so long as the presumed intention of the parties could be clearly ascertained.

General Paramount Clauses

What is the effect of a charterparty that purports to incorporate into itself the **8–015** provisions of the Hague-Visby Rules? In *Adamastos Shipping Co Ltd v Anglo Saxon Petroleum Co Ltd* [1959] A.C. 133, the House of Lords by a majority held that the charterparty which carried a paramount clause was to have effect even though the Hague Rules (or indeed the Hague-Visby Rules) would not have applied ex facie to charterparties. The definition of a paramount clause is perhaps best taken from Lord Denning's judgment in the Court of Appeal [1957] 2 Q.B. 233:

"When a paramount clause is incorporated into a contract, the purpose is to give the Hague [or Hague-Visby] Rules contractual force; so that, although the bill of lading may contain very wide exceptions, the rules are paramount and make the shipowners liable for want of due diligence to make the ship seaworthy and so forth ... ".

It is however a "notorious" fact that parties to a charterparty may often wish to incorporate the Hague-Visby Rules in their agreement but do not wish to incorporate "the *ipsissima verba* of those rules".[6] They wish to import into the contractual relationship between owners and charterers the same standard of obligation, liability, right and immunity as under the rules between carrier and shipper.

That case was particularly difficult because the charter called for non-cargo carrying voyages where the rules are clearly inapplicable to non-cargo carrying voyages. According to Viscount Simonds, this was misdirecting the issue. That issue was not whether the rules would have applied in their existing form and shape but whether they were contractually incorporated into the charterparty. If they had been, then the application of those rules to the present circumstances will depend on the proper construction of the rules as contractual terms.

8-016   The issue arose subsequently in *Lauritzen Reefers v Ocean Reef Transport Ltd (The Bukhta Russkaya)* [1997] 2 Lloyd's Rep. 744. On the matter of whether the charterparty had effectively incorporated the Hague-Visby Rules by the mere reference to the words "in trades involving neither US nor Canadian ports, the general paramount clause to apply in lieu", Thomas J. applied the test laid down by Lord Denning in *The Agios Lazaros* [1976] 2 Lloyd's Rep. 47. That test was: what did the words "general paramount clause" mean to shipping men when the charterparty was entered into? If there was a specific clause to which the words referred then that clause would be incorporated and the regime (whether the Hague, Hague-Visby or Hamburg Rules) specified in the clause applied. It is readily obvious that it is always a matter of construction as to whether a clause was effective in incorporating the rules into the contract. In that case, the court found that the samples of general paramount clauses adduced showed that the true intention was the incorporation of the Hague Rules rather than the Hague-Visby Rules.

It is not always clear whether the "general paramount clause" refers to the Hague Rules or the Hague-Visby Rules. Thomas J. in *Seabridge Shipping AB v AC Orssleff's Eftf's A/S* [1999] 2 Lloyd's Rep. 685, thought that the phrase "general paramount clause" would almost invariably refer to the Hague Rules rather than the Hague-Visby Rules despite the 1971 Act having incorporated the latter rules into English law because that this is what "shipping men" have always understood the phrase to mean. Nonetheless, it remains open to the parties to make specific reference to the Hague-Visby Rules if that is their intention.

The question of construction can sometimes pose tremendous difficulties. In *The MSC Amsterdam* [2007] EWCA Civ 794,[7] cl.1(a) of the bill of lading read:

"For all trades, except for goods shipped to and from the United States of America, this B/L shall be subject to the 1924 Hague Rules with the express

---

[6] See generally H.G. Williams, *Chartering Documents*, 3rd edn (London: LLP, 1996).
[7] See Todd, "Limiting liability for misdelivery: the MSC Amsterdam" [2008] L.M.C.L.Q. 214.

exclusion of Article IX, or, if compulsorily applicable, subject to the 1968 Protocol (Hague-Visby) or any compulsory legislation based on the Hague Rules and/or the said Protocols. Where Hague-Visby or similar legislation is compulsorily applicable, the Hague-Visby 1979 Protocol ("SDR" Protocol) shall also apply whether or not mandatory".

The goods were carried from Durban, South Africa to Shanghai, China. The **8–017** goods were delivered to thieves presenting a forged bill of lading in Shanghai. On the issue of which law applied to the contract, Aikens J. thought that the clause had effectively incorporated the Hague-Visby Rules. The Court of Appeal disagreed. Longmore L.J., with whom Tuckey and Lloyd L.JJ. agreed, held that the first part of clause meant that at the very least, the Hague Rules will apply to the voyage from Durban to Shanghai. However, the same could not be said for the Hague-Visby Rules. Clause 1(a) used the words "compulsorily" and "compulsory" but, in either case, the HVR itself was not compulsory or compulsorily applicable for shipments from South Africa to China. Although South Africa had national legislation which were similar to the Hague-Visby Rules, South Africa itself was not a contracting state to the Hague-Visby Rules and as such, the Hague-Visby Rules did not apply. Furthermore, cl.1(a) did not make specific reference to the South African legislation being incorporated into the bill of lading. The conclusion was thus that the Hague-Visby Rules did not apply, but the Hague Rules 1924 did.

As long as the incorporation is effective, the relevant Rules (Hague or Hague-Visby) will be treated as any normal express term and have equal status with any other express clauses in the agreement. The charterers in *Bayoil SA v Seawind Tankers Corp (The Leonidas)* [2001] 1 Lloyd's Rep. 533, argued that the speed warranty (a contractual clause providing that the vessel is able to prosecute the laden voyage at a particular speed, which in the present case was 11 knots) was an absolute, "tailor made" warranty which could not be qualified or defeated by the limitation clauses in the Hague Rules. Langley J. rejected their argument, stating that the clause paramount which incorporated the Hague Rules exceptions were fully effective and were not subordinate to any "tailor made" terms made between the parties. The Hague Rules exceptions as incorporated must be given equal standing with any so-called "tailor made" terms of the contract without express words to the contrary.

In an appeal from the New Zealand Court of Appeal before the Privy Council, *Dairy Containers Ltd v Tasman Orient Line CV* [2004] UKPC 22, it is evident that where the Hague Rules (as applicable in New Zealand) have been properly incorporated, it would be presumed that the provisions on limitation of liability in art.IV(5) would also apply. The court said:

"There may reasonably be attributed to the parties to a contract such as this such general commercial knowledge as a party to such a transaction would ordinarily be expected to have, but with a printed form of contract, negotiable by one holder to another, no inference may be drawn as to the knowledge or intention of any particular party. The contract should be given the meaning it would convey to a reasonable person having all the background knowledge which is reasonably available to the person or class of persons to whom the [bill of lading] is addressed . . . , which would certainly include a holder such as [the claimant]".

Period Covered by the Rules

8–018   An important issue related to the scope of application of the Rules is the period within which the rules will apply. Our chief concern is when do the duties of the carrier under the Hague-Visby Rules begin and end? Article I(e) provides that "carriage of goods" covers the period from the time when the goods are loaded on to the time they are discharged from the ship. Taken strictly and literally, it could be argued that the carrier shall not be liable for any loss or damage caused before the goods are loaded or after they have been discharged. In *Pyrene Co Ltd v Scindia Navigation Co Ltd* [1954] 2 Q.B. 402 we are exhorted not to take too strict an approach. Devlin J. held that although the damage was caused before the goods had crossed the ship's rail, this did not necessarily mean the exclusion of the rules. The judge considered this argument to be fallacious

> " . . . the cause of the fallacy perhaps [lies] in the supposition inherent in it that the rights and liabilities under the rules attach to a period of time. I think that they attach to a contract or part of a contract. I say 'part of a contract' because a single contract may cover both inland and sea transport; and in that case the only part of it that falls within the rules is that which, to use the words in the definition of 'contract of carriage' in article 1(b), 'relates to the carriage of goods by sea'. Even if 'carriage of goods by sea' were given by definition the most restricted meaning possible, for example, the period of the voyage, the loading of the goods (by which I mean the whole operation of loading in both its stages and whichever side of the ship's rail) would still *relate* to the carriage on the voyage and so be within the 'contract of carriage'".

No special significance should be placed on the phrase "loaded *on*" in art.1(e); it is not intended to specify a precise moment in time. The Rules demonstrate that they are to apply not to a period of time but "in relation to and in connexion with the carriage of goods by sea" (s.1 Carriage of Goods by Sea Act 1971).

Another reason why the phrase "loaded on" should not be treated as referring strictly to a point in time is that it is not a convention universal that "loading" takes place when the goods cross the ship's rail. It would be more reasonable simply to treat the loading (and discharging) process as a continuous operation. Hence, as long as the damage or loss is caused when the goods are being loaded or discharged whether or not they have crossed the ship's rail is irrelevant as far as the Hague-Visby Rules are concerned.

8–019   This ordinary and natural meaning of art.I(e) coincides with Mr Justice Roche's examination of the notion of cargo discharge in *Goodwin v Lamport and Holt* (1929) 34 LL.LR. 192. In that case, it was held that when goods are discharged from the carrying ship into a lighter provided by the carrier, discharge within the meaning of the Rules is not complete until the lighter has been fully loaded with all the goods intended to be put into it. The discharge process is a continuous operation and is not complete for the purposes of the Rules simply because the goods have crossed the ship's rail.

Combined transport raises complicated questions for Devlin J.'s proposition in *Pyrene Co Ltd* that the rules are to apply to a contract or part of a contract and not to any specific period of time. In *Mayhew Foods Ltd v Overseas Containers Ltd* [1984] 1 Lloyd's Rep. 317, the contract called for the delivery of goods from the consignor's premises in Sussex, England to Jeddah in Saudi Arabia. The contract provided that the shipper is entitled to transship the goods and to substitute nominated vessels to deliver the goods. The goods were to be carried from the inland premises to the port of Shoreham in the south coast of England and then, on to Le Havre for transshipment for Jeddah. The bill of lading issued provided cover only for the Le Havre to Jeddah leg. The goods deteriorated just before being transshipped on to the Benalder at Le Havre.

On whether the Rules applied to the voyage from Shoreham, a port in Sussex to Le Havre, Bingham J. held that in applying *Pyrene Co Ltd v Scindia Navigation Co Ltd* the rights and liabilities under the Rules attach to a contract or part of a contract, not a period of time. In the present case, the contract was for the delivery of goods from Sussex to Jeddah. While the Rules did not apply to inland transport prior to shipment, the rules and the Act plainly applied where the contract clearly provided for shipment from a UK port and from the time of shipment as it did in this case. It does not matter that the bill of lading was issued some days after the goods had arrived in Le Havre. Bingham J. said:

"The parties clearly expected and intended a bill of lading to be issued and when issued it duly evidenced the parties' earlier contract. Since this bill was issued in a contracting state and provided for carriage from a port in contracting state, I think it plain that the Rules applied once the goods were loaded on board the vessel at Shoreham".

As long as the bill of lading issued was contemplated to cover the entire sea **8–020** voyage (from Shoreham to Jeddah) albeit a latterly issued bill, the Rules would apply.

On the alternative contention that the Rules should not apply when the goods were kept on the dock at Le Havre since the Rules only applied to the carriage of goods on water, Bingham J. distinguished the present case from *Captain v Far Eastern Steamship Co* [1979] 1 Lloyd's Rep. 595. There, a shipowner was disentitled to plead the Canadian Carriage of Goods by Water Act (containing the Hague Rules) where the goods in question were damaged on the dock at Singapore awaiting transshipment. The present case, according to Bingham J., was different because the bill of lading as contemplated provided cover for the entirety of the voyage from Shoreham to Jeddah, whilst in the Canadian case there were two legs to the voyage and two bills of lading were contemplated. It would seem therefore that where the contract anticipates the issue of a single bill of lading covering the entirety of the voyage, the fact of any re-shipment or transshipment is immaterial to whether the Rules will apply to that contract or any part of it.

In the United States decision of *The OOCL Bravery* [2000] 1 Lloyd's Rep. 394, it was held that the Hague Rules will apply although combined international transport is used where it is clear that that was the intention of the parties as evidenced by the bill of lading. In that case, the cargo of bicycles and framesets was to be shipped door to door from Oconomowoc, Wisconsin to Spijkenisse, the Netherlands. The bill of lading stated that the goods would be transported on the OOCL Bravery from a port in Montreal, Canada to a port in Antwerp, Belgium, and that the place of delivery by the participating carrier would be the consignee's warehouse in Spijkenisse. Upon arrival at Belgium, the goods were discharged into the care and custody of a road haulier. The truck driver left his truck with the cargo unattended outside his home on a public street in Antwerp.

The truck and the goods were stolen. The question was whether the Hague Rules (as contained in the US Carriage of Goods by Sea Act) or the Convention on the International Carriage of Goods by Road (CMR) should apply considering that the goods were lost whilst being carried on land. The court rejected the defendant's argument that the applicable law was the CMR. There were no references in the bill of lading or in the contract of sale between the defendants and the claimant to the CMR. The claimant should not therefore be made subject to the CMR of which he had no notice.

It is naturally open to the parties to agree to extend the application of the rules to post-discharge events. However very explicit words to that effect must be used. In *The MSC Amsterdam* [2007] EWCA Civ 794,* the goods were misdelivered after discharge at Shanghai. The question was whether the Hague Rules which had been incorporated into the bill of lading applied also to damage or loss caused post discharge. Longmore L.J. was not convinced the convoluted 650-word-long clause was sufficiently clear to indicate persuasively an intention to extend application of the Rules to post-discharge events.

Cargoes Excluded by the Rules

8–021   The Hague-Visby Rules exclude certain cargoes from their operation:

1. the carriage of live animals (art.I(c));

2. cargo which by the contract of carriage is stated as being carried on deck and is so carried (art.I(c));

3. the carriage of "particular goods" so long as the contractual terms are incorporated into a non-negotiable receipt and no bill of lading has been or will be issued (art.VI).

In these situations, the carrier and shipper are free to negotiate their own terms of carriage subject only to the operation of the common law.

Carriage of goods on deck

8–022   The Rules will only be excluded where both requirements stated in art.I(c) are satisfied:

1. the cargo must actually be stowed on deck; and

2. the bill of lading states expressly and clearly that this is indeed the case.

Where the goods have been stowed on deck but there is no reference in the bill of lading to that effect, the Rules will nonetheless apply. The matter is complicated considerably where the bill of lading does not actually state that the goods are stowed on deck but simply gives the carrier the discretion so to do.

Svenska Traktos Aktiebolaget v Maritime Agencies (Southampton) Ltd [1953] 2 Q.B.   **8–023**
295
Facts:
Svenska, the consignees of 50 tractors, sued the carriers for the loss of one tractor washed
overboard under the Hague Rules. The Hague Rules contained a provision to the effect
that goods shipped on deck shall be excluded from the operation of the rules. The bill of
lading in question provided inter alia that the "steamer has liberty to carry goods on deck
and shipowners will not be responsible for any loss damage or claim arising therefrom".
Where the Hague Rules applied, that clause would not be operative as an exclusion
clause.
Held:
Pilcher J. held that the carriers could not avail themselves to the exclusion of liability
clause. The policy of the Rules is to regulate the relationship between the shipowner and
the owner of goods; any exceptions in the Rules must be interpreted in line with the
intention of the Rules to regulate that relationship. The requirement that there should be
a statement in the bill of lading that the goods are actually to be shipped on deck is to serve
as a warning to the cargo owner and any interested party that the rules are to be excluded.
It is not a mere formal requirement but one that has a substantive role. Where there is only
a "liberty to carry on deck" clause, that warning is not explicit. Such a general liberty
clause is not a "statement in the contract of carriage that the goods are in fact being carried
on deck". The upshot is therefore that the clause in question, to the extent it limits the
carrier's liability for damage or loss caused, is contrary to art.III r.8 of the Rules as an
exclusion of liability clause.

Sideridraulic Systems SPA v BBC Chartering & Logistics Gmbh [2011] EWHC 3106   **8–024**
(Comm)
Facts:
B had carried on deck a cargo of filter tanks from Italy to Alabama. During the voyage,
one of the tanks was lost and another was damaged. On the face of the bill of lading, it
was stated under "Master's remarks": "all cargo loaded from open storage area" and "all
cargo carried on deck at shipper's risk as to perils . . . any warranty of seaworthiness of
the vessel expressly waived by the shipper . . . ".
    The central issue was whether the carriage was subject to the Hague-Visby Rules.
    The carrier argued that the carriage was not subject to the Rules because the tanks were
deck cargo as stated by the master's remarks on the bill of lading and were, therefore, not
"goods" within the definition of the Rules.
Held:
The onus was on the carrier to show that the master's remarks had actually meant that the
goods were carried on deck. Any uncertainty should be resolved against the carrier but, on
the facts, giving the master's remarks a natural reading, it was clearly was a statement of
fact as to how the goods were carried or handled. The goods were therefore deck cargo.
That was also supported by evidence of previous dealings between the parties.

    The terms of art.I(c) are very clear—the statement that the goods are carried   **8–025**
on deck must be in the bill of lading. In *Onego Shipping and Chartering v JSC
Arcadia* [2010] EWHC 777 (Comm), the fact that the charterparty, which
incorporated the Hague-Visby Rules, very expressly envisaged that the goods
would be carried on deck was not sufficient. The bill of lading was silent as to
the goods to be carried on deck. As such, the Hague-Visby Rules were not
excluded, and the goods could not be treated as deck cargo under art.I(c).
    The special risks involved as a result of the goods being stowed on deck have
always been treated as extremely serious. Whether this should give rise to an
automatic right of repudiation of the contract was considered in *Kenya Railways
v Antares Co Pte Ltd* [1987] 1 Lloyd's Rep. 424. In that case, machinery was to

be shipped from Antwerp to Mombasa in Kenya under two bills of lading which were made subject to the Hague Rules or alternatively, the Hague-Visby Rules. When the goods were discharged at Mombasa, it was found that the goods had in fact been shipped on deck and damage had been caused to them. That the goods were shipped on board was not with the consent of the cargo owners. The cargo owners sued, relying on the doctrine of fundamental breach. If the doctrine was applicable, the carriers would not be entitled to plead the one-year limitation rule in the Conventions.

The position at law is accurately set out by Lloyd L.J. as:

"The doctrine of fundamental breach on which the [claimant] relies, that is to say the doctrine that a breach of contract may be so fundamental as to displace the exception clauses altogether, no longer exists. The death knell sounded in *Suisse Atlantique Société d'Armement Maritime SA v Rotterdamsche Kolen Centrale* [1966] 1 Lloyd's Rep. 529; [1967] 1 AC 361. The corpse was buried in *Photo Production Ltd v Securicor Transport Ltd* [1980] A.C. 827".

8–026   The Court of Appeal was asked to consider the unauthorised carriage of goods on deck as a special case falling outside the general rule in *Photo Production Ltd* (as are cases on deviation, as we have seen in the preceding chapter). Lloyd L.J. rejected this contention saying that there are no special circumstances why unauthorised on-deck carriage of goods should be treated as a special case.

That said, it had been assumed by Hirst J. in *The Chanda* [1989] 2 Lloyd's Rep. 494 that as a matter of construction, a carrier who had shipped goods on deck contrary to the contract of carriage should not be entitled to the limitations of liability provided for carriers under the Hague-Visby Rules (in art.IV(5)). The judge had commented that "there is nothing in the *Antares* case which conflicts with this view". That judgment however was recently held by the Court of Appeal, in *The Kapitan Petko Voivoda* [2003] EWCA Civ 451, to be wrong. In *The Kapitan Petko Voivoda*, the cargo owners could not derive any benefit from the supposed principle (of a very serious breach resulting in the suspension of exclusion or limitation clauses) in deviation and warehouse cases decided in the nineteenth century.[8] The court's duty, it affirmed, was to construe the contract as agreed between the parties. Article IV(5) provides that:

"[U]nless the nature and value of the goods have been declared by the shipper before shipment and inserted in the bill of lading, neither the carrier nor the ship shall in any event be or become liable for any loss or damage . . . exceeding 666.67 units of account per package or unit or 2 units of account per kilogramme . . . ".

The words "in any event" were very important when construing the contract. Tuckey L.J. in *The Happy Ranger* [2002] 2 All E.R. 24 said that "in any event" should be given their natural meaning, which was unlimited in scope. That being the case, it was incorrect of Hirst J. to construe the limitation of liability as having no application where goods have been shipped on deck. It was also contrary to the principle in *Photo Productions* to say that a protective clause

---

[8] See paras 7–040—7–043.

provided for by statute could be suspended by operation of some "fundamental" or "serious" breach.[9]

Contracts for the carriage of noncommercial goods

Article VI provides that the parties   **8–027**

"shall in regard to any particular goods be at liberty to enter into any agreement in any terms as to the responsibility and liability of the carrier for such goods"

so far as the contract is not contrary to public policy or the requirement to use due care and diligence in the loading, handling, stowage, carriage and discharge of the goods. Three further qualifications:

1. the contract shall be embodied in a non-negotiable receipt;

2. no bill of lading is issued;

3. ordinary commercial shipments made in the ordinary course of trade are excluded. Only shipments where the character or condition of the goods to be carried or the circumstances, terms and conditions under which the carriage is to be performed are such as reasonably to justify a special agreement.

Article VI's counterpart in the Hague Rules was raised in *Harland & Wolff Ltd v Burns & Laird Lines Ltd* (1931) 40 Ll.L.Rep. 286 where the contract was for the carriage of Harland's machinery made by them in Scotland from Scotland to Ireland. Sailing bills, as it will be recalled, were issued which excluded the shipowners' liability for unseaworthiness. The vessel sank and with it, the machinery. The claimant cargo owner's argument that art.VI was a sort of universal prohibition against all limitations of liability in any contract of affreightment other than those contained in a charterparty permitted by the Act was rejected. The Scottish Court of Session held that art.VI's purpose was to allow

"a carrier under a contract of carriage covered by a bill of lading to limit his responsibilities by agreement with the shipper in any way 'not contrary to public policy'; provided that the bill of lading (which would otherwise have been issued at or after shipment with the agreed-on limitations embodied in it) shall not be issued, but that instead thereof a non-negotiable receipt, marked as such and embodying the limitations, shall be used".

The presumption here seems to be that the carrier has little choice in whether   **8–028** a bill of lading should be issued or not. How would art.VI be construed if that were not the case? While not disputing the result of the case, it might be said that the court's approach verges on the constrictive in the light of the language and spirit of art.IV.

---

[9] See also *The Nea Tyhi* [1982] 1 Lloyd's Rep. 606.

In *Harland & Wolff Ltd*, the goods in question were clearly not intended for ordinary commercial shipment; as Lord Clyde pointed out, "that purpose [of the agreement] was not mercantile—for the goods were neither sold nor for sale ... ". No bill of lading was ever contemplated. It would seem that for an agreement to come within the ambit of art.VI, the contract should be of a special nature, one not consistent with the normal incidences of commercial shipments. For example, where there is a "one-off" contract for the carriage of environmental waste for safe disposal elsewhere, the purpose not being commercial or mercantile there could be a case for the use of art.VI.

Dangerous goods

8–029   Article IV(6) provides that where goods of an inflammable, explosive or dangerous nature are shipped without the consent of the carrier, the master or the agent of the carrier, the carrier is entitled to land them at any place or destroy or render the goods innocuous. He shall not be liable to the shipper for any loss or damage caused in undertaking such an action. The shipper will be liable for all damages arising directly or indirectly from the shipment of dangerous goods. As Judge Diamond, QC emphasised in *The Fiona* [1993] 1 Lloyd's Rep. 257, "the indemnity is not limited to situations where the shipment of dangerous goods is the proximate or dominant cause of the carrier's loss" and is "not limited to the situation where the shipment of a dangerous cargo is either the sole cause or the dominant cause of the carrier's loss". It's *all* damages arising.

Article IV(6) further provides that if dangerous goods shipped with the knowledge and consent of the carrier become a danger to the ship or cargo, they may be landed at any place, destroyed or rendered innocuous by the carrier without liability on the part of the carrier except to general average, if any.

Whether art.IV(6) can be invoked depends on whether the nature of the goods is known to the carrier. The standard of knowledge on the part of the carrier is "that of the ordinarily experienced and skilful carrier of goods of the general kind shipped" (*The Aconcagua* [2010] EWCA Civ 1403). In *The Athanasia Comninos* [1990] 1 Lloyd's Rep. 277, Mustill J. said that in many cases the question whether or not goods were dangerous can be resolved by asking whether or not the carrier had performed the contract of carriage in a manner appropriate to their particular description. If he had, and the danger materialised, the cargo might be regarded as abnormal since in respect of the great majority of goods "normal" precautions would eliminate the risk of carrying normal goods; so that proper carriage and dangerous goods were opposite sides of the same coin. The judge, however, also added that there are cases where so simple an analysis could not be applied. Some risks might materialise despite an acceptable standard of care of the cargo; after all, there can be no total elimination of risks in certain types of cargo. In such so called, "bad luck" cases the carrier would be held responsible.

8–030   In *Chandris v Isbrandsten-Moller Co Inc* [1951] 1 K.B. 240, the charterparty was for the carriage of a cargo of "lawful general merchandise, excluding acids, explosives ... or other dangerous cargo". The master had consented to the charterer's shipping turpentine, which is a dangerous cargo. When the ship called at Liverpool to discharge her cargo, she was ordered by port authorities to leave the dock area and to discharge using lighters. This meant that the whole process was delayed considerably. The shipowners claimed damages from the charterers for the detention of the ship. The charterers argued that the shipowners having consented to the carriage of dangerous goods must be said to have waived their right to claims arising from that carriage. The court disagreed, holding that the consent did not necessarily mean a waiver of their right to claim damages.

The definition of dangerous goods is not provided for in the Hague-Visby Rules. It might be thought that an ejusdem generis approach would be taken in interpreting the phrase "inflammable, explosive or dangerous nature" (art.IV(6)). The Court of Appeal however preferred a more common sense approach in *Effort Shipping Co Ltd v Linden Management SA (The Giannis NK)* [1996] 1 Lloyd's Rep. 577, CA; [1998] 1 Lloyd's Rep. 337, HL.

The Giannis NK [1996] 1 Lloyd's Rep. 577, CA; [1998] 1 Lloyd's Rep. 337, HL   **8–031**
Facts:
A shipment of groundnuts and wheat was carried from Senegal to the Dominican Republic. The nuts were later found to be infested with the khapra beetle. The US Department of Agriculture ordered that the vessel return the cargo to their countries of origin or dump it at sea. The cargo was then dumped at sea and the vessel had to be fumigated to eliminate the pest. The shipowners sued the shippers in respect of the delay to the vessel caused by the pest and bunker and other expenses incurred during the delay. Article IV(6) was relied on by the shipowners.
Held:
The Court of Appeal held that the goods were in fact "dangerous" within the meaning of art.IV(6), Hague-Visby Rules. On appeal, the House of Lords agreed with the Court of Appeal that a cargo can be "dangerous" even though its physical attributes do not imperil the ship itself.

On the other hand, in *Bunge SA v ADM Do Brasil Ltda* [2009] EWHC 845 (Comm) the court refused to find the cargo of soy bean pellets to be dangerous simply because a rat was found in them. The fact that the presence of rats was likely to delay the carriage of the cargo did not mean that the goods were dangerous. Danger connotes some kind of physical harm to the ship, crew or cargo. The court agreed with the arbitrators that the cargo did not pose a physical danger to another maize cargo on board and it plainly posed no threat of damage to the ship itself. The arbitrators made no finding that imposition of quarantine or dumping of the entire cargo was to be expected.

In both *Bunge SA* and *The Giannis NK*, the courts were clear that the definition   **8–032**
of dangerous goods is similar to that used in common law as fleshed out by Mustill J. in *The Athanasia Comninos* in these terms

"it is essential to remember that we are here concerned, not with the labelling in the abstract of goods as 'dangerous' or 'safe' but with the distribution of risk for the consequences of a dangerous situation arising during the voyage".

The House of Lords, in *The Giannis NK*, confirmed the decision of the Court of Appeal in these terms:

"Goods could be dangerous within rule 6 if they were dangerous to other goods, even though they were not dangerous to the vessel itself. 'Dangerous' was not to be confined to goods which were liable to cause direct physical damage to other goods. . . . The groundnut cargo was of a dangerous nature on shipment because it was liable to give rise to the loss of other cargo loaded on the same vessel by dumping at sea." (per Lord Lloyd.)

The shippers then argued that their liability was negated under art.III(3) which provides that

"the shipper shall not be responsible for loss or damage sustained by the carrier or the ship arising or resulting from any cause without the act, fault, or neglect of the shipper, his agents or his servants".

8–033   American authorities were cited in support of the contention that fault must be proved. Hirst L.J., in rejecting the shipper's defence and preferring to bring the Hague-Visby Rules in line with that common law approach, relied on dicta in *The Athanasia Comninos* and *The Fiona* where strict liability was adopted. The House of Lords similarly rejected the argument stating:

"Article IV rule 6 was a freestanding provision covering the specific subject matter of dangerous goods. It was neither expressly, or by implication, subject to article IV rule 3. It imposed strict liability on shippers in relation to the shipment of dangerous goods, irrespective of fault or neglect on their part".

The use of the word "freestanding" was however objected to by Lord Cooke who though concurring in the result, held that the relationship between art.IV(3) and art.IV(6) is to be adjudged in the following manner

" . . . if there were any *prima facie* conflict between the general provisions of article IV rule 3 and the special provisions of article IV rule 6, the correct interpretation must be that the special provisions took priority over the general provisions".

That the inconsistency between the two provisions cannot be explained away easily makes the decision difficult to rationalise, at least on semantic construction. The proof of fault as required by the US courts would seem to avoid this apparent inconsistency between the art.IV(3) and IV(6) (*Serrano v US Lines Co* [1965] A.M.C. 1038 (SDNY 1965) and *The Stylianos Restis* [1974] A.M.C. 2343 (SDNY 1972).

8–034   The English law approach is deeply influenced by the common law rule (*Bamfield v Goole and Sheffield Transport Co Ltd* [1910] 2 K.B. 94) where strict liability was paramount when it came to the shipment of dangerous goods.[10] This is reflected in the dictum of Judge Diamond Q.C. in *The Fiona* which was approved by the Court of Appeal and the House of Lords in *The Giannis NK*:

"[The right to claim] does not involve any enquiry as to whether the shipper has knowledge of the dangerous nature and character of the goods or was at fault in permitting their shipment or in warning the carrier before shipment . . . None of these matters are referred to in the rule as matters on which the carrier's right to an indemnity depends . . . ".

---

[10] Panesar "The shipment of dangerous goods and strict liability" [1998] I.C.C.L.R. 136.

This is not to say that the English position is less preferable compared with the American rule which requires proof of fault. The approaches simply have different priorities. The former takes the approach that certainty in the distribution of risk and tasks is fundamental in the contract of commercial carriage. As long as the goods are considered dangerous, the shipper must bear the risk of injury or loss caused. The American approach seems to make the distinction between goods that are ostensibly dangerous and that characteristic is or ought to be known to the shipper, and goods that are not dangerous but become dangerous as a result of externalities (such as the khapra beetle). In the first, liability would be found and could not be saved by art.IV(3) because the state of his knowledge renders him at fault. In the second situation, proof of fault is required.

Article IV(6) provides that the shipper alone is liable for all damages arising directly or indirectly from the shipment of dangerous goods. It would appear that this duty however will not be activated unless the carrier has first satisfied the duty to supply a seaworthy ship.

Northern Shipping Co v Deutsche Seereederei GmbH [2000] 2 Lloyd's Rep. 255   **8–035**
Facts:
The *Kapitan Sakhariv* was carrying laden containers belonging to the defendants. A container on deck containing a dangerous cargo exploded, causing a fire on deck which spread below resulting in the sinking of the ship. The claimants lost their ship and faced claims by the dependants of two seamen and by the Iranian authorities for pollution damage. The contracts had incorporated the Hague Rules. The facts were:

1. the initial explosion occurred in undeclared dangerous cargo stowed on deck;

2. the fire spread to a cargo of isopentane inappropriately stowed below deck by the carrier; and

3. the isopentane contributed to the fire damage below deck which ultimately sank the ship.

Held:
The stowage of the isopentane below deck clearly contravened the international shipping codes on seaworthiness (such as the International Convention for Health and Safety of Life at Sea 1974, as amended (SOLAS) and the International Maritime Dangerous Goods Code (IMDG)). The bad stowage had effectively rendered the ship unseaworthy. As far as art.IV(6) is concerned, the issue is whether the carrier's failure to exercise due diligence in the stowage of the isopentane causing unseaworthiness was an effective cause of the fire in the hold and the loss of the ship. As it was, the carriers were not entitled to rely on art.IV(6) to seek an indemnity from the shippers. It was immaterial that there was another cause or as to which of them was the dominant cause or their respective timings, the principle was that the duty to supply a seaworthy ship is an overriding duty.

It is important not to treat *Northern Shipping Co v Deutsche Seereederei GmbH* as stating that where there are two operative causes, a decision as to which is the more dominant must be made. The Court of Appeal held in no uncertain terms that, in that case, the carriers could not plead art.IV(6) because they had not, in the first place, provided a seaworthy ship. That is an overriding duty and one which must pre-exist before the protective provisions in the Hague-Visby Rules could be relied on. Once that is met, where there are two operative causes, it would seem that as long as the shipper's shipment of an undeclared dangerous cargo is one of those causes the carrier is fully entitled to resort to art.IV(6).

Excluding the Application of the Rules

8–036 The overriding rule is that where the contract is subject to the Rules by virtue of the statute, the parties are not at liberty to contract out of their application. The Rules are to have the force of law according to s.1(2) Carriage of Goods by Sea Act 1971. Additionally, art.III(8) provides that any contractual term relieving or lessening the carrier's liability under the rules shall be null and void and of no effect. While it is clear that legal provisions cannot be contracted out of, it is less straightforward whether the parties are free to choose a law applicable to their contract of carriage which might derogate from those Rules.

8–037 *The Hollandia* [1983] 1 A.C. 565
Facts:
The contract was for the carriage of a road-finishing machine from Scotland to Bonaire in the Dutch Antilles. The machine was carried first to Amsterdam before being transshipped onto the Morviken. The bill of lading contained a clause providing for the incorporation of the law of the Netherlands into the contract and for the exclusive jurisdiction of the Court of Amsterdam. The machine was damaged and the cargo owners brought an Admiralty action in rem against the Hollandia, a ship owned by the carriers. Where Dutch law was to apply, the Hague Rules 1924 will apply because they form part of Dutch law. Where on the other hand English law is to apply, the Hague-Visby Rules will apply. Under the Hague Rules, the carriers would have been entitled to a more beneficial limitation of damages provision.
Held:
The House of Lords held that the carriers could not plead the limitation of damages rule in Dutch law simply by relying on the exclusive jurisdiction and choice of law clauses in the contract. It was argued that the choice of forum clause is only a contractual provision prescribing the procedure by which disputes arising under the contract of carriage are to be resolved. It does not seek to absolve the carrier from liability or to lessen his liability. This was rejected by Lord Diplock who said that this argument ignores the substance of the clause which was to evade the provisions of the Hague-Visby Rules as applicable in the United Kingdom. The carrier's submission is simply too narrow. According to Lord Diplock, to adopt that narrow interpretation:

> "would leave it open to any shipowner to evade the provisions of article III paragraph 8 by the simple device of inserting in his bills of lading issued in, or for carriage from a port in, any contracting state a clause in standard form providing as the exclusive forum for resolution of disputes what might aptly be described as a court of convenience, *viz.*, one situated in a country which did not apply the Hague-Visby rules or, for that matter, a country whose law recognised an unfettered right in a shipowner . . . to relieve himself from all liability for loss or damage to goods caused by his own negligence, fault or breach of contract".

The choice of forum clause was therefore not effective and could not be recognised.

8–038 *Pirelli Cables Ltd v United Thai Shipping Corporation Ltd* [2000] 1 Lloyd's Rep. 663
Facts:
The claimants were holders of a bill of lading which incorporated an exclusive jurisdiction clause in favour of the courts in Thailand. The claim was for damage caused to a drum of electric cable which was being carried by the defendants from Southampton to Thailand and then, onwards to Singapore. The Hague-Visby Rules were applicable to the bill by virtue of the Carriage of Goods by Sea Act 1971 and art.X of the Hague-Visby Rules. If the claim was to be tried in Thailand which was not a signatory to the Hague Rules 1924 or the Hague-Visby Rules, lower limitation figures would be applicable than those applied

under the Hague-Visby Rules. The defendants applied to set aside the English writ served on them by the claimants and/or to stay the action in favour of the courts in Thailand. *Held:*
The High Court held that the jurisdiction clause on which the claimants relied formed an effective part of the contract even though it was not quite legible. However, by choosing Thailand as the forum for claims, the defendants limited their liability to a sum lower than that to which it was entitled under the Hague-Visby Rules. Unless and until the defendants undertook not to take advantage of the lower limit, the claimants were entitled to disregard the jurisdiction clause and to bring proceedings in this country. Since there is in place a suitable undertaking not to rely on the lower limits, a stay of English proceedings would be granted. As far as the choice between England and Thailand as the appropriate forum, there is very little to go by. Although the procedure is probably more convenient in England, many of the relevant witnesses are in Thailand/Singapore. Reliance was placed on *Baghlaf Al Zafer v Pakistan National Shipping Co* [1998] Lloyd's Rep. 229 where the court held that when the evidence for *forum conveniens* is finely balanced, there must be a "strong cause" not to stay proceedings in support of a jurisdiction clause.

Much depends on whether the Hague-Visby Rules are to have mandatory effect in the first place. In the *Komninos S* as we have noted earlier (para.8–010), the choice of English law as the applicable law did not render the contract subject to the Hague-Visby Rules because the rules have no mandatory effect on bills of lading issued in a noncontracting state, Greece. It was argued that English law being the proper law of the contracts should necessarily imply the application of the Hague-Visby Rules, which would in turn make these exception clauses null and void. Bingham L.J. rejected the contention stating that since shipment was from Greece, ss.1(3), (6) Carriage of Goods by Sea Act 1971 and art.X Hague-Visby Rules plainly had no application, and consequently there was no question of UK statutes applying automatically. Instead they must be incorporated expressly. In *The Hollandia*, the Rules had mandatory effect by virtue of the carriage being from the United Kingdom. From that judgment, it naturally follows that art.III(8) must be read together with the provisions on when the Rules will have mandatory effect.

It should also be noted that following the House of Lords decision in *The Jordan II* [2004] UKHL 49, it is confirmed that a clause in the contract of carriage which transferred the liability for storing, lashing, stowing, dunnaging and discharging the cargo to the shipper, cargo interest or charterer would not be caught by art.III(8).[11]

8–039

In a Canadian case, *Timberwest Forest v Pacific Link Ocean* [2008] F.C. 801, the Canadian Federal Court ruled a waiver of subrogation clause had a similar effect and was therefore void under the Hague-Visby Rules. The claimants were insurers who had paid the cargo interest for the lost goods. They sued the carrier, in exercise of their subrogation right. The insurance policy provided cargo cover for the shipper, but it also named the carrier as an additional insured, with a full waiver of subrogation. The effect of that was that the insurer would not be allowed to sue the carrier. The court held that the waiver of subrogation clause had the effect of relieving the carrier of liability under the rules. As such it was void. However, somewhat controversially, the court allowed the clause to be relied on by other noncarrier defendants (such as master of the tug, stevedores, etc).

---

[11] See also *Renton v Palmyra* [1957] A.C. 149; and paras 8–047—8–051.

Article III(8) also states that a benefit of insurance or similar clause shall be deemed a clause relieving the carrier from liability and as such, potentially void under the Hague-Visby Rules.

Duties of the Carrier

The carrier's duty to provide a seaworthy ship—article III(1)

8–040   Article III (1) provides that the carrier shall be bound before and at the beginning of the voyage to exercise due diligence to:

1. make the ship seaworthy;

2. properly man, equip and supply the ship;

3. make the holds, refrigerating and cool chambers and all other parts of the ship in which the goods are carried fit and safe for their reception, carriage and preservation.

Article IV(1) then states that the carrier shall not be liable for loss or damage arising or resulting from unseaworthiness *unless* caused by want of due diligence on the part of the carrier to make the ship seaworthy. Whenever loss of damage has resulted from unseaworthiness the burden of proving the exercise of due diligence shall be on the carrier. In *Owners of the Cargo Lately Laden onboard the ship Torepo v Owners and/or Demise Charterers of the Ship Torepo* [2002] EWHC 1481, a claim was brought by the shippers for the grounding of the ship. It was claimed that the grounding was caused by the negligence of the pilot in the navigation of the vessel, that is to say, the ship was unseaworthy. The court found that a senior cadet had been instructed to act as lookout and he was adequately certificated for that role. The pilot's passage plans were not entirely clear but could not be condemned as being deficient. His charts were not reliable but that was not the ship's fault. There were two Chilean charts which were inconsistent with each other. It was impossible, given the ship's circumstances, to know for certain which set was accurate. On the evidence therefore the court found that the ship was not unseaworthy and if it had been unseaworthy, the master could rely on art.IV(5).

The carrier however does not discharge his burden simply by showing that he had delegated the responsibility to some other competent or specialist contractor. In *Riverstone Meat Co Pty Ltd v Lancashire Shipping Co Ltd (The Muncaster Castle)* [1961] A.C. 807, the defendants had engaged a firm of reputable repairers to repair the ship before sailing. The repairers were negligent and caused water to enter the ship's hold damaging the claimants' goods. Lord Radcliffe held that the carriers must answer for anything that has been done amiss in the repairs. Their duty is to exercise due diligence in ensuring that the ship is seaworthy, not due diligence in securing the services of a reputable and competent professional to fulfil that task. The rationale, according to His Lordship, was:

"I should regard it as unsatisfactory, where a cargo-owner has found his goods damaged through a defect in the seaworthiness of the vessel, that his rights of recovering from the carrier should depend on particular circumstances in the carrier's situation and arrangements with which the cargo-owner has nothing to do; as for instance, that liability should depend on the measure of control that the carrier had exercised over persons engaged on surveying or repairing the ship or upon such questions as whether the carrier had or could have done whatever was needed by the hands of his own servants or had been sensible or prudent in getting it done by other hands. Carriers would find themselves liable or not liable, according to circumstances quite extraneous to the sea carriage itself".

Incidentally, it would appear that the nature of the non-delegable duty of **8–041** art.III(1) would vitally prevent the cargo interest from taking action against a classification society for negligent surveys or repairs carried out on the vessel. In *Marc Rich & Co AG v Bishop Rock Marine Co Ltd (The Nicholas H)* [1995] 3 All E.R. 307, the House of Lords held, with Lord Lloyd dissenting, that where a shipowner has undertaken the nondelegable duty of ensuring the seaworthiness of the ship as regards the carriage of goods belonging to the claimant, the classification society should not be made liable for the negligent survey carried out. The House of Lords observed that for more than 150 years, classification societies had classified merchant ships in the interest of safeguarding life and ships at sea. The critical question was thus whether it would be fair, just and reasonable to impose a duty of care on marine classification societies for the careless performance of a survey of a damaged vessel given that there was a sufficient degree of proximity to fulfil the requirement in tort law for the existence of such a duty. The recognition of such a duty, it was opined by the House of Lords, would be unjust because the shipowners would ultimately have to bear the cost of the classification societies if they were held liable. Classification societies act for the collective welfare and unlike shipowners, they do not have the benefit of any limitation provisions found in the Hague-Visby Rules, in contract or other similar instruments. As a matter of policy, it would not be fair to hold them liable to cargo owners who should be content with bringing an action in contract against the shipowners. It should not be thought that this protection would extend to all independent contractors taken on by the shipowner to repair, maintain, examine or carry out other tasks on the ship. Classification societies, as the House of Lords was at pains to stress, are unique in their role in international shipping and it would be very much against policy to hold them liable thereby exposing them to liability in an indeterminate amount for an indeterminate time to an indeterminate class of claimants.

In *Eridania SpA v Rudolf A Oetker (The Fjord Wind)* [2000] 2 Lloyd's Rep. 191, the Court of Appeal in construing the requirement[12] on the carrier to take due diligence to make the ship seaworthy confirmed that test should be that as set out in *Union of India v NV Reederij Amsterdam (The Amstelslot)* [1963] 2 Lloyd's Rep. 223. The key question was whether a reasonable person in the shoes of the defendant, with the skill and knowledge which the defendant had or ought to have had, would have taken those extra precautions, or whether the independent contractors' survey had been as thorough as they could reasonably

---

[12] The clause in question in that case was cl.35 of the Norgrain form, which imposed an absolute warranty on the shipowner to exercise due diligence to ensure seaworthiness of the vessel at the beginning of the approach voyage. That clause incorporates wholesale art.III(1) of the Hague Rules.

have been expected to conduct in the circumstances. In *The Fjord Wind*, the court found that the owners had failed to demonstrate that a proper investigation was carried out following the failure of the crankpin. Under the circumstances, they could only demonstrate due diligence if they could show that they or their independent contractors did not overlook any lines of enquiry which competent experts could reasonably be expected to have pursued.

It should also be noted that compliance with the necessary international codes of shipping standards[13] as to seaworthiness is not conclusive evidence of "due diligence", so held the Court of Appeal in *Northern Shipping Co v Deutsche Seereederei GmbH* [2000] 2 Lloyd's Rep. 255. On the same basis, non compliance as a result of a misconstruction of the relevant shipping codes on seaworthiness is not determinative evidence of lack of due diligence as the court strove to point out in that case.

8–042   Seaworthiness under the Rules is defined to encompass not only the physical attributes of the ship in undertaking the sea voyage but also the carrier's duty to man, equip and supply the ship, and ensure the ship's cargoworthiness. It is not always easy to establish whether these facets of the duty of seaworthiness have been breached. A modern case faced with such a difficulty is *A Meredith Jones & Co Ltd v Vangemar Shipping Co Ltd (The Apostolis)* [1997] 2 Lloyd's Rep. 241. In that case, the welding carried out on the ship had exposed the cargo of cotton to a risk of ignition. The trial judge had found as a fact that the welding, though not done directly above an open or partly open hold, created a risk of sparks entering the hold through a gap in the hatch covers. The issue for the court was whether the exposure to the risk of ignition caused by the welding made the ship unseaworthy.

Tuckey J. at first instance held that if it was simply fire in the cargo itself which made the vessel unseaworthy, as might be the case with a fire caused by a discarded cigarette then there would be no breach of art.III(1). However, in the present case, the threat to the cargo posed by the sparks was associated with the welding carried out on the ship had made the hold unsafe and unfit for the cargo. The test Tuckey J. laid down was:

> "If one were to ask rhetorically whether the carrier had made the hold of his ship fit and safe for the preservation of an inflammable cargo when he was carrying out welding work above the hold which resulted in sparks raining into it, there could I think be only one answer: no, his hold was not fit and safe for the cargo; his ship was unseaworthy".

Reliance was placed on *Maxine Footwear Co Ltd v Canadian Government Merchant Marine Ltd* [1959] 2 Lloyd's Rep. 105 in which cargo was ignited as a result of fire in insulation in the hold caused before the cargo was loaded. There the Privy Council had held that the vessel was unseaworthy from the time that the vessel caught fire and that the damage to the cargo was therefore caused by the unseaworthiness.

8–043   The Court of Appeal disagreed with Tuckey J. and stated that there was no breach of art.III(1) merely because the welding exposed the cargo to an ephemeral risk of ignition. The holds themselves were not intrinsically unsafe. In

---

[13] In this case, it was the Russian version of the International Maritime Dangerous Goods Code (IMDG) which was in issue.

Maxine the Privy Council found it unnecessary to decide whether the ship was on fire before the cargo was loaded. It was fire in the fabric of the vessel, namely the cork lining of the hold, which rendered her unseaworthy. Here, the ship only became unseaworthy because of the fire, not as a result of some intrinsic defect in ship or system. In addition, the Court of Appeal thought that the evidence adduced was simply not sufficiently cogent to permit a finding of fact that the "welding work . . . resulted in sparks raining into the hold" but went on to hold that even if this had been the case, the test was wrong in law. Leggatt L.J. said, "even if the fire was caused as [the Judge] found, there was no breach of article III r.1, and the owners were not liable on that ground". The exposure of the cargo or ship to an avoidable risk does not make the ship unseaworthy, according to the Court of Appeal.

The dissent on the facts aside, it is submitted that the case seems to go against the grain of *Maxine Footwear Co Ltd* where the Privy Council was quite adamant that the ship could be rendered unseaworthy by a system of repairs or works being carried out onboard a vessel which exposes the vessel to certain risks of damage. It is difficult to see how the Court of Appeal could distinguish *Maxine Footwear* on the basis that it was the fabric lining in the hold there that rendered the ship unseaworthy. This does not seem to be borne out by the Privy Council's finding there that it was ultimately the negligent use of the torch to thaw the pipes that rendered the ship unseaworthy. Lord Somervell of Harrow said in that case:

"From the time when the ship caught on fire she was unseaworthy. This unseaworthiness caused the damage to and loss of the appellants' goods. The negligence of the respondents' servants which caused the fire was a failure to exercise due diligence".

Let us consider the breadth of Leggatt L.J.'s test in this context. His Lordship stated that "even if [the exposure of the cargo to the risk of fire] . . . occurred, it was not unseaworthiness that caused the fire, but the fire which rendered the vessel unseaworthy". To paraphrase, Leggatt L.J.'s analysis looks something like this:

1. the ship was physically sound;

2. fire started, regardless of whether it was caused by a cigarette or welding; and

3. damage caused by fire. No conclusion of unseaworthiness should therefore be drawn since the ship was intrinsically fit.

This equation, it is submitted, does not seem to take into account the fact that it was the welding works that brought about the risk or danger of ignition. The issue is whether that exposure of the ship to the risk of fire without any intrinsic defect could amount to unseaworthiness. The Court of Appeal evidently thought not.

Two criticisms might be made: **8–044**

1. First, there was no link drawn between the system of repairs and the fire caused as was indeed made in *Maxine Footwear Co Ltd*. This finding seems to suggest that the system of repair or welding has no relevance in

determining whether the ship is seaworthy; all that matters is whether it was the intrinsic unfitness of the hold that caused the fire under those circumstances or whether it was the fire that made the ship unseaworthy. We will recall sound authorities where a system of repairs or works could result in the ship's unseaworthiness without the requiring proof of any intrinsic defect in the physical characteristics of the ship (see *Hongkong Fir Shipping; Standard Oil Co v Clan Line* [1924] A.C. 100, etc).

2. Secondly, the Court of Appeal did not seem too concerned with the risk of exposure. Although Leggatt L.J. was swift to cover himself by stating that the risk was ephemeral or fleeting, His Lordship went on to pronounce that even if the lower court's finding that there was an appreciable risk, it would not have made any difference. It might be contended that the creation of a risk of danger to the ship and its ability to carry the cargo can amount to unseaworthiness as we see in the House of Lords' case of *Steel v State Line Steamship Co* (1877) 3 App. Cas. 72.

While it is understandable that the Court of Appeal was concerned with the probity of evidence as to whether the welding had been carried out at all, to say that the risk of exposure to the risk from the welding could not constitute unseaworthiness might be taking things somewhat too far.

8–045   Article III(1) confines the duty of seaworthiness to "before and at the beginning of the voyage". In *Maxine Footwear*, the Privy Council took a liberal approach and held that although the fire broke out after loading but before the beginning of the voyage, the carriers were still liable under the rules. The carriers had argued that "before and at the beginning of the voyage" must be construed consistent with the common law. Accordingly, the duty should attach only at two moments in time: the beginning of the loading and the beginning of the voyage. Lord Somervell of Harrow rejected the submission stating:

> "In their Lordships' opinion 'before and at the beginning of the voyage' means the period from at least the beginning of the loading until the vessel starts on her voyage. The word 'before' cannot in their opinion be read as meaning 'at the commencement of the loading'. If this had been intended it would have been said. The question when precisely the period begins does not arise in this case, hence the insertion above of the words 'at least'".

This qualification as to when the duty attaches is given a narrow reading. In *The Happy Ranger* [2006] EWHC 122, Gloster J. held that although the shipowners had been closely involved in the preparation of the ship for the voyage prior to its delivery to the cargo interest, their duty to exercise due diligence under art.III(1) would not apply until the start of the voyage.

It is important to note that when construing the terms of a multilateral convention, national courts should as far as possible take a generous approach which conforms with the broad principles of general acceptance and application. In the interests of uniformity and comity, an English court might look to the general approach taken by other contracting states. In this case, the common law approach is quite distinct from the "general acceptation" and it would therefore not be in the spirit of the Rules to restrict the scope of the Rules thus. (See *Stag Line Ltd v Foscolo, Mango & Co* [1932] A.C. 328 for an account on how the construction of the Hague Rules (and Hague-Visby Rules) is to be tackled.)

Where a breach of art.III(1) is alleged, the claimant must show that the **8–046** unseaworthiness did actually cause the loss or damage. The approach of the courts seems to be along common sense lines rather than any specially worded legal test. It is sufficient that the claimant is able to show that the unseaworthiness is a cause of the loss, he need not prove that it was the *only* cause. In *Smith Hogg & Co Ltd v Black Sea & Baltic General Insurance Co Ltd* [1940] A.C. 997, Lord Wright said, in response to the carriers' contention that without the negligence of the master, the disaster would not have occurred:

"I can draw no distinction between cases where the negligent conduct of the master is a cause and cases in which any other cause, such as perils of the seas, or fire, is a co-operating cause. A negligent act is as much a co-operating cause, if it is a cause at all, as an act which is not negligent. The question is the same in either case, it is, would the disaster not have happened if the ship had fulfilled the obligation of seaworthiness even though the disaster could not have happened if there had not also been the specific peril or action".

We see a similar result in *The Christel Vinnen* [1924] P. 208 where although it was proved that the crew had been negligent in not pumping the water out and that was an equal contributory cause to the damage as the ship's unseaworthiness, the carrier's duty to provide a seaworthy ship was nonetheless breached.

The carrier's duty to care for the cargo—article III(2)

Nature of the duty

Article III(2) provides that "subject to the provisions of art.IV, the carrier shall **8–047** properly and carefully load, handle, stow, carry, keep, care for and discharge the goods carried". This article was discussed and examined in some detail by the House of Lords in *Albacora SRL v Westcott & Laurance Line Ltd* [1966] 2 Lloyd's Rep. 53.

Albacora SRL v Westcott & Laurance Line Ltd [1966] 2 Lloyd's Rep. 53. **8–048**
Facts:
The cargo of salted fish was found on discharge to have been seriously damaged by bacteria because the temperature in the hold was not lower than 5C. It was assumed by both the shippers and carriers that refrigeration was not necessary. The contract itself did not provide for refrigeration. The issue for the House of Lords was whether the carriers were in breach of art.III(2) for not "properly" carrying the fish.
Held:
The claimants' argument was that the only proper way of carrying that particular cargo of salted fish was in refrigerated holds and that the carriers had therefore breached art.III(2).
As far as the court was concerned, the word "properly" adds nothing to the word "carefully" which was defined in *GH Renton & Co Ltd v Palmyra Trading Corporation of Panama* [1957] A.C. 149 as "upon a sound system". A sound system does not mean a system suited to all the weaknesses and idiosyncrasies of a particular cargo. It should be confined to a reasonable system in relation to the general practice of carriage of goods by sea. It would seriously detract from the demands of efficiency to adopt the claimants' contention. Furthermore, to accept the claimants' argument would be to import into the Hague Rules a revolutionary and unintended departure from the scheme of the common law. That scheme as stated in *FC Bradley & Sons Ltd v Federal Steam Navigation Co Ltd* (1927) 27 Ll. L. Rep. 395 is

" . . . the carrier answers for his ship and men, the cargo owner for his cargo. The carrier has at least some means of controlling his crew and has full opportunity of making his ship seaworthy, but of the cargo he knows little or nothing and, as the shipper has the advantage over him in this respect, he must bear the risks belonging to the cargo".

8–049   In the opinion of Lord Reid, the obligation under art.III(2) is to adopt a system which is sound in the light of all the knowledge which the carrier has or ought to have about the nature. In the present case, the carriers had no reason to suppose that the goods required any different treatment from that which the goods in fact received. The carriers were therefore not in breach.

In *International Packers London Ltd v Ocean SS Co Ltd* [1955] 2 Lloyd's Rep. 218, the cargo owners brought an action against the carriers for damage caused to their tinned meat. The damage was caused by two separate events. First, during a severe storm insecurely fastened tarpaulins were washed away resulting in water entering the holds and damaging the tins of meat. Subsequently when the ship was taken to port for repairs, a surveyor negligently advised that the tins should be left where they were. This led to the rusting of the tins.

On whether the carriers were in breach of art.III(2), McNair J. held that although the failure to properly fasten the tarpaulins was a breach, the carriers could rely on the defence in art.IV(2)(a). On the second allegation, the carriers were in breach even though it was the negligent conduct of an independent contractor. The obligation under art.III(2) to care for the goods extends to efforts taken to protect or relieve the goods from circumstances caused by an earlier accident or danger, even when that earlier danger was an excepted peril or was brought about without the carrier's fault.[14]

8–050   The carrier's duty to ensure that the goods are properly stowed and looked after during transit also extends to the master's duty to ensure that the cargo hold is in a safe state for the contracted goods at the time of loading. In *Vinmar International Ltd v Theresa Navigation SA* (March 9, 2001), the Commercial Court found that the master had played no part during the loading of the goods and had failed to observe standard tanker practice by checking that the tanks and lines at the beginning of loading should be cleaned and any contaminants from the previous cargo should be removed. That was a matter in which he should have interested himself and taken whatever steps were necessary to satisfy himself as to the extent and source of the contamination. The shipowner was therefore liable for the loss of value suffered by the cargo of ethylene.

It should also be noted that since the early case of *Renton v Palmyra* [1957] A.C. 149 a shipowner can avoid being pinned to art.III(2) for loading, stowage and discharge of the goods by inserting a clause in the contract transferring the responsibility for loading, stowage and discharge to the cargo interest (whether that be the charterer or the shipper of goods). The House of Lords in that case approved the dicta of Devlin J. in *Pyrene Co Ltd v Scindia Navigation Co Ltd* [1954] 2 Q.B. 402 below:

"The extent to which the carrier has to undertake the loading of the vessel may depend not only upon different systems of law but upon the custom and practice of the port and the nature of the cargo. It is difficult to believe that the Rules were intended to impose a universal rigidity in this respect, or to deny

---

[14] Berlingieri, "The Hague-Visby Rules and actions in tort" [1991] L.Q.R. 18.

freedom of contract to the carrier. The carrier is practically bound to play some part in the loading and discharging, so that both operations are naturally included in those covered by the contract of carriage. But I see no reason why the Rules should not leave the parties free to determine by their own contract the part which each has to play. On this view the whole contract of carriage is subject to the Rules, but the extent to which loading and discharging are brought within the carrier's obligations is left to the parties themselves to decide".

Loading, stowage, trimming, dunnage and unloading are land-side operations which the shipowner might legitimately require the charterer or shipper to perform; on the other hand, it would be difficult and unreasonable to expect a cargo interest to look after and care for the goods once they are at sea. In *The Jordan II* [2004] UKHL 49, the cargo interest attempted to argue that such a contractual device transferring the shipowner's responsibility to load, stow and discharge the goods to the cargo interest was unlawful for running foul of art.III(8). Article III(8) provides that

"any clause ... in the contract of carriage relieving the carrier ... from liability for loss or damage to, or in connection with, goods arising from negligence, fault or failure in the duties and obligations provided in this article or lessening such liability otherwise than as provided in these Rules, shall be null and void and of no effect ... ".

In that case, the clause in question provided "Shippers/charterers/receivers to **8–051** put the cargo onboard, trim and discharge cargo free of expense to the vessel". The shippers argued that as art.III(2) imposes on the shipowners a duty to load, stow and discharge the goods, the position taken in *Renton* was incorrect. The shippers attempted to rely on the *travaux preparatoire* of the Rules, and the mandatory language used in the French text of the Rules, to show that the duty in art.III(2) could not be contractually transferred. The House of Lords however found that there was no universal view on the subject; thus, without clear reasons why *Renton* was contrary to principle or commercial practicalities, it should stand in the interest of commercial certainty.

Thus far we see how art.III(2) could be undermined by a transfer of stowage and loading responsibility clause. Where the poor stowage or loading results in a loss of seaworthiness, what are the implications of such a clause? In *The ER Hamburg* [2006] EWHC 483, the contract stipulated: "Charterers are to load, stow and trim the cargo at their expense under the supervision of the Captain". The cargo of calcium hypochlorite was carried in a container which had been loaded, in accordance with the cargo plan prepared by the charterer's ship planners, directly adjacent to a tank used to contain bunker fuel. It exploded, causing damage to the ship. The charterer argued that although they were responsible for loading and stowing under the clause, the ship's Chief Officer must be held responsible for failing to spot on the computer stowage plans that the container was to be placed next to a heat source. That, it was contended, was in breach of art.III(1) and, as the charterer argued, the clause could not override the owner's duty to provide a seaworthy ship. The court rejected the charterer's argument. Morison J. relied on *The Imvros* [1999] 1 Lloyd's Rep. 848 where Langley J. said that words such as "under the supervision of the Captain" did not limit the charterers' liability. They simply denoted the shipmaster's right to be satisfied with the loading and stowing operations. Langley J. had said, "A right to intervene did not normally carry with it a liability for failure to do so, let alone relieve the actor from his liability" and further

"it would be a remarkable construction which produced the result that so long as the loading was carried out by the charterers badly enough to put the, or the other, cargo but not the vessel at risk, the charterers would be liable but the moment the loading was so badly carried out that it made the vessel unseaworthy the entire responsibility fell upon the owners and the charterers were relieved of it".

Morison J. in *The ER Hamburg*, agreed. After all no shipowner could or would safely and properly leave the stowage to the charterers. The argument therefore that art.III(1) applied was "something of a red herring"; it was entirely the charterer's fault if their improper stowage caused the vessel to become unseaworthy.

Defences

8–052   The Hague-Visby Rules provide specific defences to the duty to care for the cargo. These specific defences are contained in art.IV(2) but they may be displaced as a result of the carrier committing such a serious breach that they become estopped from pleading these defences. For example, where the ship and cargo are seized as a result of the carrier using it for illegal purposes, his right to invoke these defences is extinguished.

Some of these defences are no different to those permitted at common law as discussed in Chapter 7 and it suffices for our purpose here to deal only with those having special significance outside the common law.

8–053   **Article IV(2)(a)—Act, neglect, or default of the master, mariner, pilot, or the servants of the carrier in the navigation or in the management of the ship**   The first proposition is that the carrier or the ship shall not be responsible for damage or loss arising from the "act, neglect, or default of the master, mariner, pilot, or the servants of the carrier in the navigation or in the management of the ship". This provision refers to the acts of the ship's crew in the navigation or management of the ship. Navigation generally refers to the direction of the vessel in the route or voyage it is proceeding. It has been defined in *The Ferro* [1893] P. 38 as "something affecting the safe sailing of the ship". Management of the vessel poses a bit more of a challenge. It was argued in *Goose Millerd Ltd v Canadian Government Merchant Marine Ltd* [1929] A.C. 223 that the failure to secure the tarpaulins during repairs and cargo discharge at port was a neglect or default in ship management and the carrier was therefore exempt from liability under art.IV(2)(a). The House of Lords held that such a construction would result in depriving the shipper of goods of the protection afforded him by art.III(2). Lord Hailsham L.C. applied the rule laid down in *The Glenochil* [1896] P. 10 where Gorell Barnes J. held:

"There will be found a strong and marked contrast in the provisions which deal with the care of the cargo and those which deal with the management of the ship herself and I think that where the act done in the management of the ship is one which is necessarily done in the proper handling of the vessel, though in the particular case the handling is not properly done, but is done for the safety of the ship herself, and is not primarily done at all in connection with the cargo, that must be a matter which falls within the words 'management of the said vessel'".

A distinction must be made between "damage resulting from some act relating to the ship herself and only incidentally damaging the cargo, . . . " and "an act dealing . . . solely with the goods and not directly or indirectly with the ship herself". The removal and subsequently negligent securing of the tarpaulins were carried out so that repairs could be made and that goods could be discharged. As a matter of fact, these acts were not done for the safety of the ship but for the safety of the goods. Thus, the carriers could not avail themselves to art.IV(2)(a).

McNair J. was urged in *International Packers London Ltd v Ocean Steam Ship Co Ltd* to adopt the House of Lords' finding of fact in *Goose Millerd*. That case involved the failure of the crew to securely fasten the tarpaulins to the cargo hold of the ship. The judge declined, stating that it is not wise to try to decide case B because the part of the ship mishandled is "like" the part mishandled in case A. In any event, the facts were different. In *Goose Millerd*, the ship was docked at port. In *International Packers*, the ship was in motion and the tarpaulins were vital not simply for the protection of the cargo but for the safety of the ship herself.

A summary of the law might be taken verbatim from Greer L.J.'s judgment in **8–054** *Goose Millerd* whose minority judgment was confirmed subsequently by the House of Lords on appeal:

"If the cause of the damage is solely, or even primarily, a neglect to take reasonable care of the cargo, the ship is liable, but if the cause of the damage is a neglect to take reasonable care of the ship, or some part of it, as distinct from the cargo, the ship is relieved from liability; but if the negligence is not negligence towards the ship, but only negligent failure to use the apparatus of the ship for the protection of the cargo, the ship is not so relieved".

In *The ER Hamburg* [2006] EWHC 483, for example, it was therefore a complete defence for the owners that as the heating of the bunker oil was necessary provide fuel to the ship's propulsion engines, that was an act in ship management. The heating of the bunker oil was not an act done as part of the care of the cargo.

A further difficulty associated with art.IV(2)(a) is whether the defence should be available for carriers whose servants had behaved with indefensible bad faith. In a controversial case from New Zealand, *NZ China Clays v Tasman Orient Line* (August 31, 2007, NZ High Court), the shipmaster had taken a dangerous short cut as the ship was behind schedule. The evidence was that he was fully aware of the risk of grounding damage. The ship struck bottom and was taking water. The shipmaster nevertheless steamed at full speed for several hours. He had also fabricated the story of the ship having hit an unidentified object. At no time did he inform the Coastguard. To top it all, he put the lives of his crew at risk by failing to organise them in an effective pumping regime. After the event, he provided false information to his managers as to the time and damage in the grounding. It was obvious that the shipmaster had acted very improperly. The question, however, following a suit for lost and damaged cargo, was whether the carrier was entitled to rely on art.IV(2)(a). The judge accepted that the case fell squarely on the principle espoused in *Goose Millerd* and as such, the shipmaster's errors should be treated as acts in the navigation of the ship. However, the judge went on to say that for the defence in art.IV(2)(a) to apply, "the act, neglect or default of those in charge of the ship must be *bona fide* in the navigation or in the management of the ship". In that case, as the shipmaster's post-grounding conduct in fabricating the facts and failing to inform Coastguard promptly could not be said to be in the interest of the ship, cargo or crew. The defence should not therefore avail the carrier. It must be said that although the court was justifiably abhorred by the master's conduct, such a decision which invites an inquiry into the subjective motives of the master, mariner, pilot or servants of the carrier would render the application of art.IV(2)(a) highly problematic.

8–055   The scope of art.IV(2)(a) was critically discussed by the House of Lords in *Kawasaki Kisen Kaisha Ltd v Whistler International Ltd* [2000] 3 W.L.R. 1954 in the context of a time charter which had incorporated the Hague-Visby Rules. Although in that case the effect of art.IV(2)(a) was purely contractual rather than statutory, it does throw some light on the ever-evolving construction of art.IV(2)(a). Under the time charter in that case, the charterers gave contractual orders to the shipmaster to proceed by the "Great Circle" route but the shipmaster decided not to proceed by that route and chose instead to proceed by a more southerly route. The question was whether that decision of the master constituted an "act of neglect or default . . . in the navigation of the ship".

The House of Lords held that the exception in art.IV(2)(a) did not provide a defence for the shipowners as it could not extend to the choice not to perform the shipowner's clear obligations to proceed with despatch and to comply with the charterer's instructions on employment of the vessel.[15] Additionally, as a matter of construction, the exception did not apply because there was no error in the navigation or management of the ship. There had been no error in seamanship which is what navigational neglect or default essentially implied. This is welcome as it narrows the term "neglect or default" considerably by removing wilful disobedience to orders from its parameters.

A corollary issue worth noting is that an incompetent crew rendering the ship unseaworthy as in *The Star Sea* [1995] 1 Lloyd's Rep. 651 (at first instance), and *Hongkong Fir Shipping Co* [1962] Q.B. 26 will not be excused by this provision because art.IV(2) does not apply to the shipowner's duty to provide a seaworthy ship.

8–056   **Article IV(2)(b)—Fire, unless caused by the actual fault or privity of the carrier**   Fire will only be defence if the carrier is not at fault or privy in causing it.[16] The constraint was considered by the House of Lords in *Lennard's Carrying*

---

[15] Authority for this view in common law might be derived from *Knutsford Steamship Co v Tillmans & Co* [1908] A.C. 406 and *Suzuki v Benyon* (1926) 42 T.L.R. 269.

[16] In *Macieo Shipping Ltd v Clipper Shipping Lines Ltd (The MV Clipper Sao Luis)* [2000] 1 Lloyd's Rep. 645, fire had started in one of the ship's holds. The charterers claimed against the shipowners for surveyor's fees and other expenses incurred to ensure that the ship was able to carry on her voyage. It was held such a claim could not succeed as it fell within the exception in art.V(2)(b) of the Hague Rules which had been incorporated into the charterparty.

Co Ltd v Asiatic Petroleum Co Ltd [1915] A.C. 705. In that case, the carrier was a company—an inanimate entity. It was essential in that case to decide whether it was possible to impute the company official's knowledge of the state of affairs on to the company. The House of Lords held, consistent with the developments in company law, that the company would only be liable if the fault or privy in the knowledge of the state of affairs was on an individual who is the directing mind or brain of the company.

Where the ship is a UK registered ship, the carrier may be entitled to plead the defence contained in s.186 of the Merchant Shipping Act 1995. That section provides that the owner of a UK ship shall not be liable for any loss or damage where any property on board the ship is lost or damaged by reason of fire on board. This defence is not only available for an action under Article III(2) on the care of the cargo but also in defeating the following claims:

- an action under art.III(1) for unseaworthiness;

- an action under common law for unseaworthiness and other causes of damage or loss to goods carried;

- an action in tort; and

- an action in bailment.

It is also important to note that the term "owner" extends to a part owner, a charterer, manager or operator of the ship.

Like art.IV(2)(b), s.186 does not apply where it is proved that the loss resulted from the carrier's personal act or omission, committed with the intent to cause such loss, or recklessly and with knowledge that such loss would probably result. The burden of proof however is upon the cargo owner to rebut and attack the carrier's case.

Article IV(2)(c)—Perils, dangers and accidents of the sea or other   8–057
navigable waters   On the definition of "perils of the sea", it is highly probable that the courts will take the same approach as in the common law cases. In general, Lord Herschell's dictum is instructive. His Lordship said in *The Xantho* (1887) 12 App. Cas. 503:

"They do not protect, for example, against that natural and inevitable action of the winds and waves, which results in what may be described as wear and tear. There must be some casualty, something which could not be foreseen as one of the necessary incidents of the adventure".

It was further pointed out in that case that this does not mean that the event must be extraordinary before it constitutes a peril of the sea. That would be being excessively restrictive.

In *Canada Rice Mills Ltd v Union Marine and General Insurance Co Ltd* [1941] A.C. 55 for example, a storm though not extraordinary in ferocity and occurrence, was held to be a peril of the sea. The Privy Council stated that it is the fortuitous incursion of sea water caused by the storm which is the peril of the sea. It is of course a matter for a decider of fact to determine whether it was fortuitous that water would have entered the holds.[17]

---

[17] For a fuller account on "perils of the sea", see paras 7–060—7–062.

8–058   The following defences are similar to those provided for at common law; all of which we have considered at some length.

- Article IV(2)(d)—Act of God;

- Article IV(2)(e)—Act of war;

- Article IV(2)(f)—Act of public enemies;

- Article IV(2)(g)—Arrest or restraint of princes, rulers or people, or seizure under legal process; and

- Article IV(2)(h)—Quarantine restrictions.

8–059   **Article IV(2)(i)—Act or omission of the shipper or owner of the goods, his agent or representative**   It is possible that the damage or loss was directly or indirectly the fault or neglect of the shipper of goods. Where the shipper, for example, had labelled his goods erroneously or had given wrong instructions on the care and carriage of the goods, then any loss or damage resulting from his act or omission will fall squarely on his shoulders. That said, it is difficult see how capacious this defence is in the light of specific exceptions on insufficiency in packing and marking, latent defect in the goods and inherent vice.

- Article IV(2)(j)—Strikes or lockouts or stoppage or restraint of labour from whatever cause, whether partial or general; and

- Article IV(2)(k)—Riots and civil commotions.

8–060   **Article IV(2)(1)—Saving or attempting to save life or property at sea**   Where the ship makes an attempt to save life or property whilst prosecuting a contractual voyage and damage or loss is caused to the cargo owner's goods, the carrier may plead the exemption in this paragraph. It is however uncertain whether this provision will apply where the ship has deviated. It depends on whether the attempt to save life and property is made in pursuant to a legitimate deviation and the effects of a wrongful deviation. Where the wrongful deviation results in the carrier losing his claim on the exception clauses in the Hague-Visby Rules, then art.IV(2) will not avail him.

8–061   **Article IV(2)(m)—Wastage in bulk or weight or any other loss or damage arising from inherent defect, quality or vice of the goods**   This defence, or rather its common law counterpart, was explained in *The Barcore* [1896] P. 294:

> "[The] cargo was not damaged by reason of the shipowner committing a breach of contract, or omitting to do something which he ought to have done, but it was deteriorated in condition by its own want of power to bear the ordinary transit in a ship".

This definition was subsequently affirmed and applied to art.IV(2)(m) by Lord Reid in the House of Lords' case of *Albacora SRL v Westcott & Laurance Line Ltd* [1966] 2 Lloyd's Rep. 53.

"Ordinary transit" means the kind of transit which the contract requires the carrier to provide. The kind of transit required is crucial in determining whether the goods had in fact deteriorated as a result of an inherent vice. For example where the contract had required refrigeration and that was not provided then the resulting deterioration of the goods could not be deemed as having been caused by an inherent vice.

- Article IV(2)(n)—Insufficiency of packing; and

- Article IV(2)(o)—Insufficiency or inadequacy of marks.

Article IV(2)(p)—Latent defects not discoverable by due diligence This paragraph refers not to the latent defect in the goods, but in the ship herself. In *The Antigoni* [1991] 1 Lloyd's Rep. 209, the ship was engaged to carry goods between Northern Europe and West Africa. Bills of lading were issued for the cargo in question. During the contracted voyage, there was a major breakdown in the engine room. Attempts to repair the ship failed and the ship had to be salvaged and towed to port. While the breakdown itself did not cause damage to the cargo, the cargo owners were obliged to pay the salvors as a matter of general average.   **8–062**

The shipowners relied on two defences—first that they had exercised due diligence in ensuring that the ship was seaworthy and thus, were protected by art.IV(1) and alternatively, they were entitled to plead art.IV(2)(p) that the casualty was caused by a latent defect not discoverable by due diligence. This cases raises a vexing issue—is art.IV(2)(p) superfluous in the light of the breadth of art.IV(1)? *Scrutton on Charterparties*, 19th edn (London: Sweet & Maxwell, 1984), p.450, points to a case where art.IV(2)(p) might be important:

"Another possible meaning for these words resulting in their giving the shipowner an immunity additional to that provided in Rule 1 of this Article is that they cover defects which would not have been discovered by the exercise of due diligence even though the shipowner could not show that he had in fact exercised such diligence".

While this view has some judicial support as indicated in Branson J.'s dicta in *Corporation Argentine de Productores de Carnes v Royal Mail Lines Ltd* (1939) 64 Ll. L. Rep. 188, it might be argued that if the shipowner had exercised due diligence and could not discover the defect because it was a latent defect then he must be said to have performed his duty in providing a seaworthy ship. He should thus be entitled to rely on art.IV(1). Article IV(2)(p) would seem superfluous.

Article IV(2)(q)—Any other cause arising without the actual fault or privity of the carrier, or without the fault or neglect of the agents or servants of the carrier, but the burden of proof shall be on the person claiming the benefit of this exception to show that neither the actual fault or privity of the carrier nor the fault or neglect of the agents or servants of the carrier contributed to the loss or damage This defence is intended to be a "catch all" defence and its terms could not be construed ejusdem generis, according to *Scrutton on Charterparties* because there is no single genus in art.IV(2). Regardless, it is not exactly a favourite defence amongst carriers for two reasons: **8–063**

1. although it is a catch-all provision, the other provisions art.IV(2) are so wide that it is only the rarest occasion which has not been adequately accommodated; and

2. the burden of proof on the carrier is not a light one to discharge. The carrier will have to prove the lack of fault on his part or, fault or neglect on the part of his servants.

In *Leesh River Tea Co Ltd v British India Steam Navigation Co Ltd* [1967] 2 Q.B. 250, the Court of Appeal had occasion to deal with it. In that case, the claimants had shipped chests of tea from Calcutta to Europe on the carrier's ship. When the ship called at Port Sudan en route to Europe, stevedores removed and stole the brass cover plate of a storm valve. This led to the incursion of water and the tea in the hold was damaged. In considering whether the catch-all exception applied, the Court of Appeal held that if theft leading to the incursion of water is not to be treated as a peril of the sea, then it would be naturally covered by art.IV(2)(q). For the shipowners to succeed on the defence, they need to prove that the theft was without their fault or privity and they also have to establish that it was without the fault or neglect of their agents, the stevedoring company in Port Sudan. This, they succeeded in doing, according to the court.

The carrier's duty to issue the bill of lading—article III(3)

8–064   Under art.III(3), the carrier is obliged to issue a bill of lading containing, inter alia:

1. the leading identification marks;

2. the number of packages or pieces, the quantity or weight of the goods; and

3. the apparent order and condition of the goods.

He is, however, not obliged to offer the bill of lading unless the shipper calls on him to issue the bill. Article III(3) does not require the carrier to issue the bill of lading to anyone but the shipper. This means that the consignee of the goods under a contract of sale will not be entitled to demand the issue of the bill of lading.

Article III(4) goes on to say that the bill of lading shall be prima facie evidence of the receipt of the goods by the carrier. Proof to the contrary shall not be admissible once the bill has been transferred to a third party acting in good faith. Although in the general the carrier is bound by the information that he represents in the bill of lading, the proviso to art.III(3) states that he shall not be bound to state or show any marks, number, quantity or weight which he has reasonable ground for suspecting not accurately to represent the goods actually received or which he has had no reasonable means of checking. It is common place for shipmasters to insert in the bills of lading "weight unknown" or "quantity unknown" clauses. These clauses will negate the presumption that the bills of lading are prima facie evidence for the weight and quantity of the goods received for shipment. "Said to contain" clauses seem to have the same effect (*The River Guarara* [1998] 1 Lloyd's Rep. 225).

It might be recalled that it was held in *The Mata K* [1998] 2 Lloyd's Rep. 614 **8–065** that where a bill of lading contained the printed term "weight unknown" or "quantity unknown" the receivers and/or holders of the bill could not rely on the weights or quantities stated as conclusive evidence that the goods were shipped.

Furthermore it should be noted that the bill of lading issued under art.III(3) and (4) refers only to a received for shipment bill of lading which has little importance in documentary sales. The received bill of lading merely shows the apparent order and condition of the goods when received for shipment. The international trader is on the other hand more interested in a bill of lading which says that the goods have been shipped in apparent good order and condition. The shipped bill of lading is provided for in art.III(7). That article provides that once the goods have been loaded, the carrier shall issue a shipped bill of lading upon demand by the shipper (art.III(7)). The particulars to be stated are similar to those adumbrated in art.III(3).

An important issue arose in *Owners of the Cargo lately laden onboard the Ship David Agmashenebeli v Owners of the Ship David Agmashenebeli* [2002] EWHC 104, (Admlty)—what is the duty, if any, the law imposes on the carrier in respect of the clausing of the bill of lading unnecessarily? In that case, a bulk cargo of urea was carried from Finland to South China. Despite protests, the carrier claused the bills of lading stating "cargo discoloured also foreign materials *e.g.* Plastic, Rust, Rubber, Stone, Black particles found in cargo". It is trite law that a buyer or his bank would not pay against claused bills. The buyer refused to take delivery of the documents when presented and the goods were finally released to the buyer at a reduced price. The sellers sued the carrier. The relevant provision for consideration is necessarily art.III(3). Colman J. held that although the actual pre-loading condition of the goods did not justify the wording used by the carrier in clausing the bills of lading, it also did not justify the issue of clean bills. Therefore as a matter of causation, although the clause in those strong terms was unjustified, it did not lead to the loss as appropriately issued (and claused) bills would nonetheless have resulted in rejection of the tender. On the substantive law, the court held that the master was required to exercise his own judgment and skill on the appearance of the cargo being loaded. If he honestly took the view that it was not or not all in apparent good order and condition, and that was a view that could properly be held by a reasonably observant master, then, even if not all or even most such masters would necessarily agree with him, he was entitled to clause the bill of lading accordingly. The duty implied in art.III(3) required the master to issue a bill of lading that recorded the apparent order and condition of the goods *according to the reasonable assessment of the master*. There is not to be implied a higher duty than that, given the international regime and the nature of shipping practice. The court refused to accept any analogy in the law of tort on the basis that tort liability could prevent masters from acting expeditious in the loading and discharge of goods, and that tort liability was extraneous to the international convention and should not be introduced to qualify the application of an international regime of law.[18]

---

[18] For a critical commentary of this case, see Parker "Liability for incorrectly clausing bills of lading" [2003] L.M.C.L.Q. 201; also Todd, "Representations in bills of lading" [2003] J.B.L. 160.

8–066   Sometimes in the case of iron, steel and metal products, a Retla clause might be used. The name "Retla" comes from an American case, *Tokio Marine & Fire Insurance Co v Retla Steamship Co* [1970] 2 Lloyd's Rep. 91. A Retla clause is expressed usually in these terms:

> "RETLA CLAUSE: If the Goods as described by the Merchant are iron, steel, metal or timber products, the phrase 'apparent good order and condition' set out in the preceding paragraph does not mean the Goods were received in the case of iron, steel or metal products, free of visible rust or moisture or in the case of timber products free from warpage, breakage, chipping, moisture, split or broken ends, stains, decay or discoloration. Nor does the Carrier warrant the accuracy of any piece count provided by the Merchant or the adequacy of any banding or securing. If the Merchant so requests, a substitute Bill of Lading will be issued omitting this definition and setting forth any notations which may appear on the mate's or tally clerk's receipt."

It would follow that in the carriage of such goods, the fact that the bill of lading is made out "in apparent good order and condition" does not mean that the goods will be entirely free from visible rust and other deformities.[19] That said, it was ruled by the English High Court in *Breffka & Hehnke Gmbh v Navire Shipping Co Ltd* [2012] EWHC 3124 (Comm) that such a clause must be interpreted subject to what actually reflects the reasonable judgment of a reasonably competent and observant master. The Retla clause should be construed as a legitimate clarification of what was to be understood by the representation as to the appearance of the cargo upon shipment. It should not be construed as a contradiction of the representation about the cargo's good order and condition, but as a qualification that there was an appearance of rust or other defects which might be expected to appear on the cargo in question. Simon J. took the view that it was likely to form the basis of a determination as to whether there had been a further deterioration due to inherent quality of the goods on shipment. It followed that the Retla clause did not apply to all rust, of whatever severity. Such a construction would rob the representation as to the good order and condition of the steel cargo on shipment of all effect.

Article III(5) further allows the carrier to seek an indemnity from the shipper for inaccuracies in the bill of lading as a result of erroneous or misleading information supplied by the shipper (*The Boukadoura* [1989] 1 Lloyd's Rep. 393). This right to an indemnity from the shipper does not limit the carrier's liability under the contract of carriage to some third party (other than the shipper).

Carrier's duty not to deviate

8–067   Article IV(4) provides that

> "any deviation in saving or attempting to save life or property at sea or any reasonable deviation shall not be deemed to be an infringement or breach of these rules or of the contract of carriage, and the carrier shall not be liable for any loss or damage resulting therefrom".

---

[19] Sturley, "Carriage of Goods by Sea" (2000) (Apr.) J.M.L.C. 241.

The duty is quite different from the duty not to deviate at common law.[20] For a start, it is not in the negative. It provides for greater laxity in the handling and navigation of the vessel as far as the carrier and his shipmaster is concerned.

In *Stag Line Ltd v Foscolo, Mango & Co Ltd* [1932] A.C. 328, the ship had set sail with two engineers working on certain equipment onboard. When the work was completed, the ship deviated from the usual route to allow them to disembark at a nearby port. On her way back to the contractual route, she ran aground and the cargo was lost. It was argued by the carriers that the deviation was reasonable.[21] The House of Lords held that what was reasonable must be assessed in the light of "every condition and every circumstance" of the case. The deviation must be reasonable not only to one party but to both. Lord Atkin was, however, careful not to classify the issue as one of fact or of law. His Lordship said:

"In the present case we are judges both of law and of fact; and if the question is of fact the concurrence of the learned judges below seems to me to lose some of its value when regard is had to the meaning they attributed to the issue they were determining".

Lord Warrington and Lord Russell both thought that it was a question of fact. **8–068** Be that as it may, it was found that although the deviation to the nearest port was not unjustified deviation, the decision to sail along the coast and not resume the original route as soon as practicable made the deviation become unreasonable.

Effect of deviation

It is not clear whether deviation will cause the carrier to forfeit the exceptions and **8–069** defences in the Hague-Visby Rules, including those on a maximum financial limit on claims. In *Stag Line Ltd*, Lord Atkin commented:

"I find no substance in the contention . . . that an unauthorised deviation would not displace the statutory exceptions contained in the Carriage of Goods by Sea Act. I am satisfied that the general principles of English law are still applicable to the carriage of goods by sea except as modified by the Act: and I can find nothing in the Act which makes its statutory exceptions apply to a voyage which is not the voyage the subject of 'the contract of carriage of goods by sea' to which the Act applies . . . ".

This proposition was however made with reference to the Hague Rules. As far as the Hague-Visby Rules are concerned, the Carriage of Goods by Sea Act 1971 provides specifically in s.1(2) that they are to have the force of law, a provision absent in the Carriage of Goods by Sea Act 1924. The natural consequence seems therefore that the rules will continue to apply even though a breach has been

---

[20] Baughen, "Does deviation still matter?" [1991] L.M.C.L.Q. 70.

[21] On the weight to be attached to master's explanation as to reasonableness of the deviation for ship repairs, see *Danae Shipping Corporation of Monrovia v TPAO Guven Turkish Insurance Co (The Daffodil B)* [1983] 1 Lloyd's Rep. 498. It appears that unless the contrary is proved, the court will normally accept the competence and skill of the master in deciding whether it would be reasonable to deviate.

committed bringing an end to the contract. It will be interesting to see how this will be addressed by the courts.

Limitations of Carriers' Liability under the Rules

8–070 While on the one hand the Hague-Visby Rules provide for a number of duties on the carrier, on the other, they offer the carrier a number of exceptions and limits on his liability under the contract of carriage. We have noted some of these defences in arts.IV(1) and (2) applicable to the duty to provide a seaworthy ship and the duty to care for the cargo. Besides these specific defences, the rules also make allowance for the time limit within which an action can be brought and the financial limit on damages claimed.

Time limit

8–071 Article III(6) sets out in detail the procedure that a claimant must comply with in order to bring an action against the carrier under the Hague-Visby Rules. These rules are:

(a) Written notice of loss or damage must be given or else removal of the goods into the custody of the person entitled to take delivery of the goods shall be treated as prima facie evidence of the contractual delivery by the carrier. The notice must describe the general nature of the loss or damage.

(b) Where the loss or damage is not apparent, the notice must be given within three days or else the removal of the goods into the custody of the consignee shall be prima facie evidence of the delivery of the goods according to contract.

(c) The notice need not be given if the state of the goods has been the determined by a joint survey or inspection at the time they were received by the receiver.

(d) Action must be brought within one year from the date of delivery or the date when the goods should have been delivered if not, the carrier's liability shall be discharged from all liability relating to those goods. The period may be extended subject to the parties' agreement. Where the claim is for actual or apprehended loss or damage, the carrier and the receiver of goods must give reasonable facilities to each other for inspecting and tallying the goods.

(e) Where the contract provides for the settlement of disputes through arbitration, the time limit will also apply to the time allowed to go to arbitration (*The Merak* [1965] P. 223).

Article III(6) refers to "discharged from all liability". The implication of this provision was discussed expansively in *Aries Tanker Corp v Total Transport Ltd (The Aries)* [1977] 1 Lloyd's Rep. 334 by the House of Lords. In that case, the voyage charter for the carriage of petroleum from the Arabian Gulf to Rotterdam had incorporated the Hague Rules. The question was whether the time limit in art.III(6) in those rules (similar to art.III(6) of the Hague-Visby Rules) was merely procedural in nature or whether it had the effect of substantive law in extinguishing the claim altogether after the expiry of the one-year time limit. It is trite law under the statutes of limitation that the expiry of any limitation period simply bars the remedy but does not extinguish the claim. An action which is time barred simply means that the courts will not entertain the claimant's claim to a remedy, it does not assert that the defendant is not liable.[22] Lord Wilberforce did not think that art.III(6) fell within this general proposition though. His Lordship considered art.II(6) to be a time bar of a special kind. The charterers' claim had not only become unenforceable but had simply ceased to exist.[23] In that case, the charterers' could not raise the short delivery of petroleum as a set-off in defence of a claim brought by the shipowners for unpaid freight because their right over the short delivery had been extinguished after the expiry of the limitation period.

The time limit commences to run following the "delivery" of the goods. In most cases, this would be a fairly straightforward matter. However, as is seen in the following case, problems can arise when parties make special provisions for the movement of the cargo.

Trafigura Beheer BV v Golden Stavraetos Maritime Inc [2003] EWCA Civ 664   **8–072**
Facts:
Under the contract of carriage which was governed by the Rules, the ship loaded a cargo of jet fuel for carriage from Rabigh in Saudi Arabia to Monbasa in Kenya. The port of discharge was subsequently changed to Lagos, Nigeria, which was permitted under the contract. At Lagos, notice of readiness to unload was given but the intended receivers of the goods refused delivery alleging that the oil was off specification. The ship was then ordered to Abidjan. *After further negotiation*, the ship was ordered to sail from Abidjan to Agioi Theodori, Greece. In a claim that the oil was contaminated, the question was whether the one-year time limit started to run from the date of delivery in Greece or Lagos. If it were the former, there was still time. If it were the latter, the action would be barred.
Held:
There were three possible places of delivery in this case:

- the original contractual place of delivery (Mombasa);

- the substituted place of delivery which was permitted under the original contract (Lagos); or

- the place of delivery agreed following further negotiations (Agioi Theodori).

Both courts agreed that the relevant place was either Lagos or Agioi Theodori. Morison J. at first instance was concerned that the latter was only chosen following a new contractual arrangement; and that arrangement was not in dispute, Lagos should be the relevant place of delivery. The relevant suit was the damaging of the goods caused during the contractual voyage from the port of loading to Lagos. As such, the time limit should commence at Lagos; Lagos was the legitimate place of delivery in relation to the voyage about which the complaint was made.

The Court of Appeal however allowed the appeal. The question that should be asked was whether delivery took place in Greece, from the terms of art.III(6). From the facts, it could be fairly and reasonably said that there was delivery *under the contract of carriage* in question even though that contract had been varied in some respects in the light of the

---

[22] James, "New claims outside the time limit of the Hague Visby Rules" [1994] J.B.L. 67.
[23] This was reiterated in the more recent *Bua International Ltd v Hai Hing Shipping Co Ltd (The Hai Hing)* [2000] 1 Lloyd's Rep. 300.

problems which had arise during the voyage. The court was not persuaded that art.III(6) was confined to the original contractual place of delivery. The new arrangement here was inextricably linked to the contract of carriage. As such, the delivery at Agioi Theodori could be properly characterised as the place of delivery for the purposes of art.III(6).

8–073   When should time start running in the case of a misdelivery? In a Hong Kong Court of First Instance case, *Starlight Exports Ltd and Star Light Electronics Company Ltd v CTO (HK) Ltd* [2006] H.C.C.A. 255 (HK CFI) the goods were delivered to the FOB buyers by the carrier without production of the relevant bills of lading. The question was whether the time limit should commence when the goods were delivered. The court held that delivery should mean delivery in accordance with the bill of lading contract. It would not be right for the time limit to start from the date of the wrongful release of the goods.[24]

The limitation period applies regardless of whether the claim is founded in tort or contract.[25] In *Salmond and Spraggon (Australia) Pty Ltd v Port Jackson Stevedoring Pty Ltd (The New York Star)* [1980] 2 Lloyd's Rep. 317, Lord Wilberforce said:

> "[T]he reference to delivery of goods [in the provision] shows clearly that the clause is directed towards the carrier's obligation as bailee of the goods. It cannot be supposed that it admits of a distinction between obligations in contract and liability in tort—'all liability' means what it says".

It was further argued in that case that as art.III(6) imposes a duty on the shipper to sue within one year when there is a fundamental breach by the carrier, the shipper is released from this duty and could therefore bring an action out of time. This was rejected by the Privy Council. It is not right to equate a clause like this with provisions that deal with performance of the contract. It is a clause that comes into operation when contractual performance has become impossible or has been given up; it regulates the manner in which liability for the breach is to be determined. It is like an arbitration clause, a choice of law or forum clause which would survive the repudiatory breach. It is not displaced simply because the contract has ended or has been repudiated.

8–074   In *Kenya Railways v Antares Co Pte Ltd (The Antares)* [1987] 1 Lloyd's Rep. 424, the Court of Appeal confirmed the application of the time limit in a case of clear repudiatory breach—where the carriers had carried the shipper's goods on deck without authorisation. The time limit is expressly given the force of law and therefore would survive a serious breach of the contract.

The severe approach of the courts towards the shipper's failure to sue within the time limit was taken even further in *Compagnia Colombiana de Seguros v Pacific Steam Navigation Co Ltd* [1965] 1 Q.B. 101. In that case, the shipper had brought an action against the carrier in New York although the contract had provided for the English courts to have exclusive jurisdiction. When the mistake was discovered, the one-year limitation period had lapsed. It was held by Roskill J. that the shipper could not rely on his own mistake to extend the statutory limit and that the provision referred specifically to one year from the date of delivery

---

[24] See Leung, "Misdelivery of Cargo without Production of Bill of Lading: Applicability of the mandatory legal regime of Hague Visby and the one-year time bar" (2008) 39(2) J.M.L.C. 205.

[25] Powles, "'Time limits and misdelivery' (sea)" [1990] J.B.L. 155.

or when delivery should have taken place. The fact that he had brought the action in New York within time was immaterial.

Another unforgivable mistake besides suing in the wrong place is suing the wrong party. The end result is the same as *Compagnia Colombiana de Seguros v Pacific Steam Navigation Co.* In *Zainalabdin Payabi v Amstel Shipping Corp Ltd (The Jay Bola)* [1992] 2 Lloyd's Rep. 62, the court held that it was not possible to join the right party to the existing incorrect action so as to avoid the time limit rule. To allow the claimant to do so would be to derogate from the objectives of art.III(6).

A less dogmatic approach was taken by Parker L.J. in the *Kapetan Markos*   **8–075** [1986] 1 Lloyd's Rep. 211, whose dictum is worth reproducing:

"Although we accept the correctness of Mr Justice Roskill's decision for present purposes, we should however not be taken to have approved the proposition stated as being of universal application. It appears to us at least arguable that in certain circumstances a defence under article III r.6 might be defeated by the fact that another suit had been brought elsewhere. Suppose for example that a cargo owner were to sue in New York within time and that there was no doubt but that the New York Court had jurisdiction to hear the claim. Suppose further that the shipowner, whilst acknowledging jurisdiction, applied for a stay on the ground that New York was *forum non conveniens* and that the *forum conveniens* was London. Finally suppose that the shipowner lost at first instance but won by a majority in the Court of Appeal and that, time having expired in the meantime, the cargo owner then issued a writ in London. In such circumstances it would appear at least arguable that article III r.6 did not apply".

Parker L.J.'s approach was adopted in *The Nordglimt* [1987] 2 Lloyd's Rep. 470. There, the cargo owners had commenced action against the carriers at Antwerp within time for damage caused to their barley shipped on the carriers' vessel, the Nordkap. Two years later they took action in rem against the carriers' other ship, the Nordglimt, in England. The carriers argued that the suit in Belgium would have discharged their liability as a matter of substantive law and they could therefore not be sued in rem. The Admiralty Court held that in order to plead that their liability has been discharged, they must establish two matters:

1. First, that the goods were carried under a contract of carriage by sea; and

2. Second, the suit or action to establish liability under the rules in respect of loss or damage to the goods carried under the contract has not been brought within a year.

In the present case, art.III(6) did not apply because the action in personam commenced and pending in Belgium, had been brought within time. That meant the carriers' liability had not yet been discharged. Hobhouse J.'s judgment was later affirmed by the Court of Appeal in *Government of Sierra Leone v Marmaro Shipping Co Ltd (The Amazona and Yayamaria)* [1989] 2 Lloyd's Rep. 130.

Where, however, an earlier legal action was brought in breach of an arbitration   **8–076** clause in the bill of lading, that action would not be treated by the courts as constituting a "suit" under art.III(6). In *Thyssen Inc v Calypso Shipping Corporation* [2000] 2 Lloyd's Rep. 243, the claimants had instituted action in the

United States against the defendants for damage caused to their cargo. That action was brought immediately upon the discovery of the damage. However, it was also an action brought in breach of an arbitration agreement. The US court, therefore, quite rightly stayed proceedings to allow the arbitration in London to proceed. David Steel J. in dealing with the second set of proceedings held that where the first suit had been brought in breach of an arbitration agreement, the court would not consider that as a suit for the purposes of art.III(6).[26] It was not enough for the correct claimant to commence proceedings before a competent court against the correct defendant. The proceedings must remain valid and effective at the time when the carrier (as the defendants) sought to rely on the article in the later set of proceedings.[27]

On the definition of "commenced" Moore-Bick J. held in *Allianz Versicherungs AG v Fortuna Co Inc* [1999] 1 W.L.R. 2117 that an arbitration would be deemed to have commenced for the purposes of art.III(6) when one party serves on the other party a notice requiring them to appoint an arbitrator or to agree to an appointment. That notice must be served in writing and must require the other party to take the steps necessary to constitute the arbitral tribunal.[28] The words used in the notice need not be identical to the terms set out in the arbitration agreement as long as the intention to bring about the appointment of arbitrators is clearly expressed.

Article III(6) provides that an action for indemnity against a third party may be brought even after the expiration of the one-year limit as long as it is brought within the limitation period set out in English law. In *Lauritzen Reefers v Ocean Reef Transport Ltd SA (The Bukhta Russkaya)* [1997] 2 Lloyd's Rep. 744, whether the parties could rely on art.III(6) depended on whether their contract of carriage was governed by the Hague-Visby Rules or not. In that case, the court came to the conclusion that the contract was governed by the Hague Rules and not the Hague-Visby Rules. Therefore, the charterers were not entitled to plead art.III(6).

Financial limit

8–077   The Rules also provide for ceiling limits for recoverable damages. The rationale seems to be that carriers would be encouraged to offer lower freight charges if the

---

[26] Current English law places much emphasis on the sanctity of the arbitration agreement. As a matter of policy, David Steel J.'s decision in this case is surely justified. See *Harbour Assurance Co (UK) v Kansa General Insurance Co Ltd* [1993] 1 Lloyd's Rep. 455 on the primacy of the arbitration clause.

[27] See also *The Finnrose* [1994] 1 Lloyd's Rep. 559.

[28] See also s.14(4) of the Arbitration Act 1996 which provides that where the arbitrator or arbitrators are to be appointed by the parties, arbitral proceedings are commenced in respect of a matter when one party serves on the other party or parties notice in writing requiring him or them to appoint an arbitrator or to agree to the appointment of an arbitrator in respect of that matter. It was held in *Seabridge Shipping AB v AC Orssleff's Eftf's A/S* [1999] 2 Lloyd's Rep. 685 that s.14 should be read expansively and not as stating that an arbitration could only be commenced by means of s.14. Thomas J. said: "However, given the fact that the Arbitration Act 1996 is intended for use by laymen and is written in 'user-friendly language' capable of application by international traders and businessmen, it is difficult to see why it should have been intended that methods for commencing an arbitration other than those set out in section 14 were to be permitted". See also *Bernuth Lines Ltd v High Seas Shipping Ltd* [2005] EWHC 3020.

law allows them to limit their liability in the shipment of goods whose value is not disclosed by the shipper. Article IV(5)(a) provides that unless the nature and value of the goods have been disclosed by the shipper before shipment and inserted in the bill of lading, the carrier shall not be liable for loss or damage exceeding 666.67 units of account per package or two units of account per kilogramme of gross weight of the goods lost or damaged, whichever is the higher.

Serena Navigation Ltd v Dera Commercial Establishment (The Limnos) [2008] EWHC 1036   **8–078**
Facts:
The bill of lading contract was subject to the Hague-Visby Rules and related to a carriage of corn from Louisiana, USA to Aqaba, Jordan. Bad weather resulted in wet damage to the goods. The physical damage was small (precise figures not yet proven but claimed were made of 7 tonnes or 12 tonnes or 262 tonnes) but as a condition of allowing discharge of cargo from the damp holds, the Jordan Silos and Supply General Co required that the cargo be fumigated, chemically treated and then transferred to pre-fumigated and disinfected silos. This operation resulted in a large number of broken kernels and a depreciation in the value of the cargo amounting to $362,142. The whole cargo then acquired a reputation as a distressed cargo and its sound arrived market price was depressed by $13 per m/t resulting in a loss of $571,842.26. The cargo interest argued that this claim for consequential economic loss fell within art.5(1)(a) as "loss or damage to or *in connection with* the goods" (emphasis added), therefore the limitation of liability should be by reference to the gross weight of the whole cargo, namely, 43,999.86 tonnes. The carrier argued that "gross weight of the *goods lost or damaged*" refers to goods physically lost or physically damaged. Therefore, the reference should be only to the quantity of physically damaged goods—the 250 tonnes.
Held:
Burton J. held that the words "goods lost or damaged" should not be construed in the same way as "loss or damage" as interpreted in the field of contract and tort, where they are conventionally taken to mean that loss is economic and damage is physical and together to cover all kinds of loss, in the sense of loss incurred. According to the judge, the words "goods lost or damaged" point to two categories of goods, namely:

1. goods that are lost in the sense of being missing or destroyed; and

2. goods that are damaged in the sense of not being lost, but surviving in damaged form.

He therefore dismissed the cargo interest's contention the words "goods lost or damaged" meant the same as "loss or damage".

Although Burton J. did not give an explicit discourse on the point, the judge   **8–079**
appeared to have accepted the carrier's argument that where there is only economic or financial loss, there would be recourse to the limits of liability in art.IV(5)(a) because no goods have been "lost or damaged".

Where a container, pallet or article of transport is used to consolidate goods, the number of packages or units enumerated in the bill of lading as packed into the article of transport shall be deemed the number of packages or units. Otherwise, the article of transport itself will be considered the package or unit.

> *N.B.* The unit of account is a special drawing right (SDR) as defined by the International Monetary Fund (IMF). On April 13, 2013, 1 SDR was equivalent to £0.982701. See para.9–013.

8–080   It would appear that with the growth in container transport, where the containers are packed and sealed by the shipper and the carrier does not usually have occasion to examine the contents, vexing problems could arise in the application of this article. It is thus common practice for carriers to use "weight unknown" or "said to contain" clauses in the bill of lading when they do not have the opportunity to verify the information provided by the shippers. How should these clauses affect the operation of the rules? Article IV(5)(c) refers to "packages or units enumerated in the bill of lading". It seems to suggest therefore that regardless of the carrier's plea that he has had no opportunity to examine and verify the information given him by the shipper, he is nonetheless bound by the "packages or units enumerated" in the bill of lading. See too *The River Guarara* [1998] Q.B. 610.

The maximum liability however does not apply if the damage is the result of an act or omission of the carrier done with intent to cause damage or recklessly and with the knowledge that damage would probably result (art.IV(5)(e)). It was questioned in *Browner International Ltd v Monarch Shipping Co Ltd (The European Enterprise)* [1989] 2 Lloyd's Rep. 185, as to whether art.IV(5)(e) extended to include acts and omissions of the carrier's servants and agents. Steyn J. held that art.IV(5)(e) does not impose on a carrier a nondelegable duty and drawing an analogy from the Warsaw Convention (the international convention on carriage by air), the word "carrier" should only mean the carrier himself or his alter ego in the case of a company or association.

We should remind ourselves that art.IV(5) carries the force of law and cannot therefore be excluded from operation for the mere reason that the contract has been repudiated by the commission of a breach of conditions. As we have seen,[29] that is the case despite the fact that the carrier had carried the goods on deck contrary to his contract of carriage (*The Kapitan Petko Voivoda* [2003] EWCA Civ 451). Article IV(5) refers to the carrier's right to limit his liability "in any event"; the Court of Appeal held in *The Kapitan Petko Voivoda* that that is to be given an extensive reading. Similarly, as the Court of Appeal emphasised in *The Happy Ranger* [2002] 2 All E.R. 24, the limitation of liability clearly would apply where the breach is "serious" such as a breach of the duty to provide a seaworthy ship because of a lack of due diligence.

Third Parties and the Exceptions in the Hague-Visby Rules[30]

8–081   Consider the situation where the carrier has employed an independent contractor to load or discharge the cargo. The independent contractors are negligent and the goods are damaged. The cargo owner has two possible defendants—the carrier and the independent contractor. In an action against the carrier,[31] it is quite clear

---

[29] See para.8–026.

[30] Treitel, "Bills of lading and third parties" [1986] L.M.C.L.Q. 294.

[31] See Davies, "The Elusive Carrier" [1991] *Australian Business Law Review* 230 on what "action against a carrier" could connote.

that he will be able to rely on the exception clauses in the contract of carriage and also those in the Hague-Visby Rules. On the other hand, the independent contractor has no contractual relationship with the cargo owner. According to the doctrine of privity,[32] the independent contractor would not be entitled to rely on those exception and limitation of liability clauses. This was held in *Adler v Dickson (The Himalaya)* [1954] 2 Lloyd's Rep. 267. In that case, the passenger had sued a member of the crew personally for negligence. It was held that the crew member could not rely on an exception clause in the contract of carriage between the passenger and the defendant's employers. Article IV *bis* r.2 goes some way at alleviating this operation of the privity doctrine. Article IV *bis* r.2 provides:

"2. If such an action is brought against a servant or agent of the carrier (such servant or agent not being an independent contractor), such servant or agent shall be entitled to avail himself of the defences and limits of liability which the carrier is entitled to invoke under these rules".

Further, it is stated in art.IV *bis* r.4 that a servant or agent will not be protected where the damage resulted from an act or omission of the servant and agent done with intent to cause damage or recklessly and knowledge that damage would probably result. It is readily seen that this provision does not apply where the third party in question is an independent contractor. It only applies where that third party is a servant or agent of the carrier. A situation as that in *Scruttons v Midland Silicones* [1962] A.C. 446 will therefore not be covered by the rule.

Scruttons v Midland Silicones [1962] A.C. 446   **8–082**
Facts:
The carrier had engage independent contractors, a firm of stevedores, to unload the cargo. The stevedores were negligent and damage was caused to the goods. The cargo owners sued the firm of stevedores. The defendants wanted to rely on the exceptions in the Hague Rules as incorporated in the contract of carriage.
Held:
They were not so entitled. The contract of carriage was made between the carrier and the cargo owners; the doctrine of privity would therefore prevent the third party stevedores from relying on the Hague Rules. It was argued that the rule in *Elder, Dempster & Co Ltd v Paterson, Zochonis & Co Ltd* [1924] A.C. 522 should apply. It was held in that case that the shipowners were able to rely on a limitation clause in the contract between the shippers and the cargo owners. The exact ground for that decision is unclear. As Lord Reid said in the present case, that decision was

"an anomalous and unexplained exception to the general principle that a stranger cannot rely for his protection on provisions in a contract to which he is not a party".

Lord Reid however went on to say that an appropriately worded contractual term could extend the benefit of the exceptions in the contract of carriage and consequently, the Hague Rules to third parties in reliance on principles of agency law. The use of agency is important as it removes the need of proof of consideration flowing from the third party.

---

[32] It should be noted that the Contracts (Rights of Third Parties) Act 1999 does not apply to contracts of carriage of goods by sea generally but s.6(5) allows the third party to rely on the Act to avail himself of a limitation of liability clause between the principals.

8–083   Such a clause is seen in the highly authoritative case of *New Zealand Shipping Line Co Ltd v AM Satterthwaite & Co Ltd (The Eurymedon)* [1975] A.C. 154. In that case, a drilling machine was shipped under a bill of lading to New Zealand. During unloading, the machine was damaged as a result of the stevedores' negligence. On whether the stevedores were able to rely on the one-year time bar in the Hague Rules as incorporated into the bill of lading, the Privy Council held that the contract was quite clear that the carrier had contracted not only on his behalf but also as trustee or agent on behalf of the independent contractors. The "appropriately worded clause" also known as a Himalaya Clause reads:

> "It is hereby expressly agreed that . . . every exemption, limitation, condition and liberty herein contained and every right, exemption from liability, defence and immunity of whatsoever nature applicable to the carrier or to which the carrier is entitled hereunder shall also be available and shall extend to protect every such servant or agent of the carrier . . . and for the purpose of all the foregoing provisions of this clause the carrier is or shall be deemed to be acting as agent or trustee on behalf of and for the benefit of all persons who are or might be his servants or agents from time to time (including independent contractors as aforesaid) and all such persons shall to this extent be or be deemed to be parties to the contract . . . ".

For the agency argument to succeed through the Himalaya clause the following conditions should be met:

1. the bill of lading (contract of carriage) must make it clear that the third party is intended to be protected by the stipulated exceptions and defences;

2. the bill of lading makes it clear that the carrier, in addition to contracting for these provisions in his own capacity, is also contracting as agent for the third party; and

3. the carrier should have authority from the third party to contract on the latter's behalf, although subsequent ratification would suffice.

These principles are very aptly illustrated in the following case:

8–084   *Lotus Cars Ltd v Southampton Cargo Handling Plc and Associated British Ports (The Rigoletto)* [2000] 2 All E.R. (Comm) 705
Facts:
Southampton Cargo Handling (SCH) were the appointed cargo handlers of the ship-owners. The second defendant, Associated British Ports (ABP), owned and operated the docks and licensed SCH, amongst others, to use the compound for the storage of cars awaiting shipment. The car in question was stolen. No bill of lading was issued in relation to the car by the carrier, but it was accepted that Lotus would have been entitled to a received for shipment bill of lading which was identical in form to that issued in relation to the 11 other cars which were duly shipped. The action proceeded as if such a bill had been issued. The lower court held that SCH were bailees of the car and were bound by the terms of their conditions which accepted liability for negligence where proved. That negligence, as far as Judge Hallgarten Q.C. was concerned, was proved. The judge rejected a defence by SCH that it was entitled to rely upon the Himalaya clause contained in the bill of lading on the ground that that clause was not intended to apply to pre-loading events. ABP was exonerated by the judge on the basis that they were not bailees of the car.

Held:

The Court of Appeal affirmed the finding of Judge Hallgarten Q.C. that SCH were in fact bailees of the car. They had accepted delivery of the car on their own conditions, which made no reference to any agency. Even though SCH were the agents of the owners of the car, they were not their servants. In the acceptance and taking delivery of the car into their care and control, they were acting on their own terms and not according to any existing agency between themselves and the owners. They were thus properly classed as "bailees".

However, SCH had accepted the car on their own conditions. That meant that they had elected not to be governed by the clauses in the bill of lading issued by the carrier.

On the facts (with Chadwick L.J. dissenting), the court found that ABP was a bailee or sub-bailee having voluntarily assumed possession of the car and the duty of safekeeping. It followed that liability should be apportioned between the two defendants and the Himalaya clause could not avail SCH.

As far as the Himalaya clause issue is concerned, this case is a good **8–085** illustration of how important it is to determine the intention of the parties to benefit the third party and that the third party had in fact relied on those protective clauses in the bill of lading in the discharge of his functions under the bailment. It should be noted that the splendid analysis taken in *The Eurymedon* to overcome the doctrine of privity and the lack of consideration from the third party, has lost a little of its vigour with the passage of the Contract (Rights of Third Parties) Act 1999. Under the Act, the protection of such a clause to a third party, including an actual carrier, should be possible. Section 6(5) enables a third party in the case of a contract of carriage to enforce a limitation clause in such a contract in reliance on s.1. Section 1 provides:

"(1) Subject to the provisions of this Act, a person who is not a party to a contract (a third party) may in his own right enforce a term of the contract if—

(a) the contract expressly provides that he may, or

(b) ... the term purports to confer a benefit on him.

(3) The third party must be expressly identified in the contract by name, as a member of a class or as answering a particular description but need not be in existence when the contract is entered into".

As a contractual stipulation the Himalaya clause is very much subject to the rules of the contractual construction.[33] This is very well demonstrated in case of *The Mahkutai* [1996] A.C. 650. The contract of carriage in question was between the cargo owners and the charterers of the Mahkutai. The bill of lading provided that the contract was governed by Indonesian law and that Indonesian courts were to have exclusive jurisdiction over any dispute. The bill of lading also contained a Himalaya clause referring to "all exceptions, limitations, provisions, conditions

---

[33] In *ITO Ltd v Mida Electronics Inc* 28 D.L.R. (4th) 641 (Supreme Court of Canada), McIntyre J. commented: "Himalaya clauses have become accepted as a part of the commercial law of many of the leading trading nations, including Great Britain, the United States, Australia, New Zealand, and now in Canada. It is thus desirable that the courts avoid constructions of contractual documents which would tend to defeat them. I would therefore accept the approach taken by Lord Wilberforce [in *The Eurymedon*] and, in doing so, I observe that the court is simply giving effect to that which the parties themselves clearly agreed to in writing". See also Tetley, "The Himalaya clause—revisited" [2003] J.I.M.L. 40.

and liberties herein benefiting the Carrier as is such provisions were expressly made for their benefit". The cargo owners sued the shipowners (rather than the charterers) for damage caused. The shipowners attempted to rely on the exclusive jurisdiction clause through the agency rule.

The Privy Council held that the shipowners could not rely on the Himalaya clause in relation to the exclusive jurisdiction clause. It was not a clause within the *Eurymedon* principle because an exclusive jurisdiction clause is not one that "benefits" the carriers or a third party.[34] It simply prescribes for mutual rights and obligations, and procedures in any civil action to be taken by one party. As a matter of construction, it fell outside the Himalaya clause.

8–086   In *The Starsin* [2003] UKHL 12, the contract of carriage was found to have been made between the charterer and the shipper. There was a Himalaya clause protecting:

> "The servant and agent of the carrier (including any person who performs work on behalf of the vessel on which the goods are carried or of any of the other vessels of the carrier, their cargo, their passengers or their baggage, including towage of and assistance and repairs to the vessels and including every independent contractor from time to time employed by the carrier)".

The House of Lords held that the shipowner could be covered by that clause, as "an independent contractor" of the charterer, who was the contractual carrier. The House of Lords held that, as a matter of construction, it protected the shipowner against any liability in tort. However, as to whether the exemption clause was nullified by art.III(8) Hague Rules, the court could not agree.

Lord Hoffmann did not think that the collateral contract between shipper and independent contractor was a "contract of carriage" so as to attract the application of the Hague Rules. But His Lordship was persuaded by the fact that the clause stated that the independent contractor "shall to this extent be deemed to be parties to the contract contained in or evidenced by this Bill of Lading". His Lordship took that to mean that he was a party only for the purpose of taking the benefit of the exemption clause against the shipper and any transferee of the bill of lading. But, for that purpose only, the provisions of the bill of lading, insofar as they are relevant, should therefore apply to him. Article III(8) was one such provision that was incorporated by virtue of the paramount clause. As such, the exemption clause should be limited by art.III(8).

8–087   Lord Bingham thought that the exemption provision however was invalidated by art.III r.8. His Lordship considered that there was a difference between *The Starsin* and *The Eurymedon* in that in the former, the third party in question was the shipowner (a factual carrier) whilst in the latter, it was a stevedore. Although His Lordship was uncomfortable with drawing a legal difference from the factual difference, he felt that it was important to give effect to the paramount clause which referred clearly to the act of carriage. His Lordship added:

> "If the act performance of which brings a contract into existence between the shipowner and the cargo owners is the carrying of the cargo owners' goods it

---

[34] See also *Petrologic Capital SA v Banque Cantonale de Geneve* [2012] EWHC 453 (Comm) where it was held that a third party could not enforce a jurisdiction clause contained in the contract under the Contract (Rights of Third Parties) Act 1999 because the contract in question (a letter of credit) did not purport to confer a benefit on the third party.

would seem to me anomalous to give the shipowner the benefit of clause 5 but take no account of article III rule 8 of the Hague Rules which were incorporated into the contract by [the paramount clause]".

Lord Millett's judgment is particularly instructive. His Lordship turned first to the words of art.III(8) referring to a clause which relieves "*the carrier or the ship*" from liability for loss or damage to the cargo. His Lordship thought it clear that the word "carrier" includes the owner or demise charterer of the ship which has entered into a contract of carriage. Unless the words "or the ship" are tautologous, therefore, they must be intended to cover the case where the owner or demise charterer of the ship has *not* entered into a contract of carriage. Thus the Rule invalidates a provision contained in a contract of carriage covered by a bill of lading to which the owner or demise charterer of the ship is a party and which purports to relieve the owner or demise charterer of the ship from liability for loss or damage to the cargo even though it has not itself entered into a contract of carriage. The only way in which effect can be given to such a provision is to square the circle and accept that the owner or demise charterer of the ship can become a party to a contract of carriage covered by a bill of lading even though it is a contract under which it does not itself undertake any obligations of carriage. It is observed that Lord Millett's approach is most methodical and it is buttressed by a reasonable reading of the precise words of art.III(8) and policy.

It is nonetheless interesting to look also at the minority judgment. Lord Steyn thought that the clause was not invalidated by art.III(8) Hague Rules because it was a collateral agreement not contained in a contract of carriage. It might be recalled that art.III(8) only applied to terms in the contract of carriage governed by the Rules; Lord Steyn considered that as there was no direct contract between the shipowner and the cargo interest, art.III(8) could not apply. Lord Hobhouse rebutted this argument stating that the collateral or implied contract is nonetheless a contract, stating:

"To deny that it is a contract of carriage is to ignore the fact that the service being provided (and which makes the contract enforceable between them) and its subject matter is the carriage of the goods by the shipowners for the goods owner".

Non-contractual actions—bailment

A cargo interest who is a successor in title in bailment or sub-bailment might be able to sue on bailment. Bailment involves the transfer of possession in law in the goods by the bailor to the bailee; in the case of carriage of goods, the bailee is often the carrier or the freight forwarder. The bailee may then pass legal possession in the goods to a sub-bailee (such as a warehouseman, or another carrier). It should be noted that legal possession does not necessarily involve the physical possession of the goods.[35] As is alluded to the discussion above, the law

8–088

---

[35] *Spectra International Plc v Hayesoak Ltd* [1997] 1 Lloyd's Rep. 153 where the Central London County Court considered that although the freight forwarder did not have physical possession of the goods kept in a bonded warehouse, he was nonetheless a bailee because he was given legal authority to deal with the goods and to arrange for their delivery to a consignee.

of bailment imposes on the bailee a duty of care and this duty would be subject to the terms (contractual or otherwise) on which the bailee had accepted the goods. Such a bailment is known as a bailment on terms. In the case where the terms are provided for in the contract of carriage, it can be seen that the bailment on terms would be a cause of action no different to an action on the contract. However, the claimant cargo interest may be compelled by circumstances to sue on bailment on terms instead of the contract of carriage. First, where the claimant had actually made a contract with a charterer and has therefore received a charterer's bill[36] but then wishes to sue the shipowner. He therefore has no contract with the shipowner and the success of his claim against the shipowner must therefore be founded on a noncontractual cause, the bailment on terms. Secondly, where the contract of carriage requires the transshipment of goods and the damage or loss was caused after the transshipment. If the cargo interest wishes to sue the second carrier, he could only do so on bailment on terms because there is no contract between himself and the second carrier.

As is immediately obvious, the doctrine of bailment on terms can serve as an effective way to circumvent the privity of contract requirement in contract law—both from the bailor's and bailee's perspectives. In *Elder Dempster & Co Ltd v Paterson Zochonis & Co Ltd* [1924] A.C. 522, for example, the shipowner was held to be able to rely on the limitation of liability clauses in the charterer's bill in defending a suit by the shipper. The court considered that there had been a bailment on the terms of the charterer's bill of lading. As such, the shipowner was entitled to rely on those terms. However, although there might be a Himalaya clause which protects the shipowner and there is bailment on terms, the court would not extend the terms of the original contract to matters such as jurisdiction or choice of law when the shipowner is being sued on the bailment (*The Mahkutai* [1996] A.C. 650).

A secondary question of some importance is how sub-bailment on terms might be dealt with. In *The Pioneer Container* [1994] 2 All E.R. 250, the claimant had sued the second carrier (sub-bailee) following damage caused to his goods after transshipment. In that case, the sub-bailee was held entitled to rely on an exclusive jurisdiction clause in the sub-bailment contract when sued by the bailor. The Privy Council held that a bailor of goods was bound by terms which he has expressly or by implication consented to the bailee making a sub-bailment on those terms. Lord Goff held

" . . . the only contract created by the sub-bailment being that between the bailee and the sub-bailee. Even so, if the effect of the sub-bailment is that the sub-bailee voluntarily receives into his custody the goods of the owner and so assumes towards the owner the responsibility of the bailee, then to the extent that the terms of the sub-bailment are consented to by the owner, it can properly be said that the owner has authorised the bailee so to regulate the duties of the sub-bailee in respect of the goods entrusted to him, not only towards the bailee but also towards the owner".

8–089   It should also be stressed that the bill of lading issued by the second carrier had referred to "on any terms whatsoever". On the basis of *The Pioneer Container*,

---

[36] See paras 8–003—8–005.

it might be natural to assume that the choice of forum clause in *The Mahkutai* should similarly be incorporated. Oddly, though, the Privy Council said that that was not to be the case—it was to be distinguished on the basis that there it was a bailment not a sub-bailment. Moreover, the bailment on terms could not have introduced the exclusive jurisdiction clause because on construction, it was not a term within the Himalaya cause and was therefore not capable of being implied into the bailment. The court was careful to emphasise that such an implication would be inconsistent with the express terms of the contract of carriage as contained in the original/first bill of lading. The issue of construction is perhaps not too controversial; however, the dicta that there was a difference between bailment and sub-bailment on terms causes some doctrinal unease.

The Privy Council also clarified the state of the law by explicitly stressing that the bailor's consent to the terms of the sub-bailment, whether express or implied, was essential to the incorporation of those terms. That said, the judicial attitude to the issue of consent appears fairly relaxed—in *Spectra International Plc v Hayesoak Ltd* [1997] 1 Lloyd's Rep. 153, for example, the terms were used widely in the trade, such as the Road Haulage Association standard terms, so that they were deemed to have been consented to by the bailor when it was clear to him that sub-bailment would be involved. Similarly, in *Sonicare International Ltd v East Anglia Freight Terminal Ltd* [1997] 2 Lloyd's Rep. 48, it was considered that there was no presumption that the terms of the sub-bailment should not be more burdensome to those in the bailment; consent would nonetheless be implied where the less attractive sub-bailment terms have actually been envisaged by the relevant parties.

Another requirement, other than consent, which has long been thought to be vital prior to the establishing of a bailment on terms is attornment. In *The Aliakmon* [1986] 1 A.C. 785, Lord Brandon made it plain that a successor in title (for example, the consignee of the bill of lading) to the original bailor could only sue in bailment if the bailee or sub-bailee attorns to it—that is to say, he clearly and unequivocally recognises it as the bailor. Attornment was found to be proved in the sub-bailee's agreeing to deliver the goods to the bailor's successor in title (*Sonicare International v East Anglia Freight Terminal Ltd* [1997] 2 Lloyd's Rep. 48).[37] The attornment should not only refer to the successor in title but also to the terms of the original bailment. In *The Gudermes* [1993] 1 Lloyd's Rep. 311, the Court of Appeal held that although the shipowners had negotiated with the new cargo owners (the original bailor's consignee) and that constituted attornment, the terms considered were not those in the bill of lading but in the charterparty. Leaving aside the difficulties in proving attornment, it is still not entirely clear whether attornment is actually required. Recently, Lord Hobhouse *The Starsin* [2003] UKHL 12, for example, has suggested, in obiter, that this requirement for attornment was probably misconceived. Similarly, in Lord Goff's speech in *The Pioneer Container* [1994] 2 A.C. 324 we find the view that no attornment is required when a claim is made against a sub-bailee. That would thus suggest that although attornment might no longer be needed in relation to a

---

[37] It should however be noted that there is some doubt as to attornment could be established without more evidence of recognition of the successor in title as the successor in title to the bailor. In *The Future Express* [1993] 2 Lloyd's Rep. 542, the court took a strict approach to attornment by stating the mere naming of the consignee in the bill of lading was not attornment.

claim against a sub-bailee, it might still be required for the successor in title to sue the carrier (*The Gudermes*).[38]

Non-contractual actions—negligence

8–090 It is also open to the cargo interest to sue the carrier and/or his subcontractors in the tort of negligence provided it can be shown that the defendant owed the claimant a duty of care, a breach of that duty and that the loss or damage was not too remote.[39] It should also be noted that there is no claim in negligence for pure economic loss.[40] The claimant must also demonstrate that at the time of the loss or damage, he was the owner of the goods or that he had an immediate right to possession of them.[41] As the House of Lords has confirmed in *The Aliakmon* [1986] A.C. 785, it is not enough for the claimant to show that the risk in the goods has passed to him. The rules on ownership are dealt with elsewhere[42] and it suffices to say that in general the reader should note the different rules applicable to documentary sales and bulk goods. As regards the issue of possession or the immediate right to possession, it should be noted that possession encompasses both actual and constructive possession. It is thus open to a person who is in possession of a ship's delivery order or a bill of lading to bring an action in negligence prior to the actual physical delivery.[43]

The Hamburg Rules

8–091 The chief complaint about the Hague and Hague-Visby Rules is that they primarily favour the carrier in a contract of carriage of goods by sea. Cargo exporting countries without a strong presence of shipowners are concerned with the limitations of the Hague-Visby Rules, particularly in respect of the following:

- the Hague-Visby Rules only have mandatory application where the contract is evidenced by a bill of lading; anything less, such as a sea waybill which is used frequently for shorter voyages, is not accommodated;

- the Hague-Visby Rules only apply to contracts of carriage by sea, they do not extend to any period of storage or consolidation of the cargo at the port of shipment even though the goods have already been received into custody by the carrier;

---

[38] See Baughen "Charterers' bills and shipowners' liabilities: a black hole for cargo claimants?" [2004] J.I.M.L. 248.

[39] *Donoghue v Stevenson* [1932] A.C. 562.

[40] *Murphy v Brentwood DC* [1991] 1 AC 398; in *The Gudermes* [1991] 1 Lloyd's Rep. 456 the court considered that transshipment costs resulting from the carrier's failure to heat the cargo of oil could not be claimed because they were purely economic. Of course, such costs would be recoverable in contract.

[41] See generally *The Aliakmon* [1986] A.C. 785; *Margarine Union GmbH v Cambay Prince Steamship Co (The Wear Breeze)* [1969] 1 Q.B. 219.

[42] See paras 4–042—4–061.

[43] *The Wear Breeze* [1969] 1 Q.B. 219; it should be borne in mind that the ship's delivery order entitles the holder to demand delivery of the goods held by the ship to him. A merchant's delivery order however does not have the same effect in relation to goods carried on a ship.

- the burden of proof under the Hague-Visby Rules weighs too heavily on the shipper;

- the Hague-Visby Rules contain no rules on how jurisdiction is to be allocated[44]; and

- the low financial limits in the Hague-Visby Rules.

The United Kingdom is however not a signatory to the Hamburg Rules, and is unlikely to be in the near future. However, some contracts of carriage which are litigated or arbitrated here are those which have incorporated the Hamburg Rules, contractually or otherwise.

Scope of application

Unlike the Hague-Visby Rules which apply to contracts covered by a bill of **8–092** lading, the Hamburg Rules will govern all "contracts of carriage by sea between two different States" under art.2(1). The only exception is charterparties.[45] This would mean that unlike a self-imposed constraint in the Hague-Visby Rules to bills of lading, the Hamburg Rules apply to any contract of carriage of sea, whatever the contractual document might be.

The Rules apply where:

1. the port of loading as provided for in the contract of carriage is located in a Contracting State; or

2. the port of discharge as provided for in the contract of carriage is located in a Contracting State; or

3. one of the optional ports of discharge provided for in the contract of carriage is the actual port of discharge and such port is located in a Contracting State; or

4. the bill of lading or other document evidencing the contract of carriage is issued in a Contracting State; or

5. the bill of lading or other document evidencing the contract of carriage by sea provides that the Hamburg Rules or the legislation of any State giving effect to them are to govern the contract.

The Hamburg Rules will apply without any regard paid to the nationality of the ship, the carrier, the actual carrier, the shipper, the consignee or any other interested person.

Under the Hamburg Rules, the period for which the carrier could be held liable **8–093** appears to have been extended. Article 4(1) makes it plain that the carrier shall be held liable under the Rules not only for the period when the goods are being shipped, but also, for the period during which he is in charge of the goods at the

---

[44] Note however that this so-called defect, at least as far as English law is concerned, has been to some extent remedied by the ruling in *The Hollandia (The Morviken)* [1983] 1 A.C. 565. It was held there that a exclusive jurisdiction clause in a bill of lading which refers disputes to a jurisdiction which provides for less protection than the Hague-Visby Rules shall be void to that extent. See paras 8–036—8–039.

[45] Art.2(3).

port of loading and at the port of discharge. The carrier is deemed under art.4(2)(a)(i) to be in charge of the goods from the time he takes over the goods from the shipper or a person acting on the latter's behalf. It might be observed that with the English courts taking a less strict approach to the construction of art.1(e) of the Hague-Visby Rules (*Pyrene Co Ltd v Scindia Navigation* [1954] 2 Q.B. 402), this "extension" in the Hamburg Rules is probably less significant than originally assumed.

The main difference between the Hamburg Rules and the Hague-Visby Rules as far as the scope of application is concerned, is the extension of application to carriage documents other than the bill of lading. A minor change is that the Hamburg Rules refer not only to the port of loading but also the port of discharge. No justification could be made for the exclusion of the reference to the port of discharge once the bill of lading is not considered to be paramount.

Who is a carrier?

8–094   The Hamburg Rules refer to the "actual carrier" and the "contractual carrier" as being susceptible to liability under the Rules concurrently. Article 10(1) provides:

> "Where the performance of the carriage or part thereof has been entrusted to an actual carrier, whether or not in pursuance of a liberty under the contract of carriage by sea to do so, the carrier nevertheless remains responsible for the entire carriage ... The carrier is responsible, in relation to the carriage performed by the actual carrier, for the acts and omissions of the actual carrier and of his servants and agents acting within the scope of their employment".

However, the actual carrier is liable only for the part of the contract which he personally performs. The contractual carrier is entitled to exclude his liability for loss or damage caused to the goods while in the custody of the actual carrier, provided that the actual carrier is named and details about that part being performed by the actual carrier are given, in the contract of carriage under art.11(1). Nevertheless, there exists another impediment to the contractual carrier's right to exclude liability under these circumstances—where it is not possible for judicial proceedings to be brought against the actual carrier in a competent court (as defined in art.21(1)(2)), that exclusion clause shall be ineffective. There is however no rule which prejudices any right of recourse between the carrier and the actual carrier. There exists between themselves, a mutual right to indemnity.

This position is different from that under the Hague-Visby Rules where, whilst the charterer and the shipowner are both subject to the Hague-Visby Rules where the contract made is covered by a bill of lading, only one could be made liable at a time.

8–095   The new provision is reflective of the change in international carriage conventions—for example, the Montreal Convention 1999[46] also places concurrent liability on the actual and contractual carrier. The rationale is to ensure that the shipper or cargo owner is not disadvantaged in any way by being

---

[46] See paras 9–001—9–002.

compelled to make a choice of defendant at the outset. He should be entitled to sue both, if he is so advised.

Basis of liability

Article 5 provides that the carrier is liable for loss resulting from loss or damage **8–096** to the goods, as well as delay in delivery, if the occurrence which caused the loss, damage or delay took place while the goods were in his charge, unless the carrier proves that he, his servants or agents took all ensures that could reasonably be required to avoid the occurrence and its consequence. This is clearly a presumption of liability provision, once it has been shown by the claimant that the goods were in the carrier's charge and the loss or damage occurred during that time, the onus shifts to the carrier to prove non-negligence. This is starkly different from the Hague-Visby Rules which set out in art.IV(2) a list of exceptions to the carrier's liability. Negligence is thus removed as an exception to liability.

Where damage or loss was caused by *fire*, art.5(4) states that the carrier will be liable only if the claimant is able to prove that the fire arose from the "fault or neglect on the part of the carrier, its servants and agents". There is in substance little difference between the fire exception under the Hague-Visby Rules and the fire liability provision under the Hamburg Rules.

As for the carriage of *live animals*, which falls outside the ambit of the Hague-Visby Rules, the Hamburg Rules provide in art.5(5) that the carrier is not liable for loss, damage or delay arising out of "any special risk inherent in that kind of carriage". Thus, where the carrier is able to show that the damage was caused by such a risk and that he had adhered to any special instructions given by the shipper, then the burden passes over to the shipper or claimant to prove that the carrier was in fact negligent.

There is no special place conferred on *cargo carried on deck* in the Hamburg Rules. Article 9(1) provides that cargo may be carried on deck either in accordance with agreement with the shipper or the usage of a particular trade or if required by statutory rules or regulations.

Limits on liability

The financial limits placed on a potential claim under art.6(1) are: **8–097**

(a) for loss of or damage to goods—an amount equivalent to 835 units of account per package or other shipping unit or 2.5 units of account per kilogramme of gross weight of the goods lost or damaged, whichever is the higher;

(b) for delay in delivery—an amount equivalent to two and a half times the freight payable for the goods delayed, but not exceeding the total freight payable under the contract of carriage of goods by sea.

Article 6(2) provides that where a container, pallet or similar article of transport is used to consolidate goods, the package or other shipping units enumerated in the bill of lading of other shipping document, as packed in such article of transport are deemed packages or shipping units. If they have not been enumerated in the shipping documents, then the goods held in the article of transport will be deemed collectively as one shipping unit. In cases where the article of transport itself has been lost or damaged, that article of transport, if not owned or otherwise supplied by the carrier, is considered one separate shipping unit. The total liability of the carrier under all heads cannot exceed the maximum limit on a total loss of the goods as calculated under art.6(1)(a).

The new limits on compensation for goods lost or damaged are clearly more favourable to the shipper than those set by the Hague-Visby Rules, an increase from 666.67 units of account per packages to 835 and 2 units of account per kilogramme to 2.5

Time limit

8–098   The Hamburg Rules, like the Hague-Visby Rules, also require the claimant to commence action or lodge a complaint within a set time. Unlike the Hague-Visby Rules though, the time limit is two years. This period of two years starts running from the date of delivery or, in the case of nondelivery, on the last day on which the goods should have been delivered. Article 20(1) allows the time limit to be extended at any time within the two-year period by the defendant provided he serves a declaration in writing to the claimant.

The claimant must first make a complaint and give notice of his dissatisfaction to the defendant within set time limits. Article 19 provides that with reference to a claim:

- consignee for loss or damage, the notice should be given within 15 consecutive working days after delivery;

- by consignee for delay in delivery, the notice is to be given within 60 days after delivery; and

- by carrier/actual carrier against shipper for loss or damage, the notice to be given is within 90 consecutive days of either the occurrence or delivery of the goods.

Failure to give notice shall be construed as a tacit acceptance that the goods have been delivered in good order and condition and on time.

Excluding the Rules

8–099   Unlike art.III(8) of the Hague-Visby Rules, art.23(1) nullifies not only stipulations in the contract which derogate *directly* but also those which derogate *indirectly* from the Rules. It would be interesting to see how the courts would construe and apply this wider provision.

Duty of carrier to issue shipping documents

8–100   Under Pt IV, the carrier is required to issue a bill of lading to the shipper when the carrier or actual carrier takes the goods into his charge which as far as art.15 is concerned, should contain the following particulars:

(a)   the general nature of the goods, the leading marks necessary for identification of the goods, an express statement, if applicable, as to dangerous character of the goods, the number of packages or pieces, and the weight of the goods or their quantity otherwise expressed, all such particulars as furnished by the shipper;

(b) the apparent condition of the goods;

(c) the name and principal place of business of the carrier;

(d) the name of the shipper;

(e) the consignee if named by the shipper;

(f) the port of loading under the contract of carriage and the date on which the goods were taken over by the carrier at the port of loading;

(g) the port of discharge under the contract of carriage;

(h) the number of originals of the bill of lading;

(i) the place of issuance of the bill of lading;

(j) the signature of the carrier or a person acting on his behalf;

(k) the freight to the extent payable by the consignee or other indication that freight is payable by him;

(l) a statement that the document is subject to the Hamburg Rules and any derogation therefrom directly or indirectly shall be null and void;

(m) the statement, if applicable, that the goods shall or may be carried on deck;

(n) the date or the period of delivery of the goods at the port of discharge if expressly agreed upon between the parties; and

(o) any increased limit or limits of liability, as agreed.

These provisions are clearly much more detailed than their counterpart— art.III(3) in the Hague-Visby Rules.

Although the carrier would be in breach of the Rules if he omits to state any of the above details (where applicable), art.15(3) provides that such an omission does not affect the legality and enforceability of the bill of lading as a contract.

As for the evidential value of the bill of lading, art.16(2) marks a change from the Hague-Visby Rules by providing that a bill of lading that fails to record the apparent order and condition of the goods is deemed to have recorded their shipment in "apparent good order and condition". Omission is presumed to be a declaration that the goods have been shipped in good order and condition, ensuring that the carrier acts diligently to ensure that any apparent deficiencies or defects in the goods are properly recorded by clausing the bill of lading.

Additionally, art.16(4) states that a bill of lading which does not expressly **8–101** provide that freight is payable by the consignee and does not set forth demurrage incurred at the port of loading payable by the consignee, is prima facie evidence that no freight or such demurrage is payable by him. However, proof to the contrary by the carrier is not admissible when the bill of lading has been transferred to a third party, including a consignee, who acted in good faith and in reliance on the absence of such an indication in the bill of lading. This provision confirms the common law rule that a lawful holder of the bill of lading is liable for freight unless the bill of lading issued contains a "freight pre-paid" indorsement.

The shipper must indemnify the carrier against any loss arising from representations made in the bill of lading as supplied to the carrier by the shipper under art.17(1). A letter of indemnity provided by the shipper to the carrier against loss resulting from the issuance of the bill of lading without entering a reservation relating to particulars furnished by the shipper for insertion in the bill of lading or to the apparent condition of the goods is void and of no effect *against a third party*, including the consignee, to whom the bill of lading has been transferred. Such an indemnity to induce the carrier to issue a clean bill of lading is nevertheless enforceable against the shipper provided the letter of indemnity has not been offered to perpetrate fraud on a third party.[47]

Jurisdiction for dispute resolution

8–102   The Hamburg Rules, unlike the Hague-Visby Rules, make specific provisions for jurisdiction. Under art.21, the claimant has the option of suing the defendant in any of the following places:

1. the principal place of business or in the absence thereof, the habitual residence of the defendant; or

2. the place where the contract was made, provided that the defendant has there a place of business, branch or agency through which the contract was made; or

3. the port of loading or the port of discharge; or

4. any additional place designated for that purpose in the contract of carriage by sea.

The courts of these places are not, however, automatically seised. They will still need to decide on the basis of their own domestic law whether they have jurisdiction to entertain the claim. The Hamburg Rules merely offer the claimant the option of suing at any of these places, if the claim is admissible by the law of those places. This is however a closed list; art.21(3) disallows proceedings to be brought in a place not specified in art.21 despite that court's own jurisdictional rules.[48]

As for arbitration, art.22(3) offers on the claimant similar options—arbitral proceedings may be commenced in a place designated for that purpose in the contract or in a state within whose territory is situated:

1. the principal place of business or in the absence thereof, the habitual residence of the defendant; or

---

[47] This provision is inconsistent with *Brown Jenkinson & Co Ltd v Percy Dalton (London) Ltd* 2 Q.B. 621 where it was held that an indemnity given to support a misrepresentation that the goods were shipped in good order and condition was unenforceable, regardless of whether fraud was proved.

[48] This provision should not cause any problems with the EU Regulation on Jurisdiction and the Recognition and Enforcement of Civil and Commercial Matters 2000 which provides that international convention rules on jurisdiction shall prevail, in an event of conflict (see art.71).

2. the place where the contract was made, provided that the defendant has there a place of business, branch or agency through which the contract was made; or

3. the port of loading or the port of discharge.

Article 22 also provides that the arbitration must apply the Hamburg Rules in resolving any such dispute, and any contractual term which purports to vary this and/or any of the options made available to the claimant under the Rules shall be null and void to that extent.

The UNCITRAL Convention on the International Carriage of Goods wholly or partly by Sea (The Rotterdam Rules)

On July 3, 2008, the UNCITRAL Commission adopted officially the final draft **8–103** of a new transport convention, the "Convention on Contracts for the International Carriage of Goods wholly or partly by Sea".[49] A ceremony opening the Convention to ratification was held in Rotterdam in 2009. The Convention will come into force one year after the date of deposit of the 20th instrument of ratification, acceptance, approval or accession. Serious reservations about the Convention have been expressed by a significant number of important trading countries, including Germany, Australia, Canada, Korea and Argentina. Italy and the United Kingdom have not expressed an inclination either way. That said, not only have the USA, France, Spain and Sweden signed the Convention but there is support for the Convention from China and a number of developing countries. Two countries have ratified the Convention thus far—Spain and Togo. It would appear that it will be a little time yet before the 20 ratifications needed for the Convention to become law will be achieved. However, the momentum is picking up given the concerns that the Hague-Visby Rules and Hamburg Rules are in need of reform[50] and reform is best achieved internationally instead of by ad hoc action by countries or regions (such as the EU).

The Rotterdam Rules address more issues than the Hague-Visby Rules or the Hamburg Rules. It contains chapters dealing with electronic documents, door-to-door cover, delivery of goods, rights of the controlling party and transfer of rights, matters which have been governed largely by national law. In the United Kingdom, these are dealt with by the common law and the Carriage of Goods by Sea Act 1992,[51] for example. In general, the larger and wider scope of coverage of an international convention, the more difficult it is to secure international acceptance. The fact that it is intended to apply with mandatory effect makes international acceptance even more challenging. The Rotterdam Rules contain 96 articles, making it one of the most comprehensively drafted multilateral

---

[49] The text referred to in this book is the one published as an annex to the Working Group III, UNCITRAL, at its 21st session in Vienna January 14–25, 2008 (A/CN.9/645) dated January 30, 2008.

[50] See Sturley, "Transport law for the 21st century" [2008] 14 J.I.M.L. 461 on the philosophy behind the Rotterdam Rules.

[51] On a comparison between the 1992 Act and the Rotterdam Rules on the transfer of contractual rights under a shipping document, see Thomas, "A comparative analysis of the transfer of contractual rights under the English Carriage of Goods by Sea Act 1992 and the Rotterdam Rules" [2011] J.I.M.L. 437.

international conventions. It will thus be a tremendous challenge to persuade the international community that it is a worthwhile legal instrument to sign up to.

Rationale for the new Convention

8–104 The best starting point to assist us in appreciating the reasons behind this significant move to table a new convention before the international community of nations is perhaps the UN General Assembly General Resolution 63/122 of February 2, 2009. The UN General Assembly expressed that there was a concern that the current maritime transport conventions lacked uniformity and failed to take into account modern shipping practices including containerisation, door-to-door transport contracts, and the use of electronic transport documents. It sees the Rotterdam Rules as a further step to achieve harmonisation and unification of the law of international trade (very much consistent with the objectives of the UNCITRAL[52]) which the UN sees as particularly needful for serving the trading needs of developing countries. It also envisages that the new Rules will serve better the interests of carriers and shippers who at present do not have the benefit of a binding and balanced universal regime to support the operation of contracts of carriage involving various modes of transport.[53] These goals are lofty and that adds to the difficulty of its seeking international acceptance.

Scope of application[54]

8–105 The Convention applies to "contracts of carriage". A contract of carriage is defined in art.1(1) as "a contract in which a carrier, against the payment of freight, undertakes to carry goods from one place to another". It is also provided that the contract shall provide for carriage by sea and may provide for carriage by other modes of transport in addition to sea carriage (art.1(1)). There is a further condition before the Convention would apply—the place of receipt and the place of delivery should be in different states, and as regards the sea leg, the port of loading and port of discharge should be in different states.

It should also be clear that one of the following, as indicated in the contract, is a contracting state:

- the place of receipt, or
- the port of loading, or
- the place of delivery, or
- the port of discharge.

A few points might be said about the new rules:

1. any multimodal carriage must involve a sea leg, unlike, for example, the UN Multimodal Transport Convention[55];

---

[52] See the UN General Assembly Resolution of Resolution 2205 (XXI) of December 17, 1966 which established the UNCITRAL.

[53] See also the Preamble to the Convention.

[54] Goddard, "The application of the Rotterdam Rules" [2010] 16 J.I.M.L. 210.

[55] For more on the Rotterdam Rules and multimodal transport, see Abogado, "NYPE charter-party—early redelivery" [2012] 18 J.I.M.L. 182; also Eftestøl-Wilhelmsson, "The Rotterdam Rules in a European multimodal context" [2010] 16 J.I.M.L. 274.

2. there is no requirement that the sea leg has to be the dominant leg, or otherwise; and

3. "the contract shall provide for the carriage by sea" suggests that the sea carriage must be clear, expressly or by implication, from the contract; the actuality that the goods were carried by sea is not enough. It would appear too that it is not enough for the contract to provide for a mere liberty to use sea carriage. The duty to use sea carriage must be present, expressly or by implication.

Given their recognition of containerisation and multimodal transport, the **8–106** Rotterdam Rules try to avoid conflict with the other transport conventions, such as the CMR, CIM-COTIF and the Montreal Convention.[56] Article 84 thus provides that nothing in the convention affects the application of the international conventions on air, road, rail and inland waterways where those conventions are applicable to particular parts of the carriage. It is clear from art.84 too that those conventions should be in force at the time the carriage convention enters into force. Although the intention of the working group was to avoid conflicts with the other carriage conventions, problems might nevertheless surface. For example, in RO-RO road transport involving a sea leg. Article 2 CMR, states that the CMR would apply unless where the loss or damage is caused solely by the carriage by sea. In such a case, the carrier's liability shall be determined in accordance with the conditions prescribed by law (if any) for the carriage of goods alone by sea. Article 84(b) provides that the sea carriage convention will not apply to the extent that the CMR applied to "the carriage of goods that remain loaded on a vehicle carried on board a ship". The words however do not refer to the entirety of the carriage, only the part of the carriage when the goods "remain loaded on a vehicle on board a ship". Hence, the sea convention will only be excluded for that period and not the entirety of the carriage. Diamond comments that

> "it can only create wholly unnecessary difficulty to exclude the operation of the [sea] convention while the vehicle is on board ship but to provide for its application before the vehicle is on board the ship and after it is driven off the ship".[57]

Hence, the result would be that *both* conventions would potentially apply to the carriage before the vehicle boards and after it has driven off the ship. Conflict between the two could thus occur.

In this connection, it is useful to refer to art.27 which provides:

> "*Carriage preceding or subsequent to sea carriage*
> When loss of or damage to goods, or an event or circumstance causing a delay in their delivery, occurs during the carrier's period of responsibility but solely before their loading onto the ship or solely after their discharge from the ship, the provisions of this Convention do not prevail over those provisions of

---

[56] On conflicts with other conventions, see Røsæg, "Conflicts of conventions in the Rotterdam Rules" [2009] 15 J.I.M.L. 238.
[57] Diamond, "The Next Sea Carriage Convention" [2008] L.M.C.L.Q. 133.

another international instrument that, at the time of such loss, damage or event or circumstance causing delay:

(a) Pursuant to the provisions of such international instrument would have applied to all or any of the carrier's activities if the shipper had made a separate and direct contract with the carrier in respect of the particular stage of carriage where the loss of, or damage to goods, or an event or circumstance causing delay in their delivery occurred;

(b) Specifically provide for the carrier's liability, limitation of liability, or time for suit; and

(c) Cannot be departed from by contract either at all or to the detriment of the shipper under that instrument".

8–107   The clear objective here is to provide for a "network solution" where there might arise a conflict between the sea convention and other carriage conventions. Article 27 requires the sea convention to yield to the other relevant mandatory carriage conventions where the above conditions are met.

An important condition in art.27 is that loss or damage must be shown to have occurred before loading or after discharge. If the loss or damage had not occurred at those times, or if there is gradual and continuous damage or loss (deterioration, for example), or if the place of damage or loss could not be established, art.27 does not apply. During these other periods of transit, there could potentially be two or more conventions applying thereby increasing the risk of conflict.

In the case of roll-on/roll-off (RO-RO) carriage, it has been held in *Quantum Corp v Plane Trucking Ltd* [2002] 2 Lloyd's Rep. 200 that for the CMR to apply, the contract of carriage does not need to have the road carriage as a substantial part of the transit. It was also not material that the carrier could have used other modes of transport. It was enough that the contract (in *Quantum*, the main leg was air carriage) allowed for international road carriage which actually took place. It is therefore not inconceivable that a potential conflict might occur.

8–108   This recognition of container transport (as is always the case in multimodal transport) has also led to the replacement of the antiquated exception in the Hague-Visby Rules for deck cargo. Article 26(1) provides that the following types of deck cargo will be covered by the Rotterdam Rules

(a) deck cargo which is required by law; or

(b) the cargo is held in containers or road/railroad vehicles which are fit for deck carriage and the decks are specifically fitted to carry them; or

(c) the carriage of cargo on deck is consistent with the contract or the customs, usages and practices of the trade.

In general, for cargo falling within the above, the convention would govern the rights and obligations of the parties. However, as regards art.26(1)(a) and (b), the carrier would not be liable if the loss, damage or delay was caused by the special risks involved in such carriage. Paragraph (c) is a marked shift. As long as the contract calls for or even permits deck cargo, that would bring the Convention into operation. A third party who has acquired a negotiable transport document or a negotiable electronic transport record in good faith can expect that goods would not be carried on deck unless the contract particulars make that explicit (art.26(4)) and thus, a carrier cannot invoke art.26(1)(c) against him despite the existence of a contract or custom to that effect.

If the cargo carried on deck does not fall within any of the above, the carrier shall be estopped from relying on the defences in art.18 (see below).

Mandatory effect

The new sea Convention is intended to have mandatory effect. Article 81 **8–109** provides that any term in the contract which directly or indirectly excludes or limits the carrier's obligations under the Convention will be void. The Convention however does not apply mandatorily to all contracts of carriage (art.6). The Convention does not apply to the following contracts in liner transportation:

1. charterparties;

2. contracts for the use of a ship or any space thereon.

As regards non-liner transportation, the convention does not apply except when:

1. there is no charterparty or other contract between the parties for the use of a ship or space thereon; and

2. a transport document or an electronic transport record is issued.

Liner transportation is helpfully defined in art.1(3) as

"a transportation service that is offered to the public through publication or similar means and includes transportation by ships operating on a regular schedule between specified ports in accordance with publicly available timetables of sailing dates".

That which is not liner transportation is non-liner transportation (art.1(4)).

It should however be noted that art.6 must be read together with art.7 which makes sure that the convention would continue to apply to the relationship between the carrier and consignee, controlling party or holder who is not an original party to the charterparty or other contract excluded in art.6. The exclusion of the convention is therefore confined solely to the relationship between the consignor and the carrier where that relationship takes the form of a charterparty or similarly excluded contract under art.6.

As regards volume contracts, art.82 provides that: **8–110**

1. the volume contract as between the carrier and shipper may provide for different rights and obligations from those under the convention; and

2. There is however no derogation from

   (a) the carrier's duty to provide a seaworthy ship (art.15);
   (b) the carrier's duty properly to crew, equip and supply the ship (art.15);
   (c) the shipper's duty to provide information relating to the goods (art.30);
   (d) the shipper's duty in relation to dangerous goods (art.33);

(e) carrier's liability arising from an act or omission referred to in art.63.

There must be clear notice on the contract that it derogates from the convention and which provisions have been derogated from. The contract must be one which is "individually negotiated". This is obviously a difficult condition to apply given that in most volume contracts, there will be some pre-printed standard form. A pragmatic approach should thus be used. Individually negotiated should not be taken to mean that the contract must have been drawn up from scratch between the parties. It should suffice that the shipper has the power to vary the pre-printed terms.

So what are volume contracts? These are defined in art.1(2) as

"a contract of carriage that provides for the carriage of a specified quantity of goods in a series of shipments during an agreed period of time"

and "the specification of the quantity may include a minimum, a maximum or a certain range". The so-called "ocean liner service agreements" (OLSAs) under which the majority of trans-Atlantic liner trades are operated would thus fall within the scope of the derogation in art.82.

8–111   The convention also allows the carrier to exclude or limit liability where live animals are carried under the contract of carriage (art.83(a)). The exclusion or limitation on liability will not be enforced if the carrier is guilty of an act or omission done recklessly and with knowledge that loss, delay or damage would result.

Article 83(b) is similar to art.VI Hague-Visby Rules. It allows for special agreements to derogate from the convention mandatory application. The parties may have to make special, nonconventional agreements which are reasonably justified by the character or condition of the goods, or the circumstances and terms and conditions under which the carriage is to be performed. An important proviso is that such a contract

"must not be related to ordinary commercial shipments made in the ordinary course of trade and no negotiable transport document or negotiable electronic transport record is issued for the carriage of goods".

Finally, where the carrier has issued a single transport document or electronic transport record that includes specified transport that is not covered by the contract and in respect of which he does not assume the obligation to carry, the carrier would only be liable under the convention for that period covered by the contract. The intention here is to protect the carrier from being exposed to the convention when he issues a through bill of lading where the on-carriage is arranged by him as agent on behalf of some other carrier.

Liability of carrier[58]

8–112   The carrier is responsible for the goods from when he or a performing party receives the goods for carriage to when the goods are delivered (art.12(1)). The

---

[58] See more generally Nikaki, "The fundamental duties of the carrier under the Rotterdam Rules" [2008] 14 J.I.M.L. 512 and Thomas, "An appraisal of the liability regime established under the new UN convention" [2008] 14 J.I.M.L. 496.

parties may agree on the time and place of receipt and delivery of the goods but the contract may not stipulate that:

1. the time of receipt is subsequent to the beginning of their initial loading under the contract of carriage; or

2. the time of delivery is prior to the completion of their final unloading under the contract of carriage (art.12(3)).

It may be recalled that under the Hague-Visby Rules, the carriage of goods is defined as covering "the period from the time the goods are loaded on to the time when they are discharged from the ship" (art.1(e) Hague-Visby Rules). In art.12, that has been modified. The period of cover will be from the time the goods are received (instead of loaded) to the time they are delivered (as against discharge).

The carrier's more specific obligations are detailed in:

● art.14 (duty properly and carefully to receive, load, handle, stow, carry, keep, care for, unload and deliver the goods);

● art.15 (a duty, at the beginning of and during the voyage, to provide a seaworthy ship, properly to crew, equip and supply the ship, and make and keep the holds and containers supplied by the carrier fit and safe for the reception, carriage and preservation of the goods).

These provisions are intended to reflect those in the Hague-Visby Rules and **8–113** the Hamburg Rules on seaworthiness, and care of cargo. There is a significant feature in art.15—it is that the duty attaches not only at commencement of the voyage but endures all through the voyage. The duty is thus a continuing duty to exercise due diligence to make and *keep* the ship seaworthy.

If the carrier breaches these duties and consequential loss, damage or delay were to arise, he would be liable if the claimant is able to prove

"that the loss, damage or delay or the event or circumstance that caused or contributed to it took place during the period of the carrier's responsibility" (art.18(1)).

The reference to delay is controversial. Carriers expressed concern during consultations that the meaning of "delay" should not be unduly capacious and insisted on delay being dependent on an express agreement to deliver the goods at a specified time. That was not considered acceptable by shipper groups. The result is art.22, which provides that delay occurs "when the goods are not delivered at the place of destination provided for in the contract of carriage within the time agreed". The removal of the express term to deliver the goods at a specific time is clearly a compromise solution. How the new turn of words should be construed is specifically left to the relevant courts; the Working Group makes it plain that the convention should contain no further guidance. The difficulty, of course, is that where no time for delivery is specified (expressly or by implication), what should a court do where the ship is seriously and unjustifiably delayed? Whilst it is clear that no court would deny the claimant a remedy, it is quite opaque what are the principles and how the ascertainable principles should be applied. Another potential problem is how time for delivery might be implied, given the removal of the express stipulation suggestion by the carriers. Deviation per se will no longer be a breach and its legality is now dependent on the contract's applicable law (art.25). Even then, the carrier would not lose his defences and limits on liability (art.25).

8–114   The carrier will not be liable if it could be shown that the cause or one of the causes of the loss, damage or delay is not attributable to its fault or to the fault of any person under its control or supervision generally (art.18(2)). Unless the carrier is at fault or the carrier had failed to provide and keep the ship seaworthy, the following will also excuse the carrier from liability:

1. Act of God;

2. Perils, dangers, and accidents of the sea or other navigable waters;

3. War, hostilities, armed conflict, piracy, terrorism, riots and civil commotions;

4. Quarantine restrictions; interference by or impediments created by governments, public authorities, rulers, or people including detention, arrest or seizure not attributable to the carrier or any person referred to in art.19;

5. Strikes, lockouts, stoppages or restraints of labour;

6. Fire on the ship;

7. Latent defects not discoverable by due diligence;

8. Act or omission of the shipper, the documentary shipper, the controlling party, or any other person for whose acts the shipper or the documentary shipper;

9. Loading, handling, stowing or unloading of the goods performed by the shipper, the documentary shipper or the consignee as specifically agreed under the contract, unless the carrier or a performing party performs such activity on behalf of the shipper, the documentary shipper or the consignee;

10. Wastage in bulk or weight or any other loss or damage arising from inherent defect, quality or vice of the goods;

11. Insufficiency or defective condition of packing or marking not performed by or on behalf of the carrier;

12. Saving or attempting to save life at sea;

13. Reasonable measures to save or attempt to save property at sea;

14. Reasonable measures to avoid or attempt to avoid damage to the environment; or

15. Acts of the carrier in pursuance of the powers conferred by arts 16 and 17 (dealing with disposal of goods which have become dangerous or have to be sacrificed to save life or property).

These defences are clearly more constrictive than those in art.4(2) Hague-Visby Rules. A clear omission is the exception of ship management and navigation (art.4(2)(a), Hague-Visby Rules) from the list. The removal of one of the most potent defences for the carrier is likely to result to more claims against the carrier being settled out of court.

The carrier shall be liable for the breach of any of its obligations under the convention caused by any performing party and their employees, the master or crew, employees, or indeed, any person who acts at the carrier's request or under his supervision (art.19). A performing party is defined in art.1(6) as any person (not being the carrier) who performs or undertakes to perform any of the carrier's obligations (under a contract of carriage) with respect to the receipt, loading, handling, stowage, carriage, care, unloading or delivery of the goods, to the extent that such a person acts, either directly or indirectly, at the carrier's request or under the carrier's supervision or control. A person retained by a shipper or documentary shipper or consignee instead of by the carrier is not a performing party (art.1(6)(b)). A maritime performing party is a performing party who performs or undertakes to perform the carrier's obligations during the period between the arrival of the goods at the port of loading and their departure from the port of discharge. An inland carrier is a maritime performing party only if it performs or undertakes to perform its services *exclusively* within a port area. **8–115**

It should be noted that although the carrier is liable for the acts of the performing party, the cargo interest might also be entitled to sue the performing party directly. Article 20 provides that the performing party would be liable for loss, damage or delay if the relevant occurrence took place when he had custody of the goods or at any other time when he was participating in the performance of the contract of carriage. However, the performing party, by virtue of art.4, can rely on the defences or limits on liability available to the carrier.

Carrier's duty to deliver the goods

Other than the above duties, the carrier is also required to carry the goods to the place of destination and deliver them to the consignee (art.11). This is different from the Hague-Visby Rules; the latter do not contain an express duty to deliver the goods. This would thus mean that a claim for misdelivery could now be made based on the convention. At English law, misdelivery is treated as a strict contractual obligation for which there are no defences and where there are limitation of liability clauses, these would be construed very narrowly. In *The Sormovskiy* [1994] 2 Lloyd's Rep. 266, for example, the carrier was not relieved of liability for misdelivery of the goods when the customs authorities who were in possession of the goods had passed them on to the buyer who had not paid for them (and therefore did not have a bill of lading). That was the case despite a clause in the bill of lading providing **8–116**

> "if the carrier is obliged to hand over the goods into the custody of a customs, port of other authority, such hand over shall constitute due delivery to the Merchant under the bill of lading".

Under the Rotterdam Rules, on the other hand, it would appear that there are defences for the carrier who misdelivered the goods (art.18, see below) and the carrier would be able to rely on the limitation of liability provisions in art.61 (so long as he had not committed a personal act or omission (art.63)).

Article 11 should be read in conjunction with art.45 which requires "the consignee who exercises its rights under the contract of carriage" to accept delivery at the time or within the time period and at the location agreed in the contract of carriage. The criterion referred to in art.45 is "who exercises its rights under the contract of carriage". The emphasis on "its rights" instead of "any of its rights" seems to suggest that the consignee must exercise the entirety of its rights instead of merely some of its rights. The Working Group meeting in October 2007 states that the intention here was

> "that a consignee who wished to exercise its rights under the contract of sale, such as the right to reject the goods, should not be allowed to refuse to take delivery of the goods under the contract of carriage".

The separateness of the two contracts is stressed. For example, the consignee who takes samples from the cargo would come under art.45 and must accept delivery but a consignee who, under a contract, simply asks for information about the whereabouts of the goods would not. Another deficiency in art.45 is the omission of any mention of a remedy for breach.

The carrier's duty to deliver the goods depends largely on the type of transport document in use

8–117   Where no negotiable transport document or negotiable electronic transport record has been issued, the carrier may refuse delivery if the person claiming to be the consignee does not properly identify himself as the consignee (art.47(a)). In general, the controlling party should advise the carrier prior to arrival of the goods the name and address of the consignee (art.47(b)). Where this is not provided or where the consignee does not turn up to collect the goods, the carrier shall advise the controlling party and seek his instructions. In the event that the carrier is unable to locate the controlling party after reasonable efforts, he shall advise the shipper. Failing which, he shall inform the documentary shipper. If that too is to no avail, the carrier is discharged from his contractual obligations. It should be noted that the controlling party is a person who has the right to give or modify shipping instructions (provided that modification is within the terms of the contract)—for example, a freight forwarder.

Where a non-negotiable transport document or electronic transport record has been issued calling for goods to be delivered to a named consignee (for example a straight bill of lading), the carrier shall deliver the goods to the said consignee, upon the consignee properly identifying himself on the carrier's request and surrender of the non-negotiable instrument by the consignee (art.48). If the consignee does not claim delivery after receiving a notice of arrival, the carrier shall seek the instructions of the shipper (or the documentary shipper, if the shipper is not located) in respect of the goods. A delivery according to those instructions would discharge the carrier from his contract (art.48(c)). There is thus a danger for the consignee who fails to collect the goods to find that the shipper could order the goods to be delivered elsewhere despite having paid for the goods. Under art.48, regrettably, the onus is therefore very much on the consignee to monitor the ship's arrival.

In the case where a negotiable transport document or electronic record is issued, art.49 states that the carrier must deliver the goods upon tender of the document. In the case of an order bill which identifies the consignee (e.g. "To Joe or order"), proof of identity is also required as a precondition to delivery. Where a number of original documents have been issued and the number of originals is stated in the document, the surrender of one of the originals will enough and will extinguish the others. The carrier would no longer be under the duty to deliver once he has delivered against one of the originals (art.49(c)). As with art.47, by and large, the carrier shall advise the controlling party, shipper or documentary shipper (in that order, as in art.47) accordingly if the holder, after notice of arrival, does not present himself to accept delivery and the goods disposed of in accordance with the latter's instructions. However a major difficulty exists here—unlike art.47, here the holder may not be an identifiable person. How should the notice of arrival be given? Although the bill of lading will usually specify a "notify party", it is not clear from art.49 that this would suffice. There is also a further requirement in art.49 which differs from art.47—the person giving the instructions (controlling party, shipper or documentary shipper as the case may be) to the carrier is required to indemnify the carrier against loss arising from the delivery to a lawful holder of the transport document. The carrier is thus entitled to ask for security. The holder's rights against the carrier depend on whether he has, or is deemed to have, knowledge of the delivery of the goods at the time he became the holder. Article 49(h) states that where the contract particulars state the expected time of arrival or indicate how to obtain information as to whether the goods have been delivered, the presumption is that the holder had or could reasonably have had knowledge of the delivery.

Where the goods could not be delivered, the carrier is entitled to dispose of them (art.50) subject to his decision to retain the goods as security (art.51).

Liability of shipper and documentary shipper[59]

The Rotterdam Rules lay down specific requirements that the shipper and the **8–118** documentary shipper must comply with. Although these requirements are by no means new duties, the convention formalises their existence and clarifies them in some detail. The shipper is required to:

1. deliver the goods ready for carriage in such a condition that they will withstand the intended carriage (art.28);

2. provide responses to the carrier's requests for information (art.29);

3. provide information and documents to the carrier in a timely manner where such information is not otherwise reasonably available to the carrier and is necessary for the proper handling and carriage of goods (art.30);

4. provide timely and accurate information for the compilation of the contract particulars and the issuance of transport documents (art.32);

5. inform the carrier of the dangerous nature of any goods (art.33).

The burden of proof is however on the carrier to show that the loss was caused by a breach of the shipper's obligations (art.31). Another important observation to make is that whilst most of the obligations referred to above require proof of fault on the shipper's part, the duty to provide accurate information and the duty in relation to dangerous goods are of strict liability.

---

[59] See Baughen, "Obligations of the shipper to the carrier" [2008] 14 J.I.M.L. 555.

The Rotterdam Rules also impose on the documentary shipper the same obligations imposed on a shipper (art.34(1)). A documentary shipper is "a person, other than the shipper, that accepts to be named as "shipper" in the transport document or electronic transport record" (art.1(9)) whilst a shipper is one who "enters into a contract of carriage with a carrier" (art.1(8)). A person named as "shipper" or "shipping agent" may thus be caught by this provision. Clear words excluding the assumption of the role of a documentary shipper are best used.

Financial and time limits

8–119   Chapters 12 and 13 of the Rotterdam Rules deal with this very important subject. As regards financial limits, art.61 states that the carrier's liability shall be limited to 875 units of account per package or other shipping unit or three units of account per kilogram of the gross weight, whichever is the higher. This provision will not apply where the carrier and shipper had agreed to higher limits, or where there is a declaration of value in the contract particulars. It should be noted that art.61 refers not to "any loss or damage to or in connection with the goods" as is the case with the Hague-Visby Rules, but, "the carrier's liability for breaches of its obligations under this Convention". The reference to "breaches of it obligations under this Convention" is clearly wider. The Australian delegation expressed concern that this might be detrimental to the shipper. The example they gave is this—art.61 would thus cover a case where the carrier negligently failed to provide appropriate documents relating to the goods to customs resulting in the shipper being given a steep fine. The shipper should be able to claim compensation in tort against the carrier but the amount of damages would be limited by art 61. Much however depends on whether such an obligation to hand over documents to customs is an obligation "under [the] Convention".

Article 61(2) explains that where goods are carried in or on a container, pallet or similar article of transport used to consolidate the foods, or in or on a road or railroad cargo vehicle, the packages or shipping units enumerated in the contract particulars as packed in or on such articles of transport or vehicle are deemed packages or shipping units.[60] If not enumerated, the goods in or on such article of transport or vehicle are deemed one shipping unit (art.61(3)). This provision is substantially similar to art.4(5)(c) Hague-Visby Rules; the minor difference is that "road or railroad cargo vehicle" is made explicit.

As for compensation for delay, liability for economic loss due to delay is limited to an amount equivalent to two-and-a-half times the freight payable on the goods delayed and *in any case*, not exceeding the total loss of the goods concerned (art.62). The reference to economic loss is intentional—a claim where the delay causes physical loss or damage would normally be treated as a claim for loss or damage, not delay. However, what does "economic loss" mean? A lost contract for resale could well fall within "economic loss" but what about the loss of a highly lucrative contract not known to the carrier or a depreciation of value due to market movements? Are these to be dealt with by national law instead of the convention?

---

[60] See Huybrechts, "Package limitation in modern maritime transport treaties: a critical analysis" [2011] 17 J.I.M.L. 90 for an evaluation of the rationale for package limitations.

The benefit of the limits would be lost if the loss is attributable to a "personal **8–120** act or omission" of the defendant done "with intent to cause such loss or recklessly and with knowledge that such loss would probably result" (art.63).

As far as the time limit is concerned, art.64 provides that the claimant has two years from the time the goods were delivered or should have been delivered to sue.

Role of documents[61]

Article 37 provides that the shipper may obtain from the carrier: **8–121**

1. a non-negotiable transport document or, subject to art.8(a), a non-negotiable electronic transport record; or

2. an appropriate negotiable transport document or, subject to art.8(a), a negotiable electronic transport record,

> "unless the shipper and carrier have agreed not to use a negotiable transport document or negotiable electronic transport record, or it is the custom, usage or practice in the trade not to use one".

A negotiable transport document is defined in art.1(15) as one which

> "indicates, by wording such as "to order" or "negotiable" or other appropriate wording recognised as having the same effect by the law applicable to the document that the goods have been consigned to the order of the shipper, to the order of the consignee or to bearer, and is not explicitly stated as being "non-negotiable" or "not negotiable"".

This provision is fairly uncontroversial as far as definitions go but the legal consequences for the use of these documents are more problematic (arts 43, 47, 48, 49, 53, 56, 59, 60).

A transport document must perform the following functions (art.1(14)): **8–122**

(a) evidences the carrier's or a performing party's receipt of the goods;

(b) evidences or contains a contract of carriage.

It is interesting that the Rotterdam Rules try to avoid making the document specific to any particular mode of transport.[62] This lends to the fact that the Rotterdam Rules are expressed as door-to-door or maritime-plus rather than a straight maritime transport convention.

Where a negotiable transport document is issued, the holder may transfer the rights incorporated in the document to another person in the following manner (art.59):

---

[61] For a helpful analysis of the role of documents under the Rotterdam Rules see Mollmann, "From bills of lading to transport documents: the role of transport documents under the Rotterdam Rules" [2011] 17 J.I.M.L. 50.

[62] See Glass & Nair, "Towards flexible carriage documents? Reducing the need for modally distinct documents in international goods transport" [2009] 15 J.I.M.L. 37 for a critique of the insistence on the use of modally distinctive transport documents.

(a) duly endorsed either to such other person or in blank, if an order document; or

(b) without endorsement if

   (i) a bearer document or a blank endorsed document, or

   (ii) a document made out to the order of a named person and the transfer is between the first holder and the named person.

8–123   A holder is helpfully explained in art.1(1) in these terms:

> "a person that is in possession of a negotiable transport document and (i) if the document is an order document, is identified in it as the shipper or the consignee, or is the person to which the document is duly endorsed; or (ii) if the document is a blank endorsed order documents or bearer document, is the bearer thereof".

Article 60 states that the holder of the bill (provided he is not the shipper) who has not exercised any rights under the contract of carriage will not assume any liability under the contract of carriage. If he does exercise *any* right under the contract, he will assume any liabilities imposed on him under that contract which are incorporated in or ascertainable from the document (art.60(2)).[63] The two qualifications in art.60(2) are important. First, he will only be liable for those liabilities imposed on him under the contract. It would thus appear that liabilities which are imposed personally or specifically on the shipper would not be passed on to the holder. A question might be whether a liability arising from the shipment of dangerous goods could be said to be specific to the shipper and therefore the holder should not be held liable. The second qualification is that those liabilities must have been incorporated in the contract or ascertainable from the document. There is no guidance as to what this means. It would seem that if the document were to say "freight collect" or "demurrage payable at discharge", it could be said that there is incorporation or that the liability is ascertainable.

These provisions relate to order bills but whilst the convention recognises the role of straight bills (arts 43(b), 48, 53(2)(a)), there is no provision on the transfer of rights under straight bills. Such a matter is thus for national law to grapple with.

8–124   As far as electronic documents[64] are concerned, the transfer of a negotiable electronic transport record means the transfer of exclusive control over the record (art.1(22)). This criterion of "exclusive control" might be difficult to establish where the systems managed by the trader and persons associated with the trader are inter-operable. Also, in a sense, there is no "record" in question, especially given that every time a electronic record is transmitted, it is always new data that is passed on. The holder of the record is "the person to which a negotiable electronic transport record has been issued or transferred in accordance with the procedures in art 9(1)" (art.1(10)(b)). Article 9(1) in turn states that the use of a

---

[63] See also, s.3 Carriage of Goods by Sea Act 1992; paras 6–065—6–069.

[64] An electronic transport record is information on one or more messages issued by electronic communication under a contract of carriage which evidences the receipt of goods by the carrier or performing party and evidences or contains the contract of carriage. See Goldby, "The performance of the bill of lading's functions under UNCITRAL's draft Convention on the Carriage of Goods: unequivocal legal recognition of electronic equivalents" (2007) 13 J.I.M.L. 160.

negotiable electronic transport record shall be subject to procedures that provide for:

1. the method for the issuance and the transfer of that record to an intended holder;

2. an assurance that the negotiable electronic transport record retains its integrity;

3. the manner in which the holder is able to demonstrate that it is the holder;

4. the manner of providing confirmation to the holder has been effected, or that the electronic record has ceased to have any effect or validity.

The legal implications of the electronic record are in the main similar to those of a paper transport document.

Dispute resolution

The Rotterdam Rules allow the parties to agree to settle their disputes by arbitration. However, art.77(2) requires that the arbitration proceedings (at the option of the person asserting a claim against the carrier) take place at: **8–125**

(a) Any place designated for that purpose in the arbitration agreement; or

(b) Any other place situated in a state where any of the following places is located:

    (i) the carrier's domicile;
    (ii) place of receipt agreed in the contract;
    (iii) place of delivery agreed in the contract; or
    (iv) the port where the goods are initially loaded on a ship or the port where the goods are finally discharged from a ship.

For the agreed place of arbitration to be binding, though, the contract in question must be a volume contract between named parties (who are the ones in the dispute) which has been individually negotiated or where there is a clear statement referring to arbitration.

As regards litigation, art.68(a) provides that the plaintiff can sue the carrier in the following places:

1. the carrier's domicile;

2. place of receipt agreed in the contract;

3. place of delivery agreed in the contract;

4. the port where the goods are initially loaded on a ship or the port where the goods are finally discharged from a ship.

Additionally, where there is a freely negotiated or clearly notified jurisdiction clause, the plaintiff may sue the carrier at the place pre-agreed in the clause (art.68(b)).

CHAPTER 9

CARRIAGE OF GOODS BY AIR, ROAD AND RAIL

Carriage of Goods by Air

The law relating to the international carriage of goods by air is very much **9–001** provided for by international conventions. The Carriage by Air Act 1932 brought into English law the Convention on the Unification of Certain Rules relating to International Carriage by Air, signed in Warsaw in 1929. This is commonly known as the Warsaw Convention of 1929. That convention was subsequently subject to a number of amending measures.[1] The United Kingdom signed up to these changes and introduced the amendments into English law in the Carriage by Air Act 1961. The amended Warsaw Convention then became the main piece of air carriage law for the large part of the 20th century. However, there was dissatisfaction with the very harsh limits on liability to claims made by passengers and cargo owners, and with its failure to take into account modern carriage practices (including the use of electronic documents especially in the carriage of passengers). In 1999, a new Convention was made in Montreal and on June 28, 2004, it came into force in the United Kingdom and the European Union.[2] By virtue of the Carriage by Air Acts (Implementation of the Montreal Convention 1999) Order 2002, the Montreal Convention has now been brought into the four corners of the Carriage by Air Act 1961.

It should, however, not be imagined that the former conventions no longer apply—the Montreal Convention will only apply to carriage by air involving flights between the United Kingdom and another contracting state (known as a State Party in the Convention). In such a case, the convention has mandatory effect and cannot be derogated from whether such derogation is attempted by using a choice of law clause, or by altering the rules as to jurisdiction, or some other means (art.49). However, where the carriage is for a journey between the United Kingdom and say, a contracting state of the amended Warsaw Convention but not the Montreal Convention, then the amended convention will apply. As regards a journey between the United Kingdom and a contracting state of the old unamended Warsaw Convention, similarly the unamended convention will apply. Finally, it is also possible for a carriage contract not be governed by any of the

---

[1] First amended in The Hague in 1955, and then in Montreal in 1975.
[2] The EU also signed the Convention in its own capacity.

convention—namely, where the flight is between the United Kingdom and a state which has not signed up to any of the conventions. In such a case, an English court would ascertain the applicable law of the air carriage contract and resolve any dispute according to that applicable law. If the applicable law turns out to be English law, the court would apply the law on common carriers.[3] For intra-UK flight, the Carriage by Air Acts (Application of Provisions) Order 2004 provides that a modified version of the new Montreal Convention shall apply.

Article 1(1) of the Montreal Convention provides that the convention rules apply to all international carriage of persons, baggage or cargo performed by aircraft for reward. It applies equally to gratuitous carriage by aircraft performed by an air transport undertaking. There is, however, no definition of the term "air transport undertaking" in the Convention—presumably, a wide approach should be taken. The term "international carriage" however has a specific meaning. Article 1(2) states it means any carriage in which, according to the agreement between the parties, the place of departure and the place of destination, whether or not there be a break in the carriage or a transhipment, are situated either within the territories of two State Parties, or within the territory of a single State Party if there is an agreed stopping place within the territory of another state, even if that state is not a State Party. Carriage between two points within the territory of a single State Party (for example, a flight from London to Manchester) without an agreed stopping place within the territory of another state is, however, not international carriage.[4]

9–002   It should be noted that the Montreal and Warsaw Convention concepts are autonomous and should therefore not be interpreted in accordance with national law. It was important that the courts of the respective signatory states should try to adopt a uniform interpretation of the Convention. The Montreal Convention is an international treaty; as such, regard should also be had to the Vienna Convention on the Law of Treaties. Article 31 of the Vienna Convention provides that a treaty is to be interpreted in accordance with the ordinary meaning to be given to the terms of the treaty in their context and in the light of its object and purpose (*Deep Vein Thrombosis & Air Travel Group Litigation* [2005] UKHL 72).

The Montreal Convention, as did the Warsaw Convention, contains a provision dealing with "pre-emption", namely the Convention alone shall be relied on for claims and defences in relation to damage, loss or delay caused to transportation by air. Article 29 states that

> "In the carriage of passengers, baggage and cargo, any action for damages, however founded, whether under this Convention or in contract or in tort or otherwise, can only be brought subject to the conditions and such limits of liability as are set out in this Convention . . . ".

Lawyers in many jurisdictions have tried to circumvent this rule by, at times, arguing that the damage or loss caused was caused outside the scope of the application of the Convention (for example, damage caused prior to boarding or

---

[3] On common carriers, see generally paras 7–011—7–015.

[4] In *Grein v Imperial Airways* [1937] 1 K.B. 50 we see an example of this—there the flight from London to Antwerp in Belgium (when Belgium was not a contracting state to the Warsaw Convention) and back again to London was held to be covered by the Convention.

loading etc) with varying degrees of success. It would appear from case law in various jurisdictions that a claimant is not entitled to bring an action in local law where the claim is prima facie one covered by the Montreal Convention.[5]

Documentation

Under the original Warsaw Convention 1929, the contract of carriage is **9–003** evidenced by an air consignment note. The air consignment note is replaced with an air waybill under the amended Warsaw Convention and the Montreal Convention. Although in general an air waybill should be used, the parties may choose to use some other documentation. However, if they do, art.4(2) of the Montreal Convention provides that any other means which preserves a record of the carriage to be performed may be substituted for the delivery of an air waybill but the carrier who does so must, if so requested by the consignor, deliver to the consignor a cargo receipt permitting identification of the consignment and access to the information contained in the record preserved by such other means. In practice, the air waybill could normally be issued in sets of anything up to 15 copies but should contain at least three originals—for the carrier, consignee and consignor. The part for the carrier should be signed by the consignor. The part for the consignee should be signed by the consignor and the carrier. The last part should be signed by the carrier and handed back to consignor only after the cargo has been accepted for carriage (art.7).

It is further provided in art.8 that where there are several packages to be carried:

1. the carrier of cargo has the right to require the consignor to make out separate air waybills;

2. the consignor has the right to require the carrier to deliver separate cargo receipts when the other means referred to in art.4(2) are used.

Although it is clear from art.8 that it should be the consignor who is required to make out the waybills, in practice, that is almost invariably carried out by the carrier itself and this will be deemed to have been done on the consignor's behalf.

The air waybill or the cargo receipt should specify (art.5): **9–004**

1. an indication of the places of departure and destination;

2. if the places of departure and destination are within the territory of a single State Party, one or more agreed stopping places being within the territory of another state, an indication of at least one such stopping place; and

3. an indication of the weight of the consignment.

Under art.9, the failure of the air waybill or cargo receipt to satisfy the documentary requirements above will not affect the existence and validity of the

---

[5] See the important US Supreme Court case of *El Al Israel Airlines v Tseng* 525 US 155 (1999); and *Ugaz v Am Airlines*, 576 F. Supp. 2d 1354 (S.D. Fla. 2008). In the US pre-emption, even by means of an international convention, is likely to encounter significant constitutional law challenges.

contract of carriage. That said, art.9 does not exonerate a consignor or his agent from a breach of duty under domestic law if he fails to satisfy the documentary requirements of the convention. Such a breach of duty was considered in *Corocraft Ltd v Pan American Airways Inc* [1969] 1 Q.B. 616. There it was held that while the particulars supplied in the air waybill (in that case, it was an air consignment note) should be clear and accurate, the breach of that duty must be measured against the standards as might be expected in the light of general commercial convenience and practicality.[6] Naturally, it should be observed that under the original Warsaw Convention, an air consignment note must contain a very long list of particulars. The air waybill on the other hand is subject to only three mandatory items (see art.5 above).

Article 10 provides that the consignor will be held responsible for the correctness of the particulars and statements relating to the cargo inserted by it or on its behalf in the air waybill or furnished by it or on its behalf to the carrier for insertion in the cargo receipt or for insertion in the record preserved by the other means referred to in art.4(2). The consignor should therefore indemnify the carrier against all damage suffered by it by reason of the irregularity, incorrectness or incompleteness of the particulars furnished by the consignor or on its behalf (art.10(2)). The duty applies even if the person acting on behalf of the consignor is also the agent of the carrier. It is thus no defence for the consignor to say that as the defective information had emanated from the carrier's agent (who is also his agent), it should not be held liable. Where incorrect or irregular information is inserted in the air waybill by the carrier, it shall have to indemnify the consignor for any damage suffered by the consignor as a result.

9–005   The air waybill or the cargo receipt is prima facie evidence of the conclusion of the contract, of the acceptance of the cargo and the contents of the contract (art.11(1)) but it is not a document of title. The statements in the waybill relating to the weight, dimensions and packaging of the cargo, and to the number of packages, are prima facie evidence of the facts stated. Those relating to the quantity, volume and condition of the cargo, however, do not constitute evidence against the carrier unless the waybill or cargo receipt states that the carrier had actually checked the goods in respect of these matters in the consignor's presence or relates to the apparent condition of the goods.

Although the air waybill is not a document of title, art.12(3) provides that if the carrier carries out the *instructions* of the consignor for the disposition of the cargo without requiring the production of the part of the air waybill or the cargo receipt delivered to the latter, the carrier will be liable to the person who is lawfully entitled to delivery of the goods by virtue of his possession of the relevant waybill or cargo receipt. The carrier is, however, entitled to claim an indemnity from the consignor as it was the consignor who issued the relevant instructions to deliver the goods without requiring production of the relevant documentation. Under the amended Warsaw Convention, the word "orders" instead of "instructions" is used. In some jurisdictions, the question has arisen as to what "orders" should mean. It must be said that the word "instructions" is much clearer and would appear to cover a wider range than "orders", as is indeed the intention.

---

[6] See also *Seth v British Overseas Airways Corp* [1966] 1 Lloyd's Rep. 323.

9–005a

CSR/ECI

Shipper's Name and Address	Shipper's Account Number	Not Negotiable **Air Waybill** issued by British Airways London Member of IATA
		Copies 1, 2 and 3 of this Air Waybill are originals and have the same validity
Consignee's Name and Address	Consignee's Account Number	It is agreed that the goods described herein are accepted in apparent good order and condition (except as noted) for carriage SUBJECT TO THE CONDITIONS OF CONTRACT ON THE REVERSE HEREOF. THE SHIPPER'S ATTENTION IS DRAWN TO THE NOTICE CONCERNING CARRIER'S LIMITATION OF LIABILITY. Shipper may increase such limitation of liability by declaring a higher value for carriage and paying a supplemental charge if required. ISSUING CARRIER MAINTAINS CARGO ACCIDENT LIABILITY INSURANCE

Issuing Carrier's Agent

Accounting Information

| Agent's IATA Code | Account No. |

Airport of departure (Addr. of First Carrier) and Requested Routing

| To | By First Carrier | Routing and Destination | to | by | to | by | Currency | CHGS CODE | WT/VAL PPD COLL | Other PPD COLL | Declrd Val for Carrg. | Declrd Val for Customs |

| Airport of Destination | Flight/Date | For Carrier Use Only | Flight/Date |

Handling Information

No. of Pieces RCP	Gross Weight	kg lb	Rate Class / Commodity Item No.	Chargeable Weight	Rate / Charge	Total	Nature and Quantity of Goods (incl. Dimensions or Volume)

| Prepaid | Weight charge | Collect | Other Charges |

Valuation Charge

Tax

Total Other Charges Due Agent

Total Other Charges Due Carrier

Shipper certifies that the particulars on the face hereof are correct and that insofar as any part of the consignment contains dangerous goods, such part is properly described by name and is in proper condition for carriage by air according to the applicable Dangerous Goods Regulations.

....
Signature of Shipper or his agent

| Total prepaid | Total collect |

| Currency conversion rates | cc charges in dest. currency |

Executed on (date) .... at (place) .... Signature of Issuing Carrier or its agent

| For Carrier's Use only at Destination | Charges at Destination | Total Collect Charges |

Original 3 - (For Shipper)

It is clear that under the Convention, it is the consignor who is responsible for official formalities for the clearance of the carriage of goods. In art.16(1), the consignor must furnish such information and such documents as are necessary to meet the formalities of customs, police and any other public authorities before the cargo can be delivered to the consignee. The carrier shall not be held liable if the information or documentation is incorrect or insufficient.

Premise for liability

9–006   The basic premise for liability in the Montreal Convention is found in art.18. Article 18(1) states:

> "The carrier is liable for damage sustained in the event of the destruction or loss of, or damage to, cargo upon condition only that the event which caused the damage so sustained took place during the carriage by air."

A legal difficulty that is immediately obvious is in relation to the term "the event which caused the damage sustained took place during the carriage by air".

In *Winchester Fruit Ltd v American Airlines Inc* [2002] 2 Lloyd's Rep. 265, the claimant brought an action under art.18 of the amended Warsaw Convention[7] (which is similar to the provision in the Montreal Convention) against the defendant airline for damage caused to their cargo of peaches. The peaches had been properly prepared for a long journey by truck to Asuncion in Paraguay and were then flown to London via Sao Paulo and New York. However, the peaches had deteriorated badly by the time they arrived in London. The dominant cause of the damage was thought to be the exposure of the fruit to ambient temperatures at Asuncion and whatever conditions prevailed during the course of the various flights and stopping places prior to delivery at London. The question for the court was whether there was a damage caused by an occurrence (or event in the Montreal Convention) which took place during the carriage by air as prescribed by art.18. The Central London County Court stated that in the ordinary course of events, the claimant only needs to show that the goods had been shipped in good order and condition but had arrived damaged, but where the circumstances dictate, he must additionally show that there was an "occurrence" causing the damage during the carriage by air. The court stressed that as a matter of construction, art.18 must be read as requiring an occurrence (or event) which was something separate from the very destruction, loss or damage itself. Only when this has been achieved by the claimant, would the burden of proof shift to the carrier who has to provide some explanation exonerating or excusing himself. In the present case, the carrier was held not to be liable under art.18(2). The reasons were:

- the carrier was able to show that it had taken all reasonable measures to avoid the fruit from deteriorating;

---

[7] Article 18(2) of the amended Warsaw Convention reads: "The carrier is liable for damage sustained in the event of the destruction or loss of, or damage to, cargo upon condition only that the occurrence which caused the damage so sustained took place during the carriage by air". The main difference is in the substitution of the word "occurrence" with "event".

- it was impossible to identify a relevant failure of the part of the carrier which could be said to represent an "occurrence";

- although the claimant was able to show that the fruit had been properly treated and packed, it could not show that the loss could not have been caused by the fungi and mould pre-existing on the fruit; and

- the transit time for the goods as stated in the contract was 72 hours and that time limit had not been exceeded by the carrier.

This case is controversial—the court was persuaded by the fact that the word **9–007** "occurrence" is used distinctly in art.18 but, on a less literal reading of the provision, it might be argued that the present judgment is out of line with the general imperative of the Convention to place the onus of proof on the carrier to explain the loss or damage as he was in control of the carriage of goods by air. Additionally, without being in control of the transit or carriage of the goods, it would be extremely difficult for the claimant to suggest a relevant occurrence which led to the damage or loss. Although the court was swift to stress that it was for the court to decide on the relevance of the occurrence to the damage or loss, nonetheless, it does not make the burden any less onerous for the claimant. There is also the additional question as to whether the approach taken by the court in that case would extend to the new convention which uses the term "event". It might be suggested that "event" does not differ considerably from "occurrence", although the latter, it might be argued, seems to refer to a discrete event whilst the former could be a little wider. Nonetheless, *Winchester Fruit* is important as regards the issue of burden of proof.

The carrier will also be liable for damage caused by delays (art.19) unless it succeeds in proving that it and its servants and agents took all measures that could reasonably be required to avoid the damage or that it was impossible for it or them to take such measures.

The carrier would not be liable if it is able to show that the loss, deterioration or damage was actually caused by some event or factor beyond its control. Article 18(2) provides that

"the carrier is not liable if and to the extent it proves that the destruction, or loss of, or damage to, the cargo resulted from one or more of the following:

(a) inherent defect, quality or vice of that cargo;

(b) defective packing of that cargo performed by a person other than the carrier or its servants or agents;

(c) an act of war or an armed conflict;

(d) an act of public authority carried out in connection with the entry, exit or transit of the cargo".

The new art.18(2) is a clear improvement from the amended Warsaw **9–008** Convention—under the latter, the carrier needed to show that the damage to the cargo was caused *solely* by one or more of the factors above. The new provision dispenses with the major difficulty faced by carriers to show the exceptions above form the sole cause of damage. Under the amended Warsaw Convention, even where the excepting factor is a dominant cause, it would appear that that would not be enough to excuse the carrier. *Winchester Fruit* demonstrates this. There the court found that there was no doubt that the inherent quality of the goods represented the dominant cause of their deterioration (given the ambient temperatures), but whether it could be said to be the sole cause was doubtful, since the ultimate problem was very much tied up with the truck carriage and the transfer of the goods from aircraft to aircraft. Although it might be possible to circumvent this difficulty by reading "solely" more expansively than a literal construction would permit (as was the case in *Winchester Fruit*), that is not a preferred option.

It should also be noted that there is nothing in the Montreal Convention which prevents carriers from clarifying those defences in art.18 and adding defences not prohibited by the Convention in their standard conditions of carriage (art.27). For instance, it is stipulated in the International Air Transport Association (IATA) Conditions of Carriage that some carriers will not assume responsibility for damage caused to perishable goods.[8]

The duration of carriage for which the carrier might be held liable under the Montreal Convention includes any period during which the cargo is in the charge of the carrier whether or not the goods are actually in the air.[9] Indeed, as art.18(4) states, any damage (subject to proof to the contrary) caused during loading, delivery or transhipment will be presumed to be the result of an event which took place during the carriage by air. If a carrier, without the consent of the consignor, substitutes carriage by another mode of transport for the whole or part of a carriage intended by the agreement between the parties to be carriage by air, such carriage by another mode of transport is deemed to be within the period of carriage by air. This is an important provision. It does not allow the carrier to remove the contract from the application of the Convention simply by substituting the intended carriage with some other mode of carriage. What is crucial though is the consent of the consignor. It may, however, be questioned as to whether, considering the unequal bargaining positions of the parties, such consent should be subject to any special condition that the freight or other conditions should be varied accordingly. Very often such substitution is offered by the carrier to the consignor at very short notice, making it extremely difficult for the consignor to refuse. It would seem a little unfair for the consignor to find himself deprived of the protection of the Convention because of economic pressure from the carrier. Although it would appear that if the economic pressure amounts to economic duress, it is open to the consignor to argue that there was no proper consent but economic duress is difficult to prove.

9–009   It should be noted that if the claimant is himself at fault, the convention will permit the court to reduce the carrier's liability accordingly (art.20). Such a diminution of liability extends not only to the claimant but also the negligence or other wrongful act or omission of any person from whom the claimant derives his rights.

Naturally, the carrier would also be liable for non-delivery or wrongful delivery. Article 13(1) states that the consignee is entitled, on arrival of the cargo at the place of destination, to require the carrier to deliver the cargo to it, on payment of the charges due and on complying with the conditions of carriage. That right, however, is subject to the consignor's right of stoppage (art.12) but

---

[8] See also *Winchester Fruit Ltd v American Airlines Inc* [2002] 2 Lloyd's Rep. 265.

[9] In *Rolls Royce Plc v Heavylift Volga Ltd* [2000] 1 Lloyd's Rep. 653, Morison J. held that although the goods had not yet been loaded on to the plane, transit must be treated as having commenced when control over the goods passed to the courier's agents who took delivery of the goods into the aerodrome.

the consignor must not exercise this right of disposition in such a way as to prejudice the carrier or other consignors and must reimburse any expenses occasioned by the exercise of this right. It is also the duty of the carrier to give notice to the consignee as soon as the cargo arrives at its destination. That duty is implied by the Convention but can be varied or excluded by contract (art.13(2)). If the carrier admits the loss of the cargo, or if the cargo has not arrived at the expiration of seven days after the date on which it ought to have arrived, the consignee is entitled to enforce against the carrier the rights which flow from the contract of carriage.

Who can be sued?

A straightforward situation is one where the consignor had contracted with a **9–010** single air carrier for the international carriage of goods and non-delivery, loss, damage or delay was alleged to have been caused by the carrier. In such a case, it is plainly obvious that the lone carrier shall bear the risk of legal action. In many situations, though, there may be several carriers involved in the carriage of the goods.

In a case involving successive carriers[10] (that is to say, the goods are passed on from carrier to carrier for delivery to the consignee), art.36(1) provides that both the consignor and consignee of the goods has a right of suit. The consignor can sue the first carrier and/or the actual carrier. The consignee can sue the last carrier and/or the actual carrier. The actual carrier is the person who in fact performed that part of the carriage during which the destruction, loss, damage or delay occurred.

Article 36 is not without its difficulties. In *Western Digital Corp v British Airways Plc* [2001] Q.B. 733, the judge at first instance held that art.30 of the Warsaw Convention (which is similar to art.36) afforded no cause of action to a party who sued as owner and not as consignee or consignor, since the latter had exclusive rights of suit. In that case, the persons named as consignees were agents for the claimant. The Court of Appeal allowed the appeal, stating that although the Convention only referred expressly to consignor or consignee, that was to be interpreted flexibly. The court thought that as the Convention merely provided a set of general rules rather than a detailed code, it was permissible to look to domestic law to decide who might qualify to sue under the Convention. An assumption on the part of the drafters of the Convention was that the person with whom a carrier dealt on a principal-to-principal basis would be a party to the contract of carriage. Nevertheless, the common law recognised that both a disclosed and an undisclosed principal could sue and be sued on a contract made by his agent. There were strong considerations of commercial sense in favour of an interpretation that recognised and gave effect to: (a) the underlying contractual structure, and/or (b) the actual rights of ownership, in determining by whom the relevant damage had been sustained. As far as the Court of Appeal was

---

[10] Article 1 states, "Carriage to be performed by several successive carriers is deemed, . . . to be one undivided carriage if it has been regarded by the parties as a single operation, whether it had been agreed upon under the form of a single contract or of a series of contracts, and it does not lose its international character merely because one contract or a series of contracts is to be performed entirely within the territory of the same State".

concerned, a strict literal reading could not have been the intention of the drafters of the Convention.[11]

9-011   In Ch.V of the Montreal Convention, we find an entirely new area of law in air carriage—the allocation of liability when the air carriage is performed by a person other than the contracting carrier. Those provisions, Arts 39–48, come into play when air carriage is no longer carried out by the contracting carrier but is undertaken by a number of carriers, who might or might not be part of some airline alliance or network. Chapter V does not however deal with the situation of successive carriers (that is dealt with in art.36). It applies when

> "a person (hereinafter referred to as "the contracting carrier") as a principal makes a contract of carriage governed by this Convention with . . . a consignor or with a person acting on behalf of the . . . consignor, and another person (hereinafter referred to as the "actual carrier") performs by virtue of authority from the contracting carrier, the whole or part of the carriage but is not with respect to such part, a successive carrier . . . ".

That authority is presumed in the absence of proof to the contrary.

Article 40 states that the actual carrier shall be liable for the leg of the carriage it performs and the contracting carrier shall be liable for the whole of the carriage as contemplated in the contract. Not only is the contracting carrier liable for the acts and omissions of the actual carrier, it is also liable for the acts and omissions of the actual carrier's servants and agents provided that they were acting within the scope of their employment. Article 41 attempts to ensure that the consignor does not need to pursue all the carriers responsible for the carriage of its cargo which it had delivered to the contracting carrier. There is no injustice caused because as far as the contracting carrier is concerned, it could always seek to be indemnified by the actual carriers for any compensation it had to pay the consignor. However, where it is not feasible or possible for the consignor to sue the contracting carrier, he could nonetheless bring an action against the actual carrier for damage or loss caused during that part of the carriage for which the actual carrier was responsible. For the purposes of such an action, art.41(2) provides that the actual carrier shall be deemed to be liable for the acts and omissions of the contracting carrier and of its servants and agents acting within the scope of their employment. Article 43 also anticipates that the servants and agents themselves could be sued by the consignor, and/or any of the carriers. They could however, if they are able to prove that they were acting in the course of their employment, rely on the conditions and limits of liability under the Convention.

It should be noted that the actual carrier is however not bound by any variation made by the contracting carrier to the limits of liability (including any special declaration of interest made by the consignor and agreed to by the contracting carrier). Proof of the actual carrier's consent to any such variation is required before it could be made subject to the changed limits.

9-012   The consignor is entitled to sue either the carrier or both separately or jointly under art.45. However, if the action is brought against only one of the carriers, that carrier shall have the right to require the other carrier to be joined in the

---

[11] The claim, however, was time barred under art.26 of the amended Warsaw Convention (see art.31 Montreal Convention).

proceedings. The procedure and effects of such a course of action shall be governed by the law of the court seised of the case. As between the different carriers, nothing in Ch.V affects the rights and obligations of the carriers between themselves, including any right of recourse or indemnification (art.48).

Limitation of liability

The Montreal Convention, as with the amended and original Warsaw Conventions, provides a limit on the financial liability of the carrier but unlike the previous legal instruments, it contains a provision permitting the review of these limits are undertaken at regular intervals. This makes the law far superior to the Warsaw regimes. This ensures that the financial limits are kept up to date and realistic. The financial limits on liability cannot be reduced or excluded from by contract (art.26) but art.25 permits the parties to agree to higher financial limits than those provided for in the Convention. That said, it is a little regrettable though understandable that despite the higher financial limits set for compensation claims, these do not apply to cargo claims. The new limits are primarily to ensure that passengers are afforded better protection but as far as cargo interests are concerned, the limits in the amended Warsaw Convention are retained.

9–013

The financial limit of 17 Special Drawing Rights (SDR)[12] per kilogramme is provided for in art.22(3) in the case of destruction, loss, damage or delay. Where the consignor has made, at the time when the package was handed over to the carrier, a special declaration of interest in delivery at destination then the carrier will be liable to pay a sum not exceeding the declared sum, unless it proves that the sum is greater than the consignor's actual interest in delivery at destination. It should also be noted that if a supplementary sum had to be paid for this higher level of compensation, that sum must first have been paid before the carrier would be liable to pay the higher limit.

In the case of destruction, loss, damage or delay of part of the cargo, or of any object contained therein, the weight to be taken into consideration in determining the amount to which the carrier's liability is limited shall be only the total weight of the package or packages concerned. Nevertheless, when the destruction, loss, damage or delay of a part of the cargo, or of an object contained therein, affects

---

[12] The SDR was set up by the International Monetary Fund in 1969 as an official reserve asset to alleviate the shortages in gold and other reserve currencies. It has no physical existence. It serves only as a unit of account. The SDRs are allocated to members of the IMF according to their economic strength and size in relation to each other. The SDR is valued in terms of a basket of currencies and is used generally as a standard nit of account in international transactions involving members of the IMF. Private institutions, such as banks, frequently use the SDR for indexation purposes. See Tobolewski, "The special drawing right in liability conventions: an acceptable solution" [1979] L.M.C.L.Q. 169. It should additionally be noted that under art.23(1) of the Montreal Convention conversion of the sums into national currencies shall, in case of judicial proceedings, be made according to the value of such currencies in terms of the SDR at the *date of the judgment*. The value of a national currency, in terms of the SDR, of a State Party which is a Member of the IMF is calculated in accordance with the method of valuation applied by the IMF, in effect at the date of the judgment. The value of a national currency, in terms of the SDR, of a State Party which is not a Member of the IMF, shall be calculated in a manner determined by that state. See also art.23(2) which allows states which are not members of the IMF to fix the limits in their own national currency not exceeding certain limits prescribed in the Article. On April 13, 2013, 1SDR is equivalent to £0.982701.

the value of other packages covered by the same air waybill, or the same receipt[13] the total weight of such package or packages shall also be taken into consideration in determining the limit of liability (art.22(4)).

9–014   When calculating the financial limits, the main difficulty is finding the relevant weight of the cargo to be taken into account. In *Applied Implant Technology Ltd v Lufthansa Cargo AG* [2000] 2 Lloyd's Rep. 46, the contract was for the carriage of a machine which had been subdivided into 11 parts from England to Japan, via Germany. Damage was caused to one package in that consignment. The claim was for the entirety of the 11 packages on the basis that they formed a single unit. That claim was £189,000. However, the airline argued that as only one package was damaged, the claim could not exceed £50,000 under art.22 (of the amended Warsaw Convention which is similarly worded). The court rejected the carrier's argument and permitted the larger claim stating that that single package contained a beamline module which was essential to the proper functioning of the machine as a whole. No separation was thus justified.

A significant provision lies in art.22(6)—the financial limits shall not prevent the court from awarding, in accordance with its own domestic law, in addition, the whole or part of the court costs and of the other expenses of the litigation incurred by the plaintiff, including interest. This power shall not apply if the amount of the damages awarded, excluding court costs and other expenses of the litigation, does not exceed the sum which the carrier has offered in writing to the claimant within a period of six months from the date of the occurrence causing the damage, or before the commencement of the action, if that is later. The question as to what it meant by "damages awarded" was examined in *GKN Westland Helicopters v Korean Air* [2003] EWHC 1120. In that case there was no actual award of damages but the claimant had accepted a settlement or a payment into court made by the defendant after proceedings had commenced. The court held that that art.22(4) of the amended Warsaw Convention (equivalent to art.22(6) of the Montreal Convention) did apply. Where a payment into court has been made accepted and the proceedings brought to an end, there was an "award of damages" by the court. As far as the court was concerned, the purpose of the convention was to ensure that the carrier's liability was to be limited to a specified amount and that the claimant should be encouraged to accept their due entitlement. Consequently, if the claimant does not accept a settlement which is comparable to the financial limit imposed, they should lose their entitlement to costs. That was despite the fact that under Pt 36 of the Civil Procedure Rules 1998, acceptance of a payment into court did not remove a claimant's entitlement to costs. The court held that it would be inappropriate to apply a procedural rule in a way to conflict with the Convention.

Besides financial limits, the claimant is also subject to strict time limits to make a claim under the Convention. At first instance, art.31(2) provides that

> "in the case of damage, the person entitled to delivery must complain to the carrier forthwith after the discovery of the damage, and, at the latest, within seven days from the date of receipt in the case of checked baggage and fourteen days from the date of receipt in the case of cargo".

---

[13] Or, if these documents were not issued, but there is a record preserved by the other means referred to in art.4(2), such a record would suffice for the purposes of this provision.

In the case of delay, the complaint must be made at the latest within 21 days **9–015** from the date on which the baggage or cargo have been placed at his disposal. That complaint must be in writing and cannot be dispensed with unless the carrier is guilty of fraud (art.31(3)(4)). The question is what constitutes a proper complaint to the carrier. In *Western Digital Corp*, a letter was sent by the consignee's freight agents to the defendants was held by the Court of Appeal not to constitute a written complaint. That letter had merely stated that the goods *had been received* in a condition which would entitle the consignee to sue. That was not consistent with the subsequent complaint that the goods *had not been received*. There is, however, probably an implied term that freight forwarders would notify the carrier of any loss within the time limit under their contract of agency with the person entitled to delivery. Failure to do so could expose them to claims for contractual damages by the consignor or consignee.[14]

In the case of where the carriage was performed by a carrier other than the contracting carrier (Ch.V), any complaint made to the carrier shall have the same effect whether addressed to the contracting carrier or to the actual carrier under art.42. The consignor is thus relieved of the need to complain within the time limits to both carriers.

Article 35(1) further provides that the limitation period for claims is two years from the date of arrival at the destination, or from the date on which the aircraft ought to have arrived, or from the date on which the carriage stopped.

Where to sue

Article 33 is a new provision and clarifies a hitherto problematic issue of the **9–016** choice of jurisdiction. It brings the law on air carriage claims in line with the private international law norm in many countries—an action for damages must be brought, at the option of the plaintiff, in the territory of one of the State Parties, either before the court

- of the domicile of the carrier or of its principal place of business; or
- where it has a place of business through which the contract has been made or at the place of destination.

The Montreal Convention also makes express provision for any dispute arising from the contract of carriage to be resolved by arbitration (art.34). This too is reflective of current practice. Alternative dispute resolution is now very much perceived in commerce as a more economical and expeditious means of bringing about a settlement. The amended Warsaw Convention does not provide for arbitration expressly but neither does it prohibit arbitration if the parties so wish. In contrast, art.34 of the Montreal Convention is notable as it makes a clear statement as to the international community's commitment to arbitration as a recognised mode of dispute resolution in the aviation sector.

Carriage by Road

International road transportation of goods is generally governed by the Carriage **9–017** of Goods by Road Act 1965, which incorporates the Convention on the Contract

---

[14] See in particular *Marbrook Freight v KMI (London) Ltd* [1979] 2 Lloyd's Rep. 341.

for the International Carriage of Goods by Road 1956.[15] The Convention shall apply to every contract for the carriage of goods by road in vehicles for reward, when the place of taking over of the goods and the place designated for delivery, as specified in the contract, are situated in two different countries (art.1).[16] One of these countries should be a contracting state. The Convention applies regardless of the place of residence and the nationality of the parties as long as there is in place a relevant contract of carriage.

9–018   *Datec Electronics v United Parcels Services* [2007] UKHL 23.
Facts:
UPS agreed to carry for Datec three packages of computer processors from the United Kingdom to the Netherlands. The packages were to be carried by road to Luton airport, flown to Cologne and then carried again by road to UPS' premises in Amsterdam and onward to the consignee's warehouse at Amsterdam Airport. The packages vanished before they reached their destination. Datec and the consignee sued UPS for damages. Datec argued that carriage of the goods on the international leg of the journey between Cologne and Amsterdam was subject to the Convention on the Contract for the International Carriage of Goods by Road (CMR). One of UPS' defences was that the CMR did not apply and its own contractual terms applied. Clause 3 of UPS' terms and conditions stated that UPS would not carry (amongst other things) packages with a value over $50,000. Under its contract, in relation to such packages, UPS could refuse to carry it, could hold it to the shipper's order, or return it and claim the reasonable costs of so doing. UPS said that, had it known the value of the packages, it would have refused to carry them. Consequently, there was no sufficient consensus between the parties to create a contract of carriage. Without a contract of carriage, the CMR could not apply. It was further asserted that even if there was a contract, the effect of cl.3 was to absolve its liability for the loss of a package that exceeded the value limit.
Held:
Clearly, whether the Convention applied depended on the existence of a "contract for the carriage" of the packages. The House of Lords agreed with the court at first instance that unless and until UPS exercised its right to refuse to transport goods or to suspend carriage, there was a contract that it would carry the packages. The terms gave UPS the right to decline to carry or to suspend carriage, they were not a precondition to the making of the contract of carriage.

Such an interpretation was consistent with commercial reality and the business expectations of the parties. The natural inference was that the whole of the relevant clause in the terms and conditions provided a contractual regime governing the carriage of non-conforming goods.

The court also reasoned that to the extent cl.3 purported to exclude or limit UPS' liability, it fell foul of art.41(1) of CMR, which provides that "*any stipulation which would directly or indirectly derogate from the provisions of this Convention shall be null and void*". The commercial realities were that if UPS had wished to protect itself, it could have required the Datec to sign a declaration that the goods complied with certain restrictions. If the consignor refused, UPS could refuse to carry the goods, and if the consignor gave a false declaration, UPS could seek redress for misrepresentation. Alternatively, UPS could have relied on the CMR to require more specific information to

---

[15] That Convention is commonly known as the CMR. CMR stands for *Convention relative au contrat de transport des merchandises par route*.
[16] It should not be thought that national law has no role to play. In *Gefco (UK) Ltd v John Mason* [1998] 2 Lloyd's Rep. 585, it was held that although the CMR was intended to operate as a comprehensive code on those matters it relates to, the wording of the Convention was wide enough to permit a counterclaim not expressly mentioned in the Convention but which would normally have been permitted under common law (but cf. *Shell Chemicals UK Ltd v P&O Roadtanks Ltd* [1993] 1 Lloyd's Rep. 114).

be declared in the consignment note, including a declaration of value. Similarly, without such a declaration, UPS could refuse to carry the goods and if a false value is given, art.7 (which provides that the sender shall be responsible for loss and damage sustained by the carrier due to the inaccuracy of particulars given in the consignment note) could avail UPS.

The Convention shall not apply to carriage performed under the terms of any international postal convention, funeral consignments and furniture removal.

Interpretation Issues

The Convention is to be given a purposive reading; it is after all an international **9–019** convention despite being one which is contained in a UK statute (the Carriage of Goods by Road Act 1965). Collins L.J. in *Hatzl v XL Insurance Co Ltd* [2010] 1 W.L.R. 470 stated that the starting point for the interpretation of international transport conventions was to consider the natural meaning of the language of the provision in question, but that it was also necessary to consider the Convention as a whole and give it a purposive interpretation. Its language should be interpreted unconstrained by technical rules of English law, or by English legal precedent, but on broad principles of general acceptation. The court may have regard to the decisions of foreign courts on the Convention and the prevailing current of foreign opinion on its application. The French text is also a legitimate tool in the process of interpretation as the French and English texts of CMR carry equal weight. The court may also have regard to the decisions of foreign courts on the Convention and the prevailing current of foreign opinion on its application.

Documentation

It might thus be said that the structure of CMR envisages a CMR Consignment **9–020** Note (see art.4; also *Cummins Engine Co v Davis Freight Forwarding* [1981] 2 Lloyd's Rep. 402; *ITT Schaub-Lorenz v Birkart Johann Internationale Spedition GmbH & Co KG* [1988] 1 Lloyd's Rep. 487). Although the absence of such a consignment note does not affect the existence or the validity of the contract of carriage which will continue to be subject to CMR, art.5 envisages three copies of such a consignment note. One copy is handed by the first carrier to the sender and the second should accompany the goods. The third is to be retained by the first carrier. The copy which accompanies the goods is to be handed over by each carrier to his successive carrier and then handed over at final delivery to the consignee (see arts 13 and 35).

Incidentally, it is possible that the contract of carriage may require the production and issue of a consignment note. Hence, although art.4 may not invalidate the contract for failure to issue the consignment note, the contract itself may render such a failure a breach of contract.

Article 6(1) sets out the particulars which must be included in the consignment note whilst art.6(2) sets out those particulars which should also be contained, where applicable. Article 6(3) provides that the parties may enter in the consignment note any other particulars which they consider useful. The consignment note is to be prima facie evidence of the making of the contract of carriage, the conditions of the contract and the receipt of the goods by the carrier (art.9) and the absence of notation on the consignment notes of any damage constitutes prima facie evidence of the condition of the goods at the time the relevant consignment note is handed over with the goods to another carrier (arts 8 and 9(2)). The consignee is not only able to sue the carrier in his own name in respect of the statutory contract of carriage constituted or evidenced by the consignment note, but is also liable to pay any charges shown to be due in that note.

9–021   In the context of successive carriers the importance of the consignment note is underlined by art.34. Each succeeding carrier is responsible for the performance of the whole operation covered by the original contract contained in the consignment note, which details the collection point and designated place for delivery. Each successive carrier, by the terms of art.34 becomes a party to the contract of carriage "under the terms of the Consignment Note, by reason of his acceptance of the goods and the Consignment Note". We shall consider the subject of successive carriers later; it is however useful to note the importance of the consignment note in the case of successive carriers here.

The carrier is required by art.8 to check the accuracy of the statements in the consignment note referring to quantity, marks and numbers, and the apparent condition of the goods and their packaging. If he has no reasonable means of doing so, he should make clear in the consignment note that that was the case. The consignment note will be treated as prima facie evidence of the making of the contract of carriage (art.9); that means it will be for the person claiming that there was no contract to prove that rather than for the party saying that there was. Article 9 also makes it clear that the consignment note will be prima facie evidence of the conditions of the contract and the receipt of the goods. That would make it difficult for a party to contend that there were oral terms varying the terms of the consignment note. It is open to the carrier to enter specific reservations in the consignment note to show the quality and condition of the goods. If he omits to do so, the presumption is that the goods

"appeared to be in good condition when the carrier took them over and that the number of packages, their marks and numbers corresponded with the statements in the consignment note" (art.9(2)).

Although the consignment note is prima facie evidence of the contract of carriage, the terms on its face might actually prove that there was no contract of carriage. In *Royal and Sun Alliance Insurance v MK Digital* [2006] EWCA Civ 629, H, in Denmark, had arranged with E for the carriage of a consignment of mobile telephones to England. E had issued a CMR note naming H as sender and a French subcontractor as the carrier and putting E's stamp and signature in the box which called for the stamp and signature of the sender. The mobile telephones were lost to thieves during transit. H sued E in France alleging that E was personally liable for the loss under French law as a "commissionnaire de transport". E on the other hand claimed that was a matter for the court in England (the place of destination under art.31(1)) as the CMR applied. On a proper reading of the CMR note, the Court of Appeal found that E had regarded itself as acting as commissionnaire not as carrier. The CMR note was in the same form as previous notes issued by E in respect of transport for H and the invoices for those previous transports were consistent with E being a commissionnaire. Moreover, E had told the French court that E accepted that it had acted as a commissionnaire de transport and explained that it had claimed in England on a CMR contract only because English law did not recognise the French concept. In the circumstances E had failed to show a good arguable case for a CMR contract leading to the application of the jurisdiction code in art.31(1).

Carrier's liability

The carrier's liability runs from the time he takes over the goods until the time **9–022** of delivery, including any delay in delivery. The defences that he could raise include:

- damage or delay caused by the wrongful act or neglect of the plaintiff;

- damage or delay caused as a result of the plaintiff's instructions (unless it is proved that the carrier has acted wrongfully or negligently);

- the inherent vice of the goods; or

- circumstances which the carrier could not avoid and the consequences of which he was unable to prevent (art.17(2)).

The burden of proving these defences rests on the carrier (art.18(1)).

In *Michael Galley Footwear Ltd v Llaboni* [1982] 2 All E.R. 200, the carrier was sued for the loss of a consignment of shoes. The driver and his assistant had parked the lorry in an unattended service park to have a meal. For him to drive on to an attended or guarded lorry park would have meant driving against the driving period regulations. The lorry was properly alarmed but the thieves succeeded in avoiding the alarm and broke into the lorry. The finding of fact was that the carrier could have prevented the loss if the lorry driver and his assistant had taken turns in guarding the lorry, thus they were liable.

In addition to art.17(2), para.(4) provides for some specific defences, for example, where the loss or damage was caused by use of open unsheeted vehicles as agreed by contract, defective packing, handling and stowage by the sender or the consignee (or their agents), special propensity of the goods to deterioration, breakage, rust, etc, poor marking on the packages and the carriage of live-stock.

When the carrier establishes that, in the circumstances of the case, the loss or **9–023** damage could be attributed to one or more of the special risks referred to in art.17(4), it shall be presumed that it was so caused (art.18(2)). The claimant however is entitled to prove that the loss or damage was not, in fact, attributable either wholly or partly to one of these risks. The claimant had to show on a balance of probabilities that the matter relied upon by the carrier did not cause the loss. In *Exportadora Valle de Colina SA v AP Moller-Maersk A/S* [2010] EWHC 3224 (Comm) the claimant had established on a balance of probabilities that the damage on outturn was not caused by any of the matters relied upon by the carrier, namely inherent vice and poor packing, handling and stowage. Although the court was satisfied that the cause was, on a balance of probability, the fact that the power in the containers had been switched off for excessive periods of time, there was no requirement in law on the claimant to explain what actually caused the loss or damage once they had rebutted exceptions relied on by the carrier.

There are some qualifications to art.18(2). For example, in attempting to rely on the defence that the damage or loss was caused as a result of the goods propensity to deteriorate, rust, etc or the carriage of livestock, the carrier must further show that he has complied with any special instructions issued to him and that he has taken all steps incumbent on him to make special allowance for the goods (art.18(4)(5)).

After the goods have arrived at their destination, the consignee is entitled to require the carrier to deliver to him, against a receipt, a copy of the consignment note and the goods (art.13(1)). Article 13(1) gives him to right to sue the carrier in his own name for any damage, loss or delay caused to the goods. However, the consignee who avails himself of the rights provided for in art.13(1) shall pay the charges shown to be due on the consignment note. If there is a dispute over the charges, the carrier shall not be required to deliver the goods unless security has been furnished by the consignee. It has long been thought that this provision does not remove the carrier's right of retention under national law. However in a highly controversial decision, Judge Jonathan Hirst QC held in *T Comedy v Easy Managed Transport* [2007] EWHC 611 that a general lien clause in the contract was invalid in the context of a CMR movement. The judge thought that a general lien would derogate from the consignees' right of delivery on payment of the charges, as the consignee could only obtain delivery on payment of additional sums due in respect of other carriages. Thus, a general lien was null and void under art.41 of the CMR Convention and, where the contract provided for a specific lien, that too would be null and void if it was wider than that granted by art.13(1). It is submitted that such a position could be seriously detrimental to international road carriers and it is difficult to see how such general and specific liens are inconsistent with the statutory lien provided for in the CMR.

9–024   Where combined transport is involved (i.e. the vehicle carrying the goods is carried over part of the journey by sea, rail, inland waterways or air), art.2 provides that where the loss or damage was caused by the carriers in the other mode of transport and not by the road carrier, the liability of the road carrier is not to be determined according to the present·Convention but the provisions of any convention or regimes relevant to *that·*mode of transport.

In *Thermo Engineers v Ferrymasters Ltd* [1981] 1 W.L.R. 1470, the goods were delivered in a trailer from the United Kingdom to Denmark. As the trailer was being loaded, it struck the bulkhead and the goods were damaged. The question was whether the CMR or the Hague Rules would apply. The court held that as the trailer had already crossed the line of the stern, the road carriage had ended and the sea carriage had commenced. As such the Hague Rules applied, and not the CMR. In *Quantum Corp v Plane Trucking* [2002] 2 Lloyd's Rep. 200, the Court of Appeal made clear that it need not be made clear in the contract that road carriage was to be central or that carriage should be road specific. There, a cargo of hard disks was carried by air from Singapore to France, and then from France to Ireland by road. The goods were stolen during the road transit. As to whether the amended Warsaw Convention or the CMR applied (the limits on liability were quite different), the court held that the CMR applied. It was irrelevant that the carrier could have chosen to deliver the goods using another mode of transport. The court referred to Belgian, Dutch and German cases, all of which unequivocally accept that CMR can apply to the road leg of a larger contract for carriage involving different methods of transport. The court went on to hold that for the purposes of art.1(1), the place of taking over and delivery of the goods should be read as referring to the start and end of the contractually provided or permitted road leg. Article 1(1), of course, is relevant as to when the convention applies.

Where the road carrier is also the carrier by other means of transport, his liability shall also be determined in accordance with the provisions relevant to those modes of transport. He shall be treated as if he were two separate persons for the purposes of liability (art.2(2)).

In the event that the carriage is governed by a single contract but to be **9–025** performed by successive road carriers, each carrier shall be liable for the performance of the entire operation. The second and each successive carrier shall be presumed to be party to the contract of carriage, under the terms of the consignment note (art.4). In any action for loss, damage or delay, only the first carrier, the last carrier or the carrier who was in control of the goods during the relevant damage or loss may be sued (art.36). This does not exclude the claimant, however, from suing several carriers at the same time under different causes of action.[17] The rule in art.36 does not apply in a case of a counterclaim or a set-off, though.

In *Arctic Electronics Co (UK) Ltd v McGregor Sea & Air Services Ltd* [1985] Lloyd's Rep. 510, a single contract performed by successive carriers is held to be a contract under which a single consignment note is issued. Where the consignment has been split into several packages and separate consignment notes are issued for these units, the carriage of the goods cannot be properly termed as being governed by a single contract. In *ITT Schaub-Lorenz Vertriebsgesellschaft mbH v Birkart Johann Internationale Spedition GmbH & Co KG* [1988] 1 Lloyd's Rep. 487, it was held that a CMR carrier sued by the sender or consignee of goods can recover against another CMR carrier actually responsible for the loss or damage. It is not open to that carrier to plead that he had delegated or sub-contracted performance to a non-CMR carrier who was actually responsible. Under art.34, the CMR successor carrier remains liable for the whole operation and may therefore not plead sub-bailment as a defence.[18]

Article 34 provides:

"If carriage governed by a single contract is performed by successive road carriers, each of them shall be responsible for the performance of the whole operation, the second carrier and each succeeding carrier becoming a party to the contract of carriage, under the terms of the consignment note, by reason of his acceptance of the goods and the consignment note."

It thus creates an artificial statutory contract between parties other than the consignor and the first carrier who are in a direct contractual relationship, (*Ulster-Swift v Taunton Meat Haulage* [1977] 1 Lloyd's Rep. 346, per Megaw L.J. at 360). However, art.34 talks in terms of the second carrier and each succeeding carrier

"becoming a party to the contract of carriage, under the terms of the consignment note, by reason of his acceptance of the goods and the consignment note".

---

[17] Although an action could be brought at the same time against several of those carriers, there was nothing in art.36 which entitled the claimant goods owner to do so in one and the same jurisdiction. The issue of jurisdiction for each of the defendants is determined by art.31 and not art.36. For the text of art.31, see fn.19 below. See *British American Tobacco Switzerland v Exel Europe* [2012] EWHC 694 (Comm).

[18] On sub-bailment as a defence generally, see para.8–089.

9–026   In *Coggins t/a PC Transport v LKW Walter International Transport Organisation AG* [1999] 1 Lloyd's Rep. 255 the defendants contracted with the consignee to effect the carriage. The defendants sub-contracted the carriage to the claimants, who in turn sub-contracted the carriage to a third party. The third party was responsible for the loss of the goods. The claimants, who sued for the price of providing the carriage, faced a counterclaim from the defendants for the loss, sought to argue that they were successive carriers within the meaning of art.34, in which case art.37 applied to excuse them from liability as the defendants had not paid compensation to the consignor and they were not, in any event, the carrier responsible for the loss or damage.

H.H. Judge Hallgarten rejected the argument that because there had been no "acceptance of the goods and the consignment note" by the plaintiffs, art.34 could not apply to make the plaintiffs successive carriers. The judge said:

> "As I see it, where a CMR carrier delegated performance of his responsibility to a sub-contractor; he vests the sub-contractor with authority to do such things as he would have done had he performed the contract in person. Had the plaintiff performed the contract in person, there is no doubt that the consignment note would have been received as an unexceptional document, although perhaps what was entered into the various boxes might have been different . . . it is not . . . a question of artificially imputing agency: delegation involves rendering the sub-contractor the instrument or conduit whereby a consignment note comes into circulation, and to insist upon some party higher in the chain procuring the original consignment note makes no commercial or legal sense".

In *Flegg Transport Ltd v Brinor International Shipping and Forwarding Ltd* [2009] EWHC 3047 (QB), F had contracted with M to transport a guillotine from premises in London, England to its premises in Aylesbury, England pending delivery to Germany. F had further contracted with B for the carriage of the cargo to Germany. B subcontracted that carriage to C. A CMR consignment note identified F as the "sender", C as the "carrier", B as "successive carrier" and a German entity as the consignee. It was issued by C (the last carrier). On arrival in Germany the guillotine was found to have been damaged. F claimed that B and/or C were liable under the CMR. F compensated M for the damage caused and subsequently sought an indemnity or contribution from B and/or C. The court held that whilst there was a CMR contract between F and M for a consignment from London to Germany, B and C did not become successive road carriers thereunder because there was no acceptance of any consignment note relating to that contract. The effect of the issue of the consignment note by C was to make C a successive carrier to a *second* CMR contract between F and B, evidenced by the terms of the consignment note limited to carriage from F's premises to Germany.

9–027   Article 37 allows the carrier who has been made liable for damages to claim contribution from the carrier who was actually responsible for the damage, loss or delay. If it cannot be ascertained to which carrier liability is attributable, the compensation has to be borne by them all proportionally. Where one of them is insolvent, according to art.38, the share of the compensation due from him shall be divided among the other carriers in proportion to the share of the payment for the carriage due to them.

Rosewood Trucking v Brian Balaam [2005] EWCA Civ 1461.   **9–028**
Facts:
P&O Ferrymasters contracted with consignors to carry a consignment of televisions from
Spain to England. P&O then subcontracted the carriage to Rosewood Trucking, which in
turn, subcontracted with another carrier. That carrier had then subcontracted to Brian
Balaam. Balaam's truck was broken into and the goods stolen.

The subcontract between P&O and Rosewood expressly prohibited further subcontract-
ing without consent. It did however provide that, in any event, Rosewood would remain
liable to P&O *"as if it had itself performed or failed to perform the carriage"*. P&O paid
the consignors' claim and Rosewood indemnified P&O as required by the subcontract.
Rosewood then relied on art.37 of CMR to seek indemnification from Balaam.
Held:
The Court of Appeal held that under the Convention, Rosewood had no liability to P&O
or the sender since, under art.36 of the Convention, proceedings in respect of liability for
loss could only be brought by the sender against the first carrier, the last carrier or the
carrier who was performing that portion of the carriage during which the event causing the
loss occurred. Accordingly, whilst Balaam would have been liable to be sued under the
terms of arts 36 and 37 by the sender or P&O, Rosewood had no entitlement to bring its
action against Balaam under the terms of the Convention since it was neither the sender
nor the original carrier. In short, Rosewood did not pay P&O compensation *"in
compliance with the provisions of the Convention"*. It had simply paid according to the
terms of the contract. Under CMR, Rosewood had no liability either to the sender or to
P&O. Its liability arose under a contract to which Balaam was not a party.

If needed, Rosewood could have protected itself by its own contract with its subcontractor by taking as assignment of P&O's claim against Balaam or possibly by way of
subrogation.

Limitation of liability and defences

Under the Convention, there is a limitation of liability provision to the effect that   **9–029**
the carrier shall not be liable for any loss, damage or delay in any amount
exceeding 8.33 units of account (SDR) per kilogramme of gross weight short. In
addition the carrier is to refund in full the carriage charges incurred in respect of
the carriage of goods (art.23).

It should be noted that any exclusion or limitation of liability provision in the
CMR cannot be relied on if the damage was caused by the carrier's wilful
misconduct or by such default on his part

"as, in accordance with the law of the court or tribunal seised of the case, is
considered as equivalent to wilful misconduct" (art.29(1)).

The same shall apply where the wilful misconduct was committed by his agent,
servant or an independent contractor engaged by him (art.29(2)). This provision
was discussed by the Court of Appeal in the case of *Laceys Footwear v Bowler
International Freight Ltd*.

Laceys Footwear (Wholesale) Ltd v Bowler International Freight Ltd [1997] 2 Lloyd's   **9–030**
Rep. 369.
Facts:
Bowler, the carriers, agreed under a contract of carriage to deliver a consignment of shoes
from Spain to the claimants' premises in London. The carriers were also contractually
required to take out insurance on the goods. The driver, in breach of his instructions
delivered the goods to thieves. Laceys, the claimants, claimed damages from the carriers

at market value of the goods at destination or in the alternative, the amount which, had the goods been insured, would have been recovered on the insurance policy. The carriers however argued that arts 23 and 27 should apply to the effect that any damages payable were to be calculated with reference to the value of the goods at Alicante, Spain at the date on which the goods were collected and by reference to the value of the goods in pesetas converted at the rate of exchange at the date of judgment in London. This was objected to by the claimants.

The contract was governed by the CMR. Bowler argued that their liability was therefore subject to the exceptions and limitations in the CMR. The claimants submitted that Bowler's right to rely on the rules of calculation of damages in the CMR had been forfeited as a result of the wilful misconduct of the driver within the meaning of art.29.

Held:

The Court of Appeal agreed with the lower court that the driver had been guilty of wilful misconduct. A driver of his experience must have known that to allow persons whose identity he had made no effort to establish to unload the goods into an unmarked lorry in the road would expose the goods to risk of theft. His actions were deliberate in the sense that he plainly intended to do what he did even though he did not intend the goods to be stolen. His deliberate actions exposed the goods to a risk of which he must have been aware. No doubt he "hoped for the best", but in the absence of any evidence from the driver to explain his conduct, Judge Anthony Thompson, QC was entitled to conclude that he behaved recklessly.

9-031   As to the carrier's argument that even if the judge at first instance was right in finding the driver guilty of wilful misconduct, art.29 could not affect their rights under Arts 23 and 27 which "*fix*" their liability rather than "*exclude or limit*" it, the Court of Appeal could find no grounds to disagree. Arts 23(1) and (2) provide that compensation is to be calculated by reference to the value of the goods at the time and place they were collected for carriage (i.e. Spain and not England, as the claimants alleged) and determine how the value is to be fixed. Article 27(2) provides that where compensation is calculated in a foreign currency conversion shall be at the rate applicable on the day and at the place compensation is payable. These are obviously not exclusion or limitation of liability provisions, thus the carriers succeeded on this point.

A good though not exhaustive definition of "wilful misconduct" in English law might be taken from Lord Alverstone in *Forder v Great Western Railway Co* [1905] 2 K.B. 532:

> "means misconduct to which the will is party as contradistinguished from accident, and is far beyond any negligence, even gross or culpable negligence, and involves that a person wilfully misconducts himself, who knows and appreciates that it is wrong conduct in his part in the existing circumstances to do, or to fail or to omit to do (as the case may be), a particular thing, and yet intentionally does or fails or omits to do it, or persists in the act, failure or omission, regardless of the consequences".

Thus, in *TNT Global v Denfleet* [2007] EWCA Civ 405, the mere fact that the lorry driver had admitted to feeling drowsy and then falling asleep at the wheels was not enough to justify a finding of "wilful misconduct". Such conduct might constitute negligence, but it is not wilful misconduct for the purposes of art.29. Similarly, in *Micro Anvika v TNT Express Worldwide (Euro Hub) NV* [2006] EWHC 230, the driver was duped into delivering the lorry to "round the corner" of the destination where the goods were stolen. The court held that as nobody had given him instructions that he was only to deliver the goods at the premises in question, he could not be guilty of wilful misconduct. In *Laceys Footwear*, on the other hand, the driver was specifically warned that the consignment "was not to be off-loaded anywhere but 263–265 Hackney Road E2".

The general principles, as Cresswell J. summarised in *Thomas Cook v Air*   **9–032** *Malta* [1997] 2 Lloyd's Rep. 399, are:

"1. The starting point when considering whether in any given circumstances the acts or omissions of a person entrusted with goods of another amounted to wilful misconduct is an enquiry about the conduct ordinarily to be expected in the particular circumstances.

2. The next step is to ask whether the acts or omissions of the defendant were so far outside the range of such conduct as to be properly regarded as "misconduct". (An important circumstance would be a deliberate disregard of express instructions clearly given and understood.)

3. It is next necessary to consider whether the misconduct was wilful.

4. What does not amount to wilful misconduct? Wilful misconduct is far beyond negligence, even gross or culpable negligence.

5. What does amount to wilful misconduct? A person wilfully misconducts himself if he knows and appreciates that it is misconduct on his part in the circumstances to do or to fail or omit to do something and yet (a) intentionally does or fails or omits to do it or (b) persists in the act, failure or omission regardless of the consequences or (c) acts with reckless carelessness, not caring what the results of his carelessness may be. (A person acts with reckless carelessness if, aware of a risk that goods in his care may be lost or damaged, he deliberately goes ahead and takes the risk, when it is unreasonable in all the circumstances for him to do so.)

6. The final step is to consider whether the wilful misconduct (if established) caused the loss of or damage to the goods."

Under the Convention, it is left to the court seised with jurisdiction[19] to decide what constitutes "wilful misconduct". Although the CMR is an international convention, there is no universally or internationally recognised definition of wilful misconduct. The test at English law seems to be this—the court should ascertain first the nature of the ordinary duty and responsibility of a driver in those circumstances, the instructions given to him and then to make an inference

---

[19] As to the question of jurisdiction, art.31 provides: "In legal proceedings arising out of carriage under this Convention, the plaintiff may bring an action in any court or tribunal of a contracting country designated by agreement between the parties and, in addition, in the courts or tribunals of a country within whose territory: (a) the defendant is ordinarily resident, or has his principal place of business, or the branch or agency through which the contract of carriage was made, or (b) the place where the goods were taken over by the carrier or the place designated for delivery is situated, and in no other courts or tribunals". As to the meaning of "defendant" see *Hatzl v XL Insurance* [2010] EWCA Civ 223, where it was held that an assignee (a person to whom the consignor or consignee had assigned their rights) could not be treated as the defendant for the purposes of art.31. For the purposes of art.31, the original consignee's or consignor's place of business was crucial.

whether the driver by his actions has departed from that standard wilfully or recklessly. Wilful blindness is also clearly included.

In *Circle Freight International Ltd v Medeast Gulf Exports Ltd* [1988] 2 Lloyd's Rep. 427, Taylor L.J. (as he then was) rejected the distinction between a driver who had wilfully, in the sense of deliberately, committed an act of neglect and a driver who was wilfully negligent:

> "[It was submitted] that although [the driver] wilfully, in the sense of deliberately, left the van unlocked and the keys in the ignition, he was not wilfully negligent or in breach of duty. I cannot accept this. On the learned Judge's findings, [the driver] was fully conscious not only that he was leaving the vehicle unsecured but that in doing so he was acting in breach of his instructions and in such circumstances as to expose the goods to risk of theft. He deliberately took a chance knowing he was acting in breach of his duty but hoping for the best. In so doing, he was in my judgment clearly guilty of wilful neglect".

9–033   What is less clear is whether a distinction should be made between a driver who sees a risk and decides to chance it and hopes for the best, and one who is so incompetent that he is totally oblivious to the serious and obvious risk to which the goods are exposed.

In *Circle Freight*, the carriers' second argument succeeded on two bases. First, it was submitted that the rationale of the CMR is to produce a uniform basis for calculating the liability of carriers from countries who are parties to the Convention. The Convention applies to carriage of goods across national borders and it is therefore important that carriers should have a fixed point of reference to establish liability not only to the owner of goods but also between themselves. Article 23 provides for this point of reference. It does not therefore seek to limit or exclude the liability of the carrier. Secondly, the object of art.29 is to prevent a carrier who is guilty of wilful misconduct to plead any provisions in the Convention which are beneficial to him. The provisions in art.23 are not intended to benefit the carrier or otherwise; they are mere neutral mechanistic tools.

In conclusion, whether there was wilful misconduct on the facts must be properly proved. In *Datec Electronics v UPS* [2007] UKHL 23 the House of Lords held that the correct standard of proof is that on a balance of probabilities. In that case, the House of Lords reiterated the trite rule that appellate courts, without the benefit of oral evidence, should always be slow to interfere with the trial court's findings of fact.

9–034   A brief word about procedures and Convention limits on liability. Under art.30(1), the consignee who takes delivery of a consignment which appears to be incomplete or damaged, and omits to send the carrier a notice of reservations, is deemed to have taken delivery of the goods in the condition described in the consignment note. As for delays, a notice of reservations must be sent to the carrier within 21 days from the time that the goods were placed at the disposal of the consignee.[20]

The limitation period for any claim under a contract of carriage governed by the CMR is one year. The one-year period becomes suspended when a written

---

[20] Art.30(3).

claim is made by the owner of the goods or his agent/proxy against the carrier. Time runs from:

1. the date of delivery in the case of partial loss, damage or delay in delivery;

2. the 30th day after the expiry of any *agreed* time limit for delivery in the case of total loss;

3. the 60th day after the date when the goods were taken over by the carrier in the case of total loss where there is no pre-agreed time limit for delivery; or

4. on the expiry of three months after the making of the contract of carriage in all other cases.[21]

The CMR imposes a maximum financial limit on claims made. Article 23(3) provides that the compensation which the carrier is liable to pay in respect of total or partial loss of the goods is subject to the ceiling of 8.33 SDRs per. kilogram of gross weight short.[22] In the case of delays, the carrier's liability is limited to the carriage charges, provided the claimant is able to prove that damage was sustained to that amount.

The carrier is also entitled to rely on quite a number of defences[23]—where the **9–035** damage, loss or delay was in fact caused by:

1. the wrongful act or negligence of the claimant;

2. instructions given by the claimant;

3. the inherent vice of the goods;

4. unavoidable circumstances and consequences outside the control of the carrier[24];

5. special risk measures as pre-agreed between the parties under the consignment note (e.g. the use of open unsheeted vehicles, special air conditioned vehicles, etc) provided the carrier demonstrates that he had taken necessary steps consistent with those "special risk measures" and complied with any special instructions issued to him.

---

[21] Art.32(1).

[22] In addition, art.23(4) permits the claimant to demand from the carrier a repayment of all carriage charges, customs duties and charges incurred in respect of the carriage of the goods. See *James Buchanan & Co Ltd v Babco Forwarding and Shipping (U.K.) Ltd* [1978] A.C. 141 where the House of Lords ordered the carriers to repay the consignors excise duty paid to the authorities as charges incurred in respect of the carriage of the consignment of whisky which was stolen whilst under the care and control of the carriers.

[23] Arts 17 and 18.

[24] In *Silber v Islander Trucking* [1985] 2 Lloyd's Rep. 243, Mustill J. held that as to whether the carrier could rely on arts 17(2) and 18(1) to exonerate him from liability if loss was caused "through circumstances which the carrier could not avoid and the consequences of which he was unable to prevent", the burden of proof on the carrier is of a higher standard than that of just acting reasonably. He must establish that the loss occurred through unavoidable circumstances.

These rights and defences (including the weight and financial limits in art.23) can be waived by the carrier as is consistent with general English law. However, as was pointed out by the Court of Appeal in *Fatme Ghandour v Circle International Ltd* (November 2, 1999), the waiver must be clear and unambiguous. The test seems more difficult to meet where the waiver is to be implied from a set of representations and statements made by the carrier without any one statement referring directly to the alleged waiver.

As is similar to the air carriage regime, the carrier loses his defences and limits if he is guilty of wilful misconduct as discussed above.

Carriage by Rail

Introduction

9–036 In the United Kingdom, the volume of goods being carried by international rail has become more important since the opening of the Channel Tunnel in 1994. The carriage of goods under a through consignment note made out for a route over the territories of at least two countries, of which one is a Member State, is generally governed by the Convention concerning International Carriage by Rail 1980 (including the CIM Uniform Rules), as amended by the Protocol for the Modification of the Convention concerning International Carriage by Rail (COTIF) 1999, also known as the Vilnius Protocol 1999. The international rules are the handiwork of the Intergovernmental Organisation for International Carriage by Rail (OTIF). There are currently 47 Member States (all the European states, excluding the successor states of the Soviet Union which are members of the SMGS Convention of Cargo Transport by Rail, but including Lithuania, Latvia, Estonia and the Ukraine, four near Eastern states and three North African states). The membership of two other countries, Iraq and Lebanon, is suspended until international rail traffic is resumed. The OTIF thus covers around 250,000km of railways.

The European Union has also joined OTIF when it signed COTIF on June 23, 2011 in Bern, Switzerland. The accession agreement came into force on July 1, 2011.

The United Kingdom has adopted the Vilnius Protocol (and thus the amendments to the current 1980 Convention) through the making of the Railways (Convention on International Carriage by Rail) Regulations 2005 on July 26, 2005. The Protocol came into force in the UK on July 1, 2006. The amended convention is accompanied by a number of "Regulations" and "Uniform Rules". As regards goods, the Uniform Rules Concerning the Contract of International Carriage of Goods by Rail (CIM—Appendix B to the Convention) are especially relevant. Other relevant instruments, but falling outside this book's consideration, are rules on the carriage of dangerous goods, the use of infrastructure in rail, etc. Under an international agreement with France, the Uniform Rules will not apply to shuttle services carrying road vehicles (including lorries and RO/RO vehicles) and passengers performed by rail exclusively between the Channel Tunnel terminals at Cheriton in Kent and Coquelles in the Pas-de-Calais. It is obvious that these are stations situated on either side of a frontier where there are no other stations between them.

The CIM—Appendix B to the Convention

Scope of application

International carriage by rail which is covered by the CIM is rail carriage for **9–037** reward involving movement over two countries, one of which is a Member State, and the parties have agreed to rely on the Rules (art.1). It should also be noted that the CIM will also apply where the international carriage contained in a single contract includes road or inland waterway carriage in the territory of a Member State if these are merely a "supplement to transfrontier carriage by rail" (art.1(3)). Hence, if A and B agree to carry goods by rail from the United Kingdom to France and the goods are anticipated in the contract to have to be transhipped on to waterway barges in France, the CIM will nevertheless apply.

The CIM shall have the force of mandatory law—the rules cannot be contracted out of or derogated from unless as otherwise provided for in the Rules themselves (art.5). However, where a stipulation is a derogation from the Rules, only that stipulation will be null and inapplicable, the contract with other conforming stipulations will survive. Also, the contract may impose on the carrier obligations more stringent than those in the CIM.

The contract of carriage is defined in art.6(1) as a contract whereby the carrier undertakes to carry the goods for reward to the place of destination and to deliver them there to the consignee. The contract must be confirmed by a consignment note. The consignment note must satisfy certain requirements under the CIM:

1. it must be signed by the consignor and carrier (though the signature can be replaced by a stamp, a machine entry or other appropriate manner);

2. on the duplicate copy which is returned to the consignor, the carrier must certify receipt of the goods;

3. one consignment note is to be made out for each consignment and indeed, a consignment note cannot relate to more than one wagon load;

4. in carriage involving transit through the EU customs territory, each consignment note must meet the requirements of art.7 (which states that information on relevant names, quantity, addresses, places, identification marks, documents required by customs, etc should be provided).

Failure to meet these requirements however would not invalidate the contract **9–038** (art.6(2)). The consignment note does not have the same status or legal effect as a bill of lading (art.6(5)). The consignor however will be liable to the carrier for loss or damage caused if he does not disclose any dangerous goods being shipped in the consignment note (art.8). The consignment note issued for cover in any part of the European Union should also alert the holder to its submission to the CIM (art.7(1)(p)).

The consignment note operates as prima facie evidence of the conclusion of the contract, and indeed, its terms and conditions. It is also evidence of the fact that the carrier has received into his custody, the relevant goods (art.12).

As against a carrier loaded the goods, the consignment note shall be prima facie evidence of the condition and their packaging as indicated. If there is no such indication on the consignment note, the note will be prima facie evidence of their apparently good condition at the time they were taken over by the carrier.

The consignment note is also prima facie evidence of the accuracy of statements on number of packages, marks, numbers, gross mass or quantity (art.12(2)). Article 12(3) goes on to state that the consignment note shall be prima facie evidence of the condition of the goods and of their packaging indicated in the consignment note or, in the absence of such indication, of their apparently good condition and of the accuracy of statements made, solely in the case where the carrier has examined them and recorded on the consignment note a result of his examination which tallies.

9–039   Where a reasoned reservation is expressed on the consignment note, the consignment note will not constitute prima facie evidence. A reason for a reservation could be that the carrier does not have the appropriate means to examine whether the goods correspond to the entries in the consignment note (art.12(4)). The carrier is entitled, under art.11 to examine the goods. He has to perform the examination under the presence of the consignor or independent witnesses, unless this is not required by local laws or some other conditions are required by local laws.

Performance of the contract of carriage

The relationship between the carrier and consignor/consignee

9–040   Many of the duties related to the carriage are to be performed by the carrier. Hence, a failure to perform will attract liability on the carrier. However, given the long distances involved in the carriage and the different rolling stocks and different rolling stock companies involved, who is the carrier, as far as the consignor is concerned? Article 3 defines the carrier as

> "the contractual carrier with whom the consignor has concluded the contract of carriage pursuant to these Uniform Rules, or a subsequent carrier who is liable on the basis of this contract".

If carriage governed by a *single* contract is performed by several successive carriers, each carrier, by the very act of taking over the goods with the consignment note, shall become a party to the contract of carriage in accordance with the terms of that document and shall assume the obligations arising therefrom. In such a case each carrier shall be responsible in respect of carriage over the entire route up to delivery (art.26).

Where the carrier has entrusted the performance of the carriage, in whole or in part, to a substitute carrier, whether or not the contract of carriage allows him to do so, the carrier shall nevertheless remain liable in respect of the entire carriage (art.27(1)). Under art.27(2), the substitute carrier will also be subject to the duties set out in the CIM for the carriage performed by him. Where and to the extent that both the carrier and the substitute carrier are liable, their liability shall be joint and several (art.27(4)).

9–041   The carrier's contract is with the consignor at first instance. Under art.18(1)(2), the consignor has the right to change his instructions even after the contract has been made. He can order the carrier to deliver the goods to another consignee, or delay the delivery of the goods, or stop delivery of the goods, or deliver the goods to another place of delivery. He loses this entitlement once the consignment note has been delivered to the consignee or when the consignee has accepted the goods or when the consignee has instituted action against the carrier for loss. He would also lose his right to modify the contract by subsequent orders if the *consignee* has exercised his right to order the carrier to deliver the goods to someone else or to some other place, or to discontinue delivery (arts 18(2)(d) and (3)). Indeed, the consignee too has the right to modify the contract as soon as the consignment note has been drawn up. Article 18(3) states that this right could however be excluded by the consignor in the consignment note. Further, the consignee's right to modify the contract is extinguished when he takes delivery of the consignment note or the goods or sues for lost goods. He will also lose his right to modify the contract if the goods were ordered by him to be delivered to a third party and that third party exercises his rights against the carrier for lost goods (art.18(4)). That third party, however does not have a right to modify the contract. It seems clear that privity of contract does not feature highly for the CIM. The pragmatic approach is desirable in that, given jurisdictional and logistical problems, it would be useful for either the consignor or consignee to be able to modify the delivery terms. However as the rules make clear, these rights are not absolute and there is clarity that as soon as the consignee exercises his right to modify the contract, the consignor's own entitlement to change the contract terms ends. Any change must not entail the splitting of the consignment (art.19(4)) and must be reasonable and lawful (art.19(3)). The person modifying the terms must bear the cost of compensating the carrier if additional expenses are incurred or consequential loss is sustained (art.19(2)).

It is stressed in art.19(1) that the consignor or consignee making the modifications by subsequent orders should produce to the carrier the duplicate of the consignment note on which the modifications are entered.

Carrier's duties

As far as loading and unloading are concerned, this is usually a matter of contract **9–042** for the parties. However, where the contract is silent, art.13 states that in the case of *packages*, the carrier shall be responsible for the loading and unloading. For full wagon loads (containers), the consignor shall be responsible for the loading and unloading. Where loading and unloading are to be performed by the consignor, he shall be liable to the carrier for any loss or damage caused by defective loading or unloading but it is for the carrier to discharge the burden of proof (art.13(2)). Similarly, as packing is best done by the consignor, any loss or damage caused by defective packaging shall be borne by him (art.14).

Administrative and customs documents are to be completed by the consignor (art.15) and the carrier shall not be liable for any accuracy of the information contained and is not required to check the information (art.15(2)). If he does undertake to check the documents and the information contained therein, then he assumes responsibility for them and would be held liable if they turn out to be incorrect and loss or damage is caused. Article 15(3) further provides that the carrier shall be liable for loss or damage arising from the loss or misuse of the documents referred to in the consignment note and accompanying it (or deposited with the carrier) unless the loss or damage was caused by circumstances which the carrier could not avoid or prevent. The general understanding here is that as the carrier has acknowledged the existence of those documents in the consignment note or his custody of them, he should be responsible for their safekeeping and use. In any case, the compensation shall not be more than that provided for in the event of loss of the goods.

The carrier is liable for delay (art.16). This is an important provision. The contract of carriage may specify the transit time and if this is stated, failure to comply with it will naturally constitute a breach and under art.33(1), the carrier must pay compensation not exceeding four times the carriage charges. However, art.33(6) allows the parties to agree as to the amount of damages or forms of remedy. Where no time is stipulated in the contract, art.16(2)–(4) lays down certain time or transit periods. These are presumed to apply to the contract of carriage and any failure to comply with these times will attract the same legal consequences.

9–043   The carrier is obliged to deliver the goods and the consignment note to the consignee at the place designated for delivery under the contract (art.17(1)). If the goods are lost or have not arrived after 30 days from the end of the transit period, the consignee "may assert, in his own name, his rights against the carrier under the contract of carriage" (art.17(3)). This provision is intended to give the consignee the sort of right of action a holder of bill of lading would normally have but it should nevertheless be remembered that the consignment note is not a document of title like the bill of lading (art.6(5)). Under art.17(3), the reference to "his rights . . . under the contract of carriage" is troubling. It does not state that the consignee is entitled to sue the carrier as if he was a party to the contract but that he is entitled to assert *his* rights under the contract in his own name. The problem arises when the contract does not actually provide for any of *his* rights (even assuming that he is able to be possessed of rights under the contract) and the rights and obligations are only expressed in terms of the consignor and carrier.

The carrier is deemed to have discharged his obligation to deliver if:

1. the goods are handed over to customs or octroi[25] authorities at their premises or warehouses, when these are not subject to the carrier's supervision; or

2. the goods have been deposited for storage with the carrier, with a forwarding agent or in a public warehouse,

as required by local legal or administrative conditions.

The consignee may insist on an examination to establish the alleged loss or damage even though he had paid the charges and accepted the consignment note (art.17(4)). If a claim is to be brought for loss or damage caused to the goods, liability shall be determined according to the provisions of art.23. Article 23(1) provides that the carrier shall be liable for loss or damage resulting from the total or partial loss of or damage to the goods caused:

1. between the time of taking over of the goods and the time of delivery; or

2. as a result of the transit period (art.16) being exceeded.

Loss is presumed when the goods have not been delivered or put at the consignee's disposal 30 days after expiry of the transit period (art.29(1)).

9–044   The carrier shall, however not be liable where the loss or damage or delay was caused by:

---

[25] "Octroi" refers to local taxes imposed on goods brought into a particular locality for consumption. Octroi has largely been abolished in all of Europe.

- the fault of the person entitled, or by an order given by him, other than as a result of the fault of the carrier;

- an inherent defect in the goods; or

- circumstances which the carrier could not avoid and the consequences of which he was unable to prevent (art.23(2)).

One observation might be offered. The provision is not entirely clear where there is contributory fault from both the person entitled and the carrier. It is submitted that "other than as a result of the fault of the carrier" (art.23(2)) seems to suggest that if there is some contributory fault of the carrier, he would not be entitled to rely on the defence.

Where the consignment has been re-consigned and that re-consignment also falls under the coverage of the Uniform Rules, and partial loss of damage has been ascertained after that re-consignment, it shall be presumed that it occurred under the latest contract of carriage (art.28(1)). The proviso is that the consignment should have remained in the carrier's charge and been re-consigned in the same condition as when it arrived at the place from which it was re-consigned. The presumption of loss rule in art.28 is very important to the person entitled. In the past, where the consignment was re-consigned and damage or loss arose, it was difficult for the claimant to prove which of the two immediately consecutive contracts of carriage was being carried out at the time of the loss or damage. Initially, the plan was to presume that the loss or damage had occurred during the performance of the latest contract of carriage. However this was clearly unsatisfactory. It only covered a small number of cases where it was not possible to ascertain during which of consecutive contracts of carriage the loss or damage occurred. Thus, now, art.28 makes clear that the presumption only applied if both the previous and subsequent transport operations were subject to the CIM. Article 28(3) also provides:

> "[T]his presumption shall also apply when the contract of carriage prior to the re-consignment was subject to a convention concerning international through carriage of goods by rail comparable with these Uniform Rules, and when this convention contains the same presumption of law in favour of consignments consigned in accordance with these Uniform Rules".

This means that where the re-consignment is governed by another international **9–045** rail carriage convention (such as the SMGS Convention, which applies to international rail carriage mainly through the countries of the former Soviet Union) and the consignment is governed by the CIM, the presumption in art.28 will nevertheless apply.

Limitation of liability

As with the other international carriage conventions, the CIM places a financial **9–046** limit on the carrier's liability. It has already been mentioned above that the financial limit on delays is no more than four times the carriage charges (art.33(1)).

As for loss of goods, art.30(2) states that the compensation shall not exceed 17 units of account per kilogramme of gross mass short (net). Other than that, the measure of damages shall be:

"in case of total or partial loss of the goods, the carrier must pay, to the exclusion of all other damages, compensation calculated according to the current market price, or if there is neither such quotation, according to the usual value of the goods of the same kind and quality on the day and at the place where the goods were taken over" (art.30(1)).

The carrier is also liable for wastage in transit but the liability is limited to:

1. Two per cent of the mass for liquid goods or goods consigned in a moist condition;

2. One per cent of the mass for dry goods (art.31(1)).

Obviously, the limits could only apply to partial loss. In the case of several packages being consigned, the wastage in transit shall be calculated separately for each package if its mass on consignment is shown separately on the consignment note or can be ascertained otherwise (for example, in a packing or shipping list).

9–047   If it is proved that the loss was not due to causes which would justify the allowance above, the limitation of liability provisions in art.31(1) could not be relied on (art.31(2)). This is a difficult provision to apply—there is limited guidance as to what causes would qualify.

As for damage caused to the goods, art.32(2) limits the carrier's liability to:

1. if the *whole* consignment has lost value through the damage, the amount which would have been payable in case of total loss;

2. if only part of the consignment has lost value through damage, the amount which would have been payable in case of partial loss.

Article 32(2) thus refers back to art.31 for its financial limits. An example might be this—a consignment of machine parts is carried and one part is damaged. If that part is central and *unique* (cannot be replaced) to the assembly of the entire machine, this should fall under 1. On the other hand, if it is a replaceable part, para.2. will apply.

9–048   Understandably where a declaration as to the value of the goods has been made in the consignment note, the declared value will supersede the financial limits provided for in the CIM (art.34). The financial limits will also be ignored if the loss or damage or delay was caused by an act or omission of the carrier committed with "intent to cause such loss or damage, or recklessly and with knowledge that such loss or damage would probably result" (art.36). It should be mentioned that the act or omission should relate to "such loss or damage" but art.36 encompasses "arts 32 to 35" which clearly includes the financial limits for delay. It would seem to follow that the intent or recklessness required must be directed at causing loss or damage, but not delay.

All claims must be made in writing to the carrier. Claims by the consignor must be supported by the duplicate of the consignment note whilst claims by the consignee must be backed by production of the consignment note if it had handed over to him (art.43). Article 44(1) provides that the consignor may bring an action based on the contract until such time as the consignee has:

1. taken possession of the consignment note;

2. accepted the goods; and

3. exercised his rights to assert his rights against the carrier for loss (art.17(3)), or to modify the contract (art.18(3)).

Article 44(2) then states that the consignee's right to sue the carrier on the contract attaches from the time he has:

1. taken possession of the consignment note;

2. accepted the goods; or

3. asserted his rights pursuant to art.17(3) or art.18(3).

Where a claim, however is for the return of sums paid, that could only be brought by the person who made the payment (art.44(3)) and only against the person to whom that payment was made (art.45(3)).

Claims based on the contract could only be brought against the first carrier, or **9–049** the last carrier, or the carrier actually performing that part of the carriage where liability is said to arise (art.45(1)). In the case of successive carriers in art.45(2) an action may be brought against "the carrier who must deliver the goods [as named] with his consent on the consignment note" in accordance with art.45(1) even if he has received neither the goods nor the consignment note.

Time limits are also important. Article 48(1) states that actions based on the contract shall be one year. It will be two years for claims where the carrier had acted with intent or recklessness to cause the loss or damage, or for cash on delivery made to the carrier, or for proceeds of sale made by the carrier (art.48(1)). Article 48(2) provides for when time shall commence:

1. for compensation for total loss, from the 30th day after expiry of the transit period;

2. for compensation for partial loss, damage or exceeding of the transit period, from the day when delivery took place; and

3. in all other cases, from the day when the right of action may be exercised.

All rights of action, subject to a few exceptions, will also be extinguished if the person entitled accepted the goods (art.47(1)(2)).

Jurisdictional rules

The CIM makes explicit provision for the forum to be seised with jurisdiction to **9–050** hear claims based on the CIM. Article 46 states:

"Actions based on these Uniform Rules may be brought before the courts or tribunals of Member States designated by agreement between the parties or before the courts or tribunals of a State on whose territory,

a) the defendant has his domicile or habitual residence, his principal place of business or the branch or agency which concluded the contract of carriage, or

b)   the place where the goods were taken over by the carrier or the place designated for delivery is situated.

Other courts or tribunals may not be seized".

This provision forms an exception from the general private international law rules (detailed in Chapter 12).

Containerisation

9–051   Containerisation has made more common the practice of using multimodal transport agreements. Containerisation is a method of distributing the goods in a unitised form, thereby permitting the use of different modes of transport for carriage. Containerisation allows a door-to-door service which, with the International Standards Organisation (ISO) or International Air Transport Association (IATA) container, may be conveyed from the factory to the retailer's site with no intermediate handling at terminal transhipment points and little risk of cargo damage or pilferage. The reduction of these risks will generally be taken into account by the insurers and should therefore result in lower premium rates. Warehouse space becomes less of a problem with containerisation in that these containers need not be "stored". They may be left where there are open spaces.

With the reduction of handling at transshipment points, substantial dock labour costs could be trimmed. Less packing is needed and in the case of specialised ISO containers, packing is not even required because these containers come either in a tank unit (for the shipment of liquefied or powdered goods) or as an air-conditioned unit. Less packing means lower costs. Containerisation therefore enhances and speeds up the transit of goods and encourages the rationalisation of ports of call.

There are however several legal issues surrounding the use of multimodal transport.

- First, it is felt that the current legal framework for the carriage of goods is over-dependent on the traditional delineation made between the different modes of transport. This means that as it becomes more difficult to determine at which point in transit liability arises, the corresponding difficulty is identifying which legal regime or convention is applicable.[26] In addition, there is the problem of how and to what extent some of the pre-container transport conventions will and should apply to containerisation. For instance, such a problem was encountered in *Owners of Cargo lately aboard the River Guarara v Nigerian National Shipping Line Ltd* [1998] 1 Lloyd's Rep. 225. In that case, the claimants sued for the damage caused to their goods as a result of the ship's sinking. The defendants argued that their liability was limited to £100 per container by virtue of the 1922 Hague Rules. The Hague Rules (as in the Hague-Visby Rules) refer to the limitation of liability to an amount "per package or unit". The problem was whether each container was to be treated

---

[26] See for example the complications in *Quantum Corp v Plane Trucking Ltd* [2002] EWCA Civ 350 discussed above (para.9–024).

as a unit or whether the items packed in the container should be considered. The court held that where a bill of lading listed a number of containers said to contain a specified number of separately packed items, then the reference point has to be the number of items packed in the containers. It is evident from the judgment that containerisation had never been reckoned on by the Hague Rules.

- Secondly, containerisation employs, as a feature, the use of through documentation (consignment note), namely an air waybill or combined transport bill of lading. It is often uncertain as to the acceptability of these documents as far as the terms of the international trade agreements are concerned. It must however be said that the Carriage of Goods by Sea Act 1992 and the Uniform Customs and Practice for Documentary Credits 2007 (UCP 600) go some way towards ameliorating these problems. Article 19 of the UCP 600, for example, stipulates the type of transport document to be furnished by the shipper, the details which these documents should contain and other incidents resulting from the tender of documents representing multi-modal transport.

- Finally, the application of combined transport may raise issues as to whether the parties have successfully performed their part of the bargain. In traditional uni-modal transport contracts, the position is quite clear in that the proper discharge of these duties is usually judged against usage and practice. An example is determining when delivery of the goods has taken place. Time of delivery is of course an important element in determining whether the seller has performed his part of the bargain satisfactorily. With container transport, the goods are usually delivered either by the seller or the freight forwarder to a combined transport operator at an inland depot. Does this then constitute delivery? These and other questions are, however, becoming less difficult to resolve as popularity in multi-modal transport gathers momentum, but they do still trouble the lawyer.

In view of these problems, there is now an international convention on the use **9–052** of multimodal transport—the UN Convention on International Multi-modal Transport of Goods, Geneva 1980. The Convention however is unlikely to come into force. However if the new UN Convention for the International Carriage of Goods Wholly or Partly by Sea (Rotterdam Rules) comes into effect,[27] there will be specific provisions dealing with multi-modal transport.

Agents in the Carriage of Goods

Forwarding agent

As far as the law is concerned, the duties of the freight forwarding agent are **9–053** determined by contract. Almost everything is open to agreement.[28] However, any limitation of liability clause will be subject to the Unfair Contract Terms Act

---

[27] See para.8–103 onwards.
[28] See *Maersk Air Ltd v Expeditors International (UK) Ltd* [2003] 1 Lloyd's Rep. 491 where the court noted that as the defendant forwarder had agreed to do no more than provide a payment and invoicing service, it could not be held liable as a bailee or haulier of the goods.

1977 (*Schenkers Ltd v Overland Shoes Ltd* [1998] 1 Lloyd's Rep. 498). Certain general duties may be assumed of the freight forwarding agent as stated by Devlin J. in *Heskell v Continental Express Ltd* [1950] 1 All E.R. 1033:

- to ascertain the date and place of sailing;

- to obtain a space allocation if that is required;

- to prepare the bill of lading by filling in the relevant standard form bills of lading issued by the shipping lines; and

- to send the draft bill of lading to the loading broker.

Where the forwarder issues a bill of lading, that should not be confused with the carrier's own bill of lading. The forwarder's bill is in law not a bill of lading properly so called. Indeed, as the court held in *Gagniere v Eastern Co* [1921] 7 Lloyd's Rep. 188, a document is not a bill of lading merely because that is what it was called on its face. The forwarder's bill, also known as a "house bill of lading" is, at most, a receipt for the goods coupled with an authority to enter into a contract of carriage on behalf of the shipper.[29]

Loading broker

9–054 Devlin J. in *Heskell* referred to trade practice for an appropriate description of a "loading broker" and concluded that a loading broker is an agent employed:

1. to arrange for the goods to be brought alongside the vessel;

2. to make the customs entry for the cargo;

3. to pay any dues on the cargo (these dues are not customs duties bearing in mind that duty is paid for goods entering the country not goods leaving); and

4. after shipment, to collect the completed bill of lading and send it to the shipper.

Most regular shipping lines appear to entrust the business of arranging for cargo to a loading broker. The broker will then advertise the date of sailings in shipping papers and journals or elsewhere. He will also issue and circulate to his customers a sailing card either physically or electronically. The sailing card will usually state the name of the carrying ship, the place where the goods should be sent for loading and the time when the ship becomes ready to load. It will also stipulate the closing date for loading. This is the last date on which the goods can be loaded. If the shipper delivers the goods late, i.e. after the closing date, the shipmaster is entitled to refuse to load even though the ship is still in port. The closing date is usually a few days before actual sailing so as to allow the ship to prepare herself for sea.

It is his business to supervise the arrangements for loading. Actual stowage though is decided on by the cargo superintendent who is in the direct service of

---

[29] A. Burrows, D. Foxton and S.C. Boyd, *Scrutton on Charterparties*, 19th edn (London: Sweet & Maxwell, 1984), p.384.

the shipowner. The broker will also usually sign bills of lading and to issue them to the shipper of his agent in exchange for freight. His remuneration is by way of commission on freight to be paid by the shipowner.

The freight forwarding agent or the loading broker is likely to take custody, **9–055** handle and carry the cargo; it is in respect of these operations that he may be held liable to the cargo owner in damages for any loss, deterioration of damage caused. There are three main constraints to the success of such an action by the claimant.

First, the claimant must show that he indeed has the entitlement to sue. In *Euro cellular (Distribution) Plc v Danzas* [2004] EWHC 11 (Comm.), the court held that proving the title to sue is to be on a balance of probabilities, no different from any other civil cases. In that case, E was a mobile phone distributor whilst D was a warehouse company acting as freight forwarders. The goods had disappeared from D's warehouse in Spain. E had argued that the goods had been paid for by them and were subsequently received by them in England for carriage to Spain by D. D, however disputed the claim that E was in fact the owner of the goods that went missing. A movement order was used for the carriage but it was not clear from the order that the carriage related to the goods claimed by E. The court held that although the documentary evidence was unpersuasive, it could rely on testimony from warehouse workers and evidence of the credit facilities held by E with the phone supplier to conclude that the goods did belong to E. Ownership, as this case shows, is important.

Secondly, he must show that the loss or damage was caused by the agent. This is not to say that the claimant must be able to explain fully what occurred during the time the goods were in the care and custody of the agent. Obviously that would be unrealistic and unfair, as it is the agent who must be deemed to have knowledge of the full facts as he had the closest proximity to the goods when the goods were damaged or lost. However, the claimant needs to show that the goods were handed over to the agent if the claim is for loss of the goods, and that they were handed over in good condition if the claim was for damage or deterioration of the goods. In *Eurocellular Distribution Plc v Danzas* [2003] EWHC 3161 (Comm.), the court emphasised this, stating that the claimant only needs to allege and prove a loss of (or damage to) the goods whilst in the possession of the defendant in the latter's warehouse. The burden of proving what in fact happened to the goods lay upon the defendant.

Finally, he will only succeed if the agent's exception or limitation of liability **9–056** clauses do not remove or reduce his claim. The limitation clause must first have been properly incorporated into the contract and, additionally, it will be construed narrowly. In *Eurocellular Distribution* the contract had incorporated the relevant British International Freight Association (BIFA) clause which limits the defendant's liability to two SDRs per kilogramme. The claimant had wanted to use their own freight forwarders guide which the defendant agreed, in addition to the BIFA clauses. The combined effect was that the defendant would bear the liability of loss caused by negligent release; whilst the claimant undertook to claim from their own insurers if the loss was caused by some other event. The court held that once a claimant has established that the goods were lost whilst in the defendant's possession, there would arise an inference of negligence which the defendant must rebut. In the present case, the defendant had not been able to do so. Thus, it was unable to rely on the limitation of liability clause despite the fact that it had been properly incorporated.

It should be noted that although the freight forwarder and loading broker perform two distinct functions, they are usually the same company or firm.

Whether the firm is acting as either forwarding agent or loading broker or both, is crucial to any potential conflict between the shipper of goods, the carrier and the agent. In *James v European West Indies Lines (UK) Ltd* (October 9, 1997) the appellant had retained the services of ESA to ship second-hand vehicles from Felixstowe to Ghana. The vessel used was operated by the respondent, EWIL, an international carrier. During the voyage the ship encountered a storm and the cargo was badly damaged. The goods had been loaded on deck and were not insured. The appellant argued that ESA had breached their duties as his forwarding agent despite the fact that they were also the loading broker for EWIL, the carrier. ESA disputed the appellant's suggestion that it was acting as the appellant's forwarding agent. They claimed that they had acted solely as EWIL's loading broker. The Court of Appeal found, from the contract and the surrounding circumstances, that it was clear to all parties that the ship was owned by EWIL and there was no separate charge made for services rendered by ESA who had merely made arrangements for the goods to be carried to Ghana on EWIL's behalf. They had arranged for the goods to be collected from where they were being stored awaiting shipment and had invoiced the appellant for the carriage. They were, as such, not forwarding agents for the appellants, but merely loading brokers for the actual carriers.[30]

9–057   In *FH Bertling Ltd v Tube Developments Ltd* (*Lawtel*, September 29, 1999) the Scottish Court of Session held that whilst it was possible for a freight forwarder (or loading broker) to have two principals, it was prima facie improbable where only party had responsibility for transport. In that case, where the buyer had expressly committed himself to arranging carriage for the goods under the sale of goods contract as principal with the freight forwarder, it was difficult to envisage how the seller could be deemed as another probable principal who should bear the unpaid freight charges owed by the freight forwarder to the carrier. The only exception might be where the buyer and seller both agree to accept joint and several liability for freight to the freight forwarder.

---

[30] See also *HSBC Bank USA v Securicor Cash Services* [2002] EWHC 2674, QBD on the problems of identifying the relevant parties with the contractual rights and liabilities.

CHAPTER 10

MARINE INSURANCE FOR CARGO

Insurance is about the trader's aversion to risk. Exporters and importers are **10–001** aware that the goods being shipped are subject to risks of damage or loss as a result of the long distances undertaken. There is also the risk of the goods being delayed and thereby resulting in a lost market. The trader knows that while he is able to sue the carrier or the shipper of the goods for any such loss, by insuring the goods he has recourse to the insurers without needing to go to litigation. By having insurance taken out on the goods, the trader knows for certain or at least to a substantial degree that if the goods are damaged or lost, he will be entitled to be indemnified by the insurers. This certainty is something he is prepared to pay for as long as the price for this peace of mind is reasonable. This chapter examines the law relating to insurance for goods carried by sea, given that the majority of international trade involves maritime transportation.

Nature of the Insurance Contract

A contract of indemnity

The insurance contract is one of indemnity. This characteristic is fundamental to **10–002** the validity or enforceability of an insurance contract. As far as the marine insurance contract is concerned, s.1 of the Marine Insurance Act 1906 (hereafter referred to as the MIA) states:

"A contract of marine insurance is a contract whereby the insurer undertakes to indemnify the assured, in manner and to the extent thereby agreed, against marine losses, that is to say, losses incident to the marine adventure".

An undertaking to indemnify means a duty to cover a loss suffered by the assured to the extent, and only to the extent of his actual loss. As Brett J. said in *Castellain v Preston* (1883) 11 Q.B.D. 380:

"The contract of insurance contained in a marine . . . policy is a contract of indemnity, and of indemnity only, and this contract means that the assured on case of a loss against which the policy has been made, shall be fully indemnified, but shall never be more than fully indemnified".

It should be remembered that the principle of indemnity in insurance contracts, though fundamental, does not always bring about a complete indemnity. This is seen in certain types of marine policy; for example when the parties agree to a valued policy, the intention is that the insurer will pay the agreed sum as fixed by contract regardless of the actual loss. Section 27(3) provides that in the absence of fraud, the value fixed in a valued policy shall be conclusive of the insurable value of the subject matter, whether the loss be total or partial.

Marine adventure

10–003 The contract of marine insurance must relate to marine losses, "that is to say, losses incident to a marine adventure". A marine adventure exists when:

1. any ship or goods are exposed to maritime perils;

2. the earning or acquisition of any freight, passage money, commission, profit or other pecuniary benefit or the security for any advances is endangered by the exposure of insurable property to maritime perils;

3. liability to a third party may be incurred by the owner of or any other person interested in insurable property by reason of maritime perils.

Maritime perils are perils consequent on or incidental to the navigation of the sea, including:

"perils of the seas, fire, war, war perils, pirates, rovers, thieves, captures, seizures, restraints and detainments of princes and peoples, jettisons, barratry and any other like perils".

While "maritime perils" may have a similar connotation with the term "perils of the sea" used in carriage of goods by sea, there is one important distinction. Lord Herschell made this clear in *The Xantho* (1887) 12 App. Cas. 503:

"Now, I quite agree that in the case of a marine policy the *causa proxima* alone is considered. If that which immediately caused the loss was a peril of the sea, it matters not how it was induced, even if it were by negligence of those navigating the vessel. It is equally clear that in the case of a bill of lading you may sometimes look behind the immediate cause, and the shipowner is not protected by the exception of perils of the sea in every case he would be entitled to recover on his policy, on the ground that there has been a loss by such perils".

It all depends on the facts and the contractual terms how those words "perils of the sea" might be construed.

Capacity to Contract—Insurable Interest

10–004 It is immediately obvious that the insurance contract is similar in genus to the wagering or gaming agreement. They both deal with contingencies and payment upon the occurrence of those events. The common law has a natural and moral aversion to wagering contracts and it is trite principle therefore that wagering contracts are not lawful. One way to overcome this "immorality" of insurance contracts is to require that only people with an appropriate or insurable interest in the property or subject matter should be entitled to insure. Indeed, s.4 provides that a contract of marine insurance by way of a gaming or wagering contract is void. A contract is deemed to be a gaming or wagering contract:

1. where the assured has not an insurable interest, and the contract is entered into with no expectation of acquiring such an interest;

2. where the policy is made "interest or non interest" or "without further proof of interest than the policy itself" or "without benefit of salvage to the insurer" or subject to any other like term.

The morality rationale has of course been the subject of much criticism in the light of relativism as a prevailing school of thought in business and economic theories. A more "rational" reason needs to be found for preserving the requirement of insurable interest. Economics might be able to provide that rational basis. The assumption that economists make is that people are likely to look after their own property with more care than they would with somebody else's property. Where insurance exists without calling for insurable interest, this will gradually lead to less incentive on the assured to take care (whether in relation to the insured's property or some other subject matter). This will result in greater cost and less efficiency. Whether this is borne out by evidence is debatable.

Be that as it may, it remains the law that insurable interest must be proved. Insurable interest is defined in s.5 in these terms:

(a) Every person has an insurable interest who is interested in the marine adventure.

(b) A person is interested in a marine adventure if he stands in any legal or equitable relation to the adventure or any insurable property at risk in that adventure. This relationship may be evidenced by:

   (i) the fact that he may benefit from the safety or due arrival of the insurable property;
   (ii) the fact that he may be prejudiced by its loss, or damage, or detention;
   (iii) the fact that he may incur liability as a result of the loss, damage or detention.

We might wish to compare this provision with the general definition adopted **10–005** by the House of Lords in *Lucena v Craufurd* (1806) 2 B.&P.N.R. 269:

"[I]nterest does not necessarily imply a right to the whole or a part of a thing, nor necessarily and exclusively that which may be the subject of privation, but the having some relation to, or concern in the subject matter of the insurance, which relation or concern by the happening of the perils insured against may be so affected as to produce a damage, detriment or prejudice to the person insuring: and where a man is so circumstanced with respect to matters exposed to certain risks or dangers, as to have a moral certainty of advantage or benefit, but for those risks or dangers he may be said to be interested in the safety of the thing. To be interested in the preservation of a thing, is to be so circumstanced with respect to it as to have benefit from its existence, prejudice from its destruction".

In that case, the assured were appointed as custodians of vessels detained by British forces. They wanted to insure the safe passage of the ships and goods to be detained and brought back to port. The House of Lords held that they had no insurable interest pending the arrival of the ships. They only had an expectation of advantage or benefit in the safe detention and seizure of the vessels. They did not have "a moral certainty of advantage or benefit".

In *Macaura v Northern Assurance Co Ltd* [1925] A.C. 619, it was held that a shareholder or simple creditor of a company has no insurable interest in the company's assets.

10–006   *Macaura v Northern Assurance Co Ltd* [1925] A.C. 619
Facts:
The assured was both the principal shareholder and main creditor in the company, having sold his timber on credit terms to the company in exchange for shares. A fire destroyed the timber which was subject to the insurance in question. The assured made a claim under his policy but was rejected by the insurer on the basis that the timber had belonged to the company and only the company had insurable interest over the timber.
Held:
It might be useful to set out the assured's arguments before considering the approach taken by the House of Lords. The assured argued that legal ownership in the subject matter is not necessary for establishing insurable interest. He contended in reliance on the test in *Lucena*, he should be deemed to have insurable interest if there is a legal certainty of loss in that as the sole shareholder of the company, he would inevitably suffer from the loss of the company's assets. To this argument, the House of Lords held that a shareholder has no legal or equitable interest in the company's assets. He might be entitled to a share in the profits generated by the company's assets and even a share in the distribution of the assets following the winding-up of the company, but this does not stand him in a legal or equitable relationship with the property itself. His relationship was with the company, not the company's property.
The assured then went on to argue that as creditor to the company he had an interest in the company's assets out of which his debt was to be paid. The example cited was that of a creditor being entitled to insure his debtor's life to the extent of the debt. A fortiori, it was contended that the assured was the only substantial creditor and the company had no other assets out of which the debt could be paid. Hence, the assured should be entitled to insure against the loss of that only asset, the timber. The House of Lords rejected this contention as well saying that the debt was not exposed to the fire. As a creditor, he stood in no legal or equitable relation to the timber at all. Although there was a moral certainty of the loss being suffered by the assured in the event of the timber being destroyed, Lord Buckmaster said:

"[T]his moral certainty becomes dissipated and lost if the asset be regarded as only one in an innumerable number of items in a company's assets and the shareholding be spread over a large number of individual shareholders".

10–007   It is obvious that in *Macaura*,[1] the House of Lords gave the term "legal or equitable relation" a somewhat literal reading. This restrictive approach reflects

---

[1] See also Bockrath, "Insurable Interest in maritime law" (1977) 8 J.M.L.C. 81.

the conservatism to prevent insurance contracts from taking on a gaming character. While not questioning the rightness or wrongness of this condemnation of gaming and wagering contracts, it might be opined that the principle of indemnity applied together with the rule on full disclosure should serve the purpose of preventing fraud and gaming better than a strict rule on insurable interest.

The insurable interest must be in relation to the goods, not the owner or anyone in possession of them as is pointed out in *Macaura*. In the area of sales, this raises the question as to when the seller or buyer will have an insurable interest in the goods for the purposes of taking out suitable cover for the goods and consequently, the risk in the sale transaction. According to s.6, the interest must attach at the time of the loss only. The assured need not be in the relationship with the adventure as described in s.5 at the time the insurance was taken out. Where the goods are insured on "lost or not lost" terms, he may recover although he may not have acquired his interest until after the loss, unless of course when the insurance was taken out the assured was aware of the loss and the insurer was not. The rule is that the assured who does not have insurable interest at the time of the loss cannot subsequently acquire interest by any act or election after he is aware of the loss.

In general, sellers will have insurable interest not only as owners but also as:

1. risk bearers—as long as title or any security interest in the goods remains with him, (for example by reserving title to the goods by means of a conditional sale agreement or by retaining the bill of lading or by exercising a possessory lien) he stands in a legal or equitable relation to the insurable property;

2. unpaid sellers having security rights. It should be noted that the mere right of stoppage in transit does confer on the sellers any insurable interest. The insurable interest only arises when the right of stoppage is exercised.

The buyer does not have insurable interest in the goods simply by entering into the contract of sale. His insurable interest usually arises:

1. when he takes possession of the goods; or

2. when the risk in the goods has passed to him; or

3. when he has made an advance payment for the goods.

In *Anderson v Morice* (1876) 1 App. Cas. 713, the buyer had taken out an **10–008** insurance for a "cargo of new crop Rangoon rice, per Sunbeam". Payment was to be by sellers' draft drawn on the buyer at six months' sight with documents attached. The Sunbeam sank during loading and with it part of the cargo. On whether the buyer had insurable interest in the subject matter at the time of the claim, the Court of Exchequer Chamber held that the contract had required risk to pass not on each bag of rice crossing the rail of the ship but on the loading of the entire cargo. Of course if the buyer had made advance payment for the goods, he would have been entitled to sue on his policy.

In *John Gillanders Inglis v William Ravenhill Stock* (1885) 10 App. Cas. 263, the insurable interest of an FOB buyer was considered at some length.

10–009   *John Gillanders Inglis v William Ravenhill Stock* (1885) 10 App. Cas. 263
Facts:
A sold to B German sugar FOB Hamburg, payment by cash in London in exchange for bill of lading. The sugar was shipped in bags on one vessel at Hamburg bound for Bristol. B had insured his sugar on floating policies for that voyage. The ship sailed from Hamburg and was lost. The assured then made a claim on those policies.
Held:
The House of Lords held that the sugar was at B's risk after shipment as the contract was on FOB terms, the risk having passed when the goods were taken over the rail of the ship. B could therefore claim on the insurance.

Section 7 states that a buyer who has insured goods will remain to have an insurable interest in them although he might have elected to reject the goods or treated them as remaining at the seller's risk because the seller had made a defective or delayed delivery. This coincides with the dictum of Lord Ellenborough C.J. in *Sirling v Vaughan* (1809) 11 Ea. 619 that while a contingent interest can be insured, a mere expectation of benefit cannot. It might also be suggested that a seller who has parted with goods has insurable interest in goods contingent on rejection of the goods or documents by the buyer. It would seem however that the buyer would have no insurable interest prior to his rejection of the goods or stoppage in transit.

10–010   It is customary for buyers and sellers to rely on agents in the sale transaction. The issue of insurable interest becomes highly relevant where the agent has taken out an insurance policy on the goods. It might be said that since the agent has only an interest in the commission from the performance of the sale agreement, he has no insurable interest in the goods. Case law seems to take a more generous view. In *Ebsworth v Alliance Marine* (1873) L.R. 8 C.P. 596, the issue was whether agents who had acted as consignees of the cargo of cotton intended for resale could enforce a floating policy, having accepted a bill of exchange drawn on them by the seller. The seller then negotiated the bill of exchange with the Bank of India. The insurer argued that the agents had no insurable interest as they only had a mere expectancy of profit or benefit from the resale resting on a contingency. There was no equitable or legal relation between the agents and the cotton. The court disagreed stating that the consignment immediately became an equitable security to the agents for the amount accepted by them on the bill of exchange. Although there was no legal interest in the goods (which was with the Bank of India) because they were not entitled to the documents or the cotton, they had beneficial interest to the amount of £3000, the value of the bill of exchange.

As for bailees, the case of *Tomlinson v Hepburn* [1966] A.C. 451 states that although the bailee or carrier of goods has an insurable interest in the goods as a result of their legal duty to the goods, they must hold the excess of their interest for the owners of the goods. In that case although the carriers had suffered no loss as a result of the damage or loss to the goods, the House of Lords held that they could sue the insurers and hold the payout for the owners of the goods who had insisted on the carriers' bringing the action. This case raises the two inconsistencies. First, it could be construed as a wagering contract in that he could recover an amount in excess of the actual loss to the owners. Secondly, it offends the principle of indemnity in that he should not recover a loss he had not suffered.

Making insurance contracts

It would be appropriate to consider how a normal contract of marine insurance **10–011** is made. The broker who acts as the trader's agent will approach an underwriter with a memorandum of agreement, also known as the slip.[2] This first underwriter the broker approaches is usually the leading underwriter. The leading underwriter, according to Lord Diplock in *American Airlines v Hope* [1974] 2 Lloyd's Rep. 301, is:

> "one who has a reputation in the market as an expert in the kind of cover required and whose lead is likely to be followed by other insurers in the market".

The broker and the leading underwriter will go through the slip together and agree on any amendments to the broker's draft terms and fix the premium. Once agreement is reached the leading underwriter will initial the slip, generally known as writing a line on the slip as to the proportion of risk he is prepared to accept. The broker then takes the slip to other underwriters who will write a line as to the proportion of the cover they accept. For practical reasons, the terms and premium of the insurance cover will be agreed on between the leading underwriter and broker alone. Once the required cover is reached, the slip is closed. The issue of the formal policy will then follow, though not necessarily immediately. Indeed s.22 of the Marine Insurance Act 1906 provides that the policy may be executed and issued either at the time when the contract is concluded or afterwards.[3] There is no legal requirement that the policy must be issued at the same time the contract was made.

An initial issue is whether the contract of insurance is made when the slip is initialled and accepted pro tanto or whether it depends on the final issue of the policy. It was held in *Ionides v Pacific Fire & Marine Insurance Co* (1871) L.R. 6 Q.B. 674; (1872) L.R. 7 Q.B. 517 that the law recognises the accepted practice amongst businessmen that the slip constitutes a binding contract. This is reinforced in the Marine Insurance Act 1906 which provides in s.21 that

> "a contract of marine insurance is deemed to be concluded when the proposal of the assured is accepted by the insurer, whether the policy be then issued or not".

In addition, that section goes on to say that the slip or covering note or other **10–012** customary memorandum of the contract of insurance (whether stamped or unstamped) may be used to show when the proposal was accepted. There is one

---

[2] See Bennett, "The role of the slip in marine insurance law" [1994] L.M.C.L.Q. 94 on the legal implications of the slip.

[3] The Law Commissions have proposed that the requirement for a policy should be removed. After all, the evidence is that the industry and market tend to operate on the basis that evidence of the insurance contract may reliably be drawn from other documents, not necessarily the policy. (see the Law Commission Consultation Paper No.201 and the Scottish Law Commission Consultation Paper No.152 (2011).)

set-back though. Section 22 provides that a contract of marine insurance is inadmissible in evidence unless it is embodied in a policy. The slip cannot be sued upon, but where there is a duly stamped policy s.89 provides that reference may be made to it in any legal proceedings.

The fact that when the underwriter writes a line in the slip, the risk has yet to be fully covered raises the issue as to whether the insurer should only be bound until the entirety of the risk has been underwritten. In *General Reinsurance Corp v Forsakringsaktiebolaget Fennia Patria* [1983] 3 W.L.R. 318, F, a Finnish insurance company wanted to amend its reinsurance of a risk at Lloyd's. The amendment slip was accepted by G for a certain proportion of the amount. The loss occurred before the full amount had been underwritten. F wanted to cancel the amendment note and rely on the original agreement. It was held that the amended agreement was concluded when it was initialled and F could not resile from it on the ground that the entire amended cover had yet been underwritten. As far as Kerr L.J. was concerned

> "the presentation of the slip by the broker constitutes the offer, and the writing of each line constitutes an acceptance of this offer by the underwriter pro tanto".

The acceptance was conclusive and was not conditional upon the full subscription of the risk. This is bolstered by the stipulation in s.24(2) that

> "where a policy is subscribed by or on behalf of two or more insurers, each subscription, unless the contrary is expressed, constitutes a distinct contract with the assured".

Indeed full subscription is not a feature of market practice. Brokers are known to solicit over-subscription as part of their business strategy. The practice is that once the slip is closed and the risk has been oversubscribed, the process of signing down takes place. This means that the cover will be reduced pro rata between the underwriters.

NON-NEGOTIABLE COPY

CLAIMS SETTLEMENT
INSTRUCTIONS

THIS CERTIFICATE
REQUIRES ENDORSEMENT IN
THE EVENT OF ASSIGNMENT

1. Lloyd's Settling Agent nearest destination is authorised to adjust and settle on behalf of the Underwriters, in accordance with Lloyd's Standing Regulations for the Settlement of Claims Abroad, any claim which may arise on this Certificate.

2. If Lloyd's Agents are not to deal with claims, it should be clearly marked by an 'X' in the adjacent box and claim papers sent to :- 1234 Brokers Ltd., 1 London Road, London EC99 1AB.

CERTIFICATE OF INSURANCE NO. C 0000/

This is to Certify that there has been deposited with the Council of Lloyd's a Contract effected by *1234 Brokers Ltd.,* of Lloyd's, acting on behalf of *New Business Supplier Ltd.,* with **Underwriters at Lloyd's, for insurances attaching thereto during the period commencing the** *First day of January, 2005,* **and ending the** *Thirty-first* **day of** *December, 2005,* **both days inclusive, and that the said Underwriters have undertaken to issue to** *1234 Brokers Ltd.,* **Policy/Policies of Insurance at Lloyd's to cover, up to** *USD5,000,000 (or equivalent in other currencies),* **in all by any one** *steamer and/or conveyances, or sending by air and/or post, General Merchandise and/or Goods and/or Equipment of any nature whatsoever including but not limited to Rice, Sugar, Motor Spare Parts, Bicycles, Generator Sets, Raw Jute, Jute Goods,* **from any port or ports, place or places in** *the World,* **to any** *ports, place or places* **in** *the World,* **including all transhipments as and when occurring, and that** *New Business Supplier Ltd.,* **are entitled to declare against the said Contract insurances attaching thereto.**

Conveyance	From	

for the Council of Lloyd's.
Dated at Lloyd's, London, 7th March, 2006.

Via/To	To		INSURED VALUE Currency

Marks and Numbers   Interest

We hereby declare for Insurance under the said Contract interest as specified above so valued subject to the special conditions stated below and on the back hereof.

Institute Cargo Clauses (A) or Institute Cargo Clauses (Air) (excluding sendings by Post) as applicable. Excluding rust, oxidisation, discolouration, twisting and bending.
Institute War Clauses (Cargo) or Institute War Clauses (Air Cargo) (excluding sendings by Post) or Institute War Clauses (sendings by Post) as applicable.
Institute Strikes Clauses (Cargo) or Institute Strikes Clauses (Air Cargo) as applicable.
Institute Classification Clause.
Institute Radioactive Contamination Exclusion Clause.
Institute Replacement Clause.

Underwriters agree losses, if any, shall be payable to the order of **NEW BUSINESS SUPPLIER LTD.,** on surrender of this Certificate.

In the event of loss or damage which may result in a claim under this Insurance, immediate notice must be given to the Lloyd's Agent at the port or place where the loss or damage is discovered in order that they may examine the goods and issue a survey report. The survey agent will normally be the Agent authorised to adjust and settle claims in accordance with the terms and conditions set forth herein, but where such Agent does not hold the requisite authority, he will be able to supply the name and address of the appropriate Settling Agent.
A full list of Lloyd's Agents can be found at www.lloydsagency.com
(Survey fee is customarily paid by claimant and included in valid claim against Underwriters.)

SEE IMPORTANT INSTRUCTIONS ON REVERSE

This Certificate not valid unless the Declaration be signed by
NEW BUSINESS SUPPLIER LTD.

Dated

Signed

Brokers : 1234 Brokers Ltd.,
1 London Road, London EC99 1AB.

LLOYD'S

Authorised Signatory
7489CM
© Lloyd's. 2006.

Consent and Uberrimae Fidei

Duty of disclosure

10–013   The contract of marine insurance is dependent on the consent of the parties, as
with most contracts. Unlike most contracts though, the marine policy rests on the
presumption that both parties are contracting in good faith and in order that good
faith is preserved throughout, the assured is required to disclose all material facts.
This duty of good faith characterises the contract of insurance as a contract
uberrimae fidei. The duty of utmost good faith is imposed on the assured and the
insurer by virtue of the general law and is independent of the contract of
insurance itself. That was held by the Court of Appeal in *Banque Keyser Ullman
SA v Skandia (UK) Insurance Co Ltd* [1990] 1 Q.B. 665, rejecting a submission
that the duty of utmost good faith prior to the conclusion of a contract of
insurance was based on an implied term in the contract. The House of Lords
affirmed the Court of Appeal on that issue generally.[4] That is however not to say
that a breach of the duty is not "a matter arising out of the contract" of insurance
for jurisdictional and procedural purposes.[5] It should be noted that the duty is
imposed on both the assured and the insurer; although the majority of cases tend
to be those where the insurer declines payment on the grounds of breach of the
duty of utmost good faith by the assured, it is indeed open to the assured to claim
that an insurer could likewise be in breach. In the Australian High Court case of
CGU Insurance v AMP Financial Planning [2007] H.C.A. 36, the court
considered that in the case of a professional indemnity policy, the insurer who
fails to make a timely decision on whether claims by third parties against the
insured person should be paid might in appropriate circumstances be held to be
in breach of the duty of utmost good faith. The court also added that a lack of
duty of good faith is not to be equated with dishonesty only, and considered that
regard should be had to both the assured's legitimate interests as well as the
insurer's interests. It may also require an insurer to act with commercial
standards of decency and fairness and those seeking relief must come with "clean
hands" in the sense. On this last point, Callinan and Heydon J.J. suggest that
even if there is conduct by the insurer which on its own could amount to a breach
of the duty of utmost good faith, the conduct of the assured also needs to be
examined and the issue looked at in the context of all of the circumstances to
decide if, in fact, there has been such a breach. There was however no
comprehensive definition—the categories of what constitutes a breach of utmost
good faith are not closed. It should however be noted that this view has not been
adopted in any English decisions.

As far as the Marine Insurance Act 1906 is concerned, s.17 provides that a
contract of marine insurance is a contract based on the utmost good faith and
where utmost good faith has not been observed, the contract may be avoided by
either party. The presumption is that where one party has been given inaccurate
or insufficient information, there is no consent upon which the contract could

---

[4] [1991] A.C. 249.
[5] e.g., for the purposes of art.5(1) EU Regulation on Jurisdiction and the Recognition and
Enforcement of Judgments in Civil and Commercial Matters 2000, the duty of utmost good faith is
treated as a matter arising out of the contract of insurance.

survive. Of course consent could also fail where there is a fundamental mistake as to the subject matter. This is however not common occurrence.

Where insufficient information is given, this is a case of nondisclosure. Where inaccurate information is given, we treat this as a case of misrepresentation. The former is governed by s.18 whilst the latter, by s.20. Section 18 provides that the assured must disclose to the insurer before the contract is concluded every material circumstance which is known to him. The assured is deemed to know every circumstance which in the ordinary course of business ought to be known by him. Section 20, on the other hand, states that every material representation made by the assured or his agent to the insurer during negotiations and before the contract is concluded must be true.

These provisions have one paradigm in common—the concept of materiality. **10–014**
Sections 18(2) and 20(2) state that

"every circumstance is material which would influence the judgment of a prudent insurer in fixing the premium, or determining whether he will take the risk".

Section 18(5) provides that the term "circumstance" includes any communication made to or information received by the insured. The materiality of a particular circumstance had to be judged when the risk had been placed (*Brotherton Aseguradora Colseguros SA* [2003] EWCA Civ 705). But what does "influence the judgment of a prudent insurer" mean?

In *Container Transport International Inc v Oceanus Mutual Underwriting Association (Bermuda)* [1984] 1 Lloyd's Rep. 476, CA; [1982] 2 Lloyd's Rep. 178, HC, Lloyd J. considered two possible interpretations to the clause. First, the circumstance will be material if it is one which the prudent insurer would wish to know of because it might have led him to decline the risk or to fix a higher premium. Secondly, it could be taken to mean that the circumstance is material only if it is one which would have led the prudent insurer so to act. Lloyd J. preferred the latter approach. The judge held that the nondisclosure must have decisively influenced the prudent insurer or have brought about a different decision on his part.

This was reversed by the Court of Appeal. Kerr L.J. held that the test must **10–015**
refer to whether the circumstance would have had an impact on the insurer's decision in taking the risk and not a decisive influence on his ultimate decision. Further, the test is to be applied on a hypothetical insurer and not the particular insurer in question. In so holding, His Lordship overruled his own judgment in *Berger & Light Diffusers Ltd v Pollock* [1973] 2 Lloyd's Rep. 442, where emphasis had been placed on the actual insurer's response to the circumstance. Closely linked with this notion is whether it should be proved that the insurer was in fact induced into offering cover on those terms. Parker L.J. set out the preferred test in these terms:

"The very choice of a prudent underwriter as the yardstick . . . indicates that the test intended was one which could sensibly be answered in relation to prudent underwriters in general. It is possible to say that prudent underwriters in general would consider a particular circumstance as bearing on the risk and exercising an influence on their judgment towards declining the risk or loading the premium. It is not possible to say, save in extreme cases, that prudent underwriters would have acted differently, because there is no absolute standard by which they would have acted in the first place or as to the precise weight they would give to the undisclosed circumstance".

From this it is clear that the insurer need not prove that he had actually been induced into the contract. But is it correct?

The matter came up to be considered by the House of Lords in *Pan Atlantic Insurance Co Ltd v Pine Top Insurance Co Ltd* [1995] 1 A.C. 501. The majority held that the although the "prudent insurer" in s.18 refers to a hypothetical insurer and that the "influence" need not be so decisive that a prudent insurer would have been led to accept the risk or change the premium, the insurer must show that he was in fact induced. This latter limb overrules the judgment of the Court of Appeal in *Container Transport International*. The new test has two components:

1. the objective element—the phrase "influencing the judgment of the prudent insurer" must clearly denote an effect on the thought process of the insurer in weighing up the risk. It is quite different from words which might have been used but were not, such as "influencing the insurer *to take* the risk". (per Lord Mustill) It might be useful to note Lord Templeman's (one of the minority) concern that with this line of approach, the insurer will be able to avoid a contract simply by adducing some "vague evidence" of influence.[6] This concern is countered by the requirement of the subjective element, i.e. the proof of actual inducement.

2. the subjective element—if misrepresentation or nondisclosure of a material fact did not in fact induce the contract then the underwriter is not entitled to rely on it as a ground for avoiding the contract. Although inducement is not expressly provided for in the MIA, the common law requirement of inducement up to 1906 must be deemed to have been codified by the Act.[7] Ordinary rules of misrepresentation at common law (not the Misrepresentation Act 1967) must apply to complement ss.18 and 20 (per Lord Mustill).

10–016   An illustration of the objective element might be seen in *Brotherton Aseguradora Colseguros SA* [2003] EWCA Civ 705. There, the insurer had agreed to provide professional indemnity insurance to a bank in Colombia. There had been press reports in Colombia about the probity of the bank's president. On the issue as to whether the insured should have disclosed that information to the insurer, the insured argued that there was no duty to disclose a rumour or allegation which if true would be material, unless it was also proved to be true. They had also adduced evidence before the High Court[8] to show that the reports about the bank's president were unfounded. The High Court held that the fact that the evidence produced showed that the allegations about the bank's president were untrue did not change the finding that the information (in the press reports) was not material. The material time for the test of materiality was the time of placement of the risk—at that time, the rumours were significant enough to

---

[6] McGee, "The proposer's duty of utmost good faith after *Pine Top*" (1995) 4 Insurance Law and Practice 95.

[7] Schoenbaum, "The duty of utmost good faith in marine insurance law: a comparative analysis of American and English Law" (1998) J.M.L.C. 1.

[8] Judgment of February 26, 2003.

warrant their disclosure. The Court of Appeal agreed with Moore-Bick J. and said that rumours or reports, so long as they were not "mere speculations, vague rumours" constitute material facts or circumstances which need to be disclosed. The Court of Appeal was also asked to follow the suggestion of Colman J. in *The Grecia Express* [2002] 2 Lloyd's Rep. 88 that the remedy of avoidance should not be granted where for reason or another it was inequitable or unconscionable for the insurer to rely on the nondisclosure. It refused, stating that avoidance, like rescission in the law of contract, takes place immediately following the breach without needing any intervention by the courts.[9] There is no authority for saying that the court retained some sort of equitable power of intervention to control the use of avoidance retrospectively. The court stressed

> "it would be an unsound step to introduce into UK law a principle of law that would enable an insured either not to disclose intelligence that a prudent insurer would regard as material or subsequently to resist avoidance by insisting on a trial . . . to investigate its correctness".[10]

North Star Shipping Ltd v Sphere Drake Insurance Plc [2006] EWCA Civ 378   **10–017**
Facts:
The North Star was a bulk carrier which was damaged by an underwater explosive device. The ship was insured under a war risk policy. The insurers refused to pay alleging, inter alia, nondisclosure of civil and criminal proceedings pending against the owners in Panama and Greece. The owners argued that expert evidence showed that moral hazard considerations played only a peripheral role in war risk insurance and had little practical significance. They subsequently also produced a letter from the Serious Fraud Office which showed that the one of the owners in question was in fact a victim of a fraud perpetrated by others (which was the subject of the proceedings in Panama and Greece). Colman J. however held that when the placement was made, the fact of civil and criminal proceedings in Panama and Greece would no doubt have an influence the decision of a prudent underwriter.
Held:
The problem was what is the correct response where there is no disclosure of an allegation of dishonesty which, at the time of placement, the assured says is false and which, after placement, turns out to be false. Waller L.J. thought that there was something unjust in the notion that insurers should be allowed avoid a policy in such circumstances. On the other hand, it is difficult to contradict an insurer who gives evidence that an allegation of fraud (whether proved or not) would have had an influence on his decision to underwrite the risk. Different judges have come to divergent conclusions on the issue. In *Reynolds and Anderson v Phoenix Assurance Co Ltd* [1978] 2 Lloyd's Rep. 440, an assured was held not have to disclose unproven allegations especially when the assured believed them to be false. But in *March Cabaret Club & Casino Ltd v The London Assurance* [1975] 1 Lloyd's Rep. 169, and *The Dora* [1989] 1 Lloyd's Rep. 69, the position was that unresolved allegations should be disclosed. Waller L.J. opined that an insurer was unlikely to spend much time considering the strength or otherwise of an allegation and, in many instances, would simply decide there was no smoke without fire.

These issues however did not affect the decision. The Court of Appeal unanimously held as this was a war risk cover, the allegations were not material. That said, the SFO

---

[9] See Soyer, "Insurance—pre-contractual duty of utmost good faith—material non-disclosure —right of avoidance" [2003] J.I.M.L. 427; Gay, "Non disclosure and avoidance: lies, damned lies and intelligence" [2004] L.M.C.L.Q. 1.

[10] See Rose, "Informational asymmetry and the myth of good faith: back to basis" [2007] L.M.C.L.Q. 181.

letter did not prove that the allegations were untrue. As evidence, it was therefore of little relevancy.

10–018   Although industry practice and expectations are clearly relevant to the objective element issue, it should not be assumed that just because the industry thinks it is good practice to disclose a particular fact, that would necessary be "material". In *Sealion Shipping v Valiant Insurance (The Toisa Pisces)* [2012] EWHC 50 (Comm), it was held that whilst disclosure of previous hull claims is good practice, in the present case they were not material to the hull and machinery policy. The materiality of the hull incidents was linked to the extent to which they caused loss of hire. The undisclosed event took place nearly four years before the policy with the insurers was entered into and was so insignificant (it did not result in a claim) that it could not be seen as material. The question of materiality thus depends on more than simply whether the fact is one routinely disclosed; it should also be relevant and significant.

As to the House of Lords' second requirement, the subjective element of inducement, it seems clear that the onus has shifted to the insurer to show an absence of consent. The presumption had always been that consent is properly provided for in the concept of good faith, that is to say, if it is proved that a material circumstance had been misrepresented or concealed the contract could be avoided without any further requirements. The House of Lords clearly evinces in *Pan Atlantic* that such a presumption is not only impractical but unjust to the assured. The *Pan Atlantic* rule that inducement must be proved might however be read with *St Paul Fire v McConnell Dowell* [1996] All E.R. 96 where the Court of Appeal held that the insurer can rely on a presumption of inducement by proving materiality. It is difficult to reconcile the two cases; it appears that while *Pan Atlantic* favours the assured, *St Paul Fire* adopts the contrary position. As a matter of evidence though, it might be suggested that in *St Paul Fire*, the inducement of the insurer in question could be presumed because actual inducement had been proved vis-à-vis the other three co-insurers involved.

In the controversial *Far Eastern Shipping Co Ltd v Scales Trading Ltd & Geo H Scales Ltd* [2001] All E.R. (Comm) 319 the Privy Council held, in an appeal from the New Zealand Court of Appeal, that where a trade guarantee agreement required full disclosure of material facts and the beneficiary had failed to make full disclosure, there was no room to argue that as the guarantor would have given the guarantee even if he was aware of the true position, he was not entitled to repudiate. There was no equitable rule allowing the court to exercise discretion to prevent the guarantor from exercising the right of repudiation. Although this is a decision of the Privy Council and is technically not binding in England and Wales, it carries much persuasive authority. It raises some doubt as to whether inducement needs to be proved where nondisclosure is made a strict duty and carries a right of repudiation for the "innocent" party. Naturally, it could be contended that no analogy can be drawn as this is a case involving a guarantee agreement and is therefore outside the purview of the Marine Insurance Act 1906. Nevertheless, it does raise the tantalising issue as to whether *Pan Atlantic* was correct to link actual inducement to the duty of disclosure.

10–019   The requirement of actual inducement may cause problems with evidence. It remains unclear which party is to bear the burden of proof in relation to inducement. In *Pan Atlantic*, Lord Mustill referred to a presumption of inducement resulting in a heavier burden on the insured to show that the insurer was not actually induced into making the contract. Indeed, in *St Paul's Fire &*

Marine Insurance the Court of Appeal presumed the inducement of one of the underwriters who had not given evidence in court. That case took place when *Pan Atlantic* was being decided, so we should not read too much into the "presumption" applied by the Court of Appeal but it serves to show how a problem with evidence can surface with the presumption of inducement approach. There can also be problems with proving what the actual insurer would have done if he had been aware of the circumstances not disclosed to them and the terms on which he would have been prepared to accept the risk.

The subject of consumer and business insurance law in the United Kingdom has been reviewed by various quarters, including the Law Commission. One of the proposals being seriously considered by the Commission is that other than actual inducement, the test of materiality should be one that asks "whether a reasonable insured would have considered the undisclosed matter to be material to a prudent insurer". This has the advantage of turning the lenses on the assured rather the insurer—given the problems of current formulation in *Pan Atlantic*, this more objective test makes it harder for insurers to claim the defence of utmost good faith to reject a claim. The Law Commission considers that the "reasonable insured test" is flexible to cope with variety of policyholders, including those in the marine, aviation and transport sectors. They also reason that in the more sophisticated markets, where both insurers and assured are professionally represented (say, by brokers), there is unlikely to be any real difference between the current test of the reasonable insurer compared with the proposed reasonable insured test.[11] Less satisfactory however is the provisional recommendation of the Law Commission that:

"In assessing what a reasonable insured in the circumstances would understand to be material to the underwriter in question, a court could also take into account whether the policyholder had received professional advice from an intermediary".[12]

This begs the question: what does "take into account" imply?

Excluding or limiting liability for breach of the duty of good faith

Notwithstanding the potency of the duty of good faith, it is possible for the **10–020** parties to agree to limit or exclude by contract the right to avoid the contract for a breach of the duty of good faith, including the duty of disclosure.[13] In *HIH Casualty and General Insurance Ltd v Chase Manhattan Bank* [2001] 1 All E.R. (Comm) 719, the Commercial Court went so far as to say that whilst as a matter of public policy the parties cannot exclude, by contract, liability for one of the

---

[11] See the Law Commission's Issues Paper 1: Misrepresentation and Non-Disclosure (September 2006) para.7.51 (*http://www.lawcom.gov.uk/docs/insurance_contact_law_issues_paper_1.pdf*); see also the Law Commission's Summary of Responses (October 2008) following the consultation on business insurance at *http://www.lawcom.gov.uk/docs/ICL_summary_of_responses_business-issues.pdf*

[12] See above, para.7.52.

[13] *Pan Atlantic Insurance Co Ltd v Pine Top Insurance Co Ltd* [1993] 1 Lloyd's Rep. 496; *Toomey v Eagle Star Insurance Co Ltd (No.2)* [1995] 2 Lloyd's Rep. 88.

parties' fraudulent misrepresentation inducing that contract of insurance, it is possible for a contractual clause to exclude a party's liability for the fraudulent misrepresentation of its agent. Such exclusion or limitation of liability clauses would be given effect to provided they are clearly drafted.

In *S Pearson & Son Ltd v Dublin Corporation* [1907] A.C. 351, the agent of Dublin Corporation, an engineer, supplied S. Pearson & Sons Limited with drawings which contained information about the existence and position of a certain wall. There was evidence that the engineer knew that the plans were false. Pearson entered into a contract to do sewage works; performed the contract but found that the plans were inaccurate, necessitating further work. Pearson sued the Dublin Corporation in deceit, claiming the cost of the additional work. The corporation relied on cl.43 of the contract which provided that the corporation did not hold itself responsible for the accuracy of the information as to the sections or foundations of existing walls; and that no charges for extra work or otherwise would be allowed in consequence of incorrect information or inaccuracies in the drawings or specifications. The House of Lords held that the Corporation could not rely on the clause in the event of proof of fraud by the engineer and the question of fact (fraud or not) had to go to the jury. Lord Loreburn L.C. stated that no one could escape from his own fraudulent statements "*by inserting a clause in a contract that the other party shall not rely upon them*". However His Lordship accepted that an innocent principal could "*guard himself by apt and express clauses from liability for the fraud of his own agents*". He considered that cl.43 was not effective to do that. So Lord Loreburn accepted that there could be clauses that exempted an innocent principal from liability for the fraud of his agent. However he then said that it would not matter whether the agent or the principal made the fraudulent statement. The Earl of Halsbury took this point up as the basis for the opposite view, i.e. that if the agent has committed fraud then liability for that cannot be excluded by contract. Lord Halsbury appears to conclude that, whether the fraud is that of the agent or the principal, it cannot be excluded by contract. Lord Ashbourne approached the matter as one of construction. Lord James of Hereford left open the issue of whether "*an express term that fraud shall not vitiate a contract would be bad in law*", although he inclined to the view that it would be so. Lord Atkinson stated that he was inclined to think that cl.43 would be "*illegal in point of law*". However, in one of the cases His Lordship relied upon, *Tunis v Jackson* [1892] 3 Ch. 441, Chitty J. had decided that parties to a building contract could expressly agree that a valuation certificate could not be set aside for the fraud of a third party, an architect. The judge then considered the clause as a matter of construction. The overall effect of the case is difficult to state. It would appear that the majority took the view that the issue of whether a clause in a contract can exclude liability or remedies for the fraud of an agent that has induced the contract containing the clause is a matter of construction. There is no public policy bar to such a clause, although there may well be a public policy bar to enforcing a clause that purports to exclude liability for the fraud of the principal party itself.[14]

---

[14] Support might also be drawn from *Boyd & Forrest v The Glasgow & South Western Railway* [1915] S.C. (HL) 20.

What to disclose

In general, material risks fall into two categories:

10–021

1. Physical hazard;
2. Moral hazard.

The physical hazard may be described as circumstances material to the subject matter insured, namely the goods in cargo insurance. For example, the packing of the goods, the quantity and condition of the goods, etc are all circumstances in the subject matter insured. The moral hazard on the other hand refers to the relationship between the assured and the subject matter insured as a matter of risk. For example where the assured is a convicted arsonist, the insurer will want to know that before accepting the risk. In *PCW Syndicates v PCW Reinsurers* [1996] 1 Lloyd's Rep. 241, the moral hazard in question turned on the dishonesty of the assured or his agents, as a material circumstance to be disclosed. In the law of non-marine insurance, the fact that the assured had been rejected by other insurers before was a material risk (*Glicksman v Lancashire & General Assurance Co Ltd* [1927] A.C. 139). In marine insurance though, it was held in the old case of *Glasgow Assurance Corp Ltd v Symondson & Co* (1911) 104 L.T. 254 that this was not material on the facts of the case.

In *Strive Shipping Corp v Hellenic Mutual War Risks Association (The Grecia Express)* [2002] EWHC 203, the insurer refused to pay on the basis that the assured had not disclosed the fact that the owner of the assured was complicit in the fraudulent sinking of his luxury yacht two months before the placement of the risk on the insured vessel. This was the first time the English court had come across a case on nondisclosure and scuttling. It was obvious that the fact of an assured's (or its owner's) role in a scuttling was a matter of moral hazard that needed to be disclosed. That indeed was conceded in this case; but the assured argued that there was actually no proof that its owner had any complicity in the sinking in the past. The court agreed that the assured should be protected from the serious allegation of the commission of a criminal offence. The standard of proof and the weight of evidence required in relation to the alleged scuttling should therefore be greater than that which would otherwise be required in an ordinary civil case. The defendant was unable to satisfy the court that on the evidence it was highly unlikely that the vessels were lost accidentally or that the evidence of complicity was strong enough to justify the serious conclusion of scuttling.[15] The defendant was unable to establish that the assured's owner had caused or connived at the casting away of his power boat. There was therefore no duty of disclosure. The case however does not quite make clear what type of allegations of misconduct or dishonesty should be disclosed—the test preferred by Colman J. is that it depended on the seriousness of the allegations. Where they are of a criminal nature, the weight of evidence had to be stronger than normal before disclosure could be compelled. The problem though is that insurers deal with the issue of risk not certainty—to them, the fact that there are allegations of dishonesty (serious or otherwise) would be a material issue. The balance is

---

[15] See Aitken, "Skeletons in the cupboard" (2004) Bus. L.R. 26 where the approach taken by the court is explained; and Midwinter, "The duty of disclosure and material rumours" (2003) L.M.C.L.Q. 158 on whether an insurer had a right to know about doubtful reports which might affect the level of risk to the moral risk of the insured.

difficult to achieve as between the right of the insurer to make a business decision taking into account all relevant risks and the right of the assured not to have its integrity questioned on the basis of mere allegations.

10–022   As far as the Act is concerned, s.18(3) provides that in the absence of inquiry, the following need not be disclosed:

(a) Any circumstance which diminishes the risk;

(b) Any circumstance which is known or presumed to be known to the insurer; (Note that the insurer is presumed to know matters of common notoriety or knowledge, and matters which an insurer in the ordinary course of his business, as such, ought to know.)

(c) Any information as to which information is waived by the insurer;

(d) Any circumstance which it is superfluous to disclose by reason of any express or implied warranty.

The interpretation and application of these provisions should be consistent with the spirit of good faith. Where a fact is material, the assured's duty to disclose arises. He should only be excused from disclosing where the material circumstance is so obvious and notorious to all that it falls within s.18(3). Where the fact though known is not known for its impact on the policy, the assured must still disclose. Thus in *Bates v Hewitt* (1867) L.R. 2 Q.B. 595, although the insured ship The Georgia was well known as a former Confederate vessel and this was known to the insurer, the assured's failure to disclose was not excusable. The duty of good faith is to be applied strictly. The insurer is not required to rely on his own devices, such as memory or reasoning to arrive at the knowledge of the material fact.

10–023

Provisional Proposals of the Law Commission

Disclosure should be a two-way process. The assured should make a fair presentation of the risk, and the insurer should make clear in appropriately worded questions what they are concerned to know in order to make a fair evaluation of the risk. There should be a burden on the insurer to make further enquiries if the information received reveals material gaps and concerns. Failure to do so should prevent the insurer from repudiating the contract on the basis of non-disclosure.

The Law Commission takes the view that avoidance in general is too harsh a remedy. They propose that avoidance only be available where the assured has acted dishonestly. Dishonesty is taken to connote deliberate or reckless behaviour. Where there is no dishonesty, the law should only be concerned with putting the insurer back to the position they would have been in had full and accurate information been provided by the insured. For example, if the insurer would have charged a higher premium had such information been available, then the assured should be required to pay the extra sums to bring the insurer back to where they would have been had they been given the appropriate information.

The parties to a business insurance contract should be allowed to contract out of these remedies as long as the contract purporting to do so is explicit and clear.

Source: *http://lawcommission.justice.gov.uk/consultations/business_disclosure.htm* [accessed April 13, 2013].

A waiver must be obvious or be communicated to the assured. Silence by the **10–024** insurer should not be taken at face value as a waiver. Whether there is a waiver depends on the circumstances of the case. In *New Hampshire Insurance Co v Oil Refineries Ltd* (April 10, 2002, Q.B.D.), the assured had taken out a liability insurance. The insurer required the insured to disclose their claims history for the period of August 1989 to July 1994. In early 1989 and late 1988, the assured was sued for damage caused to some 380 greenhouse flower growers. They did not disclose this fact to the insurer. The assured argued that as the claims history required by the insurer did not relate to late 1988 and early 1989, they had no duty to disclose. The court held that the claims history did not constitute the limit of the assured's duty to disclose. The obligation to disclose all material circumstances was an active one and silence on the part of the person seeking cover was not disclosure. Similarly, silence by an insurer in the face of silence by the assured could not be taken as a waiver. The waiver must relate specifically (directly or indirectly) to the fact in question; in the case of the insurer's silence, that is not readily established.

The insurer's conduct in the light of general usage and trade practice is central in establishing whether there has been a waiver on his part so as to allow the assured to plead s.18(3)(c). This is an objective test as applied in *L'Alsacienne Premiere Société Alsacienne v Unistorebrand International Insurance AS* [1995] L.R.L.R. 333. In that case, Rix J. held, on the assumption that there was an insurance contract, that the insurer had waived their right to disclosure under s.18(3)(c). The court found that they were aware of an underwriting agency agreement and instead of making inquiries as a prudent insurer would, they had accepted the risk without investigating the erroneous business portfolio as presented. A fortiori, the information was easily accessible and had not been deliberately concealed. They must therefore bear the consequences of their carelessness and neglect.

Although the insurers very often deal in an international arena, the fact that certain material information might be widely available at a particular locality does not necessarily lead to the conclusion that they would be deemed to be aware of such information. In *Brotherton Aseguradora Colseguros SA* [2003] EWHC 1741, Morison J. considered that allegations about the impropriety of the insured's president, although widely reported by the Colombian press, could not be deemed to be within the general and common knowledge of an underwriter in England.

In *Marc Rich & Co AG (now Glencore International AG) v Portman* [1997] 1 **10–025** Lloyd's Rep. 225, the Court of Appeal was persuaded to consider finding a waiver of disclosure where the material information was easily accessible. In that case the underwriters of a demurrage cover (i.e. an insurance cover providing cover for any risk of liability arising from any delays caused to the ship) relied on the following nondisclosures:

1. any demurrage claims made or paid by them to other shipowners for vessels performing that voyage in the past;

2. the particular features of the port of Ain Sukna which were likely to cause delays (for example, difficult tides, bad weather, congestion, etc);

3. the fact that the average turnaround time at that port was exceptionally lengthy (exceeding six days); and

4. the fact that the charterparties concerned did not the underwriters to recover demurrage from shippers or operators.

The assured on the other hand argued that the underwriters had waived the necessity of such disclosure since, in general terms, such information was obviously and to the knowledge of the underwriters available to them and could have been requested by them. It was claimed that an underwriter who insures a risk within a particular industry ought to know or find out the practices of the industry or trade, and that the matters which are in general well known by persons in that trade. It was further submitted that if an underwriter is writing a class of business he should be conversant with the course of losses affecting the types of risk which fall within that class, although he cannot be presumed to know about particular losses which specially affect particular insured persons. This submission was based on the principle set out by Rowlatt J. in *North British Fishing Boat Insurance Co Ltd v Starr* (1922) 13 Ll. L. Rep. 206:

> "I must look at the underwriter in this case as a person doing the business of insuring ships and as necessarily conversant with the course of losses affecting particular classes of ships. What he is not bound to know in the ordinary course of his business are particular circumstances specially affecting ships or lines of ships, and specially affecting some limited number of ships".

They further argued that their nondisclosures had made no difference to insurers who would have written the risk in any event and were not induced to enter the contract of insurance by the nondisclosures.

10–026   The Court of Appeal gave judgment to the underwriters and stated that the assured's duty of disclosure is strict, and except in matters that the underwriter is bound to know, he may abstain absolutely from asking questions and may leave the assured to fulfil his duty of good faith and to make full disclosure without being asked. In that case, nothing about the assured's loss experience was of common notoriety or knowledge. There was nothing about the circumstances of the voyage and the port which an insurer in the ordinary course of his business, as such, ought to know.

As far as the alleged waiver is concerned, the Court of Appeal applied Parker L.J.'s formula in *CTI v Oceanus*:

> "In order to establish waiver by implication from non-enquiry of the facts by the underwriters, the insurer must be put on enquiry by the disclosure of facts which would raise in the mind of a reasonable insurer at least a suspicion that there were other circumstances which would or might vitiate the presentation made to him".

There could be no waiver in the present case where the underwriter was being shown a risk for the first time and had no idea that there was a history of losses due to demurrage liability. In *Greenhill v Federal Insurance Co Ltd* [1927] 1K.B. 65 the trite rule is that there could be no waiver merely because the insurer was aware of the possibility of the existence of other material circumstances.

> "If this is permitted, the duty of disclosure would be emasculated to the point of extinction and waiver would become an instrument of fraud",

according to Parker L.J.

Where there are unusual facts, for example, where the port is subject to delays **10–027** lengthier than similar ports or that the charterparty contained a no-recourse clause against shippers for demurrage, it cannot be said that the insurer is on notice so as to put him on enquiry. The presentation of the risk made by the assured to the underwriter must be fair before it could be properly said that the insurer might be put on notice to make enquiries. A presentation, according to Waller L.J. in *Marc Rich & Co*, cannot be fair if there is silence as to material particulars not commonly known.

In *WISE Underwriting Ltd v Grupo Nacional Provincial SA* [2004] EWCA Civ 962, it was emphasised that where waiver is claimed, it required the making out of a clear case. It could not be established merely by proving that a prudent insurer would, by enquiry, have elicited the fact in question. In that case, the assured attempted to avoid the policy on the ground that there had been nondisclosure of material information. The assured had omitted, it would appear by an accident of translation, the fact that the goods insured were clocks when they were actually Rolex watches. The assured argued that the insurer had waived any disclosure about the watches as they had been put on enquiry by information in other documents presented to them which clearly indicated that watches were being shipped. By a majority, the Court of Appeal held that waiver had not been established.

It was obvious that the information was material and should have been properly disclosed. The fact that an insurer was entitled to assume that the presentation of the risk to him was a fair presentation meant that he must be entitled to take at face value what was said to him. In the present case, the insurer was entitled therefore to assume that he was being told what the particularly valuable items to be carried were. A presumption of a fair presentation of risk must suggest, if anything, that the insurer would be put off enquiry rather than on enquiry. The lower court was right to hold, on the facts, that the use of the word "clocks" should not have raised suspicion in the mind of the reasonable insurer that there were other circumstances which would or might vitiate the presentation of the risk.

The general view is that an insurer can limit the duty of disclosure by the **10–028** questions it asks in a proposal form. Where the questions are confined to a particular subject or a particular context, an inference might be made that the insurer has waived his right to related information. For instance, details of accidents within the last three years are asked for in the form, the insurer could be taken as having waived details of accidents outside that time range. The test is whether a reasonable man would be justified in thinking that the insurer had made such a limitation or constraint in the form. Much depends on the construction of the proposal form (*Hair v The Prudential Assurance Co Ltd* [1983] 2 Lloyd's Rep. 667). Given that the questions on the form are prepared by the insurers, the courts will thus not hesitate to use the contra proferentem rule against them where the wording is ambiguous (*R&R developments v AXA Insurance* [2009] EWHC 2429 (Ch)) but it should not be forgotten that the court's duty is not "to punish insurers guilty of unclear and inaccurate wording as to find out . . . what the parties intended to say". (*Doheny v New India Assurance Co Ltd* [2004] EWCA Civ 1705, per Longmore L.J.)

Misrepresentation

10–029   Misrepresentation goes to the heart of consent and consumes it. The failure to provide accurate information destroys the basis on which the marine policy, and indeed ordinary contracts are built. Section 20 provides that every material representation made by the assured or his agent during negotiations must be true. The insurer may avoid the contract if the material representation turns out to be false. The limit on this rule is that the representation must be material. Materiality is to be determined in the same way as in the preceding paragraphs.

Section 20(3) provides that a representation may be either a representation as to a matter of fact or as to a matter of expectation or belief. However, they are to be treated differently under the Act. Where the representation is only a matter of expectation or belief, it is unimpeachable as long as it was made in good faith (s.20(5)). That section deems an honest representation as to a matter of expectation or belief to be true and this leaves no room for an implied representation that that there were reasonable grounds for that belief (*Economides v Commercial Union* [1998] Lloyd's Rep. IR 9). There must, however, be *some* basis for the representation before it can be said to be made in good faith (*Rendall v Combined Insurance Co* [2005] EWHC 678). In general, valuation of the subject matter by the insured would be treated as a matter of opinion. In *Eagle Star Insurance Co Ltd v Games Video* [2004] EWHC 15[16] the assured had known all along that the vessel's value was no more than $150,000 but nonetheless insured her for £1,800,000. It was considered that where the valuation is excessive so as to constitute the risk speculative, that can be evidence of a lack of good faith or genuine belief in the opinion. However, the burden of proof is on the insurer to show that there was a lack of good faith. The insurer succeeded in doing so by adducing evidence of documents which had been concocted by the assured falsely to represent the value of the vessel. A representation as to fact is true only if it is substantially correct, that is to say, if the difference between what is represented and what is actually correct would not be considered material by a prudent insurer.

In *Dennistoun v Lillie* (1821) 3 Bli. 202, the assured had made a representation to the insurer on June 18 that the ship would sail on May 1. Unknown to him, the ship had actually set sail on April 23. The House of Lords held that the insurers were entitled to avoid the marine policy on the basis that the statement was a representation of fact not of expectation or belief. Contrast this with *Bowden v Vaughan* (1809) 10 Ea. 415. There, the assured's statement as to the future date of shipment was held to be a representation of expectation only since the assured, as the cargo owners, had no control over when the ship will sail.

10–030   In general law, negligent misrepresentation could lead to the rescission of a contract. The MIA is silent as to the effect of negligence on representations of expectation or belief. The issue depends largely on whether the good faith principle underlining s.20 encompasses lack of negligence. Where negligence is looked upon as a breach of duty to one's neighbour, it might be possible to suggest that that should indicate a breach of the good faith principle. This

---

[16] See Soyer (2004) J.I.M.L. 127.

approach, it is submitted, should bring the law on misrepresentation in marine insurance in line with that of general contracts.

As far as a claim in damages is concerned, the Misrepresentation Act 1967 is particularly relevant. Up until the Law Reform Committee recommendations in 1962,[17] the common law rule was that damages were recoverable for misrepresentation only if it had been made fraudulently or if it was made in breach of a relationship of confidence.[18] The ensuing recommendation was that damages should be recoverable even where the misrepresentation was innocent unless the misrepresentor could show that he believed the representation to be true and had reasonable grounds for his belief.[19] This was soon made into law—s.2 of the Misrepresentation Act 1967 provides that where a person has entered into a contract after a misrepresentation has been made to him by another party and as a result thereof he has suffered loss, then, if the person making the misrepresentation would be liable to damages in respect thereof had the misrepresentation been made fraudulently, that person shall be liable notwithstanding that the misrepresentation was not made fraudulently, unless he proves that he had reasonable grounds to believe and did believe up to the time the contract was made that the facts represented were true. This so-called "fiction of fraud" means that damages shall be assessed on the basis of fraud or deceit (that is to say, as a head of damages under tort law and not contract law) as was clearly set out in *Royscot Trust Ltd v Rogerson* [1991] 3 All E.R. 294 by the Court of Appeal. The measure for damages for the tort of deceit and for breach of contract are different; damages for deceit are not awarded on the basis that the claimant is to be put in as good a position as if the statement had been true, they are to be assessed on a basis which would compensate the claimant for all the loss he has suffered, so far as money can achieve it. That would suggest that not only could foreseeable losses be recovered, but unforeseeable losses as well.[20] Negligent misrepresentation on the other hand carries its own measure of damages—in *Hedley Byrne & Co Ltd v Heller & Parters Ltd* [1964] A.C. 465, which is based on the principle of foreseeable loss.[21]

In *Avon Insurance Plc v Swire Fraser Ltd* [2000] C.L.C. 665 the claimants, stop loss insurers[22] of Lloyd's names for the 1990 and 1991 years of account,

---

[17] Law Reform Committee (10th Report (Innocent Misrepresentation) Cmnd 1782 (1962).

[18] On fraud, see *Derry v Peek* (1889) 14 App. Cas. 337 and on fiduciary relationships, see *Nocton v Ashburton* [1914] A.C. 932.

[19] Law Reform Committee Report p.334.

[20] It should however be noted that although Balcombe L.J. held in *Royscot* that the loss did not have to be foreseeable for it to be recoverable, His Lordship curiously went on to say: "the [misrepresentor] should reasonably have foreseen the possibility that the customer might wrongfully sell the car". See also Hooley, "Damages and the Misrepresentation Act 1967" (1991) 107 L.Q.R. 547 for more general criticisms of the case.

[21] See also *South Australia Asset Management Corp v York Montagu Ltd* [1996] 3 W.L.R. 87 and *Smith New Court Securities Ltd v Citibank NA* [1996] 3 W.L.R. 1051. These cases however left undecided the question of innocent misrepresentation under the 1967 Act. The only real authority on innocent misrepresentation is thus *Royscot Trust Ltd v Rogerson* [1991] 3 All E.R. 294.

[22] Personal stop loss (or PSL) policies are a type of stop loss policy specifically designed for Lloyd's names under which they can protect themselves against their net underwriting losses for a given underwriting year (or in respect of their aggregate losses over a three-year period). They are generally written on an excess of loss basis. In *Society of Lloyd's v Robinson* [1999] 1 W.L.R. 756 Lord Steyn described them as: " . . . a form of reinsurance which reinsures aggregate losses of a [name's] underwriting in a given year and indemnifies [the name] in respect of a certain limit . . . ".

claimed damages under s.2(1) of the Misrepresentation Act 1967 in respect of certain losses allegedly suffered as a result of having made binding arrangements with the defendant insurance brokers. Rix J. held that there was some room for the exercise of judgment and a misrepresentation should not be too easily found and a broad approach should be taken. The court refused "to chop into small slices the representation, and turn up the microscope to investigate each slice". In order to establish the inaccuracy of a representation it would be preferable that the matter is looked at more broadly. A fortiori, it may be that the smaller the slice, even on the assumption of materiality, the weaker is the inference of inducement. On the facts, no misrepresentation was proved using the "truth" test in s.20(4) MIA 1906. Thus a representation may be true without being entirely correct, provided it is substantially correct and the difference between what is represented and what is actually correct would not have been likely to induce a reasonable person in the position of the claimants to enter into the contracts.

10–031   A result of this piece-meal historical development of the law on damages for misrepresentation is that tests developed for one situation may not operate adequately or fairly in another situation. Another result is that the inadequacy of existing remedies at any one time to deal with the pressure of facts in one case may have led to the development of doctrine which may not operate as well in different circumstances and against the background of a wider range of remedies.

An overriding duty on section 17?

10–032   In *Manifest Shipping Co Ltd v Uni-Polaris Insurance Co Ltd (The Star Sea)* [2001] 2 W.L.R. 170, the issue of whether s.17 had an autonomous application outside ss.18–20 and to what extent it could apply *after* the contract of insurance had been made. In that case, the Star Sea was one of three vessels owned by the claimants but managed by K. The other two vessels had been damaged by fire aboard at separate occasions, the result of a deficient firefighting system operated by K. The Star Sea herself was badly damaged by fire owing to the same problems. The assured made a claim under their marine policy with the defendants. The defendants resisted the claim and sought to avoid the policy on the basis that the claimants were in breach of their duty of good faith by failing to disclose the deficient firefighting system or alternatively, by culpably misleading them by

> "impliedly representing that they were unaware of any significant deficiencies in the fire fighting system or the condition of the fire and safety equipment on those ships".

Fraud was not pleaded.

At the Court of Appeal, although Tuckey J.'s conclusion that the s.17 duty came to an end when court proceedings began was rejected as not representing the law, the appellate judges arrived at the same conclusion for different reasons that the defendants could not rely s.17. The Court of Appeal held that at the claim stage, and after the claim had been made, the s.17 duty required no more than that the claim should not be made, or persisted in, fraudulently:

> "When the assured makes his claim, the duty of utmost good faith requires that it should not be made fraudulently; and we are prepared to contemplate that the

duty not to present a fraudulent claim subsumes a duty not to prosecute a claim fraudulently in litigation. There is no need to demand more of the assured than that, if the Draconian remedy is to apply."[23]

The issues before the House of Lords were thus:

1. the duration of the s.17 duty—does it continue beyond the making of the claim and the issue of court proceedings prosecuting the claim?

2. the content of the duty at the claim stage and thereafter—was the Court of Appeal right in confining the duty to a duty to refrain from the fraudulent presentation or prosecution of a claim and, more particularly, can the matters on which the insurers rely suffice to constitute a breach of the assured's s.17 duty?

There is a line of authorities suggesting that s.17 does operate post contractually[24]—the answer to question 1. is therefore that there is a continuing duty of good faith post contract. It is the content of that duty which is not clear. **10–033**

(a) A duty not to make fraudulent claims?   It is clear that there is a duty on **10–034**
the assured not to make a fraudulent claim. In *Goulstone v Royal Ins Co* (1858) 1 F.&F. 276, which concerned a fire policy and a plea that the claim was fraudulently exaggerated, Pollock C.B. directed the jury that if the claim "was wilfully false in any substantial respect", they should find for the defendant as the claimant had in that case "forfeited all benefit under the policy". A common fraudulent claim is one where the claim is made on a policy which had been taken out only after the loss or damage had arisen (*Joseph Fielding Properties (Blackpool) v Aviva* [2010] EWHC 2192 (QB)). In *Britton v Royal Ins. Co* (1866) 4 F.&F. 905, also a fire insurance case where it was alleged that the assured was making a fraudulent claim, Willes J. directed the jury:

"The law upon such a case is in accordance with justice, and also with sound policy. The law is, that a person who has made such a fraudulent claim could not be permitted to recover at all. The contract of insurance is one of perfect good faith on both sides, and it is most important that such good faith should be maintained. It is the common practice to insert in fire policies conditions that they shall be void in the event of a fraudulent claim; and there was such a condition in the present case. Such a condition is only in accord with legal principle and sound policy. It would be most dangerous to permit parties to practise such frauds, and then, notwithstanding their falsehood and fraud, to recover the real value of the goods consumed. And if there is wilful falsehood and fraud in the claim, the insured forfeits all claim whatever upon the policy. This, therefore, was an independent defence; quite distinct from that of arson".

---

[23] [1997] 1 Lloyd's Rep. 360 at 371.
[24] The House of Lords cited *Cory v Patton* (1872) 7 Q.B. 304, *Niger Co Ltd v The Guardian Assurance Co Ltd* (1922) Ll. Rep. 75, *Britton v Royal Insurance Co* (1866) 4 F.&F. 905, *Orakpo v Barclays Insurance Services* [1995] L.R.L.R. 443, *Galloway v Guardian Royal Exchange (UK) Ltd* [1999] Lloyd's Rep. I.R. 209 amongst others.

When a fraudulent claim is made, what are the legal consequences? There are three possible solutions:

1. the fraudulent claim might be treated as a breach of the post-contractual duty of utmost good faith entitling the insurer to avoid the policy from the beginning[25] (so that all claims paid under the policy could be recovered by the insurer);

2. adhere to normal contract law and proceed on the basis of a repudiation of contract (*The Captain Panagos DP* [1986] 2 Lloyd's Rep. 511) and possibly, for breach of a warranty under the policy; or

3. use a special, common law rule for dealing with such claims as is favoured by Lord Hobhouse in *The Star Sea*.

On this third approach, it would mean that the entire claim would be treated as void even if part of it was actually genuine. Lord Hobhouse said:

"The law will not allow an insured who has made a fraudulent claim to recover. The logic is simple. The fraudulent insured must not be allowed to think: if the fraud is successful, then I will gain; if it is unsuccessful, I will lose nothing".

10–035   A similar approach is seen in Mance L.J.'s judgment in *Agapitos v Agnew* [2002] EWCA Civ 247. The consequences would be that the insurer would be able to reclaim all sums paid out in ignorance of the fraud, including sums relating to the genuine part of the claim (*Direct Line Insurance v Khan* [2002] Lloyd's Rep. 364).

If the juridical basis for legal remedies lies solely in s.17, this would mean that the insurer would only be entitled to avoid the contract in its entirety. There would be no entitlement to sue for damages. Hence, in *Axa General Insurance v Gottlieb* [2005] EWCA Civ 112, Mance L.J. giving the lead judgment considered that the most appropriate way to deal with fraudulent insurance claims is under the special common law rule, rather than as a breach of the duty of utmost good faith.

As to the juridical bases, it might thus be concluded that the duty not to make a fraudulent claim has been characterised:

(a)   as an implied term of the contract (*Orakpo v Barclays Insurance Services Co Ltd* [1994] C.L.C. 373);

(b)   as a breach of s.17, (*The Mercandian Continent*) [2001] EWCA Civ 1275; and

(c)   as a stand-alone common law rule, based on public policy (*Agapitos v Agnew (No.1) (The Aegeon)* [2003] Q.B. 556.).

The current position of the law is that although forfeiture of the claim is the correct remedy to the making of a fraudulent claim, the question as to the right

---

[25] The House of Lords has severely criticised the idea that an insurer may avoid the contract from the start, without definitely deciding that the clear words of s.17 do not apply. (*The Star Sea* [2001] 2 W.L.R. 170; also see Law Commission's Issues Paper No.7, July 2010).

juridical basis for this remedy remains open. That said, the Law Commission does not see this open-ended controversy to cause any practical problems and does not recommend any introduction of legislation to address this question.[26] However, it does consider that forfeiture should not be the only remedy.

At common law, there are however two points on which the scope of the law **10–036** rule is not entirely clear. The first is whether a claim, which is honestly believed in when initially presented, may become fraudulent for the purposes of the rule, if the insured subsequently realises that it is exaggerated, but continues to maintain it. The second is whether the fraud must relate, in some narrow sense, to the subject matter of the claim, or may go to any aspect of its validity, including therefore a defence. Although the first point was left open by Lord Scott in *The Star Sea*, there appears to be good reason to reject, on the basis of fraud, such a claim under the policy. As Mance L.J. said in *Agapitos v Agnew* [2002] EWCA Civ 247:

"[A]s a matter of principle, it would be strange if an insured who thought at the time of his initial claim that he had lost property in a theft, but then discovered it in a drawer, could happily maintain both the genuine and the now knowingly false part of his claim, without risk of application of the rule".

As to the second point, a claim should not be regarded as valid, if there is a known defence to it which the insured deliberately suppresses. To that extent, at least, fraud in relation to a defence should fall within the fraudulent claim rule.

There is a distinction between making a fraudulent claim and using fraudulent devices to further a claim.[27] In *Agapitos*, the assured had embellished his claim under the insurance but it subsequently transpired that he nonetheless had a good claim. The question was thus whether the insurer could avoid the contract of insurance ab initio and not make payment as a result of the use of fraudulent devices by the assured. Mance L.J. said:

"The view could, in this situation, be taken that, where fraudulent devices or means have been used to promote a claim, that by itself is sufficient to justify the application of the sanction of forfeiture. The insured's own perception of the value of the lie would suffice. Probably, however, some limited objective element is also required. The requirement, where a claim includes a non-existent or exaggerated element of loss, that that element must be not immaterial, "unsubstantial" or insignificant in itself offers a parallel. In the context of use of a fraudulent device or means, one can contemplate the possibility of an obviously irrelevant lie—one which, whatever the insured may have thought, could not sensibly have had any significant impact on any insurer or judge. Tentatively, I would suggest that the courts should only apply the fraudulent claim rule to the use of fraudulent devices or means which would, if believed, have tended, objectively but prior to any final determination at trial of the parties' rights, to yield a not insignificant improvement in the insured's prospects—whether they be prospects of obtaining a settlement, or a better settlement, or of winning at trial".

---

[26] Law Commission's Issues Paper No.7 (July, 2010).
[27] per Longmore L.J. *The Mercandian Continent* [2001] EWCA Civ 1275.

10-037   The judge's hesitation is understandable. The dicta recognise the fallibility of human nature to embellish a case in a dispute but at the same time, try to be true to principle. The judgment achieves this by first making it plain that as far as principle is concerned, the fraudulent claim rule should apply to the furtherance of a claim using fraudulent devices, and secondly, that some requirement of materiality or proportionality should be applied. Nonetheless, in order to achieve such a delicate balance, commercial certainty had to be compromised to some degree.

10-038   **(b) A continuing general duty of disclosure?**   In *The Star Sea* [2001] 2 W.L.R. 170, the House of Lords endorsed the view that there was no breach of the s.17 duty for the assured to fail to disclose facts within his knowledge which, if disclosed, might have induced the insurer to terminate the policy. Authority is derived from *Cory v Patton* (1872) 7 Q.B. 304 which established the general proposition that the duty on the assured to disclose a fact material to the risk being undertaken by the insurer does not continue after the assured has become bound by the insurance contract and *Niger Co Ltd v Guardian Assurance Co Ltd* (1922) 13 L.I.L.R. 75 where the House of Lords held that no duty lay on the assured to disclose to the insurers post-contract facts which, if known, might have induced the insurer to exercise its right to terminate the contract. Viscount Sumner said this:

> "The object of disclosure being to inform the underwriter's mind on matters immediately under his consideration, with reference to the taking or refusing of a risk then offered to him, I think it would be going beyond the principle to say that each and every change in an insurance contract creates an occasion on which a general disclosure becomes obligatory, merely because the altered contract is not the unaltered contract, and therefore the alteration is a transaction as the result of which a new contract of insurance comes into existence. This would turn what is an indispensable shield for the underwriter into an engine of oppression against the assured".

In the same case at the Court of Appeal, Bankes L.J. had commented:

> "[I]f people enter into contracts of insurance for long periods, it would be a wise precaution to insert some provision requiring notice to be given them if the nature of the risk does alter or vary appreciably".[28]

It was argued in *New Hampshire Insurance Co v MGN Ltd* [1997] L.R.L.R. 24 that where under a policy there was continuing cover subject to a right on the insurers to cancel on notice, an obligation of disclosure lay on the assured and extended to facts relevant to a decision by the insurer whether or not to cancel. Potter J., at first instance, described it as "an unwarranted extension of the principle of disclosure". The Court of Appeal too rejected the submission. These

---

[28] The Court of Appeal's judgment is reported in (1921) 6 L.I.L.R. 239. These two decisions were followed in New South Wales by Rogers J. in *NSW Medical Defence Union Ltd v Transport Industries Insurance Co Ltd* (1985) 4 N.S.W.L.R. 107 where the judge affirmed that it was not a breach of the continuing duty of good faith for an assured to fail to volunteer to the insurer information material to whether the assured would exercise a right to give notice terminating the contract.

authorities make clear that the content of the duty of good faith owed by an assured post-contract is not the same as the duty owed in the pre-contract stage.

(c) A continuing duty not to act in a culpable manner? It was argued **10–039** before the Court of Appeal and Tuckey J. that the post-contractual duty of utmost good faith must extend beyond the mere proscription against making a fraudulent claim to the duty not to make *culpable* misrepresentation or nondisclosure. Authority for this proposition was taken from Hirst J.'s dicta in *The Litsion Pride* [1985] 1 Lloyd's Rep. 437

> " . . . in contrast to the pre-contract situation, the precise ambit of the duty in the claims context has not been developed by authorities, indeed no case had been cited . . . where it has been considered outside the fraud context in relation to claims. It must be right, I think . . . to go so far as to hold that the duty in the claims sphere extends to *culpable* misrepresentation or non-disclosure" (emphasis added).

In *The Litsion Pride*, the vessel was insured against war risks but, in the event of the vessel sailing to certain specified destinations, the insurers could exact an additional premium at their discretion. The time was the Gulf War. Bandar Khomeini in the Persian Gulf was, it was agreed, the most dangerous port in the Gulf. A voyage there was bound to attract an additional premium at a very high rate. The vessel sailed to Bandar Khomeini without notification being given to the insurers. It came under attack and sank. A letter purporting to pre-date the voyage and to give notice of the vessel's destination was concocted by the assured in order to deceive the insurers into believing that the failure to give notice of the voyage before its commencement was due to an innocent oversight. Hirst J. held that the falsely dated letter was a fraud directly connected to the claim *and* a breach of the s.17 duty of utmost good faith. Given these circumstances, the Court of Appeal in *The Star Sea* felt that Hirst J.'s statement should not be taken as a statement of principle. Indeed, the word "culpable" used by Hirst J. should, according to the Court of Appeal, be read as "fraudulent" and should not be given any other connotations. The House of Lords agreed with the Court of Appeal:

> "[Hirst J.'s statement] should not any longer be treated as a sound statement of the law. In so far as it decouples the obligation of good faith both from s.17 and the remedy of avoidance and from the contractual principles which would apply to a breach of contract it is clearly unsound . . . . In so far as it is based upon the principle of the irrecoverability of fraudulent claims, the decision is questionable upon the facts since the actual claim made was a valid claim for a loss which had occurred and had been caused by a peril insured against when the vessel was covered by a held covered clause".

The House of Lords went on to say that, at most, only a general requirement that the assured should act honestly when presenting a claim could be implied. Some reliance was place on *The Michael* [1979] 2 Lloyd's Rep. 1. In that case, a claim under a policy of marine insurance had been presented honestly. But after the claim had been presented the assured became aware, or had grounds to suspect, that the loss of the insured vessel had been caused not, as had been thought, by perils of the seas, but by scuttling. This information had not been passed on to the insurers. The insurers' reliance on this nondisclosure to avoid the policy failed on the facts. The court was not prepared to find or infer that the claim, honestly presented, had subsequently been dishonestly maintained. Roskill L.J. said:

"As to the allegation of subsequently maintaining a fraudulent claim, [the assured] are not to be found guilty of fraud merely because, with the wisdom of hindsight, they had information which might, if appreciated at its true value, have led them to the truth at an earlier date. A plaintiff in litigation is not maintaining a fraudulent claim merely because during interlocutory proceedings he or his solicitors become aware of evidence which may militate against the correctness of the plaintiff's case and its likelihood of ultimate success. The relevant test must be honest belief".

10–040   Additionally, the requirement of honesty should not be applied without specific reference to the issue of materiality because it would be severely unjust to allow the insurer to resort to the Draconian remedy of repudiation regardless of the materiality of the misrepresentations or nondisclosures alleged. This is consistent with Rix J.'s concerns in *Royal Boskalis Westminster NV v Mountain* [1997] L.R.L.R. 523 that the post-contractual duty of good faith could extend beyond fraud to some unspecified degree of culpability. On the facts of that case he found that "non-fraudulent but culpable and deliberate misrepresentation and non-disclosure have been proved, albeit they were subsequently repented of and remedied". He held that the insurers had failed to establish that the misrepresentations and nondisclosures had been material and that the insurers were not entitled under s.17 to avoid the policy.

But what is to be the yardstick by which materiality is assessed? Lord Scott of Foscote seems to take the view that assistance might be drawn from the civil procedure rule on the discovery of documents that

"a document, which, it is not unreasonable to suppose, may tend either to advance the case of the party seeking discovery, or to damage the case of his adversary"

should be disclosed (*Compagnie Financiere et Commerciale du Pacifique v Peruvian Guano Co* (1882), 60 11 Q.B.D. 55, 60). In short, a fact is material if it is "determinative of any issue in the claim". While this test is consistent with the growing insistence of the courts to prevent the avoidance of insurance policies on the flimsiest of reasons as very radically espoused in *Pan Atlantic*, its scope is by no means clear. Does it, for instance, require some degree of inducement? If it does, is it merely an objective test or should it require a subjective element as well?

The Mercandian Continent [2001] EWCA Civ 1275 is useful reminder of how materiality should be taken into account. The assured were a firm of ship repairers and they were found liable to a shipowner for repairs carried out. The assured made a claim on their liability policy. The shipowners brought proceedings in England on the basis of a jurisdiction agreement signed by the assured's employee. The assured then forged a document which they used to challenge jurisdiction but the forgery was actually ineffectual. The forgery was soon discovered. The insurers sought to avoid the policy on the basis of the breach of the duty of utmost good faith. It is obvious that the use of the forged document was dishonest but it was equally clear that the forgery did not contribute to any perversion of justice. Atkin J. at first instance held that there was no breach of the duty of utmost good faith unless the fact "deliberately and culpably" concealed or misrepresented was legally relevant to the claim itself, not some collateral matter.[29]

The Court of Appeal, in dismissing the appeal by the insurer, considered that **10–041** although there was a continuing duty of utmost good faith, that did not mean that the insurer was not justified in avoiding the contract in every case of non-observance of good faith by the insured. Before a contract could be avoided, the fact misrepresented or not disclosed must be material for a prudent underwriter to know when he was assessing the risk and must have induced the actual underwriter to write the risk. Those requirements of materiality and inducement must also apply, making due allowance for the change of context, in cases of post-contract lack of good faith. That required the insurer to show that the fraud was material in that it would have an effect on the underwriter's ultimate liability and the gravity of the fraud or its consequences must be such as would enable the insurer to terminate the contract, if he so wished. The court considered that on the facts it would be totally and absurdly disproportionate that the insurer be allowed to avoid the insurance policy. That too was the view of the court in *Agapitos v Agnew* [2002] EWCA Civ 247 although the Court of Appeal in that case was careful to add that it would be difficult to require proof of actual inducement; preferring to confine materiality to the requirement that "the part of the claim which is non-existent or exaggerated should not itself be immaterial or unsubstantial". In *Agapitos*, it was held that where the assured gives a false statement to embellish or improve the claim, there are two tests that should be met before the claim could be defeated. The false statement must be related to the claim, intended to improve the prospects of the claim and, if believed by the insurer, capable of giving a not insignificant improvement in the prospects of the claim. The second limb appears highly subjective, thus, proof can be very difficult.

On the issue of inducement, it was held in *Danepoint Ltd v Underwriting Insurance Ltd* [2005] EWHC 2318 that for the exaggerated claim to be treated as fraudulent it needs to be shown that the insurer had been induced to pay the assured. Hence, if the insurer actually knows that the claim does not match the damage or loss claimed to have been suffered by the claimant there can be no fraud. This proposition however was doubted in a Privy Council decision, *Stemson v AMP General Insurance (NZ) Ltd* [2006] UKPC 30 where the insurer did not need to prove it was induced. It might perhaps be suggested that *Danepoint* should only be limited to circumstances where the assured's claim is one so outrageous that it is disregarded by the insurer.

There is however an important difference between the two cases—in *Agapitos*, it was the making of fraudulent claim or using a fraudulent device or means to promote a claim whilst in *The Mercandian Continent* it was a case of deceitful conduct towards insurers which was not designed to promote the insurance claim or to prejudice the insurers, but was committed in an "over-enthusiastic" attempt to promote both their interests by defeating or minimising the third party claim

---

[29] See also *Royal Boskalis Westminster NV v Mountain* [1997] L.R.L.R. 523.

against the insured. The latter situation (conduct not designed to promote a claim) can only be considered under s.17.

10–042   **(d) The duty of utmost good faith in section 17 does not apply during litigation**   It was argued in *The Star Sea* that the parties were still bound by the duty of utmost good faith even after litigation has commenced. The argument was that if it was a continuing duty, it should necessarily extend to the stage of litigation. Lord Hobhouse disagreed, stating that once the parties are in litigation it is the procedural rules which govern the extent of the disclosure which should be given in the litigation, not s.17 as such, though s.17 may influence the court in the exercise of its discretion.

The Star Sea thus contains most powerful dicta to the effect that the duty of good faith under s.17 is superseded or exhausted by the rules of litigation, once litigation has begun.[30]

It would appear that the duty of utmost good faith does not operate post-contract other than where:

1. the insurer was being invited to renew or vary his "speculation" or "risk"; or

2. the assured was presenting or pursuing a claim on the policy (for example, where the assured is attempting to make a fraudulent claim).

As regards 1., the assured's duty is bound by the standard prohibitions against misrepresentation and nondisclosure. As regards 2., the House of Lords in *The Star Sea* stated that the duty of utmost good faith is to be more generally expressed as the duty to present the claim honestly.

These three cases, *The Mercandian Continent, Agapitos* and *The Star Sea* all demonstrate the difficulty the courts face in drawing the boundaries for whether and to what extent materiality and inducement are required when dealing with a continuing duty to act in utmost good faith. The courts are clearly reluctant to strike the contract of insurance down when the circumstances are such as those in *The Mercandian Continent* but very often the courts have no choice as the only remedy available in law is the avoidance of contract. However, as is amply demonstrated in these cases, the reluctance to use a blunt instrument, such as avoidance of contract, has resulted in three decisions with rather fine distinctions. In 2002, the British Insurance Law Association submitted a report to the Law Commission recommending that legislation on *non-marine insurance* should introduce an implied term to the effect that the parties must act towards each other with utmost good faith. The remedy for breach would thus be damages to compensate the wronged party for actual loss caused. Avoidance should not be available unless there is a fraudulent and material breach. In the case of the continuing duty of good faith, a breach would only be a materially fraudulent breach if the fraud would have an effect on the underwriter's ultimate liability and the gravity of the fraud or its consequences were sufficient. Whether any resulting reform will follow such a recommendation remains to be seen.

---

[30] See also *Agapitos v Agnew* [2002] EWCA Civ 247; also Longmore, "Good faith and breach of warranty: are we moving forwards or backwards?" (2004) L.M.C.L.Q. 158; Yeo, "Post-contractual good faith—change in judicial attitude?" (2003) M.L.R. 425.

Contractual requirements associated with a duty of good faith

Some marine policies stipulate that where the assured becomes aware of a change **10–043** in circumstances (whether or not that change has a unfavourable impact on the risk insured) which is not known to the insurers, he should notify the insurers promptly. The Institute Cargo Clauses provide for example that

> "it is necessary for the Assured when they become aware of an event which is 'held covered' under [the] insurance to give prompt notice to the Underwriters and the right to such cover is dependent upon compliance with this obligation".

Not only is such a requirement a contractual term, it appears to be a manifestation of the general overriding post-contract duty of good faith as defined in *The Star Sea*. In a non-marine insurance case, *Alfred McAlpine Plc v Bai (Run-Off) Ltd* [2000] 1 Lloyd's Rep. 437, the Court of Appeal held that it was possible that a breach of a condition of an insurance policy requiring the insured to give notice of any occurrence which might give rise to a claim "as soon as possible . . . in writing, with full details" might in some circumstances be so serious as to give a right to reject the claim albeit it was not repudiatory in the sense of enabling the insurer to accept a repudiation of the whole contract. That term is a mere innominate term; where the breach demonstrates an intention not to continue to make a claim, or has very serious consequences for the insurers, then the insurer should be entitled to defeat the entirety of the claim. As to whether the breach of the notice requirement could constitute a breach of the duty of good faith, the court indicated that it could but in that case, there was no such breach because all the insured was guilty of was negligence to notify the insurer. There was no evidence of dishonesty or wilful blindness.[31]

Agents and the duty of good faith

The issue here is whether the assured will be barred from claiming under his **10–044** policy where the failure to disclose a material fact was in fact the result of his agent's act or omission. Agents who are so closely allied with their principal that they might be properly described as their principal's alter ego, like ship agents, are clearly subject to the operation of s.18. Section 18 refers to the knowledge of the assured. Where this knowledge is possessed by the agent who is involved in every part of the principal's transaction, that knowledge could appropriately be imputed to the principal. Where the agent in question has simply been employed to secure certain information about the goods to be insured, the duty is individual and personal. The insurer's right to rescind is based not on any knowledge (or lack of it) imputed on the principal but because the marine policy was effected on the basis that such agents would perform their duties honestly and efficiently.

In *Proudfoot v Montefiore* (1867) L.R. 2 Q.B. 511, the court held that where the agent who has undertaken the duty to communicate information to his

---

[31] See *The Star Sea*, above, on the requirement of dishonesty and more generally, the Australian case of *Trans-Pacific Insurance Co (Australia) Ltd v Grand Union Insurance Co Ltd* (1989) 18 N.S.W. LR 675 for a similar approach.

principal as to the state of the cargo fails to do so, and his principal effects an insurance without such material information, the contract is voidable on the ground of nondisclosure or misrepresentation. The insurer is entitled to assume that the assured will communicate to him every material fact of which the assured has, or in the course of business, ought to have knowledge and that the assured will take the necessary measures by employing competent and honest agents to obtain all such information.

This rule was further explained by the House of Lords in *Blackburn, Low & Co Ltd v Vigors* (1887) 12 App. Cas. 531 where Lord Watson had this to say about "agents to know" (or agents whose business it is to know):

"In the ordinary course of business, the owner of a trading vessel employs a master and ship-agents, whose special function it is to keep their employer duly informed of all casualties encountered by his ship, which would materially influence the judgment of the insurer. On that ground it has been ruled that the insurer must be held to have transacted in reliance upon the well-known usage of the shipping trade, and that he is consequently entitled to assume that every circumstance material to the risk insured has been communicated to him, which ought in due course to have been made known to the shipowner before the insurance was effected. Accordingly if a master of ship-agent, whether wilfully or unintentionally fail in their duty to their employer, their suppression of a material fact will, notwithstanding his ignorance of the fact, vitiate his contract".[32]

10–045   The MIA makes specific provision for "agents to insure", that is to say, agents employed to enter into insurance contracts on behalf of their principals. Section 19 provides that where an insurance is effected for the assured by an agent, the agent must disclose to the insurer:

1. every material circumstance which is known to himself, and an agent to insure is deemed to know every circumstance which in the ordinary course of business ought to be known by, or to have been communicated to him; and

2. every material circumstance which the assured is bound to disclose, unless it came to his knowledge too late to be communicated to the agent.

This section was considered in *PCW Syndicates v PCW Reinsurers* [1996] 1 Lloyd's Rep. 241.

10–046   *PCW Syndicates v PCW Reinsurers* [1996] 1 Lloyd's Rep. 241.
Facts:
Through an unfortunate course of events, the reinsurers were faced with massive claims following the calamity on Lloyd's syndicates and "names". In an ingenious attempt to avoid paying out these claims, the reinsurers argued that the reinsured's agents who negotiated with them had not disclosed the fact that they were defrauding their principals. Although this would not have affected the incidence of the risks, the reinsurers considered this a "moral hazard".

---

[32] See also *Simner v New India Assurance Co Ltd* [1995] L.R.L.R. 240.

Held:

The Court of Appeal rejected arguments founded on s.19 on the basis that "agents to insure" only covered brokers employed to contract with the reinsurers, not intermediate agents who look after the insurance side of things for their principals. Saville L.J. held that "agents to insure" are persons who actually placed the business with the insurer or reinsurer. In the present case, the agents who were defrauding their principals were only intermediate agents who looked after certain affairs of their principal and had themselves obtained the policies through some other agent. Where liability could not be founded on s.19, the only remaining provision is s.18. The Court of Appeal relied on *Re Hampshire Land* [1896] 2 Ch. 743 which held that someone who employs an agent is not deemed to have knowledge of a fraud committed by his agent on him. Reliance could also be placed on Buckley L.J.'s definitive statement that:

"It is a well recognised exception from the general rule that a principal is affected by notice received by his agent that, if the agent is acting in fraud of his principal and the matter of which he has knowledge is relevant to the fraud, that knowledge is not to be attributed to the principal".

Section 18(1) had therefore not been breached because it is distinctly implausible that an agent would disclose to his principal that he was defrauding him.

It would follow that under these circumstances, the assured need only disclose what he actually knows. Where there is fraud being committed on the assured, s.18 cannot avail the insurer who wishes to rescind the policy on the basis of that moral hazard because the assured cannot be said to know of the fraud. As far as s.19 is concerned, the rule is that the duty will only append itself on the last agent in chain of agents. Only that agent can properly be said to be an agent to insure.

10–047

Agents for the assured or insurance brokers may also subject to a duty to advise their clients. Such agents, especially regulated insurance brokers, hold themselves out as experts in their relevant insurance sector will be held to account if they fail in their professional duties. In *HIH Casualty & General Insurance Ltd v JLT Risk Solutions Ltd* [2007] EWCA Civ 710, the Court of Appeal held that the insurance broker under the circumstances of the case owed a continuing post-placement duty to alert their client (the assured) to potential coverage issues and draw attention to unusual warranties in the policy. Whilst the question of breach of the post-placement duty by the broker is fact dependent, the law is quite clear that he does owe a duty of care to his client. In that case which involved a reinsurance contract that had gone awry, the court said, the broker had been "at the centre of devising and structuring a risky scheme for insurers and reinsurers", as such, it should take care to give adequate advice to the clients. In reinsurance it is common for brokers to act for both the insured and reinsured. Auld L.J. said in *HIH Casualty*, "the role of the insurance broker is notoriously anomalous for its inherent scope for engendering conflict of interest". The Court of Appeal made clear, however, that the fact that a broker may owe conflicting duties to various parties does not mean that it is exempt from carrying out those duties. Thus, even though informing a reinsured client of potential problems with a cover may be disadvantageous to an insured client, the broker must nevertheless perform that duty.

This duty to advise their clients is largely founded on the law of professional negligence—namely that a professional duty of care, breach of that duty and causation must all be demonstrated for the client to succeed in a claim for damages. For instance, in *Ground Gibley Ltd v Jardine Lloyd Thompson* [2011] EWHC 124 (Comm), Blair J. dealt with the failure of a broker to inform the assured about the insurer's recommendation that the assured should remove certain portable heaters as a risk prevention measure as a matter of negligence. G owned Camden Market in North London which suffered serious damage as a result of a fire started by a portable liquefied petroleum gas heater which had been left on in one of the market stalls. The insurers paid out under a settlement but only 70 per cent of the loss; the reason given was that G had not implemented the risk prevention measure suggested. G thus sought to recover the remainder from their brokers who they alleged had not drawn to their attention the insurer's recommendations. The broker's duty extended to advising the assured about the risk prevention measures and the consequences of failing to implement those measures. G thus succeeded.

Types of Policy

10–048   The policy must meet several formal requirements:

1. it must specify the name of the assured, or the person who effects the insurance on his behalf (s.23);

2. it must be signed by or on behalf of the insurer, provided that in the case of a corporation the corporate seal may be sufficient (s.24(1)); and

3. it must describe the subject matter insured with reasonable certainty, although where the policy describes the subject matter in general terms, it shall be construed to apply to the interest intended by the assured to be covered. Trade usage may be relied on in determining whether the description or designation of the subject matter is reasonably certain and in establishing the intention of the assured (s.26).

A model policy is set out in Schedule 1 of the MIA—the Lloyd's S.G. Policy and the Rules for Construction of Policy. Although this model policy makes for interesting reading, our concern is with its modern counterpart—the Lloyd's Marine Policy. That policy is intended to go hand in hand with any of the Institute Cargo Clauses (ICC) A, B or C. The Construction Rules should still have some use in the application and construction of the new standard forms. The Lloyd's Marine Policy states that the insurance is subject to English jurisdiction and is essentially the link between the standard ICC and the MIA (including Sch.1).

Whilst these standard clauses may be relied on generally for the terms of cover, specific terms agreed between the insurer and assured will result in the policy being classified as one of the following types:

Voyage policy

10–049   A voyage policy is defined by s.25 as one where the subject matter is insured "at and from" or "from" one place to another or other places. It is the norm for goods to be insured for a particular sea voyage, but in the light of combined transport and convenience, traders will often take a mixed land-sea policy to cover the land or inland waters leg of the carriage. This is possible under the MIA. According to s.2(1) a contract of marine insurance may by its express terms or by trade usage be extended to protect the assured against losses on inland waters or on any land risk which may be incidental to the sea voyage. Indeed the ICC(A) envisage this by setting out a transit clause. Clause 8 states:

> "This insurance attaches—from the time the goods leave the warehouse of place of storage at the place named herein for the commencement of the transit, continues during the ordinary course of transit and terminates either—
>
> 8.1.1 on delivery to the Consignees' or other final warehouse or place of storage at the destination named herein,
> 8.1.2 on delivery to any other warehouse or place of storage, whether prior to or at the destination named herein, which the Assured elect to use either—
> 8.1.2.1 for storage other than in the ordinary course of transit or
> 8.1.2.2 for allocation or distribution, or
> 8.1.2.3 on the expiry of 60 days after completion of discharge overside of the goods hereby insured from the oversea vessel at the final port of discharge, whichever shall first occur".

Clause 8 is also commonly known as a warehouse to warehouse clause.

Transit insurance is not new. Clause 8 is only a standard term embracing many of the principles applied by the courts in the past to similarly drafted contracts of marine insurance. Clause 8 was consequently held in *Nima SARL v Deves Insurance Public Co Ltd* [2002] EWCA Civ 1132 not to displace the provisions of s.44 MIA. Section 44 provides that where the destination is specified in the policy, and the ship, instead of sailing for that destination, sails for any other destination, the risk does not attach. In that case, the insurance related to a cargo of rice shipped from Thailand to Dakar. The insurance was under the terms of the ICC (A). The vessel never arrived at Dakar. No trace of her or her cargo had been found. The defendants argued that the loss resulted from the cargo being stolen by those who had control of the vessel and that they had formed a conspiracy to steal it by the time the ship sailed. It was a "phantom vessel"[33] and as such the risk never attached under s.44. The claimants argued that the implication of the policy (especially in cl.8) was that s.44 was displaced and that cover attached when the cargo left the warehouse. The Court of Appeal agreed with the lower court to rule that the warehouse to warehouse clause in cl.8 did not displace s.44. It was obvious, according to the court, from *Simon Israel* (1892) 62 LTMS 352 that, despite the effective extension of the voyage insured "from" the moment of sailing, back to the moment of leaving the warehouse for the purpose of the attachment of the risk, the overall adventure assured was still properly characterised as a voyage from A to B and, if that adventure was never embarked upon, the insurer would not be liable.[34] While the determination of the period of cover

---

[33] It should be noted that on the evidence, the court of fact (the High Court) was unable to conclude whether it was indeed a case of "phantom vessels" (per Andrew Smith J., November 29, 2001).

[34] Where an insurer invoked s.44, the court would normally carry out an ex post facto exercise to determine not simply the contractual, but the actual destination of the ship at the time of sailing. That exercise, it is clear, would take into account the acts and intentions of the owners and/or ship master at the time of departure.

under a voyage policy is essentially a matter of construction of the policy, there are several enduring factors. The court is concerned that movement of the goods must begin before there is transit. It has been held in *Sadler Brothers Co v Meredith* (1963) 2 Lloyd's Rep. 293, that "transit" has in its nature the element of carriage, and carriage starts when the goods are placed on the vehicle for movement. This view does not however take into account the process of consolidation of cargo as is usually the case in combined transport. Consider the following example.

10–050   *Example*: Consignor has a cargo of hats in his factory warehouse in Town A. The goods are consolidated into containers to be taken to Port B for loading onto a ship bound for State C. When does transit begin? Taking the test in *Sadler Brothers Co*, it would depend on whether the containers are to be treated as "vehicle for movement". If we consider the containers to be simply part of the packaging or packing, then transit begins when the containers are attached to trucks or trains to be carried to Port B. On the other hand where the containers are deemed to be the vehicle itself then transit starts when the goods are being consolidated into containers.

It must also be added that in *Sadler Brothers Co*, the clause under consideration was a "beginning the adventure" clause and not a general transit clause. In the case of a transit clause or warehouse to warehouse clause, the scope seems to be wider. In *Crow's Transport Ltd v Phoenix Assurance Co Ltd* (1965) 1 Lloyd's Rep. 139, the Court of Appeal held that transit does not only begin when some step has been taken by the carrier towards the loading of the goods. Lord Denning went on to say that the goods should be considered as being "in transit" even though they were sitting in the assured's vehicles awaiting loading by the carrier because from the moment they were placed in the vehicles everything else done is purely incidental to the transit. Furthermore although the vehicles belonged to the assured, the custody and control of the goods in those vehicles were with the carrier. This raises the other factor in determining whether transit has commenced. Where custody and control of the goods stay with the assured, then there is no transit. For example where the goods have been placed in vehicles but these vehicles are still kept in the assured's garages and no access to them is allowed.

There is incorporated in cl.8 a specific requirement that the goods must have left the warehouse or place of storage. American courts have construed such clauses very literally, so where the goods have left the warehouse but are still within the compound of the assured's premises, the transit insurance is said to have commenced (*Brammer Corp v Holland America Insurance Co* 1962 A.M.C. 1584 (NY 1962); *Plata American Trading Inc v Lancashire* (1957) 2 Lloyd's Rep. 347 (Sup Ct NY 1957)). As to what constitutes the terminus warehouse, the following case is instructive.

10–051   *Bayview Motors Ltd v Mitsui Marine & Fire Insurance Co* [2002] EWCA Civ 1605
Facts:
The cars were shipped from Japan to Santa Domingo in the Dominican Republic where they would be transshipped to the Turks and Caicos islands. The cars were insured under the Institute Cargo Clauses which contained a warehouse to warehouse clause—stating that transit

"terminates ... at delivery (a) to the Consignee's or other final warehouse or place of storage at the destination named in the policy ... (c) on the expiry of 60 days after completion of discharge overside of the goods hereby insured from the overseas vessel at the final port of discharge whichever shall first occur . . . ; If after discharge overside from the overseas vessel at the final port of discharge but prior to termination of this insurance the goods are to be forwarded to a destination other than that to which they are insured hereunder, thus insurance whilst remaining subject to termination as provided for above, shall not extend beyond the commencement of transit to such destination".

The cars were taken into the Dominican customs area because their documentation was not in order. Whilst the cars were in customs control at a car park, they were stolen by a few customs officers. The insured made a claim on their policy. The insurers resisted arguing that the cover terminated when the cars were discharged from the ship because the quay at Santa Domingo was "the final place of storage".

Held:
The Court of Appeal upheld the decision at first instance that the warehouse to warehouse clause would only apply where the final destination of the goods was the destination named in the policy. The court said that the relevant paragraph was (c) not (a) above. In cases where the goods were intended to go to the destination named in the policy (as is the present case), and then on to some other destination, cover is extended up to 60 days by para.(c). On that construction, the goods were covered when they were stolen.

Bayview Motors is a useful decision in that it clarifies the scope of a duration **10–052** clause in the Institute Cargo Clauses. The natural and contractual extension of the insurance cover makes "good commercial sense"[35] because it would be somewhat impractical to expect cargo interests to arrange separate cover for the period before transshipment and after discharge to the warehouse/storage area at the destination port, if cover ceased at the final destination. It might also be noted that, as far as the notion of transit is concerned, there was no end of transit from the facts. The cars were kept by the authorities in an area obviously intended as a transit area (such as a transit shed)[36]; transit could not therefore be said to have ended.

Another important qualification in cl.8 and similar transit clauses is that the cover will continue "during the ordinary course of transit". All things done during this time must be usual to the trade or circumstances. Where the loading or discharge methods are unusual to the port in question or the trade, it was held by the Australian court in *Helicopter Resources Pty Ltd v Sun Alliance Australia Ltd (The Icebird)* (1991) 312 L.M.L.N.[37] that the risk would not attach. The rationale is probably best explained using the words of Lord Mansfield:

"The insurer, in estimating the price at which he is willing to indemnify the trader against all risques, must have under his consideration the nature of the voyage to be performed, and the usual course and manner of doing it. Every thing done in the usual course must have been foreseen and in contemplation, at the time he was engaged. He took the risk upon a supposition that what was usual or necessary would be done".

Where the transit terminates will depend on the wording of the policy. In cl.8 several possibilities are provided for. The principles upon which the terms should

---

[35] Thomas, (2003) J.I.M.L. 19.
[36] *John Martin of London v Russell* [1960] 1 L.T. 554.
[37] As discussed by Hetherington, "Non-disclosure in marine insurance of aircraft" [1992] L.M.C.L.Q. 21.

be construed are essentially those used in defining the moment in time transit commences. It is clear from cl.8 and case law (*Overseas Commodities Ltd v Style* [1958] 1 Lloyd's Rep. 546 and *Deutsch-Australiasche Dampfschiffsgesellschaft v Sturge* (1913) 30 T.L.R. 137) though that the point at which transit terminates need not necessarily be the contractual delivery point of the goods under the contracts of sale or carriage.

Time policy

10–053   Section 25(1) provides that where the contract is to insure the subject matter for a definite period of time the policy is called a "time policy". The policy will specify the time of cover. Where this is not reasonably certain, the contract will not be classed as a time policy. The duration of cover is a matter for the contract. In *Scottish Metropolitan Assurance Co Ltd v Stewart* (1923) 39 T.L.R. 497, the policy stated that the indicated days will usually be treated as inclusive if no words to the contrary is set out. That term must be enforced.

It is possible to provide cover on the basis of a mixed policy, i.e. one that includes both voyage and time in its terms (s.25). Where that is the case, the underwriter will only be liable where the loss occurs within the time specified and during the contemplated voyage. It is however a question of construction as to whether ultimately the policy is a time policy qualified by geographical limits or whether it is a voyage policy effective during a specified time.

Where no specific date is set, this raises difficulty in establishing whether the policy in question is a time policy or not. In *Compania Maritime San Basilio SA v Oceanus Mutual Underwriting Association (Bermuda) Ltd (The Eurysthenes)* [1977] Q.B. 49, the policy stated that cover will "remain in force until expiry or cancellation". The rules of the club provided that all such policies would expire after one year. It was argued that as the policy was open to cancellation by any one party at any time, the policy was not for a "definite period of time". The court disagreed, holding that "definite" was added to emphasise the difference between a period of time measured by time and a period of time measured by the duration of a voyage. That one party could bring the policy to an end does not change the fact that the policy was measured by time.

Valued policy

10–054   The valued policy as pointed out earlier is one where the parties agree to the limit or amount of cover regardless of the actual value of the goods. Section 27 states, perhaps somewhat superfluously, that the value fixed is conclusive whether or not the loss is partial or total as long as there is no fraud. The value is however not conclusive in determining whether there has been a constructive loss. It should also be pointed out that where there is no fraud, the mere over-valuation of the goods is no ground to repudiate the contract of insurance (*Berger & Light Diffusers Pty v Pollock* [1973] 2 Lloyd's Rep. 442).

It is not essential that the words "valued at" a particular figure be used in a valued policy as long as it is clear that there was a specific agreed value proposed by the assured and accepted by the underwriter. In *Kyzuna Investments Ltd v Ocean Marine Mutual Insurance Association (Europe)* [2000] 1 Lloyd's Rep. 505, the insurers had insisted on a valuation survey before the insurance for a yacht was issued. The survey gave a guideline figure of £100,000 and this was the figure given by the insured as the "value to be insured" in the proposal form. The policy, which incorporated the Institute Yacht Clauses 1/11/85, stated in the schedule "£100,000 for hull, machinery, gear, equipment etc." under "sum insured". The vessel was damaged and the valuation of the yacht was £65,000–75,000. As to whether this was a valued or unvalued policy, the court found that as a matter of construction there was nothing that pointed to the intention of the parties that the sums stated in the schedule were to be the agreed value of the yacht and her equipment. The words "sum insured" ordinarily indicated a ceiling on recovery in an unvalued policy. There was nothing which displaced this ordinary meaning and the policy did not specify, in accordance with s.27(2), the agreed value of the yacht. It was therefore an unvalued policy. The practical lesson from this case is that the court will only consider a "sum insured" on the proposal form as indicating the value of the insured subject if the rest of the documentation (including the proposal form) points to such an intent unequivocally.

It is clear that whether a marine policy is a valued or unvalued policy depends almost entirely on the actual words used but there is no special import in using the words "sum insured" as indicating whether the policy was valued or not. In *Thor Navigation Inc v Ingosstrakh Insurance Co Ltd* [2005] EWHC 19, the hull and machinery insurance policy referred to the cover of the vessel with a "sum insured" of $1.5 million. The policy was made under the Institute Time Clauses—Hulls 1/11/95, which provided that English law and practice shall apply. As to whether the policy was valued or unvalued,[38] the court confirmed that the use of the words "sum insured" without any further reference to words of valuation would normally denote a unvalued policy. That was the clear guidance from ss.27 and 28 of the Act; it was not enough that the policy remained silent. The parties were required to specify the agreed value. The court also found that there was no evidence of a custom and practice in the English marine insurance market to the effect that use of the words "sum insured" meant that the policy was to be treated as a valued policy, even in the absence of any words in the policy that could be regarded as a specification of an agreed value (namely, the reference to the $1.5 million). Clear words of description of the value or valuation are required.

Unvalued policy

An unvalued policy is valued only at cost price to shipper thereby eliminating **10–055** any profit element incorporated in the invoice price. Section 28 describes the unvalued policy as one which does not specify the value of the subject matter insured and leaves the insurable value to be subsequently ascertained in the manner set out in s.16. Section 16(3) provides that the insurable value of the goods is the prime cost of the property insured, plus expenses of and incidental to shipping and the charges of insurance.

Prime cost was described by Scrutton L.J. in *Williams v Atlantic Assurance Co Ltd* [1933] 1 K.B. 81, as referring to the manufacturing costs of the goods at the time the "adventure" or risk commences. This usually reflects the invoice *value*

---

[38] The issue was important because if the policy was valued, the insurer would be obliged to pay out $1.5 million; where if it was unvalued, the quantum of loss might be in the region of $800,000 (subject to further issues of fact to be resolved).

of the goods. The prime cost does not refer to "loss or a profit or rise in the market price which was expected to be made or to occur in the future".

Floating policy

10–056 According to s.29, a floating policy describes the insurance in general terms, but leaves the name of the ship or ships and other particulars to be defined by subsequent declaration. Unless the policy otherwise provides, the declarations must be made in the order of dispatch or shipment. They must comprise all consignments within the terms of the policy. The value of the goods must be honestly stated, although an omission or erroneous declaration may be rectified even after the loss or arrival as long as the omission or declaration was made in good faith and within the terms of the policy. Where a declaration of value is not made until after notice of loss or arrival, the policy will be treated as an unvalued policy as regards the insurable value of the subject matter.

The floating policy is immediately binding in contrast to an *open cover* which is merely an agreement to issue an appropriate policy on agreed terms. Although the floating policy leaves certain details of cover to be filled by declaration, this does not render its terms so uncertain that it does not constitute a binding contract. The insurer agrees to underwrite risk/s up to a maximum aggregate value and will usually specify what sort of goods the assured is entitled to declare.

Insurance Cover

Proximate loss

10–057 The insurers are not liable to pay under the cover unless the loss or damage suffered is the result of an insured peril. This requirement gives rise to one of the more difficult issues in insurance law—that of causation. How do we prove that a loss or damage is in fact caused by the insured peril? Are there any legal tests? The matter is exacerbated when there are several causes of the damage or loss. Where there are contributory causes, the courts will have to consider whether there exists any one main or operative proximate cause or whether the other causes are equally relevant in bringing about the loss. The MIA does not offer much assistance in this regard. It states in s.55 that the insurer shall be liable under the policy for any loss proximately caused by a peril insured against, but subject to the policy, is not liable for any loss which is not proximately caused by a peril insured against. In particular:

1. the insurer is not liable for any loss attributable to the wilful misconduct of the assured but, unless the policy otherwise provides, he is liable for any loss proximately caused by a peril insured against, even though the loss would not have happened but for the misconduct or negligence of the master or crew;

2. unless the policy otherwise provides, the insurer is not liable for any loss proximately caused by delay, although the delay be caused by a peril insured against; and

3. unless the policy otherwise provides, the insurer shall not be liable for ordinary wear and tear, ordinary leakage and breakage, inherent vice or nature of the goods, or for any loss proximately caused by rats or vermin, or for any injury to machinery not proximately caused by maritime perils.

How the judges have construed and applied this concept of the proximate cause has been more a matter of common sense than any specific legal tests.[39] As Viscount Simon said in *Yorkshire Dale Steamship Co Ltd v Minister of War Transport (The Coxwold)* [1942] A.C. 691, "the interpretation to be applied does not involve any metaphysical or scientific view of causation". Much depends on judicial creativity in distinguishing the causal link between the peril and the loss. How this decision is to be made depends on the nature of the inquiry. Where the nature of the inquiry is to ascertain the truth as to what went wrong, the law's duty would be to look for unexpected causes and explain the whole chain of events. Where the inquiry has its purpose the determination of fault as in the law of tort, human culpability and causes will have a strong bearing. The purpose in the law of marine insurance is however not the attribution of fault or the determination of the truth but simply the construction of the cover and perils insured against and then the consideration whether the causes are covered.

The House of Lords case of *Leyland Shipping v Norwich Union* [1918] A.C. 350 is perhaps the best starting point. This 1918 case anatomises the *maxim causa proxima, non remota, spectatur* or the concept of proximate causes.

Leyland Shipping v Norwich Union [1918] A.C. 350   **10–058**
Facts:
The insured ship was torpedoed. She was taken by tugs to the outer harbour to be docked. She then sprang a leak after knocking against the quay. Fearing gale, she was then ordered to a berth where she moored. Her bulkheads gave way and sank. The assured claimed under the policy arguing that although the ship had suffered a particular average loss after being torpedoed, there was total loss caused by the operation of waves. The aggravation of the original injury by bumping against the outer quay and the successive grounding converted the partial loss to a total loss for which the claim is made.

The insurers resisted on the premise of the excepted hostilities clause contending that there had been no intervening cause to the damage. The subsequent events in the harbour must be taken as having been generated by the torpedo damage. If she had not been so badly damaged, she would not have broken up as she did. The whole network of circumstances was the direct result of the torpedoing.
Held:
The House of Lords held the ship was in imminent risk of sinking from the moment should was injured by the torpedo. She was never out of immediate danger. The operative cause therefore remained the torpedo attack. Lord Shaw said:

"To treat the *proxima causa* as the cause which is nearest in time is out of the question. Causes are spoken of as if they were as distinct from one another as beads in a row or links in a chain, but—if this metaphysical topic has to be referred to—it is not wholly so. The chain of causation is a handy expression, but the figure is inadequate. Causation is not a chain, but a net. At each point influences, forces, events, precedent and simultaneous, meet; and the radiation from each point extends infinitely. At the point where these various influences meet it is for the judgment as upon a matter of fact to

---

[39] See Clarke, "Insurance: The proximate cause in English Law" [1981] C.L.J. 284; Forte, "The materiality test in insurance" [1993] L.M.C.L.Q. 557.

declare which of the causes thus joined at the point of effect was the proximate and which was the remote cause . . . ".

His Lordship went on to assert that "proximate cause is an expression referring to the efficiency as an operating factor upon such the result". Where there are various concurrent factors or causes, the matter is that of fact and common sense.

10–059   Indeed, as is confirmed by Lord Denning M.R. in *Gray v Barr, Prudential Assurance Co Ltd (Third Party)* [1971] 2 Lloyd's Rep. 1

> "since . . . 1918 it has been settled in insurance law that the 'cause' is that which is the efficient or dominant cause of the occurrence or, as it is sometimes put, what is in substance the cause; even though, it is more remote in point of time, such cause to be determined by common sense".

In *Global Maritime Systems Inc v Syarkat Takaful Malaysia Berhad (The Cendor Mopu)* [2011] UKSC 5, the Supreme Court confirmed that it is the efficiency of cause that mattered. Establishing what is an efficient cause, as Bingham L.J. said in *T M Noten BV v Harding* [1990] Lloyd's Rep. 283, requires us to apply "the common sense of a business or seafaring man".

Where the loss was caused by a peril insured which might or might not occur if the assured had taken steps to prevent it, the courts would not consider the failure to prevent it to be a proximate cause. The evidence had to be less equivocal. In *The Grecia Express* [2002] EWHC 203, the ship was sunk by "persons acting maliciously" who cut the mooring ropes and set the engine room on fire, a risk provided for in the war risk insurance. However, it was argued that had the watchman actually returned and boarded the vessel immediately after the fire started, he could have prevented the total loss of the vessel. The court did not accept that argument stating that the proximate cause remained the cutting of the mooring ropes and the fire, that chain of causation remained operative throughout.

10–060   The issue of causation cannot be severed from the question of construction of the cover. In *IF P&C Insurance Ltd v Silversea Cruises Ltd* [2004] EWCA Civ 769, the cruise shipowner had taken out an insurance cover for "loss of income and extraordinary costs". After the terrorist attacks in the United States on September 11, 2001, the shipowner suffered serious loss of income as a result of warnings of terrorism posted by the US State Department which had discouraged passengers from cruising. The assured had to establish that there was a proximate cause of the loss which was an insured peril. The peril insured was interruptions in the operations of the assured's vessels. The Court of Appeal disallowed the claim because it considered that the cancellations were not due to safety concerns or other interruptions to operations of the fleet, but only to market conditions.

Summary of principles:

● Only where the peril insured against is the proximate cause of the loss will the insurer have to pay under the policy.

● Proximate cause means that which is the efficient or dominant in bringing about the loss, not that which is the nearest in time to the loss.

● The issue is a question of fact and is to be ascertained by applying common sense.

Where there are causes of equal dominance of efficiency with one cause being a peril insured against and the other an excepted peril like in *Miss Jay Jay* [1987] 1 Lloyd's Rep. 32 new difficulties arise. The general rule is that where there are two concurrent and equally effective causes of a marine loss, and one comes within the policy and the other does not, the insurer will still have to pay as long as one is a covered peril and the other is not expressly excluded (though not expressly covered as well). Where one is expressly excluded then the insurer is not liable (*Wayne Tank & Pump Co Ltd v Employers Liability Association Corp Ltd* [1974] Q.B. 57; *Tektrol v International Company of Hanover Ltd* [2005] EWCA Civ 845). Much however will depend on the terms of the policy.

Miss Jay Jay [1987] 1 Lloyd's Rep. 32   **10–061**
Facts:
The yacht insured was defectively designed. The yacht was taken on a voyage in July under ordinary weather conditions. On its return journey, the hull was damaged by waves. The marine engineer put forward the following causes of the loss:

1. the defective structure of the vessel;

2. the operation of waves on the vessel.

The insurer argued that the loss was not by "accidental external means" as provided for in the cover, and that the loss would not have occurred but for the defective design which was not a peril insured against. The assured contended that the action of the waves and the defective design were concurrent and effective causes, hence it could be said properly that the loss was caused by a peril insured against.
Held:
On whether the damage or loss was covered by the insurance, Mustill J. held at first instance that it was on the basis that the proximate cause was the incursion of water and not the defect. The Court of Appeal held that the one cause without the other would not have caused the loss. It was considered that while Mustill J.'s decision was right, the reasoning was not. The incursion of water in itself might be the direct cause,[40] but it was not the single operative cause. According to Slade L.J., both were proximate causes; consequently the insurers were to pay for the following two reasons:

1. there were no exclusions or warranties removing the insurer's liability to pay where one of the causes was an excepted peril;

2. the terms of the policy were wide enough to entitle the assured to make the claim.

In *Global Maritime Systems Inc v Syarikat Takaful Malaysia Berhad (The*   **10–062** *Cendor Mopu)* [2011] UKSC 5, the legs of an oil rig which was being towed from the US to Malaysia had fallen off. The insurers refused to pay arguing that the cause of the loss was the inherent vice of the rig; the assured on the other hand argued that the fracture was caused by perils of the sea. The High Court perceived two proximate causes—the inability of the rig to undertake the voyage and the normal stresses of the voyage. The judge then formed the view that the efficient cause was the failure of the rig to undertake the voyage; as such the insurers were covered by the inherent vice exception in the policy. Some have argued that if the High Court was right, that would limit the purpose of marine

---

[40] It should be noted that in *The Cendor Mopu* [2011] UKSC 5 Lord Mance stressed that the mere incursion of water is not a peril of the seas. The assured must be able to show a fortuitous event which led to the incursion of water.

cover as for the cover because only loss or damage caused by perils of the sea that were exceptional, unforeseen or unforeseeable would be covered by insurance. That might frustrate the very purpose of all risks cargo insurance, which is to provide an indemnity in respect of loss or damage caused by, among other things, all perils of the sea.

At the Supreme Court, Lord Saville took the view that it was incorrect to see this case as having two proximate causes. There was really only one efficient cause—perils of the sea. The lower court had misunderstood the nature and scope of the notion of inherent vice and had given that concept too wide a meaning.[41] For more on inherent vice, see below (paras 10–075—10–081).

Action taken to avoid a peril is part of the peril. An excellent example of the rule is found in *Canada Rice Mills Ltd v Union Marine & General Insurance Co Ltd* [1941] A.C. 55. In that case, the shipmaster fearing that the rough seas would result in the cargo of rice becoming wet, ordered that the vents to the holds be shut. This led to condensation within the holds and the rice was damaged. The question was whether the loss was caused by "perils of the sea". It was argued by the insurer that there was no loss by perils of the sea because the loss was in fact caused by condensation and not seawater. The Privy Council rejected the contention and held in the assured's favour. The action of the shipmaster to avoid the peril of the sea was to be treated as part of the peril itself. It was not a separate cause but a routine of seamanship in response to a peril of the sea.

10–063   *Example*: Fire breaks out onboard the ship and threatens the insured cargo. The shipmaster orders that water be used to fight the spreading fire. The water damages the cargo. Is this damage by fire or water? (see *Symington & Co v Union Insurance Society of Canton Ltd* (1928) 34 Com. Cas. 23).

"All Risks" cover in the ICC(A)

10–064   We now turn to one of the more common standard policies, the Institute Cargo Clauses (A), partly as an illustration of the general practice in cargo insurance and partly to examine how the law views and deals with an "all risks" policy. The ICC(A) are termed an "all risks" policy, quite unlike the ICC(B) and ICC(C) where the perils insured against are specifically adumbrated and described.[42] It should be remembered that the Clauses by their nature as an insurance policy are subject to a conceptual limitation on their so-called "all risks" cover. As an indemnity contract, they will only cover loss or damage caused by a risk or fortuitous event, not a certainty. Additionally the risk must be lawful to insure. A second limitation is found in the ICC(A) themselves. Clause 1 of the ICC(A) states that the insurance covers all risks of loss of or damage to the subject matter insured except as provided in Clauses 4, 5, 6 and 7 below. With these contractual exceptions it becomes quite clear that the ICC(A) do not cover every conceivable risk of loss. There is of course that overriding limitation that the insurer undertakes to cover only a specified duration or location for the loss as discussed above.[43]

---

[41] The court also overruled another case which was relied heavily on by the lower court in *The Cendor Mopu: Mayban v Alstom* [2004] EWHC 1038 (Comm).

[42] These clauses may be found at *http://www.jus.uio.no/lm/private.international.commercial.law/insurance.html*; See also George, "The new Institute Cargo Clauses" [1986] L.M.C.L.Q. 438.

[43] See paras 10–049—10–053.

Limitation 1: risk not certainty

The "all risks" insurance cover as described above is subject to the limitation **10–065** that insurance covers only a risk not a certainty. This rule is not based on some public policy as in some countries (e.g. the United States) but on the notion of risk as determined by the courts. Where the loss or damage is a certainty right from the outset, there can be no insurable risk. Certainty however is not to be tested with hindsight but at the beginning of the cover. In contrast a risk is often described as a fortuitous event, namely an accident or casualty.

British & Foreign Marine Insurance Co v Gaunt [1921] 2 A.C. 41 **10–066**
Facts:
The cargo of wool was insured under an "all risks" marine policy. It was damaged not by sea water but rain. No specific evidence was adduced to show how the wetting actually took place. The court of first instance held that the policy insures against an "operative risk". If evidence does not show that damage was caused by fortuitous cause then no claim may be made under the policy. Rowland J. said:

> "[T]he policy insures only against risks and any evidence which does not show that the damage was due to something fortuitous does not support the case when the underwriter are sued".

The Court of Appeal held that the damage caused was exceptional, such as would not have arisen under normal conditions of the transit. It was therefore to infer that the loss had proceeded from a casualty or something accidental.
Held:
On appeal the House of Lords held that while there is a need to show that the damage was fortuitous or accidental, the claimants need not show that there was exceptionally or unusually heavy rainfall. For an "all risks" policy to apply, so long as there is proof of some casualty or accident, that will suffice. Lord Sumner said:

> "There are, of course, limits to 'all risks'. There are risks and risks insured against. Accordingly, the expression does not cover inherent vice or wear and tear or British capture. It covers a risk, not a certainty; it is something which happens to the subject-matter from without, not the natural behaviour of that subject-matter, being what it is, in the circumstances under which it is carried. Nor is it a loss which the assured brings about by his own act, for then he has not merely exposed the goods to the chance of injury, he has injured them himself".

On the burden of proof, it was held that all the assured had to show was that the loss was occasioned by a casualty or something accidental. He need not show what the exact nature of that casualty consisted.

Where the loss or damage is caused by the inherent defect or vice of the goods **10–067** themselves, the law treats this as a certainty as we saw in *Gaunt*. The assured is presumed to be aware of the propensity of his cargo.
The certainty or fortuity of loss is assessed from the assured's standpoint—if he knows at the outset that the loss will occur as a matter of course, that renders the loss a certainty. Where for example, the cargo owner knows that under normal circumstances his cargo is combustible and will explode during the voyage, there can be no claim under an "all risks" policy. That was extensively discussed in the next case.

10–068   *London and Provincial Leather Process Ltd v Hudson* [1939] 3 All E.R. 857
Facts:
The claimants had entrusted his skins to P to be processed. The skins were insured for "all and every risk whatsoever . . . however arising". P then went into liquidation and his assets including the skins were seized. The claimants claimed under the insurance to which the insurer resisted on the ground that there had been no accidental seizure, the goods were seized intentionally by the creditors.
Held:
In reliance on *Gaunt*, the court held that the goods had indeed suffered a casualty because the seizure was an act from without causing the goods to be lost. There was also a loss within the terms of the policy in that the claimants were denied retrieval of the goods. What is fortuitous must be tested from the assured's standpoint. Thus, although the act of seizure was intentional, as far as the insured claimants were concerned it was a loss through an unforeseen event. The rationale for the requirement of fortuity is to prevent the assured from destroying his own goods to get insurance monies. That is not the case here.

It was held in *Gaunt* that the assured need not prove the exact nature of the peril that caused the loss. The burden of proof is favourable to the assured and in this connection, the ICC(A) are perhaps preferable to the ICC(B) and ICC(C) as far as the assured is concerned. In policies where particular risks are specified, the assured has the burden in proving the loss within the perils covered. That general test is set out in *Rhesa Shipping Co SA v Edmunds (The Popi M)* [1985] 1 W.L.R. 948.

10–069   *The Popi M* [1985] W.L.R. 948
Facts:
The insured ship sank in calm weather conditions following the incursion of water through an opening in the shell plating. The shipowners' contention that the ship was hit by a submarine was found to be untenable. The insurer on the other hand argued that the ship sank as a result of ordinary wear and tear. This too was unsubstantiated by evidence.
Held:
The House of Lords gave judgment for the insurers. The assured had not been able to prove either collision or other perils. The only fact they were able to show was the sinking of the ship. That was not sufficient to bring the claim within the terms of the policy. The burden of proof that the ship was lost through some insured peril remained on the assured. Although it was open to the underwriters to suggest some other causes of loss (excepted perils), there is no general obligation on them so to do. It is entirely available to the court to consider that the proximate cause is in doubt and therefore the burden of proof has not been discharged. Lord Brandon said:

> "[The judge] has open to him the third alternative of saying that the party on whom the burden of proof lies in relation to any averment made by him has failed to discharge that burden. No judge likes to decide cases on burden of proof if he can legitimately avoid having to do so. There are cases, however, in which, owing to the unsatisfactory state of the evidence or otherwise, deciding on the burden of proof is the only just course for him to take".

As far as an "all risks" policy is concerned, Lord Sumner described the burden of proof in this way:

> "[The assured] need only give evidence reasonably showing that the loss was due to a casualty, not to a certainty . . . I do not think he has to go further and pick up one of the

multitude of risks covered, so as to show exactly how this loss was caused. If he did so, he would not bring it any the more within the policy".

We see a similar approach in *Re Application of National Benefit Assurance Co Ltd* (1933) 45 Lloyd's List Lloyd's Rep. 147. In that case, the goods under insurance cover were to be carried from warehouse to port. En route the goods vanished. There were at that time some local hostilities. The insurer argued that it was up to the assured to show what actually happened to the goods. The court disagreed, holding that all the claimant had to do is to show loss of the insured goods suggesting that it was accidental. The onus then will shift to the assured to show that the loss was caused by an excepted peril or disprove the loss as claimed by the assured.   **10–070**

Limitation 2: contractual exceptions

Clauses 4, 5, 6 and 7 in the ICC(A) are risks or perils that the insurer will not cover generally. We shall highlight a few of the more popular exceptions and examine them in the light of the provisions of the MIA and case law.   **10–071**

Wilful misconduct of the assured   Clause 4.1 provides in conjunction with s.55(2)(a) that any loss, damage or expense caused by the wilful misconduct of the assured shall not be covered by the insurance. The exception reinforces the general requirement that the loss or damage must be fortuitous. Where the loss is caused by the assured's own wilful act, the loss as from his standpoint is no longer fortuitous but a certainty. Furthermore no man is entitled to benefit from his own wrong.   **10–072**

The term "wilful misconduct" is essentially a term of common sense, bearing in mind the notion of risk in insurance law. Where the act of the assured reduces the risk to a certainty (or virtual certainty) and is done intentionally to bring about a certain loss, that should be sufficient for the purposes of the clause and s.55(2)(a). This concept is applied in a non-marine case, *Patrick v Royal London Mutual Insurance Society* [2006] EWCA Civ 421. There, the legal liabilities cover in home contents insurance policy excluded loss arising from "any wilful, malicious or criminal acts". The insurers refused to pay for liabilities arising from fire damage to a derelict property caused by the assured's 11-year-old son in reliance on the "wilful act" exception. The Court of Appeal held that wilful act must be something blameworthy and, if so, it had to be more than deliberate. But it did not have to go as far as an intention to cause damage of the kind in question. The assured's recklessness as to the consequences of his act would be enough. If the assured was aware that he was about to do something that risked causing damage of the kind that gave rise to the claim, or did not care whether there was such a risk or not, he would be acting recklessly if he went ahead and did it. Equating wilfulness with recklessness in this way focused upon the state of the assured's mind when he carried out the act rather than on its intended consequences. The 11-year-old boy's conduct might be described as stupid, but it was not wilful. The exception did not therefore apply. The court however also emphasised the fact any construction of contractual exceptions must be made within the context of the policy in question. That element of wilfulness must not be taken in isolation from the qualification "misconduct". The act must be wrongful, to the extent that it was calculated to bring about a benefit under the insurance.

In *Papadimitriou v Henderson* (1939) 64 Ll. L. Rep. 345, the element of wrongfulness was considered in the context of a war risk policy (i.e. a policy that affords protection from loss or damage caused by war or hostilities). The court held that the shipmaster could not be penalised for prosecuting on the voyage even though there was a high risk of capture by enemy forces because that was precisely the risk the ship was insured against. There was no wrongfulness in the shipmaster's conduct.

10–073 It should be noted that negligence or even misconduct (though not wilful) may be covered subject to the terms of the policy according to s.55(2)(a). A resulting issue is whether without a stipulation in the policy, negligence or misconduct could still be covered as a risk insured against. It would seem clear that negligence would be covered because it does not detract from the concept of a risk in the insurance contract or the fact that the insurance is intended to indemnify and not unjustly enrich the assured. Cotton L.J. commented in *Lewis v Great Western Ry Co* (1877) 3 Q.B. 195 that:

> "Wilful misconduct is something more . . . [it is] entirely different from negligence, and far beyond it, whether the negligence be culpable, or gross, or howsoever denominated".

As for misconduct, for example recklessness of the assured, the matter is less clear. Academic writing has emphasised the Australian case of *Wood v Associated National Insurance Co Ltd* [1985] 1 Qd. R. 297 in this regard.[44] That case concerns shipowners who sent the ship out knowing full well that the crew was inadequately competent for the voyage. That reckless act was considered by the Supreme Court of Queensland as "wilful misconduct" and as such there was no cover for the loss. The court was particularly swayed by the fact that the shipowners would not have sent the ship out in that condition if not for their belief that they were protected by insurance nonetheless. This approach of the court places much emphasis on the economic function of insurance. The court concluded that it would not be in the interest of the social economy for the shipowners to rely on insurance in acting recklessly and not caring for their property.

A case that is particularly instructive as to the burden of proof when wilful misconduct is pleaded is *National Justice Compania Naviera SA v Prudential Assurance Co Ltd (The Ikarian Reefer)* [1995] 1 Lloyd's Rep. 455. In that case the vessel was grounded and following this, fire broke out in the engine room. The fire then quickly spread to the rest of the ship. The crew subsequently abandoned ship. The vessel was insured under a policy covering inter alia the risks of the sea, barratry and fire. The claimants' owners claimed under the insurance policy. The underwriters contended that the vessel had actually been cast away by the crew with the connivance of the claimants. The court at first instance held that the grounding of the vessel was caused by the master's negligence and that the defendant had failed to prove satisfactorily that the ship had been deliberately set fire on. That court considered that even if the vessel had been deliberately set on fire, the owners were not privy to the act. The Court of Appeal differed on the interpretation of facts and held that the owners had indeed connived at the scuttling of the vessel.

---

[44] See Bennett, *The Law of Marine Insurance* (Oxford: OUP, 1996), pp.218–220.

As far as the cover for barratry is concerned, the Court of Appeal held that **10–074** once the owners have proved a casting away by a deliberate act of the crew or master, the onus shifts to the insurers to show that the owners had consented to it. The assured were also unable to rely on the fire cover because although deliberate and accidental fire were both covered, the fire was caused by the owners' own wilful misconduct. The court gave particular bearing on the underlying motive of the owners. It is submitted that this is insufficient without actual proof of connivance as demonstrated in *Continental Illinois National Bank & Trust Co of Chicago v Alliance Assurance Co Ltd (The Captain Panagos DP (No.2))* [1989] 1 Lloyd's Rep. 33. The gravity of the allegation must be reflected in the standard of proof required. This seems to be missing in *The Ikarian Reefer*. In *Lemos v British & Foreign Marine Insurance Co Ltd* (1931) 39 Ll. L. Rep. 275, it was held that the court must be especially sensitive to the fact that there is a criminal or quasi-criminal element involved and should therefore assess the evidence in this light. The issue of standard of proof seems unsettled but there is authority in *Anonima Petroli Italiana SpA v Marlucidez Armadora SA (The Filiatra Legacy)* [1991] 2 Lloyd's Rep. 337 that while the courts should adhere to the civil standard of a balance of preponderance, they should remind themselves of the seriousness of the allegations and the inevitable grave consequences of the finding of such conduct on the parties involved.

Where the policy has been assigned by the assured to a third party and the loss is caused by the wilful misconduct of the original insured, the third party claiming under that policy can be defeated on the basis of the exception (*Graham Joint Stock Shipping Co Ltd v Merchants Marine Insurance Co Ltd* (1923) 17 Ll. L. Rep. 241). On the other hand the rule is that where a third party has taken out insurance in his own name on a subject matter owned by another, the fact that the loss or damage was caused by the wilful misconduct of the owner does not affect the third party's claim because, from the third party's standpoint, the loss is nevertheless fortuitous. Their claim is however subject to the terms of the policy. Thus, in *P Samuel & Co Ltd v Dumas* [1924] A.C. 431, the mortgagees of a ship failed in their action. They had made a claim under the marine cover to the amount of the debt owing to them as secured on the scuttled vessel. There was no dispute that the vessel had indeed been scuttled by the crew with the owners' connivance. The question was whether the mortgagees could claim under the contractual cover for loss by a "peril of the sea". The House of Lords held by a majority of 4–1 that the mortgagees could not succeed. The fact that the mortgagees were not themselves guilty of "wilful misconduct" was not relevant for purposes of the claim. The scuttling being the real and operative cause was not a fortuitous event. Viscount Finlay said:

"Storms are fortuitous, the ordinary action of the waves is not and fraudulent scuttling is even more decisively out of the region of accident".

Condition of the subject matter Clause 4.2 provides that there shall be no **10–075** insurance cover for ordinary leakage, ordinary loss in weight or volume, or ordinary wear and tear of the goods insured whilst Clause 4.3 refers to damage or loss caused by insufficiency of or unsuitability of packing. In addition Clause 4.4 excludes cover for loss, damage or expense caused by inherent vice or nature of the goods. Where the policy itself is silent as to these exceptions, not only could the insurer rely on the general exclusion of such loss but s.55(2)(c), MIA may also avail him. Section 55(2)(c) provides inter alia that the insurer is not liable for loss or damage caused by ordinary wear and tear, ordinary leakage and breakage, inherent vice or nature of the goods insured, and rats and vermin.[45]

It might be said that these provisions add little to the general requirement that an insurance policy covers only risks and fortuitous losses not a certainty. Where the condition of the goods is such that it is inevitable that damage, loss or expense will occur, the law is that there could be no insurance cover. This is of course a mere presumption which is not entirely reliable—for instance, it could not be said that where there is some inherent defect in the goods which is unknown to the assured, that defect will inevitably result in loss, damage or expense. Be that as it may, the law operates on the basis that there are some acceptable exceptions regardless of their justification under the general parameters of insurance law. It is possible after all to insure against such perils as long as the assured is prepared to pay the requisite premium.

Ordinary wear and tear generally refers to damage or loss sustained through the ordinary conditions of the voyage insured. In describing what constituted cover, Roche J. said in *Whiting v New Zealand Co Ltd* (1932) 44 Ll. L. Rep. 179:

> "Moist atmosphere is not an accident or peril that is covered. It is more or less a natural test or incident which the goods have to suffer and which the underwriter has not insured against".

10–076   It is always a question of fact as to what constitutes "ordinary wear and tear" and there is little guidance as to how this assessment should be made. In *ED Sasson & Co Ltd v Yorkshire Insurance Co* (1923) 16 Ll.LR. 129, the damage caused by mildew to the goods was held to be "the result of something unusual and not the ordinary consequence of the voyage". The burden of proof that the loss or damage was caused by ordinary wear and tear is on the insurer. What is "ordinary" will largely depend on the circumstances and conditions of the voyage as envisaged by the parties.

The Clauses and s.55(2)(c) also refer to ordinary leakage and breakage. Much depends on the construction of the policies and the nature of the subject matter. In *De Monchy v Phoenix Insurance Co of Hartford* (1929) 34 Lloyd's List Lloyd's Rep. 201, we are given a rough working description of leakage. Viscount Dunedin in deciding whether there was "leakage" of the cargo of turpentine, said that leakage means

> "any stealthy escape either through a small hole which might be discernible, or through the pores of the material of which the cask is composed".

In that case, the policy provided cover for leakage from any cause in excess of one per cent on each invoice. The House of Lords held that the policy must be construed as excepting cover where the leakage is inevitable. Only leakage which is fortuitous will be covered unless the contract expressly provides for it. The one

---

[45] Bennett, "Fortuity in the law of marine insurance" [2007] L.M.C.L.Q. 315; s.55(2)(c) of the Act operates not as an implied contractual exclusion but as a clarification on the scope of cover.

per cent excess prescribed by the contract is indicative that only fortuitous
leakages are covered.

It is also worth mentioning that where the insured cargo has been damaged by   **10–077**
the ordinary leakage or breakage of another cargo, that is covered under the
ICC(A). Such a loss is however not prescribed for under the ICC(B) and (C).

Ordinary loss of weight or volume is generally excepted from cover (Clause
4.2) because it is not a fortuity. However, it is open to insurers to provide cover
for "shortage in weight" but such a "shortage in weight" clause is to be
construed strictly. In *Coven SpA v Hong Kong Chinese Insurance Co Ltd* [1999]
C.L.C. 223, the Court of Appeal held that a "shortage in weight" clause should
not be construed as covering a shortage caused by a difference between
documented loading weight and the actual loading weight. It only covered
shortage in weight caused by physical loss or damage to goods; "shortage"
meant shortage between the quantity of goods which actually embarked in the
adventure and the delivered quantity.

Clause 4.3 talks about "insufficiency or unsuitability of packing or preparation
of the subject matter insured". For the purposes of this clause, "packing" shall
include stowage in a container or liftvan but only when such stowage is carried
out prior to the attachment of the insurance or by the assured or their servants.
Again what constitutes suitability or sufficiency is a question of fact with
particular reference to be made to standard and accepted practice in industry. In
FW Berk & Co Ltd v Style [1956] 1 Q.B. 180, it was considered that where the
packing is such that the cargo becomes unable to withstand the normal conditions
of the insured voyage, the assured is barred from claiming expenses incurred in
repacking the goods or replacing the inadequate packaging.

Damage or loss by an inherent vice in the goods may be defined as that which   **10–078**
is caused by the natural tendencies of the goods. Where the goods are such that
they could spontaneously combust, any resultant damage or loss will be treated
as loss or damage caused by the inherent nature or vice of the goods. It does not
have to be an abnormal weakness of the goods, a general and normal tendency
of goods to self-degenerate suffices. In *Blower v Great Western Railway Co*
(1872) L.R. 7 C.P. 655, the claimant had delivered a bullock to the Great Western
Railway Co to be carried on the latter's train. During the journey, the animal
escaped and was killed. In discussing the definition of inherent vice in a contract
of carriage, the court held that inherent vice is "that sort of vice which by its
internal development tends to the destruction or injury of the thing". And more
recently, in *Soya GmbH Mainz Kommanditgesellschaft v White* [1983] 1 Lloyd's
Rep. 122, Lord Diplock described it in these words:

"It means the risk of deterioration of the goods shipped as a result of their
natural behaviour in the ordinary course of the contemplated voyage without
the intervention of any fortuitous external accident or casualty".

What is key from Lord Diplock's dictum is that the deterioration occurred in the
ordinary course of the contractual voyage. That proposition needs to be read in
conjunction with the spirit and purpose of marine cover, though. In *The Cendo
Mopu* [2011] UKSC 5, the Supreme Court in discussing that case cautioned
that

"the purpose of insurance is to afford protection against contingencies and
dangers which may or may not occur; it cannot properly apply to a case where

the loss or injury must inevitably take place in the ordinary course of things".[46]

We find a good example is *Noten v Harding* (see below). It may be recalled that in that case, the gloves contained moisture which led to condensation. The condensation meant that the moisture which had accumulated in the containers then dripped back on the gloves damaging them. There was nothing external to cause the damage. Lord Mance emphasised that the damage was entirely foreseeable but the reason that there was no recovery was because the gloves had effectively damaged themselves and had not sustained any fortuitous external accident. Consequently, it might be said that a loss is caused by inherent vice where the sole reason for that loss is the nature of the cargo, in that it would suffer loss *irrespective* of external fortuitous events

10–079   It would also seem that where the goods are damaged as a result of insufficiency of packing, that insufficiency in itself could amount to an inherent vice in the goods as was pointed out in *FW Berk & Co Ltd v Style*. In that case Sellers J. considered that the kieselguhr as packed in bags could not have withstood the contemplated voyage and that condition was tantamount to an inherent defect of the goods.

Where the inherent vice is generated by an external cause, we are faced with two possible causes: the inherent vice as developed and the original cause of the inherent defect. How should the matter be resolved?

10–080   *TM Noten BV v Harding* [1990] 2 Lloyd's Rep. 283
Facts:
The goods insured were a consignment of industrial leather gloves. On out-turn the gloves were found to be wet, stained, mouldy and discoloured. It was proved that the leather had absorbed moisture before packaging and during the course of the voyage, temperature outside the containers had fallen. This resulted in warm air in the containers lifting the moisture from the gloves to the ceiling of the containers where condensation took place causing the moisture to fall back on to the gloves as water droplets. It was argued that the damage was the result of the inherent vice of the gloves.
Held:
At the Commercial Court, Phillips J. held that there was no inherent vice because the damage was actually caused by the dropping of water from an external source. The Court of Appeal disagreed, holding that the real or dominant cause was that the gloves had contained excessive moisture. Thus, it was the natural behaviour of the gloves in the ordinary course of the voyage without the intervention of any fortuitous external accident or casualty that caused the water droplets to form and in due course, the resultant damage. The fact that the gloves had themselves absorbed moisture before packaging was immaterial to the finding of the goods' inherent vice.

A contrast might be had in *CT Bowring & Co Ltd v Amsterdam London Insurance Co* (1930) 36 Ll. L.R. 309. In that case Wright J. held that if moisture which originated from the goods had become condensed and fallen back on the goods, "such sweat water would have set up a life of its own and achieved an identity of its own" and was thus an "external cause" of the damage. The statement understandably puzzled Bingham L.J. in *Noten* but on the facts, we can say that it is distinguishable on the basis that in *Bowring* it was clearly

---

[46] See *Paterson v Harris* (1861) 1 B & S 336.

unforeseeable that the sweat water which had gathered on the beams would fall. It was a fortuity.

It was also held in *Noten* that just because the damage or loss was not **10–081** inevitable, it did not mean that the damage or loss was not caused by the inherent vice of the goods. The defendants had argued in that case that the same absorption of moisture had taken place in previous voyages but no damage or loss was caused in those voyages, hence even if the loss had been caused by the inherent vice of the goods, that loss was not inevitable. The argument was essentially that inherent vice would only be a exception to the marine policy if the loss was a certainty or inevitability. The Court of Appeal rejected this equation made between the concept of inevitable loss and the concept of inherent vice. This reinforces our earlier observation that the rationale for these provisions being the inevitability or certainty of loss cannot hold true.

Delay Clause 4.5 excludes loss, damage or expense proximately caused by **10–082** delay even though the delay be caused by a risk insured against (except expenses payable under the general average clause). This mirrors the statutory provision in s.55(2)(b) which provides:

"Unless the policy otherwise provides, the insurer on ship or goods is not liable for any loss proximately caused by delay, although the delay be caused by a peril insured against".

The genesis of the rule is not entirely clear, and save for academic interest, it is not entirely important considering that parties are generally free to contract out of this rule.

An example of how the rule applies is seen in *Federal Insurance Co of Canada v Coret* [1968] 2 Lloyd's Rep. 109. The defendants had taken out an open cargo policy with the claimant insurers. The standard cover excluded "damage or deterioration arising from delay". The insured goods were a consignment of handbag parts and accessories. The consignment was lost but found later. They were seasonal goods and by that time, had become substantially less saleable. The defendants rejected the goods and made a claim under the policy. It was held that this was a loss occasioned by delay and came within the ambit of the exception.

War clause Clause 6 of the ICC(A) provides that in no case shall the **10–083** insurance cover loss, damage or expense caused by:

"6.1—war, civil war, revolution, rebellion, insurrection, or civil strife arising therefrom, or any hostile act by or against a belligerent power;

6.2—capture, seizure, arrest, restraint or detainment (piracy excepted) and, the consequences thereof or any attempt threat;

6.3—derelict mines, torpedoes, bombs or other derelict weapons of war".

It should be recognised that these exceptions may be expressly covered where the parties have agreed to extend the insurance cover to war risks. This extension may take the form of a separate policy or an appendage to the existing policy. The standard Institute War Clauses (Cargo) may be used. Clause 1 of the Clauses provides for the express cover of these very perils. Incidentally, it might be noted that s.3 of the MIA considers these perils to be maritime perils. Hence, it could be said that War Risk cover is probably the norm rather than the exception. Semantics aside, we shall consider the definition of the terms used in Clause 6 of the ICC(A) and Clause 1 of the Institute War Clauses (Cargo). We do well to remember that in some of the following cases, the perils described are applied as perils insured whilst in others, they are perils excepted.

War and civil war We are instructed in *Kawasaki Kisen Kabushiki Kaisha of Kobe v Bantham Steamship Co Ltd* [1939] 2 K.B. 544, that the law of insurance will ascertain the meaning of war, etc, as a matter of construction of the contract rather than by reference to some definition ascribed to war by international law. In that case the charterparty provided that the contract may be cancelled "if war breaks out involving Japan". The shipowners cancelled the contract when fighting broke out between China and Japan. There was however no formal declaration of war. The question was whether the shipowners were right to do so. The Court of Appeal held that although the Foreign Office was unable to certify that a state of war was in existence between China and Japan, that was irrelevant for the purposes of the action. "War" according to the court was not to be given a legal technical meaning as prescribed by international law, but be construed according to what the parties would ordinarily understood it to be within the context of their commercial dealings. Furthermore

"to say that English law recognises some technical and ascertainable description of what is meant by 'war' appears . . . to be a quite impossible proposition".

10–084   Lord Greene added, "Nobody would have the temerity to suggest in these days that war cannot exist without a declaration of war".

In the context of insurance, we might seek assistance from the American case of *Pan American World Airways Inc v Aetna Casualty & Surety Co* [1974] 1 Lloyd's Rep. 207. In that case, the "all risks" insurance cover excepted "war . . . civil war, revolution, rebellion, insurrection or warlike operations whether there be a declaration of war or not". The insured plane was hijacked and subsequently destroyed by terrorists. The US District Court of New York held that an interpretative approach which favours inclusion rather than exclusion of cover should be generally preferred. However, "war" should necessarily imply the use of force between governments. "Warlike operations" should not be extended to the infliction of intentional violence by political groups on civilians and their property far removed from the locale of any warfare. The purpose of the terrorism was not conquest or coercion but the striking of spectacular blows for propaganda effect. It is unclear whether at English law there is such a requirement that the parties in the conflict should possess some sort of sovereign attributes as suggested by the American case.

The nature of the violence also plays an significant role in defining the term "war". In *Spinney's (1948) Ltd v Royal Insurance* [1980] 1 Lloyd's Rep. 406, Mustill J. held that there was no civil war in Beirut because at that time fighting was random, inconsistent in purpose, and sporadic. There was no ascertainable sides, making the situation more akin to public order strife than a state of war.

10–085   *Revolution, rebellion and insurrection* In general, the term "revolution" is to be given its natural common sense depiction, i.e. the intention of the action is to bring about the overthrow of an existing regime. As far as "rebellion" and "insurrection" are concerned, Saville J. in *National Oil Co of Zimbabwe (Private) Ltd v Sturge* [1991] 2 Lloyd's Rep. 281, remarked that the two terms have "somewhat similar meanings to each other". The judge considered that both refer to an organised and violent internal uprising in a country with, as a main purpose, the object of trying to overthrow or supplant the government of that country, although it should be said that "insurrection" denotes a lesser degree of organisation and size than "rebellion". It would seem that all three terms are sufficiently wide to cover all stages of civil upheaval with the purpose of replacing or changing the existing governing regime.

Civil strife arising therefrom The phrase refers to civil commotion or disturbance arising after the event of war, civil war, revolution, rebellion or insurrection. Where for example, the rebelling forces had successfully overthrown the previous government but continued looting the country, this should amount to civil strife arising from the rebellion.

Any hostile act by or against a belligerent power It was described by Bailhache J. in *Atlantic Mutual Insurance Co Ltd v King* [1919] 1 K.B. 309, that "hostilities" means hostile acts by persons acting as agents of sovereign powers or such organised and considerable forces as are entitled to the dignified name of rebels as contrasted with mobs or rioters. The acts of a private individual acting entirely on his own initiative do not attract the term "hostilities" however hostile his actions may be. This element of belligerent powers should not however be thought to extend to "war". The House of Lords made this clear in *British Steamship Co v R. (The Petersham)* [1921] 1 A.C. 99. According to Lord Wrenbury, to extend the word "hostilities" to a state of war "would give the expression a scope far beyond anything which one can conceive as intended". In that case, although the merchant ships were sailing in convoy without lights in time of war as a precautionary measure, that could not be considered as a hostile act.

Capture and seizure "Capture" and "seizure" are to be classed as maritime **10–086** perils according to s.3 MIA. Under the ICC(A) they are expressly excluded. In general, "capture" includes the act of seizure of the subject matter insured and any act leading up to the seizure carried out by a belligerent force. "Seizure" according to Lord Fitzgerald in *Cory v Burr* (1883) 8 App. Cas. 393, is wider and should be interpreted as embracing "every act of taking forcible possession either by a lawful authority or by overpowering force". The confiscation of diseased cattle by health authorities in *Miller v Law Accident Insurance Society* [1903] 1 K.B. 712, for example, was a seizure within the purposes of exception but not a "capture". The term is so wide that it includes even the seizure of the insured ship by those on board as was the case in *Cory v Burr*. In *Republic of China et al v National Union Fire Insurance Co of Pittsburgh (The Hai Hsuan)* [1958] 1 Lloyd's Rep. 351, though, it was observed that where the seizure was carried out by the ship's crew entrusted to looking after the vessel, this was not "seizure".

The restrictive construction of the term "capture and seizure" is again confirmed in the more recent case of *Bayview Motors Ltd v Mitsui Marine and Fire Insurance Co Ltd* [2002] EWCA Civ 1605. In that case, the goods were stolen by customs officers in the port at Santa Domingo, Dominican Republic. The Court of Appeal held that such a loss could not be characterised as "seizure" because the goods had already been voluntarily placed in their custody. It was necessary to establish non-consensual dispossession in seizure.

Arrest, restraint and detainment This phrase resembles the old SG policy clause "arrest, restrains, and detainments of all kings, princes, and people" contained in Sch.1 to the MIA. The phrase in the MIA as defined in Rule 10 of the Rules for Construction of the SG (Ship and Goods) Policy "refers to political or executive acts, and does not include a loss caused by riot or by ordinary judicial process". The omission of the words "of all kings, princes, and people" would seem to suggest that the intention of the drafters of the ICC is to extend the exception to non-political acts or acts done by non-executive agents. Case law however has yet to develop this "new" description of the exception. It remains unclear how far Clause 6.2 should and could be construed to match the tincture in Rule 10.

In *Miller v Law Accident Insurance Co* it was established that force is not a prerequisite to operation of the phrase "arrest, restraint and detainment". In that case, the ship carrying a cargo of diseased cattle was prevented from entering port by an executive decree issued by the authorities. It had been argued that there had been no use of force and as such there could not be an arrest, restraint and detainment of the people. The Court of Appeal disagreed and held unanimously that as long as the decree emanated from the state concerned and the effect of the decree was the restraint and detainment of the cattle, that was sufficient to constitute an act by the people. The court however went on to say that even though no force was actually used, the authorities concerned would not have hesitated in using force if the shipmaster had resisted.

10–087   In *Ikerigi Compania Naviera SA v Palmer (The Wondrus)* [1991] 1 Lloyd's Rep. 400, *The Wondrus* had been prevented from leaving port because port dues and freight tax had not been paid. She was served an order instructing her to remain in port until all dues had been paid. If this was a detention, the assured would be able to claim under their insurance for war and related risks. At first instance, Hobhouse J. held that there was in a sense a detention.[47] Although the ship was not in fact physically detained, she would be if she had tried to leave without paying. However the judge went on to say:

"[I]n the absence of an express agreement to the contrary, a policy should not be construed as covering the ordinary consequences of voluntary conduct of the assured arising out of the ordinary incidents of trading; it is not a risk".

In *Sunport Shipping Ltd v Tryg-Balica International (UK) Ltd (The Kleovoulos of Rhodes)* [2003] EWCA Civ 12, the vessel was insured under the terms of war risks insurance that included the Institute War and Strikes Clauses, Hulls-Time of 1.10.83. Clause 4.1.5 of the Institute Clauses excluded loss arising from detainment by reason of infringement of customs regulations. The vessel had sailed from Colombia to Greece, where she was detained following the discovery of cocaine in a sea chest below the waterline. The master and crew were charged with drug offences but eventually acquitted. Meanwhile the vessel was detained under the provisions of Greek criminal law. The assured decided to make a claim for a constructive total loss under the policy. The question was whether "detainment by reason of infringement of customs regulations" included

---

[47] In a carriage of goods by sea case, *Great Elephant v Trafigura Beheer* [2012] EWHC 1745 (Comm) it was held the authorities by insisting on a "fine" and improperly refusing the ship its cargo papers was a restraint. The legality or illegality of the restraint was irrelevant.

prohibitions on imports.[48] Creswell J. had disallowed the claim stating that the loss was excluded by clause 4.1.5. The Court of Appeal dismissed the claimant's appeal. It held that the term should not be confined to dutiable goods but extended to goods whose import was prohibited. The court was not prepared to overrule the view taken in *The Anita* [1971] 1 Lloyd's Rep. 487 that it was within the common trade understanding to consider the prohibition of the importation of drugs and other narcotics as forming part of customs regulations. Giving the words a commercially informed interpretation, the Court of Appeal found that there was no material difference between smuggling and infringement of customs regulations. Given the longstanding view in *The Anita*, it would not be appropriate to detract from commercial certainty by changing the meaning of the words.

Derelict mines, torpedoes, bombs or other derelict weapons of war This provision was thought essential by the drafters of the Institute clauses to abrogate the effects of *Costain-Blankevoort (UK) Dredging Co Ltd v Davenport (The Nassau Bay)* [1979] 1 Lloyd's Rep. 395. In that case the insured dredger had sucked up a number of Oerlikon shells dumped at the sea by British forces after the Second World War exploded. The court was asked to decide whether the explosion was a consequence of hostilities or warlike operations. Walton J. held that it was not, on the ground that the dumping of ammunition after the end of war could not constitute an act of hostility; if anything at all, it was in the interest of pacification that ammunition was discarded. This ruling contradicted the then accepted practice that derelict mines or ammunition should form part of the war risk and consequently express provision has been introduced in war clauses to counter the effect of that ruling.

Strikes Clause 7 of the ICC(A) provides that there shall be no insurance cover for loss, damage or expense:　　　　　　　　　　　　　　　　**10–088**

"7.1—caused by strikers locked-out workmen, or persons taking part in labour disturbances, riots or civil commotions,

7.2—resulting from strikes, lock-outs, labour, disturbances, riots or civil commotions,

7.3—caused by any terrorist or any person acting from a political motive".

Again, these exceptions like the war exception may be expressly insured against by the parties. The Institute Strikes Clauses (Cargo) for example provide in Clause 1 that:

"This insurance covers, except as provided in Clauses 3 and 4 below, loss of or damage to the subject-matter insured caused by,

1.1 strikers, locked-out workmen, or persons taking part in labour disturbances, riots or civil commotions

---

[48] In order to rely on cl.4.1.5 which excluded loss or damage arising from the detention of a vessel by reason of, among other things, an infringement of customs regulations, underwriters did not have to show that there was privity or complicity on the part of the insured or its servants or agents in such an infringement. *Atlasnavios-Navegacăo LDA (formerly Bnavios-Navegacao LDA) v Navigators Insurance Co Ltd* [2012] EWHC 802 (Comm).

1.2 any terrorist or any person acting from a political motive".

It is immediately noticeable that cover under the Institute Strikes Clauses (Cargo) is only provided for loss or damage caused by strikers, not the strike action itself. Indeed Clause 3.7 of these strikes clauses states that

"in no case shall this insurance cover loss damage or expense arising from the absence shortage or withholding of labour of any description whatsoever resulting from any strike, lockout, labour disturbance, riot or civil commotion".

10–089 Clause 7.2 in its adoption of the phrase "resulting from" seems to indicate that even if the loss or damage is not proximately caused by strikes, lock-outs, labour disturbances, riots or civil commotions, the exception will apply so long as that loss or damage did result from them.

These provisions in the ICC(A) and the ISC(Cargo) are not to be construed as if they are technical terms of the law. We must bear in mind that they are contractual terms as understood by commercial people. As far as strikes are concerned we may use Lord Denning's description in *Tramp Shipping Corp v Greenwich Maritime Inc* [1975] I.C.R. 261 as a guide:

"[A] strike is a concerted stoppage of work by men done with a view to improving their wages or conditions, or giving vent to a grievance or making a protest about something or other, or supporting or sympathising with other workmen in such endeavour. It is distinct from a stoppage brought about by an external event such as a bomb scare or by apprehension of danger".

The ambit of the term is wide as we see in the case of *Williams Brothers (Hull) Ltd v Naamlooze Vennootschap WH Berghuys Kolenhaandel* (1916) 21 Com. Cas. 253.

10–090 *Williams Brothers (Hull) Ltd v Naamlooze Vennootschap WH Berghuys Kolenhaandel* (1916) 21 Com. Cas. 253
Facts:
The ship's crew refused to take the ship into the North Sea for fear that the German forces would attack their ship. The Germans had issued a warning that all neutral ships would be attacked if they entered the North Sea area. The question for the court was whether this refusal by the crew was a strike within the terms of the insurance cover.
Held:
The court considered that this amounted to a strike even though there was no direct dispute or grievance between the employers and the crew. It is sufficient that the crew was taking action over a safety or political cause rather than an employment matter.

A "lock-out" was considered by the Court of Appeal in *Express & Star Ltd v Bunday* [1988] I.C.R. 379, an employment case. There, May L.J. adopted the definition as:

"[A]n act of locking out a body of operatives; *i.e.* a refusal on the part of an employer, or employers acting in concert, to furnish work to their operatives except on conditions to be accepted by the latter collectively".

10–091 Again this is not a definition at law. The court must adopt a view which is generally and widely perceived as referring to a lock-out.

The term "riot" is slightly more problematic in that it does possess an express legal meaning. The question for us is whether that legal definition should be applied when construing insurance policies. In *London & Lancashire Fire Insurance Co Ltd v Bolands Ltd* [1924] A.C. 836, the House of Lords preferred a technical definition of the term when construing a commercial contract. "Riot" was defined at common law by *Field v Receiver of Metropolitan Police* [1907] 2 K.B. 853 as requiring the following elements:

1. the involvement of not less than three participants;

2. all pursuing a common purpose;

3. that common purpose being executed;

4. there is evidence that the participants are prepared to assist one another, and use force if necessary; and

5. force or violence if used was such that a person of reasonable firmness would have been put to fear for his personal safety.

The House of Lords in *London & Lancashire* applied that definition to the facts and held that the assured baker could not make a claim under his insurance after his shop was robbed by four armed men because the robbery constituted a "riot" and fell within the exceptions in the policy. Lord Sumner said:

"It is true that the uninstructed layman probably does not think, in connection with the word 'riot', of such a scene as is described in the case stated. How he would describe it I know not, but he probably thinks of something, if not more picturesque at any rate more noisy. There is, however, no warrant here for saying that, when the proviso uses a word which is emphatically a term of art, it is to be confined, in the interpretation of the policy, to circumstances which are only within popular notions on the subject, but are not within the technical meaning of the word".

At any rate the Public Order Act 1986 provides in s.10(2) that Rules 8 and 10 **10–092** of the Rules for Construction of Policy in Sch.1 to the MIA shall be construed in accordance with the definition set out in the 1986 Act for "riot". That Act defines "riot" in s.1 as:

"(1) Where 12 or more persons who are present together use or threaten unlawful violence for a common purpose and the conduct of them (taken together) is such as would cause a person of reasonable firmness present at the scene to fear for his personal safety, each of the persons using violence for the common purpose is guilty of riot.

(2) It is immaterial whether or not the 12 or more use or threaten violence simultaneously.

(3) The common purpose may be inferred from conduct.

(4) No person of reasonable firmness need actually be, or likely to be, present at the scene".

"Riot" must be an operative cause of the loss or damage before it falls within the exception in the ICC(A) or the peril insured against in the ISC(Cargo). In *Athens*

Maritime Enterprises Corp v Hellenic Mutual War Risks Association (Bermuda) Ltd (The Andreas Lemos) [1983] 1 All E.R. 590, the assured tried to claim for loss of equipment under his policy for loss or damage "arising from riot or piracy". The thieves had taken the insured equipment and had threatened to use force when attempting to flee. The court considered that for the purposes of construction, a "riot" should be given the meaning ascribed to it by the House of Lords in *London & Lancashire Fire Insurance Co Ltd v Bolands Ltd.* However there is no recoverable loss here because the thieves had not used force or threatened to use force when removing the equipment; they had merely threatened force to make an escape. There was no proximate cause.

The fundamental difficulty with using the legal definition in describing "riot" in a marine insurance policy is whether the court should adopt the definition in law at the time the policy was agreed on or at the time when the dispute arises. Some assistance might be derived from Staughton J.'s judgment in *The Andreas Lemos*. The judge observed that when construing archaic expressions, we cannot apply their ordinary meaning in our language today but should instead treat them as terms of art and interpret them in accordance with their original meaning. This would suggest that although we refer to the law for the definition of a particular term, the term remains a matter of construction and not of law. Its original meaning would refer to the state of the law when the policy was made and not at the prospective time of the dispute.

10–093   "Civil commotions" was described by the Privy Council in *Levy v Assicurazioni Generali* [1940] A.C. 791, as that stage between a riot and civil war.

"It has been defined to mean an insurrection of the people *for general purposes*, though not amounting to rebellion; but it is probably not capable of any precise definition." (emphasis added.)

The element of turbulence or tumult is necessary for there to be a "commotion". Where the participants are part of an organised conspiracy to commit crimes and there is no tumult or turbulence, there is no civil commotion. The term "civil" should imply that the disturbances must have some cohesion to prevent them from being the work of a mere mindless mob.

Clause 7.3 refers to acts of any terrorist or any person acting from a political motive resulting in the loss or damage. This seems straightforward enough but there is some controversy as to what "political" means. Three observations might be made in this connection. First, the standard clauses refer to "acting from a political motive" and not "a political act". This distinction suggests that the drafters of the ICC intend the clause to be liberal and wide. It must be shown that a political motive in involved. There is no requirement that the act must be wrongful. Motive is also different from intention and is less easy to prove, although it is possible to infer that motive from the actual conduct. Secondly, while there is much case law on the term "political character" in criminal and extradition law (for example *Schtraks v Government of Israel* [1964] A.C. 556; *R. v Governor of Brixton Prison Ex p. Kolcynski* [1955] 1 Q.B. 540; *Re Extradition Act 1870, Ex p. Treasury Solicitor* [1969] 1 W.L.R. 12; *Cheng v Governor of Pentonville Prison* [1973] A.C. 931; *T v Secretary of State for the Home Department* [1995] 1 W.L.R. 545), it is submitted that these decisions are not entirely instructive. They deal primarily with public and criminal law matters such as extradition, political asylum, political refugee status, etc. Their concern is not with the formulation of a term of art to be applied in construing commercial documents. As such, the parameters of the term are naturally kept within strict limits and bounds. The ends of those cases are of tremendous import, life and liberty. The courts when addressing the term "political" as provided for in such public law statutes and international conventions must take into account considerations different from those of a commercial people. It is advisable to adopt the approach of the American court in *Pan American World v Aetna* [1975] 1 Lloyd's Rep. 77 where the first rule is to apply a natural meaning to the term, one which uses "an ordinary man's understanding of the term". Thirdly, the courts should adopt a *contra proferentem* rule whenever possible—where there is an ambiguity, the court should opt for an interpretation which would provide cover for the assured instead of one which does not.

As far as terrorism is concerned, s.1 Terrorism Act 2000 defines it as the use **10–094** or threat of violence designed to influence the government or an international governmental organisation or to intimidate the public in furtherance of a political, religious or ideological cause. Again, the debate is whether it should be ascribed this technical definition or whether some common sense understanding of the term should be embraced. Nevertheless it remains helpful to cite the legal definition—terrorism is the use of violence for political ends, and includes any use of violence for the purpose of putting the public or any section of the public in fear. That said, it should be noted that following September 11, 2001, many insurers have insisted on a contractual definition of "terrorism" for better clarity.

Limitation 3: duration of cover

This is usually stipulated in the policy; in the ICC(A) for example, Clause 8.1 **10–095** provides that:

"this insurance attaches from the time the goods leave the warehouse or place of storage at the place named herein for the commencement of the transit, continues during the ordinary course of transit and terminates either

— on delivery to the Consignees' or other final warehouse or place of storage at the destination named herein,
— on delivery to any other warehouse or place of storage, whether prior to or at the destination named herein, which the Assured elect to use either

— for storage other that in the ordinary course of transit or
— for allocation or distribution

— on the expiry of 60 days after completion of discharge overside of the goods hereby insured from the oversea vessel at the final port of discharge,

whichever shall first occur".

The insurance cover is intended to operate over a period where the risk remains fairly constant. That constancy of risk is usually based on who has control over the insured interest. From Clause 8.1 for example, we can see that the goods are protected from the time may leave the warehouse and control is passed to the carrier until the time they are delivered to the consignee or some other place where the carrier is divested of his control over the goods. The presumption is that as long as the goods remain in the control of the carrier, that risk is fairly stable. The policy is issued on the basis that there are no major fluctuations in the risk factor. As far as the insurers are concerned, any change in control of the goods represents a significant or material change for which, a different premium for cover should be considered.

In a Hong Kong case, *E.L.A.Z. International Co v Hong Kong & Shanghai Insurance Co Ltd* [2006] HKCFI 406, the court held that where the goods were held at a yard awaiting customs clearance and the assured had done all that they could to facilitate the on-carriage of the goods to the final destination, Clause 8.1 could not be said to have been breached by the assured. The ordinary course of transit did not end *simply* because the delay pending on-shipment or transshipment was unduly long. It had to be shown that the assured had caused the undue delay or that during the delay, there was an interruption to his control of the cargo.

10-096 The ICC(A) are very explicit in their definition of the duration of cover. Some policies are less graphic. In many a case, they are merely described as "transit insurance" or "warehouse to warehouse cover". Where this is the case, the court's task will be to examine when control over the insured subject matter was transferred, thereby resulting in either suspension or termination of the insurance cover. As far as the transit is concerned, the general view is that transit does not end where the journey has been interrupted temporarily (*Sadler Brothers Co v Meredith* (1963) 2 Lloyd's Rep. 293). However, when there is a significant change in the risk as in *SCA (Freight) Ltd* [1974] 2 Lloyd's Rep. 533 where the driver of the assured's goods took the loaded vehicle on a frolic of his own, then there would be a break in transit. Transit may not be deemed to have ended where the goods have merely been placed under temporary seizure by the relevant authorities, particularly the carrier retains notional control over the goods (*Marten v Nippon Sea & Land Insurance* (1898) 3 Com. Cas. 164).

10-097 *Wunsche Handelgesellschaft International mBH v Tai Ping Insurance Co Ltd* [1998] 2 Lloyd's Rep. 8
Facts:
The claimant, W, was the CIF buyer of canned vegetables from China. W was the assignee of the relevant policies of insurance (as consistent with a CIF sale) issued by the defendants (Tai Ping). The policies identified the voyage as "From Shenzhen, China to Hamburg with transhipment at Hong Kong" and provided cover: "ex factory in the People's Republic of China to warehouse in Hamburg—warehouse to warehouse clause and risks of transhipment included".

The vegetables were canned at various plants around China and the cans were put in cardboard cartons at their respective canning plants which were then transported by rail, truck or barge to Shenzhen. There, the goods would be made up into consignments and put into containers for carriage to Europe, shipment being from China (that is to say, the goods are consolidated in Shenzhen and carried to Hong Kong for shipment to Europe).

The goods arrived damaged by rust and dents, and some were lost as a result of theft. It was established that most of the damage and loss occurred whilst the goods were on transit between the canning plants and Shenzhen. The High Court held that W had a good claim because:

● the words "ex factory in the PR China" clearly included inland transport from the canning plants to Shenzhen;

● by appropriating the goods to a particular voyage at the time of shipment, cover was obtained retrospectively for the goods in respect of the risks of inland transport;

- there was no implied term in the policies that the goods were only covered whilst being carried in containers.

Held: **10–098**

The Court of Appeal held, dismissing the appeal, that "ex factory PRC" could not be construed as being limited to only warehouses in Shenzhen or its immediate hinterland. The use of the word "factory" as against "warehouse" was significant. The reference was to the places where the goods were produced rather than the places where they were re-packed. It therefore extended the various canning factories/plants around the People's Republic of China. The fact that the cover was a "marine cover" should not be taken to mean the exclusion of inland transport risks.

   Moore-Bick J. at first instance was correct to hold that when the goods were appropriated (setting aside) to a particular voyage at the time of shipment in pursuant to the terms of the insurance, cover was obtained retrospectively for the goods in respect of inland risks, even though some of the goods were already missing (having been stolen) at the time of shipment. There was furthermore no implied term that the goods would only be covered if they were containerised. The references in the policy to containerisation were simply a means of identifying the goods covered by the policies and were not a restriction on cover in the period when they were not in containers.

This is a classic case of how poorly drafted terms resulted in substantial losses. If the insurers had intended to exclude cover for goods from inland transport risks, that should be made explicitly clear. In the present case, the words "PR of China" were obviously a reference to the time when the goods left their place of production, namely, the factories or canning plants. That express term should naturally be given prominence despite a very persuasive argument from Jonathan Gilman QC for the appellants that references in the policy to containerisation must be intended for more than mere identification purposes.

Insurance Warranties

Warranties by the assured

The contractual relationship between assured and insurer is governed by certain   **10–099**
important terms known as "warranties". These warranties may be express or implied. The parties are free to incorporate any warranty expressly into their policy subject only to the requirement that they be lawful terms.[49] As regards vessel insurance, the general rule, stated in para.681 of *Arnould* (vol.II, 16th edn), is that every statement of fact contained in a policy related to the ship insured "amounted to a warranty and as such must be fulfilled". Indeed, in *Sun Alliance & London Assurance v PT Asuransri Dayin Mitra TBK (The No.1 Dae Bu)* [2006] EWHC 812 the fact that the vessel's class was stated to be "KR", referring to the Korean Registry of Shipping, was enough for the court to treat it as a warranty. Soon after the time the policy was taken out, the ship's class with

---

[49] In *Konstantinos Agapitos v Ian Charles Agnew* [2002] EWHC 1558, the contractually prescribed warranties in a marine cover included "London Salvage Association approval of location, fire fighting . . . arrangements and all recommendations complied with" and "no hot work". The insured had carried out hot work on the vessel, resulting in a fire to some seating on the vessel. There was also no survey certificate relating to the vessel in the insured's possession. As such, the assured was in breach of warranties and the cover could be avoided.

KR expired. The owners then entered the vessel with the International Maritime Bureau Inc (the IMB) of Panama, and received interim class certificates for the ship. It is common knowledge that unlike the KR classification society which is amongst the best in the world, the IMB is in the lowest category of classification societies. The fact that the ship was no longer "KR" meant that the warranty had been breached. The insurers were therefore not required to pay under the policy. As far as the MIA is concerned certain warranties will be implied subject to any express contractual stipulation to the contrary. There are three such implied warranties in the Act:

1. warranty of seaworthiness;

2. warranty of cargoworthiness; and

3. warranty of legality.

We should not confuse the term "warranty" used in marine insurance with that used in ordinary contract law. In the law of contract, a breach of warranty is a breach of a term of minor importance. The remedy for such a breach is damages. In marine insurance, the breach of warranty could result in the termination of the policy. Lord Mansfield described the warranty in insurance law as "a condition on which the contract is founded" (see *Bean v Stupart* (1778) 1 Doug. 11)). The effect of such a breach, as explained by the House of Lords in *Bank of Nova Scotia v Hellenic Mutual War Risks Association (Bermuda) Ltd (The Good Luck)* [1992] 2 A.C. 233, is that the warranty is a condition precedent in the marine policy and a breach will automatically discharge the insurer from liability from the date of the breach. Section 33 echoes this. It states that a warranty means a promissory warranty, that is to say, a warranty by which the assured undertakes that some particular thing shall or shall not be done, or that some condition shall be fulfilled, or whereby he affirms or negatives the existence of a particular state of facts. It is a condition which must be exactly complied with, whether it be material to the risk or not. If it is not so complied, the insurer is discharged from liability as from the date of the breach of warranty. This is however without prejudice to any liability incurred by him before that date, that is to say, accrued liabilities will naturally not be discharged.

The freedom of the parties to contract on the terms of the policy however is preserved. Any implied (*Quebec Marine Insurance Co Ltd v Commercial Bank of Canada* (1870) L.R. 3 P.C. 234) or express warranty (*Liberty Insurance v Argo Systems* [2011] EWCA Civ 1572) may be excluded, waived or limited by contract but it should be remembered that contract must be properly worded. Any ambiguities will be construed to accommodate the statutory implied warranties rather than not. This freedom of contract is also seen in s.34(3) where it is provided that the insurer may waive the breach of any warranty.[50] An example of this is Clause 5 of the ICC(A), which allows the assured to make a claim under the policy even though there might have been a breach of the implied warranty of seaworthiness. It was raised in *The Good Luck* that s.34(3) is superfluous because under s.33(3) the contract becomes automatically discharged anyway following a breach of warranty. Lord Goff explained away this dissonance by asserting that s.34(3) refers to how the contract remains binding on the insurer as

---

[50] See Clarke, "Insurance warranties: the absolute end?" [2007] L.M.C.L.Q. 474.

a result of his waiving his right to an automatic discharge or an equitable estoppel preventing him from relying on his right to an automatic discharge.

The Good Luck [1992] 2 A.C. 233   **10–100**
Facts:
The owners of the Good Luck had insured the ship with R. The ship was mortgaged to A Bank. As between R and A, R had undertaken to inform A "promptly if [R] ceases to insure" the ship. The owners had breached a warranty by using the ship in a prohibited area. In fact the ship was rendered a total loss as a result of the breach. In November 1981 R became aware of the breach. In July 1982, the owners made a claim under their insurance policy feigning ignorance that they had used the ship in the prohibited area. At the same time, they made an application for more credit and made out an assignment of the insurance monies to the bank as security. R rejected the claim in August 1982. The bank sued R for breach of the undertaking to inform them. The question is whether the insurance ceases when R discovered the breach in November 1981 or when R formally rejected the claim in August 1982. The question is how s.33(3) should be applied. If it means that the insurance came to end the minute there arises a breach of warranty, then R's undertaking to inform A would have become effective in November 1981. The counter argument was that consistent with the law of contract, a repudiatory breach allows the innocent party to decide to accept the breach and thus, terminating the contract.
Held:
As far as the House of Lords was concerned, s.33(3) is clear in its effect. It provides that the policy comes to an end automatically when the breach is committed. This automatic discharge is not inconsistent with the provisions of s.34(3) which allow the insurer to waive the breach. It was argued that s.34(3) would be rendered redundant if s.33(3) is construed as resulting in the automatic discharge of the contract. If the breach of warranty terminates the contract automatically, there is nothing left for the insurer to waive. Lord Goff considered that there was nothing inconsistent here in that s.34(3) applies to bind the insurer to the contract if through his conduct he is deemed to have waived his right to automatic discharge.

Apart from a waiver, s.34(1) allows the breach of a warranty (whether implied or express) to be excused when

> "by reason of a change of circumstances, the warranty ceases to be applicable to the circumstances of the contract, or when compliance with the warranty is rendered unlawful by any subsequent law".

We might contrast this with the old common law position as set out in *Hore v*   **10–101**
Whitmore (1778) 2 Cowp. 784 where it was held that although the breach of warranty is not brought about by the default of the assured but by a change in circumstances or intervening event, the assured is nonetheless held responsible and must bear the consequences.
Example:
There is an express warranty that the ship shall sail before a particular date. It fails to do so because a legal restriction has been placed on the ship from sailing by the port authorities (circumstances similar to those in *Hore v Whitmore*). According to s.34(1) it might be argued that there has been a radical change in the circumstances or that compliance with the warranty to sail on the agreed date has been made unlawful.

Where the assured could not prove a change in circumstances or a subsequent illegality, the common law rule of strict compliance applies. In *Douglas v*

Scougall (1816) 4 Dow 278, Lord Eldon had this to say about the strictness required:

"It is not necessary to inquire whether the owners acted honestly and fairly in the transaction, for it is clear law that, however just and honest the intentions and conduct of the owner may be, if he is mistaken in the fact, and the vessel is in fact not seaworthy, the underwriter is not liable".

10–102   Section 34(2) buttresses the common law rule that a breach of warranty cannot be cured by providing that:

"Where a warranty is broken, the assured cannot avail himself of the defence that the breach has been remedied, and the warranty complied with, before loss".

Compliance is strict. In *De Hahn v Hartley* (1786) 1 T.R. 343, the assured had warranted that "50 hands or upwards" would man the Juno. Fifty men had actually been employed but when the ship commenced the insured voyage, there were only 46 men on board. Lord Mansfield held that a warranty must be strictly complied with and it was no defence for the assured to say that they had in fact taken on 50 men. No excuse would be tolerated. The warranty was for 50 hands and that had not been provided.

The strictness operates almost at all costs; the insurer is fully entitled to rely on the exact performance of the warranty. In *Overseas Commodities Ltd v Style* [1958] 1 Lloyd's Rep. 546, the cargo of tinned pork was insured under an "all risks" policy in which the assured had warranted that "all tins [will be] marked by manufacturers with a code for verification of date of manufacture". A number of cans had not been so marked. The assured claimed cover if not for the entire consignment, at least for those tins properly marked. The question was whether the contract was severable to enable the claim pro rata. McNair J. held against the assured. The judge observed that there was only a single policy for the consignment; the presumed intention must therefore be for the protection of the cargo as a single entity. The contract of insurance could not be severed to accommodate the assured's claim. To do so would be to go against the integrity of the policy.[51]

10–103   The strictness of the express warranties would not be assailed unless, following the conventional rules of contractual interpretation, qualifications or provisos must be read into the warranties to give the policy commercial sense.[52] In The *Resolute* [2008] EWCA Civ 1314 the Court of Appeal confirmed that the correct approach has to be for the court firstly to consider the ordinary and natural meaning of the warranty and, secondly, to consider the commercial purpose of

---

[51] See also *Brownsville Holdings Ltd & Khalid Abbar v Adamjee Insurance Co Ltd* [2000] 2 All E.R. (Comm) 803. In that case, there was a warranty that the assured was to employ a suitably qualified skipper on board the yacht at all times. By failing to do so for about nine months, the claimants were in breach of warranty. That breach discharged the insurers from all liability in pursuant to s.33(3) MIA 1906. It was also found that there was no waiver by the insurers of that breach of warranty.

[52] *Argo Systems v Liberty Insurance Pte Ltd* [2010] EWHC 540 (QB).

the warranty in the context of the policy as a whole.[53] The court would thus be prepared to apply any common sense qualifications to the otherwise strict terms of the warranty and in the event of ambiguity, a *contra proferentem* reading. In that case, the policy stipulated " . . . Warranted Owner and/or Owner's experienced Skipper on board and in charge at all times and one experienced crew member . . . ". On the night in question, the skipper of the assured fishing vessel went out for a drink with his friends after landing a good catch. During his absence of two hours, the vessel caught fire and was damaged. The insurers refused to pay, arguing that there was a breach of warranty. The warranty was for the vessel's protection but it was not an unqualified provision. If the insurers had wanted the crew on board continuously without being allowed to go ashore in all circumstances, they should have clearly so stipulated. "At all times" has been interpreted by previous authorities (*The Newfoundland* [2006] Lloyd's Rep. IR 704 and *The Milasan* [2000] 2 Lloyd's Rep. 458) to mean presence of the skipper is required to ensure that the ship is properly looked after and that it would not be exposed to unnecessary security risks. However, as those cases also assert, there are situations where the skipper's absence might be justified—for example, emergencies, such as the need to evacuate the vessel for safety reasons, and the performance of crewing duties to achieve the proper management of the vessel, such as collecting necessary crew and vessel supplies. It would also follow that where the skipper is required by the authorities to leave the ship to attend to any statutory duties or legal requirements, the warranty could not be said to have been broken. In the present case, however, the skipper was absent from the ship not because of an emergency or necessity.

All things considered, given the strictness of compliance, the courts will always construe express warranties narrowly. In *Elafonissos Fishing & Shipping Co v Aigion Insurance Co SA* [2012] EWHC 1512 (Comm), for example, the policy contained a warranty that the fishing vessel should be "laid up from 1/11/06 until 20/02/07 in the port of Mahajanga". Whilst in port it was damaged during a cyclone. The insurers refused to pay arguing that: (a) "warranted in the port of Mahajanga" required lay up to be in accordance with the regulations of that port; (b) that such regulations required the vessel to have four crew members on board and operational main and auxiliary engines; and (c) that the vessel's owner was in breach of the warranty. The High Court disagreed; it refused to imply in the warranty that the lay up had to be in accordance with port regulations.

One final word about warranties in general before we embark on an examination of the three implied warranties set out in the MIA—the distinction between warranties and representations should be recalled. The latter usually falls to be discussed within the duty to disclose and not to misrepresent. The latter is subject therefore to the test of materiality. A warranty is not subject to the test of materiality. In s.33(3) it is expressly stated that the warranty "is a condition which must be exactly complied with, *whether it be material to the risk or not*". As Lord Eldon said in *Newcastle Fire Insurance Co v Macmorran & Co* (1815) 3 Dow 255

" . . . where a representation is material it must be complied with—if immaterial, that immateriality may be inquired into and shown; but if there is

---

[53] See also *AC Ward v Catlin (Five) Ltd* [2009] EWHC 3122 (Comm).

a warranty it is part of the contract the matter is such as it is represented to be. Therefore the materiality or immateriality signifies nothing. The only question is as to the mere fact".

10–104　　In their final Consultation Paper on reforming business insurance,[54] the Law Commission tentatively proposes that:

* breach of a warranty should suspend, rather than discharge, the insurer's liability. A remedy of the breach should restore the insurer's liability; and

* where a term is designed to reduce a particular type of risk, liability should be suspended only in relation to that risk.

The Law Commission had thought the law on warranties is too inflexible and the all or nothing outcome is not always fair or economically efficient.

Warranty of seaworthiness

10–105　　The ICC(A) provide in Clause 5 that in no case shall the insurance cover loss, damage or expense arising from:

* unseaworthiness of vessel or craft;

* unfitness of vessel, craft, conveyance, container or liftvan for the safe carriage of the subject matter insured

where the assured or their servants are privy to such unseaworthiness or unfitness, at the time the goods insured are loaded therein. That provision is important. The ICC(A) being an "all risks" policy allows the assured to claim for loss or damage caused by unseaworthiness or unfitness of the conveyance unless the assured or their servants are privy to the unseaworthiness or unfitness.

This provision is a restatement of the duties of the assured set out in ss.39 and 40 of the MIA. Section 39(1) provides that in a voyage policy there is an implied warranty that at the commencement of the voyage the ship shall be seaworthy for the purpose of the particular adventure insured.[55] In the case of a time policy, s.39(5) states that there is no implied warranty that the ship shall be seaworthy at any stage of the adventure, but where the ship has been sent to sea in an unseaworthy state with the privity of the assured, the insurer is relieved of his duty to pay against any loss occasioned by the unseaworthiness.[56]

It might be mentioned that the meaning of the term "seaworthiness" should broadly coincide with that understood in the law of carriage of goods by sea.

---

[54] Consultation Paper "Insurance Contract Law: The Business Insured's Duty of Disclosure and the Law of Warranties" (June 2012) (*http://lawcommission.justice.gov.uk/areas/insurance-contract-law.htm*), accessed April 13, 2013.

[55] The fact that the ship was seaworthy when the risk was placed is immaterial; s.39 requires that the ship be seaworthy at the start of the insured voyage (see *The Pride of Donegal* [2002] EWHC 24). In that case, the court also stated that where there were two defects which were relied on as causing the ship's lack of seaworthiness, they should be looked at together and not separately to ascertain whether the risk was such that the vessel was not reasonably fit to encounter the perils of the voyage on which she was embarking.

[56] See also *Gibson v Small* (1853) 4 H.L. Cas. 353; *Marina Offshore v China Insurance (The Marina Isis)* [2006] S.G.C.A. 28 (Singapore Court of Appeal).

There is thus no need to go through those principles again. However it should be pointed out that s.39 does offer some statutory guidance to the term, albeit not exhaustively. For instance, s.39(2) states that where the policy attaches while the ship is at port, the warranty extends to the ship's fitness in encountering the ordinary perils of the port in question. Furthermore, where the policy relates to a voyage which is to be performed in different stages, during which the ship requires different kinds of or further preparation or equipment, there is an implied term that at the commencement of each stage the ship is seaworthy in respect of such preparation or equipment for the purposes of that stage. This of course is the statutory equivalent of the doctrine of stages we encountered in Chapter 7. What constitutes seaworthiness is also set out in the Act but only in the most general of terms. Section 39(4) states:

"A ship is deemed to be seaworthy when she is reasonably fit in all respects to encounter the ordinary perils of the seas of the adventure insured".

It was held in *Pickup v Thames & Mersey Marine Insurance Co Ltd* (1878) 3 **10–106** Q.B.D. 594, that the insurer generally bears the burden of proof that the vessel is unseaworthy at the relevant time when relying on the warranty as a defence. In that case, it was affirmed by the Court of Appeal that there was a presumption at law of seaworthiness and the presumption has to be disproved by the insurer. It is a reflection of the time honoured maxim "he who asserts must prove". It was further laid down as a matter of principle by the House of Lords in *Parker v Potts* (1815) 3 Dow 23 that it must be taken prima facie that a ship is seaworthy at the commencement of the risk, but that, if soon after her sailing it appears that she is not sound or fit at sea, without adequate reason to account for it, we might infer quite rationally that she was not seaworthy when the voyage commenced. The onus seems to move back to the assured to show that the vessel was in fact seaworthy.

Where privity of the assured is alleged, Roskill L.J. in *The Eurysthenes* [1977] Q.B. 49 offers this test:

"If the facts amounting to unseaworthiness are there staring the assured in the face so that he must, had he thought of it. Having realised their implication upon the seaworthiness of his ship, he cannot escape from being held privy to that unseaworthiness by blindly or blandly ignoring these facts or by refraining from asking relevant questions regarding them in the hope that by his lack of inquiry he will not know for certain that which any inquiry must have made plain beyond possibility of doubt".

Central to this test is the level or degree of knowledge possessed by the assured as regards the seaworthiness of the ship. There is no defence in saying that there was no actual knowledge. As far as *The Eurysthenes* was concerned, constructive knowledge would be sufficient.

This test was clarified in the human unseaworthiness case of *Manifest Shipping* **10–107** *& Co Ltd v Uni-Polaris Insurance Co Ltd and La Réunion Européne (The Star Sea)* [2001] 2 W.L.R. 170. The ship in question was considered to be unseaworthy in that it did not have an adequate firefighting system and her crew were not properly trained in handling the firefighting system. The policy concerned was a time policy and seaworthiness was customarily not a warranty and so the contract could not be avoided unless the insurer could prove privity on the part of the assured as to the unseaworthiness of the ship. Although the ship was owned by the claimants she was managed by an independent company, K Ltd.

It was accepted that the assured did not have actual direct knowledge of the relevant unseaworthiness. But it was argued that the assured's state of mind was equivalent to knowledge—so-called "blind eye knowledge". As far as Tuckey J. was concerned, that had been proved. The House of Lords however disagreed, stating that the insurers had to establish a suspicion or realisation in the mind of the assured that the ship was unseaworthy in the relevant aspects and a deliberate decision not to check whether that was so for fear of having certain knowledge about it. In order for there to be blind-eye knowledge, the suspicion must be firmly grounded and targeted on specific facts.

This is clearly the view taken by Lord Denning M.R. in *The Eurysthenes* [1977] Q.B. 49 at 68 who said:

> "To disentitle the shipowner, he must, I think, have knowledge not only of the facts constituting the unseaworthiness, but also knowledge that those facts rendered the ship unseaworthy, that is, not reasonably fit to encounter the ordinary perils of the sea. And, when I speak of knowledge, I mean not only positive knowledge, but also the sort of knowledge expressed in the phrase 'turning a blind eye'. If a man, suspicious of the truth, turns a blind eye to it, and refrains from inquiry—so that he should not know it for certain—then he is to be regarded as knowing the truth. This 'turning a blind eye' is far more blameworthy than mere negligence. Negligence in not knowing the truth is not equivalent to knowledge of it".

10–108   Geoffrey Lane L.J. in the same case stressed that privity meant knowledge and consent and was not equivalent to negligence.

In *The Star Sea*, as far as the House of Lords was concerned, the test of privity is extremely high—even gross negligence will not suffice if there is no deliberate decision not to pursue the facts for fear of discovering that the ship is in fact unseaworthy. Where the assured does not enquire because he is too lazy or he is grossly negligent or believes that there was nothing wrong, then privity has not been made out.

The test of privity is thus, to some extent, subjective: did the assured have direct knowledge of the unseaworthiness or an actual state of mind which the law treats as equivalent to such knowledge?

10–109   The section refers to the privity of the assured; the privity must be of an individual who is to be identified with the assured. In *The Star Sea* Manifest Shipping Co Ltd (the owners in the action) was a Cypriot company beneficially owned by the Kollakis family. The management of the vessel was in fact delegated to an English company based in London, Kappa Maritime Ltd. At the material times the directors of Kappa were Captain Stefanos Kollakis and his sons Pantelis and George, who were concerned with commercial and operational matters, and Mr Nicholaidis, the technical director. The registered managers were a Greek company, Charterwell Maritime SA, based in the Piraeus. Its directors were Captain Stefanos and a Mr Faraklas (who was also the sole director of Manifest). The House of Lords proceeded on the basis that the state of mind of any of these individuals may have been relevant to the question of privity but laid down no general test as to how the "relatedness" of these individuals to the company is to be ascertained. It would suffice to state that this is probably a question of fact to be decided based on how closely they are to the facts.

The knowledge required of the assured is that of the shipowner personally or of his alter ego, or in the case of a company, of its directors or whoever may be considered their alter ego. In *The Pacific Queen* [1963] 2 Lloyd's Rep. 201, the fact that two partners of the firm were aware of the ship's condition was sufficient. According to Lord Denning in *The Eurythenes* the assured must

"have knowledge not only of the facts constituting the unseaworthiness, but also knowledge that those facts rendered the ship unseaworthy, that is, not reasonably fit to encounter the ordinary perils of the sea".

Furthermore the state of knowledge must relate to the state of unseaworthiness that brings about the loss. In *Thomas v Tyne and Wear Steamship Freight Insurance Association Ltd* [1917] K.B. 938, the ship was unseaworthy for two reasons—a defective hull and an insufficient crew. Where the loss was caused by the defective hull which was not within the knowledge of the assured, the insurer could not plead breach of warranty on the basis that the assured was privy to the failure in supplying sufficient crew to man the ship. Atkin J. said:

"Where a ship is sent to sea in a state of unseaworthiness in two respects, the assured being privy to the one and privy to the other, the insurer is only protected if the loss was attributable to the particular unseaworthiness to which the assured was privy".

Warranty of cargoworthiness

Section 40(2) of the MIA provides that there shall be an implied warranty in a **10–110** voyage policy that the ship on which the insured goods are carried is not only seaworthy at the commencement of the voyage but is reasonably fit to carry the goods or other moveables to the agreed destination. This is reiterated by the ICC(A) in Clause 5 as set out above (para.10–105) with the all important qualification that the all risks cover will afford protection to the assured unless he is privy to the unfitness of the ship to receive and carry the cargo. It should also be noted that the words "arising from" in Clause 5 require that the causal link between the damage, loss or expense and the lack of seaworthiness or cargoworthiness be made.

The goods shipped need not however satisfy any requirement of seaworthiness. Section 40(1) provides that in a policy on goods or other moveables there is no implied warranty that the goods or moveables are seaworthy. The failure of the goods to withstand or encounter the ordinary incidents of the voyage could however be an inherent defect or vice of the goods. Where the goods perish or become lost as a result of that unseaworthiness, it is possible for the underwriter to argue that there should be no cover for loss or damage caused by an inherent defect. In *Koebel v Saunders* (1864) 17 C.B. (N.S.) 71, such a plea was accepted but the burden is on the insurer to prove that there is a causal link the loss and the unfitness of the goods for the voyage.

It is however open to the insurer to require the assured to make a warranty that the goods will be held in a container at all times. In a Hong Kong case, *E.L.A.Z.*

International Co v Hong Kong & Shanghai Insurance Company Ltd [2006] H.K.C.F.I. 406 for example, we see a policy expressed in the standard ICC(A) form but it also contained an express warranty that the policy was issued on a "subject to full container load" basis. That meant that the goods should at all times be held in the container. The facts were that the consignment of ladies wear had been carried by sea from Dongguan to Los Angeles via Hong Kong and thereafter, by train and road, to Laredo, Texas. The goods remained there until the necessary customs clearance to import the goods into Mexico could be obtained. On arrival in Laredo, the goods were placed in the custody of the ocean carrier's agents. The goods appeared to have been unloaded from the container and re-loaded into a trailer. That trailer was then stolen. The insurers refused to pay, arguing that as the goods had been unloaded from the container, there was a breach of the express warranty. The Hong Kong Court of First Instance held that there was no breach. It found no authority in Hong Kong law or English law for the proposition that the term "subject to full container load" meant that there could be no transshipment between containers. The literal meaning of this term is simply that there can be no intermingling with other shipments and that only the same shipment of goods would be in a container. There is merit in this judgment in that the transfer of the goods to a trailer would not actually expose the goods to a higher risk of damage customarily envisaged as being prevented by containers.

10–111   It is also too common for insurers to extract a warranty that the goods would be carried below deck. In *Geofizika DD v MMB International Ltd* [2010] EWCA Civ 459, the freight forwarder had warranted to the seller that the goods would be carried below deck without first checking the facts. The insurers quite rightly rejected the claim for breach of warranty. The only recourse open to the assured was to try and seek compensation from the freight forwarder.

Warranty of legality

10–112   It is trite law that all contracts, including those of marine insurance, must be legal and consistent with public policy. Indeed s.3 MIA refers to the prosecution of "a lawful marine adventure". In *Redmond v Smith* (1844) 7 Man. & G. 457, Tindal C.J. said of the nature of illegality:

> "A policy on an illegal voyage cannot be enforced; for it would be singular, if, the original contract being invalid and incapable to be enforced, a collateral contract founded upon it could be enforced. It may be laid down, therefore, as a general rule, that, where a voyage is illegal, an insurance upon such voyage is illegal".

Section 41 expands on this by prescribing that there is an implied warranty that the adventure is a lawful one, and that so far as the assured can control the matter, the adventure shall be carried out in a lawful manner. It does not however specify that the contract shall be void ab initio per se. Instead it has its ligature in s.33(3) which releases the insurer from liability as from the date of the breach. Liability already accrued will not be discharged. Where the adventure is illegal at the outset, then no valid contract of marine insurance is made. Where the adventure subsequently becomes illegal, the insurer is not liable from the time of the illegality.

Section 41 preserves the law of contract rules on *ex turpi causa non oritur actio* to the extent that where the adventure itself is unlawful the contract becomes null and void, but where merely the manner of performance is unlawful, the contract will be cancelled only if the assured is privy to the illegality.

On the first rule that the essence and object of the contract must be lawful, **10–113** reference to the relevant statutory or legal provision must be made. In *Redmond v Smith*, the statute prohibited the ship master from taking out seamen who were not under articles. The fact that the captain breached this law did not render the marine policy bad because according to Tindal C.J., the relevant law was

"passed for a collateral purpose only; its inte...on being to give to merchant seamen a readier mode of enforcing their contracts and to prevent their being imposed upon".

That statute did not state that noncompliance shall make the voyage illegal. It only provided a remedy for the seamen against his master.

Where the assured has the ability to steer the performance of the adventure away from illegality, he must do so according to the second limb of s.41. This is illustrated in the *Sanday Case* [1915] 2 K.B. 781, where the assured had abandoned the voyage upon its becoming illegal following the outbreak of war. The insurer claimed that to pay would be to contravene the illegality principle, for after all the voyage insured had become illegal. This was rejected. It is clear that if the assured had proceeded with the voyage, he would be deemed to have failed to exercise control to ensure that the adventure was carried out in a lawful manner.

Motives and extraneous factors will not on their own render the adventure **10–114** unlawful as we see in *Bird v Appleton* (1800) 8 T.R. 562. There, the cargo insured had been bought using unclean money but as far as the court was concerned this did not cause the adventure which in itself was lawful to become unlawful.

The more difficult question where a breach of the warranty has been established is whether the insurer could waive that breach under s.34(3). There is authority in *Gedge v Royal Exchange Assurance Corp* [1900] 2 Q.B. 214 that a breach of the implied warranty of legality cannot be waived. In that case, the policy was unlawful and unenforceable but the insurer had attempted to circumvent the effects of automatic discharge by treating the contract as if it were effective. They had resisted the claim made by the assured on the basis that there was nondisclosure of material facts instead of alleging that the contract was illegal. The court refused itself to be led into treating the contract as alive and well. It held:

"No court ought to enforce an illegal contract or allow itself to be made the instrument of enforcing obligations alleged to arise out of a contract or transaction which is illegal, if the illegality is duly brought to the notice of the court, and if the person invoking the aid of the court is himself implicated in the illegality".

Held covered clauses

In order to avoid the automatic discharge of the insurance cover, traders tend to **10–115** rely on a contractual device called the "held covered clause". An example of a held covered clause in the ICC(A) is Clause 10 which refers to a change of destination. The rule is that where there is a change of destination, the cover immediately ceases. However, according to Clause 10:

"where, after attachment of [the] insurance, the destination is changed by the Assured, held covered at a premium and on conditions to be arranged subject to prompt notice being given to the Underwriters".

Such a clause was considered judicially in *Greenock Steamship Co v Maritime Insurance Co Ltd* [1903] 1 K.B. 367. In that case, the assured was "held covered in case of any breach of warranty . . . at a premium to be hereafter arranged". The assured had sent their ship to sea in an unseaworthy condition. On whether this breach may be held covered, Bingham J. held that contractually the clause was effective in extending insurance cover to the subject matter even though there was a breach of warranty. The phrase "any breach of warranty" was wide enough to accommodate the event.

Held covered clauses usually have an appendage which provides that the extension of cover is subject to a "premium and conditions to be arranged". At contract law, a term could be rendered unenforceable if it is uncertain and vague. The question is whether such a "to be arranged" (TBA) clause suffers the same fate. The other issue is how should premium be measured or calculated in that event. Section 31(1) provides that where an insurance is effected at a premium to be arranged, and no arrangement is made, a reasonable premium is payable. Subsection (2) goes on to state that where an insurance is effected on the terms that an additional premium is to be arranged in a given event, and that event happens but no arrangement is made, then a reasonable additional premium is payable.

10–116 In *Greenock*, although no additional premium to cover the breach of warranty was set, it was not fatal to the claim. However, the court held that as the breach was only discovered after the loss, the fact of the loss may be taken into account when calculating the reasonable premium. The reasonable premium in such a case where the risk has become a certainty must thus necessarily be equal to the value of the loss.

Clause 10 requires that the assured gives prompt notice to the insurer. Such a "prompt notice" clause is fairly standard and many modern policies actually state precisely how prompt that notice should be. For example, the Institute Hulls and Freight Clauses expressly stipulate that the assured is to give notice "immediately after receipt of advices". Where the precise timing is not stipulated in the policy, the House of Lords held in *Thames & Mersey Marine Insurance Co Ltd v HT van Laun & Co* (1905) (1917) 23 Com. Cas. 104 that it would be subject to the requirement of reasonableness.

As to whether such a clause is a condition precedent to the reliance on the held covered clause, again that would depend on the precise terms of the policy. In a non-held covered case, *K/S Merc-Scandia XXXXII v Underwriters of Lloyds Policy No.25T 1054 87 & Ocean Marine Insurance Co Ltd* [2000] 2 Lloyd's Rep. 357, it was held that a prompt notice of claim clause is not a condition precedent but a mere innominate term. In that case, the policy provided that the assured was to give prompt written notice "in the event of any occurrence which may result in a claim". In that case, the insurer would not be prejudiced by the failure to give prompt notice as they would eventually have had to pay under the policy regardless. As such, it was an innominate term the breach of which should *not* result in avoidance of the policy and was not a condition precedent to the making of the claim. The nature of a notice clause in a held covered situation is quite different from that of a notice of potential claim. The former would clearly affect the insurer's preparedness to accommodate change in an insured risk.

Even if we were to say that it is an innominate term, it would seem invariably   **10–117** the case that the breach would result in serious consequences thereby entitling the insurer to avoid liability under the held covered clause.

Duty to pay premium

Section 52 MIA provides that the duty of the assured or his agent to pay premium   **10–118** and the duty of the insurer to issue the policy are concurrent conditions. The insurer is thus not obliged to issue the policy until payment or tender of the premium. Where premium is payable by instalments, it was made clear by the Court of Appeal in *Kadigra Denizcilik Ve Ticaret AS v Chapman & Co Ltd (In Liquidation)* (March 5, 1998) that although the premium might be payable by instalments, there was only one single premium. That meant that although the insurers were released from liability following an unpaid instalment, there remained a liability on the insured to pay the instalments that had not become due at the date of the breach, unless there is a waiver from the insurers. A waiver would be found if the insurers had demanded payment of the lapsed instalment or if they had accepted late payment as was the case in *Cia Tirrena di Assicurazioni v Grand Union Insurance Co Ltd* [1992] 2 Lloyd's Rep. 143.

Where the policy is effected through a broker, unless otherwise agreed, the assured discharges his payment obligation by paying the broker and the broker becomes directly responsible to the insurer for the premium (s.53(1)). In *Heath Lambert Ltd v Sociedad de Corretaje de Seguros* [2004] EWCA Civ 792, H, the broker, had paid the premiums to the insurer well before it was due to be paid. H however was not reimbursed by the assured. H then sued the assured. The question was whether the action was time barred—it would be time barred if time ran from the time the premium was actually paid, but not if time started to run from the time when premium was finally due. It should be noted that in such a case, the broker's action for premium is not for an indemnity in respect of the actual premium paid, but for an indemnity in respect of premium deemed to have been paid. It followed that its cause of action did not accrue on payment but when the broker was deemed to have paid the premium. The policy made it plain that premium was payable not when the risk was placed and the contract was made, but only 90 days later. H's action was not therefore time barred.

As a general rule, the assured is individually responsible for ensuring that premiums, especially those to be paid under a held covered agreement or by instalments, are paid in time. However, where the insurers have promised, expressly or by implication, to collect payments of the premium and failed to do so, they could be held liable to the assured for any lapses in cover. In *Betty Weldon v GRE Linked Life Assurance Ltd & Paragon Finance Plc* [2000] 2 All E.R. (Comm) 914, the High Court held that an insurer could be liable in contract or tort where an insurance policy had lapsed because of its failure to collect premiums through the direct debit system. Under the insurance contract, the insurers were under a duty to implement the direct debit mandate and could not therefore rely on its own failure as constituting nonpayment under the policy or as rendering the policy void or lapsed. By so doing, they were in breach of an implied term of the contract. It is no defence to argue that the assured should have taken steps to check that the necessary instalments have been collected. As far as a tortious claim is concerned, there was a real prospect of the claimant succeeding in showing a duty of care on the insurers—it was a reasonably foreseeable consequence of failing to implement the direct debit mandate properly, and a subsequent wrongful reliance upon that failure to avoid the policy, that the assured or his successors/assignees would be deprived of the benefit of the policy and thereby suffer loss. It should however be noted that this was a non-marine consumer insurance case. Whether the same is applicable to marine cases remains to be seen.

10–119   In *Glencore International AG v Alpina Insurance Co Ltd* [2004] EWHC 66, where cover was free for 30 days, as long as that is supported by consideration,[57] any loss suffered during that time can be claimed against the insurer. The court went on to say that the fact that the contract referred to 30 days' free cover was not necessarily an indication that the cover was merely for 30 days. The court concluded from the circumstances of the case that the cover was intended to be indefinite and the 30 days reference was only relevant for the calculation of the premium payable for the full cover. If the insurer wanted to terminate the cover after (or during) the 30 days, they could only do so by giving proper notice, clearly and unambiguously.

The English and Scottish Law Commissions have proposed to reform the law on the broker's liability for premium. The Law Commissions reasoned:

> "Section 53(1) makes a marine broker liable to pay premiums to the insurer. It is a complex provision. It appears to reflect the common law position, in which the insured was not liable to pay premiums to the insurer. This could have surprising consequences if a marine broker were to become insolvent. We think the position needs to be clarified, to state that policyholders are liable to pay premiums to the insurer."

The Commissions suggest that, in the marine market, the default rule should be that the broker is jointly responsible for the premiums, but that it should be simple for the parties to contract out of that provision.[58]

Loss

10–120   We have observed that before a claim may be made, the following criteria must be met:

1. the insurance covers the risks the assured alleges;

2. the loss is proximately caused by the risk insured against;

---

[57] The consideration, for example, might be the setting up of a direct debit or other particular payment mechanism to pay future premiums, or a promise to continue with the policy after the free period.

[58] See Law Commission's Issues Paper No.8 "The Broker's Liability for Premiums (Section 53)" (July 2010); also England Consultation Paper No.201, and Scotland, Consultation Paper No.152; for comments on the proposal see in particular the Bar Council's response to consultations at *http:/ /www.barcouncil.org.uk*.

3. the assured has the capacity to claim under the policy, that is to say, he has properly acquired the policy and he has insurable interest to claim;

4. the assured's claim is not defeated by any breach of good faith; and

5. the assured has committed no breach of express or implied warranties.

Furthermore the assured's entitlement to the insurance monies is dependent on the type of loss he has suffered. According to s.56, a loss may be total or partial. Where the assured brings an action for a total loss and the evidence proves only a partial loss, he may, unless the policy otherwise provides, recover for a partial loss. A total loss can take the form of an actual total loss or a constructive total loss.

Actual total loss

There is deemed to be an actual total loss when the goods are destroyed, so **10–121** damaged as to cease to be the thing insured, or where the assured is irretrievably deprived of them (s.57). The case *Asfar & Co Ltd v Blundell* [1896] 1 Q.B. 123 illustrates how this definition should be applied.

Asfar & Co Ltd v Blundell [1896] 1 Q.B. 123 **10–122**
Facts:
A barge had sunk in shallow waters with a cargo of dates. The vessel was subsequently raised but the dates had deteriorated so much that they were no longer fit for human consumption. They were however fit to be distilled to make industrial alcohol. The question was whether the dates were to be treated as total loss or not.
Held:
Lord Esher held that where the nature of the thing is altered and it has become for business purposes something else, so that it is not dealt with by business people as the thing it originally was, then there is a total loss. If the goods have changed character as to become an unmerchantable thing, then there is total loss. The dates had ceased to be merchantable as edible dates and were therefore to be regarded as a total loss.

This may be contrasted with *Francis v Boulton* (1895) 65 L.J.Q.B. 153.

Francis v Boulton (1895) 65 L.J.Q.B. 153 **10–123**
Facts:
A barge had sunk with a consignment of rice. The rice was valued at £450. The barge was subsequently raised but the assured decided to reject the cargo and to treat it as a total loss. The rice was then kiln-dried at a cost of £68 and sold at a loss.
Held:
The court held that there was no total loss in this case; the rice was damaged but still merchantable albeit at a lesser quality. Its nature had not changed insofar as business people were concerned.

Where the second limb of s.57(1) is concerned, irretrievable deprivation amounting to a loss means that although the goods are not totally lost at the time the claim is made, that loss is certainty. It is not about the reasonable abandonment of the goods where the total loss *appears* to be inevitable, as is the case with a constructive total loss. In s.57(1), the test required is more stringent—the loss must be shown to be a certainty, not merely appearing to be. This distinction might be lifted from Lord Abinger C.B.'s speech in *Roux v Salvador* (1836) 3 Bing., N.C. 266, a case involving the sale at an intermediate port of the insured hides which were deteriorating fast

" . . . the jury have found that the hides were so far damaged by a peril of the sea, that they never could have arrived in the form of hides. By the process of fermentation and putrefaction, which had commenced, a total destruction of them before their arrival at the port of destination, became as inevitable as if they had been cast into the sea or consumed by fire. Their destruction not being consummated at the time they were taken out of the vessel, they became in that state a salvage for the benefit of the party who was to sustain the loss, and were accordingly sold; and the facts of the loss and the sale were made known at the same time to the assured. Neither he nor the underwriters could at that time exercise any control over them, or by any interference alter the consequences. It appears to us, therefore, that this was not the case of what has been called a constructive loss, but of an absolute total loss of the goods: they could never arrive; and at the same moment when the intelligence of the loss arrived, all speculation was at an end".

10–124 It was held that the circumstances of fact must be such that the loss is an inevitability. Where the goods are not of a perishable nature for example, then the mere fact that they require re-shipment and further expenses to fortify their fitness for the voyage does not render them an actual total loss.

The application of the exception is strict as we see in *Masefield AG v Amlin Corporate Member Ltd (The Bunga Melati Dua)* [2011] EWCA Civ 24. There, the *Bunga Melati Dua*, a chemical/palm oil tanker, was seized by Somali pirates in the Gulf of Aden on August 19, 2008. The Somali pirates, true to form, demanded a ransom for the vessel's safe return. The issue was whether capture by pirates rendered a vessel and its cargo an actual total loss for the purposes of the marine cover. At the court of first instance, Steel J. held that there was no deprivation of property unless it was physically and legally[59] *impossible* to recover it (recovery which could be achieved by disproportionate effort and expense will not be enough). As is clear in *Roux* above, the difference between an ATL and CTL is essentially a matter of the distinction between physical impossibility and mercantile impossibility. The Court of Appeal accepted that to be a correct pronouncement of the law; it added that as there was a strong likelihood that payment of a ransom would secure recovery, there was automatic ATL. The enquiry was ultimately a "wait and see" situation based on the factual circumstances.[60]

Also, in *Bensaude v Thames & Mersey Marine Insurance Co Ltd* [1897] A.C. 609. In that case the vessel's main shaft broke whilst at sea. She had therefore returned to port for repairs. The delay caused led to the charterer's termination of the charterparty. A claim was made under the freight insurance for loss of freight. This was rejected on the basis that

---

[59] In that case, as the payment of ransom money is not illegal generally, there was no legal impossibility.

[60] See also *Clothing Management Technology v Beazley Solutions* [2012] EWHC 727 (QB).

"although the subject matter has been lost, and although it has been lost by a peril insured against, if the claim depends on loss of time in the prosecution of voyage so that the adventure cannot be completed within the time contemplated, then the underwriter is to be exempt from liability".

Much depends on the exact wording in the policy. The courts will attempt to **10–125** give the clause a meaning which most closely reflects trade practice and the common sense of seafaring men. In the ICC(A), the phrase used is "proximately caused by delay". This is to be distinguished from policies like the Institute Time and Voyage Clauses that adopt the phrase "loss consequent on delay". In *Naviera de Canarias SA v Nacional Hispanica Aseguradora SA (The Playa de las Nieves)* [1978] A.C. 853, the House of Lords rejected the assured's argument that "consequent on" meant "proximately caused". In that case, the assured had taken out a freight policy which excluded inter alia "any claim consequent on loss of time whether arising from a peril of the sea or otherwise". The ship's machinery broke down and required repairs. The delay resulted in the suspension of the charterparty and consequently, a loss of freight to the shipowners. According to Lord Diplock, the proper construction was that the delay need not be the proximate cause of the loss. It is sufficient that the delay was an intermediate cause of the loss. His Lordship said:

"[the exception] expressly makes the operation of the clause dependent upon the presence in the chain of an intermediate event (viz. 'loss of time') between the loss for which the claim is made (viz. 'loss of freight') and the event which in insurance law is the 'proximate cause' of that loss (viz. a peril insured against). The intermediate event, 'loss of time', is not itself a peril though it may be the result of a peril. That is why the words 'whether arising from a peril of the sea or otherwise' are not mere surplusage . . . They are there to make it plain that the clause is concerned with an intermediate event between the occurrence of a peril insured against and the loss of freight of which the peril was, in insurance law, the proximate cause".

If on the other hand, the policy had adopted a clause like that in the ICC(A), the position would be quite different.

Section 58 provides that where the ship concerned in the adventure is missing, and after a lapse of a reasonable time no news of her has been received, an actual total loss may be presumed. As far as goods carried on the vessel are concerned, the presumption will apply, rendering the goods a total loss as well. What constitutes a reasonable time, according to s.88, is a matter of fact. In *Houstman v Thornton* (1816) Holt N.P. 242, we are reminded that the presumption is subject to the proviso implicit in all insurance contracts that where the ship is subsequently found, the insurers will have a direct claim to her and her cargo to the extent of the pay-out.

Where the goods have actually reached their destination but due to marks on the packing having been obliterated, they are incapable of identification, the loss, if any, is partial and not total (s.56(5)). In *Spence v The Union Marine Insurance* (1868) L.R. 3 C.P. 427, the assured's cotton had been shipped together with cotton belonging to other owners. Part of the cargo was lost when the ship was wrecked. The remainder were damaged but were nevertheless carried to their destination by another vessel. The identification marks on the bales had been obliterated by seawater and it was not possible to identify the assured's bales. The market in cotton had then fallen. The assured claimed under his policy for a total loss.

10–126   The rule of law as far as the court was concerned is this:

> "... when goods of different owners become by accident so mixed together as to be indistinguishable, the owners of the goods so mixed become tenants in common of the whole, in the proportion in which they have severally contributed to".

Each owner was therefore entitled to a proportion of the value of the goods lost and of the damage to the remainder which could not be identified. The loss was to be treated as a partial loss.

Constructive total loss

10–127   Section 60(1) provides that there is a constructive total loss where the subject matter is reasonably abandoned on account of its actual total loss appearing unavoidable, or because it could not be preserved from actual total loss without an expenditure which would exceed its value when the expenditure had been incurred. This is mirrored in Clause 13 of the ICC(A) which provides that no claim for constructive total loss shall be recoverable unless the subject matter insured is reasonably abandoned either on account of its actual total loss appearing to be unavoidable or because the cost of recovering, reconditioning and forwarding the subject matter to the destination to which it is insured would exceed its value on arrival.

Below is a general example of how constructive total loss is established.

10–128   *Vacuum Oil Co Ltd v Union Insurance Society of Canton* (1926) 25 Ll. L. Rep. 546
Facts:
The vessel carrying a cargo of petroleum was stranded. The petroleum was contained in tins. Although a large number of tins were recovered, they were beginning to show signs of stress and some were indeed leaking. Some of the leaking tins were crudely repaired and filled with the contents of tins which were irreparably damaged. In total, about half the amount was saved. Was this a constructive total loss?
Held:
The Court of Appeal considered that there was a constructive total loss on the basis that it would have been impossible to get a ship to carry a cargo of leaking petroleum tins. Expert evidence adduced showed that about 900 tins might have leaked in the time it would have taken to complete the voyage and 900 tins represents between 3500 and 4000 gallons of petroleum, "which during this time would have flowed and leaked into the hold of the unfortunate vessel which was supposed to be carrying them". That is to say that assured was right to abandon the cargo since its actual total loss is unavoidable.

"Unavoidable" was also discussed in *Court Line Ltd v R. (The Lavington Court)* [1945] 2 All E.R. 357, where the court at first instance held that the term

> "connotes a very high degree of probability, with the additional element that there is no course of action, project or plan, present at the time or place in the mind of the person concerned which offers any reasonable possibility of averting the anticipated event".

It does not mean that the actual total loss is an inevitability—a high degree **10–129** probability is required but not inevitability. It is however unclear whether this statement imports an objective or subjective test. It is submitted that the appropriate test should be objective to the extent that the requirement for reasonableness in the decision must be accounted for but at the same time taking into account the assured's or his agents' state of mind. It is the test of how the objective assured would react considering the exigencies and peculiar circumstances of the situation.

The loss could also be generated by the voyage being frustrated by a peril insured against. Where the goods are prevented from arriving at their destination because of a peril insured against, the assured may make a claim for a constructive total loss as is demonstrated in *Rodocanachi v Elliot* (1874) L.R. 9 C.P. 518. There, the insured cargo of silk was shipped under a contract that required the goods to be carried from China through France and on to England. When the goods arrived in France, war between Germany and France had broken out and it was not possible for the goods to be transported to England. Shipment of the goods was to be effected by the owners who were insured under a standard policy with the underwriter. The goods were not damaged and possession remained with the owners, but could not reach their destination. On whether the assured could claim a constructive total loss, the court held that the restraint imposed on the goods is a peril insured and the assured were entitled to abandon them. Bramwell B. held:

> "It is well established that there may be a loss of the goods by a loss of voyage in which the goods are being transported, if it amounts, to use the words of Lord Ellenborough, 'to a destruction of the contemplated adventure'".

Besides the general rule in s.60(1), it is provided specifically in s.60(2) that in particular there is to be a constructive total loss of the goods insured where the assured is deprived of the possession of his goods by a peril insured against and:

1. it is unlikely that he can recover the goods; or

2. the cost of recovering the goods would exceed their value when recovered; or

3. the cost of repairing the damage and forwarding the goods to their destination would exceed their value on arrival.

"Unlikely to recover the goods"

Section 60(2)(i) refers to reasonable abandonment of the goods where it is **10–130** unlikely that the goods could be recovered. The difficulty here is time relevant in determining whether the goods are unlikely to recovered.
Example:
Assume that the carrying vessel has been stranded. War has broken out in the area and it appears unlikely that the ship could be retrieved. The assured decides to abandon the ship and goods insured, and to make a claim under their marine policies. Six weeks later the war ends, and it seems likely that the vessel could

be retrieved. At what point in time should they be regarded as unlikely to recover the goods and ship?

10–131   *Polurrian Steamship Co Ltd v Young* [1915] 1 K.B. 922
Facts:
When hostilities broke out between Turkey and Greece, the insured vessel was seized for carrying coal for Turkish consignees. The assured decided to give notice of abandonment. Six weeks later, the ship was released.
Held:
The relevant date for determining whether the ship was a constructive total loss was that of the commencement of the action. That date was *in this case* the date on which the notice of abandonment was given. The assured failed to succeed in their claim though. They had failed to prove that recovery of the vessel was *unlikely* within a reasonable time, all they were able to establish was that it was *uncertain* whether the vessel could be recovered within a reasonable time. The court said:

> "[I]t is indisputable that, according to the law of England, in deciding upon the validity of claims of this nature between the assured and the insurer, the matters must be considered as they stood on the date of the commencement of the action. That is the governing date. If there then existed a right to maintain a claim for a constructive total loss by capture, that right would not be affected by a subsequent recovery or restoration of the insured vessel".

If at the time of action brought the circumstances are such that a notice of abandonment would not be justifiable, the assured can only recover for a partial loss.

10–132   The claimants had argued that "unlikely to recover" should be given the same meaning as "uncertain to recover" which was the requirement under the law merchant. That argument rested on the basis of s.91(2) MIA which provides that the rules of the common law including the law merchant, save in so far as they are inconsistent with the express provisions of the Act, shall continue to apply. This was rejected by the court which held that the MIA had expressly modified the law merchant by substituting "uncertain to recover" with "unlikely to recover". Under the new law, the assured will have to show: (i) that he is deprived of possession of his ship or goods, and (ii) that he is unlikely to recover them, not merely uncertain that they could recover in reasonable time. This rule has been criticised on the basis that it is an extremely difficult test to satisfy because it involved conjecture and speculation. The old test, it is argued, is more practical.
Section 60(2)(i) is given capacious airing in the case below.

10–133   *The Bamburi* [1982] 1 Lloyd's Rep. 312
Facts:
The Bamburi was docked at Shatt-al-Arab. Before permission to leave was granted, the Iran-Iraq war broke out. The harbour master informed the ship that she was not to leave in the interests of safety. The ship was covered by a war risk policy. Three issues arose:

1. whether the detention was proximately caused by a peril insured against;

2. whether the assured was deprived of possession of the ship;

3. if so, whether it was unlikely to recover.

Held:

1. The order by the harbour master instructing the vessel to remain at port constituted a restraint by princes. Where the only reason is for the ship's safety would not render the act a restraint by princes, the true motive was that the Iraqis wanted to avoid political embarrassment from the ship's being sunk by enemy forces. This was therefore an insured peril, the policy being one for war risks. However it is important that the proximate cause remained an operative cause until the notice of abandonment and was likely to remain the proximate cause until the expiry of a reasonable time. This was sufficiently proved from the diplomatic notes and repeated refusal to release the ship by the authorities.

2. The concept of possession should be taken to refer to whether the assured retained the right to control and use, and the right of disposal vis-à-vis the vessel. The assured had been deprived of possession even though their crew was still aboard the insured vessel because they were unable to control her fate.

3. What constitutes a reasonable time is a question of fact. In this case expert evidence showed that it was not likely that the vessel would be released within the next 12 months from the date of the notice of abandonment. Twelve months, according to the court, was a reasonable time.

The assured's burden of proof is not light. In *Marstrand Fishing Co Ltd v Beer* **10–134** [1937] 1 All E.R. 158, the crew had taken possession of and sailed away with the ship unlawfully. Although the ship had been sighted at various places, she successfully evaded capture. It was left to Porter J. to decide whether there had been a constructive total loss. The judge decided that the true test was whether the ship was more likely to be lost than to be recovered. The probability of the ship being recovered was not so remote that the judge had to concede that he was unable to decide whether the ship was more likely to be lost than recovered. Under such circumstances, it was not a constructive total loss.

"Cost of recovering, or cost of repairing the damage and forwarding the goods to their destination exceeding their value"

Section 60(2)(i) also states that there is a constructive total loss where the cost of **10–135** recovering the goods would exceed their value when recovered. Section 60(2)(iii) adds to this by providing that the goods will be considered a constructive total loss if the cost of repairing the goods and then forwarding them to the destination would exceed their value on arrival.

A manifest example is the case *Vacuum Oil Co v Union Insurance Society of Canton* (1926) 25 Lloyd's List Lloyd's Rep. 546, where the Court of Appeal considered that the cost of buying new tins and shipping them to the stranded ship, together with the cost of reconditioning the unclean petroleum, would clearly exceed the value of the petroleum. There was therefore a constructive total loss. The assured is not however entitled to add to the overall cost, the original freight which would have been payable anyway (see too *Farnworth v Hyde* (1866) L.R. 2 C.P. 204).

In the House of Lords' case of *Sailing Ship "Blairmore" Co Ltd v MacRedie* [1898] A.C. 583, the insured ship had sunk in harbour and a notice of abandonment was given to the insurer. The insurers managed to raise the ship, albeit at substantial expense. They then claimed that the ship could be repaired for less than her value and thus the loss was only a partial loss. It was held that the insurers could not convert a constructive total loss to a partial loss by incurring substantial expenditure which an ordinary prudent and uninsured owner would not have incurred. The cost of raising the vessel so exceeded the value of the ship that she must be treated as a total loss. It is not open to say that only the cost of repairing need to be taken into account.

Abandonment and its effects

10–136   Section 61 sets out the effect of a constructive total loss generally—where there is a constructive total loss, the assured may either treat the loss as a partial loss, or abandon the subject matter insured to the insurer and treat it as if it were a total loss. In order to make a claim for total loss in these circumstances, the assured needs to give a notice of abandonment to the insurer. Failure to do so will result in the loss being treated as a partial loss (s.62(1)). The notice must be given with reasonable diligence after the receipt of reliable information of the loss, but where the information is of doubtful character, the assured is entitled to a reasonable time to make inquiry (s.62(3)). We could rely on Lord Chelmsford's description in *MR Currie & Co v Bombay Native Insurance Co* (1869) L.R. 3 P.C. 72:

> "What is a reasonable time . . . must depend upon the particular circumstances of each case. On the one hand, the assured is not to delay his notice when a total loss occurs, in order to keep his chance of doing better for himself by keeping the subject insured, and then, when he finds it will be more to his advantage to do so, throwing the burden upon the underwriters; while, on the other, the underwriters cannot complain of a suspense of judgment fairly exercised on the part of the assured, to enable him to determine whether the circumstances are such as to entitle him to abandon".

Once the notice has been given properly, the fact that the insurer refuses to accept it is immaterial to the claim (s.62(4)). Acceptance of the notice may be express acknowledgement or by conduct. Mere silence however does not amount to acceptance. Once the notice has been accepted, it becomes irrevocable. This means that the acceptance confirms that the notice has been sufficiently and properly given and the liability for the loss is admitted. As with other requirements in the Act, the notice of abandonment may be waived by the insurer. Further, s.62(7) provides that the notice of abandonment is not necessary where, at the time when the assured receives information about the loss, there would be no benefit to the insurer if notice were given to him. That section is generally applied to situations where the subject matter insured is freight or demurrage. In *Rankin v Potter* (1873) L.R. 6 HL83, notice for a constructive total loss of freight need not be given not only because there was no benefit to the insurer to be given a notice of abandonment but that there was nothing to abandon anyway.

In relation to cargo insurance, s.62(7) was also examined in *Vacuum Oil* where Bankes L.J. considered that "possibility of benefit" arises when the circumstances are such that

> "the underwriter, if the goods had been abandoned and he had had the absolute control over them, could have exercised that control and done what he thought best under the circumstances"

or that the insurer is able to convert the lost property into some sort of advantage, physical or otherwise. In *The Litsion Pride* [1985] 1 Lloyd's Rep. 437, it was held that abandonment was not necessary because the ship had been lost in war time circumstances and it was impossible to salvage it. There was thus no possibility of benefit to the insurer.

Kastor Navigation Co Ltd v AGM M A T [2004] EWCA Civ 277   **10–137**
Facts:
K's ship sank 15 hours after a fire had started in her engine room. K then claimed on the insurance on the basis of an ATL. One of the insurer's defence was that before the sinking of the vessel, she was so badly damaged by the fire that she was a CTL because the cost of repairing her would have exceeded her value when repaired. The question was whether K, having lost a claim for an ATL, he could claim on a CTL. The lower court decided that the fire could not have caused the sinking but that it had led to a CTL that preceded the ATL at a time when the vessel was not bound to become an ATL. The judge went on to say that the CTL became an accrued cause of action before the ATL and the ATL did not prevent the action for a CTL to be maintained.

The insurer argued that:

- there was no claim for a CTL because there was no abandonment under s.61 MIA 1906;

- there was only one loss because the vessel was doomed to become an ATL when she became a CTL;

- the assured had elected to claim for an ATL and could not thereafter claim for a CTL.

The parties had agreed that the notice of abandonment was to be dispensed with.
Held:
The Court of Appeal held that under s.62(1) unless notice of abandonment was given or excused, the loss could only be treated as a partial loss. K's claim for an ATL could not amount to treatment of the CTL as a partial loss. By claiming for a total loss K indicated a willingness to abandon the vessel to the insurer. It was not impossible to make a claim for a CTL after an ATL of the vessel. The right to claim for a CTL did not disappear if the ATL preceded the assured's opportunity to elect to treat the casualty as a total loss.

The trial judge was fully entitled to find that the fire was an independent cause of loss from the ingress of water. A CTL could be claimed where an ATL had occurred shortly afterwards by operation of a peril other than the cause of the CTL, even though no notice of abandonment had been served.

There had been no irrevocable election by reason of the initial claim for an ATL.

It should however be noted that the notice of abandonment is not an essential   **10–138**
condition to the characterisation of a loss as a constructive total loss, that is to say, the existence of a constructive total loss is not dependent on the notice. Hence, there can be a constructive total loss even though there is no proper notice given. However, the assured may not make a claim for total loss if he does not give notice. In *Robertson v Petros Nomikos Ltd* [1939] A.C. 371, Lord Wright held:

"[A] notice of abandonment is not an essential ingredient of a constructive total loss. The Appellant's argument confuses two different concepts, because it confuses constructive total loss with the right to claim for a constructive total loss. The right to claim ... depends on due notice of abandonment under section 62 of the Act. The distinction is explicitly stated in section 61 ...

[which] makes it clear that the right to abandon only arises when there is a constructive total loss in fact. That is the necessary precondition to a right to abandon".

In *Bank of America National Trust & Savings Association v Christmas (The Kyriaki)* [1993] 1 Lloyd's Rep. 137, for example, limitation period will run from the date of the constructive total loss and not from the date of the notice of abandonment.

Section 63(1) provides that where there is a valid abandonment the insurer is entitled to take over the interest of the assured in whatever may remain of the subject matter insured and all proprietary rights incidental thereto. The common law position is that the insured property upon abandonment becomes the property of the insurer and with it the rights and liabilities of ownership. It does not appear that this rule has been modified by the Act even though the Act makes no express reference to liabilities incidental to ownership of the subject matter.

10–139   Where the notice has been rejected by the insurer which he is entitled to do, what will become of the property? Does it remain with the assured? In *Roux v Salvador* (1836) 3 Bing. N.C. 266, although the matter was raised, it was not decided on. There are three possibilities, the first being that the subject matter should remain the property of the assured, the second being that property regardless should pass to the insurer, and thirdly, the goods should be treated as *res nullius*. It is important to establish for the purposes of liabilities as to whom property should vest. Take for example a case where the cargo of dangerous substances has become a constructive total loss. If the notice is accepted by the insurer, the insurer becomes liable for any potential tortious damage. If the notice is not accepted, should the assured remain liable? Should it be treated as *res nullius*? Clarity is needed.

It should, however, be remembered that, as was pointed out in *Dornoch Ltd v Westminster International BV* [2009] EWHC 889 (Admlty), the mere fact that underwriters declined notice of abandonment could not without more in the ordinary way deprive them of their right to take over the insured's interest in the subject-matter insured, which is derived from other provisions of the MIA (and not s.63). In that case, the insurer had rejected the notice of abandonment but had subsequently paid for the constructive total loss. The court held that they, therefore, retained their rights of subrogation despite having rejected the notice of abandonment. This takes us back to the earlier proposition—abandonment and the notice of abandonment are not the same thing.

General average

10–140   If a general average loss has been incurred in connection with a peril insured against, the assured may recover the whole amount from the insurer without having recourse to the other parties liable to contribute (s.66). It may be left to the insurer to recover this amount from the others. First, a brief word about general average. In the course of sea voyage there are three particular interests at risk:

• the vessel;

• the cargo; and

- the freight.

Where a peril affects any of these interests resulting in a loss, that loss is borne by that interest alone. For example where the cargo spontaneously combusts, that loss is borne by the cargo owner specifically and no one else. However, where "extraordinary sacrifices" are made or expenditure is incurred to save the entire adventure, the loss is to be borne by all pro rata. That sacrifice or expenditure is known as a general average loss. In this case, the particular interest which has suffered the loss is entitled to a contribution from the other interests—this is called a general average contribution. The following conditions must be met before the court would find a general average:

1. there must be a common danger to all relevant interests. For instance, a severe storm that affects not only the ship, but the cargo and the potential freight to be earned;

2. the danger must not be caused by the default of the interest claiming contribution. Where the goods are thrown overboard because they are becoming dangerous, the cargo owner is not entitled to claim general average contribution;

3. there must be a real danger. In *Joseph, Watson & Son Ltd v Fireman's Fund Insurance Co* [1922] 2 K.B. 355, the crew had mistakenly thought the ship's hold to be on fire and so steam was streamed into the hold causing damage to the goods. That damage could not be classed as a general average loss;

4. any sacrifice incurred must be reasonable;

5. there must be a link between the incurring of extraordinary expenditure with the danger or event. For example, where extraordinary large amount of fuel is used to refloat a ship may be treated as a general average loss; and

6. the interest seeking contribution must have actually been saved.

Where the assured has incurred a general average expenditure, he may recover **10–141** from the insurer in respect of the proportion of the loss which falls on him. In the case of a general average loss, he may recover from the insurer in respect of the whole loss without having enforced his right of contribution from the other parties liable to contribute. Where the assured has paid or is liable to pay a general average contribution in respect of the subject matter insured, he may recover that amount from the insurer. In the case where the ship, freight and cargo or any two of these interests are owned by the same assured, s.66(7) provides that the liability of the insurer in respect of general average losses or contribution is to be determined as if those subjects were owned by different persons.

It is open to the relevant parties to enter into an agreement limiting or excluding the proportion of the expenses payable as regards liability in general average. However the court will require evidence that s.66 MIA 1906 is to be departed from (*Comatra Ltd & Arabian Bulk Trade v Various Underwriters as Specified on the Original Writ* (2000) C.L.C. 354).

A particular average loss according to s.64 is a partial loss. It therefore does not give rise to any right of contribution from the other parties interested in the adventure.

Measure of indemnity

10–142 The insurance being a contract of indemnity means that the assured is only entitled to recover the extent of his actual loss. Where there is a total loss (whether actual total loss or constructive total loss), the assured recovers value prescribed in a valued policy or the insurable value of the subject matter in the case of an unvalued policy.

Where there exists a partial loss of goods, the measure of indemnity is set out in s.71:

"(1) Where part of the goods, merchandise or other moveables insured by a valued policy is totally lost, the measure of indemnity is such proportion of the sum fixed by the policy as the insurable value of the part lost bears to the insurable value of the whole, ascertained as in the case of an unvalued policy".

This takes the form of the mathematical formula below:

$$\text{Agreed Value} \times \frac{\text{Insurable Value of the Part}}{\text{Insurable Value of the Whole}}$$

> *N.B.* The insurable value is defined in s.16 as the "prime cost of the property insured, plus the expenses of and incidental to shipping and the charges of insurance upon the whole".

10–143 "(2) Where part of the goods, merchandise or other moveables insured by an unvalued policy is totally lost, the measure of indemnity is the insurable value of the part lost, ascertained as in the case of total loss.

(3) Where the whole or any part of the goods or merchandise insured has been delivered damaged at its destination, the measure of indemnity is such proportion of the sum fixed by the policy in the case of a valued policy, or of the insurable value in the case of an unvalued policy, as the difference between the gross sound and damaged values at the place of arrival bears to the gross sound value . . . ".

In the valued policy, the measure of indemnity shall be:

$$\text{Agreed Value} \times \frac{(\text{Gross Sound Value—Gross Damaged Value})}{\text{Gross Sound Value}}$$

In an unvalued policy, the measure of indemnity shall be:

$$\text{Insurable Value} \times \frac{(\text{Gross Sound Value—Gross Damaged Value})}{\text{Gross Sound Value}}$$

10–144 In *Michael Kusel v Charles Neville Rupert Atkin (The Catariba)* [1997] 2 Lloyd's Rep. 749, the application of s.69(3) was raised. Section 69(3) is similar in terms to s.71(3) but unlike s.71(3), which applies to a cargo claim, it refers to the partial loss of a ship. Nevertheless, the approach taken by the court in *The*

Catariba should be equally applicable to cargo claims under s.71(3) as vessel claims under s.69(3). In that case, the insured vessel sustained damage after running aground. At this point in time, the insurance expired. However, there was a "held covered" clause which came into operation thereby keeping the cover alive. The vessel was then towed to safety at the Virgin Islands. The island was unfortunately struck by Hurricane Luis and the vessel was more severely damaged. The claimant rejected the underwriter's offer of a Constructive Total Loss and argued that he was therefore entitled to recover the aggregate cost of repairs caused by the two accidents notwithstanding that the aggregate exceeded the insured value of the vessel. Colman J. held that a partial loss which is left unrepaired is for the purposes of the measure of indemnity superseded or obliterated by a subsequent total loss, so successive partial losses unrepaired at the date of termination of cover, must, by analogy be treated as having caused to the assured only such actual pecuniary loss as is measured by reference to the cumulative depreciation of the vessel's value at the time of termination of cover by the express terms of s.69(3). Accordingly, assuming that there was no constructive total loss, the aggregate amount was limited to the insured value of the vessel less the amounts for which the claimant must give credit. The insurer's liability was thus to be limited to the insured value of the vessel regardless of the number of successive losses there might have been and whatever effect those losses had in diminishing the value of the vessel.

"s.71 (4) 'Gross value' means the wholesale price or, if there be no such price, the estimated value, with, in either case, freight, landing charges, and duty paid beforehand; provided that, in the case of goods or merchandise customarily sold in bond, the bonded price is deemed to be the gross value. 'Gross proceeds' means the actual price obtained at a sale where all charges on sale are paid by the sellers.

s.72 (1) Where different species of property are insured under a single valuation, the valuation must be apportioned over the different species in proportion to their respective insurable values, as in the case of an unvalued policy. The insured value of any part of a species is such proportion of the total insured value of the same as the insurable value of the part bears to the insurable value of the whole, ascertained in both cases as provided by this Act."

There is an overriding duty on the assured to take measures to minimise the loss (s.78(4))[61] and in order to ensure that the assured is not prejudiced by anything he does to minimise loss after the peril, a "suing and labouring" clause is usually inserted in the policy. Such a clause will require the assured and his agents "to take and to continue to take all such steps as may be reasonable for the purpose

---

[61] Section 78(4) reads: "it is the duty of the assured and his agents, in all cases, to take such measures as may be reasonable for the purpose of averting or minimising a loss". In *The Grecia Express* [2002] EWHC 203 the marine insurer could not avoid the policy on the basis of a breach of s.78(4) when it could not be proved that the proximate cause of the loss was the ship's watchman's misconduct in failing to be on the ship to prevent the complete loss. The proximate cause was, according to the court in that case, the cutting of the mooring ropes and the flooding of the engine room.

of averting or minimising any loss, damage, liability, cost or expense" in respect of the insured risk. The test as to whether the assured had taken the requisite reasonable measures requires us to ask what should have been done "in all the circumstances", and it makes it essential, therefore, to consider whether any other suggested action would have had any realistic prospect of success in achieving a different result. It also means that the court must take into account the reason why the assured (or his agent) did not take such a step. (*Melinda Holdings v Hellenic Mutual War Risks Association Bermuda* [2011] EWHC 181 (Comm)).

10–145   Section 78(1) states that where there is incorporated a "sue and labour" clause:

> "the engagement thereby entered into is deemed to be supplementary to the contract of insurance, and the assured may recover from the insurer any expenses properly incurred pursuant to the clause".

This is not prejudiced or affected by the fact that the insurer might have already paid for the loss. Clause 16 of the ICC(A) for example stipulates that while it is the duty of the assured to take reasonable measures to avert or minimise loss, the underwriter will, in addition to any loss recoverable under the policy, reimburse the assured for any charges properly and reasonably incurred. In conjunction with the general duty to avert or minimise loss, the assured must ensure that all rights against carriers, bailees or other third parties are properly preserved and exercised.

10–146   *The State of the Netherlands v Youell* [1998] 1 Lloyd's Rep. 236
Facts:
The Dutch Royal Navy had insured two of their submarines which were being built at a shipyard against builders' risks. The builders' work was not up to scratch, resulting in the debonding and cracking of the paintwork. The underwriters argued that s.78(4) MIA 1906 applied as the shipyard, as the navy's agents, had failed to take reasonable measures to avert or minimise the loss in respect of which the claim was made.
Held:
There was no agency between the shipyard and the navy. The shipyard was dealing with the submarines not as the navy's agent but as the submarines' builder under a building contract. The builder cannot be an agent for the purposes of s.78(4) by virtue, simply and only, of his status under the building contract.

This case raises the issue as to whether s.78(4) can be reconciled with s.55(2)(a), which provides that it is no bar to the insurance cover that the proximate cause of the loss was in fact the negligence or misconduct of the assured and/or his agent. On the one hand, s.78(4) suggests that the claim could be defeated where the assured or his agent is at fault. On the other, s.55(2)(a) clearly anticipates the assured's or his agent's fault as an insurable peril.

10–147   As far as Phillips L.J. was concerned,[62] there is no conflict between the two provisions. In fact, Phillips L.J. held that s.78(4) should be construed in the light

---

[62] The other two judges, Butler-Sloss and Buxton L.JJ., did not take up the issue of s.55(2)(a). The latter preferred to confine his judgment to the fact that the shipyard was not an agent for the purposes of s.78(4). The former dismissed the appeal without giving any reasons.

of the provisions of s.55(2)(a). That being the case, s.78(4) should and could only apply where the misconduct or breach of duty is so significant that it must displace the prior insured peril (namely, negligence and misconduct of the assured or his agents). Section 55(2)(a) should generally prevail unless the circumstances are such that the breach or misconduct committed by the assured and/or his agents is so blatantly outside what was envisaged in s.55(2)(a). It was considered in that case that the shipyard's failure to minimise the risk of damage was an insured peril and as such the insurance cover should not be displaced.

In *Astrovlanis Compania Naviera SA v Linard (The Gold Sky)* [1972] 2 Lloyd's Rep. 187, Mocatta J. suggested that s.78(4) covered the acts of the assured and his agents but not those of his servants. The latter is thus to be accommodated by s.55(2)(a). This view was affirmed in *The Vasso* [1993] 2 Lloyds Rep. 203. Phillips L.J. in *The State of the Netherlands v Youell* however disagreed with this analysis stating:

"If the approach in these cases is correct, then it would seem to follow that whenever agents of the assured, by negligence or misconduct, fail to take steps which would avert or minimise the consequences of an assured peril, underwriters can by defence or counterclaim, avoid liability for such consequences. Thus, in effect, the policy would exclude liability for loss attributable to negligence or misconduct of the assured's agents after, but not before, the casualty".

The view in *National Oilwell (UK) Ltd v Davy Offshore Ltd* [1993] 2 Lloyd's Rep. 582 that it is a mere question of causation, that is to say, if negligence of the assured is an insured peril then s.55(2)(a) should apply displacing s.78(4) but if negligence is not a stipulated peril then s.78(4) should apply. That too is to be doubted in the light of the Court of Appeal's decision in *The State of the Netherlands v Youell*. It must be said that the approach taken by Phillips L.J., though lacking a strong basis on principle, has pragmatic appeal. The clear intention of the Act is that the two provisions should not be construed as being in conflict one with the other. That is a trite rule of construction; that being the case, it does seem right that the two sections should operate side by side and they should be taken as referring to different perils. As far as Phillips L.J. was concerned, that was about the degree of the misconduct.

Assignment and Third Parties

There must be made a distinction between an assignment of the insured goods **10–148** and an assignment of the insurance policy. The Act provides in s.15 that where the assured assigns his interest in the goods insured, he does not thereby transfer to the assignee his rights under the contract of the insurance, unless there exists an express or implied agreement with the assignee to that effect. The assured will not therefore be able to claim under the policy once his interest in the goods has been assigned—he will not have the insurable interest to claim. It is possible however for him to make a claim as trustee of the assignee where there is between them an agreement that the policy will be held for the assignee's benefit (*Powles v Innes* (1843) 11 M.&W. 10).

Such an assignment must be distinguished from what we see in CIF sales where the insurance policy is assigned to the buyer in the tender of sale documents. Section 50(1) allows the assignment of an insurance policy subject to any express terms to the contrary. The assignment may take place before or after loss. According to s.50(3) an assignment may be effected by indorsement or in any customary manner. As far as the CIF contract is concerned, the mere delivery of the policy to the buyer will be sufficient as the customary mode of assignment. Once the policy is properly assigned, the assignee is entitled to sue on the policy in his own name and the defendant is entitled to make any defence arising out of the contract which he would have been entitled to make if the action had been brought in the name of the original assured.

The phrase "arising out of the contract" is usually taken to refer to any implied terms or warranty the insurance is subject to. Where the original assured is in breach of a warranty, for example that of seaworthiness, the insurer may set that up as a defence against the third party now in possession of the insurance rights. The phrase was further extended in *The Litsion Pride* where Hirst J. considered it to encompass

> "fraudulent claims made under the very contract of insurance itself, even if the obligation not to make them were not to be treated strictly as an implied term".

10–149   Section 50(2) exists to protect the insurer from being placed in a prejudiced position following the assignment of the policy. Similarly, at common law, any assignment whether statutory or equitable will render the assignee subject to the liabilities of the assignor. Where only the benefit in the insurance policy is assigned as opposed to the assignment of the entire policy, the matter is not entirely clear. Such an assignment is possible either at equity (*Walter & Sullivan Ltd v Murphy* [1955] 2 Q.B. 584) or at law as contained in s.136 of the Law of Property Act 1925 but while it confers on the assignee the benefit in the insurance, it does not make him a full party to the contract of insurance. All the assignee is entitled to is the benefit of the insurer's undertaking to indemnify against the insured loss. But what happens if the assured assigns the benefit in the insurance to the person who is responsible for causing the loss? This was what transpired in *Colonia Versicherung AG v Amoco Oil Co* [1997] 1 Lloyd's Rep. 261.

10–150   *Colonia Versicherung AG v Amoco Oil Co* [1997] 1 Lloyd's Rep. 261.
Facts:
A cargo of naphtha was sold under FOB terms and delivered to Teesport in the United Kingdom. It was found to be contaminated as a result of the sellers' failure to maintain industrial standards or negligence. The goods were insured under the ICC (All Risks). The buyers then notified their insurers of their intention to claim under the insurance and also filed an action against the sellers. The sellers agreed to pay all the buyers' damages in consideration of their being granted an unconditional release from any and all claims by the buyers as well as an assignment of the buyers' rights under the insurance policy. The sellers then notified the insurers and claimed under the policy for loss caused by themselves as assignees of the benefit in the original insurance or as co-assured.
Held:
The insurers argued that the insurance was an indemnity and could not be extended through such an assignment of rights. It was also argued that the insurance contract as an indemnity contract entitled the insurer to deduct from the claim any payment already made

in satisfaction to the assured (the buyers in this case). The sellers countered this by contending that the payment made was only a gift which could not be used to diminish the insurer's liability under the cover. At first instance, Potter J. held that a payment ex gratia could be used to diminish the measure of indemnity unless it was intended by the donor that the payment was to benefit the assured to the exclusion of the insurers. The sellers also argued in the alternative that they were entitled to claim as co-assured.

The Court of Appeal did not consider the argument as to when a gift could be set against the indemnity payable by the insurer, but felt that the deeds could not be construed as permitting the sellers an outright assignment of the benefit of insurance. The court affirmed the lower court's decision that the sellers were not co-assured because they "had failed to establish that the policy was effected on their behalf or that they were intended to benefit thereunder". The case was thus disposed of by a stroke of contractual construction.

The case leaves open the possibility of assigning the benefit of an insurance to **10–151** a third party who is responsible for the loss and who as a result may be entitled to materialise that benefit to the detriment of the insurer. It might be argued that such an assignment should be subject to two prevailing principles. First, that in all forms of assignment, the insurer is not to be prejudiced thereby and second, that all insurance contracts are indemnity contracts and must therefore not result in any unjust enrichment of the assignee. Be that as it may, has the insurer been prejudiced and is there, as alleged by the insurer, a breach of the indemnity rule in this case? A loss has occurred. That loss is covered by a peril insured against; it is immaterial that the loss was caused by the assured or the assignee. Furthermore the insurance contract agreed by the insurer allowed the buyers to assign their rights under it. That they did, to the sellers, lawfully. If the insurers were concerned that the rights in the policy should not be assigned away, they could have made provision for that. On the issue of unjust enrichment, it is submitted that there is none in the present case. It was always open to the insurer once subrogated to the buyers' rights to take action against the sellers for causing damage to the cargo. This is notwithstanding the undertaking given by the buyers to release the sellers unconditionally from all liabilities because Clause 16 of the ICC(A) as incorporated provides specifically that it is the duty of the assured and their agents to "ensure that all rights against carriers, bailees or other third parties are properly preserved and exercised". That undertaking is invalid if it deprives the insurer of their claim in tort or contract against the sellers.

As observed above, it is always open to insurers to restrict certain assignments. Rule 15 of the UK P&I Club for instance stipulates that:

"No insurance given by the Association and no interest under these Rules or under any contract between the Association and any Owners may be assigned without written consent of the managers who shall have the right in their discretion to give or refuse such consent without stating any reason or to give such consent upon such terms or conditions as they may think fit. Any purported assignment made without such consent or without there being due compliance with any such terms and conditions as the Managers may impose shall, unless the Managers in their discretion otherwise decide, be void and of no effect".

Much, however, is dictated by the construction of the terms as we saw in *Colonia v Amoco*.

Subrogation and Contribution

10–152 The doctrine of subrogation,[63] the hint of which we saw earlier in *Colonia v Amoco*, is applicable only to insurance contracts which are also contracts of indemnity. It does not apply to non-indemnity insurance contracts such as life assurance, personal injury cover, etc. The doctrine states that the insurer may step into the shoes of the assured and enforce any claim, defence or set-off the assured possesses against any third party. The right arises only after the insurer has paid for the loss. Section 79 explains this in further detail:

"(1) Where the insurer pays for a total loss, either of the whole, or in the case of goods of any apportionable part, of the subject matter insured, he thereupon becomes entitled to take over the interest of the assured in whatever may remain of the subject matter so paid for. He is thereby subrogated to all the rights and remedies of the assured in and in respect of the subject matter as from the time of the casualty causing the loss.

(2) Where he pays for a partial loss, he gets no title to the goods insured, or such part of the goods as may remain. He is however subrogated to all rights and remedies of the assured in and in respect of the goods insured as from the time of the casualty causing the loss, in so far as the assured has been indemnified by the insurer's payment for the loss."

The doctrine at common law is perhaps best taken from Lord Blackburn's judgment in *Burnard v Rodocanachi* (1882) 7 App. Cas. 333:

"The general rule of law (and it is obvious justice) is that where there is a contract of indemnity . . . and a loss happens, anything which reduces or diminishes that loss reduces or diminishes the amount which the indemnifier is bound to pay; and if the indemnifier has already paid it, then, if anything which diminishes the loss comes into the hands of the person to whom he has paid it, it becomes an equity that the person who has already paid the full indemnity is entitled to be recouped by having that amount back".

In that case, the House of Lords refused to allow the insurer to claim an ex gratia payment made to the assured under a compensation fund on the basis that that payment was a gift made not for the purpose of reducing the loss but to compensate the assured for the loss personally suffered to the exclusion of the insurer. In *Colonia v Amoco*, the trial judge considered that the payment made by the sellers in consideration of the buyers' assigning to them the insurance and undertaking to release them from all liabilities was not such a payment. It was made as consideration in settlement of the dispute and therefore far from being a gift, it had been made pursuant to an enforceable agreement.

10–153 It should be noted that subrogation cannot be used by the insurer against the co-assured or a third party who is clearly intended to benefit from the insurance taken out by the assured, for example, where the tenant of the insured property had paid part or all of the premium even though the insurance has been effected

---

[63] Hasson, "Subrogation in insurance law—a critical evaluation". (1985) 5 O.J.L.S. 416.

in the landlord's name (see *Mark Rowlands Ltd v Berni Inns Ltd* [1986] Q.B. 211).

Where the same interest in the same adventure is insured for the benefit the same assured, and the sums insured exceed the indemnity allowed by the MIA, there is a case of double insurance (s.32(1)). Where the assured is over-insured by double insurance, s.32(2) states:

(a) The assured may claim payment from the insurers in such order as he may think fit. Two provisos apply:

    (i) that the policy does not provide otherwise, and
    (ii) that he is not entitled to receive any sum in excess of the indemnity allowed in the Act;

(b) Where the policy is a valued policy, the assured must give credit as against the valuation for any sum received by him under the policy without regard to the actual value of the goods insured.

Example:

In *Irving v Richardson* (1831) 1 M.&Rob. 153, the assured had taken out two insurance policies. One policy insured the ship to the amount of £2000 whilst the other, £1700. The actual value of the ship was £3000. The total the assured may claim is therefore only £3000, not £3700.

(c) A similar rule applies where the policy is an unvalued policy. The assured must give credit as against the full insurable value for any sum received by him under any other policy;

(d) Where the assured receives any sum exceeding the indemnity allowed by the Act, he is deemed to hold such sum in trust for the insurers according to their right of contribution among themselves.

This right of contribution has its genesis in equity (*Deering v Earl of* **10–154** *Winchelsea* (1787) 2 Bos. & Pul. 270) but the parties may vary its operation by contract. In *Commercial Union Assurance Co Ltd v Hayden* [1977] Q.B. 804, for example, the parties have incorporated a rateable proportion clause in their policies specifying exactly how contribution is to be made.

Section 80 constrains each insurer, as between himself and the other insurers, to contribute rateably to the loss in proportion to the amount for which he liable under his policy when the assured is over-insured by double insurance. Contribution is therefore a duty upon which an insurer who has paid less than his proportion of the loss to make good to his co-insurers. His co-insurers are entitled to a court order instructing him to contribute rateably.

Chris O'Kane v Jonathan Jones [2004] 1 Lloyd's Rep. 389   **10–155**
Facts:
The Martin P was owned by D2 and managed by D3. She ran aground and became a CTL. D2 and D3 held separate policies on the ship, policy A and policy B respectively. Policy A was issued by C, whilst Policy B was issued by J. Policy B however was cancelled a day after the ship ran aground. C claimed a contribution from J. C argued that at the time of the casualty, there was over insurance by double insurance within the meaning of ss.32 and 80. It was argued that following its payment of the insured value of $5 million it was entitled to a contribution from J who had insured the vessel for $2.5 million.

J refused, submitting that even if there was such over insurance, it was not liable to pay any contribution because its policy had been cancelled when the claim was made. It was also questioned as to whether D2 was insured under Policy B (so as to suggest a case of double insurance).

Held:

The court concluded that Policy B was intended to cover D2; as D3 had actual authority to agree to Policy B on D2's behalf. There was therefore over-insurance by double insurance. The liability created under s.80 was for each insurer to contribute rateably in cases of over insurance arose at the time of the loss and post-loss consensual cancellation of one policy could not affect this obligation to contribute. C was thus entitled to a contribution of $1,67 million from J.

10–156   Trade practice and the law merchant suggest that where one policy is valid whilst the second is void, the assured could still be considered to be over-insured by double insurance. This means that contribution may still be claimed by one insurer from the other (*Thames & Mersey Marine Insurance Co Ltd v "Gunford" Ship Co Ltd* [1911] A.C. 529). Where the second insurer has a valid defence against the assured whilst the first does not, the position was examined in *Monksfield v Vehicle & General Insurance Co Ltd* [1971] 1 Lloyd's Rep. 139. The second insurer was able to defeat the assured's claim because the assured had failed to give the requisite notice. The issue was whether the first insurer could make a claim for contribution from the second insurer. It was held that he could not. That case was overruled in *Legal & General Assurance Society Ltd v Drake Insurance Co Ltd* [1992] Q.B. 887, by a majority in the Court of Appeal. The facts are essentially the same in these cases. They were dependent on how the court construed the operation of equity as between the parties. It had been held in *Monksfield* that there cannot be

> "an equitable result that an insurance company which had no notice of an accident, had no say in the handling of the claim and . . . no opportunity to investigate the rights and wrongs of it should be called upon to make a contribution in a case in which it would quite clearly have had the right to repudiate if the claim had been brought under the terms of its own policy".

The majority in *Legal & General Assurance Society Ltd*, however, considered that the balance of equity was in the favour of the first insurer because the procedural breach was committed by the assured in whom they had no control. Lloyd and Nourse L.JJ. did not consider the procedural defence to be on the same footing as substantive defences; the technical breach should therefore not be applied to the detriment of the innocent first insurer. A distinction was therefore made between a procedural defence and a substantive one. The latter nullifies the policy whilst the former does not. In a case of a substantive breach, the right of contribution depends on whether that breach has been accepted by the insurer concerned.

In 1994 when the matter arose in a motor insurance case, in *Eagle Star Insurance Co Ltd v Provincial Insurance Plc* [1994] 1 A.C. 130 the Privy Council held that *Monksfield* was the correct enunciation of the law. Equity should favour the insurer who has suffered the breach of the procedural requirement of notice because according to Lord Woolf, the very basis of the second insurer's contract is that these substantive and procedural requirements are met by the assured. The second insurer is fully entitled to expect compliance with these terms and requirements by the assured. Contribution should be determined according to each of the insurer's respective contractual relationship with the assured. This is not unfair because

"it is unlikely that the existence of the other insurer would have been known at the time that the contract of insurance was made".

It remains to be seen how this so-called "equity" will further develop. The two **10–157** cases are clearly inconsistent both in result and rationale. We need perhaps to ask what that relevant equity is before the dilemma could be resolved. Is the equity to ensure that the second insurer should retain his procedural right to examine the "rights and wrongs" of the claim or to spread the risk amongst the two insurers? It would seem that equity with its emphasis on individual justice and fairness should reflect the former.

Where the assured is insured for an amount less than the insurable value or in the case of a valued policy, for an amount less than the policy valuation, he will not be covered for the uninsured balance (s.81).

Following a claim under a cover with multiple insurers, it is conceivable that one insurer is more prepared to pay whilst his co-insurer might be less so inclined and would be more prepared to challenge the assured's claim. This would no doubt lead to inconvenience and even acrimony between the various co-insurers. In an attempt to avoid the bad publicity and inconvenience this could cause, co-insurers might make a "follow the leader" agreement between themselves. Under a "follow the leader" agreement, all the co-insurers agree to accept and not dispute any settlement or course of action proposed or in fact, taken by the lead underwriter. It is immediately obvious that the agreement should clearly identify who the "leader" is. Failure to do so would invariably lead to aggravation and worse still, possible litigation. In *Roar Marine Ltd v Bimeh Iran Insurance Co* [1998] 1 Lloyd's Rep. 423, the High Court was called upon to interpret a "follow the leader" clause. The lead insurer in that case was described as "leading British Underwriters". The claimant argued that the leading British Underwriters were Lloyd's Syndicate 724 and as Lloyd's Syndicate 724 had settled their claim in respect of the vessel's engine damage, the defendants' who were co-insurers should follow suit. The claimants in that case were assignees of the insurance benefit and mortgagees of the vessel. The defendants argued that Lloyd's Syndicate 724 had settled wrongfully because the loss was not caused by an insured peril. Mance J. held that on the evidence it was clear that Lloyd's Syndicate 724 were the "leader" and the defendants' attempts to contradict the "follow the leader" clause were illegitimate not only as a matter of law but as a matter of custom. The defendants' attempts would undermine the very rationale of a "follow the leader" clause which is to ensure commercial certainty and simplicity in the administration of claims settlements.

CHAPTER 11

PAYMENT AND FINANCE FOR INTERNATIONAL TRADE

In international sales, it is not true to assume that success depends only on the **11–001** quality, delivery and price of the goods or services. There is now a factor of equal importance—the ability to give and willingness to take credit. This has naturally led to the creation of new problems for the traders. As far as the seller is concerned, he may be without payment for longer periods. This in turn could reduce cash flow and liquidity of the seller. In order to compensate any potential reduced cash flow, the seller will need to pitch his price at the right level. The seller will quote a price that will take the period of payment into account amongst other things. In making this decision on his price policy, other than the traditional costs (for example labour, manufacturing, storage, raw materials, publicity, delivery, charges, etc) the seller will also take into account:

- the risks involved in the transaction;

- the duration of the payment term;

- the strength of the currency involved;

- competition in product or geographic market; and

- goodwill and loyalty of customer.

In the UK the global credit crisis in 2008 led to substantial government borrowing and massive cuts in the interest rate. This, in turn, caused sterling to plummet. The suddenness in the change of fortunes for the pound emphasises the importance of minimising the foreign exchange risk. As a matter of policy, it is sometimes recommended that the sale should be made in the buyer's currency. It is deemed good practice in marketing strategy and a courtesy to the buyer. By selling in a foreign currency the seller is assuming the exchange risk himself. He could however reduce his risk and exposure by using the forward exchange market. The method works like this:

Example:
The seller will enter into a forward exchange contract with his bank. That contract will involve inter alia, an undertaking on the bank's part to sell or purchase currency at a rate of exchange agreed at the time of entering into the

contract, for delivery at a fixed future date or between two fixed dates in the future. The seller thus avoids the risk of any fluctuations by fixing the amount he will receive in sterling—and if he is paid in the buyer's currency, he could sell that to the bank at the agreed rate of exchange.

11–002   As between the seller and buyer, it is entirely open to them to agree a fixed exchange rate if that would make the transaction more commercially certain. This must be properly committed through an express term. The court would not imply such a term even if it appears to be fair; in such commercial transactions, a term would only be implied if it satisfies the business efficacy or necessity test. In *Proctor & Gamble v Svenska Cellulosa Aktiebolaget SCA* [2012] EWCA Civ 1413 the contract provided for the prices of the goods to be fixed. It listed the prices in euros but stated that payment should be made in sterling, which was the seller's operating currency. There was no mention of any sterling prices. Appended to the contract was a document setting out the seller's manufacturing budgets and how the fixed costs had been calculated. It contained a footnote which read "£/Euro exchange rate 1.49164". The issue was whether, on its true construction, the contract provided, expressly or implicitly, for an agreed exchange rate of £1 to €1.49164 for payment by S of the fixed price for the goods and, if not, what was the appropriate exchange rate to be applied. The Court of Appeal agreed with the lower court that that footnote at the bottom of the budget document could not sensibly be read as an express term mandating the use of that exchange rate. The document's purpose was to explain how the fixed prices had been established, and to record the basis on which sterling costs had been translated into euro costs. It was not intended to regulate the parties' performance. If the annotation had been intended as an express term, it was unlikely that it would have been done in such a casual and elliptical way.

As to whether a term should be implied, the High Court commented that any court should be very wary of implying or interpolating a term that altered the allocation of an exchange rate risk, (relying on the Supreme Court's decision in *Sigma Finance Corp (In Administration), Re* [2009] UKSC 2). The Court of Appeal, whilst agreeing with the lower court, noted additionally "invoices were rendered in Euros, a practice that would have had little purpose if the parties had agreed a fixed rate of exchange".

Price Policy and Payment Tools

Open Account and Pre-payment

11–003   The price policy of any trader should also take into account the payment method or any credit terms agreed by contract. If the relationship between the buyer and seller is good, they may choose to trade on "open account" terms. Open account is quite the norm between parties who have been trading with each other for a long time and there is implicit trust between them. It is particularly popular in intra-EU trade. Where the seller is selling to a subsidiary or associated company abroad, open account terms will keep the costs low.

It is usually a cheaper form of payment method because with bank involvement kept to a minimum, bank charges will be considerably reduced. This means that the seller will deliver the goods to the buyer directly and send him an invoice calling for payment of the purchase price. The buyer then remits payment using one of the following methods:

Buyer's own cheque

As far as the seller is concerned this is not entirely satisfactory because quite apart from the normal risks that the cheque may bounce, the cheque is drawn in the buyer's currency which means that it has to be sent back through the international banking clearing processes for it to be cleared and paid by the buyer's bank. This means the incurring of additional banking charges which the open account system is intended to avoid. **11–004**

Banker's draft

This is a draft drawn by the buyer's bank on its correspondent bank in the seller's country. The seller clearly would prefer such a method of payment in that he does not usually bear the cost of the transaction and payment is guaranteed once the draft has been issued. The buyer on the other hand might find it less attractive in that the draft could not be revoked once issued. Banks are extremely reluctant to re-issue any drafts lost in transit. They will also usually require the applicant (buyer) to provide an indemnity for wrongful payment and other liabilities. **11–005**

International Money Orders (IMO)

The buyer could buy an IMO from a bank which he could then remit to the seller in the same way as a banker's draft. The difference between a banker's draft and an IMO is that an IMO may be purchased over the counter and the types of currencies available are limited while the banker's draft may be made out in any recognised currency. The latter however requires detailed form filling and other formalities. **11–006**

Mail or telegraphic transfer

The buyer instructs his bank to request a correspondent bank in the seller's country to pay the agreed amount to the seller. The procedure works through the system of debiting and crediting various accounts. The buyer's bank debits the buyer's account and then credits the amount in the seller's bank. The seller's bank then credits the seller's account. Where instructions are sent by mail, the transfer is called a mail transfer. On the other hand, a telegraphic transfer relies on instructions sent by cable. Such transfers are becoming less popular in the advent of computerised systems such as SWIFT transfers and the international direct debit system. **11–007**

SWIFT transfers

SWIFT stands for the Society for Worldwide Inter-bank Financial Telecommunication. It is fast replacing the remittance of instructions by cable or post. The remitting bank will make payment through a bank in the seller's country (usually in a cheque drawn locally), or credit the seller's account consistent with instructions given by the buyer. Banks will charge a fee for the transaction and **11–008** to avoid any misunderstanding, they will stipulate that charges will be paid by the seller unless the contrary is spelt out.

International Direct Debit

11–009   The International Direct Debit System (IDDS) works in very much the same way as a domestic direct debit system operates. The seller gains authorisation from the buyer or his agent, and transmits an electronic message to the principal bank for the amount to be debited. The bank then remits the message to the destination country where the money is collected usually through the local bank automated clearing system (ACS). Where possible this will be accessed by the principal bank. It is most efficient where the exporter is invoicing in local currency because the local ACS is permitted generally only to accept payment instructions in its local currency. Where the seller wishes to collect payment in sterling, he is obliged to convert sterling to local currency before commencing the transmission of collection instruction. Be that as it may, it is always the case that the payer (buyer) is debited in local currency. The seller would also normally operate an account with the local bank into which monies could be paid.

Documentary collection or draft

Where "open account" terms are deemed not suitable, it is up to the seller to arrange for payment to be collected from the buyer. The usual way is by using bills of exchange. What happens here is that instead of sending merely the sale documents to the buyer, the seller draws a bill of exchange on the buyer for the sum due and attaches it to the documents. The bundle of documents is then sent through the banking channels for presentation to the buyer. The seller does this by giving clear and precise instructions to his bank as to what action should be taken. For example:

1. whether the documents are to be sent electronically, by airmail or other means;

2. whether the documents are to be released against payment or acceptance of the bill;

3. whether the bill is to be "protested" if dishonoured;

4. whether the goods should be kept in warehouses and insured if they are not accepted by the buyer; and

5. whether rebate should be given for early payment.

The seller's bank will then forward the bill and documents to its correspondent bank in the buyer's country. The correspondent bank will then present the bill and documents to the buyer according to the instructions given.

11–010   If the bill of exchange provides for payment to be made on sight, this means that no credit period has been given. The buyer will have to pay on sight of conforming documents (the trade acronym being D/P or documents against payment). On the other hand where there has been a credit period agreed between the parties, the bill will be drawn to reflect this. It might say "At 90 days' after sight, pay to the order of Sellers Ten Thousand US Dollars value received". Here documents will be released to the buyer upon his acceptance of the bill (D/A or documents against acceptance). He signs or indorses his acceptance across the face of the bill making the bill actionable for payment in 90 days' time and property in the goods passes to him.

Once the bill has been accepted, the correspondent or collecting bank will advise the seller's bank of the date of acceptance and hold the bill until it matures. When it matures, the collecting bank will present it to the buyer for full payment. If payment is not made, the collecting bank will arrange a "protest" to be made, usually by their lawyers or a notary. This is deemed to be summary evidence of the presentation of the bill and its subsequent dishonour by the buyer and is intended to speed up any litigation or arbitration on the matter.

11–011

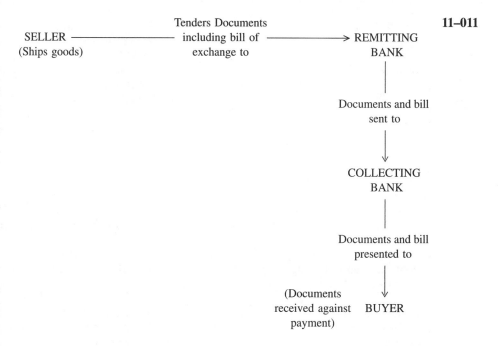

Bills of Exchange

The bill of exchange or draft is defined in s.3 of the Bills of Exchange Act 1882. **11–012**

"(1) A bill of exchange or draft is an unconditional order in writing, addressed by one person to another, signed by the person giving it, requiring the person to whom it is addressed to pay on demand or at a fixed or determinable future time a sum certain in money to or to the order of a specified person, or to bearer.

(2) An instrument which does not comply with these conditions, or which orders any act to be done in addition to the payment of money, is not a bill of exchange."

In order to examine the bill of exchange satisfactorily, it would be useful to refer to the following examples.

Example of a sight bill of exchange:

11–013

No 1111	for £3000	Date: December 24, 2012

At sight pay this sole Bill of Exchange to the order of IM Sellers Ltd the sum of Three Thousand pounds value received

To: UR Buyers
13 Thisthat Road
Utopia
Republic of Utopia

For and on behalf of
IM Sellers Ltd
1 Old Road
London
ENGLAND
Isabelle M Sellers
Director

Example of a usance bill of exchange

11–014

No 2222	for €3000	Date: December 24, 2012

At 90 days after sight pay this first of exchange second of the same date and tenor being unpaid to the order of IM Sellers Ltd Three Thousand euro value received

To: UR Buyers
13 Thisthat Road
Utopia
Republic of Utopia

For and on behalf of
IM Sellers Ltd
1 Old Road
London
ENGLAND
Isabelle M Sellers
Director

Accepted payable at VR Bank, City Street, Utopia, Republic of Utopia. For and on behalf of UR Buyers,
Usman Rakesh
Director

There are generally four personalities to the bill of exchange:

1. The Drawer—this is the seller issuing or drawing the bill of exchange and in our example, IM Sellers Ltd.

2. The Drawee—the party on whom the bill of exchange is drawn and in our context the importer or buyer.

3. The Payee—this is the person to whom the amount of the bill is to be paid. In our examples, the drawer and payee are the same, namely IM Sellers Ltd.

4. The Acceptor—this is the person who has accepted the bill. In our case, once the drawee has accepted the bill, he is then called the acceptor.

An unconditional order

It is immediately obvious that in our specimen bills, the term used is "pay"—this **11–015** signifies that the bill is an order. It must be unequivocal in that the payer is ordered to make payment according to the tenor of the bill; he has no discretion in the matter. It was held in *Hamilton v Spottiswoode* (1894) 4 Ex. 200, that an instrument with the words "We hereby authorise you to pay on our account to the order of G £6000" could not be classed a bill of exchange, there being no order, only a liberty. Additionally, that order must be unconditional. A bill would be improperly drawn if a condition is introduced, for example, "pay provided that shipment is made before December 5, 2012" or "pay provided goods delivered in accordance with pro forma invoice", etc. The stipulation in specimen No.2222 that "second of the same date and tenor being unpaid" is valid. That stipulation merely confines payment to be made against the first bill where bills have been issued in a set or in duplicates and does not subject the payment to a condition. The drawing of bills in sets is to allow for the possible loss of documents in transit.

In *Korea Exchange Bank v Debenhams (Central Buying) Ltd* [1979] 1 Lloyd's Rep. 548, it was unclear as to whether a bill requiring the drawee to "pay at 90 days D/A of this First Bill of Exchange" was conditional since the condition was not directed at the drawee. It would seem that an order to pay provided that certain documents are tendered must be construed as conditional but a stipulation "documents against acceptance" (or "D/A") in *Korea Exchange Bank* is less clear.

It should also be noted that s.3(3) provides that the following conditions do not make the bill conditional for the purposes of subs.(1):

(a) an order in the bill that the drawee is to reimburse himself from a specific fund or a particular account to be debited with the amount;

(b) a statement of the transaction which gives rise to the bill. The term "for value received" for example does not import a condition into the bill—it merely underlines the transaction giving rise to the bill, albeit not too clearly. Similarly a description of the sale bringing about the bill does not constitute a condition.

Addressed by one person to another

It must be clear in the bill as to who the parties are. The drawee and the payee **11–016** must be named or at least be ascertainable. Where there exists a misspelling of names, or typographical error, it is open to the drawer to correct it. Where there is an ambiguity as to who the parties are, it may be possible for the claimant to adduce extrinsic evidence to explain the ambiguity (*Bird & Co (London) Ltd v Thomas Cook & Son Ltd* [1937] 2 All E.R. 227) as long as the ambiguity is latent. Where the name has been misspelt for example, it is possible to adduce evidence to show who the drawer intended to be the payee.

Example:

Bill is drawn "pay M Herrett £2000". Where there are two possible persons, Matthew Herrett and Mark Herrett who could qualify, extrinsic evidence can be adduced to show which of the two is intended as the payee. This is an ambiguity which is latent. Where the drawer intends to pay M Smith, then the bill is said to contain an error on its face or a patent error. Such an error cannot be explained away by extrinsic evidence.

Where the payee is a fictitious or non-existing person, s.7(3) states that the bill may be treated as payable to bearer. A fictitious person is an existing person who is not intended to be the payee.

11–017 *Bank of England v Vagliano Brothers* [1891] A.C. 107
Facts:
V's clerk, G, had forged the signature of Z in a bill drawn in favour of P. The forged bill was accepted by V (the drawee). G then forged P's indorsement and when the bill matured, he presented it for payment at V's bank. The bank paid. V, upon discovery of the fraud, claimed that the bank was not entitled to debit their account with the amount paid out.
Held:
P was never intended to be the payee and was therefore a fictitious person for the purposes of the Bills of Exchange Act 1882. The bill was to be treated as a bill payable to bearer for which the bank had lawfully paid; a bearer bill being capable of being indorsed by the bearer (in this case, the forger). v could not therefore succeed. Lord Herschell said:

> "Do the words, 'where the payee is a fictitious person', apply only where the payee named never had a real existence? I take it to be clear that by the word 'payee' must be understood the payee named on the fact of the bill; for of course by the hypothesis there is no intention that payment should be made to such person. Where, then, the payee named is so named by way of pretence only, without the intention that he shall be the person to receive payment, is it doing violence to language to say that the payee is a fictitious person? I think not. I do not think that the word 'fictitious' is exclusively used to qualify that which has no real existence. When we speak of a fictitious entry in a book of accounts, we do not mean that the entry has no real existence, but only that it purports to be that which it is not—that it is an entry made for the purpose of pretending that the transaction took place which is represented by it . . . ".

The drawer's intention is hence essential in determining whether a payee is fictitious.

11–018   The importance of the drawer's intention is again evident in this next case. In *Vinden v Hughes* [1905] 1 K.B. 795, the fact was that the drawer had indeed intended the named person be the payee, the cheque was not to be treated as a bearer bill even though the cheques were sold off fraudulently. In that case, V, the drawer, was induced by his clerk into making cheques out to customers to whom he thought he owed money. The clerk then sold the cheques to H. On whether the cheques were to be treated as bearer bills, the court held that they were not. The payees were persons V did intend to pay, although that intention had been brought about by the clerk's fraud. The indorsements made by the clerk were not valid because the cheque had been made out to the named persons' order and was not a bearer bill. V could therefore recover the proceeds of the cheques from Hughes who had sold them on without lawful title to them.

The result is similar in the House of Lords' case below.

North and South Wales Bank v Macbeth [1908] A.C. 137   **11–019**

Facts:
M was induced by W's fraud to draw a cheque in favour of K or order intending to benefit K. W then forged K's indorsement and paid the cheque into his bank account. M sued the bank for conversion.

Held:
On whether the cheque was a bearer bill under s.7(3), the House of Lords held that as M did intend K to benefit under the bill, the bill was not a bearer bill. It was made payable to K or his order and as such the indorsement made was not operative. The bank was therefore not entitled to receive payment under it.

Where the payee is non-existent, the drawer's intention becomes irrelevant (*Clutton v Attenborough & Son* [1897] A.C. 90).

A bill made to order is valid but it must be clear who the parties are. An instrument that states "pay cash or order" though is not a bill of exchange because it is not addressed to or to the order of a specified person. In *Chamberlain v Young & Tower* [1893] 2 Q.B. 206, however, an instrument drawn "pay to . . . order" was construed as a bill drawn "pay to my order". The case however does not state whether such an instrument is a good bill of exchange; its decision is centred on the construction of the relevant bill within the specific circumstances of the case. Where the instrument is drawn without specifying the name of the payee, s.20(1) provides that the holder may insert the name of the payee so long as he does so within a reasonable time and strictly in accordance with the authority given him.

Signed by the person giving it

The bill must be signed by the drawer and in the two examples above, we see that   **11–020**
they have been signed by Isabelle M Sellers, the director of the company. Under s.23 of the Act, a person is liable as drawer only if he has signed it as such. This of course does not mean that it must be signed by him personally. He could be represented by an agent or an authorised official. In our example, the company is represented by Isabelle M Sellers, the director. Under s.91(1), it is sufficient that her signature is written on the bill by some other person "by or under his authority".

There are special rules relating to bills drawn by companies. Section 91(2) states that it is sufficient that the bill is sealed with the corporate seal, a signature can be dispensed with. In most cases, though, a signature will be applied. Who should sign the company's bill? Section 52 Companies Act 2006 provides that a bill will be deemed to have been made, accepted or endorsed by a company if signed by a person acting under its authority. The person signing the bill binds the company, and not himself personally. He will however be liable personally if he does not make clear that he signs for and on behalf of the company (*Rolfe Lubell v Keith* [1979] 1 All E.R. 860). Where there is doubt as to whether the person had signed the bill representatively or personally, the court will normally adopt a construction which is most favourable to the validity of the bill (s.26(2)).

Section 25 provides that a signature by procuration operates as notice that the agent has but a limited authority to sign, and the principal is only bound by such signature if the agent in so signing was acting within the actual limits of his authority. Signing by procuration is done by the agent entering a clause in the bill that he signs "per pro", or "pp" or "per procurationem". A possible effect of s.25 is that a principal who has misled a third party by suggesting that his agent had authority can avoid liability by relying on the notice.

11–021   Where the agent lacks authority to sign the bill but does so anyway, it was held in *Starkey v Bank of England* [1903] A.C. 114 that the principal is nonetheless bound. The agent is himself not liable under the bill but he could be sued for a false representation of authority. If the agent signs the bill in his own name, he alone is bound regardless of the fact that every party knows that he was doing so as agent (*Leadbitter v Farrow* (1816) 5 M.&S. 345).

Where *any* of the signatures on the bill is unauthorised or forged, that signature in question becomes wholly inoperative. No person, even acting in good faith and having provided consideration for the bill, could derive any rights under it. In *Kreditbank Cassel v Schenkers Ltd* [1927] 1 K.B. 826, the unauthorised signature of the defendant's manager was held to be totally inoperative and the holder in due course was barred from claiming on the bill. However, if the bill has a non-existent or fictitious payee, it can be treated as a bearer's bill (s.7(3)). Thus, a person in possession of that bill is a "holder" who could enforce it if he has given value; following s.59, a person or a bank accepting and paying it gets a good discharge.

The defence of non est factum within its narrow confines may also apply in a similar way nullifying the signature. This old common law defence permits a person who had executed a written document in ignorance of its character to plead that "it is not his deed" (*Saunders (Executrix in the Estate of Rose Maud Gallie) v Anglia Building Society* [1971] A.C. 1004).

To pay on demand or at a fixed or determinable future time

11–022   A bill is payable on demand if it states that payment is to be made "on demand" or "on sight" or "on presentation" as we see in specimen bill No.1111. Where it states that payment is to be made 90 days after sight, the order is that payment is to be made a fixed or determinable future time. Where the instrument states that payment is to be made "when the ship arrives", it does not qualify as a bill of exchange because it does not order payment to be made at a fixed or determinable future time. It is not determinable when the ship will arrive and even if any estimated time of arrival is made, it is by no means certain that the ship will arrive. Section 11 clarifies this requirement by providing:

"A bill is payable at a determinable future time within the meaning of this Act which is expressed to be payable—"

1. At a fixed period after date or sight;
2. On or at a fixed period after the occurrence of a specified event which is certain to happen, though the time of happening may be uncertain.

"An instrument expressed to be payable on a contingency is not a bill, and the happening of the event does not cure the defect."

In *Korea Exchange Bank v Debenhams (Central Buying) Ltd* [1979] 1 Lloyd's Rep. 548, the bill was erroneously expressed "at 90 days D/A of this First Bill of Exchange". It should have read "at 90 days *sight* D/A of this First Bill of Exchange". The Court of Appeal was asked to consider whether the bill as expressed was one payable at a fixed or determinable future time. It held that a bill payable 90 days after "acceptance" could not be a valid bill of exchange. Megaw L.J. was quite convinced that it does not qualify under s.11(2) because according to His Lordship, "the bill may never be accepted". As for s.11(1) it is equally clear that this was not a bill payable "after date", no date had been stated. On whether it was a bill payable "after sight", His Lordship said:

> "90 days is a fixed period. But 'after acceptance' is a different expression from 'after sight'. It is, to my mind, a bold submission that in a document in which the word 'sight' has been struck out and 'acceptance' put in, the document is nevertheless to be 'payable at a fixed period after sight'".

His Lordship continued;   **11–023**

> "Even if the position were . . . that . . . 'sight' and 'acceptance' mean the same thing, I should not be prepared to accept that the statutory phrase 'expressed to be payable . . . after sight' [in s.11] could be interpreted as though it permitted the bill to be expressed otherwise than by the use of the word 'sight'. But, in any event, while it may be right to say that for the purposes of section 11 sight *includes* acceptance, there can be sight without acceptance. For a bill can be seen but not accepted. Therefore, while '90 days after acceptance' provides a fixed period in respect of an accepted bill which would coincide with the fixed period after sight, it provides no fixed period if the bill, as may well happen, is not accepted".

There is, according to Megaw L.J. insufficient certainty in that stipulation.

A sum certain in money

The rule is that there should be no uncertainty as to the amount payable. Where   **11–024**
an instrument stipulates payment "up to" or "not exceeding" or "at least" a certain amount, that instrument does not qualify to be bill of exchange. There are however a few exceptions. Section 9(1) provides for example that a sum is considered certain in money even though it may be payable:

(a) with interest;

(b) by instalments, with or without a provision that upon default in payment of any instalment the whole shall be due;

(c) according to an indicated rate of exchange.

There is no requirement that the bill should be expressed in the currency of the law governing the bill. Where it is governed by English law, for example, there is no requirement that it should be expressed in sterling. Our specimen bill No.2222 which expresses the sum in euro is nonetheless valid at English law.

Negotiation of a bill

11–025 A bill is negotiated when it is transferred from one person to another in such a manner as to constitute the transferee the holder of the bill (s.31(1)). A bill payable to bearer or a bearer bill is negotiated by delivery. Delivery is defined in s.2 as the transfer of possession, whether actual or constructive, from one person to another. A bearer bill according to s.8(3) is one which is described as payable to bearer or one which has its only or last indorsement in blank. An indorsement in blank is made when the indorser signs the bill without specifying who the indorsee is to be.

A bill payable to order is on the other hand negotiated by the indorsement of the holder completed by delivery. Section 8(4) defines a bill payable to order as one which is expressed to be so payable, or which is expressed to be payable to a particular person and does not contain words prohibiting transfer or indicating an intention that it should not be transferable.

Example:

Where the bill of exchange is expressed "pay J Smith £5000", it is expressed to be payable to a particular person. That makes it a bill payable to order.

11–026 Where the bill states "pay J Smith only £5000", the bill is not an order bill because although it is expressed to be payable to a particular person, it contains the word "only" which prohibits transfer of the bill and indicates an intention that the bill should not be transferable.

A bill which is payable to the order of a particular person is also an order bill (for example, "Pay to the order of J Smith"). A bill can also be converted to an order bill through a special indorsement. When a bill has been indorsed in blank, a holder can convert the blank indorsement into a special indorsement by writing above the indorser's signature a direction to pay the bill to or to the order of himself or some other person. A special indorsement specifies the person to who, or to whose order, the bill is to be payable (s.34(2)).

An indorsement must be in relation to the entire bill, that is to say, the indorser is not entitled to indorse a part of the amount stipulated in the bill. He must indorse all of it or nothing at all. He is therefore the first person entitled to the sum stated in the bill, i.e. the payee usually. Section 32 also provides that the indorsement must be written on the bill itself and be signed by the indorser. Any indorsement must be unconditional, although if a condition is stated it does not render the bill a nullity. The indorsee is entitled to disregard the condition and still claim under the bill.

11–027 The effect of negotiation of the bill is to pass to the transferee a good title to the bill and where the transferee takes it as a holder in due course, his title is indefeasible regardless of any defects in title sustained by his predecessor holders. Section 29(1) defines a holder in due course as one who has taken a bill:

(a) which is complete and regular on the face of it;

Example:
Arab Bank Ltd v Ross [1952] 2 Q.B. 216
Where the bill is drawn in favour of "Fathi and Faysal Nabulsy Company" as payees, but is subsequently indorsed to "Fathi and Faysal Nabulsy", the bill is not complete and regular on its face. Denning L.J. said:

"Regularity is a different thing from validity . . . Thus, by a misnomer, a payee may be described on the face of the bill by the wrong name, nevertheless, if it is quite plain that the drawer intended him as payee, then an indorsement on the back by the payee in his own true name is valid and sufficient to pass the property in the bill . . . , but the difference between front and back makes the indorsement irregular unless the payee adds also the misnomer by which he was described on the front of the bill".

As far as Denning L.J. was concerned, the missing word "company" was not mere description. It was part of the name of the payee. It was therefore a patent error which could not be ignored.

This approach reflects the strict attitude that bankers adopt in such transac-   **11–028**
tions. The strictness is justified both in the bank's interest and their customers' own interests. It would be quite impossible for banks to make inquiries to see that all the indorsements on the bill of exchange are in fact genuine. All that suffices is that they should at least see that it is regular on its face. That is all the requisite safeguard in the interest of efficiency and certainty in commercial transactions.

(b) before it was overdue;

(c) without notice that it had been previously dishonoured, where such is the case;

(d) in good faith and for value;

A thing done in good faith is described in s.90 as that which is in fact done honestly, regardless of whether it was negligent or not. In *Bank of Credit and Commerce SA v Dawson and Wright* [1987] F.L.R. 342, the claimant bank was considered not to have acted in good faith in the light of evidence that the bank manager had in the past credited cheques to a customer's account knowing full well that they would be dishonoured just to keep that customer's account in credit. There is a presumption in s.30 that every party whose signature appears on a bill of exchange is prima facie deemed to have become a party thereto. Every holder is therefore prima facie deemed to be a holder in due course and it is up to the party alleging otherwise to prove any defect in title.

"For value" is generally defined in s.27(1) as any consideration sufficient to support a simple contract or antecedent debt or liability. The second limb clearly includes past consideration. In *MK International Development Co Ltd v The Housing Bank* [1991] 1 Bank L.R. 74, the payee is deemed to have provided good consideration for a bill of exchange by agreeing to give up a debt owed only in part to him. The fact that the debt was owed to other creditors was irrelevant as far as the issue of consideration was concerned. That release was good and sufficient consideration for the cheque. He was therefore entitled to sue the drawer bank when the cheque was subsequently dishonoured.

It is important not to confuse the issue of consideration for the promissory note   **11–029**
with the issue of consideration for any associated or related contract. In *Oxigen Environmental Ltd v Shaun Mullan* [2012] NIQB 17, X and M were involved in a joint venture to develop a landfill site. In the course of their dealings, X made a payment of £200,000 to M. In return, M executed a a promissory note, under which M promised to pay X on demand the sum of £200,000 for value received. X subsequently withdrew from the joint venture and sought the return of the

£200,000 under the terms of the promissory note. M refused to pay alleging that X was in breach of the joint venture contract. M claimed that there had been a total failure of consideration therefore the promissory note need not be honoured. The Northern Irish court held, however, that the consideration for the promissory note was the payment of the £200,000. It was not appropriate to link the agreements; the reality was that the arrangement for the payment of the money was made by way of a promissory note and a promissory note is treated as cash and is a free-standing, independent agreement. What M contended for was not a total failure of consideration for the promissory note but a total failure of consideration in respect of the joint venture agreement. Therefore, even if X had wrongfully withdrawn from the joint venture, that was a separate issue. The promissory note was made in exchange for the £200,000 paid. There was no failure of consideration in respect of the promissory note.

If, on the other hand, the £200,000 cash paid in exchange for the promissory note was made in forged bank notes, for example, that then would have been a total failure of consideration for the promissory note.

It should be pointed out that the reference to an antecedent debt or liability is that of the drawer. A bill drawn to pay an existing debt owed by the drawer is drawn for value but one drawn to pay another's debt is not (*Oliver v Davis* [1949] 2 K.B. 727).

(e) without notice at the time the bill was negotiated to him of any defect in the title of the person who negotiated it to him.

11–030   Notice means either the actual knowledge possessed by the holder of a fact or a strong suspicion that things are not proper. The definition should cover wilful blindness as to the fact but does not include constructive knowledge. Notice could be imputed as is demonstrated in *Bank of Credit and Commerce International SA v Dawson and Wright* where the knowledge of the bank manager of the customer's fraud was imputed to the bank. Section 29(2) catalogues a list of defects of title. It states that the title of a person who negotiates a bill is defective if:

- he obtained or accepted the bill through fraud, duress, force or fear, or any other unlawful means;

- the consideration he provided was illegal;

- he negotiates the bill in breach of faith;

- he obtained or accepted the bill through "such circumstances as amount to fraud".

In *Jones v Gordon* (1877) 2 App. Cas. 616, Jones who bought bills issued under questionable circumstances, had known that the seller of the bills was in serious financial difficulties. He could have verified matters about the seller's standing from people he knew but did not do so. The seller then became bankrupt and Jones tried to prove against his estate for the sum total of the bills. The House of Lords refused to treat Jones as bona fide purchaser. He was wilfully blind—it was more than carelessness. Lord Blackburn had this to say:

"But if the facts and circumstances are such that the jury... came to the conclusion that he was not honestly blundering and careless, but that he must have had a suspicion that there was something wrong, and that he refrained from asking questions, not because he was an honest blunderer or a stupid man, but because he thought in his own secret mind—I suspect there is something wrong, but if I ask questions and make farther inquiry, it will no longer be my suspecting it, but my knowing it, and then I shall not be able to recover—I think that is dishonesty. I think, my Lords, that that is established, not only by good sense and reason, but by the authority of the cases themselves".

Rights of the holder

Any person (whether for value or not) who derives the bill through the holder in due course will acquire a good title to the bill as long as he is not privy to any fraud or illegality affecting the bill and will have all the rights of that holder in due course as regards the acceptor and all parties to the bill prior to that holder (s.29(3)). While the original payee cannot be a holder in due course (*Re Jones Ltd v Waring & Gillow Ltd* [1926] A.C. 670), he (or the drawer) can derive the rights of a holder in due course where the dishonoured bill was subsequently returned to him through recourse or derivation. **11–031**

Re Jones Ltd v Waring & Gillow Ltd [1926] A.C. 670   **11–032**
Facts:
A fraudster had induced the appellants to draw two cheques payable to the order of the respondents. The fraudster then tendered the cheques to the respondents as payment of his debt to them. The cheques were returned to the appellants on the basis that the signature was irregular. The appellants then issued the respondents with a single cheque containing the sum total of the two returned cheques. The respondents were not privy to the fraud.
Held:
On whether the respondents were required to repay the money paid out, the House of Lords held that they were. The respondents' argument was that they were holders in due course and were therefore protected from the defects in title. Viscount Cave L.C. considered that while it might be true to say that s.2 of the Act seems to extend the term "holder in due course" to the payee of a bill, s.29(1) refers specifically to "a person to whom a bill has been *negotiated*". By virtue of s.31, "negotiation" provides that a bill is negotiated when it is transferred from one person to another and (if payable to order) by indorsement and delivery. It was not possible therefore to treat an original payee of the bill as a holder in due course because the bill was never "negotiated" to him.

Jade International Stahl und Eisen GmbH & Co KG v Robert Nicolas [1978] Q.B. 917   **11–033**
Facts:
J had drawn on N a bill payable to themselves or order as payment for steel sold to N. J then indorsed the bill and discounted it to S Bank. The bill was discounted further to a bank which then discounted it to M Bank. M Bank presented the bill to N for payment. N accepted the bill but dishonoured it because of a dispute with J as to the quality of the steel. M Bank then indorsed the bill in blank and, as each of the other banks exercised their rights of recourse, the bill was returned down the chain to J. J's account had already been debited by S Bank originally. They then sued N on the bill as holder in due course.
Held:
The Court of Appeal held that they could. Once they had discounted the bill to S Bank, they lost their status as drawers. Then when in the effluxion of time they once again

become holders of the bill, it is in that new fresh capacity of holders in due course. It would be inappropriate, according to Geoffrey Lane L.J., to regard J as having a dual capacity (i.e. as both holders and drawers) when the bill was returned to them by recourse.

It should be noted that s.29(3) only offers protection to the holder by derivation to the same extent as that given the holder in due course. This means that defences applicable to defeat the title of the holder in due course such as forged signature, incapacity, *non est factum*, etc, are equally potent in affecting the holder in due course by derivation.

Acceptance of the bill and payment

11–034 Once the acceptor has accepted the bill, he becomes liable to pay according to the tenor of the bill (s.54(1)). In international trade transactions, acceptance of the bill is accomplished by the drawee writing "accepted payable on the [date]" on the face of the bill and signing it. That date is the maturity date of the bill and is determined or calculated according to the usance of the bill. Where for example, the bill is drawn payable 90 days after sight, then the date will be that 90 days after the date the drawee first sighted the bill. A usance bill which has been accepted by the drawee is vital because the act of acceptance binds the drawee to pay according to the tenor of the bill.[1] After acceptance, the bill may be returned to the seller for safekeeping until its maturity date. If the seller requires immediate payment, he could discount it to a bank or any third party willing to take the bill. The bank will pay the face value of the bill, less discount. That discount constitutes the bank's commission for "credit" given. The bank then becomes a holder in due course and enjoys the protection afforded by s.29. The discounting of the bill is usually "with recourse" to the drawer. This means that the bank reserves the right under s.55 to have full recourse against its customer (the seller). Discounting is known as "negotiation" in business circles but should not be confused with the legal definition of negotiation in s.31(1).

It is of course trite that whether or not the bank will discount a bill depends very much on the commercial soundness of the customer, the drawee and the transaction involved. Although the right of recourse entitles the bank to take action against its customer, it must be fairly certain that the customer will not abscond. Some banks are prepared to discount a bill "without recourse" where the standing of the drawee is unquestionably secure and subject to a higher discount charge. It is also not uncommon for certain banks, especially merchant

---

[1] It might be noted that in *Bimal Kumar v United Bank Ltd* [2001] EWCA Civ 1651 the arrangement was that payment would be made against documents which would come forward with bills of exchange for acceptance by the company. The defendant bank had presented the bills to the claimants for signing for acceptance. The bank did not advise the claimants that the claimants should sign the bills for and on behalf of the company (of which they were managers). Under s.349(1) Companies Act 1985 (see now ss.82 and 83 of the new Companies Act 2006 where this provision for personal civil liability has been removed), anyone signing on a bill of exchange in respect of a company whose full and proper name was not on the document would be personally liable for the bill. That was what happened in this case, for the company's full name, Kumar Brothers International Limited, was not on the bills, thus, the claimants were deemed liable for the bill. The Court of Appeal agreed with the lower court that the bank did not owe a duty of care in this connection to the claimants.

banks, to lend their name as drawee and acceptor of a bill to enable the drawer to raise funds by discounting the bill. Such a bill is known as an accommodation bill.

Although it is not common in international trade for a bill of exchange to be discounted more than once, it is not unlawful (see e.g., *Jade International Stahl und Eisen GmbH & Co KG v Robert Nicolas* (above) where the bill was discounted three times). When it does happen, the holder who presents it for payment has the right of recourse not only against the drawer but to all subsequent holders who have indorsed the bill if the bill is dishonoured.

Where the bill is dishonoured by a non-acceptance, the holder may turn to a **11–035** third party prepared to accept the bill for the honour of the drawer. Where the bill states the name of this third party, that named person is called the referee in case of need. According to s.15, there is however no obligation on the holder to seek out the referee in case of need.

An acceptance for honour, as the procedure is known, can only take place after the bill has been protested for non-acceptance and is not overdue. Section 65 requires that the acceptance for honour supra protest is to:

(a)   be written on the bill and indicate that it is an acceptance for honour; and

(b)   be signed by the acceptor for honour.

It may also state for whose honour the bill has been accepted, but if no such statement is inserted the presumption is that the bill has been accepted for the honour of the drawer. Under s.66, the acceptor for honour is liable to pay according to the tenor of the bill once he has accepted the bill, provided that:

(a)   it is presented to the drawee for payment;

(b)   it has not been paid by the drawee;

(c)   it is protested for nonpayment; and

(d)   the acceptor in honour has notice of these matters.

Presentment of the bill for payment is distinct from the act of acceptance. **11–036** Acceptance is the indication that the acceptor is bound to pay according to the tenor of the bill. Presentment on the other hand is the formality the payee must perform in order to be paid. Presentment may be made to any person liable to pay; that person can be the drawee, acceptor, indorsers or acceptor in honour. Presentment is the exhibiting of the bill to the person from whom payment is to be exacted. On payment the holder must surrender the bill to the payer. When the bill is payable on demand, s.45(2) states that presentment to the *drawer* must be made within a reasonable time from issue of the bill. Where presentment of a bill payable on demand is to be made to the indorser, that presentment must be within a reasonable time from indorsement. What constitutes a reasonable time depends on the nature of the bills, trade custom relating to similar bills and other circumstances of the case. In the case of a bill not payable on demand (a usance bill, for example) presentment must be on the date payment is due (s.45(1)).

Section 45(3) stipulates that presentment must be made at a reasonable hour of the business day to the payer or some other person authorised to make payment on his behalf. It must also be made at the place specified in the bill. Where no specific place is stated, it should be made at the drawer's or acceptor's address as stated in the bill. Where no address is stated at all, it should be presented at the acceptor's place of business, if known. If that too is unknown, presentment can be made at his ordinary residence. In any other case, s.45(4)(d) states that the bill may be presented to the acceptor wherever he can be found or at his last place of business or residence. Presentment may be made through the post only if the agreement or usage authorises it. Any delay in presentment may be excused if it is imputable to circumstances beyond the holder's control as long as the presentment has been effected with reasonable diligence after the cause of the delay has ceased to operate.

According to s.46, presentment for payment may be dispensed with:

(a)   where, after the exercise of reasonable diligence, it cannot be effected;

(b)   where the drawer is a fictitious person;

(c)   as regards the drawer, where the drawee is not bound as between himself and the drawer to accept the bill, and the drawer has no reason to believe that the bill would be paid if presented;

(d)   as regards an indorser, where the bill was accepted or made for the accommodation of that indorser, and he has no reason to expect that the bill would be paid if presented; and

(e)   by waiver if presentment, express or implied.

11–037   A bill is considered to have been dishonoured:

(a)   when it is duly presented for payment and payment is refused or cannot be obtained; or

(b)   when presentment is dispensed with and the bill falls overdue and remains unpaid.

Once the bill is dishonoured by nonpayment or non-acceptance, a notice of dishonour should be given to the drawer and each indorser in accordance with the rules in s.49. Any drawer or indorser not given the notice shall be discharged from liability.

It should also be noted that a bill can be discharged where:

● the holder waives or renounces his rights under it (s.62);

● the holder cancels the bill and makes the cancellation apparent on the bill (s.63); or

● the bill has been materially altered without the assent of all parties liable on it (s.64).[2]

---

[2] It might be noted that where a bill of exchange had been fraudulently altered by the deletion of the name of the true payee and substitution of the name of a different payee, and the bill of exchange is then presented or paid, neither the payer nor a collecting bank would be liable in conversion for the full value of the instrument. Section 64 rendered the instrument worthless, such that only nominal damages were recoverable (*Smith & Hayward v Lloyds TSB Bank Plc* [2001] 1 All E.R. 424).

Instructions to the bank for documentary collections

We have observed earlier that when sending the bills to the bank for collection **11–038** certain instructions must be given clearly on such matters like:

1. whether documents against acceptance or payment;
2. procedure to be used in the event of dishonour;
3. storage of goods delivered;
4. insurance of the goods following the termination of transit; and
5. to whom the bank should refer in case of need.

These instructions are to be inserted in a form, known in the export trade as the bank's lodgement form. This form is also called a collection order, under the ICC Uniform Rules for Collection Publication No.522 (1995). The Uniform Rules will normally apply to complement any instructions given for the collection of bills of exchange by banks as they are often incorporated in the relevant contract (the so-called Collection Instructions). Article 2 defines "collection" as

"the handling by banks of documents, in accordance with instructions received, in order to:
 (i) obtain payment and/or acceptance, or
 (ii) deliver documents against payment and/or against acceptance, or
 (iii) deliver documents on other terms and conditions".

There are essentially two types of documents the Rules deal with—financial documents and commercial documents. The former includes cheques, bills of exchange, promissory notes and any other document used to obtain money. Commercial documents are those documents which relate to the underlying commercial transaction (for example, a sale) such as transport documents, insurance documents, invoices, etc.

In general, all documents sent for collection must be accompanied by a **11–039** collection instruction. The collection instruction must indicate clearly that the collection is subject to URC522 and give complete and precise instructions (art.4). Banks are only permitted to act upon the instructions given in such collection instruction, and in accordance with the Rules. The instructions must be found only in the collection instruction—banks will not therefore examine documents in order to ascertain the instructions.

It is the duty of the presenting bank to make the documents available to the relevant trader. This is called presentation and the person to whom the presentation is made is called the drawee (art.5). Where the documents are payable at sight the presenting bank must make presentation for payment without delay. As for documents payable at a tenor, the presenting bank must, where acceptance is called for, make presentation for acceptance without delay, and where payment is called for, make presentation for payment not later than the appropriate maturity date (art.6). In discharging its functions, the bank is required to act with good faith and reasonable care (art.9). This is a matter left to the national court seised with jurisdiction to decide, using the applicable law of the contract. As far as reasonable care is concerned, international banking practice is quite established. That makes ascertaining the appropriate thresholds of care much more achievable than finding the content of a general duty of good faith.

Article 7 is particularly significant. It states that a collection should not contain bills of exchange payable at a future date (usance bill) with the instruction that commercial documents are to be delivered against payment. If a collection contains a bill of exchange payable at a future date, the collection instruction should state whether the commercial documents are to be released to the drawee against acceptance (D/A) or against payment (D/P). In the absence of such statement, commercial documents will be released only against payment and the collecting bank will not be responsible for any consequences arising out of any delay in the delivery of documents. If a collection contains a bill of exchange payable at a future date and the collection instruction indicates that commercial documents are to be released against payment, documents will be released only against such payment and the collecting bank will not be responsible for any consequences arising out of any delay in the delivery of documents. All this is to ensure that the bank does not contribute to any fraud or breach of contract which might be practised on the seller and buyer, bearing in mind the fact that in a sale, whoever is in possession of the appropriate commercial documents could well take delivery of the goods from the carrier.

11–040   The collecting bank is responsible for informing the bank from which the collection instruction came about any payment or acceptance made against the documents (art.26). The presenting bank on the other hand is required to give advice to the bank from which it received the collection instruction as to whether and why a payment or acceptance had been refused. Upon receiving this information, the remitting bank must give further instructions on how the documents should be handled (art.26).

The bank is not interested in the performance of the underlying commercial transaction, such as the sale. Therefore, it will not undertake to deliver, collect or even receive the goods as the buyer's agent (art.10). The bank will not be responsible for any goods consigned or sent to it without its consent.

A bank must make sure that the documents received appear to be as listed in the collection instruction and must advise by telecommunication or, if that is not possible, by other expeditious means, without delay, the party from whom the collection instruction was received of any documents missing, or found to be other than listed. Banks have no further obligation in this respect. If the documents do not appear to be listed, the remitting bank shall be precluded from disputing the type and number of documents received by the collecting bank (art.12). The bank is not usually responsible for the form of words in any of the documents unless it has expressly undertaken that responsibility. However, where there is a bill of exchange which has to be accepted, a presenting bank shall ensure that the form of the *acceptance* of a bill of exchange appears to be complete and correct (art.22). It is nevertheless not responsible for the genuineness of any signature or for the authority of any signatory to sign the acceptance.

11–041   As regards payment, art.16 stressed that the amounts collected (less charges and/or disbursements and/or expenses where applicable) must be made available without delay to the relevant party as identified in the collection instruction. That said, unless otherwise agreed, the collecting bank will effect payment of the amounts collected in favour of the remitting bank only.

Documentary Credit[3]

It is not unusual for the seller to want payment before he gives up control of **11–042** goods. Unfortunately, on the other hand, the buyer would wish to ensure that the goods will be delivered according to the contract before making payment. The tension is made worse because:

- the parties may not know each other at all or as well as in a domestic arrangement;
- there will be a delay while goods in transit, so capital is tied up; and
- if things go wrong, the parties will have a cross-border dispute on their hands.

By introducing the bank/s as a "reliable and solvent paymaster", the documentary credit or letter of credit system reduces the risk of bankruptcy as far as the seller is concerned (and it also reduces jurisdiction and enforcement if the seller insists on being allowed to deal with a bank in his own country). Secondly, it allows the buyer to stipulate what documents he wants to see before payment is made, and to insist on seeing certificates of quality/quantity produced by an independent third party whom he trusts. This could reduce the risk of fraud as far as the buyer is concerned. Thirdly, and more significantly, documentary credits can assist both the buyer and seller in the financing of the transaction. The seller may use the letter of credit to finance the transaction by:

- using a transferable credit or back to back credit in favour of his supplier; or
- discounting the credit with a bank and using the proceeds to purchase/ manufacture goods.

As regards the buyer, he may use documentary credit to finance his purchase by obtaining an advance from his bank, secured

- by letter of charge or hypothecation to issuing bank; or,
- by a pledge of bill of lading and other shipping documents.

The buyer could also raise finance by a resale of goods (but giving the issuing **11–043** bank a trust receipt for the documents to ensure its security)).

The documentary credit system usually involves the following steps:

1. After the sale has been agreed, the buyer (referred to as the "applicant") approaches his own bank (the "issuing bank") and asks it to issue a documentary credit in favour of the seller (often referred to as the "beneficiary"). The issuing bank will usually ask the buyer to complete its

---

[3] See generally, P. Todd, *Bills of Lading and Documentary Credits,* 3rd edn (London: LLP, 1998); F.M. Ventris, *Bankers Documentary Credits,* 3rd edn (London: LLP, 1998); B. Wunnicke, *Standby and Commercial Letters of Credit,* 2nd edn (New York, Chichester: Wiley, 1996); W. Hedley, *Bills of Exchange and Banker's Documentary Credits,* 4th edn (London: Informa, 2001), Malek and Quest, *Jack: Documentary Credits,* 4th edn (London: Butterworths, 2009).

standard form. If the issuing bank agrees to issue the letter of credit, the application form will form the basis of the contract between the buyer and the issuing bank.

2. The seller needs to be advised of the letter of credit. This may be done directly by the issuing bank. But it is more commonly done through a bank in the seller's own country (the "advising bank"). It is also usual for the advising bank to be asked by the seller to confirm the letter of credit. If the bank does so, it becomes the "confirming bank" and there now emerges a contract between the confirming bank and the seller. The terms of the contract are set out in the fax or telex evidencing the documentary credit.

3. In order to be paid, the seller will tender the documents stipulated in the credit, at the place stipulated in the documentary credit (usually the counters of the issuing or confirming bank during normal banking hours), prior to the expiry of the credit. The issuing or confirming bank then checks that the documents conform with those stipulated in the credit and within five banking days makes a decision to accept or reject the documents. If the documents are rejected, the seller may then re-tender valid documents as long as the credit has not expired. It is also possible for the bank to waive certain discrepancies.

4. If the documents are accepted, the seller will be paid:

   (a) in cash;
   (b) electronic funds transfer; or
   (c) by the bank's acceptance of bills of exchange ("drafts").

   In the case of an unconfirmed letter of credit, the issuing bank will make payment to the beneficiary. Where there is confirmation, the confirming bank will make payment at first instance. It will then tender the documents to the issuing bank for reimbursement. The issuing bank will reimburse the confirming bank if the documents are in conformity.

5. Finally, the issuing bank will tender the documents to the buyer and seek reimbursement. The buyer will then check the documents to see if they conform, and if they do, will reimburse the issuing bank. Armed with the documents, the buyer can then seek delivery of the goods from the carrier or sell the goods on to a sub-buyer.

11–044   Where the credit provides that the seller is to be paid on presentation of the documents, it is known as a sight payment credit. Where it entitles the seller to present with the documents a draft (bill of exchange) for acceptance and payment at maturity, it is called an acceptance credit. The third possibility is that it may enable the seller to negotiate or sell the draft and/or documents to an authorised bank. That bank then becomes the beneficiary of the documentary credit.

The difference between payment by documentary collection and documentary credit is that in the case of a documentary collection, by the time the buyer has accepted the bill of exchange, the goods may have arrived or at least be about to arrive at the buyer's premises. If the buyer fails to honour the bill, the seller is left in a disadvantaged position and much expense and inconvenience will have to be incurred to rectify the situation. Even if the bill of exchange has been discounted by a bank, this dishonour of the bill could mean that the bank could have recourse against the seller (the bank's customer). This is why the standing of the buyer is of great importance in the documentary collection system. With the documentary credit system, the seller obtains payment from the bank as soon as he tenders conforming documents to the bank.

The documentary credit system does not command popularity in trade within the EU Single Market, partly as a result of the substantial charges involved and partly because trade risk in the single market is relatively lower. With trade outside the single market where trade risks are considerably higher or at least perceived to be, documentary credits are more widely used. There is also the added factor that some traders by convention prefer using the documentary credit system. In some countries in Asia and Africa, exchange control rules might require the use of the letter of credit to ensure that cross-border payment in any currency is better monitored by the governments concerned since payment is ultimately made by banks which are directly or indirectly regulated.[4]

Letters of credit are generally governed by the Uniform Customs and Practice for Documentary Credits (2007 Revision, ICC Publication No.600) (hereafter referred to as the UCP). The rules are usually incorporated into the letter of credit by reference. As contractual terms they shall naturally have precedence over common law rules where any inconsistencies exist, the common law being applicable only to the extent of any gaps in the letter of credit.[5]

---

[4] Some governments also view the letter of credit as a source of revenue through the imposition of stamp duty on the letter of credit.

[5] Buckley, "The 1993 Revision of the Uniform Customs and practice for documentary credits" (1995) 6 Journal of Banking and Finance Law and Practice 77.

11–045

FOREIGN BILL AND/OR DOCUMENTS FOR COLLECTION

Drawer/exporter	Drawer's/exporter's reference(s) (to be quoted by bank in all correspondence)
Consignee	**Drawee (if not consignee)**
To (bank)	**For bank use only**

FORWARD DOCUMENTS ENUMERATED BELOW BY AIRMAIL. FOLLOW SPECIAL INSTRUCTIONS AND THOSE MARKED X

Bill of exchange	Commercial invoice	Certified/consular invoice	Certificate of origin	Insurance policy/certificate	Bill of lading	Parcel post receipt	Air waybill

Combined transport document	Other documents and whereabouts of any missing original bill of lading

RELEASE DOCUMENTS ON	ACCEPTANCE	PAYMENT	If unaccepted ➤	Protest	do not protest
If documents are not taken up on arrival of goods	warehouse goods	do not warehouse	and advise reason by	telex/cable	airmail
	insure against fire	do not insure	If unpaid ➤	protest	do not protest
			and advise reason by	telex/cable	airmail
Collect ALL charges				telex/cable	airmail
Collect correspondent's charges ONLY			Advise acceptance and due date by	telex/cable	airmail
Return accepted bill by airmail			Remit proceeds by	telex/cable	airmail
In case of need refer to				for guidance	accept their instructions

SPECIAL INSTRUCTIONS   1 Represent on arrival of goods if not honoured on first presentation

Date of bill of exchange	Bill of exchange value/amount of collection
Tenor of bill of exchange	
Bill of exchange claused	Please collect the above-mentioned bill and/or documents subject to the Uniform Rules for Collections (1978 Revision), International Chamber of Commerce, Publication No. 322. I/We agree that you shall not be liable for any loss, damage, or delay however caused which is not directly due to the negligence of your own officers or servants.
	Date and signature

Establishing the letter of credit

The law requires the buyer to open a letter of credit in time to enable the **11–046** shipment of the goods. In *Garcia v Page & Co Ltd* (1936) 55 Ll.LR. 391 it was held that the buyer's duty to open a letter of credit in time is usually a condition precedent to the seller's duty to ship the goods. In that case, the contract of sale required the buyer to "open immediately a confirmed credit in London" in the seller's favour. The contract was made in May and stipulated that shipment was to be in September. The letter of credit was not properly set up until September 3. The question for the court was whether the buyer was in breach entitling the seller to terminate the contract. Porter J. said in giving judgment for the seller:

" . . . under the original contract there was a contract by which a confirmed credit in the terms specified was a condition precedent and it had to be opened immediately. That means that the buyer must have such time as is needed by a person of reasonable diligence to get that credit established".

It therefore follows that where a date for the opening of the credit is stipulated in the contract, the buyer must comply with that date. Failure to do so is tantamount to a repudiatory breach which allows the seller to treat the contract as having been discharged. The seller is therefore freed from delivering the goods under the contract.

That said, it is only a condition precedent to the seller performing his part of the bargain. It is not a condition precedent to the formation of the contract of sale itself. This means the validity and existence of a contract of sale itself is not dependent on whether the letter of credit had been opened or not (*Vitol SA v Conoil* [2009] EWHC 1144 (Comm)). In *Vitol*, C had agreed to buy oil from V but, failing to secure a sub-buyer for the oil, wanted to cancel the contract. C failed to take delivery and V sued C for non-acceptance of goods. C, however, countered by submitting that as a confirmed irrevocable letter of credit had not been issued no contract had been concluded between the parties. The court held that although without a letter of credit in place the seller is not required to ship the goods, the absence of the letter of credit did not affect the validity and existence of the contract.

What does "opening a letter of credit" mean? It was authoritatively held in **11–047** *Bunge Corp v Vegetable Vitamin Foods (Pte) Ltd* [1985] 1 Lloyd's Rep. 613 that a credit is only "opened" when the advice of the opening of the letter of credit or the confirmation of the letter of credit is communicated to the beneficiary.[6]

Where no time is stipulated, as in *Pavia & Co SpA v Thurmann-Nielsen* [1952] 2 Q.B. 84, the Court of Appeal held that the credit must be made available to the seller *at the beginning* of the shipment period. The reason is because the seller is entitled to be assured before he actually ships the goods that he will be paid on shipment. He is not bound to tell the buyer the precise date of shipment and when he does ship the goods, he must be able to draw on the credit. Denning L.J. explained:

---

[6] This coincides with the general rule in *Brinkibon Ltd v Stahag Stahl und Stahlwarenhandels GmbH* [1983] 2 A.C. 34 which states that acceptance and revocation notices would only take effect upon their communication to the respondent. The mere act of sending the notice is insufficient.

"[The seller] may ship on the very first day of the shipment period. If, therefore, the buyer is to fulfil his obligations he must make the credit available to the seller at the very first date when the goods maybe lawfully shipped in compliance with the contract."

Where as in *Plasticmoda SpA v Davidsons (Manchester) Ltd* [1952] 1 Lloyd's Rep. 527 the contract provides for a shipment date instead of a period of time, the buyers are required to open the credit a reasonable time before that date.[7]

11–048   In *Ian Stach Ltd v Baker Bosley Ltd* [1958] 2 Q.B. 130, shipment of the goods was stipulated to be in August-September at the buyers' option. The buyers failed to open the credit by August 1. They argued that the contract in question was an FOB contract whereby the buyers had the duty and right to nominate the shipment date and as such, there was no breach so long as the credit was opened in a reasonable before the date to be nominated. The court rejected the submission and held that to allow the buyers to do so would be to create an uncertainty in an already established practice. Hence, in line with *Pavia & Co SpA*, it was held that the buyers were in breach. It should also be noted that the duty to open the credit in time is strict. In *AE Lindsay & Co Ltd v Cook* [1953] 1 Lloyd's Rep. 328, the buyers were not excused even though their failure was caused by circumstances beyond their control.

These essential requirements are neatly summarised in the case of *Glencore Grain Rotterdam BV v Lebanese Organisation for International Commerce* [1997] 4 All E.R. 514. The Court of Appeal held that in the absence of any special agreement, the sellers under a sale contract on normal FOB terms (and indeed any other trade term) were entitled to see a conforming letter of credit in place before they began shipment of the goods, and their obligation was to ship the contract goods on board the vessel provided by the buyers for carriage regardless of the terms as to freight or otherwise that the buyers had agreed with the shipowner. In that case it had been raised in defence that payment was on terms that the sellers presented bills of lading issued as "freight pre-paid". As far as the court was concerned that made little difference. The sellers were expressly free of any obligation to pay freight, since freight pre-paid bills of lading were contrary both to the underlying concept of an FOB contract (with the buyers as shippers) and to the essential commercial purpose of the letter of credit machinery. Accordingly the buyers were not entitled to require the sellers to procure and produce freight pre-paid bills of lading in order to receive payment.

The buyer who has undertaken to open the credit according to the terms of the contract of sale, will instruct his bank as to what documents must be presented, time for presentment, the description of the goods and other conditions to be met by the beneficiary seller (see specimen application form). Article 6(d)(ii) states the place of the bank with which the credit is available is the place of presentation. The buyer will also specify an expiry date on which the documents may be presented to the bank for payment. That date may also be the latest shipment date but an earlier shipment date is usually inserted to give the seller

---

[7] See also *Sinason-Teicher Inter-American Grain Corp v Oil Cakes & Oil Seeds Trading Co Ltd* [1954] 1 W.L.R. 1394 where it was held that a reasonable time refers to a reasonable time calculated back from the first date of the shipment and not to be calculated forward from the time the contract was first made between the parties.

time for presentation by expiry. Article 6(d)(i) provides that all credits must stipulate an expiry date and a place for presentation of documents for payment, acceptance or, with the exception of freely negotiable credits, a place for presentation of documents for negotiation. An expiry date stipulated for payment, acceptance or negotiation will generally be construed as the expiry date for presentation of documents. Where the credit calls for the tender of transport documents, art.14(c) states that the presentation must be made no later than 21 calendar days after the date of shipment and, in any event, not later than the expiry date.

Incidentally, it might be added that a letter of credit can be extended—that is **11–049** a matter of agreement between the applicant and the issuing bank; however, it is important to note that an extension of the letter of credit in the event that documents had not been tendered on time or delivery deadlines had not been met may be construed by the courts as a waiver of the applicant buyer's right to insist on timely presentment/delivery.[8]

Article 29(a) provides inter alia that if the letter of credit expired on a day the banks were closed then the date of expiry was extended to the first following day on which the bank was open. Article 29(b) then states that the bank to which presentation is made on such business day must provide a statement that the documents were presented within the time limits as extended. The chief difficulty in applying this practical provision is whether the Issuing Bank can disclaim liability if the Confirming or Advising Bank fails to provide this statement of extension. This was precisely what the next case dealt with.

---

[8] See *South Caribbean Trading Ltd v Trafigura Beheer BV* [2004] EWHC 2676—although it should be noted that there the court found the extension of the letter of credit to be a variation of the contract given that the buyer had agreed to extend the letter of credit in consideration the seller's additional promises.

11–050

LETTER OF CREDIT PRESENTATION FORM

Drawer/exporter	Drawer's/exporters reference(s)	
	Issuing bank L/C no.	Your reference no.
	Issuing bank	
To (bank)	Value of the drawing	

DOCUMENTS ENCLOSED (state no. of copies)

Bill of exchange	Commercial invoice	Certified Consular Invoice	Certificate of origin	
Insurance policy/certificate	Transport documents	L/C for endorsement	OTHER DOCUMENTS	
			Document	Copies

Dear Sirs,

We have much pleaseure in enclosing the above documents related to the
Letter of Credit referred to above.
We trust you will find the documents to be in order and look forward to
receiving your settlement as shown below.
Should you discover any discrepancies, please contact us as shown
below BEFORE taking any action.

FOR TERM DRAFTS
We request you to *discount/negotiate (less interest)
Please *retain/return accepted draft(s) to us
*Delete as appropriate

PAYMENT INSTRUCTIONS

	For GBP sterling items please remit proceeds to our account no. :
	held with :
	  :
	  :
	Sort code no. :
			For GBP sterling items please remit proceeds to us by cheque.

	For currency items - (please specify) : : : Forward contract reference (if any) :		OTHER - (please specify) : : : :

DISREPANCIES/SPECIAL INSTRUCTIONS

Contact details (eg fax, telex nos)	Company/telephone no.
	Name of signatory
	Place & date
	Signature

Bayerische Vereinsbank Aktiengesellschaft v National Bank of Pakistan [1997] 1   **11–051**
Lloyd's Rep. 59
Facts:
The London branch of the Confirming Bank (claimants) was closed on Saturday and
Sunday, July 30 and 31, 1994. By virtue of art.44(a) UCP 500 (now art.29(a), UCP 600)
the expiry date of the credit was extended to the following Monday. No statement of the
extension was given by the Confirming Bank to the Issuing Bank (defendants) although
it was stated that "the beneficiary has presented in order and *in time*" (emphasis
added).
Held:
It would not be appropriate to treat art.44(c) (now art.29(b)) as introducing a condition
precedent to a Correspondent Bank's right to be reimbursed by the Issuing Bank. If the
Issuing Bank suffered any loss as a result of the failure of the Correspondent Bank to
provide that statement, it would be entitled to claim damages but not, repudiation. Even
if this proposition is incorrect, Mance J. said:

"On the hypothesis that article 44(c) introduces a condition precedent, the defendants
were justified so long as there was no such statement; the justification would exist
although this was not an objection of which they were aware or which they took at the
time and they had in fact received an express assurance that the documents had been
presented 'in time'. The mere initial presentation of the documents without a statement
could not, however, constitute a repudiatory breach. Nor could the mere initial rejection
of the documents by the defendants discharge them from any further obligation to take
up the documents if and when a statement was provided in accordance with article
44(c). Just as the bank's initial rejection of non-conforming documents . . . does not
preclude a beneficiary from remedying the defects and re-presenting complying
documents within the period of validity of the credit, so here it would clearly be open
to a confirming bank to rectify the omission of any statement required by article
44(c)".

The instructions for the issue of a credit must be complete and precise and   **11–052**
should state precisely the documents against which payment, acceptance or
negotiation is to be made. The buyer's instructions are of paramount importance.
A bank that has paid out contrary to given instructions has no recourse against the
applicant buyer but where the instructions are not clear, it cannot be blamed for
adopting a sensible or reasonable interpretation. As Lord Diplock said in
Commercial Banking Co of Sydney Ltd v Jalsard Pty Ltd [1973] A.C. 279:

"Both the issuing banker and his correspondent bank have to make quick
decisions as to whether a document which has been tendered by the seller
complies with the requirements of the credit at the risk of incurring liability to
one or other of the parties to the transaction if the decision is wrong. Delay in
deciding may in itself result in a breach of his contractual obligations to the
buyer or to the seller. This is the reason for the rule that where the banker's
instructions from his customer are ambiguous or unclear he commits no breach
of his contract with the buyer if he has construed them in a reasonable sense,
even though upon closer consideration which can be given to questions of
construction in an action in a court of law, it is possible to say that some other
meaning is to be preferred".

Where it is reasonable and convenient to contact the buyer for clarification
especially where there is an obvious ambiguity, the bank should do so (*European
Asian Bank AG v Punjab and Sind Bank (No.2)* [1983] 1 W.L.R. 642).

The buyer's bank (Issuing Bank) might require that the buyer put it in funds to meet the purchase price represented in the letter of credit. More usually, the bank will rely on the buyer's creditworthiness and/or the likelihood of funds being put in place before the documents are presented for payment.

Once the credit is set up by the Issuing Bank, the buyer may then issue the letter of credit to the seller directly or, more conventionally, arrange for a bank in the seller's country to notify the seller as to the opening of the credit. That bank is called an Advising Bank. The notification issued to the seller by the Advising Bank is, for all intents and purposes, the letter of credit. The Issuing Bank becomes bound to honour the letter of credit as soon as the letter is received by the seller.

Irrevocability, confirmation, acceptance and deferred payment

11–053 A letter of credit is any arrangement, however named or described, that is irrevocable and thereby constitutes the issuing bank's definite undertaking to honour a complying presentation (art.2). Irrevocability means that the letter of credit cannot be cancelled or amended without the agreement the issuing bank, confirming bank if any) and the beneficiary (art.10(a)). If however an amendment or cancellation is made, the terms of the original credit will remain in force for the beneficiary until he communicates his acceptance of the amendment to the bank that advised him of the amendment (art.10(c)). The beneficiary is duty bound to inform the relevant bank as to his acceptance or rejection of the amendment. If he fails to give proper notification, a presentation that complies with the credit and to any not yet accepted amendment will be deemed to be notification of acceptance. At that moment of the presentation, the credit is deemed to have been amended (art.10(c)).

Although the Issuing Bank owes a duty to the beneficiary to pay against conforming documents as required by the credit, a beneficiary may nevertheless wish for a bank which he trusts more or which is more convenient to undertake to pay him directly. This undertaking is independent of the issuing bank. Confirmation is defined in art.2 as a definite undertaking of the Confirming Bank, in addition to that of the Issuing Bank, to honour or negotiate a complying presentation. As such, if the Confirming Bank pays but the Issuing Bank refuses to, the Confirming Bank cannot normally have recourse against the seller to whom it had paid. The Confirming Bank's right to be reimbursed depends largely on its contract with the Issuing Bank. It is therefore advisable to obtain the Issuing Bank's consent for the letter of credit to be confirmed.

What constitutes a confirmation is strictly construed.[9] Any ambiguity will be construed as indicating an unconfirmed credit. In *Wahbe Tamari & Sons Ltd v Colprogeca-Sociedada Geral de Fibras, Cafes e Products Colonias Lda* [1969] 2 Lloyd's Rep. 18, the advising bank had inserted a right of recourse against the beneficiary in the advice. That, according to the court, did not constitute a confirmation of the credit.

Let us consider a few examples of Documentary Credits.

---

[9] Schmitthoff, "Confirmation in export transactions" [1957] J.B.L. 17.

Example 1: Advice to Seller of an Unconfirmed, Irrevocable Credit:

11–054

Kingstown Bank Plc
Documentary Credits Section
PO Box 11
High Street
London
Great Britain

2 January 2013

ADVICE OF AN UNCONFIRMED DOCUMENTARY CREDIT

IM Sellers Ltd
1 Old Road
London
Great Britain

Dear Sirs
Documentary Credit No 123/4/567 F

We have been advised by Big Malaysian Bank, Port Kelang, Malaysia that they have opened an irrevocable Documentary Credit Number 123/4/567 F in your favour for GBP 25,000.00 (say) Twenty Five Thousand Pounds Sterling for account of Malay Importers Sdn. Bhd.

This credit is to be available by draft(s) drawn at sight for 100 per cent CIF Invoice Value on Kingstown Bank Plc, Documentary Credits Section, PO Box 11, High Street, London, ENGLAND clearly marked that it is/they are' drawn under Credit No.123/4/567 F and accompanied by the undermentioned documents.

Invoices in triplicate indicating the goods are of UK origin.

Packing List in Triplicate.

Inspection Certificate signed and dated at the port of shipment issued by Good Liverpool Inspection Co Ltd.

Insurance Policy or Certificate in duplicate covering Institute Cargo Clauses (A) for CIF Invoice Value plus 10 per cent.

Complete set clean "on board" ocean bills of lading issued to order, blank indorsed marked "freight paid" and "notify Malay Importers Sdn. Bhd.".

Covering the shipment of:

300 road drills as Proforma Invoice No.999 dated 29 December 2012 Price CIF Port Kelang From Liverpool to Port Kelang not later than 28 February 2013 Part Shipments not allowed Transshipment allowed.

The credit is available for presentation until 15 March 2013 in the UK.

We reserve the right to make a charge not exceeding GBP 50 for additional costs arising should documents be presented which do not comply with the terms of this credit.

This letter is solely an advice of the credit established by the bank and conveys no engagement on our part.

Except so far as otherwise expressly stated, this credit is subject to Uniform Customs and Practice for Documentary Credits 2007 Revision International Chamber of Commerce Publication No.600.

Yours faithfully

T.H.E. Banker

Kingstown Bank Plc
Documentary Credits Section
PO Box 11
High Street
London
Great Britain

Comment:

11–055   Example 1 is an irrevocable documentary credit by virtue of art.3 UCP 600 which states that a credit is irrevocable even if there is no indication to that effect. It is expressed in GBP to the sum of £25,000. The seller is required to draw a sight bill of exchange (draft) to be paid.

The parties to the documentary credit are as follows:

1. the beneficiary is IM Sellers Ltd;

2. the applicant is Malay Importers Sdn Bhd;

3. the Issuing Bank is Big Malaysian Bank;

4. the Advising Bank is Kingstown Bank Plc.

It is readily seen that the credit is valid as between the seller and buyer because it has been opened in time for shipment. Shipment is agreed by contract to be in February 2013. The advice of the credit is issued in January predating the start of shipment period.

The credit will expire on March 15, 2013.

Example 2: Advice of Seller of a Confirmed, Irrevocable Credit

11–056

Kingstown Bank Plc
Documentary Credits Section
PO Box 11
High Street
London
Great Britain

2 February 2013

ADVICE OF A CONFIRMED DOCUMENTARY CREDIT

IM Sellers Ltd
1 Old Road
London
Great Britain

Dear Sirs

Documentary Credit No.333/4/555 G

We have been advised by Secure Singaporean Bank, Long Road, Republic of Singapore that they have opened an irrevocable Documentary Credit Number 123/4/567 F in your favour for US 30,000.00 (say) Thirty Thousand US Dollars for account of Buyers Ltd.

This credit is to be available by draft(s) at 90 days after sight on Kingstown Bank Plc, Documentary Credits Section, PO Box 11, High Street, London, Great Britain clearly marked that it is/they are drawn under Credit No.333/4/555 G and accompanied by the documents stipulated below.

Draft(s) is/are to be drawn to the extent of 100 per cent of the full invoice value.

Documents required

Invoices in triplicate indicating the goods are of UK origin and certifying goods in accordance with Proforma Invoice No.111/01.

Certificate of UK origin issued by a Chamber of Commerce and countersigned by the Singapore High Commission.

Air Consignment Note indicating goods consigned to Buyers Ltd marked "freight paid" and despatch from London Heathrow Airport (LHR) to Singapore Changi Airport (SIN). Part shipments allowed Transshipment prohibited.

Covering:

100,000 Class A widgets

This credit expires 17 April 2013.

The description of the merchandise on the invoice must appear exactly as shown in the documentary credit.

If, due to discrepancies, we are unable to honour documents when presented, we reserve the right to make a handling charge for additional costs.

Charges are for your account including:
ADVISING COMMISSION GBP 40.00
CONFIRMATION COMMISSION GBP 50.00
PAYMENT COMMISSION OF 0.1 per cent MINIMUM GBP 50.00 PER PAYMENT.

We shall be pleased to receive your remittance in settlement of the above charges, alternatively they will be deducted from the proceeds following presentation of documents.

This credit is confirmed by Kingstown Bank Plc, PO Box 11, High Street, London in accordance with the terms of the undertaking expressed in the Uniform Customs and Practice for Documentary Credits, ICC Publication No.600.

Except so far as otherwise expressly stated, this credit is subject to Uniform Customs and Practice for Documentary Credits 2007 Revision International Chamber of Commerce Publication No.600.

Yours faithfully

T.H.E. Banker

Kingstown Bank Plc
Documentary Credits Section
PO Box 11
High Street
London
Great Britain

Comment:

11–057   Here we have an irrevocable credit (art.3 UCP 600) confirmed by the seller's bank in England but with drafts drawn at 90 days' sight. Payment is not made against the presentation of documents, but at a specified time after the event. In the meantime the documents will be remitted to the buyer. This is called a deferred payment credit.

A deferred payment credit gives the buyer and any issuing, nominated or confirming bank a period of time before payment must be made to the seller. The credit would normally state when the future payment should be made (for example payment to be made "on 30 September 2013" or "within 90 days after the date of shipment as shown in the bill of lading"). Although payment under a deferred payment credit is for a later date, the seller will often ask the nominated or confirming bank to "discount" the documentary credit by making an earlier and reduced payment to the seller in return for an assignment to the bank of the proceeds of the letter of credit.

A deferred payment credit should be distinguished from an acceptance credit. An acceptance credit requires the seller to present a usance draft to the Correspondent Bank (or the Issuing Bank where there is no Correspondent Bank) for acceptance against documents and subsequently payment by the accepting bank at maturity. The seller will not necessarily hold the bill until maturity. He may decide to negotiate it for earlier payment, albeit at a discount. Below is an example of an undertaking to honour an acceptance credit:

"This credit is available with Kingstown Bank Plc by acceptance of IM Sellers' drafts at 90 days after date of bills of lading drawn on Kingstown Bank Plc, PO Box 11, High Street, London, Great Britain for 100% of Invoice Value marked "drawn under Documentary Credit Number 222/3/444" and accompanied by documents stipulated below".

Where the credit is an acceptance credit, the Advising Bank will accept it and **11–058** will pay at maturity and then debit the Issuing Bank with the face value of the bill plus commission.

Confirmed letters of credit have not only the advantage of security as far as the seller is concerned, but also of speed. The seller is able to claim payment as soon as documents are presented to his bank in the United Kingdom. They are also unfortunately the most expensive method. The commissions payable include the opening, amendment, negotiation and confirmation commissions. "Country exposure" is a term applied by banks to the extent of facilities they allow to a country and where the country risk is high, the "exposure" is a limited commodity and as such the commission for such facilities will be quite considerable. While the opening of a credit is usually the responsibility of the buyer, it is not unusual for the seller to agree to defray some of the banking charges. Where the country exposure involved is scarce, the seller should be aware that the commission involved is likely to be very high and should therefore ascertain the full facts before agreeing to contribute to the cost.

Silent confirmations

In order to obtain even greater security as to payment, a UK seller might resort **11–059** to a silent confirmation. This involves the seller asking his own bank in the United Kingdom to add their confirmation to letters of credit issued by a foreign bank without the latter's knowledge. Technically, the silent confirmation is not a confirmation in the sense of the confirmed documentary credit arrangement. It is in fact a separate undertaking by a bank in the seller's country to pay in the event of documents in compliance with the terms being presented under an irrevocable letter of credit opened by the buyer's bank being dishonoured. That undertaking is given not in pursuant of any contract between the Confirming Bank and the Issuing Bank or the Applicant. The undertaking produces an effect similar to that of a confirmed letter of credit, save the fact that the buyer is not told of the confirmation.

Silent confirmations are based on the understanding that the bank will be able to claim reimbursement from the Issuing Bank notwithstanding the absence of a contract between itself and the Issuing Bank. As the Confirming Bank does not have proper authority from the Issuing Bank to "confirm" the letter of credit, the Issuing Bank would not be under a contractual duty to reimburse the Confirming Bank directly. The silent confirmation may serve a purpose similar to that of a confirmation by providing the beneficiary with an additional source of payment. However, it involves different parties and necessarily creates different rights and obligations in law. In fact, there can be a commitment silently to confirm even before the letter of credit is issued where on the other hand, in a proper case of confirmation, the letter of must be issued before confirmation can arise. Clearly, a silent confirmation is not confirmation. Indeed, this is what the American Bar Association Task Force has to say about silent confirmations:

"A confirmation made without the authority of the issuer is not a true confirmation. While a so- called silent confirmation may itself constitute a new and separate letter of credit, commitment to purchase, guarantee, or other obligation binding on the one making it, *vis-à-vis* the beneficiary, the silent confirmer does not acquire the rights of an issuer on the original credit and is not a confirmer in any sense of the term. The use of the term 'confirmer' . . . should never be construed to imply a reference to a silent confirmer".

So, it is therefore clear that the Confirming Bank cannot seek reimbursement *under its contract* with the Issuing Bank.

11–060   Moreover, it is not entirely clear if the Confirming Bank would be able to require the beneficiary to claim for its reimbursement from the Issuing Bank. The reason for this is because it might be difficult to imply such a term from the silent confirmation arrangement. Where there is an express term, naturally that could be enforced against the beneficiary. Another controversial solution might lie in the bank acting as the beneficiary's assignee. The argument goes like this—there exists an assignment of the beneficiary's rights under the letter of credit to the Confirming Bank. There are difficulties with this argument as is indicated in *Marathon Electrical Manufacturing Corp v Mashreqbank PSC* (May 13, 1997)—there are potential problems with the lawfulness of an assignment being made of a future or contingent debt, the validity of notice given to interested parties, any relevant applicable law, etc.

A more natural solution might be for the bank to exercise its rights against the Issuing Bank as a negotiating bank under the letter of credit. This was a problem under the old UCP 500, because negotiation was defined in art.10(b)(ii) UCP 500 as "the giving of value for Draft(s) and/or documents by the bank authorised to negotiate". The emphasis on "authorised to negotiate" might exclude the silent Confirming Bank. The UCP 500's position also seemed to be that the silent confirmation is no more than an agreement to negotiate, and not the negotiation itself. As such, there was no duty on the Issuing Bank to reimburse the silent Confirming Bank even though that bank had given value to the documents. The UCP 600 provides, on the other hand, that "negotiation" means the purchase of drafts or documents or an agreement to advance funds prior to the date of actual payment by the issuer (art.2). This, it would appear, extends to silent confirmations. The new definition attempts to do away with this dichotomy.

It should also be noted that unlike the accepted view of the UCP 500 (see in particular the American Bar Association Task Force's description above), it appears from art.2 UCP 600 that the concept of confirmation itself can accommodate silent confirmation. Article 2 defines confirmation as "a definite undertaking of the confirming bank, in addition to that of the issuing bank, to honour or negotiate a complying presentation". It does not seem to require authorisation from the Issuing Bank. That said, art.2 also defines a Confirming Bank as one authorised or requested by the Issuing Bank to confirm the credit. There is no real conflict; the silent confirmer is not a Confirming Bank for the purposes of the UCP but where silent confirmation exists, the Issuing Bank may be required to reimburse the silent confirmer (which art.12(b) refers to as the Nominated Bank).

11–061   The UCP 600 requires the Issuing Bank to honour drafts and/or documents drawn under letters of credit but it is equally emphasised that credits must not call for drafts drawn on the applicant, and not just that they should not. This responsibility is further underlined in art.12 which for the first time makes clear that nomination should mean the authorisation to pre-pay or purchase a draft accepted, or a deferred payment undertaking incurred, by that nominated bank. This removes all doubt as to the right of the nominated bank to be reimbursed having pre-paid their acceptances or deferred payment undertakings.

Straight and negotiation credits

The letter of credit is not a negotiable instrument in itself; the obligation to pay **11–062** under it is given by the Issuing Bank (or Confirming Bank) to the seller alone. If the beneficiary were to sell it to a third party, that third party does not have a claim against the bank/s involved, because there is no contractual relationship between them. Such a credit is called a "straight" or "specially advised" credit.

A negotiation credit on the other hand is an undertaking given by the Paying Bank (whether Issuing or Nominated Bank) to a third party who buys the bill of exchange drawn by the seller under the documentary credit (art.2). The third party, usually a bank which has purchased the documents from the seller, can then present them under the credit and receive payment in due course (art.2).

What constitutes negotiation is not always clear. The mere examination of documents without giving valuable consideration is not negotiation. Banks paying against documents will also collect the documents on behalf of the Issuing Bank or buyer. This collection of the documents in exchange for payment does not however constitute negotiation, there being no value given. So too is the mere promise to give money for the bill of exchange at a later date following the receipt of funds (*European Asian Bank AG v Punjab and Sind Bank (No.2)* [1983] 1 W.L.R. 642). Negotiation only takes place when value is given for the drafts and/or documents by the bank authorised to negotiate.

A negotiation credit could further be classified as open or restricted. An open **11–063** negotiation credit allows negotiation by any bank which is prepared to do so. The open negotiation credit will usually state that the credit is available with any bank by negotiation of the drafts drawn on the Issuing Bank accompanied by conforming documents specified in the credit. A restricted negotiation credit limits negotiation to only bank/s selected by the Issuing Bank.

Red clause and green clause credits

A red clause credit requires payment in advance, that is to say, before shipment **11–064** takes place. Payment is usually made against a warehouseman's receipt. A green clause credit is a similar anticipatory credit; it requires payment in advance and, further, that the goods be kept in the bank's name. An anticipatory credit is particularly needful where the supply of certain goods requires the purchasing of other goods to make up the total quantity required by the buyer.

Example:

The buyer requires a very large quantity of wool. To make up the quantity, the seller will have to buy from various suppliers over a wide area. The outlay is not only substantial but will endure for quite some time. In order to facilitate the seller to put together the order, the buyer could open an anticipatory credit which allows the seller to draw down from before the eventual shipment. The amount is to be repaid through a deduction from payment ultimately made against those documents. In the event that the documents are not presented to the bank making the advance, that bank is entitled to claim reimbursement from the Issuing Bank.

Such credits are becoming less popular. Traders are more inclined to insert in a documentary credit the stipulation that a stated amount or percentage may be drawn down in advance of the receipt of documents, against presentation of a banker's guarantee that it will be refunded in the event of the failure on the seller's part to present conforming documents. The bank acts as a guarantor that the seller will perform his part of the bargain.

Transferable and back-to-back credits

11–065   Where the sellers are in fact middlemen buying from suppliers to sell to buyers abroad, they might require credits that are transferable so that their suppliers could be paid in the same secure manner. The transferable credit allows the beneficiary (seller) to request the Advising Bank to make the credit available in whole or part to one or more other parties (art.38(b)).[10] Although there is no obligation on the bank to do so, it would not normally refuse as long as adequate transfer charges are paid. The second beneficiary could then obtain payment by presenting the specified documents in his own name. Consent from the bank however must be express according to *Bank Negara Indonesia 1946 v Lariza (Singapore) Pte Ltd* [1988] A.C. 583 and relate to the extent and manner of the transfer.

A transferable credit may be transferred once only (art.38(d)) although this may be to two or more "second" beneficiaries or transferees. The transfer must be on the same terms as prescribed in the original credit with several exceptions (art.38(g)). The amount or unit prices may, for example, be reduced. The expiry date and the last date for presentation of documents could be amended within the permitted time in the original credit. It is of course permissible to have the name of the first beneficiary substituted for that of the applicant for the original credit, but if the applicant's name is required by the original credit to appear in any document other than the invoice, this requirement shall also apply in the transferable credit. The prudent seller should take care to ensure that no document other than the invoice requires the original applicant's name to be disclosed under the terms of the original credit. If this is not so, the second beneficiary could contact the applicant (buyer) directly to solicit further business, thus cutting out the need of the "seller" as middleman. In order to prevent such a consequence, the first beneficiary (seller) has the right to substitute his invoices for those of the second beneficiary and to claim the difference under the original credit as profit.

The back-to-back credit operates in a similar way. The middleman seller approaches his bank with the credit in his favour and requests that the bank accept it as security for a credit to be issued in his supplier's favour. That second credit shall usually be on similar terms but for a reduced amount, reflecting the profit to be made by the middleman. Banks are however not enthusiastic about offering back-to-back credits because they have no recourse against anyone but the middleman who normally does not have a strong capital base. The middleman's main asset is his expert knowledge of markets to "buy and sell". He is not directly involved in the manufacturing or production of goods and it is not surprising therefore to find him without the sort of capital base that the banks would find assurance in.

11–066   It should also be noted that the bank generally owes their customer, the middleman, a duty of confidentiality not to disclose the details of the middleman's purchase terms with the exporter to the middleman's buyer. The bank in

---

[10] Schmitthoff, "The transferable credit" [1988] J.B.L. 49.

Jackson v Royal Bank of Scotland [2005] UKHL 3 had disclosed to the middleman's (their customer) buyers the details of the original supplier in Thailand through bills of lading and other documents. The House of Lords agreed with the lower courts that the bank, being aware of the object of a transferable letter of credit, owed their customer a duty of confidentiality.

Revolving credits

Where goods are shipped and paid for by instalments, it is usually convenient to open a single credit to cover the entire transaction. The buyer does not have to raise a separate credit for each shipment. The revolving credit is one in which the amount payable is renewed or reinstated for the next shipment, after each payment. The beneficiary is therefore entitled to present documents and obtain payment as often as he wishes during the credit period and within the financial limit specified. As each payment is drawn, the applicant's account will be debited to replace that which has been paid out.

11–067

Securing payment

Autonomy of the letter of credit[11]

When the seller presents the documents under the letter of credit for payment, he is assured of payment as long as the documents are conforming and all other conditions in the credit have been properly met. It is not open to anyone (including the buyer) to argue that there has been a breach of the underlying contract of sale and hence, deny the seller payment under the letter of credit. The buyer is not entitled to prevent payment. His only recourse is to take legal action subsequently. This separation between the contract and the letter of credit is known as the principle of the autonomy of the credit. Article 4(a) UCP explains the principle in this way:

11–068

"A credit by its nature is a separate transaction from the sale or other contract on which it may be based. Banks are in no way concerned with or bound by such contract, even if any reference whatsoever to it is included in the credit. Consequently, the undertaking of a bank to honour, to negotiate or to fulfil any other obligation under the credit is not subject to claims or defences by the applicant resulting from its relationships with the issuing bank or the beneficiary. A beneficiary can in no case avail itself of the contractual relationships existing between banks or between the applicant and the issuing bank".

In *Hamzeh Malas & Sons v British Imex Industries Ltd* [1958] 2 Q.B. 127, the buyer claimed that the goods were defective. Thus, they applied for an injunction to prevent the bank from paying under the letter of credit. The injunction would not be granted. Jenkins L.J. remarked:

---

[11] Goode, "Abstract Payment Undertakings" in (P. Cane and J. Stapleton (eds), *Essays for Patrick Atiyah* (New York: Oxford University Press, 1991).

"[I]t seems to be plain enough that the opening of a confirmed letter of credit constitutes a bargain between the banker and the vendor of goods, which imposes upon the banker an absolute obligation to pay, irrespective of any dispute there may be between the parties as to whether the goods are up to contract or not".

The reason is that "an elaborate commercial system had been built up on the footing that bankers' confirmed credits are of that character". It would be wrong to interfere with the legitimate mercantile desire for certainty.[12]

11–069   Indeed, art.5 stressed thus that banks deal with documents and not with goods, services or performance to which the documents may relate. We should also remember that in many international trade transactions, there are more parties involved than just the buyer or seller. The seller usually has to obtain goods or raw materials from a supplier before he is able to meet the contract made with the buyer. The seller will need to be financed in making payments to their suppliers. That financing comes from the negotiation or discounting of drafts drawn under the documentary credit arrangement. That system of financing would break down completely if a dispute between the seller and buyer was to have the effect of "freezing" the sum in respect of which the letter of credit was opened.

Article 34 reflects this approach and states that the bank shall not be liable for the sufficiency, accuracy, genuineness, falsification or legal effect of any documents it is required to receive from the beneficiary. The bank is protected as long as it makes payment upon the presentation of conforming documents. It is not duty bound to inquire into whether there is a tainted presentation or whether the underlying contract was fraudulent or whether the documents are a forgery. In *Gian Singh & Co Ltd v Banque de l'Indochine* [1974] 1 W.L.R. 1234, the Privy Council held that the bank could not be held responsible for paying upon the tender of a forged document. As far as the law was concerned, the bank had acted within the remit of its obligations to the applicant and beneficiary. It was not obliged to investigate the genuineness of a signature which on its face purports to be the signature of the person named or described in the letter of credit. In the ordinary case without any specific instructions to the contrary, visual inspection of the documents presented is all that is called for.

Fraud however can destroy the autonomy of the credit. Where the payer (whether the Issuing or Nominated Bank) can prove fraud or forgery, he does not have to pay the beneficiary. The narrowness of this exception or defence was extensively explored by the House of Lords in the next case.

11–070   *United City Merchants (Investments) Ltd v Royal Bank of Canada (The American Accord)* [1983] 1 A.C. 168
Facts:
Payment for the sale of manufacturing equipment was by confirmed irrevocable credit. The carrier's agent had fraudulently issued a bill of lading showing shipment to be within shipment period. That bill of lading was incorrect and false. This was not known to the sellers. The confirming bank refused to pay on the basis that it had information suggesting that shipment had not taken place as indicated in the bill of lading.

---

[12] Davidson, "The evolution of letters of credit transactions" [1995] Butterworth's Journal of International Banking and Financial Law 128.

Held:

The general rule following authorities from the United States is that where the seller, for the purpose of drawing on the credit, fraudulently presents to the confirming bank documents that contain, expressly or by implication, material representations of fact that to his knowledge are untrue, that presentation should not be honoured. Lord Diplock said:

> "The exception for fraud on the part of the beneficiary seeking to avail himself of the credit is a clear application of the maxim *ex turpi causa non oritur actio* or, if plain English is to be preferred, 'fraud unravels all'. The courts will not allow their process to be used by a dishonest person to carry out a fraud".

The instant case however does not fall within the fraud exception to payment. The sellers were unaware of the inaccuracy of the notation in the bill of lading. They had in fact believed it to be true. They were therefore not perpetrators of the fraud.

It was also argued in that case that the knowledge on the part of the sellers is **11–071** not required because the fraud rendered the entire transaction a nullity. This was rejected by the court with Lord Diplock saying that such a proposition would seriously undermine the whole system of financing international trade by means of documentary credit. That said, it should not be assumed that an invalid instrument would be enforced (*Solo Industries v Canara Bank* [2001] EWCA Civ 1041). In *Solo Industries*, the surety attempted to avoid the performance guarantee on the ground that its issue had been procured by a fraudulent conspiracy and/or misrepresentation to which the beneficiary was a party. The trial judge held that the test to be applied in determining whether the surety should be permitted to defend the claim was not the so-called "fraud exception" test[13] but whether under r.24.2(a)(ii) of the Civil Procedure Rules 1998, it would have a real prospect of successfully defending the claim. He found that the test to be satisfied and dismissed the beneficiary's application for summary judgment. The Court of Appeal agreed with him. It stated that although the general principle was that performance guarantees, bills of exchange, letters of credit and the like were to be treated as the equivalent of cash, that principle only applied where the issue between the parties related to the enforcement of obligations under such instruments, rather than to the validity of such instruments.

Contrast however:

Montrod Ltd v Grundkotter Fleischvertriebs GmbH, Fifi Bank (UK) Plc and Standard **11–072**
Chartered Bank [2001] C.L.C. 466
Facts:

The letter of credit was issued by SCB in favour of G at the request of F Bank which undertook to indemnify SCB. It was required that one of the documents to be presented under the letter of credit should be an "inspection certificate" to be signed by M. M was financing the buyer's purchase of the goods. The buyer then asked G to sign the certificates by misrepresenting to them that M had authorised G to sign the certificates. Consequently G signed the documents and presented them for payment at SCB. Both SCB and F accepted the documents but M objected to them on the grounds that it had not issued them. SCB paid out and sought to be paid by F but M refused to reimburse F.

The question was whether M was right to object to the acceptance.

---

[13] See paras 11–124—11–131 in relation to the "fraud exception" and performance guarantees.

Held:

Judge Raymond Jack QC held that it was not dishonest for the beneficiary of a letter of credit to seek payment against documents which it had presented honestly even if by the time of payment it was known that a document was not truthful in a material respect. On the evidence, the court found that G had honestly believed that it had M's authority to sign the certificates.

The court also discussed whether the certificates should be treated as "nullities" because they were made without proper authorisation. That was rejected by the court which held that there was nothing at English law which allowed the so-called "nullity exception".[14] That would add a further complication where simplicity and clarity are needed. Also there are problems defining when a document is a nullity.

11–073 These authorities (see also *Gian Singh v Banque de l'Indochine* [1974] 1 W.L.R. 1234) seem to suggest that there is a no definitive answer as to whether there exists in law a nullity defence. It must however be said that the reasons given by Judge Raymond Jack QC in *Montrod* are very persuasive and that the principle of autonomy should generally prevail.[15]

Fraud involves dishonesty as is evident from Lord Diplock's speech in *The American Accord*. It is therefore important to identify a false act or statement done knowingly or without belief in its truth or recklessly (*Derry v Peek* (1889) 14 App. Cas. 337). The fraud could be either in relation to the documents as is the case in *The American Accord* or in relation to the credit itself or the underlying contractual transaction, but the fraud must have been perpetrated by the seller or his agent.

It is noteworthy that dishonesty on the part of the beneficiary is given such prominence, even in cases of forgery (as against fraud). Hence, in *The American Accord*, it was considered that the bank should pay the beneficiary under the letter of credit despite the forged documents because the beneficiary was not privy to the forgery.

11–074 What happens where the forged documents are not tendered by the beneficiary but an innocent third party, such as a negotiating or discounting bank? In *Discount Records Ltd v Barclays Bank Ltd* [1975] 1 W.L.R. 315, it was held that the fraud principle should not apply to such a third party because they, as holder in due course of the bill of exchange, should not be made to suffer the consequences of the beneficiary's fraud. The main difficulty with this argument is that the bill of exchange drawn under a letter of credit does not usually carry the Issuing Bank's acceptance; as such, it is unable to pass any rights against the Issuing Bank to the holder.

The bank in refusing to pay on grounds of fraud or forgery must plead and prove actual fraud.[16] It was held in *Society of Lloyd's v Canadian Imperial Bank of Commerce* [1993] 2 Lloyd's Rep. 579, that evidence from which a reasonable bank would consider the beneficiary to have committed fraud was not enough.

---

[14] Neo, "A nullity exception in letter of credit transactions?" [2004] Singapore J.L.S. 46.
[15] See Low, "Confusion and difficulties surrounding the fraud rule in letters of credit: an English perspective" [2011] 17 J.I.M.L. 462; Todd, "Non-genuine shipping documents and nullities" [2008] L.M.C.L.Q. 547; Hooley, "Fraud and letters of credit: Is there a nullity exception?" [2002] C.L.J. 279; Donnelly, "Nothing for nothing: a nullity exception in letters of credit?" [2008] J.B.L. 316; and also the Singapore case of *Beam Technologies v Standard Chartered Bank* [2002] 2 S.L.R 155; affirmed [2003] 1 S.L.R. 597
[16] Arora [1984] L.M.C.L.Q. 81; Ellinger [1981] J.B.L. 258.

Actual fraud must be proved. This is no small burden, as Sir John Donaldson M.R. said in *Bolivinter Oil SA v Manhattan Bank* [1984] 1 Lloyd's Rep. 251:

"But the evidence must be clear, both as to the fact of fraud and as to the bank's knowledge. It would certainly not normally be sufficient that this rests upon the uncorroborated statement of the customer [buyer], for irreparable damage can be done to a bank's credit in the relatively brief time [involved] . . . ".

This is further explained by the Court of Appeal in a case involving a performance guarantee, *United Trading Corp SA and Murray Clayton Ltd v Allied Arab Bank Ltd* [1985] 2 Lloyd's Rep. 554n, where Ackner L.J. said:

"We would expect the court to require strong corroborative evidence of the allegation, usually in the form of contemporary documents, particularly those emanating from the buyer. In general, for the evidence of fraud to be clear, we would also expect the buyer to have been given an opportunity to answer the allegation and to have failed to provide any, or any adequate answer in circumstances where one could properly be expected. If the Court considers that on the material before it the only realistic inference to draw is that of fraud, then the seller would have made out a sufficient case of fraud".

It is not required that all possible explanations must be excluded in order for the court to infer fraud. It hinges on what is reasonable and cogent under the particular circumstances of the case.

Where fraud is suspected, the usual course of action for the applicant is to **11–075** apply for an injunction to prevent other banks from making payment under to the letter of credit or to prevent the beneficiary from making claim for payment. This injunction is normally sought before any litigation on the substantive issue between beneficiary and applicant begins and as such is known as a pre-trial injunction (called an interim injunction before the advent of the Civil Procedure Rules 1998). There are two conditions which must be met before such an injunction could be granted. These were set out by Kerr J. in the well known case of *RD Harbottle (Mercantile) Ltd v National Westminster Bank Ltd* [1978] Q.B. 146 as:

- an injunction will only be available if the Issuing Bank is threatening to make a payment in breach of its contract with the applicant; and

- the balance of convenience is in favour of the applicant.

The latter condition is hardly ever satisfied because of the potential for greater damage to the bank than the applicant could make good and because the applicant would normally have an adequate remedy in damages.

Czarnikow v Standard Chartered Bank (London) Ltd [1999] C.L.C. 1148 **11–076**
Facts:
Three confirmed letters of credit had been issued by SCB. The beneficiary had presented the documents for early payment to the confirming bank. Before maturity of the letters of credit, the applicant sought an injunction to restrain Standard Bank from reimbursing the confirming banks on the basis that they had been induced into entering the contracts with the beneficiary by fraud.

Held:

Rix J. reiterated the two conditions set out by Kerr J. in *RD Harbottle* and said that there had to be a threatened breach of the applicant's contract with the Issuing Bank by the Issuing Bank. Fraud in the underlying sale contract is not enough—it must be clearly shown that the Issuing Bank is aware of the fraud (the onus of which is not easily met as was held in *United City Merchants*) before payment was made. The letter of credit must be given full autonomy—it must be insulated from the disputes between traders. As far as the banks are concerned, even fraud can only affect matters if payment had not been made.

These cases demonstrate how difficult it is to secure an injunction to prevent the banks from paying under a validly issued letter of credit. Such an approach would clearly detract from the "pay now argue later" rule which is considered to be the vital element in autonomous payment undertakings.[17]

11–077

Excerpt from *The Observer* newspaper, October 31, 1999:
Global trade in phantom cargoes swindles banks of £500 million

Last May two investigators arrived at a nondescript office block overlooking an ugly dual carriageway in Rayleigh, Essex, and knocked on the door of a company bearing the nameplate Simetal. Acting for a consortium of 17 international banks, including some of the biggest institutions in the City of London, the husband-and-wife team of investigators had come to interrogate the company's director, Milton Kounnou, about £190 million of the banks' money that appeared to have gone missing. On paper Simetal, and its associated company, TSA Shipping, were major importers of metals—mainly aluminium and zinc—from the Middle East. For months they had been providing blue-chip banks, including Barclays, Citibank and ABN Amro, with bills of lading and other documents needed to satisfy the banks that cargoes shipped from the Middle East had arrived in Britain and elsewhere. As a result, the banks had extended millions of dollars in credit to the exporter, Solo Industries, a smelting company in Dubai owned by a charismatic young Indian businessman, Madhav Patel. There was just one problem: it now appeared that many of the cargoes had never existed, while others were not nearly as valuable as the documents had stated. Worse, Solo had collapsed and Patel and his family had suddenly left Dubai for Britain.

The banks' investigators, Eric Ellen, the former director of the International Chamber of Commerce, and his wife Lin, wanted to know what light, if any, Kounnou could shed on the mystery. But no sooner had they crossed the threshold of Simetal than the alarm bells began ringing. Instead of ranks of traders and the serried glow of computer screens, they found a few dusty filing cabinets and a printer which had been working overtime. Simetal did not actually buy and sell metals itself, explained Kounnou. It simply prepared the shipping documents necessary to support letters of credit issued by Solo's bankers in the Middle East. According to Kounnou, he would be "shocked" to discover that the documents were false and the cargoes never existed. Five months later, that is still his answer and the banks are having to face the probability that they are the victims of one of the biggest frauds in the history of maritime finance.

---

[17] See Montague, "Letters of credit—some recent decisions on fraud, injunctions and construction" [1999] 1(5) Finance & Credit Law 1.

Patel was brought up in Iran and educated at one of New Delhi's top public schools. After the fall of the Shah in 1979, his father, B.M. Patel, returned to India and established the Hamco Group, a mining and metals company listed on the Bombay Stock Exchange. At the same time, Patel set up Solo Industries and lived an executive lifestyle, shuttling between India, the Middle East and his luxury flat in Bayswater, London. Solo also kept an office at a prestigious address in the City.

When Patel's deals finally came under the spotlight in May he hurriedly left Dubai for London, where he was hauled before the High Court by Crédit Agricole, France's biggest bank. The case collapsed.

Soon afterwards he met a very worried Citibank, Barclays and ABN Amro in the City and assured them that he would sort the problems out. But no sooner was the meeting over than he fled again. That was in June. Despite a worldwide manhunt by the Serious Fraud Office, the City of London police and Interpol, he has not been seen since.

To add to the mystery, in August his number two, Solo's financial controller, Paul Thotten, was found dead in the southern Indian state of Kerala after appearing to swallow poison. Meanwhile, the disputed letters of credit continue to grow. The latest estimate puts the banks' losses at more than £300m, a sum that could rise to £500m, according to investigators. "Every day we turn up fresh evidence of what appears to be false documentation. In retrospect it seems that Patel and his associates were turning this stuff out like confetti," said one source close to the fraud inquiry. In May, Kounnou was arrested by the SFO. Investigators had found that, at the time of Solo's collapse, just four of its 159 bills of lading were genuine. Kounnou strenuously denied knowledge of the alleged fraud and was released on police bail without being charged. Last week he did not return calls from The Observer.

In the next fortnight, officers from the SFO are due to visit Dubai to take statements from 11 Middle Eastern banks, which together account for a third of the losses. But the biggest individual losers are Citibank, down £30m, followed by ABN Amro (£16m) and Barclays (£13m). The half-billion-pound question is: how did a modest smelting plant in the Dubai port of Sharjah manage to deceive maritime, customs and banking authorities for so long and why—when suspicion began to fall on Patel—was he allowed to slip the police net?

To understand how Patel is alleged to have scammed the international banking system, it is necessary to know something of maritime finance. Because of the time it takes for cargoes shipped from foreign ports to reach their destination, importers have to find a way of guaranteeing payment to exporters before the goods are received. The answer is a letter of credit—an instruction by the importer's bank to an overseas bank to pay the exporting company in advance. The banks naturally charge interest for this service.

Without such arrangements, world trade would grind to a halt. The problem is, for the system to work banks have to be reassured the cargoes actually exist.

In Solo's case, however, many of the cargoes were fictitious. According to investigators, they were loaded for customs purposes only to be surreptitiously removed before the ships left port. In other cases, boats were packed with aluminium scrap rather than the valuable lead silver alloy stated on the bills of lading. And in a third variation on the alleged scam, genuine cargoes were loaded only to be diverted to destinations other than those on the export declaration. The result was an endless merry-go-round: container ships circling the globe in the illusion of healthy trade when in reality those cargoes which existed were worth a fraction of their stated value.

Letter of credit scams are nothing new. But usually it is the genuine importer who bears the grief when the banks come looking for their money. The beauty of Patel's scheme was that he controlled the exporter Solo and, secretly, the importers, too: a web of firms stretching from India and the Middle East to Britain, France, Switzerland and the Netherlands Antilles. When the music stopped, Patel left the banks squabbling among themselves as to who would pick up the losses.

In retrospect, the alarm should have been ringing in September 1998, when Indian tax authorities began investigating Hamco for suspected import and export fraud. The company's premises were raided, but it wasn't until June of this year that Patel's father was arrested. Patel was quick to distance himself, but despite his assurances to the bankers, it is alleged that he was secretly preparing one final sting. Astonishingly, by the beginning of the year, Citibank, Barclays and ABN Amro had nearly doubled their exposure, according to banking sources.

When Patel's father confessed to defrauding Indian banks and implicated his son, Solo and various associates, the banks were horrified. But by then it was too late. Patel had fled.

The end result is that in London Simetal's bank accounts have been frozen. In Dubai police have arrested Patel's brother-in-law, Ashok Verma. And in Switzerland the Geneva prosecutor has launched a criminal investigation into Solo's dealings with Frobevia and Alcuivre, alleged front companies. Meanwhile investigators hired by the banks hardest hit by the alleged fraud are scouring the world looking for Patel. Some reports put him in Brazil, others in the United States. And while accountants have begun asset-tracing, the fear is that any money that is left is already safely hidden in offshore accounts.

"Patel knows that half the world is looking for him and that it is only a matter of time before we find him," said a source close to the investigation. "If he is sensible he will try to strike a deal with the banks first. The question is, is there any money left?" In their hearts, bankers already know the answer to that question. As they fight among themselves over who should pay for the letters of credit, the only issue now is whether they, or Patel, will blink first.

11–078   Other than fraud, the bank may also refuse payment if the credit is inherently void because of a fundamental mistake or illegality. It may be rendered illegal by a law in the place where it is to be honoured prohibiting payment under it. That illegality can be an existing or supervening event; either case will render the credit null and void.

11–079   *Mahonia Ltd v JP Morgan Chase Bank* [2003] EWHC 1927 (Comm)
Facts:
In 2001, Mahonia, Chase Bank and a subsidiary of Enron entered into three swap transactions. Under those transactions, Mahonia lent Enron through Chase Bank's intermediation a sum of about $350 million. The sum was to be repaid with interest in six months' time. Repayment by Enron was partly secured by the issue of a letter of credit by West LB AG. The overall effect of the three swaps was that Enron was to receive the use of $350 million for six months. West LB argued that the transaction was a cosmetic device to provide Enron with a loan of $350 million at a rate of interest of roughly 3.4 per cent per annum which Enron did not have to record in its accounts as a debt. Enron had also paid Chase an arrangement fee of $1 million.

Enron defaulted on the repayment and Mahonia claimed payment under the letter of credit from West LB. West LB refused to pay arguing that the letter of credit was in support of an illegal arrangement (to allow Enron to commit an accounting misdemeanour under US law). West asserted that it was not aware of the illegal nature of the underlying transactions until after the claim for payment under the letter of credit was made by Mahonia.
Held:
The court held that the letter of credit was an essential requirement of Chase Bank to set up the cosmetic scheme. It could not be severed from the illegal underlying transactions. Thus, if the three swaps were illegal, the letter of credit must also be deemed to be illegal. English law, according to Colman J., would not enforce a letter of credit that is significantly operative in assisting the commission of an illegal act in another jurisdiction.

If Mahonia was permitted to rely on the letter of credit that would be tantamount to allowing it.

The court's approach is very similar to that in the piercing of the corporate **11–080** veil; it refused to accept the argument that the principle of autonomy prevented it from making such inquiries into the legality of the underlying transactions. It would also appear that the fact the illegality was under a foreign law, and not English law, is immaterial as a matter of international judicial comity. Naturally, where the foreign law was contrary to English public policy, the "illegality" would be disregarded and the letter of credit would be enforced.

In many cases of illegality, it is often virtually impossible to claim that the letter of credit is not significant to the underlying illegal transaction. It is thus to be welcomed that the judgment emphasises the letter of credit as "an essential requirement to illegality" in the scheme of things resulting in its non-enforceability. What is less certain, though, is the question of degree. How serious should the illegality be? For example, if in *Mahonia*, the underlying transaction was not to commit a serious offence to pass off Enron's accounts as healthy but a mere technical offence with only minor consequences, would a bank be entitled to refuse payment? This demonstrates how problematic it can be once the principle of autonomy has to be derogated from.

After resolution of the preliminary issue of law, the matter was subsequently remitted to another judge of the Commercial Court (*Mahonia Ltd v JP Morgan Chase Bank & West LB* [2004] EWHC 1938) to decide on whether, on the facts, there was an actionable illegality and whether the beneficiary was tainted. That court decided that on the evidence it was unable to decide whether there was indeed the commission of an offence under the relevant US Securities Exchange Act 1934 (and the US Generally Accepted Accounting Principles (GAAP)). As a result, although a letter of credit could be defeated by the illegality of the underlying transaction, there was in this case no such illegality proved. The letter of credit was thus enforceable.

A related question of some importance is whether and to what extent is a bank **11–081** required to make inquiries as to whether payment under the letter of credit was to serve an illegal purpose? Colman J. in *Mahonia Ltd* held that the fact that the bank did not have clear evidence of the illegality at the time when payment was due should not prevent it from having a good defence if it could be shown subsequently at trial that its suspicions were founded.[18]

Any monies paid out under a void or voidable credit will be dealt with in the same way as the normal rules of contract law dictate. Where the bank has paid against forged or fraudulent documents, it may sue for damages from the beneficiary under the tort of deceit or claim the proceeds back as money paid out through a mistake of fact (*Bank Russo-Iran v Gordon Woodroffe & Co Ltd* (1972) 116 Sol. J. 921).

In *KBC Bank v Industrial Steels (UK) Ltd* [2001] 1 All E.R. (Comm) 409, the Commercial Court held that as the defendants had provided a certificate which contained a false statement and they were either aware of it or were reckless as to whether or not it was false, the claimants were entitled to recover from the

---

[18] The procedure recommended by the Court of Appeal in *Balfour Beatty Civil Engineering Ltd v Technical & General Guarantee Company Ltd* (2000) 68 Con. L.R. 180 (see also para.11–124) would appear to apply.

defendants the sums paid out by them in reliance on that certificate under the letter of credit. The claimants were also entitled to claim the costs of separate proceedings instituted by them against the banks that had rejected the certificate, so as to put them back in the position they would have enjoyed if the false certificate had not been issued.[19] The fact that the claimants failed (negligently) to spot that the documents were noncompliant thereby contributing to their own loss was irrelevant.

11–082   Similarly in *Standard Chartered Bank v Pakistan National Shipping Corp* [2002] UKHL 43, although the Confirming Bank had failed to spot the discrepancies in the documents which were subsequently relied on by the Issuing Bank to refuse to reimburse the Confirming Bank, the Confirming Bank was not denied the opportunity to sue the beneficiary and carrier for fraud.[20] Further, their failure to spot the discrepancies did not amount to contributory negligence for which any quantum of damages might be reduced under the Law Reform (Contributory Negligence) Act 1945.

Where the bank has a right of set-off against the sum due under the credit to seller, it can lawfully withhold payment (see *Hongkong and Shanghai Banking Corp v Kloeckner & Co AG* [1990] 2 Q.B. 514; and *Marathon Electrical Manufacturing Corp and Detroit Diesel Overseas Distribution Corp v Mash-reqbank PSC and Munradtech Industrial Generators Ltd* (High Court, May 13, 1997).

An ally of the principle of autonomy of credits is the doctrine of strict compliance. That doctrine states that unless the documents presented are in strict compliance with their description in the letter of credit and are conforming as having performed the contract, no payment need to be made. We have seen in art.5 that banks are not concerned with the underlying contractual performance. Only the documents are of any material interest to the paying bank. This pivotal role played by the documents is demonstrated in the doctrine of strict compliance.

Strict compliance

11–083   Article 14, UCP states that upon receipt of the documents, the Issuing Bank and/ or Nominated Bank must determine on the basis of the documents alone whether or not they appear on their face to be in compliance with the terms and conditions of the credit. If the documents appear on their face not to be in compliance or conformity, the bank may refuse to take up the documents. The bank is not required to make inquiries as to any ambiguities or discrepancy.[21] This is illustrated in the case below.

11–084   *JH Rayner & Co Ltd v Hambro's Bank Ltd* [1943] K.B. 37
Facts:
The credit described the goods as "Coromandel groundnuts". The sellers had tendered a bill of lading referring to the goods as "machine-shelled groundnut kernels" and an invoice for "Coromandel groundnuts".

---

[19] See *Smith New Court Securities v Scrimgeour Vickers Asset Management & Citibank NA* [1996] 3 W.L.R. 1051 on the measure of damages for an action in deceit.

[20] *N.B.* the Confirming Bank's action did not rest on the failure of these individuals to tender conforming documents, but on fraudulent misrepresentation.

[21] See Bennett, "Strict compliance under UCP 500" [1997] L.M.C.L.Q. 7 and Buckley, "Potential pitfalls with letters of credit" (1996) 70 A.L.J. 217.

Held:
Although it was well known in the trade that the two terms were one and the same, the Court of Appeal held that the bank was entitled to reject the documents and refuse payment. This was because

"it was quite impossible to suggest that a banker is to be affected with knowledge of the customs and customary terms of every one of the thousands of trades for whose dealings he may issue a letter of credit".

The principle must be strictly observed because, as was pointed out by Viscount Sumner in *Equitable Trust Company of New York v Dawson Partners Ltd* (1927) 27 Lloyd's Rep. 49:

"It is both common ground and common sense that in such a transaction the accepting bank can only claim indemnity if the conditions on which it is authorised to accept are in the matter of the accompanying documents strictly observed. There is no room for documents which are almost the same, or which will do just as well. Business could not proceed securely on any other lines. The bank's branch abroad, which knows nothing officially of the details of the transaction thus financed, cannot take upon itself to decide what will do well enough and what will not. If it does as it is told, it is safe; if it declines to do anything else, it is safe; if it departs from the conditions laid down, it acts at its own risk".

In *Seaconsar Far East Ltd v Bank Markazi Jomhouri Islami Iran* [1993] 1 **11–085** Lloyd's Rep. 236, CA; [1993] 3 W.L.R. 756, H.L., there is no room for a de minimis effect argument. Nothing is trivial because the banks are not expected to test the materiality of the information or particulars required under the credit and contract between buyer and seller. The letter of credit in that case stipulated that all documents presented to the bank should carry the credit number and the buyer's name. One of the documents tendered omitted to state the credit number and the buyer's name. It was considered by the Court of Appeal that the bank was right to reject the documents even though the discrepancy might be trivial. The tender was therefore potentially invalid. On appeal this point was not discussed by the House of Lords.

Where the UCP apply, art.30 allows the bank to disregard certain minor variations subject to the express provisions of the credit. It states that the quantity specified in the documents may be five per cent more or less than that specified in the credit as long as the credit does not refer to the quantity in terms of a stated number of packing units or individual items. Hence, where the credit refers to 1000kg and the document tendered specifies 1005kg, that document may be accepted. Where the credit refers to 1000 sacks, no variation will be allowed. Article 30(a) provides that where the words "about" or "approximately" are used in connection with the amount of the credit or quantity or unit price of the goods, they are to be construed as allowing a tolerance not exceeding 10 per cent more or less than the amount or quantity to which they refer.

This might be contrasted with *Moralice (London) Ltd v ED & F Man* [1954] 2 Lloyd's Rep. 526, where the UCP did not apply. The common law position is that *de minimis non curat lex* cannot apply where certainty is of paramount importance. In that case the credit called for proof of shipment of 500 metric tons of sugar. The bank was entitled to documents describing the quantity as 499.7

metric tons. It should be borne in mind that while the de minimis rule might not apply generally between the bank and the beneficiary, it should apply to the extent permitted under the law of sale of goods between the buyer and seller (*Bunge Corp v Vegetable Vitamin Foods (Private) Ltd* [1985] 1 Lloyd's Rep. 613).

11–086   As stated before, the paying bank is only concerned with the documentary requirements of the letter of credit; they are not interested in any non-documentary requirements or conditions. Hence, where a letter of credit contains a non-documentary requirement or condition that the beneficiary must satisfy, it should be disregarded by the paying or negotiating bank (art.14(h)). In *Chailease Finance Corp v Credit Agricole Indosuez* [2000] 1 All E.R. (Comm) 399, the letter of credit related to a contract for the sale of a ship for delivery in Taipei during the period August 17–20, 1998. The documents reveal that delivery date was August 21. The question for Judge Stephen Tomlinson QC was whether the bank was justified in not paying because the documents clearly showed that the ship had been delivered outside the agreed shipment period.

The judge held that the documents did not have to state the delivery took place between August 17–20, they merely had to give the delivery date. It could not have been a condition of the letter of credit that shipment must take place between August 17–20—such a condition would have been a non-documentary condition and must necessarily be disregarded by the court (and the paying bank) under art.13(c) UCP 500 (now art.14(h) UCP 600).

In *Credit Agricole Indosuez v Generale Bank and Seco Steel Trading Inc and Cosnidar Inc* [2000] 1 Lloyd's Rep. 123, the buyer purported to reject the documents on the basis that the relevant dates (for notice of readiness) did not match in the documents tendered. The defence argued that the date requirement was a nondocumentary condition and as such should be disregarded. The court observed that although a date specification could very well be treated as a nondocumentary condition, where the dates stated on the documents are clearly inconsistent one with the other, the presentment could be rejected for documentary discrepancy. Documents which are mutually inconsistent on their face are clearly not acceptable.

11–087   In a controversial case, *Sirius International Insurance Co Ltd v FAI General Insurance* [2003] EWCA Civ 470, the letter of credit was issued to provide some form of guarantee to the reinsurer, S. A, a Lloyd's syndicate, had wanted to reinsure their risks and F was suggested as a possible reinsurer. A, however, wanted a reinsurer with a stronger standing. The resultant arrangement was that F would act as de facto reinsurer whilst S, a stronger party, would front the agreement. S agreed to do so only if F would provide for the issuing of a letter of credit in their favour. The letter of credit was to be governed by the UCP 500. The agreement drawn up between S and F provided that S would not draw down under the letter of credit unless:

1. F had agreed that S should pay a claim but had not put S in funds; or

2. The syndicate obtained a judgment or an arbitration award against S and S was obliged to pay.

It should be immediately obvious that these are not documentary conditions. F then went into provisional liquidation and acknowledged in judicial proceedings (a Tomlin order) that it owed S $22.5 million. S's claim was that the Tomlin order satisfied the first condition entitling it to draw down under the letter of credit. S also argued that the letter of credit was autonomous and as such the Tomlin order did not preclude its right of drawdown. The Issuing Bank paid against the call. At first instance, Jacob J. agreed with S. F appealed, arguing that the Tomlin order preserved the terms of the letter of credit and thus precluded the drawdown without its consent. That consent, as is obvious, could no longer be forthcoming following F's provisional liquidation. The Court of Appeal disagreed with the lower court as to the construction of the conditions for drawdown. However, for our purposes, the two issues before the Court of Appeal which are especially relevant were:

1. whether the condition for drawdown was satisfied; and

2. whether the principle of autonomy meant that the issuing bank should have paid without inquiring into the underlying transactions.

The two issues are clearly connected—conditions for drawdown which have **11–088** not been incorporated in the letter of credit should normally be disregarded, that is to say, as non documentary conditions, they cannot be binding on the beneficiary. The Court of Appeal held that given that the circumstances were so unusual, it should be read into the contract between the issuing bank and the beneficiary that payment would not be made unless consent was forthcoming from F. May L.J. said:

> "The present case is in more than one important respect a *variant of the more typical.* Here the relevant underlying agreement is, not the commercial transaction that the letter of credit was intended to support, as in the typical case, the contract of sale or in the present case, the retrocession treaties, but *a related agreement at regulating as between F and S terms on which the letter of credit would be established.*" (emphasis added).

It is not entirely clear what the court was suggesting there. Was it saying that in the present agreement there was an express stipulation which overrode the letter of credit's autonomy? Was it suggesting that there was a collateral agreement overriding the principle of autonomy? Are not preconditions to making a demand under the letter of credit generally undertakings "related" to the letter of credit? The uncertainties are clearly problematic. Moreover, there is little guidance as to what constitutes unusual circumstances. Regrettably, when the case went on appeal to the House of Lords, this matter of the principle of autonomy was no longer in issue.[22] It would appear that outside the domain of international sales (at least, conventional international sales), the courts may be slower to support of autonomy and the stricture of documentary conditions.

Documentary requirements are, by their nature, necessarily open to interpretation. In the case of an ambiguity, as was held by the Court of Appeal in *Credit Agricole Indosuez v Muslim Commercial Bank Ltd* [2000] 1 Lloyd's Rep. 275, it should be construed in the light of standard international banking practice. In that case, the letter of credit stated that:

---

[22] [2004] UKHL 54 dealt solely with whether the condition for drawdown was satisfied by the Tomlin order. It overruled the Court of Appeal, holding that it did.

"Original documents along with eight copies each of invoice, packing list, weight and measurement list, Bill of lading and certificate of origin should be sent to us by Courier at the cost of beneficiary".

11–089   The weight and measurement list and the certificate of origin were not sent by the Confirming Bank to the Issuing Bank. The issue for the court was whether those documents were essential documents against which negotiation and payment were agreed to be made under the letter of credit or whether they were merely documents to be forwarded, after negotiation had taken place, to the Issuing Bank. The Court of Appeal held that even though a court might arrive at a different construction a banker could safely act upon a reasonable construction of ambiguous or unclear terms. It could not be said that the Confirming Bank's construction of the letter of credit was unreasonable. The bank was not under a duty to make enquiry before payment is made to the beneficiary. It should be noted though that in this case, the issue of contention was between the Issuing Bank and the Confirming Bank, and not between the paying bank and the beneficiary. The beneficiary was clearly under a duty to present all the above stated documents in order to be paid—that was provided for in the advice of the letter of credit sent to him. On the other hand, the issue here was whether the Confirming Bank, in order to be reimbursed by the Issuing Bank, should have sent those documents on to the Issuing Bank.

In *Credit Agricole Indosuez v Muslim Commercial Bank Ltd*, the instructions were not clear as to whether the weight and measurement list and the certificate of origin were essential documents against which payment or reimbursement by Muslim Commercial Bank would be made.

Any requirement in the credit that documents should be marked has always been construed strictly in accordance with the general presumption that banks are not expected to distinguish between important and unimportant markings. In *Seaconsar Far East Ltd v Bank Markazi Jomhouri Islami Iran* we see how the omission to insert the credit number and the buyer's name could be fatal to the beneficiary's entitlement under the credit.

Original documents

11–090   Article 17 states that at least one original of each document stipulated in the credit must be presented. A bank shall treat as an original any document bearing an apparently original signature, mark, stamp, or label of the issuer of the document, unless the document itself states that it is not an original. Unless a document states otherwise, a bank will also accept a document as original if it:

1. appears to be written typed, perforated, or stamped by the document issuers hand; or

2. appears to be on the document issuer's original stationery; or

3. states that it is original, unless the statement appears not to apply to the document presented.

If a credit requires presentation of copies of documents, presentation of either originals or copies as permitted. If a credit calls for multiple documents (e.g.

words like "in duplicate", or "in two copies" are used), this will be satisfied by the presentation of at least one original and the remaining number in copies.

How should the documents be examined by the bank? In *Bank Melli Iran v Barclays Bank DCO* [1951] 2 Lloyd's Rep. 367,[23] the credit had called for documents showing the shipment of "sixty new Chevrolet trucks". The invoice referred to the goods as "in new condition", the delivery order described them as "new-good" and a certificate stated that the goods shipped were "new, good, Chevrolet trucks". On whether the documents had been properly accepted and paid for, the court held that the tender was bad because the documents were clearly inconsistent with each other. When construing the documents required by the credit, the bank must note all such inconsistencies. The documents must however be construed in their entirety and within their specific contexts (art.14(d), (e), (f)). In *Kredietbank NV v Midland Bank Plc* where the court held that in considering whether documents conform, banks must be careful to steer between too literal or rigid an approach on the one hand and on the other, applying a version of reasonableness, equity or good faith which could only lead to uncertainty. The bank's examination of the documents and compliance shall accord with international standard banking practice. The lesson from this case is that documents which appear on their face to be inconsistent with one another will be considered as not appearing to be in conformity but they must be examined as a whole.

Midland Bank Ltd v Seymour [1955] 2 Lloyd's Rep. 147   **11–091**
Facts:
Payment for a consignment of duck feathers was to be by confirmed irrevocable credit. The sellers were rogues and the buyer never received his feathers. His bank had paid out under the letter of credit. The buyer refused to reimburse the bank on the ground, amongst others, that the bill of lading did not state the description, quantity and price of the goods. These were however specified in other accompanying documents.
Held:
The documents were conforming because when read together there was no inconsistency. If the buyer had wanted plainly to specify that the bill of lading should contain full description of the goods, he could have done so. He had not.

Where the inconsistency is detected between a document contractually required and one not required by the credit, it can be ignored (art.14(g)) unless it gives rise to a strong suspicion of fraud. Documents not stipulated by the credit will be disregarded and returned to the beneficiary or delivered to the applicant by the receiving bank without attracting liability.

Banks required to examine the documents must do so within a reasonable time.   **11–092**
Delays are costly and if they are guilty of serious lapses, an action could lie against them. Indeed it is stated in art.14(b) that the banks (Issuing, Confirming or any other Nominated Bank) shall each have a maximum of five banking days following the date of receipt of the documents to examine them and determine whether to take up or refuse the documents. They should then inform the party from which they received the documents accordingly.

---

[23] See also Ellinger, "New problems of strict compliance in letters of credit" [1988] J.I.B.L. 320.

11–093

The International Standard Banking Practice for the Examination of Documents under Documentary Credits (ISBP) 2007, ICC Publication No.681

The International Standard Banking Practice for the Examination of Documents under Documentary Credits (the "ISBP"), drafted by an ICC Task Force in 2002 and revised in 2007, is intended to clarify the bank's duty in examining the documents presented for payment under a letter of credit. Whether the documents are in compliance is to be determined in accordance with "international standard banking practice" (art.2 UCP 600). The ICC was concerned that the different interpretations applied by different countries and their banks as to what constitutes "international standard banking practice" and the failure of beneficiaries to appreciate what constitutes acceptable standard banking practice in connection with the documents prepared by themselves have led to the rejection of documents. It has been estimated that discrepancies in documents presented under Documentary Credits have led to 60–70 per cent of those documents being rejected on first presentation.

The ISBP has been drafted to help resolve these difficulties. It contains 185 paragraphs of best practice, setting out the steps that document-checkers should take when reviewing documents and explains the commercial practices implied and indicated in the UCP 600. It should be noted that the ISBP does not amend the UCP 600; it merely serves to explain how commercial parties might accept international standard banking practice in the area of documentary credit.

As a general principle, the ISBP states that in discharging the duty in art.13, what is required is not that the terms in the documents be identical but simply that there should not be any inconsistency.

The ISBP deals a large number of technical issues:

• The provision that drafts, certificates and declarations, even if not stated in the credit, require a signature as that represents good banking practice.
• Under what conditions can drafts drawn on the applicant be issued? Here the position is that credits should not be issued requiring drafts be drawn on the applicant.
• It also clarifies when a document might be said to indicate that the goods have been shipped on board. It makes it plain that if a document contains the words "shipped apparent good order", "laden on board" and "clean on board" or other phrases incorporating words such as "shipped" or "on board" should be assumed to have the same effect as "shipped on board".
• Another issue of some controversy is how to determine where the place of taking in charge, dispatch, loading on board and destination on a multi-modal transport document is.[24] The ISBP states that if a credit gives a geographical range for the

---

[24] In *Swotbooks.com v Royal Bank of Scotland* [2011] EWHC 2025, the court had to deal with a road transport document. It held that although the UCP 600 does not offer a generic definition of "transport document" and the letter of credit in question did not specify the type of transport document required, the nature and type of document required is well established. According to Malik & Quest, *Jack: Documentary Credits* 4th edn (London: Bloomsbury Professional, 2009) at 8.82: "A transport document is issued by the carrier when the goods are consigned. In the documentary credit transaction it performs three main functions: (1) It evidences receipt of the goods in the charge of the carrier for delivery as specified in the document. This gives the bank and the buyer the assurance when paying against the document that the goods have been despatched. (2) In the case of negotiable marine bill of lading (and, possibly, certain other transport documents), it acts as what can loosely be described as a document of title giving rights of ownership or possession to the holder. (3) It evidences the existence and terms of the contract of carriage between the consignor and the carrier. . . . ". In that case, a letter issued by the courier stating that the goods had been consigned was held not to be a transport document.

place of taking in charge, dispatch, loading on board and destination (e.g. "Any European Port"), the multi-modal transport document must indicate the *actual* place of taking in charge, dispatch, loading on board and destination, which must be within the geographical area or range quoted.

- The ISBP also deals with air transport documents as to whether the document should state that the goods have been accepted for carriage. That has been an issue of some controversy for some time with some banks dispensing with the notation and others, not. The ISBP now makes it clear that an air transport document must indicate that the goods have been accepted for carriage.
- There has also been some difficulty encountered by banks as to what it means by "within a certain time"—for example, if the credit requires an act to be done "within 2 days of", what does that mean? The ISBP states that that refers to a period two days prior to the event until two days after the event. "Within" in relation to a date excludes that date in the calculation of the period. As is immediately obvious these are technical provisions but are nevertheless, very important and deserve to be clarified.
- Another issue of great significance is whether typographical errors would render a document discrepant. The ISBP position is that they do not provided they do not affect the meaning of a word. So "Cntainer" instead of "Container" is fine, but "Container 123" instead of "Container 132" would not be acceptable.

It should be noted that there are a large number of such provisions in the ISBP; it is not the place here to refer to all of them. It suffices to say that the reader should be aware that banks and traders will frequently refer to the ISBP as a guide to the UCP 600. The ISBP does not replace the UCP 600. It is to assist in clarifying what constitutes international standard banking practice. As it refers to good practice, it would be unreasonable for international traders and banks to disregard it.

Acceptance without examining the documents

Whilst the standard documentary credit arrangement requires that the relevant **11–094** banks accept the presentment of documents to check that they are in conformity, this requirement may be waived by agreement. It is not inconceivable that certain documents presented would not be in a language that the document checkers could understand. Under such conditions, it would seem commercially absurd not to permit the parties to agree that documents be "accepted as presented".

Although the validity of such clauses in the letter of credit is usually not in doubt, it might cause difficulties with other "standard" provisions of the letter of credit as was highlighted in *Credit Agricole v Credit Suisse* (2001) Lawtel C–0100616 (judgment of January 24, 2001). In that case, the letter of credit related to the sale of a consignment of rolled steel plates for delivery by rail (DDU Polish/Ukraine Border Moscika). The credit stipulated that the railway bills issued could be completed in English or Cyrillic language and should be accepted as presented. However, the letter of credit goes on to state that the period for presentation of the required documents was "20 days after date of transport documents". The bills presented did not bear any date stamp and as such must necessarily be deemed to have failed to meet the time requirement. The question was whether the "accepted as presented" clause overrode the 20-day period of presentation requirement. The court held that the time requirement was so fundamental that the provision "accepted as presented" clause could not properly be taken to mean that an undated transport bill had to be accepted.

Refusing the documents

11–095   Article 16 requires a bank which decides to refuse the documents to give notice by telecommunication or other expeditious means, without delay but no later than the close of the fifth banking day following the day of presentation. The notice should state all discrepancies in respect of which the bank refuses the documents. It should also state whether it is holding the documents at the disposal of or is returning them to the presenter. Article 16(f) underlines the importance of the notice by stating:

> "If an issuing bank or a confirming bank fails to act in accordance with . . . this article, it shall be precluded from claiming that the documents do not constitute a complying presentation".

What constitutes "without delay" was the subject of discussion in *Bayerische Vereinsbank Aktiengesellschaft v National Bank of Pakistan* [1997] 1 Lloyd's Rep. 59 (which concerned the old art.14(c) UCP 500 which is similar to art.16(f) UCP 600). In that case, the credit was made available against presentation of drafts drawn on the Confirming Bank at 150 days' sight from the bill of lading date together with specified shipping documents. The bank duly accepted the documents and paid against them on August 4. The documents were passed on to the defendant Issuing Bank who did not take them up on the grounds of discrepancies in the documents. The Confirming Bank subsequently sold off their interest in the cargo of cotton to the beneficiary at a loss. They then took action against the Issuing Bank. One of the several grounds on which the Issuing Bank was not entitled to refuse payment was because they had not objected to the discrepancies in the manner prescribed in art.14(d) UCP 500 (now arts 16(c), (d) UCP 600). The notice sent by the bank had been delivered by courier instead of by telecommunication. By so doing, Mance J. considered them not to have acted "without delay" as required by art.14(d) UCP 500. The court was clearly concerned that the Issuing Bank had at its disposal fax and telex access but had chosen not to use them.

This approach to art.16 is consistent with *Seaconsar Far East v Bank Markazi Jombouri Islami Iran* [1997] 3 All E.R. 628, when it was finally decided on the merits by the High Court (after the House of Lords overruled the Court of Appeal on the point of jurisdiction and gave leave to serve out). The Confirming Bank had identified discrepancies in the tender. They discussed this with the beneficiary at a meeting where the beneficiary attempted to cure a few of the deficiencies. He managed to cure four out of seven. However, the bank rejected the documents. The issue was whether the bank had acted in compliance with the UCP which required the notice to be given by telecommunication or, if that were not possible, by other expeditious means. Tuckey J. held that the documents had been properly rejected at the meeting between the bank and the beneficiary. No particular form of words need to be used. Although a strict interpretation of art.16 would indicate that face-to-face oral communication is only permissible where it would not have been possible to give notice by telecommunication, a rigid approach appears to be inconsistent with accepted banking practice. Whilst telecommunication might be available to the bank, it might not be the most expeditious means of communication to the beneficiary. If oral notice is more expeditious there should be no reason to deny the bank that liberty.

Article 16(c) also requires the notice clearly to state what the bank intends to **11–096** do with the non-conforming documents. It should inform the beneficiary:

(a) that the bank is holding the documents pending further instructions from the presenter; or

(b) that the issuing bank is holding the documents until it receives a waiver from the applicant and agrees to accept it, or receives further instructions from the presenter prior to agreeing to accept a waiver; or

(c) that the bank is returning the documents; or

(d) that the bank is acting in accordance with instructions previously received from the presenter.

If the bank tells the beneficiary that the documents will be returned, they must be returned promptly.

Fortis Bank v Stemcor [2011] EWCA Civ 58   **11–097**
Facts:
The letters of credit in question were issued by B and made available by negotiation with F's London branch. F was the confirming bank. S was the beneficiary. F accepted the documents presented by S and paid S the amount due; the documents were forwarded by F to B. B rejected the documents presented on the basis of discrepancies and refused to reimburse F or pay S. It gave notice under art.16(c)(iii)(c) of UCP 600 stating that it was returning the documents or as regards one set of documents, it was exercising the option under art.16(c)(iii)(a) to hold pending further instructions from the presenter. B did not return the documents until after F had indicated that B's failure to return them meant that it was precluding (by art.16(f) of UCP 600) from claiming that the documents did not comply. S and F commenced proceedings against B under the letters of credit.

S and F contended that if the issuing bank gave notice it would return the documents then, on the proper construction of art.16, it was under an obligation to return them promptly and, if it failed to do so, then by virtue of art.16(f) it was precluded from claiming that the documents did not constitute a complying presentation.

B, the issuing bank, argued that an issuing bank was under no obligation on a proper construction of art.16 to return the documents. The only obligation of the issuing bank was to give a notice; nor should any term be implied into art.16 of the UCP to that effect. Therefore any obligation to return the documents was outside the scope of the UCP.
Held: **11–098**
The Court of Appeal rejected B's approach to the interpretation of art.16(c) which was too narrow. The Court held that an internationalist mercantile approach should be taken, parochial and national legal concepts should be avoided. From a survey of DOCDEX decisions (these are decisions by experts selected by an ICC committee from a list maintained by the ICC Banking Commission on disputes referred for non-binding resolution according to the ICC DOCDEX Rules), there is clear evidence that the ICC Banking Commission's approach is to treat art.16 as applying to the duty to return rejected documents. One such decision, Decision 242 pointed out that:

"Notwithstanding the absence of a specific requirement or specific guidance in this regard, there is a market expectation that . . . international standard banking practice and the importance associated with possession of the documents, especially title documents, the timely return of dishonoured commercial documents requires priority processing, as delay in returning the documents may prejudice the beneficiary's rights and security . . . . While the Experts do not have the authority to establish such a standard concerning an exact time period to return the documents once notice is sent, the Experts agree that once the notice is sent stating that the documents are being returned, documents should be returned without delay and by expeditious means."

There was no need to imply a term using national English law because it is clear from the ICC decisions that a duty to return the documents with reasonable promptness exists. Thomas L.J. commented:

"It is not necessary to reach a concluded view in this case on this issue, though in my view there would be real difficulties in using a rule of national law as to the implication of terms (if distinct from a method of construction) to write an obligation into the UCP."

The delay was clearly substantial. B was thus barred by art.16(f) from relying on the discrepancy in the documents.

11–099   In a follow-up to that case, the claims were then re-introduced at the High Court (before Hurst J.) [2011] EWHC 538 (Comm). The court fleshed out in more clarity what is meant by reasonable promptness. The judge held that

"in the absence of special extenuating circumstances, a bank which failed to despatch the documents within *three banking days* would have failed to act within [sic] reasonable promptness."

This is a helpful clarification as the Court of Appeal's requirement of reasonable promptness was susceptible to various interpretations. The period of three banking days is fairly short; banks should bear this in mind when considering discrepant documents. There is, however, a difficulty with the Commercial Court imposing such a specific time limit—the time limit which the judge assumed reflected international mercantile and banking practice may not be seen in the same light by tribunals in other jurisdictions. The matter is perhaps best taken up by the ICC so that a more uniform and internationalist understanding can be reached.

Article 16(c)(ii) requires that the notice or refusal must state each discrepancy in respect of which the bank refuses to honour or negotiate.[25] It would appear that the bank in failing to enumerate each and every discrepancy it wishes to rely on, could subsequently be estopped from raising new grounds for refusal.

11–100   It is not unusual for a Confirming Bank to be asked to pay against documents which in its view do not fully comply with the terms of the credit. The bank will then have to decide whether:

1. to refuse payment; or

2. to pay, but extract an indemnity from the beneficiary in respect of any loss or damage resulting from the defect in documentation; or

3. to pay the beneficiary "under reserve".

---

[25] For an evaluation of the judicial application of this requirement, see Chatterjee, "Letters of credit transactions and discrepant documents: an analysis of the judicial guidelines developed by the English courts" (1996) 12 J.I.B.L. 510.

The expression "under reserve" is not defined in the UCP 600. According to Kerr L.J. in *Banque de l'Indochine et de Suez SA v JH Rayner (Mincing Lane) Ltd* [1983] Q.B. 711, the term suggests

"that payment was to be made . . . in the sense that the beneficiary would be bound to repay the money [to the Confirming Bank] on demand if the issuing bank should reject the documents, whether on its own initiative or on the buyer's instructions. I would regard this as a binding agreement made between the confirming bank and the beneficiary by way of a compromise to resolve the impasse created by the uncertainty of their respective legal obligations and rights".

The beneficiary could take action against a Correspondent Bank for failing to pay against conforming documents in damages for a repudiatory breach of the latter's undertaking. Where there is yet time to tender conforming documents, they could alternatively take action for the amount of the credit including interest. In the event that the beneficiary chooses to sue for breach of contract, the bank is entitled to prove against him remoteness of damage and/or the beneficiary's failure to mitigate the loss.

Payment "under reserve" is not likely to be treated as "honour" (art.2).

Issuing Bank's obligation to honour

The Issuing Bank's duty to honour the letter of credit is set out in art.7 UCP 600. **11–101** It states that provided that the documents are complying, the issuing bank must honour if the credit is available by:

1. sight payment, deferred payment or acceptance with the issuing bank;

2. sight payment with a nominated bank and that nominated bank does not pay;

3. deferred payment with a nominated bank and that nominated bank does not incur its deferred payment undertaking or, having incurred its deferred payment undertaking, does not pay at maturity;

4. acceptance with a nominated bank and that nominated bank does not accept a bill of exchange drawn on it or, having accepted a draft drawn on it, does not pay at maturity;

5. negotiation with a nominated bank and that nominated bank does not negotiate.

This provision thus places the Issuing Bank as the ultimate payor, where other parties obliged to pay do not.

As regards the Issuing Bank's duty to reimburse other banks that have paid out, art.7(c) provides that the issuing bank undertakes to reimburse a nominated bank that has honoured or negotiated a complying presentation and forwarded the documents to the Issuing Bank. There are two pre-conditions in art.7(c)

(i) the nominated bank must have honoured or negotiated a complying presentation; and

(ii) it must have forwarded the documents to the issuing bank.

In the case of (ii), the nominated bank must forward all the documents specified; it is not entitled to withhold any document including the bill of exchange which had been drawn on and accepted by the nominated bank (*Societe Generale SA v Saad Trading* [2011] EWHC 2424 (Comm)).

In the case of acceptance or deferred payment credits, reimbursement by the Issuing Bank is only due at maturity. It is immaterial that the nominated bank had made prepayment or purchased before maturity. The Issuing Bank's relationship to the nominated bank is independent of its relationship with the beneficiary.

11–102   Article 7 makes an important change when compared with the UCP 500. It makes no distinction between deferred payment credits and sight credits as regards the Issuing Bank's duty to honour. This overcomes a difficult problem raised in *Banco Santander v Bayfern* [2000] 1 All E.R. (Comm) 776. As the deferred payment credit calls for payment to be made at a later date, a seller will often ask the nominated or confirming bank to "discount" the documentary credit by making an earlier and reduced payment to the seller in return for an assignment to the bank of the proceeds of the letter of credit. In that case, the Court of Appeal held that that a bank entering into such an arrangement without express authority from the issuing bank to pay early bore the risk of fraud discovered between the time of early payment and the credit's maturity date. Article 7 removes that problem by placing the deferred payment credit on par with a sight or acceptance credit; under the UCP 500, the deferred payment credit lacked the protection conferred on the acceptance credit (which required the production of a bill of exchange) by negotiable instruments law and the immediacy of payment in a sight credit.

Where the Issuing Bank has agreed that the letter of credit will be confirmed by another bank, there is to be implied a contract between the Issuing Bank and the Confirming Bank. That contract will normally be subject to the UCP 600. It would appear that the agreement is one of agency, with the Confirming Bank acting as the Issuing Bank's agent in the transaction.[26] What the Confirming Bank does will therefore bind the Issuing Bank for all intents and purposes. Thus, if an invalid acceptance of the documents was made to the beneficiary by the Confirming Bank, the Issuing Bank is similarly bound as far as the beneficiary is concerned but not as far as the Confirming Bank is concerned (art.13).

As far as damages are concerned, in *Bayerische Aktiengesellschaft v National Bank of Pakistan*, it was held that if an Issuing Bank fails to reimburse the Confirming Bank and to take up documents, it could be liable to the Confirming Bank in damages for the difference between the amount paid out to the beneficiary and the amount recovered on the sale of the goods in question following the Issuing Bank's refusal to accept the documents.

11–103   On the other hand, where the Issuing Bank is induced to reimburse the Confirming Bank when the latter had in fact acted in breach of its agency (for example, as in *Bayerische Aktiengesellschaft* by paying on a late presentation of documents without any appropriate time extension) the former can recover the

---

[26] The relationship between the Confirming Bank and the beneficiary, however, is one between principals as described by Mance J. in *Bank of Baroda v Vysya Bank Ltd* [1994] 2 Lloyd's Rep. 87 at 90.

monies paid as monies paid under a mistake of fact,[27] or sue for damages in breach of contract or tort. In the event that the Confirming Bank has misrepresented to the Issuing Bank that the presentation was technically fine when it was not and this was done in wilful blindness or with intent to deceive, the Issuing Bank could very well have an action in deceit/fraud against the Confirming Bank.[28]

Whilst the Confirming Bank will not be entitled to be reimbursed by the Issuing Bank where it is clearly at fault in accepting a nonconforming presentation, this does not necessarily prevent them from taking action against the beneficiary and other parties who might have caused the bank's loss. In *Standard Chartered Bank v Pakistan National Shipping Corp* [2003] 1 A.C. 959, a letter of credit was issued by IB and confirmed by S in favour of O. O's managing director, M, arranged for the bills of lading to be backdated by the carriers (P) in order to obtain payment under the letter of credit. S knew that the documents were presented late but decided to waive late presentation. It then made payment of around $1.1 million. S then sought reimbursement from IB, stating falsely that the documents had been presented before the expiry date. IB rejected the documents, not because of the late presentation which it did not know, but on other grounds. S then sued P, O and M for deceit. The defendants argued that S's loss was partly caused by its own "fault" and that under s.1(1) of the Law Reform (Contributory Negligence) Act 1945, the amount of damages should be reduced accordingly. The Court of Appeal held that S's conduct was not "fault" as defined in s.4 of the Act because it was not at common law a defence to an action in deceit. The House of Lords held that under s.4 conduct by a claimant could not be "fault" unless it gave rise to a defence of contributory negligence at common law. The court also considered that contributory negligence could not be a defence to a claim in deceit.[29] The House of Lords agreed that the test for the maxim *ex turpi causa non oritur actio* had to be applied narrowly. In reliance on *Tinsley v Milligan* [1994] 1 A.C. 340, it might be said that S's conduct was not so flagrant that it should be denied the right to sue the original perpetrators of the illegality (P, M and O).[30]

---

[27] See *Barclays Bank v Simms* [1980] Q.B. 677 and *Lloyds Bank Plc v Independent Insurance Co Ltd* [1999] 1 All E.R. (Comm) 8. In *Bayerische Aktiengesellschaft v National Bank of Pakistan* [1997] 1 Lloyd's Rep. 59, Mance J. held that if a Confirming Bank pays on a late presentation of documents where time had not been properly extended under art.44(a) UCP 500 or by agreement, the Issuing Bank could clearly recover any money paid to the Confirming Bank as money paid under a mistake of fact.

[28] See generally Warne and Elliott, *Banking Litigation*, 1st edn (London: Sweet & Maxwell, 1999), para.6–16.

[29] See also *Alliance & Leicester Building Society v Edgestop* [1993] 1 W.L.R. 1462; *Corporacion Nacionale del Cobre de Chile v Sogemin Metals Ltd* [1997] 1 W.L.R. 1396; *Nationwide Building Society v Thimbleby* [1999] E.G.C.S. 34.

[30] On the liability of the managing director, the Court of Appeal had held that M had made the fraudulent misrepresentation on behalf of O and not personally. He was therefore not liable. That point was however reversed by the House of Lords, which held that the fact that M had made the representation on behalf of O was irrelevant. The fact remained that he was the only human being involved in the making of the representation to S. He was thus personally liable. The court rejected any analogy to be made with cases on negligent misrepresentation (*Williams v Natural Life Health Foods* [1998] 2 All E.R. 577); the present case being one on fraudulent misrepresentation. See Parker, "Fraudulent bills of lading and bankers' commercial credits: deceit, contributory negligence and directors' personal liability" [2003] L.M.C.L.Q. 1, Chuah, "Contributory negligence of the confirming bank in a documentary credit arrangement" [2003] 9 J.I.M.L. 17.

It was also argued that as S had itself failed to spot those discrepancies relied on by IB to refuse payment, S was guilty of contributory negligence and accordingly, any claim in damages should be reduced. On this issue, the Court of Appeal found that this failure was not weighty enough to constitute significant contributory negligence.

Bank-to-bank reimbursement

11–104　The ICC Uniform Rules for Bank-to-bank Reimbursement (URR) 725 came into effect on October 1, 2008. They make detailed provisions for the rights and obligations of the banks when a bank that has accepted drafts, drawn a letter of credit or paid the beneficiary seeks reimbursement from a bank nominated by the Issuing Bank. The Rules envisage, therefore, three possible banks in the matrix—the Reimbursing Bank, the Claiming Bank and the Issuing Bank. The Claiming Bank is the bank that has paid or negotiated a credit. It will then present its claim for reimbursement directly to the Issuing Bank or sometimes, for convenience, to a Reimbursing Bank (usually a bank with which it has good commercial relations). The Reimbursing Bank is one which has been authorised by the issuing bank to make the payment or reimbursement.

For the URR 725 to apply, the Issuing Bank must indicate in the letter of credit that the rules are to apply (art.1).

It cannot be over-emphasised that the reimbursement authorisation given by the Issuing Bank to the Reimbursing Bank is separate from the letter of credit itself (art.3). Therefore, the Reimbursing Bank is not concerned with or bound by the terms and conditions of the letter of credit even if these are referred to in the reimbursement authorisation. Where the letter of credit is not subject to the URR 725, bank-to-bank reimbursements will be governed by art.13 UCP 600.

The Issuing Bank must ensure that any conditions for the reimbursement to be made should be clearly set out in the authorisation given to the Reimbursing Bank (art.5). The authorisation should specify an expiry date, if needed (art.7) but if this is not stated, the authorisation will not lapse until honoured. The authorisation must state the following:

1. credit number;

2. currency and amount;

3. additional amounts payable and tolerance, if any;

4. claiming Bank or, in the case of a credit available with any bank, that claims can be made by any bank. (In the absence of any such indication, the reimbursing bank is authorised to pay any Claiming Bank); and

5. parties responsible for charges (art.6(d)).

11–105　If the Reimbursing Bank is requested to accept and pay a time draft, the reimbursement authorisation must indicate the following, in addition to the information specified in art.6(d) above:

1. tenor of draft to be drawn;

2. drawer; and

3. party responsible for acceptance and discount charges, if any.

An Issuing bank should not require a sight draft to be drawn on the Reimbursing Bank. This is because it is not the Reimbursing Bank that is primarily liable for the payment, but the Issuing Bank.

In some cases, the Reimbursing Bank may add its own independent undertaking to pay the Claiming Bank—this is a little like the role played by the Confirming Bank in the credit. This undertaking is separate and independent from the Issuing Bank's undertaking to reimburse. However, the Reimbursing Bank's independent undertaking must be authorised by the Issuing Bank. The Rules do not protect silent undertakings from the Reimbursing Bank. The Reimbursing Bank, if it adds its own undertaking to pay or accept drafts, should set out clearly in the "reimbursement undertaking" the terms for reimbursement (art.9).

Article 11 provides that the Reimbursing Bank shall have a maximum of three banking days following the day of receipt of the reimbursement claim to process the claim. If the bank refuses to pay, it must communicate that refusal and the reasons to the Claiming Bank and the Issuing Bank. A reimbursement claim received outside banking hours will be deemed to be received on the next following banking day.

These rules are intended to provide acceptable international standards for **11–106** banks seeking reimbursement from issuing banks. However, it should not be thought that they must *always* be used. Indeed, it is possible and not necessarily risky for Issuing Banks to make their letters of credit available at the counters of a nominated bank and then to allow the nominated bank to claim reimbursement by sending by SWIFT a demand directly to itself. This does away with Reimbursing Banks and could save costs. However, as stated above, if the URR 725 does not apply, art.13 UCP 600 would (unless expressly contracted out of). That article states that the Issuing Bank must provide the Reimbursing Bank with a reimbursement authorisation that conforms with the availability stated in the letter of credit but there can be no expiry date. There is some sort of autonomy principle at work too—the Claiming Bank shall not be required to produce any certificate of compliance to the Reimbursing Bank (art.13(b)(ii)). An Issuing Bank is responsible for any loss of interest, together with any expenses incurred, if reimbursement is not provided on first (complying) demand by a Reimbursing Bank (art.13(b)(iii)). Article 13(c) provides that the Issuing Bank's duty to reimburse does not cease if the Reimbursing Bank did not reimburse a Claiming Bank on first demand. Article 13 does not provide for the sort of information required in a reimbursement authorisation and a claim, unlike the URR 725. There is no provision for the expected time for reimbursement once a claim has been received. It is thus obvious that art.13 is intended to be no more than a default provision and offers the banks little more than a minimal degree of certainty.

Performance Guarantees

The documentary credit system focuses attention on the seller's insecurity that **11–107** payment might not be forthcoming. Where the insecurity is with the buyer that the seller might break his promise and not deliver the goods or services as agreed, he could require the seller to procure a guarantee or promise from a bank or third party to pay a certain amount if performance is not made by the seller. Similarly, the seller could also require the buyer to obtain a guarantee from a third party guaranteeing his contractual performance to the seller.

Many potential buyers when buying goods will open the order to tender. The buyers favour this form of trading because it allows them to ascertain the best price for the goods and the best available service for the order. The main disadvantage is that the seller might decide to renege on the tender. Considering the magnitude of some of these transactions, this will place the buyers in a very vulnerable position. In order to reduce the risk of the sellers not performing, buyers have frequently relied on a requirement that the tenderers accompany their bids with a cash deposit or earnest money. This is however inconvenient and could be quite expensive for firms with cash flow ailments. Furthermore, the large majority of the tenderers are bona fide potential sellers who are genuinely interested in the order. A more effective method is requiring them to obtain a performance guarantee from their bank that they will perform if the tender is accepted. The guarantor (bank) undertakes to pay the sum, usually expressed as a percentage of the tender amount, if the tenderer fails to proceed with the order. The performance guarantee must be able to afford the buyers the same level of protection as the cash deposit accompanying tender will.[31] That protection is the ability of the buyers simply to retain the cash if the order is not acted on by the sellers/tenderers. In order to offer this level of protection, the performance guarantee is usually expressed as payable upon first demand of the buyer (beneficiary) without requiring proof or conditions. In banking terms, this is known as payable on demand without contestation. Such a performance guarantee is called a demand guarantee or a stand-by letter of credit. The demand guarantee should be contrasted against a simple or "see to it"[32] guarantee. The simple guarantee is a promise by the guarantor or surety to pay upon satisfaction that there has been a default by the trader whose performance is guaranteed. It is clear that the surety would not be required to pay unless there is evidence of default. That degree and nature of evidence required is normally contractually prescribed—for example, the guarantee might require that the beneficiary obtain a court judgment or an arbitral award against the other party (applicant) before the surety would be obliged to pay, or it might require a sworn statement by some expert that the contractual specifications have not been met, etc. In some industries, such as the construction sector, it is vital that the demand should not be made until the quantum of damages has been ascertained (*Paddington Churches Housing Association v Technical & General Guarantee Co Ltd* (1999) B.L.R. 244[33]). It should also be noted that simple guarantees are subject to s.4 of the Statute of Frauds 1677 (An Act for prevention of Frauds and Perjuries) which provides that:

---

[31] Despite its similarity in function to a deposit or other pre-agreed remedies, the performance guarantee is not subject to the rule against penalties. It was decisively held by the Court of Appeal in *Comdel Commodities Ltd v Siporex SA* [1997] 1 Lloyd's Rep. 424 that a performance guarantee is a "a guarantee of due performance" and not a "pre-estimate of damages" which would be endured as a result of a breach of the underlying contract. It would therefore follow that if the guarantee exceeds the damages payable, the guarantor may be able to recover the excess on the restitutionary grounds.

[32] See generally the use of the term "see to it" in *Caja de Ahorros del Mediterraneo v Gold Coast Ltd* [2001] EWCA Civ 1086, and *TTI Team Telecom International Ltd v Hutchison 3G UK Ltd* (January 23, 2003). See also *Marubeni Hong Kong and South China Ltd v Mongolia* [2005] EWCA Civ 395.

[33] For a commentary of this case, see McMilan (1999) May Issue No.20 Building 79.

"No action shall be brought . . . whereby to charge the Defendant upon any special promise to answer for the debt default or miscarriages of another person unless the Agreement upon which such Action shall be brought or some Memorandum or Note thereof shall be in Writing and signed by the party to be charged therewith or some other person there unto by him lawfully authorised".

Demand guarantees (and indemnities) are not subject to the Act.[34]

A demand guarantee that is expressed as a tender guarantee might look like this:

Example 3: Tender Guarantee

11–108

Kingstown Bank Plc
PO Box 11
High Street
London
Great Britain

3 January 2013

The Government of Utopia
PO Box 22
Utopia City
The Republic of Utopia

Dear Sirs,

Our Guarantee No.111/222A

Your invitation to Tender UT 101/01 closing date 15 January 2013

With reference to Tender No.3/44/55 dated 3 January 2013 submitted against the above the invitation by IM Sellers Ltd, 1 Old Road, London, Great Britain we hereby undertake to pay to you on your first demand on us in writing being received at this office and bearing our reference Guarantee No.111/222A complying with the terms hereof any sum or sums not exceeding in aggregate £20,000 (twenty thousand pounds sterling).

---

[34] In *WS Tankship II BV v Kwangju Bank* [2011] EWHC 3103, the surety tried to suggest that the writing requirement had not been met. Blair J. found that the instrument was a demand guarantee so the writing requirement did not apply. That said, even if there was a writing requirement, that had been properly met. The facts were that Kwangju Bank had sent a message by SWIFT message containing the guarantee to the buyers' bank. It accepted that the word "signed" in the Statute of Frauds "does not necessarily involve signature by an individual using an ink pen and that it suffices that the guarantor's name is written or printed in the document". However, in the body of the guarantee the words "Kwangju Bank" did not appear. The bank is referred to as "we". The defence was to the effect that it was thereby unsigned, and the bank was not bound. It was sent by conventional means by way of the secure messaging system used between banks. Blair J. said, "as a matter of common sense, authentication by sending was equivalent (in modern terms) to authentication by signing, and so within the spirit, if not the letter of section 4 of the Statute of Frauds."

Your demand must state the amount payable and confirm that IM Sellers Ltd, 1 Old Road, London, Great Britain have refused to sign the contract awarded to them in response to their Tender No.3/44/55 for the supply of electrical equipment for the North-South Power Plant or have withdrawn their tender prior to adjudication.

Provided that this undertaking is personal to you and not assignable.

Our liability limited to an aggregate sum not exceeding £20,000 (twenty thousand pounds sterling).

This undertaking shall expire on 1 June 2013 except in respect of valid claims received by us on or before that date after which our undertaking shall become null and void whether or not it has been returned to us.

This undertaking shall be subject to English law and your acceptance of the undertaking shall be regarded as your agreement that you accept the jurisdiction of the English Courts to adjudicate on claims thereunder. The undertaking is also issued subject to ICC Uniform Rules for Demand Guarantees, 2010

Yours faithfully,

T.H.E. Banker
Manager, Kingstown Bank Plc

11–109   *Comment*

It is readily obvious that the efficacy of the facility depends very much on the proper construction of its terms. It is standard practice to stick closely to accepted phraseology as evidencing when and how payment may be exacted from the guarantor. Performance guarantees almost invariably require that banks will pay on first demand without contestation as we have discussed above. This unfortunately raises particular problems for the parties. Where the demand is based on the tenderer's non-acceptance of the tender, the position is quite straightforward. The buyer in the situation described in example 3 merely needs to "confirm" that the seller has not taken up the tender. Some performance guarantees provide that the bank will pay the buyer a sum of money if the seller "does not perform the contract". That is more complicated; the issue of whether there has been non-performance of the contract is usually a matter of opinion. Differences in opinion could occur in the interpretation of the terms of the contract, the quality of the goods delivered and the efficiency of delivery and other related services. For this reason, sellers or suppliers might be reluctant to obtain an on-demand performance guarantee. However, if he does not, the buyer is not interested in his tender. This sort of impasse is overcome to a certain extent through the use of a Conditional or Arbitration Guarantee:

Example 4: Conditional or Arbitration Guarantee

11–110

> The operative words of such a guarantee are:
>
> "We hereby undertake to pay to you any sum or sums not exceeding in aggregate £30,000 (thirty thousand pounds sterling) being 5 per cent of the contract price for the supply of 1,000 generators by IM Sellers Ltd under contract number JB 123/34 dated 4 January 2013 upon your first demand to us in writing stating that the seller has become liable to pay the sum to you as a result of non-performance of the contract and has not made such payment the amount payable and the liability being evidenced by:
>
> (a) A notarially certified copy of the judgment of a competent Court of Law in your favour which must accompany your claim under this Guarantee.
>
> Or
>
> (b) A notarially certified copy of an arbitrator's award in your favour which must accompany your claim under this Guarantee
>
> Or
>
> (c) A written confirmation addressed to us by the seller stating that the terms of the said contract have not been complied with which must accompany your claim under this guarantee."

Demand guarantees are also sometimes used as refund guarantees. Refund **11–111** guarantees are given to secure the return of monies paid by the buyer as deposit or earnest money if the supplier is unable or unwilling to continue with the contract.[35] It should however be noted that refund guarantees can also take the form of a simple guarantee.

A claim on the refund guarantee for pre-paid monies can sometimes amount to a waiver of the claimant's rights under the common law to seek damages for repudiation of contracts. However, clear words in the underlying contract must be present before a court would consider that a claim on a refund guarantee had ousted the claimant's common law remedies (*Stocznia Gydnia SA v Gearbulk Holdings* [2008] EWHC 944).

In the US, banks were in the past prohibited from issuing guarantees of performance and in order to avoid breaking the law, many US banks adapted the letter of credit to do just that. Such an instrument is generally referred to as a "standby letter of credit". Under a standby letter of credit, the beneficiary will be paid a sum of money if the applicant fails to perform the contract. For example, if the supplier (applicant) fails to supply the contract goods, the buyer (beneficiary) can demand satisfaction from the bank issuing the standby letter of credit. In the US, standby letters of credit are usually issued subject to the UCP 600. However, the UCP is more suited for letters of credit as a means of payment, not as a default undertaking. Recognising the problem, the International Chamber of Commerce put together a set of special rules called the Uniform Rules for Demand Guarantees (URDG) ICC Publication No. 758 (2010) to serve the use of such default undertakings. The URDG 758 will apply where they have been

---

[35] See generally *Caja de Ahorros del Mediterraneo v Gold Coast Ltd* [2001] EWCA Civ 1806.

expressly incorporated by reference in a guarantee or counter-guarantee. Where this is the case the URDG 758 applies entirely unless specific articles are explicitly ruled out or amended. Also, the URDG 758 may apply even if they are not expressly incorporated by reference to the text of a guarantee or counter-guarantee:

(i) in the event of indirect, asymmetrical guarantees[36]; and

(ii) as a result of trade usage or a consistent course of dealing. (art.1).

11–112   The URDG 758 are very flexible because they are essentially a matter of contract. The parties can exclude or alter different provisions of the URDG when agreeing upon a guarantee or counter-guarantee. The old URDG 458 (the predecessor to the URDG 758) were not widely used because many felt that the provisions did not accurately reflect standard guarantee practice. The ICC, however, is ambitious and optimistic for the acceptance of URDG 758 which came into effect on July 1, 2010.

When should the performance guarantee be set up?

11–113   We have seen that in the case of documentary credits, unless the contrary is stipulated in the contract, the letter of credit must be opened in time for the seller to perform his side of the bargain—that meant that the letter of credit should normally be opened prior to shipment period.[37] Should the same rule apply in respect of performance guarantees? In *Ruchi International Ltd v Agri Marketing Co SARL* (January 13, 2000) the CIF contract called for shipment of the cargo of soya bean meal commencing April 10, 1996. The performance guarantee was to be provided against shipment for approximately six per cent of the contract value. The seller failed to load within the shipment period and the buyer declared the seller in default and sued for damages for nondelivery. The seller argued that the buyer had failed to provide the performance guarantee before the shipment period commenced. Longmore J. considered that no analogy should be drawn from letters of credit as far as this is concerned. The judge said that in the absence of a provision in the contract as to the time by which the performance guarantee had to be provided, it had to be provided in reasonable time. That does not however mean that it must be provided before shipment period commences. If time was to be of the essence, that should have been made clear in the contract between the merchants.

What amounts to "opening" or "providing" a bank guarantee is the communication of that fact to the beneficiary, despite Evans J.'s obiter dictum in *State Trading Corp of India v M Golodetz Ltd (The Sara D)* [1988] 2 Lloyd's Rep. 182 that the "opening" of a bank guarantee required the person so obliged to take "appropriate steps" with the bank. As a matter of general principle, no

---

[36] The Rules provide that where the counter-guarantor had requested that the guarantee be subject to the URDG, the counter-guarantee would automatically also be subject to the URDG. However, a demand guarantee does not become subject to the URDG simply because the counter-guarantee is subject to the URDG.

[37] See in particular, *Ian Stach Ltd v Baker Bosley Ltd* [1958] 2 Q.B. 130 and *Chiemgauer Membran und Zeltbau GmbH v New Millenium Experience Co Ltd* (November 3, 1999, CA); (2000) C.I.L.L. 1595.

performance guarantee would and should be effective without proper notice being given to the beneficiary so as to enable him to conduct himself in the assurance that the applicant has performed his side of the agreement.

Nature of a performance guarantee

At the outset it should be noted that a performance guarantee is not intended to **11–114** enrich, but to indemnify, the beneficiary. There is therefore an implied term that there would be an accounting for the proceeds of the performance guarantee and that the party in breach was entitled to recover any surplus over and above the actual loss suffered by the other party. In *Cargill International SA v Bangladesh Sugar & Food Industries Corp* [1998] 1 W.L.R. 461, the Court of Appeal held that the seller who was in breach of contract and payment under a performance guarantee had followed), was entitled to recover the full payment made because the buyer had suffered no loss from the seller's breach.[38]

The practice of using performance guarantees is widespread, especially in the construction and manufacturing sector. In recent years we have also seen an upsurge in the number of cases involving performance guarantees going to court. The phenomenon may be explained partly by the fact that there is now greater use of the facility, partly because the terms are capable of various interpretations by lawyers and partly by the legal uncertainties surrounding the use of a relatively novel financing tool. So how does the law regard the effect and role of the performance guarantee?

In *Edward Owen Engineering Ltd v Barclays Bank International Ltd* [1978] Q.B. 159, the suppliers obtained a performance guarantee for 10 per cent of the contract price, and in return the buyers agreed to open a confirmed irrevocable credit in the suppliers' favour. The contract called for the supply of glasshouses in Libya. The guarantee or bond was issued "on demand without proof or conditions". The buyers then failed to open the letter of credit as agreed and so the suppliers terminated the contract. The buyers then claimed the 10 per cent under the guarantee from the suppliers' bank. The suppliers applied for an injunction to prevent the bank from paying.

Lord Denning in considering this "new creature" said: **11–115**

"All this leads to the conclusion that the performance guarantee stands on a similar footing to a letter of credit. A bank which gives a performance guarantee must honour that guarantee according to its terms. It is not concerned in the least with the relations between the supplier and the customer; nor with the question whether the supplier has performed his contracted obligation or not; nor with the question whether the supplier is in default or not. The bank must pay according to its guarantee, on demand, if so stipulated, without proof or conditions. The only exception is when there is a clear fraud of which the bank has notice".

The reference in Lord Denning's dicta to "without proof or condition" is exceedingly important.[39] As we discussed above, in a simple guarantee, the

---

[38] See G. McMeel, "Pay now, argue later" (1999) L.M.C.L.Q. 5; Akenhead (2002) October Issue No.40 *Building* 52.
[39] See also *Caja de Ahorros del Mediterraneo v Gold Coast Ltd* [2001] EWCA Civ 1806; *Carey Value Added SL v Grupo Urvasco SA* [2010] EWHC 1905 (Comm).

surety's liability is not triggered until the beneficiary is able to prove default. On the other hand, the demand guarantee will usually simply require the surety to pay on mere demand or assertion, by the beneficiary, of default.

The demand guarantee is usually said to possess four attributes:

(a) the underlying transactions are between parties in different jurisdictions;

(b) the guarantees do not contain clauses excluding or limiting the defences available to a surety in a classic guarantee where the surety's liability is secondary;

(c) the undertaking is to pay on demand; and

(d) the instrument is usually issued by a bank.

11–116   As far as the URDG 758 are concerned,[40] in order to fall within their scope, the instrument must meet the following conditions.

(i) It must consist of a single undertaking for the payment of money.

(ii) The payment undertaking must be for a specified or maximum amount.

(iii) The guarantee or counter-guarantee must be made conditional only upon presentation of a demand in a single document, without the need for proof of actual default on the part of the applicant.

(iv) The sole purpose of the guarantee must consist only on being relied upon in the event of default in the underlying relationship.

(v) As stated above, the instrument must expressly state it is subject to URDG 758. Alternatively, URDG 758 must in some other way have effect under applicable law.

Whether an instrument is a demand or simple guarantee (or meets the definition requirements above) can sometimes be a difficult matter of construction.[41]

11–117   *Trafalgar House Construction (Regions) Ltd v General Surety and Guarantee Co Ltd* [1995] 3 All E.R. 737
Facts:
Under a subcontract for the construction of a leisure complex, the subcontractor undertook jointly with G to provide the main contractors (claimants) with a bond of £101,285. The subcontractors then went into receivership and became unable to perform the construction contract. The claimants completed the project and sued under the performance bond. The question was whether the bond was a demand guarantee or a simple common law guarantee; bearing in mind that if it were the latter, actual proof of nonperformance would be required. The bond stipulated that, "if on default by the Subcontractor the Surety shall satisfy and discharge the damages sustained".
Held:
The construction of the instrument should proceed on the premise that without any clear words to the contrary it shall be treated as a simple guarantee. In this case, the words

---

[40] Not all demand guarantees will be subject to the URDG.

[41] Guarantees are subject to the same rules of construction as simple contracts (*Fairstate v General Enterprise and Management* [2010] EWHC 3072 (QB)); on rules on construction see paras 1–011—1–016.

"damages sustained" indicated that proof of actual loss would be required. Therefore the mere assertion of nonperformance was not enough.

In contrast, where the bond is expressed in the following terms

"we . . . hereby guarantee, waiving all right of objection and defence, the payment to yourselves a sum not exceeding [£500,000] on your first demand . . . Your claims should be received by us in writing stating therein that the Principals have failed to pay you under their contractual obligations",

the court did not have any hesitation in finding that it is a demand guarantee.[42]

As a matter of construction, the factual matrix is highly relevant.[43] In **11–118** *Marubeni Hong Kong & South China Ltd v Mongolia* [2005] EWCA Civ 395, for example, the Court of Appeal placed some emphasis on the fact that the guarantee had not been given by a bank but a foreign governmental body. It held that as the surety was not a bank, it could not be presumed to have consented to the far reaching consequences a demand guarantee would naturally attract.[44] It considered that in a noncommercial banking context, the presumption should therefore be against the finding of a demand guarantee where the words are not entirely clear.[45] Similarly where the instrument is a personal guarantee, the presumption would be against the guarantee being a demand guarantee. However, the presumption can be rebutted where the documents read within their factual context demonstrate a clear intention to pay simply on demand or notice of default. In *IIG Capital Llc v Van Der Merwe* [2008] EWCA Civ 542, the "Deed of Guarantee" stipulated that

"if . . . the guaranteed moneys are not paid in full on their due date . . . it (the guarantor) will immediately upon demand unconditionally pay to the Lender (IIG) the Guaranteed moneys which have not been so paid".

That and other terms dispensing with proof of default strongly indicated that the parties had contracted for a demand guarantee; for example where the instrument simply calls for payment against the presentation of a document (*Meritz Fire*).[46] In *Meritz Fire*, the fact that the parties had chosen to incorporate the ICC

---

[42] *Frans Maas v Habib Bank* [2001] Lloyd's Rep. Bank 14.

[43] It has been stressed time and time again that a guarantee is subject to the same rules of construction as a contract; therefore the factual matrix is just as important when interpreting the terms of a guarantee—*Fairstate v General Enterprise and Management* [2010] EWHC 3072 (QB).

[44] Although commentators have often referred to the on demand guarantee as being characterised (partly) by the fact that the surety is a bank, this is not always necessary as long as the terms are clear and the parties are clearly involved in a transnational commercial transaction. See *Meritz Fire & Marine v Jan de Nul* [2011] 1 All E.R. (Comm) 1049 ([2012] 1 All E.R. (Comm) 182 before the Court of Appeal) where the surety was an insurance company.

[45] See also, *Carey Value Added SL v Grupo Urvasco SA* [2010] EWHC 1905 (Comm) where the guarantee was issued by the parent company of a property development company. This is a classic case of a performance guarantee given in a non-banking context; the court refused to find the instrument to be a demand guarantee; also *Vossloh Aktiengesellschaft v Alpha Trains (UK) Ltd* [2010] EWHC 2443 (Ch) (a guarantee issued by the locomotive manufacturer was clearly one given in a non-banking context).

[46] *Meritz Fire & Marine v Jan de Nul* [2011] 1 All E.R. (Comm) 1049.

Uniform Rules for Demand Guarantees (URDG) was likely to be treated as conclusive evidence that the instrument is a demand guarantee. However, Blair J. in *WS Tankship II BV v Kwangju Bank* [2011] EWHC 3103, considered rightly that its omission is in itself a neutral factor.

In *Rainy Sky SA v Kookmin Bank* [2011] UKSC 50, the Supreme Court reminded us that the exercise of construction of demand guarantee (as with other commercial instruments) was essentially one unitary exercise in which the Court had to consider the language used and ascertain what a reasonable person (being a person who had all the background knowledge which would reasonably have been available to the parties in the situation in which they were at the time of the contract) would have understood the parties to have meant. In undertaking that exercise, the Court had to have regard to all the relevant surrounding circumstances. If there were two possible constructions, the Court was entitled to prefer the construction which was consistent with business common sense, and to reject the other. In that case, the bond was an undertaking by K to pay to R "all such sums due to [R] under the Contract". The bond underpinned a shipbuilding contract. When the shipbuilder became insolvent, the vessels could not be delivered. R then called K to reimburse them for sums paid as "pre-delivery instalments". K argued, however, that that the expression "such sums" referred to the repayment of the pre-delivery instalments in the event of the contract terminating or a total loss of the vessels, not the shipbuilder's insolvency. The bank relied on another part of the bond to support this interpretation. The Court of Appeal accepted the argument but the Supreme Court held that R's construction was to be preferred because it was consistent with the commercial purpose of the bonds in a way in which K's construction was not. After all, the insolvency of the builder was the situation for which the security of an advance payment bond was most likely to be needed. As Sir Simon Tuckey, the judge at first instance, said

"it defies commercial common sense to think that this, among all other such obligations, was the only one which the parties intended should not be secured. Had the parties intended this surprising result I would have expected the contracts and the bonds to have spelt this out clearly but they do not do so."

11–119   It is an unfortunate reality that given the reach of the demand guarantee, some parties would try their best to challenge it on grounds of construction—that is to say, the party refusing to pay would always try to argue that the true meaning of the guarantee was something contrary to what the beneficiary was attempting to rely on. As a matter of procedure, this could very well lead to protracted proceedings to decide on the true construction of the instrument but the courts are careful not to allow this. In *TTI Team Telecom International Ltd v Hutchison 3G UK Ltd* (January 23, 2003), A promised contractually to supply B with a software which would monitor and manage B's mobile phone network. A guarantee was provided for by C in relation to the contract. B then made a call under the guarantee following an allegation that A was in breach. The grounds relied on by C for refusal to pay were varied—they range from the allegation that the demand was made in bad faith to the failure to meet the formalities of the demand. The court found itself unable to decide summarily the validity of the demand because the factual and technical issues were clearly complicated and could only be determined properly at trial.[47] However, as the court could see that the guarantee was a demand guarantee, it ruled that it would be contrary to the presumed intention of the parties to allow the bank to refuse to pay. It should thus be noted that the pay first argue later maxim should apply in such a case.

Indeed as the Court of Appeal stressed in *Wuhan Guoyu Logistics v Emporiki Bank of Greece SA* [2012] EWCA Civ 1629, the courts should not over-complicate the matter of construction. At the lower court, the judge had cited no fewer than 20 authorities and written a 93-paragraph judgment to find that the instrument was a simple guarantee and not a demand guarantee. Longmore L.J. had this to say:

"But something has surely gone wrong if this comparatively simple question of construction requires such lengthy consideration. It is a problem of our system of precedent, that as more and more cases get decided, it seems to be necessary for judges at first instance to consider each case and determine how near or how far the document in question differs from the document construed in each past case. The commercial community deserves better than this, if better can be done."

The Court of Appeal reaffirmed the virtual presumption that an instrument would be treated as a demand guarantee if it:

(i) relates to an underlying transaction between the parties in different jurisdictions;

(ii) is issued by a bank;

(iii) contains an undertaking to pay "on demand" (with or without the words "first" and/or "written"); and

(iv) does not contain clauses excluding or limiting the defences available to a guarantor, it will almost always be construed as a demand guarantee.

Courts should not be unduly swayed by the fact that the instrument refers to the underlying obligation; after all, most demand guarantee can hardly avoid making reference to the obligation for whose performance the guarantee is security. Indeed, as Paget's Law on Banking states,[48]

"a bare promise to pay on demand without any reference to the principal's obligation would leave the principal even more exposed in the event of a fraudulent demand because there would be room for argument as to which obligations were being secured".

---

[47] Where the underlying contract clearly and expressly prevented the beneficiary from making a demand under the bond, the court could restrain it from doing so. That is usually a matter for the court at a "without notice" or interim injunction stage. At such stage in the proceedings, it would be rare for a court to form a final view as to the meaning of the contract. Thus, as it could not be expected to make a final ruling, it would be acceptable and natural for the court to make the injunction simply on being satisfied that the party seeking the injunction had a strong case. (*Simon Carves v Ensus UK Ltd* [2011] EWHC 657 (TCC).)

[48] J. Paget and M. Hapgood, *Paget's Law of Banking*, 11th edn (London: Butterworths, 1995), see para.26 of the judgment.

The fact that the parties have subjected the instrument to the Uniform Rules for Demand Guarantees is also evidence that the instrument is intended to be a demand guarantee (*Meritz Fire*).

Principle of strict compliance

11–120 The next question is whether the documentary and notice requirements under the performance guarantee are to be strictly complied with, as is the case with letters of credit. The issue is not entirely clear; although contemporary cases seem to take the view that performance guarantees are to be treated, on this issue, differently to letters of credit. In *Siporex Trade SA v Banque Indosuez* [1986] 2 Lloyd's Rep. 146 for example, Hirst J. took the view that the doctrine of strict compliance which prevails in letter of credit was not to be applied in considering the validity of the demands made in pursuant to a performance guarantee. The argument seems to be this—in letters of credit banks are dealing with the documents themselves and as such, precise compliance is vital. On the other hand, in the case of a performance guarantee, the bank is dealing with no more than a statement in the form of a declaration to the effect that a certain event or default has occurred. This was applied by Sir Christopher Bellamy QC sitting as High Court judge in *Frans Maas v Habib Bank* [2001] Lloyd's Rep. Bank 14. In that case, the guarantee required a statement that P had "failed to pay" whilst the demand notice served on the surety referred to a "failure to meet contractual obligations". The surety refused to pay arguing that the precise terms of the demand had not been satisfied. Whilst accepting that strictly compliant words are not necessary, the judge found that the demand was not sufficiently consistent with the requirement in the demand guarantee. The natural scope of the guarantee, according to the court, was limited to the failure to pay the liquidated and ascertained sums falling due under the agreement from time to time, however the demand was wide enough to cover *any* claim for damages for unliquidated and unascertained sums arising from any breach of the agreement. The demand was therefore unable to trigger the bank's liability under the guarantee.

The matter, however, does not appear to have been fully resolved. Each of the two cases, whilst supporting the view that the doctrine of strict compliance need not be applied invariably, actually relied on the precise terms of the demand guarantee for its decision. In *Siporex*, Hirst J. said: " . . . precise wording is not essential, particularly where the bond itself specifies no more than a requirement for [the] *declaration to that effect*". The court's position was very much that even if it was wrong to say that the doctrine did not apply, the end result was right because the bond required no more than a declaration *to the effect* that there had been a default. The bond itself permitted a less than precise requirement. Similarly, although the court in *Frans Maas* reasoned that there was strong justification for treating the performance guarantee as being on a different footing than the letter of credit, it again felt bound to give effect to the true reading of the demand guarantee which would not be content with *any* contractual failure other than a failure to pay liquidated and ascertained sums under the agreement. As far as the Court of Appeal was concerned, while it held in *IE Contractors Ltd v Lloyds Bank Plc* [1990] 2 Lloyd's Rep. 496 that there is "less need for a doctrine of strict compliance in the case of performance bonds", it also considered that the pivotal question was whether the promise made by the bank to the beneficiary under the bond required strict compliance and whether the beneficiary could avail himself of that promise. Staughton L.J. (with whom Sir Denys Buckley and Purchas L.J. agreed) said:

> "[T]he degree of compliance required by a performance bond may be strict or not so strict. It is a question of construction of the bond. If that view of the law is unattractive to banks, their remedy lies in their own hands".

It is submitted that there is no convincing rationale for the doctrine in performance guarantees. However, given the expectations of participants in international banking and the long passage of time where the principle of strict compliance has been applied to performance guarantees, it is difficult for judges, even if they might desire it, to turn the tide.

In *Ermis Skai Radio and Television v Banque Indosuez Europa SRL* (judgment **11–121** of February 26, 1997), ERTV entered into an agreement with P for the acquisition of entertainment programmes. A performance bond was issued by Banque Indosuez on ERTV's application in favour of P to the amount of $500,000. Relations broke down between ERTV and P. P then claimed under the bond from the bank. It was alleged that the beneficiary's demand had inserted a wrong reference date. This, according to Thomas J. was sufficient to defeat their claim under the bond. Materiality or de minimis effect is not a defence or excuse for failure to adhere to the conditions.

It was then argued by the beneficiary that as the bank had conceded that it would have paid if the demand did not refer to any date at all, the inclusion of the date (albeit a wrong date) was mere additional information and could be disregarded for the purposes of payment. This too was rejected by Thomas J. who held that if a demand contained a statement that added to or qualified what was required, the banker was entitled to reject the demand. In this case, the bond clearly stated that payment was only to be made in respect of a demand under the contract "concluded after the making of the Bond on 14 September 1995". The demand as presented had referred to a contract signed on September 13, 1995; that was clearly inconsistent with the requirement in the Bond. The date was no mere additional information which could be disregarded.

In *Odebrecht Oil & Gas Services Ltd v North Sea Production Co Ltd* [1999] 2 All E.R. (Comm) 405, the court said that on a true construction of the performance bond, all that was required from the beneficiary's formal demand was a description of the alleged breach. There was no requirement for full details of the breach to be set out. Similarly, the beneficiary was not required under the terms of the bond to state precisely the quantum claimed. An approximation was sufficient. The surety was thus not entitled to refuse payment. On the other hand, where the performance bond requires that the "net established and ascertained damages" sustained by the claimant be established by expert assessment until those calculations were effected, there was no liability on the defendant to make any payment to the claimant.[49] These cases demonstrate the centrality of careful and precise draftsmanship in performance guarantees. Where the words are clear as to what is required, the court has no option but to support that intention and

---

[49] *Paddington Churches Housing Association v Technical & General Guarantee Co Ltd* [1999] 65 Con. L.R. 132.

enforce the performance guarantee accordingly, however harsh it might appear.[50] It was thus held in *State Trading Corp of India v ED & F Man (Sugar) Ltd, The Times*, July 22, 1981 that it was not possible to imply a term in the contractual relationship between the buyer and seller that the beneficiary of a performance guarantee should only give notice of default for a reasonable and just cause. Such a term would strike at efficacy and purpose of performance guarantees. The only term that could be imported was that notice would not be given unless the buyer honestly believed that there was default.

11–122   The courts are not prepared to allow the implied term device to damage the autonomy principle so highly venerated by the law on demand guarantees. In *Uzinterimpex J.S.C. v Standard Bank* [2008] EWCA Civ 819 the Court of Appeal refused to imply a term into the demand guarantee that if the beneficiary made a demand that turned out to be excessive, they should repay the excess. In this connection, it is useful to refer to the URDG (ICC publication 758) to which the demand guarantee in the case was subject. The URDG clearly recognise the guarantor's independent role, as detailed in art.5, which emphasises that a guarantee is independent of the underlying relationship. Moreover, art.6 states that guarantors deal with documents and not with the goods, services or performance to which the documents may relate. Under art.7 a guarantee should not contain a condition (other than a date or the lapse of a period) without specifying a document to indicate compliance with that condition. If the guarantee does not specify any such document and the fulfilment of the condition cannot be determined from the guarantor's own records or from an index specified in the guarantee, then the guarantor will deem such condition as not stated and will disregard it except for the purpose of determining whether data that may appear in a document specified in and presented under the guarantee does not conflict with data in the guarantee.

Any implied term has to be subject to the dominant principle of autonomy. Business efficacy arguments could not override the presumption of autonomy. Any claim that the beneficiary had received a windfall should be dealt with as a separate claim, and not be tied to the demand guarantee whose very raison d'être has to be its autonomy.

Be that as it may, the URDG try to discourage beneficiaries from making unfair calls. Article 15 requires that demands must be accompanied by such documents as the guarantee specifies and contain a statement setting out "in what respect the applicant is in breach of its obligations under the underlying relationship". The expectation is that beneficiaries will think twice about making a false statement. This provision might be seen as a pro-applicant/guarantor because it provides a basis upon which a guarantor can challenge a demand claim in court by alleging that an accompanying statement is false. As in the old URDG 458 it remains open to the parties expressly to exclude this provision.

Who is the beneficiary?

11–123   Another important aspect of a valid demand is that the demand should be made by the properly authorised beneficiary. This was stressed in *Maridive & Oil*

---

[50] See *De Montfort Insurance Co Plc v Justin Cooke & Balbir Singh Sidhu* (February 18, 1999) where Garland J. refused to entertain an application to set aside the performance guarantee which was claimed to be "draconian".

Services (SAE) v CNA Insurance Co (Europe) Ltd [2002] EWCA Civ 369 that the contractual description of the beneficiary must be construed narrowly. In that case, a Lease Bond (performance guarantee) was provided by the surety for the charterer's obligations to M, the shipowner. The beneficiary was to be M's P&I Club. A claim was made in M's name but when the surety refused to pay, M's solicitors then sent another demand, this time in both names (M and the P&I Club). The court noted in passing that the guarantee was a clear agreement that the beneficiary was to be the P&I Club and the P&I Club alone. The terms of the guarantee must be taken at face value. Thus, a contractually valid demand could only be made by the Club as beneficiary in the same capacity. It was thus, on the basis that the beneficiary must be the person properly authorised to make a call, that the applicant in *Consolidated Oil Ltd v American Express Bank* (2002) C.L.C. 488[51] argued that following the military coup in the Ivory Coast, the beneficiary was no longer properly authorised to claim.

Fraud as a defence

Fraud is a possible defence to a call on the guarantee but it is usually very tightly controlled as a defence.[52] The court in *Kvaerner John Brown Ltd v Midland Bank Plc* (1998) C.L.C. 446 stated that for the court to interfere with payment under an irrevocable stand-by letter of credit (performance guarantee) was a very serious step and the court would only do so, if it could be clearly demonstrated that the application for payment was fraudulent and that the bank must be on notice of the fraud. In that case, the performance guarantee required the beneficiary to give 14 days' written notice prior to the demand. The demand made wrongly certified that the required notice had been given when it was patently clear that it had not been. On that basis, the court considered that such a demand was fraudulent and an injunction could be granted to prevent the surety from paying. A similar approach was taken in case on counter-guarantee —*Turkiye IS Bankasi AS v Bank of China* (*The Times*, December 17, 1997). There, the Court of Appeal held that such is the exactitude of the principle of autonomy that only where the bank has proper notice of fraud at the time when the demand is made, could it refuse to pay. **11–124**

The reference to "at the time when the demand was made" is troublesome as we see in *Balfour Beatty Civil Engineering Ltd v Technical & General Guarantee Co Ltd* [2000] 68 Con. L.R. 108. In that case, the beneficiary of a demand guarantee made a claim under the guarantee on the basis that as the applicant had become insolvent and consequently unable to perform the contract, the surety was liable to pay them under the performance bond. Before legal proceedings commenced, the surety was uncertain about fraud but nevertheless resisted payment. It was not until an application for summary judgment was made by the claimant that the issue of fraud became clearer. These circumstances could give rise to this oddity—if the court had concluded on the evidence available at the summary judgment hearing that the demand was fraudulent, should judgment

---

[51] Below, para.11–025.

[52] In *Solo Industries (UK) Ltd v Canara Bank* (July 3, 2001) the CA made clear that the fraud payment exception may only be applied where the guarantee is in fact valid. It can thus be resisted on the basis that the guarantee itself is invalid.

nevertheless be given to the fraudster because *at the time of the demand*, there was no such evidence of fraud? Waller L.J. giving judgment for the Court of Appeal set out the following principles.

"(a) When the demand was made, did the surety or the bank have clear evidence from which the only inference to be drawn was fraud? If the answer was no then prima facie the beneficiary was entitled to judgment.

(b) What, on the information available at the time of the application for summary judgment, was the strength of the surety's case that the demand was fraudulent?

   (i) If the evidence was now clear, then no judgment would be given in favour of the beneficiary because of the fact that the surety would be entitled to a judgment for the equivalent sum.
  (ii) If the evidence was powerful but not quite sufficient to enable summary judgment to be entered in favour of the surety on the basis that the demand was fraudulent, then either judgment would be entered with a stay of execution or probably no judgment would be entered at all until what was in effect the counterclaim had been fought out at trial.
 (iii) If the evidence was less than powerful, judgment would be entered in favour of the beneficiary and the surety would be left either to pursue his remedy against the applicant (customer) or pursue a claim or counterclaim for reimbursement for monies paid if it subsequently transpired that there was indeed fraud. (N.B.: That case was decided with reference to the old RSC Ord. 14 rules; although the court doubted that the position under the new Civil Procedure Rules 1998 would be different, it did not consider it.)".

11–125   This solution attempts to negotiate the procedural rights of the surety or bank around the necessity to maintain the sanctity of the performance guarantee. The question is whether it derogates too much from the philosophy of a performance guarantee which is to ensure that payment is made merely upon a plea of default by the beneficiary. The "pay now argue later" rule, it could be argued, should normally predominate. In contrast, the other view is that the performance guarantee should not be elevated to a role which transcends substantive justice and substantive justice requires an examination into the pleas made in preventing an abuse of the surety's goodwill. *Balfour Beatty* is a difficult case and this is reflected in the reluctance of the court ultimately to find fraud in the circumstances, despite its concession to the bank's procedural rights.

But how should courts approach the matter when it is not the bank that refuses to pay but the applicant who seeks an injunction or temporary restraining order on grounds of fraud to prevent the bank from paying?[53] The law insists that the applicant seeking an injunction must be able to prove a cause of action against the bank (i.e. the bank is in breach of a duty to him) before an injunction can be granted (*American Cynamid Co v Ethicon Ltd* [1975] A.C. 396). In addition, the

---

[53] Arora, "The legal position of banks in performance bond cases" [1981] L.M.C.L.Q. 264.

applicant must establish that it is seriously arguable on the materials available that the beneficiary is not entitled to the money.[54]

In general, that means that on documentary evidence it should be clear that the ground on which the injunction was sought (for example, fraud, illegality or invalid demand) was the only realistic inference. In *Consolidated Oil Ltd v American Express Bank* (2002) C.L.C. 488, the claimant applied for an injunction to prevent the bank from paying under a performance guarantee which had been provided to back a bid for shareholding in a company owned largely by the government of the Ivory Coast. The beneficiary of the performance guarantee was a committee set up by the then Prime Minister's office. That committee subsequently made a call on the guarantee. The claimant argued that the bank should not make any payments until it had been properly ascertained that the beneficiary was actually authorised to make the demand, stressing that following the overthrow of the prime minister's office in the military coup, the committee was set up under his auspices also ceased to exist. The court refused to grant the injunction stating that the only obligation for the bank was to consider the demand and decide whether it complied with the requirements of the guarantee. Only if the applicant is able to show that the only realistic inference from the facts was that the demand was invalid, or that the committee no longer existed or that the committee had not been authorised to make the call, would a court consider the grant of the injunction. Even then, it must be remembered that the court would not order an injunction if damages would be an adequate remedy.

By and large, no difference in approach is perceived in cases where the **11–126** injunction is sought by the applicant against the bank and cases where the bank of its accord refuses to pay and is thus challenged by the beneficiary in court. After all, the raison d'être is that

"performance bonds are part of the essential machinery of international commerce and to delay payment under such documents strikes not only at the proper working of international commerce but also at the reputation and standing of the international banking community".

In *United Trading Corp v Allied Arab Bank Ltd* [1985] 2 Lloyd's Rep. 554n, Ackner L.J. considered that the impact of the proposition should not be over-stated. His Lordship made reference to practice in the United States saying:

"It is interesting to observe that in America, where concern to avoid irreparable damage to international commerce is hardly likely to be lacking, interlocutory relief appears to be more easily obtainable. A temporary restraining order is made essentially on the basis of suspicion of fraud, followed some months later by a further hearing, during which time the applicant has an opportunity of adding to the material which he first put before the Court. Moreover, their conception of fraud is far wider than ours and would appear to include ordinary breach of contract. (See *Dynamics Corp. of America v Citizens and Southern National Bank* 356 F Supp. 991 (1973); *Harris Corp. v NIRT* 691 F 2d 1344 (1982); and *Itek Corp v FN Bank of Boston* 566 F Supp. 1210 (1983)). These cases indicate that, for the purpose of obtaining relief in such cases, it is not necessary for an American plaintiff to

---

[54] Bennett, "Performance bonds and the principle of autonomy" [1994] J.B.L. 574.

demonstrate a cause of action against a bank, whereas it is . . . common ground that a plaintiff must in this country show a cause of action. There is no suggestion that this more liberal approach has resulted in the commercial dislocation which has, by implication at least, been suggested would result . . .".

This approach was approved, albeit in a limited way, in *Themehelp Ltd v West* [1995] 4 All E.R. 215, by the majority of the Court of Appeal.

11–127   *Themehelp Ltd v West* [1995] 4 All E.R. 215
Facts:
The claimants' intended purchase of the defendants' share capital in a trading company was guaranteed by a performance guarantee obtained from a third party. Under the guarantee the defendants were entitled to give notice to the guarantors to make good any default on the part of the claimants. The claimants in turn were to indemnify the guarantors. The purchase price for the share capital was to be made in several instalments. The claimants argued that the defendants had falsely and fraudulently misrepresented to them, thereby inducing them to buy the share capital. They then stopped payment. Notice was given by the defendants to the guarantors for payment. The claimants applied for a injunction to stop the guarantors from paying under the bond.
Held:
The Court of Appeal in a majority decision held that since the issue of fraud arose at the early stages and the beneficiary's conscience could not yet be established, the injunction did not interfere with the autonomy of the bond. Additionally, the claimants should not be made to run the appreciable risk of being unable to recover the sum guaranteed in the event they succeeded in the action later on.

This case highlights the problem of proof in an interlocutory action attempting to prevent the execution and performance of the bond as perceived by Ackner L.J. in *United Trading Corp*. The majority in the Court of Appeal did not adopt *in toto* the American solution; they simply could not in the light of our rules on injunctions as set out by the House of Lords in *American Cynamid v Ethicon Ltd*.

11–128   This ruling also leaves it open to banks doubting the bona fides of the beneficiary's demand to encourage the customer to undertake the lighter burden applying for a temporary injunction by showing that

> "it is seriously arguable that, on the materials available, the only realistic inference is that the beneficiary could not honestly have believed in the validity of its demands on the performance bond".

This saves the bank from the conventionally onerous task of showing that there is not only fraud but the fraud is evident to them on the face of the documentation and that they have notice of the fraud. Surely such a consequence would render the "pay now argue later" rationale quite ineffective. On that basis, it was argued in the first edition of this book that *Themehelp* was probably not correctly decided.[55]
There is no distinction to be made of the fraud exception between an injunction to restrain the bank as against the beneficiary. Although the majority in

---

[55] See Chuah, *Law of International Trade*, 1st edn (London: Sweet & Maxwell, 1998), p.350.

Themehelp suggested that such a distinction could be made, its correctness is to be doubted, as Staughton L.J. pointed out in *Deutsche Ruckversicherung AG v Walbrook Insurance Co Ltd* [1994] 4 All E.R. 181:

" . . . The effect of the lifeblood of commerce will be precisely the same whether the bank is restrained from paying or the beneficiary is restrained from asking for payment. That was the view of Donaldson M.R. in *Bolivinter Oil SA v Chase Manhattan Bank* [1984] 1 Lloyd's Rep. 251, of Donaldson L.J. in *Intraco Ltd v Notis Shipping Corp (The Bhoja Trader)* [1981] 2 Lloyd's Rep. 256 . . . ".

In *Czarnikow-Rionda Sugar Trading Inc v Standard Bank London Ltd* [1999] **11–129** 1 All E.R. (Comm) 890, Rix J., in refusing to grant an injunction to restrain the beneficiary from making a demand, said that the fact that the policy reasons for restricting the scope of the fraud exception must apply equally to injunctions sought against the beneficiary as they do to applications against the bank.

Finally, it might be recalled that an injunction would only be granted where the balance of convenience lies in the favour of the grant (*American Cynamid Co v Ethicon Ltd* [1975] 1 All E.R. 504). In the case of a performance guarantee, that balance is almost always decisive against the grant of an injunction.

11–130

In *Simon Carves v Ensus UK Ltd* [2011] EWHC 657 (TCC) the court helpfully summarised the principles in these terms:

(a) in the absence of fraud, a bank would not be prevented from paying out under an on-demand bond provided that there had been compliance with the bond conditions;

(b) the same applied where a beneficiary sought payment under a bond;

(c) there was no legal authority permitting a beneficiary to make a call on a bond when it was expressly disentitled from doing so;

(d) if the contract in relation to which the bond had been provided as security clearly and expressly prevented the beneficiary to the contract from making a demand under the bond, the court could restrain it from doing so (in that case, the bond had stipulated that upon the acceptance of a particular certificate, the bond will lapse and indeed, the certificate had been issued and accepted); and,

(e) at a without notice or interim injunction stage, it would be rare for a court to form a final view as to the meaning and performance of the underlying contract. It could not be expected to make a final ruling and had only to be satisfied that the party seeking the injunction had a strong case. At this stage there is no trial of the issues.

In that case, the injunction was given because the court found on an arguable case that the bond had expired in relation to the claim in question.

An alternative solution might be for the claimant to apply for a freezing **11–131** injunction restraining the beneficiary from using the funds he has received from the performance bond. This remedy has the advantage of not derogating from the principle of autonomy of the bond. With this approach, the bank is not freed from its separate and distinct duty to honour the undertaking, thus preserving good commercial sense.

PAYMENT AND FINANCE FOR INTERNATIONAL TRADE

It should however be remembered despite the strict autonomy of performance guarantee, it is not the law's intention to allow any of the parties involved in the underlying transaction to be unjustly enriched as a result. It was resolutely held by the Court of Appeal in *Cargill International SA v Bangladesh Sugar & Food Industries Corp* [1998] 2 All E.R. 406 that in a performance bond guaranteeing performance of the contract by one party and indemnifying the other against any loss caused by default of performance or breach of the contract, there must necessarily be an implied term that there would be an accounting for the proceeds of the bond and that the party in default or breach should be entitled to recover any surplus over and above the actual loss suffered by the other party. The beneficiary of the bond in that case could only retain that amount which represented loss suffered from the claimant's breach. As there was no loss the claimant was entitled to recover the full amount of the bond. However, as an implied term, it is inevitably open to variation or exclusion by the clear agreement of the parties as is likely to be the case in many demand guarantees, subject only to any limitations placed on such agreement by, for example, the Unfair Contract Terms Act 1977.[56]

We see in the above cases that fraud and the bank's notice of fraud must be established. A novel approach to the issue was raised in *Ermis Skai Radio and Television v Banque Indosuez Europa SRL* in an attempt to circumvent this severity. While notice of fraud could not be proved, the applicant argued that no payment need be made because the beneficiary had not complied with an implied term of honesty. That term was expressed as being the requirement that the claim must be made in the honest belief that they, the beneficiary, were actually entitled to the sum demanded. Failure to do so was therefore improper and dishonest. Thomas J. held that there was no such term in the undertaking, nor could it be implied. To imply a term that the claimants must honestly believe that they were entitled to the demanded sums is to dilute the doctrine of strict compliance. That would be inconsistent with the autonomy of the guarantee. The implying of such a term would surely be antithetical to the business efficacy of an independent guarantee.

Discharge and termination of a performance guarantee

11–132   Naturally, once payment is made under a performance guarantee, the guarantee becomes discharged and it lapses. It is then up to the surety to make a claim for reimbursement (to the extent as permitted under his contract with the applicant) from the applicant or some third party (where, for example, there is a counter guarantee or indemnity[57]). More problematic is when the guarantee provides for a period of time that it is active and operative or for the occurrence of an event which would then bring the guarantee to an end; when that prescribed the guarantee should come to a natural end when that time is up or the event takes place. It is clear that as the issue as to when the guarantee lapses is a matter of construction, it can easily lend itself to dispute as to the correct interpretation. In *Alstom Combined Cycles Ltd v Henry Boot Construction Plc* (May 1, 2001), the

---

[56] See *Oval Ltd v Aegon Insurance Co (UK) Ltd* [1998] 85 B.L.R. 97 where the performance bond in issue was construed in the light of s.3 of the Unfair Contract Terms Act 1977. The bond was held by Recorder Colin Reese QC to satisfy the requirement of reasonableness.
[57] See *Shanning International Ltd v Lloyds TSB Bank Plc* [2001] UKHL 31.

performance bond in the building project provided that it should become null and void "upon the Engineer under the contract issuing a defects correction certificate". The question was whether that meant the bond was terminated, not only from the time the certificate was issued, but also with retrospective effect. The beneficiary argued that the issue of the certificate did not mean that they could not make a demand on the bank for breaches committed prior to the issuing of the certificate. The court agreed with the beneficiary and stated that it was not an appropriate interpretation that the bond had no effect with reference to breaches committed prior to event which bring an end to the bond.[58]

Where the performance guarantee prescribes that the demand should be made before the guarantee lapses, that requirement would be construed and applied strictly (*Lorne Stewart Plc v Hermes Krediversicherungs AG* (October 22, 2001). In that case, Lorne was a subcontractor in a construction project for which Amey was the main contractor. The performance bond taken out by Lorne with the surety, Hermes, provided that in the event of default by Lorne on its obligations, Amey was entitled to make a demand for payment on Hermes for 10 per cent of the subcontract fee. There were two main provisos:

1. the "longstop date" of October 11, 2001 had not passed; and

2. Amey had previously served notice of default on Lorne.

The bond also stipulated Hermes was not required to accept any requirement for payment unless it was made "before" the "termination date" as defined by the bond. On October 11, 2001, Amey sent a requirement for payment to Hermes but the demand which was drafted the day before stated "the longstop date has not yet occurred" and "notice of default has been served on [Lorne]".

Lorne applied for an injunction to restrain Hermes from paying arguing that **11–133** the demand for payment was invalid because it should have been made *before* October 11, 2001. Garland J. construed the time clause strictly against the beneficiary. The judge found that the "termination date" was the "longstop date" and the bond required that the demand be made before the termination date. The demand was therefore out of time and there is no room for a de minimis exemption. All demand conditions must be met precisely.

There is an unresolved issue in this context. What if the performance guarantee does not provide that a claim should be made within its lifespan. Is there an implied term that a demand could not be made after the expiry of the guarantee? In the case of letters of credit, it might be recalled that the expiry date of the letter of credit is also deemed to be the expiry date for the presentation of the documents for payment (art.6(d) UCP 600). Naturally, where the performance guarantee is expressed to be governed by the UCP 600 art.6(d) could apply but where that is not clear, the position is less clear. What if the guarantee is subject to the URDG 758?

Under the URDG, sub-article 25 (b) states:

"Whether or not the guarantee document is returned to the guarantor, the guarantee shall terminate:

i. on expiry,

---

[58] See also, *Simon Carves v Ensus UK Ltd* [2011] EWHC 657 (TCC).

    ii. when no amount remains payable under it, or

    iii. on presentation to the guarantor of the beneficiary's signed release from liability under the guarantee."

That should be read in conjunction with art.25 (c) which states:

"If the guarantee or the counter-guarantee states neither an expiry date nor an expiry event, the guarantee shall terminate after the lapse of three years from the date of issue and the counter-guarantee shall terminate 30 calendar days after the guarantee terminates."

A presentation made after expiry shall not be honoured.

11–134   Article 2 defines "expiry" as "the expiry date or the expiry event or, if both are specified, the earlier of the two; expiry date means the date specified in the guarantee on or before which a presentation may be made". An expiry event is further defined as

"an event which under the terms of the guarantee results in its expiry, whether immediately or within a specified time after the event occurs, for which purpose the event is deemed to occur *only*:

    a. when a document specified in the guarantee as indicating the occurrence of the event is presented to the guarantor, or

    b. if no such document is specified in the guarantee, when the occurrence of the event becomes determinable from the guarantor's own records" (emphasis added)

The so-called "extend or pay" rule, where the beneficiary makes a demand close to the expiry date and permits the guarantor to extend the validity of the guarantee as an alternative to immediate payment, is covered by art.23. That article provides for the possibility to suspend payment of the demand to allow the principal and the beneficiary of the guarantee to agree to an extension of the expiry date. Article 23 states that the guarantor may suspend payment for a period not exceeding 30 calendar days following receipt of the demand (though the condition is that the demand must be complying). If it refuses to extend, then it must pay (given that the presentation is complying).

    Nothing in art.23 should be read as preventing the surety from rejecting the demand if the demand is not complying—and in those circumstances the guarantor would neither be obligated to pay nor extend the expiry.

Forfaiting as a Method of Financing International Trade

11–135   Forfaiting operates on the basis that a bill of exchange or series of bills will be used as payment instruments in the trade transaction. It was first designed by Swiss bankers to meet the demand from sellers of capital goods on medium credit terms (between one and five years) for finance on a "without recourse" basis. The seller draws a usance bill on the buyer 'without recourse' to himself. The buyer is then accepted by the buyer and "backed" by the buyer's bank. That backing may be given either by way of an "aval" or a guarantee i.e. the bank simply appends its signature on the bill. The seller could then indorse the bill again "without recourse" and discount it to his bank. His bank acts as the forfaiter.

11–136

N.B. The definition of an aval may be borrowed from the Geneva Convention providing a Uniform Law for Bills of Exchange and Promissory Notes 1930.
Article 30
Payment of a bill of exchange may be guaranteed by an "aval" as to the whole or part of its amount. This guarantee may be given by a third person or even by a person who has signed as a party to the bill.
Article 31
The "aval" is given either on the bill itself or an "allonge". It is expressed by the words "good as aval" ("*bon pour aval*") or by any equivalent formula. It is signed by the giver of the "aval". It is deemed to be constituted by the mere signature of the giver of the "aval" placed on the face of the bill, except in the case of the signature of the drawee or of the drawer. An "aval" must specify for whose account it is given. In default of this, it is deemed to be given for the drawer.
Article 32
The giver of an "aval" is bound in the same manner as the person for whom he has become guarantor. His undertaking is valid even if the liability which he has guaranteed is inoperative for any reason other than defect of form. He has, when he pays a bill of exchange, the rights arising out of a bill of exchange against the person guaranteed and against those who are liable to the latter on the bill of exchange.

Thus, the person who has given the "aval" for the acceptor (the buyer) is liable to the drawer (seller), without the need to establish a guarantee in writing or to create retrospectively, through the notion of the bill being "incomplete", an unbroken chain of indorsements (see *G&H Montage GmbH v Irvani* [1990] 2 All E.R. 225). The guarantee given by way of an aval is not specially catered for in the Bills of Exchange Act 1882. This would suggest that liability will be determined according to the general rules on holders and signatories of a bill of exchange under the Act and rules on guarantees at common law (see *Gerald MacDonald & Co v Nash & Co* [1924] A.C. 625), resulting in a less than satisfactory state of affairs.

Forfaiting can also be applied to promissory notes. The buyer issues a   **11–137** promissory note which is similarly purchased at a discount by the forfaiting bank "without recourse". Whether bills of exchange or promissory notes are used, it is customary that they be drawn in a series over the duration of the contract; hence providing payment by instalments. The forfaiting process is perhaps best explained by way of an example.

Example:
The agreement between S and B provides that S shall deliver capital goods to B over a period of five years. Payment is to be made over 10 equal instalments. The series of bills (promissory notes) drawn will mature at every six month respectively, the last bill should mature by the completion of the contract period. B then accepts the 10 bills "without recourse" and these are "avalised" or guaranteed by a bank deemed acceptable to S's bank (the forfaiting bank). The forfaiting bank's only recourse is the avalising bank, therefore it must satisfy itself as to the creditworthiness of the buyer and the avalising bank before agreeing to forfait. The bills may be expressed in any currency acceptable to the forfaiting bank. These bills will then be purchased by the forfaiting bank at a price which will cover the interest over that credit period of five years, expenses and any margin of profit commensurate with the risk involved. The purchase, as

stated before, is without recourse to S. Upon maturity of each bill, the forfaiting bank presents it for payment.

11–138

> The International Forfaiter Association describes the steps (without mentioning the aval) like this.
>
> 1. During the course of negotiations between an exporter and an importer for the supply of goods, the importer asks for credit terms.
>
> 2. The exporter approaches a forfaiter and asks for an indication of whether the forfaiter is willing to provide this credit and how much it is likely to cost. At this stage the forfaiter will need to know:
>
>   a. The country of the importer;
>   b. The importer's name;
>   c. The type of goods;
>   d. The value of the goods;
>   e. The expected shipment date;
>   f. The repayment terms sought by the importer; and
>   g. Whether the importer's obligations will be guaranteed by a bank, and if so, who?
>
> 3. The forfaiter provides the exporter with an indication of the costs involved. At this stage neither party is committed in any way.
>
> 4. When the details of the commercial contract have been agreed, but usually before it has been signed, the exporter asks the forfaiter for a commitment to purchase the debt obligations (bills of exchange, promissory notes, etc) created under the export transaction.
>
> 5. The information required for this is the same as for an indication.
>
> 6. The forfaiter issues a commitment which is accepted by the exporter and which is binding on both parties. This commitment will contain the following points:
>
>   a. The details of the underlying commercial transaction;
>   b. The nature of the debt instruments to be purchased by the forfaiter;
>   c. The discount (interest) rate to be applied, together with any other charges;
>   d. The documents that the forfaiter will require in order to be satisfied that the debt being purchased is valid and enforceable; and
>   e. The latest date that the exporter can deliver these documents to the forfaiter.
>
> 7. The exporter signs the commercial contract with the importer and delivers the goods.
>
> 8. In return, if required, the importer obtains a guarantee from his bank provides the documents that the exporter requires in order to complete the forfaiting. This exchange of documents is usually handled by a bank, often using a Letter of Credit, in order to minimise the risk to the exporter.
>
> 9. The exporter delivers the documents to the forfaiter who checks them and pays for them as agreed in the commitment.
>
> 10. Since this payment is without recourse, the exporter has no further interest in the transaction. It is the forfaiter who collects the future payments due from the importer and it is the forfaiter who runs all the risks of non-payment.[59]

---

[59] http://www.forfaiters.org.

Forfaiting is popular in the continent where it has been in existence for a very **11–139** long time. The three major advantages in forfaiting are:

1. that the burden of collecting payment is passed on to the forfaiter;

2. that any currency exchange risk is minimised; and

3. that the seller need not worry about any recourse against a dishonoured bill since the forfaiting is always expressed as "without recourse".

The forfaiter bears these risks but not without a price. Banks are also not prepared to forfait unless at least a part of the purchase price has actually been paid. It is customary for merchant banks to stipulate that at least 15 per cent of the purchase price has been paid before they are prepared to forfait.

Uniform Rules on Forfaiting

On January 1, 2013, the International Chamber of Commerce's new uniform **11–140** rules on forfaiting (URF 800) entered into effect. These rules have taken a long time to draft but they should provide some degree of consistency of practice and approach to forfaiting agreements. They define a forfaiting transaction as the sale by the seller and the purchase by the buyer of the payment claim on a without recourse basis on the terms of the URF 800 (art.2). They may be modified by contract. The contract between the primary forfaiter and initial seller must specify precisely the terms on which the payment claim is to be sold (art.5). Those terms include:

- details about the payment claim and any credit support documents including the amount, currency, due date and obligors;

- a list of documents required to be presented;

- the availability date[60];

- the purchase price;

- the settlement date or anticipated settlement date; and

- its governing law and jurisdiction.

Similar to the documentary credit procedure, the initial seller must deliver documents which comply with the forfaiting agreement and the primary forfaiter must examine them and decide whether they conform to the contract requirements (including authenticity of the documents). If he is not satisfied, he must notify the seller (art.7(f)). Payment of the purchase price will mean acceptance unless the forfaiter makes clear he is paying under reserve[61] (art.7(f)).

---

[60] Art.2 defines availability date to mean "the last day on which the seller must deliver to the buyer satisfactory documents and satisfy any other condition. If the availability date is described in the forfaiting confirmation or forfaiting agreement as 'immediately available' or similar terms, that means the day falling 10 business days after the trade date".

[61] Defined in art.2 as conditional payment. Under art.12, the buyer is entitled to lay down reserve points (namely, conditions) for the seller to satisfy. If the seller fails to meet these reserve points, the buyer can require the seller to repurchase the claim on repurchase terms. The buyer will then return all documents received.

The payment claim could further be sold on.When it is sold by the primary forfaiter or another seller to a buyer, this is called a forfaiting transaction in the secondary market. Article 8 provides that in order to create a forfaiting transaction in the secondary market, there must be an agreement on the trade date[62] between the primary forfaiter or a subsequent buyer and another buyer to sell the payment claim. They are required to deliver to the buyer a signed forfaiting confirmation within two business days of the trade date. Failure to do so will entitle the buyer not to proceed with the transaction by notice to the seller. The forfaiting confirmation must set out the sale terms including terms which may have been changed after the trade date. After receipt of the forfaiting confirmation, the buyer must, within two business days from the date of receipt, either sign and return it to the seller or notify the seller of his disagreement with any of the terms. If the buyer does not take either of the steps mentioned above, the seller is free not to proceed and will not be prejudiced for not proceeding with the contract.

11–141   The parties shall be held liable to each other if they actually did not have the authority or power to make the transactions in question (art.13(a)) or if they did not have ownership of the payment claim which they purported to sell (art.13(b)(ii)). There is also imposed on the initial seller, a duty to disclose to the primary forfaiter any fact which could affect the right to be paid under the underlying agreement (the sale of goods agreement for example) or any credit underpinning the original agreement (e.g. payment by instalments). This is close to a general duty of good faith but is not expressed as such. These terms are open to modification by the parties.

These rules are intended to support the typical forfaiting arrangement. It remains to be seen how uniformly these rules will be interpreted and applied by national courts and arbitral tribunals. However, the rules have received much support from the sector and many favour the internationalist and pro-contract approach taken by the ICC.

Factoring

11–142   Factoring companies take on the book debts of a customer at a price, which they will then arrange to collect from the buyers. They also take on board the associated exchange, status and transaction risks. This naturally is an extremely convenient option for the sellers who should be able to save time and expense on debt collection and credit control. The factor charges a commission usually based on turnover, for taking over an agreed set of book debts or a sales ledger. In order to preserve the public profile of the sellers and to maintain the goodwill and relationship between buyer and seller, the factor will usually offer an invoice discount service. This means that the customer retains control over the sales ledger and the factor simply advances payment against invoices and underwrites any existing debt. The finance provided by the factor may be either with or without recourse.

Recourse financing allows the customer to receive payment from the factor against invoices but if the buyer fails to pay, the seller must reimburse the factor. The factor does not underwrite the risk or debt involved.

---

[62] Art.2 defines this as the date the parties make the agreement.

Without recourse factoring affords the seller absolute protection from credit risk. That is to say, if the buyer fails to pay according to the contract, the seller is not compelled to reimburse the factor. The factor will have to pursue the debt against the buyer himself.

Given the importance of the factoring facility, the International Institute for the **11–143** Unification of Private Law (UNIDROIT) has adopted a draft convention on international factoring in 1988. The Convention will apply (*N.B.* the Convention is not in force in the United Kingdom where the rights and liabilities of the parties are governed by the contract alone) if:

1. the parties to the contract of sale have places of business in different states and those states and the state in which the factor has its place of business are Contracting States or both the contract of sale and the factoring contract are governed by the law of a Contracting State (art.2(1));

2. the factoring agreement is one which the supplier may or will assign to the factor receivables (book debts) arising from contracts of sale of goods, but excluding contracts for goods bought primarily for personal, family or household use. (art.1(2)(a));

3. the factor performs at least two of the following functions (art.1(2)(b)):

   (a) finance for the supplier, including loans and advance payment;
   (b) maintenance of accounts (ledgering) relating to the receivables;
   (c) collection of receivables; or
   (d) protection against default in payment of debtors; and

4. notice of the assignment of the receivables is given to the debtors.

The Convention may be excluded in its totality by the parties to the factoring agreement or the sale agreement. In the latter, notice must be given to the factor. It also appears that the Convention may not be excluded in part; it has to be all or nothing.

Chapter II of the Convention sets out the rights and duties of the parties to the factoring agreement. Article 7 states that as between the parties, it is possible to provide in the contract for the transfer all or any of the supplier's rights under the contract of sale with or without a new act of transfer. The transfer can include any benefit the seller has vis-à-vis retention of title, liens, or any other security interest.

The debtor (buyer) is under a duty to pay the factor, if and only if, he does not **11–144** have knowledge of any other person's superior right to payment and notice in writing of the assignment:

1. is given to the debtor by the supplier or by the factor with the seller's authority;

2. reasonably identifies the receivables which have been assigned and the factor to whom or for whose account the debtor is required to make payment; and

3. relates to receivable arising under a contract of sale of goods made at or before the time the notice is give (art.8).

In any claim by the factor against the debtor for payment of a receivable, the debtor may invoke any defence (including any right of set-off) he might have if the action had been brought by the seller (art.9).

Credit Insurance

11–145 Factoring has its genesis in the United States, and forfaiting, the European continent; in the United Kingdom, a similar facility is found in the provision of credit insurance. The seller obtains, by payment of a premium to the insurer, protection against political and commercial risks of nonpayment or default. In many countries, the state would act as the insurer. As diversification in the insurance sector took hold, some of these state agencies were prepared to pass on that mantle to private insurers. In the United Kingdom, the Export Credit Guarantee Department (ECGD) was set up in 1919 to assist British exporters to re-establish their trading strengths after the disruption caused by the First World War but its remit has changed in recent times. In 1991, the arm of ECGD which dealt with exporters who traded on short terms of credit (i.e. up to two years) was sold to NCM Credit Insurance Ltd. Short-term transactions involving ordinary (or consumable) goods naturally are less risky compared with a medium- or long-term transaction involving large investment projects or capital goods. Thus, it was deemed appropriate by the Government to "privatise" that segment of the ECGD's business. Soon, further liberalisation followed and other private insurers were invited to participate in offering exporters short term export and investment protection. The ECGD has however retained its power under the Export and Investment Guarantees Act 1991 to provide exporters of British capital goods and services with finance and insurance packages to help them win valuable overseas orders. The ECGD also insures British companies who invest abroad against the political risks of a nonreturn on their investments.

There are in general two types of facilities offered to British exporters and investors:

Insurance facilities

Export Insurance Policy

11–146 The Export Insurance Policy (EXIP) from the ECGD protects the exporter against the political and commercial risks of not being paid in connection with individual capital goods or services contracts. The insurance can cover up to 95 per cent of the value of any loss suffered.

Bond Insurance Policy

11–147 It is not unusual for a buyer to require the seller to take out a performance guarantee or bond to guarantee the seller's performance under the contract. However, as we have observed earlier in this Chapter, performance guarantees or bonds expressed as demand guarantees carry a very high risk of unfair calls by the buyer or overseas trader. The ECGD would be prepared to insure the exporter against the risk of such bonding liabilities provided the exporter has already taken out a form of basic cover from the ECGD such as a Buyer Credit, or an Export Insurance Policy.

Tender to Contract/Forward Exchange Supplement (TTC/FES)

It is sometimes good marketing strategy to sell in the buyer's currency. **11–148** Sometimes, it is required by the buyer or his country's laws that a tender price be submitted using a foreign currency. In such an event, the seller might stand to lose a considerable sum if the exchange rates move against him before the contract is signed. The ECGD's TTC/FES schemes are particularly useful in this regard. They protect the seller against adverse exchange rate movements thereby ensuring that the exporter can commit himself to a firm foreign currency price.

Finance facilities

The ECGD is also empowered to provide exporters with finance facilities, **11–149** subject to EU rules on state aid and unfair competition. The trade finance facilities on offer include:

Buyer credit

Buyer credit is particularly useful in transactions involving high-value capital **11–150** goods. Foreign buyers rarely want to pay in cash for major projects or imports of high-value capital goods and services. However, not many exporters can cope with the cashflow difficulties or the risks of extending long-term credit for such contracts. Such finance can naturally be sought from the banks but lenders are not prepared to lend without any collateral or security. Security, however, is hard to come by. This is where the ECGD can offer assistance; it can step in to guarantee the loan.

With Buyer Credit the exporter is paid as though it has a cash contract with the buyer. The buyer, on the other hand, has time to pay and can borrow at favourable fixed or floating rates. The loans can be denominated in a wide range of currencies thereby making them even more convenient and attractive to the buyer. The lending bank has little to fear because the loan is backed by the UK government through the ECGD.

It should however be noted that the loan must be made in support of a contract with a value of at least £1 million (or the foreign currency equivalent) and the credit, or repayment, period must be at least two years. In practice, though, Buyer Credits are more suitable for contracts of £5 million or more. For contracts which are less than £1 million, a more appropriate form of finance would be the Lines of Credit (or Supplier Credit Financing Facility).

The exporter, however, must provide at least 15 per cent of the contract value **11–151** himself. The Buyer Credit Loan will only finance up to 85 per cent of the contract value.

There are four contracts involved:

• the Sale or Supply Contract between the seller and the buyer;
• the Premium Agreement between the seller and the ECGD;

- the Support Agreement between the ECGD and the financing bank; and

- the Loan Agreement between the bank and the buyer.

11–152   **Sale or Supply Contract**   The seller is required by the ECGD to ensure that the Supply Contract provides explicit terms on direct payments to be made by the bank (on behalf of the buyer/borrower) to the seller, and methods and regularity of payment. It should also provide for an alternative means of payment in the event that the loan is withdrawn. In certain cases, such as project finance, the ECGD will also want to scrutinise the terms of the contract to ensure that the terms are in compliant with the ECGD's own support criteria—such as the risks, issues of governance, and possibly, wider policy issues on international development and corruption, etc.

11–153   **Premium Agreement**   The Premium Agreement is the agreement between the ECGD and the seller under which the seller undertakes to pay a premium and to act in accordance with the ECGD's requirements. An application form for such a facility will, for example, require that the seller undertakes to comply with guidelines for combating illegal practices and money laundering. The agreement will naturally also include recourse provisions. For added protection from being liable to the ECGD, the seller can take out an Export Insurance Policy in conjunction with a Buyer Credit Loan.

11–154

Recourse

The ECGD in both the insurance and finance facilities it offers will customarily reserve a right of recourse. If the seller fails to perform his part of the contract with the overseas buyer, there is a likelihood that the buyer would not pay, either to the seller or to a bank financing the transaction. In the case of insurance cover (e.g. an Export Insurance Policy), the ECGD reserves the right to decline liability if an exporter's nonperformance leads the buyer to default on payment, or to suspend consideration of a claim whilst a dispute exists between an exporter and a buyer. In the case of a finance facility such as a Buyer Credit or Supplier Credit Finance facility, whilst the ECGD would pay the financing bank if the overseas borrower does not repay the loan regardless of the reason for nonpayment, it reserves the right in such circumstances to claim from the exporter some or all of the money paid to the bank.

Recourse is reserved almost as a matter of course. Only in very limited circumstances, would recourse not be sought. For example, where finance is provided unil the Supplier Credit Finance facility by means of a bank purchasing the bills or notes securing payment under the seller's contract, or where the contract is for the supply of goods for which the seller has an established track record, and where any related services do not constitute more than five per cent of the contract value.

Under the terms of the facility, no causal link between the contractual default and the bank's failure to receive payment needs to be proved for recourse to be taken. Be that as it may, the ECGD would not take recourse if it is satisfied that the seller's default is neither material nor substantial or has been caused by one of the following events:

- an act or omission by the buyer not induced or provoked by the seller;

- the prevention of, or delay in, the transfer of funds in respect of the contract resulting from the occurrence outside the United Kingdom of political events, economic difficulties, legislative or administrative measures, or a general moratorium;

- any measure or decision (including the nonrenewal of an export licence) of any government other than that of the United Kingdom which, in whole or in part, prevents performance of the contract;

- the occurrence outside the United Kingdom of hostilities, civil disturbance or natural disaster which, in whole or in part, prevents performance of the contract;

- the cancellation or nonrenewal of a United Kingdom export licence; and

- any restrictions introduced in the United Kingdom after the date of the contract which prevent performance of the contract, other than the refusal to grant a UK export licence or other authorisation necessary for performance of the contract if such authorisation was required at the date of the contract.

The seller would be freed from his recourse obligations once it is clear that a contract has been completed or performed to an agreed standard. There are two types of release procedure: either the seller obtains certification from the buyer that the contract has been performed satisfactorily or he makes such a certification himself (i.e. he asserts that the contract has been performed satisfactorily). In the latter case, if the seller's certification turns out to be untrue or incorrect, the ECGD retains a right to enforce the original recourse obligations on the seller.

This self-certification can be problematic especially where the seller is unable to certify that all his obligations have been fully performed but can certify that there are only minor areas still to complete. In such a case, the underwriter would have to examine the evidence underlying the certification and the seller could still be freed from his recourse obligations if the underwriter is satisfied that any failures in performance relate solely to minor and residual responsibilities.

Release from Recourse while the borrower is in default under the Loan Agreement
There is no release from recourse, where the loan is in default, until the circumstances of that default have been fully ascertained. However, where the default under the loan is for reasons extraneous to the contract (for example, where the foreign government has passed a law or taken measures preventing debt repayment) and the exporter has satisfied the conditions for release and given the relevant certification, a release might nonetheless be given.

Smaller exporters are entitled to take out a Recourse Indemnity Policy with Lloyd's of London to cover their recourse obligations to ECGD.

Support Agreement The Support Agreement is essentially the ECGD's **11–155** contract of guarantee to the lending bank(s). It contains certain responsibilities on the bank(s) to operate the loan in accordance with the ECGD's instructions.

Loan Agreement The Loan Agreement is between the lending bank(s) in the **11–156** United Kingdom and the overseas buyer. It sets out the terms on which the money is being lent, when it has to be repaid and at what interest rate. It will also contain certain conditions which have to be fulfilled before any money can be drawn from the loan. These preconditions may include requirements such as confirmation from the exporter that direct payments have been received for the goods, any guarantees required have been obtained, together with legal opinions as to the validity of the contract and loan, etc.

Buyer Credit loans normally operate on a disbursement basis—that means, when the applicant makes a shipment, or performs services under the contract, or reaches a certain stage of work, he should present a Qualifying Certificate (QC) to the bank certifying that he has fulfilled that part of his contract with the buyer. The QC must be supported by evidence that the contract has been performed and may need to be countersigned by the buyer. On satisfaction that the QC is valid and payment is due, the bank will authorise the disbursement.

An alternative method of payment is reimbursement. Payment is made to the buyer. The buyer pays first and then submits a Reimbursement Certificate to the bank supported by a receipt of payment from the seller.

Supplier Credit Financing Facility

11–157   For smaller transactions, the Supplier Credit Financing Facility might be useful in bridging the two opposing concerns of the traders—extended credit being sought by the buyer, and the seller not wishing to wait for his money. The Supplier Credit Financing Facility gives the buyer at least two years' credit and the seller payment in cash. The scheme places the payment risk on the seller's bank and if the buyer defaults on the credit, the bank would have recourse to the ECGD who acts as guarantor. Given the small sums involved, it might also be possible for the seller to be granted Supplier Credit Financing Facility without recourse—meaning that the ECGD would not pursue the seller in the event of the buyer's default.

Lines of Credit

11–158   An exporter may also wish to consider applying for an ECGD-supported "Line of Credit", especially when selling capital and project goods or services. The seller will be paid cash following shipment of the goods whilst the overseas buyer will be able to pay for them over a period of time. With minimum contract values as low as $25,000, it is envisaged by the ECGD that British exporters could better penetrate new markets overseas. A Line of Credit is an arrangement between a bank in the UK and a bank (or other borrower) overseas to make finance available for a series of contracts. The Line will be put in place before the supply contract between the buyer and seller is made, ensuring that the seller and the buyer gain access to the facility fairly promptly. The Line will specify the currency (or currencies) and overall amount of finance that may be made available, together with any conditions, for example, the minimum contract value. The seller will be paid from the loan by the UK bank and if the borrower fails subsequently to repay any part of the finance, the UK bank can enforce their guarantee from the ECGD.

Policy Considerations

11–159   The ECGD having been given wider powers in 1991 is able to make special financing arrangements which might draw on the capital markets, or to denominate a loan in a foreign currency (Local Currency Financing Scheme), or to enter into arrangements with private banks and syndicates of banks to offer a variety of trade finance facilities to exporters of different complexion, including smaller exporters. These powers give the ECGD a great deal of commercial discretion and proficiency in participating in the export process. Many of its decisions are thus made on a commercial assessment of the risks and opportunities.[63] However, it should not be forgotten that the ECGD is a governmental

---

[63] See *Credit Lyonnais Bank Nederland NV v Export Credit Guarantee Department* [1998] 1 Lloyd's Rep. 19 for a discussion about the ECGD's commercial practices and procedures.

agency and is more than a commercial entity. Its public remit not only involves the narrowing of any trade deficit of the UK and to assist British traders, but also, the contribution to appropriate standards in international development. In 2000, the ECGD issued a new procedural code which laid down more stringent requirements on applicants for ECGD support, especially, in connection with money laundering and corruption. Applicants are required to make a "no bribery declaration" when completing the application form. They are also warned about money laundering on the application form. It would also be relevant whether or not the company making the application subscribes to a code regulating responsible conduct, internal or otherwise.

As far as the OECD is concerned, its Working Party on Export Credits and Credit Guarantees (ECG) issued a document in November 2003 on "Best Practices to deter and combat bribery in officially supported export credits" which led to the issuing of the OECD Recommendation on Bribery and Officially Supported Export Credits 2006. Some of the good practices for Export Credit Agencies suggested are:

- require companies to provide details of agents' commissions that amount to more than five per cent of a project's cost and should consider introducing a cap on commissions and applying enhanced due diligence for commissions over five per cent of a project's cost;

- require companies to state on application for export credit support whether they have been debarred by any multilateral or bilateral financial institutions, such as the World Bank, from contracts with that institution or found guilty in a national court of bribery, with a view to the export credit agencies withholding support or applying enhanced due diligence (investigating the history, performance and value of a company before investing in it or extending financial support to it);

- require export credit agencies to inform national investigative authorities of any suspicion or evidence of corruption both before and after support has been given;

- apply enhanced due diligence and suspend an application if suspicion or sufficient evidence of bribery arises;

- suspend payments to a company and deny access to further support if there is evidence of corruption until an official investigation has been concluded;

- apply all possible measures, such as suspending payment to a company, seeking compensation from it, and debarring it from further support for a certain number of years, where there is a legal judgment of bribery.

The ECG has also reached agreements on the environment (the OECD **11–160** Common Approaches for Officially Supported Export Credits and Environmental and Social Due Diligence 2012) and Sustainable Lending (Principles and Guidelines to Promote Sustainable Lending to Low Income Countries 2008).

These are important standards of good practice but it is equally obvious that international cooperation between export credit agencies is necessary to combat corruption. A number of export credit agencies, including the United Kingdom, Australia, Belgium, Germany and Japan, have taken positive steps to implement these standards. It is encouraging but there is some concern from businesses that the measures taken should not be too disproportionate at the expense of commercial competitiveness.

Private insurers are necessarily guided by commercial and market considerations. However, public disquiet and pressure groups have ensured that private insurers can no longer seek refuge behind a cloak of commerciality.[64] Membership of transnational organisations such as the Berne Union (the Berne Union admits both public and private export credit agencies) has also bound these private ECAs to certain common ethical principles.

---

[64] Chuah, "Export credit and credit guarantee institutions: balancing values in the legal and regulatory environment" [2010] Int.T.L.R. 155.

CHAPTER 12

CIVIL AND COMMERCIAL JURISDICTION

Transnational commercial disputes will normally give rise to issues requiring the **12–001** court to decide:

1. which country's courts should have jurisdiction to try the dispute;

2. which country's laws should be applied to resolve the dispute; and

3. whether any foreign judgment obtained abroad might be enforceable in England.

Consider the following situation:

> Seller, who is based in England, is in dispute with Buyer who has his place of business in Country B. Seller wishes to enforce a contract which he has entered into with Buyer against Buyer. The contract provides that the goods are to be delivered to Country C and payment is to be made in Country D. Seller wishes to know whether he could initiate action in England or whether he needs to proceed in Country B or a third country, possibly Country C or D. Furthermore, he needs to know to which of these or other countries' laws the contract is subject. Finally, if he succeeds in obtaining judgment in Country B against Buyer, he would like to know whether he is entitled to enforce that judgment in England and the procedures involved to that end.

Where there is a personal action containing an international element, the jurisdiction of the English court is dependent on whether the defendant is domiciled in the European Union or the European Free Trade Association (EFTA) or elsewhere. If he is domiciled in the European Union the EU Council Regulation on Jurisdiction and the Recognition and Enforcement of Judgments in Civil and Commercial Matters 2000 (Reg.44/2001) will apply. If the defendant is domiciled in an EFTA country, the relevant law is found in the Lugano Convention. That Convention is similar but not identical to Regulation 44/2001. Where the defendant is not domiciled in either an EU or EFTA country, then the common law rules on jurisdiction will apply.

This chapter considers primarily the provisions of Regulation 44/2001 and the **12–002** rules at common law. Before delving into the issues of jurisdiction, it is needful to examine the circumstances under which an entity might be immune from English jurisdiction as a matter of international law and/or the State Immunity Act 1978.

Immunity from Jurisdiction

12–003 Certain foreign nationals are afforded special jurisdictional privileges as a result of their status. For example, it is a trite rule of international law that foreign diplomats and consular officials are given certain immunities from criminal and civil action in their receiving states generally. In the realm of international trade, the focus is usually on foreign states trading as private parties in a commercial transaction. The question is whether these trading states and their agencies are afforded any degree of immunity from suit if they were to breach their contractual obligations.

This brings us into the area of state immunity. The traditional international law rule is that the foreign state must be absolutely immune from the jurisdiction of the receiving state's courts. This is based on the principle of equality between states. In *The Schooner Exchange v McFaddon* (1812) 7 Cranch. 116 (US), Marshall C.J. delivering the judgment of the US Supreme Court, said:

> "One sovereign being in no respect amenable to another, and being bound by obligations of the highest character not to degrade the dignity of his nation, by placing himself or its sovereign rights within the jurisdiction of another, can be supposed to enter a foreign territory only under an express license, or in the confidence that the immunities belonging to his independent sovereign station, though not expressly stipulated, are reserved by implication, and will be extended to him. This perfect equality and absolute independence of sovereigns, and this common interest compelling them to mutual intercourse, and an interchange of good offices with each other, have given rise to a class of cases in which every sovereign is understood to waive the exercise of a part of that complete exclusive territorial jurisdiction, which has been stated to be the attribute of every nation".

However, as international commerce grew, commercial disputes involving state agencies and bodies also gained greater prominence and occurrence. It was felt that these agencies should not be allowed to plead state immunity to avoid performing their commercial obligations. The Belgian and Italian courts were amongst the first to make a distinction between acts of government (*jure imperii*) and acts of a commercial nature (*jure gestionis*). The former would be subject to ordinary rules of state immunity; the latter not. This approach is known as the restrictive immunity principle.

12–004 The principle is adopted by the United Kingdom in its State Immunity Act 1978.[1] The Act takes the approach that there should at first instance, a general

---

[1] For an account of the practice of other European countries, see Reinisch, "European Court Practice Concerning State Immunity from Enforcement Measures" (2006) 17 E.J.I.L. 803. The State Immunity Act 1978 takes its cue from the European Convention on State Immunity 1976 though there are differences between the two. The Convention left contracting states free to give effect to the restrictive principle of sovereign immunity, "without prejudice to the immunity from jurisdiction which foreign States enjoy in respect of acts performed in the exercise of sovereign authority (*acta jure imperii*)", while art.27 provided that: "(1) For the purposes of the present Convention, the expression 'Contracting State' shall not include any legal entity of a Contracting State which is distinct therefrom and is capable of suing or being sued, even if that entity has been entrusted with public functions. (2) Proceedings may be instituted against any entity referred to in paragraph 1 before the courts of another Contracting State in the same manner as against a private person; however, the courts may not entertain proceedings in respect of acts performed by the entity in the exercise of sovereign authority (acta jure imperii)." The European Convention thus excludes from the

principle of state immunity. It therefore provides in s.1 that a state is immune from the jurisdiction of the UK courts. This is then followed by a catalogue of exceptions:

1. Section 2 which deals with submission to jurisdiction by the foreign state;

2. Section 3 which refers to commercial transactions and contracts to be performed in the United Kingdom;

3. Section 4 on contracts of employment;

4. Section 5 which addresses personal injury, death and damage to property caused by the foreign state;

5. Section 6 on rights to property;

6. Section 7 on intellectual property rights;

7. Section 8 which deals with proceedings arising from the foreign state's membership of bodies corporate;

8. Section 9 which refers to arbitration agreements entered into by the foreign state (see *Tsavliris Salvage (International) Ltd v The Grain Board of Iraq* [2008] EWHC 612 where the fact that the manager of the Grain Board of Iraq had signed the Lloyd's Standard Form of Salvage Agreement 2000 Edition which contained an arbitration clause was enough to bind the Grain Board under s.9. Gross J. rejected the argument that something more was needed);

9. Section 10 which turns on admiralty proceedings involving ships used for commercial purposes (see *Bridge Oil Ltd v Owners and/or Demise Charterers of the Ship Giuseppe di Vittorio, The Times*, November 10, 1997 on state succession and state immunity under the State Immunity Orders).

For our purposes the most important section is s.3. It provides that a state is not immune as respects proceedings relating to:

1. a commercial transaction entered into by the state; or

2. an obligation of the State which by virtue of a contract (whether a commercial transaction or not) falls to be performed wholly or partly in the United Kingdom.

"Commercial transactions" means: **12–005**

1. any contract for the supply of goods or services;

---

scope of the State any distinct legal entity capable of suing or being sued, even if entrusted with public functions including activities involving the exercise of sovereign authority. In return, however, the European Convention took an entirely new step, in giving to any such entity a particular immunity in respect of acts in the exercise of sovereign authority, identified with *acta jure imperii*. Previously, such an entity could only have any immunity if regarded as part of the State. (For an account of the history of the law on state immunity see *La Generale des Carrieres et des Mines v FG Hemisphere Associates LLC* [2012] UKPC 27).

2. any loan or other transaction for the provision of finance and any guarantee or indemnity in respect of any such transaction or of any other financial obligation; and

3. any other transaction or activity (whether commercial, industrial, financial, professional or other similar character) into which a state enters or in which it engages otherwise than in the exercise of sovereign authority. Contracts of employment between a state and an individual are expressly excluded from the definition.

In *Kuwait Airways Corp v Iraq Airways Co* [1995] 1 Lloyd's Rep. 25, Kuwait Airways took action against Iraqi Airways Co for the conversion of their aircraft which was seized by the latter. The House of Lords held by a majority of 3–2 that although Iraqi Airways enjoyed state immunity for its acts of taking the aeroplanes belonging to Kuwait Airways and removing them to Iraq as directed by the Iraqi government, that immunity dissipated following a resolution of the Iraqi government to dissolve Kuwait Airways and to transfer their assets to Iraqi Airways. The retention and use of the aircraft after that date were not acts done in the exercise of sovereign authority and were therefore not covered by state immunity. That resolution was clearly in breach of international law and the United Nations resolutions passed following the unlawful invasion of Kuwait by Iraq.

The Court of Appeal has held that whenever the issue of immunity arises under the Act, this question must be decided as a preliminary issue in favour of the claimant before the substantive action can proceed (*International Tin Council Appeals (Direct Actions)* [1988] 3 All E.R. 257).

12–006   Section 14(1) states that state immunity would apply to:

(b) the government of a foreign State; and

(c) any department of that government,

but not to any entity (referred to as a "separate entity") which is distinct from the executive organs of the government of the State and capable of suing or being sued.

Under s.14(2) a "separate entity" of the state is immune only if:

(a) the proceedings relate to anything done by it in the exercise of sovereign authority; and

(b) the circumstances are such that a state would have been immune from those proceedings. A "separate entity" is any entity which is distinct from the executive organs of the government of the state and capable of suing and being sued.

Section 14 was in issue in *Tsavliris Salvage (International) Ltd v The Grain Board of Iraq* [2008] EWHC 612 where it was argued that the Iraqi Grain Board was a separate entity of the state of Iraq. Gross J. held that although the Grain Board was established, owned and capitalised by the state of Iraq and not required to make a profit, it nevertheless had financial and administrative independence. Its relationship to the Iraqi government was more akin to that between an autonomous subsidiary and head office, rather than that of a branch office and head office (see also *Czarnikow Ltd v Rolimpex* [1979] A.C. 351). In addition, it had separate legal personality. A further question was whether it should nevertheless be entitled to immunity under s.14(2), in that the proceedings related to "anything done by it in the exercise of sovereign authority". As far as the judge was concerned, the making of the contract of salvage (Lloyd's Standard Form of Salvage Agreement 2000 Edition) by the Grain Board "did not have the character of and was not a governmental act".

In *La Generale des Carrieres et des Mines v FG Hemisphere Associates LLC* **12–007** [2012] UKPC 27, the Privy Council however stressed that a separate juridical status is not conclusive. Lord Mance said that an entity's constitution, control and functions remain relevant but

> "constitutional and factual control and the exercise of sovereign functions do not without more convert a separate entity into an organ of the State"

especially where a separate juridical entity is formed by the state for what are on the face of it commercial or industrial purposes, with its own management and budget, the strong presumption is that its separate corporate status should be respected, and that it and the state forming it should not have to bear each other's liabilities. It will take quite extreme circumstances to displace that presumption. The presumption will be displaced if in fact the entity has, despite its juridical personality, no effective separate existence and is in effect entirely controlled by the state. An important question is whether the affairs of the entity and the state are so closely intertwined and confused that the entity could not properly be regarded for any significant purpose as distinct from the state and vice versa.

Very often the issue of state immunity is invoked when the foreign state is not the defendant to the action but when the proceedings could affect property interests of the foreign state (*The Cristina* [1938] A.C. 485, for example). This is generally known as indirect impleading. While the Act is silent on this matter, the practical effect is that the position of indirect impleading before the Act is maintained (ss.2(4) and 6(4)).

On the right of any claimant or party invoking a process of enforcement **12–008** against the foreign state, the law as contained in s.13(2) is that the property of the state shall not be subject to any process for the enforcement of a judgment or arbitration award, or, in an action in rem, for its arrest, detention or sale. This immunity may be claimed not only by the foreign state but its central bank or monetary authority. Under s.13(3) injunctive relief or the issue of any process of enforcement may however be given with the written consent of the state concerned. This written consent may be contained in a prior agreement. The section goes on to state however that a jurisdiction clause will not suffice.

It is of course possible for the foreign state to waive its immunity. The fact of the waiver is a question of fact, not of law. It may be made in a variety of ways. The state may communicate its waiver through a treaty, a diplomatic communication or simply by voluntarily submitting to the proceedings of the local court. Voluntary submission however must not be taken to mean submission or agreeing to measures of execution. It should be noted that an application to stay proceedings in the local court on the ground of want of jurisdiction is not submission for this purpose.

Lastly it should be noted that "state" is given a narrow construction. It does not include constituent "states" in a federalised country. So, the state of New York in the USA is not a state for the purposes of the Act.[2]

Jurisdiction at Common Law

Presence of the defendant in the territory

12–009 Civil procedure is now largely governed by the Civil Procedure Rules 1998 (CPR) which replace the former Rules of the Supreme Court (RSC). This is a very large body of law and it should be said at the outset that our discussion will only focus on the allocation and distribution of jurisdiction by the High Court (including the Commercial Court) and not other civil courts (such as the County Court).

At common law, jurisdiction might be founded if the claim form is properly served on the defendant who is in the country (CPR 1998 r.6). The claim form may be served lawfully on the defendant who is present in the country however fleeting his or her visit. In *Maharanee of Baroda v Wildenstein* [1972] 2 Q.B. 283, the writ (or the claim form following the CPR 1998) was deemed to have been properly served on the defendant, a French national, who was in the country for the Ascot races. Once jurisdiction is founded, it will continue despite the fact that the defendant might have left the country subsequently.

The same principle will apply to legal entities. In *South India Shipping Corp v The Import Export Bank of Korea* [1985] 1 Lloyd's Rep. 413, the defendant bank was registered in Korea but had kept a small publicity office in London, it was held that this was sufficient for the purpose of service.

12–010 As far as the CPR[3] are concerned, service can be effected by:

(a) personal service[4];

(b) first class post, document exchange or other service which provides for delivery on the next business day[5];

(c) leaving it with the defendant's lawyer,[6] or place of business,[7] or if his address is not provided by the defendant the place of his residence or business place[8];

(d) fax or other means of electronic communication; or

---

[2] *R v Secretary of State for the Home Department* [2011] EWCA Civ 616, (the state of Pahang in Malaysia is not a state for the purposes of the Act); [2009] EWHC 2529 (Ch) (neither is Kentucky in the USA).

[3] Generally r.6.3.

[4] See r.6.5 which provides that in the majority of claims, the claim form must be served personally and a claim form is served personally on: (a) an individual by leaving it with that individual; (b) a company or other corporation by leaving it with a person holding a senior position within the company or corporation; or (c) a partnership (where partners are being sued in the name of their firm) by leaving it with: (i) a partner; or (ii) a person who, at the time of service, has the control or management of the partnership business at its principal place of business.

[5] See Practice Direction (PD) 6A.

[6] r.6.7.

[7] r.6.8.

[8] r.6.9.

(e) any method authorised by the court under r.6.15.

A company may be served:

(a) by any method referred to above; or

(b) by any of the methods of service permitted under the Companies Act 2006.

A limited liability partnership may be served:

(a) by any method referred to above; or

(b) by any of the methods of service permitted under the Companies Act 2006 as applied with modification by regulations made under the Limited Liability Partnerships Act 2000.

Submission to jurisdiction

The jurisdiction of the High Court would also be established if the defendant **12–011** submits voluntarily to its jurisdiction by accepting the claim form or making an appearance to defend the action in court. He will however not be deemed to have submitted to jurisdiction simply by appearing to apply for a stay of proceedings on the ground of want of jurisdiction (*Kuwait Airways Corp v Iraqi Airways* [1994] 1 Lloyd's Rep. 25). However, if he applies to stay proceedings on other grounds, for example, forum non conveniens, that act may be deemed as acknowledgement that the local court has jurisdiction (*The Messianiki Tolmi* [1984] 1 Lloyd's Rep. 266).

One of the most common ways of attracting jurisdiction is the express act of the defendant in making a contractual clause with the claimant to refer disputes exclusively to the jurisdiction of the English court. This is known as a choice of forum clause. It should be distinguished from a choice of law clause. The latter deals with the parties' chosen law to govern their legal relationship whilst the former attempts to place jurisdiction over their dispute with the courts of a particular country.

Submission by appearance may also occur in the following ways:

1. at common law, if the defendant's solicitor endorses on the writ (or claim form) an acknowledgement of service (*Manta Line v Sofianites* [1984] 1 Lloyd's Rep. 14). That has now been changed by the CPR—r.11 provides that the defendant will not be presumed to have submitted to jurisdiction if he acknowledges service of the claim form but makes an application to contest the court's jurisdiction. The situation in *Baghlaf Al Safer Factory Co v Pakistan National Shipping Co* [1998] 2 Lloyd's Rep. 229 should not re-surface. In that case, the shipowners' solicitors were instructed to accept service of the writ in circumstances where the shipowners were vigorously protesting against proceedings being brought in England but where the cargo owners were on the verge of arresting one of their ships. That acknowledgement of service was made under tremendous pressures. There was, as the Court of Appeal found, no implication that the shipowners were abandoning their insistence that the dispute should be litigated in Pakistan.

2. the defendant applying for an order requiring the claimant to give security for costs (*Lebonex Limon v Hong Kong Banking Corp* (1886) 33 Ch D 446).

3. the defendant applying for an order to set aside a default judgment and to order the claimant to deliver a statement of case (*Fry v Moore* (1889) 23 Q.B.D. 395). The application by the defendant to extend time for serving a defence does not however amount to submission according to the Court of Appeal in *Hewden Stuart v Gottwald* Unreported May 13, 1992.

4. the defendant consenting to the continuance of a freezing injunction (*Esal v Pujara* [1989] 2 Lloyd's Rep. 479). This must be distinguished from the rule in *Obikoya v Silvernorth, The Times*, July 6, 1983 where the defendant's appearance to challenge the application for a freezing injunction was held not to be submission.

12–012   It should also be noted that where the defendant has submitted to the court's jurisdiction in one matter, this could not be taken to mean that jurisdiction may be founded over other related actions which have yet to commence (*Adams v Cape Industries* [1991] 1 All E.R. 929).

In general, the claim form must be served on the defendant within jurisdiction, however, where the conditions in *Practice Direction* PD6B (see also r.6.36) are met, service can be made abroad.

Service out of jurisdiction—CPR PD6B

12–013   Service out of jurisdiction is possible either with or without permission of the court under the CPR 1998. Service without permission generally applies to claims to be brought against defendants domiciled in a country within the EU or EFTA. Service out of jurisdiction under the Brussels regime will be looked at later. The reason permission of the court is required for non-EU/EFTA countries is because traditionally, a country has no jurisdiction outside its territory. As far as non-EU/EFTA domiciliaries are concerned, permission to serve the claim form outside the jurisdiction pursuant to CPR r.6.36 is required. The claimant must first establish that each cause of action in respect of which he claims stands a reasonable prospect of success. CPR 6.37(1)(b) requires the claimant to state his belief that his claim has such a prospect. This is a relatively low threshold. In substance it is the same test as that of asking whether, on the written evidence, there is a serious issue to be tried (*Seaconsar Ltd v Bank Markazi* [1994] 1 A.C. 438; *Bas Capital Funding Corp v Mediaco Ltd* [2004] 1 Lloyd's L.R. 253) or of determining whether the claimant has a realistic prospect of succeeding on the claim (see also *De Molestina v Ponton* [2002] 1 Lloyd's Rep. 271). The claimant must then show that, in respect of each of his claims, he has a good arguable case that the claim falls within one or more of the types of claim specified in CPR PD6B. Waller L.J. in Canada *Trust v Stolzenberg (No.2)* [1998] 1 W.L.R. 547 described a good arguable case in these terms:

"Good arguable case" reflects in that context that one side has a much better argument on the material available. It is the concept which the phrase reflects on which it is important to concentrate i.e. of the court being satisfied or as satisfied as it can be having regard to the limitations which an interlocutory process imposes that factors exist which allow the court to take jurisdiction".

However making the right decision can be difficult at this early stage of litigation because there is usually insufficient evidence. Christopher Clarke J. in *Cherney v Deripaska* [2008] EWHC 1530 stressed that where it is virtually impossible to decide which side had a better argument given the limited facts, the temptation to require proof on a balance of probabilities should be resisted. That should not be undertaken at this stage of proceedings. Finally, the claimant must show that England is proper place for the trial. (r.6.37(3)) see below.

The grounds listed in PD6B include:

Claims made in relation to a contract

Where the claimant is instituting action against an overseas defendant in relation   **12–014**
to a contract made between themselves, special rules will apply before permission would be granted by the court for service outside the jurisdiction. PD6B para.3.1(6) provides that permission may be granted in such claims where the contract in issue:

(i) was made within the jurisdiction;

(ii) was made by or through an agent trading or residing within the jurisdiction;

(iii) is governed by English law; or

(iv) contains a term to the effect that the court shall have jurisdiction to determine any claim in respect of the contract.

PD6B para.3.1(7) allows the claimant to ask for permission to serve outside the jurisdiction if the claim is made in respect of a breach of contract committed within the jurisdiction. Finally, PD6B para 3.1(8) states that where the claimant seeks a court declaration that no contract existed, if that contract was presumed to exist it would satisfy the requirements of PD6B para.3.1(6), then the court may grant permission to serve abroad.

These provisions do not specify any particular remedies sought in relation to the contract—the claimant may seek to enforce, rescind, dissolve or annul the contract. He could also be granted permission to serve abroad for a claim for damages or some other relief in relation to the contract under this head of PD6B.

(i) Where the contract was made in jurisdiction The place where the   **12–015**
contract was made is to be determined by English contract law. English domestic legal principles on the communication of offer, acceptance and revocation, the postal rule, and rules on instantaneous communications will be used to determine where the contract was made. In *Brinkibon v Stalag Stahl* [1983] 2 A.C. 34 for example, permission to serve outside the jurisdiction was denied because the contract was made not in England but in Austria. There, an offer was made to the sellers by the buyers. The sellers in Austria had sent a telex to the buyers in England purportedly accepting the offer subject to some amendments to the original offer. This was accepted by the buyers who sent an advising telex to the

sellers. The sellers then decided to withdraw from the sale. The House of Lords held that the sellers' telex was a counter offer and not an acceptance as the buyers alleged. This counter offer was accepted by the buyers' advising telex which was received in Austria. The postal rule not being applicable to telex or other forms of instantaneous communications meant that the contract was made in Austria (the place where the telex was received) and not England (the place of transmission).

12–016   **(ii) Where the contract was made by or through an agent trading or residing within the jurisdiction**   This rule's original ego in ord.11 r.1(1)(d)(ii) RSC provided that where the contract was made by or through an agent trading or residing within the jurisdiction on behalf of a principal trading or residing out of jurisdiction, leave or permission to serve abroad may be granted by the court. The rationale was to ensure that the claimant who made a contract with a foreign principal with a presence in the jurisdiction could rely on that presence as a connecting factor to require the defendant to appear in the jurisdiction to answer allegations and claims founded on that contract.

It is readily seen that the CPR provision has done away with the clause "on behalf of a principal trading or residing out of jurisdiction". The new rule dispenses with the need to establish that the principal is in fact a foreign defendant—all that is required is that the defendant is acting through the embodiment of his agent within the jurisdiction. The new rule deems quite rightly that the agent is the extension of the defendant's presence.

12–017   **(iii) Where the contract is governed by English law**   Where the contract provides specifically that English law shall govern the contract or that it is ascertained that the applicable law of the contract is in fact English law, that choice made by the parties could also be taken by the court as constituting a sufficiently strong connecting factor to require the defendant to appear before an English court to respond to a claim made in relation to that contract. The question as to whether a contract is governed by English law is to be assessed according to the rules set out in the EU Reg.593/08 (Rome I).[9]

12–018   **(iv) Where the contract contains a term to the effect that the court shall have jurisdiction to determine any claim in respect of the contract**   This provides one of the strongest connecting factors between the defendant and the English forum. Although it is by no means mandatory that if there exists such a choice of forum agreement, the court will grant permission to the claimant to serve the claim form on the defendant abroad, where the court is satisfied that the parties have freely consented to using England and Wales as the place to have jurisdiction over the claim, it will usually give force to that agreement. It is however always a matter of judicial discretion whether permission would be granted.[10] Where the choice of forum points to another forum other than England, on the same basis, permission to serve abroad to bring the defendant into English jurisdiction would not normally be granted. In *Insurance Co "Ingosstrakh" Ltd v Latvian Shipping Co* [2000] I.L. Pr.164 the Court of Appeal refused to allow the applicant to serve out of jurisdiction because to do so would

---

[9] See *Gan Insurance Co Ltd v Tai Ping Insurance Co Ltd* [1999] C.L.C. 1270.
[10] *The Chaparral* [1968] 2 Lloyd's Rep. 158.

have been inconsistent with the choice of forum clause in the contract. A clause in the insurance contract provided that "all disputed claims" between the insurer and the insured were to be litigated in Moscow. The claimant (insurer) sought to recover sums received by the defendants from a third party. Langley J. at first instance considered that the exclusive jurisdiction clause should be construed narrowly and held therefore that the provision was only limited to disputes in relation to insurance monies paid out by the insurer and not monies received by the insured from a third party in which the insurer alleged to have an interest. This was rejected by the Court of Appeal as lacking commercial logic. The Court of Appeal held that the exclusive jurisdiction clause dealt with all the most common disputes between insurer and insured without limitation. In those circumstances, and given that neither party had any connection with England, leave to serve out was to be refused. Moreover, Soviet law was the proper or applicable law of the contract. The insurer's claims fell outside rules on service outside the jurisdiction.

(v) Where the claim is brought in respect of a breach of the contract committed within the jurisdiction It does not matter that the contract was 12–019 made within or without the jurisdiction. As long as the contract requires that performance is to be in England and the other party has failed to perform the obligation in England or has tendered defective performance in England, then permission to serve abroad may be granted. Much depends on the proper construction of the contract in deciding where the breach actually takes place. The connecting factor is the defendant's duty to tender proper performance of the contract within jurisdiction; as that duty is claimed to have been breached in jurisdiction, it provides a genuine link between the court, and the dispute and the defendant.

(vi) Where the claim is made for a declaration that no contract exists where, if the contract was found to exist, it would comply with the conditions set out in PD6B para.3.1(6) The problem with a claim for a declaration that 12–020 a contract is void ab initio is this—if the contract is indeed void, then the claim could simply not be a claim made in relation to a contract. On the other hand, what if there does indeed exist a contract between the parties, to disallow it at the time of commencement of the action as a claim made in relation to a contract would not be fair. The new PD6B para.3.1(8) overcomes the problem by relying on the notion of a putative contract. Under PD6B para.3.1(8), the court will examine the contract in question and decide whether it would satisfy the requirements set out in PD6B para.3.1(6) assuming that it was not void ab initio. If it meets those requirements despite the possibility of the contract being declared as non-existent subsequently, permission to serve out of the jurisdiction could be granted under this head.

Claims in tort

PD6B para.3.1(9) provides that where the claimant's action is founded on a tort 12–021 and the damage was sustained within the jurisdiction or the damage sustained was the result of an act committed within the jurisdiction, then permission to serve out of the jurisdiction may be granted by the court. The approach of the

English courts to how jurisdiction might be assumed on this basis is neatly expressed by the Court of Appeal in *Metall und Rohstoff v Donaldson Lufkin & Jenrette* [1990] Q.B. 391:

"Where some significant damage has occurred in England or damage has resulted from substantial and efficacious acts committed by the defendants in England, English jurisdiction would have been founded. This is regardless of the fact that there are other related substantial and efficacious acts having been committed elsewhere".

Accordingly, it was held that where the defendant who was domiciled in the state of New York in the United States was alleged to have induced its subsidiary to breach contracts with the claimant resulting in financial loss and the latter's accounts being closed in England, an English court could be seised under this rule.

It should be noted that the "damage" required in PD6B para.3.1(9) to have been sustained in the jurisdiction meant harm (whether economic or physical) that had been sustained by the claimant and not the damage that completed the cause of action in tort. In *Booth v Phillips* [2004] EWHC 1437, the claimant was the widow of an engineer who was killed in an accident whilst working abroad. The engineer was employed by the defendant. The widow applied for permission to serve the claim form out of jurisdiction on the defendants. The defendants argued that permission should not be granted because Jordan was the more appropriate forum. The claimant argued that she had sustained damage within English jurisdiction in the form of the loss of her dependency on her husband and the payment of his funeral expenses. The court held that her loss of financial dependency on her husband was damage that was sustained in England where she lived. Additionally, her husband's funeral expenses constituted damage sustained in England. The court rejected the defendants' argument that the damage in PD6B para.3.1(9) should mean where the alleged tort was committed or where the damage which determined the tort was first caused.

Miscellaneous

12–022   The other heads of jurisdiction under PD6B will not usually apply to an international trade transaction or dispute. They refer generally to matters in relation to property, trusts, taxation, etc.

Doctrine of forum conveniens

12–023   The court will not give permission unless it is satisfied that England and Wales is the proper place in which to bring the claim or the forum conveniens (r.6.36). This is particularly problematic when there exists another relevant forum for the same set of facts as was held in *Seaconsar Far East Ltd v Bank Markazi Jombouri Islami Iran* [1994] 1 Lloyd's Rep. 1.

In deciding whether England and Wales is the "proper place in which to bring the claim", the court will consider factors such as the nationality and residence of the parties, the witnesses and where they are located, the nature of the dispute, any applicable law of the contract, any legal or practical difficulties, evidence and expenses, etc.[11] These factors may at times even supersede any choice of jurisdiction agreement (*Alliance Bank JSC v Aquanta Corp* [2011] EWHC 3281 (Comm)). In *Evans Marshall v Bertola SA* [1973] 1 W.L.R. 349, for example, leave to serve out under the now defunct ord.11 r.1 R.S.C. was granted despite the existence of a choice of forum clause in favour of the Spanish courts because most of the factors in the case were connected with England. The court placed considerable importance on the fact that all the witnesses were English, the claim was based substantially in England, delivery of the goods was to be made in England and the Spanish civil procedure was much slower than the English system. Conversely but based on the same principle, in *Alliance Bank JSC v Aquanta Corp*, the English court did not think it should be seised despite the presence of an English jurisdiction clause. Almost all the events took place in Kazakhstan. Kazakh law might have an important role to play; almost all the documents were in Kazakhstan; there had been proceedings in Kazakhstan which had resulted in the conviction of one of the defendants and important findings of fact; the evidence to establish conspiracy would be overwhelmingly in Kazakhstan; and the appeal court in Kazakhstan had plainly encouraged the bringing of civil proceedings which would overlap the subject matter of the proposed English proceedings. These were overwhelming factors justifying the court's decision to depart from the English jurisdiction clause.

In *Mackender v Feldia* [1967] 2 Q.B. 590, however, the court was careful to add that judicial discretion must be exercised in the light of international judicial comity. This means that the court should avoid making any judgment as regards the quality of justice abroad. Indeed, the Privy Council stressed in *AK Investment CJSC v Kyrgyz Mobil Tel Ltd* [2011] UKPC 7 the court should not pronounce on the independence of a foreign judicial system but if there is cogent evidence that there is a real risk that justice will not be obtained in the foreign court by reason of incompetence or lack of independence or corruption, the court may be minded to grant permission to serve abroad.[12] Of course, if it can be shown that justice "will not" be obtained that will weigh more heavily in the exercise of the discretion in the light of all other circumstances.

As the grant of permission to serve the claim form out of jurisdiction is **12–024** discretionary, the court could also take into account evidence of the parties' bona fides. It is however not easily proved that bad faith is present. In *Bristow Helicopters Ltd v Sikorsky Aircraft Corp* [2004] EWHC 401, the personal representatives of a deceased helicopter crew applied to have proceedings commenced by B and S in England stayed. They had argued that B had contrived with S to force them to litigate in England. It was alleged that if they were to litigate in England, they could be barred from certain remedies in the United States. Morison J. however held that there was nothing in English law that prevented a litigant from "fixing" the timing and venue of litigation in a potential

---

[11] See e.g. the recent case of *Peer International Corp v Termidor Music Publishers Ltd* (November 22, 2004, Ch.D.) where the court refused to grant a stay of English proceedings accepting the evidence that Cuban proceedings would be more inconvenient, lengthy and uncertain. Although some aspects of the case would be better tried in Cuba, the court was not prepared to accept jurisdiction for certain aspects and to pass on the others to the foreign jurisdiction. Judge Weeks QC was not convinced that the doctrine of forum conveniens permitted this. In *Golden Ocean Group v Salgaocar Mining* [2011] EWHC 56 (Comm) the High Court stressed that personal issues such as the party's health are not relevant to the question of forum conveniens.

[12] See also *Ferrexpo AG v Gilson Investments Ltd* [2012] EWHC 721 (Comm).

transnational dispute. The fact that the claimants were fully entitled to commence proceedings in England in the light of the close connection the dispute has with England and the fact that the applicable law was obviously English law, the burden on the applicants to show that B and S acted improperly was especially high. They had failed to discharge that burden.

Stay of proceedings

12–025 Closely allied to the application to serve abroad is the defendant's right of challenge when there is another country's court which would be a more appropriate forum. For example, where the defendant has instituted action against the claimant in South Africa at the same time the claimant starts proceedings against the defendant in England, the defendant can resist the English court's jurisdiction over the dispute by applying for a stay of the English court's proceedings on the grounds of forum non conveniens (that is to say, that the English court is not the forum conveniens for the dispute and should therefore decline jurisdiction). In *Spiliada*, Lord Goff laid down the following guidelines for the stay to be granted:

> "the burden resting on the defendant is not just to show that England is not the natural or appropriate forum but to establish that there is another available forum which is clearly or distinctly more appropriate . . . [where] the connection of the defendant with the English forum is fragile one (for example, if he is served with proceedings during a short visit to this country), it should be all the easier for him to prove that there is another clearly more appropriate forum for the trial overseas.
>
> . . . [t]he court will look first to see what factors there are which point in the direction of another forum . . . So it is for connecting factors . . . that the court must first .look; and these will include not only factors affecting the convenience or expense (such as the availability of witnesses), but also other factors such as the law governing the relevant transaction . . . and the places where the parties respectively reside or carry on business.
>
> . . . If the court concludes at that stage that there is no other available forum which is clearly more appropriate for the trial of the action, it will ordinarily refuse a stay.
>
> . . . If, however, the court concludes at that stage that there is some other forum which prima facie is clearly more appropriate for the trial of the action, it will ordinarily grant a stay unless there are circumstances by reason of which justice requires that a stay should nevertheless not be granted. In this inquiry, the court will consider all circumstances of the case, including circumstances which go beyond those taken into account when considering connecting factors with the other jurisdiction. One such factor can be the fact, if established objectively by cogent evidence, that the [claimant] will not obtain justice in the foreign jurisdiction . . . [but here] the burden shifts to the [claimant]".

An illustration of how these connecting factors are applied is seen in:

Governor and Company of the Bank of Ireland v State Bank of India [2011] NIQB 22 **12–026**
Facts:
G was the confirming bank in a transaction involving the sale of goods by a United Kingdom-based seller to an India-based buyer. S was the issuing bank for the letter of credit and had agreed to reimburse G for payments made to the seller. However, when G sought reimbursement, S refused to pay. S's defence was that there were discrepancies in the documents. It issued proceedings in India against G, the buyer and the seller, seeking a declaration that the documents did not comply with the requirements in the letter of credit. G subsequently began proceedings in Northern Ireland claiming damages from S for breach of contract. The primary question was whether India or Northern Ireland was the appropriate forum. If India was the more appropriate forum, the court should stay proceedings in Northern Ireland.
Held:
The court placed much emphasis on the place of performance of the contract—the court concluded that the characteristic performance of the contract was the reimbursement on receipt of the appropriate documents. Which party was to effect that characteristic performance? It was obvious that the issuing bank was that party and as its principal place of business is India, India was the place of performance of the contract. The court did not accept that civil proceedings in India would be so unduly lengthy that it would cause an injustice. Taking the connecting factors together, the court concluded that on a balance of convenience, despite the fact that the witnesses were largely in Northern Ireland, a stay of proceedings should be granted. After all, India was the country with which the contract is most closely associated given that it was the place of performance of the contract, the Indian proceedings were already dealing with the same issues and involving the same parties and the matter was advancing steadily without undue delay.

No one connecting factor should be taken as pivotal—all the circumstances should be assessed objectively and be given appropriate weighting.[13] Assessing the connecting factors objectively would entail the court taking into account, not only all evidence of fact, but also any common law presumptions on the legal action—for example, the common law might presume the damage or loss to have been caused in a particular place. That said, the court would nevertheless exercise its discretion in deciding whether there are more connecting factors pointing to another forum.[14] That discretion includes the judge's discretion in allocating the appropriate weight to the different factors put to him. Indeed, as the Court of Appeal confirmed in *DSM Anti-Infectives BV v Smithkline Beecham Plc* [2004] EWCA Civ 1199, matters of weight were for the judgment of the judge exercising his discretion and the appeal court would rarely interfere with that judgment. In that case, it was argued that the lower court had not given sufficient weight to the likelihood of conflicting judgments if a stay of English proceedings was not granted when the proceedings in the United States were progressing.

---

[13] This was stressed in the recent case of *Royal & Sun Alliance Insurance Plc v Retail Brand Alliance Inc* [2004] EWHC 2139 where although it was recognised that English law might be relevant to the construction of the master policy, other commercial and legal connecting factors clearly pointed to New York. As there was no evidence that New York law would not be able adequately to deal with the construction of the document, the forum conveniens was New York. See also *Golden Ocean Group v Salgaocar Mining* [2011] EWHC 56 (Comm).

[14] See *Don King v Lennox Lewis* [2004] EWCA Civ 1329 where the court considered that although the common law presumes the tort of libel to have been committed at the place where the libellous statement was published, that did not prevent the court from taking a more "open textured" approach in exercising its discretion vis-à-vis internet libel (where a separate tort was committed every time the libellous statement was downloaded).

12–027   The court will also consider the legitimate personal or juridical advantage of the claimant which might be lost if the stay of proceedings was granted to the defendant (*MacShannon v Rockware Glass Ltd* [1978] A.C. 795) but that factor does not carry any special weight. The court will always assess the entirety of the circumstances. In *Owners of the Ship Herceg Novi v Owners of the Ship Ming Galaxy (The Herceg Novi)* [1998] 2 Lloyd's Rep. 454, the court held that the fact that if English proceedings were allowed, the claim would have been subject to a higher limitation of liability provision in the Convention on the Limitation of Liability or Maritime Claims 1976 and not the lower limits set out in the Convention Relating to the Limitation of the Liability of Owners of Seagoing Ships 1957 was not to be treated as conferring a juridical advantage.

On the other hand, the House of Lords held in *Lubbe v Cape Plc* [2000] 1 W.L.R. 1545, that a stay would not be granted for the following grounds:

- there was no legal aid available to the claimants in South Africa, unlike in England;

- there was little possibility of a contingency fee arrangement open to the claimants in South Africa;

- the South African system did not have developed procedures for dealing with group actions.[15] It should however not be thought that the fact there is no legal aid or contingency arrangement available in the foreign forum is necessarily a cause to refuse a stay (*Conolly v RTZ Corp* [1997] 3 W.L.R. 373), provided substantial justice is available abroad.

The court would also consider the ability of the claimant to enforce a judgment to be an important factor in determining the personal and juridical advantage a forum proffers the claimant. In *Inter-Tel Inc v OCIS Plc* [2004] EWHC 2269, for example, the competing jurisdictions were Arizonan and English and whilst all the connecting factors pointed to Arizona, the court permitted the claimant (an Arizonan company) to bring proceedings in England to restrain the defendant (established in England) from making insulting and threatening telephone calls and emails. The reason given was that enforcement was not available to the claimant in any meaningful sense in Arizona. All it could expect to obtain in Arizona was an empty judgment. As the defendant was based in England and the threatening communications were sent from England, the restraining order would really be best obtained in England.[16]

12–028   Where there is a foreign jurisdiction clause, the defendant may rely on it to secure a stay of proceedings. However that does not necessarily mean that the English court must stay its proceedings. The case is more compelling if it is an exclusive jurisdiction clause but that too in itself is not decisive. Naturally, whether the clause is an exclusive or non-exclusive clause is a matter of construction. In *Celltech v Medimmune* [2004] EWHC 1522 (Pat), for example, despite the fact that the clause made no mention of the exclusivity of English jurisdiction, the court concluded that it was necessarily one of exclusive

---

[15] That ground alone though would not have constituted a ground for refusing a stay.
[16] See also *International Credit and Investment Co (Overseas) Ltd v Sheikh Kamal Ad Ham* [1999] I.L.Pr. 302.

jurisdiction on the circumstances.[17] What is the effect of a non-exclusive jurisdiction clause? In *Breams Trustee v Upstream Downstream Simulation Services Inc* [2004] EWHC 211, the parties had entered into a non-exclusive English jurisdiction agreement. The court held that although, technically speaking, the defendants were free to litigate in Florida (instead of in England), when the claimants had instituted action in the chosen jurisdiction, England, the defendants were bound to accept that selection under the jurisdiction agreement. The court would not relieve the defendants of that obligation by granting a stay of English proceedings or setting aside service out of jurisdiction unless there were strong and compelling reasons for doing so. It was set out in *The Eleftheria* [1970] P. 94 that the English court will always give effect to the clause subject to the claimant's showing that there is strong cause for not doing so. Some of the factors the court may consider include:

- in what country the evidence on the issues of fact is situated, or more readily available, and the effect of that on the relative convenience and expense of trial as between the English and foreign courts;

- whether the law of the foreign court applies and if so, whether it differs materially from English law;

- the extent of the parties' connection with the foreign country;

- whether the defendant genuinely desires trial in the foreign country or is only seeking procedural advantages; and

- whether the claimant would be prejudiced by having to sue in the foreign court because they would be deprived of security for their claim, be unable to enforce any judgment obtained, be faced with a time bar not applicable in England or be unlikely to get a fair trial for political, racial, religious or other reasons.

The fact that foreign proceedings might have started and have been progressing elsewhere is not determinative of the court's exercise of discretion (*OT Africa Line Ltd v Magic Sportwear Corp* [2005] 1 Lloyds Rep. 252; *DSM Anti-Infectives BV v Smithkline Beecham Plc* [2004] EWCA Civ 1199). The issue of staying proceedings, under the common law, is always a matter of judicial discretion.

Sinochem International Oil (London) Ltd v Mobil Sales and Supply Corp [2000] 1 Lloyd's Rep. 670   **12–029**
Facts:
Sinochem (London) contracted to sell a cargo of crude oil to Mobil (Delaware) on FOB terms. Mobil (Delaware) refused to pay arguing that they were contractually entitled to set off against the price, monies owed to their affiliate Mobil (HK) by Sinochem (Beijing), an affiliate of Sinochem (London). The contract between Sinochem (London) and Mobil (Delaware) contained an English applicable law and jurisdiction clause, whilst the contract between Sinochem (Beijing) and Mobil (HK) contained a Chinese law and jurisdiction clause. The issue for the Court of Appeal was whether English proceedings

---

[17] See also *DSM Anti-Infectives BV v Smithkline Beecham Plc* [2004] EWCA Civ 1199 and *Craft Enterprises (International) Ltd v AXA Insurance Co* [2004] EWCA Civ 171; and *Aizkir Navigation Inc v Al Wathba National Insurance Co PSC* [2011] EWHC 3940 (Comm).

commenced by Sinochem (London) should be stayed on the basis of the various related actions and the Chinese law and jurisdiction clause in the contract between Mobil (HK) and Sinochem (Beijing).
Held:
The court could, applying the rule in *Re Harrods (Buenos Aires) Ltd* [1992] Ch. 72 if it deemed appropriate, stay English proceedings pending litigation in Hong Kong of the issues under the contract between Mobil (HK) and Sinochem (Beijing). However, it was not sufficient that there was the possibility of the multiplicity proceedings. There must be strong reasons of justice why Sinochem (London) should be relieved of their contractual right to litigate disputes under English law and jurisdiction. It was clear that Sinochem (London) and Mobil (Delaware) had entered into the English law and jurisdiction agreement in the light of the contract between their affiliates in China. That being the case, the presumed intention of the parties must have been to subject their contract to English law and jurisdiction despite what was agreed between their affiliates.

In *Baghlaf Al Safer Factory Co v Pakistan National Shipping Co* [1998] 2 Lloyd's Rep. 229, the court was asked whether the fact that the claim in the forum conveniens or the chosen jurisdiction (in that case, Pakistan) had become time barred should influence an application for a stay of English proceedings. The Court of Appeal considered two Commercial Court cases, *Citi-March Ltd v Neptune Orient Lines* [1996] 1 W.L.R. 1367 and *The MC Pearl* [1997] 1 Lloyd's Rep. 556, and held the test to be:

> "where the [claimant] has acted reasonably in commencing proceedings in England and in allowing time to expire in the agreed foreign jurisdiction, a stay of English proceedings should only be granted on terms that the defendant waives the time bar in the foreign jurisdiction".

12–030   Whether the claimant has acted reasonably in bringing the action in England depends on various questions of fact, including any legitimate advantage he was hoping to obtain. In that case, it was to secure a higher financial limit under English law as against Pakistani law.

In cases involving questions of law with important and pressing consequences, the English court may decide not to stay its own proceedings despite the fact that foreign court proceedings have been instituted. In *AWB (Geneva) SA v North America Steamships Ltd* [2007] EWCA Civ 739 the Court of Appeal held that proceedings should not be stayed pending the outcome of insolvency proceedings in Canada because the contract terms in dispute, the International Swaps and Derivatives Association master agreement, could have serious ramifications for the financial markets. Thus, the sooner the issues raised were determined the better. It should however be noted that the insolvency proceedings in Canada were not identical in nature to the dispute in England over the meaning of the contract. They were only related actions. Additionally, there was no exclusive jurisdiction clause subjecting a dispute over the contract to the Canadian courts.

Stay of foreign proceedings or anti-suit injunctions

12–031   As far as English law is concerned, the English court has the power not only to stay its own proceedings but to issue an injunction against any party from instituting or continuing proceedings in a foreign court. This power of the court can be exercised either as being founded on an independent cause of action or as the court's jurisdiction to make ancillary orders (*Masri v Consolidated Contractors International Co SAL* [2008] EWCA Civ 625). Ancillary orders are orders given by the court to support the integrity and expediency of its proceedings. Anti-suit injunctions, in principle, should not be granted in cases where the EU rules apply *Turner* (C-159/02) [2004] E.C.R. I-3565; see also *The Front Comor* [2007] UKHL 4 where the issue as to whether the English court can grant an anti-suit injunction where one party is threatening to sue or suing in another Member State in breach of an arbitration agreement was discussed[18]). The following rules however are only applicable where the Brussels regime (or the Lugano Convention) does not apply.

Clearly this is a form of indirect interference with the judicial sovereignty of another state and as such great care must be exercised before a stay of foreign proceedings or anti-suit injunction is granted. The case in point is *Société Nationale Industrielle Aerospatiale v Lee Kui Jak* [1987] A.C. 871 where Lord Goff set forth the following principles:

1. the stay should only be granted where the "ends of justice" require it;

2. the stay is not issued against the foreign court (that would be tantamount to direct interference with the sovereignty of another state) but against the litigant/s;

3. the stay should be an appropriate and effective remedy against the person; and

4. any such power must be exercised with caution.

It is not unusual for applicants to plead that the quality of justice abroad is not satisfactory and as such the matter should proceed in England and an anti-suit injunction be granted. The court would be especially careful when this is pleaded and would not consider simply that as the overseas court does not apply the rules of fundamental freedom as they would be applied in England, that would a presumption of poor quality of justice. In *Al-Bassam v Al-Bassam* [2004] EWCA Civ 857 the trial judge had expressed concern that although there was no good ground to prevent the claimant from proceeding in Saudi Arabia, a consequent judgment from that country might not subsequently qualify for recognition and enforcement in England because it would not meet the requirements of the Human Rights Act 1998. The Court of Appeal, in allowing the appeal in part, held that an English court's restraint of a party from continuing foreign proceedings could not and should not be founded on its perception as to the fairness or unfairness of the proceedings in the other jurisdiction where the country in which the party sought to sue was not itself bound by the European Convention on Human Rights. The court went on to emphasise that the question of fairness in these circumstances could not arise until after the foreign judgment had been given. By looking at it before the event, the Court of Appeal considered that the lower court had acted prematurely and that had flawed the reasoning behind the granting of the anti-suit injunction. This is particularly interesting because the grant of an anti-suit injunction will invariably entail assessing the quality of justice abroad and whilst, it should not admit conjecture and

---

[18] See para.12–046.

guesswork, the very high likelihood (if any, and it is not argued that that is the case here) of a failure to recognise and enforce the foreign judgment in English jurisdiction must surely be significant. This case serves as a reminder that the rules in *Aerospatiale* should be applied with circumspection.

12–032   As far as the conditions for an anti-suit injunction to be given, the House of Lords set out the following exhaustive list:

1. England is one of the available for a for the action or dispute in question;

2. the party by bringing the action abroad has infringed a legal or equitable right of the other party not to be sued abroad; and

3. it is unconscionable for the party to sue the other abroad.[19]

It should however be noted that whilst these categories are closed, the content and detail of the law are constantly evolving. Indeed, it was held in *Airbus Industrie GIE v Patel* [1998] 2 W.L.R. 686 by the House of Lords that the above guidelines should be applied with the principle of international judicial comity in mind. In that case, it was argued before the English court that Texas was a forum non conveniens and proceedings in Texas would be oppressive to the defendant and the claim should have been brought in India which provided the closest connection to the claim. However, the House of Lords pointed out that judicial comity required that before an English court could interfere, it must be shown that the English court should have a sufficient interest in or in connection with the matter in question. That was not present in the case and as such, no stay of foreign proceeding may be granted.

Judicial comity, however, does not mean that the English court would not grant an anti-suit injunction simply because proceedings have commenced in a foreign court and the foreign court had refused to stay its own proceedings on the grounds that there was an exclusive jurisdiction agreement. After all there may be serious doubts as to whether the exclusive jurisdiction agreement had been freely entered into or whether the exclusive jurisdiction agreement actually extended to the subject matter of the claim abroad. In *Akai Pty Ltd v People Insurance Co Ltd* [1998] 1 Lloyd's Rep. 90, PIC issued an insurance policy to Akai which contained an English exclusive jurisdiction clause. Akai began proceedings in Australia and England. On December 23, 1996 the High Court of Australia, reversing the New South Wales Court, refused to stay the Australian proceedings on the ground that the exclusive jurisdiction clause was contrary to Australian statute law and therefore void. Thomas J. however refused to stay the English proceedings and granted an anti-suit injunction restraining Akai from pursuing the Australian proceedings. The judge's comments, which were subsequently approved by the Court of Appeal in *Donohue v Armco Inc* [2000] 1 Lloyd's Rep. 579 where a similar situation arose, are particularly noteworthy:

---

[19] In *A/S D/S Svendborg v Wansa* [1996] 2 Lloyd's Rep. 559, it was clearly unconscionable for the defendant to insist on action in Sierra Leone when he had boasted that he had the ability to manipulate the Sierra Leone legal system to his advantage. That was evidence of vexation and oppression and even though the claimant had submitted to jurisdiction in Sierra Leone, an anti-suit injunction should be granted.

"Finally I have taken into account the fact that in refusing to stay these proceedings, the effect may be that there is simultaneous litigation here and in New South Wales with the inevitable and undesirable consequences that follow. Although the Court will always lean against that, it is the consequence of Akai not abiding by a freely negotiated jurisdiction clause; it would not be just that they should be entitled to take advantage of their own breach of contract to achieve this result".

Where there is an exclusive English jurisdiction clause, the court may grant an anti-suit injunction to prevent the party from suing abroad thereby ensuring that he does not breach his contract with the defendant.[20] The position is quite different from that held by EU Regulation on Jurisdiction and the Recognition and Enforcement of Judgments in Civil and Commercial Matters 2000 (and also, the Lugano Convention) where there is no room for the exercise of judicial discretion. The court shall prorogate jurisdiction accordingly (that is to say, decline jurisdiction in favour of the court/s chosen by the parties—art.23 of the Regulation).[21] **12–033**

Where there is an *exclusive* jurisdiction clause subjecting the dispute to English jurisdiction or English arbitration,[22] the court may hold that this is an indication that it would satisfy the ends of justice to enforce the jurisdiction clause and stay foreign proceedings in favour of the relevant English proceedings (*The Chaparral* [1968] 2 Lloyd's Rep. 158 and *The Angelic Grace* [1995] 1 Lloyd's Rep. 87). It might also be observed that the "continuing or bringing of foreign proceedings in breach of contract may well in itself be vexatious or oppressive", according to Staughton L.J. in *Sohio Gatoil* [1989] 1 Lloyd's Rep. 588.

This is not to say that the exercise of judicial discretion is the exception rather than the rule when the application is made at common law. As Rix J. said in *Credit Suisse First Boston (Europe) Ltd v MLC (Bermuda) Ltd* [1999] 1 All E.R. (Comm) 237:

" . . . [In] the case of an exclusive jurisdiction clause the jurisdiction to enforce by injunction is discretionary and is not to be exercised as a matter of course, but good reason needs to be shown why it should not be exercised; [and . . . in other cases the ultimate test is that of the interests of justice]. That does not of course mean that in the former case the interests of justice are not sought, merely that as a general rule and barring good reason to the contrary it is thought to be just that the agreement of an exclusive jurisdiction clause should be upheld".

Clearly, as a matter of judicial discretion, an application for an anti-suit injunction based on the presence of a jurisdiction clause becomes less cogent **12–034**

---

[20] See generally *OT Africa Line Ltd v Magic Sportwear Corp* [2004] EWHC 2441; also Peel, "Exclusive jurisdiction agreements: priority and pragmatism in the conflict of laws" [1998] L.M.C.L.Q. 182.

[21] See discussion on art.23 below paras 12–082—12–090.

[22] In *Tryggingarfelagio Foroyar P/F v CPT Empresas Maritimas SA* [2011] EWHC 589 (Admlty) for example, an antisuit injunction was given to prevent the pursuit of proceedings in Chile where it was established that the agreement between the parties was on the BIMCO Wreckhire form containing an English law and arbitration clause.

where the clause is merely a non-exclusive jurisdiction clause. In *Royal Bank of Canada v Co-operative Centrale Raiffeisen-Boerenleenbank BA* [2004] EWCA Civ 7 where the court emphasised the presumed intention behind a non-exclusive jurisdiction clause to be the contemplation of "the possibility of virtually simultaneous trials with all the additional burdens . . . [of] parallel proceedings". The anti-suit injunction was thus not granted.

The exclusive jurisdiction clause will always be trumped by evidence that the "ends of justice" required that the litigation be conducted at some other jurisdiction. The House of Lords in *Donohue v Armco* [2001] UKHL 64 reminded the parties that it should not be lost sight of that the matter of granting the anti-suit injunction is matter of judicial discretion despite the presence of an exclusive jurisdiction clause. The court held that where there are many litigants and competing claims, the court would give much emphasis to where it is most appropriate and fair to hold a composite trial—that is to say, if there are many related claims and most of these are best heard in country X, despite the fact that the dispute in question is to subject to an exclusive English jurisdiction clause, the court would not enforce it on the ground that it would not serve the ends of justice criterion laid down in *Aerospatiale*.

The second principle in relation to the grant of an anti suit injunction to support an exclusive English jurisdiction clause is this—if an English exclusive jurisdiction clause is present, the party seeking to avoid its effect must show *strong* cause for being permitted to do so. However, the words "show good reason" seem to have crept into the case law by way of illustrating the fact that the court's jurisdiction to grant an injunction is discretionary. They were used by Millett L.J. in *The Angelic Grace* [1995] 1 Lloyd's Rep. 87 when the Court of Appeal was concerned to turn the tide of judicial non-intervention which was tending to give greater primacy to "the tender feelings of a foreign court" (where proceedings had been started in defiance of an exclusive jurisdiction clause) than to the bargain made by the parties. Buxton L.J. in *Mediterranean Shipping Co SA v Atlantic Container Line AB* (CAT December 3, 1998) commented that:

"In my judgment when Millett L.J. referred to 'good reason' he was referring to good reasons not to grant injunctive relief, that is, discretionary relief. No doubt what His Lordship said is an indication that the court should tend to consider that relief should be granted unless the circumstances are unusual, and should look with care at the reasons given for not granting relief. But that, in my judgment, is as far as it goes".

12–035   In *Andrew Beazley v Horizon Offshore Contractors Inc* [2004] EWHC 2555 (a case on the stay of English proceedings rather than for the grant of an anti-suit injunction) it was argued that as a matter of judicial comity, the court should exercise its discretion not to enforce the English jurisdiction clause. Judge Chambers QC said that in international commerce, jurisdiction agreements could not be seen as offending the sensibilities of a foreign court. The foreign courts must have naturally foreseen and expected that international commercial matters might be litigated outside their jurisdiction as a result of a binding jurisdiction agreement between the litigants. A foreign tribunal which is cognisant of the practicalities of international commerce and the need for international litigation cannot afford to take offence to their nationals participating in litigation elsewhere.

In *OT Africa Line v Magic Sportswear* [2005] EWCA Civ 710 the Court of Appeal, whilst recognising that there is a doctrine of international comity, said that does not mean that the English court would not intervene to prevent a litigant from bringing foreign proceedings which are oppressive or vexatious, such as where, for instance, they are brought in breach of a binding jurisdiction clause. Longmore L.J. commented:

> "[T]he maintenance of the principle that parties should be free to choose the courts where their disputes are to be resolved must be of paramount importance and cannot be reduced to a mere legal aspiration".

The third governing principle is that the applicants for an anti-suit injunction relying on their rights under an English exclusive jurisdiction clause should apply promptly for the relief they seek.[23] An injunction is an equitable remedy and it is trite law that equity will not come to the assistance of those who sleep on their rights. In *The Angelic Grace* [1995] 1 Lloyd's Rep. 87 Millett L.J. articulated this principle when he said that in such a case the English Court need feel no diffidence in granting the injunction "provided that it is sought promptly and before the foreign proceedings are too far advanced". In *Donohue v Armco Inc* [2000] 1 Lloyd's Rep. 579, the majority of the Court of Appeal found that the applicant had not been guilty of delay because he had had to deal with ancillary proceedings instituted in four other jurisdictions. It is a question of fact whether the applicant was guilty of unreasonable delay.[24]

The judicial discretion referred to in the *Aerospatiale* guidelines will thus also **12–036** mean that the English court would grant an anti-suit injunction if the litigant is proceeding abroad in an attempt to re-litigate issues already determined by the English court (*Masri v Consolidated Contractors International Co SAL* [2008] EWCA Civ 625).

Jurisdiction under the EC Regulation on Jurisdiction and the Recognition and Enforcement of Judgments in Civil and Commercial Matters 2000

On September 27, 1968, the original six members of the EEC made a treaty **12–037** providing for the mutual recognition and enforcement of judgments given in any of their courts as far as these judgments relate to civil and commercial matters. That Convention also provided for specific rules on how jurisdiction is to be allocated between the Contracting States. The intention was to reduce the problem of forum shopping within the EEC, which the original Member States clearly saw as antithetical to the spirit of judicial cooperation. As far as English law is concerned, the new regime attempted to do away with the doctrine of

---

[23] On whether and to what extent damages could be claimed for breach of an exclusive jurisdiction clause, see *Union Discount Co Ltd v Zoller (Costs)* [2001] EWCA Civ 1755 and *A/S D/S Svendborg v Akar* [2003] EWHC 797. Also, Tan and Yeo, "Breaking Promises to Litigate in a Particular Forum: Are Damages an appropriate remedy?" [2003] L.M.C.L.Q. 435; and Tham, "Damages for Breach of English Jurisdiction Clauses: More than Meets the Eye" [2004] L.M.C.L.Q. 46.

[24] Although on appeal ([2001] UKHL 64) the Court of Appeal's decision was overturned, this point was not dealt with by the House of Lords and should, it is submitted, be treated as correct.

forum non conveniens in relation to defendants who are domiciled in an EU[25] Member State. The United Kingdom acceded to it in 1978 and it was incorporated into English law through the Civil Jurisdiction and Judgments Act 1982.

The Lugano Convention modelled after the Brussels Convention applies to Member States of the EU and the EFTA.

It was intended right from the outset of the drafting of the Brussels Convention in the 1960s that revision of its provisions needs to be made as EU integration becomes ever closer. In 1998 the EU launched into a formal revision programme of the Convention. That has finally resulted in the publication of the EU Council Regulation on Jurisdiction and the Recognition and Enforcement of Judgments in Civil and Commercial Matters (hereafter referred to as "Regulation 44/2001") in 2000. It came into force on March 1, 2002.

12–038   Article 66 provides that the Regulation shall apply only to legal proceedings instituted and to documents formally drawn up or registered as authentic instruments after the date it comes into force. What is an "authentic document"? Article 57 deems it to be a document which has been formally drawn up or registered as an authentic instrument in a Member State and is enforceable there. It would normally refer to any judicial instrument or certification issued indicating a certain procedural requirement, consequence or entitlement. It should bear the seal or authority of a court or other competent authority in that Member State.

Although it was originally conceived that a new Treaty would be made to replace the Brussels Convention, it became possible with the entry into force of the Treaty of Amsterdam on May 1, 1999 for the reform to be expedited by means of a Council Regulation. A Council Regulation is directly applicable and is of universal application. That means that it does not need to be "transposed" into national law before it becomes effective.

The Council Regulation does not affect the general operation of the Lugano Convention.

It might also be mentioned that as far as intra-UK jurisdiction (jurisdiction between Scotland, Northern Ireland, and England and Wales) is concerned, Sch.4 of the Civil Jurisdiction and Judgments Act 1982 (as amended by the Civil Jurisdiction and Judgments Order 2001) would apply. That schedule is largely identical to the Council Regulation (with relevant modifications for internal jurisdiction). What is important to note though is that although the provisions of Sch.4 are similar to those in the Council Regulation, they are not subject to the CJEU's[26] jurisdiction. Thus, where there arises a question of interpretation, the appropriate UK court cannot refer the matter to the CJEU for a preliminary ruling because it is a matter of wholly domestic nature.[27]

12–039   For legal proceedings instituted after March 1, 2002, as far as the United Kingdom is concerned, the issue of jurisdiction in civil and commercial matters might be ascertained in the following manner:

---

[25] Following *Mahme Trust v Lloyds TSB Bank Plc* [2004] EWHC 1931, Ch., it has now been affirmed that the doctrine of forum non conveniens has no place in the scheme of the Lugano Convention.

[26] The new name "Court of Justice of the European Union" (CJEU) replaces the old "European Court of Justice" (ECJ) following the Treaty of Lisbon's coming into effect. In this book, pre-Lisbon cases will continue to refer to the ECJ, as the presiding court, not the CJEU.

[27] *Kleinwort Benson Ltd v Glasgow City Council* (C–346/93) [1995] All E.R. (E.C.) 514.

- where the defendant is domiciled in an EU country, the new Council Regulation;

- where the defendant is domiciled in an EFTA country which is not an EU Member State, the Lugano Convention;

- where the defendant is domiciled in any other country, the rules of common law as discussed earlier.

Our emphasis shall be the Council Regulation, given its importance as far as intra-EU relations are concerned.

Interpretation and scope of application

Section 3(1) of the Civil Jurisdiction and Judgments Act 1982 provides that any **12–040** question as to the meaning or effect of any provision of the Brussels Convention shall, if it is not referred to the European Court of Justice under the relevant protocol, be determined in accordance with the principles laid down by any relevant decision of that Court. A similar provision need not be provided for specifically as far as the new Regulation is concerned because as a Council Regulation, Member States have the right or indeed, under certain circumstances, the duty to seek a preliminary ruling from the CJEU matters of interpretation and application arising from a measure of secondary legislation under art.234, EU.[28]

The CJEU has made it plain that when interpreting the provisions of the Brussels rules, regard must be had to their objectives. The following have been expressed in the Regulation as constituting the objectives of the law:

- the promotion of judicial cooperation between the Member States[29] consistent with the principle of mutual trust[30];

- the removal of differences between national rules on jurisdiction and recognition of judgments which the EU considers to hamper the sound operation of the internal market[31];

- to provide individuals domiciled in the EU to have certainty as to where they might be sued in civil and commercial matters[32];

---

[28] It might be observed that, as the ECJ held in *Erich Gasser GmbH and MISAT Srl* (C–116/02) December 9, 2003 [2003] ECJ CELEX LEXIS 607, a national court may, under the Brussels Convention, make a reference to the ECJ even where it is relying on submissions of a party to the main proceedings of which it has not yet examined the merits. The proviso is that that national court must have regard to the particular circumstances of the case, that a preliminary ruling is necessary to enable it to give judgment and that the questions on which it seeks a ruling are actually relevant. It is however incumbent on the national court to provide the CJEU with factual and legal information so as to enable the CJEU to give a useful and relevant interpretation.

[29] Paras (1) and (3), Preamble to Regulation 44/01.

[30] Paras (16) and (17), above, see, e.g., *Owusu v Jackson* (C–281/02) March 1, 2005 [2005] ECJ CELEX LEXIS 75, *Turner* (C–159/02) [2004] ECJ CELEX LEXIS 150 and *GIE Groupe Concorde* (C–440/97) [1999] E.C.R. I–6307.

[31] Para.(2), above; see e.g. *Gmurzynska-Bscher* (C–231/89) [1990] E.C.R. I–4003, *Djabali* (C–314/96) [1998] E.C.R. I–1149, and *Bacardi-Martini and Cellier des Dauphins* (C–318/00) [2003] E.C.R. I–905.

[32] Para.(10), above, see especially the following recent cases—*Besix* (C–256/00) [2002] E.C.R. I–1699, DFDS *Torline* (C–18/02) [2004] ECJ CELEX LEXIS 38 and *Kronhofer v Maier* (C–168/02) June 10, 2004.

- protection of the individual who is in a weaker position contractually such as insured persons, employees and consumers[33];

- to support international commitments, especially treaty obligations, entered into by Member States.[34]

It will be readily seen that in almost every controversial decision, the CJEU will go to great lengths to reason that the decision was justified on one of the above objectives. Although cross-border harmonisation is seen as important, the Regulation does make clear that some degree of flexibility should be admitted to take into account the different procedural rules of certain Member States.[35]

12–041   The Lugano Convention is not subject to interpretation by the CJEU in the same way, but an English court is obliged to take into account any principles laid down in a relevant decision of the court in another Contracting State (s.31B Civil Jurisdiction and Judgments Act 1982).

The Regulation applies in civil and commercial matters whatever the nature of the court or tribunal. It shall not extend, in particular, to revenue, customs or administrative matter (art.1(1)). It shall also not apply to (art.1(2)):

1. the status or legal capacity of natural persons, rights in property arising out of a matrimonial relationship, wills and succession;

2. bankruptcy, proceedings relating to the winding-up of insolvent companies or other legal persons, judicial arrangements compositions and analogous proceedings[36];

3. social security; or

4. arbitration.[37]

---

[33] Para.(13) above.

[34] Para.(25) above, see for example *Nürnberger Allgemeine Versicherungs AG v Portbridge Transport International BV* (C–148/03) October 28, 2004 [2004] ECJ CELEX LEXIS 506 and *Tatry* (C–406/92) [1994] E.C.R. I–5439.

[35] Para.(26) Preamble to Regulation 44/01, and see *Mærsk Olie & Gas A/S v Firma M. de Haan* (C–39/02) October 14, 2004 where the ECJ took account of the special features in procedure in the Netherlands for setting up a limitation of liability fund for shipowners.

[36] There is now a specific Regulation on resolving jurisdiction and recognition and enforcement of judgments in insolvency matters. The EU Regulation on Insolvency Proceedings ([2000] O.J 1346 2000) L160/1) which came into force in May 2002 provides specifically for the mutual respect between Member States as regards insolvency judgments and orders. The bankruptcy exception in art.1(2)(b) of Regulation 44/2001 was to be narrowly construed; the excluded proceedings had to derive directly from the bankruptcy or winding-up and be closely connected with them; the fact that the trustee in bankruptcy was a party to the proceedings was insufficient to engage the exception, *Gourdain v Nadler* (133/78) [1979] E.C.R. 733. On the other hand, proceedings seeking damages for misrepresentation and/or breach of contract against a Dutch bankruptcy trustee were found to be sufficiently closely connected with the bankruptcy in question to be within the exception for bankruptcy in art.1(2)(b) (*Polymer Vision R & D Ltd v Sebastiaan Maarten Marie van Dooren* [2011] EWHC 2951 (Comm)).

[37] It should be noted that proceedings brought to enforce an arbitration clause or to question the validity of an arbitration clause would fall within the arbitration exception in this article. See *The Ivan Zagubanski* (November 6, 2000) and also *The Xing Su Hai* [1995] 2 Lloyd's Rep. 15; but cf. *The Heidberg* [1994] 2 Lloyd's Rep. 287. See also *The Front Comor* [2007] UKHL 4 but cf. *Allianz SpA v West Tankers* (C–185/07) February 10, 2009 (see below, para.12–046).

What does "civil and commercial matters" mean?

The Regulation does not offer a definition for the phrase "civil and commercial **12–042** matters" but as far as the Brussels Convention is concerned, given the international nature of the convention, an autonomous definition has frequently been applied. According to the ECJ in *LTU GmbH v Eurocontrol* (29/76) [1976] E.C.R. 1541, it applies to claims under private law, as distinct from public law. It would therefore not apply to a dispute between a private person and a public authority which arises from acts done by the public authority in the exercise of public powers. In that case, there arose a legal dispute over route charges owed between Lufthansa and Eurocontrol, an international body which supplied air traffic control services to civil aviation in Europe. It was clear that Eurocontrol was a public body but that did not necessarily remove the action out of the Brussels Convention. The question that must be asked is whether the relevant public body had been acting in the exercise of its public powers or functions.

This does not mean that we are required to establish whether the body was acting in an *ultra vires* fashion; the notion of public powers here refers to activities performed specific to the purposes of the organisation. As long as the legal relationship entered into by the public body is one which is not specifically related to its principal official objects, it could constitute a "civil and commercial" relationship. For example, if Eurocontrol in the case above were to buy pencils for their offices, that should be properly classed a "civil and commercial matter".

The general rule—article 2

The dominant requirement of the Regulation (and the Brussels and Lugano **12–043** Conventions) is that a claimant should sue his or her defendant in the country where the latter is domiciled. Article 2(1) provides that persons domiciled in a Member State shall, whatever their nationality, be sued in the courts of that Member State. The rule is dependent on the domicile of the defendant, not of the claimant. This was made clear in *Societe Group Josi Reinsurance Company SA v (Compagnie D'Assurances Universal) General Insurance Co* (C–412/98) [2000] E.C.R. I–5925 where the fact that the claimant was domiciled in Canada which was not a contracting state was held to be immaterial for the purposes of art.2.

There is no need for the claimant to apply for permission to serve on a defendant domiciled in any of the EU or EFTA countries (CPR PD6B para.2.1; r.6.33–34). This is clearly different to the position where the defendant is domiciled in a non-EU or non-EFTA country as we have seen above.

Mandatory application of article 2 and the doctrine of forum non conveniens

It has been mentioned earlier that the new regime intends to do away with the **12–044** English doctrine of forum non conveniens. That doctrine, it may be recalled, places much discretion on the court to decide whether permission to serve out should be given, or whether a stay of English proceedings should be granted or whether an anti-suit injunction should be given. The doctrine's potency was to a very large extent reduced by the Brussels Convention and now, Reg.44/2001. There is strong indication in *UGIC v Group Josi Reinsurance Co SA* (C–412/98)

[2000] E.C.R. I–5925 that there should be no room for discretion in matters of jurisdiction which are dealt with by art.2 of the Brussels Convention.

Moreover, it was considered in *S & W Berisford Plc v New Hampshire Insurance Co* [1990] 2 All E.R. 321 and *Arkwright Mutual Insurance Co v Bryanston Insurance Co Ltd* [1990] 2 All E.R. 335 that the English court has no discretionary power to stay proceedings when jurisdiction is ascertained by the Brussels (Lugano) regime. That would be the case, even when the competing jurisdiction in question is not a Member State of the EU (or EFTA, as the case may be). A controversial exception however was applied by the Court of Appeal in *Re Harrods (Buenos Aires) Ltd* [1992] Ch.72 in an attempt to retain the discretionary powers possessed of the court in the doctrine of forum non conveniens. There, proceedings had been brought in England for the winding-up of an English company. That company had exclusively carried on business in Argentina. It was argued that the most appropriate forum was Argentina. However, England too had jurisdiction under art.2 of the Brussels Convention as the place where the company had its domicile. The Court of Appeal concluded that as the issue was not over the allocation of jurisdiction between contracting states, the Brussels Convention had no application. It is difficult to justify and defend the decision in *Re Harrods* given the clear rationale of the Brussels regime to do away with the doctrine of forum non conveniens.[38]

A reference for a preliminary ruling on a similar issue was made to the ECJ by the Court of Appeal in *Andrew Owusu v Nugent B Jackson* [2002] EWCA Civ 877. In that case, the claimant had been seriously injured whilst on a holiday in Jamaica organised and arranged by the defendants. All the defendants, except for D1, were domiciled in Jamaica. D1 was domiciled in England. The claimant commenced action in tort and contract against all the defendants in England. The defendants, including D1, applied for a declaration from the court that it had no jurisdiction to entertain the claim. The argument was essentially that as all the relevant events had occurred in Jamaica and that is where the evidence is located, the English court should decline jurisdiction in the light of the doctrine of forum non conveniens. The trial judge held that in the light of *UGIC v Group Josi Reinsurance Co SA* (C–412/98) [2000] E.C.R. I–5925, he had no discretion to stay the action although it was obvious that Jamaica was clearly the forum conveniens. The Court of Appeal concluded that there was no ruling by the ECJ on the effect of art.2 in such a context. There were conflicting previous opinions of Advocate-Generals on the matter. The Court of Appeal found that it was unable to make any pronouncement on how art.2 should be interpreted and a reference was made to the ECJ asking whether it was inconsistent with the Brussels rules where a claimant contended that jurisdiction was founded on art.2, for a court of a Member State, to exercise a discretionary power to decline hear proceedings brought against a person domiciled in that state in favour of the courts of a non-Member State, where the jurisdiction of no other Member State was in issue and the proceedings had no connecting factors with any Member State. This was a hard case because whilst there was a need to sanction the

---

[38] The court relied, in part, on s.49 CJJA, which provides that a stay of proceedings on the ground of forum non conveniens is permissible, "where to do so is not inconsistent with the 1968 Convention". Section 49 does not however refer to Reg.44/2001. See Briggs, "Spiliada and the Brussels Convention" [1991] L.M.C.L.Q. 10; Briggs, "Forum Non Conveniens and the Brussels Convention Again" [1991] 107 L.Q.R. 180 and Kaye, "The EEC Judgments Convention and the outer world: goodbye to forum non conveniens?" [1992] J.B.L. 47.

mandatory effect of art.2 and the Brussels rules, it would seem exorbitant for the English court to assume jurisdiction over all the defendants who were not domiciled in England (or another Member State) in a case where almost all the connecting factors point to Jamaica.

The ruling was made on March 1, 2005 confirming the rationale of the **12–045** Brussels regime to remove the element of discretion of the national courts when the technical rules of allocation of jurisdiction in the Brussels regime are satisfied. The ECJ ruled that the Brussels rules

"preclude a court of a Contracting State from declining the jurisdiction conferred on it by art.2 of that convention on the ground that a court of a non-Contracting State would be a more appropriate forum for the trial of the action even if the jurisdiction of no other Contracting State is in issue or the proceedings have no connecting factors to any other Contracting State".

The ECJ also stressed that there was nothing in the Brussels rules requiring a connecting link between the country of jurisdiction and the litigants. Additionally, the court held that the doctrine of forum non conveniens if permitted to apply in cases involving the Brussels regime would invariably result in uncertainty. That was to be avoided. The court drew support from *Turner v Grovit* (C–159/02) [2004] E.C.R. I–3565, April 27, 2004.[39]

In that case, the ECJ ruled that even where there is clear evidence of bad faith in an action commenced by the claimant, so long as that action is brought in Member State X against the defendant in accordance with the Brussels rules, a more appropriate forum in Member State Y has no discretion to grant an anti-suit injunction. In that case, T was domiciled in Spain and was consequently sued in Spain in pursuant to art.2. He however disputed the jurisdiction of the Spanish court and applied for a injunction from an English court ordering the respondents to discontinue proceedings in Spain. It was contended that the respondents had commenced action in Spain in bad faith to obstruct legitimate proceedings in England. The ECJ however said that the grant of such an injunction would impede and impair the effectiveness of the Brussels rules. The court said that such an interference by a national court cannot be justified by the fact that it was only indirect and was intended to prevent an abuse of process by the defendant in the proceedings in the forum State. The court added:

"In so far as the conduct for which the defendant is criticised consists in recourse to the jurisdiction of the court of another Member State, the judgment made as to the abusive nature of that conduct implies an assessment of the appropriateness of bringing proceedings before a court of another Member State. Such an assessment runs counter to the principle of mutual trust which, . . . , underpins the Convention and prohibits a court, except in special circumstances which are not applicable in this case, from reviewing the jurisdiction of the court of another Member State".

It is obvious that the ECJ considered such a derogation from art.2 was **12–046** effectively the casting of an aspersion that another Member State's court was

---

[39] See also *Through Transport Mutual v New India Assurance* [2005] 1 Lloyd's Rep. 67 and *The Front Comor* [2007] UKHL 4.

unable or unwilling to prevent an abuse of process. It is obvious that the rationale here could not be applied in *Owusu*; in *Owusu*, there would be no aspersions cast on the ability or willingness of another Member State's court to prevent an abuse of process.[40] There, the problem is how art.2 when used in a context involving the jurisdiction of the home state (of the defendant and the claimant) and a non-Member State should be applied; and no Member States are involved.

It might also be pointed out that the ECJ was asked an additional question in *Owusu*—that was whether there were some instances where the doctrine of forum non conveniens might apply alongside the Brussels rules. Essentially, this was the Court of Appeal's concern as to how s.49 CJJA (see fn.28 above) should be construed. The ECJ however refused to answer the question on the basis that the facts giving rise to the dispute in *Owusu* did not necessitate the tackling of this largely theoretical question. It might of course be recalled the procedure under art.267, TFEU only permitted the CJEU to give a preliminary ruling on a question directly relevant to the underlying facts. It is not enabled by that provision to give guidance on general questions of law. It should be noted that although the above cases concerned the Brussels Convention, the same principles would apply to Reg.44/2001.

Another problem has arisen of late. How should a conflict between the Regulation and the English court's inherent jurisdiction to grant an anti-suit injunction to prevent a litigant from commencing action in another state in breach of an arbitration clause? We have seen how the ECJ in *Turner* has effectively ruled against anti-suit injunctions in cases involving a conflict of jurisdiction under Reg.44/2001. However, in *Through Transport Mutual Assurance Association (Eurasia) Ltd v India Assurance Co Ltd* [2005] 1 Lloyd's Rep. 67, the English judges have continued to grant anti-suit injunctions in arbitration cases because in their opinion, as arbitration falls outside Reg.44/2001, the English court's inherent jurisdiction is not affected where the arbitral seat chosen is clearly in England.[41] In *The Front Comor* [2007] UKHL 4, a similar problem arose. The litigant in question was clearly entitled to bring an action in Italy under the Regulation but under the charterparty, they were committed to participating in arbitration in London. The question was whether the English court could grant an anti-suit injunction preventing the litigant in question from proceeding in Italy until at least after the arbitration. The House of Lords decided that the matter should be referred to the ECJ for clarification (as *Allianz SpA v West Tankers* (C–185/07) February 10, 2009). The ECJ held that the grant of anti-suit injunctions in Regulation cases is antithetical to the spirit of the EU law. By adhering to the tenor of the judgment in *Turner*, the ECJ considered that it was a matter for the Member State court seised, namely the Italian court, to decide whether proceedings in Italy should continue. It would be contrary to the spirit of the Regulation to allow the English court to grant an anti-suit injunction. Lastly as to the question of whether the matter was an arbitration matter thus falling outside the Regulation, the ECJ concluded that as the claim in Italy was an action in tort and/or contract for damages and not on the arbitration agreement, this was a case for Reg.44/2001. The ECJ added that although such proceedings for an anti-suit injunction might fall outside Reg.44/2001 by virtue

---

[40] See also 889457 *Alberta Inc v Katanga Mining* [2008] EWHC 2679.
[41] See also *Verity Shipping SA v NV Norexa* [2008] EWHC 213.

of art.1(2)(d), they may nevertheless have consequences which undermine its effectiveness.

Determining the domicile of the defendant

The concept of domicile is central to the application of the Regulation (and **12–047** indeed the Brussels and Lugano Conventions) as is evident in the terms of art.2(1). The Regulation provides guidance as to how it should be decided. As far as individuals are concerned, art.59 of the Regulation provides that in order to determine whether a party is domiciled in the Member State whose courts are seised of a matter, the court shall apply its internal law. Thus, where proceedings are being brought before an English court, it shall be up to the English court applying its internal law on domicile to establish the domicile of the defendant. Article 59(2) however goes on to say that where the party is not domiciled in the Member State whose courts are seised of the matter, then in order to determine whether the party is domiciled in another Member State, the court shall apply the law of that Member State. For example, in a particular case, the English court finds, by applying English law, that the defendant is not domiciled in England then in order to determine whether the defendant is domiciled in France, that English court should apply French law.

As for corporate persons, art.60(1) provides that a company or legal person or association of natural or legal persons is domiciled at a place where it has:

1. statutory seat; or

2. central administration; or

3. principal place of business.

This is not found in the Brussels or Lugano Conventions (art.52 of both Conventions) which rely on the application of internal law of the country of the courts seised to ascertain the domicile of corporate entities.

The Regulation provides in art.60(2) that as far as the United Kingdom is concerned, "statutory seat" is to mean the registered office or, where there is no such office anywhere, the place of incorporation or where there is no such place anywhere, the place under the law of which the formation took place.

Returning to the domicile of an individual, art.59(1) refers to the Member **12–048** State's internal law. That internal law in the United Kingdom is s.41 CJJA. That section provides that an individual is domiciled in the United Kingdom if and only if he is resident in the United Kingdom and the nature and circumstances of his residence indicate that he has a substantial connection with the United Kingdom. There is no definition of "residence" or "substantial connection", but the Act states that in the case of an individual resident in the United Kingdom and has been so resident for the last three months or more, it shall be presumed that he has a substantial connection with the United Kingdom, unless the contrary is proved. This is to reduce the adversity in assessing what would constitute "substantial connection".

In *Cherney v Deripaska* [2007] EWHC 965 (QB), although D was present at the London address when service was effected, the court found that he was not resident there. He travelled all over the world in pursuit of his business interests and had a number of residences in several countries. He spent less than 10 per cent of the nights in the year at the London address. There was no pattern to his visits. The majority were for one night only and involved business meetings. He had significant business interests in England but they formed a minimal part of his total interests which were largely Russian. He spent the majority of his time in Russia. He was resident in Russia. He was not also resident in England. Despite the permanence of the establishment at the London address, it was not his "settled or usual place of abode" (see also *High Tech International AG v Deripaska* [2006] EWHC 3276).

According to s.41(6), an individual is domiciled in a particular part of the United Kingdom if and only if:

(a) he is a resident in that part; and

(b) the nature and circumstances of his residence indicate that he has a substantial connection with that part.

If he is domiciled in the United Kingdom but has no substantial connection with any part, he is to be treated as domiciled in the part of the United Kingdom where he is resident.

Special jurisdiction

12–049   Section 2 of the Regulation makes provision for cases which could be exempt from the general rule set out in art.2, that is to say, a defendant domiciled in one Member State could be sued in another Member State. We shall concern ourselves with only the following "special cases":

(a) matters relating to contract (art.5(1));

(b) matters relating to tort, delict or quasi-delict (art.5(3));

(c) disputes arising from the operations of a branch, agency or other establishment (art.5(5));

(d) trusts (art.5(6));

(e) disputes concerning the payment of remuneration claimed under the salvage of a cargo or freight (art.5(7));

(f) claims against co-defendants (art.6(1));

(g) third party proceedings (art.6(2));

(h) counterclaim arising from the same contract or facts (art.6(3)).

(a) Matters relating to a contract

12–050   Article 5(1) provides that a person domiciled in a Member State may be sued in another Member State in matters relating to a contract, in the courts for the place of performance of the obligation in question. This provision is vulnerable to construction difficulties. One of the first problems is the definition of "contract". In *Arcado Sprl v Haviland SA* (9/87) [1988] E.C.R. 1539, the ECJ made it quite clear that the concept of a contract must be given an autonomous meaning under the Convention. In that case, the agent claimed damages from a manufacturer for the latter's deliberate and wrongful termination of the latter's contract with the agent's principal thereby causing the agent a loss of commission. It was unclear whether there was in fact a contract between the agent and the defendant but the ECJ stated that the approach should not be unduly constrictive. Not only could an implied relationship suffice, but also one where the claimant is not a privy to the principal contract. The various concepts of a contract in the different national legal systems are of no direct relevance.

The ECJ in *Jakob Handte & Co GmbH v Traitements Mecano-chimiques des Surfaces* SA (C–26/91) [1992] E.C.R. I–3967 additionally held that "contract" should not be extended to a "situation in which there is no obligation freely assumed by one party towards another". A claim arising from such a relationship is what English law normally deems to be a tortious claim. In that case, an action by an ultimate purchaser of goods in a chain transaction against the manufacturer could not be sustained by art.5(1) because the liabilities of the various sellers may differ (depending on their contracts) and the manufacturer could not have been aware of the identity or domicile of the ultimate purchaser.

Another related issue is how the court should apply art.5(1) when a defendant pleads that there was no contract in the first place, whilst the claimant is arguing that the defendant had breached that "contract". In *Effer v Kantner* (38/81) [1982] E.C.R. 825, the ECJ held that art.5(1) should and could apply even where one party is seeking to prove the contract's nullity.

As for pre-contractual liability claims, the position in *Agnew v Länsförsäk-*   **12–051**
ringsbolagens [2001] 1 A.C. 223 was that a claim for non disclosure and misrepresentation which resulted in an insurance contract being made was held by the House of Lords to be a claim relating to contract for the purposes of art.5(1). However, that view has been rejected by the ECJ. In *Fonderie Officine Meccaniche Tacconi SpA v HWS Heinrich Wagner Sinto Maschinenfabrik GmbH* (C–334/00) [2002] E.C.R. I–7357, September 17, 2002, the position as to pre-contractual liability claims is that these would fall under art.5(3) and not art.5(1). In *Tacconi*, the Italian suit in question also involved a claim for damages for breach of the duty to act in good faith and the duty to act honestly (a cause of action available under art.1337 of the Italian Civil Code). The ECJ said:

"[W]hile Art 5(1) . . . does not require a contract to have been concluded, it is nevertheless essential, for that provision to apply, to identify an obligation, since the jurisdiction of the national court is determined, in matters relating to a contract, by the place of performance of the obligation in question".

In *Kleinwort Benson v Glasgow City Council* [1997] 4 All E.R. 641, the majority of the House of Lords held that where the action is a restitution claim, it must be established whether the claim was based on unjust enrichment or a contractual obligation. In that case, the "contract" was never in existence being void ab initio. The claimant bank's claim was based on unjust enrichment. That was not in the contemplation of art.5(1) and as such the general rule that action must be commenced at the Member State of the defendant's domicile must prevail. Lord Goff was concerned that the approach to art.5(1) should not be too wide. His Lordship turned to *Shenavai v Kreischer* (266/85) [1987] 1 E.C.R. 239 where the ECJ recommended that regard should be had "solely to the contractual obligation whose performance is sought in the judicial proceedings". The ECJ also stated:

"The place in which that obligation is to be performed usually constitutes the closest connecting factor between the dispute and the court having jurisdiction over it, and it is this connecting factor which explains why, in contractual matters, it is the court of the place of performance of the obligation which has jurisdiction".

That obligation is, it would seem, the "obligation in question". The position seems to be this—once this criterion is abandoned, the justification for jurisdiction being vested in a court of the place of performance of the obligation in question expires. If there is no obligation in question as in the case of a restitution claim based on unjust enrichment, there cannot be distending of art.5(1) to accommodate the claimant's action. This is of course not to deprive the claimant of his claim—he would simply have to bring the claim at the place of the defendant's domicile unless he could satisfy any of the other special jurisdiction exceptions.

12–052   **"The place of performance of the obligation in question"** Subject to agreement, the place of performance of the obligation in question shall be in the case of the sale of goods, the place in a Member State where, under the contract, the goods were delivered or should have been delivered. In the case of the provision of services, where under the contract the services were provided or should have been provided. This definition set out in art.5(1)(b) is an improvement from the Brussels Convention which left the notion of "place of performance of the obligation in question" undefined resulting in much controversy.

The ECJ made it clear in *Color Drack GmbH v Lexx International Vertriebs GmbH* [2010] 1 W.L.R. 1909 that art.5(1)(b) is a rule of special jurisdiction establishing the place of delivery as the autonomous linking factor to apply to all claims founded on a contract for the sale of goods. The purpose of art.5(1)(b) is to unify the rules of conflict of jurisdiction and to designate the court having jurisdiction directly, without reference to the domestic rules of the Member States. At para.39 the ECJ said this:

" . . . By designating autonomously as "the place of performance" the place where the obligation which characterises the contract is to be performed, the Community legislature sought to centralise at its place of performance jurisdiction over disputes concerning all the contractual obligations and to determine sole jurisdiction for all claims arising out of the contract".

The wording of art.5.1(b) could not be clearer. It does not say that the place of delivery will be the place of performance only when it is the delivery obligation which is in issue in a claim arising out of a contract for the sale of goods. The place of delivery will always be the place for performance where the claim arises out of a contract for the sale of goods—unless the parties "otherwise agreed". (*Cube Lighting v Afcon* [2011] EWHC 2565 (Ch)).

12–053   However, it is submitted that the definition does not go far enough. First, it only refers to sale and supply of goods and services. Article 5(1)(c) makes it plain that the old position would have to be resorted to in cases which fall outside "goods and services".

As far as the old law is concerned, it was held in *De Bloos Sprl v Bouyer SA* (14/76) [1976] E.C.R.1497 that the obligation in question is that which the claimant is relying on as the basis of his claim. In that case, the obligation in question was the sole distributorship purportedly granted to the claimant, and since that obligation was to be performed in Belgium, the Belgian court could seise itself of jurisdiction under art.5(1) of the Brussels Convention. It was immaterial that other obligations were to be performed in France.

The ECJ also suggested in *De Bloos* that a claim to damages could in certain cases be based on an independent contractual obligation to pay damages and need not be founded on a breach of a duty to perform some other act. It appears that this proposition has no place in convention law as discussed in the later case of *Arcado v Haviland* (9/87) [1988] E.C.R. 1539. This want of clarity has not been rectified in the Regulation although *Custom Made Commercial Ltd v Stawa Metalbau GmbH* (C–288/92) [1994] E.C.R. I–2913 has confirmed that, in general, the test is dependent on which obligation the claimant is suing. As far as the international sale of goods is concerned, that ruling would mean that if the buyer sues the seller for goods not meeting the contractual description, the obligation in issue is the duty to deliver goods but where the seller sues the buyer for failure to pay the contract price for the goods, the relevant obligation is the buyer's duty to pay. Under the Regulation, that would be different. A perfunctory reading of art.5(1)(b) seems to suggest that regardless of which obligation is in dispute, as long as it is a case of the sale of goods or the provision of services, the place of performance of the obligation shall be deemed to be the place where the goods or services under the contract were delivered or should have been delivered.

Example: **12–054**

Buyer is domiciled in England. Seller is domiciled in Spain. The contract is expressed as "FOB Hamburg, Germany". Payment is to be made in Spain. If Buyer is alleging that goods were not delivered on time, he could either sue the defendant in Spain, where the latter is domiciled under art.2 or Germany, where the goods were delivered under art.5(1)(a)(b). Under the Brussels Convention a similar result would be reached. If it is the seller who is suing the buyer for failure to pay, under the Brussels Convention, he could sue the buyer either in England as the latter's place of domicile or in Spain where payment was due. Indeed it was held in *Custom Made Commercial Ltd* that the place where the goods are to be delivered is immaterial to a claim for unpaid money under a contract of sale where art.5(1) (of the Brussels Convention) is concerned. Under the new Regulation, though, does it mean that the seller would have to sue either England or Germany and not Spain because art.5(1)(b) presumes the place of obligation in question in a contract for the sale of goods to be the place where delivery was due or should have been made?

An associated problem is what law should be used to interpret the precise nature of the contract. In *Scottish & Newcastle International Ltd v Ghalanos* [2008] UKHL 11, the House of Lords relied on English law to construe the terms of a contract expressed as a CFR contract. The contract was expressed as CFR Limassol, Cyprus but it was the buyer who nominated and designated the carrying vessel. That, as readers will appreciate, is inconsistent with the contract being a CFR contract. The court also turned to s.32(1) Sale of Goods Act 1979 to deem the seller as having made delivery when the goods were loaded on to a vessel designated by the buyer at Liverpool, UK. The court thus concluded that the contract was in fact an FOB contract whereby delivery took place at

Liverpool and according to art.5(1)(b), the contract was performed in England. It is interesting to observe that the court did not see it fit to refer to "autonomous concepts" to construe the contract.

It should be noted that art.5(1)(b) inserts the proviso "unless otherwise agreed". The precise scope of this proviso is not quite clear. It would seem to allow the parties to vary the scope of application of art.5(1) either by pre-agreeing in their contract as to the relevant place of performance of certain obligations, or by agreeing, *after the dispute has arisen*, that a particular place should be deemed as the place of performance of the relevant obligation in question. It might be observed that if the agreed place of performance is used principally to fix the jurisdiction rather than to determine the actual place of performance, such an agreement must, it would seem, also satisfy the requirements under art.17.[42]

12–055   The more vital issue is whether it could be raised in objection to any Member State's court's jurisdiction that "otherwise agreed" could also be taken to mean a tacit agreement. Where, for example, the obligation to pay in our illustration above was clearly intended to have been performed in Spain, Spain must surely be the intended place of performance of the obligation in question. It is submitted that this is probably the correct interpretation of art.5(1)(b) as there is little justification for differentiating an implied agreement from an express agreement in such a context. That being the case, the Regulation in art.5(1)(b) will only apply where it is unclear from the express terms of the contract or the circumstances what the place of performance of the obligation in question in a contract for the sale of goods is. The scope of its application is therefore somewhat limited; however art.5(1)(b) would be useful in cases where it is quite obvious that the place of performance is not clear.

Where the claimant makes a claim based on several obligations, the ECJ held in *Shenavai v Kreischer* (266/85) [1987] E.C.R. 239 that art.5(1) of the Brussels Convention should be taken as referring to the most significant or important obligation. In *Union Transport v Continental Lines* [1992] 1 All E.R. 161, the charterer sued the shipowner for not nominating a suitable vessel and/or providing a vessel. The obligation characteristic of the charterparty is making the ship available for loading in Florida, United States. However, the essential duty alleged to have been breached was the failure to nominate a vessel to satisfy the charterparty. That duty, according to Lord Goff, was to be performed in England since the nomination was to be received there, and consequently, the English court had jurisdiction over the claim.

In the event that it is impossible to apply either the presumption in art.5(1)(b) or the intention of the parties as regards the place of performance (having identified the obligation in question), the court should apply the applicable law of the contract to decide where the place of performance should be. It was held in *Industrie Tessili Italiana Como v Dunlop AG* (12/76) [1976] E.C.R. 1473 that the court where the claimant seeks to pursues the action under art.5(1) must apply its own private international law rules to ascertain the applicable or proper law of the contract and then apply that applicable law to determine where performance was due. In *Mercury Publicity Ltd v Wolfgang Loerke GmbH, The Times,* October 21, 1991, the claim was over a repayment of a contractual debt. The

---

[42] *Genossenschaft AG (MSG) v Les Gravières Rhénanes Sar,* (C–106/95), *The Times,* February 25, 1997.

Court of Appeal decided using English rules of conflict that the contract was to be governed by English law and consequently, as English law deemed that repayment of a debt should be made at the place of the creditor's residence, that was the place of performance for the purposes of art.5(1). The competing law in that case was German law; had the English rules of conflict pointed to German law as the applicable or proper law of the contractual debt, then matters would have been quite different. German law, unlike English law, referred to the place of debtor's residence as the place where debt repayment was due.

The prescription that the court seised should apply its own rules of private **12–056** international law is by no means clear, especially where the circumstances are quite clear as to where performance in fact is due or ought to be due. It was asked of the ECJ in *GIE Groupe Concorde v The Master of the Vessel, Suhadiwarno Panjan* (C–440/97) September 29, 1999:

> "[M]ust the place of performance of the obligation be determined in accordance with the law which, pursuant to the rules on conflict of laws of the court seised, governs the obligation at issue or should the national courts determine the place of performance of that obligation by seeking to establish, having regard to the nature of the relationship creating the obligation and the circumstances of the case, the place where performance actually took place or should have taken place, without having to refer to the law which, under the rules on conflict of laws, governs the obligation in issue".

In that case, the carriers were being sued by the cargo owner's insurers (having been subrogated to the cargo owner's rights) for wine which was found to be damaged. The wine was delivered to Le Havre in France for loading on a ship bound for Brazil. It was claimed that action could be commenced in France because the contract called for the delivery of the wine to the ship docked at Le Havre. The insurer's action was dismissed by the French court in Rouen on the basis that it lacked jurisdiction. The insurers appealed arguing that the Cour d'Appel in Rouen was wrong to rule that the place of performance of the obligation at issue was not Le Havre without first investigating which law governed the contract of carriage.

Several Member States made submissions to the ECJ, concerned at the potential impact of this preliminary ruling. The German and UK governments and the Commission argued very strongly that the objectives of the Brussels Convention, which were to enable potential litigants to foresee which courts will have jurisdiction and to provide legal certainty and equal treatment favour the establishment of uniform criteria so that the concept of the place of performance for the purposes of art.5(1) could be determined independently.[43] France and Italy however argued that while the recourse to the private international law of each Member State might cause difficulties and the loss of certainty, the adoption of an autonomous definition which is what the Commission, the United Kingdom and Germany (and the defendants in *GIE Groupe*) were arguing for, could only work in the case of a few simple contracts and that this solution would be

---

[43] In the case of employment contracts, the CJEU has advocated an "autonomous" approach. In *GIE Groupe*, it was argued by the defendants and the Commission that this approach should be extended to the case of art.5(1).

incompatible with the constant evolution of contractual practice in international trade.

12–057   The ECJ held that whilst an autonomous approach would support legal certainty, it cannot provide a satisfactory result because to use an autonomous concept would be to deprive the parties of their right to choose an applicable law to their contract. Hence, the ECJ accepted the argument that recourse may be had to the Member State's own private international law to determine the nature of the obligation in question. Indeed, as all Member States were signatories to the Rome Convention, the risk of any serious inconsistency in the application of the conflict rules to ascertain the place of performance of the obligation in question was likely to be minimal. The same reasoning should apply in the context of the Rome I Regulation.

Naturally, as far as a simple contract for goods or services is concerned, the position under the Regulation is set out in the autonomous Community law presumptions in art.5(1)(b). Nevertheless, in other types of contract, the decision in *GIE Groupe* should prevail.

Lastly, art.5(1) is an exception to a general rule (art.2) and should not be thought of as ever being able to assume a larger scope of application than the general provision. It has thus been made clear that although words such as "contract" are to be given some degree of flexibility, the article itself could not be construed to allow a court, not one naturally seised under art.2, from assuming jurisdiction over all the different obligations of a contract under dispute where these obligations are to be performed elsewhere. In *Leathertex Divisione Sintetici SpA v Bodetex* (C-420/97) October 5, 1999 there were two obligations of equal rank—a duty to pay commission in Belgium and a duty to pay commission in Italy. It was not permissible for the Belgian court to assume jurisdiction for both claims under art.5(1). The ECJ said:

> "[W]hile there are disadvantages in having different courts ruling on different aspects of the same dispute, the plaintiff always has the option, under Article 2 of the Convention, of bringing his entire claim before the courts for the place where the defendant is domiciled".

12–058   There is no room for an argument based on the maxim *accessorium sequitur principale* or the claim is to be directed by the principal claim where there are two or more competing courts of equal competence.

12–059   **Article 5(1) and letters of credit**   Article 5(1) of the Brussels Convention had in the past thrown up difficult problems for disputes arising from a documentary credit arrangement. Given that the Regulation does not depart far from the original Brussels Convention equivalent, these problems are not likely to attract different treatment under the Regulation. In a conventional doc-umentary credit transaction, it is important to ascertain the relevant contracts in question:

- there is a contract between the issuing bank and the applicant;

- a contract between (the letter of credit) between the issuing bank and the beneficiary (*Petrologic Capital SA v Banque Cantonale de Geneve* [2012] EWHC 453 (Comm))·

- if the letter of credit is confirmed, a contract between the confirming bank and the seller;

- a contract to pay and be reimbursed between the issuing bank and the confirming bank and any negotiating bank;

- a contract between the confirming bank and a properly authorised negotiating bank who has paid the beneficiary under the letter of credit; or

- a contract of agency between the issuing bank and an advising bank.

Given the various possible contracts involved, it should be clear as to which relationship we are concerned with in any dispute.

In determining where the place for performance is, we need to be clear as to which of the above relationships we are concerned with. For example, a letter of credit may provide for the letter of credit to be discharged by a negotiating bank who seeks reimbursement from the confirming bank, who in turn wants to be reimbursed by the issuing bank. In such an instance, if the claim is made by the confirming bank against the issuing bank, the relevant contract is that between the issuing bank and the confirming bank. Where is the place of performance of the obligation in question? Is it the place of business of the issuing bank, or the third bank, or the confirming bank? The Court of Appeal held in *Royal Bank of Scotland v Cassa di Risparmio delle Provincie Lombard, Financial Times*, January 21, 1992 that the place of performance was at the specified place of business of the third bank because the obligation in question was the payment to the beneficiary by the third bank (an agent of the confirming bank) and it was there that the duty becomes fully discharged.[44] The essence of the contract between the issuing bank and confirming bank is the confirming bank's duty to pay the beneficiary.

Where the place for performance is not expressly stated in the contract, the court will ascertain from the facts where that place was intended by the parties to be.

Chailease Finance Corporation v Credit Agricole Indosuez [2000] 1 Lloyd's Rep. 348   **12–060**
Facts:
The dispute arose out of an irrevocable standby letter of credit issued by the defendant French bank from its Geneva branch in the favour of the claimant Panamanian company. The terms of the letter of credit were that on presentation of certain specified documents to the defendant's offices, they would pay the claimant "as per your instructions". The underlying contract was a contract for the purchase of a ship. The claimant was the first mortgagee of the ship at the time of the sale. When presented with the relevant documents, the defendant rejected them three times. The claimant said that its claim was based upon the failure of the bank to pay. They also alleged that the place for payment was London and as such that was the place where the obligation was to be performed for the purposes of jurisdiction under art.5(1). The defendant argued that art.2 should apply and it should be sued in France as it is domiciled there. The defendant also disagreed that the letter of credit required performance in London. They claimed that the place for the performance of the obligation in question should have been in Switzerland. Alternatively, as the payment obligation depended on the conduct of the claimant in presenting the documents at a place of their choosing and the "as per your instructions" clause meant that the

---

[44] See also *Governor & Company of the Bank of Ireland v State Bank of India* [2011] NIQB 22; and *Bank of Baroda v Vysya Bank* (1994) 4 C.L.C. 41.

claimant could have asked for payment in any country, the place of performance was a "floating" place because which would fall outside the ambit of art.5(1).
Held:
The general rule is that for the purposes of art.5(1) where the claim for nonpayment, the obligation in question was the obligation to pay money and the place of payment was the place of performance. *Custom Made Commercial v Stawa Metlbau* (C–288/92) [1994] E.C.R. I–2913 should be followed. The Court of Appeal held that art.5(1) should not be avoided simply on the basis that the place of performance of the obligation has yet to crystallise. On construction of the terms of the letter of credit, it would appear that the claimant was entitled to nominate London as the place of payment. As this was the case, the fact that the letter of credit might stipulate a "floating" place of performance would not alter the fact it was in London where the obligation in question was to be performed. As long as that place was ascertainable, that was sufficient.

The legal effect of the words "we shall pay you as per your instructions" was not entirely clear from *Chailease* but, it suffices to state that such a clause does create "floating" place of performance which the court would attempt to "crystallise" at least for the purposes of allocating jurisdiction under art.5(1).

(b) Matters relating to tort

12–061 In matters relating to tort, delict or quasi-delict, a person domiciled in a Member State may be sued in another Member State, namely the courts of the place where the harmful event occurred or may occur could be seised. An autonomous definition of "tort, delict or quasi-delict" is essential, according to the ECJ in *Kalfelis v Schroder, Munchmeyer, Heuqst & Co* (189/87) [1988] E.C.R. 565:

> "The term 'matters relating to tort, delict or quasi-delict' used in Art.5(3) must be regarded as an independent concept covering all actions which seek to establish the liability of a defendant and which are not related to a 'contract' within the meaning of article 5(1)".

This would suggest that in order to determine whether an action is tortious, the court should consider first whether the issue is one relating to civil obligations, and if it is, it will decide whether it is related to a "contract" and if it considers that it is not, then, it will be treated as falling prima facie within art.5(3). A good example of this approach is seen in *Reunion Europeenne SA v Spliethoff's Bevrachtingskantoor BV and The Master of the Vessel Albasgracht V002* (C–51/97) [1998] E.C.R. I–6511. The ECJ held that in an action by a consignee of goods and/or his insurer who has become subrogated to his rights against a carrier under a bill of lading, at first instance, it would seem that there is a contract on which the action is based thus satisfying art.5(1). But on closer inspection, the carrier who was being sued in that case was not the carrier who issued the bill of lading. As against the carrier who issued the bill of lading, it could not be said that there exists a contract on which the claim could be based. Article 5(3) should therefore apply. The ECJ said:

> "It must therefore be held that that bill of lading discloses no contractual relationship freely entered into between [the consignee] on the one hand and, on the other, [the defendants] who, according to the insurers, were the actual maritime carriers of the goods".

This is a difficult case to reconcile with English law and practice on carriage of goods. English law often employs the fiction of an implied contract as we have seen in earlier chapters. Although the ECJ's emphasis on the lack of a direct relationship between the holder of the bill of lading and the sea carrier who had not issued the bill of lading might be criticised as not recognising the notion of implied contracts, some consolation might be derived from the fact that as far as jurisdiction is concerned, there is no real deprivation of legitimate choice as the claimant is still entitled to rely on art.5(3), also an exception to the general rule of art.2. It would appear that in the light of this decision, much depends on whether the bill of lading issued is an owner's or charterer's bill.

It might be noted that this mutual exclusivity of claims in tort and contract **12–062** roughly resembles the French doctrine of noncumulation of remedies which states that a claim in contract precludes a parallel remedy in tort. While an action may be framed in either contract or tort before the courts of law, the distinction must be made for jurisdictional purposes under the Regulation.

In *Kalfelis*, the ECJ extended art.5(3) to cover noncontractual actions founded on unjust enrichment. Taking its cue from the ECJ, the Court of Appeal held in the recent case of *Casio Computer v Eugen Kaiser* [2001] EWCA Civ 661 that a claim for restitution based on dishonest assistance and knowing receipt should necessarily fall within art.5(3). It is perhaps needful to remind ourselves that there are no hard and fast rules as to whether a claim falls within art.5(3) and not art.5(1). Indeed, as the court said in *Sarrio SA v Kuwait Investment Authority* [1999] A.C. 32, a wide, common sense approach should be adopted.

In *Kleinwort Benson v Glasgow City Council* [1997] 4 All E.R. 641, Glasgow City Council appealed against the decision of the Court of Appeal that the English courts had jurisdiction over a claim made by Kleinwort Benson for restitution. The bank had instituted action in England following a ruling from the House of Lords that certain interest rate swap transactions entered into with local authorities were null and void. The bank claimed inter alia that the matter was within the jurisdiction of the English courts on the basis of art.5(3). The House of Lords held that art.5(3) could not be applied to a claim arising from a void contract.[45] This was because such a claim did not, apart from exceptional circumstances, presuppose either a harmful event or a threatened wrong.[46] It was therefore held that the English courts did not have jurisdiction under art.5(3). That reading of art.5(3) is however not entirely satisfactory in the light of the opinion of Advocate General Darmon in *Shearson Lehamn Hutton Inc v Treuhand für Vermögensverwaltung und Beteiligungen (TVB) mbH* (C–89/91)

---

[45] See *Casio Computer Co Ltd v Sayo* (*Times LR* February 6, 2001) where Anthony Mann QC, sitting as High Court judge, held that art.5(3) was however wide enough to accommodate a claim for damages for breach of a constructive trust and knowing assistance. The judge said that unlike unjust enrichment, an act of knowing assistance had parallels with the tortious wrong. A wrong was committed and loss was caused. Also, see *Dexter Ltd v Harley* (*Times LR* April 2, 2001) where Lloyd J. held that when applying the concept of "harmful event" to a constructive trust claim based on knowing receipt or dishonest assistance, it was not sufficient simply to point to acts done in the jurisdiction if those acts had nothing to do with the defendant. The harmful event had to be a harmful event on the part of the defendant.

[46] In the Scottish case of *Bonnier Media Ltd v Greg Lloyd Smith & Kestrel Trading Corp* (Court of Session; *Times LR* July 10, 2002), the action was for an injunction to prevent the defendants from abusing the applicant's domain name. The Court of Session held that art.5(3) clearly applied to threatened wrongs as much as to completed wrongs, provided that a harmful event was likely to occur in the jurisdiction.

[1993] E.C.R. I–139. In that case, the Advocate General construed a passage in the judgment of *Kalfelis* as enabling a claim for unjust enrichment to fall within art.5(3). Lord Clyde considered that proposition to have been founded on a misreading of an imprecise translation of the passage in *Kalfelis*. Further, the ECJ had held in that case that the term "matters relating to tort, delict or quasi-delict" must be regarded as an independent concept covering all actions which are not related to contract under art.5(1). In so holding, the ECJ stressed that the special jurisdiction in arts 5 and 6 are to be construed restrictively and further emphasised that while disadvantages may arise from different aspects of the same dispute being adjudicated upon by different courts, the claimants is always entitled to bring his action in its entirety before the courts of the defendant's place of domicile. It is however observed that in *Tacconi v Wagner* (C–334/00) [2002] E.C.R. I–7357, the ECJ clearly stressed that art.5(3) could include restitutionary claims, whether arising from contract or not, despite a restrictive reading.

12–063 Moving on to the second limb of art.5(3), it might be useful to use an illustration to highlight its potential construction difficulties.

Example:

A has a factory in France. He imported a consignment of machines from B, the manufacturer, who is based in Germany. A week after taking delivery of the goods, the machines exploded causing damage to A's premises. The cause of the explosion was a faulty part in the machines. A wishes to sue B in tort. Under art.5(3), it is necessary for the court to decide where the harmful event occurred. There appear to be several possible interpretations to art.5(3) in this respect:

1. the place where the wrongful event giving rise to the damage occurred; or

2. the place where the damage results; or

3. the place where the damage becomes apparent; or

4. the place where the effect of the damage continues to be suffered.

In our example, there are two possible candidates—France, where the explosion took place or Germany, where the faulty machines were made.

12–064 The leading case on the subject is *Handelskwekeij GJ Bier BV v Mines de Potasse d'Alsace SA* (21/76) [1976] E.C.R. 1735. The Dutch claimant sued a French mining company in the Dutch court for damage caused to his plants in the Netherlands. The damage was allegedly caused by the defendant discharging waste materials into the Rhine in France which were subsequently carried into the Netherlands downstream. The Court stated that:

"[W]here the place of happening of the event which may give rise to liability in tort, delict or quasi-delict and the place where that event results in damage are not identical, the expression 'place where the harmful event occurred', in article 5(3) . . . must be understood as being intended to cover both the place where the damage occurred and the place of the event giving rise to it".

From *Bier*, it is quite clear that A has a choice to sue B in France where the damage resulted or in Germany where the harmful event originated.

There is some circumscription on the general rule in cases involving financial harm. In *Dumez Bâtiment and Tracona v Hessische Landesbank* (C–220/88)

[1990] 1 E.C.R. 49, the ECJ held that where a parent company was injured as a result of losses suffered by its subsidiary situated elsewhere it could not bring an action in the courts of the place where it, the parent company, discovered the consequential financial loss to its assets. There, the French claimant was prevented from taking action against a German bank in France whose withdrawal of credit to a German property developer had resulted in the collapse of the claimant's subsidiary which in turn led to consequential financial loss in France by the claimant. Article 5(3) could not be extended to cover actions founded on consequential financial loss by an indirect victim.[47]

This restrictive interpretation has been confirmed in the later case of *Marinari* **12–065** *v Lloyds Bank* (C–364/93) [1995] E.C.R. I–2719. In *Marinari*, the claimant, an Italian domiciliary, had lodged promissory notes of an exchange value of $752,500 with a branch of Lloyds Bank in England. The promissory notes were issued by the Negros Oriental province of the Philippines in favour of a company in Beirut. The staff at Lloyds Bank refused to return the promissory notes and advised the police of their existence and uncertain origin. As a result, the claimant was arrested and the promissory notes seized. The claimant, upon his release without having been prosecuted, brought an action against Lloyds Bank in Italy. He sought compensation for the bank's refusal to pay the exchange value of the notes, damage suffered as a result of his arrest, breach of several related contracts and damage to his reputation. Lloyds Bank challenged the Italian court's jurisdiction arguing that the alleged damage and losses had occurred in England. The ECJ adopted a restrictive stance and held that the term "place where the harmful event occurred" could not be interpreted as referring to the place where the victim claims to have suffered financial loss consequential upon initial damage arising and suffered by him in another Member State.[48]

On very much the same basis, in *Kronhofer v Maier* (C–168/02) [2004] E.C.R. I–6009, June 10, 2004, the ECJ ruled that the expression "place where the harmful event occurred" could not refer to the place where the claimant is domiciled or where "his assets are concentrated" by reason only of the fact that he has suffered financial damage there resulting from the loss of part of his assets which arose and was incurred in another Contracting State. In that case, the claimant was domiciled in Austria and the defendants in Germany. He claimed damages against the defendants for causing him to suffer serious financial loss to some investments placed in Germany and England. He brought proceedings in Austria. The Austrian declined jurisdiction. The ECJ agreed with the Austrian court that Austria was not the place where the harmful event occurred. The court reiterated the view taken in *Kalfelis* (189/87) [1988] E.C.R. 5565 that art.5(3) should not be given too expansive a reading.

In international trade, a cause of action in misrepresentation is not unforeseeable. The question is where the harmful event occurred when the misstatement was made in one country and acted upon in another. In *Alfred Dunhill Ltd v Diffusion Internationale de Maroquinerie de Prestige SARL* [2002] 2 All E.R. (Comm) 950, the claimant sued the defendant for damages under the Misrepresentation Act 1967 or at common law on the ground that the defendant had

---

[47] See also *Shevill v Presse Alliance* (C–68/93) [1995] E.C.R. I–415.
[48] In *Shevill v Presse Alliance* (C–68/93) [1995] E.C.R. I–415, the ECJ reiterated the point that the Brussels Convention does not provide criteria for assessing whether the event in question is harmful. That must be a matter for the national court applying its own substantive law.

made negligent and false oral misrepresentations at meetings in Italy and/or telephone calls from Italy to England concerning the fitness of the goods. The court followed the lead in *Marinari* and held that England could not be the place where the harmful event occurred.[49]

Where the claim is founded on unjust enrichment rather than a tort, the connection between the action and the "place where the harmful event occurred" is less obvious.

12–066   *Dexter Ltd (in Administrative Receivership) v Edwina Amethysts Harley, The Times,* April 2, 2001
Facts:
D Ltd, the claimant, claimed to have suffered substantial loss as a result of breaches of fiduciary duties on the part of a former director, who was H's son. D Ltd asserted that part of a substantial sum of money wrongfully removed from its possession had passed through an account in the name of H at a bank in Guernsey. That, they alleged, made H a constructive trustee of that money or rendered her liable to account for the money on the basis of unjust enrichment. H was domiciled in Spain and none of the acts or omissions alleged as against her in relation to the money had happened within the jurisdiction. The issue was whether art.5(3) allowed H, the domiciliary of Spain, to be sued in England.
Held:
The court held that although a claim for unjust enrichment did not ordinarily give rise to a harmful event or a threatened wrong for the purposes of art.5(3) (per Lord Goff in *Kleinwort Benson v Glasgow City Council* [1999] 1 A.C. 153), it was conceded by H that a constructive trust did. Nevertheless, and notwithstanding that a harmful event had occurred within the jurisdiction which was part of the chain of events which had to be pleaded and proved in order to establish liability against H, it was not sufficient simply to point to acts done within the jurisdiction, if those acts had nothing to do with her.

As far as Lloyd J. was concerned, the harmful event, be it an act or omission, had to be a harmful event on the part of the defendant. Alleged acts or omissions which caused the defendant to be liable as a constructive trustee which were undertaken by persons other than those under the defendant's control or authority could not be said to be a harmful event linking the defendant with that place.

12–067   In *Casio Computer v Eugen Kaiser* (April 11, 2001) the claimant alleged that K had dishonestly assisted in the dissipation of its monies and had knowingly received monies belonging to itself. K was domiciled in Spain. The question was whether the claimant could rely on art.5(3) to sue K in England. The Court of Appeal held that the company account into which money was paid was carried out in England. The place of the event giving rise to the damage was England. The breach of trust and the dishonest assistance could possibly be characterised as "harmful events" within the meaning of art.5(3) and as such, it was clear that under art.5(3), the defendant could be sued in England.

In these cases, the courts have taken the view that "harmful events" do not only include the consequences of breach suffered by the claimant but also events or acts and omissions bringing about the damage.

A final note on the subject. The House of Lords held in *Shevill v Presse Alliance* [1996] 3 All E.R. 929 that art.5(3) will apply even though there is no actual harm or damage suffered if there is a presumption at law of some nominal damage. In that case, the defendant had argued that "harmful event" connotes

---

[49] See also *Domicrest v Swiss Bank Corp* [1999] Q.B. 548.

actual harm and therefore art.5(3) should have no place in a libel action where the claimant relied solely on the presumption of harm, a liberty nourished by English law. Lord Jauncey, speaking for the House of Lords, held that what constitutes a "harmful event" must necessarily be a matter for the national court applying its own substantive law. It is thus abundantly clear that where English law presumes the publication of a defamatory statement to be harmful to the claimant without specific proof thereof, that would be sufficient for the application of art.5(3).

The Regulation has affixed a third limb to art.5(3) by stating that not only **12–068** could jurisdiction be founded by the courts of a Member State where the harmful event occurred as is the case under the Brussels Convention but also the courts of a Member State where the harmful event *may occur*. This means that where preventive measures have been taken to confine the damage caused in a particular place and these measures have been successful, the courts of that place could also be seised with jurisdiction, providing, of course, that there is a substantive cause of action under any applicable law. A tort which is actionable per se but has the potential to cause harm is an obvious example.

(c) Disputes arising from the operations of a branch, agency or other establishment

Article 5(5) provides that as regards a dispute arising out of the operations of a **12–069** branch, agency or other establishment, the action could be commenced at the courts for the place in which the branch, agency or other establishment is situated. This article only applies where the defendant is domiciled in a Member State—where the defendant is not so domiciled, the common law rules on jurisdiction will apply.

On the definition of "branch, agency or other establishment", *De Bloos Sprl v Bouyer SA* (14/76) [1976] E.C.R. 1497 sets out the following criteria:

1. whether it acts as an extension of the parent body;

2. whether it is subject to the parent body's control and direction; and

3. whether it has the appearance of some degree of permanence.

Hence, in *Blanckaert & Willems v Trost* (139/80) [1981] E.C.R. 819, the ECJ decided that an independent commercial agent who merely carried out negotiations on behalf of the principal and has the liberty to conduct the nature and amount of work for the principal, does not fall within the definition of art.5(5). On the other hand, in *Dinkha Latchin v General Mediterranean Holdings SA* (December 4, 2001, Commercial Court) although it was obvious that the subsidiary office had done little more than organising meetings between the principal parties, art.5(5) could apply. It was an extension of the parent, was subject to the parent's direction and had the appearance of some degree of permanence.

On the application of the term "operations", a restrictive construction was **12–070** adopted by the ECJ in *Somafer SA v Saar-Ferngas AG* (33/78) [1978] E.C.R. 2183. It held that art.5(5) applied only to matters relating to:

1. the management of the branch (e.g. its premises and staff);

2. tortious or delictual acts committed arising from activities in which the branch or agency has engaged on behalf of the parent body at the place where it is located;

3. undertakings which have been entered into at the establishment in the name or authority of the parent body and which must be performed in the Member State where the agency or branch is situated.

This last requirement that the relevant undertakings are to be performed in the Member State where the agency, branch or other establishment is situated was subsequently rejected by the ECJ in:

12–071 *Lloyd's Shipping Register v Société Campenon Bernard* (C–439/93) [1995] 2 C.E.C. 3
Facts:
A French company (claimant) arranged with the French branch of Lloyd's Register (a registered charity in England) for the testing and certification of certain concrete reinforcing steel to be carried out by the latter. The contract later specified that the testing would take place in Spain, and would be carried out by the Spanish branch of Lloyd's Register. The French branch accepted the terms of the contract. Alleging that Lloyd's Register had wrongly certified the steel, the claimant company sued Lloyd's Register for damages in France (i.e. through the intermediary of the French branch). Lloyd's Register pleaded that the French courts lacked jurisdiction on the basis that the undertakings negotiated by the French branch did not take place in France, but in Spain.
Held:
The ECJ in agreeing with the mantle of academic opinion dismissed Lloyd's Register's arguments on the following grounds:

1. The actual wording of art.5(5) in no way requires that the undertakings negotiated by a branch should be performed in the Member State where it is established.

2. Since art.5(1) already allows the claimant to sue in contract in the courts of the place of performance of the obligation in question, art.5(5) would simply duplicate that provision if it applied solely to undertakings entered into by a branch which were to be performed in the Member State in which the branch was established. At the very most, it would create a second head of special jurisdiction where, within the Member State of the branch, the place of performance of the obligation in question was situated in a judicial area other than that of the branch.

3. The notion of an ancillary establishment in art.5(5) as a place of business implies that it should have some semblance of permanence as the extension of a parent body, to negotiate and deal directly with third parties. As far as the ECJ was concerned,

   "there does not necessarily have to be a close link between the entity with which a customer conducts negotiation and places an order and the place where the order will be performed".

   Undertakings may therefore form part of the operations of an ancillary establishment even though they are to be performed outside the Member State where it is situated, possibly by another ancillary establishment.

(d) Trusts

12–072 The courts of the Member State in which the trust is domiciled will have jurisdiction in an action against a person in his capacity as settlor, trustee or beneficiary. The trust must have its genesis in statute or a written instrument, excluding wills. If the trust was made orally, before this article could apply, the court must be satisfied that the trust is properly evidenced in writing. Trusts emanating from wills and intestacies are excluded from the Regulation which applies only to civil and commercial matters.

(e) Salvage

As regards a dispute concerning the payment of remuneration claimed in respect   **12–073** of the salvage of a cargo or freight, the court under the authority of which the cargo or freight in question has been arrested to secure such payment or the court under whose jurisdiction, the cargo or freight could have been arrested to secure payment but bail or other security had been given. The proviso to both limbs is that the action in question should claim that the defendant has an interest in the cargo or freight or had such an interest at the time of salvage.

(f) Co-defendants

Where the defendant is one of several defendants, he may be sued in another   **12–074** Member State if any of the defendants is domiciled there. It is, thus, entirely permissible for the claimant to sue one defendant who is domiciled in a Member State and join to that action defendants who may or may not be domiciled in an EU Member State. Article 6 is therefore quite a controversial provision because it allows EU jurisdiction to be extended to non-domiciliaries. Article 6 however (at least as far as the English courts are concerned) is limited to cases where the same claimant was bringing proceedings against both the defendant domiciled in a Member State and the non-domiciled defendant and did not confer jurisdiction where one claimant is suing the EU domiciled defendant and another is suing the non-domiciled defendant (*Madoff Securities v Stephen Ernest John Raven* [2011] EWHC 3102 (Comm)).

The relevant time for ascertaining the domicile of any one of the defendants is at the time the claim form is issued not when it is actually served if *Petrograde v Smith* [1998] 2 All E.R. 346 is to be followed. Support for this approach might also be found in *Canada Trust v Stolzenberg (No.2)* [1998] 1 W.L.R. 547. Article 6 also provides that it must be demonstrated that the claims are so closely connected that it is expedient to hear and determine them together to avoid the risk of irreconcilable judgments resulting from separate proceedings.

This proviso is an incorporation of the ECJ's ruling in *Kalfelis v Schroder, Munchmeyer, Hengst & Co* (189/87) [1988] E.C.R. 5565 that there must be a genuine connection between the claims made against the different defendants and consequently, any application under art.6 must be read in conjunction with art.22 of the Brussels Convention (now, art.28 under the Regulation). The application of art.6(1), it would appear, should be dictated by the need to avoid the danger of conflicting judgments between different Member States. In *La Réunion Européenne v Spliethoff's Bevrachtingskantoor* (C–51/97) [1998] E.C.R. I–6511, the ECJ found that there was no risk of irreconcilable judgments where there were two claims in one action against different defendants and one based in contract and the other on tort. The implication there is thus that there was insufficient connection between the claims as one was founded on contract whilst the other was in tort, despite the fact that the claims were brought by the same claimant against two defendants over the same loss. The correctness of this statement was called into question in the following case. In *Brian Watson v First*

Choice Holidays & Flights Ltd [2001] EWCA Civ 972, the Court of Appeal was troubled by the possible implications of the rule in *La Réunion Européenne*. In *Watson*, the claimant sustained serious injuries whilst on holiday in Tenerife, part of the Kingdom of Spain. He sued D1, the tour operator, in England and attempted to join D2, the hotel owner established in Spain, to proceedings in England in pursuant to art.6(1). The action against D1 was in contract whilst the claim against D2 was in tort. If the two actions were deemed to be so closely connected that it would be more expedient to hear and determine them together to avoid the risk of irreconcilable judgments, then the English court should assume jurisdiction over both D1 and D2. However, it was argued by D2 that in the light of *La Réunion Européenne*, as a claim in tort was distinct from an action in contract, there was no risk of irreconcilable judgments and therefore, D2 should be sued in Spain where it is domiciled. The Court of Appeal was unable to decide and a reference for a preliminary ruling was made to the ECJ on this question. It is submitted that the opinion in *La Réunion Européenne* was not intended to set out a technical point that where there are two different causes of action based on the same facts, there is no risk of irreconcilable judgments. What seems to be more important is the court's finding that there was indeed a risk of irreconcilable judgments because the two claims are so closely related. Nonetheless, there is the argument that art.6(1) as an exception to art.2 should be construed and applied strictly, hence, the statement in *La Réunion Européenne* should be taken as unequivocally narrow. The reference was subsequently abandoned, presumably as a result of a settlement between the parties.

12–075   In 2007 the ECJ had a renewed opportunity to discuss its decision in *Réunion*. In Case-98/06 *Freeport Plc v Arnoldsson* (October 11, 2007), A tried joining F1 to proceedings against F2 in Sweden. F1 was domiciled in the United Kingdom whilst F2, in Sweden. The claim against F1 was in contract and the claim against F2 was in tort, delict or quasi delict. F1 resisted being joined arguing that the claims were not connected and as such, there was little risk of irreconcilable judgments. The ECJ held that the wording in art.6(1) does not suggest that the multiple claims should share an identical legal basis. The court went on to say:

> "It is for the national court to assess whether there is a connection between the different claims brought before it, that is to say, a risk of irreconcilable judgments if those claims were determined separately and, in that regard, to take account of all the necessary factors in the case-file, which may, if appropriate yet without its being necessary for the assessment, lead it to take into consideration the legal bases of the actions brought before that court".

The ECJ however said that this was not inconsistent with *Réunion* whose facts were unique and that F1 had misread *Réunion*. It seems more convincing simply to say that *Réunion* was not wrong. That said, the position now is preferable to the confusion caused by *Réunion*.

The ECJ also added that, unlike the case of art.6(2), in order to apply art.6(1) there is no need to show that the joinder was brought with the *purpose* of excluding the jurisdiction of the court at the Member State where one of the parties is domiciled. It would be inappropriate to restrict the scope of art.6(1).

12–076   In *Messier Dowty Ltd v Sabena SA* [2000] 1 Lloyd's Rep. 428, Dowty had manufactured certain aircraft parts for Airbus, an aeroplane manufacturer. An

Airbus plane owned by Sabena was involved in an incident when landing at Brussels Airport. Dowty, in anticipation of legal action being taken against themselves, claimed against Sabena, BAA (who designed the landing gear) and/ or Airbus before the English court asking for nonliability declarations. They had applied to join Sabena to the proceedings in England. Sabena objected on the basis that they were domiciled in Belgium and consequently, under art.2 of the Brussels Convention, that was the proper place for them to be sued. Dowty argued that there was a considerable advantage in Sabena being joined in the proceedings because it would enable a consistent determination of all questions of responsibility and fault concerning the incident at Brussels Airport. They also relied on art.6(1) of the Brussels Convention contending that Sabena was "one of a number of defendants in the courts of the place where any one of them is domiciled". The Court of Appeal held that art.6 must be read in conjunction with the provisions on *lis pendens* so that art.6 only applied where the actions brought against the various defendants were related when the proceedings were instituted, that is to say, where it was expedient to hear and determine them together in order to avoid the risk of irreconcilable judgments resulting from separate proceedings. At the stage when Sabena had made no claim against Dowty, Dowty could not establish that the joinder of Sabena met that additional requirement. Such a case should no longer be a cause of controversy given the proviso in art.6 of the new Regulation, which is not found in the existing Brussels and Lugano Conventions.

The existence of genuine link does not mean that the claimant must identify an anchor defendant and institute action against him first before art.6 could be used.

Canada Trust Co v Stolzenberg and Gambazi [2000] 3 W.L.R. 1376   **12–077**
Facts:
The respondent, CTC, issued a writ on August 1, 1996 against S and 36 other defendants. They alleged that they had been induced by S's fraud to invest in a group of companies all of which had become insolvent. At the time of the issue of the writ, S was domiciled in England. However, at the time of the service of the writ, he had already moved to live in Germany. It was uncertain where S was domiciled at the time of the service of the writ. CTC wished to sue S in England and use S as the "anchor defendant" to join the other 36 defendants, domiciled elsewhere, to proceedings in England under art.6 of the Lugano Convention. However, two of the 36 defendants had been served before S had been served. It was therefore argued that under art.6(1), S should have been served first before he could be used as an "anchor defendant".
Held:
In establishing whether S was domiciled in England at the critical time, it was not necessary to adopt a test which was more than a good arguable case. If a more stringent test were to be applied, this could well lead to greater expense and delay in circumstances where the jurisdictional issues ought to be decided with due despatch. The House of Lords also construed the word "sued" as referring to the time the writ was issued, not when it was served. On whether art.6(1) could only be relied on if S had already been served before the issue or service of the proceedings on the co-defendants, the House of Lords held that there was no such requirement from the scheme of the Convention. Support could not be drawn from RSC ord.11 r.1(i)(c) which had express provisions for such a requirement.

The House of Lords rejected the argument that the anchor defendant should have been served first.

(g) Third parties

12–078   Article 6(2) states that a person domiciled in a Member State may also be sued as third party in an action on a warranty or guarantee or in any other third party proceedings in the court seised of the original proceedings. The exception is that where those proceedings were instituted solely with the object of removing him from the jurisdiction of the court which would be competent in his case. A third party is generally one who is a stranger to the proceedings. It was confirmed in *GIE v Zurich Espana* (C-77/04) May 26, 2005 that in cases of multiple insurers or co-insurers where contribution is sought, art.6(2) could be used.

(h) Counterclaim

12–079   Article 6(3) states that a person domiciled in a Member State may also be sued, on the counterclaim arising from the same contract or facts on which the original claim was based, in the court in which the original claim is pending. A counterclaim is a claim made by the defendant who alleges that he is entitled to any relief or remedy against a claimant, instead of bringing a separate action. A counterclaim must be separately pleaded.

It was held in *National Justice Compania Naviera SA v Prudential Assurance Co Ltd (The Ikarian Reefer) (No.2)* [2000] 1 Lloyd's Rep. 129 that the requirement that the counterclaim arises "from the same contract or facts" was designed to ensure that it was not any kind of counterclaim which a defendant was to be permitted to bring against the claimant in the same jurisdiction but only one which was significantly connected with the original claim.

Jurisdiction in matters relating to insurance

12–080   The protective rules of jurisdiction in s.3 of the Regulation (arts 8–14) relate to actions based on a contract of insurance. These rules assume that the insured is generally in a weaker bargaining position and thus, needs special protection. It follows therefore that the insured should be given a wider choice of fora in which to bring an action against the insurer. Article 9 enables the insured to sue the insurer in the courts of the place where he is domiciled as well as in the courts of the place where the insurer is domiciled. Furthermore, an insurer who is not domiciled in a Member State but has a branch, agency or other establishment in one of the Member States shall, in disputes arising out of the operations of the branch, agency or other establishment, be deemed to be domiciled in that Member State.[50] On the other hand, the insurer is generally required to sue the insured at the place of the insured's domicile. Contracting out of these special rules is severely curtailed.[51]

---

[50] Art.9(2), Regulation.

[51] Art.13 provides that the provisions of this section may only be departed from by an agreement: 1. which is entered into after the dispute has arisen; or 2. which allows the policyholder, the insured or a beneficiary to bring proceedings in courts other than those indicated in this section; or 3. which is concluded between a policyholder and an insurer, both of whom are at the time of conclusion of the contract domiciled or habitually resident in the same Member State, and which has the effect of conferring jurisdiction on the courts of that State even if the harmful event were to occur abroad, provided that such an agreement is not contrary to the law of that State; or 4. which is concluded with a policyholder who is not domiciled in a Member State, except in so far as the insurance is compulsory or relates to immovable property in a Member State; or 5. which relates to a contract of insurance in so far as it covers one or more the risks set out in art.14.

For the purposes of marine insurance in international trade, art.13 read together with art.14 provides that the protective jurisdiction rules could be departed from by a jurisdiction agreement between the parties, provided that the insurance contract relates to any of the following risks:

1. loss or damage to sea-going ships, installations situated offshore or on the high seas, or aircraft arising from perils which relate to their use for commercial purposes;

2. goods in transit other than passengers' baggage where the transit consists of or includes carriage by such ships or aircraft;

3. any liability arising out of the use of or operation of ships, installations or aircraft or for loss or damage caused by goods in transit (except where such liability relates to bodily injury to passengers or loss of or damage to their baggage);

4. any financial loss connected with the use or operations of ships, installations or aircraft in a particular loss of freight or charter-hire;

5. any risk or interest connected with any of the above.

This effectively removes all marine risks, other than those relating to passenger carriage, from the operation of s.3. In marine policies, the insurers would thus be free to impose a jurisdiction clause on the insured which departed from the protective rules of s.3.

In *Charman v WOC Offshore* [1993] 1 Lloyd's Rep. 378 though, the court held **12–081** that the exceptions on maritime risks above do not apply where the insurance and the jurisdiction agreement cover both marine and non-marine risks, unless the non-marine risks are simply secondary to the marine risks. In that case, the court refused to accept an English jurisdiction clause contained in an insurance contract which referred to equipment used to reconstruct a breakwater. Some of the equipment carried a certificate of seaworthiness and could be rightly made the subject of a marine cover. Other machinery parts though were harbour items. They were therefore land-based and could not be protected by a marine cover. These items were important pieces to the project and as such their risk was not ancillary or secondary to the marine risks. The clause could not thus be enforced in the light of s.3.

Exclusive jurisdiction clauses

Article 23[52] provides that if the parties, one or more of whom is domiciled in a **12–082** Member State, have agreed that a court or courts of a Member State are to have jurisdiction to settle any disputes which have arisen or which may arise in connection with a particular legal relationship, that court or those courts shall have jurisdiction over those disputes. Such jurisdiction shall be exclusive unless the parties have agreed otherwise. This is a departure from the common law where a jurisdiction clause, whilst generally effective in conferring jurisdiction on the chosen forum, does not necessarily confer *exclusive* jurisdiction on that

---

[52] The new art.23 replaces art.17 of the Brussels and Lugano Conventions.

court.[53] It is also an improvement to art.17 of the Brussels and Lugano Conventions which, although it provides for the exclusivity of jurisdiction, does not make it clear that the parties could agree to derogate from that exclusivity of jurisdiction.

The choice of forum agreement shall be either:

1. in writing or evidenced in writing; or

2. in a form which accords with practices which the parties have established between themselves[54]; or

3. in international trade or commerce, in a form which accords with a usage of which the parties are, or ought to have been, aware and which in such trade or commerce is widely known to, and regularly observed by, parties to contracts of the type involved in the particular trade or commerce concerned.

Unlike art.17 in the Brussels and Lugano Conventions, it is additionally stipulated, as a concession to electronic commerce, that any communication by electronic means which provides a durable record of the agreement shall be equivalent to "writing". This is probably not quite necessary as the EU Directive on Electronic Commerce very adequately ensures that Member States recognise and enforce electronic contracts (and a jurisdiction agreement should be included) and not discriminate against contracts made electronically and it seems very unlikely that even under the old provision "in writing" would not have been construed to include electronic communications which could be reproduced in hard copy.

12–083   Where the jurisdiction agreement is concluded between parties, *none of whom is domiciled in a Member State*, the courts of other Member States shall have no jurisdiction over their disputes unless the court or courts chosen have declined jurisdiction.[55]

The exclusive jurisdiction agreement must be clear. There is imposed on the court before which the matter is brought the duty of first examining whether the clause conferring jurisdiction upon it was in fact the subject of consensus between the parties. Clear evidence of consensus is required as was held in *Estasis Salotti v RUWA* (24/76) [1976] E.C.R. 1831 and *New Hampshire Insurance Co v Strabag* [1992] 1 Lloyd's Rep. 361. This test should not be taken meaning that only express terms are admissible. Indeed as the ECJ pointed out in *Coreck Maritime GmbH v Handelsveem BV* (C–386/98) ([2001] OJ C28/07) (it should be noted that discussions surrounding art.17 of the Brussels Convention are usually compatible with art.23 of the Regulation):

---

[53] At common law whether a jurisdiction clause is exclusive or not is a matter of construction of the contract against the background of its factual matrix (*Aizkir Navigation Inc v Al Wathba National Insurance Co* [2011] EWHC 3940 (Comm)). See para.12–028.

[54] In *Kolmar Group v Visen* [2009] EWHC 3765 (QB), of the five contracts between the parties, three were made in the same way, namely by way of an oral agreement over the telephone, followed by email confirmation and then an email/fax setting out the terms and conditions including the jurisdiction clause. The High Court concluded that that was a course of dealing sufficient to satisfy art.17(1)(b) (see also *Partenreederei M/S Tilly Russ v Haven & Vervoerbedrijf Nova* (71/83) [1985] Q.B. 931). The court took the view that the more uniform the practice of the parties the less often they needed to have dealt with each other to establish a course of dealing.

[55] Art.23(3).

"However, if the purpose of article 17 is to protect the wishes of the parties concerned, it must be construed in a manner consistent with those wishes where they are established. Article 17 is based on a recognition of the independent will of the parties to a contract in deciding which courts are to have jurisdiction to settle disputes falling within the scope of the [Brussels] Convention, other than those which are expressly excluded pursuant to the fourth paragraph of article 17 (*Meeth v Glacetal* (23/78) [1978] E.C.R. 2133, paragraph 5).

It follows that the words 'have agreed' in the first sentence of the first paragraph of article 17 of the [Brussels] Convention cannot be interpreted as meaning that it is necessary for a jurisdiction clause to be formulated in such a way that the competent court can be determined on its wording alone. It is sufficient that the clause state the objective factors on the basis of which the parties have agreed to choose a court or the courts to which they wish to submit disputes which have arisen or which may arise between them".

On this basis, incorporation by reference is permissible as long as such an **12–084** intention is expressed in writing and preferably, signed by both parties. That reference must be express and reasonable steps must be taken by the party attempting to rely on it to bring the contents of that provision to the knowledge of the other party. This might be done simply by sending that other party a copy of the signed document before the signing of the main agreement. It might further be noted that in *Estasis Salotti*, the notice requirement could be dispensed with if it could be properly inferred that the other party is already aware of or familiar with its terms.[56] In that case, both parties belonged to the same trade association. That suggested that they must both be aware of the incorporated standard terms as recommended by the association.

These requirements were clearly not satisfied in *Lafarge Plasterboard Ltd v Fritz Peters & Co* [2000] 2 Lloyd's Rep. 689. It was contended by L that an exclusive jurisdiction agreement was to be found in the fact that FP had delivered goods against written orders placed by it. On the reverse of each order form were a number of standard terms and conditions, one of which provided that the contract thereby created was to be governed by English law and that both parties submitted to the jurisdiction of the English court. FP alleged that orders were only faxed to it, with only the face (and not the reverse) of the order form ever being faxed, and that any top-copy order forms which might have been sent subsequently were never received. In delivering the goods, FP would send an order confirmation on a printed form, which provided for German law and jurisdiction to apply. The court was not persuaded that the fact that there has been a continuing trading relationship between the parties was of any help to L, since the evidence indicated no more than that L habitually sent orders on its conditions to FP, and FP habitually delivered goods under confirmations on its conditions. There was, therefore, no established practice between the parties of contracting on L's conditions. L's claim that the dispute to be litigated in England could not therefore succeed.

In contrast, the court was convinced in *SSQ Europe SA v Johann & Backes* [2002] 1 Lloyd's Rep. 465 that with over 672 invoices, all bearing the claimant's exclusive jurisdiction clause on the reverse, having been processed, it was not

---

[56] See also *MSG v Gravières Rhénanes* (C–106/95) [1997] E.C.R. I–911.

open to the defendant to argue that there was no consent to the exclusive jurisdiction clause. It was irrelevant whether the contracts were concluded in writing or orally and later confirmed in writing; there was a good arguable case that the defendant was aware of the exclusive jurisdiction.

12–085   Agreement to the jurisdiction clause is difficult to prove in cases involving subcontracts and a network of contracts. In *AIG Europe SA v QBE International Insurance Ltd* [2001] 2 Lloyd's Rep. 268 for example although the reinsurance contract in question contained a provision that "all terms, clauses and conditions as original and to follow the original in all respects including settlements . . . ", the court ruled that that was not enough to incorporate the exclusive French jurisdiction clause in the original contract of insurance into the reinsurance relationship. The court said that it did not necessarily follow that general words of incorporation would be taken as demonstrating clearly and precisely the existence of a consensus in relation to clauses, such as jurisdiction and law clauses, which are ancillary to the contract. The commercial context too was not of sufficient weight to make good the deficiency in the language of the general incorporation clause.[57] So too in *Siboti K/SV v BP France* [2003] EWHC 1278, it was held that a bill of lading which provided that the goods were "carried under and pursuant to all terms whatsoever of the charterparty" was not sufficiently precise to incorporate the exclusive jurisdiction in the charterparty into the bill of lading contract. The starting point in a case of a bill of lading was the contract contained in or evidenced by the bill of lading. The fact that the holder of a bill of lading had notice of the terms of the charterparty did not mean that they were incorporated into the bill of lading. General words of incorporation could only incorporate into the bill of lading those provisions which were directly germane to the shipment, carriage and delivery of the goods. Ancillary provisions of the charterparty would not be incorporated by general words.

So long as there is full consent, it is not possible for a litigant to argue that he nonetheless retained an unfettered right to choose the forum for his legal proceedings under art.6 of the European Convention on Human Rights and/or ss.3 and 6 of the Human Rights Act 1998 which provide for the general right to fair trial (*OT Africa Line Ltd v Fayad Hijazy* [2001] 1 Lloyd's Rep. 76). He is to be strictly bound by the jurisdiction clause. The fact that the exclusive jurisdiction had been made in a commercial context means that the parties' consent will normally be deemed to be present and despite the fact that it might become burdensome, the court would not consider the inconvenience to be a relevant factor. In *Andrew Beazley v Horizon Offshore Contractors Inc* [2004] EWHC 2555, the slip policy contained an English jurisdiction clause. The court refused to ignore the choice of jurisdiction clause stating that as a matter of contract the defendants had bound themselves to English jurisdiction. Where the parties have freely agreed on a place for the resolution of their disputes, the presumption must be that they have done so with full understanding that circumstances might make keeping true to such an agreement far more onerous than what was normally the case. Consent in a commercial context is not easily challenged.

---

[57] See also *Timothy Prifti v Musini Socciedad Anonima de Seguros y Reaseguros* [2003] EWHC 2796 where the court held that a jurisdiction clause in a slip agreement could only be incorporated by reference into the full insurance contract if the terms were properly identified and the parties had reached a clear consensus on jurisdiction at the time of entry into the contract.

Deutsche Bank v Asia Pacific Broadband Wireless Communications [2008] EWCA Civ   **12–086**
1091
Facts:
D agreed to give A a credit facility. A was controlled by the W family. Some of the W
family were indicted for fraud in Taiwan. A failed to make repayments. D sued A in
England relying on a jurisdiction clause. A argued that the jurisdiction clause could not be
relied on as the credit facility was signed, without proper authority, by members of the W
family who used it to perpetrate large-scale fraud. As such, the agreement and the
jurisdiction clause were tainted by fraud and want of authority and could not be enforced
under art.23(1).
Held:
The High Court held the jurisdiction was tainted and could not be enforced. However, the
Court of Appeal allowed the appeal. It is for the claimant to prove consensus ad
idem—but this is satisfied by:

1. the agreement confirming jurisdiction was in writing and was contained in a written
   agreement; and

2. the latter agreement had been signed or "chopped" (rubber-stamped) by all parties.

The Court of Appeal also held that the doctrine of separability can be applied to
jurisdiction clauses. According to the court, it is as much a part of English law as it is
European law. A jurisdiction clause (like an arbitration clause) can be treated distinctly
from the rest of the agreement containing it. It is only where the jurisdiction clause is
under *specific* challenge, that the question as to whether it is right to invoke it (e.g., where
fraud or duress is alleged specifically in relation to the clause) should be addressed.

A couple of observations might be made. The Court of Appeal in this case
borrowed largely from cases involving the separability of arbitration clauses
from the main agreement. Arbitration agreements however do expressly benefit
from s.7 Arbitration Act 1996 which clearly codified the doctrine of separability.
There is no equivalent for jurisdiction clauses. Secondly, be that as it may, a
distinction should be made, as Lord Hoffmann suggested in *Premium Nafta
Products v Fili Shipping* [2007] UKHL 40 (also known as *Fiona Trust v Privalov*
[2008] 1 Lloyd's Rep. 254) which involved an arbitration clause, between cases
where there was "no authority whatever" (e.g. an agreement signed by the office
cleaner) and cases of "excess of authority". In the former, the allegation of lack
of consent strikes at both the agreement and the arbitration (jurisdiction) clause.
On the other hand, the claim is that the agent had exceeded his authority by

> "entering into a main agreement in terms which were not authorised or for
> improper reasons, that is not necessarily an attack on the arbitration agreement.
> It would have to be shown that whatever the terms of the main agreement or
> the reasons for which the agent concluded it, he would have had no authority
> to enter into an arbitration agreement" (per Lord Hoffmann).

He is however free to question whether the exclusive jurisdiction clause does   **12–087**
extend to the dispute in issue. This is usually a matter of construction. That
however means that in a commercial law context, the court would take a narrow
view as to the ambit of the clause; the assumption being that if the parties had
intended to adopt a wide exclusive jurisdiction clause, they would have made it
explicitly clear. In *Mazur Media Ltd v Mazur Media GmbH* [2004] EWHC 1566
(Ch), for example, the relevant exclusive jurisdiction clause did not extend to

tortious, only contractual, claims. Thus, it could not relied on for furthering a claim in tort in the jurisdiction in question.

In *Donohue v Armco Inc* [2001] UKHL 64, a case decided on the doctrine of forum non conveniens, the relevant exclusive jurisdiction was expressed in the following terms: "the parties hereby irrevocably submit themselves to the exclusive jurisdiction of the English courts to settle any dispute which may arise out of or in connection with this agreement". It was argued that the clause only applied to contractual disputes. The House of Lords disagreed, affirming the ambit of the clause as extending to tortious actions. Lord Scott said:

> "The exclusive jurisdiction clause is expressed to cover '*any dispute* which may arise out of or in connection with' the agreement. It is not limited to 'any claim against' the party to the agreement. To give the clause that limited construction would very substantially reduce the protection afforded by the clause to the party to the agreement. The non-party, if he remained alone as a defendant in the foreign proceedings, would be entitled to claim from his co-tortfeasor a contribution to any damages awarded. He could join the co-tortfeasor, the party entitled to the protection of the exclusive jurisdiction clause, in third party proceedings for that purpose".

A party who has instituted proceedings in country contrary to the jurisdiction clause could not be prevented from subsequently suspending those proceedings and instituting action in the country specified in the jurisdiction clause unless there is clear evidence that he has clearly and unequivocally abandoned the jurisdiction clause (*Dubai Islamic Bank v PSI Energy* [2011] EWHC 1019 (Comm)). Where parties had bound themselves by a jurisdiction agreement, a party who wished to depart from it would need to show strong reasons for so doing. Whether there were such reasons sufficient to displace the other parties' prima facie entitlement to enforce the agreement would depend on all the facts and circumstances of the particular case (*Donohue v Armco Inc* [2001] UKHL 64).

12–088   An exclusive jurisdiction clause will also bind a third party who has succeeded to those rights and obligations under the original contract under the applicable national law.[58] For example, a holder of a bill of lading will be bound by the choice of forum clause agreed between the original shipper and carrier of goods and a third party beneficiary may rely on a choice of forum clause inserted in a contract of insurance (which falls within the exemptions in art.14) taken out wholly or in part for his benefit.[59]

In *Coreck Maritime GmbH v Handelsveem BV* [2001] O.J. C28 07 a preliminary ruling was sought from the ECJ as to whether a jurisdiction clause which has been agreed between a carrier and a shipper and appears in a bill of lading is valid as against *any* third party bearer of the bill of lading or whether it is only valid as against a third party bearer of the bill of lading who succeeded by virtue of the applicable national law to the shipper's rights and obligations when he acquired the bill of lading. The ECJ had held in the past that, in so far

---

[58] *Donohue v Armco Inc* [2001] UKHL 64.
[59] See Case 71/83 *Russ v Haven* [1984] E.C.R. 241, Case 201/82 *Gerling v Treasury Administration* [1983] E.C.R. 2503 and *Coreck Maritime GmbH v Handelsveem BV* (C–387/98) [2000] E.C.R. I–9337.

as the jurisdiction clause incorporated in a bill of lading is valid under the Convention rules (art.17) as between the shipper and the carrier, it can be pleaded against the third party holding the bill of lading so long as, under the relevant national law, the holder of the bill of lading succeeds to the shipper's rights and obligations.[60] It would seem to follow then that the question whether a party not privy to the original contract against whom a jurisdiction clause is relied on has succeeded to the rights and obligations of one of the original parties must be determined according to the applicable national law. If he did, it would not be necessary to ascertain whether he accepted the jurisdiction clause in the original contract. In such circumstances, acquisition of the bill of lading could not confer upon the third party more rights than those attaching to the shipper under it. The third party holding the bill of lading thus becomes vested with all the rights, and at the same time becomes subject to all the obligations, mentioned in the bill of lading, including those relating to the agreement on jurisdiction. However, if on the other hand, under the applicable national law, the party not privy to the original contract did not succeed to the rights and obligations of one of the original parties, the court seised must ascertain whether he actually accepted the jurisdiction clause relied on against him. The ECJ thus held that:

" . . . a jurisdiction clause agreed between a carrier and a shipper which appears in a bill of lading is enforceable against a third party bearer of the bill of lading if he succeeded to the rights and obligations of the shipper under the applicable national law when he acquired the bill of lading. If he did not, it must be ascertained whether he accepted that clause having regard to the requirements laid down in the first paragraph of [art.23] of the Convention".

In cases where the jurisdiction clause is contained in a contract made for the benefit of a third party, the ECJ stressed in *Société Financière et Industrielle du Peloux v Axa Belgium* ((C–112/03) [2005] E.C.R. I–3707 May 12, 2005) the third party would not be bound by that clause if he had not expressly consented to it. In that case, the insured and insurer had made a policy intended to provide cover for a third party. The exclusive jurisdiction clause in the policy did not therefore bind the third party beneficiary, despite the clause being in compliance with s.III (which provides for protective jurisdiction rules for an insured person).

It has also been recently confirmed by the CJEU that a sub-buyer is not bound by a jurisdiction clause contained in the seller-buyer agreement (*RefComp SpA v Axa Corporate Solutions Assurance SA* (C–543/10) February 7, 2013).

It might be noted that the Court of Appeal in *Dresser v Falcongate* [1992]   **12–089** Q.B. 502 considered that a choice of forum clause in the bill of lading has no effect on the relationship between a bailor and a sub-bailee because that relationship was not contractual, but was in fact a consensual bailment on terms. It would appear that the approach of the Court of Appeal is not contrary to the guidelines set out by the ECJ in *Coreck Maritime GmbH*.

Where the choice of forum agreement is formally defective according to the requirements in art.23:

---

[60] *Tilly Russ v Nova* (71/83) [1984] E.C.R. 2417 and *Castelletti v Trumpy* (C–159/97) [1999] E.C.R. I–1597.

(a) it will be void for all intents and purposes;

(b) it may however be possible to remit the jurisdiction issue to the *lex fori* where the defendant is not a domiciliary of any of the Member States.

Article 4 is specifically relevant in this regard. It provides:

> "If the defendant is not domiciled in a Member State, the jurisdiction of the courts of each Member State shall, subject to [art.23], be determined by the law of that State. As against such a defendant, any person domiciled in a Member State may, whatever his nationality, avail himself in that State of the rules of jurisdiction there in force . . . in the same way as the nationals of that State".

12–090   As far as the substantive validity of the jurisdiction clause is concerned, it would seem that this will be a matter for the national law applicable to the agreement as determined by the private international law rules of the lex fori. In *Benincasa v Dentalkit* (C–269/95) [1997] E.C.R. I–3767, the ECJ held that the courts of a Member State, which have been designated by the jurisdiction clause contained in an allegedly void contract, have jurisdiction to determine the validity of the contract in its entirety despite that allegation. A distinction should be drawn between a jurisdiction clause and the substantive provisions of the contract in which it is incorporated. A jurisdiction clause serves a procedural purpose and will be governed by the Convention/Regulation. The substantive provisions and any dispute as to the validity of the agreement (including the jurisdiction clause), on the other hand, are to be governed by the lex causae as determined by the private international law of the state of the forum. It is consonant with that aim of legal certainty and harmonisation that the court seised should be able readily to decide whether it has jurisdiction on the basis of the rules of the Convention (Regulation), without having to consider the substance of the case. The ECJ said:

> "The aim of securing legal certainty by making it possible reliably to foresee which court will have jurisdiction has been interpreted in connection with Article 17 of the Convention, which accords with the intentions of the parties to the contract and provides for exclusive jurisdiction by dispensing with any objective connection between the relationship in dispute and the court designated, by fixing strict conditions as to form".

Under art.24, jurisdiction may also be assumed by a court of a Member State where the defendant enters an appearance before it. That rule will not apply where appearance was entered solely to contest the court's jurisdiction over the claim.

Lis pendens—related actions

Article 27

12–091   Lis alibi pendens refers to the situation where there are simultaneously pending actions in the courts of different Member States over similar or related disputes. Article 27 of the Regulation (replacing art.21 of the Brussels Convention) provides that where proceedings involving the same cause of action and between the same parties are brought in the courts of different Member States, any court other than the court first seised shall stay proceedings by its own motion. That stay shall remain until such time as the jurisdiction of the court first seised is established. Once the jurisdiction of the court first seised is established, the court which has stayed proceedings should then decline jurisdiction completely. In *Erich Gasser GmbH and MISAT Srl* (C–116/02) December 9, 2003, the ECJ held that art.27 cannot be derogated from even where the proceedings in the court first seised is excessively long and might result in injustice. The court of any Member States which could also be seised has no power to interfere (*J.P. Morgan Europe v Primacon AG* [2005] EWHC 508).

At which point in legal proceedings does a court become "first seised"? The traditional rule in English law is that the English court was not seised until service of the proceedings on the defendant (*Dresser v Falcongate* [1992] 2 All E.R. 450). This, arguably, placed England at a serious disadvantage when in many other jurisdictions, the court became seised under the national law when a document was lodged with the court for service on the defendant.

That approach has now yielded to a Community-wide definition under the Regulation. Article 30 provides that a court shall be deemed to be seised:

"(i)   at the time when the document instituting the proceedings or an equivalent document is lodged with the court, provided that the plaintiff has not subsequently failed to take steps he was required to take to have service effected on the defendant, or:

(ii) if the document has to be served before being lodged with the court at the time when it is received by the authority responsible for service, provided that the plaintiff has not subsequently failed to take the steps he was required to take to have the document lodged with the court".

Thus, under art.30, the English court will be seised when the claim form is   **12–092**
issued because that is the time when a document instituting proceedings (the claim form) is lodged with the court. If the claim form is not subsequently served on the defendant, the court would not be seised under the proviso in art.30. The seisin is defeated by the claimant's omission to take reasonable steps to serve the claim form on the defendant.

This is clearly an improvement on the rule in *Zelger v Salinitri*—national and domestic peculiarities of service and seisin are removed by the Regulation. In place of these idiosyncratic approaches is a Community-wide harmonised approach.

Article 27 does not apply unless the parties involved are the same in the action pending in another Member State's court. In *Mecklermedia Corp v DC Congress GmbH* [1998] 1 All E.R. 148, the claimants alleged that they had established goodwill in the United Kingdom in their product name "Internet World". They claimed that the defendants, a German company, were committing the tort of passing off. The defendants applied to have the proceedings stayed on the grounds that a German court was first seised of a related action between the claimants' German licensee and the defendants. The application was dismissed by Jacob J. It was held that a mere licensee who happened to be working for the claimants could not be regarded as the "same party" as the claimants because it was a wholly different enterprise. Moreover in that case, the causes of action were different—the cause of action in the German court was alleged infringement of the German trademark registration and hardly any of the facts relevant to the English passing off claim would be relevant to the action there. It followed that the English court would not be required under art.27 to stay the proceedings. The requirement that the parties must be the same in both actions is absolutely essential. For example, what if the licensee decided not to contest the proceedings in Germany or decided to fight them in some way contrary to the claimants' interests? There is nothing the claimants could do to stop this because they are not the same party. In *Kvarner Masa-Yards Inc v Barrett* [2002] 2 B.C.L.C. 61, K was given a guarantee by C for the liabilities of A to K. K brought action in England against C to prove his debt. Proceedings in Italy were commenced against K by A and C to challenge the validity of the guarantee. The Companies Court in England held that although A was not a party to the English proceedings, that was merely a procedural matter that could be cured in due course and would not derogate from the effectiveness of art.27.

12–093   In international trade, an important issue in this connection is whether an insurer would be treated as the same party as the insured person when the insurer having paid out is subrogated to the insured's cause of action. In *Sony Computer Entertainment v RH Freight Services* [2007] EWHC 302, the court held that S and S's insurer could not be treated as the same party for the purposes of art.27[61] even though the claims in the Netherlands and England are mirror claims. Both claims related to the theft of S's goods carried under the Convention on the Contract for the International Carriage of Goods by Road (CMR). That said, the court conceded that the claims were related actions under art.28.

On the interpretation of "proceedings involving the same cause of action and between the same parties", *Gubisch Faschinenfabrik v Palumbo* (144/86) [1987] E.C.R. 4861 is particularly useful. The facts of that case revolved around the sale of a moulding machine by a German company to an Italian domiciliary. The seller sued the buyer in Germany claiming payment of the contract price. The buyer then instituted action in Italy seeking a declaration that the contract never existed because his offer to buy had been revoked. Alternative claims were framed based on allegations of fraud, mistake and late delivery.

There were two actions in this case—one brought by the buyer claiming annulment or rescission in Italy and the other the seller's pending action in Germany instituted to claim payment for the sale. The question was whether art.27 (or art.21 under the Brussels Convention on which this case was founded) could apply. The ECJ held that it should apply because:

1. the actions involved the same parties—here, the German seller and the Italian buyer;

2. the actions relate to the same subject matter—the contractual relationship for the sale and purchase of the moulding machine;

3. the object of the two actions is the same since both actions turned on the validity and enforcement of the contract. The second action must be treated as a mere defence to the first;

---

[61] See also *Drouot Assurances SA v Consolidated Metallurgical Industries (CMI Industrial Sites)* (C–351/96) (1999) Q.B. 497 ECJ.

4. the purpose of the Convention (and similarly, the Regulation) is to reduce the risk of one Member State deciding that the contract was enforceable and another deciding that it was not, the provision must therefore be construed accordingly.

The test as to whether the two sets of pending proceedings are the same **12–094** depends on how closely their interests in the proceedings are connected. In *Drouot Assurances SA v Consolidated Metallurgical Industries (CMI Industrial Sites)* (C–351/96) [1998] E.C.R. I–3075, one action was brought by the insurer of a vessel which had foundered against the cargo owner and the insurer of the cargo which the vessel was carrying when it sank. The other was brought by the latter two parties against the shipowner and the charterer. The ECJ held that there was no lis pendens in the case of two actions for contribution to general average unless it was established that with regard to the subject matter of the two disputes, the interests of the insurer of the hull of the vessel were identical to and could not be dissociated from those of its insured, the ship owner and the charterer. It was further held by the ECJ in *The Maciej Rataj* [1994] E.C.R. I–5439 that actions had the same "*objet*" if they had the same end in view. As far as Moore-Bick J. in *Glencore International AG v Metro Trading International Inc* [2000] C.L.C. 83 was concerned, art.21 of the Brussels Convention (art.27, Regulation) extended to third party proceedings. In that case, Itochu wished to join Trad-Credit Lyonnais as third parties to the proceedings in England. Itochu were themselves being sued by Trad-Credit Lyonnais in France. The court held that the court must examine the case by reference to the position of individual defendants, even though that might give rise to some fragmentation of proceedings. Whether the actions in issue were third party claims, counterclaims, or main proceedings, the crucial factor for the court was whether the parties were the same and had the same end in view, applying the test in *The Maciej Rataj*.

That test was applied in *Maersk Olie & Gas A/S v Firma M de Haan* (C–39/02) October 14, 2004 where the ECJ held that a shipowner's application to set up a limitation of liability fund[62] in one Member State was not a same action as a claim for damages by a claimant against that shipowner even though the claimant might be a person provided for under the limitation of liability fund. The ECJ held that in one action was the assertion that the shipowner was liable whilst in the other, what was sought was merely a declaration that if the shipowner is found liable, his liability shall be limited accordingly. The two subject matters were not the same.

Although a case based primarily on the CMR, *Andrea Merzario Ltd v Internationale Spedition Leitner Gesellschaft GmbH, The Times*, February 27, 2001 does demonstrate the court's approach to the phrase "pending action". There, the claimants commenced proceedings in England against the defendant on October 15, 1999 by which time the defendant had already commenced its own action in the commercial court of Vienna, Austria for a declaration of non-liability against the claimants. Although the Austrian proceedings were commenced first, service was effected after service in the English proceedings. The

---

[62] This is an application to set up a fund to pay out potential claimants against a shipowner for damage caused by the ship; the fund will take into account any limitation on the shipowner's liability as prescribed under a relevant limitation of liability convention. In this case, it was the International Convention relating to the Limitation of the Liability of Owners of Sea-Going Ships of October 10, 1957.

defendant contended that the Austrian action became a "pending action" for the purposes of art.31(2) of the CMR. Article 31(2) provides:

> "Where ... an action is pending before a court or tribunal competent ... no new action shall be started between the same parties on the same grounds unless the judgment of the court or tribunal before which the first action was brought is not enforceable in the country in which the fresh proceedings are brought".

12–095   It was argued that the proceedings in Austria were not an "action" for the purposes of art.31(2) of the CMR (which is substantially similar to the lis pendens provision in art.27) because it was only a plea for a negative declaration from the Austrian court. In a related road carriage case, *Frans Maas Logistics (UK) Ltd v CDR Trucking BV* [1999] 2 Lloyd's Rep. 179, Colman J. had held that an action for a negative declaration is nonetheless an action for the purposes of art.31(2). It is obvious that the qualification "on the same grounds" did not exclude the case of a negative declaration which mirrored a substantive claim. As Rix L.J. in the present case said:

> " ... it was unrealistic to think that a substantive claim in one jurisdiction followed by a claim for a negative declaration in another jurisdiction should not be within the scope of a *lis pendens* provision such as article 31(2)".

It should be remembered that these cases are not about art.28 and therefore care should be exercised in making any direct comparison.

Article 28

12–096   Article 28 on the other hand refers to "related actions". These are actions

> "so closely connected that it is expedient to hear and determine them together to avoid the risk of irreconcilable judgments resulting from separate proceedings".

The court subsequently seised *may* suspend jurisdiction (i.e. stay proceedings) to allow the first court seised to decide on the matter so that its (the second court's) potential judgment on the matter will have the benefit of the first court's decision, thereby avoiding any irreconcilability in outcomes. The court subsequently seised could also decline jurisdiction entirely under art.28(2) if:

1. one of the parties applies for such an order;

2. the law of the country to which the first court belongs allows for the consolidation of related actions; and

3. the first court has jurisdiction generally to entertain both actions.

"Related actions" was discussed quite extensively in *Sarrio SA v Kuwait Investment Authority* [1997] 4 All E.R. 929.

Sarrio SA v Kuwait Investment Authority [1997] 4 All E.R. 929   **12–097**
Facts:
The claimant, a Spanish company, entered into a contract for the sale of its special paper business with G and its subsidiary company, T. G was controlled by the defendant. G then breached the contract and became insolvent. The claimant commenced proceedings against the defendant, and G and its subsidiary in Spain on the basis that they had undercapitalised G and had wrongfully abused its legal entity causing damage to the claimant who were G's creditors. While those proceedings were pending, the claimant commenced action in England against the defendant for negligent misrepresentations which it alleged to have been made on the defendant's behalf to induce it to enter into the sale agreement. It was argued that there was little likelihood of a conflict of judgments because the "primary" issues were quite different from each other.
Held:
On whether the court latterly seised (namely, the English court) should stay its proceedings under art.22 of the Brussels Convention (which is similar in substance to art.28 of the Regulation), the House of Lords held that having regard to the objective of that article, which was to facilitate the proper administration of justice in the EC (now EU), its application was not limited to cases where there was a potential conflict between "primary" issues. Rather, the court should apply a wide test which would cover a range of circumstances, from cases where matters before the courts were virtually identical, to cases where the connection was close enough to make it expedient for them to be heard and determined together to avoid the risk in question. In this case, the allegations of misrepresentation were common to both proceedings. They related to negotiations leading to the sale contract and the defendant's relationship with the claimant thereunder. There was therefore a risk of irreconcilable judgments or findings. Accordingly, the two proceedings should be heard and determined together.

The court referred to *Tatry (Cargo Owners) v Maciej Rataj (Owners) (The Maciej Rataj)* (C–406/92) [1994] E.C.R. I–5439 where the Advocate-General stated:

> "The court second seised should therefore be able to have recourse to the machinery envisaged by that provision [art.22 of the Brussels Convention] whenever it considers that the reasoning adopted by the court hearing the earlier proceedings may concern issues likely to be relevant to its own decision".

At the Court of Appeal, Evans L.J. interpreted that statement as requiring that   **12–098**
art.22 of the Brussels Convention be restricted to cases concerning similar or related "primary issues". His Lordship defined "primary issues" as issues of fact or law limited to those facts necessary to establish a cause of action and do not include other issues of fact which the court may or may not decide and which are not essential to its conclusion in this way. This approach was rejected by the House of Lords on the grounds that it was too restrictive and did not reflect the general policy statements in *The Maciej Rataj*.

In *Mecklermedia Corp v DC Congress GmbH* [1998] 1 All E.R. 148, the court would not exercise its discretion to stay proceedings because the action in Germany was not a "related action" in that there was no risk of irreconcilable judgments between the trademark infringement action in Germany and the English passing off claim. It was clear that the most convenient forum for deciding an English trademark or passing off case was the English court following guidelines laid down by the ECJ in *The Maciej Rataj*. In *The Maciej Rataj*, the two actions in question were:

1. an action brought in a Member State by one group of cargo owners against a shipowner seeking damages for damage caused to part of the cargo carried in bulk under separate but identical contracts of carriage;

2. an action in damages brought in another Member State against the same shipowner by owners of another part of the cargo shipped under the same conditions and under contracts which were separate from but identical to those between the first group and the shipowner.

The ECJ held that "related actions" should not be interpreted as being confined to a situation where there is a real risk of the two actions giving rise to mutually exclusive legal consequences. It suffices that a separate trial and judgment would run the risk of conflicting decisions; it is not necessary for the court to inquire as to whether different or conflicting legal consequences would result.

12–099   However, it is plain that there must be present a real risk of conflicting judgments (*WMS Gaming Inc v B Plus Giocolegale Ltd* [2011] EWHC 2620 (Comm)). What is required, as stated in *Research in Motion UK Ltd v Visto Corp* [2008] EWCA Civ 153, is to make:

" . . . an assessment of the degree of connection, and then a value judgment as to the expediency of hearing the two actions together (assuming they could be so heard) in order to avoid the risk of inconsistent judgments. It does not say that any possibility of inconsistent judgments means that they are inevitably related. It seems to us that the Article leaves it open to the court to acknowledge a connection, or a risk of inconsistent judgments, but to say that the connection is not sufficiently close, or the risk is not sufficiently great, to make the actions related for the purpose of the Article."

In *WMS Gaming Inc*, the facts were that claim number 1 (brought in Italy) concerned W's termination of the supply contract on the basis that there were serious doubts about B's beneficial ownership.[63] In claim number 2 (brought in England), the issue was whether W's parent company by ending negotiations with B for a further supply contract was in breach of contract. The court considered that although the two claims were connected, there was no appreciable risk of irreconcilable judgments since in the Italian proceedings the issue would be whether W was liable for ending the discussions, whereas in the English proceedings the issue would be whether W's parent company was responsible for ending discussions.

The exercise of judicial discretion to stay proceedings in support for related proceedings in the courts of another Member State is naturally made less difficult where there exists a jurisdiction clause conferring jurisdiction on that other court. The added value of the jurisdiction clause should invariably result in a stay of local proceedings.[64]

12–100   Whilst the courts have striven to give art.28 a wide construction, it must be wondered, in the light of the equally capacious reading of the term "same object" in art.27, how the two provisions are actually distinctive from each other.

---

[63] The contract was for the supply of gaming machines where the buyer's standing and reputation are important.

[64] *Glencore International AG v Metro Trading International Inc* [2000] C.L.C. 83; *ABKCO Music & Records Inc v Alejandro Jodocowski* (February 21, 2002, Ch.D.).

Nevertheless, for practical reasons both provisions are usually pleaded concurrently when a stay of local proceedings is sought.

Lis pendens and forum non conveniens

These articles attempt to do away with the doctrine of forum non conveniens and **12–101** simply allocate jurisdiction on the basis of the court first seised with jurisdiction. There should be no evaluation of the appropriateness of any forum. As long as the court first seised is lawfully seised, it shall have priority over the dispute. It was pointed out by the ECJ in *Overseas Union Insurance Ltd v New Hampshire Insurance Co* (C–351/89) [1991] 1 E.C.R. 3317 that art.21 of the Brussels Convention (art.27 of the Regulation) does not allow any court of the Member State to assess or determine the jurisdiction of the first court even where the jurisdiction of that first court appears uncertain and is being contested. This is to ensure that the spirit of cooperation and judicial comity will be preserved. Be that as it may, s.49 of the Civil Jurisdiction and Judgments Act 1982 very pointedly provides that the doctrine *may* be applied to the extent that it is not inconsistent with the Brussels and Lugano Conventions. In *Re Harrods (Buenos Aires) Ltd* [1992] Ch. 72, proceedings were instituted in England and Argentina, a non-contracting state. The defendant was in fact domiciled in England. That being the case, the applicable law would have been the Brussels Convention but as the Brussels Convention was silent as to whether a stay of English proceedings should be granted in such circumstances, the court applied the doctrine of forum non conveniens and ordered a stay of English proceedings. The correctness of this ruling must now be doubted in light of *Owusu* (March 1, 2005; ECJ).

In *Von Horn v Cinnamond* (C–163/95) [1997] E.C.R. I–5451, the ECJ however recognised a special exception to the rule. In that case, the defendant had taken an action in Portugal where the claimant was domiciled for a declaration clarifying his rights against the claimant. This was done before Portugal acceded to the Brussels Convention. Soon after the Portuguese accession to the Convention, the claimant took action in the United Kingdom on the same subject matter. The question was how art.21 (art.27, Regulation) should be construed in the light of art.29 of the Accession Convention (the San Sebastian Convention) which provided that the Brussels Convention applied only to legal proceedings instituted after the entry into force of the Accession Convention. The ECJ considered that in applying art.29 of the Accession Convention (which was a transitional measure) a national court attempting to apply those provisions was entitled to

"review the jurisdiction of a court of another contracting state outside the cases expressly listed in Art.28 and the second paragraph of Art.34 of the Brussels Convention".

The exception to the rule is justifiable. Accordingly, the court seised had assumed jurisdiction on the basis of a national rule which accorded with the jurisdiction provisions in the Brussels Convention or another convention in force between the two states concerned when the proceedings were instituted. It had to do so provisionally if the court first seised had not yet ruled on whether it had jurisdiction.

12–102   Such a situation would indeed be rare as far as the Regulation is concerned. The doctrine of forum non conveniens, it seems, has finally been severed from EU jurisprudence on civil and commercial jurisdiction. The doctrine however will continue to apply in non-EU related jurisdiction matters. However, where the relevant defendant is domiciled in a Member State but the competing jurisdiction is a non-Member State, as was the case in *Re Harrods (Buenos Aires) Ltd* and *Owusu*, it is now clear that, with *Owusu*, judicial discretion should be substantially restrained.

Lis pendens and exclusive jurisdiction clauses

12–103   What is the relationship between art.23 and s.9 of the Regulation? Article 23 provides generally that Member States' courts should give effect to the parties' exclusive jurisdiction agreements. However, it is not inconceivable that the parties have chosen the courts of one Member State to have jurisdiction but the court of another Member State is the court first seised to try the same action or a related action between the two parties under the terms of s.9 of the Regulation. How should the conflict between the two provisions be reconciled?

12–104   *JP Morgan v Primacom AG* [2005] EWHC 508
Facts:
JP Morgan had acted as agent for several banks in providing a term loan facility to P, a German company. The loan agreement was expressed to be governed by English law and subject to exclusive English jurisdiction. P had failed to make two repayments. Amid concerns over its capacity to repay, it pre-emptively sought a declaration in a German court that it owed no interest under the agreement because the interest provisions were contrary to German public policy. JP Morgan responded by initiating proceedings in England, in part, for a declaration that the contractual provisions on interest were enforceable.
Held:
Cooke J. held that following the ECJ's decision in *Erich Gasser* (C–116/02) [2003] E.C.R. I–14693, as the German court was first seised, despite the exclusive jurisdiction clause, the English proceedings should be stayed. It is for the German court to decide whether its proceedings should be stayed because of the exclusive English jurisdiction clause.

This thus poses a serious risk of pre-emptive strikes using art.27 to defeat the object of an exclusive jurisdiction clause. In the present case, it is clear that the lender (JP Morgan) thus faced the prospect of further unwelcome litigation and might be pressured into settling. That said, it is quite clear in *Erich Gasser* that in the interest of certainty, it has to be for the court first seised to pronounce on its jurisdictional competence in the light of art.17. The ECJ added:

"the difficulties of the kind referred to by the United Kingdom Government, stemming from delaying tactics by parties who, with the intention of delaying settlement of the substantive dispute, commence proceedings before a court which they know to lack jurisdiction by reason of the existence of a jurisdiction clause are not such as to call in question the interpretation of any provision of the Brussels Convention, as deduced from its wording and its purpose".

12–105   In *OT Africa Line Ltd v Hijazy (The Kribi)* [2001] 1 Lloyd's Rep. 76, the claimants had instituted action in Antwerp, Belgium despite the existence of an exclusive English jurisdiction clause in the bill of lading. However, the defendants, instead of contesting the Antwerp court's jurisdiction, made an application in England for an anti-suit injunction against the claimants. This case seems to fall all fours on *Continental Bank NA*. The argument put forward by the claimants (in the Belgian action) was that an anti-suit injunction would contravene his right under art.6 of the European Convention on Human Rights to go before an independent and impartial tribunal established by law, in this case the Belgian court. It was also argued that s.37 of the Senior Courts Act 1981 on which an application for an anti-suit injunction is sought should be construed in a manner prescribed by s.3 of the Human Rights Act 1998. Section 3 of the 1998 Act provides that

> "so far as it is possible to do so primary legislation and subordinate legislation must be read and given effect in a way which is compatible with Convention rights".

The court was urged to construe s.37 of the Senior Courts Act 1981 so as not to deprive the claimants of their right to resort to a fair and public hearing of their case within a reasonable time by an "independent and impartial tribunal established by law" (which again was the Belgian court, as far as the claimants were concerned). The human rights arguments were unsurprisingly dismissed on the basis that the article does not confer on the party an unfettered right to choose his tribunal.

Jurisdiction under other conventions

There are other international conventions providing for rules on the allocation of **12–106** jurisdiction between litigants in a private international legal dispute—for instance, the CMR as we saw above. Under the Regulation, art.71, which replaces art.57 of the Brussels Convention, refers to a closed list of specific conventions to which Member States are already party and which will continue to apply so that there will be no risk of conflict between the Regulation and these conventions. However, unlike art.57 of the Brussels Convention, art.71 does not make any provision for future conventions. Article 57 states that the Brussels Convention

> "shall not affect any conventions to which the Contracting States *are or will be* parties and which in relation to particular matters, govern jurisdiction or the recognition or enforcement of judgments".

On the other hand, art.71 merely states:

> "This Regulation shall not affect any conventions to which the Member States *are* parties and which in relation to particular matters, govern jurisdiction or the recognition or enforcement of judgments".

It remains to be seen how this provision will be construed to encompass future international conventions which Member States might accede to.

Article 71 (or the original art.57) was intended to introduce an exception to the **12–107** general rule that the Brussels rules would take precedence over other conventions signed by the Contracting States on jurisdiction and the recognition and enforcement of judgments. The purpose of that exception is to ensure compliance with the rules of jurisdiction laid down by specialised conventions, since when those rules were enacted account was taken of the specific features of the matters to which they relate (see *Tatry* (C–406/92) [1994] E.C.R. I–5439). For example, it is presumed that the CMR provisions on jurisdiction should take precedence over the Brussels rules when the subject matter relates to the international carriage of goods by road. That does not however mean that the Brussels rules would always be displaced—it is envisaged that the general provisions in the Brussels rules can be applied alongside more specialised rules in specialised conventions; a fortiori where the application of the Brussels rules would support the specialised convention.

12–108 *Nürnberger Allgemeine Versicherungs AG v Portbridge Transport International BV* (C–148/03) [2004] E.C.R. I–10327, October 28, 2004
Facts:
P, a company in the Netherlands, had contracted with N, a German company, for the carriage of goods by road from Germany to the United Kingdom. N sued P for loss caused to the goods. The claim was brought in Germany under the terms of the Convention on the Contract for the International Carriage of Goods by Road (CMR). It might be recalled that under art.31(1) of the CMR:

"In legal proceedings arising out of carriage under this Convention, the plaintiff may bring an action in any court or tribunal of a contracting country designated by agreement between the parties and, in addition, in the courts or tribunals of a country within whose territory:

(a) the defendant is ordinarily resident, or has his principal place of business, or the branch or agency through which the contract of carriage was made, or

(b) the place where the goods were taken over by the carrier or the place designated for delivery is situated".

P, however, contested the jurisdiction of the German court and did not submit any defence. P relied on art.57(1) and (2)(a) of the Brussels Convention.

The German court held that, notwithstanding the provisions of the CMR, and the second sentence of art.57(2)(a) of the Brussels Convention, art.20 Brussels Convention (or art.26 Reg.44/01) should be applied where a defendant did not enter an appearance or refused to submit any pleas on the merits of the case.

Article 20 provides:

"Where a defendant domiciled in one Contracting State is sued in a court of another Contracting State and does not enter an appearance, the court *shall* declare of its own motion that it has no jurisdiction unless its jurisdiction is derived *from the provisions of the Convention*" (emphases added).

The German court was of the opinion that it could not be seised because there is no derivation of jurisdiction under the Brussels regime for the CMR action.

12–109 *Held:*
The ECJ disagreed and ruled that it was not appropriate to take a literal approach to art.20 and that despite the fact that the claim for jurisdiction was based on the CMR and not technically the Brussels Convention, it should nonetheless be deemed as a matter under which jurisdiction for the German court was derived from "*the provisions of the convention*". The German court should thus have jurisdiction to entertain the matter.

It might be noted that art.57 (or the new art.71) suffers from the deficiency of uncertainty; the ECJ's ruling is thus welcome to the extent that it clarifies when generalised Brussels regime could operate alongside the specialised international carriage regime. However, although the court has confirmed that a side-by-side existence and application could be reconciled, the approach taken by the court means that the full import and remit of art.71 remains unclear. Further guidance by the ECJ on an area still fraught with difficulties would be useful.[65]

Proposed reform of Regulation 44/2001

On December 14, 2010, the European Commission published its proposal to revise Regulation (EC) 44/2001 (The so-called Recast Brussels Regulation). The Commission's proposal can be found at *http://ec.europa.eu/justice/policies/ civil/docs/com_2010_748_en.pdf.*   **12–110**
Some of the proposals for reform include:

1. Exequatur The Commission's proposal is to abolish *exequatur* (the **12–111** procedure by which a court authorises enforcement of a foreign judgment). The procedure as it stands is already seldom used. However, certain practical matters are agreed:

* the requirement of a standard form of certification of authenticity; and

* that, to save costs, only a translation of the final order (operative parts and summary of grounds) will be required, unless an application is made for review in respect of this proposal, in which case a full translation is required.

2. Choice of court agreements and *lis pendens* The concern here is that the **12–112** lack of commercial and legal certainty and the danger of a torpedo action (see the problem caused by *Erich Gasser GmbH v MISAT* (C–116/02) [2003] E.C.R. I–14693).
Two proposals are made:

* the court designated in a jurisdiction clause should not be required to stay its proceedings if proceedings are commenced in another court. There should be an associated requirement that any jurisdictional disputes should be decided expeditiously by the chosen court; and

* the court designated in a jurisdiction clause should have the option to stay its proceedings where another court is better placed to hear the case.

This is a welcome proposal given how unjust and economically inefficient the outcome in *Gasser* can be.

3. Third state matters Key areas for reform: **12–113**

  (i) in relation to rights in rem in respect of immovable property or tenancies of immovable properties in third states, the rules on exclusive jurisdiction

---

[65] See, e.g. the problems with ship arrest in *The Anna H* [1995] 1 Lloyd's Rep. 11; *The Deichland* [1990] 1 Q.B. 361; *The Prinsengracht* [1993] 1 Lloyd's Rep. 41.

with regard to these matters could be extended to cover such properties (art.22, Brussels Regulation);

(ii) extension of jurisdiction to defendants domiciled in third states where justice requires it (*forum necessitatis*). The proposed draft recast Regulation provides "Where no court of a Member State has jurisdiction under this Regulation, the courts of a Member State may, on an exceptional basis, hear the case if the right to a fair trial or the right to access to justice so requires, in particular:

(a) if proceedings cannot reasonably be brought or conducted or would be impossible in a third State with which the dispute is closely connected; or

(b) if a judgment given on the claim in a third State would not be entitled to recognition and enforcement in the Member State of the court seised under the law of that State and such recognition and enforcement is necessary to ensure that the rights of the claimant are satisfied;

and the dispute has a sufficient connection with the Member State of the court seised".

Such an extension might very well lead to the final abolition of the common law rules on jurisdiction (which currently apply to defendants domiciled in non EU/EFTA countries). The implications are therefore extremely serious for those who see merit in the common law framework.

(iii) amend the Brussels Regulation to give effect to exclusive jurisdiction for third states' courts (this would solve the *Owusu* problem in a limited way) In the Rapporteur's Report, it was suggested that the courts of a Member State having jurisdiction (as to the substance) may stay proceedings if they consider that the court of another Member State or the courts of a third state: "would be better placed to hear the case, or a specific part thereof, thus enabling parties to bring an application before that court or to enable the court seized to transfer the case to that court with the agreement of the parties".

12–114   **4. Arbitration**   The proposals on arbitration are highly controversial.

Currently, arbitration is excluded from the scope of the Brussels Regulation. The arbitration exception would not be deleted. Instead the exception should make it clear that judicial procedures relating to the validity or extent of arbitral competence are excluded from the scope of the Regulation. The objective was to give priority to the courts of the Member State where an arbitration takes place (that is, the seat of arbitration) to decide on the existence, validity and scope of the arbitration agreement. This of course seems inconsistent with the *kompetenz-kompetenz* doctrine where the arbitral tribunal should be free to determine its one competence.

The proposed draft Regulation (art.29(4)) states:

"a court seised of a dispute should be obliged to stay its proceedings on the basis that certain conditions are satisfied:

(a) that those proceedings contravene an arbitration agreement; and

(b) that either an arbitral tribunal has already been seised of the dispute or that court proceedings have been commenced in the Member State where the arbitration has its seat."

5. Interim Measures   There will also be specific guidance on when a court **12–115** should grant interim measures in support of proceedings elsewhere. There will be limitation on the circulation of such measures ordered by a court other than the court with jurisdiction over the substance of the dispute. The Commission argues that given the wide divergence of national laws in this area, the effect of such measures should be limited to the territory of the Member State where they were granted. The Commission's justification for this proposal is that it would prevent the risk of abusive forum-shopping

Interim relief

The English court is endowed with certain powers to prevent either litigant from **12–116** doing anything which renders the proceedings ineffective or pointless. For example, it would be a travesty of justice if the claimant can claim successfully that the English court has jurisdiction over a dispute between himself and the defendant but in the meantime is unable to prevent the defendant from removing and disposing of assets which could be used to settle the potential judgment debt. The power to grant interim relief could be exercised both, in relation to matters falling under the court's common law jurisdiction and to those under the court's powers provided for by the Brussels (and Lugano) rules. As far as Reg.44/2001 is concerned, art.31 provides that application may be made to the courts of a Member State for such provisional and protective measures as may be available under the law of that state to support judicial proceedings brought in line with the Regulation in that or another Member State. That power may be exercised even though the court being asked to provide interim relief does not have jurisdiction over the substance of the matter.

In this section, we shall consider two interim remedies:

1. the freezing injunction; and

2. the search order.

Freezing injunction

The freezing injunction is issued to prevent a party from removing from the **12–117** jurisdiction assets which are located there and/or to prevent him from dealing with any assets, whether located within the jurisdiction or not. Its purpose as was stated in *Mareva Compania Naviera SA v International Bulkcarriers SA* [1975] 2 Lloyd's Rep. 509 was to ensure that the defendant does not cause the a judgment made against him to be nugatory by denying the claimant a legitimate right to have his judgment debt discharged by the defendant. The discretionary power of the High Court to grant a freezing injunction is provided for in s.37, Senior Courts Act 1981. That section should be read together with Pt 25 of the CPR 1998.[66]

---

[66] For a history of freezing injunctions, see Lord Bingham's speech in *Comm. of Customs & Excise v Barclays Bank Plc* [2006] 3 W.L.R. 1.

Rule 25.2(1) provides that a freezing injunction may be made at any time, including the time before the action is actually commenced and the time after judgment has been made. The expansive scope of that rule would have given some considerable cause for concern but for the constraints placed on the court's power under rr.25.2(2) and (3). Those provisions state that a freezing injunction would only be granted before a claim form is lodged if the matter is urgent or it is otherwise necessary to do so in the interests of justice, and if granted the court may direct that proceedings be brought as soon as practicable.

At common law, there was yet another constraint—it was held in *The Siskina* [1979] A.C. 210 that no Mareva injunction (as a freezing injunction was known before the CPR) could be granted if the English court had no jurisdiction over the substantive claim. Where the new Regulation applies, that common law rule has yielded to art.31:

"Application may be made to the courts of a Member State for such provisional, including protective measures as may be available under the law of that State, even if, under this Regulation, the courts of another Member State have jurisdiction as to the substance of the matter".

12–118   That provision is identical to art.24 of the Brussels and Lugano Conventions. The court's power to grant freezing injunctions is reinforced by ss.24 and 25 of the Civil Jurisdiction and Judgments Act 1982. Section 25(1) enables the English court to grant interim relief to support proceedings in other Member States. As for proceedings falling outside the EU and EFTA regimes, s.25(3) gives the English court a similar power.[67] Although the lack of a substantive jurisdictional link is not an impediment to the court's power to grant a freezing injunction, it does affect the way the court exercises its discretion under s.25 or art.31 Regulation. The court might find that without that substantive jurisdictional link, it might be inexpedient to grant the injunction.

The application for a freezing injunction is usually made without notice to the defendant but must be supported by written statements of evidence[68] which should set out the facts on which the applicant relies, including all material facts of which the court should be made aware. The injunction is granted against an undertaking by the applicant that if he loses the action subsequently, he would indemnify all parties concerned and in order to ensure the enforceability of the indemnity, the applicant may be ordered to provide a bank guarantee.[69]

As for how discretion should be exercised by the court when granting the freezing injunction, the CPR are silent but general guidance might be had from rr.1.1 and 1.2 of the CPR. These two rules deal with the general duty of the court "to deal with cases justly". Rule 1.1(2), in particular, provides that dealing with a case justly includes, so far as is practicable:

(a) ensuring that the parties are on an equal footing;

(b) saving expense;

(c) dealing with the case in ways which are proportionate—

    (i) to the amount of money involved;

---

[67] See also CPR r.25.4.
[68] CPR Pt 25 *Practice Direction—Interim Injunctions* para.25 PD–3.
[69] above, para.25 PD–4.

    (ii) to the importance of the case;

    (iii) to the complexity of the issues; and

    (iv) to the financial position of each party;

(d) ensuring that it is dealt with expeditiously and fairly; and

(e) allotting to it an appropriate share of the court's resources, while taking into account the need to allot resources to other cases.

It is submitted that these criteria would serve to guide the exercise of judicial **12–119** discretion in the grant of interim remedies. An illustration of how these principles might work could be had from *Gulf Interstate Oil Co v Ant Trade and Transport Ltd of Malta (Owners of the Vessel Giovanna)* [1999] 1 Lloyd's Rep. 867. In that case, Rix J. considered that in deciding whether a Mareva injunction should be given, the court must be satisfied that the applicant has made or would be making full and fair disclosure of all the material facts known so as to ensure that no one party is given an unfair advantage. Additionally, where the applicant's legal cause of action has yet to accrue, he has no standing to bring an application for a freezing injunction. In *Gulf Interstate Oil*, for example, the claimants were expecting to become holders of the bill of lading on which they hope to sue, but as theirs was only an inchoate title to sue, the court refused to grant them their application for a Mareva injunction. It should be noted though that cases prior to the CPR 1998 are not directly binding and could only be used as a guide of how judicial discretion might be exercised. The CPR must be construed in their own right.

A particular concern is with the extensive powers of the court to grant a freezing order, not only in relation to assets in the United Kingdom, but also to assets held worldwide. The circumstances under which such a potent weapon would be deployed are quite narrow. Guidelines are provided by the Court of Appeal in *Dadourian Group International v Simms* [2006] EWCA Civ 399:

Guideline 1: The principle applying to the grant of permission to enforce a worldwide freezing order abroad is that the grant of that permission should be just and convenient for the purpose of ensuring the effectiveness of the worldwide freezing order, and in addition that it is not oppressive to the parties to the English proceedings or to third parties who may be joined to the foreign proceedings.

Guideline 2: All the relevant circumstances and options need to be considered. In particular consideration should be given to granting relief on terms, for example terms as to the extension to third parties of the undertaking to compensate for costs incurred as a result of the worldwide freezing order and as to the type of proceedings that may be commenced abroad. Consideration should also be given to the proportionality of the steps proposed to be taken abroad, and in addition to the form of any order.

Guideline 3: The interests of the applicant should be balanced against the interests of the other parties to the proceedings and any new party likely to be joined to the foreign proceedings.

Guideline 4: Permission should not normally be given in terms that would enable the applicant to obtain relief in the foreign proceedings which is superior to the relief given by the worldwide freezing order.

Guideline 5: The evidence in support of the application for permission should contain all the information (so far as it can reasonably be obtained in the time available) necessary to enable the judge to reach an informed decision, including evidence as to the applicable law and practice in the foreign court, evidence as to the nature of the proposed proceedings to be commenced and evidence as to the assets believed to be located in the jurisdiction of the foreign court and the names of the parties by whom such assets are held.

Guideline 6: The standard of proof as to the existence of assets that are both within the worldwide freezing order and within the jurisdiction of the foreign court is a real prospect, that is the applicant must show that there is a real prospect that such assets are located within the jurisdiction of the foreign court in question.

Guideline 7: There must be evidence of a risk of dissipation of the assets in question.

Guideline 8: Normally the application should be made on notice to the respondent, but in cases of urgency, where it is just to do so, the permission may be given without notice to the party against whom relief will be sought in the foreign proceedings but that party should have the earliest practicable opportunity of having the matter reconsidered by the court at a hearing of which he is given notice.

12–120   The *Dadourian* guidelines are very welcome. The reputation and standing of the English court could only be enhanced as a result of these guidelines. Foreign and domestic litigants need to have confidence that when English courts despatch a hugely formidable tool such as the worldwide freezing order, they would do so judiciously.

Search order

12–121   A search order or *Anton Piller* order,[70] as it was known before the advent of the CPR, is issued to require a party to admit to another party to premises to ensure that property or evidence is properly preserved for the trial or the execution of any potential judgment. Section 7 of the Civil Procedure Act 1997 and CPR Pt 25 relate specifically to how search orders might be made and the procedures to be adhered to by the applicant. It is generally granted without the need for notice on the defendant. As with a freezing injunction, the court has discretion to grant the order and to impose relevant conditions to the grant based on the evidence supplied by the applicant. The exercise of discretion should similarly be guided by the principles set out in rr.1.1 and 1.2 CPR.

---

[70] Name taken from *Anton Piller KG v Manufacturing Processes Ltd* [1976] Ch. 55.

CHAPTER 13

CHOICE OF LAW FOR CONTRACTUAL AND NON-CONTRACTUAL OBLIGATIONS

In the last chapter, we dealt with the issue of whether and when an English court **13–001** might assume jurisdiction over a civil and commercial claim. Once an English court has successfully assumed jurisdiction, whether under the Reg.44/01, or the Lugano Convention or the common law, the next question it has to deal with is what law should be applied to resolve the claim. In transnational commercial law, that question is usually confined to the parties' obligations in private law towards each other, hence in this chapter, we shall concern ourselves mainly with the applicable law of the contract, tort and restitution.

As regards contractual claims, the issue of applicable law is governed by EU Regulation 593/08 on the law applicable to contractual obligations (Rome I). Prior to Rome I, the law was contained in the Contracts (Applicable Law) Act 1990 which in turn had incorporated the EU-engineered Rome Convention on the Law Applicable to Contractual Obligations 1980, and prior to that, the common law proper law doctrine.

As far as non-contractual obligations cases are concerned, these are now governed by Reg.864/07 on the law applicable to non-contractual obligations (Rome II) which applies to proceedings commenced after January 11, 2009. Its rules will apply to non-contractual events giving rise to damage occurring after August 19, 2007. Non-contractual obligations are those duties in tort, restitution, delict or quasi-delict.

Regulation 593/2008 of the European Parliament and of the Council of June 17, 2008 on the Law Applicable to Contractual Obligations (Rome I)

It should be remembered that the European Commission did not intend for Rome **13–002** I to be starkly different from the Rome Convention. The new law thus reinforces the tenor of the provisions of the Rome Convention but provides clarification on a number of the complexities and uncertainties case law on the Convention had thrown up.

The Regulation is expressed as applying to contractual obligations in civil and commercial matters. It does not apply to revenue, customs or administrative matters. Article 1(2) excludes a number of matters from the Regulation. These are:

(a) questions about the status or legal capacity of natural persons;

(b) matters relating to a family or similar relationship, including maintenance obligations;

(c) obligations arising from a matrimonial property regime including wills and succession;

(d) obligations arising under bills of exchange, cheques and promissory notes and other negotiable instruments to the extent that the obligations under such other negotiable instruments arise out of their negotiable character;

(e) arbitration agreements and agreements on the choice of court;

(f) questions governed by the law of companies and other bodies, corporate or unincorporated;

(g) the question whether an agent is able to bind a principal, or an organ to bind a company or other body corporate or unincorporated, in relation to a third party;

(h) the constitution of trusts and the relationship between settlors, trustees and beneficiaries;

(i) obligations arising out of dealings prior to the conclusion of a contract;

(j) contracts of insurance for the protection of workers and self-employed for work related death or injury or curtailment of work; and

(k) matters relating to evidence and procedure.

There is a matter of some controversy as regards bills of lading. Article 1(2)(d) repeats essentially what was in the Rome Convention but it now has to be read alongside Recital 9 of the Preamble. That Recital states:

"[O]bligations under bills of exchange, cheques and promissory notes and other negotiable instruments should also cover bills of lading to the extent that the obligations under the bill of lading arise out of its negotiable character".

13–003 It would thus follow that where a bill of lading does not give rise to obligations from its negotiability, it would continue to be governed by the Regulation. For example, it appears that a straight bill of lading would not come under the exception. The preparatory documents relating to this exception are not very clear as to what is meant by "the extent that the obligations under the bill of lading arise out of its negotiable character". Does that mean all order bills? Or what if the claim is in relation to the nature of the bill as a document of title? What is the connection between art.5(1) Rome I and the exception here? These are not easy questions. In the interest of legal certainty, proper guidance from the EU would be useful with reference to the Rome Convention, the Giuliano-Lagarde Report (the official commentary to the Convention) states that it is for the private international law of the forum to determine whether a document is to be characterised as being negotiable. The new Regulation does not have a similar provision. It is difficult to see why bills of lading should be excluded from the Regulation. Unlike negotiable instruments which have been subject to special rules including those contained in the Bills of Exchange Act 1882, the Geneva Convention providing a uniform law for bills of exchange and promissory notes of June 7, 1930 and the Geneva Convention providing a uniform law for cheques of March 19, 1931 instead of the proper law, bills of lading have never had that special treatment as far as the issue of proper law was concerned.

Another important change is in art.1(2)(i) which provides that matters relating to pre-contractual obligations are to be excluded from the Regulation. For example, matters relating to misrepresentation, duress, coercion, etc. will fall outside the Regulation. These will now be remitted to the Regulation 864/07 on Non-Contractual Obligations (Rome II).

Ascertaining the applicable law

Party autonomy

Rome I, like the Rome Convention, gives effect to the principle of party **13–004** autonomy. It provides in art.3 that the parties' contract shall be governed by their choice of law. The choice shall be made expressly or clearly demonstrated by the terms of the contract or the circumstances of the case. Selection need not be express as long as it is clear from the contract terms or circumstances. However, it should not be assumed the use of a trade term such as INCOTERMS 2010 will imply a choice of law. In *Sapporo Breweries v Lupofresh*[1] the court refused to find that a CIF UK port term indicated that English law was the chosen applicable law.

It might also be noted that reading art.3 with Recital 12 of the Preamble, a relevant circumstance supporting the implied choice of law is an exclusive jurisdiction clause. Recital 12 reads:

"An agreement between the parties to confer on one or more courts or tribunals of a Member State exclusive jurisdiction to determine disputes under the contract should be one of the factors to be taken into account in determining whether a choice of law has been clearly demonstrated".

This is an improvement to the current position whereby choice of exclusive jurisdiction does not necessarily mean an alignment with the applicable law question. So, if the parties chose English exclusive jurisdiction but the contract is silent as to choice of law, under the current law, it is not entirely conclusive that English law is also selected.

In the Giuliano-Lagarde Report, the words "circumstances of the case" are **13–005** explained by means of two examples. First, where a court finds that there has been an express selection in a related transaction, it could legitimately draw the conclusion that it is the parties' intention that the same choice of law would apply to the contract in question. Secondly, where there is a pre-existing or previous course of contractual dealings, an omission in one of the contracts to select an applicable law should not be taken as a departure from the chosen law applicable to the other contracts. However, where there was an active act of deletion of the law clause, that will be treated as evidence of an absence of a choice of law. In *Samcrete Egypt Engineers v Land Rover*,[2] one of the parties had expressly deleted the English choice of law reference offered to them by the other party and

---

[1] *Sapporo Breweries v Lupofresh* [2012] EWHC 2013 (QB).
[2] *Samcrete Egypt Engineers v Land Rover* [2001] EWCA Civ 2019.

no replacement was agreed to by the parties. The court thus concluded rightly that there was no selection.

Recital 12 also states that the "Regulation does not preclude parties from incorporating by reference into their contract a non-State body of law or an international convention". This would however be subject to the test of certainty—where the non-country specific law cannot be clearly ascertained, say Shari'a law (which, as the Court of Appeal stated in *Bank Shamil of Bahrain v Beximco* [2004] EWCA Civ 19, was a mixture of legal and religious principles), it should not be applied. The provision however would seem arguably to allow the parties to select, say, the CISG to govern their sale contract, for example. This recital is intended to provide for the adoption of EU autonomous rules, such as the European Contract Law.

Article 22 provides that where a State comprises several territorial units, each of which has its own rules of law in respect of contractual obligations, each territorial unit shall be considered as a country for the purposes of identifying applicable law. It would not be advisable therefore to provide for the "law of the UK" as the applicable law.

13–006   The parties are also free to select the law applicable to the whole contract or just a part of the contract. Clearly the latter course of action would only work if there is no conflict between the different parts of the contract. It is also not possible to use what is commonly called floating choice of law clauses. A floating choice of law clause might look something like this: "Chinese or English law at the defendant's option". The contract cannot be without a clearly known applicable law at the outset (*Dubai Electricity Co v Islamic Republic of Iran Shipping Lines (The Iran Vojdan)* [1984] 2 Lloyd's Rep. 380); in our example, the defendant is not identifiable at the start of the contract (since there is no legal dispute as yet) which means we do not know what the applicable law is when the contract is made. It would seem that although the regulation does not recognise floating choice of law clauses, there is nothing to prevent the parties from changing the applicable law during the currency of the contract as long as the new agreement meets the formal validity requirements of the relevant law (art.11)[3] and does not prejudice the rights of third parties (art.3(2)).

Like the Rome Convention, the parties may agree to change the applicable law during the currency of the contract but art.3(2) states that that should not adversely affect the rights of any third parties and that it should not prejudice its formal validity under the provisions of art.11.

Presumptions in the absence of choice

13–007   Here, as with the Rome Convention, there are special presumptions to help ascertain the applicable law of the contract where there is no selection by the parties. Article 4(1) states

"... without prejudice to Articles 5 to 8, the law governing the contract shall be determined as follows:

---

[3] In cases of international commercial transactions (where the parties are in different countries), art.11(2) provides that the choice of law agreement will be deemed to be formally valid if it satisfies the formal requirements of the applicable law of the underlying contract, or of the law of either of the countries where either of the parties or their agent is present at the time of conclusion, or of the law of the country where either of the parties had his habitual residence at that time.

(a) a contract for the sale of goods shall be governed by the law of the country where the seller has his habitual residence;

(b) a contract for the provision of services shall be governed by the law of the country where the service provider has his habitual residence;

(c) a contract relating to a right *in rem* in immovable property or to a tenancy of immovable property shall be governed by the law of the country where the property is situated;

(d) a contract for a short term (no more than 6 months) temporary tenancy of immovable property shall be governed by the law of the country where the landlord has his habitual residence, provided that the tenant is a natural person and has his habitual residence in the same country;

(e) a franchise contract shall be governed by the law of the country where the franchisee has his habitual residence;

(f) a distribution contract shall be governed by the law of the country where the distributor has his habitual residence;

(g) contract for the sale of goods by auction shall be governed by the law of the country where the auction takes place, if such a place can be determined;

(h) a contract concluded within a multilateral system which brings together or facilitates the bringing together of multiple third-party buying and selling interests in financial instruments, as defined by art.4(1), point (17) of Directive 2004/39 (the Markets in Financial Instruments Directive), in accordance with non-discretionary rules and governed by a single law, shall be governed by that law".

In cases not falling within any of the above or where the contract straddles **13–008** more than one of the above paragraphs, the contract shall be governed by the law of the country where the party who is required to effect the performance of the contract which is characteristic of the contract has his habitual residence (art.4(2)). Habitual residence however is given a special definition in art.19. As regards companies and other corporate or unincorporated bodies, their habitual residence shall be the place of central administration. For a natural person acting in the course of his business activity, this shall be his principal place of business. Article 19(2) then provides that where the contract is concluded in the course of the operations of a branch, agency or any other establishment, the place where the branch, agency or other establishment is located shall be deemed the place of habitual residence. Similarly, where the contract provides that performance is the responsibility of the branch, agency or other establishment, the place where the branch, agency or other establishment is located shall be treated as the place of habitual residence. Lastly, for good measure, the Regulation states in art.19(3) that when determining the habitual residence, the relevant point in time is the time of the conclusion of the contract. Thus, the time at which the dispute arises is immaterial to this question. One problem is immediately apparent—what law should be used to decide when a contract is concluded? Presumably, an autonomous definition would be applied but this is not especially clear in the Regulation.

What do the words "performance of the contract which is characteristic of the contract" mean? The same words were used in the Rome Convention. In that connection, the Giuliano-Lagarde Report described this phrase as that which "essentially links the contract to the social and economic environment of which it will form a part". It cannot escape the astute reader's attention that the special presumptions have removed the need to make this evaluation in conventional contracts. In less conventional cases, this is that part of the obligation which is the principal plank of the contract. In *Bank of Baroda v Vysya Bank* [1994] 2 Lloyd's Rep. 87, a case pre-dating Rome I, in the relationship between a confirming bank and issuing bank of a letter of credit,[4] the performance which is characteristic of the contract is the act of the confirming bank honouring the confirmation of the letter of credit in favour of the beneficiary. As that had to be performed by the London bank, the presumption under art.4(2) would be that English law was the applicable law.

The new provisions, though structurally different to art.4 of the Rome Convention, essentially do not deviate, in practical terms, too far from how the English courts have applied the presumptions in art.4, Rome Convention. The new law takes a more schematic approach; offering a step-by-step approach to establishing the applicable law. Particular contracts such as those in art.4(1) are given a simple straightforward test. Where art.4(1) proves inconclusive, another presumption will apply—that of art.4(2). Only when art.4(2) fails to provide a satisfactory answer, should the courts be allowed to consider, on the facts, the country with which the contract is most closely connected (art.4(4)).

13–009   The presumed applicable law as identified by art.4(1) or (2) may be rejected if it is clear from all the circumstances of the case that the contract is *manifestly* more closely connected with another country (art.4(3)). It should be noted that unlike art.4(5) Rome Convention, here there is a requirement of "manifestly". This reinforces the judgment of the High Court in *Waldwiese Stiftung v Lewis* [2004] EWHC 2589 (Ch) where it was held that the mere fact of the subject matter (the promised gift) was an asset in Switzerland was not sufficient to exclude application of the special presumptions.[5] The intention of the European Commission is to create a better balance between the closest connection test and the presumptions. It has been a criticism of the English courts that they had tended to give more emphasis to the test of "closest connection" in art.4(5) Rome Convention than the presumptions in art.4(2) Rome Convention.[6] Whilst on the other hand, continental and Scottish courts have been thought to have given too much weight to the presumptions at the expense of the test of "closest connection". The clear indication in art.4(3) is that courts should not lightly depart from the presumptions.

---

[4] It is also important to bear in mind that when an act of confirmation is given to the beneficiary, the contract is between the confirming bank and the seller. Similarly when a letter of credit is issued by the issuing bank to the beneficiary, the contract (letter of credit) is made between the issuing bank and the beneficiary not between the issuing bank and the buyer even though it was the buyer who applied to have the letter of credit opened (*Petrologic Capital SA v Banque Cantonale de Geneve* [2012] EWHC 453 (Comm)).

[5] Namely the presumptions in art.4(1)–(2).

[6] See for example *Marconi Communications v PT Pan Indonesia Bank* [2005] EWCA (Civ) 422. In that case, the confirming bank was in Indonesia and as the confirmation was the performance which is characteristic of the contract, the presumed applicable law under the Rome Convention was Indonesian law. However the court considered that as the letter of credit was communicated to the beneficiary in England, the documents were to be negotiated in England and that payment was to be made through a negotiating bank in England, the contract was more closely connected to England. English law was therefore held to be the applicable law. The outcome in this case may well be different under the new regulation depending on how the English courts construe the word "manifestly" in art.4(3).

Article 4(3) would clearly be relevant where the characteristic performance of the contract is a payment obligation which exists in a large matrix of connected contracts, such as in documentary credits or performance guarantees. In such cases, it would be useful to have a single applicable law for the entire network of contracts rather than different applicable laws for the constituent parts of the network. For example, in documentary credits, it would be more straightforward and commercially sensible for there to be one applicable law for the contract between the Issuing Bank and Advising Bank, and the contract between Issuing Bank and Negotiating Bank, and the contract between the Issuing Bank and beneficiary, etc. As Potter L.J. said in *PT Pan Indonesia Bank v Marconi* [2005] EWCA Civ 422:

> "The question of the weight to be accorded to the presumption under Article 4(2), [Rome Convention] as against other features of the contract and its surrounding circumstances which indicate a closer connection with a country other than that which is the place of business of the party which is to effect the performance characteristic of the contract, gives rise to considerations of some complexity in relation to letter of credit transactions. That is because they involve various contractual relationships which may give rise to a 'wholly undesirable multiplicity of potentially conflicting laws".

Indeed, this is recognised in Recitals 20 and 21 of Rome I which provides that in determining whether the contract is most closely connected to a country other than the one presumed, "account should be taken, *inter alia*, of whether the contract in question has a very close relationship with another contract or contracts".

As alluded to above, where art.4(1) and (2) cannot apply—for example, where **13–010** the performance which is characteristic of the contract cannot be ascertained —the court will look to the law of the country which is most closely connected to the contract. It is quite conceivable that the performance which is characteristic of the contract is incapable of ascertainment. In *Apple Corp v Apple Computer Inc*,[7] where both parties had agreed to desist from taking certain positive acts, the inevitable conclusion had to be that there was no performance which might be properly said to be characteristic of the contract.

Special presumptions

Special rules apply to contracts of carriage of goods. Where there is an applicable **13–011** law clause, that will prevail. Where there is no agreement, art.5(1) states that the law applicable to such contracts shall be the law of the country of the habitual residence of the carrier, provided that the place of receipt or the place of delivery or the habitual residence of the consignor is also situated in that country. If those requirements are not met, the law of the country where the place of delivery as agreed by the parties is situated shall apply. As said before, what is the position of bills of lading under this provision in the light of art.1(2)(d)?

The presumed applicable law however would be disapplied if it is clear from all the circumstances of the case that the contract is manifestly more closely connected with another country; the law of that other country shall apply.

---

[7] *Apple Corp v Apple Computer Inc* [2004] EWHC 768 (Ch).

Large risk insurance contracts[8] (but not reinsurance contracts) are also governed by special rules. It does not matter that the risk covered is not inside the EU. Article 6(2) provides that in general, the choice of law clause in the insurance contract will prevail. Where there is no choice, the insurance contract shall be governed by the law of the country where the insurer has his habitual residence. However, where it is clear from all the circumstances of the case that the contract is *manifestly* more closely connected with another country, the law of that other country shall apply (art.6(2)).

13–012   Other contracts governed by special presumptions include contracts for the carriage of passengers, consumer contracts, small risk insurance contracts and employment contracts.

Limitations on the applicable law

13–013   Article 3(3) states that where all other elements relevant to the situation at the time of the choice are located in a country other than the country whose law has been chosen, parties choice of law could not avoid the mandatory rules of that country. This is largely the same as art.3(3) Rome Convention. The same criticism as to what is meant by "all other elements" might thus apply.

Mandatory rules are defined (unlike the case of the Rome Convention). Article 9(1) describes them as provisions the respect for which is regarded as crucial by a country for safeguarding its public interests, such as its political, social or economic organisation, to such an extent that they are applicable to any situation falling within their scope, irrespective of the law otherwise applicable to the contract under this Regulation. Recital 37 stresses that the concept of "overriding mandatory provisions" should be distinguished from the expression "provisions which cannot be derogated from by agreement" and should be construed more restrictively.

Article 3(4) goes on to introduce a proscription against the contracting out of mandatory provisions of EU law using an applicable law clause. It states that where all other elements relevant to the situation at the time of the choice are located in one or more Member States, the parties' choice of applicable law *other than that of a Member State* shall not prejudice the application of mandatory rules of Community law, where appropriate as implemented in the Member State of the forum. It would appear that even if the mandatory EU law had not been implemented in any Member States, including the Member State of the forum, there could be no derogation.

13–014   Article 9(2) reiterates the well established principle both in the Rome Convention and the common law that the mandatory rules of the forum could not be derogated from by virtue of a choice of law clause. Article 21 goes on to require that the applicable law should be disapplied only if "such application is manifestly incompatible with the public policy ('ordre public') of the forum".

Article 9(3) is the replacement to the poorly worded art.7(1) Rome Convention. Article 9(3) states that

"effect may be given to the overriding mandatory provisions of the law of the country where the obligations arising out of the contract have to be or have

---

[8] For a definition, see art.5(d) of the First Council Directive 73/239/EEC of July 24, 1973.

been performed, in so far as those overriding mandatory provisions render the performance of the contract unlawful . . . ".

Although it is clear that the United Kingdom's position was that such a provision should not be incorporated at all into the Rome I, the wording in art.9(3) has the advantage of being much more narrow and as such, does not suffer from the sort of uncertainty which beset art.7(1) Rome Convention. The provision now prohibits non-derogation only as regards mandatory rules of the place of performance of the contract. That said, art.9(3) would have an impact on existing law. Under English law, *Foster v Driscoll* [1929] 1 K.B. 470 is authority for the proposition that an English court would not enforce a contract, the performance of which is prohibited by applicable law (a foreign law), in the light of comity of nations and as such enforcement would be contrary to English public policy. *Foster v Driscoll* however does not specifically address a case where the applicable law is the law of country A whilst the place of performance is country B. In such a case, art.9(3) makes clear that a relevant supervening illegality would be measured using the law of the place of performance rather than the applicable law.

Another issue of some controversy is how should "effect may be given" be   **13–015**
interpreted. Clearly, discretion is envisaged and the only guidance provided is in art.9(3). The article suggests:

"In considering whether to give effect to those provisions, regard shall be had to their nature and purpose and to the consequences of their application or non-application".

The list of factors for consideration is not exhaustive. Other than the problem of achieving uniformity of approach amongst the many courts of the different Member States, there is also the issue of what effect should be given. Other than applying and not applying the mandatory rule, the judicial discretion would seem to stretch to making a partial application. It is not far from the probable that these different permutations would result in a loss of legal certainty.

That said, the UK government had expressed satisfaction (Consultation Paper CP05/08; April 2, 2008) that art.9(3) represented such an improvement from art.7(1) that the United Kingdom would not be averse to opting into the provision.

Issues of validity of the contract

Article 10 provides that the existence and validity of a contract (or a term in it)   **13–016**
shall be determined by the law which would govern it under the Regulation *if* the contract or term were valid. This is a reiteration of the putative contract rule adopted in the Rome Convention. The Regulation also recognises the difficulties with one of the parties (usually a consumer) who might not be aware of the material validity requirements of the applicable law where the applicable law is not the law of the country of his habitual residence. It thus sets out in art.10(2) that a party may rely on the law of the country of his habitual residence to show that he did not actually consent if it appears from the circumstances that it would not be reasonable to determine the effect of his conduct using the applicable law. There is no change here to the Rome Convention.

As regards formal validity, art.11 makes three important categorisations:

(a) contracts made by parties (or their agents) who are in the same country when the contract was made;

(b) contracts made by parties (or their agents) who are in different countries at the time contract was concluded; and

(c) a unilateral act intended to have legal effect relating to an existing or contemplated contract.

In the case of (a), the contract will be formally valid if it meets the formal requirements of that country where the parties were in when the contract was made OR the applicable law. In the case of (b), the contract will be formally valid if it satisfies the formal requirements of *any* of the following:

1. the applicable law;

2. the law of either of the places where the parties (or their agents) were present when contract was made; and

3. the law of either of the places where the parties had their habitual residence.

13–017   The Commission also felt that the Rome Convention did not properly address formal validity rules relating to distance contracts (such as those made in e-commerce). Article 11(3) therefore provides that an unilateral act intended to have legal effect relating to an existing or contemplated contract is formally valid if it satisfies the formal requirements of:

(a) the applicable law;

(b) the law of the country where the act was done; and

(c) the law of the country where the person doing the unilateral act has his habitual residence at that time.

Scope of the applicable law

Article 12

13–018   Article 12 is largely the same as art.10 Rome Convention. It provides that the applicable law will govern:

(a) interpretation;

(b) performance;

(c) within the limits of the powers conferred on the court by its procedural law, the consequences of a total or partial breach of obligations, including the assessment of damages in so far as it is governed by rules of law;

(d) the various ways of extinguishing obligations, and prescription and limitation of actions; and

(e) the consequences of nullity of the contract.

Article 12(2) repeats art.10(2)—as regards the manner of performance and the steps to be taken in the event of defective performance, regard shall be had to the law of the country where performance takes place. The same problem occurs here—what does "regard" entail?

Article 14—assignment and subrogation

Article 12 Rome Convention, allocates: **13–019**

1. questions about the relationship between assignor and assignee to the applicable law of the assignment; and

2. questions about the relationship between debtor and assignee to the applicable law of the debt.

The original draft of Rome I for the most part reproduced these provisions. Problematically, there was also introduced a highly contentious rule for dealing with the proprietary aspects of the assignment of debts. It provided that priority questions arising for an assignee vis-à-vis third parties to the debts should be governed by the law of the assignor's habitual residence. This proposal had not gone down very well for those involved in the financial sector. Although such a proposal would have been useful for financing instruments such as factoring, it could cause all manner of difficulties for other types of financing contracts. The rule would make it difficult to ascertain the applicable law, especially where there are successive assignments. A debtor does not always know to whom the debt was owed, thus it would be impractical to refer to the law of the assignor's habitual residence. It was thus to the relief of many that the proposal was subsequently dropped. The current provisions are materially similar to those in art.12 Rome Convention:

- The relationship between assignor and assignee under a voluntary assignment or contractual subrogation of a claim against a debtor (a third party) shall be governed by the applicable law of the assignment contract (art.14(1));

- The law governing the assigned or subrogated claim shall determine its assignability, the relationship between the assignee and the debtor, the conditions under which the assignment or subrogation can be invoked against the debtor and whether the debtor's obligations have been discharged (art.14(2)).

That said, the problem has not entirely gone away. The Commission is required to submit a report two years after the adoption of the Regulation (that is to say, six months after it comes into force) addressing the issue as to the effectiveness of an assignment and subrogation of a claim against third parties and the priority of the assigned or subrogated claim over another person's right. Where appropriate, the Commission will publish proposed amendments to the current text. Hence, there is the possibility of the current position being changed.

Article 14 however has one clear positive feature, compared with art.12 Rome   **13–020**
Convention. It provides that the concept of assignment shall include outright transfers of claims, transfers of claims by way of security and pledges or other security rights over claims. This adds some clarity, by providing a uniform EU-wide definition to the concept of assignment.

As regards legal subrogation, art.15 repeats the terms of art.13 Rome Convention. Where a creditor has a contractual claim upon the debtor, but a third party has a duty to satisfy the creditor, the law that governs the third party's duty shall also determine whether the third party is entitled to exercise against the debtor the rights which the creditor had against the debtor under the law governing their relationship.

Regulation 864/07 on the Law Applicable to Non-contractual Obligations (Rome II)

13–021   Prior to January 2009,[9] the question as to the proper law governing claims for breach of duty in tort law with an international element is essentially a matter of national private international law. In England and Wales, that would be largely an aggregation of the principles in common law and the Private International Law (Miscellaneous Provisions) Act 1995. However, with the coming into force of Reg.864/07 on the law applicable to non-contractual obligations (Rome II), the issue is now a matter of EU law.[10] As a regulation, Rome II has direct application in all Member States (except for Denmark (art.1(4)). Recital 14 of the Preamble states:

> "The requirement of legal certainty and the need to do justice in individual cases are essential elements of an area of justice. This Regulation provides for the connecting factors which are the most appropriate to achieve these objectives . . . ".

The intention is to unify choice of law rules for non-contractual obligations to ensure that there is "forseeability of solutions regarding the applicable law" for all such litigations in the Member States.[11]

The Regulation provides special choice of law rules for:

1. non-contractual obligations arising out of tort (Ch.II); and

2. non-contractual obligations arising out of unjust enrichment, *negotiorum gestio* and *culpa in contrahendo* (Ch.III).

---

[9] There is some uncertainly about the date from which the Rome II Regulation applies. Art.31 of the Regulation, which is titled "Application in time", provides that "This Regulation shall apply to events giving rise to damage which occur after its entry into force". However no date is specified for when the Regulation entered into force and in these circumstances, under art.254(1) of the EC Treaty, it came into force on the 20th day following publication in the Official Gazette, that is to say on August 19, 2007. However, art.32, which is headed "Date of application" provides that "This Regulation shall apply from January 11, 2009 . . . ". In *Bacon v Nacional Suiza Cia Seguros Y Reseguros SA*, [2010] EWHC 2017 (QB), Tomlinson J. thought that this meant that events giving rise to damage after August 19, 2007 are subject to the Regulation *if* the law applicable to the obligation is determined on or after January 19, 2009. However, in *Homawoo v GMF Assurance SA*, [2010] EWHC 1941 (QB), Slade J., while stating that she was inclined to the view that the date of January 11, 2009 did not refer to the date on which proceedings were brought, directed a reference to interpret arts 31–32 to the Court of Justice of the EU.

[10] See generally Rushworth and Scott, "Rome II: Choice of law for non-contractual obligations" [2008] L.M.C.L.Q. 274.

[11] See COM/2003/427 final: Explanatory Memorandum..

As for the definition of "non-contractual", Recital 11 of the Preamble states that it is an autonomous concept and thus is not a creature of either the common law or civil law or indeed, any national law. It also extends to strict liability obligations. Lastly, from the provisions in Ch.III, we also see non-contractual obligations encompassing pre-contractual obligations and obligations giving rise to claims in unjust enrichment.

Scope of the Regulation

Article 1(1) states that the Regulation applies in "situations involving a conflict **13–022** of laws, to non-contractual obligations in civil and commercial matters". It does not apply to revenue, customs or administrative matters or matters of state liability for acts in exercise of state authority. Article 1(2), like art.1 in Rome I, also excludes a number of special civil and commercial matters from the scope of the Regulation. However there are a few differences. First, there is no exclusion from the Regulation of questions relating to the status or legal capacity of natural persons. Secondly, where Rome I talks about "the constitution of trusts and the relationship between settlors, trustees and beneficiaries", Rome II refers to "non-contractual obligations arising out of the relations between settlors, trustees and beneficiaries of a trust created *voluntarily*" (emphasis added). Hence, a trust not voluntarily created (e.g. one imposed by law), the Regulation will apply to non-contractual obligations arising from it. There are also exceptions referring to non-contractual arising from nuclear damage, privacy breaches and defamation. The latter two will continue thus to be dealt with by the Private International Law (Miscellaneous Provisions) Act 1995 and for those matters not covered by the 1995, by the common law.

For students of international trade law, art.1(2)(c) also excludes non-contractual obligations arising under bills of exchange, cheques and promissory notes and other negotiable instruments to the extent that the obligations under such other negotiable instruments arise out of their negotiable character. Unlike Rome I, there is no reference to bills of lading in the preamble but given the expressed desire of the EU to apply the two regulations in a manner consistent with each other, it is highly likely that bills of lading (where the obligations arise out of their negotiability) would also be excluded. There are, as discussed above, difficulties with placing bills of lading within the same exception as bills of exchange and other negotiable instruments.[12]

Choice of law for tort and delict

General rule

The general rule in art.4(1) the applicable law of a non-contractual obligation **13–023** arising out of a tort or delict shall be:

"[T]he law of the country in which the damage occurs irrespective of the country in which the event giving rise to the damage occurred and irrespective of the country or countries in which the indirect consequences of that event occur".

---

[12] See above para.13–003.

That country in question can be any country, not only a Member State of the EU (art.3). It is the country where direct damage occurs.

There are two exceptions:

(a) where the claimant and defendant have their habitual residence in the same country at the time the damage occurs, the law of that country will apply (art.4(2)); and

(b) where it is clear from all the circumstances of the case that the tort or delict is manifestly more closely connected with a country other than that indicated in art.4(1) or (2), the law of that other country will apply (art.4(3)).

On what it means by direct or indirect damage, it would appear that some help might be derived from *Marinari v Lloyds Bank Plc* (364/93) [1995] E.C.R. I–2719, a case concerning the application of art.5(3) Convention (the predecessor to the Brussels Regulation 44/01). There, the Italian claimant had lodged some promissory notes with the bank in England. The English bank, suspecting that the notes might have been obtained through fraud, confiscated them. As a result, the claimant allegedly suffered damage including the loss of reputation and financial loss as a result of the inability to use the notes to pay certain debts. The question as to where the damage was caused was important to the application of art.5(3). The ECJ considered that the relevant place of harm was England and not Italy. The place where consequential losses are suffered is immaterial. An example given by the 2003 Explanatory Memorandum[13] might be useful. In a case of traffic accident, the place of direct damage or injury is the place where the collision occurs and it is immaterial that consequential financial loss, pain or other forms of suffering arise or emerge elsewhere. In a shipping context where non-contractual obligations are in issue (for example, *Réunion Européenne* (C–51/97) [1998] E.C.R. I–6511), if the carrier causes damage to the consignee's goods the direct damage occurs at the place where the carrier had to deliver the goods, and not at the consignee's residence where the damage was discovered or where he suffers consequential financial loss.

13–024   Where the single harmful event causes damage to occur in multiple countries, art.4(1) would apply the law of each of those countries to the damage that occurs there. Thus, where goods are carried by the carrier through several countries—the Unite Kingdom, France, Spain and Portugal—if his lack of care causes the goods to deteriorate as he goes through each country, the applicable law for claims relating to the local damage will be the law of that country.

As regards art.4(2), the key criterion there is what constitutes habitual residence. The definition of "habitual residence" is similar to that in Rome I. Article 23 states that the habitual residence of corporate entities and other associations is the place of central administration. For a natural person acting in the course of his business activity, that shall be the principal place of his business. Article 23(1) adds that as far as corporations and associations are concerned, where the event giving rise to the damage occurs, or the damage arises, in the course of operation of a branch, agency or any other establishment, the place where the branch, agency or any other establishment is located shall be treated as the place of habitual residence.

---

[13] COM/2003/427 final: Explanatory Memorandum.

Article 4(3) acts very much as an escape provision from the presumed applicable law. It allows the court to consider, on the facts, whether there is another country which is more closely connected to the tort. If there is, that country's law will be the applicable law. Article 4(3) emphasises when making this assessment, a court should consider the pre-existing relationship between the parties, such as a contract, which is closely connected with the tort in question. The Explanatory Memorandum states that the pre-existing relationship need not consist of an actual contract; it may simply be an anticipated or contemplated contractual relationship (which did not materialise)—for example, where the parties entered into negotiations to make a sale contract but the negotiations broke down. The relationship, as evidenced by the course of negotiations, might be relevant factor.

Article 4(3) refers to "a country *other* than that indicated in paragraphs (1) or 13–025 (2)". The emphasis on "other" can cause problems where the country which is more closely connected is also the country where the damage occurs but is not the country where the parties share habitual residence. An example might be used to explain this. A and B are both habitual residents in England. A makes a boat in Spain. She gives the boat to B in Spain. The boat explodes as a result of a defect injuring B. Article 4(1) would indicate the applicable law as Spanish law where the direct damage occurred. However, art.4(1) yields to art.4(2) and thus, English law applies. The question then is whether art.4(3) could apply directing the applicable law back to Spain which is clearly more closely connected to the tort. It has been suggested that art.4(3) would not be able to do this because the tort is not "manifestly more closely connected with a country *other* than that indicated" in art.4(1) and (2).[14]

Lastly, whatever the applicable law might be under these provisions, art.16 stressed that

"nothing in this Regulation shall restrict the application of the provisions of the law of the forum in a situation where they are mandatory irrespective of the law otherwise applicable to the non-contractual obligation".

Special rules

There are two types of special rules—namely rules which deviate from 13–026 art.4—first, those which select a law that cannot be derogated from by contract and secondly, those which select a law that can. It is not the intention to discuss these rules in any great detail here as they do not frequently relate to international trade transactions.

Nevertheless, as regards the first type of special rules, there are two notable provisions—arts 6 and 8. Article 6 provides that the applicable law for an obligation arising out of an act of unfair competition shall be the law of the country where competitive relations or the collective interests of consumers are, or are likely to be, affected. However where the act of unfair competition affects exclusively the interests of a specific competitor, art.4 shall apply. Unfair competition would include the sort of activities prohibited by arts 81 and 82 EC.

---

[14] See discussion in Rushworth & Scott, "Rome II: Choice of law for non-contractual obligations" [2008] L.M.C.L.Q. 274. Also, *Hillside New Media v Bjarte Baasland* [2010] EWHC 3336 (Comm).

Article 6 cannot be derogated from by a choice of law agreement between the parties made pursuant to art.14. Article 8 also relates to rules which cannot be derogated from by contract. Article 8(1) states that where an infringement of intellectual property right is claimed, the applicable law shall be the law of the country for which protection is claimed. Where the right is provided for by a unitary EU intellectual property law, the applicable law shall be the law of the country where the infringement was committed (art.8(2)).

The second type of rules can be contracted out of using a choice of law agreement which satisfies the requirements of art.14. These include:

- art.5 on product liability claims;

- art.7 on environmental damage claims; and

- art.9 on liability for damage caused by an industrial action.

13–027   Article 5 seems extremely capacious; it relates to non-contractual obligations "arising out of damage caused by a product". Whether this should be given a narrow reading is not entirely clear but in the interest of legal certainty, it is submitted that a more restrictive approach would be welcome, especially, as regards commercial relations. A more appropriate reading would thus confine art.5 to so-called product liability cases. Article 5 explicitly excludes the application of art.4(2). The applicable law is the law of the country in which the claimant has his habitual residence when the damage occurred *if the product was marketed in that country* (art.5(1)(a)). If the product was not marketed in that country, the applicable law will be the law of the country where the product was acquired (art.5(1)(b)). If that cannot be established, the applicable law shall be the law of the country in which the damage occurred, if the product was marketed there. A further proviso exists—where the defendant could not reasonably foresee the marketing of the product or a product of the same type, the applicable law shall be the law of the country of the defendant's habitual residence. As if these different steps are not already complicated, art.5(2) states that where from all the circumstances of the case it is clear that the tort is manifestly more closely connected with a country other than the above, that country's law shall apply. A manifestly closer connection with another country, according to art.5(2), might be based on a pre-existing relationship between the parties, such as a contract, that is closely connected with the tort in question. However, art.5 can be derogated from under a properly executed agreement (art.14).

As regards environmental damage, art.7 states quite simply that the applicable law shall be the law of the place where the direct damage occurs unless the claimant seeks compensation under the law of the country in which the event resulting in the environmental damage occurred. Recital 25 justifies this provision by referring to "the precautionary principle and the principle of priority for corrective action at source and the principle that the polluter pays". This provision raises a difficult problem of characterisation. The regulation is silent as to what constitutes a non-contractual obligation arising out of environmental damage. Is a claim for negligence by the defendant leading to environmental damage be subject to art.7? What law is to be used by the forum tribunal to decide what a "non-contractual obligation arising out of environmental damage" is? Consider this—in English law, the tort of negligence does not require environmental damage for there to be liability. Does this therefore mean that a claim in negligence would not fall within art.7? It is not clear how, even if permitted, an autonomous approach would help given the legal complexities such a question entails.

Article 9 which deals with industrial action states that the applicable law of a non-contractual obligation in respect of damage caused by industrial action is the law of the country where the action is or has been taken.

Article 14—Choice of law to derogate from the presumptive rules

Article 14, as alluded to earlier, allows the parties to make an agreement to select   **13–028**
their own law to govern a non-contractual claim. The following conditions must be observed (art.14(1)):

- the agreement is made after the even giving rise to the damage;

- in cases where all the parties concerned are pursuing a commercial activity, a freely negotiated agreement made prior to the event giving rise to the damage will suffice;

- the choice must be expressed or demonstrated with reasonable certainty by the circumstances of the case; and

- the agreement shall not prejudice the rights of third parties.

A selection or choice inferred from the circumstances of the case (as against an explicit clause) would seem to suffice and unlike Rome I, all that is required is that this is demonstrated with reasonable certainty. Under Rome I, in contrast, it had to be "clearly demonstrated by... the circumstances of the case" (art.3(1)).

Legal rules of the country to which "all the elements relevant to the situation at the time of the event giving rise to the damage" are located which cannot be contracted out of will prevail over the parties choice of law (art.14(2)). Also, the parties' agreement cannot derogate from the rules of Community law which cannot be contracted out of where all the relevant elements are located in one or more Member States (art.14(3)).

On the issue of commercial agreements made before the event, two points are   **13–029**
worth stressing. First, there is no definition anywhere in the Regulation of "commercial activity". The natural antonym of "commercial" is usually "consumer". In this regard, some guidance might be had from the Rome Convention and/or the Brussels regime where a consumer is defined as a person who acts outside his trade or profession. Commercial activity would presumably be activities between parties who both act in the course of their trade or profession. What about contracts involving both commercial and noncommercial purposes? In *Gruber* (C–464/01) [2005] E.C.R. I–439, a farmer had purchased tiles for his farm building. The building was used both as his private residence and his agricultural business. The ECJ said:

"... [I]nasmuch as a contract is entered into for the person's trade or professional purposes, he must be deemed to be on an equal footing with the other party to the contract, so that the special protection reserved by the Brussels Convention for consumers is not justified in such a case. That is in no way altered by the fact that the contract at issue also has a private purpose, and it remains relevant whatever the relationship between the private and professional use of the goods or service concerned, and even though the private use is predominant, as long as the proportion of the professional usage is not negligible".

Thus, such a person would not be entitled to rely on the special rules relating to the consumer unless

"the trade or professional purpose is so limited as to be negligible in the overall context of the supply, the fact that the private element is predominant being irrelevant in that respect".

The same approach, it is submitted, would apply to art.14(1).

The second point relates to "freely negotiated". At a simplistic level, it would exclude standard form contracts. This raises a practical problem—most commercial agreements are expressed in standard form contracts and are rarely individually negotiated. The intention is to prevent any abuse of a person with a weaker bargaining position but where commercial parties of presumptive equal bargaining strengths are concerned, art.14(1) fails abysmally to take into account how commercial contracts are actually made. This is a serious cause for concern.

Scope of application of the applicable law

13–030   Article 15 provides that it will be for the applicable law to govern:

(a)   the basis and extent of liability, including the determination of persons who may be held liable for acts performed by them;

(b)   the grounds for exemption from liability, any limitation of liability and any division of liability;

(c)   the existence, the nature and the assessment of damage or the remedy claimed;

(d)   within the limits of powers conferred on the court by its procedural law, the measures which a court may take to prevent or terminate injury or damage or to ensure the provision of compensation;

(e)   the question whether a right to claim damages or a remedy may be transferred, including by inheritance;

(f)   persons entitled to compensation for damage sustained personally;

(g)   liability for the acts of another person; and

(h)   the manner in which an obligation may be extinguished and rules of prescription and limitation, including rules relating to the commencement, interruption and suspension of a period of prescription or limitation.

Choice of law for non-contractual obligations arising out of unjust enrichment, negotiorum gestio and culpa in contrahendo

The applicable law of claims in unjust enrichment, *negotiorum gestio* and *culpa in contrahendo* is governed by Ch.III of the Regulation. For non-contractual obligations arising out of unjust enrichment (including claims for sums "wrongly received"[15]), art.10(1) states that if those obligations concern a relationship existing between the parties, the applicable law shall be the law that governs that relationship. If that cannot be ascertained, and the parties have their habitual residence in the same country when the event giving rise to unjust enrichment occurs, the law of that country shall apply (art.10(2)). Failing that, art.10(3) states that the law of the country where the unjust enrichment takes place will be the applicable law. Lastly, where it is clear from all the circumstances of the case that the non-contractual obligation arising out of unjust enrichment is manifestly more closely connected with a country other than that indicated in arts.10(1), (2), (3), the law of that other country shall apply (art.10(4)).

There is no definition in the Regulation for "unjust enrichment". In its **13–031** proposal, the Commission was concerned that there were too many inconsistencies between the Member States' laws on unjust enrichment and recommended thus that an overly technical approach should be avoided by the national courts when addressing art.10. The key criterion, it is submitted, given the flexible and common sense approach advocated by the Commission, has to be the lack of "justice" in the enrichment using principles common to the different legal systems of the Member States.

Another issue of doubt is in relation to art.10(3). That article refers to "the country where the unjust enrichment takes place". It is unclear what that actually entails. Does it mean, for example, the entire cause of action or simply the enrichment itself? It is not uncommon for the cause of action to involve acts in a number of countries. This would make it virtually impractical to refer to the entire cause of action as the "unjust enrichment". It is more convenient only to look to the enrichment alone, for example, where acts of a related fraud are perpetrated in Spain, England and France but the defendant's account in Germany is unjustly enriched. If the reference point is the entire of cause of action, it is immediately obvious how impractical that would be to the example given. On the other hand if art.10(3) turns on the location of enrichment, that would make matters much more straightforward.

Negotiorum gestio refers to acts "performed without due authority in connection with the affairs of another". Article 11(1) states that if the obligation arises out of a relationship between the parties, it will be the law that governs that relationship which will apply to the non-contractual obligation in question. Thus, if an agent buys goods without proper authority from his principal, the law of the agency relationship will also govern any claims for restitution based on *negotiorum gestio*. Naturally, claims in contract against the agent would be governed by the applicable law of the agency contract. Where art.11(1) cannot be applied and the parties are habitually resident in the same country, art.11(2) states that that country's law will be the applicable law. Where art.11(2) also fails, art.11(3) makes the law of the country in which the act (namely, the act performed without authority) was to be performed the applicable law. These presumptions will give way to the law of another country which is manifestly more closely connected with the obligation in question (art.11(4)).

As regards *culpa in contrahendo*, the Regulation states in its preamble (Recital **13–032** 30) that these include obligations arising from "violation of the duty of

---

[15] "Wrongly received" should mean "received under a mistake" instead of "wrongfully received". The latter would connote some breach of legal duty, which would normally fall within tort/delict.

disclosure and the breakdown of contractual negotiations". It would thus include claims for damages under s.2(1) Misrepresentation Act 1967 and pre-contractual fraud. Article 12(1) states that

> "the law applicable to a non-contractual obligation arising out of dealings prior to the conclusion of a contract, regardless of whether the contract was actually concluded or not, shall be the law that applies to the contract or that would have been applicable to it had it been entered into".

Where this cannot be ascertained, art.12(2) provides that the following rules will apply:

(a) the law of the country in which the damage occurs, irrespective of the country in which the event giving rise to the damage occurred and irrespective of the country or countries in which the indirect consequences of that event occurred; or

(b) where the parties have their habitual residence in the same country at the time when the event giving rise to the damage occurs, the law of that country; or

(c) where it is clear from all the circumstances of the case that the non-contractual obligation arising out of dealings prior to the conclusion of a contract is manifestly more closely connected with a country other than that indicated in points (a) and (b), the law of that other country.

It should be borne in mind that art.12 covers only non-contractual obligations presenting a direct link with the dealings prior to the conclusion of a contract. This means, as Recital 30 reminds us, if, while a contract is being negotiated, a person suffers personal injury caused by those dealings, art.12 would not apply.

The applicable law relating to these three types of non-contractual obligations as provided for by the Regulation can be derogated from by contract as long as the contract satisfies the conditions in art.14.

CHAPTER 14

RECOGNISING AND ENFORCING FOREIGN AWARDS

Suppose a claimant has obtained judgment against a defaulting defendant in a **14–001** foreign court and is now in possession of the judicial award. The natural question that follows is whether and to what extent that foreign judgment can be recognised and enforced in this country.

The claimant is entitled to take either of the following courses of action:

1. apply to register that judgment in the English courts; or

2. sue on the judgment as a debt at common law before the English courts.

By registering the foreign judgment, the appropriate legislation attaches to that judgment the legal force which would allow the claimant to enforce it in this country. The main statutes that govern the registration of foreign judgments are:

1. Civil Jurisdiction and Judgments Act 1982 which is generally applicable to judgments emanating from the EU and EFTA Member States and other parts within the United Kingdom. Recognition of judgments governed by Regulation 44/2001 is automatic and a matter of course;

2. Administration of Justice Act 1920 which applies to judgments obtained from a few countries belonging to the Commonwealth;

3. Foreign Judgments (Reciprocal Enforcement) Act 1933 which applies with reference to all countries having a reciprocal agreement with the United Kingdom for the mutual recognition and enforcement of judgments.

At common law, a claimant who has obtained a foreign judgment may sue on **14–002** the judgment as a debt. This procedure is by means of Pt 24 of the Civil Procedure Rules 1998 which provides the procedure by which the court may decide a claim or a particular issue without a trial. Rule 24.2 states that the court may give summary judgment against a claimant or defendant on the whole of a claimant or on a particular issue if:

(a) it considers that—

    (i) that claimant has no real prospect of succeeding on the claim or issue; or

     (ii) that defendant has no real prospect of successfully defending the claim or issue; and

(b) there is no other reason why the case or issue should be disposed of at a trial.

As is evident, this procedure is ideal where the issues or claims are fairly straightforward. Where the claimant is already in possession of a judicial award, it would normally be expected that the issues have been resolved by the foreign court and that there was no real ground for the matter to go to trial in England except as a delaying tactic by the defendant. The summary judgment procedure is therefore quite a suitable tool for the enforcement of judgment debts. Once summary judgment is given, the debt would then be enforced quite simply as an English judgment.

    However, the foreign judgment debt must satisfy two conditions—first, it is not in fact an order for taxes, duties or penalties and second, the judgment given in the foreign court is final and conclusive.

14–003   Under the Civil Jurisdiction and Judgments Act 1982, ss.18 and 19 address the issue of mutual recognition and enforcement of judgments obtained in Scotland and Northern Ireland. As far as commercial judgments are concerned the procedure is relatively free from difficulty. Recognition and enforcement are given almost as a matter of course. It should however be noted that there are several exceptions to the enforcement of judgments obtained from Scotland and Northern Ireland, including judgments relating to the status or legal capacity of an individual, the management of the affairs of a person not capable of managing his own affairs and on the issue of a provisional or protective measure other than an order for the making of an interim payment (s.18(5)).

Foreign Judgments under Regulation 44/2001

14–004   Judgments obtained from another EU country are to be dealt with under Reg.44/2001. Article 33 of the Regulation provides that a judgment given in a Member State shall be recognised in the other Member States without any special procedure required. On the basis of the judgment's automatic recognition, art.38 provides that a judgment given in a Member State and enforceable in that state shall be enforced in another Member State when, on the application of any interested party, it has been declared enforceable there. That application is to be made to the relevant court or authority[1] according to the procedure laid down by that Member State.[2] It should be borne in mind that in proceedings concerned with the enforcement of judgments, the courts of the Member State in which the judgment has been or is to be enforced have exclusive jurisdiction (art.22(5)) regardless of the defendant's domicile. In *Speed Investments Ltd v Formula One Holdings Ltd* [2004] EWHC 1827 Ch), it has been held that where art. 22 is in point, the court with exclusive jurisdiction has the power to determine its own jurisdiction. It does not have to stay its own proceedings awaiting another court seised to decline jurisdiction.

---

[1] Art.39(1).
[2] Art.40(1).

But what is a "judgment" for the purposes of Reg.44/2001? Article 32 provides that "judgment" means any judgment given by a court or tribunal of a Member State, whatever that judgment may be called, including a decree, order, decision or writ of execution as well as the determination of costs or expenses by an officer of the court. Article 32 is clearly not limited to decisions which terminate a dispute in whole or in part, but must necessarily extend to provisional or interlocutory decisions. It should however bear the authority of the Member State's judicial body (*Solo Kleinmotoren* (C–414/92) [1994] E.C.R. I–2237). In *Mærsk Olie & Gas A/S v Firma M de Haan* (C–39/02) [2004] E.C.R. I–9657, (October 14, 2004) it was additionally confirmed that an order could qualify as a judgment even though it was not made uncontested as long as it could be the subject of an appeal or review in the Member State where it was made.[3]

The rules on challenging the enforceability of a judgment obtained in another Member State have now been made more restrictive—unlike the Brussels Convention, the court in which the judgment is sought to be enforced must declare the judgment enforceable immediately upon the completion of formalities and is not entitled to consider any grounds for non-enforcement (art.41).

Grounds for non-enforcement can only be considered if and when an appeal is made by the defendant against the declaration of enforceability. Another limitation is that the appeal against the declaration of enforceability must be made within one month of service of the decision. If the party against whom the enforcement is sought is domiciled in a Member State other than that in which the declaration of enforceability was given, the time for appealing shall be two months and shall run from the date of service, either on him in person or at his residence. No extension of time may be granted on account of distance. **14–005**

The grounds for non-enforcement have also been made more narrow. Article 34(1) states that if the recognition is manifestly contrary to public policy in the Member State where recognition is sought, then recognition may be refused. Under the Brussels and Lugano Conventions, the word "manifestly" is absent. This is to highlight the strictness of this exception—it is an imperative that a judgment from another EU country should not be denied recognition unless the public policy offence is manifestly significant.

Article 34(2), like art.27 of the Brussels and Lugano Conventions, also provides that where the judgment was given in default of appearance or if the defendant was not served with the document which instituted the proceedings or similar document in sufficient time and in such a way as to enable him to arrange for his defence, that judgment shall not be recognised. However, it goes further than art.27 by providing that this default of appearance exception could not be used if "the defendant failed to commence proceedings to challenge the judgment when it was possible for him to do so". Thus if a defendant fails to take the appropriate steps in the courts of the Member State where the default judgment was given to have it set aside or nullified, he will be barred from resisting its enforcement and recognition in another Member State.

In *TSN Kunststoffrecycling GmbH v Harry Maria Jurgens* (February 16, 2001), the claimant had obtained a default judgment against the defendant in Germany for the sum of DEM 520,000. That judgment was subsequently registered in the High Court under s.4 Civil Jurisdiction and Judgments Act 1982. **14–006**

---

[3] See also *Denilauler* (125/79) [1980] E.C.R. 1553 and *Hengst Import* (C–474/93) [1995] E.C.R. I–2113.

The defendant applied to set aside the registration in the High Court of the judgment obtained in Germany on the ground, inter alia, that there was no good service on him of the German proceedings and that service had not provided him sufficient time to arrange his defence. Jack J. held that as the envelope containing the German certificate of service had in fact been delivered to the defendant's house, service had duly been effected. That would have afforded him sufficient time to arrange his defence, in the ordinary course of events. The fact that the proceedings had not come to the defendant's notice did not constitute an exceptional circumstance strong enough to justify the conclusion that the period between service and the default judgment was inadequate.[4] Article 27 of the Brussels Convention was therefore satisfied but enforcement proceedings would be stayed pending an appeal by the defendant to the German court.

CJEU case law has stressed that the purpose of art.34(2) was to ensure that a judgment would not be registered if the defendant had not had an opportunity to put his defence before the court which gave the judgment (*Klomps* (166/80) [1981] E.C.R. 1593, *Sonntag* (C–172/91) [1993] E.C.R. I–1963). That means that art.34(2) is only relevant where the defendant is in default of appearance in the original proceedings. The test is whether the notification of the suit was effected in the due and proper form under the relevant national law, and in sufficient time to enable the defendant to arrange its defence effectively; account being taken of all the circumstances of the case (*Klomps* and *Debaecker and Plouvier* (49/84) [1985] E.C.R. 1779).

14–007   *Wim Harry Gerard Maronier v Bryan Larmer* [2002] EWCA Civ 774
Facts:
M had sued L for faulty dental work in the Netherlands. Proceedings were started in 1984 but the claim lapsed from 1986 to 1998. When it was reactivated, L could not be traced and the case was undefended. Judgment was given in default of his appearance. The right to appeal against the Dutch judgment expired after three months. L subsequently moved to England and M brought proceedings in England to enforce the Dutch judgment. The High Court held that the judgment had been obtained contrary to English public policy as L had been denied the right to defend himself. It therefore declined to recognise and enforce it.
Held:
The Court of Appeal dismissed the appeal and affirmed the lower court's decision. It held that although there should be a strong presumption that court procedures in other Member States were compliant with the European Convention on Human Rights, on the facts available to the English court, it was impossible not to conclude that L had been denied his right of defence.

Article 34 also allows a court to refuse to recognise or enforce the foreign judgment if the service of the claim had not been served on the defendant in "sufficient time to enable him to arrange for his defence". The question as to what that means was considered in *TSN Kunststoffrecycling GmbH v Harry Maria Jurgens* [2002] EWCA Civ 11. There, service of German proceedings was effected on the defendant by the posting of a sealed envelope through his letter at home. He failed to make an appearance within the two weeks allowed for doing so. As a result, judgment in default was entered against him. That took place some five weeks from the date of service. The question was whether the

---

[4] See *Klemps v Michel* [1982] 2 C.M.L.R. 773; *Deboeker v Bouwman* [1985] E.C.R. 1779.

relevant time was the two weeks permitted for entering an appearance or five weeks between service and the issue of the default judgment. If it was the latter, J was prepared to concede that the German judgment was fine and that he would accept its registration in England. The Court of Appeal held that the requirement of sufficient time was a question of fact to be decided on all the circumstances of the case. Prima facie, it was "an empirical matter" to be assessed over the whole period starting with service and ending with the default judgment. The court was satisfied that the relevant period for the purposes of art.34 was five weeks between service and the issue of the default judgment.

Another exception is found in art.34(3). A judgment shall not be recognised if it is irreconcilable with a judgment given in a dispute between the same parties in the Member State in which recognition is sought. Finally, art.34 also provides that if the judgment is irreconcilable with an earlier judgment given in another Member State or in a third state involving the same cause of action and between the same parties, provided that the earlier judgment fulfils the conditions necessary for its recognition in the Member State addressed. This is an improvement on the Brussels Convention—under the latter, the exception only referred to judgments given by non-contracting states. There really is no good reason why that should not be extended to judgments given by other Member States. **14–008**

The fact that enforcement of judgments has been made more convenient between Member States of the EU and EFTA means that when a claimant ordinarily resident in one of these Member States brings an action in England, the English courts would not require security for costs from him because the defendant could always make a claim for costs against him at his home state with little inconvenience and expense. On the other hand where the claimant is ordinarily resident in a place outside the EU or EFTA, the English court entertaining his suit would normally require him to provide security to cover any prospective or potential costs owed to the defendant. The procedure for such an application for security for costs is laid down by the CPR 1998 Pt 25.

However, an issue of some importance has arisen following the passage of the Human Rights Act 1998. It was argued in *Amy Nasser v United Bank of Kuwait* [2001] EWCA Civ 556 before the Court of Appeal that it would be discriminatory under art.6 of the European Convention or Human Rights as incorporated into English law by virtue of the Human Rights Act 1998, for the court to require persons not ordinarily resident in EU or EFTA countries to provide security for costs whilst those who are ordinarily resident will not be so required. The Court of Appeal held that the CPR with their distinction between residents inside and outside the EU and EFTA states, raised a potential question of discrimination on the grounds of nationality which could not have arisen under the old rules.[5] The exercise of discretion conferred by rr.25.13(1) and 2(a)(i) and 2(b)(i) had therefore to be exercised by the courts in a manner that was not discriminatory. It would thus follow that the courts should not start with an inflexible assumption that any person not resident in an EU or EFTA state should provide security for costs and if the discretion to order security was to be exercised, it had to be on objectively justified grounds relating to obstacles or to the burden of enforcement in the context of the particular foreign claimant or country concerned. In that case, the court concluded that the steps needed to enforce any judgment in the

---

[5] See *Fitzgerald v Williams* [1996] Q.B. 657.

United States, where the claimant was then ordinarily resident, would involve extra delay and cost for the defendant, compared with any equivalent steps that could have been taken in England or any EU/EFTA state. As such, security for costs could be objectively justified.

Foreign Judgments outside Regulation 44/2001 and the Civil Jurisdiction and Judgments Act 1982

14–009   Where the foreign judgment requires the payment of a sum of money and it has been obtained in a country falling within the list of countries in either the Administration of Justice Act 1920 or the Foreign Judgments (Reciprocal Enforcement) Act 1933, these statutes shall govern the procedures for its recognition and enforcement.

Part II of the 1920 Act provides for the reciprocal enforcement of judgments obtained in the superior courts in certain commonwealth countries. The list of countries covered by the Act is fairly limited. It is anticipated that this Act will gradually be superseded by the Foreign Judgments (Reciprocal Enforcement) Act 1933. As it stands, it applies to the Australian states, Malawi, Bermuda, Sri Lanka, New Zealand, Malta, Newfoundland, the Falkland islands, Jamaica, Trinidad, Ghana, Nigeria, Kenya, Tanzania, Uganda, Zimbabwe, Botswana, Malaysia, Singapore, Hong Kong, Cyprus and the Gambia. Under the Act, a judgment obtained in these countries may be registered within 12 months from the date of the judgment or with leave thereafter at the discretion of the High Court. The judgment must be for a sum of money, unlike the provisions in the Civil Jurisdiction and Judgments Act 1982.

The Foreign Judgments (Reciprocal Enforcement) Act 1933 is similar in effect. It provides for the reciprocal enforcement by registration of judgments of UK courts and judgments of courts in the Commonwealth and other countries. It also applies to judgments[6] given in any of the contracting states to international conventions on carriage by rail, and road, on oil pollution and others to which the United Kingdom is also signatory. The application of the Act may be generally extended by Order in Council to countries offering reciprocity of treatment to the United Kingdom.

These foreign judgments must satisfy certain criteria before they are entitled to be registered and subsequently enforced under the 1920 and 1933 Acts. These conditions are:

(a) Jurisdiction of the foreign court must be established

14–010   It must be shown that the foreign court concerned must have jurisdiction to try and issue a judgment on the particular case, jurisdiction *as defined by the common law*. This means that unless the English High Court is satisfied that jurisdiction has been established for the following grounds, there can be no recognition or enforcement:

---

[6] The 1933 Act applied to money judgments made by a recognised court, even in insolvency proceedings, subject to the terms of the order by which the court was recognised, see *re New Cap Reinsurance* [2011] EWCA Civ 971.

(i) the defendant is resident or present in the country concerned; and

(ii) the defendant has voluntarily submitted to the jurisdiction of the foreign court either by appearance or a forum clause in any relevant contracts.

We have already seen how these requirements have been interpreted by the English courts and there is no need to go through them again.

It is not open to the English court to question either the formal or substantive validity of the foreign judgment. In *Habib Bank Ltd v Mian Aftab Ahmed* (2000) 97(43) L.S.G. 37 it was argued before Camwath J. that the claimant bank's Pakistani judgment registered in pursuant to the Foreign Judgments (Reciprocal Enforcement) Act 1933 and the Reciprocal Enforcement of Judgments (Pakistan) Order 1958 should be set aside because the Pakistan High Court which made the judgment had acted as a "Banking Court" and not as a "High Court". That was rejected by Camwath J. who made it plain that it is a trite rule at English law that an English court would not question the formal validity of a foreign court that appeared to be regular on its face. Moreover, the court was satisfied, in any event, that the High Court of Sindh although having sat as a Banking Court, it had nevertheless discharged its functions as a "High Court".

(b) Defences

It is also open to the defendant to plead certain defences that will negate the effectiveness or validity of the foreign judgments. These defences are discussed below.   **14–011**

Fraud

It goes without saying that where the foreign judgment has been obtained by means of fraud, it cannot be recognised in this country. The Acts reflect this. Section 9(2)(d) of the 1920 Act states that no judgment shall be ordered to be registered if the judgment was obtained by fraud (see also s.4(1)(a)(iv) of the 1933 Act). Fraud committed by the defendant, or by the foreign court with an interest in the matter or by both the court and the defendant will defeat the application to have the foreign judgment recognised. There are however problems in how this should be applied without infringing the unstated rule of judicial comity and without re-opening the case.   **14–012**

Owen Bank Ltd v Bracco [1992] 2 All E.R. 193   **14–013**
Facts:
The claimants alleged to have lent the defendant nine million Swiss francs. The claim was taken in St Vincent where the claimants were awarded substantial damages. They then sought to register the judgment in England under the Administration of Justice Act 1920. Fraud was pleaded by the defendant.
Held:
The House of Lords held that the fraud exception, although criticised for causing uncertainty to the mutual recognition and enforcement of foreign judgments, is operative and should be applied. The court has no choice but to review the merits of the dispute to ascertain whether fraud was in fact perpetrated and this duty remains steadfast whether or not the party pleading on the fraud defence is relying on evidence which he presented or could have adduced before that foreign court.

Public policy

14–014   If it is shown that the enforcement or recognition of the foreign judgment will mean acting contrary to our public policy then the application under the 1920 or 1933 Act must be refused (s.9(2)(f) of the 1920 Act, and s.4(1)(a)(v)). A classic example is in *Re Macartney* [1921] 1 Ch. 522.

14–015   *Re Macartney* [1921] 1 Ch. 522
Facts:
The applicant had obtained a judgment in Malta ordering the estate of a deceased father to pay perpetual maintenance to the mother of his illegitimate child. The issue was whether that judgment could be enforced and recognised in England.
Held:
It was considered that it could not be recognised. English law does not recognise an affiliation order not limited to the child's minority. This according to the court was contrary to public policy. Furthermore, the order given posthumous is not a remedy recognisable at English law. Enforcement of such an order could not be made in the interest of practicality. That element of practicality was also evident in the final ground for refusal. The court held that as the court in Malta could from time to time vary, amend or terminate the order, the judgment was so inconclusive that it is impossible for enforcement or recognition.

Where the underlying agreement subject to the foreign court's jurisdiction is illegal under English law as well as the law of the country of performance of the contract, it would follow that on the authority of *Soleimany v Soleimany* [1998] 3 W.L.R. 811 an English court would inquire into the merits of the foreign judgment or award and refuse to recognise it on the ground of public policy. Although that case involves the recognition and enforcement of a foreign arbitral award, it is submitted that it should apply mutatis mutandis to foreign judgments.

14–016   There is no room for the argument that as there has been a change in the foreign jurisdiction after the judgment was made making practical redress there impossible, it would be contrary to public policy to recognise the foreign judgment given, especially where the applicant had consented to proceedings in that foreign court. In *Habib Bank Ltd v Mian Aftab Ahmed* (2000) 97(43) L.S.G. 37, it was held that the change of regime in Pakistan was immaterial, even though it could result in the defendants losing their right to certain remedies which existed under Pakistani law before, since this did not affect the validity of a judgment that had been obtained *prior* to that change. Moreover, such an argument could not be entertained in the absence of representations from the Foreign Office, given the implication of the applicant's case in this regard.

Often associated with the defence of public policy is the application of the Protection of Trading Interest Act 1980. Section 5 of the Act provides that judgments given in a foreign country ordering the payment of multiple damages shall neither be recognised nor enforced by the courts in the United Kingdom. A judgment for multiple damages is defined in s.5(3) as a judgment for an amount arrived at by doubling, trebling or otherwise multiplying a sum assessed as compensation for the loss or damage sustained by the person in whose favour the judgment is given. Multiple damages have been known to be awarded against UK traders accused of restrictive trade practices in an overseas country. Section 6 goes further in providing that UK citizens, corporations incorporated in the United Kingdom and persons carrying on business in the United Kingdom against whom multiple damages have been awarded, have the right to recover such amounts as exceed the sum assessed by the foreign court as compensation for the loss or damage sustained. These provisions are essentially directed at courts in the United States which have applied their anti-trust laws as allowing them to "infringe" the territorial and jurisdictional sovereignty of the United Kingdom.

Breach of Human Rights law

It is now also firmly established that a foreign judgment would not be recognised **14–017** or enforced if to do so would be to disrespect the defendant's rights under the European Convention on Human Rights (ECHR) because the ECHR has the force of law in England.[7] The ECHR provides for the right to a fair trial. Where the foreign judgment had been obtained in breach of this fundamental right, it would not be recognised or enforced here in England. As pointed out by Steel J. in *Merchant International Co Ltd v Natsionalna Aktsionerna Kompania Nafto-gaz*,[8] this exception is probably better considered as arising through s.6 of the Human Rights Act, rather than through public policy alone. There is also obviously an overlap between the human rights exception and natural justice.[9]

Natural justice

Traditionally at common law, a foreign judgment obtained without due process **14–018** cannot be recognised or enforced. What constitutes "due process" or natural justice is debatable in this area of law. One clear situation is provided for in s.9(2)(c) of the 1920 Act which states that no judgment may be registered if the defendant was not duly served with the process of the court and as a result did not appear to defend himself. A similarly worded provision is found in s.4(1)(a)(iii) of the 1933 Act which states the registration of a foreign judgment must be set aside if the defendant did not receive notice of the proceedings in sufficient time to enable him to make his defence and he did not appear.

The position is clearly wider at common law. In *Adams v Cape Industries Plc* [1990] Ch. 433, damages for personal injury had been assessed by an American court without considering any evidence. That was in breach of the relevant American procedural law. It was argued that the concept of natural justice should be confined to those grounds on non-appearance or no notice. This was rejected by the Court of Appeal which held that a foreign judgment cannot be recognised or enforced if it had been given in breach of the common law's understanding of substantial justice. The assessment of damages without considering the evidence is clearly one such breach.

Where the issue of procedural injustice is raised, the person alleging that the judgment should not be recognised for breach of natural justice may be refused if he raised but failed on the issue at the foreign court. Similarly, if he could have raised it at the foreign court but did not, this could be held against him as is demonstrated in *Adams v Cape Industries Plc*. The Court of Appeal did consider

---

[7] *Pellegrini v Italy* [2002] E.H.R.R. 44.
[8] *Merchant International Co Ltd v Natsionalna Aktsionerna Kompania Naftogaz* [2011] EWHC 1820 (Comm); upheld on appeal [2012] EWCA (Civ) 196.
[9] *Joint Stock Company Aeroflot v Berezovsky* [2012] EWHC 3017 (Ch).

that it would have been detrimental to the defendants' case if they had known of the procedural breaches but did not raise it before the American court. However, as the court found that they had no reasonable means of knowing of the particular facts which could have enabled them to contest the issue in America, they were allowed to rely on the natural justice defence.

14–019　　It should be noted that whilst the defence may be construed widely, the fact of judicial restraint in the light of international judicial comity means that it will be construed reasonably and in that spirit. Hence, where the party pleading the defence relies solely on the fact that evidence adduced and accepted by the foreign court was manifestly incompatible with English rules of evidence as in *Scarpetta v Lowenfeld* (1911) 27 T.L.R. 509, there is no breach of natural justice. It must offend the English court's perception of "substantial justice" (*Adams v Cape Industries Plc*).

A foreign judgment which is obviously wrong in law or fact is not deemed to be contrary to natural justice. The standard rule is that the English court shall not reopen the case on its merits. The finality of a foreign judgment must be respected. This is so even when the foreign court acting to apply English law in a case where English law is the applicable law, has misinterpreted the relevant rule of English law (*Godard v Gray* (1870) L.R. 6 Q.B. 139).

Appeal pending

14–020　　Under s.9(2)(e) of the 1920 Act, where an appeal is pending at the foreign court or the judgment debtor satisfies the English court that he is entitled to appeal and intends to appeal against the judgment in question, then no registration of that judgment can take place. Section 5(1) of the 1933 Act offers a similar defence with the qualification that the registering court in the United Kingdom may, if it thinks fit and on such terms as it may think just, either set aside the registration or adjourn the application to set aside the registration until after the expiration of such time as appears to the court to be reasonably sufficient to enable the applicant to take the necessary steps to have the appeal disposed of by the foreign tribunal. The purpose of these provisions is to allow judgment debtors the full benefit of all local remedies in the foreign court.

State immunity

14–021　　It has been held that if the judgment sought to be recognised and enforced is one made against a country's government by a court of that country, an action brought under the 1920 Act (and also the 1933 Act)[10] is likely to be caught by s.1 of the State Immunity Act 1978 (*AIC v The Government of Nigeria* [2003] EWHC 1357 (QB)). In that case, the claimants had been given judgment against the Nigerian Government by a Nigerian court. They then attempted to enforce that judgment in England. It was held that that was contrary to the principle of state immunity. In this context, it is also not possible to claim the "commercial"

---

[10] See s.4(3) which provides that on an application to set aside the registration of a judgment under that Act: " . . . the courts of the country of the original court shall not be deemed to have had jurisdiction—(c) if the judgment debtor, being a defendant in the original proceedings, was a person who under the rules of public international law was entitled to immunity from the jurisdiction of the courts of the country of the original court and did not submit to the jurisdiction of that court."

exception in s.3 of the State Immunity Act 1978—namely the claimant is not permitted to assert that the judgment debt was in relation to a commercial matter therefore state immunity did not apply. In *AIC v Nigeria*, Stanley Burnton J. said

"if Parliament had intended the State Immunity Act to include an exception from immunity relating to the registration of foreign judgments, it would have been illogical to limit it to commercial transactions entered into by the state . . . with no provision for the registration foreign judgments where the exception to immunity before the original court was the equivalent of one of the other exceptions to immunity in that Act".[11]

Moreover, s.31(1) of the Civil Jurisdiction Act 1982 provides:

"(1) A judgment given by a court of an overseas country against a state other than the United Kingdom or the state to which that court belongs shall be recognised and enforced in the United Kingdom if, and only if—

(a) it would be so recognised and enforced if it had not been given against a state; and

(b) that court would have had jurisdiction in the matter if it had applied rules corresponding to those applicable to such matters in the United Kingdom in accordance with sections 2 to 11 of the State Immunity Act 1978."

From this section it is clear that a foreign judgment against a state will be capable of enforcement in England, if both of the following conditions are fulfilled: first, that the foreign court would have had jurisdiction if it had applied the United Kingdom rules on sovereign immunity set out in ss.2–11 of the State Immunity Act 1978, the effect of which is that a state is not immune (inter alia) where it submits to the jurisdiction, or where the proceedings relate to a commercial transaction. Second, that under United Kingdom law the state is not immune from the processes of execution. Dicey, Morris & Collins, *The Conflict of Laws* states:

"Section 31(4) of the 1982 Act gives to judgments against foreign States the benefit of (inter alia) the immunities from execution contained in ss.13 and 14(3), (4) of the 1978 Act; their effect is that there can be no execution against sovereign property without the written consent of the foreign State unless the property is in use or intended for use for commercial purposes".[12]

Enforcement of Foreign Arbitral Awards

Similar rules apply for the recognition and enforcement of awards obtained from an arbitration held outside the jurisdiction. The successful party can choose from the following options if he wishes to enforce a foreign award in this country:

14–022

---

[11] See also *Svenska Petroleum Exploration AB v Government of the Republic of Lithuania* [2006] 1 Lloyd's Rep. 181, para.[50] per Gloster J., upheld by the Court of Appeal in [2007] Q.B. 886 at paras [134]–[137] per Moore-Bick L.J.

[12] Dicey, Morris & Collins, *The Conflict of Laws*, 14th edn, Vol.1, para.14–095; see also *NML Capital v Argentina* [2009] EWHC 110 (Comm).

1. bring an action at common law on the award or apply for summary enforcement of the award (s.36(1) Arbitration Act 1950 and s.66 Arbitration Act 1996);

2. apply to enforce the award under Pt II of the Arbitration Act 1950 where the award is one made under the Geneva Convention for the Execution of Foreign Arbitral Awards 1927;

3. apply to enforce the award under Pt III of the Arbitration Act 1996 where the award is one made under the New York Convention on the Recognition and Enforcement of Foreign Arbitral Awards 1958; and

4. enforce under the Administration of Justice Act 1920, the Foreign Judgments (Reciprocal Enforcement) Act 1933 and the Civil Jurisdiction and Judgments Act 1982.

Common law enforcement

14–023 The party in whose favour the award is made may bring an action on the award at common law. That application may be via CPR Pt 24 which provides for a summary procedure. The foreign award may be enforced if the party is able to show that the arbitration has been held with the parties consent as evidenced by an arbitration agreement. It must also be demonstrated that the arbitration agreement is valid under its applicable or proper law and that the resultant award is valid and final according to the lex fori or the law governing the arbitration procedure.

It should be mentioned first of all that the parties are entirely free to choose the applicable law for their arbitration agreement. That choice of law can be distinct from the applicable law of the underlying contract. When the validity of the arbitration agreement is examined, this has to be done against the backdrop of that applicable law.

As far as English law is concerned the jurisdiction of the arbitrators stems from that agreement to arbitrate. That agreement is defined in the 1996 Act as an agreement to submit to arbitration present or future disputes (whether they are contractual or not). The agreement need not be in writing to be valid. The section clearly envisages the use of an arbitration clause in a contract providing for the arbitration of future disputes and the possibility of the parties coming together subsequent to the dispute arising to make an agreement to go to arbitration.

14–024 The validity of the arbitration agreement is to be treated as distinct and separate from the underlying contract. This is a notion not present in the old regime (namely, the 1950, 1975 and 1979 Acts). Section 7 provides that the enforceability of the arbitration agreement is not dependent on the validity or legality of the contract of which the arbitration agreement forms a part. This is known as the principle of severability. The principle was extensively discussed and applied in *Harbour Assurance Co (UK) Ltd v Kansa General Insurance Co Ltd* [1993] 1 Lloyd's Rep. 455. It suffices for our purposes to say that what the Court of Appeal decided in that case now forms part of the 1996 Act. This section is however not a mandatory provision of the Act. This means that it can be contracted out of.

As far as the second criterion is concerned, the English court must be satisfied that the award is valid and final in the eyes of the law governing the arbitration proceedings. As with the choice of law applicable to the arbitration agreement, the parties can choose the law of any country to apply to the proceedings of their arbitration. It is customary that the law of the place where the arbitration takes place will not only apply to the arbitration proceedings but also the arbitration contract itself. Where the parties agree that the law of country X shall apply to the contract but that the arbitration is to take place in country Y, then the validity of the arbitration agreement will be determined by the laws of country X but the arbitration proceedings will be governed by the laws of country Y. Where the parties have omitted to choose a law to apply to their arbitration proceedings, those proceedings shall be governed by the law of the country where the arbitration takes place. This is because the presumption at law (*Whitworth Street Estates Ltd v James Miller and Partners Ltd* [1970] A.C. 583) is that the law of the country most closely connected with the proceedings shall govern the proceedings.

It is trite law that an award, be it domestic or foreign, cannot be enforced unless it is final and conclusive as to its terms. In *Union Nationale des Coopérative Agricoles v Catterall* [1959] 2 Q.B. 272 (a case on the Geneva Convention on the Execution of Foreign Arbitral Awards 1927) it was argued that in order for a foreign award to be enforced under the Arbitration Act 1950, it must satisfy the requirement imposed on it by its governing law (or lex arbitri) to be expressed first and foremost in a judgment or decree from the supervising foreign court. The question was whether this rendered the award final and conclusive for the purposes of its enforcement. The court held that as long as the award was final by the law governing its proceedings as understood in England, that should suffice. Hence, even though the award was not final in the sense that it could not be enforced in the foreign country where it was made, if it was regarded as final by that law in the English sense, it could be enforced. The correct question to ask as suggested by Lord Evershed M.R. is:

"Has [the award] become final, as we understand that phrase, in the country in which it was made? Of course the question whether it is final in [that country] will depend no doubt upon [that country's] law, but [that law] is directed to showing whether it is final as that word is understood in English".

The defences the defendant could raise in resisting an application by the **14–025** claimant to have the arbitral award recognised and enforced by the common law include:

1. the arbitration's lack of jurisdiction;

2. the award was obtained through fraud[13];

3. public policy considerations; and

4. breach of rules of natural justice.

Other than bringing an action on the award at common law, it is also possible where the validity of the award is reasonably clear (*Re Boks & Co and Peters, Rushton & Co Ltd* [1919] 1 K.B. 491) to apply for leave to enforce the award under s.66 of the Arbitration Act 1996. It is declared in s.66(1) of the Arbitration Act 1996:

---

[13] See e.g. *Arab National Bank v El Sharif Saoud bin Masoud bi Haza'a El-Abdali* [2004] EWHC 2381.

"An award made by the tribunal pursuant to an arbitration agreement may, by leave of court, be enforced in the same manner as a judgment or order of the court to the same effect".

Where leave is given, the court will enter judgment in terms of the award. This means that the award is now expressed as a judgment of the English court concerned, and any enforcement thereafter will be made according the rules on enforcement of an English judgment. Leave to enforce an award this way shall not be given where, or to the extent that, the person against whom it is sought to be enforced shows that the tribunal lacked substantive jurisdiction to make the award. It should be noted though that if the party concerned is aware of the jurisdictional deficiency but takes part in the arbitration anyway, he is deemed to have waived the jurisdictional defence (ss.30 and 73 Arbitration Act 1996).

Enforcement under the Geneva Convention 1927—Part II Arbitration Act 1950

14–026   Section 99 of the 1996 Act provides that Pt II of the Arbitration Act 1950 shall continue to apply in relation to foreign awards subject to the Geneva Protocol on Arbitration Clauses 1923 and the Geneva Convention on the Execution of Foreign Arbitral Awards 1927 (but not the New York Convention awards). The Geneva Protocol and Convention apply as between the United Kingdom and other states signatory to them; it is stipulated in s.35(1)(b) of the 1950 Act that it applies between persons of whom one is subject to the jurisdiction of one of such contracting states as Her Majesty (being satisfied that reciprocal provisions have been made) may by Order in Council declare to be parties to the Convention set out in the Act, and of whom the other is subject to the jurisdiction of some other of the contracting states. This provision is the source of considerable controversy. It was held in *Brazendale & Co Ltd v Saint Freres SA* [1970] 2 Lloyd's Rep. 34, that the phrase "subject to the jurisdiction of" is not confined to persons of nationalities of two different contracting states. The Protocol and Convention will apply as long as the two contesting parties are resident or have their ordinary place of business in two different contracting states. There is also no restriction that one of or both parties to the arbitration should be necessarily a national of the state where the award is made (see, for example, *Union Nationale des Coopérative Agricoles v Catterall* [1959] 2 Q.B. 272).

Section 37 of the 1950 Act which survives following the massive overhaul of the Arbitration Acts, prohibits the enforcement of foreign awards (those governed by the Geneva Protocol and Convention) that do not meet the following conditions:

(a) it must have been made in pursuance of an agreement for arbitration which was valid under the law by which it was governed;

(b) it must have been made by the tribunal provided for in the agreement or constituted in manner agreed upon by the parties;

(c) it must have been made in conformity with the law governing the arbitration procedure;

(d) it must become final in the country in which it was made (s.39 states that a "final award" is not final if any proceedings for the purpose of contesting the validity of the award are pending in the country in which it was made);

(e) it must have been in respect of a matter which may lawfully be referred to arbitration under the law of England; and

(f) its enforcement must not be contrary to the public policy or the law of England. (In *Soleimany v Soleimany, The Times*, March 14, 1998, the enforcing court may inquire into the merits of the case where it is patent that the substance and enforcement of foreign award would be illegal under English law and/or the law of the country of performance. While that case involved a deliberation of s.26 of the 1950 Act, it should apply mutatis mutandis to the enforcement of awards generally, including those made under the Geneva Protocol).

Where the award has in fact been annulled in the country in which it was made, there can be enforcement granted under English law. Furthermore, the English court must be satisfied that the rules of natural justice have been complied with in the proceedings and the making of the award. For instance, where the party against whom it is sought to enforce the award was not given sufficient notice to present his case, there can be no enforcement of that award. Section 37(2)(b) goes on to state that where that person was under some legal incapacity and was not properly represented, this too would constitute a breach of the procedural justice and the enforcement of the award must be refused. Where the award does not deal with all the questions referred or contains decisions on matters outside the scope of the arbitration agreement, the award cannot be enforced under English law. The party resisting the application for enforcement of the award is given the right to raise any other ground not listed above. If he does so, the court may, if it thinks fit, either refuse to enforce the award or adjourn the hearing until after the expiration of a reasonable period to enable him to take the necessary steps to have the award annulled by the competent tribunal.

Section 36(1) states that a foreign award shall, subject to the provisions as **14–027** discussed above, be enforceable either by action or in the same manner as the award of an arbitrator is enforceable by virtue of s.66 of the new Act. Any foreign award enforceable under Pt II of the 1950 Act shall be treated as binding for all purposes on the persons as between whom it was made. It could therefore be relied on by any of those persons by way of defence, set-off, or otherwise in any legal proceedings in England.

Enforcement under New York Convention—Part III Arbitration Act 1996

Many of the signatories to the Geneva Protocol and Convention are also now **14–028** contracting states to the New York Convention on the Recognition and Enforcement of Foreign Arbitral Awards adopted by the UN Conference on International Commercial Arbitration on June 10, 1958. Foreign awards subject to the NY Convention are to be dealt with under Pt III of the 1996 Act. But what is a New York Convention award?

Section 100(1) defines it as an award made in pursuance of an arbitration agreement in the territory of a state (other than the United Kingdom) which is a party to the New York Convention. As is readily obvious, this definition overcomes the convoluted definition of a Geneva Protocol and Convention award which requires the international element that either party to the arbitration is subject to the jurisdiction of two different contracting states. This is not to suggest that the provision is free from difficulty. A problematic preliminary issue was discussed in *Kuwait Minister of Public Works v Sir Frederick Snow* [1984] A.C. 426. The House of Lords held that although the award was made before Kuwait became a contracting state to the Convention, the enforcement action could be expedited through the machinery of the New York Convention because the enforcement proceedings were fixed after ratification of the Convention. This is a very important decision in that awards made before a state became a contracting state will be enforceable provided the enforcement proceedings were started after that state has become a party to the convention.

Article II of the Convention deals with the question of form. The arbitration agreement which calls to be recognised by the contracting state must meet certain formal requirements. It must be an agreement in writing under which the parties undertake to submit to arbitration all or any differences which have arisen or which may arise between them in respect of a defined legal relationship, whether contractual or not, concerning a subject matter capable of settlement by arbitration. The term "agreement in writing" includes an arbitral clause in a contract or an arbitration agreement signed by the parties or contained in an exchange of letters or telegrams. The Convention seeks not to be construed literally and rigidly. This being the case, it seems rational to assume that other forms of communication bringing about the arbitration agreement including electronic communications should suffice so long as they are in writing. In *Zambia Steel & Building Supplies v Clark & Eaon* [1986] 2 Lloyd's Rep. 225, the Court of Appeal considered that an arbitration agreement concluded by the oral acceptance of a written offer was quite sufficient.

14–029   Article II(3) goes on to state that the court of a contracting state, when seised of an action in a matter in respect of which the parties have agreed to submit to arbitration, at the request of one of the parties, shall refer the parties to arbitration unless it finds that the arbitration agreement is null and void, inoperative or incapable of being performed. This is somewhat vexing. It is not entirely clear whether this provision refers to the formal or essential validity of the arbitration agreement. It is submitted that it should not be read as referring to the arbitrability or formal validity of the agreement. By applying the ejusdem generis rule it might be said that the requirements in that article relate directly to the performance and essence of the arbitration agreement, and not the formalities involved. As far as the term "incapable of being performed" is concerned, *The Rena K* [1978] 1 Lloyd's Rep. 545 held that it applies to the prevention of the agreement being performed by some external factors and not by the mere factor of the one of the parties becoming insolvent.

Mandatory Stay of Proceedings

14–030   The power of the court to stay proceedings brought in breach of a written arbitration agreement in art.II of the convention is expanded on in s.9 of the Arbitration Act 1996 (which re-enacts with changes the provisions of s.1 of the 1975 Act). Under the old law, the grant of a stay of proceedings was mandatory (s.1 1975 Act) in the case of a nondomestic award, while it is discretionary in the case of a domestic award (s.4 1950 Act). The new law states:

"A party to an arbitration agreement against whom legal proceedings are brought (whether by way of claim or counterclaim) in respect of a matter which under the agreement is to be referred to arbitration may (upon notice to the other parties to the proceedings) apply to the court in which the proceedings have been brought to stay the proceedings so far as they concern that matter. On an application under this section the court shall grant a stay unless satisfied that the arbitration agreement is null and void, inoperative or incapable of being performed".

Although it would seem to follow that the mandatory grant of stay applies to both domestic and nondomestic awards alike, the old preserve has been retained by s.86 of the 1996 Act. Hence, the old distinction has survived. Section 9(2) introduces a new provision that an application to stay may be made even though the contract provides that the matter should not be referred to arbitration until after some other condition for dispute resolution has been met. This is consistent with Lord Mustill's speech in *Channel Tunnel Group Ltd v Balfour Beatty Construction Ltd* [1993] A.C. 334. The burden of proving that any of the grounds in s.9(4) (or art.II(3)) is on the claimant according to *Hume v AA Mutual International Insurance* [1996] L.R.L.R. 19.

Once the award is properly constituted (as a convention award), s.101 Arbitration Act 1996 states that it shall be recognised as binding on the persons between whom it was made and may accordingly be relied on by those persons by way of defence, set-off or otherwise in any legal proceedings in England and Wales or Northern Ireland. The convention award may then by leave of court be enforced in the same manner as a judgment or order of the court to that effect. This provision simplifies the technically verbose s.3 of the Arbitration Act 1975. It might be observed that the award can be enforced not only by the High Court but also by a county court. Under the Convention, there is no distinction in terms of enforcement between a domestic award and a convention award.

A foreign award may however be refused recognition if its enforcement would **14–031** be contrary to the specified grounds in s.103. Section 103 which reproduces almost in verbatim the defences in the New York Convention (art.V), provides that recognition or enforcement may be refused if the defendant proves any of the following:

(a) that a party to the arbitration agreement was, under the law applicable to him, under some incapacity. The test of his incapacity is determined by the law applicable to him. This raises the problem as to whether the law applicable to him is his personal law or the law relating to the contract to which he is privy. The balance should be perhaps be in favour of the former so as to prevent the use of a commercial agreement to avoid the personal law restrictions on matters like infancy or mental incapacity.

(b) that the arbitration agreement was not valid under the law to which the parties subjected it (*Dallah Real Estate & Tourism Holding Co v Ministry of Religious Affairs Pakistan*[14]) or failing any indication thereon, under the law of the country where the award was made;

---

[14] *Dallah Real Estate & Tourism Holding Co v Ministry of Religious Affairs Pakistan* [2010] UKSC 46. In *Dallah*, as a matter of French law (the law of the country where the award was made), as the respondent was not a party to the arbitration agreement, the award would not be enforced.

(c) that he was not given proper notice of the appointment of the arbitrator or of the arbitration proceedings or was otherwise unable to present his case;

(d) that the award deals with a difference not contemplated by or falling within the terms of the submission to arbitration or contains decisions on maters beyond the scope of the submission to arbitration. Subsection (4) however subjects awards made on matters not submitted to arbitration to the doctrine of severability. It provides that an award that contains decisions on matters not submitted to arbitration, may be recognised or enforced to the extent that it contains decisions on matters submitted to arbitration which can be separated from those matters not so submitted;

(e) that the composition of the arbitration or the procedure was not in accordance with the agreement of the parties. In the absence of such an agreement, it is open to the defendant to plead that the composition of the arbitral tribunal or the arbitral procedure did not comply with the law of the country in which the arbitration took place; and

(f) that the award is not a final award in that it has yet to become binding on the parties. It is also an equally potent defence to say that the award has in fact been set aside or suspended by a competent authority of the country in which, or under the law of which, it was made.

A case of some interest is *C v D* [2007] EWCA Civ 1282.[15] There, the arbitration agreement provided for arbitration to be subject to the Arbitration Act but the contract in dispute (being an insurance policy) was to be governed by New York law. The US insurer argued that New York law entitled them to have the award reviewed in the United States since the arbitration had involved US corporations in relationships without a significant international element. They also contended that the award was a non-Convention award in that it was made between US corporations and as such could not be enforced under the 1958 Convention. Lastly, it was submitted that the arbitrators had made fundamental errors of New York law in the award. The High Court judge[16] (whose judgment the Court of Appeal endorsed) held that as London was the seat of arbitration and the agreement to the 1996 Act as the procedural law of the arbitration, the parties must be taken as having adopted the framework of the 1996 Act as applying to the arbitration.[17] That would include its mandatory provisions, including those relating to enforcement of the award and challenges based on substantive jurisdiction or serious irregularity. It is not unusual for contracts to contain different procedural and substantive law provisions but that should not be interpreted as allowing one party to use the substantive applicable law to override the procedural when they are dissatisfied with the award.

14–032   It is of course platitudinous to suggest that the application for enforcement of an award must be denied where to do so would be to act inconsistent with public policy (see the case of *Soleimany v Soleimany*).[18] Disputes which are not capable of being the subject matter of an arbitration are outside the purview of the

---

[15] For more on arbitrations and applicable law, see para.15–013.
[16] The High Court decision is reported in [2007] EWHC 1541.
[17] Longmore L.J., giving the judgment for the Court of Appeal, said, "a choice of seat for the arbitration must be a choice of forum for remedies seeking to attack the award".
[18] *Soleimany v Soleimany*, [1998] 3 W.L.R. 811.

Convention. This paradigm rule is catered for in s.103(3) which provides that enforcement of an award may be refused if the award is in respect of a matter which is not capable of settlement by arbitration. For example, an award made about the illegality or criminality of the transaction cannot be enforced because such matters of public law cannot be the domain of private commercial arbitration. Similarly an award made about the legal capacity of any individual will not be enforceable.

Where the claim is that the conduct of the party or arbitrators constituted a breach of public policy, the bar is set very high. In *Gater Assets Ltd v Nak Naftogaz Ukrainiy* [2008] EWHC 237, Tomlinson J. commented:

"[N]othing short of reprehensible or unconscionable conduct will suffice to invest the court with a discretion to consider denying to the award recognition or enforcement. That means conduct which we would be comfortable in describing as fraud, conduct dishonestly intended to mislead".

In a case where the party had concealed important documents maliciously (*Profilati Italia S.r.l. v Paine Webber Inc* [2001] 1 Lloyd's Rep. 715), an award made in those circumstances would be treated as one made contrary to public policy. Where the concealment was the result of mere negligence, it is submitted that that would not amount to the sort of reprehensible or unconscionable conduct referred to by Tomlinson J.

Enforcement under the Administration of Justice Act 1920, the Foreign Judgments (Reciprocal Enforcement) Act 1933 and the Civil Jurisdiction and Judgments Act 1982

It suffices to say that where an arbitral award which *under the law in force where* **14–033** *they have been made are enforceable in the same manner as judgments*, is capable of being registered under the 1920 or 1933 Act (ss.9(3)(a), 9(5) and 12(1) of the 1920 Act; and s.10A of the 1933 Act) respectively depending on the countries concerned. The procedure is essentially similar to that of recognising and enforcing foreign judgments and is subject to the same defences.

An arbitral award which has become enforceable in the part of the United Kingdom in which it was given in the same manner as a judgment given by a court of law in that part (s.18(2)(e) Civil Jurisdiction and Judgments Act 1982) shall be recognised and enforceable elsewhere in the United Kingdom. An award given in Scotland for example shall have the force and standing of a judgment given there as far as the rest of the United Kingdom is concerned. Under Sch.6 to the Act, awards for the payment of a sum of money made in Scotland or Northern Ireland can be enforced in England as a local award. Similarly, Sch.7 provides that awards for the performance of any nonpayment-related duty may be enforced as a domestic award.

CHAPTER 15

ALTERNATIVE DISPUTE RESOLUTION

In this chapter we shall consider the role of alternative dispute resolution in **15–001** international trade. As far as traders are concerned there are two forms of dispute resolution methods available—the litigation process and other less formal alternative modes of dispute resolution (ADR). The conventional description of the term "ADR" refers to the various forms of ad hoc procedure which are consensual and not subject to any coercive powers of the court, except perhaps in the enforcement of the resolution (for, e.g. arbitral awards).

ADR procedures are necessarily informal or at least less formal than the litigation process. Their chief concern is the amicable settlement of disputes between the parties; although the extent to which this is achieved depends on the type of ADR procedure chosen.[1] On the one hand, there is negotiation or conciliation where the informality of the process is self evident but the parties are free to withdraw at any time. There are no formal structures to ensure that some conclusion or result be arrived at. On the other hand, we have the arbitral process which is more formal in that the parties go before an arbitral tribunal or panel whereby rules of evidence will be adhered to, legal principles be referred to and applied, and a binding award is envisaged.

The conventional modes of ADR include:

Mediation and Conciliation

Mediation involves a third party who is normally neutral attempting to elicit a **15–002** compromised solution for the parties. His role generally includes the separate and private negotiation with each party to the dispute and will attempt to use his goodwill with both parties to ensure that some form of resolution to the problem will be reached. The resulting compromise will normally then be expressed in a binding contract or agreement to which both parties will accept. The main advantage of the mediation and conciliation process is confining the discussions privately thus avoiding bad publicity. The mediator does not offer an opinion as to the rights and wrongs of the case. His remit is to ensure that a resulting agreement be arrived at.

Conciliation on the other hand relates to the settlement of the dispute by direct reference to the merits of the dispute. The conciliator is therefore generally

---

[1] See generally Connerty, "The role of ADR in the resolution of international disputes" (1996) 12 *Arbitration International* 47; Edwards, "Alternative Dispute Resolution: Panacea or Anathema?" (1986) 99 Harv. L. Rev. 668; Glasser and Roberts, "Dispute Resolution: Civil Justice and its alternatives" (1993) 56 M.L.R. 207.

required to provide an opinion on the case, albeit normally in a provisional sense in order to allow the parties to negotiate a settlement.[2] The Institute of International Law defines conciliation in these terms in art.1 of the Regulations on the Procedure of International Conciliation:

"A method for the settlement of international disputes of any nature according to which a Commission set up by the Parties, either on a permanent basis or an ad hoc basis to deal with a dispute attempts to define the terms of a settlement susceptible of being accepted by them or affording the Parties, with a view to its settlement, such aid as they may have requested".

Conciliation should provide the parties with a better understanding of their opponent's case and an objective appraisal of the merits of their own case. The conciliator in setting out the legal strengths of either party and delineating a possible solution is central to the success of conciliation as an ADR procedure. The importance of conciliation in commercial disputes cannot be underestimated. Indeed this is envisaged in the ICC Rules of Arbitration.

Although there was in the past a general disinclination by the courts to get involved in supporting non-arbitral ADR procedures, that is no longer the case. The High Court has confirmed in *Shirayama Shokusan Co Ltd v Danovo Ltd* (December 5, 2003) that the courts have jurisdiction to direct ADR.[3] Indeed, by Pt 1 of the Civil Procedure Rules 1998, the court is required actively to manage cases and encourage the parties to use ADR. The court would not make such directions unless there is evidence of the parties' willing. In that case, the parties had been in a long-term commercial relationship and were in some profit-sharing arrangement which would benefit from mediation. A number of the issues were minor but potentially inflammatory—that being the case, mediation had obviously a tremendous advantage over litigation and if mediation worked, there would be much to be gained.

Arbitration

15–003   Mediation and conciliation as ADR procedures may be roughly termed "diplomatic means of dispute resolution". As pointed out, the approach is entirely informal and the parties are entitled to back out and refuse to carry on. The parties retain substantial control over the means and process of settlement. Arbitration, on the other hand, is more akin to judicial settlement. Once the parties have agreed to set up the arbitration for the resolution of their dispute, their right to withdraw will be construed as a breach of the arbitration agreement and that will not be looked upon by the courts of law favourably. It might be noted that under s.9 of the Arbitration Act 1996, the English courts must stay proceedings commenced before them in favour of an arbitration where there exists a valid arbitration agreement.

International commercial disputes are particularly suitable for resolution by arbitration. The technical issues and trade customs involved are not easily

---

[2] Glossner, "Enforcement of conciliation agreements" (1983) 11 *International Business Lawyer* 151.

[3] See Gerlis, "Settling on mediation" (2004) 101(27) L.S.Gaz. 36; Pliener, "At last, clarity for mediation" (2004) 154(7132) N.L.J. 878.

accessible to the non-specialist judge. An arbitrator who has substantial experience in the trade or industry in question will make a splendid umpire in disputes about reasonable conduct in business, the presumed contractual intention of the parties, chief concerns of the industry and other similar issues. In cases which hinge on the facts and specific customs, it is preferable that they be decided by arbitration. Where on the other hand, intricate questions of law are involved they are better referred to the courts of law.

In general it is assumed that arbitration has the following benefits:

- confidentiality and privacy;

- informality of the proceedings;

- lower costs;

- efficiency;

- technical specialism; and

- a final award which could be enforced at the courts.

In this chapter, we shall concern ourselves with domestic arbitration as provided for in the Arbitration Act 1996; in other words arbitrations subject to English law and jurisdiction. As far as international commercial arbitration is concerned, we have seen how English law deals with the enforcement and recognition of awards handed down by a foreign arbitral tribunal in the preceding chapter. It suffices to note here that there is no standard definition to the term "international arbitration". From the perspective of the English lawyer, the international arbitration has several aspects making it international in nature. It could involve a case conducted in a foreign country, or a case involving parties from different countries, or a case conducted in this country but subject to a chosen foreign law, etc. What matters ultimately though is whether the arbitration in question is one defined by the Geneva Convention, or the New York Convention, or any of the statutes on the enforcement of foreign judgments, or the common law.

An international arbitration may be affected by four different laws:

- the law governing the contract between the parties;

- the law governing the arbitration agreement;

- the law governing the arbitration proceedings (the procedural law); and

- the law governing the reference to arbitration.

Both the procedural and applicable law to the underlying contract and/or the **15–004** arbitration agreement may be expressly nominated by the parties. While the procedural law of the arbitration may be chosen by the parties, for the sake of convenience the procedural law will usually follow that of the seat of the arbitration. Section 3 of the 1996 Act recognises this. It defines the seat as

"the juridical seat of the arbitration designated—

(a) by the parties to the arbitration agreement; or
(b) by any arbitral or other institution or person vested by the parties with the powers in that regard; or

(c) by the arbitral tribunal if so authorised by the parties,

or determined, in the absence of any such designation, having regard to the parties' agreement and all the relevant circumstances".

In *Dubai Islamic Bank PJSC v Paymentech Merchant Services Inc* [2001] 1 Lloyd's Rep. 65, the parties' arbitration had been conducted entirely on paper (the exchange of documents). Unhappy with the decision, the Islamic bank appealed to an appeals arbitration body and the matter was heard in London. That appeal was dismissed. The Islamic bank then instituted action in England challenging the award on the basis of certain alleged defects under s.68 of the Arbitration Act 1996. Paymentech, on the other hand, argued that the English court had no jurisdiction over the arbitration because the arbitration did not have its seat in England and Wales within the terms of ss.2 and 3 of the Act. Aitkens J. made it plain that unless the arbitration had its seat in England and Wales, the English court would have no power to review the award made. Section 3 stated that the seat of the arbitration meant the juridical seat of the arbitration; it was clear the section intended to refer to some state or territory which was associated with a recognisable and distinct system of law. The juridical seat had to mean the state or territory where for legal reasons the arbitration was to be regarded as situated. In this instance, the circumstances pointed to California as having the closest connection with the transaction. Although the appeals arbitration was heard in London, that was not an obligation under the agreement. Indeed it was not contemplated by anyone in the bank, Paymentech and other relevant parties, that the appeal would necessarily be heard in London. All the preparatory work of the appeals body was made in California. The seat was therefore not in England and Wales. It was also held that the relevant time at which the juridical seat is to be determined is the time when the relevant arbitration begins.

Section 3 refers to the designation of the juridical seat but commercial parties are not always so informed that their arbitration agreement will specify explicitly where the juridical seat is. In such cases, the court will need to assess the factual circumstances and the underlying contractual relationship and terms to see whether there is a designation which can be ascertained with sufficient clarity and certainty. In *Roger Shashoua v Mukesh Sharma* [2009] EWHC 957 (Comm), the court held that although the arbitration clause had provided for the arbitration to be conducted in accordance with the ICC Arbitration Rules (a supranational body of rules), the fact that it provided that the "venue" of the arbitration would be London, that was enough to indicate a designation of a juridical seat in London. The court was persuaded by the fact that the parties had not simply provided for the location of hearings to be in London for the sake of convenience; despite the fact that the underlying shareholders agreement was governed by Indian law, and any disputes were likely to be associated with the new venture in India, they had nevertheless wanted the arbitration to take place in London. That must surely have meant that their intention was to use England as the juridical seat.

15–005   The seat will designate the procedural law for the arbitration proceedings and the court of that place will have supervisory jurisdiction generally.[4] The concept of a floating arbitration is not recognised at English law; every arbitration must

---

[4] See Park, "The Lex Loci Arbitri and International Commercial Arbitration" (1983) 32 I.C.L.Q. 21; Paulsson, "Delocalisation of International Commercial Arbitration: When And Why It Matters" (1983) 32 I.C.L.Q. 53.

have a seat from which judicial control might be exerted. Indeed as the Departmental Advisory Committee on Arbitration Law Report on the Arbitration Bill said:

> "English law does not at present recognise the concept of an arbitration which has no seat and we do not recommend that it should do so".[5]

This means that an arbitration must have a seat at the time the arbitration commences. Once arbitration starts and it has a "seat", it will not normally change unless one of the mechanisms envisaged in s.3 operates.

Applicable law and arbitration

Where the arbitration involves a cross-border element, issues of applicable law   **15–006** are likely to arise. As alluded to above, the issue can arise in four respects:

(a)   what law governs the substantive dispute;

(b)   what law governs the arbitral process;

(c)   what law governs the arbitral agreement; and

(d)   what law governs the enforcement of the award.

It should be remembered that the Rome I Regulation does not apply to arbitration; so the rules on the applicable law in relation to these four aspects of arbitration are derived largely from the common law and international law and practice.

Applicable law of the substantive dispute

The applicable law of the substantive dispute in contractual matters is usually the   **15–007** applicable law of the underlying contract (this should be contrasted against the applicable law of the arbitration agreement). Party autonomy should prevail but where there is no choice of law made by the parties, the tribunal will decide according to what it considers appropriate.

This approach is reflected in the London Court of International Arbitration (LCIA) Rules, for example. Article 22.3 of those Rules states:

> "The Arbitral Tribunal shall decide the parties' dispute in accordance with the law(s) or rules of law chosen by the parties as applicable to the merits of their dispute. If and to the extent that the Arbitral Tribunal determines that the parties have made no such choice, the Arbitral Tribunal shall apply the law(s) or rules of law which it considers appropriate."

Similarly, the ICC Rules 2012 provide in art 21.1 that:

> "The parties shall be free to agree upon the rules of law to be applied by the arbitral tribunal to the merits of the dispute. In the absence of any such

---

[5] Para.27 of the report.

agreement, the arbitral tribunal shall apply the rules of law which it determines to be appropriate."

So too in art.35, UNCITRAL Model Law:

"The arbitral tribunal shall apply the rules of law designated by the parties as applicable to the substance of the dispute. Failing such designation by the parties, the arbitral tribunal shall apply the law which it determines to be appropriate."

The term "appropriate" is open to interpretation and could result in uncertainty and arbitrariness. The expectation usually amongst English arbitrators seems to be that it should mirror closely the *proper law doctrine*—namely what is the law of the country most closely connected to the dispute. However this is not articulated in international arbitration rules. Other considerations may therefore apply though it is unclear what.

15–008   The international arbitration rules all provide that the arbitrator should take into account the contract terms and any relevant trade usage, and may assume the powers of an *amiable compositeur* or decide *ex aequo et bono* (but usually only if the parties have agreed to give it such powers) (see art.21.3 ICC Rules 2012)). *Ex aequo et bono* means "according to the right and good" or "from equity and conscience". The parties may expressly exclude from the relevant sources of applicable law, trade practice and/or *ex aequo et bono*.

As for an *amiable compositeur*, this term has its genesis in French law, namely in *amicabilis compositor* of canon law, who acted rather as conciliator than decision-maker in a dispute and was not bound to apply strict rules of civil procedure and substantive law. The concept was first enacted in the Code Napoleon and the French Code of Civil Procedure of 1806. Some commentators contend that an *amiable compositeur* must apply the law, because there is a presumption that what is in the law is fair and equitable.[6] On the other hand, the concept of *amiable compositeur* is usually adopted in international commercial arbitration. In this transnational sphere, whilst law is important, there are other equally influential norms such as general principles of law and trade practice. However, whatever these sources of the applicable law may be, they must be certain and ascertainable.

It follows that as the arbitrator must decide according to the applicable law,[7] no account can be taken of principles or maxims alien to the applicable law of the contract. In *Orion Compania Espanola de Seguros v Belfast Maatschappij Voor Algemene V* [1962] 2 Lloyd's Rep. 257, an arbitration clause that provided that the arbitrator may decide the dispute using an equitable interpretation rather than a legal construction was declared null and void to that extent. The rationale was that where the award goes for judicial review, the courts will not be able to ascertain the legal justifiability and validity of the award if it has been made outside the principles of law. This decision was subsequently affirmed in *Home & Overseas Insurance v Mentor Insurance* [1989] 1 Lloyd's Rep. 473.

15–009   An arbitration tribunal is free to apply non-legal rules from the discussion above (see also s.46(1)(b)); examples of these non-legal rules include the lex

---

[6] K.P. Berger, *International Economic Arbitration*, (Kluwer Law International, 1993), p.570.

[7] Chukwumerije, "Applicable substantive law in international commercial arbitration" [1994] Anglo-Am. L. Rev. 265.

mercatoria, public international law, the UNIDROIT Principles, trade usage, etc. In *Channel Tunnel v Balfour Beatty* [1992] Q.B. 656 the contract provided that

> "the contract shall . . . be governed by and interpreted in accordance with the principles common to both English law and French law, and in the absence of such common principles by such general principles of international trade law as have been applied by national and international tribunals."

Whilst it is clear that such a clause would fall foul of the terms of the Rome Regulation on applicable law, it is not unusual in arbitrations for the parties to apply general principles of law common to several jurisdictions and international trade law in general. The difficulty for the arbitrator is discovering what these principles are.

The lex arbitri or curial law (law that governs the arbitration)

In international arbitration law the *lex arbitri* is usually the law of the seat of the **15–010** arbitration. The seat of the arbitration is usually agreed by the parties[8]; if no agreement is found, the arbitrators decide (see art.18 UNCITRAL Model Law 2010). But sometimes place and juridical seat may not be the same. In *Braes of Doune Wind Farm* [2008] EWHC 426 (TCC) the seat was to be "Glasgow" but the parties had chosen the English Arbitration Act as the applicable procedural law. A reason why parties may do that is because whilst the seat of the arbitration is well placed to handle the dispute (e.g. it is where the witnesses are resident, where the subject matter is located, and where the contract is to be performed), the country in question may not have suitable laws on arbitration (for example, they may have rules of evidence which the parties do not find amenable or their arbitration law is not appropriate for transnational disputes, etc).

In countries where arbitration law is not fully formed, the parties and arbitral tribunal may see a need to supplement the *lex arbitri* with more detailed procedural rules (such as those adopted by the LCIA, ICC[9] etc). Even where there are in place developed procedural rules for arbitration, the parties may decide to adopt the rules of one of these international organisations because they may be perceived as being more friendly to the trade.

The *lex arbitri* provides for:

- protective measures to support, enforce and supervise the arbitration;

- procedural provisions such as statements of case, evidence, hearings;

- rules about arbitrability;

- rules about the constitution of the tribunal, challenges to arbitrators, and the entitlement of the tribunal to rule on its own jurisdiction; and

---

[8] As far as the English Arbitration Act 1996 is concerned, s.3 defines "the seat of the arbitration" as "the juridical seat of the arbitration designated—(a) by the parties to the arbitration agreement, or (b) by any arbitral or other institution or person vested by the parties with powers in that regard, or (c) by the arbitral tribunal if so authorised by the parties; or determined in the absence of any such designation, having regard to the parties' agreement and all the relevant circumstances".

[9] On the ICC Rules 2012, see below paras 15–064—15–066.

● procedural safeguards, such as rules about equal treatment of parties.

There is an emerging view that transnational or international arbitration should not be tied to the law of the seat; instead it should be delocalised and be controlled by autonomous rules. This is what is commonly called the delocalisation theory. The current UK (England) position is reflected in the Departmental Advisory Committee on Arbitration Law Report on the Arbitration Bill which is essentially to reject the adoption of such a principle in English law. The link between an arbitration and the seat of arbitration is, as far as the UK Government is concerned, central. One of the reasons is that where the country perceives itself as having a set of sound arbitration legal rules and sees international/transnational commercial arbitration as good business for the country, it is less likely to support the idea of delocalisation.

Law governing the arbitration agreement

15–011 The question as to what law governs the arbitration agreement is different from the question of what law governs the dispute, and the question of what law governs the underlying contract.

There are two possible candidates—the law of the underlying agreement and the law of the seat. The starting premise is that the proper law of the arbitration agreement is the body of law most closely connected to it where no choice of law had been made. In *Miller v Whitworth Street Estates Ltd* [1970] A.C. 583 and *Black Clawson International Ltd v Papierwerke Waldhof-Aschaffenberg AG* [1981] 2 Lloyd's Rep. 446, the body of law with the closest and most real connection to the arbitration agreement is the law of the underlying agreement where that underlying agreement does contain an express choice of law.

However, where there is no such express choice of law in either the substantive agreement or the arbitration agreement, but the venue of the arbitration is identified, it will normally, but not invariably, be concluded that the arbitration agreement and the substantive contract should both be governed by the law of that place. Although an express choice of law provision applicable to the substantive contract may be, and often is, to be found in the clause which also contains the arbitration agreement or the jurisdiction agreement, it is important to appreciate that such provisions are normally part of the substantive contract and, in the absence of express indications to the contrary, do not fall within the arbitration or jurisdiction agreement so as to invest them with the same attribute of separability of such agreements. (*Sonatrach Petroleum Corporation (BVI)* [2001] EWHC 481 (Comm)).

15–012 In *Shashoua v Sharma* [2009] EWHC 957 (Comm), the court commented that

"when therefore there is an express designation of the arbitration venue as London and no designation of any alternative place as the seat, combined with a supranational body of rules governing the arbitration and no other significant contrary indicia, the inexorable conclusion is, to my mind, that London is the juridical seat and English law the curial law."

In that case, the *lex arbitri* chosen was the ICC Rules.

As we have seen, much depends on how the judges construct the connecting factors. In *Sulamerica cia Nacional de Seguros SA v Enesa Engenharia SA* [2012] EWCA Civ 638 where a contract provided for Brazilian law and jurisdiction but contained an arbitration clause providing that the seat of arbitration was to be in London, the court refused to take that as an implied choice of Brazilian law to govern the arbitration agreement. The court held that its proper law was English law because that was the law of the seat with which the arbitration agreement had its closest and most real connection. The court relied on the Court of Appeal's decision in *C v D* [2007] EWCA Civ 1282 where it was thought that as the seat of arbitration is crucial to the enforcement of the arbitration agreement, and that provided a real and substantial connection (also *Abuja International Hotels v Meridien SAS* [2012] EWHC 87 (Comm)). This (quasi) presumption that the arbitration agreement is most closely connected to the law of the seat is obviously a departure from *Sonatrach*.

So where does all this leave us? The fundamentals are that the solution lies in the notion of which body of law is closest and has the most real connection with the arbitration agreement and how the courts have applied the test has not been consistent. There are naturally good reasons for supporting either positions. Those who favour the law of the underlying agreement rely on the argument that that creates a one stop shop and thus lends itself to better commercial certainty. Also, it will provide better clarity for non-lawyers who see the underlying agreement as the key document. On the other hand, those who favour the law of the seat find support in the fact that legal succour for the arbitration agreement must surely come from the law of the seat rather than the law of underlying contract. Moreover, there is, prima facie, a good argument that the connection between the seat (whose subject matter is the arbitration) and the arbitration agreement is stronger than the link between the arbitration agreement and the underlying agreement (whose subject matter is not the arbitration).

Law governing the award

The general principle is that the law governing the award shall be the law of the seat. In *C v D* [2007] EWCA Civ 1282, the underlying contract was a "Bermuda Form" insurance policy in the usual terms, referring disputes to arbitration in London, and applying New York law to issues arising under the policy. The defendant had argued that as the arbitration agreement was silent as to its proper law, it should not follow the seat of the arbitration (namely London) but should follow the proper law of the contract (namely New York law) thus allowing challenges to the award in the New York courts. The Court of Appeal dismissed the appeal. The Court of Appeal found that by choosing London as the seat of arbitration, the parties must be taken as having agreed that proceedings on the award should only be those permitted by English law. To allow the remedies available under New York law would be invite more litigation and inconvenience.

Even where there is no express law of the arbitration agreement, it will rarely be the case that the law of the arbitration agreement will be different from the law of the seat of the arbitration.

This case reminds us that an express choice of seat for arbitration proceedings is frequently regarded as indicating the forum in which the parties may seek remedies to challenge an award.

15–013

Arbitration and the courts

15–014 The prevailing attitude of English law is that the autonomy of arbitration cannot be achieved without some degree of judicial intervention.[10] In this regard, we might identify several areas where the courts will have to play some role, at times for the preservation of the arbitration as a mode of dispute resolution.

1. There are some matters which cannot be subject to arbitration. We have seen in the preceding chapter that matters involving the legal status or capacity of any legal or natural person, the illegality of the underlying contract and the public policy of the jurisdiction cannot be subject to arbitration.

2. The staying of proceedings before the court to ensure that the parties comply with the arbitration agreement is essential if the arbitration agreement is to remain sacrosanct.

3. The courts are the final place of appeal where an award has been made unjustly or unlawfully. The courts have the power to set aside any award made unlawfully. There is also the power to remit a matter to the arbitral tribunal or panel to re-assess a particular case in the event of any irregularity or error. We shall consider this in greater detail later.

4. The courts will also be called upon to recognise and enforce any arbitral award made so as to ensure that respect for arbitration is not disregarded.

5. The courts are also necessarily involved where specific orders or injunctions have to be made to ensure the smooth functioning of the arbitral process. The courts may be asked to extend time, appoint and remove arbitrators, etc.

Source of law

15–015 Once upon a time, arbitration was regulated by the common law and four statutes, the Arbitration Acts of 1950, 1975 and 1979, and the Consumer Arbitration Agreements Act 1988. The Arbitration Act 1996 has now repealed the latter three Acts and Pt I and s.42(3) of the 1950 Act. The new Act has been hailed as the closest thing to a definitive code of arbitration law in England. It should be remembered that this does not mean the common law and decisions on earlier legislation can be ignored. They should serve as a good guide to the interpretation and application of the new provisions. Whilst the 1996 Act takes on board many of the proposals in the United Nations Model Law on Arbitration 1985,[11] it remains distinctive in many of its own provisions. The Departmental Advisory Committee on Arbitration Law chaired by Lord Mustill had put forward these reasons for not adopting the Model Law wholesale, especially in the light of the repute and significance of the Model Law:

1. The Model Law applies and caters specifically for international commercial arbitration and not purely domestic disputes. The 1996 on the other hand represents a compromise and an integration of the two regimes.

---

[10] Roberts, "Alternative dispute resolution and civil justice: an unresolved relationship" (1993) 56 M.L.R. 452 offers an in-depth analysis into this mutually dependent relationship.

[11] P. Sanders (ed.), *UNICITRAL's Project for a Model Law on International Commercial Arbitration* (Deventer: Kluwer Publishing, 1984); see also P. Sanders, "Unity and diversity in the adoption of the Model Law" (1995) 11 *Arbitration International* 1.

2. The Model Law is essentially founded on precepts alien to English law. It would therefore cause a good deal of short-term dislocation in the English arbitration market while new procedures and principles were absorbed by lawyers and the industries.[12]

3. The Model Law was designed primarily for those jurisdictions with little or nothing in the way of developed principles of arbitration law, whereas England in this respect possessed a mature tried-and-tested system.[13]

4. There was little evidence that demonstrated any generalised call for root and branch reform.

Effect of an arbitration agreement

The arbitration is a creature of contract. This necessarily means that whatever **15–016** powers the arbitrator has are largely dependent on that agreement. The agreement to submit disputes to arbitration must be in writing (s.5(1) 1996 Act). An arbitration agreement which is not in writing is not unlawful but it will not be governed by the Act, instead it falls under the common law rules which have been preserved by the Act in s.81. There is however no definition as to what constitutes "writing" although it could be said that under s.7 of the Arbitration Act 1975, it includes an agreement contained in an exchange of letters or telegrams. An arbitration agreement concluded electronically should be permissible. Article 9 of the EU Directive on Certain Legal Aspects of Electronic Commerce in the External Market provides in no uncertain terms that Member States shall ensure that contracts are capable of being concluded electronically and shall not cause such contracts to be deprived of legal effect and validity on account of their having been made electronically. It might further be noted that in "writing" criterion should be capable of being satisfied if the electronic agreement could be reduced to a hard copy.

What is the position where the arbitration agreement is contained in a telex offer but accepted orally by the other party?

In *Fahem & Co v Mareb Yemen Insurance Co Ltd* [1997] 2 Lloyd's Rep. 738, the defendants had sent a telex to the claimants which was expressed to be an "offer" for sale of sugar with price to be advised later by separate telex. The telex contained an arbitration clause. The claimants accepted the offer by telex. Cresswell J. referred to the decision of the Court of Appeal in *Zambia Steel & Building Supplies Ltd v Clark & Eaton Ltd* [1986] 2 Lloyd's Rep. 225 where O'Connor L.J. said:

" . . . if it is established that a document with an arbitration clause in writing forms part of a contract between the parties, the assent by one party orally to the contract is sufficient".

Ralph Gibson L.J. shared that sentiment. His Lordship expanded on the approach, saying:

---

[12] Cappalletti, "Alternative dispute resolution processes within the framework of the world-wide access-to-justice movement" (1993) 56 M.L.R. 282.

[13] Steyn, "England's response to the UNCITRAL Model Law of Arbitration" (1994) 10(1) *Arbitration International* 337.

"It seems to me that the phrase 'an agreement in writing' may have two meanings at least. The first is that the terms agreed between the parties are set out in writing. On that basis, provided that the terms of agreement to submit to arbitration are contained in a document or documents, proof that those terms were agreed by the parties to be binding upon them may be given outside those documents. Such proof must be given by evidence of conduct, from which the Court is persuaded that the inference of agreement must be drawn, or by evidence of oral acceptance, or indeed any other evidence which satisfies that court that the written terms constitute or form part of an agreement between the parties".

The arbitration clause in *Fahem* must therefore necessarily constitute a valid arbitration agreement.[14]

15–017   Whether an arbitration clause has been incorporated into the contract depends on the words of incorporation used. Two scenarios should first be identified:

- where there are two autonomous contracts with one containing an arbitration clause and not the other (two-contract scenario); and

- one contract is set out in writing in a document but the arbitration agreement is contained in a written record not forming the same physical document (one-contract scenario).

In *Sea Trade Maritime v Hellenic Mutual War Risks Association* [2006] EWHC 2530, the court held that in the case of the latter, general words of incorporation. Indeed, as stated in s.6(2) Arbitration Act 1996:

"the reference in an agreement to a written form of arbitration clause of to a document containing an arbitration clause constitutes an arbitration clause if the reference is such as to make that clause part of the agreement".

In *Interserve Industrial Services Ltd v ZRE Katowice SA*, [2012] EWHC 3205 (TCC), the arbitration clause was found in the main agreement but there was no arbitration clause in the settlement agreement which had arisen out of a dispute between them. Although this is not strictly a one-contract situation in that it might be said that there are two distinct contracts, as a matter of construction, the two agreements relate to the same rights and obligations between the parties. As such, the court was prepared to imply that the arbitration clause in the main agreement was to apply to the settlement agreement too.

15–018   On the other hand, in the former, stricter rules should apply and general words of incorporation would not suffice. In *The Federal Bulker* [1989] 1 Lloyd's Rep. 103, there was an arbitration clause in the charterparty but only the following words in the bill of lading issued thereafter: "all terms . . . as per Charterparty . . .

---

[14] The approach in *Fahem* is clearly supported by the Departmental Advisory Committee Report on the Arbitration Bill which stated that "writing" included recording by any means, There is also evidence that contracts involving the sale and carriage of sugar almost always included a clause referring disputes to arbitration by the Refined Sugar Association and that all contracts over a 10-year period between the claimant and the second defendants (sellers) contained the same arbitration clause.

to be considered as fully incorporated herein as if fully written". This is clearly a two-contract case; as such, general words of incorporation were not enough to incorporate the arbitration clause into the bill of lading. On the other hand, in *Sea Trade Maritime*, the policy had referred to the Hellenic Mutual War Risk Rules of Association which contained an arbitration clause. General words were enough to incorporate the arbitration clause into the policy. The rationale for the difference in treatment is because in two-contract cases at least one party will not have been privy to first contract. For example, in *The Federal Bulker*, the charterparty was between the charterer and the shipowner whilst the bill of lading was between the charterer/shipowner (depending on whether it is an owner's or charterer's bill) and the shipper—the shipper was not privy to the first contract, the charterparty. In general, a stricter rule has been applied in charterparty/bills of lading cases (*Habas Sinai Ve Tibbi Gazlar Isthisal Endustri v Sometal Sal* [2010] EWHC 29 (Comm)).

Section 6(1) defines an arbitration agreement as an agreement to submit to arbitration present or future disputes (whether they are contractual or not). This re-enactment of s.32 of the 1950 Act however refers to "disputes" and not "differences" as s.32 did. It is submitted that there is no material difference between the two terms. Section 82(1) defines "dispute" as including any "difference" suggesting that the term is wider but it is difficult to envisage any appreciable extension. As far as the common law is concerned, a "difference" has been defined as referring to a failure to agree (see *F & G Sykes (Wessex) Ltd v Fine Fare Ltd* [1967] 1 Lloyd's Rep. 53). In *Wilky Property Holdings Plc v London & Surrey Investments Ltd* [2011] EWHC 2226 (Ch) the court found that the clause in question was one referring disputes to expert determination, not arbitration.[15] Expert determination is not the same as arbitration and will not be governed by the Arbitration Act 1996. With the many and varied means of alternative dispute resolution available, it is more important than ever to make clear that arbitration is the intended method.

Disputes as to the precise scope of an arbitration clause invariably arise when a party wishes to resist the invocation of an arbitration agreement. In the past, we have seen the courts struggle with how certain provisions should be construed—for example, is a clause stating that "all disputes arising under the agreement" to be treated as the same as one requiring "all disputes arising out of the agreement" to be referred to arbitration? The matter is particularly acute when the issue of contention is that over the validity of the agreement rather than the application of any particular provision alleged to have been breached. In *Fiona Trust v Privalov* (sub nom *Premium Nafta v Fili Shipping*) [2007] UKHL 40 the House of Lords made it plain that in the interest of expediency in international commerce fine distinctions should not be read into arbitration agreements. Lord Hoffmann noted that previous cases have frequently made a distinction between clauses requiring all disputes "arising under" and those requiring all disputes "arising out of" the agreement to be referred to arbitration. His Lordship however considered that such distinctions "reflect no credit upon English commercial law". In his view, the time had come to "draw a line under the authorities to date and to make a fresh start". His Lordship said:

---

[15] Similar facts arose in *British Telecommunications Plc v SAE Group Inc* [2009] EWHC 252 (TCC).

"In my opinion the construction of an arbitration clause should start from the assumption that the parties, as rational businessmen, are likely to have intended any dispute arising out of the relationship into which they have entered or purported to enter to be decided by the same tribunal. The clause should be construed in accordance with this presumption unless the language makes it clear that certain questions were intended to be excluded from the arbitrator's jurisdiction".

It now is clear that if the parties wish to exclude certain issues from being brought to arbitration, they should make that clear in the arbitration agreement. The new start, as Lords Hope and Hoffmann described, is consistent with the legislative object of the "new" Arbitration Act 1996.

15–019　　　An arbitration clause does not need to use words like "arbitration" or "arbitrator" where it is clear from the entirety of the agreement that an arbitration was intended. In *David Wilson Homes Ltd v Surrey Services Ltd (In Liquidation)* [2001] EWCA Civ 34, the defendants had argued that the clause in the insurance contract:

"any dispute or difference arising . . . between the assured and the insurers shall be referred to a Queen's Counsel . . . to be mutually agreed . . . or in the event of disagreement, by the Chairman of the Bar Council"

was not a properly constituted arbitration clause as it did not refer to "arbitration" or "arbitrator" or the 1996 Act. They also submitted that there was nothing in the clause which indicated that the determination by Queen's Counsel was to be final and binding and was accordingly, a nonbinding opinion that was sought and therefore did not amount to an arbitration clause. The Court of Appeal disagreed, stating that the necessary attribute was an agreement to refer a dispute to a person, other than a court, who was to resolve the dispute with binding effect on the parties; it was not vital that the agreement referred specifically to "arbitration". It was not necessary for the agreement to state that the decision of the arbitrator was to be final because s.58(1) Arbitration Act 1996 stated quite clearly that an arbitrator's decision is final and binding. As far as the construction of the agreement goes, it was plain that the role of the appointed Queen's Counsel was to hold an inquiry in the nature of a judicial inquiry and hear the dispute and resolve the issues based on the evidence before him.

Clarity of terms is essential; this is especially so when the agreement to arbitrate is "conditional" on certain preliminary steps to be taken by the parties. The rationale for such conditions (usually called dispute escalation clauses) is to ensure that the dispute does not fester and escalate to uncontrollable levels. However, as there remains a question as to the legal effect of such clauses, these preliminary steps may be compulsory or voluntary. If the latter, they are clearly not finally binding but will go some way at showing earnest and good faith. On the other hand, if they are expressed in compulsory terms, it might be assumed that they will be binding. However, as a recent case shows, this is not necessarily uncontroversial. In *Wah (also known as Tang) v Grant Thornton International Ltd* [2012] EWHC 3198 (Ch) the court was asked to consider the appropriate test for determining whether a contractual provision setting out the requirements for the conciliation of disputes prior to arbitration was sufficiently clear and certain to be given binding effect. Cases would be considered on their own terms. It should not be a case of the court mechanistically ticking off the minimum ingredients for validity.

Wah (also known as Tang) v Grant Thornton International Ltd [2012] EWHC 3198 (Ch)   **15–020**

Facts:
X's partnership had been expelled from an accountancy and audit network, of which G was the umbrella organisation. Membership of the group was governed by a master agreement, which was subject to English law. X brought arbitration proceedings in Hong Kong over the disputed expulsion. The majority partners in X (Z) subsequently agreed to a discontinuation of the arbitration. X contested their application to do so, alleging that the tribunal had no jurisdiction to determine the issue because the steps (including conciliation and amicable resolution) outlined in the master agreement had not been followed. The tribunal disagreed stating that the steps in the agreement were not sufficiently precise or certain to be contractually binding; or alternatively that they had not been intended to prevent a reference to arbitration. X then challenged the award.

Held:
On the issue as to whether the agreement was sufficiently certain, the court agreed with the tribunal. In the context of an obligation to attempt to resolve a dispute before referring it to arbitration, the test was whether the provision provided, without the need for further agreement:

(a) a sufficiently certain and unequivocal commitment to commence a process;

(b) a means of discerning the steps each party was required to take to start the process;

(c) sufficient clarity and definition to enable the court to make an objective determination of the minimum participatory requirements for each party; and

(d) an indication of how the process would be exhausted or properly terminable without breach (*Sulamerica Cia Nacional de Seguros SA v Enesa Engenharia SA* [2012] EWCA Civ 638, [2012] 2 All E.R. (Comm) 795, *Cable & Wireless Plc v IBM United Kingdom Ltd* [2002] EWHC 2059 (Comm), [2002] 2 All E.R. (Comm) 1041 and *Petromec Inc v Petroleo Brasileiro SA Petrobras (No3)* [2005] EWCA Civ 891, [2006] 1 Lloyd's Rep. 121 were considered).

Agreements to agree, and agreements to negotiate in good faith, would generally be unenforceable because good faith was too open-ended a concept to provide sufficient definition or clarity. In the present case as the agreement to use conciliation and amicable resolution was contained in a legally enforceable contract, the question was whether the terms were sufficiently clear for enforcement.

The court should consider each case on its own terms rather than ticking off minimum ingredients for validity. The test was not whether there was valid provision for a recognised process of mediation, but whether obligations imposed were sufficiently clear and certain to be given legal effect. The relevant provisions calling for amicable resolution were too equivocal and nebulous in communicating the parties' respective obligations to be given legal effect. There was no provision as to the quality or nature of such preliminary attempts to be made to resolve a dispute. There was insufficiency clarity in those provisions.

An arbitration clause in a contract is not only binding on the parties to the contract but any person claiming under or through the original contracting parties. It was so held in *Astra SA Insurance & Reinsurance Co v Yasuda Fire & Marine Insurance Co* [1999] C.L.C. 950. In that case, Astra as successors in title   **15–021** to ADAS, the original party to the arbitration contract, were bound by the arbitration clause in certain reinsurance contracts (see also *Through Transport Mutual v New India Assurance* [2005] EWHC 455).

There is some controversy where it comes to a person who was not involved in the original proceedings seeking to rely on a finding made in those proceedings in related proceedings. In *Sun Life Assurance Co of Canada v The Lincoln National Life Insurance Co* [2004] EWCA Civ 1660, L underwrote certain reinsurance risks for S's benefit. Similarly, C had also offered similar cover to S on related risks. Disputes had arisen between S and C, and between S and L. An arbitral award was made in arbitral proceedings between S and C and it was found by the arbitrator that there was misrepresentation and non-disclosure which C could rely on to refuse payment. L sought to rely on those findings in his arbitration with S. The Commercial Court held that L was entitled to do so because

"the modern tendency when tackling the problems of serial litigation involving a common issue had been to move away from technical rules towards a broader consideration of what was fair".[16]

The Court of Appeal however overturned the lower court's decision. It held that what was claimed was issue estoppel and for issue estoppel to work, the parties or at least their privies (such as successors in title or assignees) must be the same. The principle of mutuality required that someone who was not a party such as L could not take advantage of a decision in proceedings made when he was not there. It is however submitted that although the Court of Appeal's decision is very much technically correct, its emphasis on the identification of the parties raises the problem of how close the parties' privies ought to be. In a complex commercial context involving several disputes, certainty and expediency of the arbitral process could well be jeopardised.

Thus far we have been looking at parties who have relied on some succession of title to rely on the arbitration. In *The Elikon* [2003] EWCA Civ 812, there arose an equally challenging issue—who actually are the parties?

15–022   *Internaut Shipping Ltd GmbH v Fercometal Sarl (The Elikon)* [2003] EWCA Civ 812
Facts:
S was the owner of the Elikon. F was the charterer and IS was the broking firm. S was named as owner in the charterparty but IS had signed it as "owner". A dispute arose and IS commenced arbitral proceedings in the name of "owner" and it was clear that IS had proceeded on the basis that S was the owner. However, a few years later, it became obvious that S and IS had different interests and no corporate connection. Proceedings were commenced to establish the correct parties to the arbitration and charterparty. The High Court decided that IS, not S, was entitled to commence the arbitration.
Held:
The Court of Appeal held that IS had signed the charterparty as owner without qualification and there was every justification to construe the charterparty as a whole as one in which IS was accepting personal liability for the owner. On the facts, therefore, the conduct of the arbitration in the name of S could not be treated as a mere misnomer. F had unwittingly adopted the identification of S as the claimant and the arbitration had

---

[16] See also Saville J.'s judgment in *Navimprex Centrala Navala v George Moundreas & Co SA* (*The Times*, March 21, 1983).

proceeded on that basis for five years. It also appeared that the difference in the identity of the owner might affect the arguments adopted in the arbitration. As such, the arbitration in the name of the claimant who had never actually been a party to the charterparty (or the arbitration agreement) was a nullity.

It should also not be forgotten that as a contract the arbitration agreement may also be affected by Contracts (Rights of Third Parties) Act 1999, namely, that where a third party has been mentioned or alluded to the in the arbitration agreement[17], that third party may be able to rely on the arbitration agreement. Section 8 of the 1999 Act provides that the right of the third party to enforce the arbitration agreement is subject to his enforcement of the substantive rights under the underlying agreement. For example, if in the main sale contract between A and B, A agrees to pay the sale proceeds to C and that main contract contains an arbitration clause mentions C, C will be able to enforce that arbitration clause against A if it demands payment under the main contract but A refuses to pay. However, C cannot rely on the arbitration clause if it does not seek first to enforce the payment obligation under the main contract. In *Fortress Value Recovery Fund v Blue Sky Special Opportunities Fund* [2012] EWHC 1486 (Comm), Blair J. held that as the defendant did not seek an indemnity or rely on the exclusion clause in their defence and did not seek to avail themselves of a substantive term in the main contract, there was no dispute relating to the enforcement of a substantive term by them as required by s.8 of the 1999 Act. As such, they could not be treated as parties to the arbitration.

As a matter of contract, if one party does not appoint or agree to the appointment of arbitrators following the service of a notice to appoint by the other party, the former would be in breach of contract. The problem though is that it is not inconceivable for one party to serve notice to arbitrate but then do nothing for a long time. The question is then whether the notice would expire following the lapse of reasonable time. In *Indescon Ltd v Robert Ogden* [2004] EWHC 2326 (QB), the arbitration notice was given 10 years prior to the commencement of proceedings. The court held that although the notice was 10 years old, as the applicant had done nothing to show that he intended to abandon the arbitration the notice was nonetheless valid. The court held that there was no express term in the contract that the appointment of arbitrators had to take place without delay and there was no basis for implying such a term in the contract.

Severability of the arbitration clause from the underlying contract

There persisted for some time a view that arbitrators could never have jurisdiction to decide whether a contract was valid. That is because if the contract was invalid, so too was the arbitration clause. In *Overseas Union Insurance Ltd v AA Mutual International Insurance Co Ltd* [1988] 2 Lloyd's Rep. 63, 66 Evans J. said that this rule "owes as much to logic as it does to authority". But that proposition was questioned and doubted by the Court of Appeal in *Harbour Assurance Co (UK) Ltd v Kansa General International Insurance Co Ltd* [1993] Q.B. 701 and the question was put beyond doubt by s.7 of the Arbitration Act 1996:

15–023

---

[17] s.1(3) of the 1999 act states that the third party must be expressly identified in the contract by name, as a member of a class or as answering a particular description.

"Unless otherwise agreed by the parties, an arbitration agreement which forms or was intended to form part of another agreement (whether or not in writing) shall not be regarded as invalid, non-existent or ineffective because that other agreement is invalid, or did not come into existence or has become ineffective, and it shall for that purpose be treated as a distinct agreement".

This section shows a recognition by Parliament that businessmen frequently *do* intend that the question of effectiveness or existence or legality of their contracts be submitted to arbitration and that the law should not place conceptual obstacles in their way (see *Fiona Trust v Privalov* [2007] UKHL 40). This means that an arbitration might be binding even though the underlying contract had not come into existence. Whether it would be had to be determined as a question of fact and degree, depending on the circumstances of the case (*Ur Power GmbH v Kuok Oils & Grain* [2009] EWHC 1940 (Comm); *Vee Networks Ltd v Econet Wireless International Ltd* [2004] EWHC 2909 (Comm), and *Fiona Trust & Holding Corp v Privalov* [2007] UKHL 40).

That does not however mean that the arbitration clause could never be also tainted by the invalidity of the underlying contract. Section 7 requires that a separate assessment be made as to whether the factors which render the contract void also *directly* affected the arbitration clause (see *Vee Networks v Econet Wireless International Ltd* [2004] EWHC 2909 and *Harbour Assurance v Kansa General International Insurance* [1993] 1 Q.B. 701). Where for example the person signing the agreement had absolutely no authority to do so (e.g. an office cleaner signing the agreement), that would strike at the heart of consent of both the underlying contract and the arbitration clause. However, where it is merely a case of an agent exceeding his authority by signing the agreement, this is not necessarily an attack on the arbitration agreement.

Stay of court proceedings to support arbitration

15–024 We have observed that the courts will attempt to ensure that the parties abide by their agreement to go to arbitration before allowing their dispute to go to judicial process. Section 9 builds on this policy. In general when a party takes his case to court where there exists an arbitration agreement, he has committed a breach of that agreement. This means that the courts should not entertain his action, for to do so would be to back that breach. The other party wishing to arbitrate may apply to have proceedings stayed. Section 9(1) provides that a party to an arbitration agreement against whom legal proceedings are brought in respect of a matter which under the agreement which is to be referred to arbitration may apply to stay the proceedings. The question as to "a matter under which the agreement is to be referred to arbitration" was discussed in *Three Shipping Ltd v Harebell Shipping Ltd* [2004] EWHC 2001. In that case, the bareboat charter between the parties provided that disputes arising out of the charterparty were to be settled by the English courts but that *the shipowners* had the option of bringing any dispute to arbitration. A dispute arose between the charterers and the shipowners about the relevant interest rates payable. The charterers proceeded to bring action before the English High Court. The shipowners applied to stay those proceedings in pursuant of s.9(1). The charterers argued that the charterparty merely referred to the shipowners' entitlement to rely on arbitration; they, as charterers, were not bound by the charterparty to use arbitration. They therefore submitted that as there was no agreement to arbitrate, the shipowners were not entitled to apply for a stay. The court held that the charterparty was designed to give "better" rights to the shipowners. Morison J. construed the relevant clause in this way—in the normal course of events where a dispute arose, the parties would seek to resolve by agreement whether that dispute was to be arbitrated or litigated, but with a reservation of a right to the shipowners to have the dispute referred to arbitration. If the charterers tried to bypass the shipowners' determination to have disputes resolved by arbitration, then the shipowners' option of bringing the disputes to arbitration must remain. Section 9(1) therefore could apply. Once the shipowners' option to have the dispute referred to arbitration was exercised, that was a "matter which under the agreement [was] to be referred to arbitration".

A stay granted means that the parties will have to arbitrate. In the case of a non domestic arbitration agreement, stay of judicial proceedings must be granted unless the arbitration agreement is null and void, inoperative or incapable of being performed.

The court's power depends on the finding that there was in fact an arbitration agreement (*Joint Stock Company Aeroflot v Berezovsky* [2012] EWHC 1610 (Ch)) but that agreement may be "null and void, inoperative of incapable of being performed". Section 9(4) provides "on an application under this section the court shall grant a stay unless satisfied that the arbitration agreement is null and void, inoperative, or incapable of being performed." In *Albon v Naza Motor Trading Sdn Bhd (No.3)* [2007] EWHC 327 (Ch), for example, Lightman J. refused to stay proceedings under s.9 because he was not satisfied that the joint venture agreement which contained the arbitration clause had not been forged. Lightman J. went on to state that only in an exceptional case would the court exercise its power to stay proceedings to allow the arbitrator to determine jurisdictional issues. An exceptional case might be where it was virtually certain that there was a valid arbitration agreement and/or there were convincing grounds of convenience and cost. The doctrine of *Kompetenz-Kompetenz* (which states that the arbitrator has the power to decide his own competence to sit) would not prevent the court from deciding whether the arbitration agreement was valid or not (see also *Al Naimi v Islamic Press Agency* [2000] 1 Lloyd's Rep. 522).

It was also argued in *Stretford v Football Association Ltd* [2007] EWCA Civ **15–025** 238 that the court should not stay its own proceedings to allow the arbitration to proceed because the arbitration clause was "null and void or inoperative" by reason of art.6 European Convention on Human Rights (ECHR). Article 6 provides for the right to a fair and public hearing within a reasonable time by an independent tribunal established by law. The Court of Appeal held that the 1996 Act meant that an arbitration subject to the Act, for the purposes of the ECHR, is the provision of a fair hearing by an impartial tribunal established by law as long as the arbitration agreement had been entered into voluntarily and was not contrary to public policy. The stay was thus granted.

The incapability referred to in s.9(4) Arbitration Act 1996 turns on the incapability of the arbitration and not on any of the parties. In *Janos Paczy v Haendler Natermann GmbH* [1981] 1 Lloyd's Rep. 30, the claimant claimed that he should be entitled to proceed in court (i.e. that proceedings should not be stayed) because he was impecunious and the legal aid provision he was receiving for the action could not be made available for the agreed arbitration. He also claimed that he would be unable to pay the required deposit under the relevant arbitration rules. The court considered that this practical difficulty on the part of one of the parties was not relevant to the effect of the arbitration agreement which must take precedence. A stay of proceedings was therefore granted.

An application for a stay may not be made by a person before taking the appropriate procedural step (if any) to acknowledge the legal proceedings against him or after he has taken any step in those proceedings to answer the substantive claim. In *Capital Trust Investments Ltd v Radio Design TJ AB* [2002] 2 All E.R. (Comm) 514, Jacob J. (whose decision was affirmed by the Court of Appeal, [2002] EWCA Civ 135) held that the party who had initiated an application for a stay pending an arbitration had not taken a step in the proceedings within the meaning of s.9(3) if he, simultaneously or subsequently, invoked or accepted the court's jurisdiction provided he did so only conditionally on his stay application failing. In that case, the claimant brought a claim in deceit against the defendant before the English court. The defendant applied for a stay of proceedings on the grounds that the contract was subject to a Swedish arbitration clause or, alternatively, for summary judgment that the claim be struck out. The two applications were clearly inconsistent with each other—if the first is granted, the second could not stand and vice versa. On that basis, the claimant contended that the defendant's application for stay was effectively barred by s.9(3). The court however held that the defendant had not "taken [a] step in those proceedings to answer the substantive claim" by making an alternative application for summary judgment because s.9(3) was only intended to apply to applicants for stay of proceedings who have invoked or subjected themselves to the court's jurisdiction *unconditionally.*[18] Furthermore, such a conditional or alternative application by the defendant could in fact be proper case management, a requirement under the new CPR.

15–026   Section 1(1) of the Arbitration Act 1975, before it was superseded by s.9(4), provided that where proceedings were commenced in respect of any matter agreed to be referred to arbitration, the court was bound to grant a stay unless satisfied that arbitration agreement was inoperative or incapable of being performed [or that there was not in fact any dispute between the parties with regard to the matter agreed to be referred]. Those concluding words in square brackets were omitted when the new s.9(4) was enacted. That was a radical change as evidenced in *Halki Shipping Corp v Sopex Oils Ltd, The Times,* October 13, 1997; [1998] 1 Lloyd's Rep. 465, CA.

In that case it was argued by the shipowners that there was no dispute because the parties could not have intended to submit to arbitration claims to which there was obviously no answer in fact or law. In short, the owners of the *Halki* felt that the charterers who had not paid demurrage were so clearly in breach that any attempt at an arbitration would be a mere farce. Clarke J. however, felt that with the omission of those concluding words in s.9(4), the agreed arbitration should proceed. The Court of Appeal agreed holding that a dispute arose once money was claimed and the defendant refused to acknowledge it.[19]

---

[18] See also *Bilta v Muhammad Nazir* [2010] EWHC 1086 (Ch), where it was held that the defendant's application for an extension of time to serve its defence did not amount to a "step in the proceedings" to answer the substantive claim. As such, s.9(3) did not apply to bar it from making an application to stay the proceedings. It had been entirely legitimate for it to seek more information about the claim before deciding whether to submit to the court proceedings or rely upon an arbitration agreement it maintained was in place.

[19] See also *Exfin Shipping Ltd Mumbai v Tolani Shipping Co Ltd Mumbai* [2006] EWHC 1090 but note *Wealands v Contractors* [1999] 2 Ll. L.R. 739.

In the case of a domestic arbitration agreement on the other hand, English courts have always exercised some sort of discretion in granting stay of proceedings. That discretion is now contained in s.86(2)(b) of the 1996 Act. Section 86(2)(b) allows the court to take into account any "sufficient grounds for not requiring the parties to abide by the arbitration agreement" apart from the grounds of nullity and incapability of performance (as referred to above). This discretion has been preserved in the case of domestic arbitration agreements only to the extent that it does not conflict with EU law on nondiscriminatory treatment of EC nationals (*Philip Alexander v Bamberger*, [1996] C.L.C. 1757). The element of discrimination could arise in that disputes involving EC nationals will have to be prosecuted as a nondomestic arbitration, which means according them a different treatment from cases involving UK nationals only.

The exercise of that discretion not to grant a stay of proceedings is seen in this **15–027** next case (a domestic arbitration agreement, necessarily). In *Taunton-Collins v Cromie* [1964] 1 W.L.R. 633, which involved a multi-party arbitration, no stay was granted because although between the employer and the builder there was an arbitration agreement, there was no such agreement between the employer and the architect. A stay of proceedings would have the effect of imposing on the architect an arbitration to which he had not agreed.[20]

Scott v Avery clauses

Quite apart from the rules on the stay of proceedings, at common law the contract **15–028** itself can provide that the arbitration award shall be a condition precedent to legal proceedings. A *Scott v Avery* clause as it is commonly known (*Scott v Avery* (1856) 10 E.R. 1121) will say something like this:

"It is hereby declared that arbitration (as set out in clauses 2, 3, 4 and 5 above) shall be a condition precedent to the commencement of any legal action".

As a term of the contract, if the party concerned proceeds with court action without first exhausting the agreed arbitral process, he will be in breach and the court could be asked to stay proceedings on that ground. The effect of a *Scott v Avery* clause is clearly less important in the light of s.9 of the Arbitration Act 1996 and its predecessors. A *Scott v Avery* clause is referred to in s.9(5), which provides that if the court refuses to stay legal proceedings, any provision that an award is a condition precedent to the bringing of legal proceedings in respect of any matter is of no effect in relation to those proceedings. It is quite obvious that the court's power to refuse to stay proceedings is not subject to any contractual clause entered into between the parties.

Section 9(1) provides that a party to the arbitration agreement who is being sued may ask the court for a stay of legal proceedings to ensure that the arbitration agreement is respected by the other party. He will however be barred from doing so if he has "acknowledge[d] the legal proceedings against him or after he has taken any step in those proceedings to answer the substantive claim".[21]

---

[20] See also *Albert Whiting v William Halverson* [2003] EWCA Civ 403.
[21] Section 9(3), see also L. D'arcy, C. Murray & B. Cleave, *Schmitthoff's Export Trade* (London: Sweet and Maxwell, 2000), p.485.

15–029   Section 9(4) states that the court shall grant a stay unless it is satisfied that the arbitration is null and void, inoperative or incapable of being performed. The problem is that it is not always altogether clear whether the dispute or claim before the court is one which is covered by the arbitration agreement. Under those circumstances, it might be possible for the court to grant a stay of proceedings, not under s.9 of the Arbitration Act 1996, but in pursuant to the court's inherent jurisdiction to see that good case management is achieved.

The Court of Appeal held in *Ahmad Al-Naimi (T/A Buildmaster Construction Services) v Islamic Press Agency Inc* [2000] 1 Lloyd's Rep. 522 offers the following guidance:

> "[T]he court should be satisfied (a) that there was an arbitration clause and (b) that the subject of the action was within that clause before the Court could grant a stay under that section: but a stay under the inherent jurisdiction might in fact be sensible in a situation where the Court could not be sure of these matters but could see that good sense and litigation management made it desirable for an arbitrator to consider the whole matter first".

It should be remembered that the arbitrator has the competence to decide on his own competence to arbitrate the matter under the *Kompetenz-Kompetenz* doctrine.

The finality of the High Court's decision made in pursuant to s.9 of the Arbitration Act 1996 is guaranteed by s.18 of the Senior Courts Act 1981. That section states that

> "no appeal shall lie to the Court of Appeal . . . (g) except as provided by Part I of the Arbitration Act 1996, from any decision of the High Court under that Part".

A literal reading of the section would suggest that not only are decisions made under s.9 (and Pt I) of the Arbitration Act 1996 so limited but virtually any decision of the High Court unless there are specific and express provisions in Pt I to the contrary. How should the section be interpreted?

15–030   *Inco Europe Ltd v First Choice Distribution* [2000] 1 Lloyd's Rep. 467
Facts:
The main contract was for the delivery of a consignment of nickel cathodes from Rotterdam to Hereford. The claimants commenced proceedings in England despite the existence of an arbitration clause referring any potential disputes to arbitration in the Netherlands. The High Court held that the arbitration agreement was null and void and a stay of proceedings would not be granted. The defendant applied for leave to appeal to the Court of Appeal but that was denied by the High Court on the basis of s.18(1) of the Supreme Court Act 1981 (now re-named the Senior Courts Act 1981).
Held:
A literal reading of s.18(1)(g) would suggest that every decision of the High Court under Pt I of the Arbitration Act 1996 would be refused leave to appeal to the Court of Appeal, with few exceptions. That, according to the House of Lords, was clearly inconsistent with the legislative intent to ensure that s.18(1)(g) would not vary greatly from its original premise in the now defunct 1979 Arbitration Act.

The House of Lords held that the phrase "from any decision of the High Court under that Part" was to mean "from any decision of the High Court under a section in that Part which provides for an appeal from such a decision". As the appeal was not about a decision made under a section in that Part, but about the validity of the arbitration agreement, it could be brought to the Court of Appeal on appeal. The phrase in s.18(1) was only intended to give effect to the exclusions and limitations on the right of appeal to the Court of Appeal laid down in Pt I of the Arbitration Act 1996 and no more. Leave to appeal to the Court of Appeal was therefore permissible.

There was clearly a drafting flaw in the legislation but as Lord Nicholls said:

15–031

"[T]he court must be able to correct obvious drafting errors . . . [and] in suitable cases, in discharging its interpretative function the court will add words or omit words or substitute words".

That power should naturally be confined to obvious drafting errors.

As far as the House of Lords was concerned, s.18(1)(g) of the Supreme Court Act 1981 (now re-named the Senior Courts Act 1981) does not impose additional restrictions on the right to appeal to the Court of Appeal from decisions of the High Court. It merely brought into the law on leave to appeal the restrictions already expressed in the relevant sections of the Arbitration Act 1996.

Atlantic Shipping clauses

In *Atlantic Shipping & Trading Co v Louis Dreyfus & Co* [1922] 2 A.C. 250, the parties had inserted a clause which provided that no claim before the courts of law could be made under the contract unless it was in writing and an arbitrator had been appointed within a certain time. The courts can vary this clause by extending time. Section 12 Arbitration Act 1996 states that where an arbitration agreement provides that a claim shall be time barred or the claimant's right to arbitrate will be extinguished, unless the claimant takes within a time fixed by the agreement some step:

15–032

(a) to begin arbitral proceedings; or

(b) other dispute resolution procedures which must be exhausted before arbitral proceedings can be begun

the court may by order extend that time.

Section 12(3)(a) states that an order will be made only if

"the circumstances are such as were outside the parties' contemplation when they made that time bar provision and that it would be just to extend time" (*Vosnoc Ltd v Trans Global Ltd* [1998] 1 Lloyd's Rep. 711, but *cf. Grimaldi E.T.A.L. v Sekihyo Lines Ltd, The Times*, July 20, 1998).

It was held in *The Alexia M* [2005] EWHC 1345, that s.12(3) is limited to instances where the circumstances were not only beyond the reasonable contemplation of the parties but were also such that if the parties had contemplated the circumstances they would have contemplated that the time bar might not apply in such circumstances (see also *Harbour and General Works Ltd v Environment Agency* [2001] 1 Lloyd's Rep. 65, per Waller L.J.). Toulson J. went on to state that s.12(3)(a) must refer to some "sort of extraneous things which in other contexts might be considered force majeure or frustrating events". In that case, the shipowner's agents had sent an acceptance of the charterer's offer to appoint one of the three arbitrators to a wrong facsimile number. By the time the error was discovered, it was too late under the terms of the offer. The shipowner applied to extend time. Toulson J. refused their application on the basis that the circumstances in question were not those within the reasonable contemplation of the parties at the time the contract was made as the kind of circumstances which might trigger an extension. Furthermore, it would be unjust to deprive the charterer of the benefit of the contractual time bar. This reading of s.12(3)(a) is starkly different to the old approach to s.27 Arbitration Act 1950 which was much more capacious. This new approach is further evidence of the judicial policy to support the arbitration agreement and not to allow derogation from its terms too easily. In *Sos Corporacion Alimentaria SA v Inerco Trade SA* [2010] EWHC 162 (Comm) the court held that the fact that the defect in the goods which formed the substance of the dispute had not been easily discoverable was a relevant circumstance when deciding whether time should be extended. There, though, on balancing all other factors for consideration, the court did not think that time should be extended.

An alternative ground for an order to extend time is when the conduct of one party makes it unjust to insist on the time bar (s.12(3)(b)). Here, the threshold question is whether the claimants could attribute their failure to comply with the time bar to the defendant's conduct. The rationale behind s.12(3) is to prevent court interference with a contractual bargain unless the circumstances are such that, had they been drawn to the parties' attention on agreeing the provision, the parties would have contemplated that the time bar might not apply.[22] It is then for the court to decide whether justice required an extension to be given. This assessment of the facts is to be made objectively and is very much swayed by what is reasonable and common practice given the circumstances of the trade.[23]

The arbitral tribunal

15–033   The parties are free to agree on the number of arbitrators to form the tribunal. They can also agree as to whether there will be a chairman or umpire for their arbitration under s.15 of the Act. The presumption is that the parties would agree to have an odd number of arbitrators for obvious reasons. Section 15(2), in an attempt to ensure that the arbitration does not fail for mere technicality, provides that an agreement that the number of arbitrators shall be two or any other even number shall be construed as requiring the appointment of an additional arbitrator as chairman of the tribunal. If there is no agreement as to the number of arbitrators, the presumption shall be that there is only to be one arbitrator (s.15(3)).

Not only are the parties free to agree on the number of arbitrators, they have full liberty to specify how the arbitrators are to be appointed under s.16, and what should happen if the procedure is ineffective (s.18(1)). If there is no such provision made in the event of a failure of the appointment procedure, s.18(2)

---

[22] *Harbour & General Works v Environment Agency* [2000] 1 W.L.R. 950.
[23] *Thyssen Inc v Calypso Shipping Corp SA* [2000] 2 Lloyd's Rep. 243.

provides that any party to the arbitration may apply to the court to exercise any of the following powers:

1. to give directions as to the making of any necessary appointments;

2. to direct that the tribunal shall be constituted by such appointments (for any one or more of them) as have been made;

3. to revoke any appointments already made;

4. to make any necessary appointments itself.

An appointment made by the court shall have effect as if it had been made with the agreement of the parties.[24]

This power is however at the discretion of the court. The court will take into account the appropriateness of appointing an arbitrator in the light of all the evidence before it. In *Durtnell v DTI* [2001] 1 Lloyd's Rep. 275, following a dispute over certain building contracts, D sent a formal request to the Secretary of State for Trade and Industry (DTI) for arbitration to commence. The DTI rejected the claim for arbitration on the ground that there had been inordinate and inexcusable delay in making the request for arbitration. As far as they were concerned, five years after the completion of the building works was not a reasonable period. The DTI argued that the court had a discretion under s.18 of the Arbitration Act 1996 not to nominate an arbitrator where to do so would be to signify approval of D's unreasonable and inexcusable delay. The court agreed that there was a residual discretion in the court to refuse to exercise its powers under s.18 for D who had long neglected his right to seek a remedy under the Act. However, taking all the circumstances into account it could not be said that the claimants were guilty of inexcusable and inordinate delay. It would appear that the court would normally exercise its discretion in favour of appointing an arbitrator unless there is strong evidence that the arbitral process could not result in a fair resolution of the dispute. In *Atlanska Plovidba v Consignaciones Asturianas SA* [2004] EWHC 1273, there was a contract of carriage between C and D. C wrote to D following a dispute giving notice referring to "all disputes under the bill of lading concerning the carriage of and damage to the . . . [goods] to arbitration in London" and calling on D to join in the appointment of an arbitrator. D disputed the validity of the arbitration agreement and submitted that the appointment of an arbitrator would lead to unnecessary inconvenience and expense in the light of concurrent proceedings in Spain. The court held that respect for party autonomy and the desirability of holding parties to their arbitration agreement together provided strong grounds for exercising the court's discretion under s.18 in favour of constituting a tribunal. The court should also not concern itself with issues of inconvenience or expense which did not go to the heart of the arbitral process, unless they were so serious as to undermine fairness. The court would also not be interested in factors which would normally be engaged in ascertaining whether a particular forum is an appropriate forum. Reliance was placed on the House of Lords case of *Donohue v Armco Inc* [2001] UKHL 64. In the present case, the court was also keen to mention that the

---

[24] Section 18(4). See also *Federal Insurance Co v Transamerica Occidental Life Insurance Co* [1999] 2 Lloyd's Rep. 286.

existence of Spanish proceedings did not provide sufficient grounds for declining to constitute the arbitral panel. It would also be contrary to the spirit of the New York Convention 1958 to refuse to constitute the arbitral panel. It is thus obvious that it was only in very limited circumstances that the court would decline to constitute an arbitral panel.

The arbitral procedure

15–034   The conduct of the arbitration can be decided on by the parties. Where no provision is stated in the agreement, the arbitration shall be subject to the general duty in s.33. That duty imposes on the arbitral tribunal to act fairly and impartially as between the parties, giving each party a reasonable opportunity to put his case and address that of his opponent. The arbitrator shall also adopt procedures to the circumstances of the particular case with the dominant concern not to incur unnecessary delay or expense. It shall be for the tribunal to decide all procedural and evidential matters, subject naturally always to the intention and agreement of the parties.

Consent as regards the type of evidence and procedure is so important that the findings in one arbitration will not bind arbitrators dealing with a different but related transaction or dispute. It was held by Mance J. in *Sacor Maritima SA v Repsol Petroleo SA* [1998] 1 Lloyd's Rep. 518 that it was inherent in arbitration practice that each arbitration was separate as regards issues raised and evidence called and, in the absence of consent, there were no procedures for combining or trying together common issues arising between different parties with a view to avoiding inconsistent findings of fact. That is so even where it is a case of string arbitrations.[25] As a matter of commercial expediency, parties might also wish to prescribe length of time for the taking of evidence, for the hearing, etc. or whether the hearing could be conducted solely on the basis of documents. However, the parties should be aware of the merits and demerits in using a documentary process. In *Ocean Marine Navigation Ltd v Koch Carbon Inc (The Dynamic)* [2003] EWHC 1936 for example, Simon J. considered that although the arbitration, which was conducted on the basis of documents, had not resulted in any serious irregularity or injustice, it would have been much better had the arbitrator been entitled to conduct a short oral hearing.

Similarly, when it comes to legal representation, although most international commercial arbitration would be conducted with legal assistance, it is possible for the arbitration agreement to dispense with legal representation in all or part of the dispute (*Davinder Singh Virdee v Amritpal Singh Virdi* [2003] EWCA Civ 41).

15–035   The parties are also free to agree when arbitral proceedings are to be regarded as having been commenced. In the absence of such an agreement, s.14(3) states that arbitral proceedings commence when "one party serves on the other party or parties a notice in writing requiring him or them to submit [the] matter" to the named arbitrator/s. Where the arbitrators have yet to be appointed by the parties, when one party serves a notice in writing to the other party or parties requesting them to appoint an arbitrator or agree to a nominated arbitrator, proceedings are

---

[25] See also *Sun Life Assurance Co of Canada v The Lincoln National Life Insurance Co* [2004] EWCA Civ 1660.

said to have commenced (s.14(4)).[26] In commercial law generally, notice requirements are usually treated as a strict requirement and terms interpreted narrowly, however, in arbitration law, the tenor of the authorities is that some flexibility should be permitted. After all, what is more important is the fact that business people will understand the notice as one calling for arbitration. A strict and technical requirement would defeat the object of an efficient dispute resolution system. As Moore-Bick J said in *Atlanska Plovidba v Consignaciones Asturianas SA (The Lapad)* [2004] 2 Lloyd's Rep 109:

"To be effective, a notice of arbitration to identify the dispute to which it related with sufficient particularity and had also to make it clear that the person giving it was intending to refer the dispute to arbitration, not merely threatening to do so if his demands were not met. Apart from that, there was no need for any further requirements. If one party to an arbitration agreement sent a written notice to the other that made it clear that he was seeking to invoke that agreement to determine an existing dispute between them, the Court should be slow to hold that it was ineffective simply because the sender had identified the wrong document as containing or evidencing their contract if the dispute was otherwise sufficiently identified. In the present case there could have been no doubt about which arbitration agreement A was seeking to invoke, nor about which dispute it was seeking to refer."

In *Easybiz Investments v Sinograin (The Biz)* [2010] EWHC 2565 (Comm) the dispute concerned a cargo loaded pursuant to a charterparty under 10 separate bills of lading. The bills of lading all contained an English arbitration clause. S issued a notice purporting to commence arbitration under all 10 bills of lading. E argued that that notice was ineffective to commence arbitration because it purported to commence a single composite arbitration. E's view was that there should be a notice for each of the bill of lading. The court rejected that view stating that despite the fact that some of those bills of lading named another cargo claimant as notify party, they had all concerned E and S's relationship. In refusing to take a technical and strict approach to the notice requirement, the court held that the notice was sufficient as it adequately identified the dispute to which it related and made it clear that S was intending to refer the dispute to

---

[26] See *Seabridge Shipping AB v AC Orssleff's Eftf's A/S* [1999] 2 Lloyd's Rep. 685; s.14(4) of the Arbitration Act 1996 which provides in material part as follows: " . . . arbitral proceedings are commenced in respect of a matter when one party serves on the other party or parties a notice in writing requiring him or them to appoint an arbitrator or to agree to the appointment of an arbitrator in respect of that matter." In *Seabridge Shipping AB v AC Orsslef's Eftf's A/S* [1999] 2 Lloyd's Rep. 685; Thomas J. held that s.14 should be interpreted broadly and flexibly. As for Moore-Bick J. in *Atlanska Plovidba v Consignaciones Asturianas SA (The Lapad)* [2004] 2 Lloyd's Rep. 109: "To be effective, a notice of arbitration to identify the dispute to which it related with sufficient particularity and had also to make it clear that the person giving it was intending to refer the dispute to arbitration, not merely threatening to do so if his demands were not met. Apart from that, there was no need for any further requirements. If one party to an arbitration agreement sent a written notice to the other that made it clear that he was seeking to invoke that agreement to determine an existing dispute between them, the Court should be slow to hold that it was ineffective simply because the sender had identified the wrong document as containing or evidencing their contract if the dispute was otherwise sufficiently identified." That passage reflects the approach advocated in the leading textbook viz that a notice commencing arbitration will not be invalidated if (for example) the claimant refers to the wrong contractual document: see *Mustill & Boyd on Commercial Arbitration*, 2nd edn (London: Butterworths, 1989), pp.198–199.

arbitration. The substance of the notice was more important than the form. The test is how a reasonable person in the position of the recipient would have understood the notice given its terms and the context in which it was written.

15–036 Where the appointment is to be made by a third party, not privy to the dispute, arbitral proceedings commence when one party gives notice in writing to that third party asking him to make an appointment (s.14(5)). In this context, s.76 states that the parties are free to agree on a manner of service of any notice or other document. In the absence of agreement, "*a notice or other document may be served by any effective means*" (s.76(4)). Notices sent by post to the addressee's last known principal residence, principal business address, registered office or principal office will be treated as effectively served. In *Bernuth Lines v High Seas Shipping* [2005] EWHC 3020, it was held that an email sent by one party to a *general* email address of the other party (info@bernuth.com) was held to be service by any effective means. The fact that Bernuth's staff had understandably assumed that the email was spam and ignored it had no relevance on the effectiveness of service.

Removal of arbitrators

15–037 Section 24 provides specifically for the removal of an arbitrator on the ground:

(a) that circumstances exists that give rise to justifiable doubt as to his impartiality;

(b) that he does not possess the qualifications required by the arbitration agreement;

(c) that he is physically or mentally incapable of conducting the proceedings or there are justifiable doubts as to his capacity to do so;

(d) that he has refused or failed:

   (i) properly to conduct the proceedings; or
   (ii) to use all reasonable despatch in conducting the proceedings or making an award, and that substantial injustice has been or will be caused to the applicant.

The Departmental Advisory Committee in its report set out some guidelines for courts when applying this section:

"We trust that the Courts will not allow [this process] to be abused by those intent on disrupting the arbitral process . . . We have every confidence that the Courts will carry through the intent of this Part of the [Act], which is that it should only be available where the conduct of the arbitrator is such as to go so beyond anything that could reasonably be defended that substantial injustice has resulted or will result. The provision is not intended to allow the Court to substitute its own view as to how the arbitral proceedings should be conducted. Thus the choice of an arbitrator of a particular procedure, unless it breaches the duty laid on arbitrators by [s.33], should on no view justify the removal of an arbitrator, even if the Court would not itself have adopted that procedure. In short, this ground only exists to cover what we hope will be the very rare case where an arbitrator so conducts the proceedings that it can fairly be said that instead of carrying through the object of arbitration . . . he is in effect frustrating that object".

The test of "bias" is to be assessed on whether the arbitrator had a pecuniary interest or close connection to a party in the arbitration. The court has to look at the entirety of the circumstances of the case in question to ascertain whether there was any danger of conscious or unconscious bias.

In *AT&T Corp v Saudi Cable Co* [2000] 1 Lloyd's Rep. 22, the dispute was **15–038** over the termination of a pre-bid agreement between AT&T and Saudi Cable. AT&T and other telecommunications companies were invited to bid for a project in Saudi Arabia. There was a condition in the invitation to bid that the successful bidder must buy their cables from Saudi Cable. The agreement also contained an arbitration clause submitting disputes to the International Chamber of Commerce, the place of arbitration being London and English law was to be the proper law of the arbitration agreement. The arbitration set up was chaired by F; F was in fact a non-executive director of a company who competed with AT&T and that company had also bid for the project but was unsuccessful. AT&T applied to set aside the arbitration on the basis of bias.

It was argued by AT&T that this was essentially a case of assumed bias as F had a close connection with a competitor and whether or not he was in fact biased, the presumption of bias should be made. Longmore J. held that the test to be applied was whether the arbitrator must in law be presumed to have been or was actually biased. The judge said:

"[T]he present state of English law in relation to apparent or assumed bias, as it applied to Judges and inferior tribunals was that there was an automatic disqualification for any Judge who had a pecuniary interest (such as owning shares) in one of the parties or was otherwise so closely connected with a party that he could truly be said to be judge in his own cause; apart from that, it was for the Court to determine whether there was a real danger of bias in the sense that the Judge might have unfairly regarded with favour or disfavour the case of a party under consideration by him or might be pre-disposed or prejudiced against one party's case for reasons unconnected with the merits of the issue".

This is two-stage test—first, whether a presumption of bias at law should be made on the basis of a pecuniary interest or close connection (for example, as managing director) with one of the parties, and if that is not satisfied, the court should assess the circumstances of the case to ascertain whether there was real danger of unconscious bias of the arbitrator being pre-disposed or prejudiced against one of the parties for reasons unconnected with the merits of the case. In that case, no bias, real or presumed, was found.

In *Rustal Trading Ltd v Gill & Duffus SA* [2000] 1 Lloyd's Rep. 14, it was **15–039** contended by one of the parties that the award should be set aside on the basis of bias. They relied very heavily on the expert evidence of their consultant, L. They argued that the arbitrator had expressed animosity towards L and was engaged in a dispute with L two years ago. The court however felt unable to accept that the existence of that earlier dispute was sufficient in itself to raise justifiable doubts of the arbitrator's impartiality and the fact that some of the parties were involved in the earlier dispute in one capacity or another did not add anything to the force of the argument.

In international trade arbitrations, it is not uncommon for the arbitrators to be active members of the trade. It is therefore plausible that some might have conflict of interest or have an axe to grind with one of the parties. How should a court ensure that the correct balance between having expert arbitrators and preventing bias be struck? In *Rustal Trading Ltd v Gill & Duffus SA* [2000] 1 Lloyd's Rep. 14, Moore-Bick J. held that as the parties had chosen to have their disputes resolved by people who are active traders and so have direct and relevant knowledge of the trade, they must be presumed to have had that fact in mind when the arbitration agreement is made. A court should therefore be slow, without other relevant evidence, to remove an expert trade arbitrator simply on the basis that he had been involved in a previous dispute with one of the parties (*ASM Shipping Ltd of India v Harris* [2007] EWHC 1513).

It should also be noted that where one of parties is doubtful about the impartiality of the arbitrator he should act straightaway to have the arbitrator removed. Although he could later apply to have the award made by the less than impartial arbitrator set aside, he could be precluded from so doing if he does not raise the objection promptly once he has discovered the flaw in the arbitral process. The effect of s.73(1) of the Arbitration Act 1996 was that a party to an arbitration must act promptly if he considered that there were grounds on which he could challenge the effectiveness of the proceedings.[27]

Challenging arbitral awards

15–040 Where the proceedings are governed by English law, the award may be challenged by a party to the arbitration on any of the following grounds:

1. failure of substantive jurisdiction (s.67);

2. serious irregularity (s.68);

3. appeal on point of law (s.69).

The effect of challenging or appealing against an award may result in the following:

1. a confirmation of the award by the court;

2. a variation of the award;

3. the setting aside of the award either in whole or in part.

Where a point of law is appealed against (s.69(7)(c)) the court could, if it deems fit, remit the award to the tribunal, in whole or in part, for reconsideration in the light of the court's determination. The power of remittal might also be exercised in relation to a challenge on grounds of serious irregularity (s.68(3)) but in cases

---

[27] Indeed, as Moore-Bick J. said in *Rustal Trading Ltd*: " . . . there was no reason why a party who discovered grounds of objection after the conclusion of the hearing and before publication of the award should not be required to voice it promptly if he wished to pursue it later on by challenge to the award . . . ". See also *ASM Shipping v Harris* [2007] EWHC 1513.

where the court finds that the arbitration lacks substantive jurisdiction, remittal would not be appropriate. It should however be noted that the remittal of an arbitration award however does not deprive it of legal effect (*Michael Carter v Harold Simpson Associates (Architects) Ltd* [2004] UKPC 29).[28]

Section 70 provides for certain procedural requirements for an appeal of challenge to be met. Subsection (2) sets out the general parameters of the procedure:

"An application or appeal may not be brought if the applicant or appellant has not first exhausted—

(a) any available arbitral process of appeal or review, and
(b) any available recourse under s.57 (correction of award or additional award)".

Any such application or appeal must be brought within 28 days of the date of the award.[29] If there has been an arbitral process of appeal or review invoked, the 28 days will run from the date when the applicant or appellant was notified of the result of that process (s.70(3)). The court may order the arbitral tribunal to state or expand on the reasons for an award in event of need.

Section 70(2) requires that the applicant should first exhaust remedies available within the arbitration set up. For example, where the arbitration agreement provides that the arbitral panel has the power to correct an award, the applicant should naturally take that step first before going to the courts of law. In this connection, it might be observed that s.57(3) states where there is no such contractual provision, the tribunal may on its own initiative or on the application by a party:

15–041

(a) correct an award so as to remove any clerical mistake or error arising from an accidental slip or omission or clarify or remove any ambiguity in the award[30]; or

---

[28] In that case, the Privy Council held that the remittal of an arbitration award did not mean that the award stopped being valid. As such, it continued to operate so as to make the arbitrator functus officio, unable to alter his award, on those matters that were not remitted. Those other parts of the award remained valid. See also *Johnson v Latham* (1851) 20 L.J.Q.B. 236.

[29] It is naturally possible to apply to the court to extend time after the expiry of the time limit in s.70(3) but the court would be slow to grant the extension and would only do so where it would otherwise cause substantial injustice. Where the dissatisfied party does not challenge the award despite having ample opportunity to do so, the court would not be inclined to be generous; see *Peoples' Insurance Co of China, Hebei Branch v Vysanthi Shipping Co Ltd* [2003] EWHC 1655. In *Aoot Kalmneft v Glencore International AG* (July 27, 2001, Q.B.D.), the court held that discretion to extend time might be guided by: (a) length of the delay; (b) how reasonable the parties have conducted themselves; (c) whether the respondent to the arbitration or the arbitrator had contributed to the delay; (d) to what extent, the respondent would be adversely affected by an extension; (e) costs; (f) strength of the application; and (g) whether in the broadest sense it would be unfair to the applicant for him to be denied the opportunity of having the application determined. It was emphasised in that case that failure to seek legal assistance was not a reasonable excuse for the delay.

[30] See, e.g., *Gannet Shipping Ltd v Eastrade Commodities Inc* (December 6, 2001, Q.B.D. (Comm)), where an incorrect amount of costs was an "accidental slip or omission" which the arbitrator could rectify.

(b) make an additional award in respect of any claim (including a claim for
interest or costs) which was presented to the tribunal but was not dealt with
in the award.

Of course, all parties concerned would first be given a reasonable opportunity to
make representations prior to the making of such corrections or modifications.
The scope of s.57(3) however does not extend to an allegation by the party
concerned that the arbitrator had failed to attach sufficient weight to particular
evidence in arriving at a conclusion on a question of fact. It was held in *World
Trade Corp v C Czarnikow Sugar Ltd* [2004] EWHC 2332 that as the arbitrators
had failed to consider all the circumstances of the dispute and had given
insufficient weight to an important fact, the complainant could rely on s.68 to ask
the court for the remission of the award despite the fact that no effort was taken
by the complainant to refer first the award back to the arbitrators. That was
because s.57(3)(a) did not apply when the issue was not the mere correction or
the clarification of the award but a direct challenge of the arbitrators' findings of
fact. There was no issue as to the ambiguity of the award.

On the other hand, in *Omnibridge Consulting Ltd v Clearsprings (Management) Ltd* (October 12, 2004), although the arbitrator had made an error as to the
amount of compensation payable, the error was but one which the arbitrator
could rectify if an application had been made to him under s.57(3)(a). As the
claimant had not done so, the court declined to permit a remission or challenge
of the award.

15–042   It should also be noted that nonparties can also question or challenge an award
by seeking declaratory relief from the courts. Section 72 states that a person
alleged to be a party to the proceedings but takes no part in the proceedings may
question:

(a) whether there is a valid arbitration agreement;

(b) whether the tribunal is properly constituted; or

(c) what matters have been submitted to arbitration in accordance with the
arbitration agreement.

A person seeking to make an application under s.72 must be a person who has
not taken part in the arbitral proceedings prior to the determination of his
application. Nothing more about his standing is required (*Hackwood v Areen
Design Services* [2005] EWHC 2322 (TCC)).

Such a person also has the right to challenge the award on the basis of lack of
substantive jurisdiction (but only in relation to him) or serious irregularity (again
only in matters affecting him). In *Arab National Bank v El Sharif Saoud bin
Masoud bi Haza 'a El-Abdali* [2004] EWHC 2381, an arbitral award had been
made in favour of D. B, the bank, sought to restrain the publication and
enforcement of the award in pursuant to s.72. The court found that as B had
established overwhelming evidence that the arbitral award had been obtained by
fraud, that there was no arbitration agreement in force, that the arbitral tribunal
had not been properly constituted, and that there had not been any agreement on
the scope of the arbitration, the award could be challenged. B was entitled to

protection of its reputation and D would therefore be restrained from publishing the award.

(i) Failure of substantive jurisdiction

Section 67 permits the parties to challenge an award on the basis that the arbitrators did not have jurisdiction when making the award. The grounds of challenge include: **15–043**

- the lack of a valid arbitration agreement;

- the arbitration agreement does not cover the dispute in question; and

- the arbitrators have not been properly appointed.

These provisions mirror art.34(2) of the UNCITRAL Model Law on International Commercial Arbitration. These legal consequences of an award made through the want of jurisdiction were not set out in such precision prior to 1996 and should provide certainty in this difficult and fraught area of arbitration law. Under the old law, there was no express power given to the supervisory court to declare an award null and void for want of jurisdiction. In *Finzel Berry & Co v Eastcheap Dried Fruit Co* [1962] 1 Lloyd's Rep. 370, it was held that as the award was void *ab initio* there was nothing to set aside.

It should be observed though that the right to bring a challenge on the want of substantive jurisdiction may be exercised only after the arbitrators have adjudged their own jurisdiction and:

1. the party has not appeared in the arbitration; or
2. the party has appeared in the arbitration and has registered an objection within time which has not been resolved by a preliminary ruling.

Under the *Kompetenz-Kompetenz* doctrine, the tribunal itself has the power to rule on its own jurisdiction. This universal doctrine recognised in *Christopher Brown v Genossenschaft Osterreichlischer Waldbesitzer* [1954] 1 Q.B. 8, is given effect to in s.30 of the new Act. It states that unless otherwise agreed by the parties, the arbitral tribunal may rule on its own substantive jurisdiction, that is, as to: **15–044**

- whether there is a valid arbitration agreement;

- whether the tribunal is properly constituted; and

- what matters have been submitted to arbitration in accordance with the arbitration agreement.

Any such ruling is necessarily subject to review by the courts of law. Incidentally, it was held in *JSC Zestafoni G Nikoladze Ferroalloy Plant v Ronly Holdings Ltd* [2004] EWHC 245 that the principle of openness and fair dealing between the parties demanded that if jurisdiction was to be challenged under s.67, each ground of challenge to an arbitrator's jurisdiction had to have been raised before the arbitrator.

If the arbitral tribunal proceeds to determine its own substantive jurisdiction and this is not objected to by the parties, they are deemed under s.73 as having waived their right to object and hence may not rely on s.67 to challenge the award. If one party wishes to contest jurisdiction when the arbitral purports to exercise its power to decide on its own jurisdiction, he has the right either:

1. to refuse to appear and take part in the proceedings; or

2. to appear but raise an objection to the asserted jurisdiction of the tribunal as soon as he is aware of the jurisdictional issue or before he has participated in the substantive proceedings (s.31).

15–045   Following such an objection, the arbitral tribunal may under s.31(4) address it in three possible ways:

1. it may choose to make a preliminary award. If it does, this award may be appealed against on the ground of want of jurisdiction under s.67; or

2. the arbitral tribunal may proceed with the arbitration and make a final award on the entire dispute. Here too the aggrieved party may raise a challenge of the award on jurisdictional grounds under s.67; or

3. it may agree to allow an application for preliminary ruling on jurisdiction to be made to the court by any of the parties under s.32.

15–046   *LG Caltex Gas Co Ltd v China National Petroleum Co* [2001] B.L.R. 235 (January 19, 2001)
Facts:
There were disputes between the parties over whether certain contracts had actually been concluded containing arbitration clauses and whether independent agreements to arbitrate had been concluded. The arbitrator concluded that neither of the respondents was a party to the alleged contracts. Neither respondent was therefore bound. This is a case where the arbitrator decided on his own competence under any assumed contracts.

The applicants applied to the court to vary, set aside or remit the awards under s.67 and 68 of the Arbitration Act 1996.

The issues for the court were, whether,

1. under the 1996 Act, it was relevant that there had been an ad hoc submission to the arbitrator of the issue of whether the respondents were privy to the two "contracts";

2. there was an ad hoc submission of the issue of whether the parties were bound by the two contracts;

3. even if there was no ad hoc submission, had the applicants lost the right to challenge the arbitrator's lack of jurisdiction by virtue of s.73 Arbitration Act 1996;

4. the arbitrator's awards were ones as to his substantive jurisdiction within s.67(1)(a) Arbitration Act 1996;

5. the applicants could challenge the awards under s.67(1)(b) Arbitration Act 1996.
Held:
Aitkens J. held that the 1996 Act had not done away with the traditional rule that it was possible to make an ad hoc submission to the arbitrator of the initial existence of a contract. Where there exists a dispute about the jurisdiction of the arbitrator to decide an issue, then the arbitrator himself could rule on the point (ss.30 and 31(4)(a)) or the court could do so as a preliminary issue (s.32) under certain circumstances. The arbitrator's decision could naturally be challenged under s.67(1)(a) but that challenge is subject to the terms of s.73. Section 73(1) provides that a party could lose his right to raise an objection

under ss.67 and 68 if he does not do so during proceedings before the arbitrator (unless at the time he took part in the proceedings he did not know and could not with reasonable diligence have discovered the grounds for the objection).

The fact that the applicants had not protested during arbitration proceedings meant that they must lose their right to assert subsequently before the court that the arbitrator had lacked substantive jurisdiction. They could not pass the test set out in s.73(1). It would follow that the awards could not be overturned.

Issues 4. and 5. were therefore not relevant but the judge answered them as follows:

- the arbitrator's awards were not awards as to his substantive jurisdiction;

- the applicants could not challenge the awards under s.67(1)(b) even though they were awards on the merits between the parties.

That case demonstrates how important it is for the parties who submit to ad **15–047** hoc proceedings to treat those proceedings seriously and to raise any objection as to failure of compliance to the agreement, substantive jurisdiction, irregularity and impropriety during those proceedings. There is to be no second bite at the cherry under s.73.[31] The role of the court is not to support parties to an arbitration agreement who have failed to observe the terms of the Arbitration Act 1996.

N.B. The preliminary ruling entitlement is set out in s.45 which re-enacts s.2 of the Arbitration Act 1979 with minor alterations. That section enables the parties to apply to the court for a preliminary ruling on any question of law arising in the course of the proceedings which the court is satisfied substantially affects the rights of one or more of the parties. Section 45(3) introduces a new procedural requirement in that the applicant must identify the questions of law and where the application is not supported by any of the other parties, the grounds of the application.

(ii) Serious irregularity

The general duty of the tribunal under the Arbitration Act 1996 is to act fairly and **15–048** impartially as between the parties. It must ensure that the rules of natural justice are prioritised. Both parties must be given a reasonable opportunity to put their cases and defend themselves. It must however also give consideration to the spirit of an arbitration which is to avoid unnecessary delay and expense. These duties are set out in s.33 and are mandatory. Although they cannot be excluded by contract, they have been drafted according to Departmental Advisory Committee in the widest possible sense so as to give maximum manoeuvrability to the arbitral tribunal. The effect is that tribunals are not subject to any rigid procedural requirements as in judicial proceedings but a flexible requirement of fairness and impartiality.

Consistent with this general duty is the right of the aggrieved party in an arbitration to bring an action under s.68 to have an award set aside or varied on the basis of a serious irregularity, provided that the applicant has or will suffer substantial injustice from the irregularity. Any challenge must be brought within 28 days of the date of the award (s.70(3)). In addition, under s.73, if a party *"takes part, or continues to take part, in the proceedings"* without making an objection that there has been an irregularity, it may not raise it later, unless, at the time, it did not know and could not with reasonable diligence have discovered the grounds for the objection (*Thyssen Canada v Mariana Maritime* [2005] EWHC

---

[31] See also *Rustal Trading Ltd v Gill & Duffus SA* [2000] 1 Lloyd's Rep. 14.

219). This rule is underpinned by the principle of finality in arbitrations (*Nestor Maritime v Sea Anchor* [2012] EWHC 996 (Comm)). Participation in the proceedings includes the period between the end of the hearing and the publication of the award (*Profilati v Paine Webber* [2001] 1 L.L.R. 715).

In order to rely on s.68, there is no need for the court to try the material issue of the arbitration to ascertain whether substantial injustice had been caused. This was made clear in *Vee Networks Ltd v Econet Wireless International Ltd* [2004] EWHC 2909. In that case, V and E had entered into an agreement for the provision of mobile telephony services. V decided to terminate the contract prematurely. The matter was referred to arbitration and an award made. V submitted that the award should be set aside or remitted to the arbitrator under s.68 because he had relied on an argument, demonstrably wrong, that was not advanced by either party, giving no warning or opportunity to make further submissions. There was, V argued, a serious irregularity leading to substantial injustice. The court held that the arbitrator had indeed made a mistake by referring to irrelevant materials, and had not acted fairly by not giving each party a reasonable opportunity to put their case. The court stressed that in an application based on s.68, it was enough to show that:

"the irregularity caused the arbitrator to reach a conclusion unfavourable to the applicant that, but for the irregularity, he might well never have reached, provided that the opposite conclusion was at least reasonably arguable".

15–049   There is no need to prove that actual substantial injustice was caused; substantial injustice may be inferred from the importance of the irregularity. In *Buyuk Camlica Shipping Trading & Industry Co Inc v Progress Bulk Carriers Ltd* [2010] EWHC 442 (Comm) the court considered the issue which had been ignored by the tribunal as being an irregularity but that issue decided either way could not be said to have the potential of causing substantial injustice.

An irregularity can take any of the following forms:

(a) failure by the tribunal to comply with s.33. The Court of Appeal in *Fletamentos Maritimos SA v Effjohn International BV* [1997] 2 Lloyd's Rep. 302 stressed that the arbitrators has an absolute commitment to act fairly and impartially. In that case, an umpire was required to sit with the arbitrators. The umpire had intervened more frequently than other umpires might have done, but the court found that he had not overstepped the line. The test, as formulated by Lord Hope in *Porter v Magill* [2002] A.C. 357, is: "The question is whether the [court], having considered the facts, would conclude that there was a real possibility that the Tribunal was biased".

Fairness requires that if the arbitrators feel compelled to depart from issues defined, admitted or conceded to by the parties, they should ensure that the party affected has good notice of their intention and is given an opportunity to decide on the proper course of action. Indeed it was held in *Pacol Ltd v Joint Stock Co Rossakhar* [2000] 1 Lloyd's Rep. 109, that where one party has admitted liability and that the arbitration was set up principally to determine questions of quantum of compensation, arbitrators who intend to re-open issues of liability should warn the parties concerned of their intention. Failure to do so would result in the award being set aside on grounds of serious irregularity and breach of s.33.

Similarly, in *Omnibridge Consulting Ltd v Clearsprings (Management)* **15–050**
Ltd [2004] EWHC 2276 the arbitrator was found to be guilty of a serious
irregularity by not accepting the common position agreed between the
parties and proceeding on his own opinion of the issue at hand. The court
held that it was not open to the arbitrator to take a view or position different
from that which had been prescribed by the parties by agreement. The
irregularity was exacerbated by the fact that the claimant had not been given
a reasonable opportunity to address the arbitrator on the point in issue.[32]

There is however no breach of s.33 where the arbitrator had proceeded on
an alternative argument (one not proscribed by the contract) and ignored the
one submitted by the party in question, if it could be shown that no
substantial injustice was caused (*Warborough Investments Ltd v S Robinson
& Sons (Holdings) Ltd* [2003] EWCA Civ 751).

Clearly the tribunal's failure to make available to the applicant witnesses
which the other side had had an opportunity to question, preventing the
applicant to present permissible evidence and using documents which are
privileged will constitute serious irregularity. However, the reviewing court
will need to be satisfied that these allegations are actually proved by the
applicant; mere assertions or questionable evidence will be rejected.
(*Double K Oil Products 1996 Ltd v Neste Oil Oyj* [2009] EWHC 3380
(Comm)).

Another matter of some import is the growing reliance on paper-only and
online arbitration without the need for any witnesses or the parties being
present. As far as English law is concerned, it would appear that where the
parties are represented only by documents, paper or online, the arbitrator
should ensure that he does not introduce the arbitration matters not expressly
referred to by the parties or matters which have ceased to be matters in issue
as far as the parties are concerned. Arbitrators must respect the definition of
issues made or agreed by the parties. Failure to do so is a flagrant detraction
from the consent element vital to an arbitration. Colman J. said in *Pacol
Ltd*:

> "In a paper arbitration the temptation to arrive at a conclusion which
> might not have been envisaged by either party by reference to matters
> upon which the parties have not had the opportunity of adducing further
> evidence, may be a particular temptation which arbitrators should be
> careful to avoid. It is important for the continuation of the standing and
> quality of international commercial arbitrations in London, particularly in
> the commodity fields, that arbitrators should have the problem very
> clearly in mind . . . ".

The duty to allow the parties a reasonable opportunity to respond to **15–051**
matters not stated in the remit of the arbitration submitted is vital. Natural
justice requires that justice be seen to be done.

(b) the tribunal exceeding its powers (otherwise than by exceeding its substantive jurisdiction under s.67). This particular provision is concerned with
the excess of procedural powers. A case in point could be *The Kostas Melas*
[1981] 1 Lloyd's Rep. 18. In that case it was held by Goff J. that the function

---

[32] See also *Guardcliffe Properties Ltd v City & St James* [2003] EWHC 215, Ch for a similar
example of how this principle is applied.

of arbitrators is not to make temporary financial adjustments between the parties pending the resolution of the dispute unless this is what they have agreed the arbitrators can do. In *Lesotho Highlands Development Authority v Impregilo SpA* [2005] UKHL 43, the House of Lords dealing with the first case on the Arbitration Act 1996 was asked to consider whether the arbitrators had the power under s.48(4)[33] to make an award in a basket of currencies differing from that provided in the contract and under s.49(3)[34] to grant pre-award interest which was not permitted under Lesotho law. Both the High Court and the Court of Appeal had ruled that the arbitrators had exceeded their power under s.48(4) to make those awards. The House of Lords however held that under the 1996 Act, unlike the old Arbitration Acts, a more relaxed approach to evaluating the powers of the arbitrators should be adopted. Lord Steyn suggested that a natural and commercially sensible reading of s.48(4) should be adopted. On both issues, the House of Lords held that although the tribunal may made an error of law, they had not exceeded their powers. Lord Steyn said:

> "It is consistent with the legislative purpose of the 1996 Act, which is intended to promote one-stop [decision-making]. If the contrary view of the Court of Appeal had prevailed, it would have opened up many opportunities for challenging awards on the basis that the tribunal [had] exceeded its powers in ruling on the currency of the award. Such decisions are an everyday occurrence in the arbitral world. If the view of the Court of Appeal had been upheld, a very serious defect in the machinery of the 1996 Act would have been revealed. The fact that this case has been before courts at three levels and that enforcement of the award has been delayed for more than three years reinforces the importance of the point".

15–052   The case makes it plain that excess of power would be given a very narrow interpretation in light of the one-stop shop policy.

(c) failure by the tribunal to conduct the proceedings in accordance with the procedure agreed by the parties. There is clearly an overlap between this and the paragraph above, but in general it refers to the failure of the tribunal in applying or adhering to the procedural matters set out by the parties in accordance with s.34.

(d) failure of the tribunal to deal with all the issues[35] that there are to it. This is the reiteration of an established common law rule that an award that does not

---

[33] Section 48(4) states, "The tribunal may order the payment of a sum of money, in any currency".

[34] Section 49(3) states, "The tribunal may award simple or compound interest from such dates, at such rates and with such interest as it considers meets the justice of the case . . . ".

[35] The word "issues" must be distinguished from "arguments" or "points" made by the parties or indeed by another member of the tribunal (*Ispat Industries v WesternBulk* [2011] EWHC 93 (Comm)). There is no serious irregularity if the arbitrator merely failed to address every of the parties' arguments or points. Indeed, occasionally, courts have referred to "essential issues" or "key issues" or "crucial issues" or "fundamental issues" when finding serious irregularity. (see for example, *Ascot Commodities NV v Olam International Ltd*, [2002] 2 Lloyd's Rep 277; *Weldon Plant v Commission for New Towns*, [2001] 1 All E.R. 264; *Buyuk Camlica Shipping Trading and Industry Co Ltd v Progress Bulk Carriers Ltd*, [2010] EWHC 442 (Comm); and *Fidelity Management SA v Myriad International Holdings BV* [2005] EWHC 1193 (Comm)).

address all the issues referred to the arbitrators is deficient. That deficiency can however be cured by the arbitrators reopening the case and deciding on those issues (see for example, *Thomas v Countryside Council for Wales* [1994] 4 All E.R. 853) usually following a remission of the case by a court of law to the tribunal. It is important to note that the award is not necessarily defective simply because the tribunal had not given enough weight to a piece of evidence (*World Trade Corp Ltd v C Czarnikow Sugar Ltd* [2004] EWHC 2332) or the tribunal had failed to address every issue put to it (*Glencore International AG v Beogradska Plovidba (The Avala)* [1996] 2 Lloyd's Rep. 311; *Petrochemical Industries Co (KSC) v The Dow Chemical Co* [2012] EWHC 2739 (Comm)). There must first be some actual or potential substantial injustice having been practised on the applicant as a consequence of the arbitrator's failure to deal with the issues put to him. This paragraph could be relied on if the arbitrator had taken into account issues which are no longer live (issues where the parties had conceded or agreed to resolve out the arbitration or otherwise spent) or which were not actually put to the arbitrator or which were expressly agreed to be excluded from the arbitration (*Ronly Holdings Ltd v JSC Zesrafoni* [2004] EWHC 1354).

(e) any tribunal or other institution or person vested by the parties with powers in relation to the proceedings or the award exceeding its powers. This provision envisages any excess or error committed by some third party acting under the arbitration agreement for the purposes of the arbitration. An example would be a fact finding commission set up to assist the tribunal acting erroneously or in excess of its powers.

(f) uncertainty or ambiguity as to the effect of the award. This mirrors the time-honoured rule that an award could not be enforced if it is unclear as to what the resultant duties and rights are. Where the court is satisfied that the uncertainty is of scant significance, the award will naturally be entitled to be enforced. It should be noted that the reference is to the effect of the award, not the reasons for the award. Therefore where the reasons given for the award are ambiguous, there is no serious irregularity under this paragraph. (See below paras 15–062—15–063.) **15–053**

(g) the award being obtained by fraud or the award or the way in which it was procured being contrary to public policy. It is not sufficient for the objector merely to show that a witness who gave evidence during the arbitration lied or that there had been perjury and conspiracy to fabricate evidence; s.68(2)(g) only applied where the award had been obtained by the fraud of *a party to the arbitration* (*Nestor Maritime v Sea Anchor* [2012] EWHC 996 (Comm); *Elektrim SA v Vivendi Universal SA* [2007] EWHC 11 (Comm), [2007] 2 All E.R. (Comm) 365).

(h) failure to comply with the requirements as to the form of the award. The general rule is that the parties are free to negotiate as to the form of the award. Where no agreement is reached, certain minimum requirements will apply. These are set out in s.52 as requiring the award to be in writing signed by all the arbitrators or all those assenting to it, to contain the reasons for the award unless it is an agreed award or the parties have agreed to dispense with reasons, and to state the seat of the arbitration and the date when the award is made.

15–054 (i) any irregularity in the conduct of the arbitration or in the award which is admitted by the tribunal or by any arbitral or other institution or person vested by the parties with powers in relation to the proceedings or the award. This is taken from the specific ground in s.22 of the 1950 Act (now repealed) for the making of a remission which in turn is derived from the entrenched common law rule that arbitrators are free to apply to the court for a remission of an issue or award erroneously given by the arbitrators themselves where that error is admitted by them (*Anderson v Darcy* (1812) 18 Ves. Jr. 447).

(iii) Appeal on point of law

15–055 Section 69 provides that unless otherwise agreed by the parties, a party to arbitral proceedings may appeal to the court on a question of law arising out of an award made. Where there is an agreement to dispense with reasons for the award, that will be construed by law as an exclusion of the court's appellate jurisdiction. No appeal may be brought except:

1. with the agreement of all other parties to the proceedings; or

2. with the leave of the court.

As for the agreement of the parties, where they have subjected their arbitration, for example, to the appropriate International Chamber of Commerce Rules[36] or LCIA Rules[37] which contain provisions on finality, that could be construed as the parties' having agreed to dispense with their right to appeal to a court.[38] Where the parties have specifically agreed that the award shall be "final" or "conclusive" or "binding" (or a combination of these terms), the English courts have consistently held these do not mean that the parties' right to appeal in relation to a question of law under s.69 had been excluded. In order to amount to such an exclusion, sufficiently clear wording is needed (*Essex CC v Premier Recycling Ltd* [2006] EWHC 3594 (TCC); *Shell Egypt West Manzala GmbH v Dana Gas Egypt* [2009] EWHC 2097 (Comm)).

Where the parties have agreed to allow the appeal to be brought before the courts, for example, by means of a clause similar to "any party to the dispute may appeal to the court on a question of law arising out of an award made in the arbitral proceedings", leave or permission to appeal would not be required. (*Royal & Sun Alliance v BAE System* [2008] EWHC 743).

15–056 Leave or permission to appeal will be given only if the court is satisfied that the determination of the question will substantially affect the rights of one or more of the parties. This is a matter that goes to the heart of the court's

---

[36] See, e.g., ICC Rules 2012 art.34 which provides: "Every award shall be binding on the parties. By submitting the dispute to arbitration under the Rules, the parties undertake to carry out any award without delay and shall be deemed to have waived their right to any form of recourse insofar as such waiver can validly be made".

[37] Art.26 of the LCIA rules provides: " . . . the parties . . . waive irrevocably their right to any form of appeal, review or recourse to any state court or other judicial authority, in so far as such waiver may be validly made."

[38] *Sanghi Polyesters Ltd (India) v The International Investor (KCFC) (Kuwait)* [2000] 1 Lloyd's Rep. 480.

jurisdiction to reopen the case. The judgment in *President of India v Jadranska Slobodna Plovidba* [1992] 2 Lloyd's Rep. 274, is redolent of this principle. The court opined that the question of law involved must affect the outcome of the arbitration, and must not only turn on one small and severable part of the award. The appellant must also show that the question of law is one which the tribunal had been asked to consider (as opposed to an issue not discussed by the arbitrators before) and that decision given is obviously wrong (s.69(3)(b) and (c)(i)) (*The Fu Ning Hai* [2006] EWHC 3250). The error has to be so obvious that it could be grasped by perusal of the award (*Pioneer Shipping Ltd v BTP Tioxide Ltd (The Nema) (No.2)* [1982] A.C. 724). It had to be so obvious as to be classified as a major intellectual aberration (*Braes of Doune Wind Farm (Scotland) Ltd v Alfred McAlpine Business Services Ltd* [2008] EWHC 426 (TCC); *HMV UK Ltd v Propinvest* [2011] EWCA Civ 1708).

If he is unable to show that it is obviously wrong, he must prove to the satisfaction of the court that the question is a matter of general public importance and the decision of the tribunal is at least open to serious doubt (s.69(3)(c)(ii)). The success of his application to have the case reassessed by the court is subject to the overriding consideration in s.69(3)(d) that:

"despite the agreement of the parties to resolve the matter by arbitration, it is just and proper in all the circumstances for the court to determine the question".

We might contrast the new provisions with the old. Under the 1979 Act, s.1(4) merely provided that the court shall not grant leave unless it considers that, having regard to all the circumstances, the determination of the question of law could substantially affect the rights of one or more of the parties. It makes no reference to the criteria to be adopted by the court in deciding to grant leave. Until *Pioneer Shipping Ltd v BTP Tioxide Ltd (The Nema)* [1981] 2 All E.R. 1030, leave had been consistently given without much self-restraint. This was considered by the House of Lords in *The Nema* as being inconsistent with the spirit and terms of the 1979 Act which were to preserve finality in arbitral awards. Certain guidelines were outlined in that case (these guidelines were subsequently confirmed in *The Antaios* [1984] 3 All E.R. 229).

The guidelines provide that in "one-off" cases, leave to appeal should not be **15–057** granted unless the arbitrators were obviously wrong. In other general cases, leave to appeal was subject to the court's satisfaction that a strong prima facie case has made out that the arbitrators were wrong and that the appeal should provide clarity and certainty in the law. "One-off" cases are those which are peculiar and unique to the parties concerned and carry no wider or more general significance. These guidelines are recognised in the new Act by its express reference to the possibility of appealing on the grounds that the arbitrators were obviously wrong on the question of law or that the question is a matter of such public importance that it should be resolved by the appellate court.

Section 69(3)(d) introduces a requirement that the court must be satisfied that the leave to appeal should be just and proper. This subjects the matter of granting leave to the discretion of the court to consider whether it would be appropriate in the interest of ensuring that arbitration should remain a speedy option.

These principles governing permission to appeal under s.69 were given very extensive consideration by the Court of Appeal in *CMA CGM SA v Beteiligungs-*

Kommanditgesellschaft MS Northern Pioneer Schiffahrtgesellschaft mbH & Co [2002] EWCA Civ 1878.

15–058   *CMA CGM SA v Beteiligungs-Kommanditgesellschaft MS Northern Pioneer Schiffahrtgesellschaft mbH & Co* [2002] EWCA Civ 1878
Facts:
The arbitrators made an award against the charterers finding that the events in Kosovo did not constitute "war" for the purposes of the charterparty and even if they did, Germany as a member of NATO was not "involved" in that war, as such the charterers could not invoke the relevant war cancellation clause in the charterparty. They also found that the charterers had not given notice of cancellation within a reasonable time. The High Court judge refused the charterers permission to appeal on point of law because the question of law (namely the reasonableness of the notice) was not one that the arbitrators had been asked to consider (s.69(3)(b)). However, the court was also aware that the question as to the meaning of the war cancellation clause was a question of public importance. Tomlinson J. was unsure whether the new law had a different effect. As such, the charterers were permitted to appeal to the Court of Appeal for the latter to consider whether he had misapplied the statutory criteria in s.69 or had approached them inappropriately inflexibly given the importance of the question in issue.
Held:
The Court of Appeal reiterated the point that the guidelines on appeals from an arbitration were no longer judge-made but are provided for by statute. There was no scope for amplifying or adapting them in the light of changing practices or new developments (such as the changing concept of international hostilities and war cancellation clauses in the present case). Given that the judge had found that the arbitrators had not been asked the critical question of reasonableness of the notice, s.69(3)(b) must mean that no permission to appeal would be granted. The judge had therefore applied the correct principles laid down by s:69(3).
    Section 69(3)(c)(ii) however provided a broader test than that in *The Nema*—the criteria were now that the question should be one of general public importance and that the arbitrator's decision should be at least open to serious doubt. That being the case, had the arbitrators' decision on the reasonableness of the notice not rendered the question academic, it would have been open to the lower court to give permission to appeal in respect of the issue of Germany's alleged involvement in the alleged war.

15–059   Section 69 refers to a "question of law". This term is given a specific definition in the Arbitration Act 1996. Section 82(1) states that "question of law" means:

(a) for a court in England and Wales, a question of the law of England and Wales; and

(b) for a court in Northern Ireland, a question of the law of Northern Ireland.

This definition is intentionally restrictive. It does not include questions of foreign law even though the seat of the arbitration is in England and Wales and consequently, subject to the jurisdiction of the English courts.
    In *Sanghi Polyesters Ltd (India) v The International Investors (KCFC) (Kuwait)* [2000] 1 Lloyd's Rep. 480, the applicant argued that the arbitrator had misapplied the law. The arbitration agreement provided that the dispute was to be governed by the laws of England "except to the extent it may conflict with Islamic Shari'a which shall prevail". The entire dispute was about the reach of Shari'a law and whether it might conflict with English law. The court held that as the effect of English law on the contracts was not in issue, the questions raised

fell outside s.82 and leave would therefore be refused under s.69. That too was the reason given by the court in declining to entertain an application under s.69 in *Athletic Union of Constantinople v National Basketball Association* (August 7, 2001, Q.B.D. (Comm)) because the question was about the arbitrator's application and interpretation of Greek law.[39]

Where it is not clear that the tribunal had applied the relevant law, instead of a case of clear misapplying the law, the court would still remit the matter to the arbitrator. In *Ocean Marine Navigation Ltd v Koch Carbon Inc (The Dynamic)* [2003] EWHC 1936, the court was concerned that the tribunal, though asked a specific question of law, did not appear to have consulted or referred to the applicable English legal principles on the issue. It was not clear as to whether the tribunal had merely neglected to apply the law or whether he had refused to do so or whether he did apply the law but misconstrued it. That however was enough for the court to rule that that the award should be remitted.

In *Demco Investments & Commercial SA v SE Banken Forsakring Holding Aktiebolag* [2005] EWHC 1398, Cooke J. stated that the legislative intent of s.69(3) was to prevent parties seeking to dress up questions of fact as questions of law (see also *Surefire Systems v Guardian* [2005] EWHC 1860 (TCC)). **15-060**

On findings of mixed law and fact, the court will allow an appeal against the arbitrator's award if there is an error of law and there will *only* be an error of law if it could be shown that the tribunal had misdirected itself or no tribunal properly instructed as to the proper law could have come to the determination reached (*Edwards v Bairstow* [1955] UKHL 3; see also *The Mary Nour* [2007] EWHC 2340).

An application for leave to appeal on a point of law, under s.69(4), must make clear the question of law to be determined and state the grounds on which it is alleged that leave to appeal should be granted. The court shall determine such an application without a hearing unless it appears to the court that a hearing would be needful (s.69(5)). All this is to ensure that the arbitral process is not undermined by lengthy and complex judicial proceedings commenced in relation to the arbitration. In *BLCT (13096) Ltd v J. Sainsbury Plc* [2003] EWCA Civ 884, it was not open to the applicant to argue that his right under art.6 of the European Convention on Human Rights (as incorporated into English law through the Human Rights Act 1998) was infringed by s.69(5). The court held that it was not a requirement of art.6 of the Convention that there should be an oral hearing unless there were exceptional circumstances. The parties had already had a full hearing before the arbitrator. By choosing arbitration the parties had waived their right to a public hearing. In the case of an appeal on a point of law, art.6 could not be said to require an oral hearing save in exceptional circumstances. It should however be added that, be that as it may, the court would always retain a residual jurisdiction to grant permission to appeal in a case of unfairness (*North Range Shipping Ltd v Seatrans Shipping Corp* [2002] EWCA

---

[39] It should however be noted that where the question was whether the applicable law was Greek law (rather than about the interpretation of Greek law), the court would have jurisdiction under s.69 because that was an issue of English private international law and not an issue of foreign law. It is also important to bear in mind that whilst the arbitration agreement can be subject to foreign law, the English court is not precluded from finding that the agreement was void for uncertainty and could not be enforced (see, e.g., *Sonatrach Petroleum Co v Ferrell International Ltd* [2002] 1 All E.R. (Comm) 627 where the arbitration clause provided for different disputes to be subject to the law of different countries was found not to be enforceable for uncertainty).

Civ 405) and fairness would be assessed, inter alia, on whether the parties had been given a fair hearing. That discretion however is to be exercised with the care. It would not be applied to override the raison d'être of arbitration without good ground.

15–061 Where the complaint is that the court had failed to provide sufficient reasons when dealing with an application to appeal on a point of law, there is no room to argue on the basis of art.6 of the European Convention of Human Rights that the judge should give detailed reasons when refusing permission to appeal. Prior to the Arbitration Act 1996, the position was clear—a judge need not state reasons for refusal of permission to appeal from an arbitration award as a matter of practice (*The Antaios* [1984] 3 W.L.R. 592). It was however argued in *Mousaka Inc v Golden Seagull Maritime Inc* [2002] 1 All E.R. 726 that with the passage of the Human Rights Act 1998, the position should be modified to require the court to give reasons. David Steel J. disagreed and held that there was nothing in the Arbitration Act 1996 that required a court to state reasons when disposing of an application under s.69. Article 6 had not been breached because the appeal process was intended to be swift and based on the principles of finality and privacy assumed to prevail by the parties when they agreed to arbitrate. Additionally, no unfairness had been caused since the parties had been given a fully reasoned award.

An alternative means of obtaining a judicial decision on a point of law is through s.45. That section allows an application to be made during the course of the arbitral proceedings. It shall not be considered unless it has the agreement of all the other parties to the proceedings or it is made with the permission of the tribunal and the court is satisfied that the determination of the question is likely to produce substantial savings in costs and the application was made without delay. With this procedure, the arbitration proceedings could carry on while the court is considering the matter as long as it is appropriate to do so.

Reasons for the award

15–062 Under the old law, an award could be set aside for "error on the face". For this reason, many arbitrators strove to avoid stating their reasons for any awards made. This was subsequently corrected in the 1979 Act and the duty to give full reasons with the award is now standard practice. It should be noted that the arbitrator still retains a wide discretion as to the extent of his reasons to be stated. Where there are pending issues that need to be resolved, the arbitrator might wish to avoid going into too much detail and giving reasons which might prejudice the determination of those other issues yet to be decided. Reasons including findings of fact are generally relevant to an appeal on a point of law (s.69(3)(c) as we have seen above). The court has power under s.70(4) to order the arbitrator to provide reasons or further reasons for the award made.[40] And as was pointed out, where the parties agree to dispense with reasons this will be deemed as an exclusion of the right to appeal.

What is meant by a "reasoned award"? Donaldson L.J. in *Bremer v Westzucker* [1981] 2 Lloyd's Rep. 130 said that:

---

[40] It would appear that the question as to whether an award is a "reasoned award" is question of fact (*Bay Hotel & Resort Ltd v Cavalier Construction Co Ltd* [2001] UKPC 34).

"All that is necessary is that the arbitrators should set out what, on their view of the evidence, did or did not happen and should explain succinctly why, in the light of what happened, they have reached their decision and what that decision is".

An arbitral tribunal should avoid reasoning which is "so opaque that it cannot be ascertained from reading it by what evidential route they arrived at their conclusion" (see *WTC v Czarnikow* [2005] 1 Lloyd's Rep 422; also *Pace Shipping of Malta v Churchgate Nigeria Ltd* [2009] EWHC 1975 (Comm)) and bear in mind that "an award which contains inadequate rationale or incomplete reasons for a decision is likely to be ambiguous or need clarification" (see *Torch Offshore v Cable Shipping* [2004] 2 Lloyd's Rep. 446). However, when reviewing the reasons of an arbitral tribunal, the court should read the award "as a whole in a fair and reasonable way ... [and] should not engage in minute textual analysis" (see *Kershaw Mechanical Services Ltd v Kendrick Construction* [2006] EWHC 727 (TCC); [2006] 2 All E.R. (Comm) 81). The courts are not to approach awards "with a meticulous legal eye endeavouring to pick holes, inconsistencies and faults in awards and with the objective of upsetting or frustrating the process of arbitration" (see *Zermalt Holdings SA v Nu-Life Upholstery Repairs Ltd* [1985] 2 E.G.L.R. 14).

The duty to state reasons can sometimes conflict with the aim of arbitration to **15–063** limit publicity. It is not unusual for parties to an arbitration to provide expressly that reasons given are to be treated as a confidential and should not be relied on in any proceedings related to the arbitration, including an application to review the award. How should the court respond to such a contractual undertaking? Some guidance is provided in *Tame Shipping Ltd v Easy Navigation Ltd* [2004] EWHC 1862. In that case, the arbitral award did not contain the arbitrator's reasons. The reasons were published in a separate document and were given for the information of the parties only and on the understanding that no use whatsoever was made of them on or in connection with any proceedings related the award. The applicant sought to have the award remitted under s.68 on grounds derived from those confidential reasons. The respondent argued that although the court could not be prevented from looking at the arbitrator's reasons, there was a strong public interest in enabling arbitrators to publish confidential reasons which could not be deployed by a dissatisfied party. Moore-Bick J. held that precedent was that the parties are bound contractually not to use the confidential reasons in application to challenge or remit the award but such an agreement could to prevent the court from looking at those reasons if it considered it right to do so.[41] In effect, what the court is saying there was that although it was a technical breach of contract for the dissatisfied party to refer to those unpublished reasons, the court nonetheless could totally disregard that contractual commitment and proceed as normal, giving due consideration to those reasons in assessing whether the arbitrator had committed a serious irregularity. The court's prerogative to supervise arbitral proceedings must trump any contractual arrangement to the provision of reasons by the arbitrator. The duty of the arbitrator to give reasons for the award cannot be diluted by the parties' agreement—that is to be the case even when confidentiality and privacy are key considerations.

---

[41] See, e.g. *The Montan* [1985] 1 Lloyd's Rep. 198.

In the above case, the question was very much about the confidentiality of the arbitrator's reasons. What if the matter was subsequently referred to the courts, to what extent is the court's judgment or report bound by the perceived need for confidentiality and privacy? Would it be held back from publication? In *Department of Economics, Policy and Development of the City of Moscow v Bankers Trust Co* [2004] EWCA Civ 314, D sought to make public a judgment which had been held in private because it wanted to publicise the fact that it was not guilty of any of the misdemeanours which have been in circulation as a result of the conflict. The judgment was made in relation to an arbitration claim between D and T. The judgment was received by Lawtel, a law reporter, which summarised the judgment and published it on its website. T complained to Lawtel which then removed it. The Commercial Court held that a judgment made should have been kept private and not be published; the emphasis being that it was the parties' presumed intention for the proceedings to be private and confidential. The court held that the publication of such a judgment would militate against the legitimate pursuit of any challenge to an award where a fundamental basis for agreeing to arbitration was the requirement for privacy. The Court of Appeal, by and large, agreed with the lower court but stated that although the parties had elected to arbitrate confidentially and privately, that could not dictate the position in respect of arbitration claims brought to the court.[42] Such proceedings were no longer consensual and the possibility of pursuing them existed in the public interest—that is to say, it falls to be a matter of the public domain. Although the court could still take into account the parties' expectations regarding privacy and confidentiality, it would use its discretion to decide whether some details of the arbitration/judgment should be made public. As the Lawtel summary only offered brief and neutral information about the background of the case and did not disclose any private or confidential information, the court would not prevent its publication. Indeed, the court made a point about the fact that the summary was of some interest to lawyers and others interested in understanding the respective roles of an arbitrator and the court. D's appeal was therefore allowed in part.[43]

The ICC Arbitration Rules 2012—Example of a private system

15–064   Arbitration is largely driven by the parties' desire for some control over their disputes. This is recognised by the mercantile communities in general. As such, although the law regulates issues around recognition and enforceability of the arbitration agreement and awards, matters relating to the arbitration process itself are best regulated by the parties' agreement or better still, in the interest of consistency and convenience, by frameworks set up by communities of stakeholders such as the ICC or some local industry led association with an interest in ADR and arbitration more specifically. As we have seen in the preceding discussion, the law will endeavour to give effect to these rules as agreed privately between the parties or assented to by the parties.

In this section, we shall consider some of the rules of arbitration established by the ICC. The ICC Rules[44] are chosen for study because of how widely the ICC

---

[42] The relevant provisions relied on for bringing the matter to court are in CPR r.62.10.
[43] See also *Tame Shipping Ltd v Easy Navigator* [2004] EWHC 1862.
[44] The Rules are available for download at *http://www.iccwbo.org*.

Rules are adopted by arbitral tribunals across the world and how often ICC International Court of Arbitration is relied on to organise and administer arbitrations. The Court itself is not an arbitral tribunal. It assists in the setting up of an arbitral tribunal; it monitors the process and awards made and offer other administrative support. It is the only body authorised to administer the resolution of disputes in accordance with the ICC Rules (arts 1.2; 6.2).

The ICC Arbitration Rules 2012 govern the conduct of ICC arbitration proceedings—they cover, inter alia, the following matters:

- how claims are to be filed;

- the constitution of arbitral tribunals;

- the conduct of proceedings;

- the decision and award making; and

- the determination of costs.

The ICC Rules also support the parties' autonomy in choosing the arbitrators, **15–065** the place, and the language of arbitration. The new Rules replace the 1998 Arbitration Rules and are intended to be more comprehensive in their coverage.

An improvement from the old Rules is the provision for joinder of additional parties. Article 7 allows the joinder of additional parties before the confirmation or appointment of the arbitrator. Any request for joinder after such time is nevertheless possible but will require the consent of all parties. The old Rules were silent on whether additional parties could be joined. In conjunction with this new facility, art.8 also allows claims to be made by any party against any other party involved in the multiple parties arbitration. Where previously there was no provision to allow for the hearing of claims arising out of multiple contracts, now under art.9, that is possible. All claims arising out of more than one contract may be heard in a single arbitration.

The Rules are also concerned about impartiality and although under the old Rules, there was a provision requiring that every arbitrator should be independent of the parties in the arbitration, now art.11.1 takes it a step further by requiring that the arbitrator signed a declaration of impartiality and independence. That declaration also binds them to informing the Secretariat of the ICC Court of any matters affecting their independence or impartiality. A statement of availability also has to be signed by the arbitrator to avoid any conflict of interests and obligations.

The Rules provide in art.22.1 that it is an express requirement for the tribunal **15–066** and parties to conduct the arbitration in an expeditious and cost-effective manner. It is however unclear what the consequences are. Moreover, such a positive duty is difficult to enforce given the consensual nature of the process. However, as rhetoric goes, this is a clear and unequivocal expression from the ICC that cost and efficiency are key to a successful arbitration.

A power similar to that possessed by the English courts is the power conferred by the Rules on the tribunal to ensure effective case management. In the past under the 1998 Rules, no express powers were given to the tribunal to take an active role in case management. Articles 22.2, 24.1 and 24.3 empower the tribunal to adopt procedural measures as it sees fit to ensure effective case management. Case management conferences can be introduced by the arbitrator to consult with the parties on the most efficient and fair way to progress the case. The new Rules offer the arbitrator a list of tried and tested case management techniques (many derived from the practices of the English High Court), for example, identifying with the parties the key issues for resolution, agreeing with the parties as to any process of discovery and the resolving of areas of common ground.

Article 29 (and Appendix V) enables an emergency arbitrator to be appointed. This is needed if one of the parties urgently seeks interim relief before an arbitrator can be appointed. Although this is not unusual in English civil procedure and arbitration,[45] for many not familiar with English civil procedure, such a concept will be very novel. In the past where this facility was not available under the ICC Rules 1998, parties were compelled to seek interim relief from the courts. Whilst that recourse has not been removed by the 2012 Rules, it is a relief to many that they now do not need to turn to the courts and air their problems in public. The emergency arbitrator option means that their privacy is maintained. That said, it should be noted that there are two important issues around the emergency arbitrator facility. First, a decision or order made by the emergency arbitrator may not be recognised as an arbitral award for the purposes of recognition and enforcement of arbitral awards under the New York Convention. Secondly, the decision made by the emergency arbitrator will not bind the arbitral tribunal subsequently constituted.

Lastly an important provision is art.27 which requires the arbitrator to give an indication to the parties after the closure of the arbitration as to when the award might be expected. Although this obligation is not mandatory, many who have had to endure long waits before receiving awards will find this provision an improvement.

Arbitration as a default dispute settlement method in international commerce

15–067   Much of this book has been about substantive law which the common law courts will apply to resolve disputes between the trading parties. This last chapter has explored how alternative dispute resolution methods can be used to resolve disputes between traders and at times, without resorting to substantive law. It seems therefore fitting to close the book with an discussion about whether the default position when it comes to dispute resolution should be arbitration or ADR rather than litigation. Of course, it has to be recognised that parties can sometimes torpedo the arbitral process using court ordained sanctions—after all, as we have seen, judicial control of arbitration is a necessity for arbitration to work effectively. However, excessive reliance on judicial control is not pro-arbitration.

Arbitration is ideally suited to international commercial disputes. Disputes are resolved usually at neutral locations, and by neutral and qualified experts. A supposition might be made that commercial parties are predisposed to the benefits of cross border arbitration. That predisposition could in turn be taken to suggest that in international trade parties have implicitly assumed the need for arbitration. If that predisposition and recognition of the need for arbitration could stretch to include consent, it is not difficult to see how arbitration could be default

---

[45] See s.44, Arbitration Act 1996 for instance.

mechanism. That is to say, arbitration will be used unless there is an express contractual exclusion of it by the parties. Naturally this presumption of consent will be controversial but it is not too removed from the bounds of the reasonable to suggest that binding commercial parties to default rules is acceptable in international commercial law (as we have seen elsewhere, in the context of international sale both at common law and under the CISG).

A question may legitimately be asked that even if there is presumption of consent to arbitration, surely that consent cannot stretch to a presumed consent as to the appropriate procedure. Perhaps this is where the international community might be able to offer some assistance. We have already seen how the ICC Rules (though not an international treaty) may be relied on for guidance as to the appropriate procedure. At international law level, the example of the Panama Convention[46] might be useful. Article 3 of that Convention provides that in the event the parties have not agreed upon any institutional or other arbitration rules, the rules of the Inter-American Commercial Arbitration Commission (IACAC) will govern the arbitration. These provisions are largely identical to the original UNCITRAL Arbitration Rules 1976. Hence, it is not unfathomable that international commercial arbitration in the future should become the default norm rather than remain a special or alternative method of dispute resolution as is the case at present.

---

[46] The Inter-American Convention on International Commercial Arbitration (the "Panama Convention") applies to arbitration agreements between parties from contracting states within North and South America; the Panama Convention displaces the New York Convention as regards those circumstances.

INDEX

Accidents of the sea
See **Perils of the sea**
Abandonment
  marine insurance, and, 10–136—10–139
Act of God
  carriage by sea, and
    common law, 7–054
    Hague-Visby Rules, 8–058
"Act of Queen's enemies"
  carriage by sea, and
    common law, 7–055
    Hague-Visby Rules, 8–058
Act of war
See **War**
Action for price
  generally, 4–017—4–019
  late payment interest, 4–020—4–022
Actual total loss
  marine insurance, and, 10–121—10–126
Administration of Justice Act 1920
  recognition of judgments, and
    appeal pending, 14–020
    breach of human rights law, 14–017
    defences, 14–011—14–021
    establishing jurisdiction of foreign court,
      14–010
    fraud, 14–012—14–013
    generally, 14–009
    natural justice, 14–018—14–019
    public policy, 14–014—14–016
    state immunity, 14–021
Advance freight
  carriage by sea, and, 7–082—7–085
Agents
  brokers, 2–010
  carriage of goods, and
    forwarding agents, 9–053
    loading brokers, 9–054—9–057
  commercial agents, 2–014—2–015
  commission agents, 2–011
  confirming houses, 2–012
  del credere agent, 2–013
  factors, 2–009
  forwarding agents, 9–053
  loading brokers, 9–054—9–057
Agreements to sell
  generally, 3–011
Air waybills
  carriage by air, and, 9–003—9–005
All risks cover in ICC(A)
  See also **Marine insurance**
  arrest, 10–086
  capture, 10–086
  civil commotion, 10–093
  civil strife, 10–085

All risks cover in ICC(A)—*cont.*
  civil war, 10–083—10–084
  condition of the subject matter,
    10–075—10–081
  contractual exceptions, 10–071—10–094
  delay, 10–082
  derelict mines, torpedoes, bombs etc,
    10–087
  detainment, 10–086—10–087
  duration of cover, 10–095—10–098
  hostile act by or against belligerent power,
    10–085
  insurrection, 10–085
  introduction, 10–064
  limitation, 10–065—10–098
  lock-outs, 10–090
  rebellion, 10–085
  restraint, 10–086
  revolution, 10–085
  riots, 10–091—10–092
  risk not certainty, 10–065—10–070
  seizure, 10–086
  strikes, 10–088—10–090
  terrorism, 10–094
  war, 10–083—10–084
  war clause, 10–083—10–087
  weapons of war, 10–087
  wilful conduct of the assured,
    10–072—10–074
"Allonge"
  international trade finance, and, 11–136
Alternative dispute resolution
  arbitration
    See also **Arbitration**
    appeal on point of law, 15–055—15–061
    applicable law, 15–006—15–013
    arbitrators, 15–033
    Atlantic Shipping clauses, 15–032
    benefits, 15–003
    challenging awards, 15–040—15–061
    courts, and, 15–014
    default dispute settlement, as, 15–067
    effect of arbitration agreement,
      15–016—15–032
    failure of substantive jurisdiction,
      15–043—15–047
    governing law, 15–003
    ICC Arbitration Rules 2012,
      15–064—15–066
    introduction, 15–003
    juridical seat, 15–004
    procedure, 15–034—15–036
    reasons for award, 15–062—15–063
    removal of arbitrators, 15–037—15–039
    seat of the arbitration, 15–004—15–005